DISPUTES ORANGE 23

LAW AND CORPORATE BEHAVIOUR

This book examines the theories and practice of how to control corporate behaviour through legal techniques. The principal theories examined are deterrence, economic rational acting, responsive regulation, and the findings of behavioural psychology. Leading examples of the various approaches are given in order to illustrate the models: private enforcement of law through litigation in the USA, public enforcement of competition law by the European Commission, and the recent reform of policies on public enforcement of regulatory law in the United Kingdom. Noting that behavioural psychology has as yet had only limited application in legal and regulatory theory, the book then analyses various European regulatory structures where behavioural techniques can be seen or could be applied. Sectors examined include financial services, civil aviation, pharmaceuticals, and workplace health and safety. Key findings are that 'enforcement' has to focus on identifying the causes of non-compliance, so as to be able to support improved performance, rather than be based on fear motivating complete compliance. Systems in which reporting is essential for safety only function with a no-blame culture. The book concludes by proposing an holistic model for maximising compliance within large organisations, combining public regulatory and criminal controls with internal corporate systems and external influences by stakeholders, held together by a unified core of ethical principles. Hence, the book proposes a new theory of ethical regulation.

Volume 3 in the series Civil Justice Systems

Civil Justice Systems

Series General Editor, Christopher Hodges, Head, Swiss Re/CMS Research Programme, Centre for Socio-Legal Studies, University of Oxford

This series covers new theoretical and empirical research on the mechanisms for resolution of civil disputes, including courts, tribunals, arbitration, compensation schemes, ombudsmen, codes of practice, complaint mechanisms, mediation, and various forms of Alternative Dispute Resolution. It examines frameworks for dispute resolution that comprise combinations of the above mechanisms, and the parameters and conditions for selecting certain types of techniques and procedures rather than others. It also evaluates individual techniques, against parameters such as cost, duration, accessibility, and delivery of desired outcomes, and illuminates how legal rights and obligations are operated in practice.

Volume 1: *The Costs and Funding of Civil Litigation: A Comparative Perspective* edited by Christopher Hodges, Stefan Vogenauer and Magdalena Tulibacka

Volume 2: *Consumer ADR in Europe* by Christopher Hodges, Iris Benöhr and Naomi Creutzfeldt-Banda

Law and Corporate Behaviour

Integrating Theories of Regulation, Enforcement, Compliance and Ethics

Christopher Hodges

Professor of Justice Systems at the University of Oxford
Supernumerary Fellow, Wolfson College, Oxford
Head of the Swiss Re/CMS Research Programme on Civil Justice Systems,
Centre for Socio-Legal Studies, Oxford
Honorary Professor, China University of Political Science and Law,
Beijing
Solicitor (non-practising)

·HART·
PUBLISHING
OXFORD AND PORTLAND, OREGON
2015

Published in the United Kingdom by Hart Publishing Ltd
16C Worcester Place, Oxford, OX1 2JW
Telephone: +44 (0)1865 517530
Fax: +44 (0)1865 510710
E-mail: mail@hartpub.co.uk
Website: http://www.hartpub.co.uk

Published in North America (US and Canada) by
Hart Publishing
c/o International Specialized Book Services
920 NE 58th Avenue, Suite 300
Portland, OR 97213-3786
USA
Tel: +1 503 287 3093 or toll-free: (1) 800 944 6190
Fax: +1 503 280 8832
E-mail: orders@isbs.com
Website: http://www.isbs.com

British Library Cataloguing in Publication Data
Data Available

ISBN: 978-1-84946-653-0 (Hart Publishing)
978-3-406-689 43-5 (Verlag CH Beck)

Typeset by Compuscript Ltd, Shannon
Printed and bound in Great Britain by
CPI Group (UK) Ltd, Croydon CR0 4YY

ACKNOWLEDGEMENTS

This book rests on 25 years of experience as a practising lawyer followed by ten years as a scholar. Very many people have contributed to my knowledge and understanding during this period—far too many to be acknowledged by name, and I hope they will accept this public expression of thanks and understand that a few deserve particular mention.

I owe particularly warm thanks to the following. My wife Fiona has provided continuous unstinting support throughout the past five years (and the last four decades) without which this book could not have been written. Writing a book like this requires enormous concentration, and many normal aspects of family life suffer as a result, but Fiona has been wonderfully understanding and supportive.

Ian Dodds-Smith of Arnold & Porter taught me all about pharmaceutical regulation. The late Malcolm Carlisle of Smiths Industries and later Eschmann did the same for management systems and medical device regulation. Mark Tyler of Salutaris collaborated over many years on general product safety and product liability, and has provided invaluable comments on draft text on health and safety in the workplace. Invaluable education on competition law has been provided by discussion with David Marks of CMS Cameron McKenna, Ken Daly of Sidley Austin LLP, Kaarli Eichhorn of GE, Arundel McDougall of the European Justice Forum and Eddy De Smijter of the European Commission. Andrew Mills of Experian has kindly provided a series of objective comments on an advanced draft of various sections.

Graham Russell, Chief Executive, Helen Kirkman and various colleagues at the Better Regulation Development Office of the UK's Department for Business, Innovation & Skills have reviewed and commented on aspects of UK regulatory policy and history, not least in highlighting important aspects of the Primary Authority scheme. Comments on drafts on financial services, which identified numerous errors and misunderstandings on my part, have been made by Clive Adamson, then Director of Supervision at the Financial Conduct Agency, and his senior colleagues Celyn Armstrong, Sean Martin, Daniel Thornton and John O'Hara; and by Simon Hills, Executive Director, Prudential Capital, Risk & Regulatory at the British Bankers Association. The crucial material on aviation safety owes much in practical understanding to help from Captain John Monks, Elizabeth Hichens and an anonymous First Officer of British Airways, and on regulatory policy to Dominic Marino of the Civil Aviation Authority. Numerous conversations with officers of regulatory agencies in different sectors have been invaluable: especially Sir Kent Woods and John Wilkinson of the Medicines and Healthcare products Regulatory Agency.

Conversations with academic colleagues too numerous to mention have stirred intellectual response. Especial thanks to Hans Micklitz, Burkhard Hess, Steve Weatherill, Simon Whittaker, Willem van Boom, Astrid Stadler, Gerhard Wagner and John Armour. Julian Roberts and Johan Boucht have kindly given assistance on criminal law aspects.

Various members of our Oxford research team have, of course, contributed in many ways: Naomi Creutzfeldt and Iris Benöhr on our work on ADR and in understanding how the legal system works in various countries; Stefaan Voet of Gent University on numerous aspects of European procedural developments and especially on the Belgian piggy-back technique; Franziska Weber formerly of Erasmus University, Rotterdam and now Hamburg University on advertising.

This book could not have been written without my enjoying the ability to concentrate fully on research and thinking. Grateful thanks for making this possible are to funders of our academic research programmes. Funding of my post at the Centre for Socio-Legal Studies, Oxford has kindly been provided by the Swiss Reinsurance Company Limited, for my post for four years in Rotterdam by the Erasmus University, and research funding by the European Justice Forum and the international law firm group CMS. All of these entities have throughout maintained scrupulous arm's length distance, allowing personal academic intellectual independence, whilst individuals in them have given invaluable personal support. I am particularly grateful to Urs Leimbacher, Lorenz Ködderitzsch, Arundel McDougall and David Marks for listening to ideas and responding with critical comments. A Visiting Professorship in 2013 at the Catholic University of Leuven allowed me to start to bring the ideas together, for which I am grateful to Professors Jules Stuyck, Evelyne Terryn and Vincent Sagaert and Dean Bernard Tilleman. I have the good fortune to have been given considerable support by Oxford colleagues, especially Denis Galligan, Timothy Endicott, Fernanda Pirie, Marina Kurkchiyan and Katie Hayward.

I am grateful to the excellent team at Hart Publishing. Richard Hart has provided huge encouragement for many years; it has been a delight to work with his successor Sinead Moloney and colleagues Mel Hamill, Emily Braggins and copy editor Helen Kitto.

The usual disclaimers apply. None of the people named above should be landed with responsibility for any of the views expressed here, but all have prevented numerous errors from appearing.

AMDG

Oxford
February 2014

TABLE OF CONTENTS

Part F: Conclusions

DETAILED TABLE OF CONTENTS

Part D: Regulation and Compliance by Business

LIST OF TABLES, FIGURES AND BOXES

LIST OF ABBREVIATIONS

ABPI	Association of the British Pharmaceutical Industry
ABTA	Association of British Travel Agents (now the Travel Association)
ACCC	Australian Competition and Consumer Commission
ACD	assumed consumer detriment
ADR	alternative dispute resolution
AIFMD	Alternative Investment Fund Managers Directive (2011/61/EU)
ARROW	Advanced Risk-Responsive Operating framework
ASA	Advertising Standards Authority
ASAP	as soon as possible
ASRS	Aviation Safety Reporting System
ATM	automatic teller machine *or* air traffic management
ATVOD	Authority for Television on Demand
AVMS	Audio Visual Media Service
B2B	business-to-business
BBA	British Bankers Association
BCAP	British Code of Advertising Practice
BCSB	Basel Committee on Banking Supervision
BFA	British Franchise Association
BIS	Department for Business, Innovation & Skills
BRI	Bristol Royal Infirmary
BRRD	Banking Recovery and Resolution Directive (2014/59/EU)
BS	British Standard
BSI	British Standards Institute
CAA	Civil Aviation Authority
CAP	Code of Advertising Practice

CAT	Competition Appeal Tribunal
CCAB	Consumer Codes Approval Board
CCEB	Competition and Consumer Enforcement Bulletin (of Ofcom)
CCP	central counterparty
CDO	Competition Disqualification Order under the Company Directors Disqualification Act 1986, s 9A
CDR	Consumer Dispute Resolution
CE (marking)	The marking 'CE' applied to products certified under EU Directives of the NLF type
CEBS	Committee of European Banking Supervisors
CEO	Chief Executive Officer
CHIRP	Confidential Human Factors Incident Reporting Programme
CHMP	Committee on Human Medicinal Products
CHP	complaint handling procedure
CMA	Competition and Markets Authority
CMAR	Control of Misleading Advertising Regulations 1988/915
CMCB	Compensation Monitoring Contact Group
CMO	Chief Medical Officer
COMAH	Control of Major Accident Hazards Regulations 1999/743 as amended
COSHH	Control of Substances Hazardous to Health Regulations
CP	communications provider
CPP	Consumer Protection Partnership
CQC	Care Quality Commission
CR	corporate responsibility
CRD3	Third Capital Requirements Directive (2010/76/EU)
CRO	Civil Recovery Order
CSR	corporate social responsibility
D&O	Directors and Officers
DEPP	Decision Procedure and Penalties Manual of the FCA
DG COMP	The European Commission's Directorate General on Competition
DHPC	direct healthcare professional communications

DIY	do-it-yourself
DOJ	Department of Justice (USA)
DPA	Deferred Prosecution Agreement
DSIB	domestically systemically important bank
EASA	European Aviation Safety Agency
EASP	European Aviation Safety Plan
EBA	European Banking Authority
ECR	European Central Repository
EEA	European Economic Area
EFPIA	European Federation of Pharmaceutical Industry Associations
EIOPA	European Insurance and Occupational Pensions Authority
EMA	European Medicines Agency
EMM	Enforcement Manual Model
EN	European Standards
ERR	Enterprise and Regulatory Reform Act 2013
ESA	European Supervisory Authority
ESARR	Eurocontrol Safety and Regulatory Requirement
ESMA	European Securities and Markets Authority
ESRB	European Systemic Risk Board
EU	The European Union
FAA	Federal Aviation Authority (USA)
FATF	Financial Action Task Force
FCA	Financial Conduct Authority
FCPA	Foreign Corrupt Practices Act (USA)
FOS	Financial Ombudsman Service
FPC	Financial Policy Committee
FSA	Financial Services Authority *and* Food Standards Agency
FSB	Financial Stability Board
FSMA	Financial Services and Markets Act 2000
FTSE 100	London Stock Exchange index of share prices of the top 100 listed companies

FX	foreign exchange
G20	Group of 20 major economies
G30	Group of 30 major economies
GDP	Gross Domestic Product
GEMA	Gas and Electricity Markets Authority
GHS	globally harmonised system
GMC	General Medical Council
GPS	general product safety
G-SIB	globally systematically important bank
GSIE	Global Safety Information Exchange
GVA	gross value added
HACCP	Hazard Analysis Critical Control Point
H&S	health and safety
HSE	Health and Safety Executive
IAIS	International Association of Insurance Supervisors
IATA	International Air Transport Association
ICAO	International Civil Aviation Organisation
ICASS	International Confidential Aviation Safety System
IEC	International Electrical Commission
IMF	International Monetary Fund
IOSA	IATA Operational Safety Audit
IOSCO	International Organisation of Securities Commissions
IRHP	interest rate hedging product
ISO	International Standards Organisation
IVDMD	in vitro diagnostic medical device
LA	Local Authority
LAATSN	Local Authority Assured Trader Scheme Network
LACORS	Local Authority Coordinators of Regulatory Services
LAPFF	Local Authority Pension Fund Forum
LATTS	Local Authority Trading Standards Service

LBRO	Local Better Regulation Office
LIBOR	London Inter-Bank Offered Rate
MAPP	major accident prevention policy
MBA	Master of Business Administration
MHRA	Medicines and Healthcare products Agency
MiFID	Markets in Financial Instruments Directive (2004/39/EC)
MSA	market surveillance authority
NAA	National Aviation Authority
NAO	National Audit Office
NCA	National Competent Authority (EU) *or* National Crime Agency (UK)
NHS	National Health Service
NICE	National Institute for Health and Care Excellence
NLF	New Legislative Framework
NMAC	near mid-air collision
NMC	Nursing and Midwifery Council
NPA	Non-Prosecution Agreement
NTLS	National Reporting and Learning System
NTSB	National Trading Standards Board
OCB	organisational citizenship behaviour
ODA	Olympic Delivery Authority
OECD	Organisation for Economic Cooperation and Development
Ofcom	Office of Communications
Ofgem	Office of Gas and Electricity Markets
Ofwat	Water Services Regulatory Authority
OFT	Office of Fair Trading
OJ	Official Journal of the European Union
ORR	Office of Rail Regulation
OTC	over-the-counter
PAGB	Proprietary Association of Great Britain
PAS	Publicly Available Specification

PBR	performance based regulation
PCT	Primary Care Trust
PMCPA	Prescription Medicines Code of Practice Authority
PoCA	Proceeds of Crime Act 2002
PPI	Payment protection insurance
PRA	Prudential Regulatory Authority
PSLRA	Private Securities Litigation Reform Act (USA)
PSUR	periodic safety update report
QMS	quality management system
QOCS	qualified one way cost shift
RAPEX	Rapid Alert System for non-food dangerous products (EU)
REMIT	Regulation (EU) No 1227/2011 on wholesale energy market integrity and transparency
RESA	Regulatory Enforcement and Sanctions Act 2008
RIDDOR	Reporting of Injuries, Diseases and Dangerous Occurrences Regulations 2013
RIPA	Regulation of Investigatory Powers Act 2000
RIU	Regulated Industries Unit
SAFA	Safety of Foreign Aircraft Programme
SARP	standards and recommended practice
SEC	Securities and Exchange Commission (USA)
SFAIRP	so far as is reasonably practicable
SFO	Serious Fraud Office
SIPEP	Strategic Intelligence, Prevention and Enforcement Partnership
SLC	standard licence condition
SME	Small and Medium Sized Entities
SmPC	Summary of Product Characteristics
SMS	safety management system
SOP	standard operating procedure
SRB	single resolution board
SRF	single resolution fund

SSM	Single Supervisory Mechanism
SSP	State Safety Programme
TCF	treating customers fairly
TSPB	Trading Standards Policy Board
TSI	Trading Standards Institute
TSS	Trading Standards Service
TV	television
UK	United Kingdom
UKAS	United Kingdom Accreditation Service
UN	United Nations
USA	United States of America
UTCCR	Unfair Terms in Consumer Contracts Regulations 1999/2083
UWG	Gesetz gegen den unlauteren Wettbewerb (Germany)
VZBV	Verbraucherzentrale Bunbdesverband e.V. (Germany)
WBZ	Wettbewerbszentrale
WHO	World Health Organisation
WYSIATI	what you see is all there is

Introduction

How do legal techniques affect corporate behaviour? *Do* legal techniques affect corporate behaviour? *Which* legal techniques affect corporate behaviour—and *how*? A cursory glance across various areas of law reveals considerable diversity in the answers to the first question, and not much evidence on the second.

I have had the advantage of spending most of my working life as a lawyer advising companies. The companies were of all shapes and sizes, and based all over the world—from the USA to Japan, and Australia to Finland. In exposure to extensive litigation, large and small, I never felt that companies or the people working in them were worried about whether outcomes might affect what they would do in future. It was regulation that could keep firms off the market; it was the risk criminal sanctions and threats to professional reputations that affected their behaviour. In most of the sectors I worked with, financial incentives had no noticeable effect on behaviour, but we now know that money can powerfully affect behaviour, although possibly more as a token of success than to satisfy intrinsic greed. It is the *love* of money that corrupts.

Having now spent 10 years happily immersed full-time in academic thinking, I quickly became surprised to find how great is the gulf between influential theories and the reality of the commercial and regulatory worlds. That is the spur for this book. If theories of deterrence and economic rational acting are not well founded, where are reliable theories about what actually affects corporate behaviour? If policies relating to regulation and enforcement systems are based on inadequate theories, should they not be reformed?

This book aims to examine how legal techniques seek to affect corporate behaviour, and how legal systems can support and affect desired behaviour. It looks across a wide range of legal subjects to seek illumination. It focuses primarily on techniques that have traditionally been categorised as regulatory, and also notes the influence of private law techniques such as contract and tort law. Thus, the scope of the inquiry encompasses both public and private law.

I. Regulation and Enforcement

It may be helpful to start with a general definition of 'regulation' and 'enforcement'. Regulatory scholars have debated this issue in detail.[1] Drawing on their work, the concept

---

[1] For some leading recent definitions see A Ogus, *Regulation: Legal Form and Economic Theory* (Oxford, Oxford University Press, 1994); R Baldwin, C Scott and C Hood, *A Reader on Regulation* (Oxford, Oxford University Press, 1998); R Baldwin and M Cave, *Understanding Regulation: Theory, Strategy, and Practice* (Oxford, Oxford

of regulation that I address here is any public means of control over an activity that is essentially lawful but which the state wishes to be undertaken subject to certain constraints. In simple terms, the state adopts the attitude: please feel free to continue your activity, but perform it subject to specified constraints. As appears from the descriptions of regulatory systems and architectures in Parts C to E below, regulatory systems in Europe (and elsewhere) have grown, particularly in the past 50 years, and are now highly extensive, complex and sophisticated. Essential features of regulatory systems are a set of requirements to be observed (usually in relation to processes to be adopted and outputs to be achieved), a public authority whose function is to monitor the requirements of the system and the fact that businesses comply with the rules, and a system of 'enforcing' the rules.

In looking at regulation, it is easy to concentrate on what public officials do. But, as will be seen below, regulatory systems are not just about how public officials perform their functions. The whole purpose of regulation is to attempt to control how businesses perform their functions. In looking at that aspect, scholars have primarily focused on some negative aspects, such as that some businesses will game the system and engage in 'creative compliance' such that they can claim to comply with the letter of important rules whilst in fact primarily acting in ways that suit them but which are contrary to the spirit of the law.[2] Such evasive phenomena are, of course, relevant, especially in designing and operating regulatory and enforcement structures. But the line of thought that most businesses seek to break the rules most of the time might not engage with how most businesses in fact seek to operate, or with how they can be assisted to comply all of the time. It follows from the fact that the wide scope and deep complexity of regulatory systems now reaches deeply into how businesses operate and organise themselves that serious effort should be directed at understanding how businesses operate and how they can be assisted to comply with society's norms. After all, the vast majority of the people who apply regulatory systems in practice are employed by the businesses themselves, either in-house or on an outsourced contract basis. Serious attention needs to be directed at how they work, and can be helped to do their job.

Enforcement in its classical sense is limited to taking formal action against those who breach the rules, such as a prosecution or serving an improvement notice. The OECD (Organisation for Economic Co-operation Development) definition of regulation and inspection says:

> '[E]nforcement' will be taken in its broad meaning, covering all activities of state structures (or structures delegated by the state) aimed at promoting compliance and reaching regulations' outcomes—eg lowering risks to safety, health and the environment, ensuring the achievement of some public goods including state revenue collection, safeguarding certain legally recognised rights, ensuring transparent functioning of markets etc. These activities may include: information, guidance and prevention; data collection and analysis; inspections; enforcement actions in the narrower

---

University Press, 1999); K Yeung, *Securing Compliance. A Principled Approach* (Oxford, Hart Publishing, 2004); B Morgan and K Yeung, *An Introduction to Law and Regulation* (Cambridge University Press, 2007); T Prosser, *The Regulatory Enterprise: Government, Regulation, and Legitimacy* (Oxford, Oxford University Press, 2010); M Cave, R Baldwin, M Lodge (eds), *The Oxford Handbook of Regulation* (Oxford, Oxford University Press, 2010); J Black and R Baldwin, 'Really Responsive Risk-Based Regulation' (2010) 32(2) *Law & Policy* 181.

[2] D McBarnet and C Whelan, 'The Elusive Spirit of the Law: Formalism and the Struggle for Legal Control' (1991) 54 *MLR* 848; D McBarnett, *Crime, Compliance and Control* (Aldershot, Dartmouth, 2004).

sense, ie warnings, improvement notices, fines, prosecutions etc. To distinguish the two meanings of enforcement, 'regulatory enforcement' will refer to the broad understanding, and 'enforcement actions' to the narrower sense.

'Inspections' will be understood as any type of visit or check conducted by authorised officials on products or business premises, activities, documents etc.[3]

This book tries to address two inter-related issues. First, what affects the behaviour of individuals and businesses (ie groups of individuals)? Second, what enforcement policy or policies are effective, and why, and in what circumstances? This involves an examination of the enforcement policies that are currently adopted and applied by public enforcement bodies in a number of different sectors. Historically, the second question has received far more attention than the first question. Indeed, very little legal writing has addressed the first question. But it appears logical that it is the 'behaviour' question that should be answered before the 'enforcement' question, since the former will dictate the answer to the latter.

A whole series of different approaches exist towards enforcement. The traditional distinction is between public enforcement and private enforcement. However, that juxtaposition of supposed opposites in fact contains several variables: The nature of the actor (a public body or a private body, but in some instances some form of hybrid, such as a non-governmental organisation exercising public or private powers); the nature of the tribunal, forum or third party (the paradigm is a court, but it could be official tribunals, public or private alternative dispute resolution entities such as ombudsmen, private arbitrators or mediators, or something else); and the nature of the law or remedies (possibly public, administrative or private).

For example, criminal law is traditionally enforced by public officers through techniques such as fining, imprisonment and even execution; but private persons may sometimes institute criminal proceedings. Tort law is typically enforced through private litigation initiated by private individuals, or other intermediaries, adopting techniques named injunctions or actions for damages; but is increasingly resolved through alternative dispute resolution (arbitration, mediation, ombudsmen or other means). Public administrative regulatory systems are predominantly enforced by public officials, using techniques such as licensing regimes backed ultimately by cessation or disqualification orders and criminal sanctions; but there are extensive systems of self-regulation or co-regulation in which compliance is achieved by private parties, often employees of a large corporation or external audit or accreditation bodies.

In examining legal rules, this inquiry analyses both systemic and enforcement issues. The principal systemic aspect is whether the design of the regulatory system is optimal in achieving compliance with the norms set by society, or even of exceeding them. The principal enforcement issue is whether the activities of a regulatory body, and of any other actor who may be involved, achieve the same goal of compliance.

Some legal systems are built on favouring a particular mode of enforcement. For example, the United States of America strongly favours private enforcement of not only private rights but also of public norms, and the idea is widely quoted that public agencies cannot be trusted or are captured or have insufficient resources. In contrast, European jurisdictions maintain a different balance between public and private enforcement, and regulatory

---

[3] *OECD Best Practice Principles for Regulatory Policy: Regulatory Enforcement and Inspections* (Paris, OECD, 2014).

systems have become extensive and strong in the past 60 years, and is central to the EU's harmonisation of pan-EU markets. The UK, despite sharing a common law legal system with the USA, is clearly part of the European model in having strong public regulation, with private litigation in a secondary role as a means of delivering compensatory damages and not behaviour control.

II. Affecting Behaviour

In setting out to examine how law might influence or control corporate behaviour, we will need to examine several aspects. We will need to look at the major competing theories by which law is claimed to control behaviour. We will then examine some of the regulatory policies adopted by the UK and some leading regulatory systems in some detail. Given the diversity of approaches, the additional question then arises of how well these various techniques work, and which are best? That evaluative question has hitherto received little attention. So we will examine the empirical evidence for how, and how well, the competing theories work.

The design of the systems of regulation, enforcement and private law that currently exist has evolved over time—in the case of private law, a long time—without there having been a widely-based review of how society can and should use all legal techniques so as to achieve optimal compliance with its rules and standards. This book constitutes a first attempt at such an inquiry. The basic question is whether our systems actually work, whether they can be improved, and whether the diversity of different techniques can be drawn together into a holistic theory and practical framework. This may point to the advisability of making alterations in priorities and techniques.

This book traverses a series of different areas of law, such as the theory of private and tort liability, economic analysis of law, civil procedure, theories of regulation and enforcement, government policy on regulation and enforcement both in general and in a series of different business sectors, behavioural psychology, business organisation and compliance, and cultural issues. It is a long list of different specialist topics. It is striking how each area exists in its own silo, with its own internal debate or culture amongst opinion leaders (whether academic, governmental, business, practitioner or consumer) and often with limited or even no knowledge of the landscape or of similar debates in other silos. This phenomenon conforms to the closed or autopoietic view of law, and of subsidiary areas of law, theorised by Teubner[4] and Luhmann.[5] The extent to which the series of conversations are internalised

---

[4] G Teubner, 'Substantive and Reflexive Elements in Modern Law' (1983) 17 *Law and Society Review* 239; G Teubner (ed), *Dilemmas of Law in the Welfare State* (Berlin, De Gruyter, 1986); G Teubner (ed), *Juridification of Social Spheres: A Comparative Analysis of the Areas of Labor, Antitrust and Social Welfare Law* (Berlin, De Gruyter, 1987); G Teubner (ed), *Autopoietic Law: A New Approach to Law and Society* (Berlin, De Gruyter, 1988); G Teubner and A Febbraio (eds), *State, Law and Economy as Autopoietic Systems* (Milano, Giuffrè, 1991); G Teubner, L Farmer and D Murphy, *Environmental Law and Ecological Responsibility* (Chichester, Wiley, 1994); RJ in 't Veld, CJAM Termeer, L Schaap and MJW Van Twist (eds), *Autopoiesis and Configuration Theory: New Approaches to Societal Steering* (Dordrecht, Kluwer Academic Publishers, 1991).
[5] N Luhmann, *The Differentiation of Society* (New York NY, Columbia University Press, 1982); N Luhmann, *Social Systems* (Redwood CA, Stanford University Press, 1995); R Nobles and D Schiff, *Observing Law through Systems Theory* (Oxford, Hart Publishing, 2012).

and take little account of thinking, or perceived reality, in other areas is in fact alarming. A major purpose of this book is to open up some of these different internalised worlds to wider scrutiny and other ideas, and to begin to take an overview of the thinking that exists, so that comparisons can be drawn, and ideas, justifications and approaches be tested.

I feel personally on thin ice on several of these areas, but that is not the point. The real point is to take a fresh and wide-ranging look at the relevant thinking and evidence. Some of the evidence included here may itself be wrong, or quickly superceded. I will be entirely content if experts in the various fields produce better and more accurate summaries of what appears to be the truth on individual aspects, with the result that the overview has to be reassessed. But I believe that it is extremely important to start to see all of the evidence, covering all of the relevant specialist areas, and to overcome silo vision. Without such a wide approach, we do not stand much of a chance of getting to the truth about what works and where we should want to go next. This belief is strengthened by the fact that I believe that the current evidence shows that several highly influential theories about how law is supposed to affect behaviour, on which entire regulatory policies, liability systems and even legal systems are based, are clearly wrong, that other theories are correct and preferable, and therefore that adjustments in policy and legal structures are manifestly needed. In the rest of the book, I have tried to be scrupulously objective and to state a great deal of evidence in a scientifically objective manner, with extensive substantiation and references. But here and in the final chapter I will speak more freely.

III. The Thesis

I believe that businesses are nothing more than collections of human beings. It is also valid to speak of more inanimate corporate culture, and systemic effects, but all decisions are taken ultimately by humans: Even if trading decisions, for example, are taken by computers, the programming and decisions to rely on the programmes are clear human choices. Thus, if we wish to understand what drives the behaviour of individuals we need to look at cognitive and behavioural psychology. A significant amount of psychological research is now available, and it has begun to percolate into economics and political spheres (in order to 'nudge' people in certain directions). But its findings have not been applied 'head on' in legal and regulatory systems. Similarly, if we wish to understand how decisions are made in organisations, we should look at learning on how organisations are structured and how they operate.

If we look at these areas, we find that the conclusions form a flat rejection of the theories of deterrence and economic rational actors that have dominated tort law, criminal law, regulatory systems and regulatory enforcement in recent decades. If that conclusion is even half true, it has huge implications for tort law and systems of private or public enforcement of law that claim to have regulatory effect. The current approaches and even architectures of such systems should logically be revised.

The issue of how to ensure businesses observe the rules has become highly important and topical. Mass production can affect the safety of multitudes of people, banks can mis-sell products to millions of people who do not want or need them, and the entire viability of the global economic system can be put at risk. So it is important to worry about how

regulation or liability systems work, and to be sure that they do work. Did the global financial crisis demonstrate that regulation does not work? I do not think so: I think that the
prior regulatory system was not going to be effective because it was not designed to be so,
as explained in chapter 20. We need to look in detail at regulatory systems to see if they
need improving, and this book aims to compare a number of different regulatory systems,
and self-regulatory systems. It also looks at a number of different enforcement policies of
regulatory agencies, to compare them. Lessons can be learned from comparing all these
systems and policies.

But the realisation that systems of rules, whether liability or regulatory rules, might not
be enough to ensure our ongoing safety raises the question of what would do so. At that
point, the issue of culture arises. We have gone beyond a question of whether an individual
trader, such as Enron or BCCI, might have a defective culture. We are now having to address
the fact that entire industries, such as finance, might have a rotten culture, and on a global
scale. Can law affect culture? Not much. It's really the other way round. So what can? It
has to come from inside. So, if we want corporate behaviour to protect our economies and
civilisation, what should we do?

So this inquiry seems timely, and there are at least five further reasons. First, extensive
and sophisticated regulatory systems have been constructed over the past 50 years or so, led
at EU level by measures aimed at effecting a single EU market and at UK national level by
the need to regulate industries as they were privatised. But no systemic overview analysis
has been undertaken.

Second, the past 10 years or so have seen a period of very significant change in British
policy and practice on enforcement, its techniques and objectives. Major reforms have led
to the appearance in the past three years of new enforcement powers, and new enforcement
policies by many public regulatory bodies. Although the general policies have been set by
government, they have led to a diversity of approaches between regulators, and this book
seeks to take overarching review. One of the purposes of this book is to examine the numerous changes that have occurred.

Third, the approaches to enforcement that different enforcers have taken emerged
historically out of assumptions on the relevance of policies such as deterrence and criminal
sanctions, but have evolved over time towards softer and more multi-layered approaches.
Some agencies have undertaken research (usually merely surveys) on the effectiveness of
either their enforcement activities or of what drives compliance by the targets that they seek
to influence. There is a need to undertake a holistic review of both that research and of the
scientific evidence base on compliance and enforcement. Such a review may in turn highlight
gaps in knowledge, and in the evidence for certain regulatory and enforcement practices.
One aspect may be whether there is a disconnect between, on the one hand, enforcement
design and practice and, on the other hand, academic theory that much regulation is now
de-centered, involving multiple influences and stakeholders.

Fourth, long-running and largely unresolved debates, at both EU and national levels,
have occurred on redress, especially collective redress, which have highlighted the question
of whether better means of delivering redress can be identified than cumbersome, slow
and expensive collective private actions that are ineffective in delivering mass redress to
multiple individuals, especially consumers who typically incur levels of detriment that are
individually small. Given that some enforcers in UK have developed highly effective mass
redress techniques and policies in the past three years, it is timely to investigate them.

Overall, and the fifth reason for undertaking the current inquiry, it can be seen that a significant amount of change has occurred in recent years. Enforcement policy has been both officially stated and changed, moving clearly from an authoritarian approach to an approach based on responsive and restorative justice, and focusing on outcomes, achieving desired behaviour and redress. The focus of many regulatory bodies has significantly widened, and new means of bringing about redress have emerged through a combined deployment of regulatory powers and ombudsmen schemes. In some sectors, no blame cultures have been found to be vital in supporting the sharing of information that is vital for collective learning, performance and improvement. That lesson has been applied effectively in civil aviation but it seems that it cannot be applied in healthcare. Yet an authoritarian deterrent approach is still clung to in some sectors, without producing notable improvements in behaviour. In financial services, a lax regulatory system has been found wanting, and has been strengthened, but regulators realise that it is business culture that is vital to achieving acceptable behaviour, and not regulatory requirements. So how can the right sorts of culture be achieved? The objective is, therefore, to evaluate the changes, both individually and on a comparative and collective basis across different sectors and authorities. This leads on to seeing if general lessons can be learned that could apply to all business sectors as a general policy on regulation, enforcement, compliance, culture and ethics.

IV. Structure of the Book

Part A summarises the findings of cognitive and behavioural psychology that seem relevant to how human beings make decisions, individually and in groups. A central finding is that people obey rules if the rule is created and applied in a fair manner, and if the substance of the rule corresponds to a value system that an individual holds.

Part B begins with an examination of the theory of deterrence, in relation to individual human activity and especially in economic theory in relation to corporate entities. It also notes criticisms of both deterrence theory as a sole basis for enforcement and of economic theory as a sole basis for understanding the behaviour of entities and the people who work in them. Two examples of the application deterrence theory in legal systems are then examined. First, the phenomenon of private enforcement of law being a priority in a legal system, as illustrated by the United States of America. Second, the public enforcement of competition law, as exemplified by the European Commission's current policy.

Part C examines public regulation, as it exists in the United Kingdom. Chapter eight outlines the purposes of public regulation, noting the basic objective of affecting the way in which certain legal activities are performed, and then identifying the principal means by which regulation is enforced. Chapter nine outlines the extensive landscape of public regulatory bodies in the UK, and the development of regulatory policy in recent years, leading to the adoption of formal enforcement policies by the leading regulatory authorities. It charts the Better Regulation movement through the 2005 Hampton Report and the Macrory Report on enforcement, involving a widening of the goals of enforcement to support compliance and redress. It then notes a series of changes in the regulatory landscape, and further changes in obligations imposed on regulators by law and by the Regulators' Code.

Chapter 10 notes various aspects of how policy on criminal enforcement has evolved in the UK in ways that parallel and complement developments in regulatory enforcement policy. The purpose of sentencing in criminal law has widened the focus from punishment to reducing re-offending, and to take account of the position and needs of victims. It also notes the development of policy on expanding criminal enforcement to cover not just sanctions on offenders but also ensuring the delivery of compensation to victims.

Chapter 11 sets out the distinctive theory of enforcement that is widely used by public regulatory authorities, responsive regulation, and some examples of how it is applied, before noting the expansion of the concepts into open and meta regulation. In theories developed over the past three decades especially by Australian and British scholars, the focus has changed from deterrence and enforcement to strategies and means to support compliance with rules. In particular, it notes various parallels in moving away from command and control and deterrent approaches to more responsive approaches. Chapter 12 examines the policies issued by the OECD on regulatory enforcement, which similarly mirror, and largely adopt, those of the UK. A major development in UK regulatory policy has been a requirement for regulatory authorities to issue statements of their regulatory and enforcement policies. Chapters 13 to 15 examine the enforcement policies of individual agencies. The issue is to see what enforcement policies they adopt, and how their approaches conform to general theories and to government policy. Many policies and official approaches to enforcement have been reformed as a result of the changes noted in the previous chapter. The analysis identifies some broadly similar approaches but the absence of a uniform approach. Competition enforcement policy is almost alone in adhering firmly to deterrence, whereas others adopt responsive, soft and outcomes-based approaches. It also notes that some authorities have had notable success in delivering redress where particular powers and policies have been adopted. Chapter 13 covers environmental protection, financial services, communications, energy, water, railways, civil aviation, legal services, and health and safety in the workplace. Chapters 14 and 15 cover consumer protection and competition respectively, against the background of a series of research studies undertaken by the two halves of the same agency. The research is set out at some length, partly because it is not widely known, and partly because its findings somewhat contradict the enforcement policies that the relevant agency subsequently issued, whereas the findings are consistent with much of the psychology literature. Chapter 16 draws conclusions from the evidence set out in this Part.

Regulatory systems frequently have significant involvement of groups of businesses, especially through trade associations or other structures (co-regulation) or rest largely on structures operated by trade associations with minimal involvement of public agencies (self-regulation). Part D examines these types of structures in chapter 17, along with the use of external official standards and accreditation techniques. Leading examples are the Advertising Standards Authority, the Pharmaceutical Medicines Code of Practice Authority, the Franchise and Leasing association, and a series of sectoral Codes of Practice, subject to the Consumer Codes Approval Scheme. In view of the fact that 'regulation' by external public agencies only provides half of the picture, the other half, of how companies aim to achieve compliance through internal means, is examined in chapter 18.

Part E looks at a series of regulatory systems by describing their architectural features and techniques. Chapter 19 focuses on some contrasting systems that all aim at achieving safety, such as general product safety, medicines, health and safety in the workplace and civil aviation. It also notes that regulatory systems are built around business management systems. Almost all of these systems have evolved to operate on the basis of a constant flow and evaluation of data. Regulatory systems that have been designed to operate on an ex ante or ex post basis are obsolete: These systems can only operate effectively by using both approaches, and by involving *all* actors, at every level, as essential cogs in a large holistic system. The systems illustrate the reality of meta and decentered regulation. The civil aviation sector is highly relevant. That sector has learnt that safety can only be underpinned if every individual feeds back all relevant pieces of information on a constant basis, and that behaviour can only be achieved in a 'no blame' environment. This observation and practice have huge implications for the design and operation of regulatory systems, and their compliance and 'enforcement' components.

By contrast, chapter 20 examines the steps that have been taken to address the global financial crisis after its 2008 near meltdown. A series of regulatory changes were instituted, but the striking conclusion is that a regulatory system cannot operate effectively unless it functions in the context of a satisfactory culture.

Accordingly, we examine in chapter 21 learning on business cultures, and how they ultimately seem to come down to ethics. Thus, a series of steps recommend themselves in relation to building an ethical culture for business, on which regulatory systems can be founded with greater confidence. Chapter 22 summarises the findings and recommendations.

Since many markets are now global, regulatory and enforcement systems have to operate globally. Much more needs to be done to recognise and build globally effective regulatory operation. In relation to enforcement and compliance, markedly different enforcement systems operate, for example as between the USA and Europe. This book views enforcement and compliance as being based on the values of the society within which the system operates. It advocates particular values in relation to Europe. In so doing, it explains why different (more punitive) values exist in the USA, but it inherently challenges such values. Given the fact that culture is a localised phenomenon, it focuses essentially on the UK, and does not assume that the same approach should necessarily apply elsewhere. However, it does provoke questions about whether and why different approaches might be justified elsewhere.

This book is not a complete exegesis of the way in which legal rules and systems act on the behaviour of organisations. It will not set out every public power (such as regulatory enforcement powers and sanctions) and rules of private law (such as the law of tort). Its primary concern is to note a series of major changes that have occurred in many different relevant fields, and to identify general trends so as try to knit broad techniques and strands together as revealing a way forward in understanding and designing control of corporate behaviour in the twenty-first century.

V. Illustrations

The problems that need to be answered can be illustrated by a series of vignettes taken from my personal experience. Whilst this book follows an academic trajectory, in undertaking the research reproduced here I have kept in mind practical problems such as these, in order to seek to ensure that the scholarly thought produces outcomes that can provide practical answers to the real life problems that people faced in these situations.

The first story was in the 1980s, when the senior management UK subsidiary of a pharmaceutical company headquartered in another European state (that no longer exists in its then form) decided to withdraw a licenced product since it appeared that the information that was filtering in from practitioners (in various countries) about its use indicated that it probably gave rise to an unexpected but serious adverse risk. At that stage, the pharmacovigilance system was not as sophisticated as it has since become in a number of respects, including the extent of the involvement of regulators, but the basic situation was that the drug was clearly effective for the condition for which it was licenced and data had begun to emerge that it might not be adequately safe. Interpretation of the available data was at that stage a matter of sophisticated technical judgement. The UK management discussed it with the foreign headquarters, which initially disagreed with the UK managers' views, as did the US headquarters. After a long struggle, the drug was about to be licenced in USA. The commercial implications of withdrawing the drug were significant for the company. There was a major internal battle between senior managers. The views of the UK management prevailed, as they insisted that they were responsible for drug safety in the UK and it was their decision that the drug should be withdrawn in the UK. It was therefore withdrawn worldwide, which provoked many objections from doctors and patients. Why did the UK management prevail in this decision? Firstly, the UK management comprised three individuals, who were all medically qualified and formed the same professional view on the safety issue. As a 'gang of three' they supported each other and formed a combined and unmoveable front with more senior colleagues abroad. As medical professionals, they felt that the ethical values that had been instilled in them all their professional lives were fundamental and non-negotiable and trumped the commercial considerations of their employment. Such values were supported by a peer group of colleagues, which was then emerging as the Faculty of Pharmaceutical Physicians, in which it was no accident that the three of them played a prominent role. Their reputations, and those of the company, were enhanced by their 'difficult' decision.

The second story remains in the pharmaceutical sector and contrasts attitudes between firms and regulators in the USA and EU at around the mid-1990s. I attended a large internal conference in an American drug company, at which one of the speakers was a senior official of the Federal Drug Administration (FDA). He began his remarks by congratulating the company on the close working relationship between the FDA and the company. At that point, an in-house lawyer leant over to me and said 'We escort them onto the campus and we escort them off. They only get to see and discuss what is agreed in advance. We don't share things with them unless we have to.' That approach contrasts with what I had observed in numerous different contexts of the relationship between the UK regulator (now MHRA) and firms in the UK (even the same firm as just mentioned in its US context). The relationship was based on professional respect and trust, since most of those taking part on both sides were qualified in medicine or pharmacy. They had no difficulty in sharing and openly discussing the technical information, and agreeing the right course of action. The problem that both sides faced was more to do with the inexpert attitudes of politicians and the media, and how best to explain their technical decisions to such non-experts. The first question that those interlocutors would ask was 'Who is to blame?' To those who were grappling with complex technical issues, lack of complete data, and a serious gap in comprehension and communication, a simplistic framing of an issue in terms of blame was simply irrelevant, and did nothing to aid public understanding, reassurance or protection.

The third story was a conversation with a senior lawyer in a multinational company arising out of my questioning on how they tried to prevent cartels and how they detected them. He (and many others) said that they have extensive internal education, compliance and checking programmes. He said that, despite their best efforts, they do very occasionally uncover cartels. In his particular industry, it appeared that such illegal behaviour might occur as instigated by the manager of a subsidiary—other sectors appear to produce different behaviour, including some that have very low risk of cartels or foreign bribery. His company had learnt that such behaviour could sometimes be identified by internal due diligence, such as on corporate structure reconstructions or sales. I asked him if the company sacked the managers concerned. He said that they absolutely wanted to do that—the managers' behaviour was completely contrary to company policy and shared morality—but they were in fact *prevented* from doing so, because there would ensue years of dealing with enforcement authorities over fines on the company (which they thought would have little benefit) and litigation over paying damages, and it was necessary for the company to retain the knowledge of the only individuals who knew what had happened. He was incensed at the injustice of this situation. Things would be better if the authorities could adopt a collaborative approach with the company in finding and responding to wrongdoing, and support swift action in which every aspect was resolved quickly and at the same time. These factors still seem significant in how to support an ethical decision.

The fourth story concerns a partner in an Australian law firm, again in the 1980s. One of his major clients faced a possible serious safety risk with one of its major products (say in the food industry). The available data was, as usual, unclear in establishing the size of the risk. The issue was whether the product line should be withdrawn or not. This was before legislation emerged on notifications to the regulatory authority and recall obligations. The commercial implications of withdrawal were immense. The managing director of the company refused to take the decision on whether the product should be withdrawn or not, and insisted that his external lawyer took it, by looking solely at the safety and legal information and risks, and not at the commercial aspects. The lawyer and his partners were highly uncomfortable over their own risk of negligence liability and insurance cover. But he took the decision. Again, such an arrangement still appears valid in supporting an ethical decision, by avoiding a conflict of interest, although more sophisticated standing arrangements might be in place now.

The fifth story concerns a transport company in which two engineers who were working on a high platform fell off and were badly injured. Subsequent investigation found that neither of them were wearing safety harnesses, in clear breach of company policy and rules. Further, it transpired that the senior engineer habitually failed to wear safety harnesses, since he believed that they interfered with his work. The other engineer was a junior person who was heavily influenced by the more senior colleague. The company was concerned that its internal procedures had allowed the fact that failure to wear safety harnesses had gone unchecked, especially over some time, and 'put its hands up', responding openly in its dealings with the Health and Safety Executive to improve its system and performance in future. It concluded that the senior engineer's attitude was unacceptable and fired him, whilst retaining and supporting the junior one.

The sixth and seventh stories are contrasts. One occurred recently in the operating theatre of a well-known provincial hospital. A trainee doctor asked the consultant surgeon 'Are you sure you are taking out the correct kidney?' The senior male consultant shouted at the junior female and continued what he was doing. No-one else present said anything further or checked the position—but the junior was correct, and the healthy kidney was removed whilst the diseased one was left untouched. That situation can be compared with a conversation I had recently with a middle-ranking pilot. He confirmed that pilots are free to fly a large commercial airliner virtually in any way they see fit, but their decisions are supported by highly sophisticated information technology systems, operating parameters and reminders. Crucially, it is expected that any pilot of any seniority can question and check with a colleague, including a very senior colleague, and this would not be taken as criticism but as normal and expected behaviour. Language would be used that is low key and non-critical. The exchange could operate as a learning opportunity for a junior person or an opportunity for a more senior person to review and justify an action. The prevailing culture was regarded as the critical component. This was confirmed by the experience of the pilot to whom I spoke that when he went home and questioned why his wife had taken a certain action when she drove their car, the same language would be taken as critical!

The final story takes the issue of culture further. It is the well-known one of the financial services industry over the past decade or so, which needs little elaboration. Many have questioned how a whole industry can lose contact with the morality of the society in which it is embedded, such that so much everyday practice (systematic behaviour, such as lending mortgages that could never realistically be repaid, then selling and buying such worthless securities; selling payment protection insurance products to those who did not need them; fixing foreign exchange and other dealing rates; claiming that culture had been 'fixed' when it had not and serious infringements were still being carried on) that was internally regarded as normal and laudable was what the external society viewed as being blatantly immoral. Further, how did such practice escape both internal and external attention, and as adding up to behaviour that was so risky as to endanger the integrity of the global financial system? The response has to include strengthening the regulatory system, but that is not enough to affect the day-to-day behaviour of so many workers in an entire industry. How can regulators or others affect mass behaviour? Will it be adequate for global regulatory bodies or an impressively large group of judges[6] to insist that bankers adopt an ethical culture? Will preaching at bankers be enough? Will establishing a professional institute for bankers be enough? Will the morale of those involved in the industry be undermined by an extended period of public vilification, such that the quantity and quality of recruitment will suffer, and bankers will drown under a regulatory burden and prefer to take the low risk option of not lending? There are signs that all these problems remain unsolved in the financial services sector.

The purpose of these vignettes is to give some granularity to the theoretical analyses that follow, and to challenge the theoretical and policy ideas that emerge so that they have relevance to real life situations. How can society ensure that extensive business activities of many differing kinds are performed well and appropriately? How can people in businesses be supported so that they do the right thing? Is a repressive approach the answer to every situation, or just extreme situations that cannot otherwise be controlled or that demonstrate moral failure? If a deterrent policy is at best of limited relevance, what policy should support the vast majority of business activities, systems and people in doing the right thing? I ask readers to re-read the above vignettes after they have read this book, and see if their ideas have changed, and if there are strong pointers to ways forward—as I believe there are. What then needs to change?

---

[6] Meeting of the Law and Ethics in Finance Project, Bank of England, 20 January 2015.

Part A

Psychology

1

The Findings of Social Psychology

The invaluable contribution of psychology to law is centred on illuminating why humans either observe rules or break them. From there, it sheds light on the question of how best to motivate public rule-following behaviour, both in general and with respect to specific encounters with authorities, such as public regulators and employers.[1]

Evidence from psychological observation and experiments has accumulated over past decades, but has yet to be fully recognised in legal scholarship and systems. It percolated into the theory of economics (as behavioural economics) and was to some extent implicit in the compliance theories of the 2000s. However, it is important to consider the psychology literature on its own terms,[2] since it prompts fresh ideas about enforcement, and particularly about the design of regulatory systems. This is particularly so since, in general, the evidence lends little support to the notion that the external imposition of 'command and control' or deterrent sanctions is particularly successful in generating compliance, save, as noted below, where supervision and surveillance are virtually continual and the perceived identification of an infringement will be identified and lead to adverse consequences.

We will first summarise research findings on relevant aspects of general behaviour and then look specifically at the conditions for maximising compliance. The first striking observation, which challenges the rational choice theory discussed in chapter two below, is that people tend to comply with the law even when a rational calculus would predict differently, when the threat of sanctions is significantly low.[3] Widespread compliance occurs 'just because it is the law'.[4] There is, therefore, a fundamental conflict over whether humans are naturally, or principally, creatures who have law-abiding normative commitment[5] or are cold self-motivated calculators, or something else.

---

[1] J Darley, TR Tyler and K Bilz, 'Enacting Justice: The Interplay of Individual and Institutional Perspectives' in M Hogg and J Cooper (eds), *The SAGE Handbook of Social Psychology* (London, Sage, 2003); TR Tyler, *Why People Obey the Law* (Newhaven CT, Yale University Press, 2006).

[2] See generally T Gilovich, D Griffin and D Kahneman (eds), *Heuristics and Biases: The Psychology of Intuitive Judgment* (Cambridge, Cambridge University Press, 2002) (compiling research on how people make judgements); D Kahneman and A Tversky (eds), *Choices, Values, and Frames* (Cambridge, Cambridge University Press, 2000).

[3] HL Ross, *Deterring the Drinking Driver: Legal Policy and Social Control. Reviewed and updated Edition.* (Lexington MA, Lexington Books, 1984); TR Tyler, 'Justice and Leadership Endorsement' in R Lau and D Sears (eds), *Political Cognition* (Hillsdale NJ, Lawrence Erlbaum and Associates, 1986) 257–78; Tyler (n 1).

[4] I Ayres and J Braithwaite, *Responsive Regulation: Transcending the Deregulation Debate* (New York, Oxford University Press, 1992).

[5] D Easton, 'The Perception of Authority and Political Change' in CJ Friedrich (ed), *Authority* (Cambridge MA, Harvard University Press, 1958); JR French, Jr and B Raven, 'The Bases of Social Power' in D Cartwright (ed), *Studies in Social Power* (Ann Arbor MI, University of Michigan Press, 1959); TR Tyler and EA Lind, 'A Relational Model of Authority in Groups' in MP Zanna (ed), *Advances in Experimental Social Psychology*, Vol 25 (New York, Academic Press, 1992) 115–91; TR Tyler, 'The Psychology of Legitimacy: A Relational Perspective on Voluntary Deference to Authorities' (1997) 1(4) *Personality and Social Psychology Review* 323–45.

I. Individuals Learning the Law

It has long been thought that individuals' capacity for moral understanding develops and is capable of development, as does physical capacity. Kohlberg proposed six levels of development, grouped into three levels: Pre-conventional morality (obedience and punishment orientation, and self-interest orientation), conventional morality (inter-personal accord and conformity, and authority and social-order maintaining orientation), and post-conventional morality (social contract orientation, and universal ethical principles).[6]

Engel has summarised the evidence on how humans learn and apply law.[7] He concludes that institutions are crucial in the process of transmitting both procedural knowledge (normative proficiency) and declarative knowledge (normative expectations). It is not the case, as many legal theorists have asserted, that addressees must know the rules. It has been empirically demonstrated that the degree of knowledge is not correlated with a high degree of implementation.[8] Some human beings' behaviour is guided by custom rather than law.[9]

Engel noted that both the individual and society benefit from the willingness of the individual to be guided by what she merely infers to be normative expectations originating in the legal order. He notes that this finding is consistent with three findings on how humans develop primary learning. First, neurobiology suggests that the brain gradually constructs models of the physical world. Second, developmental psychology suggests that a child tries to make sense of a new element from the environment by assimilating it to categories it already possesses. Third, learning psychology suggests the development of use of language and the capacity for abstract reasoning, planned experiment and explicit instruction. Learning also occurs by observation: This is vicarious and involves learning through behavioural patterns, judgemental standards, cognitive competences and generic rules for creating new types of behaviour. Declaratory knowledge is addictive. Procedural knowledge is integrative.

Engel continues that primary learning of norms is part and parcel of general primary learning. Consequently, it would be inappropriate to analyse the law in isolation. Primary learning is iterative: Later steps build on earlier ones. In order to be effective, institutions must be present over an extended period of time.

Since primary learning is associative, Engel notes that this implies that successful institutions do not teach abstract rules, but present the addressee with graphic situations. Institutions can manipulate attention, and can affect the storage of what has been learned in memory. The two critical parameters are elaboration and retrieval. Information is stored better the more intensely it has been elaborated. Specifically, the number of associative clues is critical.[10] Institutions therefore work best if they provide the addressee with several

---

[6] L Kohlberg, *Essays in Moral Development 1-II* (London, Harper and Row, 1981, 1984). But see also C Gilligan, *In a Different Voice* (Cambridge MA, Harvard University Press, 1982).

[7] The following section is based on C Engel, 'Learning the Law' (2008) 4(3) *Journal of Institutional Economics* 275–97.

[8] A Diekmann, *Die Befolgung von Gesetzen. Empirische Untersuchungen zu einer rechtssoziologischen Theorie* (Berlin, Duncker & Humbolt, 1980) 38, 125f.

[9] WG Sumner, *Folkways: A Study of the Sociological Importance of Usages, Manners, Customs, Mores, and Morals* (Boston MA, Ginn, 1907); E Schlicht, *On Custom in the Economy* (Oxford, Clarendon Press, 1998).

[10] JR Anderson, *Learning and Memory: An Integrated Approach* (New York, Wiley, 2000) 213, 70f.

occasions for rehearsal. While the law does have an influence on primary learning, the key institutional forces that affect it are different: The family;[11] kindergarten and school; the church; the institutions for professional training,[12] universities or apprenticeships; and institutions for non-professional training like driving schools, dancing schools, military or social service.

Engel notes that primary learning must be accompanied by secondary learning, to account for situations in which rules change or individuals leave their contexts of origin. Retrieval is more likely the more associative cues are attached to a particular piece of knowledge. Memory is reconstructive, not merely recalling.[13] The storage of the new normative expectations can be impeded by interference.[14] Ironically, interference is more likely the closer the new normative expectation resembles its predecessor. Consequently, where new expectations are significantly different from previous rules, legal reform is more promising if the expectations can still be handled by the existing normative proficiency (and the new rules do not trigger reactance).[15]

It is not necessary that humans are familiar with every legal rule, or with the many intricacies that arise in the interpretation of rules, many of which may be complex: That is the job of lawyers. The addressees' knowledge of the law can therefore be tacit, implicit and practical.[16] What is necessary, Engel concludes, is that humans have gained a sense of justice and an understanding that legal intervention aims at governance of behaviour in the society, as one means of communication between citizens and the state. Given the existence of pluralism in a state, individuals' views must be negotiated and an accommodation reached, that will command general commitment. Hence, the existence of formal procedures for deliberation and rule production are crucial, as are the fact that they must be transparent and fair.

When faced with a particular situation, the individual may draw on exemplars of a social norm or custom as a means of guiding social compliance and normative orientation.[17] Thus, she knows what the law expects her to do in a certain context. She can extend this knowledge to different contexts by way of analogy. The negligence standard is a clear example of a guide for 'appropriate' behaviour. The predominant mechanism for learning for normative expectations is observation. Engel concludes that transaction costs would sky-rocket if formal judicial action were the major enforcement technology.[18]

---

[11] K Kreppner, 'Einfluss von Familienkommunikation auf das Entstahen von Vorläufern des Rechtsempfindens bei Kleinstkindern' in E-J Lamoe (ed), *Zur Entwisklung von Rechtsbewusstsein* (Frankfurt, Suhrkamp, 1997) 341–70.

[12] TM Newcomb, *Personality and Social Change* (New York, Dryden, 1943).

[13] FC Bartlett, *Remembering: A Study in Experimental and Social Psychology* (Cambridge, Cambridge University Press, 1932) 204, 206; Anderson (n 10) 285–87.

[14] Anderson (n 10) 240f, 249.

[15] SS Brehm and JW Brehm, *Psychological Reactance: A Theory of Freedom and Control* (New York, Academic Press, 1981).

[16] M Polanyi, *Personal Knowledge: Towards a Post-Critical Philosophy* (Chicago, University of Chicago Press, 1958).

[17] A Bandura, *Social Foundations of Thought and Action: A Social Cognitive Theory* (Englewood Cliffs NJ, Prentice-Hall, 1986) 103; Anderson (n 10) 348.

[18] Engel (n 7) 275–97.

II. Making Decisions

Tversky and Kahneman identify two 'systems' of thinking found in the human brain: A fast heuristic approach (System 1) and a slower system that is capable of reasoning, is cautious, but at least in some people is also lazy (System 2).[19] Dividing types into Econs and Humans, they state that Econs do not have a System 1, but Humans do.

The brain uses resources in as economical a manner as possible. If it realises that the individual faces similar tasks, the brain reacts with expertisation. Instead of composing all of the individual steps separately each time an individual is confronted with a situation, the brain stores the entire chain of mental or physical steps as one unit. The heuristic associative shortcut is described by Kahneman as the impulsive and intuitive System 1.[20] Even a single cue may be enough to set the entire programme into motion,[21] so a particular prime may produce particular behaviour. Behaviour is, therefore, patterned[22] or even automated.[23] Hence, after a legal reform, or after a learned pattern of non-compliance, a previous regime must be deactivated. Conscious control is required to override System 2 when a task is novel; when a task is critical, difficult or dangerous; when a habitual approach to a task needs over-riding; and when prioritising competing tasks.[24]

However, in repeated decision making, individuals who have learned a repetitive heuristic routine do change it when confronted with new information on choice.[25] The new evidence has to compensate prior knowledge before individuals decide to abandon their routine.

Sunstein has summarised the central findings[26] of recent social science research on how people make decisions. He organises the findings under four headings: Inertia and procrastination; framing and presenting; social influences; and difficulties in assessing probability.[27] In addition to prompting ideas on compliance with rules, Sunstein notes that these[28] empirical findings suggest choices for the appropriate design of effective, low-cost,

---

[19] A Tversky and D Kahneman, 'Judgment under Uncertainty: Heuristics and Biases' (1974) 185 no 4157 *Science* 1124–31; D Kahneman, *Thinking, Fast and Slow* (London, Allen Lane, 2011).

[20] Kahneman, ibid 48.

[21] DO Hebb, *The Organization of Behavior: A Neuropsychological Theory* (New York, Wiley, 1949) 157; Anderson (n 10) 324f; W Singer, 'Hirnentwicklung—neuronale Plastiztät—Lernen' in R Klinke and S Silbernagl (eds), *Lehrbuch der Physiologie* (Stuttgart, Thieme, 2005) 743–56, 751.

[22] JR Anderson, D Bothell, MD Byrne and C Lebiere, 'An Integrated Theory of the Mind' (2004) 111 *Psychological Review* 1036–60, 1038.

[23] Anderson (n 10) 310.

[24] LD Loukopoulos, RK Dismukes and I Barshi, *The Multitasking Myth. Handling Complexity in Real-World Operations* (Farnham, Ashgate, 2009).

[25] T Betsch and S Haberstroh, 'The Routines of Decision Making' Preface in T Betsch and S Haberstroh (eds), *The Routines of Decision Making* (Mahway NJ, Lawrence Erlbaum, 2005); T Betsch, S Lindow, C Engel, C Ulshöfer and J Kleber, 'Has The World Changed? My Neighbor Might Know: Effects of Social Context on Routine Deviation' (manuscript, 2012) 2012.

[26] See generally Gilovich, Griffin and Kahneman (n 2) (compiling research on how people make judgements); Kahneman and Tversky (n 2).

[27] The following summary is taken from CR Sunstein, 'Empirically Informed Regulation' (2011) 78(4) *University of Chicago Law Review*.

[28] Sunstein, ibid.

choice-preserving approaches to disclosure requirements, default rules and simplification.[29] The key findings are:

A. Inertia and Procrastination

Individuals will go to great lengths to conform to the attitudes and beliefs of those around them, even when conforming violates known facts or one's own ideological worldview.[30] Default rules often have a large effect on social outcomes. People have a preference for the status quo.[31] When people are asked whether they want to opt in to a retirement plan, the level of participation is far lower than if they are asked whether they want to opt out. Procrastination can have significant adverse effects. When people are informed of the benefits or risks of engaging in certain actions, they are far more likely to act in accordance with that information if they are simultaneously provided with clear, explicit information about how to do so.[32] The inertia affect is linked to finding that preferences are influenced by the temporal distance between costs and benefits.[33]

B. Framing and Presentation

People can be influenced by how information is presented or 'framed'. Information that is vivid and salient can have a larger impact on behaviour than information that is statistical

[29] Sunstein, ibid.
He refers to WJ Congdon, JR Kling and S Mullainathan, *Policy and Choice: Public Finance through the Lens of Behavioral Economics* (Brookings Institute, 2011) (describing implications of behavioural economics for public finance); P Diamond and H Vartiainen (eds), *Behavioral Economics and Its Applications* (Princeton, 2007) (examining behavioural dimensions of public economics; economic development; law and economics; health, wage determination, and organisation economics); H Schwartz, *A Guide to Behavioral Economics* (Higher Education, 2008) (providing an introduction to behavioural economics for a general audience). Office of Information and Regulatory Affairs (OIRA) has provided guidance on disclosure and simplification as regulatory tools: See CR Sunstein, Administrator, ORIA, *Memorandum for the Heads of Executive Departments and Agencies, Disclosure and Simplification as Regulatory Tools*, online at http://www.whitehouse.gov/sites/default/files/omb/assets/inforeg/disclosure_principles.pdf.
[30] SE Asch, 'Effects of Group Pressure Upon the Modification and Distortion of Judgments' in H Guetzkow (ed), *Groups, Leadership and Men* (Pittsburgh PA, Carnegie Press, 1951) 177–81, 186 (demonstrating that roughly one-third of individuals will give an obviously incorrect answer to a simple line judgement task when that answer is given by the others in the room); GL Cohen, 'Party Over Policy: The Dominating Impact of Group Influence on Political Beliefs' (2003) 85 *Journal of Personality & Social Psychology* 808, 819 (support of a welfare policy among liberals and conservatives depended more on whether the policy was endorsed by a Republican or Democrat than on the content of the policy).
[31] W Samuelson and R Zeckhauser, 'Status Quo Bias in Decision Making' (1988) 1(7) *Journal of Risk & Uncertainty* 31–33.
[32] See H Leventhal, R Singer and S Jones, 'Effects of Fear and Specificity of Recommendation upon Attitudes and Behavior' (1965) 2 *Journal of Personality & Social Psychology* 20, 27; DW Nickerson and T Rogers, 'Do You Have a Voting Plan? Implementation Intentions, Voter Turnout, and Organic Plan Making' (2010) 21 *Psychological Science* 194, 198 (showing that people are significantly more likely to vote if asked to identify when and where they will vote); C Heath and D Heath, *Switch: How to Change Things When Change Is Hard* (New York, Broadway Books, 2010) 15–17.
[33] See SJ Hoch and GF Loewenstein, 'Time-Inconsistent Preferences and Consumer Self-Control' (1991) 17 *Journal of Consumer Research* 492, 497; D Kahneman and A Tversky, 'Choices, Values and Frames' (1984) 39 *American Psychologist* 341, at 143–44 (discussing how the framing of possible outcomes may change individual preferences); A Tversky and D Kahneman, 'The Framing of Decisions and the Psychology of Choice' (1985) 211 *Science* 453, 453–58 (discussing how the framing of prospects, contingencies and outcomes can lead to preference reversals).

and abstract. People often display loss aversion; they may well dislike losses more than they like corresponding gains.[34] Whether a change counts as a loss or a gain depends on the reference point, which can be affected by policy decisions, and which is often the status quo. In part for this reason, the initial allocation of a legal entitlement can affect people's valuations; those who have the initial allocation may value a good more than they would if the allocation were originally elsewhere, thus showing an endowment effect.[35]

Evidence suggests that people are averse to ambiguity: Accordingly, a policing response to this would be to increase random patrols in high risk areas, and to make them well publicised so as to influence people's 'perceived availability heuristics'.[36]

C. Social Influences

In multiple domains, individual behaviour is greatly influenced by the perceived behaviour of other people.[37] Perception of the norm in the pertinent community can affect risk taking, safety and health.[38] The norm conveys significant information about what ought to be done; for that reason, those who lack private information may follow the apparent beliefs

[34] See RH Thaler, D Kahneman, and JL Knetsch, 'Experimental Tests of the Endowment Effect and the Coase Theorem', in RH Thaler, *Quasi Rational Economics* 167, 169 (Russell Sage, 1991); AP McGraw, et al, 'Comparing Gains and Losses', (2010) 21 *Psychological Science* 1438, 1444; D Card and GB Dahl, 'Family Violence and Football: The Effect of Unexpected Emotional Cues on Violent Behavior' (2011) 126 *Quarterly Journal of Economics* 103, 105–06, 130–35 (finding an increase in domestic violence after a favoured team suffers from an upset loss in football).

[35] See Thaler, Kahneman and Knetsch, ibid at 167. A detailed literature discusses the mechanisms behind the endowment effect and the circumstances in which it will be found. See, for example, KM Marzilli Ericson and A Fuster, 'Expectations as Endowments: Evidence on Reference-Dependent Preferences from Exchange and Valuation Experiments' (2011) 126(4) *The Quarterly Journal of Economics* 1879–907; DG Pope and ME Schweitzer, 'Is Tiger Woods Loss Averse? Persistent Bias in the Face of Experience, Competition, and High Stakes' (2011) 101 *American Economic Review* 129, 132 (concluding that loss aversion costs each of the top twenty golfers in the world $640,000 a year on average).

[36] A Harel and U Segal, 'Criminal Law and Behavioural Law and Economics: Observations on the Neglected Role of Uncertainty in Deterring Crime' (1999) 1(12) *American Law and Economics Review* 276–312.

[37] See D Hirshleifer, 'The Blind Leading the Blind: Social Influence, Fads, and Informational Cascades', in M Tommasi and K Ierulli (eds), *The New Economics of Human Behavior* (Cambridge, Cambridge University Press, 1995) ('When people can observe one another's behavior, they very often end up making the same choices.') 188, 189; E Duflo and E Saez, 'The Role of Information and Social Interactions in Retirement Plan Decisions: Evidence from a Randomized Experiment' 118 *Quarterly Journal of Economics* 815, 839 (2003) (discussing retirement plan decisions); H Allcott, 'Social Norms and Energy Conservation' 5 (MIT Center for Energy and Environmental Policy Research Working Paper No 09-014, Oct 2009), online at http://web.mit.edu/ceepr/www/publications/workingpapers/2009-014.pdf (visited Apr 5, 2011) (discussing energy conservation); SE Carrell, M Hoekstra and JE West, *Is Poor Fitness Contagious? Evidence from Randomly Assigned Friends* 17 (NBER Working Paper No 16518, Nov 2010), online at http://www.nber.org/papers/w16518 (concluding that peers influence personal fitness and the likelihood of failing fitness requirements); AV Banerjee and E Duflo, 'Poor Economics: A Radical Rethinking of the Way to Fight Poverty' (New York, Public Affairs, 2011) 267–73 at 68 (noting that 'knowledge travels' and that friends and neighbours of those given a free bed net 'were also more likely to buy a net themselves'). For a general treatment with a great deal of evidence, including the finding that the probability of becoming obese increases when a close friend becomes obese, and that siblings and spouses were less powerful, see NA Christakis and JH Fowler, *Connected: The Surprising Power of Our Social Networks and How They Shape Our Lives* (London, Little, Brown, 2009).

[38] See US Department of Agriculture and US Department of Health and Human Sciences, Dietary Guidelines for Americans 2010 56, at http://www.health.gov/dietaryguidelines/dga2010/DietaryGuidelines2010.pdf (emphasising the relevance of 'social and cultural norms and values' for 'nutrition and physical activity').

and behaviour of relevant others, sometimes creating informational cascades.[39] In addition, people care about their reputations, and for that reason, they may be influenced by others so as not to incur their disapproval.[40] In some contexts, social norms can help create a phenomenon of compliance without enforcement—as, for example, when people comply with laws forbidding indoor smoking or requiring buckling of seat belts, in part because of social norms or the expressive function of those laws. People who act in groups do not attribute responsibility or blame to themselves, nor do they apportion it equally to each member of the group: They tend to see the group as being separate from themselves.[41]

In part because of social influences, people are more likely to cooperate with one another, and to contribute to the solution of collective action problems, than standard economic theory predicts.[42] People's willingness to cooperate is partly a product of an independent commitment to fairness; but it is partly a product of a belief that others will see and punish a failure to cooperate or to act fairly. Norms of reciprocity can be exceedingly important. In many contexts, the result is a situation in which people cooperate on the assumption that others are cooperating as well and might punish those who fail to do so.[43]

Further, Engel has pointed out that governance by law crucially depends on the activities of the, mostly non-legal, intermediaries who generate these compressions that inform the populace.[44] Legal institutions may have the option to bypass learning. This can be done in three ways: By switching to a different governance tool, by switching to a different addressee, or by redefining the governance task. The need for learning is eclipsed if the governance tool is self-enforcing. This is most prominent in regulation by technical code.[45]

Obtaining feedback is important. Thaler and Sunstein base an important design feature on this finding: 'Learning is most likely if people get immediate, clear feedback after each try. Long-term processes rarely provide good feedback.'[46] They suggest that the best way to help Humans improve their performance is to provide feedback. Well-designed systems tell people when they are doing well and when they are making mistakes.

---

[39] See D Hirshleifer (n 37) at 191 ('[A]n informational cascade occurs when the information implicit in predecessors' actions—or resulting payoffs—is so conclusive that a rational follower will unconditionally imitate them, without regard to information from other sources.'). See also Duflo and Saez (n 37) 815 at 819 (suggesting that social influences affect participation in retirement plans).

[40] T Kuran, *Private Truths, Public Lies: The Social Consequences of Preference Falsification* (Cambridge MA, Harvard University Press, 1997) 35–38.

[41] AG Greenwald and MR Banaji, *Blindspot: Hidden Biases of Good People* (New York, Delacorte Press, 2013); S Fein and S Spencer, 'Prejudice as Self-image Maintenance: Affirming the Self through Derogating Others' (1997) 73(1) *Journal of Personality and Social Psychology* 31–44; C Stangor (ed), *Stereotypes and Prejudice: Essential Readings* (Abingdon, Taylor & Francis, 2000).

[42] See CF Camerer, *Behavioral Game Theory: Experiments in Strategic Interaction* (Princeton, Princeton University Press, 2003) 46.

[43] See J Habyarimana et al, *Coethnicity: Diversity and the Dilemmas of Collective Action* (London, Russell Sage, 2009) 108–09; H Gintis et al, 'Moral Sentiments and Material Interests: Origins, Evidence, and Consequences' in H Gintis et al (eds), *Moral Sentiments and Material Interests: The Foundations of Cooperation in Economic Life* (Cambridge MA, MIT, 2005) 3, 8.

[44] Engel (n 7) 275–97.

[45] J Reidenberg, 'Governing Networks and Rule-Making in Cyberspace' (1996) 76 *Emory Law Journal* 911–30; J Boyle, 'Foucault in Cyberspace: Surveillance, Sovereignty, and Hardwired Censors' (1997) 66 *University of Cincinnati Law Review* 177–205; J Reidenberg, 'Lex Informatica: The Formulation of Information Policy Rules Through Technology' (1998) 76 *Texas Law Review* 553–93; L Lessig, *Code and Other Laws of Cyberspace* (New York, Basic Books, 1999).

[46] RH Thaler and CR Sunstein, *Nudge* (Newhaven CT, Yale University Press, 2008) 82.

Laboratory experiments find that use of a threat of punishment to enforce high returns in the trust game backfires.[47] Threat of sanctions also led to less return when the sanctions were imposed by the experimenter without the knowledge of the trusters.[48] In contrast, those subjects who forewent the punishment option in favour of strong trust found that their trust was rewarded.[49] People believe that others are more motivated by extrinsic incentives than they are themselves,[50] and the majority of experimental subjects threatened sanctions, even though the threats decreased their expected earnings.[51] Thus, there is a strong popular belief in the value of punishment, but it is in fact of little value.

Awrey and Kershaw suggest that studies on ranchers,[52] diamond merchants,[53] cotton merchants[54] and other traders,[55] engaged in long-term, repeat-play arrangements supports the intuition that the norms generating the most powerful behavioural constraints will be those where: (1) Violations are easily observable; (2) news of violations is easily disseminated within the relevant group; and (3) the group possesses the capacity and incentives to impose meaningful sanctions on violators.[56]

D. Difficulties in Assessing Probability

In some domains, people show unrealistic optimism.[57] The 'above average' effect is common;[58] many people believe that they are less likely than others to suffer from various misfortunes, including automobile accidents and adverse health outcomes.

As noted above, people often use heuristics, or mental shortcuts, when assessing risks.[59] For example, judgements about probability are often affected by whether a recent event comes readily to mind.[60] If an event is cognitively 'available', people may well overestimate

---

[47]   E Fehr and B Rockenbach, 'Detrimental Effects of Sanctions on Human Altruism' (2003) 422 (6928) *Nature* 137–40; E Fehr and JA List, 'The Hidden Costs and Returns of Incentives—Trust and Trustworthiness among CEOs' (2004) 2(5) *Journal of the European Economic Association* 743–71.

[48]   D Houser, E Xiao, K McCabe and V Smith, 'When Punishment Fails: Research on Sanctions, Intentions and Non-Cooperation' (2008) 62(2) *Games and Economic behavior* (2008) 509–32.

[49]   Fehr and Rockenbach (n 47) 137–40; Fehr and List (n 47) 743–71.

[50]   C Heath, 'On the Social Psychology of Agency Relationships: Lay Theories of Motivation Overemphasize Extrinsic Incentives' (1999) 78(1) *Organizational Behavior and Human Decision Processes* 25–62.

[51]   Fehr and List (n 47) 743–71.

[52]   R Ellickson, *Order Without Law: How Neighbors Settle Disputes* (Cambridge MA, Harvard University Press, 1994).

[53]   L Bernstein, 'Opting Out of the Legal System: Extralegal Contractual Relations in the Diamond Industry' (1992) 21(1) *The Journal of Legal Studies* 115–57.

[54]   L Bernstein, 'Private Commercial Law in the Cotton Industry: Creating Cooperation through Rules, Norms and Institutions' (2001) 99 *Michigan Law Review* 1724–90.

[55]   A Greif, 'Contract Enforceability and Economic Institutions in Early Trade: The Maghribi Traders' Coalition' (1993) 83. *American Economic Review* 525–48.

[56]   D Awrey and D Kershaw, 'Toward a More Ethical Culture in Finance: Regulatory and Governance Strategies' in N Morris and D Vines (eds), *Capital Failure; Rebuilding Trust in Financial Services* (Oxford, Oxford University Press, 2014).

[57]   See C Jolls, 'Behavioral Economics Analysis of Redistributive Legal Rules' (1998) 51 *Vanderbilt Law Review* 1653, 1659. See generally T Sharot, *The Optimism Bias: A Tour of the Irrationally Positive Brain* (Toronto, Knopf, 2011).

[58]   See ND Weinstein, 'Unrealistic Optimism about Susceptibility to Health Problems: Conclusions from a Community-Wide Sample' (1987) 10 *Journal of Behavioral Medicine* 481, 494.

[59]   See generally D Kahneman and S Frederick, 'Representativeness Revisited: Attribute Substitution in Intuitive Judgment' in Gilovich, Griffin and Kahneman (n 2) 49.

[60]   See A Tversky and D Kahneman, 'Availability: A Heuristic for Judging Frequency and Probability' (1973) 5 *Cognitive Psychology* 207, 221.

the risk. If an event is not cognitively available, people might well underestimate the risk.[61] In short, 'availability bias' can lead to inaccurate judgements about the probability of undesirable outcomes.[62]

In making judgements, people may neglect or disregard the issue of probability, especially when strong emotions are triggered.[63] When emotions are strongly felt, people may focus on the outcome and not on the probability that it will occur.[64]

III. Risk Taking

The problem of assessing probability leads on to various findings that suggest why risk taking occurs, which is relevant to contexts where the culture is to achieve particular goals (such as high profits or other targets). Ariely has suggested that many people are prepared to cheat, by fudging opposing emotions, especially on other people's behalf rather than their own, or if it reinforces their belief that they are more intelligent or popular than is objectively the case.[65] Nisbett and Borgida noted subjects' 'unwillingness to deduce the particular from the general was matched only by their willingness to infer the general from the particular.'[66] This leads to the illusion of validity, referred to by Tversky and Kahneman as WYSIATI, the phenomenon of concluding that What You See Is All There Is, and basing decisions on information that is immediately perceived.[67]

Studies of investment traders show that the most active traders had the poorest results, while the investors who traded least earned the highest returns.[68] Langevoort suggests that examination of the psychological motivations for insider trading have more to do with unconscious misperception or rationalisation than with greed or fraud, and that traditional legal definitions and responses should be reanalysed.[69] Kahneman notes:

> In the standard economic model, people take risks because the odds are favourable. But executives too easily fall victim to the planning fallacy. They make decisions based on delusional optimism, rather than on rational weighting of gains, losses, and probabilities. They overestimate the benefits

---

[61] See EU Weber, 'Experience-Based and Description-Based Perceptions of Long-Term Risk: Why Global Warming Does Not Scare Us (Yet)' (2006) 77 *Climatic Change* 103, 107–08.

[62] See P Slovic, B Fischhoff and S Lichtenstein, 'Cognitive Processes and Societal Risk Taking' in P Slovic (ed), *The Perception of Risk* 32, 37–38 (London, Earthscan, 2000); L Dubé-Rioux and JE Russo, 'An Availability Bias in Professional Judgment' (1988) 1 *Journal of Behavioral Decision Making* 223, 234.

[63] See GF Loewenstein et al, 'Risk as Feelings' (2001) 127 *Psychological Bulletin* 267, 280.

[64] See Y Rottenstreich and CK Hsee, 'Money, Kisses, and Electric Shocks: On the Affective Psychology of Risk' (2001) 12 *Psychological Science* 185, 185. For a demonstration that probability is often neglected with respect to things, but not with respect to money (without, however, emphasising the role of emotions), see AP McGraw, E Shafir and A Todorov, 'Valuing Money and Things: Why a $20 Item Can Be Worth More and Less than $20' (2010) 56 *Management Science* 816, 827. For a discussion of emotions and risk, see generally P Slovic (ed), *The Feeling of Risk: New Perspectives on Risk Perception* (London, Earthscan, 2010).

[65] D Ariely, *The (Honest) Truth about Dishonesty* (New York, HarperCollins, 2012).

[66] RE Nisbett and E Borgida, 'Attribution and the Psychology of Prediction' (1975) 32 *Journal of Personality and Social Psychology* 932–43.

[67] Kahneman (n 19) 85–88.

[68] BM Barber and T Odean, 'Trading is Hazardous to Your Wealth: The Common Stock Investment Performance of Individual Investors' (2002) 55 *Journal of Finance* 773–806.

[69] DC Langevoort, 'What Were They Thinking? Insider Trading and the Scienter Requirement' in SM Bainbridge (ed), *Research Handbook on Insider Trading* (Cheltenham, Edward Elgar Publishing, 2013).

and underestimate costs. They spin scenarios of success while overlooking the potential for mistakes and miscalculations. As a result, they pursue initiatives that are unlikely to come in on budget or on time or to deliver the expected returns—or even to be completed.[70,71]

The evidence suggests that optimistic bias plays a role—sometimes the dominant role—whenever individuals or institutions voluntarily take on significant risks. More often than not, risk takers underestimate the odds they face, and do not invest sufficient effort to find out what the odds are. Because they misread the risks, optimistic entrepreneurs often believe they are prudent, even when they are not. Their confidence in their future success sustains a positive mood that helps them obtain resources from others, raise the morale of their employees, and enhance their prospects of prevailing. When action is needed, optimism, even of the mildly delusional variety, may be a good thing.[72]

In explaining entrepreneurial delusions, Tversky and Kahneman describe Humans as being guided by the immediate emotional impact of gains and losses, not by long-term prospects of wealth and global utility (Prospect Theory).[73] Evaluation of gains and losses is relative to a neutral reference point (sometimes called an 'adaptation level'). A principle of diminishing sensitivity applies to both sensory dimensions and the evaluation of changes of wealth. A principle of loss aversion also applies: When directly compared or weighed against each other, losses loom larger than gains. There is asymmetry between the power of positive and negative expectations or experiences. This has an evolutionary history, since organisms that treat threats as more urgent then opportunities have a better chance to survive and reproduce.

The brain responds quickly even to purely symbolic threats. Bad emotions, bad parents, and bad feedback have more impact than good ones, and bad information is processed more thoroughly than good. The self is more motivated to avoid bad self-definitions than to pursue good ones. Bad impressions and bad stereotypes are quicker to form and more resistant to discontinuation than good ones.[74]

Goals are reference points, and affected by the fact that we are driven more strongly to avoid losses than to achieve gains. 'The ultimate currency that rewards or punishes is often emotional, a form of mental self-dealing that inevitably creates conflicts of interest when the individual acts as an agent on behalf of an organization.'[75]

Similarly, Thaler refers to 'mental accounts', noting that regret is an emotion and also a punishment that we administer to ourselves.

The only test of rationality is not whether a person's beliefs and preferences are reasonable, but whether they are internally consistent … Rationality is logical coherence—reasonable or not. Econs are rational by this definition, but there is overhwlming evidence that Humans cannot be. An Econ would not be susceptible to priming, WYSIATI, narrow framing, the inside view, or preference reversals, which Humans cannot consistently avoid.[76]

---

[70] Footnote from source material: D Kahneman and D Lovallo, 'Delusions of Success: How Optimism Undermines Executives' Decisions' (2003) 81 *Harvard Business Review* 56–63.

[71] Kahneman (n 19) 252.

[72] ibid 256.

[73] Kahneman (n 19) 271ff.

[74] RF Baumeister, E Bratislovasky, C Finkenauer and KD Vohs, 'Bad is Stronger Than Good' (2001) 5 *Review of General Psychology* 323.

[75] Kahneman (n 19) 342.

[76] Kahneman, ibid 411.

Overall, the findings of Tversky, Kahneman, Thaler, Sunstein and others constitute a fundamental challenge to the 'law and economics' approach (discussed in chapter two) of defining human rationality as coherent. The law and economics approach appears impossibly restrictive in demanding adherence to rules of logic that a finite mind is not able to implement. Instead, they point to research showing that Humans are not well described by the rational-agent model. That raises major implications over the rationality of deterrence theory (also discussed in chapter two).

IV. Conditions for Maximising Compliance

Stopping to think can overcome the operation of the short-cut heuristic: Contemplation or reflection can enhance decision making.[77]

Kagan, Gunningham and Thornton have summarised the socio-legal evidence on personal motivation and behaviour as follows:

> Sociological explanations of law-abidingness in individuals (among taxpayers, for example) suggest three basic motivations.[78] One is fear of detection and punishment by government enforcement agents. The second is fear of humiliation or disgrace in the eyes of family members or social peers. The third is an internalized sense of duty, that is the desire to conform to internalized norms and beliefs about the right thing to do.[79]

Not all of these explanations may operate in individuals at the same time. Studies of taxpayer behaviour find that in deciding whether to report non-salary income on their returns, some taxpayers respond primarily to fear of being caught and punished while others are more motivated by a sense of legal or civic duty.[80] When personal values of individual taxpayers or corporate employees are consistent with particular laws, regulations and company policies, they are much more inclined to comply voluntarily,[81] whereas normative disagreement undermines compliance.[82]

Considerable evidence has accumulated that humans can be motivated to obey rules where one or more of certain conditions apply, and that the effect is cumulative if more

---

[77] B Gunia et al, 'Contemplation and Conversation: Subtle Influences on Moral Decision Making' (2012) 55(1) *Academy of Management Journal* 13; K Murnighan, D Cantelon, and T Elyashic, 'Bounded Personal Ethics and the Tap Dance of the Real Estate Agency' in J Wagner, J Bartunek and K Elsbach (eds), *Advances in Qualitative Organizational Research* (Oxford, Elsevier/JAI Press, 2001).

[78] Footnote from source material: L Friedman, *The Legal System: A Social Science Perspective* (New York, Russell Sage Foundation, 1975) 105–13.

[79] RA Kagan, N Gunningham and D Thornton, 'Fear, Duty, and Regulatory Compliance: Lessons from Three Research Projects' in C Parker and VL Nielsen (eds), *Explaining Compliance. Business Responses to Regulation* (Cheltenham, Edward Elgar, 2012).

[80] JT Scholz and N Pinney, 'Duty, Fear and Tax Compliance: The Heuristic Basis of Citizenship Behaviour' (1995) 39 *American Journal of Political Science* 490–512; RD Schwartz and S Orleans, 'On Legal Sanctions' (1967) 34 *University of Chicago Law Review* 274–300.

[81] K Murphy, TR Tyler and A Curtis, 'Nurturing Regulatory Compliance: Is Procedural Justice Effective when People Question the Legitimacy of the Law?' (2009) 3 *Regulation & Governance* 3; TR Tyler, J Dienhart and T Thomas, 'The Ethical Commitment to Compliance: Building Value-based Cultures' (2008) 5 *California Management Review* 31–51.

[82] TR Tyler and JM Darley, 'Building a Law-abiding Society: Taking Public Views about Morality and the Legitimacy of Law into Account when Formulating Substantive Law' (2000) 28 *Hofstra Law Review* 707–39.

than one condition applies. This self-motivation to comply can occur in all social situations, such as families, social groups, work environments, and the public sphere of the state's law.

One finding is that the substance of the rule must align with the personal, internalised moral values of the individual. A second finding is that individuals who view the processes by which the rules are made and applied as being fair imbue the legal system with legitimacy and will voluntarily abide by laws and defer to authorities.[83] A third finding notes the influence of the social context. Individuals have a strong tendency to conform to the rules of their peer group. Thus, a group culture can be identified that will influence the tendency to comply or infringe internal or external rules.

The above three observational findings of human social behaviour prompt design conditions in which rule compliance is enhanced and non-compliance is minimised. We will look at the application of those design issues in chapters 19 to 22 below. Here, we continue by summarising the main research findings from the psychology research literature in relation to the three issues of the internalisation of moral values, legitimacy and culture. It will be seen that these issues can be bound together by the concept of fairness.

V. Application of Internalised Moral Values

Moral values are a source of motivation to support or oppose the law because they are based on internalised feelings of responsibility to follow certain personally held moral principles.[84] Tyler notes that a 'key feature of moral values is that people feel personally obligated to adhere to them, and they feel guilty when they fail to do so. Hence, moral values—once they exist—are self-regulatory in nature; people who possess them are strongly motivated to bring their conduct into line with normative standards.'[85] This approach chimes with Habermas' positioning of law in its moral context.[86] Studies demonstrate that people's views about appropriate sentencing decisions in criminal cases are driven by moral judgements about deservingness rather than by instrumental judgements concerning how to deter future criminal conduct.[87]

---

[83] Darley, Tyler and Bilz (n 1); JT Jost and B Major (eds), *The Psychology of Legitimacy* (Cambridge, Cambridge University Press, 2001); Tyler (n 1); TR Tyler and SL Blader, *Cooperation in Groups: Procedural Justice, Social Identity, and Behavioral Engagement* (Philadelphia, Psychology Press, 2000); TR Tyler and SL Blader, 'Can Businesses Effectively Regulate Employee Conduct? The Antecedents of Rule Following in Work Settings' (2005) 48 *Academy of Management Journal* 1143–58; J Jackson, B Bradford, M Hough, A Myhill, P Quinton and TR Tyler, 'Why Do People Comply with the Law? Legitimacy and the Influence of Legal Institutions' (manuscript, 2013) (a survey of 7,434 respondents' attitudes to the police and the criminal law in the United Kingdom).

[84] See PH Robinson and J Darley, *Justice, Liability, and Blame* (Boulder CO, Westview, 1995); Tyler and Darley (n 82) 707–39.

[85] TR Tyler, 'Psychology and the Law' in KE Whittington, RD Kelemen and GA Caldeira (eds), *The Oxford Handbook of Law and Politics* (Oxford, Oxford University Press, 2008).

[86] J Habermas, *Between Facts and Norms* (Cambridge MA, MIT Press, 1996).

[87] KM Carlsmith, JM Darley and PH Robinson, 'Why Do We Punish? Deterrence and Just Deserts as Motives for Punishment' (2002) 83(2) *Journal of Personality and Social Psychology* 284; JM Darley, KM Carlsmith and PH Robinson, 'Incapacitation and Just Deserts as Motives for Punishment' (2000) 24 *Law and Human Behaviour* 659.

Summarising the literature, Tyler concluded[88] that studies focused on legitimacy,[89] on morality,[90] and on the general role of fairness in shaping social behaviour[91] all suggest that ethical values may shape employee behaviour. Research also suggests that ethical concerns motivate self-regulatory behaviour in organisational settings.[92] Ethical values shape behaviour when people believe that the rules of their organisation are legitimate, and hence ought to be obeyed, or that the values defining the organisation are congruent with their own moral values, thus leading people to feel that they ought to support the organisation.

VI. Legitimacy and Fairness

The focus here is on the concept of the legitimacy of, first, the legal (or social, or work) system within which people operate and, second, the substance of the rules themselves (in general and individual manifestations). By the legitimacy of the system, we mean the processes by which the rules are made, applied, observed, enforced and sanctioned. Every aspect should be perceived to be fair. This requires there to be fairness in fact (compliance with the individuals' personal ethics, as noted above) and for the practices to be perceived as fair, which requires transparency in the procedures.

Tyler notes[93] that this concept of legitimacy is a quality that can be possessed by an authority, a law or an institution that leads others to feel obligated to accept its directives,

---

[88] TR Tyler, 'The Psychology of Self-regulation: Normative Motivations for Compliance' in C Parker and VL Nielsen (eds), *Explaining Compliance. Business Responses to Regulation* (Cheltenham, Edward Elgar, 2012).

[89] S Human and K Provan, 'Legitimacy Building in the Evolution of Small-firm Multilateral Networks: A Comparative Study of Success and Demise' (2000) 45 *Administrative Science Quarterly* 327–65; M Suchman, 'Managing Legitimacy: Strategic and Institutional Approaches' (1995) 20 *Academy of Management Review* 571–610; TR Tyler, 'Promoting Employee Policy Adherence and Rule Following in Work Settings: The Value of Self-regulatory Approaches' (2005) 70 *Brooklyn Law Review* 1287–312; Tyler (n 1); Tyler and Blader, *Cooperation in Groups: Procedural Justice, Social Identity, and Behavioral Engagement* (n 83); Tyler and Blader, 'Can Businesses Effectively Regulate Employee Conduct? The Antecedents of Rule Following in Work Settings' (n 83) 1143–58; TR Tyler, P Callahan and J Frost, 'Armed, and Dangerous (?): Can Self-regulatory Approaches Shape Rule Adherence among Agents of Social Control' (2007) 41 *Law & Society Review* 457–92; M Zimmerman and G Zeitz, 'Beyond Survival: Achieving New Venture Growth by Building Legitimacy' (2002) 27 *Academy of Management Review* 414–31.

[90] R Paternoster and SS Simpson, 'Sanction Threats and Appeals to Morality: Testing a Rational Choice Model of Corporate Crime' (1996) 30 *Law & Society Review* 549–84; Tyler (n 1); Tyler and Blader, *Cooperation in Groups: Procedural Justice, Social Identity, and Behavioral Engagement* (n 83); Tyler and Blader, 'Can Businesses Effectively Regulate Employee Conduct? The Antecedents of Rule Following in Work Settings' (n 83) 1143–58.

[91] M Rabin, 'Incorporating Fairness into Game Theory and Economics' (1993) 83 *American Economic Review* 1281–302; Tyler and Blader, *Cooperation in Groups: Procedural Justice, Social Identity, and Behavioral Engagement* (n 83); M Vandenbergh, 'Beyond Elegance: A Testable Typology of Social Norms in Corporate Environmental Compliance' (2003) 22 *Stanford Environmental Law Journal* 55–144.

[92] M Aalders and T Wilthagen, 'Moving Beyond Command-and-Control: Reflexivity in the Regulation of Occupational Safety and Health and the Environment' (1997) 19 *Law & Policy* 415–43; N Gunningham and J Rees, 'Industry Self-regulation: An Institutional Perspective' (1997) 19 *Law & Policy* 363–414; A King and M Lenox, 'Industry Self-regulation without Sanctions: The Chemical Industry's Responsible Care Program' (2000) 43 *Academy of Management Journal* 698–716; C Rechtschaffen, 'Deterrence vs Cooperation and the Evolving Theory of Environmental Enforcement' (1998) 71 *Southern California Law Review* 1181–272.

[93] Tyler (n 88).

generating their self-regulatory responses.[94] Further, if a system enjoys widespread legitimacy, authorities can appeal to members based upon their shared purposes and values, providing the system with long-term stability.[95]

Research, initially by Tyler and now supported by others, demonstrates that perceptions of system legitimacy shape everyday compliance with the law, and that perceived legitimacy seems to have more influence on compliance than do subjective assessments of the likely risk of punishment.[96] It has been found that behavioural choices are directly linked to the level of fairness involved in decision making and in the execution of decisions.[97] People who perceive themselves unfairly treated tend to confront decisions and act uncooperatively.[98] Perceptions of legitimacy by regulatees can generate a higher level of compliance with state regulation.[99] Regulatees have higher compliance where they perceive that inspectors treat them with respect and trust.[100] Employees' ethical values are shaped primarily by employee perceptions of how fairly they are treated by management.[101] Procedural fairness is identified as important in shaping the behaviour of employees in all types of work settings.[102]

[94]   D Gottfredson, B Kearley, S Najaka and C Rocha, 'How Drug Treatment Courts Work: An Analysis of Mediators' (2007) 44 *Journal of Research in Crime and Delinquency* 3–35; TR Tyler, *Psychology and the Design of Legal Institutions* (Nijmegen, Wolf Legal Publishers, 2007); TR Tyler, 'Psychology and Institutional Design' (2008) 4 *Review of Law and Economics* 801–87.

[95]   R Paternoster, R Brame, R Bacjman and LW Sherman, 'Do Fair Procedures Matter? The Effect of Procedural Justice on Spouse Assault (1997) 17 *Law and Society Review* 457–79; DG Pruitt, RS Pierce NB McGillicuddy, GL Welton and LM Castrianno, 'Long Term Success in Mediation' (1993) 17 *Law and Human Behavior* 313–30.

[96]   Tyler (n 1); J Sunshine and TR Tyler, 'The Role of Procedural Justice and Legitimacy in Shaping Public Support for Policing' (2003) 37 *Law and Society Review* 513–48; TR Tyler and YJ Huo, *Trust in the Law* (New York, Russell Sage Foundation, 2002).

[97]   TR Tyler and HJ Smith, 'Social Justice and Social Movements' ch 101, in DT Gilbert, ST Fiske and G Lindzey (eds), *The Handbook of Social Psychology*, Vol II, 4th edn (New York NY, Oxford University Press, 1998) 595–629; JW Thibaut and L Walker, *Procedural Justice: A Psychological Analysis* (Hillsdale NJ, Erlbaum, 1975); EA Lind and TR Tyler, *The Social Psychology of Procedural Justice. Critical Issues in Social Justice* (New York NY, Plenum, 1988); Tyler and Blader, *Cooperation in Groups: Procedural Justice, Social Identity, and Behavioral Engagement* (n 83).

[98]   Tyler and Smith, ibid; TR Tyler and P Degoey, 'Trust in Organizational Authorities: The Influence of Motive Attributions on Willingness to Accept Decisions' in RM Kramer and TR Tyler (eds), *Trust in Organizational Authorities* (Thousand Oaks CA, Sage Publications Inc, 1996) 331; K Murphy, '"Trust Me, I'm the Taxman": The Role of Trust in Nurturing Compliance' (2002) *Centre for Tax System Integrity Working Paper no 43* 1–31.

[99]   J Braithwaite, *Restorative Justice and Responsive Regulation* (Studies in Crime and Public Policy. New York NY, Oxford University Press, 2002); Tyler and Degoey, ibid; Tyler (n 1); E Bardach and RA Kagan, *Going by the Book: The Problem of Regulatory Unreasonableness* (Philadelphia PA, Temple University Press, 1982); Tyler and Lind (n 5) 115–91; Tyler (n 5) 323–45; K Murphy, 'Procedural Justice and Tax Compliance' (2003) 38(3) *Australian Journal of Social Issues* 379–407.

[100]   J Braithwaite and T Makkai, 'Trust and Compliance' (1994) 4(1) *Policing and Society* 1–12; K Aoki, L Axelrad and RA Kagan, 'Industrial Effluent Control in the United States and Japan' in RA Kagan and L Axelrad, *Regulatory Encounters* (Berkeley, Los Angeles, London, University of California Press, 2000) 64–95; M Wenzel, 'The Impact of Outcome Orientation and Justice Concerns on Tax Compliance: The Role of Taxpayers' Identity; *Journal of Applied Psychology* 87, no.4 (2002): 629–645; M Wenzel, 'Principles of Procedural Fairness in Reminder Letters: A Field-Experiment' *Center for Tax System Integrity Working Paper no 42* (2002); Murphy, ibid 379–407.

[101]   Tyler and Blader, *Cooperation in Groups: Procedural Justice, Social Identity, and Behavioral Engagement* (n 83); TR Tyler and SL Blader, 'The Group Engagement Model: Procedural Justice, Social Identity, and Cooperative Behaviour' (2003) 7 *Personality and Social Psychology Review* 349 (finding that over 80% of compliance decisions are driven by the credibility of the organisation's leadership message and congruence of organisational and personal values, and less than 20% are driven by formal rewards and punishments).

[102]   WC Kim and R Mauborgne, 'Procedural Justice, Attitudes, and Subsidiary Top Management Compliance with Multinationals' Corporate Strategic Decisions' (1993) 36 *Academy of Management Journal* 502–26; J Greenberg and R Cropanzano (eds), *Advances in Organizational Justice* (Lexington, New Lexington Press, 2001); EA Lind and TR Tyler, *The Social Psychology of Procedural Justice* (New York, Springer, 1988); Tyler, Callahan and Frost (n 89) 457–92.

These findings apply to the relationship between both state and citizens or enterprises, and to that between employers or other group leaders and the employees or members of the groups.[103] It suggest that it is important for achievement of maximising observance of their rules that government, regulators and private sector organisations ensure that their processes of making and applying rules are perceived to be fair. Procedural fairness[104] plays a crucial role in supporting both legitimacy of authority and moral cohesion of society. Fair application of regulatory enforcement serves a 'reassurance function' for firms that have made normative commitments to be law-abiding.[105] The importance of procedural justice in shaping legitimacy has recently been confirmed in a large US survey that found lower levels of support for formal authority amongst Anglo-Americans[106] than Europeans,[107] and that legitimacy is more important than police effectiveness. The researchers suggested that legitimacy is based upon the fairness of the manner through which legal authorities manage their authority, and that fair interpersonal treatment is more centrally involved than fair decision making, and that outcome favourability is not a key factor.[108]

These findings are consistent with a shift in political theory away from the location of power in a sovereign who rules by imposing will downwards on a cascade of subjects[109] to the notion that autonomous power held by all individuals in a society is conferred on the society's delegated representatives to be exercised in a legitimate, transparent and accountable manner.[110] Ferguson has noted recognition of the need in China for morality to support the requirements for economic growth of a foundation of property rights and a safeguard of law.[111]

The extension of legitimacy by public bodies is seen in their increased transparency and the widening involvement of businesses and stakeholders in the formulation and implementation of regulatory policy.[112] Tyler notes that[113] such involvement includes negotiation to reach consensus on administrative regulations,[114] cooperative arrangements for

---

[103] C Perrow, 'Economic Theories of Organization' (1986) 15 *Theory & Society* 11–45.

[104] DJ Galligan, *Due Process and Fair Procedures* (Oxford, Clarendon Press, 1996).

[105] D Thornton, RA Kagan and N Gunningham, 'General Deterrence and Corporate Environmental Behaviour' (2005) 27 *Law & Policy* 266.

[106] TR Tyler and J Jackson, 'Popular Legitimacy and the Exercise of Legal Authority: Motivating Compliance, Cooperation and Engagement' (2014) 20(1) *Psychology, Public Policy and Law* 78–95.

[107] M Hough, J Jackson and B Bradford, 'Legitimacy, Trust and Compliance' in J Tankebe and A Liebling (eds), *Legitimacy and Criminal Justice: An International Exploration* (Oxford, Oxford University Press, 2013).

[108] Also found in TR Tyler and YJ Huo, *Trust in the Law: Encouraging Public Cooperation with the Police and Courts* (New York, Russell-Sage Foundation, 2001).

[109] Even Machiavelli suggested that successful leaders should strive to win the consent of the governed in addition to use of brute force to execute their will, so that their commands would be voluntarily obeyed: N Machiavelli, *The Prince* (1531, English translation G Bull, London, Penguin Books, 1961). See M Weber, *Economy and Society* ed G Roth and C Wittich (Berkeley, University of California Press, 1968); M Zelditch Jr, 'Theories of Legitimacy' in JT Jost and B Major (eds), *The Psychology of Legitimacy* (Cambridge, Cambridge University Press, 2001) (on the social dynamics of authority); HC Kelmaan, 'Patterns of Personal Involvement in the National System: A Social-psychological Analysis of Political Legitimacy' in J Rosenau (ed), *International Politics and Foreign Policy* (New York, Free Press, 1969); Tyler (n 1).

[110] RJ Merelman, 'Learning and Legitimacy' (1966) 60 *American Political Science Review* 548–51, 548 (legitimacy is 'a quality attributed to a regime by a population').

[111] N Ferguson, *Civilisation. The Six Killer Apps of Western Power* (London, Penguin, 2011) 288.

[112] See chs 9 and 13.

[113] Tyler (n 85).

[114] C Coglianese, 'Assessing Consensus: The Promise and Performance of Negotiated Rulemaking' (1997) 78 *Duke Law Journal* 1255–349.

delivering social services[115] and joint efforts to manage wildlife and wildlands.[116] He also notes that these policies decentralise power to 'enable citizens and other actors to utilize their local knowledge to fit solutions to their individual circumstances'.[117]

VII. Individuality

The findings above are, of course, about people generally. Around one per cent of the population are individuals who lack empathy and conscience—psychopaths.[118] Psychopaths are over-represented in the prison population, estimated at 15–25 per cent,[119] and among business leaders (four per cent).[120] Gold argues that such persons will only ever be weakly trustworthy, and material incentives are needed to affect their behaviour.[121] We discuss trust further in chapter 22.

For now, it is necessary to note that some researchers divide people into those who tend to be 'good faith people' or 'bad faith people', and they respond to different approaches to external control.[122] People who are high on moral identity (in our terminology, good faith people) are likely to be affected by moral priming, whereas moral priming was found to have no effect on people who are low on moral identity (in our terminology, bad faith people).[123]

Good faith people[124] are responsible for most opportunistic deeds,[125] and many fail to recognise that their deeds are opportunistic.[126] In considering employee misbehaviour,

[115] R Stewart, 'Administrative Law in the Twenty-first Century' (2003) 78 *New York University Law Review* 437–60.

[116] B Karkkainen, 'Collaborative Ecosystem Governance: Scale, Complexity and Dynamism' (2002) 21 *Virginia Environmental Law Journal* 189–243; A Lin, 'Participants' Experiences with Habitat Conservation Plans and Suggestions for Streamlining the Process' (1996) 23 *Ecology Law Quarterly* 369–439.

[117] M Dorf and C Sabel, 'A Constitution of Democratic Experimentalism' (1998) 98 *Columbia Law Review* 267.

[118] N Gold, 'Trustworthiness and Motivations' in N Morris and D Vines (eds), *Capital Failure; Rebuilding Trust in Financial Services* (Oxford, Oxford University Press, 2014) 146.

[119] RD Hare, 'Psychopathy: A Clinical Construct Whose Time Has Come' (1996) 23(1) *Criminal Justice and Behavior* 25.

[120] P Babiak and RD Hare, *Snakes in Suits: When Psychopaths Go to Work* (New York, HarperCollins, 2009); P Babiak, CS Neumann and RD Hare, 'Corporate Psychopathy: Talking the Walk' (2010) 28(2) *Behavioral Sciences and the Law* 174; BJ Board and K Frtizon, 'Disordered Personalities at Work' (2005) 11(1) *Psychology, Crime & Law* 17.

[121] Gold (n 118) 146.

[122] Y Feldman and HE Smith, 'Behavioral Equity' (2014) 170 *Journal of Institutional and Theoretical Economics* 137–59.

[123] K Aquino, D Freeman, A Reed II, VKG Lim and W Felps, 'Testing a Social-cognitive Model of Moral Behavior: The Interactive Influence of Situations and Moral Identity Centrality' (2009) 97(1) *Journal of Personality and Social Psychology* 123.

[124] See also LA Stout, *Cultivating Conscience: How Good Laws Make Good People* (Princeton NJ, Princeton University Press, 2011); Y Benkler, *The Penguin and the Leviathan: The Triumph of Cooperation over Self-Interest* (New York, Crown Publishing Group, 2011).

[125] J Hollis, *Why Good People Do Bad Things: Understanding Our Darker Selves* (New York, Gotham Books, 2008); RM Kidder, *How Good People Make Tough Choices: Resolving the Dilemmas of Ethical Living* (New York, HarperCollins, 2009); DM Bersoff, 'Why Good People Sometimes Do Bad Things: Motivated Reasoning and Unethical Behavior' (1999) 25(1) *Personality & Social Psychology Bulletin* 28; N Mazar, O Amir and D Ariely, 'The Dishonesty of Honest People: A Theory of Self-Concept Maintenance' (2008) 45(6) *Journal of Marketing Research* 633; MM Pillutla, 'When Good People Do Wrong: Morality, Social Identity, and Ethical Behavior' in D De Cremer, R van Dijk and K Murnighan (eds), *Social Psychology and Organizations* (New York, Routledge, 2011) 353–56; Greenwald and Banaji (n 41).

[126] MH Bazerman and AE Tenbrunsel, *Blind Spots: Why We Fail to Do What's Right and What to Do about It* (Princeton NJ, Princeton University Press, 2011); Greenwald and Banaji (n 41).

Bandura notes the active role that the self plays in allowing people to engage in inhumane behaviour through moral disengagement with the ethics of the organisation.[127] He suggests eight mechanisms by which individuals are able to convince themselves that their actions are not immoral. Feldman and Smith[128] suggest that exploiting ambiguity in rules is central to people's ability to justify immoral behaviour, relying on work by Moore et al,[129] and Ashforth and Anand.[130] People frequently construct self-serving interpretations of the legal and organisational requirements they must follow. Haisley and Weber[131] found that people prefer to take ambiguous risks when this allows them to justify unfair behaviour, and Dana et al found that people are less generous in situations in which they can appeal to moral ambiguity in explaining their actions. Similarly, Hsee found that people make choices that satisfy their preferences, at the cost of best achieving an assigned goal, if they can exploit existing ambiguity about which decision may complete the assignment.[132] Yeldman and Teichman have shown that people use legal ambiguity strategically to formulate a minimal interpretation of what is required from them by laws or contracts.[133]

On the other hand, ambiguity in rules can be helpful. A number of studies indicate that incentives,[134] or overly-specific rules for example in contracts,[135] can crowd out ethics. Studies also find that strict enforcement, sanctions and specificity can harm cooperation.[136]

The same message can be received differently by different audiences: This has been called 'acoustic separation'.[137] Feldman and Smith argue that the law can afford not to achieve exact compliance by good faith people, who may not be aware of the rule or not be focused on it.[138] But they argue that a literal message can have a differential effect by serving both

---

[127] A Bandura, 'Moral Disengagement in The Perpetration of Inhumanities' (1999) 3(3) *Personality and Social Psychology Review* (Special Issue on Evil and Violence) 193.

[128] Feldman and Smith (n 122) 137–59.

[129] C Moore, JR Detert, LK Treviño, VL Baker and DM Mayer, 'Employees Do Bad Things: Moral Disengagement and Unethical Organizational Behavior' (2012) 65(1) *Personnel Psychology* 1.

[130] BE Ashforth and V Anand, 'The Normalization of Corruption in Organizations' in RM Kramer and BM Staw (eds), *Research in Organizational behavior* Vol 25 (Oxford, Jai Press, 2003) 1.

[131] E Haisley and RA Weber, 'Self-serving Interpretations of Ambiguity in Other-regarding Behavior' (2010) 68(2) *Games and Economic Behavior* 634.

[132] CK Hsee, 'Elastic Justification: How Tempting but Task-Irrelevant Factors Influence Decisions' (1995) 62(3) *Organizational Behavior and Human Decision Processes* 330.

[133] Y Feldman and D Teichman, 'Are all Legal Probabilities Created Equal?' (2009) 84(4) *New York University Law Review* 980–1022; Y Feldman, 'The Complexity of Disentangling Intrinsic and Extrinsic Compliance Motivations: Theoretical and Empirical Insights from the Behavioral Analysis of Law' (2011) 35 *Washington University Journal of Law & Policy* 11; Y Feldman, 'Bounded Ethicality and the Law: A Proposed Framework for the Incorporation of Ethical Decision Making Research into Behavioral Law and Economics' in E Zamir and D Teichman (eds), *The Oxford Handbook of Behavioral Economics and the Law* (Oxford, Oxford University Press, 2014).

[134] S Bowles, 'Policies Designed for Self-Interested Citizens May Undermine "The Moral Sentiments": Evidence from Economic Experiments' (2008) 320(5883) *Science* 1605.

[135] EY Chou, N Halevy and K Murnighan, 'The Hidden Cost of Contracts on Relationships and Performance' (2010), IACM 23rd Annual Conference Paper, available at http://papers.ssrn.com/sol3/papers.cfm?abstract_id=1612376; E Fehr and S Gächter, 'Fairness and Retaliation: The Economics of Reciprocity' (2000) 14(3) *Journal of Economics Perspectives* 159.

[136] AE Tenbrunsel and DM Messick, 'Sanctioning Systems, Decision Frames, and Cooperation' (1999) 44(4) *Administrative Science Quarterly* 684; A Falk and M Kosfeld, 'The Hidden Costs of Control' (1996) 96(5) *The American Economic Review* 1161.

[137] M Dan-Cohen, 'Decision Rules and Conduct Rules: On Acoustic Separation in Criminal Law' (1984) 97(3) *Harvard Law Review* 625.

[138] Feldman and Smith (n 122) 137–59.

as an anti-evasion device for bad faith actors, even if it has little effect on good faith actors (behavioural equity).[139]

Engel and Nagin have found that certainty of punishment did have an effect, and it was explained by risk preferences, if risk preferences and the expected value of stealing are considered separately.[140] They found that if, but only if, stealing did not pay, risk seeking participants were more deterred by higher certainty than by higher severity. Risk averse participants were always more deterred by higher severity. Interestingly this also held for risk seeking participants, provided stealing paid. It even held if the expected value of any stolen unit was zero.

Engel and Weber observe that the choice of decision-making mechanism impacts outcomes.[141] They note that visibly raising stakes will have the effect of focusing self-critical attention on the Stage 2 decision-making process,[142] since higher stakes induce people to prepare more intensely,[143] to be more open to facts,[144] to take more of the available information into account,[145] to show greater internal consistency,[146] and to become more risk averse.[147] They also conclude that having to justify a decision has the same effect, since it makes the individual aware of the actual complexity of the task,[148] as does having to observe a cooling-off period.[149]

VIII. Culture: The Behaviour and Support of Others

As noted above, humans apply their personal values within the social contexts that they operate—home, work, society, public sphere. Thus, people can be expected to apply their internal norms to their own behaviour and in evaluating the behaviour of others, such as in assessing the reputability of a government or an employer. But humans will also be

---

[139] ibid.

[140] C Engel and D Nagin, 'Who is Afraid of the Stick? Experimentally Testing the Deterrent Effect of Sanction Certainty' (June 30, 2012) 7th Annual Conference on Empirical Legal Studies Paper. Available at SSRN: http://ssrn.com/abstract=2097055.

[141] C Engel and EU Weber, 'The Impact of Institutions on the Decision how to Decide' (2007) 3(3) *Journal of Institutional Economics* 323.

[142] HR Arkes, 'Costs and Benefits of Judgment Errors—Implications for Debiasing' (1991) 110 *Psychological Bulletin* 486.

[143] PE Tetlock, 'Accountability and Complexity of Thought' (1983) 45 *Journal of Personality and Social Psychology* 74.

[144] JS Lerner, JH Goldberg and PE Tetlock, 'Sober Second Thought: The Effects of Accountability, Anger, and Authoritarianism on Attributions of Responsibility' (1998) 24 *Personality and Social Psychology Bulletin* 563.

[145] PE Tetlock, 'Accountability and the Perseverance of First Impressions' (1983) 46 *Social Psychology Quarterly* 285; PE Tetlock and R Boettger, 'Accountability: A Social Magnifier of the Dilution Effect' (1989) 57 *Journal of Personality and Social Psychology* 388.

[146] R Hagafors and B Brehmer, 'Does Having to Justify one's Judgments Change the Nature of the Judgment Process?' (1983) 31 *Organizational Behavior and Human Decision Processes* 223; RH Ashton, 'Effects of Justification and a Mechanical Aid on Judgment Performance' (1992) 52 *Organizational Behavior and Human Decision Processes* 292.

[147] JM Blatt, 'The Utility of Being Hanged on the Gallows' (1979) 2 *Journal of Post Keynesian Economics* 231.

[148] G Cvetkovich, 'Cognitive Accommodation, Language, and Social Responsibility' (1978) 41 *Social Psychology* 149; Hagafors and Brehmer (n 146); E Weldon and GM Gargano, 'Cognitive Loafing: The Effects of Accountability and Shared Responsibility on Cognitive Effort' (1988) 14 *Personality and Social Psychology Bulletin* 159.

[149] Engel and Weber (n 141) 323.

influenced in their behaviour by the values and behaviour of others, and by the norms observed by the social group to which they belong.[150]

Humans tend to follow paths that they believe others have previously taken in similar situations (a herd instinct).[151] This is similar to the idea of a Type 1 heuristic in the brain. Sunstein's summary of the findings of social influences on people has been noted above.[152] He summarises the relevance of social norms thus:[153]

Social scientists have emphasized the importance of social practices and norms, which have a significant influence on individual decisions.[154] If people learn that they are using more energy than similarly situated others, their energy use may decline—saving money while also reducing pollution.[155] The same point applies to health-related behavior. It has long been understood that people are more likely to engage in healthy behavior if they live or work with others who so engage.[156] And if people are in a social network with other people who are obese, they are significantly more likely to become obese themselves.[157] The behavior of relevant others can provide valuable information about sensible or appropriate courses of action. As noted above, informational cascades are a possible consequence, as people rely on, and thus amplify, the informational signals produced by the actions of their predecessors. Similarly, those actions can provide information about what others will approve and disapprove.[158]

Human behaviour can change in an organisational context, since a wider range of effects come into play, such as economics, psychology, organisational effects[159] and law.[160] Owner-managers may tend to behave in a similar fashion to individuals, whereas individuals in

[150] DM Kahan, 'Social Influence, Social Meaning, and Deterrence' (1997) 83 *Virginia Law Review* 349.

[151] S Coleman, 'The Minnesota Income Tax Compliance Experiment State Tax Results' Minnesota Department of Revenue (1996), at http://www.revenue.state.mn.us/research_stats/research_reports/19xx/research_reports_content_complnce.pdf. This reported a striking experiment in which a significant rate of compliance with tax laws was achieved where people were told that more than 90% of Minnesotans already comply in full with their tax obligations; but no effect on compliance was found where targets were told one of three other statements: their taxes went to various good works, including education, police protection, and fire protection; they were threatened with information about the risks of punishment for non-compliance; they were given information about how to get help to fill in their tax forms if confused or uncertain.

[152] From Sunstein (n 27).

[153] Sunstein, ibid.

[154] Footnote from original source: For general overviews, see Christakis and Fowler (n 37); S Bikhchandani, D Hirshleifer and I Welch, 'Learning from the Behavior of Others: Conformity, Fads, and Informational Cascades' (1998) 12 *Journal of Economic Perspectives* 151. See also PW Schultz, et al, 'The Constructive, Destructive, and Reconstructive Power of Social Norms' (2007) 18 *Psychological Science* 429, 432–33; RB Cialdini, et al, 'Managing Social Norms for Persuasive Impact' (2006) 1 *Soc Influence* 3, 10–12 (finding that drawing public attention to the existence or pervasiveness of undesirable behaviour can increase such behaviour).

[155] Footnote from original source: See Allcott (n 37) (discussing energy conservation) at 16–17. See also generally PJ Ferraro and MK Price, 'Using Nonpecuniary Strategies to Influence Behavior: Evidence from a Large Scale Field Experiment' (2013) 95(1) *The Review of Economics and Statistics* 64–73 (finding that social comparison information significantly decreased water consumption).

[156] Footnote from original source: See JK Langlie, 'Social Networks, Health Beliefs, and Preventive Health Behavior' (1977) 18 *J Health & Soc Behav* 244, 244–45.

[157] Christakis and Fowler (n 37) at 105–12.

[158] For a relevant discussion, see Kuran (n 40) at 61.

[159] RM Cyert and JG March, *A Behavioral Theory of the Firm* (Oxford, Blackwell, 1992); WR Scott, *Organizations. Rational, Natural, and Open Systems* (Upper Saddle River NJ, Prentice Hall, 2003); U Berger and I Bernhard-Mehlich *Die verhaltenswissenschaftliche Entscheidungstheorie. Organisationstheorien* (Alfred Kieser Stuttgart, Kohlhammer, 2006) 169–85.

[160] For a comprehensive survey see C Engel, 'The Behaviour of Corporate Actors: A Survey of the Empirical Literature' (2010) 4 *Journal of Institutional Economics* 445.

larger organisations can exhibit a wide range of effects.[161] Corporate culture plays a critical role.[162] Data from railroad accidents shows that railroad companies basically only learn from their own experience as long as their performance is close to aspiration levels. They become sensitive to others' experiences only if they are far enough away from the aspiration level.[163] Managers have been clearly shown to suffer from over-optimism,[164] especially if there are no clear benchmarks.[165] This effect is much stronger in managers than in ordinary subjects.[166]

Kagan, Gunningham and Thornton have emphasised[167] the consistent finding of socio-legal research that 'compliance' within regulated enterprises is socially constructed, some-times in a dialogue with regulatory enforcement officials.[168] They conclude that effective regulation requires imaginative cooperation as much or even more than it requires govern-ment monitoring and legal coercion.[169]

Those scholars also note that regulatory enforcement has an important 'reminder func-tion'. A significant number of regulatory violations also violate official company policies.

> In most regulatory programs, enforcement officials find that only a tiny fraction of detected vio-lations entail sufficient evidence of willfulness, deception or gross negligence to justify criminal prosecution. Rather, the violations stem from inattention or miscalculation of risks by particular company subunits or employees, or by unexpected technical or business pressures that induce harried subunit managers or employees to postpone or modify time-consuming regulatory compliance routines.[170]

---

[161] JME Pennings and A Smidts, 'The Shape of Utility Functions and Organizational Behavior' (2003) 49 *Management Science* 1251.

[162] TE Deal and AA Kennedy, *Corporate Cultures. The Rites and Rituals of Corporate Life* (Reading MA, Addison-Wesley Pub Co, 1982); JP Kotter and JL Heskett, *Corporate Culture and Performance* (New York Toronto, Free Press, 1992); J Crémer, 'Corporate Culture and Shared Knowledge' (1993) 3 *Industrial and Corporate Change* 351; GM Hodgson, *Corporate Culture and the Nature of the Firm. Transaction Cost Economics and Beyond* (Boston, Kluwer, John Groenewegen, 1996) 249–69; BE Hermalin, 'Economics and Corporate Culture' in CL Cooper, S Cartwright und PC Earley (eds), *The International Handbook of Organizational Culture and Climate* (Chichester, New York, Wiley, 1996); DC Langevoort, 'Opening the Black Box of "Corporate Culture" in Law and Economics' (2006) 162 *Journal of Institutional and Theoretical Economics* 80; C Cordes, PJ Richerson, R McElreath and P Strimling, 'A Naturalistic Approach to the Theory of the Firm: The Role of Cooperation and Cultural Evolution' (2008) 68 *Journal of Economic Behavior & Organization* 125.

[163] JAC Baum and KB Dahlin, 'Aspiration Performance and Railroads' Patterns of Learning from Train Wrecks and Crashes' (2007) 18 *Organization Science* 368.

[164] PG Moors, 'The Manager's Struggles with Uncertainty' (1977) 140 *Journal of the Royal Statistical Society* 129; DC Langevoort, 'Organized Illusions. A Behavioral Theory of Why Corporations Mislead Stock Market Investors (and Cause Other Social Harms)' (1997) 146 *University of Pennsylvania Law Review* 101.

[165] MD Alicke, ML Klotz, DL Breitenbecher, TJ Yurak and DS Vredenburg, 'Personal Contact, Individuation, and the Better-Than-Average Effect' (1995) 68 *Journal of Personality and Social* Psychology 804–25.

[166] LE Palich, LE and DR Bagby, 'Using Cognitive Theory to Explain Entrepreneurial Risk-Taking. Challenging Conventional Wisdom' (1995) 10 *Journal of Business Venturing* 425.

[167] Kagan, Gunningham and Thornton (n 79) 37.

[168] BM Hutter, *Compliance: Regulation and Environment* (Oxford, Oxford University Press, 1997); LB Edelman, S Petterson, E Chambliss and HS Erlanger, 'Legal Ambiguity and the Politics of Compliance: Affirmative Action Officers' Dilemma' (1991) 13 *Law & Society Review* 73–97.

[169] Kagan, Gunningham and Thornton (n 79) 39.

[170] RA Kagan and J Scholz, 'The "Criminology of the Corporation" and Regulatory Enforcement Styles' in K Hawkins and J Thomas (eds), *Enforcing Regulation* (Boston, Kluwer Nijhoff Publishing, 1984) 67–69; D Spence, 'The Shadow of the Rational Polluter: Rethinking the Role of Rational Actor Models in Environmental Law' (2001) 89 *California Law Review* 972–73; T Malloy, 'Regulation, Compliance and the Firm' (2003) 76 *Temple Law Review* 451–531.

Consequently, in well-established regulatory regimes in which a significant level of enforcement is taken as inevitable, the primary function of most enforcement action is consciousness raising, reminding business managers to try harder to achieve the regulatory goals that they had already promised to work toward.[171,172]

These findings suggest that legal cultures and the culture of social or business organisations are important in supporting moral congruence, building consensus on the ethical content of rules and processes, and hence motivating adherence and reducing deviancy. In the context of regulation, the concept arises of understanding the dynamics of a particular industrial context,[173] so as to apply an appropriate 'regulatory character' that combines effective interaction between the external regulatory framework and the internal social context. Regulatory character is informed by an understanding of the importance of cultural ordering to regulatory change and regulatory compliance.[174] Findings that employees can be motivated by perceptions of fairness and legitimacy to feel personal responsibility for bringing their behaviour into line with corporate rules and policies (deference, rather than mere compliance) suggest value in self-regulatory models.[175] Team accountability reinforces the message that safety is not an individual responsibility.[176]

IX. Managers' Decisions: Protecting Firms' Multiple Licences

So far, the focus has been on how individual humans make decisions. How does the analysis change when the context in which the decisions are made is that of an organisation? The economic, command and control, and deterrence approaches to regulation and enforcement that are considered in chapter two below treat firms as the relevant entity to be addressed,

---

[171] Footnote from original source: J Mendeloff and WB Gray, 'Inside the Black Box: How do OSHA Inspections Lead to Reductions in Workplace Injuries?' (2005) 27 *Law & Policy* 219–37, finding that health and safety inspections and penalties induced firms to direct more attention to the normative goals of safety in general, not merely toward compliance with legal rules.

[172] Kagan, Gunningham and Thornton (n 79) 47.

[173] F Haines, *Corporate Regulation. Beyond 'Punish or Persuade'* (Oxford, Clarendon Press, 1997); Tyler, Dienhart and Thomas (n 81) 31–51; S Killingsworth, 'Modeling the Message: Communicating Compliance Through Organizational Values and Culture' (2012) XXV(4) *Georgetown Journal of Legal Ethics* 961.

[174] C Hood, *The Art of the State: Culture, Rhetoric and Public Management* (Oxford, Clarendon Press, 1998); P Selznick, *The Moral Commonwealth: Social Theory and the Promise of Community* (Berkeley, University of California Press, 1992) (arguing that cultural order is moulded by the economic and political dependencies; Hood identifies four types of administrative contexts: hierarchist, fatalist, egalitarian, individualist); F Haines, 'Regulatory Reform in Light of Regulatory Character: Assessing Industrial Safety Change in the Aftermath of the Kader Toy Factory Fire in Bangkok, Thailand' (2003) 12 *Social and Legal Studies* 461–87; reprinted in F Haines (ed), *Crime and Regulation* (Farnham, Ashgate, 2007).

[175] P Selznick, *Law, Society, and Industrial Justice* (New York, Russell-Sage Foundation, 1969); Aalders and Wilthagen (n 92) 415–43; Darley, Tyler and Bilz (n 1) 458–76; Gunningham and Rees (n 92) 363–414; King and Lenox (n 92) 698–716; Rechtschaffen (n 92) 1181–272; Suchman (n 89) 571–610; TR Tyler, 'Trust and Lawabidingness: A Proactive Model of Social Regulation' (2001) 81 *Boston University Law Review* 361–406; Tyler and Darley (n 82) 707–39.

[176] P McCulloch, A Mishra, A Handa, T Dale, G Hirst, K Catchpole, 'The Effects of Aviation-style Non-technical Skills Training on Technical Performance and Outcome in the Operating Theatre' (2009) 18(2) *Quality and Safety in Healthcare* 109.

rather than looking at the individuals who operate within the social structure created by the business. Reference to a firm's culture is a shorthand heuristic for the collection of relevant decisions taken by the relevant influential humans. As Wells noted, centrality within criminal law of notions of individualism leads to difficulties in making corporations criminally accountable.[177] However, different insights emerge when one approaches 'the firm's behaviour' by analysing the individual decisions and actions of the humans that are its directors and managers, even if they are made legally on behalf of the company.

Business managers have been shown to respond to a variety of motivational factors. An important study of pulp mills showed that managers felt constrained and pressured by three 'licences to operate': First, the firm's 'economic licence', its obligations to meet the financial expectations of investors and creditors; second, the facility's 'legal' or 'regulatory licence', encompassing applicable laws, regulation, and permit conditions; and third, the 'social licence', the pressures for responsible environmental performance that managers felt from neighbours, employees, community groups, the news media and environmental advocacy groups.[178]

Clearly, the economic incentives for both individuals and firms, coupled with over-enthusiastic risk-taking attitudes, have powerful effects on behaviour. Yet all of the external groups just noted can generate adverse publicity that might enhance or damage a firm's reputation.[179] Wells has noted the attempts to bolster brand image in advertising and the efforts of corporations to regain a clean image after a disaster as showing the commercial importance of status and image.[180] Damage to reputation made it harder to retain and attract employees, to get permits, and win contracts.

Gunningham, Kagan and Thornton suggest that there is a significant interaction between an enterprise's legal and social licences. Perceived changes in any one of the licences would affect managerial decisions. For example, the facilities' environmental performance varied more in relation to the intensity of the social licence pressures than the legal licence. Social licence pressures help explain why larger regulated firms, especially those which deal directly with the consuming public, tend to have better regulatory compliance records than smaller firms.[181] But they also tend to have tighter legal licences, that is they are more closely monitored.[182] In addition, large firms with widely recognised brand names are more fearful of the adverse publicity that can flow from a serious environmental accident or regulatory prosecution.[183]

---

[177] C Wells, *Corporations and Criminal Responsibility* (Oxford, Clarendon Press, 1993).

[178] N Gunningham, RA Kagan and D Thornton, *Shades of Green: Business, Regulation and Environment* (Stanford, Stanford University Press, 2003) 20–40; N Gunningham, RA Kagan and D Thornton, 'Social Licence and Environmental Protection: Why Businesses go Beyond Compliance' (2004) 29 *Law and Social Inquiry* 307–41.

[179] C Davis, 'Making Companies Safe: What Works', Presentation to Health and Safety Executive Conference on "Director Responsibility for Health and Safety: What the Evidence Shows", London, 6 October 2005. This study notes that members of senior management in responsible companies are significantly influenced by the twin goals of regulating positive company credibility, and preventing the loss of that credibility, and employees who may have directly caused the offending behaviour may not be singled out as the cause.

[180] Wells (n 177) 37.

[181] This and the following sentences are from Kagan, Gunningham and Thornton (n 79).

[182] N Shover, J Lynxwiler, S Groce and D Clelland, 'Regional Variation in Regulatory Law Enforcement: The Surface Mining Control and Reclamation Act' in K Hawkins and J Thomas (eds), *Enforcing Regulation* (Boston, Kluwer-Nijhoff, 1984) 121–46.

[183] A Mehta and K Hawkins, 'Integrated Pollution Control and its Impact: Perspectives from Industry' (1998) 10 *Journal of Environmental Law* 61–77; RA Kagan, 'The Consequences of Adversarial Legalism' in RA Kagan and L Axelrad (eds), *Regulatory Encounters: Multinational Corporations and American Adversarial Legalism* (Berkeley, University of California Press, 2000) 372–74.

There do not appear to have been behavioural studies reporting that individuals' or firms' behaviour changed as a result of damages awards being imposed on firms.

Vogel has summarised evidence that social and normative pressures often engender a 'market for virtue' in which particular firms can prosper by investing in socially and normatively desired, but not legally required, products and processes. However, Kagan, Gunningham and Thornton describe the effect as rather limited and always constrained by the companies' economic licences.[184] They suggest that only specific regulatory requirements and the threat of enforcement could trump tight economic constraints by making a credible implicit promise: You will have to make a huge investment, but your competitors will have to do it too.

Kagan, Gunningham and Thornton conclude that[185] even within each single regulatory regime, the mix of 'licence pressures' and dispositions to comply often differ from nation to nation,[186] from region to region within nations,[187] from firm to firm,[188] and sometimes from facility to facility within the same corporation.[189]

Hutter's detailed study of compliance with safety laws in the British railway system[190] concluded that compliance is a continually creative process, and that in many important respects full compliance may be elusive.[191] She found that where regulatory ambitions were not being met the main obstacles emerged as:

— The fragmentation of the company, both organisationally and geographically;[192]
— serious communication difficulties;[193]

---

[184] D Vogel, *The Market for Virtue: The Potential and Limits of Corporate Social Responsibility* (Washington DC, Brookings Institution, 2005); D Thornton, RA Kagan and N Gunningham, 'When Social Norms and Pressures Are Not Enough: Environmental Performance in the Trucking Industry' (2009) 43 *Law & Society Review* 405–36.

[185] Kagan, Gunningham and Thornton (n 79) 53.

[186] Kagan (n 183) 372–74.

[187] Shover, Lynxwiler, Groce and Clelland (n 182) 121–46.

[188] J Howard-Grenville, J Nash and C Coglianese, 'Constructing the Licence to Operate: Internal Factors and their Influence on Corporate Environmental Decisions' (2008) 30 *Law & Policy* 73–107.

[189] N Gunningham and D Sinclair, 'Organizational Trust and the Limits of Management-based Regulation' (2009) 43 *Law & Society Review* 865–90.

[190] BM Hutter, *Regulation and Risk: Occupational Health and Safety on the Railways* (Oxford, Oxford University Press, 2001). At the time of the study, the single operating company had 130,000 personnel and was responsible for 23,000 miles of track; subsequent privatisation that created more operating companies and introduced more tiers involved in risk-control and enforcement itself produced different challenges of regulatory control, and a more distant and adversarial relationship with the public regulator.

[191] Hutter (n 168).

[192] Key findings were: Non-compliance may be the result of incompetence or a lack of communication. Indeed large organisations may be extremely difficult to control precisely because of their size; thus communication emerges as a key factor in the ability of companies to self-regulate and manage risk. The complexity of large companies lends itself to conflicting goals, misunderstood messages and unintended consequences. There is considerable variability between companies and also within companies. See ibid, pp 307–15.

[193] In this case, the major challenges included the sheer scale of activities and the large number of people involved, the need to cascade information down managerial tiers to the workforce, problems the workforce had in assimilating written information, individuals' tendencies to undervalue safety messages and avoid using safety equipment because it was personally inconvenient and hindered 'getting the job done', and mechanisms for data to be channelled back up to relevant managers so that it could be collated and conclusions learned. Ignorance or lack of awareness did not emerge as a major explanation of non-compliance. Baldwin's general study of the health and safety regulatory system concluded that rules do not produce compliance when those willing to comply do not know what compliance involves and when those less willing are not informed or stimulated in the appropriate manner. He suggested that finding the right rule for the job makes a big difference to regulation: R Baldwin, *Rules and Government* (Oxford, Clarendon Press, 1995).

— inequalities in knowledge of regulation and risk; and
— difficulties in the perceived legitimacy of state regulation and corporate risk management efforts.

A positive relationship between firm size and non-compliance is a consistent finding, such as with American antitrust law,[194] and some scholars conclude that 'this relationship has less to do with size *per se* than with opportunities for non-compliance to occur.'[195] Research in environmental compliance[196] has found significant differences based on the size and resource capacity of firms, and their public visibility and hence openness to external stakeholder and reputational pressures.[197] Haines' study of work-related deaths found that large organisations tended to act in a virtuous manner, small ones tended to lack virtue, and in the exceptions where large organisations responded in a blinkered manner their response was related to culture not structure.[198]

Small and medium sized enterprises (SMEs) are often not converted beyond compliance,[199] whereas large companies were most likely participants in the US voluntary compliance programme, driven by gaining public recognition rather than compliance reasons.[200] Stakeholders such as NGOs can have a huge potential to influence organisational behaviour.[201] But external stakeholders have also little interest in, and insufficient power to influence, SMEs.[202] Visibility increases as firm size increases. Social legitimacy expectations have a greater impact on large firms due to them being more visible to the pressures that induce ethical behaviour.[203] SMEs are more likely to be influenced by

---

[194] SS Simpson, 'The Decomposition of Antitrust: Testing a Multi-level, Longitudinal Model of Profit-squeeze' (1986) 51 *American Sociological Review* 859–75.

[195] SS Simpson and M Rorie, 'Motivating Compliance: Economic and Material Motives for Compliance' in C Parker and VL Nielsen (eds), *Explaining Compliance. Business Responses to Regulation* (Cheltenham, Edward Elgar, 2012).

[196] See summary in G Lynch-Wood and D Williamson, 'Regulatory Compliance: Organizational Capacities and Regulatory Strategies for Environmental Protection' in H Quirk, T Seddon and G Smith (eds), *Regulation and Criminal Justice* (Cambridge, Cambridge University Press, 2013) 134–61.

[197] J Barney, 'Firm Resources and Sustained Competitive Advantage' (1991) 17(1) *Journal of Management* 33–46; M Peteraf, 'The Cornerstones of Competitive Advantage: A Resource-Based View' (1993) 14 *Strategic Management Journal* 179–88; A Hutchinson and I Chaston, 'Environmental Management in Devon and Cornwall's Small and Medium Sized Enterprise Sector' (1994) 3(1) *Business Strategy and the Environment* 15–22; A Gerstenfeld and H Roberts, 'Size Matters: Barriers and Prospects for Environmental Management in Small and Medium-Sized Enterprises' in R Hillary (ed), *Small and Medium-sized Enterprises and the Environment: Business Imperatives* (Sheffield, Greenleaf Publishing, 2000); D Hitchens, S Thankappan, M Trainor, J Clausen and B de Marchi, 'Environmental Performance, Competitiveness and Management of SMEs' (2004) 96(5) *Tijdschrift voor Economische en Sociale Geografie* 541–57.

[198] Haines (n 173).

[199] I Worthington and D Patton, 'Researching the Drivers of SME Environmental Behaviour: A Study of the UK Screen-printing Sector' (2005) 12(5) *Business Strategy and the Environment* 352–62.

[200] S Arora and T Cason, 'Why Do Firms Volunteer to Exceed Environmental Regulations? Understanding Participation in EPA's 3/50 Program' (1996) 72(4) *Land Economics* 413–32.

[201] R Freeman, *Strategic Management: A Stakeholder Approach* (Cambridge MA, MIT Press, 1994).

[202] J Rowe and R Enticott, 'Evaluating the Links between Locality and Environmental Performance of SMEs: Some Observations from Survey and Partnership Programmes in the Greater Bristol Area' (1998) 5(3) *Eco-Management and Auditing* 112–25; D Williamson and G Lynch-Wood, 'A New Paradigm for SME Environmental Practice' (2001) 13(6) *International Journal of Total Quality Management* 424–32; G Lynch-Wood and D Williamson, 'The Social Licence as a Form of Regulation for Small and Medium Enterprises' (2007) 34(3) *Journal of Law and Society* 321–41.

[203] P DiMaggio and W Powell, 'The Iron Cage Revisited: Institutional Isomorphism and Collective Rationality' in W Powell and P DiMaggio (eds), *The New Institutionalism on Organizational Analysis* (Chicago, University of Chicago Press, 1991) 63–82; D Wood, 'Corporate Social Performance Revisited' (1991) 16(4) *Academy of*

the ethics of their owner-managers, which are in turn influenced by market values, and prioritise revenue-based activities.[204] Fairman and Yapp found that many SMEs studied in the food sector believe they comply with the law even when they do not.[205] They noted that for a deterrence strategy based on local prosecutions of similar businesses to succeed, small businesses would have to relate the reasons for a prosecution in another business to the problems that exist in their own, which they failed to do. Hence, when the lack of knowledge and awareness of hazards within businesses is considered alongside their general belief that they comply, the report noted that it is clear that deterrence may not be effective. In various contexts, enforcers have found that small businesses may be more responsive to advice, education and 'rehabilitative' approaches than to authoritarian policies.[206]

These differences in the receptive capacity of business structures have led Lynch-Wood and Williamson to suggest a resource-based model for enforcement, which directs regulatory resources to where they are most needed.[207] The argument runs that the typical approach of targeting large firms is unnecessary and overlooks the location of the primary problem, which rests with SMEs. SMEs comprise 99 per cent of all firms[208] and are estimated to produce 60 per cent of all business carbon dioxide emissions, 70 per cent of business pollution, 60 per cent of commercial waste, and 43 per cent of serious pollution incidents.[209] The pluralist analysis and receptive capacity model are not, however, without critics, arguing that concentrations of capital whose essential purpose is to make profits[210] cannot be either trusted to act morally or be controlled by public authorities with limited resources.[211]

There are suggestions that (at least in most economically advanced democracies) most business firms, particularly large ones, substantially comply with most kinds of regulations most of the time.[212]

> Sociolegal research indicates that managers in regulated business firms do not resemble those pictured in the economic model of the firm, carefully calculating the probabilities of detection and the cost of legal sanctions to determine what they can get away with. Amidst the cacophony of information and urgent demands that business managers receive, the deterrent messages sent by legal penalties often do not get through or soon drift out of consciousness.[213]

Management Review 691–718; D Greening and B Gray, 'Testing a Model of Organizational Response to Social and Political Issues' (1994) 37(3) *Academy of Management Journal* 467–98; R Marshall, M Cordano and M Silverman, 'Exploring Individual and Institutional Drivers of Proactive Environmentalism in the US Wine Industry' (2005) 14(2) *Business Strategy and the Environment* 92–109.

[204] D Williamson, G Lynch-Wood and J Ramsey, 'Drivers of Environmental Behaviour in Manufacturing SMEs and the Implications for CSR' (2006) 67 *Journal of Business Ethics* 317–30; R Lewicki, D Saunders and J Minton, *Negotiation* (New York NY, McGraw-Hill, 1999).

[205] R Fairman and C Yapp, 'Compliance with Food Safety Legislation in Small and Micro-businesses: Enforcement as an External Motivator' (2004) 3(2) *Journal of Environmental Health Research* 40.

[206] H Croall, 'Combating Financial Crime: Regulatory Versus Crime Control Approaches' (2003) 11 *Journal of Financial Crime* 45–55, reprinted in Haines (ed), *Crime and Regulation* (n 174).

[207] Lynch-Wood and Williamson (n 196) 134–61.

[208] Marshall Report, *Economic Instruments and the Business Use of Energy. Report to the Chancellor of the Exchequer* (London, HM Treasury, 1998).

[209] NetRegs, *SME-nvironment 2006* (Bristol, Environment Agency, 2006).

[210] M Friedman, 'The Social Responsibility of Business is to Increase Its Profits' *New York Times Magazine* (New York, 1973) 13.

[211] D Whyte, 'An Intoxicated politics of Regulation' in H Quirk, T Seddon and G Smith (eds), *Regulation and Criminal Justice* (Cambridge, Cambridge University Press, 2013).

[212] Mehta and Hawkins (n 183) 61–77; Vandenbergh (n 91) 55–144.

[213] Kagan, Gunningham and Thornton (n 79) 40.

Indeed, contrary to the legal deterrence model, Kagan and colleagues note that hundreds of large corporations have voluntarily instituted formal, externally certified environmental management systems,[214] participated in industry-run self-regulation systems,[215] joined compliance programmes, or undertaken fairly costly environmental and workplace safety improvements that are not required by legal regulations at all, even when those improvements do not clearly save the firm money.[216]

Large corporations typically maintain extensive legal, compliance, audit and risk functions, employing in-house and outside consultants, who operate as 'shadow regulators'. Such 'gatekeepers' often have firm commitments to the basic regulatory norms they work with every day and refer to in their discussions with operations departments.[217] Compliance systems are discussed at chapter 18 below.

Belcher's examination of the annual reports of 106 companies in the period immediately preceding and after the publication of the Cadbury Code (the first iteration of the 'comply or explain' formula in the UK) found a correlation between the size of the corporation and compliance statements.[218] While 77 per cent of the firms she looked at complied, the most common stated reason for non-compliance was the small size of the firm. She praised the degree of compliance in the period immediately after the Code was issued but drew attention to a huge variation in the detail given by companies.

Macneil and Li studied seventeen FTSE100 corporations that were serial non-compliers with the corporate governance Code in 2000 to 2005.[219] They concluded that in the absence of usable information from the corporation, investors constructed their own proxy measure of the importance of non-compliance, and that measure was financial performance.

There is evidence that 'tick box' procedures for declaring non-compliance have limited effect.[220] Thus, people who disclose conflicts may actually subsequently feel freer to act selfishly, because the disclosure gives them moral licence by warning the counterparties of the risk.[221] However, research in laboratory settings of repeat play, where there are greater

---

[214] MA Delmas and MW Toffel, 'Organizational Responses to Environmental Demands: Opening the Black Box' (2008) 29 *Strategic Management Journal* 1027–55; C Coglianese and J Nash, *Leveraging the Private Sector: Management-Based Strategies for Improving Environmental Performance* (Washington DC, Resources for the Future, 2006); A Prakash and M Potoski, *The Voluntary Environmentalists: Green Clubs, ISO 14001, and Voluntary Environmental Regulations* (New York, Cambridge University Press, 2006); A Prakash, *Greening the Firm: The Politics of Corporate Environmentalism* (Cambridge, Cambridge University Press, 2000);

[215] J Rees, 'Development of Communitarian Regulation in the Chemical Industry' (1997) 19 *Law & Policy* 477–528; J Rees, *Hostages of Each Other: The Transformation of Nuclear Safety Since Three Mile Island* (Chicago, University of Chicago Press, 1994); Gunningham and Sinclair (n 189) 865–90.

[216] Gunningham, Kagan and Thornton (n 178) 20–40; Prakash (n 214); S Konar and M Cohen, 'Information as Regulation: The Effect of Community Right to Know Laws on Toxic Emissions' (1997) 32 *Journal of Environmental Economics and Management* 109–24.

[217] RH Kraakman, 'Gatekeepers: The Anatomy of a Third-Party Enforcement Strategy' (1986) 2 *Journal of Law, Economics and Organization* 53–104; C Parker and VL Nielsen, 'Corporate Compliance Systems: Could they Make any Difference?' (2009) 41 *Administration and Society* 3–37. CJ Coffee Jr, *Gatekeepers: The Professions and Corporate Governance* (Oxford, Oxford University Press, 2006).

[218] A Belcher, 'Compliance with the Cadbury Code and the Reporting of Corporate Governance' (1996) 17 *Company Lawyer* 11–17.

[219] I Macneil and X Li, 'Comply or Explain: Market Discipline and Non-compliance with the Combined Code' (2006) 14 *Corporate Governance* 486–96.

[220] DC Langevoort, 'Behavioral Approaches to Corporate Law' in CA Hill and BH McDonnell (eds), *Research Handbook on the Economics of Corporate Law* (Northampton, Edward Elgar, 2012).

[221] D Cain, G Loewenstein and D Moore, 'The Dirt on Coming Clean: Perverse Effects of Disclosing Conflicts of Interest' (2005) 34 *Journal of Legal Studies* 1–25.

opportunities for those hurt by the selfishness to punish it later on, has found that the opportunism diminishes.[222]

Although corporate cultures that develop a strong sense of shared goals and the need for cooperation can be very efficient and effective in achieving common goals, where the nature of such goals is principally task-driven, the 'burden of perceived reality' can override non-core ethical values and challenges.[223] Summarising the evidence, Langevoort suggests that the notion of 'corporate scienter' or culture is likely to be very difficult to assess.[224] He suggests that it is difficult to change embedded corporate cultures through corporate governance or shareholder pressure, and that external directors should hold regular meetings with key managers so as to challenge authoritarian control from the Chief Executive. However, the burden of the psychological evidence above is that another approach may be to operate corporate structures in which ethical values are instilled amongst the staff.

X. Conclusions

These findings of cognitive and behavioural psychology collectively comprise a substantial and coherent body of knowledge about how and why human beings learn, make decisions, and tend to comply or not with norms. We note first that human reasoning and minds develop, and perhaps various stages can be identified, but not everyone might achieve the stage of wide-seeing wisdom, at least not without developmental assistance. The findings show that merely because a rule has been declared for a society or group it will not necessarily be obeyed by some or all of the group members. Thus, making a law is only a first step for a society to generally comply with its substance. Further, the findings show why a theory that people will obey a rule because of fear of potentially adverse consequences, or because they make calculations about the potential costs and benefits of disobedience, are not major causes of compliance. Thus, we might expect to find that empirical evidence of the extent to which theories about deterrence and rational economic actors do not show strongly successful results. We examine those two theories and empirical evidence about them in Part B, and the findings are as may be anticipated here.

What features should a society construct in order to maximise compliance with its norms? Note that we are talking about a society here, and are not asking the question 'What features should a legal system have in order to achieve maximal compliance?', since it is clear that the architecture and features of a legal system will themselves probably be inadequate to achieve the goal. The legal mechanisms should, instead, be seen as part of a larger construct of the social system—itself made up of a collection of social systems, such as overlapping family, business, social and political groups—of which the legal system forms a part.

---

[222] B Church and X Kuang, 'Conflicts of Interest, Disclosure and (Costly) Sanctions: Experimental Evidence' (2009) 38 *Journal of Legal Studies* 505–32; C Koch and C Schmidt, 'Disclosing Conflicts of Interest—Do Experience and Reputation Matter?' (2010) 35 *Accounting, Organizations and Society* 95–107.

[223] G Akerlof and R Kranton, 'Identity and the Economics of Organizations' (2005) 19 *Journal of Economic Perspectives* 9–32; D Kreps, 'Corporate Culture and Economic Theory' in J Alt and K Shepsle (eds), *Perspectives on Positive Political Economy* (Cambridge and New York, Cambridge University Press, 1990) 90–114; Langevoort (n 162) 80–96.

[224] Langevoort (n 220).

The empirical research outlined above suggests that the following features are advisable to maximise compliance.

Rules should conform to the moral principles of members of the group, and be made and applied in a fair and consistent way. Fair processes for making and applying rules have to apply. Possible transgressions should be identified, acknowledged and resolved in a fair and consistent manner. Issues should not be dealt with on a selective basis, ignored or left to fester. Norms of groups need to be informed by principles, moral feelings and negotiated by discussion. Whilst some organisations need leaders who run them, their mandate is to serve the goals and ethics of the group, so wholly authoritative structures will be counter-productive.

People should be given opportunities to develop their minds and critical thinking. Education plays a large part here, including moral education. They should also be given ongoing opportunities to identify moral or unusual problems that need more than swift thought, and should then be encouraged to take time, and be allowed time, to think through the answers, through discussion with colleagues and outside thinkers whose moral reasoning and judgement is valued. This means ongoing training, involving discussion on solutions to applying morality to hard problems, rather than just cold learning of the principles alone. It also needs availability of access to internal and external fora in which moral issues can be discussed.

Decisions and debates should guard against mis-framing and mis-presentation of issues, so should encourage looking at issues from different perspectives and accept challenge. They should also guard against the tendency to follow the perceived behaviour of others. Where the general behaviour is morally acceptable, and Type II decisions are not needed, this can reinforce ethical behaviour. But where the situations are reversed, it will reinforce unethical behaviour. Hence, transparency, openness to challenge, and openness to contemplating change will be important.

Behaviours can be reinforced and will tend to increase in frequency when recognised, rewarded, given air time, incentivised, and bring personal gratification in financial or reputational terms.[225] So behaviours that are desired should be reinforced accordingly; behaviours that are not so enforced will fade. In order to change organisational behaviour it is necessary to adopt strategies that involve both issuing information, training or a communications cascade and also engaging the social influence and support of small groups of 'people like me' affinities.[226]

Constant feedback, especially positive feedback but also negative, helps learning. This means that people should feel able to raise and question issues, without fear of adverse consequences, including where they themselves have done something wrong or stupid. Repression of information will not assist group or individual learning. Neither will a tendency to make decisions on inadequate information, in view of the tendency to infer the general from the particular. However, fear of embarrassment and loss of reputation can support compliance, but a culture of fear, as opposed to open sharing of information, will not be ideal. In contrast, imposition of severe sanctions will have a limited effect on improving compliance. However, a sense of fairness in relation to those sanctions that are imposed

---

[225] L Herrero, *Homo Imitans: The Art of Social Infection: Viral Change*™ *in action* (meetingminds, 2011) 61.
[226] ibid.

would support the requirement that any sanctions that are imposed should be fair, and hence proportionate and tariff-based.

Where fast decisions are needed, without time for reflection and consultation, it is preferable for them to be taken by one or more individuals who possess good judgement, and for the reasons for the decision to be subsequently reviewed, not so that it need necessarily be reversed but so that all can learn from it.

The norms and procedures of a legal system should be aligned with those of all relevant groups. Hence, messages and support from families, work colleagues, leisure activities, and society generally, should be aligned and mutually enforcing. They should not be misaligned. If they are aligned, it should be possible to achieve efficient results. For example, learning and sanctioning within a supportive work environment may avoid any need to rely on the systems of the wider society, such as its legal system.

In the following chapters we will see to what extent these ideas are found in theories of law and enforcement, in regulatory systems, in criminal and regulatory enforcement policies, and in business behaviour. We will then revert to these ideas in the Conclusions in Part F.

Part B

Deterrence

2

Deterrence Theory

I. Deterrence in Criminal Enforcement Theory

The identification of an act as a crime is based on prohibitions that have been so declared, and are enforced, by the state as the result of specific defined processes. This typically involves legislation, criminal investigation and conviction by a court. In the absence of such process, action by the state would be illegal. In distinguishing crimes from non-crimes, there are competing theories, none of which is wholly satisfactory.[1] On one approach, legal moralism links the criminalisation of certain acts to their immorality.[2] This can involve consideration of whether crimes are *mala in se*, which would be considered to be wrong irrespective of the law, or *mala prohibita*, which would be wrong because the state prohibits them. The latter would not attract the same degree of moral condemnation.[3] On the other approach, criminalisation is based on the prevention of harm to others or to society.[4]

Differing approaches are held to justify criminal enforcement. A lengthy deontological tradition places primary emphasis on punishment as censure for a wrongful act, and stresses the need for the sanction to be proportionate to the seriousness of that act.[5] The imposition of punitive sanctions is essentially retrospective, constituting retribution imposed by a powerful society for breaking its laws, and so constituting an affront to the good order and rules of that society. Indeed, punishment should only be imposed by a state[6] (as opposed to any other originator) in response to breach of that state's law.[7] In order to be principled,

---

[1] See T Brooks, *Punishment* (London, Routledge, 2012).

[2] RA Duff, 'Towards a Theory of Criminal Law?' *Proceedings of the Aristotelian Society: Supplementary Volume LXXXIV* (2010) 1–28; RA Duff, *Trials and Punishments* (Cambridge, Cambridge University Press, 1896).

[3] K Yeung, *Securing Compliance. A Principled Approach* (Oxford, Hart Publishing, 2004) 83–85.

[4] Classically expressed by JS Mill, On Liberty, ed E Rapaport (Indianapolis, Hackett, [1895] 1978).

[5] A Bottoms and A von Hirsch, 'The Crime-Preventive Impact of Penal Sanctions' in P Cane and HM Kritzer, *The Oxford Handbook of Empirical Legal Research* (Oxford, Oxford University Press, 2010); A Ashworth and L Zedner, 'Defending the Criminal Law: Reflections on the Changing Character of Crime, Procedure, and Sanctions' (2008) 2 *Criminal Law and Philosophy* 21–51, 22.

[6] See L Green, *The Authority of the State* (Oxford, Oxford University Press, 1989); J Raz, *The Authority of Law: Essays on Law and Morality* (Oxford, Clarendon Press, 1983); A Guinchard, 'Fixing the Boundaries of the Concept of Crime: The Challenges for Human Rights' (2004) 54 *International and Comparative Law Quarterly* 719; SJ Shapiro, *Legality* (Cambridge, Belknap/Harvard University Press, 2011).

[7] J Feinberg, 'The Expressive Function of Punishment' in J Feinberg (ed), *Doing and Deserving: Essays in the Theory of Responsibility* (Princeton, Princeton University Press, 1970) 95–98 (arguing that imprisonment expresses public censure to a criminal); Brooks (n 1).

punishment should be 'justly deserved', proportionate to the crime, so as to cancel out the offender's debt to society[8] by paying the appropriate 'price' for the offence (desert theory).[9]

The mere public condemnation of an offender for having committed an offence may constitute punishment, especially if it produces damage to reputation or other social consequences.[10] In contrast, a utilitarian approach focuses on the forward looking goal of deterring future unlawful behaviour.[11] A more recent consequentialist approach evaluates the appropriateness of penal sanctions by their results, particularly by the extent to which they reduce overall levels of crime.

Each of the above approaches can be argued to support three particular techniques that are used as responses to crime committed by individuals:[12] *Incapacitation* (disablement); *special deterrence* aimed at reducing the risk that the particular offender will re-offend in the future (which may be preventative and/or reformatory, such as rehabilitation);[13] and *general deterrence*, aimed at reducing the risk that others will commit the same offence for which a particular offender is being sanctioned (often invoking the principle of *pour encourager les autres*). Let us examine these three techniques a little more closely.

Incapacitation, removing an offender from circulation,[14] can be both a proportionate response in certain circumstances and can protect society from those who are thought to be at greatest risk of committing further serious offence.

Deterrence refers to an intention to prevent future offence. The objective is the prevention of future non-compliance, especially by those who have been found to have committed an infringement, or, to put the objective more positively, to induce future compliance. It is said to justify imposition of a sanction on a person who has been found guilty of having committed an offence. Deterrence has certainly been said to be the task of criminal law: 'To induce people not to cause harm of serious kinds'.[15]

Deterrence is theoretically divided into two types. First, it can be 'special', when directed at the individual who is being sanctioned for having committed a prior offence and who it is hoped will be deterred from re-offending by the imposition of a particular sanction. Second, deterrence can be 'general', when an individual offender is sanctioned for a particular breach and it is hoped that the news of the prosecution of the particular offence, the

---

[8] GWF Hegel, *The Science of Logic* (AV Millers trans, Amherst, Humanity Press, 1999); a problem in reconciling the principles of equal treatment, consistency and proportionality is that the amount of pain that any punishment causes to an individual varies with his temperament and circumstances: TH Green, *Lectures on the Principles of Political Obligation* (London, Longmans, 1941), quoted in T Brooks, 'Punishment and British Idealism' in J Ryberg and JA Corlett, *Punishment and Ethics: New Perspectives* (Basingstoke, Palgrave Macmillan, 2010) 16–32.

[9] I Kant, *The Philosophy of Law: An Exposition of the Fundamental Principles of Jurisprudence as the Science of Right* (repr Clifton, NJ, Augustus M Kelly Publishers, 1974); Hegel, ibid; A Ashworth, 'Is the Criminal Law a Lost Cause?' (2000) 116 *LQR* 225, 253–56; Yeung (n 3).

[10] An instrumental conception of law as a powerful normative order that can regulate social actors' behaviour and thus facilitate social change: P Legrand and R Munday (eds) *Comparative Legal Studies: Traditions and Transitions* (Cambridge, Cambridge University Press, 2003).

[11] J Bentham, *An Introduction to the Principles of Morals and Legislation* (1789, NY Anchor Books, 1973).

[12] Bottoms and von Hirsch (n 5).

[13] Brooks (n 8).

[14] Execution, imprisonment, removal of freedom or licence, such as restriction to a particular location, disqualification as a director or, in the corporate context, removal of a marketing authorisation of restriction of its conditions.

[15] A Ashworth, *The Criminal Process: An Evaluative Study* (Oxford, Oxford University Press, 1994) 24; J Gardner, 'Ashworth on Principles' in J Roberts and L Zedner (eds), *Principles and Values in Criminal Law and Criminal Justice: Essays in Honour of Andrew Ashworth* (Oxford, Oxford University Press, 2012).

conviction for the behaviour involved and the imposition of a particular penalty, will have an impact on others who may thereby be influenced not to commit the offence.

The use of deterrence as a theoretical justification for imposing sanctions or punishment goes further than the objective of seeking the prevention of future offending. The claim is that the imposition of official sanctions *can and will* influence future behaviour, both of the particular offender and of everyone else, and will prevent future offences being committed. Generations of philosophers have asserted this claim to have substance. For example, it has long been asserted that penal sanctions can influence an offender's will.[16] Thus, the police seek to control individuals' behaviour 'by manipulating an individual's calculus regarding whether "crime pays" in any particular instance'.[17] But in evaluating contemporary policy, we should look beyond philosophical assertion to empirical evidence. However, as discussed below, empirical findings are less convincing in supporting the effectiveness of deterrence as a mechanism of affecting human behaviour.

II.　Deterrence in Liability Law Theory

Deterrence has also been used as one of the objectives and justifications of the law of obligations. There is little doubt that an important purpose of contract law is to support people fulfilling the actions that they promise, and so the expectation that enforcement action will follow breach is a key component of a legal system. Contractual governance through networks is being extensively used along supply chains, nationally and internationally.[18] It is well established that pressure from (usually large) purchasers on (often smaller) suppliers can assist in specifying service levels and quality standards, and quality systems to achieve them.[19] Commercial consequences follow for a firm that is found to have produced goods which do not meet mandated standards of quality, or to have been at fault in accidents in which it was involved, or to have issued false advertising or financial statements.[20] Potential

---

[16] J Bentham, *An Introduction to the Principles of Morals and Legislation* (JH Burns and HLA Hart, eds) (London, Methuen, 1789/1982) 158, referring to 'reformation'.

[17] TL Meares, 'Norms, Legitimacy, and Law Enforcement' (2000) 79 *Oregon Law Review* 391–415, 396.

[18] F Cafaggi and H Muir Watt (eds), *The Regulatory Function of European Private Law* (Cheltenham, Edward Elgar, 2009); F Cafaggi, *The Challenge of Transnational Private Regulations: Conceptual and Constitutional Debates* (Oxford, Wiley-Blackwell, 2011); F Cafaggi, 'New Foundations of Transnational Private Regulation' (2011) 38(1) *Journal of Law and Society* 1; F Cafaggi, *Enforcement of Transnational Regulation: Ensuring Compliance in a Global World* (Cheltenham, Edward Elgar, 2012); F Cafaggi, 'Transnational Governance by Contract. Private Regulation and Contractual Networks in Food Safety' in J Swinnen, J Wouters, M Maertens and A Marx (eds), *Private Standards And Global Governance: Economic, Legal and Political Perspectives* (Cheltenham, Edward Elgar, 2012).

[19] H Collins, *Regulating Contracts* (Oxford, Oxford University Press, 2002).

[20] S Peltzman, 'The Effects of FTC Advertising Regulation' (1981) 24 *Journal of Law & Economics* 405–48; G Jarrell and S Peltzman, 'The Impact of Product Recalls on the Wealth of Sellers' (1985) 93 *Journal of Political Economy* 512–36; ML Mitchell and MT Maloney, 'Crisis in the Cockpit? The Role of Market Forces in Promoting Air Travel Safety' (1989) 32 *Journal of Law & Economics* 329–55; JM Karpoff and JR Lott, Jr, 'The Reputational Penalty Firms Bear from Committing Criminal Fraud' (1993) 36 *Journal of Law & Economics* 757–802; CR Alexander, 'On the Nature of the Reputational Penalty for Corporate Crime: Evidence' (1999) 42 *Journal of Law & Economics* 489–526; JM Karpoff, D Scott Lee and GS Martin, 'The Cost to Firms of Cooking the Books' (2008) 43 *Journal of Financial and Quantitative Analysis* 581–611; J Armour, C Mayer and A Polo, 'Regulatory Sanctions and Reputational Damage in Financial Markets' (2010) Oxford Legal Studies Research Paper No 62/2010.

customers may refuse to trade, or impose more onerous conditions, such as less generous terms.[21]

The primary focus of this chapter is, however, on tort law. Here, it is necessary to distinguish objectives from justifications. First, it might be a theoretical *objective* of tort law that the imposition of liability, and payment of compensatory damages, should deter the particular defendant, and perhaps also others, from repeating the action that gave rise to the liability. Whether such an effect on future behaviour in fact occurs can only be measured empirically. Second, it might be a *rational justification* of tort law that it has a deterrent effect. But if that justification is to be rational, and if it is justifiable as a policy, it ought (similarly) to be supported by empirical evidence that tort law does in fact affect future behaviour. However, centuries of philosophical assertion have taken place that have both confused the issues of objectives and justifications, and also been undertaken without any illumination by empirical evidence.

Analysis of ancient law and the findings of evolutionary psychology by Parisi, Luppi and Fargnoli support an evolutionary view of a changing mix of retaliatory, punitive and compensatory objectives.[22] They found an early disposition for retaliatory behaviour as a deterrent against other tribes causing harm later transformed into punitive justice, as a social norm, constrained by kind-for-kind limitations of discretionary magnitude. Later, this transformed to compensatory justice, as an additional measure-for-measure constraint developed to limit spirals of escalating blood feuds. Concomitant with these changes, liability shifted from tribes to individuals. More specialised tools for effecting deterrence were developed, and the monolithic liability of *lex talionis* branched out on two separate paths: Tort liability and criminal liability. These ideas might suggest that the mix of techniques, effects, objectives and justifications continue to vary as societies evolve.

There has been virtually universal agreement that the principal aim of tort law is compensatory justice—a responsibility to make good harm caused.[23] In addition, some scholars have claimed that tort law does have a deterrent effect, but few now seem to support that.[24] In 1951, Glanville Williams claimed that the principal *aims* of tort law were appeasement, justice, deterrence and compensation.[25] In 1999, Honoré argued that the two general justifying aims of tort were to discourage undesirable behaviour and therefore to protect rights and award compensation when they have been violated.[26] However, in 2010 Lord Bingham,

[21] JR Graham, Si Li and Jiaping Qiu, 'Corporate Misreporting and Bank Loan Contracting' (2008) 89 *Journal of Financial Economics* 44–61.

[22] F Parisi, B Luppi and I Fargnoli, 'Deterrence of Wrongdoing in Ancient Law' (2014) Minnesota Legal Studies Research Paper No 14-38.

[23] Aristotle, *Nichomachean Ethics, Book V* (T Irwin tr, Indianapolis, Hackett Publishing, 1999) paras 1131b-1134a; T Aquinas, *Summa Theologica* (Fathers of English Dominican Province trs, New York, Benziger Bros, 1947), part 2(2) question 62 arts 1–3; H Grotius, *De Jure Belli ac Pacis Libri tres* (FW Kelsey tr, Oxford, Clarendon Press, 1925) book 2 ch 17 para I; S Pufendorf, *Of the Law of Nature and Nations* (HC Oldfather and WA Oldfather trs, Oxford, Clarendon Press, 1934) book 3 ch 1 § 2; A Beever, *Rediscovering the Law of Negligence* (Oxford, Hart Publishing, 2007); A Beever, 'Our Most Fundamental Rights' in D Nolan and A Robertson (eds), *Rights and Private Law* (Oxford, Hart Publishing, 2012) ch 3.

[24] Standard text books note deterrence as one of the aims of tort law, but without expanding on why, and state that it is 'subsidiary' and subject to doubt: S Deakin, A Johnston and B Markesinis, *Markesinis and Deakin's Tort Law* 5th edn (Oxford, Oxford University Press, 2003) 37–38.

[25] G Williams, 'The Aims of Tort Law' (1951) 4 *Current Legal Problems* 137. Noted in P Cartwright, *Consumer Protection and the Criminal Law. Law, Theory and Policy in the UK* (Cambridge, Cambridge University Press, 2001).

[26] T Honoré, 'The Morality of Tort Law: Questions and Answers' in DG Owen (ed), *Philosophical Foundations of Tort Law* (Oxford, Oxford University Press, 1995), reprinted in T Honoré, *Responsibility and Fault* (1999), 71 ff. Adopted by J Bell, 'The Development of Tort Law' in H Koziol and B Steininger (eds) *European Tort Law 2008*

one of the most distinguished British judges of recent years, expressly disagreed with that view, and asserted that securing compensation is the primary function of tort.[27] Nevertheless, the truth of one or other of these differing viewpoints has not been supported by empirical evidence. In 2013 Cane agreed that the purpose of tort in English law is to compensate, not punish, and supported that position with the fact that compensation bears no relation to the means of the tortfeasor. He concludes that tort law focuses primarily on the obligation of the defendant to pay rather than the entitlement of the claimant to be paid compensation, and that its fundamental goal is corrective justice or reducing the balance of fairness between two parties.[28]

It is interesting that, although deterrence was frequently cited by American tort and economics scholars some decades ago, the major debates amongst tort theorists over the past 30 or more years have been over whether tort law is primarily about corrective justice[29] or distributive justice,[30] or whether it is based on duties or rights.[31] All of these debates contain almost no reference to tort itself having any deterrent goal or practical effect. In the USA, civil recourse theory asserts that a person who has been wronged by another is awarded by the state a private right of action and an enforcement mechanism as a proportionate response.[32] This focuses on a state controlled system of law, as providing a more socially acceptable solution to disputes, permitting individual freedom to exact retribution through taking the law into one's own hands, on the assumption that public regulation is of little relevance.[33]

The assertion that tort law and private enforcement generally 'deters' future behaviour is based on three principal arguments. These are that: The vindication of rights and the articulation of law has an intrinsic effect on behaviour; the belief that increasing the force of

---

(Berlin/Boston, De Gruyter, 2009) 213 ff (no 21 ff). Honoré argues from the philosophical position that a person who causes harm is responsible for such an outcome, even if the outcomes was not intended or foreseen and in the absence of fault (outcome responsibility).

[27] Lord Bingham of Cornhill, 'The Uses of Tort' (2010) 1 *Journal of European Tort Law* 3.

[28] P Cane, *Atiyah's Accidents, Compensation and the Law* 8th edn (Cambridge, Cambridge University Press, 2013) 477. Cane, unlike most previous private law scholars, takes into account some important empirical evaluations, notably DN Dewees, D Duff and M Trebilcock, *Exploring the Domain of Accident Law: Taking the Facts Seriously* (Oxford, Oxford University Press, 1996) (discussed below).

[29] EJ Weinrib, *The Idea of Private Law* (Oxford, Oxford University Press, 1995); EJ Weinrib, *Corrective Justice* (Oxford, Oxford University Press, 2012).

[30] AI Ogus, *Regulation: Legal Form and Economic Theory* (Oxford, Clarendon Press, 1994) 46–51; Cane (n 28); A Ogus, 'Shifts in Governance for Compensation to Damage: A Framework for Analysis' in WH van Boom and M Faure (eds), *Shifts in Compensation between Private and Public Systems* (New York, Springer, 2007).

[31] R Stevens, *Torts and Rights* (Oxford, Oxford University Press, 2007); R Stevens, 'Rights and Other Things' Law' in Nolan and Robertson (n 23). See generally Nolan and Robertson (n 23).

[32] B Zipursky, 'Rights, Wrongs, and Recourse' (1998) 51 *Vanderbilt Law Review* 1; B Zipursky, 'Philosophy of Private Law' in J Coleman and S Shiro (eds), *The Oxford Handbook of Jurisprudence and Philosophy of Law* (Oxford, Oxford University Press, 2002); B Zipursky, 'Civil Recourse, Not Corrective Justice' (2003) 91 *Georgetown Law Journal* 695; JCP Goldberg, 'The Constitutional Status of Tort Law: Due Process and the Right to a Law for the Redress of Wrongs' (2005) 115 *Yale Law Journal* 524 (suggesting a constitutional grounding for a right to redress); AJ Sebok, 'Punitive Damages: From Myth to Theory' (2007) 92 *Iowa Law Review* 957 (suggesting a recourse-based account of punitive damages); J Solomon, 'Equal Accountability Through Tort Law' (2009) 103 *Northwestern University Law Review* 1765; JCP Goldberg and BC Zipursky, 'Civil Recourse Revisited' (2011) 39 *Florida State University Law Review* 341; JCP Goldberg and BC Zipursky, 'Rights and Responsibility in the Law of Torts' in Nolan and Robertson (n 23) ch 9; JCP Goldberg and BC Zipursky, 'Tort Law and Responsibility' in J Oberdiek (ed), *Philosophical Foundations of the Law of Torts* (Oxford, Oxford University Press, 2014).

[33] EL Sherwin, 'Interpreting Tort Law' (2011) 39(1) *Florida State University Law Review* 227 (civil recourse reflects the need for the not entirely laudable function of a peaceful alternative to private revenge).

the legal consequences increases the effect on behaviour, and hence the effect on behaviour itself exists; and the economic argument that any rational actor who seeks to maximise self-interest will adjust future behaviour in the light of the risk of a liability to pay damages, and the assumption that everyone is a rational economic actor. Let us note the main arguments on these three points.

A. Articulation of Law

The argument that law and legal processes deter falls into two parts. First, it is argued that the activity of articulating law increases compliance. It is said that the mere public declaration of a particular standard of behaviour promotes observance by society of that standard, and will *ipso facto* affect the future behaviour of many.[34] Liability rules establish standards of conduct, and court judgments uphold such standards, expressing disapproval of undesirable activity,[35] and amplify the detailed requirements in particular situations.

The second argument is the refinement to assert that the fact that legal rules are *enforced* affects behaviour. Thus, the imposition of *any* ex post financial sanction will affect future behaviour to some extent. Actors will note that the law is being enforced, and that society is thereby not only declaring the intrinsic value of the standard set but also signalling that all of the society's legal standards will be enforced, and that non-compliance gives rise to the risk of adverse consequences. In relation to tort decisions against businesses, judgments are said to have the particular mechanistic effect of 'inducing organizations to develop claims management capabilities' and thereby 'improve safety, reduce risk, and increase compliance with external legal requirements.'[36] Organisations' internal claims management operations can, though they need not, facilitate care-taking in four important ways: (a) Promoting the gathering and analysis of claims information; (b) requiring the hiring of specialised personnel with a mission to reduce claim payouts; (c) encouraging bureaucratised procedures that may be harm-reducing, and (d) increasing the salience of claims to various actors within the organisation.[37]

But, on the other hand, the effect of individual legal cases may be expected to have limited effect. People may have a general awareness that the legal and court system exists, and that the law is upheld, so their conduct should conform to the standards that the law requires and, if it does not, they may be held liable. But how much of an effect does that have on behaviour? How many members of society are capable of articulating the substance of even the principal laws? Common perceptions may be that the outcome of legal cases, if they are known, can be unpredictable and seemingly irrational and unfair (the law is an ass).[38] Cane highlights the disconnection between popular and legal ideas of causation and liability, and

---

[34] WM Landes and RA Posner, *The Economic Structure of Tort Law* (Cambridge MA, Harvard University Press, 1987).

[35] P Cane, *The Anatomy of Tort Law* (Oxford, Hart Publishing, 1997) 119.

[36] M Schlanger, 'Operational Deterrence: Claims Management (In Hospitals, a Large Retailer, and Jails and Prisons)' (2008) 2 *Journal of Tort Law* 1.

[37] ibid.

[38] There are too many cases in which an activity does contribute (in a statistical sense) to accident causation, but in which the law's concepts of fault and cause operate in such a way that one 'causer' of an accident may be charged with too high a proportion of the costs, and another 'causer' with too small a proportion: Cane (n 28) 477.

distribution of the costs of accidents between victims and causers of accidents in a manner inconsistent with general deterrence theory.[39] To what extent will people know the details of particular decisions, so they can adjust their behaviour accordingly? It has always been the case in common law jurisdictions that the vast majority of civil cases settle and receive little publicity.[40] We saw in chapter one that behavioural psychology does find that messaging and reminders have an effect on behaviour, but an isolated instance may only produce a limited effect.

The broad deterrence approach has been developed—especially in the USA—into the argument that tort law provides a public regulatory function,[41] although such an approach encounters difficulties in being based essentially on ex post decisions that present difficulties of anticipation by complex commercial enterprises who seek far more detailed ex ante clarity of behavioural rules and certainty. Nevertheless, the 'litigation as regulation' notion has been extensively developed through economic analysis.[42]

A prerequisite for a deterrent effect is that actors must be able to control their actions, have the capacity to anticipate that certain actions will cause harm and the potential for liability, and be able to take steps to avoid that harm. All of these issues are problematic in life. In 1997, Cane noted that punitive damages and even compensatory damages *might* have, as one of their rationales, the expression of disapproval of and discouragement of certain kinds of conduct, and that one of the multifarious extrinsic (and opposed to intrinsic) functions of tort law might be deterring people generally from engaging in the sort of conduct for which the defendant is sanctioned.[43] However, he also argued that deterrence of future conduct by defendants generally is problematic as a justification for the imposition of tort liability to pay damages for two reasons. First, deterrence of future tortious conduct by a person depends on how he reacts to the award of the remedy after the damages have been paid. The other extrinsic goals of tort remedies can typically be secured by state enforcement procedures, but there is no state machinery to ensure that the desired deterrent effect of monetary tort liability is realised. Second, he recognised that relatively little is

[39] G Calabresi, 'Does the Fault System Optimally Control Primary Accident Costs?' (1968) 33 *Law and Contemporary Problems* 429.

[40] C Hodges, 'Settlement and its Pitfalls in England and Wales' in C Hodges and A Stadler (eds), *Resolving Mass Disputes: ADR and Settlement of Mass Claims* (Cheltenham, Edward Elgar, 2013). Her Majesty's Court Service figures to 2010 suggested that 2.5% of all fast and multi track claims were decided at trial, but this figure included a large number of undefended money claims that proceeded straight to judgment without a trial. Of claims that were defended in the fast and multi track, around 25% were decided at trial, but the percentage varied between different types of claim. *Proposals for Reform of Civil Litigation Funding and Costs in England and Wales. Implementation of Lord Justice Jackson's Recommendations*, Ministry of Justice, Consultation Paper CP 13/10, November 2010, para 115, available at https://www.gov.uk/government/uploads/system/uploads/attachment_data/file/238368/7947.pdf.

[41] AZ Roisman et al, 'Preserving Justice: Defending Toxic Tort Litigation' (2004) 15 *Fordham Environmental Law Review* 191 (tort liability changes the behaviour of others); AF Popper, 'In Defense of Deterrence' (2012) 75(1) *Albany Law Review* 101: The impact or quantum force of messaging—the deterrent value—is difficult to calculate. 'My fundamental conclusion is that modern American negligence law regulates activity levels to a considerably greater extent than has previously been recognized.' SG Gilles, 'Rule-Based Negligence and the Regulation of Activity Levels' (1992) 21 *Journal of Legal Studies* 319, 320.

[42] WK Viscusi (ed), *Regulation through Litigation* (Washington, Brookings Institution Press, 2002).

[43] Cane (n 35) 116, 119, 207. Other extrinsic functions he identified include the protection of property, reinforcement of contract, the preservation of competition, loss spreading, the protection of life and property, law enforcement, the due administration of justice and preserving freedom of contract.

known about how effective tort remedies are in deterring tort defendants from future tortious conduct, and that 'it would be unwise to pronounce the tort system either justified or
unjustified in terms of its deterrence function'.[44]

Similarly, Stapleton's response to an invitation to consider the extent to which tort law
has a regulatory effect was to reject the proposition that it does.[45] She concluded that tort
law has not been called upon to play any significant role in accountability regimes or societal governance mechanisms. She noted that most tort doctrines, having been created by
common law, have no definitive stated purpose, and are motivated by a complex and diverse
set of concerns.[46] Tort entitlements never impose a strict obligation of affirmative action
to achieve a result, and can realistically be seen as minor negative restraints on freedoms of
action.[47]

There may be various possible disadvantages of a deterrence policy. First, Cane notes
the arguments that, by focusing attention on accidents that generate compensation claims,
the tort system diverts attention away from the majority of accidents that do not, and so
discourages the formation of systematic and thorough accident-prevention strategies.[48]
Second, it has long been argued that fear of liability can be counter-productive by encouraging excessive caution and unnecessary precautions—what an economist would term
over-deterrence. This is most often suggested in relation to medical treatment,[49] although
evidence is unclear.[50]

---

[44] ibid, 217–21. As noted below, his 2013 analysis took into account empirical evidence from Dewees et al and
concluded that there are strong reasons to doubt the effectiveness of the tort system as a deterrent or accident
prevention mechanism: Cane (n 28) 477.

[45] J Stapleton, 'Regulating Torts' in C Parker, C Scott, N Lacey and J Braithwaite, *Regulating Law* (Oxford,
Oxford University Press, 2004).

[46] ibid, 132.

[47] ibid, 129.

[48] eg M Brazier, 'NHS Indemnity: The Implications For Medical Litigation' [1990] *Professional Negligence* 88,
90; H Genn and S Lloyd-Bostock, 'Medical Negligence—Major New Research in Progress' [1990] *Journal of Medical Defence Union* 42. On the shortcomings of studies of litigated medical mishaps as aids to accident prevention,
see C Vincent, 'The Study of Errors and Accidents in Medicine' in CA Vincent, M Ennis and RJ Audley, *Medical
Accidents* (Oxford, Oxford University Press, 1993) 21–23.

[49] For evidence of defensive medical practices see eg D Kessler and M McClellan, 'Do Doctors Practice
Defensive Medicine?' [1996] *Quarterly Journal of Economics* 353; K Clark, 'Litigation: A Threat to Obstetric
Practice?' (2002) 9 *Journal of Law and Medicine* 303; LM Nash, MM Walton, MG Daly et al, 'Perceived Practice
Change in Australian Doctors as a Result of Medicolegal Concerns' (2010) 193 *Medical Journal of Australia* 579.
For an overview see R Dingwall, P Fenn and L Quam, *Medical Negligence: A Review and Bibliography* (Oxford,
Oxford University Press, 1991) 41–56. See also MA Jones and AE Morris, 'Defensive Medicine: Myths and Facts'
(1989) 5 *Journal of Medical Defence Union* 40; D Tribe and G Korgaonkar, 'The Impact of Litigation on Patient
Care: An Enquiry into Defensive Medical Practices' [1991] *Professional Negligence* 2; Dewees (n 28) 96–112;
B Dickens, 'The Effects of Legal Liability on Physicians' Services' (1991) 41 *University of Toronto Law Journal* 168;
Factors Influencing Clinical Decisions in General Practice (London, Office of Health Economics, 1991); M Ennis,
A Clark and JG Grudzinskas, 'Change in Obstetric Practice in Response to Fear of Litigation in the British Isles'
(1991) 338 *The Lancet* 616; YT Yang, DM Studdert and SV Subramanian, 'Does Tort Law Improve the Health of
Newborns, Or Miscarry? A Longitudinal Analysis of the Effect of Liability Pressure on Birth Outcomes' (2012) 9
Journal of Legal Studies 217.

[50] A survey reported in 1992 showed that, although 85% of British obstetricians were or had been involved in
litigation, the more significant deterrent to recruitment was long working hours, residency conditions and the job
prospects of junior hospital doctors: P Saunders, 'Recruitment in Obstetrics and Gynaecology: RCOG Sets Initiatives' (1992) 99 *British Journal of Obstetrics and Gynaecology* 538; see further *A Career in Obstetrics and Gynaecology: Recruitment and Retention in the Specialty* (Royal College of Obstetricians and Gynaecologists, 2006). See
also YT Yang, DM Studdert, SV Subramanian and MM Mello, 'A Longitudinal Analysis of the Impact of Liability
Pressure on the Supply of Obstetrician-Gynaecologists' (2008) 5 *Journal of Empirical Legal Studies* 21; FA Sloan,
SS Entman, BA Reilly, CA Glass, GB Hickson and HH Zhang, 'Tort Liability and Obstetricians' Care Levels' (1997)
17 *International Review of Law and Economics* 245.

Third, fear of sanctions may induce people not to own up, or even to conceal, information about when problems might have occurred. This is viewed as a serious concern in healthcare.[51] The fear of liability may make potential defendants unwilling to investigate injury-causing accidents,[52] may induce tampering with evidence,[53] and delay or prevent taking remedial measures before any claim is settled for fear that this may be interpreted as an admission.[54] Where achieving safety is critically important, some industries have developed a no-blame culture specifically so as to overcome the fear of criticism and adverse consequences and to promote the sharing and reporting of essential information. The achievements of the aviation industry in this respect are noted in chapter 19. Calls to remove blame from healthcare have been made regularly.[55]

B. Incremental Deterrence

The argument here is that it is rational to expect that the threat or fear of imposing more significant penalties will increase the effect on behaviour. There is assumed to be a linear magnifying effect. Hence, the more severe the sanction, the more intense the fear experienced by individuals, and the greater the likelihood that they will comply. We are not concerned here with arguments of fairness that sanctions should relate to offences on some sort of proportionate or tariff basis, and not be arbitrary or completely incommensurate.

If some incremental effect exists, the argument follows that there must be a deterrent effect, at least above some threshold. The magnification argument therefore theoretically supports a policy of producing or increasing a deterrent effect by imposing more than compensatory damages, and adding punitive damages.

There is a range of potential sanctions that might be imposed, such as capital punishment, removal of licence to operate or of liberty (imprisonment), and orders to pay a fine or damages. Some criminologists argue that having to pay damages has less force than capital punishment or imprisonment: Indeed, the amount of force exerted on behaviour by

---

[51] Sir D Dalton and N Williams, *Building a culture of candour: A review of the threshold for the duty of candour and of the incentives for care organisations to be candid* (Royal College of Surgeons, 2014), at http://www.rcseng. ac.uk/policy/documents/CandourreviewFinal.pdf. ('We know that levels of reporting do not reflect the actual level of harm that occurs in healthcare, and that there are significant differences in reporting culture between different kinds of health care services.' Para 1.20. The challenges identified in implementing systemic approach to candour in the NHS are: Definitions and thresholds (including what counts as a safety incident); ascription of what is reportable; the bureaucratic burden of sharing/reporting; fear of litigation; potential for/fear of excessive regulatory response; and potential for adverse effect on organisational reputation. Ch 2); H Marsh, *Do No Harm. Stories of Life, Death and Brain Surgery* (London, Weidenfeld & Nicolson, 2014) ('Although there is much talk of the need for doctors to work in a 'blame free' culture it is very difficult in practice to achieve this. Only if the doctors hate each other, or are locked in furious competition (usually over private practice, which means money) will they criticise each other more openly, and even then it is more behind each other's backs.')

[52] 'It's one of the painful truths of neurosurgery that you only get good at doing the really difficult cases if you get lots of practice, but that means making lots of mistakes at first and leaving a trail of injured patients behind you.' Marsh, ibid 210 in paperback edition.

[53] Marsh, ibid. ('It's quite easy to lie if things go wrong with an operation. It would be impossible for anybody to know after the operation in what way it had gone wrong.' 173).

[54] EA Webb, *Industrial Injuries: A New Approach* (London, Fabian Society, 1974) 11. For this reason, the Compensation Act 2006, s 2 provided that an apology, an offer of treatment or other redress, shall not of itself amount to an admission of negligence or breach of statutory duty.

[55] LT Kohn et al, *To Err Is Human: A Safer Health System* (Institute of Medicine, 1999).

compensatory damages may be minimal.[56] Cane notes that it seems unlikely that tort law provides people with significant incentives to take care for their *own* safety.[57] He cites data that shows that between 1973 and 1980 only 30 per cent of the UK population used car seat belts, but when not wearing them became a criminal offence in 1983 the compliance rate rose to 95 per cent for cars and over 80 per cent for vans, leading to an estimated 20–25 per cent fewer accidents.

As was seen in chapter one, behavioural psychology research significantly undermines the proposition that the degree of severity of a threatened sanction has much effect on behaviour. Instead, the more relevant findings are that people act and make decisions on all sorts of unpredictable bases, and that it is the perception of the likelihood of being identified that affects most rational people (but not those who have limited emotional responses).

A policy of deterrence underpinned the arms race in the cold war, and the competitive development of nuclear weapons and 'star wars' technology. It is worth placing that debate as occurring at the top of the Ayers-Braithwaite pyramid of sanction responses discussed in chapter 11. However, Freedman has concluded that it is important in strategic international deterrence to demonstrate not only how the deterrent will work if challenged but also the nature of the interest to be defended, that is, to reinforce the norms-based values that are being protected.[58]

C. The Economic Argument: Rational Choice, Rational Actors and Cost Internalisation

It was noted above that a mathematical approach can be taken towards calculating the risks and benefits of offending as against the risk of future sanctions. Economists have devoted extensive effort to developing an economic theory of law, in which deterrence plays a central role. Economic analysis of law has deep roots.[59] Indeed, 'law and economics' theories have come to dominate academic literature on enforcement in the United States and in relation to competition law globally.

The 'law and economics' analysis starts from a theory of how efficient competitive *markets* work. It has then been expanded to a theory on how individual economic traders behave, and how the law should treat them. The core propositions are that all actors make rational decisions based on their self-interest, so that if their activities cause external costs, the law should ensure that such costs are imposed on their originator. That cost internalisation mechanism will have the effect that it will be rational for actors to make future decisions in the expectation that their externalities need to be calculated, and hence undesirable future behaviour will be deterred. Liability law and/or regulators should impose a penalty or 'tax' on an activity that generates negative externalities, such that the full social cost of its activities are imposed upon the firm.[60]

---

[56] See T Brooks (ed), *Deterrence* (Farnham, Ashgate, 2014).

[57] Cane (n 28) 428.

[58] L Freedman, *Deterrence* (Malden MA, Polity Press, 2004) 4, 118.

[59] C de Secondat, Baron de Montesquieu, *The Spirit of Laws* (1748, repr Univ California Press, 1977); C Beccaria, *On Crime and Punishment, and Other Writings 1767* (ed R Bellamy, R Davies trans, Cambridge, Cambridge University Press, 1995); Bentham (n 11).

[60] AC Pigou, *The Economics of Welfare* (London, MacMillan, 1920) 168–71.

Let us examine the key assumptions that have been put forward more closely. First, it is said that all actors will (choose to) act as 'amoral calculators'[61] in assessing the likely costs and benefits of the options before them. All alternative courses of action can be ranked in order of preference, but an actor's indifference between two or more options is also possible (completeness assumption).[62] Second, all actors can and will seek all information relevant to a decision, so all decisions can be and are taken on the basis of full knowledge of all potential costs. Third, and critically, every actor is motivated solely by economic self-interest and utility maximisation. Fourth, firms exist in a capitalist system to make profits, so the profit maximisation theory clearly applies to their activities.

The expanded argument is that, in a free society, every actor will choose to base every action (transitivity assumption) on such rational and disinterested assessments of whichever option provides the largest net gain for him, so as to achieve his own greatest satisfaction (utility maximisation assumption).[63] Thus, businesses will base decisions on a calculation of the total costs and benefits,[64] and will rationally calculate whether it will pay them to engage in conduct that breaks the law. Actors 'carefully determine the means to achieve illegal ends, without restraint by guilt or internalized morality.'[65] The legal system should, therefore, function so that, in markets that operate in conditions of perfect competition, commercial costs accurately include all the costs of production *and of liability compensation*. This produces the result that the activity level of production of goods and services is optimal, in the sense that it inherently exhibits the optimally efficient levels of production, quality and safety, and accidents are reduced to the optimal level. In other words, commercial activities will be optimally safe—but not absolutely safe.[66]

A fifth assumption in relation to organisations is that the organisation can be viewed as a single economic and organic entity. Since a business exists to make profits, the analysis applies at the level of the organisation. It follows that corporations are able to control all the activities of their employees.[67] Since individuals initiate wrongdoing, it is cost-effective

---

[61] R Kagan and J Scholz, 'The "Criminology of the Corporation" and Regulatory Enforcement Styles' in K Hawkins and J Thomas (eds), *Enforcing Regulation* (Boston, Kluwer-Nijhoff, 1984) 67–95.

[62] JH Turner, *The Structure of Sociological Theory* 7th edn (Belmont CA, Wadsworth Publishing Company, 2003).

[63] M Allingham, *Rational Choice* (New York, St Martin's Press Inc, 1999); MS Archer and JQ Tritter. *Rational Choice Theory: Resisting Colonization.* (New York, Routledge, 2001).

[64] Allingham, ibid; Archer and Tritter, ibid.

[65] See R Cooter and TS Ulen, *Law and Economics* 5th edn (Boston MA, Addison-Wesley, 2007) 494.

[66] G Calabresi, *The Costs of Accidents: A Legal and Economic Analysis* (New Haven CT, Yale University Press, 1970); R Bowles, *Law and Economy* (Oxford, Oxford University Press, 1982) ch 7; AM Polinsky, *An Introduction to Law and Economics* 2nd edn (Boston, Little Brown & Co, 1989) chs 6 and 7; RA Posner, *Economic Analysis of Law* 8th edn (New York, Aspen Publishers, 2011) ch 6.

[67] J Arlen and R Kraakman, 'Controlling Corporate Misconduct: An Analysis of Corporate Liability Regimes' *NYU Law Review* 72, no 4 (1997) 687–779; CJ Walshand A Pyrich, 'Corporate Compliance Programs as a Defense to Criminal Liability: Can a Corporation Save Its Soul?' (1995) 47 *Rutgers Law Review* 605–92; VS Khanna and TL Dickinson, 'The Corporate Monitor: The New Corporate Czar' (2007) 105 *Michigan Law Review* 1713–56; BW Heineman Jr, 'Caught in the Middle' (2007) *Corporate Counsel* (April) 84–89; R Kraakman, 'Vicarious and Corporate Liability' in M Faure (ed) *Tort Law and Economics* 2nd edn (Cheltenham and Northampton MA, Edward Elgar, 2009) 669–81; S Shavell, *Economic Analysis of Accident Law* (Cambridge MA, Harvard University Press, 1987); J Arlen, 'The Potentially Perverse Effects of Corporate Criminal Liability' (1994) 23(2) *Journal of Legal Studies* 833–67; KB Huff, 'The Role of Corporate Compliance Programs in Determining Corporate Criminal Liability: A Suggested Approach' (996) 96 *Columbia Law Review* 1252–98; VS Khanna, 'Corporate Liability Standards: When Should Corporations Be Held Criminally Liable?' (2002) 37 *American Criminal Law Review* 1239–83.

to ascribe the wrongdoing to the company, which will usually benefit financially from the wrongdoing. This will also induce firms to police their employees and prevent them from committing misconduct.[68]

Since complying with requirements imposed by public policy (such as liability or regulatory costs) involves extra cost above the level that is commercially necessary, firms will only pay that marginal extra price when they believe that non-compliance is likely to be detected and penalised, such that it is likely to be cheaper to comply than to infringe.[69] Hence, the claim is that punishment will efficiently deter actors from committing crimes by changing the cost of the crime.[70] Abbott (drawing on Becker) argues that a deterrence strategy should be explicitly adopted for regulatory crime: His insight is that there is no contradiction between a compliance approach that seeks genuine compliance and the use of deterrent sanctions, for the threat of the latter is often necessary in order to secure the former.[71] The question is simply one of effectiveness.

In short, rational choice theory claims to assert a true and universal explanation for all human behaviour, and hence provides a series of conclusions as to ways in which behaviour can be controlled. It dictates that the appropriate enforcement response to non-compliance with law is to deter breaches by ensuring that cost–benefit calculations need to take into account the cost of punishment, so that it is not economically rational to defy the law.[72] Accordingly, this theory is claimed to supply a 'public law' vision of tort,[73] under which tort is said to provide inherent general deterrence. As Cane points out, general deterrence is a theory about who should bear the costs of 'accidents'. It is not a theory about who should be paid compensation.[74]

It is accepted that seeking maximal deterrence is harmful, and the objective is to produce an efficient level of deterrence (optimal deterrence). There are competing approaches to how optimal deterrence should be calculated:[75]

— A gain-based sanction, which forces the infringer to disgorge the gains achieved through the violation; or
— a harm-based sanction, which sets the liability at the level of the social harm created by the violation.

Both approaches are referred to, although the latter is generally preferred. Each may lead in practice to figures that differ from the other.

---

[68] VS Khanna, 'Corporate Criminal Liability: What Purpose Does It Serve?' (1996) 109 *Harvard Law Review* 1477.
[69] G Becker, 'Crime and Punishment: An Economic Approach' (1968) 76 *Journal of Political Economy* 169–217; GJ Stigler, 'The Theory of Economic Regulation' (1971) 2 *Bell Journal of Economics and Management Science* 3–21; M Faure, A Ogus and N Philipsen, 'Curbing Consumer Financial Losses: The Economics of Regulatory Enforcement' (2009) 31 *Law & Policy* 161–91.
[70] WK Estes, *An Experimental Study of Punishment* (Evanston IL, The American Psychological Association, Inc, 1944); A Bandura, *Principles of Behaviour Modification* (New York, Hole, Rinehart and Winston, 1969); B Schwartz, *Psychology of Learning and Behaviour* (New York, Norton, 1989).
[71] C Abbott, *Enforcing Pollution Control Regulation* (Oxford, Hart Publishing, 2009).
[72] Becker (n 69) 169–217.
[73] RL Rabin, 'The John G Fleming Lecture: A Brief History of Accident Law—Tort and the Administrative State' (2012) 20 *Tort Law Review* 1.
[74] Cane (n 28) 435.
[75] See S Oded, *Corporate Compliance: New Approaches to Regulatory Enforcement* (Cheltenham, Edward Elgar, 2013).

Under the gain-based theory, the rational actor will be deterred if the expected financial consequences (fine and/or damages and transactional costs) *equal or exceed* the expected *gain* from the violation. If the sanction is a fine, the minimum fine that will deter the individual will therefore be the expected gain multiplied by the inverse of the probability of a fine being effectively imposed.[76]

Under the harm-based approach, the theoretically optimal fine should *equal* the estimated calculation of the expected *net harm* caused to persons other than the offender from the violation, divided by the probability of detection (ie multiplied by the inverse of the probability of a fine being effectively imposed).[77] It is assumed that this will make the offender *internalise* all the costs and benefits of the violation,[78] including the *social* cost of their activities. It should, therefore, efficiently determine the level of precautions, as well as the level of activity.[79] This will lead the offender to commit 'efficient violations' the total benefits of which exceed the total costs, while deterring 'inefficient violations' the total costs of which exceed the total benefits. A consensus has applied since the 1970s that antitrust law, for example, should only condemn practices that reduce economic efficiency.[80] Under the internalisation approach, it is important that the total costs created by the misconduct should be taken into account, including not only the direct harm created in the market but also relevant enforcement costs, associated with enforcement actions related to the specific misconduct.[81] However, analysis reveals that it is important that accurate calculations of risks and benefits are undertaken, since both under- and over-deterrence adversely affect social welfare.[82]

---

[76] WPJ Wils, *Efficiency and Justice in European Antitrust Enforcement* (Oxford, Hart Publishing, 2008). See Y Katsoulacos, E Motchevenkova and D Ulph, 'Penalizing Cartels: The Case for Basing Penalties on Price Overcharge' *TILEC Discussion Paper DP 2-14-037* (Tilburg University, 2014).

[77] AM Polinsky and S Shavell, 'The Economic Theory of Public Enforcement of Law' [2000] XXXVIII *Journal of Economic Literature* 45.

[78] Becker (n 69) 169; WM Landes, 'Optimal Sanctions for Antitrust Violations' (1983) 50 *The University of Chicago Law Review* 652.

[79] MA Polinsky and S Shavell, 'Punitive Damages: An Economic Analysis' (1998) *Harvard Law Review* 111(4) 869–962.

[80] RA Posner, *Antitrust Law* 2nd edn (Chicago, University of Chicago Press, 2001) vii–ix; WH Page, 'Optimal Antitrust Remedies: A Synthesis' in RD Blair and DD Sokol (eds), *The Oxford Handbook of International Antitrust Economics* (Oxford, Oxford University Press, 2012).

[81] GJ Stigler, 'The Optimum Enforcement of Laws' (1970) 70 *Journal of Political Economy* 526–36, 533.

[82] The main issue is that over-zealous enforcement can deter firms from innovating, investing or from forms of vigorous (but beneficial) competition. The US Supreme Court referred to this in a predatory pricing case (*Monsanto*), noting that 'Mistaken inferences in cases such as this one are especially costly, because they chill the very conduct that the antitrust laws are designed to protect'. Posner (n 80) 222; M Polinsky, 'Private Versus Public Enforcement of Fines' (1980) 9(1) *The Journal of Legal Studies* 105–27; FH Easterbrook, 'Detrebling Antitrust Damages' (1985) 28 *Journal of Law & Economics* 462–63, 450; AM Polinsky and S Shavell, *The Economic Theory of Public Enforcement of Law*, Stanford Law School, John M Olin Programme in Law and Economics, Working Paper No 159 (2000); MA Polinsky and S Shavell, 'Public Enforcement of Law' in N Garoupa (ed), *Criminal Law and Economics* 2nd Edition (Cheltenham and Northampton MA, Edward Elgar Publishing Limited, 2009); R Bowles, M Faure and N Garoupa, 'The Scope of Criminal Law and Criminal Sanctions: An Economic View and Policy Implications' *Journal of Law and Society* (2008) 35(3) 389–416; R Van den Bergh, 'Should Consumer Protection Law be Publicly Enforced? An Economic Perspective on EC Regulation 2006/2004 and its Implementation in the Consumer Protection Laws of the Member States' in W van Boom and M Loos (eds), *Collective Enforcement of Consumer Law: Securing Compliance in Europe through Collective Group Action and Public Authority Intervention* (Groningen, Netherlands, Europa Law Publishing, 2007) eds; RA Bierschbach and A Stein, 'Over-enforcement' (2005) 93(6) *The Georgetown Law Journal* 1743–81.

In making a calculation of future costs and risks, the variables that are relevant under a deterrence theory are: The kind of sanction imposed; the *severity* of the sanction that is likely to be imposed, which might vary with different types of sanction; and the *probability* of a future violation being detected and a sanction being imposed. Nine explanatory factors of corporate crime have been identified,[83] although the economic variables have been found not to be consistent at a firm level in their effects across the studies:[84]

1. Perceived certainty and severity of formal legal sanctions
2. Perceived certainty and severity of informal sanctions
3. Perceived certainty and severity of loss of self-respect
4. Perceived cost of rule compliance
5. Perceived benefits of noncompliance
6. Moral inhibitions
7. Perceived sense of legitimacy or fairness of law
8. Situational context of the criminal event
9. Prior offending record of the individual decision maker.

In order to overcome the objection that it may not be possible to calculate the cost and benefit of every alternative course of future conduct, the theory is assumed to be applied on the basis of an assumed probabilistic evaluation, estimating expected[85] outcomes (known as modified rational choice theory).

Criminal sentencing theory does not require that potential offenders act as fully rational, self-interested calculators, but that they possess 'bounded rationality', that is, 'they consider benefits and costs, to some degree, within parameters influenced by their attitudes, beliefs, and preferences, and by the information (however complete or inaccurate) available to them.'[86] The concept of 'bounded rationality' accepts that individuals differ in their knowledge and ability to evaluate the future risks of certainty and severity of punishment. Hence the imposition of sanctions should differ between individuals. But it can be challenging to define accurately the perceptions and beliefs of every potential offender, and adopting a differentiated approach involves a risk of inconsistency. Deterrence is irrelevant for those who do not have potential to offend. Questions of injustice arise if a sentence with general deterrent severity is imposed on an offender who is unlikely to re-offend. Further, people can be influenced by factors other than pure monetary self-interest, and non-monetary benefits can be relevant, such as social inclusion or environmental advantages.[87]

---

[83] R Paternoster and SS Simpson, 'A Rational Choice Theory of Corporate Crime' in RV Clarke and M Felson (eds), *Routine Activity and Rational Choice: Advances in Criminological Theory Vol. 5* (New Jersey, Transaction Publishers, 1993) 37–58; see SS Simpson and M Rorie, 'Motivating Compliance: Economic and Material Motives for Compliance' in C Parker and VL Nielsen (eds), *Explaining Compliance. Business Responses to Regulation* (Cheltenham, Edward Elgar, 2012).

[84] Simpson and Rorie, ibid.

[85] The evidence indicates that regulated business firms' *perceptions* of legal risk (primarily of prosecution) play a far more important role in shaping firm behaviour than the objective likelihood of legal sanctions: S Simpson, *Corporate Crime and Social Control* (Cambridge, Cambridge University Press, 2002) ch 2.

[86] Bottoms and von Hirsch (n 5) 99; see G Gigenrenzer and R Selten (eds), *Bounded Rationality: The Adaptive Toolbox* (Cambridge MA, MIT Press, 2001).

[87] MD Adler, 'Bounded Rationality and Legal Scholarship' in MD White (ed), *Theoretical Foundations of Law and Economics* (Cambridge, Cambridge University Press, 2009); RB Korobkin and TS Ulen, 'Law and Behavioural Science: Removing the Rationality Assumption from Law and Economics' (2000) 88 *California Law Review* 1051, at 1064–65; AE Carlson, 'Recycling Norms' (2001) 89 *California Law Review* 1231, at 1237–38.

In addition to increasing the cost of detected and sanctioned non-compliance through sanctions, a positive incentive can be created to encourage desirable behaviour. Some schemes aim to incentivise compliance, or to inform the authorities of wrongdoing that may be difficult for those not involved to discover (the leniency policy in competition law),[88] or to plead guilty at an early stage of an investigation or otherwise cooperate with the authorities (the plea bargaining system).[89]

As with the approach in criminal law discussed above, it is assumed that both general and individual deterrence through actual sanctions imposed on those offenders who are caught will make a substantial positive contribution to reducing the social harm proscribed by regulation.[90] An approach widely argued in the United States of America holds that individual deterrence is less important than general deterrence, and so the level of fines (and costs) may have little relationship to the level of loss suffered or illicit gain made, as long as they are sufficiently high as to achieve sufficient attention by market actors.[91] Such an approach has obvious tensions with constitutional rights and justice that apply in relation to the specific wrongdoer.

One advantage of the cost internalisation theory is that the currency in which risks and benefits are calculated can be the same under both private and public means of enforcement—namely money, whether penalties are expressed as damages or fines. This enables the legal system to choose and switch between operating public and/or private enforcement systems, since they are substitutes.

III. Dilution of Liability Deterrence by Insurance

If there is any deterrent effect of tort liability, it is widely accepted that it is significantly diluted, if not extinguished, by the effect of liability insurance. Liability insurance acts as a series of pooling mechanisms to spread the financial impact of the cost of compensating a particular claimant across multiple payers and across time.[92] An individual payment of compensation, or part of it, will be passed on from the defendant to his insurance company (or companies) under a contract of liability insurance, then further partly shared between all other insureds of the insurance company and the reinsurance companies with which the primary insurance company has contracts. To some extent, at least, the cost of annual premiums is also shared between all customers, shareholders and employees of the defendant. Hence, the insurance system spreads risk widely, thereby diluting the impact of the cost to an injured party of any single adverse event. It also inherently dilutes the financial effect

---

[88] *Revised Leniency Policy* (European Competition Network, November 2012), available at http://ec.europa.eu/competition/ecn/mlp_revised_2012_en.pdf.

[89] For US DPAs see Oded (n 75). For UK DPAs see ch 10 below.

[90] Simpson (n 85).

[91] M Gilles and G Friedman, 'Exploding the Class Action Agency Costs Myth: The Social Utility of Entrepreneurial Lawyers' [2006] *University of Pennsylvania Law Review* 105.

[92] G Calabresi, 'Some Thoughts on Risk Distribution and the Law of Torts' (1961) 70 *Yale Law Journal* 499; S Shavell, *Foundations of Economic Analysis of Law* (Cambridge MA, Harvard University Press, 2004) 261–64.

on any defendant of having to pay any damages. That reduction in financial liability clearly reduces any deterrent effect.[93]

On the other hand, a defendant who has a poor claims record might in future have to pay increased premiums or have to bear an increased deductible (a sum that is deducted from the liability of an insurer in the event of a claim). However, increased premiums may equally arise through the inherent riskiness of the industry involved, or from the state of the insurance market.[94] These factors therefore also dilute any individual deterrent effect.

Indeed, while Wagner asserts that both delict and criminal law serve a deterrence function, in addition to compensating, he accepts that the shifting of costs of harm from tortfeasors to liability insurers and to the public at large 'obviously destroys the incentives that tort law generates'.[95] In reviewing the fluctuations in esteem of the deterrence and compensation models in European liability theory, Wagner noted a 'deep scepticism towards the deterrent function of tort law' which was partially rescued by the rise of interest in the law and economics movement, but which 'does nothing to prove that this [deterrent] effect actually exists'.[96]

A further theoretical concern is that a business that has some insurance cover will be incentivised to act less carefully than it otherwise might. This is known as moral hazard.[97] Insurers have various techniques to combat moral hazard.[98] Indeed, in theory, insurance operates as a private sector regulatory mechanism on insureds' behaviour.[99] Relevant techniques include monitoring the insured's behaviour in order to increase the premium if the insured relaxes his safety measures, requiring evidence of satisfactory risk reduction mechanisms by the insured such as third party certifications, adapting after the fact on a bonus/malus scheme, limiting cover and leaving parts of the risk of liability lying with the insured, applying caps, deductibles and exclusions on liability cover only offered cover based a high premium or, in extreme circumstances, refusing cover.[100] In practice, it will be seen that the effects of insurance are not causatively linear in relation to affecting behaviour, and can

---

[93] P O'Malley, 'Fines, Risks and Damages: Money Sanctions and Justice in Control Societies' (2010) *Sydney Law School Research Paper No 10/40*.

[94] T Baker and SJ Griffith, *Ensuring Corporate Misconduct: How Liability Insurance Transforms Shareholder Litigation* (Chicago, University of Chicago Press, 2010). The insurance market has been shown to be cyclical, with periodic crises that produce significant disruption.

[95] G Wagner, 'Tort Law and Liability Insurance' (2006) 31 *The Geneva Papers* 277. No empirical evidence is produced to support the initial assertion, and the analysis omits consideration of the effect on behaviour of regulation, or the findings of psychology.

[96] ibid.

[97] T Baker and P Siegelman, 'The Law and Economics of Liability Insurance: A Theoretical and Empirical Review' University of Pennsylvania, Institute for Law & Economics Research Paper No 11-09 'The Law and Economics of Liability Insurance: A Theoretical and Empirical Review'; SJ Chandler, 'The Interaction of the Tort System and Liability Insurance Regulation: Understanding Moral Hazard' (1996) 2 *Connecticut Insurance Law Journal* 91.

[98] ibid; Cane (n 35) 220.

[99] RV Ericson, A Doyle and D Barry, *Insurance as Governance* (Toronto, University of Toronto Press, 2003); RV Ericson and A Doyle, *Uncertain Business: Risk, Insurance and the Limits of Knowledge* (Toronto, University of Toronto Press, 2004); T Baker, 'Insurance in Sociolegal Research' (2010) 6 *Annual Review of Law and Social Science* 433.

[100] Wagner (n 95) 277–92. See also C Heimer, *Reactive Risk and Rational Action: Managing Moral Hazard in Insurance Contracts* (Berkeley, University of California Press, 1985); Baker and Griffith (n 94); T Baker, 'Risk, insurance and the social construction of responsibility' in T Baker and J Simon (eds), *Embracing Risk: The Changing Culture of Insurance and Responsibility* (Chicago, University of Chicago Press, 2002); KS Abraham, *Distributing Risk: Insurance, Legal Theory, and Public Policy* (New Haven, Yale University Press, 1986).

be highly complex and difficult to generalise about. In addition, insurance markets do not operate in such a way that risk relates to price, and prices can vary significantly depending on market circumstances.[101]

The dilution effect has given rise to significant debate amongst tort scholars and economists over whether judicial decisions on imposition of liability are, or should be,[102] taken regardless of whether the defendant has cover. Leading scholars have denied that there is any consistent pattern in the law which reflects such a close relationship with insurance, and that such considerations should be irrelevant,[103] since tort law is based on ideas of personal responsibility and a 'bipolar' relationship between injurer and injured.[104] Others have argued that judges appear more ready to impose liability when insurance enables the cost of compensation to be more widely distributed.[105] Tort rules are said to have been developed in favour of claimants, at least in situations where they have been less able to protect themselves by taking out their own first party insurance. Merkin and Steele have recently argued that the way in which insurance in fact operates is far more integral and widespread than many have realised, that its role in the law of obligations is therefore integral, and that its loss-spreading function is so pervasive as to completely undermine the orthodox view of tort law.[106] It follows that theories that deny the relevance of insurance to decisions on the existence of a duty of care rely strongly on a deterrence argument: But if tort liability does in fact rest on the extensive risk-spreading mechanisms of insurance, both the role and any functional effect of deterrence lose relevance.

Claims statistics in England and Wales clearly establish that the existence of third party liability insurance drives claiming behaviour.[107] That is, a claim is likely to be made against a defendant who has adequate insurance, and not made against an insolvent and uninsured defendant. Lewis found that almost all claims brought are insured: Personal injury claims overwhelmingly concern road traffic incidents (53 per cent) and work (33 per cent) accidents, and not home or leisure accidents.[108] In the late 2000s, insurers paid £984 million annually to claimant solicitors in relation to costs for motor related claims, as opposed to £171 million for costs in employees' liability claims.[109]

Further, the processes of insurance are applied instead of those of the law. Insurers process the overwhelming majority of claims outside court procedures, applying their own simplified liability criteria since tort criteria are too uncertain when applied in an administrative

---

[101] Wagner (n 95) 277–92.

[102] MG Faure, 'The View from Law and Economics' in G Wagner (ed), *Tort Law and Liability Insurance* (Wien, Springer, 2005).

[103] J Stapleton, 'Tort, insurance and ideology' (1995) 58 *Modern Law Review* 820; WL Prosser, *The Law of Torts* 4th edn (St Paul MN, West Publishing Co, 1971) 547: 'A dispassionate observer, if such a one is to be found in this area, might … conclude that the "impact" of insurance upon the law of torts has been amazingly slight…'

[104] Weinrib, *The Idea of Private Law* (n 29); Weinrib, *Corrective Justice* (n 29).

[105] J Fleming, 'Accident Liability Reconsidered: The Impact of Liability Insurance' (1948) 57 *Yale Law Journal* 549; M Davies, 'The End of the Affair: Duty of Care and Liability Insurance' (1989) 9 *Legal Studies* 67; J Morgan, 'Tort, Insurance and Incoherence' (2004) 67 *Modern Law Review* 384.

[106] R Merkin and J Steele, *Insurance and the Law of Obligations* (Oxford, Oxford University Press, 2013); R Merkin, 'Tort, Insurance and Ideology: Further Thoughts' (2012) 75(3) *The Modern Law Review* 301.

[107] R Lewis, 'How Important are Insurers in Compensating Claims for Personal Injury in the UK?' (2006) 31 *The Geneva Papers* 323–39.

[108] ibid.

[109] Lord Justice Jackson, *Review of Civil Litigation Costs: Preliminary Report* (The Stationery Office, 2009) ch 24, para 2.1.

procedure.[110] Most tort awards are for very limited sums—little more than £2,500.[111] In 2002, it was estimated that one per cent of cases resulted in a payment of £100,000 or more, and these comprised 32 per cent of the total damages paid out.[112] Hence, tort law plays only a marginal role in the legal system.

Similarly, a rare study on claims against local authorities in Scotland and Ireland, in respect of harm attributed to alleged negligent maintenance of roads and footpaths, found that the law was significantly simplified in the bureaucratic processes that applied.[113] This simplification applied both where decision making was contracted-out to insurance companies, and determined irrespective of whether they fell below or above the authorities' deductible limits (as in Scotland), or involved public officials (as in Ireland, where claims handlers and local engineers exercised considerable discretion in assessing liability, with almost no input from lawyers). It did not appear that this 'street-level decision-making'[114] had much impact on authorities' actions in reducing their exposure.

A similar position is found in the United States. Tort claiming is almost entirely coextensive with liability insurance across a wide range of subfields. Potential tort defendants without liability insurance are rarely sued,[115] except if they have substantial assets. Liability insurance is a bureaucratic claims processing mechanism that renders large swaths of tort law into an administrable, simplified set of compensation rules and procedures.[116] The simplifying effect of the liability insurance claim processing mechanism varies inversely with the size of the claim.[117] For claims against individuals, claims liability insurance policy limits have become a de facto cap on tort damages.[118] Individual defendants might pay 'blood money' from their own pockets, but the aggregate amounts paid are trivial proportion of overall tort payments.[119] Exclusions very nearly eliminate entire categories of claims. The exclusion of intentional injury explains why the civil justice system has not played a significant role in addressing domestic violence.[120] To recover, victims must shape their tort claims to match the available insurance. H Laurence Ross stated in his pioneering study of automobile insurance adjusters in the 1960s that 'legal philosophy has lost contact with the reality of modern society'.[121]

---

[110] It is unusual for insurers to contest liability: A study found that insurers' files 'contained remarkably little discussion of liability', and it was initially denied in only 20% of cases. 'In nine out of ten cases, the real defendants are insurance companies, with the remainder comprising large self-insured organizations or public bodies': T Goriely, R Moorhead and P Abrams, *More Civil Justice? The Impact of the Woolf Reforms on Pre-Action Behaviour* (London, The Law Society and the Civil Justice Council, 2002) 103.

[111] P Pleasance, *Personal Injury Litigation in Practice* (London, Legal Aid Board Research Unit, 1998) 40 Figure 3.17.

[112] Lord Chancellor's Department (2002) Table 1.

[113] S Halliday, J Ilan and C Scott, 'Street-Level Tort Law: The Bureaucratic Justice of Liability Decision-Making' (2012) 75(3) *Modern Law Review* 347.

[114] M Lipsky, *Street-Level Bureaucracy: Dilemmas of the Individual in Public Services* (New York, Russell Sage, 1980).

[115] T Baker, 'Blood Money, New Money and the Moral Economy of Tort Law in Action' (2001) 35 *Law & Society Review* 275–319; J Wriggins, 'Domestic Violence Torts' (2001) 75 *Southern California Law Review* 121–84.

[116] Baker (n 99).

[117] T Baker, 'Insurance as Tort Regulation: Six Ways that Liability Insurance Shapes Tort Law' (2006) 12 *Connecticut Insurance Law Journal* 1–16.

[118] Baker, ibid 1.

[119] K Zeiler, BS Black, CM Silver, DA Hyman and WM Sage, 'Physicians' Insurance Limits and Malpractice Payments: Evidence from Texas Closed Claims, 1990–2003' (2008) *Journal of Legal Studies* 36.

[120] Wriggins (n 115) 121.

[121] HL Ross, *Settled Out of Court: The Social Process of Insurance Claims Adjustments* (Chicago, Aldine Publishing Company, 1970).

In the United States, the effect of insurance is restricted to individual liability decisions by various means. First, jurors are not to be told whether the plaintiff has insurance coverage. Second, under the collateral source rule the plaintiff does not need to offset any benefits received from a third-party against the compensatory amount owed to her by a liable defendant. One of the justifications for this rule, in addition to the policy that the insured is entitled to the benefit of a contract bargain, is that the effect on future health care might be lost, in view of the effective absence of universal health coverage in the USA.[122]

Business and the insurance industry have lobbied for tort reform in the USA since at least the 1990s. Those who support claimants and their rights view this movement as a cynical attempt to reduce the risk of liability. In contrast, an insurance perspective would be that the objective has been to reduce the legal ambiguity generated by the tort system and reduce the unpredictability of the liability costs covered by insurance, making it easier to set premiums, and also to reduce them.[123]

Punitive damages have a far greater influence on tort claims and settlements in the USA than in Europe.[124] Even if US awards are relatively rare,[125] they have an effect on inflating damages and settlements to levels far in excess of European compensatory damages. The use of punitive damages specifically reflects the regulatory purpose of private litigation in the USA. They are awarded to punish outrageous conduct and 'deter [defendants] and others ... from similar conduct in future'.[126] Thus the US Supreme Court says that they are 'imposed for purposes of ... deterrence'.[127] However, there is a paucity of empirical evidence on whether punitive damages in fact affect behaviour. Viscusi's examination of differences in risk levels between states that permit punitive damages awards and those that do not found no evidence of such a deterrent influence.[128]

Weinrib says punitive damages have no place in private law since they 'are geared, not to restoring the plaintiff's rights, but to punishing the defendant'.[129] In the English context, Stevens has argued that punitive damages are justified not by deterrence considerations, but on the basis that 'the contumacious infringement of a right is more serious' than a less culpable infringement, notwithstanding the fact that the degree of culpability does not affect the value of the right infringed.[130]

---

[122] TS Ulen, 'The View from Abroad: Tort Law and Liability Insurance in the United States' in G Wagner (ed), *Tort Law and Liability Insurance* (Vienna, Springer, 2005).

[123] M Geistfeld, 'Legal Ambiguity, Liability Insurance, and Tort Reform' (2011) 60 *DePaul Law Review, NYU School of Law, Public Law Research Paper No 11-49*.

[124] Popper (n 41) 101. C Hodges, S Vogenauer and M Tulibacka (eds), *The Costs and Funding of Civil Litigation: A Comparative Approach* (Oxford, Hart Publishing, 2010).

[125] CR Sunstein, R Hastie, JW Payne, DA Schkade and WK Viscusi, *Punitive Damages: How Juries decide* (Chicago, University of Chicago Press, 2002) (noting empirical studies that found that judges' instructions to juries were brief and frequently not remembered by juries, who often adopted common sense conceptions of blameworthiness, tended to increase amounts of awards after joint deliberation, did not think coherently about deterrence and did not apply theories of optimal deterrence).

[126] Restatement (Second) of Torts § 908.

[127] *Pacific Mutual Life Insurance Company v Haslip*, 499 US 1, 19 (1991). *State Farm Mutual Automobile Insurance Company v Campbell*, 538 US 408, 416 (2003).

[128] WK Viscusi, 'Does Product Liability Make Us Safer?' (2012) 35(1) *Regulation* 24.

[129] EJ Weinrib, 'Two Conceptions of Remedies' in CEF Rickett (ed), *Justifying Private Law Remedies* (Oxford, Hart Publishing, 2008) 3, 24. But see A Burrows, 'Damages and Rights' in Nolan and Robertson (n 23)).

[130] Stevens, *Torts and Rights* (n 31).

3

Private Enforcement in the USA

I. Private Enforcement: The US Model

In contrast to its virtual absence from the literature on English law, the claim that tort law and civil enforcement have deterrent effect and justification is found extensively in American scholarly literature.[1] The reason for American interest clearly lies in the important role that private enforcement plays in the legal architecture of the United States of America, which is somewhat unique.

Enforcement of law by private actors in the United States is specifically intended to enforce not only private rights but also—and especially—public norms.[2] Hence, private litigation seeks to deliver not only compensation for damage caused in breach of private rights but also punishment for breach of public regulatory norms, as a matter of controlling individual and corporate behaviour, expressly based on the theory of deterrence.[3] In emphasising the purpose of private enforcement of public norms, the American legal system is distinct from many other legal systems, and constitutes what has been known as American 'exceptionalism'.[4]

The right to assert claims in the courts is a deeply cultural phenomenon in the USA. From the origins of the country in the seventeenth century, emphasis has been placed on the ability for individuals to assert their individual freedoms and rights. Kagan has vividly charted a system of 'adversarial legalism', with free access to civil courts and unimpeded right to challenge the powers and actions of Federal government and big corporations.[5] Key factors he identified are the enshrinement of individualism in the US Constitution, a tendency to distrust distant powers,[6] notably Federal authority and large corporations, reliance on local

---

[1] Recent example: WK Viscusi and J Hersch, 'Assessing the Insurance Role of Tort Liability after Calabresi' Vanderbilt Law and Economics Research Paper No 12-35 (tort compensation also serves a deterrence role).

[2] See S Farhang, *The Litigation State: Public Regulation and Private Lawsuits in the United States* (Princeton, Princeton University Press, 2010).

[3] Amongst many papers see JC Coffee Jr, 'Paradigms Lost: The Blurring of the Criminal and Civil Law Models—And What Can Be Done About It' (1991) 101 *Yale Law Journal* 1875; JC Coffee, Jr, 'Reforming the Securities Class Action: An Essay on Deterrence and its Implementation' (2006) 106 *Columbia Law Review* 1534–86.

[4] R Marcus, 'Exceptionalism and Convergence: Form versus Content and Categorical Views of Procedure' (2010) 49 *Supreme Court Law Review* (2d) 521; R Marcus, '"American Exceptionalism" in Goals for Civil Litigation' Goals of Civil Justice and Civil Procedure in Contemporary Judicial Systems' in A Uzelac (ed), *Goals of Civil Justice and Civil Procedure in Contemporary Judicial Systems* (Vienna, Springer, 2014).

[5] RA Kagan, *Adversarial Legalism. The American Way of Law* (Cambridge, Harvard University Press, 2001); D Kelemen, 'Suing for Europe. Adversarial Legalism and European Governance' (2006) 39(1) *Comparative Political Studies* 101. See also Farhang (n 2); SB Burbank, S Farhang and H Kritzer, 'Private Enforcement' (2013) 17 *Lewis & Clark Law Review* 637.

[6] The Boston Tea Party was an early manifestation of this tendency.

courts with locally elected judges and local juries as sources of authority. Farhang's recent analysis noted that persistent conflict between Congress and the president over control of bureaucracy, a perennial feature of the American state, creates incentives for Congress to bypass the bureaucracy and provide for enforcement via private litigation.[7]

The choice of relying on private enforcement in place of public enforcement as a means of behaviour control was made deliberately in the United States.[8] In a seminal scholarly analysis in 1941, which profoundly influenced later development of policy, Kalven and Rosenfield noted the theoretical option of empowering a number of then newly-created public agencies to deliver enforcement and behaviour control.[9] Concerns also existed in relation to the effectiveness of existing agencies, so the authors explained a vision of class litigation serving a regulatory function.

> This power of administrative bodies, to act affirmatively after the injury, is still in the tentative stage, and there are, of course, many fields in which administrative bodies have not made an appearance. As a consequence, whether it is desirable or not, private litigation must still police large areas of modern law and provide the exclusive remedy for many large-scale group injuries.[10]

They explored the possibilities of revitalising private litigation to fashion an effective means of redress for mass issues. In relation to the options for who should be the initiating actors, they noted:

> The choice seems to be between the public official and the amateur volunteer representative. But the more basic choice is between lawyers on a public pay-roll and lawyers in private practice, and this choice is by no means so simple.[11]

Hence, the choice emerged in favour of private lawyers and litigation, and that mode of behaviour control became entrenched despite the subsequent growth of federal and state public regulation. As American federal agencies emerged during the twentieth century,[12] they tended to adopt a policy of only taking enforcement action in a small minority of cases, and this avoided significant expense. Between 2006 and 2009 the number of organisations sentenced annually under the Organizational Sentencing Guidelines fell from 217 to 177, although there has been an increase in use of deferred- or non-prosecution agreements, to 30 in 2010.[13] Public regulation in the USA and private litigation have remained largely separate domains, and those working in the latter have strenuously maintained that a primary purpose of litigation is deterrence and hence regulation of business. The phenomenon is

---

[7] Farhang (n 2) 5.

[8] This and the following paragraph are reproduced from C Hodges, 'Collectivism: Evaluating the Effectiveness of Public and Private Models for Regulating Consumer Protection' in W van Boom and M Loos (eds), *Collective Consumer Interests and How They Are Best Served in Europe* (Vienna, Kluwer, 2007).

[9] H Kalven Jr and M Rosenfield, 'The Contemporary Function of the Class Suit' (1941) 8 *University of Chicago Law Review* 684, 687.

[10] ibid.

[11] ibid.

[12] The first significant antitrust legislation was the Federal Sherman Act of 1890, and the Food and Drug legislation emerged from the 1930s. There are various powerful US Federal regulatory agencies, such as the Department of Justice, the Securities and Exchange Commission, the Federal Trade Commission, the Food and Drug Administration and the Office of Safety and Health Administration. All of these agencies are largely mirrored in European states. The extent of regulatory requirements and the agencies' powers of market surveillance, inspection, enforcement and sanctioning are also extensive and largely similar in both USA and the EU (whether at state or EU levels).

[13] J Arlen, 'Corporate Criminal Liability: Theory and Evidence' in A Harel and KN Hylton (eds), *Research Handbook on the Economics of Criminal Law* (Cheltenham, Edward Elgar, 2012) 15, Tables 7.1 and 7.5. DPAS and NPAS are discussed in ch 10 below.

described as 'regulation through litigation'.[14] Although extensive public regulation now exists in America, the vast majority of 'enforcement' is left to private actors enforcing private law rights through the civil justice system.

Sean Farhang's analysis highlighted the role of private litigation in many important areas of federal policy in the United States as 'massive both in absolute terms and relative to enforcement by the national government.'[15] He found that in the 2000s decade, around 165,000 lawsuits were filed per year to enforce federal statutes in United States district courts.[16] These suits spanned the waterfront of federal policy, including antitrust, civil rights, labour and employment, environmental, banking and securities/commodities exchange regulation. More than 97 per cent of the suits were private filed. After petitions by prisoners to be set free, job discrimination lawsuits were the single largest category of litigation in federal courts, at around 20,000 annually in the 2000s decade, of which two per cent were prosecuted by the federal government and 98 per cent by private parties.[17]

Farhang outlined the seminal creation of an unconditional private right of action under the Civil Rights Act of 1964, as a response to an underfunded Equal Employment Opportunity Commission, the move being supported by Republicans as a policy of derailing liberal efforts at bureaucratic state-building, imposing private litigation as an alternative instrument to regulation.[18] His detailed historical analysis of federal statutes from 1887 to 2004 that created exceptions to the 'no cost shifting' rule, by providing for enforcement of specific statutes to be subject to a no-way cost shifting rule, concluded that such instances constituted clear legislative choice to proactively mobilise private litigants and attorneys in policy implementation. He noted a strikingly close association between a rise in fee shifts *and* the private rate under statutorily-created rights of action (as opposed to only a modest rise in tort claims) from end of 1960s. In his cohort of legislation, only nine per cent of the incentives provided for by Congress provided for actions against states, while 17 per cent did so against federal government, and 84 per cent apply against private sector entities.[19]

The US civil procedure system has various features that specifically support a role of aiming to deter through litigation. The model aims to encourage private actors generally, and especially private intermediaries, to take action against businesses so as to investigate and challenge potential wrongdoing and negotiate the imposition of deterrent penalties under the authority of the court system, as a means of maintaining constant scrutiny in behaviour and of imposing high penalties, mirroring what would otherwise be the role of enforcement by public bodies, but replacing them.[20]

---

[14] WK Viscusi (ed), *Regulation through Litigation* (Washington, Brookings Institution Press, 2002).

[15] Farhang (n 2) 10, and see chs 4 to 6.

[16] ibid.

[17] *Annual Report of the Administrative Office of the United States Courts*, 1997–2007, table C2.

[18] Farhang (n 2) 118. In contrast, he noted that, while creating a wide array of rights for workers, neither the National Labor Relations Act of 1935 nor the Occupational Safety and Health Act of 1970 allowed private enforcement.

[19] ibid, 55, 67.

[20] S Shavell, *Economic Analysis of Accident Law* (Cambridge MA, Harvard University Press, 1987) 277–86 (comparing and contrasting ex ante vs ex post, and privately initiated vs state initiated approaches to risk regulation); S Issacharoff, 'Regulating after the Fact' (2007) 56 *DePaul Law Review* 375, 377 ('What really sets the United States apart is the fact that its basic regulatory model is *ex post* rather than *ex ante*'); David Rosenberg, 'The Causal Connection in Mass Exposure Cases: A "Public Law" Vision of the Tort System' (1984) 97 *Harvard Law Review* 849, 853 ('Society has for the most part relied on the tort system both to prevent mass exposure accidents and to compensate their victims' and identifying five advantages of the tort system 'over the conventional administrative process').

Important features of this model are extensive discovery of documents, depositions of witnesses, no legal costs for claimants because of contingency or court-awarded fees, no risk to claimants of paying defendants' costs if they lose, but the benefit of a one-way fee shifting from defendants to claimants under many statutes if claimants win, jury decisions on liability and quantum of damages, high levels of damages and the ability to award punitive damages.

The system is designed so that the impact of litigation on the 'private attorneys general'[21] who are the principal actors, and on the courts, should be minimal. In contrast, the impact on the defendant, and on the population of defendants generally, should be financially significant. Hence, the system's principal features are an absence of barriers to investigation, and incentives to litigate and to succeed in settlements.

A system designed to deliver widespread *general* deterrence through an ex post facto mechanism involving mass non-specialist enforcers should logically aim at facilitating the achievement of results that have a high impact on the market at large, possibly at the expense of fairness in individual cases. A similar approach has focused on the deterrent effect of legislation or administrative rules. For example, based on a finding that traffic density increases accident costs substantially, Edlin and Karaca-Mandic suggested that insurance premiums should be tied to miles driven instead of per car per year so as to reduce accidents.[22]

II. Empirical Evidence on How US Private Enforcement Operates

It has been said above that philosophical assertions on whether tort law does or should deter need to be proved by empirical evidence. In view of the strong adherence in the United States to the ideologies of deterrence and private enforcement, and the considerable volume of tort liability claims and general private enforcement through litigation in the USA over a lengthy period of time, if litigation were to have a significant effect on corporate behaviour, the jurisdiction where this effect should be most visible ought to be the United States. It might be expected that empirical evidence of the effect of liability law, or lack of it, on behaviour would have emerged. In contrast to the vast doctrinal literature on the theory and practice of private enforcement and class actions in the USA, there is only a limited

---

[21] See JC Coffee, Jr, 'Rescuing the Private Attorney General: Why the Model of the Lawyer as Bounty Hunter is not Working' (1983) 42 *Maryland Law Review* 215; JC Coffee, Jr, 'Understanding the Plaintiff's Attorney: The Implications of Economic Theory for Private Enforcement of Law Through Class and Derivative Actions' (1986) 86 *Columbia Law Review* 669; B Garth, IH Nagel and SJ Plager, 'The Institution of the Private Attorney General: Perspectives from an Empirical Study of Class Action Litigation' (1987–88) 61 *Southern California Law Review* 353; LM Grosberg, 'Class Actions and Client-Centered Decisionmaking' (1989) 40 *Syracuse Law Review* 709 (arguing that it is a delusion to suggest that the 'client' is the decision maker in class actions, and that class action lawyers act like public officials). SN Subrin and MYK Woo, *Litigating in America* (New York, Aspen Publishers, 2006).

[22] A Edlin and P Karaca-Mandic, 'The Accident Externality from Driving' (1999) Public Law Research Paper No 130, University of California, Berkeley.

quantity of reliable empirical research on the *outcomes* of litigation.[23] There is almost no direct evidence on the *actual* effect of private enforcement of law, or on *how* litigation actually affects corporate decisions. The basic assumption is that since economic theory postulates that the imposition of a financial penalty *will* deter later wrongdoing, it must be so.

Significant points are that a significant number of class actions are dismissed, and of those that are certified, the vast majority settle. Thus, Willging, Hooper and Niemic collected data in four federal district courts on all types of class actions.[24] They identified 407 class actions, of which 152 (37 per cent) were certified as class actions, 59 of which (39 per cent) being certified for settlement purposes only. The most frequently certified class was the Rule 23(b)(3) or 'opt-out class', of which securities cases were the most likely, which occurred in roughly 50 per cent to 85 per cent of the certified classes in the four districts. The second most frequently certified class was the Rule 23(b)(2) or 'injunctive class', of which civil rights cases of various types were the most likely, which occurred in 17 per cent to 44 per cent of the certified classes. There was some evidence of tactical activity, which might produce inefficiency, since at least one form of multiple filing occurred in 20 per cent to 39 per cent of the class actions in the four districts.

It appears that the types of case that are or are not instigated are driven by incentives related to whether the desired outcome is cessation of objectionable activity (through an injunction) or payment of money (whether fines or damages[25]). Fitzpatrick found that the vast majority of federal class action settlements in 2006 and 2007 provided cash relief (82 per cent), but a substantial number provided injunctive or declaratory relief (23 per cent) or in-kind relief (six per cent).[26] Every single securities settlement provided cash to the class and almost none of them provided in-kind, injunctive, or declaratory relief. Consumer cases had the greatest percentage of settlements providing for in-kind relief (30 per cent), reflecting the CAFA debate. Civil rights cases had the greatest percentage of settlements providing for injunctive or declaratory relief (75 per cent), though almost half of civil rights cases also provided some cash relief (49 per cent).

A. Securities Actions

Shareholder class actions have dominated the scene in terms of numbers, and have received particular attention. Formal approval of the policy of deterrence was given in the Supreme Court's recognition of private rights of action under the securities laws.[27]

---

[23] A summary of the empirical research on various aspects of US class actions, including some aspects not covered below, is NM Pace, 'Group and Aggregate Litigation in the United States' (2009) 622 *Annals of the American Academy of Political and Social Science* 32. He also noted a number of reasons why little data has been collected, and the limitations of existing data. A later study found outcomes of class actions to be difficult to identify: NM Pace and WB Rubenstein, 'How Transparent are Class Action Outcomes?' Empirical Research on the Availability of Class Action Claims Data' Working Paper (RAND Institute for Civil Justice, 2008).

[24] TE Willging, LL Hooper and RJ Niemic, *Empirical Study of Class Actions in Four Federal District Courts: Final Report to the Advisory Committee on Civil Rules* (Washington DC, Federal Judicial Centre, 1996).

[25] T Eisenberg and C Engel, 'Assuring Adequate Deterrence in Tort: A Public Good Experiment' (2014) 11(2) *Journal of Empirical Legal Studies* 301–49 (finding that damages and fines have the same deterrent effect of sanctioned participants).

[26] BT Fitzpatrick, 'An Empirical Study of Class Action Settlements and their Fee Awards' (2010) 7 *Journal of Empirical Legal Studies* 1–41.

[27] *Herman & MacLean v Huddleston*, 459 US 375, 380 (1983).

A strong attack was made on securities class actions by Janet Cooper Alexander in 1991.[28] Alexander asserted that recovery depended essentially on the occurrence of a large loss and did not require proof that a securities violation had actually occurred, akin to no fault insurance. The result was that securities class actions operated as insurance against market losses but only benefited a small number of institutional investors against market losses from a speculative investment, and benefited small investors little, whilst destroying shareholder value.

After Alexander's charge that merits were irrelevant in securities class actions amendments were made to private securities class actions by the Private Securities Litigation Reform Act of 1995 (PSLRA).[29]

Alexander returned to the attack in 1996 with a critique of the regulatory aspects of the securities class action system.[30] She started with the premise that the system is a primary enforcement mechanism for a regulatory regime whose purpose is to protect the public interest in the integrity of the capital markets. In considering what sanction would be optimal for achieving the regulatory purposes, she argued that class-based compensatory damages are ineffective and inefficient, and that an alternative regime of civil penalties for superior fraud deterrence, enforced through a bounty system for successful private plaintiffs, would be preferable. Alternatively, there should be procedural reforms to improve the monitoring of class counsel's performance, and better alignment of the incentives of class counsel with the interests of the class.

Choi argued in 2004 that without a class action, many potential fraud lawsuits might simply not get litigated,[31] but he did not consider public enforcement alternatives. His review of empirical studies identified three problems with the mechanism: Frivolous suits; lack of incentives for plaintiff attorneys to focus on smaller companies; and the agency problem between plaintiffs' attorneys and the plaintiff class. Frivolous suits appeared to be encouraged by the fact that Directors' and Officers' insurance policies would not pay if directors or officers were found guilty of violating the securities laws, so cases often settle irrespective of merits in order to maintain insurance cover.

Coffee has written extensively on securities class actions. In 2006, he asserted that they impose enormous penalties but achieve little compensation and limited deterrence, because of basic circularity: Damages imposed on a corporation fall on diversified shareholders.[32] This induces 'pocket-shifting' wealth transfers among shareholders. The equilibrium benefits corporate insiders, insurers and plaintiffs' attorneys but not investors, especially employees or smaller 'buy and hold' investors. Such an enforcement policy was contrary to public policy, which was that large financial penalties should be avoided when they fall inequitably on innocent shareholders.[33] Instead, the official policy was to seek penalties from culpable individual offenders.

---

[28] JC Alexander, 'Do the Merits Matter? A Study of Settlements in Securities Class Actions' (1991) 43 *Stanford Law Review* 497.

[29] Pub L No 104–67, 109 Stat 737 (1995) (codified in scattered sections of 15 USC). This amended the Securities Act of 1933 and the Securities Exchange Act of 1934.

[30] JC Alexander, 'Rethinking Damages in Securities Class Actions' (1996) 48 *Stanford Law Review* 1487.

[31] SJ Choi, 'The Evidence on Securities Class Actions' (2004) 57 *Vanderbilt Law Review* 1465–525.

[32] Coffee, 'Reforming the Securities Class Action: An Essay on Deterrence and its Implementation' (n 3). See also EJ Weiss and LJ White, 'File Early, then Free Ride: How Delaware Law (Mis)shapes Shareholder Class Actions' (2004) 57 *Vanderbilt Law Review* 1797.

[33] Press Release, US Securities & Exch Commission, Statement of the Securities and Exchange Commission Concerning Financial Penalties (January 4, 2006).

Coffee based his argument on various statistics. First, securities class actions dwarfed all other types: The former were 47 to 48 per cent of federal class actions between 2002 and 2004 (in 2004, 2480 ex 5179).[34] Second, senior management were highly likely to be named as defendants, but not outside directors or auditors (4 per cent) or underwriters. But such insiders rarely contributed financially to the settlement.[35] Where the defendant was a solvent corporation, its insurer would cover everything up to the policy limits, and the corporation would pick up the balance. The cost of insurance falls on shareholders. So the deterrent rationale was undercut; it rested at best on enterprise liability, inducing increased monitoring of the corporate officials. There was some evidence of turnover amongst CEOs. Coffee considered that insiders do not pay more because:

— Executives want to settle their liability with funds from the corporation: This constitutes an agency cost.
— State corporate law authorises indemnification; the Securities and Exchange Commission (SEC) does not permit this under federal rules but the ban was ineffective. There
   is powerful pressure to settle.
— Directors and Officers (D&O) insurance coverage issues: Original D&O corporate
   policies were supplemented by policies covering the company, so the same insurer
   pays under both.

There is evidence that control of securities class actions rests with major institutional investors instead of class counsel, but only if the stakes are sufficiently high.[36]

Bauer and Braun noted that equity-linked incentives constitute a major part of American directors' and officers' total compensation,[37] so shareholder litigation also materially affects their overall pay package.[38] In addition, there was a significant amount of reputational risk at stake for managers of sued corporations.[39]

Bauer and Braun examined the database of Stanford Law School and Cornerstone Research, which had operated since 1996 and then included over 2800 listed companies. This showed that a portfolio of all sued companies underperformed over long horizons of up to 48 months after litigation, after correcting for conventional risk factors. However, if shareholders sued only selected directors rather than the entire corporate entity, then underperformance was not observed. They explained this result as direct evidence of a disciplining effect on individual corporate decision makers. They contended that that result did not come at the expense of creditors in the form of a higher probability of default.

---

[34] Table X-4 to the annual Judicial Business of the United States Courts reports.

[35] Dunbar NERA study 1995 found that insurers paid 68.2% and corporations 31.4%, so at most 0.4% was paid by individual directors: BS Black, BR Cheffins and M Klausner, 'Outside Director Liability' (2006) 58 *Stanford Law Review* 1055.

[36] JD Cox and RS Thomas, with D Kiku, 'Does the Plaintiff Really Matter? An Empirical Analysis of Lead Plaintiffs in Securities Class Actions' (2006) 106 *Columbia Law Review* 1587–640.

[37] BJ Hall and JB Liebman, 'Are CEOs Really Paid Like Bureaucrats?' (1998) 113(3) *Quarterly Journal of Economics* 653–91.

[38] R Bauer and R Braun, 'Long-Term Performance of Distressed Firms: The Role of Class Action Lawsuits' Netspar, Discussion paper 10/2010-007, January 21, 2010 at http://arno.uvt.nl/show.cgi?fid=100123.

[39] EM Fich and A Shivdasani, 'Financial Fraud, Director Reputation, and Shareholder Wealth' (2007) 86 *Journal of Financial Economics* 306–36.

Bauer and Braun confirmed that lawsuits occur in response to bad stock price performance, as predicted.[40] They suggested that if stock prices do not recover over medium to long horizons this implies that shareholders in the aggregate market lose out and only plaintiffs gain. If share prices recover but bankruptcy risk increases, there is a wealth transfer from creditors to shareholders. They concluded that class action lawsuits are a powerful tool to discipline managers, and have a reasonable ability to exert influence on distressed firms without any wealth transfer being involved.

They identified seven main reasons for shareholders to go to court against the corporation totals over 1996–2007:

false/misleading statements/failure to disclose	391
stock price manipulation	331
illegal business practices	220
insider trading of directors& officers	127
Governance-/compensation related	124
accounting fraud/errors in financial statements	95
SEC-/IPO (Initial Public Offering)/acquisition-related	90
Annual number of class action lawsuits	650

These reasons were not mutually exclusive. A 'triggering event' (material correction of management's earnings forecasts) preceded the filing of the lawsuit in over 55 per cent of cases. Claims had peaked in 2002 after the bubble burst.

The most litigation-vulnerable sectors in the cohort were[41]

Retail (FF9)	148
Manufacturing (FF3)	133
Consumer durables (FF2)	87
Energy (FF4)	70
All others (FF12)	67
Financial institutions (FF11)	32
Business equipment (FF6)	31
Healthcare, medical equipment, drugs (FF10)	28
Consumer non-durables (FF1)	27
Chemicals (FF5)	12
Business utilities (FF8)	9
Telecoms (FF7)	6

The top four categories tended to be mostly capital-intensive and large industries. The researchers were surprised that business equipment did not show up higher. They confirmed that large firms were sued for their deep pockets.[42] An out-of-court settlement was proposed in 91 per cent of cases.[43] The involvement of a top plaintiff's law firm is significantly associated with a higher probability of success (settlement).[44]

---

[40] P Povel, R Singh and A Winton, 'Booms, Busts and Fraud' (2007) 20(4) *Review of Financial Studies* 1219–54.
[41] Giving Fama-French classifications.
[42] LL DuCharme, PH Malatesta and SE Sefcik, 'Earnings Management, Stock Isues, and Shareholder Lawsuits' (2004) 71 *Journal of Financial Economics* 27–49.
[43] Fich and Shivdasani (n 39).
[44] CNV Krishnan, SD Solomon and RS Thomas, 'Zealous Advocates of Self-interested Actors? Assessing the Value of Plaintiffs' Law Firms in Merger Litigation' ECGI Working Paper No 265/2014.

Bauer and Braun's conclusions were as follows. First, a recovery of the stock price highly depends on the type of allegation, the time horizon, and the estimation technique of long-term performance. In relation to the type of allegations:

— Accounting fraud: Negative abnormal financial returns persist significantly for up to 30 months.
— Illegal business practices: Alpha reverses as long as stocks are held longer than 24 months.
— Insider trading: Recovery occurs within one month. If allegations of illegal insider trading are made against individuals rather than the firm,
— Governance problems: Returns stay negative, but to a limited extent.

They concluded that illegal business practices and accounting fraud are de facto systematically adverse events that affect the entire corporation, which seems to erode investor confidence on a permanent basis. For insider trading, the observed action of the lawsuit or reputational costs disciplines existing managers, or a more efficient and ethical management replaces the incumbent managers. After accounting fraud, firms typically shed labour and capital to become more productive.

Second, for allegations involving the corporate entity as a whole, a class action is highly disruptive. In the short run, the filing of a class action is a materially adverse corporate event, and long-term economic and financial effects depend on the nature of the allegations. There is a slight recovery in stock price immediately after filing, and the price then sharply reverses and gradually declines (to a minimum of −23 per cent CAR) remaining down over the following three years. 'On average, shareholder litigation does not seem to pay off in terms of stock price recovery'.[45] The researchers inferred that shareholders aim for the settlement amount and dispose of any equity share in the company.

Third, filing a class action had a disciplining effect in terms of stock market performance. There was no statistically significant difference in their alphas from firms with and without a triggering event before the filing date. It was not fundamental events before the filing that made investors lose faith in the company and directors. It seemed to be the official filing of a lawsuit by shareholders that eroded confidence.

Fourth, any potential recovery and/or long term disciplining effect did not come at the expense of creditor groups. Thus, there was a disciplining effect. A lower market valuation suggests that firms are shunned by investors. There was a sharp decrease in profitability and net worth. Firms facing litigation were significantly distressed.

Bai, Cox and Thomas considered the effect of class actions alleging financial fraud.[46] They first noted that other studies had found that executives linked to misrepresentations were frequently terminated,[47] and there was extensive literature on the perverse effects of stock-based compensation.[48] Some studies had found that there was no significant long

[45] Bauer and Braun (n 38) 10.

[46] L Bai, JD Cox, RS Thomas, 'Lying and Getting Caught: An Empirical Study of the Effect of Securities Class Action Settlements on Targeted Firms' (2010) 158 *University of Pennsylvania Law Review* 1877.

[47] JM Karpoff et al, 'The Consequences to Managers for Financial Misrepresentation' (2008) 88 *Journal of Financial Economics* 193, 201, 208, funding that 93.61% of those identified in the government prosecution lose their job, and for responsible parties who are officers, 92.39% lose their jobs; firing occurs more quickly when the board chair is not held by the firm's chief executive officer.

[48] See T Baker et al, 'Stock Option Compensation and Earnings Management Incentives' (2003) 18 *Journal of Accounting, Auditing & Finance* 557, 559 (noting decreasing earnings accruals associated with periods before options are granted to executives); E Bartov and P Mohanran, 'Private Information, Earnings Manipulation

term effect on stock price or operating performance for firms sued for fraud.[49] Studies do report a substantial reputational loss as measured by declines in the short term market values of their securities.[50] A consistent finding was that the disclosure of a financial fraud yields a large negative market reaction.[51]

Bai, Cox and Thomas then reviewed 480 companies which had settled securities class actions since 1996. They found notable and statistically significant negative changes, particularly with respect to their operations in terms of efficiency, short-term liquidity, overall financial health and stock market performance. For post-settlement periods, defendants with high settlement amounts had higher probability of under-performing. There was an indication that insurance did not provide full coverage of the settlement. The market price plummeted immediately after the start of the lawsuit, and did not recover even three years afterwards. Firms experience statistically greater risks of financial stress than others. The researchers concluded that there was strong support for the view that suits are better directed towards the officers, advisors and other individuals who bear responsibility for the fraudulent representations than against companies.

Cox et al found that since PSLRA was enacted, institutions were more likely to intervene in cases with larger estimated provable losses, and against firms with greater total assets, and where the SEC has previously taken enforcement action.[52] They expressed disquiet at finding that 20.5 per cent of the settlements in their cohort were below $2 million, and those cases involved shorter class action periods, significantly lower provable losses and quicker settlements than the norm, and yielded investors lower recovery on their provable losses than in larger settlements. Such cases indicated characteristics of 'strike suits', that is opportunistic claims that raised concerns over merits. The activism of hedge funds in commencing litigation has increased hyperbolically, and they now form 'wolf packs'.[53]

It has been commented that many securities frauds are committed by managers who fear they are in a last period because the firm is in financial trouble.[54]

and Executive Stock-Option Exercises' (2004) 79 *The Accounting Review* 889, 891 (finding that income increasing accruals are systematically associated with higher levels of executive stock options); DB Bergstresser and T Philippon, 'CEO Incentives and Earnings Management' (2006) 80 *Journal of Financial Economics* 511, 513 (finding that discretionary earnings accruals are associated with wealth gains associated with executive options); J Francis, P Olsson and K Schipper, *Stockholm Institute for Financial Research*, Call options and Accrual Quality 3–4 (2005) available at http://sifr.org/wp-content/uploads/research/sifr-wp34.pdf (finding that the presence of option-based compensation worsens the quality of earnings accruals).

[49] D Marciukaityte et al, 'Governance and Performance Changes after Accusations of Corporate Fraud' (2006) May–June 62 *Financial Analysts Journal* 40.

[50] JM Karpoff et al, 'The Cost to Firms of Cooking the Books' (2008) 43 *Journal of Financial & Qualitative Analysis* 581.

[51] See eg SP Ferris & AC Pritchard, 'Stock Price Reactions to Securities Fraud Class Actions Under the Private Securities Litigation Reform Act' 1 *University of Michigan John M Olin Center for Law & Economics*, Paper No 01-009, 2001, available at http://papers.ssrn.com/sol3/papers.cfm?abstract_id=288216 (finding 'a large and statistically negative [stock market] reaction' to 'the revelation of potential fraud'); see also S Bhagat, J Bizjak and JL Coles, 'The Shareholder Wealth Implications of Corporate Lawsuits' (Winter 1998) *Financial Management* 6–7 (reporting a loss of 0.97% of the market value of defendant firms' equity during the two day period following the announcement of the lawsuit, but no significant loss in the two day period following settlement).

[52] JD Cox, RS Thomas, L Bai, 'There Are Plaintiffs and … There Are Plaintiffs: An Empirical Analysis of Securities Class Action Settlements' (2008) 61 (2) *Vanderbilt Law Review* 355.

[53] JC Coffee Jr and D Palia, 'The Impact of Hedge Fund Activism: Evidence and Implications' ECGI Working Paper No 266/2014.

[54] J Arlen and W Carney, 'Vicarious Liability for Fraud on Securities Markets: Theory and Evidence' (1992) *University of Illinois Law Review* 691; see Karpoff et al (n 50) (finding that many firms with financial misstatements delisted or went bankrupt during the enforcement period).

B. *Qui Tam* Actions

Private citizens (known as relators) may bring an action in the USA in respect of loss caused to the State under various statutes, known as a *qui tam* action.[55] This mechanism was permitted by Congress in 1986 under the False Claims Act, which created liability for any person who knowingly submits a false money claim to the government, uses a false statement to induce the government to pay a false claim, conspires to defraud the government into paying a false claim, or uses a false statement to reduce an obligation to pay money to the government.[56]

David Freeman Engstrom's recent detailed empirical research has illuminated the practice of *qui tam* litigation.[57] Since 1986, *qui tam* litigation under the False Claims Act has grown significantly with a total of about 6,000 unsealed actions (and an unknown number of sealed or pending actions). In the period 1999–2014 there were around 3,000 such lawsuits, in which a total of $20 billion was recovered.[58] In 2013 there were almost 700 actions, of which around 500 were claims related to health, and around 50 related to defence, with a wide range of other claims, such as oil and gas royalty claims. One False Claims Act case was settled in 2013 for $2.2 billion,[59] following which a number of former employee whistleblowers shared $169 million.[60] Recoveries have grown in parallel with filings, roughly doubling in the period 2000–2014 as a result of a handful of large settlements involving pharmaceutical companies, with substantial growth in high-value claims, and peaking around 2012 at an annual total of $3 billion.[61] Since 1986, however, success rates have steadily declined, in 2004–2013 being in the range of 20 per cent to zero.

Freeman Engstrom shows that the types of case have changed, starting from uncontroversial frauds such as overbilling for Medicare services and expanding in innovative fashion to exploit ambiguities in a wide range of regulatory legislation. The rise in health claims occurred alongside a rise in health spending from roughly $150 billion to $500 billion in the period 1986–2013, which indicates that an allegation that there has been explosion in litigation cannot be supported. However, it has been commented that the 'swamp' of fraud opportunities has grown substantially.[62]

The volume of *qui tam* litigation provokes polarised viewpoints in the USA.[63] A positive view notes the volume of alleged wrongdoing that is discovered, enforced against and deterred by means of a wholly privatised mechanism. A critical view regards *qui tam* litigation as a product of large bounties incentivising speculative lawsuits that result in uncontrolled

---

[55] The following information is based largely on: D Freeman Engstrom, 'Private Enforcement's Pathways: Lessons from Qui Tam Litigation' (2014) 114(8) *Columbia Law Review* 1913.

[56] False Claims Act, 31 USC §§ 3729–3733 (2012, esp § 3729(a) (2012)).

[57] Freeman Engstrom (n 55).

[58] *US Dep't of Justice, Fraud Statistics—Overview: Oct 1, 1987–Sept 30, 2013* (2013) available at http://www.justice.gov/civil/docs_forms/C-FRAUDS_FCA_Statistics.pdf.

[59] *Press Release: Johnson & Johnson to Pay More than £2.2 Billion to Resolve Criminal and Civil Investigations* (Department of Justice, Nov 4, 2013) at http://www.justice.gov/opa/pr/johnson-johnson-pay-more-22-billion-resolve-criminal-and-civil-investigations.

[60] G Wallace, '$168 Million Payout to Johnson & Johnson Whistleblowers' CNN Money (Nov 4, 2013, 5:04 PM), http://money.cnn.com/2013/11/04/news/johnson-and-johnson-whistleblower-payout/.

[61] Freeman Engstrom (n 55) 1957–59.

[62] Patrick Burns, quoted in 'Pharma Qui Tam Caseload Jumps to 180', *Rx Compliance Rep*, Jan 16, 2007, at 1, 8, available at http://rxcompliancereport.com/issues/2007/RxComp0116.pdf.

[63] See Freeman Engstrom (n 55).

institutional blackmail, socially inefficient and even democratically illegitimate.[64] To European eyes, the *qui tam* jurisdiction is a striking phenomenon that has no European equivalent. If the theory deterrence by litigation has an effect, one may wonder at the level of wrongdoing that is reflected in the level of litigation in the USA. Does a similar level of wrongdoing exist in Europe, and why or why not?

C. The Effect of High Economic Costs

It is clear that many cases in the US litigation system are selective, in relation to type of case instigated and defendant selected, and many cases settle. Does a high rate of settlement evidence a high rate of wrongdoing by corporations? The problem in reaching a conclusion here is that the financial incentives for both sides in American litigation are of such force that they distort the extent to which settlements reflect wrongdoing/liability or avoidance of the irrecoverable cost of discovery/litigation (the 'blackmail settlement' issue). As noted, several studies considered the issue of whether merits matter in settlements, or whether the private enforcement technique of a class action merely attracts attorneys to claim against companies over a threshold size with cases then being settled favourably to the claimants irrespective of the underlying merits (see Alexander[65] and Cox et al,[66] both examining securities cases).

It is plausible that defendants facing large damages payments and litigation costs, and likely targets of litigation with such consequences, will seek to minimise their liability or exposure to such payments. But what is not obvious is whether—and how—such financial exposures will induce companies to change their behaviours so as to comply with the law in all desired respects. In simple terms, the risk of having to make damages payments may induce companies to minimise the extent of such financial risk, but not necessarily to do the right thing in complying fully with the underlying substantive rules, breach of which may give rise to the liability. Equally, the irrecoverable very high cost of discovery in US civil procedure has been identified as a major incentive to settle.[67]

Figures are available for total tort costs: The distinction between tort and the types of cases enforced through class actions should be noted. Over the past 50 years, direct tort costs in the US grew more than 100-fold from less than $2 billion in 1950 to $254.7 billion in 2008, exceeding Gross Domestic Product (GDP) growth by an average of over two percentage points.[68] The authors estimated that in 2008 personal tort costs were $94.2 per person and commercial tort costs were $160.5. 'Commercial' reflected torts alleged against businesses and included all medical malpractice tort costs. 'Personal' tort costs included torts alleged against individuals, excluding medical malpractice. Personal tort costs stemmed from automobile accidents.

---

[64] MH Redish, *Wholesale Justice: Constitutional Democracy and the Problem of the Class Action Lawsuit* (Stanford CA, Stanford University Press, 2009), 228.

[65] Alexander (n 28).

[66] Cox, Thomas, Bai (n 52).

[67] Conversations between the author and a number of lawyers in companies and law firms in USA since the 1980s.

[68] *2009 Update on US Tort Costs Trends* (New York, Towers Perrin, 2009).

The 2006 figure equated to a 'litigation tax' of $825 per person, compared to $12 in 1950. In 2009 total tort costs were equal to 1.79 per cent of the GDP of the United States: That percentage fell since a high of 2.24 per cent in 2003. In 2006 nearly one in six jury awards were $1 million or more, and over 7 per cent of businesses experienced a liability loss of $5 million or more during the previous five years.[69]

In 2005 the annual tort cost for small United States businesses was $98 billion. This equated to $20 per $1,000 of revenue. Small businesses bore 69 per cent of US business tort liability but took only 19 per cent of revenues. They paid $20 billion of their tort costs out of pocket, as opposed to through insurance.[70]

Some sources allege that the full cost of the US system is $865.37 billion, which is equivalent to an eight per cent tax on consumption, or a 13 percent tax on wages.[71] There has been strong criticism of these figures[72] but, whatever the true figures may be,[73] the cost of the US civil justice system is clearly high and is argued by industry to constitute an unnecessary and debilitation tax on business and the economy, with disproportionately little benefit to competition, consumers or the economy.[74]

In 2006, 40 per cent of the largest companies spent $5m or more on litigation, excluding settlements and awards.[75] A 2009 poll of top American business lawyers found that 97 per cent consider that the American civil justice system is 'too expensive'.[76] A survey of 500 US Chief Executives by the Conference Board found that lawsuits caused 36 per cent of their companies to discontinue products, 15 per cent to lay off workers, and eight per cent to close plants.[77] A Gallup survey of US small businesses found that 26 per cent of owners said that fear of liability kept them from releasing new products, services or operations to the market.[78] Over 200 insurance companies failed in the United States in the decade prior to 2006.[79]

A United States federal government analysis in 2002 concluded that excessive tort litigation costs in 2000 were an $87 billion drag on the national economy.[80] The study estimated

---

[69] *US Tort Costs and Cross-Border Perspectives; 2005 Update* (New York, Towers Perrin-Tillinghast, 2006).

[70] *Tort Liability Costs For Small Business* (US Chamber Institute for Legal Reform, 2007). Small businesses are defined here as those with less than £10 million annual revenues and at least one employee in addition to the owner. The tort cost increased 13% from 2002 to 2005.

[71] *Jackpot Justice: The True Cost of America's Tort System* (San Francisco, Pacific Research Institute, 2007). The authors calculated that the excess (ie unnecessary) annual social cost in 2006 was $588.63 billion, and the excess annual accounting cost is $664.15 billion. They also asserted that the annual wealth loss to US stockholders is $684 billion; 60,000 workers have been displaced through asbestos bankruptcies, at an economic cost of $226 million in 2006 $s; each worker losing up to $50,000 over his career. Human capital losses total up to $3.16 billion in lost wages, and $559 million capital lost to pensions.

[72] See R Posner at http://www.becker-posner-blog.com/2007/04/is-the-tort-system-costing-the-united-states-865-billion-a-year--posner.html.

[73] See the overview by C Silver, 'Does Civil Litigation Cost Too Much?' (2002) 80 *Texas Law Review* 2073.

[74] The state of Mississippi, for example, passed reform legislation in 2003, after which levels of claims fell, industry started to reinvest, employment levels rose, and doctors returned to practice in the state. See C Ross, 'Jackson Action: In Mississippi Tort Reform Works' *The Wall Street Journal*, 15 September 2005.

[75] *Fourth Annual Litigation Trends Survey Findings* (New York, Fulbright & Jaworski, 2007).

[76] *Civil Litigation Survey of Chief Legal Officers and General Counsel belonging to the Association of Corporate Counsel* (Denver, Institute for the Advancement of the American Legal System, 2010).

[77] US Senate Commerce Committee Report on Product Liability Reform Act of 1997.

[78] National Small Business Poll (Washington, National Federation of Independent Businesses, 2002).

[79] AM Best, 'Rising Number of P/C Company Impairments Continues Trend' March 10, 2003, quoted in D Deal et al, *Tort Excess 2005: The Necessity for Reform from a Policy, Legal and Risk Management Perspective* (Washington, US Chamber of Commerce, 2005).

[80] *An Economic Analysis of the US Tort Liability System* (Washington, US Council of Economic Advisers, 2002).

that the impact of wasteful legal expenditures equated to a 1.3 per cent tax on consumption, or a 2.1 per cent tax on wages. High litigation risks and stringent regulations were the principal factors in a 2007 Report that New York is in danger of losing its status as world financial centre.[81]

It has been asserted that 19 per cent of tort costs go to claimant lawyers and the total in the early 2000s was almost $40 billion a year, which was 50 per cent more than Microsoft or Intel and twice that of Coca-Cola, so the combined cost would be somewhat more than that.[82]

In the important 2000 study by Hensler et al, total transaction costs could not be discovered, partly because defendants were reluctant to reveal their costs.[83] Estimated total costs in their ten cases, excluding defendants' own legal expenses, ranged from about $1 million to over $1 billion. Eight of the cases cost more than $10 million; four cost more than $50 million; three cost more than half a billion dollars. But in three cases, class members received one-third or less of the funds set aside, and in three cases class counsel received more than the total received by class members altogether.

The issues of how collective processes transform both claimants and their lawyers have been studied by Meili.[84] Studies on dispute transformation[85] of individual cases have found that lawyers shape their clients' expectations and goals to what is realistically attainable within the legal system, often to only recovering money. Meili has found that in consumer class actions, rather than *de* flating the unrealistic expectations of clients in individual cases, lawyers deliberately *in* flate the expectations of their clients, encouraging them to look beyond individual monetary compensation and focus on relief of the entire class. If their clients refuse to be so encouraged, the lawyers do not adopt them as named plaintiffs. Named plaintiffs who give a deposition are given an incentive award ranging between $500 and a few thousand dollars. Class lawyers felt that the process has been unfairly maligned, and attributed negative public perception to lawyers in securities and mass torts. Most were proud of their work, whilst a few attorneys were cynical about the potential of class actions to bring about any kind of meaningful social change. It appeared that representative claimants evidenced wider motivations than class action attorneys in relation to issues of enforcement.

In contrast to the United States' tort costs, European tort costs as a percentage of GDP in 2003 were said to be 0.6 per cent in Poland and Denmark, 0.7 per cent in France and UK, 1.1 per cent in Germany and 1.7 per cent in Italy.[86] However, one should be careful to make the right comparisons. If the US litigation system is intended to include a significant element

---

[81] MR Bloomberg and CE Schumer, *Sustaining New York's and the US's Global Financial Services Leadership*, 2007, available at http://www.nyc.gov/html/om/pdf/ny_report_final.pdf. Significantly, the authors were political opponents.

[82] *Trial Lawyers, Inc* (Centre for Legal Policy, Manhattan Institute, 2003) at http://www.triallawyersinc.com.

[83] DR Hensler, B Dombey-Moore, B Giddens, J Gross, EK Moller and NM Pace, *Class Action Dilemmas. Pursuing Public Goals for Private Gain* (RAND Institute for Civil Justice, 2000).

[84] S Meili, 'Perceptions of Consumer Class Actions: The Views of Plaintiffs' Lawyers and their Clients' unpublished, February 2010.

[85] T Relis, 'It's Not About the Money!: A Theory on Misconceptions of Plaintiffs' Litigation Aims' (2007) 68 *University of Pittsburgh Law Review* 341–85.

[86] *US Tort Costs and Cross-Border Perspectives; 2005 Update* (New York, Towers Perrin-Tillinghast, 2006). The data in this analysis was obtained from the insurance industry, but the basis for these European figures is not transparent. Although the authors have produced an annual assessment of US tort costs, they have not produced figures for Europe since those quoted here.

of public enforcement, then it is illogical to compare the total costs of litigation or tort in USA (ie damages and transactional costs) with the costs of litigation in other jurisdictions. It would be more relevant to compare first the total costs of public and private enforcement of different jurisdictions, and second the ratios of public to private enforcement costs.

Nevertheless, illuminating differences have been shown in litigation practice between, for example, the USA and UK. Data from the mid-2000s showed that securities litigation generally, and the risk of a director of a company being sued for breach of duty in UK, is almost zero, compared with a 1.1 per cent annual chance in the USA.[87] Compared with the 150–200 US federal securities class actions brought annually,[88] plus some in state courts, only three cases were found in the UK from 1990 to 2006.[89] Armour and Gordon's analysis of 341 US cases between 2001 and January 2011 showed that where the wrongdoing affected third parties there were no statistically significant abnormal returns beyond the amount of financial payments required, but where misconduct involved harm to trading partners, for example, mis-selling financial products and mis-statements in financial reports, the penalised firms' stock prices experienced statistically significant abnormal losses of approximately nine times the fines and compensation paid.[90] Armour and Gordon noted that penalties are much larger in the US than the UK, raising the possibility that they may be excessive when combined with reputational losses in cases involving second party wrongs.[91]

D. Merits and Outcomes of Class Litigation

A key point is to be able to assess the merits of individual cases and thus conclude whether they are justified, or whether settlements have been reached at levels that were justifiable. However, Hensler at al's detailed 2000 study of ten class actions concluded that benefits and costs are very difficult to assess.[92]

> At the time of settlement, considerable uncertainty remained about the defendants' culpability and plaintiff class members' damages. It remained unclear which cases 'just ain't worth it' and which were … Viewed from one perspective, the claims appear meritorious and the behaviour of the defendant blameworthy, but viewed from another, the claims appear trivial or even trumped up, and the defendant's behaviour seems proper.[93]

This echoed Garth's 1992 observation that there is no general agreement on what constitutes success or failure in lawsuits that typically end in negotiated settlements.[94] Instead, Hensler et al found that the process of reaching these outcomes suggested that class counsel

---

[87] J Armour, B Black, B Cheffins and R Nolan, 'Private Enforcement of Corporate Law: An Empirical Comparison of the United Kingdom and the United States' (2009) 6 *Journal of Empirical Legal Studies* 687. The UK situation is attributable to differences in substantive law and litigation funding rules: P Davies, *Davies Review of Issuer Liability: Final Report* (London, HM Treasury, 2007).

[88] *Securities Class Action Filings 2013 Year in Review* (Menlo Park CA, Cornerstone Research, 2014).

[89] Armour, Black, Cheffins and Nolan (n 87).

[90] J Armour, C Mayer and A Polo, 'Regulatory Sanctions and Reputational Damage in Financial Markets' (2010) Oxford Legal Studies Research Paper No 62/2010.

[91] ibid.

[92] Hensler et al (n 83).

[93] ibid, 417.

[94] BG Garth, 'Power and Legal Artifice: The Federal Class Action' (1992) 26 *Law & Society Review* 237–72.

were sometimes simply interested in finding a settlement price that the defendants would agree to—rather than in finding out what class members had lost, what defendants had gained, and how likely it was that defendants would actually be held liable if the suit were to go to trial, and negotiating a fair settlement based on the answers to these questions. They commented that such instances undermine the social utility of class actions, which depends on how effectively the lawsuits compensate injured consumers and—many would argue—deter wrongful practices. Moreover, among the class actions studied, some settlements appeared at first reading to provide more for class members and consumers than they actually did, and class action attorneys' financial rewards sometimes were based on the settlements' apparent value rather than on the real outcomes of the cases.[95] Such outcomes contribute to public cynicism about the actual goals of damage class actions as compared to the aspirations articulated for them by class action advocates.

Hensler et al also found that in all of the six consumer cases studied, litigation was associated with changes in the defendants' practice, although some of the changes may be explainable independently of the class action itself. In four of the six cases, the evidence strongly suggested that the litigation directly or indirectly produced the changes in practice. In the other two cases, the evidence was more ambiguous.

Concerns have been noted above that securities claims are made without merits (Alexander), and that although Cox et al found that the strength of the complaint mattered, small cases seem to involve a significant number of strike suits, and larger settlements may simply reflect the size of the fall in share price, the extent of insurance cover, and, as Hensler found, 'what the company will pay'. Armour, Black and Cheffins found that the rate of class action litigation approaches 100 per cent in large US merger and acquisition transactions, which they said implies a lot of nuisance litigation.[96]

Given the size of the financial consequences of liability suits on corporations, it is inconceivable that they have no effect on the behaviour of corporations. Thus, as noted above, some corporations have ceased to market some products because the costs of liability, and particularly of liability insurance, have become unaffordable. Examples include light aircraft, vaccines and sports equipment. For similar reasons, product information leaflets have grown very long, in view of the legal need to restrict liability by referring to extensive possible risks. One question is whether these consequences are desirable or effective in reducing actual risk, or whether they merely serve to open a pathway to the defendant's insurance as an alternative to self-insurance or wider healthcare coverage. Viscusi's overview of the evidence was that the safety-inducing potential of product liability fails to be realised, and that risks from new and innovative products are especially uncontrollable by liability.[97]

Does litigation induce social change? A principal finding of Garth's 1992 study was that litigation tends to narrow the dispute that gives rise to it and that individual initiators take a more prominent role in certain types of cases than in others. Thus, Garth found, first, that securities and antitrust cases were brought predominantly by entrepreneurial plaintiffs' attorneys (Garth described securities cases as often involving small investors, but more

---

[95] The position may subsequently have been affected by the Class Action Fairness Act of 2005.

[96] J Armour, B Black and BR Cheffins, 'Is Delaware Losing its Cases?' (2012) 9 *Journal of Empirical Legal Studies* 605–56.

[97] WK Viscusi, 'Does Product Liability Make Us Safer?' (2012) 35(1) *Regulation* 24.

recent cases have involved large corporate investors, as discussed above).[98] Second, welfare cases are frequently initiated by public organisations so as to raise topical welfare and political issues. Third, individuals often initiate employment discrimination cases, in which a sense of grievance or public fairness is often a necessary motivator. The process can transform employment discrimination victims into activists, but they do not always personally benefit from the outcome in the way initially envisaged.

It appears that many outcomes are not transparent in the sense of monitoring who gets paid what.[99] Further, there is almost no evidence on whether defendants' behaviour is affected by the litigation, and how it may be affected. Class counsel do not appear to monitor the enforcement of 'behaviour control' aspects of settlements, such as compliance with agreements to change business practices or with injunctions.

E. Relationship Between Private and Public Enforcement

Although the US system is designed to facilitate private enforcement, it has to be seen in the context of such public enforcement as occurs. The arguments for private enforcement and against public enforcement can be circular. Private enforcement is said to be essential because public agencies can be captured (by both the communities that they are intended to regulate, and by the political policies of the Executive, which holds the purse strings),[100] such that the resources and enthusiasm for enforcement, and its force and extent, are compromised and sub-optimal. On the other hand, the existence of an active private enforcement industry can be used by public agencies and those who fund or dislike them to justify maintaining a limited public enforcement role. It appears that the enforcement budgets, policies and activities of major agencies such as the Department of Justice and SEC are more limited than in some other jurisdictions (but this needs to be tested) and are targeted at taking criminal and/or civil action against high profile cases. It is unclear to what extent public agencies enforce against cases that private attorneys general would not consider worth it.

---

[98] JC Coffee, Jr, 'Accountability and Competition in Securities Class Actions: Why "Exit" Works Better Than "Voice"' (2008) 30 *Cardozo Law Review* 407–44.

[99] Pace and Rubenstein (n 23).

[100] EA Bardach and RA Kagan, *Going by the Book: The Problem of Regulatory Unreasonableness* (Philadelphia PA, Temple University Press, 1982). SP Huntington, 'The Marasmus of the ICC: The Commission, the Railroads, and the Public Interest' (1952) 61(4) *The Yale Law Journal* 467; MH Bernstein, *Regulating Business by Independent Commission* (Princeton NJ, Princeton University Press, 1955); TJ Lowi, *The End of Liberalism: Ideology, Policy, and the Crisis of Public Authority* (New York, Norton, 1969); GJ Stigler, 'The Theory of Economic Regulation' (1971) 3 *Bell Journal of Economics and Management Science* 3; M Derthick and P Quirk, *The Politics of Deregulation* (Washington DC, The Brookings Institution, 1985); ME Levine and JL Forrence, 'Regulatory Capture, Public Interest, and the Public Agenda: Toward a Synthesis' (1990) 6(1) *Journal of Law, Economics, & Organization* 167; J-J Laffont and J Tirole, 'The Politics of Government Decision-Making: A Theory of Regulatory Capture' (1991) 106(4) *Quarterly Journal of Economics* 1089; PJ May and S Winter, 'Regulatory Enforcement and Compliance: Examining Danish Agro-Environmental Policy' (1999) 18(4) *Journal of Political Analysis and Management* 25; C Coglianese and RA Kagan, *Regulation and Regulatory Processes* (Aldershot, Ashgate, 2007); MA Lovermore and RL Revesz, 'Regulatory Review, Capture, and Agency Inaction' (2013) 101 *Georgetown Law Journal* 1337. In the UK there is a dearth of scholarly empirical evidence on capture, whilst there are some statements that it is rare: K Hawkins, *Environment and Enforcement: Regulation and the Social Definition of Pollution* (Oxford, Clarendon Press, 1984) 192; I Ramsay, *Consumer Law and Policy. Text and Materials on regulating Consumer Markets* (Oxford, Hart Publishing, 2012).

As may be expected, there is evidence of some connection between public and private enforcement activity. Thus, private attorneys general will be attracted to cases where an agency has pre-determined the fact that an illegal infringement has occurred, or has carried out the initial investigation of evidence that would prove breach. The former 'piggyback' situation occurs in antitrust cases, financial fraud and some consumer fraud cases. The latter situation is illustrated by the US Equal Employment Opportunity Commission making available complex information and analysis to support employment discrimination cases.[101] In securities cases, there seems to be limited overlap between SEC enforcement and private class actions:[102] Instead, the latter are filed merely if a significant fall in the stock price occurs. Such an event is immediately transparent to private enforcers, and the 'race to file' may be triggered.

Farhang has noted that many scholars suggest that, compared to administrative regulation, private enforcement regimes (1) produce inconsistency and uncertainty (since policy emanates from a multitude of litigants and judges); (2) mobilise less policy expertise; (3) are needlessly adversarial, subverting cooperation and voluntary compliance; (4) are extremely costly; and (5) are painfully slow and cumbersome.[103]

Garth, Nagel and Plager's analysis of all federal class actions in the Northern District of California certified between 1979 and 1984 found that there had been a 'dramatic shift' from the initial model of the Lone Ranger or bounty hunter engaged in private law enforcement to a preoccupation with economic logic over incentives to sue.[104] The private attorney general model does not support advocacy before administrative agencies, only courts.[105] They found that a significant number of class action private attorneys tended to 'piggyback' their cases on governmental investigations, even to the extent of copying the government's complaint. For example, antitrust and securities cases depended largely on the investigative activities of governmental agencies.

> A lawyer dependent on fees from a successful lawsuit naturally looks for the easy victories; creativity and innovation in the generation of the lawsuit are unlikely. Indeed, it looks as if the mercenary lawyers limit themselves largely to 'no research' lawsuits because of the efficiency of such a strategy.... The mercenary lawyer takes fewer risks in defining the scope of the class. Accordingly, the attorney's goal is to reduce the reach of the suit and the breadth of the defendants' exposure so as to both maximise class certification and the probability of an expeditious and favourable settlement.[106]

In the result, Garth et al concluded that the 'legal mercenary' model of private attorneys 'cannot fully realize the ideals implicit in the model of a private, institutional antidote to, or substitute for, governmental machinery'. By contrast, they found that the 'social advocate' model, involving publicly paid lawyers, delivered the best enforcement of public law goals.

---

[101] Garth, Nagel and Plager (n 21).

[102] J Larsen, E Buckberg and B Lev, 'SEC Settlements: A New era Post-SOX' (*NERA*, 2008); Cox, Thomas, Bai (n 52).

[103] S Farhang, 'Public Regulation and Private Lawsuits in the American Separation of Powers System' (2008) 52 *American Journal of Political Science* 821, citing E Bardan and R Kagan, *Going by the Book. The Problem of Regulatory Unreasonableness* 1st edn 1982 (New Brunswick, Transaction Publishers, 2002); FB Cross, 'Rethinking Environmental Citizen Suits' (1989) 8(Fall) *Temple Environmental Law & Technology Journal* 55–76; Kagan (n 5); RB Stewart and CR Sunstein, 'Public Programs and Private Rights' (1981–1982) 95 *Harvard Law Review* 1193.

[104] Garth, Nagel and Plager (n 21).

[105] *Webb v Board of Education of Dyer County*, 471 US 234 (1985).

[106] Garth, Nagel and Plager (n 21) at 377.

A federally funded legal services programme was established in 1965 as part of the 'War on Poverty', and ran in parallel with a notable stream of civil liberties and environmental cases.[107] Garth et al found that 50 per cent of the certified class actions in their 1979–1984 cohort was the product of law firms created directly by broad funding agencies[108] trying to generate legal power for the unrepresented and underrepresented in society. But there the private foundations had retreated and federal funding had shrunk for the Legal Services Corporation, whose cases had fallen from 3,584 in 1976 to 736 in 1986.[109] Garth et al concluded that the 'private attorney general' model works well when there is either subsidised social advocacy or a genuine governmental commitment to promote strong efforts by mercenary law enforcers. They suggested that efforts to reform the model and to create an antidote or substitute for governmental machinery—an effective enforcement institution independent of the vagaries of government—would fail unless they confront this basic proposition.

Garth et al did identify some examples of private enforcement independent of government, but they concluded that there were very few such cases and the limiting conditions were 'severe indeed'.[110] The most important characteristic of such cases was that there were one or more aggrieved plaintiffs who sought legal representation and who were armed at the outset with the facts necessary to prove a violation of the law affecting a large but easily identifiable group of persons. These facts were simple and largely undisputed in the crucial respects; the lawyers could proceed much as they would in a relatively simple private lawsuit, without investing in significant research.

---

[107] Such as *Associated Industries v Ickes*, 134 F.2d 694, 704 (2d Cir 1943); *NAACP v Button*, 371 US 415 (1963); *Newman v Piggie Park*, 390 US 400, 402 (1968); *Alyeska Pipeline Service Co v Wilderness Society*, 421 US 240 (1975).
[108] Notably ACLU, NAACP, the Sierra Club.
[109] *In Camera*, 10 Class Action Rep 93 (1987).
[110] The cohort contained six out of 46 such cases, dealing with length of pretrial detention, a pension plan, a company acquisition, insurance provisions restricting access on basis of race, and medication for mental patients.

4

Enforcement of Competition Law[1]

The focus of this chapter is deterrence and rational actor theory as the foundation of enforcement of competition law. Such a policy is central to competition enforcement across the world. Indeed, the 'competition world' is a closed network of insiders—public officials, economists and lawyers—who adhere to the same orthodoxy of deterrence and (modified) rational actor theory. This chapter will use as an example competition enforcement of the EU (European Union). That model is based, in contrast to the enforcement model of the previous chapter, on the primacy of enforcement by *public* bodies.

I. Public Enforcement: Deterrence and Fines

Maintaining competition is a vital objective of the EU single market project.[2] Competition drives innovation, competitiveness (attractive and responsive offerings, including low prices), economic health and therefore prosperity employment and stability. There are four basic areas covered by EU competition law:[3] Anti-competitive agreements (typically of two types: Horizontal agreements between competitors, for example to fix prices, to share markets or to restrict output, which are severely punished, and vertical agreements between firms at different levels of the market which may be harmful to competition, such as where a supplier instructs its retailers not to resell goods at less than a certain price); abusive behaviour (by a monopolist or firm that has dominant market power, such as to reduce prices to less than cost in order to drive a competitor out of the market or to deter a competitor from entering the market); mergers between firms that could harm competition (for example by restricting consumer choice or creating a dominant firm); and public restrictions of competition by the State.

Cartels are regarded as the most serious abuses, and can have a highly detrimental impact on consumers and cause substantial harm.[4] Of the 61 Commission enforcement decisions

---

[1] This section is updated from CJS Hodges, *The Reform of Class and Representative Actions in European Legal Systems: A New Framework for Collective Redress in Europe* (Oxford, Hart Publishing, 2008); CJS Hodges, 'A Market-Based Competition Enforcement Policy' [2011] *European Business Law Review* 261–91; and CJS Hodges, 'European Competition Enforcement Policy: Integrating Restitution and Behaviour Control' [2011] *World Competition* 385–96.

[2] TFEU, arts 101–03; Council Reg (EC) No 1/2003, recital 1 (a system which ensures that competition in the common market is not distorted). *Report on Competition Policy 2013* COM(2014) 249, 6.5.2014.

[3] R Whish and D Bailey, *Competition Law* 7th edn (Oxford, Oxford University Press, 2012) 2–3.

[4] OECD, *Report on the Nature and Impact of Hard Core Cartels and Sanctions Against Cartels under National Competition Laws*, 2002.

under the 1988 Guidelines up to 2005, 51 were cartel decisions and only 10 were abuses of dominance.[5] A 2005 study found the median 'mark-up' (the amount in excess of the competitive price) commanded by international cartels to be 25 per cent.[6] Such price rises occur across substantial areas of economic activity, and companies involved in international cartels between 1990 and 2003 had sales of approximately US$436 billion.[7] In 2013 the Commission fined banks €1.71 billion for participating in cartels in interest rate derivatives.[8]

Competition law is primarily enforced in the EU by public authorities at both European and national levels. The European Commission, acting through its Directorate-General for Competition (DG COMP), has overarching enforcement powers, conferred in 1962,[9] and is the apex of a system of trans-EU and national enforcement, involving national competent authorities (NCAs) and national courts. In no other area does the European Commission have a similar enforcement function.[10] EU substantive competition law is harmonised from 1 May 2004 under the Modernisation Regulation.[11]

The EU enforcement system 'relies on market players assessing the compatibility of their conduct with EU competition rules and on targeted *ex post* enforcement action by competition authorities'.[12] The Commission's enforcement policy in relation to breaches of EU competition law[13] is designed to 'ensure compliance with the prohibitions ... by making provision for fines and periodic penalty payments'.[14] According to the Court of Justice, fines 'have as their objective to suppress illegal conduct as well as to prevent it being repeated'.[15] The Commission has stated that 'the purpose of the fines is twofold: to impose a pecuniary sanction on the undertaking for the infringement and prevent a repetition of the offence, and to make the prohibition in the Treaty more effective'.[16] The Court of Justice considers

[5]   D Geradin and D Henry, 'The EC Fining Policy for Violations of Competition Law: An Empirical Review of the Commission Decisional Practice and the Community Courts' Judgments' (2005) 1 *European Competition Journal* 401.

[6]   JM Connor and RH Lande, 'How High Do Cartels Raise Prices? Implications for Optimal Cartel Fines' (2005) 80 *Tulane Law Review* 513–70.

[7]   JM Connor, 'Global Antitrust Prosecutions of Modern International Cartels' (2004) 4 *Journal of Industry, Competition and Trade* 239–67.

[8]   Press release, *Commission fines banks €1.71 billion for participating in cartels in the interest rate derivatives industry* (European Commission, 4 December 2013).

[9]   Council Reg No 17 of 1962.

[10]   Significant constitutional and fundamental rights arguments have been advanced that decisions should not be made by Commissioners but by a separate body. See IS Forrester, 'Due Process in EC Competition Cases: A Distinguished Institution with Flawed Procedures' (2009) 34 *EL Rev* 817.

[11]   Reg (EC) No 1/2003 of 16 December 2002 on the implementation of the rules on competition laid down in Arts 81 and 82 of the EC Treaty. See JS Venit, 'Brave New World: The Modernisation and Decentralisation of Enforcement under Articles 81 and 82 of the EC Treaty' (2003) 40 *CML Rev* 545, 554; AP Komninos, 'Public and Private Antitrust Enforcement in Europe: Complement? Overlap?' (2006) 3(1) *Competition Law Rev iew* 5 (referring to a culture of diverse enforcement).

[12]   Communication from the Commission to the European Parliament and the Council, Ten Years of Antitrust Enforcement under Reg 1/2003: Achievements and Future Perspectives, COM(2014) 453, 6.5.2014, para 6.

[13]   TFEU, arts 101 and 102.

[14]   TFEU, art 103(2)(a). *Guidelines on the Method of Setting Fines Pursuant to Article 23(2)(a) of Regulation No 1/2003*, 2006/C 210/02: hereafter '*Guidelines*'. Undertakings can also be accepted. For the purposes of this paper, periodic penalty payments are included within the concept of a fine.

[15]   Case 41/69 *Chemiefarma v Commission* [1970] ECR 661, para 173 (Wils' translation of '*ont pour objet de réprimer des comportements illicites aussi bien que d'en prévenir le renouvellement*'). See WPJ Wils, *Efficiency and Justice in European Antitrust Enforcement* (Oxford, Hart Publishing, 2008) 80.

[16]   *Thirteenth Report on Competition Policy 1983*, para 62.

intentional and negligent infringements to be equally serious.[17] Actual consumer detriment does not have to be established.

There is no democratically authorised statement of enforcement policy in EU legislation. Deterrence—alone—is viewed as the primary purpose of European enforcement of competition law by scholars,[18] the OECD (Organisation for Economic Co-operation and Development),[19] and the European Court.[20] In this respect, EU enforcement policy was influenced by the prior and well-established tradition of deterrence as the enforcement policy of the United States. The approach has only recently been challenged.[21] The Commission uses fines alone on the sole basis of achieving deterrence. The Commission's enforcement policy, set out in its Fining Guidelines, states that

> Fines should have a sufficiently deterrent effect, not only in order to sanction the undertakings concerned (specific deterrence) but also in order to deter other undertakings from engaging in, or continuing, behaviour that is contrary to articles [101, then 81] and [102, then 82] of the EC Treaty (general deterrence).[22]

General deterrence operates ex ante, whereas specific deterrence is ex post.[23] The 2006 Fining Guidelines specify that the basic amount of a fine (based primarily on the gravity and

---

[17] Case C-137/95 P, *SPO* [1996] ECR I-1611, para 55.

[18] K Yeung, *Securing Compliance. A Principled Approach* (Oxford, Hart Publishing, 2004) 86; Wils (n 15) 57 (who defined the three tasks of competition law enforcement as clarifying the content of the antitrust prohibitions, preventing violations and dealing with the consequences of violations); P Buccirossi, L Ciari, T Duso, G Spagnolo and C Vitale (2009) 'Deterrence in Competition Law', No 285, Discussion Papers, SFB/TR 15 Governance and the Efficiency of Economic Systems, Free University of Berlin, Humboldt University of Berlin, University of Bonn, University of Mannheim, University of Munich, http://econpapers.repec.org/RePEc:trf:wpaper:285; C Harding, 'Cartel Deterrence: The Search for Evidence and Argument' (2011) 56(2) *The Antitrust Bulletin* 345–76 (noting a rhetoric of deterrence).

[19] *Report on the Nature and Impact of Hard Core Cartels and Sanctions against cartels under National Competition Laws*, OECD, DAFFE/COMP (2002) 7, 9.4.2002, at http://www.oecd.org/competition/cartels/2081831. pdf; *Promoting Compliance with Competition Law* (OECD, August 2012) at http://www.oecd.org/daf/competition/ Promotingcompliancewithcompetitionlaw2011.pdf. The latter concluded: 'Drivers of compliance include: financial penalties, director disqualification orders, criminal sanctions, fear of damage to corporate or individual reputation, morality and a strong culture of compliance. Drivers of non-compliance include: an ambiguous commitment—or no commitment—to compliance by management, uncertainty about legal requirements, employee naiveté and/or simple error, rogue employees, arrogance, and competing interests from other compliance areas.'

[20] *Chemiefarma v Commission* (n 15); Joined Cases 100/80 to 103/80 *Musique Diffusion française and others v Commission* [1983] ECR 1825, para 106; Case C-453/99, *Courage and Crehan* [2001] ECR I-6297; Cases C-295-298/04 *Manfredi* [2006] ECR I-6619; Case C-289/04 P *Showa Denko v Commission* [2006] ECR I-5859, para 16; Case C-413/08 P *Lafarge v Commission* [2010] ECR I-5361, para 102; Case C-679/11P *Alliance One International Inc v Commission* judgement of 26.9.2013, paras 73–75.

[21] AP Reindl, 'How Strong is the Case for Criminal Sanctions in Cartel Cases?' in KJ Cseres, MP Schinkel and FOW Vogelaar (eds), *Criminalisation of Competition Law Enforcement: Economic and Legal Implications* (Cheltenham, Edward Elgar, 2006) 116; Hodges, 'A Market-Based Competition Enforcement Policy' (n 1) 261–91; Hodges, 'European Competition Enforcement Policy: Integrating Restitution and Behaviour Control' (n 1).

[22] *Guidelines on the method of setting fines imposed pursuant to Article 23(2)(a) of Regulation N0 1/2003*, para 4, referring to *Musique Diffusion française and others v Commission* (n 20) para 106. Almost the same wording appears at Communication from the Commission on quantifying harm in actions for damages based on breaches of Arts 101 and 102 of the Treaty on the Functioning of the European Union, OJ C 167/07, 13.6.2013, para 1. The twin aims of specific and general deterrence were underlined by the court: Case T-13/03, *Nintendo* [2009] ECR II-975, para 73. Analysis of the 39 cartels listed by the Commission between 1999 and 2006 reveals that once the gravity of the offence is set, the basic fine increases most as a result of the application of the 'sufficient deterrence' uplift an duration: C Veljanovski, 'Cartel Fines in Europe: Law, Practice and Deterrence' (2007) 30 *World Competition* 65–86.

[23] Buccirossi, Ciari, Duso, Spagnolo and Vitale (n 18).

duration of an offence) may be increased 'to ensure that fines have a sufficiently deterrent effect ... on undertakings which have a particularly large turnover beyond the sales of
goods or services to which the infringement relates' or 'in order to exceed the amount of
gains improperly made as a result of the infringement.'[24]

As noted in chapter two, theoretical literature contains two somewhat differing
approaches towards calculating fines that will induce a rational actor not to break the law:
The calculation can either be based on *removing illicit gains (deterrence)* or on *internalising
all net harms caused* (inducing *optimally efficient* behaviour and precautions). Thus, the
former focuses on disgorgement of illicit profits and the latter on removal of a sum equal
to the net costs caused. Hence, both theories focus on *removal* of money from the infringer,
rather than on *restoration* of the market and victims, although restoration is implied in the
second approach. Wils recognises that 'fines will normally have disgorgement of the unjust
enrichment as one of their effects, [but] the proceeds of fines normally go into the public
budget rather than to the victims of the antitrust violations, and fines could thus at most be
said to contribute to the pursuit of corrective justice through compensation in an abstract
and indirect way.'[25] Thus, compensation of victims is not the primary focus under either
approach, although it might (but might not) be a consequence, in particular under the
second approach.

Academic consensus since the 1970s has been that antitrust law should only condemn
practices that reduce economic efficiency.[26] The theory postulates that optimal deterrence
will be achieved through different combinations of the level of fines and of the probability
of detection and punishment.[27] Thus, the gain or net harm should be discounted by the
probability of detection.[28] The optimal level of deterrence should avoid preventing agents
from undertaking actions that improve social welfare, and hence there should never be
over-deterrence.[29] Over-deterrence occurs when the sanction is set too high or the enforcement effort is excessive.[30]

There is no formal statement by an EU level authority on which of the two theoretical
approaches (gain-deterrence or harm-internalisation) is adopted as official policy: Neither
approach is referred to, save the general concept of 'deterrence'. The imposition of deterrent fines is said to serve the two objectives of (i) the suppression of illegal activity (general deterrence) and (ii) the prevention of recidivism (specific deterrence).[31] Hylton has

---

[24]   *Guidelines*, paras 30 and 31.

[25]   Wils (n 15) 55. See also WPJ Wils, 'The Relationship between Public Antitrust Enforcement and Private
Actions for Damages' (2009) 32(1) *World Competition* 3–26.

[26]   RA Posner, *Antitrust Law* 2nd edn (Chicago, University of Chicago Press, 2001) vii–ix; WH Page, 'Optimal
Antitrust Remedies: A Synthesis' in RD Blair and DD Sokol (eds), *The Oxford Handbook of International Antitrust
Economics, Volume 1* (Oxford, Oxford University Press, 2012) ch 11.

[27]   Wils (n 15) 61.

[28]   KN Hylton and H Lin, 'Optimal Antitrust Enforcement, Dynamic Competition, and Changing Economic
Conditions' (2010) 77 *Antitrust Law Journal* 247–76 (arguing that once the probability of private enforcement
reaches 100%, there is no need to multiply damages by three in the USA, and that it follows that the optimal
multiplier for private lawsuits efficiently balances the supply of lawsuits with the 'demand' required by the optimal
deterrence goal).

[29]   Buccirossi, Ciari, Duso, Spagnolo and Vitale (n 18); DH Ginsburg and JD Wright, 'Antitrust Sanctions'
(2010) 6(2) *Competition Policy International* 3–39; George Mason University Law and Economics Research Paper
Series available at http://papers.ssrn.com/sol3/papers.cfm?abstract_id=1705701.

[30]   AM Polinsky and S Shavell, *The Economic Theory of Public Enforcement of Law*, Stanford Law School, John M
Olin Programme in Law and Economics, Working Paper No 159 (2000).

[31]   Geradin and Henry (n 5).

suggested that the policies of US and EU authorities on antitrust fines differ.[32] He argues that EU penalties are designed to deter by eliminating profits, but are *not* designed to vary directly with the amount of consumer harm, since they are structured to vary directly with the amount of profit that a firm gains from conduct deemed to violate EU competition law. In contrast, the US has adopted the harm internalisation approach. Thus, for cartel cases, the EU reflects a social welfare approach whereas the US is a penalty system, and Hylton prefers the former. However, for monopolisation cases, the EU fine system appears to be inferior on welfare grounds to the US punishment system, since in stripping gains from monopolising conduct, the former deters both efficient as well as inefficient conduct.

The level of fines imposed has increased significantly and continuously.[33] Combe and Monnier found that average fines per cartel rose in the period 1996–2005, and did so significantly from 2006 to 2008, which they explained by a change in the Commission's policy.[34] Between 1990 and 2009 the increase was eight per cent, and 107 per cent since the introduction of the Commission's 2006 Guidelines.[35] Fines averaged €356.77m per cartel in the period 2005–2009.[36] Well known examples are Intel 2009 €1.06 billion,[37] Heineken 2007 €219 million,[38] Interbrew 2001 €46 million,[39] €1.3 billion in 2008 to the Carglass cartel,[40] and the largest fine of €1.47 billion in 2012 to seven members of the ten year cathode ray tube cartel.[41] The Commission has to a significant extent focused its resources on the fight against cartels,[42] adopting five and 10 major cartel decisions a year, and fines running into billions of euros. Combe and Monnier found that between 1975 and 2009 the Commission imposed fines on 110 cartels, for which aggregate fines, after leniency but prior to revision on appeal, were €12 billion.[43]

There is ongoing academic debate over whether the level of fines is or is not high enough to deter. The debate is based solely on theoretical economic calculations of the fine necessary for optimal deterrence and not on empirical evidence of what effect particular penalties have in practice. Some scholars have supported the view that a clear majority of fines imposed by the European Commission in recent years meet the deterrence objective,[44]

[32] KN Hylton, 'Antitrust Enforcement Regimes: Fundamental Differences' *Boston University School of Law, Law and Economics Research Paper No 12-41.*

[33] See http://ec.europa.eu/comm/competition/cartels/statistics/statistics.pdf, relied on by Ginsburg and Wright (n 29); George Mason University Law and Economics Research Paper Series available at http://papers.ssrn.com/sol3/papers.cfm?abstract_id=1705701.

[34] E Combe and C Monnier, 'Fines Against Hard Core Cartels in Europe: The Myth of Over Enforcement' Cahiers de Recherche PRISM-Sorbonne, June 2009, at http://ssrn.com/abstract=1431644http://ssrn.com/abstract=1431644.

[35] JM Connor and DJ Miller, 'Determinants of EC Antitrust Fines for Members of Global Cartels' paper presented at the 3rd LEAR Conference on The Economics of Competition Law (Rome, 25–26 June 2009), http://papers.ssrn.com/sol3/papers.cfm?abstract_id=2229358.

[36] JK Ashton and AD Pressey, 'Who Manages Cartels? The Role of Sales and Marketing Managers within International Cartels: Evidence from the European Union 1990–2009' CCP Working Paper 12-11 (2012).

[37] See http://europa.eu/rapid/pressReleasesAction.do?reference=IP/09/745&format=HTML&aged=0&language=EN&guiLanguage=fr.

[38] See http://europa.eu/rapid/pressReleasesAction.do?reference=IP/07/509&format=HTML&aged=0&language=EN&guiLanguage=en.

[39] See http://europa.eu/rapid/pressReleasesAction.do?reference=IP/01/1739&format=HTML&aged=0&language=EN&guiLanguage=en.

[40] See http://europa.eu/rapid/pressReleasesAction.do?reference=IP/08/1685&guiLanguage=en.

[41] See http://europa.eu/rapid/press-release_IP-12-1317_en.htm.

[42] Wils (n 15) iii.

[43] Combe and Monnier (n 34).

[44] M Boyer, M-L Allain, R Kotchoni and J-P Ponssard, 'The Determination of Optimal Fines in Cartel Cases: The Myth of Underdeterrence' at http://papers.ssrn.com/sol3/papers.cfm?abstract_id=1987107.

whereas others have argued that fines are too low, in general[45] or to achieve deterrence of price-fixing.[46] It has been argued that the arbitrary 10 per cent cap on fines for firms is far too low to provide deterrence at the margin and introduces an asymmetry in punishment between diversified and non-diversified firms.[47] American scholars have argued that the multiplier for US antitrust damages is too low to constitute an effective deterrent, and should be increased from three to five times the actual loss.[48] Assertions by both sides are based on mathematical calculations based on assumptions, notably what constitutes the level of illicit gains, and not on any empirical research into what might affect the future behaviour of any person or business who was involved or might in future be involved. Industry has argued that the level of fines imposed by the Commission is so high as to be stifling business and innovation, rather than encouraging competition.[49]

Connor's analysis of the first 22 cartel decisions of the European Commission (EC) under the 2006 fining Guidelines regarding 128 cartel participants found that the severity of the cartel fines relative to affected sales was about double that of the fines decided under the 1998 Guidelines.[50] Severity varied only modestly across companies in the same cartel. A large minority of EC fines now disgorge the monopoly profits accumulated by cartelists. The mean average final fine imposed on the 22 cartels in the sample was $383 million (99 per cent higher than under the 1998 Guidelines), but because the fines were highly skewed, the *median* average cartel fine was much lower ($178 million). His calculation on measurement of severity of fines was based on dividing by the annual global sales in the relevant market and by total affected cartel sales in the EU, both of which measures showed high variation across cartels and cartel participants. He applied a formula to the 128 defendants that were fined under the 2006 Guidelines, which calculated that the medial severity was 80 per cent, but 45 (36 per cent) of them displayed annual-sales severities above 100 per cent. Three firms in *Marine Hose* ranged as high as 500 per cent to 650 per cent of affected sales, which he described as possible (but rare) examples of supra-deterrence. He concluded that the European Commission fines regularly disgorge the monopoly profits accumulated by most cartelists. However, the more conventional index of severity shows that median fines were only 26 per cent of affected sales.

Veljanovski also analysed the fines imposed on 168 firms in the same cohort of 22 cartels prosecuted by European Commission under the 2006 Penalty Guidelines over the period 2007 to 2010. He found that fines were considerably *less* than provided for under the

[45] Combe and Monnier, (n 34) (finding that half of the fines fell below the company's illicit gain); C Veljanovski, 'Are European Cartel Fines Ridiculously High?' *Casenotes* (London, Case Associates, Feb 2012) (50 of the 168 firms prosecuted under the 2006 Guidelines, about 69% of firms received fines at or in excess of 67% of annual sales, so some fines were excessive, while others were inadequate).

[46] Veljanovski (n 22); Combe and Monnier, (n 34) above.

[47] I Bos and MP Schinkel, 'On the Scope for the European Commission's 2006 Fining Guidelines under the Legal Maximum Fine' (2006) 2(4) *Journal of Competition Law and Economics* 673.

[48] RH Lande and JM Connor, 'Optimal Cartel Deterrence: An Empirical Comparison of Sanctions to Overcharges' available at http://papers.ssrn.com/sol3/papers.cfm?abstract_id=1917657 (arguing that if mean average figures are used, the imposed sanctions have only been 16% to 21% (based on mean average figures) or 9% to 12% (based on median average figures) as large as they should have been to protect victims of cartelisation optimally).

[49] N Tait, 'Brussels urged to cut cartel fines' *Financial Times* (London, January 24 2008).

[50] JM Connor, 'Cartel Fine Severity and the European Commission: 2007–2011' (2013) 34 *European Competition Law Review* 58–77. His review of the first 13 cartel decisions of the European Commission under the 2006 fining guidelines is JM Connor, 'Has the European Commission Become More Severe in Punishing Cartels? Effects of the 2006 Guidelines' (2011) 32 *European Competition Law Review* 27.

Guidelines.[51] He found that the average fine per firm declined significantly after 2007, that repeat offenders were let off lightly, and that the Commission's published decision often redacted key information on the fining procedure. During the period, fines totalled €7.6 billion, averaging €73 million per cartelist before leniency and €60 million after leniency. Average duration of cartel was nine years (the longest was 35 years), with 7.6 participating firms. Cases were concentrated in the industrial inputs (45 per cent), chemicals (32 per cent) and services (14 per cent) sectors. The average post-leniency fine was 9.6 per cent of world-wide turnover for small and medium sized enterprises (SMEs) and 0.5 per cent for very large companies. There were two settlement decisions. The most prevalent aggravating circumstance was recidivism (14 firms in 11 cartels had their basic amount increased by between 50 per cent to 100 per cent for having participated in prior cartels). A 'specific deterrence increase' was applied to six firms out of the 13 decisions that had been then published in full. In all of the 13 decisions fines were reduced as a result of leniency: The total reduction was €911 million (18 per cent), with seven firms receiving full immunity (€355.8 million) and 40 firms receiving some reduction (and €555.6 reduced for cooperation during the investigation). The Commission took between two and seven years (average 4.3 years) in investigating these cartels.

Veljanovski later analysed the four cartels prosecuted by the Commission in each of 2011 and 2012. In 2011 he found that the average fine per firm remained similar (€43.9 million) and that data on 50 of the 168 firms prosecuted under the 2006 Guidelines showed that about 69 per cent of firms received fines at or in excess of 67 per cent of annual sales.[52] Given that Allain argued that the fine necessary for optimal deterrence is 28–67 per cent of annual sales,[53] it followed that some fines were excessive, while others were inadequate. For 2012 he found that the average fine per firm rose considerably (€51 million) but remained similar before leniency (€58 million in 2012, €61 million in 2011).[54] Average duration of the cartels increased from 3.3 years in 2011 to 6.1 years in 2012.

In 2014, the Commission concluded 10 cartel investigations, fining 45 firms a total of almost €1.7 billion, with an average fine of €36 million per cartel, around €3.9 million per firm and €9.6 million per cartel year.[55] The cap that fines do not exceed 10 per cent of the previous year's annual worldwide turnover[56] was applied to at least 15 undertakings. Eight (80 per cent) of the 10 prosecutions were initiated by a full leniency applicant. These whistleblowers collectively avoided fines of €372 million. In addition the 37 partial leniency applicants received discounts of between 10 per cent and 60 per cent which reduced their fines in aggregate by an additional €402 million. In total the leniency programme 'saved' cartelists, or cost the Commission, a total of €774 million in avoided fines. The average cartel duration was 3.9 years compared to nearly 5.5 years in 2013.

---

[51] C Veljanovski, 'European Cartel Fines Under the 2006 Penalty Guidelines—A Statistical Analysis' (London, Case Associates, 2010) available at http://ssrn.com/abstract=1723843.

[52] Veljanovski (n 45).

[53] M-L Allain, M Boyer and J-P Ponssard, 'The Determination Of Optimal Fines in Cartel Cases: Theory and Practice' (2011) 4 *Concurrences* 32–40.

[54] C Veljanovski, *European Cartel Fines in 2012* (London, Case Associates, 2013).

[55] C Veljanovski, *European Cartel Fines in 2014* (London, Case Associates, 2015).

[56] 2006 Penalty Guidelines, para 37.

II. Private Enforcement

A. Antitrust Enforcement in the USA

Private antitrust enforcement has far greater significance, and led to a far greater volume of litigation, in the USA than in Europe.[57] Private enforcement is argued to provide both compensation and deterrence,[58] to save scarce public funds on enforcement, to maintain enforcement from the vagaries of fluctuations in the attitude of public enforcers or public budgetary processes, and to help ensure the stability of legal norms by preventing abrupt transitions in enforcement policy.[59]

In introducing the illegality of antitrust behaviour into USA in 1890, the Sherman Act[60] and its successor the Clayton Act[61] expressly provided for private rights of action for damages by any injured person in addition to criminal penalties, and that private claims would recover triple damages.[62] The Clayton Act also gave private parties the right to seek injunctive relief,[63] and any finding of violation in civil or criminal proceedings would be prima facie evidence of violation in private civil cases.[64] The US government has throughout maintained a restricted policy on taking enforcement action.[65] Recent enforcement policy by the US Department of Justice has been to concentrate on cases involving larger amounts of commerce and seeking increased fines and longer terms of imprisonment.[66] As a result, it is said that in the USA private enforcement represents the vast majority of all antitrust court actions: A ratio of private to public cases ranging from 10 to one to 20 to one,[67] at least 90 per cent in the 1980s[68] and arguably over 95 per cent recently.[69]

---

[57] AE Foer and JW Cuneo (eds), *The International Handbook on Private Enforcement of Competition Law* (Cheltenham, Edward Elgar, 2010); CA Jones, *Private Enforcement of Competition Law in the EU, UK and USA* (Oxford, Oxford University Press, 1999); RH Lande and JP Davis, 'Benefits from Private Antitrust Enforcement: An Analysis of Forty Cases' (2008) 42 *University of San Francisco Law Review* 879.

[58] See Supreme Court judgments in *Perma-Life Mufflers, Inc v International Parts Co*, 392 US 134, 139 (1968); *Brunswick Corp v Pueblo Bowl-O-Mat, Inc*, 429 US 477 (1977); *Illinois Brick v State of Illinois*, 431 US 720, 748 (1977) (Brennan J dissenting).

[59] JC Coffee, Jr, 'Rescuing the Private Attorney General: Why the Model of the Lawyer as Bounty Hunter is not Working' (1983) 42 *Maryland Law Review* 215, 217.

[60] Act of 2 July 1890, c 617, 25 Stat 209, 15 USC §§ 1–7.

[61] Act of 15 Oct 1914, c 323, 38 Stat 730, 15 USC §§ 12–27.

[62] Clayton Antitrust Act, s 7 as amended. Ironically, the triple damages rule was inspired by the English Statute of Monopolies, 21 Jac I c 3(1623). There has been criticism that triple damages are objectionable in principle as constituting unfair windfalls to claimants of penalties that should be paid to the state: *Conference of Studio Unions v Loew's, Inc*, 193 F 2d 51, 55 (9th Cir 1951). It is widely considered that the US rule on recovery of triple damages and the EU rule on interest on judgments being backdated to dates of infringement effectively equate to similar sums of money: See Jones (n 57) ch 19.

[63] Sect 26, 15 USC § 16.

[64] Sect 5(a), 15 USC § 16(a).

[65] The Justice Department received no funds at all for enforcement for the first 13 years: HB Thorelli, *The Federal Antitrust Policy: Origination of an American Tradition* (Baltimore, Johns Hopkins Press, 1954) 588, 590.

[66] AK Bingham, 'The Clinton Administration: Trends in Criminal Antitrust Enforcement', Address to Corporate Counsel Institute, San Francisco, California, 30 November 1995.

[67] Jones (n 57) 85.

[68] S Salop and L White, 'Private Antitrust Litigation: An Introduction and Framework' in L White (ed), *Private Antitrust Litigation: New Evidence, New Learning* (Cambridge MA, MIT Press, 1988) 3.

[69] K Bernard, 'Private Damages Actions: A US Perspective on Importing US Damages Actions to the EU' eCCP, October 2007 at https://www.competitionpolicyinternational.com/private-damages-actions-a-us-perspective-

B. Private Enforcement in the EU

As noted above, the principal means of enforcement of competition law in the EU has from the start continued to be enforcement by a public agency. However, after the Court of Justice held that a right to damages exists under EU law for those who have suffered loss from infringements of EU competition law,[70] the European Commission has proposed to support 'private enforcement' actions. The Commission's 2008 White Paper on damages[71] clarified that its goal was that of achieving increased payment of damages rather than filling any regulatory enforcement gap, but the two aspects are in reality viewed as completely inter-linked.[72] It referred to the 'current ineffectiveness of antitrust damages actions'[73] and asserted that the 'current legal framework for competition damages actions is ineffective: [there exist] major difficulties for victims to obtain compensation'.[74] What appeared to be a low level of competition damages in Europe[75] contrasts with the primacy of private enforcement in the United States of America.[76] However, evidence has since emerged that the level of private enforcement is much higher than was at first thought.[77] Peyer's study found that a large number of private cases were concluded in Germany, including when compared with public investigations.[78] Mateus' review found that in the UK follow-on actions have

---

on-importing-us-damages-actions-to-the-eu. Jones (n 57) states that the number of private actions between 1985 and 1999 was in the range of 600 and 1,000 annually.

[70] The ECJ referred to 'the practical effect of the prohibition being put at risk' in *Courage and Crehan* (n 20) paras 26 and 27, and to damages actions making 'a significant contribution to the maintenance of effective competition' in *Manfredi* (n 20).

[71] White Paper on damages actions for breach of the EC antitrust rules, COM(2008) 165, 2.4.2008. See also Commission Staff Working Document accompanying the White Paper on damages actions for breach of the EC antitrust rules: Impact assessment, SEC(2008) 405, 2.4.2008 ('Impact Assessment Report'); Green Paper: Damages actions for breach of the EC antitrust rules, COM (2005) 672, 19.12.2005; Commission Staff Working Paper: Annex to the Green Paper 'Damages actions for breach of the EC antitrust rules', SEC(2005) 1732, 19.12.2005; A Renda, J Peysner, A Riley, R Van den Bergh, S Keske, R Pardolesi, E Camilli and P Caprile, *Making Antitrust Damages Actions More Effective in the EU: Welfare Impact and Potential Scenarios*, final report submitted to the Commission on 21 December 2007 ('Impact Study').

[72] CJS Hodges, 'Competition Enforcement, Regulation and Civil Justice: What is the Case?' (2006) 43 *Common Market Law Review* 1381–407.

[73] White Paper on damages actions for breach of the EC antitrust rules, COM(2008) 165 final, 2.4.2008, para 1.1.

[74] Commission Staff Working Document accompanying the White Paper on damages actions for breach of the EC antitrust rules: Impact assessment, SEC(2008) 405, 2.4.2008 ('Impact Assessment Report') 2.1.

[75] D Waelbroeck, D Slater and G Even-Shoshan, *Study on the Conditions of Claims for Damages in Case of Infringement of EC Competition Rules* (Brussels, Ashurst, 2004); Impact Assessment para 42 and Impact Study para 2.1.1.

[76] Antitrust cases filed in US District Courts 1975–2007, Table 5.41.2012 shows that the percentage of private to public cases has only fallen below 90% in 10 of the 36 years (mainly around 1990, lowest 83.4%); the percentage has risen since 2000, and generally been around 94%. *Sourcebook of Criminal Justice Statistics Online*, http://www.albany.edu/sourcebook/pdf/t5412012.pdf.

[77] *Private Enforcement in the European Union—Pitfalls and Opportunities* (Bundesverband der Deutschen Industrie eV and Freshfields Bruckhaus Deringer, 2007); BJ Rodger, 'Private Enforcement of Competition Law, the Hidden Story: Competition Litigation Settlements in the United Kingdom, 2000–2005' [2008] *European Competition Law Review* 2; U Böge and K Ost, 'Up and Running, or is it? Private Enforcement—the Situation in Germany and Policy Perspectives' [2006] *European Competition Law Reviewer* 197; S Peyer, 'Injunctive Relief and Private Antitrust Enforcement' UEA WP 11-7 ssrn (finding a conservative estimate of an average of 200 private antitrust cases a year in Germany in 2004 to 2009, most injunctions or removal claims).

[78] S Peyer, 'Private Antitrust Litigation in Germany from 2005 to 2007: Empirical Evidence' (2012) 8(2) *Journal of Competition Law and Economics* 331.

become systematic, mostly with settlements, and in Germany a number of damages claims were progressed through the model of being assigned to a private enforcement house.[79]

A large study led by Rodger has recently found that the level of competition damages claims is very much higher than the very low level suggested by the European Commission, notably in Germany, Spain, France, UK, Netherlands, Belgium, Italy, Portugal and Sweden.[80] Rodger's pan-EU study found a total of 1268 court judgments in competition cases in the period 1 May 1999 to 1 May 2012,[81] thereby excluding a significant number of cases that are known to be resolved through settlement, mediation or arbitration.[82] It identified a very mixed landscape of private enforcement of competition law across the Member States, with national culture, and national rules on competition architecture and civil procedure, clearly affecting rates of litigation in many Member States. In new or small states, in particular, the effectiveness of both authorities and courts was impeded by limited procedures.

It was found that competition law was mostly used by businesses in commercial contract disputes, often as one of a number of arguments that are primarily about contract law rather than competition law. A significant number of competition issues were raised as shields rather than swords, that is as defences to business-to-business (B2B) breach of contract claims. The highest impact that competition law can have is in deploying an interim remedy quickly (injunction, nullity) so as to stop an infringement and limit the ongoing damage. But in some jurisdictions (an exemplar being the UK) there are significant barriers in obtaining an injunction through the cost and need to give a cross-undertaking for wrongful damages caused.

Importantly, the Rodger study noted that making a determination of dominance is difficult and requires serious evidence, which is a specialist task that many lawyers and courts are just not equipped to undertake, whereas the body that is best placed to decide it is a competition authority. In the B2B context, many cases ought to settle (and do in some but not all Member States), but there are barriers, such as asymmetrical information or civil procedure systems that do not facilitate settlement (in the Continental system, the judge has all the information, not the parties), or the need for claimants to interact in future with restrainers or abusers. A possible conclusion from the study is that competition law might be being over-used and the focus should rather be on business behaviour and remedies. In contrast, in consumer-to-business (C2B) situations, there were almost no small value mass consumer claims based on competition law.

Stand-alone actions dominated (1,075, representing 85.3 per cent of the total), with only (85) 14.7 per cent of judgments in follow-on actions. Many of the States with more case

---

[79] AM Mateus, 'Ensuring a More Level Playing Field in Competition Enforcement throughout the European Union' [2010] *European Competition Law Review* 514.

[80] The AHRC Research Project on EU Competition Law: Comparative Private Enforcement and Collective Redress in the EU 1999–2012, reported in B Rodger (ed), *Competition Law: Comparative Private Enforcement and Collective Redress Across the EU* (Alphen aan den Rijn, WoltersKluwer, 2014).

[81] It found very limited enforcement experience in 2004 accession states (Bulgaria (0), Cyprus, Estonia and Latvia (1), Romania (3), Czech republic (4), Lithuania, Slovakia and Slovenia (5), and Poland (6)); some states with limited private enforcement experience (Finland (4), Luxembourg (4), Malta (7)); some states with developing private enforcement experience (Austria (64), Denmark (10), Greece (27), Ireland (24), Portugal (24) and Sweden (25)); and some states with considerable private enforcement experience (Belgium (128), France (71), Germany, Italy (98), the Netherlands (308), Spain (323) and UK (106)).

[82] See G Blanke, 'The Role of EC Competition Law in International Arbitration: A Plaidover' [2005] *European Business Law Review* 170; A Komninos, 'Arbitration and EU Competition Law' in J Basedow, S Francq and L Idot (eds), *Conflict of Laws and Coordination* (Oxford, Hart Publishing, 2011).

law had significantly lower levels of follow-on claims: For example, Belgium only one case (0.8 per cent); Sweden one case ex 25 (four per cent: It was thought that follow-on proceedings in Sweden settled out of court). In the UK follow-on claims constituted 36.8 per cent (111), but with a noticeable increase in the period 2009–2012 (29 judgments). Germany had 25 follow-on cases (4.11 per cent) and 583 stand-alone cases (95.89 per cent).

It was found that the vast majority of judgments, over two-thirds (67 per cent) were unsuccessful. Of the combined total of 33 per cent successful cases, only 21.7 per cent were fully successful and 11.3 per cent were partially successful.[83] Although follow-on actions were considerably less frequent (185 compared with 1062 stand-alone actions) they had a relatively much higher combined success rate at 56.8 per cent (37.8 per cent successful and 18.9 per cent partially successful) than stand-alone actions, which had a combined success rate of 28.9 per cent (18.9 per cent successful and 10 per cent partially successful). The difference is striking—an overall success rate in follow-on actions at virtually double that of stand-alone actions.

III. Public Sanctioning and Leniency

Given that breach of European competition law is regarded as a matter of serious public concern and the principal means of enforcement is by public authorities, it is curious that the European Commission is not empowered to impose or seek criminal penalties on to individuals. The EU enforcement approach contrasts starkly with the 'formidable congeries of US weapons'[84] (see chapter three). Some Member States have introduced criminal penalties but there is no power to do so at EU level and the issue is contentious.[85] The evidence does indicate very different levels of enforcement among countries (greatest in the Netherlands, France, Denmark, Germany and UK), associated with variations in endowment of national authorities (the better endowed being the Nordic countries, UK, and the Netherlands, followed by France and Hungary), although enforcement activities are of long duration in many states.[86]

Some competition infringements, especially cartels, are very difficult to identify. Summarising the evidence, Peyer notes that price fixing is difficult to detect, most cartels are broken up by a competition authority, and private litigants often lack the resources and compulsory process (by means of power) to discover cartel violations.[87]

A specific technique has been developed to identify such breaches, which the EU copied in 1996 from prior practice of the US Department of Justice Antitrust Division first

---

[83] Komninos, ibid, 150.

[84] Geradin and Henry (n 5).

[85] Criminal sanctions for competition breaches have been introduced in the United Kingdom, Ireland, France and Estonia, and for bid-rigging in Germany, [Hungary, Cyprus, Malta and Poland]: See T Calvani and TH Calvani, 'Cartel Sanctions and Deterrence' (2011) 56(2) *The Antitrust Bulletin* 185, 187; also Cseres, Schinkel and Vogelaar (n 21). Extra-EU countries with criminal sanctions include Brazil, Canada, Israel, the republic of Korea, Japan, Russia, the USA, and recently Australia.

[86] Mateus (n 79).

[87] Peyer (n 78) 331. Private follow-on actions are far more likely than independently initiated cases to focus on horizontal price-fixing, the most egregious and economically significant antitrust violation. Peyer notes that an injunction or nullity of a contract may suffice to remediate future problems with cases of vertical restraints or unilateral conduct.

introduced in 1978.[88] Under the European Commission's leniency programme,[89] infringers who are first to notify the authorities of wrongdoing by their employees can obtain immunity from fines, and other companies that provide additional information that has significant additional value for the authority can seek reduced fines.[90] The theoretical basis for creating a significant incentive for firms to be the first to own up is based on the belief that conspiracies have an inherent internal stability problem, under which the rational assessment of the classic conundrum of the 'prisoners' dilemma' can be exploited both to incentivise members to own up first so as to 'buy' exemption from punishment and to lower detection and enforcement costs through achieving deterrence at lower levels of sanction.[91]

Although authorities possess power to gather evidence through coercive investigations (dawn raids), the leniency programme is considered to be essential in discovering cartels. The discovery of a cartel infringement occurs almost exclusively as a result of the 'leniency' policy.[92]

Combe and Monnier found an increase in the rate of detection of cartels after the introduction of the leniency policy in 1996: In the 28 years pre-1996 there were 35 detected

---

[88]   US Department of Justice, *Corporate Leniency Policy* (10 August 1993), accessible at http://www.usdoj.gov/ atr/public/guidelines/0091.pdf and SD Hammond, 'Measuring the Value of Second-In Cooperation in Corporate Plea Negotiations', address to the 54th Annual American Bar Association Section of Antitrust Law Spring Meeting (Washington DC, 29 March 2006), accessible at http://www.usdoj.gov/atr/public/speeches/215514.pdf.

[89]   Commission Notice on Immunity from fines and reduction of fines in cartel cases, OJ 2006 C207/4-6. Leniency programmes exist in every Member State except Malta: 1207 Lear report for EP *Collective Redress in Antitrust* IP/A/ECON/ST/2001-19, June 2012. See W Wils, 'Leniency in Antitrust Enforcement: Theory and Practice' (2007) 30 *World Competition* 25.

[90]   *Revised Leniency Policy* (European Competition Network, November 2012), available at http://ec.europa.eu/ competition/ecn/mlp_revised_2012_en.pdf; updating Commission Notice on Immunity from fines and reduction of fines in cartel cases, OJ C 298/17, 8.12.2008, available at http://eur-lex.europa.eu/LexUriServ/LexUriServ. do?uri=COM:2008:0165:FIN:EN:PDF.

[91]   GJ Stigler, 'A Theory of Oligopoly' (1964) 72 *The Journal of Political Economy* 44–61; G Spagnolo, 'Optimal Leniency Programs' FEEM Nota di Lavoro No 42.00, Fondazione ENI 'Enrico Mattei' Milano (2000) (at http:// papers.ssrn.com/sol3/papers.cfm?abstract_id=235092; G Spagnolo, 'Cartels Criminalization and Their Internal Organization' in M Schinkel et al (eds), *Remedies and Sanctions in Competition Policy: Economic and Legal Implications of the Tendency to Criminalize Antitrust Enforcement in the EU Member States* (Cheltenham, Edward Elgar, 2005); G Spagnolo, 'Self-Defeating Antitrust Laws: How Leniency Programs Solve Bertrand's Paradox and Enforce Collusion in Auctions' FEEM Nota di Lavoro No 52.00, Fondazione ENI 'Mattei' Milano (2008) (at www.ssrn. com and www.feem.it); M Motta and M Polo, 'Leniency Programs and Cartel Prosecution' (2003) 21 *International Journal of Industrial Organization* 347–79; P Rey, 'Towards a Theory of Competition Policy' in *Advances in Economics and Econometrics: Theory and Applications—Eight World Congress*, (Cambridge, Cambridge University Press, 2003).

[92]   See Dir 2014/104/EU on certain rules governing actions for damages under national law for infringements of the competition law provisions of the Member States and of the European Union, recital 26: 'Leniency programmes and settlement procedures are important tools for the public enforcement of Union competition law as they contribute to the detection and efficient prosecution of, and the imposition of penalties for, the most serious infringements of competition law. Furthermore, as many decisions of competition authorities in cartel cases are based on a leniency application, and damages actions in cartel cases generally follow on from those decisions, leniency programmes are also important for the effectiveness of actions for damages in cartel cases. Undertakings might be deterred from cooperating with competition authorities under leniency programmes and settlement procedures if self-incriminating statements such as leniency statements and settlement submissions, which are produced for the sole purpose of cooperating with the competition authorities, were to be disclosed....' The proposal was echoed by the UK: 'Given the critical importance of the leniency regime in cartel detection and enforcement, the OFT very much welcomes the recognition that it is important to safeguard leniency incentives.': *Private Actions in Competition Law: a consultation on options for reform: The OFT's response to the Government's Consultation* (London, Office of Fair Trading, 2012), OFT1434resp, para 1.16, available at http://hb.betterregulation. com/external/Private%20Actions%20in%20Competition%20Law%20a%20consultation%20on%20options%20 for%20reform%20-%20The%20OFTs%20response%20to%20the%20Governments%20Consultation.pdf.

cartels, but in the subsequent 12 years (to 2008) 75 cartels were detected (an average of 6.25 per year).[93] There appear to have been 26 cases of leniency between 1996 and 2002, and 32 from 2002 to 2007.[94] In Ashton and Pressey's analysis of 56 cartels dealt with by DG COMP between 1990 and 2009, the majority (64 per cent) were identified by whistle-blowers and leniency was involved in 64.3 per cent.[95] Leniency was applied to one or more cartelists in all but one of the first 22 cartels dealt with under the 2006 Guidelines between 2007 and 2011, and reduced the level of final fines significantly (post-leniency fines were 33 per cent to 35 per cent lower than those that would have been imposed).[96] All four cartels sanctioned by the Commission in 2012 were triggered by a whistleblower and involved leniency discounts to 15 of the 34 firms (44 per cent).[97] Similarly, in the USA, over 90 per cent of fines imposed for Sherman Act violations since 1996 can be traced to investigations assisted by leniency applicants.[98] The detection rate may have increased by as much as 60 per cent in recent years as a result of the leniency programme.[99]

Scholars note that leniency increases constitutional problems over fairness, leaves infringers free to offend again, and is undermined where an infringer has a prospect of having to pay substantial damages irrespective of any fine.[100] The leniency policy treats firms as integral entities, and as able to control the behaviour of all staff. But some have noted that firms' ability to ensure that all staff abide by the law depends on internal mechanisms such as compliance mechanisms, and that the official position here is notably unhelpful and unjust.

Since firms operate on the basis of systems, a compliance programme is an essential internal mechanism to maximise compliance by staff, even if it cannot realistically expect to eliminate all wrongdoing.[101]

The Commission 'welcomes and supports all compliance efforts by companies.... But the mere existence of a compliance programme will not be considered as an attenuating circumstance. Nor will the setting-up of a compliance programme be considered as a valid argument justifying a reduction of the fine in the wake of investigation of an infringement'.[102] Wils notes that the European Commission has never granted a reduction of a fine because of the existence of a compliance programme at the time of the infringement.[103] He identifies that in seven decisions, adopted between 1982 and 1992, the Commission granted a fine reduction because the companies concerned had set up a compliance programme after

---

[93] Combe and Monnier (n 34).

[94] M Motta, 'On EU Antitrust Fines and Cartel Deterrence' at http://ec.europa.eu/dgs/competition/economist/motta.pdf.

[95] Ashton and Pressey (n 36). 26.8% were also investigated by US authorities. Other sources were customer complaint (9%), identified by another antitrust authority (6%), information disclosed by a third party (3%), uncovered during a separate investigation (3%).

[96] Connor, 'Cartel Fine Severity and the European Commission: 2007–2011' (n 50); Veljanovski (n 51).

[97] Veljanovski (n 54).

[98] GJ Werden, SC Hammond and BA Barnett, 'Deterrence and Detection of Cartels: Using All the Tools and Sanctions' (2011) 56(2) *The Antitrust Bulletin* 207–34.

[99] NH Miller, 'Strategic Leniency and Cartel Enforcement' (2009) 99 *American Economic Review* 750, 760.

[100] Wils (n 15) ch 5.

[101] P Puri, 'Judgment Proofing the Profession' (2001) 15(1) *Georgetown Journal of Legal Ethics* 9–10 (listing rapid growth, globalisation and increased specialisation as factors that explain the inability of law firms to monitor their members); A Hamadi and A Klement, 'Corporate Crime and Deterrence' (2008) 61 *Stanford Law Review* 271.

[102] European Commission, *Compliance Matters—What Companies can do Better to Respect EU Competition Rules* (November 2011) accessible at http://ec.europa.eu/competition/antitrust/compliance/, at 19–20.

[103] WPJ Wils, 'Antitrust Compliance Programmes & Optimal Antitrust Enforcement' (2013) 1(1) *Journal of Antitrust Enforcement* 52.

the start of the Commission's investigations.[104] But since then the Commission has never granted any reductions because of compliance programmes.[105] Further, he notes that the EU Courts have consistently upheld this policy, pointing out that the implementation of a competition compliance programme 'does not alter the reality of the infringement and does not oblige the Commission to grant a reduction in the amount of the fine'.[106]

This European Commission policy of refusing formally to incentivise compliance measures is similar to the long-standing policy of the US Department of Justice Antitrust Division.[107] The policy has been criticised by some authors, who call for 'a substantial fine reduction for firms with effective compliance programs'.[108] A few authors have gone further, arguing that, 'if a company has made a reasonable effort to comply with the antitrust law, and an employee nevertheless engages in price-fixing, then it makes no sense to fine the corporation'.[109] Their idea would thus be that a company with a compliance programme

---

[104] Commission Decisions of 7 December 1982, *National Panasonic* [1982] L 354/28; of 14 December 1984, *John Deere* [1985] OJ L 35/58; of 16 December 1985, *Sperry New Holland* [1985] OJ L376/21; of 18 December 1987, *Fisher-Price/Quaker Oats–Toyco* [1988] OJ L 49/19; of 22 December 1987, *Eurofix-Bauco/Hilti* [1988] OJ L65/19; of 18 July 1988, *British Sugar* [1988] OJ L 284/41; of 5 June 1991, *Viho/Toshiba* [1991] OJ L 287/39; and of 15 July 1992, *Viho/Parker Pen* [1992] OJ L233/27; all these decisions concerned vertical agreements or abuse of a dominant position, which were the main types of cases the Commission prosecuted in those years. When British Sugar was later found to have committed another infringement, the Commission took the violation of the compliance programme, together with the fact of the recidivism, into account as an aggravating factor leading to a higher second fine; Commission Decision of 14 October 1998, *British Sugar* [1999] OJ L 76/1; see further my paper 'Recidivism in EU Antitrust Enforcement: A Legal and Economic Analysis' (2012) 35 *World Competition* 5.

[105] In a decision in 2001 the Commission took into account the introduction of a compliance programme as one of a number of elements indicating that the infringement had been terminated and that there was thus no need for the Commission to order its termination; Commission Decision of 5 December 2001, *Interbrew and Alken-Maes* [2003] OJ L 200/1, para 291. More importantly, since 1996, the Commission grants fine reductions and even immunity from fines to companies that put an end or have put an end to their participation in a secret cartel and cooperate with the Commission in providing intelligence and evidence of the cartel under the conditions set out in the Commission's Leniency Notice; see text accompanying n 89 above.

[106] Judgment of the General Court of 6 March 2012 in Case T-53/06 *UPM-Kymmene v European Commission* [2012] ECR I-000, paras 123–24; Judgment of the Court of Justice of 28 June 2005 in Joined Cases C-189/02 P etc, *Dansk Rørindustri and Others v Commission* [2005] ECR I-5488, para 373; Judgment of the General Court of 12 December 2007 in Joined Cases T101/05 and T-111/05, *BASF and UCB v Commission* [2007] ECR II-4959, para 52; and Judgment of 13 July 2011 in Case T-138/07, *Schindler v Commission*, [2011] ECR II-4819, para 88.

[107] Under the US Sentencing Guidelines, which give the courts advice on sentencing (*United States v Booker*, 125 S Ct 738 (2005)), corporate fines are reduced if the company had in place at the time of the infringement an 'effective compliance and ethics program', but this does not apply if 'high-level personnel' or 'substantial authority personnel' participated in the infringement, which is in practice always the case for antitrust infringements, as these categories include all individuals who within the scope of their authority exercise a substantial measure of discretion, for instance individuals with authority to negotiate or set price levels or to negotiate or approve significant contracts (§8C2.5(f) and §8A1.2 of the Guidelines Manual (November 1, 2011), accessible at www.ussc.gov/guidelines). The US Department of Justice Antitrust Division does not either take into account the existence of a compliance programme in its decisions whether or not to prosecute a case; see US Attorney's Manual 9-28.400 Special Policy Concerns, Comment B, accessible at http://www.justice.gov/usao/eousa/foia_reading_room/usam/title9/28mcrm.htm, and 'Antitrust Compliance Programs: The Government Perspective', address by WJ Kolasky, Deputy Assistant Attorney General, before the Corporate Compliance 2002 Conference (San Francisco, July 12, 2002), accessible at http://www.justice.gov/atr/public/speeches/, and JH Shenefield and RJ Favretto, 'Compliance Programs as Viewed from the Antitrust Division' (1979) 48 *Antitrust Law Journal* 73.

[108] F Brunet, 'The Role of Antitrust Compliance Programs in Competition Law Enforcement', New Frontiers of Antitrust Conference (Paris, 10 February 2012), *Concurrences* N° 2-2012, www.concurrences.com, 16 at 22.

[109] Ginsburg and Wright (n 29) 18; WPJ Wils, 'Does the Effective Enforcement of Articles 81 and 82 EC Require Not Only Fines on Undertakings But Also Individual Penalties, In Particular Imprisonment?' in CD Ehlermann and I Atanasiu (eds), *European Competition Law Annual 2001: Effective Private Enforcement of EC Antitrust Law* (Oxford, Hart Publishing, 2002); WPJ Wils, *The Optimal Enforcement of EC Antitrust Law* (Vienna, Kluwer, 2002)

should not merely receive reduced fines for antitrust infringements, but immunity from such fines.[110]

Like the European Commission and most national competition authorities of the EU Member States, the French competition authority (*Autorité de la concurrence*) does not grant any reduction in the amount of fines to companies that had a compliance programme at the time of the infringement.[111] However, French law provides for a settlement proce-dure (*procédure de non-contestation des griefs*), under which companies that do not contest the statement of objections sent to them by the *Autorité de la concurrence* may obtain a fine reduction.[112] In the context of this specific procedure, the *Autorité de la concurrence* is willing to grant, in addition to a 10 per cent fine reduction corresponding to the settlement proper, and to a further five per cent reduction that may be awarded in return of other com-mitments, a fine reduction of up to 10 per cent to companies that did not have a compliance programme in place at the time of the issuing of the statement of objections and that com-mit to set up a compliance programme meeting the best practices set out by the *Autorité de la concurrence*. A similar fine reduction is available if the company already had a compliance programme that did not meet these best practices and commits to upgrade it according to these best practices.[113]

Among the national competition authorities of the EU Member States, there is just one authority, the UK Office of Fair Trading (OFT), which regularly grants fine reductions of up to 10 per cent on the ground of 'adequate steps having been taken with a view to ensuring compliance'.[114] A similar approach is taken in Australia, where the Australian Competition and Consumer Commission's Enforcement and Compliance Project refers to 'commitment to the values of the rules and motivation to comply with them'.[115]

Current enforcement policy of the European Commission and many other agen-cies focuses exclusively on fining corporations. As discussed in chapter 15 below, the UK

---

chs 8 and 9; WPJ Wils, 'Is Criminalization of EU Competition Law the Answer?' (2005) 28 *World Competition* 117; WPJ Wils, 'Optimal Antitrust Fines: Theory and Practice' (2006) 29 *World Competition* 183; Wils (n 15); WPJ Wils, 'Recidivism in EU Antitrust Enforcement: A Legal and Economic Analysis' (2012) 35 *World Competition* 5.

[110] See also K Hofstetter and M Ludescher, 'Fines against Parent Companies in EU Antitrust Law: Setting Incen-tives for "Best Practice Compliance"' (2010) 33 *World Competition* 55.

[111] Framework-Document of 10 February 2012 on Antitrust Compliance Programmes, accessible at http://www.autoritedelaconcurrence.fr/user/standard.php?id_rub=260, paragraphs 24-28; see also Cour d'appel de Paris (Paris Court of Appeal), Judgment of 26 January 2010, Adecco France.

[112] Art L.464-2, III of the French Commercial Code.

[113] Framework-Document of 10 February 2012 on Antitrust Compliance Programmes, paras 29–31, and Communiqué de procedure du 10 février 2012 relatif à la non-contestation des griefs, accessible at http://www.autoritedelaconcurrence.fr/user/standard.php?id_rub=260.

[114] This policy was recently reaffirmed by the Office of Fair Trading (OFT) in OFT's *Guidance as to the appro-priate amount of a penalty* (OFT423, September 2012) at 2.15 and fn 26; see also *How your business can achieve compliance with competition law* (OFT1341, June 2011) at 7.2. The OFT has indeed granted compliance discounts in many of the cases in which it imposed fines for antitrust infringements in the past decade (*Arriva/First Group*, Case CA98/9/2002; *Hasbro and Distributors*, Case CA98/18/2002; *Replica Kit*, Case CA98/6/2003; *Toys*, Case CA98/8/2003; *West Midlands Roofing*, Case CA98/1/2004; *Desiccant*, Case CA98/8/2004; *Scottish Roofing I*, Case CA98/1/2005; *North East Roofing*, Case CA98/2/2005; *Scottish Roofing II*, Case CA98/4/2005; *England and Scotland Roofing*, Case CA98/1/2006; *Stock Check Pads*, Case CA98/3/2006; *Spacer Bars*, Case CA98/4/2006; *Construction Recruitment Forum*, Case CA98/01/2009; *Construction*, Case CE/432704; *Tobacco*, Case CA98/01/2010; *Gaviscon*, Case CA98/02/2011; *Dairy Retail Price Initiatives*, Case CA98/03/2011).

[115] Cartel Project, at http://cartel.law.unimelb.edu.au.

authority has recently included individuals in its enforcement efforts as well. The need to focus on individual behaviour, rather than firms' behaviour, is only a recent realisation in competition literature,[116] and one that is far from widely understood or accepted. Yet relevant pointers clearly exist. The OFT research noted at chapter 15 clearly points to the importance of sanctioning consequences on individuals. The US Antitrust Division believes 'individual accountability through imposition of jail sentences is the single greatest deterrent' to cartel activity.[117] In his 2011 review of the evidence on deterrence, Harding noted:

> Yet it remains far from clear what amounts to effective deterrence ... or indeed how deterrence may be measured. A major problem resides in the fact that, while the rhetoric is strong, it remains inexact. What (or what exactly) should be deterred, beyond a broad sense of cartel activity? And when is it known whether something or somebody has been deterred, and by what?

> ... [The critique from behavioural economists] ... separates the human and corporate elements of business activity and questions the relevance of predications based upon neo-classical economic theory and the latter's 'unrealistic and simplifying assumptions about human nature.'[118] Viewed in particular in the light of such a critical onslaught, the limitations of optimal deterrence argument appear clear enough.[119]

IV. The Creation and Discovery of Cartels

There have been very limited attempts to study the reasons for non-compliance. There is far greater emphasis on sanctioning and enforcement than on looking at the real causes of behaviour. For example, one of the few pieces of evidence is merely a 2011 survey of 501 responses from large firms and 308 from small firms, with responses from two business organisations and 27 telephone interviews with professionals.[120] On the basis of these limited findings, the UK OFT concluded:

> The results of the business survey clearly indicate that, while other sanctions and enforcement tools also have significant deterrence effects, the three most important factors deterring potentially anti-competitive behaviour are, in order of importance:

> — the risk of reputational damage for the company
> — criminal sanctions for individuals, and
> — financial penalties for the company.[121]

---

[116] See Ginsburg and Wright (n 29); George Mason University Law and Economics Research Paper Series available at http://papers.ssrn.com/sol3/papers.cfm?abstract_id=1705701; DA Crane, *The Institutional Structure of Antitrust Enforcement* (Oxford, Oxford University Press, 2011) 177.

[117] SD Hammond, 'Ten Strategies for Winning the Fight Against Hardcore Cartels', Oct 18, 2005 (Paris Working Party No 3 Prosecutors Program).

[118] Footnote from original source: MS Stucke, 'Behavioral Economists at the Gate: Antitrust in the twenty-First Century' (2007) 38 *Loyola University of Chicago Law Journal* 513.

[119] Harding (n 18).

[120] *The deterrent effect of competition enforcement by the OFT. A report prepared for the OFT by Deloitte* (Office of Fair Trading, 2007) OFT962.

[121] *The impact of competition interventions on compliance and deterrence* (OFT, 2011) OFT1391, paras 6.5 and 6.6, available at http://www.oft.gov.uk/shared_oft/reports/Evaluating-OFTs-work/oft1391.pdf.

The OFT further concluded that it had identified three key pillars of compliance: Knowledge and awareness of competition law, sanctions and enforcement, and voluntary compliance measures.[122] It noted academic suggestions that reputational damage from competition enforcement is an important deterrent for businesses.[123] Further, it noted that, contrary to the predictions of the literature,[124] private damages were ranked relatively low by respondents in terms of being an effective deterrent.[125] However, it contrasted this with an earlier finding that sanctions at the individual level are the most important.[126]

The OFT's conclusions relate to motivations and behaviours of *both* business entities and individuals, mixing up the two, against the background assumption that what is relevant is the 'behaviour' of businesses. However, it is important to analyse separately what influences the behaviour of the individual human actors from what generalisations might be made about how the combination of behaviours of the individuals who work within a particular structure could be said to represent their unified or aggregate behaviour, and therefore the behaviour of the incorporeal structure within which they work, namely their business entity. The question arises whether competition enforcement policy has been focusing on the correct targets.

A. How are Cartels Created?

As noted above, cartels are conspiracies that are secret crimes.[127] Cartels usually do not occur by mistake.[128] The number of executives involved in the group has risen from an average of 13 in the 1990s to 19 in the 2000s.[129] Offenders act with great care and in secrecy to avoid detection and punishment.[130] Cartel meetings are normally disguised,[131] transmitted information is encrypted sometimes[132] and evidence of illegal agreements may be destroyed.[133]

---

[122] ibid, para 1.10.

[123] JC Bosch and EW Eckard, 'The Profit of Price Fixing: Evidence From Stock Market Reaction to Federal Indictments' (1991) 73(2) *The Review of Economics and Statistics* 309–17; A Gunster and MA van Dijk, 'The Impact of European Antitrust Policy: Evidence from the Stock Market' Working Paper (2011).

[124] For example, UK Department of Trade 2001, and S Calkin, 'Corporate Compliance and the Antitrust Agencies' Bi-modal Penalties' (2007) 60(3) *Law and Contemporary Problems* 127–67.

[125] *The Deterrent Effect of Competition Enforcement by the OFT: Discussion Paper 963* (London, Office of Fair Trading, 2007) para 6.10: 'Our survey suggests that at present the threat of private actions is not seen as a serious deterrent in comparison to the possibility of public enforcement action.'

[126] ibid, para 6.14, referring to Deloitte and Touche, *The Deterrent Effect of Competition Enforcement by the OFT*, OFT Report No 962 (London, OFT, 2007).

[127] RR Faulkner, ER Cheney, GA Fisher and WE Baker, 'Crime by Committee: Conspirators and Company Men in the Illegal Electrical Industry Cartel' (2003) 41 *Criminology* 511–54.

[128] S Peyer, 'Myths and Untold Stories—Private Antitrust Enforcement in Germany', University of East Anglia, Centre for Public Policy, Working Paper 10-12, July 2010, at http://ssrn.com/abstract=1672695; Peyer (n 78) 331–59.

[129] JM Connor, *Global Price Fixing* 2nd edn (Berlin, Springer-Verlag, 2008).

[130] H Hovenkamp, *The Antitrust Enterprise: Principle and Execution* (Cambridge MA, Harvard University Press, 2005) 66.

[131] For instance, 'budget meetings' in the Vitamin cartel, European Commission, Case COMP/E-1/37.512 *Vitamins* [2001] OJ L6/1.

[132] European Commission, Case COMP/F/38.899 *Gas Insulated Switchgear* [2007] OJ C75/19.

[133] European Commission, Case COMP/38354 *Industrial Bags* [2005] OJ L282/41.

Ashton and Pressey's analysis of all 433 investigations made by DG COMP under EU antitrust laws over the period 1990–2009 identified 74 cartels, 18 of which were domestic cartels occurring within a single member state and were not selected, leaving a final sample of 56 international cartels.[134] They found that the average number of firms involved was 8.2 (the figure was stable across each of the five year periods involved). Only 35.7 per cent of cases had only one level of managerial hierarchy in the cartel and 19.7 per cent of cartels had three or more levels of hierarchy. Almost half of the cartels (48.2 per cent) involved management at the highest level within the firm.[135] Over half of the cartels (51.8 per cent) that had involvement of marketing and sales managers involved the highest level of such managers within the firm. There was also a substantial proportion of cartels (24 cartels, 42.9 per cent) where the most senior marketing and sales manager was the fourth tier of management in the firm.[136] Ashton and Pressey concluded that half of all cartels used 'buffers'[137] within the cartel organisation to be 'thrown under the bus' to insulate senior management from legal prosecution.[138] They also noted that research examining how cartel offences are presented in the media also reflects this organisational practice, where firms often attribute blame on middle managers and imply middle managers have a lower morality than senior staff.[139] Recognition of these organisational and behavioural realities prompted Ashton and Pressey to advocate greater education within management professions to counter the causative normative and empirical perceptions involved.

Ashton and Pressey have noted that the relationship between the individuals is based on trust and camaraderie, and these features tend to prolong cartel duration.[140] They cite the following points. First, sales and marketing managers employed to assist discussions can discover they have much in common with persons from other firms, identify with mutual interests and often desire to achieve 'fair' outcomes in cartel agreements.[141] Second, the competitive culture of marketing and sales staff in some organisations might consider team-crime such as price-fixing as an acceptable option in lean times.[142] Third,

---

[134] Ashton and Pressey (n 36). Four cases were excluded from the sample and analysis for the following reasons: no English language version (Alloy Surcharge (2006), Sodium Gluconate II (2004), E.ON-GdF Collusion (2009)), no final report (Aluminium Fluoride Producers (2008)).

[135] See DC Klawiter and JM Driscoll, 'Antitrust Compliance in the Age of Multi-jurisdictional Leniency: New Ideas and New Challenges' [2009] *Global Competition Review Supplement* (Antitrust Review of the Americas, 2009) 24.

[136] This was consistent with the view that the sales and marketing managers are relatively junior in comparison to other managers within the firm participating in cartel maintenance: SS Simpson and CS Koper, 'The Changing of the Guard: Top Management Characteristics, Organizational Strain and Antitrust Offending' (1997) 13 *Journal of Quantitative Criminology* 373–404.

[137] E Goffman, *Strategic Interaction* (Oxford, Basil Blackwell, 1970).

[138] RA Robson, 'Crime and Punishment: Rehabilitating Retribution as a Justification for Organizational Criminal Activity' (2010) 47 *American Business Law Journal* 109–44. This finding supported the view that senior management are central to the formation of cartels: Faulkner, Cheney, Fisher and Baker (n 127). It contradicted a view that cartels are mostly led by more junior employees: J Sonnenfeld and PR Lawrence, 'Why do Companies Succumb to Price Fixing?' (1978) 56 *Harvard Business Review* 145–57.

[139] ME Siltaoja and MJ Vehkaperä, 'Constructing Illegitimacy? Cartels and Cartel Agreements in Finnish Business Media Form Critical Discursive Perspective' (2010) 92 *Journal of Business Ethics* 493–511.

[140] Ashton and Pressey (n 36). One British businessman imprisoned for a cartel in the USA commented: 'it doesn't seem right that by dumping everybody else in the mud you can get away with it. Especially when, clearly in some of these incidents, the people that have gone to the authorities in the first place were by far the most culpable participants in this illegal activity': M O'Kane, 'Does Prison Work for Cartelists? The View from Behind Bars. An Interview with Bryan Allison' (2011) 56(2) *The Antitrust Bulletin* 483–500, 490–91.

[141] Faulkner, Cheney, Fisher and Baker (n 127).

[142] G Mars, *Cheats at Work: An Anthropology of Workplace Crime* (London, Unwin Paperbacks, 1982).

such influences may be amplified if marketing and sales managers lack awareness of the illegality of cartels,[143] or succumb to narcissism and flattery when being asked to undertake actions that facilitate organisational survival.[144] Fourth, lower ranked managers can be the victim of coercive senior managers when certain management philosophies, such as a 'profit-making at all costs' approach.[145] Ashton and Pressey describe the approach: 'Senior managers may focus on quick profits, maximum growth and high levels of managerial remuneration, creating organizational strains leading to criminal outcomes such as cartels. Financial and socioeconomic benefits may also be accrued by the employee for illegal corporate behaviours including bonuses, promotions and the goodwill of colleagues. Alternatively, not participating in cartel activity could lead to lack of promotion, demotion, ostracism or even dismissal.'[146] The best predictor of whether a person or firm indulges in cartel behaviour may be past cartel behaviour.[147]

Market structure (the structure–conduct–performance paradigm)[148] and market conditions (the 'bounds' approach) have both been suggested as economic theories on why cartels form.[149] The latter identifies that cartels may develop where the market has overcapacity, declining prices, steady and adverse economic conditions,[150] homogenous products, clearly defined markets, less powerful buyers and barriers to entry.[151] In Ashton and Pressey's sample the vast majority of cartel cases in the sample originated from the chemical and manufacturing industries, with a limited number of distribution cases and a very low level of cases in services and food industries.[152] A majority of the cartels involved price-fixing and market sharing.

B. How are Cartels Discovered?

The authorities place enormous—in effect complete—reliance on the leniency system to discover cartels. The public authority advertises a policy of major remission of fines on firms that inform it of its involvement in a cartel and cooperate in its break up. Yet public authorities do not discover cartels in Europe through their own actions—companies involved tell them or, in a limited number of cases, foreign authorities pass on the information from cartelists that they have discovered, usually by being told about them by the

---

[143] D Bush and BD Gelb, 'When Marketing Practices Raise Antitrust Concerns' (2005) 46 *MITSloan Management Review* 73–81; DT Le Clair, 'Marketing Planning and the Policy Environment in the European Union' (2000) 17 *International Marketing Review* 193–215.

[144] HS Schwartz, 'Anti-social Actions of Committed Organizational Participants: An Existential Psychoanalytic Perspective' (1987) 8 *Organization Studies* 327–40.

[145] Simpson and Koper (n 136).

[146] WE Baker and RR Faulkner, 'The Social Organization of Conspiracy: Illegal Networks in the Heavy Electrical Equipment Industry' (1993) 58 *American Sociological Review* 837–60.

[147] Simpson and Koper (n 136).

[148] JS Bain, 'Relation of Profit-Rate to Industry Concentration: American Manufacturing, 1936–1940' (1951) 65 *Quarterly Journal of Economics* 293–324.

[149] J Sutton, *Technology and Market Structure* (Cambridge MA, MIT Press, 1998).

[150] AG Kenwood and AL Lougheed, *The Growth of the International Economy,1820–1980* (London, George Allen & Unwin, 1984); M Neumann, *Competition Policy: History, Theory and Practice* (Cheltenham, Edward Elgar, 2001).

[151] MC Levenstein and V Suslow, 'What Determines Cartel Success?' (2006) 44 *Journal of Economic Literature* 43–95.

[152] Ashton and Pressey (n 36).

corporations involved.[153] Private litigation is never brought on the basis of discovery of a cartel by a third party not involved in it.

Yet the important question that needs to be addressed is: How do the firms find out? In small businesses, there may be a close relationship between a controlling manager and the direction and ownership of the business—they may even be the same person—such that it is easier to equate involvement in a conspiracy with 'the business', although there is no evidence that even small businesses formally 'adopt' illegality as a formal business goal or practice. Small businesses can certainly have a distorting effect on competition, but usually on localised markets. In contrast, larger businesses can have widespread and significant impact on competition, so are worth greater attention in the current context.

The firms involved in large cartels are large corporate entities with complex internal structures. They do not formally adopt involvement in any cartel as a matter of formal, transparent company business policy, such as through a recorded Board resolution, internal statement of policy or standing operating practice, or specific decision at any lower level. The evidence quoted above indicates that the few individuals involved in a cartel go to great lengths to keep the conspiracy secret from the official channels of the company just as much as from any external disclosure. Anecdotal evidence from those involved in compliance, legal affairs and management within large corporations indicates that they are as annoyed at the discovery of a conspiracy as any external public or ethical commentator.[154] Large corporations appear to expend considerable resource in compliance systems and achievement of compliance.[155]

There is some suspicion that a significant proportion of cartels are only revealed when they have ceased to provide benefits. There is no research on how companies uncover the conspiracies, including whether one of the participating employees owns up, but there is anecdotal evidence that a number are revealed by internal compliance or auditing staff of the company.[156]

---

[153] CT Hoang, K Hüschelrath, U Laitenberger and F Smuda, 'Determinants of Self-Reporting under the European Corporate Leniency Program' (Zentrum für Europäische Wirtschaftsforschung GmbH, 2014), Discussion paper No 14-043: a data set of 442 firms that participated in 76 cartels found that the probability of a firm becoming the chief witness increased with its character as a repeat offender, the size of the expected basic fine, the number of countries active in one group, and the size of the firm's share in the cartelised market.

[154] Conversations between the author and ten officers of multinationals, Brussels, 2012.

[155] See ch 18 below.

[156] Communications to the author by legal personnel in various large companies.

5

Criticisms of Deterrence

I. Criticisms of Economic Analysis of Liability Law

The idea of basing law on economic theory has dominated scholarship and the judiciary in the USA, but has been far less influential in any European jurisdiction, whose traditions are far more concerned with philosophy and ethics.[1] Over time, economic liability theory has been subject to a series of major attacks, such as the following issues, which arise in extrapolating the general theory of markets to individual cost–benefit decisions that are notionally made by actors or after the event by judges and juries.

The limitations of the rational choice theory were recognised by law and economics scholars themselves.[2] Shavell, for example, argued in his paper on law versus morality as regulators of conduct[3] that morality has many advantages over external sanctions, in particular because it is likely to provide more accurate sanctions for every misconduct.

We list here some of the criticisms on the classic economic approach. First, it must be possible to identify the actor to whom the particular costs of injuries ought to be allocated, such as the cheapest cost-avoider or some other actor.[4] However, this may be difficult, controversial, and itself involve excessive cost. Keating argues that

> economic theory is hard pressed to explain why plaintiffs always have rights against and only against those who have wronged them. To induce efficient precaution going forward, we ought to pin liability on cheapest cost-avoiders going forward. The economic theory of tort can explain tort law's backward-looking focus on past wrongdoers only by saying that we have good reason to think that past wrongdoers probably are the cheapest cost-avoiders going forward. This argument fits tort practice poorly and justifies it only very weakly.[5]

Second, application of the theory depends on identification of all costs. This is unachievable since there is wide agreement that this involves either ignoring non-economic losses or placing some arbitrary conventional value on them.[6]

---

[1] For England and Wales, see PS Atiyah, *The Damages Lottery* (Oxford, Hart Publishing, 1997) and works by Cane cited here. Note JG Fleming, *The American Tort Process* (Oxford, Oxford University Press, 1988).

[2] Y Feldman and HE Smith, 'Behavioral Equity' [2014] 170 *Journal of Institutional and Theoretical Economics* 137.

[3] A Shavell, 'Law Versus Morality as Regulators of Conduct' (2002) 4(2) *American Law and Economics Review* 227–57.

[4] P Cane, *Atiyah's Accidents, Compensation and the Law* 8th edn (Cambridge, Cambridge University Press, 2013) 442.

[5] GC Keating, 'Is the Role of Tort to Repair Wrongful Losses?' in D Nolan and A Robertson (eds), *Rights and Private Law* (Oxford, Hart Publishing, 2012) 378.

[6] Cane (n 4) 454.

Third, the theory requires detailed and accurate calculation of the relative costs and benefits of activities, which will often be impossible because of lack of relevant or complete information.[7] The calculations must include all production and liability costs. Whilst production costs may be calculable before marketing, the reality is that liability costs cannot be calculated at that stage, but emerge only over time, and the relevant time period may be difficult to anticipate and may be long or short. It is true that decisions on the amount of insurance cover can be taken before marketing, but they may prove to be either under- or over-estimates, and be subject to constant fluctuation during the period of market exposure.

It follows, fourth, that the theory that future activity will be affected by uncertain future costs that will only be incurred, and be quantified ex post, appears to have significant flaws. In other words, the theory that economic factors will influence *future* behaviour through 'deterrence' is likely to be unreliable.[8]

Fifth, Cane points out that the party to whom accident costs are allocated must, to some extent at least, be sensitive to increased costs.[9] Most amenable to price control are activities that have high elasticity of demand. Less so diseases, which take a long time to develop, and the person responsible for the activity may no longer be engaged in it.[10] Sensitivity to accident costs is weakened by insurance. One group concluded that in the case of auto accidents, 'there are no adequate grounds for believing that the proper cost allocation would either reduce accidents or change the total amount of driving appreciably'.[11]

Sixth, the theory assumes that a rational cost-benefit calculation is undertaken in relation to every decision. In 1997, Cane considered that relatively little is known about how effective tort remedies are in deterring tort defendants from future tortuous conduct, and that 'it would be unwise to pronounce the tort system either justified or unjustified in terms of its deterrence function'.[12] He also argued that deterrence of future tortuous conduct by a person depends on how he reacts to the award of the remedy after the damages have been paid. The other extrinsic goals of tort remedies can typically be secured by state enforcement procedures, but there is no state machinery to ensure that the desired deterrent effect of monetary tort liability is realised.[13]

Seventh, it is not the job of courts to seek the 'best loss spreader' in each case, and they are not equipped to do so.[14]

Eighth, non-compliance is essentially initiated by individuals rather than organisations,[15] and most individuals make decisions for reasons other than on grounds of rational calculation or fear of adverse consequences as a result of deterrence. The evidence from cognitive

---

[7] Cane (n 4) 454.

[8] D Dewees, D Duff and M Trebilcock, *Exploring the Domain of Accident Law. Taking the Facts Seriously* (Oxford, Oxford University Press, 1996) asking at 8: If tort liability is deterrent, why wait for a death before attempting to deter it?

[9] Cane (n 4) 442.

[10] J Stapleton, *Disease and the Compensation Debate* (Oxford, Clarendon Press, 1986) 126–28.

[11] AF Conrad et al, *Automobile Accident Costs and Payment* (Ann Arbor MI, University of Michigan Press, 1964) 127.

[12] P Cane, *The Anatomy of Tort Law* (Oxford, Hart Publishing, 1997) 217–21.

[13] Cane, ibid 116, 119, 207. Other extrinsic functions he identified include the protection of property, reinforcement of contract, the preservation of competition, loss spreading, the protection of life and property, law enforcement, the due administration of justice and preserving freedom of contract.

[14] R Merkin and J Steele, *Insurance and the Law of Obligations* (Oxford, Oxford University Press, 2013).

[15] A Hamadi and A Klement, 'Corporate Crime and Deterrence' (2008) 61 *Stanford Law Review* 271, 282.

psychology and behavioural sociology has indicated that economic factors and calculations, and a rational calculation of the economic costs and benefits, play at best a limited role in decisions made by individuals, groups and even commercial organisations. This is discussed in chapter one above.[16]

Ninth, the behavioural evidence has questioned the ability of organisations to control the behaviour of all of their employees. This undermines the theoretical assertion that all external costs can be internalised, and raises an issue of the justice of imposing sanctions on actors who are not fully morally responsible or might not be able to take steps to prevent the non-compliance.

Tenth, an effective deterrence policy rests on maximising the perception of being caught. That requires constant surveillance, and considerable cost.

Eleventh, continuous surveillance of behaviour and enforcement by authoritarian figures tends to be accusatory, confrontational, punitive and coercive and produces a culture of mistrust and resentment.[17] Tyler comments:

> The use of surveillance implies distrust, which decreases people's ability to feel positively about themselves, their groups, and the system itself.[18] Furthermore, people may experience intrusions into their lives as procedurally unfair, leading to anger and other negative emotions often associated with perceptions of injustice.[19] America ... has created an adversarial relationship between legal authorities and members of the communities they serve ... leading the public to grow less compliant with the law and less willing to help the police to fight crime.[20,21]

There is overwhelming evidence from Cold War Communist states of cultures involving entire populations living in constant fear of spies, surveillance and informers.[22]

Twelfth, the operational costs of delivering compensation are universally high in relation to tort liability, and usually far lower under compensation schemes. The costs of the US litigation system are recognised to be particularly high.[23] In the UK, the total cost of the tort system is nearly double the amount paid out in compensation because the tort liability insurance system is staggeringly expensive to operate in comparison with the benefits

---

[16] Some leading sources are TR Tyler, *Why People Obey the Law* (Hartford CT, Yale University Press, 2006); A Tversky and D Kahneman, 'Judgment under Uncertainty: Heuristics and Biases' (1974) 185 no 4157 *Science* 1124–31; D Kahneman and A Tversky (eds), *Choices, Values, and Frames* (Cambridge, Cambridge University Press, 2000). For an accessible summary see D Kahneman, *Thinking, Fast and Slow* (London, Allen Lane, 2011).

[17] B Hutter, 'Regulating Employers and Employees: Health and Safety in the Workplace' (1983) 20 *Journal of Law and Society* 452–70; B Hutter, *Regulation and Risk: Occupational Health and Safety on the Railways* (Oxford, Oxford University Press, 2001).

[18] Footnote from original source: RM Kramer and TR Tyler (eds), *Trust in Organizational Authorities* (Thousand Oaks CA, Sage Publications Inc, 1996) 1006.

[19] Footnote from original source: eg TR Gurr, *Why Men Rebel* (Princeton NJ, Princeton University Press, 1970); TR Tyler and HJ Smith, 'Social Justice and Social Movements' ch 101, in DT Gilbert, ST Fiske and G Lindzey (eds), *The Handbook of Social Psychology*, Vol II 4th edn (New York, Oxford University Press, 1998) 595–629.

[20] Footnote from original source: J Sunshine and TR Tyler, 'The Role of Procedural Justice and Legitimacy in Shaping Public Support for Policing' (2003) 37 *Law and Society Review* 513–48.

[21] TR Tyler, 'Psychology and the Law' in KE Whittington, RD Kelemen and GA Caldeira (eds), *The Oxford Handbook of Law and Politics* (Oxford, Oxford University Press, 2008) 715.

[22] M Glennie, *The Balkans: Nationalism, War and the Great Powers, 1804–1999* (London, Penguin Books, 1999); M Glennie, *The Rebirth Of History: Eastern Europe in the Age of Democracy* (London, Penguin Books, 1990); D Galligan and M Kurkchiyan, *Law and Informal Practices: The Post-communist Experience* (Oxford, Oxford University Press, 2003).

[23] Dewees, Duff and Trebilcock (n 8).

paid.[24] Leading up to 2001, 65 per cent of medical negligence claims settled for £50,000 or less, and their costs exceeded the compensation paid.[25]

Thirteenth, any deterrent effect of liability is diminished through the practical consequences of how insurance operates. As noted above, difficulties arise in risk-identification, pricing, market forces, effective pooling of separate risks and so on, such that the relationship between allocation of the true cost of injuries and a rational cost–benefit calculation evaporates.

Fourteenth, empirical evidence significantly undermines the idea that deterrence theory produces deterrence: This is discussed in chapter six below. Hamadi and Klement argue that harsh penalties discourage firms from monitoring for misconduct and undermine compliance incentives within professional firms.[26] They argue that sanctions on firms can have serious collateral consequences, and should be limited because of the risk of triggering insolvency,[27] and greater reliance should be placed on purely financial corporate penalties and no criminal penalties, and subjecting culpable individuals within the firm to liability.

Fifteenth, in the light of the global financial crisis from 2008, Armour and Gordon consider the extent to which traditional private law mechanisms—in particular, the law of tort—fail to internalise systemic harms.[28] They consider that the activities of certain sorts of firms—vividly exemplified by large financial institutions—can cause economic losses to large numbers of parties through indirect and diffuse causal channels. In contrast, tort law is primarily concerned with direct physical harms to individual plaintiffs. Purely financial or 'economic' losses are generally not recoverable.[29] Tort law only applies liability ex post for harm actually suffered, and does not address probabilistic harms. Armour and Gordon concluded that private law does not do an imperfect job of internalising systemic harms, it does no meaningful job at all.

II. Criticisms of Competition Enforcement

Regulatory techniques can be categorised into ex ante and ex post techniques. The EU (European Union) competition regulatory architecture that is the primary focus of this chapter adopts an exclusive ex post approach towards cartels. But some elements of ex ante techniques are utilised in other situations, and it is instructive to review these.

The control of mergers requires concentrations with a Community dimension to be notified to the Commission prior to their implementation and following the conclusion of the agreement, the announcement of the public bid, or the acquisition of a controlling

---

[24] Cane (n 4) 391. The total estimated cost as at 2011 was £7.5 billion.

[25] National Audit Office, *Handling Clinical Negligence Claims in England* (2001).

[26] Hamadi and Klement (n 15) 271.

[27] More than one-third of all organisations convicted in USA do not have sufficient assets to pay the entire criminal fine imposed: J Arlen, 'Corporate Criminal Liability: Theory and Evidence' in A Harel and KN Hylton (eds), *Research Handbook on the Economics of Criminal Law* (Cheltenham, Edward Elgar, 2012) 20.

[28] J Armour and JN Gordon, 'Systemic Harms and Shareholder Value' (2014) 6(1) *Journal of Legal Analysis* 35.

[29] See H Bernstein, 'Civil Liability for Pure Economic Loss Under American Tort Law' (1998) 46 *American Journal of Comparative Law Supplement* 111 (position in US); J Stapleton, 'Comparative Economic Loss: Lessons from Case-Law Focused "Middle Theory"' (2002) 50 *UCLA Law Review* 531 (position in UK, Australia and Canada).

interest, coupled with extensive requirements for filing full disclosure.[30] Applications can be refused, or, as regularly occurs, granted subject to undertakings or conditions, such as to divest certain parts of the business so as to prevent concentrations.[31] The evidence is that this system largely worked: There was no evidence of enforcement for failure to notify, or providing incomplete disclosure. If companies broke the conditions, the Commission may immediately impose an enforcement sanction. However, it was changed because of the volume of applications and preference by policymakers not to fund the necessary resources, and replaced with a self-regulatory system, under which firms must notify mergers that require approval. Future compliance is now typically ensured by requiring the appointment, at the company's expense, of an external monitoring trustee, such as boutique banks or economists.

This notification system is difficult to categorise as either ex ante or ex post, since it occurs at the moment that the first state transforms into the second state.[32] The approach is workable because mergers are essentially a structural question, not (as is the case with cartels) a question about future behaviour.

Merger control was fully ex ante until 2004, when it was removed at EU level,[33] although still remains in some National Competition Authorities (NCAs). The system was changed because it became an uninsurable insurance, and unworkable in practice. Mere notification gave immunity from fines, so vast numbers of notifications were made and the Commission and NCAs were swamped and did not have resource to process them, so rarely gave a response. The switch was to self-assessment, accompanied by a severe penalty if you get it wrong. Companies can theoretically still approach an authority and request clearance, but no reply is ever given. The Notice said that the Commission would give guidance on novel questions,[34] but it has not yet done so.

In contrast, identifying abuse of dominance is a difficult exercise. Few behaviours can be said to be outright abuse. It all depends on the context: The market, behaviour, economic effects. The Commission has issued guidance on the types of behaviour that it considers more serious for enforcement purposes.[35]

The sanctioning response would usually be a fine and prohibition on behaviour. Commitment decisions are increasingly used. The Commission has wide investigative powers to gain access to evidence held by any sources. A power to order structural divestment was

---

[30] Council Reg (EC) No 139/2004 of 20 January 2004 on the control of concentrations between undertakings, art 4. Surveys in the UK have consistently found that the 'deterrent effect' of merger decisions is higher than for general competition law: *The deterrent effect of competition enforcement by the OFT. A report prepared for the OFT by Deloitte*. Office of Fair Trading, 2007, OFT962, para 1.19, available at http://www.oft.gov.uk/shared_oft/reports/Evaluating-OFTs-work/oft962.pdf; *The Impact of Competition Interventions on Compliance and Deterrence* (OFT, December 2011) OFT1391, para 1.33, available at http://www.oft.gov.uk/shared_oft/reports/Evaluating-OFTs-work/oft1391.pdf.

[31] Reg 139/2004, ibid, art 8.2.

[32] The Merger Regulation allows the merging parties to request, during the pre-notification period, the referral of mergers to the Commission that do not fall within the Regulation's thresholds and are notifiable in at least three Member States: Reg 139/2004, art 4(5).

[33] Council Reg (EC) No 139/2004 of 20 January 2004 on the control of concentrations between undertakings (the EC Merger Regulation), OJ L 24, 29.1.2004. See Commission Staff Working Document: Towards more effective EU merger control, SWD(2013) 239, 25.6.2013.

[34] Guidelines on the assessment of horizontal mergers under the Council Regulation on the control of concentrations between undertakings, OJ C 31, 05.02.2004, 5–18.

[35] See also Communication from the Commission—Guidance on the Commission's enforcement priorities in applying Article 82 of the EC treaty to abusive exclusionary conduct by dominant undertakings, 2009/C 45/02.

considered for inclusion in the Third Energy Directive but ended up being rejected by the European Parliament, although the Commission has such power in any event. Injunctions can be used, in the form of Commission Orders. Monitors can be appointed.

Business has raised serious objections to the rules being impossible to comply with. A company should look at its market, evidence and behaviour, and make a judgement. In contrast, the Commission can typically take perhaps eight years to complete investigation of a market and a possible infringement and issue a Decision, for example on whether there has been overpricing or discounting to an illegal extent. The Commission would assemble evidence from every player in the market, to compile a complete picture, but such a width of material would be unavailable to individual companies when they have to make their own internal decisions. Companies have argued that it is impossible for them to work out what answer the Commission might ultimately come to, without access to such comprehensive information and lengthy availability of time.[36] Commissioner Almunia therefore adopted a policy of resolving things by negotiation,[37] so as to be somewhat more reasonable and less aggressive about enforcement.[38] However, the shift to negotiated remedies has been criticised as unable to ensure the design of efficient remedies.[39]

It is the adoption of an exclusively ex post approach for cartels, outlined in greater detail above, that gives rise to a series of major concerns. Listed below are 10 significant criticisms of current EU competition enforcement policy, some of which are generic and some directed principally at the ex post enforcement policy. These all ultimately flow from a single source, namely the adherence to an enforcement policy based solely on attempting to deter through imposing significant fines. This policy is focused exclusively, in the case of the EU, on firms, with no option of imposing sanctions on employees, whereas some Member States have sensibly adopted the ability to sanction individuals, which has become the primary approach in the United States.[40] The change in the US approach recognises the finding noted in chapter 11 below that there should be Braithwaite pillars for *both* corporations and individuals. The conclusion will be that enforcement of EU competition law is both an unprincipled and dysfunctional system. We proceed to discuss the sequence of problems with the EU approach.

A. The Determination of Fines is not Transparent or Fair

Serious concerns arise inherently from the nature of the application of the deterrence policy, rather than some imprecision in the Guidelines themselves. Geradin and Henry have

---

[36] KH Eichhorn, 'EU Sanctions Policy and the Encouragement of Private Enforcement in Article 102 Cases' paper at the Union des Avocats Européens Symposium, IX Antitrust between EU and National Law (Brussels, Bruylant, 2011) 467.

[37] Commission Reg (EC) No 622/2008 of 30 June 2008 amending Reg (EC) No 773/2004, as regards the conduct of settlement procedures in cartel cases (Text with EEA relevance), OJ L 171, 1.7.2008; Commission Notice on the conduct of settlement procedures in view of the adoption of decisions pursuant to Art 7 and Art 23 of Council Reg (EC) No 1/2003 in cartel cases, 2008/C 167/01, 2.7.2008.

[38] An example is the Samsung patent infringement: IP/14/490 *Press release. Antitrust: Commission accepts legally binding commitments by Samsung Electronics on standard essential patent injunctions*, 29 April 2014.

[39] DMB Gerard, 'Negotiated Remedies in the Modernization Era: The Limits of Effectiveness' in P Lowe and M Marquis (eds), *European Competition Law Annual 2013: Effective and Legitimate Enforcement* (Oxford, Hart Publishing, 2014).

[40] See chs 3 and 4 above.

concluded that the Guidelines are linguistically vague, and that the calculation of the fine is remarkably imprecise and bears little if any relation to the size of the detriment produced by the particular infringer.[41] They maintain that it is often difficult to understand the logic of the fines that have been imposed by the Commission. Identical factual scenarios will be treated differently, while different factual scenarios will be offered the same treatment.[42] Different start amounts are given for the same anti-competitive infringements; the Guidelines are only a very rough indication of how to calculate start amount, with no indication of an economic test which is to be applied when assessing gravity; the start amount is to a considerable extent chosen arbitrarily and at random; there is a lack of clarity of the method used by the Commission to calculate fine; conclusions given are 'laconic'; factors relied upon by the Commission and the Court of First Instance to impose or review fines tend to vary from one case to another; and this situation encourages increased litigation.[43]

The Commission's fines are based on a supposedly arithmetic approach: The basic amount is related to a proportion of the value of sales of the entity (normally up to 30 per cent), depending on the degree of gravity of the infringement, multiplied by the number of years of infringement.[44] The basic amount may be increased or decreased where there are aggravating or mitigating circumstances, the latter including instances such as where the undertaking terminated the conduct on being found out, or owned up voluntarily.[45] It will be seen that such an approach is inherently imprecise, and it is acknowledged to involve a wide margin of discretion,[46] subject to the final sum not exceeding 10 per cent of the undertaking's turnover.[47]

Thus, the approach of the Commission, which is mirrored by many national authorities,[48] is that, in basing the fine on an undertaking's turnover, competition enforcement is aimed at maximising *general* deterrence. Fines for a company that has been caught are, therefore, multiples of the calculation of the risk that a company that has been caught will be caught.

Since the approach is founded on the undertaking's financial performance, it does *not directly take into account the level of damage actually suffered* by other undertakings, customers or the market, nor the gain actually made by the undertaking.[49] If the illicit gain is small

---

[41] D Geradin and D Henry, 'The EC Fining Policy for Violations of Competition Law: An Empirical Review of the Commission Decisional Practice and the Community Courts' Judgments' (2005) 1 *European Competition Journal* 401.

[42] ibid, 403.

[43] ibid, 413, 472 and 473.

[44] *Guidelines on the method of setting fines pursuant to Article 23(2)(a) of Regulation No 1/2003, 2006/C 210/02*: hereafter 'Guidelines', paras 19 and 21.

[45] *Guidelines*, paras 27–34. Commission Notice on Immunity from fines and reduction of fines in cartel cases, 2006/C 298/11.

[46] *Guidelines*, para 2.

[47] *Guidelines*, para 32.

[48] But not all: It is unnecessary to undertake a comprehensive analysis for the purposes of this inquiry into collective redress. However it was said that the 'calculation of gain is crucial for sanctioning policy' in *Sanctioning pursuant to the Norwegian Competition Act*, English translation of a report by the committee of the Norwegian Competition Authority, 25 March 2001, at http://www.konkurransetilsynet.no/iKnowBase/Content/415989/SANCTIONING%20PURSUANT%20TO%20THE%20NORWEGIAN%20COMPETITION%20ACT.PDF. The reasons given were that gain should be a starting point for estimation of optimal sanctions, being more effective, and furthering deterrence.

[49] As can be seen from the *JJB Sports plc* case, in some cases there may be no gain for the undertaking, which highlights issues of justice and proportionality: see C Hodges, *The Reform of Class and Representative Actions in European Legal Systems: A New Framework for Collective Redress in Europe* (Oxford, Hart Publishing, 2008) 24–26.

or negligible, a fine based on turnover may clearly exceed the gain. This absence of a link between the severity of either the harm caused or the illicit profit gained is a remarkable feature.

The policy imposes fines on a theory of optimising general deterrence, which may be unjust in relation to particular firms or individuals that are sanctioned (individual deterrence). In not linking sentencing to the extent of harm caused or the extent of culpability of the offender, issues arise of the extent to which the system observes principles of fundamental rights and of justice, and should deserve respect. The approach starts from the policy that all cartels are bad, and deserve to be punished irrespective of whether they actually caused harm.

It is impossible to 'calibrate' a deterrent sanction. The likelihood of future re-offending varies from person to person, and may be influenced by future circumstances. In the corporate context, the position is complicated further by the existence of multiple factors: Multiple individuals who may or may not get involved in wrongdoing, the organisational architecture and 'culture' of each firm that might be involved, and the external market forces that might exert pressure to form a conspiracy or abuse a dominant position. Various individual factors are included in the Guidelines that may be taken into account in increasing or decreasing a fine, but the system as a whole gives rise to considerable discomfort over its achievement of fairness and consistency.

Further, the policy does not take into account the undertaking's actual behaviour in the past and future, such as the extent to which the undertaking could have influenced the activity, or intended not to commit the offence.[50] It does not take into account the ability of a firm to affect the behaviour of employees in future. Fines are approached solely as supposed economic levers, and whilst the behavioural consequence of deterrence plays a strong part in the official process, it is curious that deterrence is not approached in behavioural terms (individual deterrence) but on the basis of economic theory (general deterrence).

Further, the frequency and size of recidivism discounts went up markedly under the revised 2006 Guidelines. The studies cited above by Combe and Monnier and Veljanovski found ample evidence that the Commission had been inconsistent in applying recidivism penalties in the manner promised it its 2006 Guidelines. In particular, it had been lenient by failing to account for numerous previous violations.

The system has also been criticised on the constitutional grounds that the adoption of a decision finding guilt is made by 27 political appointees (the Commissioners) who have not heard or studied the evidence; that there is no hearing before a decision maker; and that the same case team in the Commission handles both the investigation of the case and the reaching of a decision.[51]

In short, the European fine has been described as an arbitrary administrative figure.[52] These criticisms raise significant concerns over whether the system breaches the principles of justice and proportionality.

---

[50] Save that evidence of negligence is a mitigating factor; *Guidelines*, para 29, third indent.

[51] IS Forrester, 'Due Process in EC Competition Cases: A Distinguished Institution with Flawed Procedures' (2009) 34 *EL Rev* 817.

[52] C Veljanovski, 'Cartel Fines in Europe: Law, Practice and Deterrence' (2007) 30 *World Competition* 65–86. See also SB Völker, 'Rough Justice? An Analysis of the European Commission's New Fining Guidelines' (2007) 44 *Common Market Law Review* 1285; I Kilbey, 'Financial Penalties under Article 228(2) EC: Excessive Complexity?' (2007) 44 *Common Market Law Review* 743.

B. Encouraging Perverse Behaviour

A policy of waiving or reducing fines respectively for the first couple of companies that own up raises serious concerns that it is intrinsically unjust. Perversely, it introduces a *positive* incentive for conspirators to undertake cynical calculations to break the law, and retain illicit gains by being first or second to squeal on the others. The leniency policy does not encourage compliance, or the introduction of internal controls to guard against non-compliance. It merely incentivises firms who discover infringements to inform the authorities quickly. In applying the 'prisoners' dilemma' to disrupt the conspiracy by encouraging one of the parties to maximise his resources by owning up, it fails to direct the offered benefit at the right targets (the individual conspirators).

The moral basis of leniency is unattractive: Rather than affirming positive values it is 'sin, snitch and escape' rather than comply. Retributive justice or deterrence are ignored here: The company has infringed, may keep illicit gains, and may infringe again. Thus, market distortion is perpetuated, particularly since some but not all infringers are subjected to fines.

Furthermore, the current leniency policy is perverse in encouraging all subsequent damages claims to be made against that company, since unlike all the other alleged cartelists, it cannot deny liability, and is joint and severally liable.[53] That result does not encourage people to own up, and cries out for a 'collective' solution, by involving all companies in the cartel. It has been argued that increasing the number of damages actions risks undermining national and EU leniency programmes, because the risk of follow-on damages actions may discourage potential leniency applicants from coming forward.[54] So unless the current leniency policy is reviewed, there may be complete failure of the current enforcement policy.

C. Current Policy does not Encourage Rectification of Unbalanced Markets

A focus on deterrence entails imposition of sanctions on infringers, rather than measures, justified on the principle of corrective justice, on maintaining level playing fields with healthy competition. Fines are paid to public exchequers rather than to those who have suffered detriment. Fines are unrelated to the amount of illicit gain. How is it known whether the result may be a net advantage for the infringer or not? How is it known whether over- or under-deterrence occurs?

Restoring market balance has rarely been referred to in theoretical literature or official policy statements.[55] However, it should be the primary objective of a competition

---

[53] This occurred in relation to civil claims against Lufthansa arising out of the air cargo cartel. Altering the rules by, for example, making liability not joint and several would introduce yet further distance from reality and basic concepts of fairness.

[54] C Caufmann, 'The Interaction of Leniency Programmes and Actions for Damages' (2011) 7(12) *The Competition Law Review* 181–220.

[55] Recital 1 to Reg 1/2003 states the principle of establishing 'a system which ensures that competition in the common market is not distorted'. The European Parliament recently emphasised that 'EU competition policy based on the principles of open markets and a level playing field in all sectors is a cornerstone of a successful internal market and a precondition for the creation of sustainable and knowledge-based jobs': European Parliament

regulatory to maintain a competitive market.[56] That goal is self-evident in a market-based theory and system, in which the whole focus of the European Union is on the market. It is also enshrined in the Treaty on the Functioning of the EU (TFEU). Article 3 TFEU states the competence of coordination of economic policies, and the objective of maintaining a competitive internal market is implicit in the prohibitions of Articles 101 and 102. Article 101.1 TFEU requires the 'prevention, restriction or distortion of competition within the internal market'. The first recital of Regulation 1/2003 states the principle of establishing 'a system which ensures that competition in the common market is not distorted' and of a 'competition culture'. The Commission's 2008 Enforcement Priorities refer to 'safeguarding the competitive process in the internal market' and 'what really matters is to protect an effective competitive process'.[57]

Maintaining a balanced market automatically includes three functions: Ending unlawful conduct, removal of illicit gain (disgorgement), and restoration of losses to those harmed (restitution).[58] By omitting the second and third of these functions from an enforcement policy, the result has been to direct enforcement action instead at the narrower goals of ending infringements and achieving future 'deterrence', whilst leaving historic imbalances unrectified, unless it be rectified to some extent by private enforcement.

Figure 5.1 shows a balanced market (the horizontal line) and the effect of illegal activity, producing illicit gain to the infringers (here cartelists) and the total loss to others (who may, in a cartel, be customers in a series of tiers, such as distributors, then retailers, then consumers).

The payment of full compensation by those who have benefited from wrongdoing to those who have suffered loss or damage should (almost) achieve the rebalancing of the market. This is what often occurs in the United States, either as a result of payment of private damages or payment by a public enforcer of sums recovered (whether as fines or otherwise) to victims.[59] Functionally, the effect on the left hand side of the graph constitutes the removal of illicit profits (sometimes known as 'skimming off') and should roughly balance the reparation made on the right hand side.

However, sums actually paid may well be reduced. The total that should in fact be due may be reduced through negotiation and settlement or (plea) bargaining. If reparation is paid as damages, sums due to victims may be reduced by fees payable to intermediaries (lawyers, funders, experts, courts).

Resolution of 20 January 2011 on the Report on Competition Policy 2009, (2010/2137(INI)) para 5. The goal of the UK OFT is 'to make markets work well for consumers': see http://www.oft.gov.uk/about-the-oft/;jsessionid=2 FB93FF154E35E381F3D818DFE00BEA0.

[56] A recent summary of the purposes of antitrust enforcement in the USA does include *restoring* competition to the market: Compensation of victims of unlawful conduct, punishment and deterrence of unlawful conduct, termination and preventing the recurrence of unlawful conduct and restoring competitive conditions to the market harmed by the unlawful conduct: AD Melamed, 'Afterword: The Purposes of Antitrust Remedies' (2009) 76(1) *Antitrust Law Journal* 359. The American approach to 'restoring competitive conditions to the market' is somewhat different from the approach analysed here, and includes remedies such as requiring firms to disclose relevant information to competitors, which Melamed notes are difficult and controversial.

[57] Communication from the Commission, Guidance on the Commission's Enforcement Priorities in Applying Article 82 EC Treaty to Abusive Exclusionary Conduct by Dominant Undertakings, 3.12.2008.

[58] The Court of Justice referred in *Courage v Crehan* to how actions for damages can make a significant contribution to 'the maintenance of effective competition': Case C-453/99 [2001] ECR I-6297, para 27.

[59] See chs 3 and 4 above.

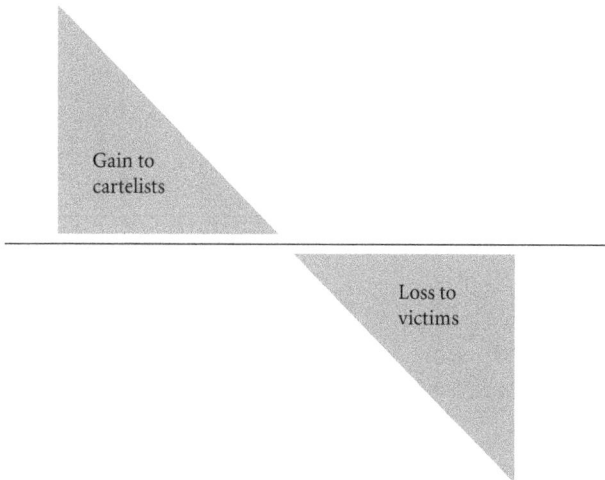

Figure 5.1: The Effect of a Cartel on the Market

Competition fines will normally have disgorgement of the unjust enrichment as one of their *effects*,[60] but this is not an official goal of current policy in competition enforcement.[61] The policy is based on public enforcement solely involving fines, based on a deterrence theory, and has been related, arbitrarily, to the sales of an infringing company.[62] This produces two effects. First, a fine will reduce the infringers' resources by an amount that is unrelated to the size of their illicit gains, hence it is unknown whether the left hand side of the graph returns to balance. Second, the fine has no effect in reducing the victims' losses. The result is that the historical imbalance in the market that was created by the illegality remains unrectified. This is illustrated in Figure 5.2: The fine on the left hand side of the graph reduces the gain to some (unquantified) extent (assuming there to have been a gain), whilst the total aggregate loss on the right hand side remains untouched.

Where fines are waived or reduced for the first to own up, the effect is clearly unfair as between infringers, and does nothing for restoration of the market or victims. The leniency policy is held up to be the only effective way of identifying cartels. But if the detection rate is so low, just how effective is the enforcement policy?

The current separation in EU competition policy between public sanctioning and subsequent private damages actions does not enable the authorities to deliver, or even be aware of to what extent there has been delivered, a retrospective rectification in the imbalance of the market that was created by the infringement.[63] There are two core aspects to this problem. First, public and private enforcement are kept separate activities and, second,

---

[60] WPJ Wils, *Efficiency and Justice in European Antitrust Enforcement* (Oxford, Hart Publishing, 2008) 55.

[61] Germany has a law under which the Bundeskartelamt may seek disgorgement of 'skimmed off' profits, but it has never used it: Information kindly supplied by S Peyer on his contacts with the Bundeskartelamt in 2013.

[62] Guidelines on the method of setting fines pursuant to Art 23(2)(a) of Reg No 1/2003, 2006/C 210/02, paras 19 and 21.

[63] C Hodges, 'European Competition Enforcement Policy: Integrating Restitution and Behaviour Control' [2011] *World Competition* 385–96; C Hodges, 'A Market-Based Competition Enforcement Policy' [2011] *European Business Law Review* 261–91.

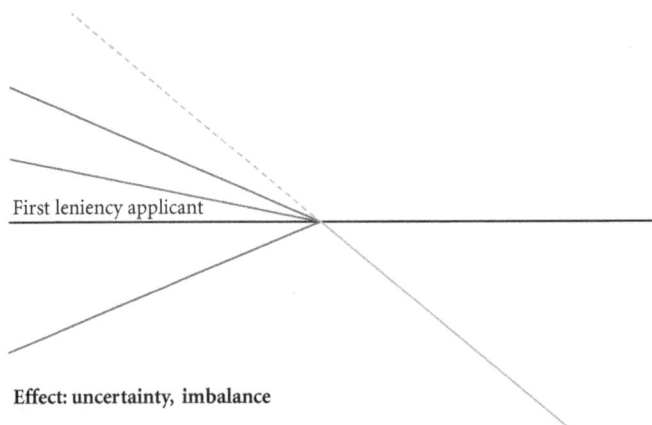

First leniency applicant

Effect: uncertainty, imbalance

Figure 5.2: The Consequence of Public Enforcement

public enforcement precedes private enforcement. However, the problem could be solved if payment of compensatory damages were to occur before or contemporaneously with the imposition of a fine: The fine could then reflect the retrospective aspect of the degree of seriousness of the illegal conduct and the prospective aspect of the level of deterrent sanction likely to prevent future wrongdoing.

D. Problems of Coordinating Public and Private Enforcement, and Achieving Deterrence

Under the EU system of enforcement of competition law, public and private enforcement are prioritised and sequenced in that order.[64] A fine is imposed as the public response to wrongdoing and it is subsequently open to any private party to seek damages for their loss that was caused by the wrongdoing.

The effect of sequencing the two procedures in this way almost always produces consequences that are uncoordinated and unfair—and not return the market to balance. There may be circumstances in which damages are paid, and some circumstances in which they are due but not paid, for various reasons. If the effect of a fine (the left hand side of Figure 5.3) is added to uncertainty over the extent of paid damages (a similar range of results on the right hand side below the line), it will be seen, first, that the result rarely achieves the flat line of a balanced market and, second, that the overall outcome on the market at the time of imposition of the fine is unpredictable, since many possible outcomes are possible on both sides of the graph, and what occurs on the left is unconnected with what occurs on the right (see Figure 5.3).

---

[64] See Proposal for a Directive of the European Parliament and of the Council on certain rules governing actions for damages under national law for infringements of the competition law provisions of the Member States and of the European Union, COM(2013) 404, 11.6.2013, recital 2 and Explanatory Memorandum 2, 4.

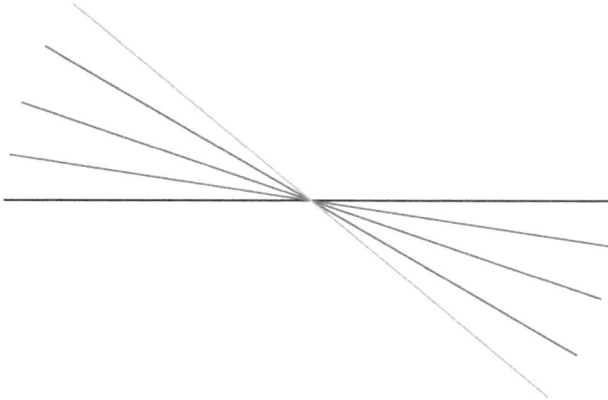

Figure 5.3: The Effect of Lack of Coordination Between Fines and Damages: Widely Differing Possible Results on Both Sides

Thus, when a system of private compensation is added to a system of public fines, difficult issues of justice arise. It is unarguable that victims of infringements should not be compensated for their losses. But is it not also unfair that defendants should be forced to pay both a large fine based on turnover and subsequently private damages? In addition to constituting economic over-deterrence, might that not breach Article 6 ECHR (European Convention on Human Rights) rights of fair treatment, in both individual and comparative cases? Some defendants might end up paying twice or three times more than others for similar infringements. Might that not offend the principle of equal treatment?

Much of the theoretical literature is directed to ensuring that the level of the public fine should be calculated to achieve deterrence. Such an approach is based on the paradigm, as far as the EU system is concerned, that only public enforcement occurs, that is that private enforcement does not occur. Indeed, it was assumed until recently that private enforcement did not occur other than at a minimal level.[65] Achieving the right level of fine is important not only so as to achieve optimal deterrence, but also to avoid producing either under- or over-deterrence, both of which states have been identified as undesirable.[66] It is theoretically important, therefore, to calibrate the 'perfectly deterrent' fine with accuracy.

Yet, if fines and damages are decided sequentially, at the time of imposing the fine, it cannot be known whether damages will subsequently be paid, nor how much and to whom. Private actions are usually settled, and a figure is paid that is negotiated, and which rarely if ever involves payment of full compensation. There is always some settlement discount. Settlement negotiations take into account a range of factors, such as the relative bargaining power of the parties, their individual availability of and need for funds, the anticipated costs

---

[65] See B Rodger (ed), *Competition Law: Comparative Private Enforcement and Collective Redress Across the EU* (Alphen aan den Rijn, WoltersKluwer, 2014).

[66] ch 4 above. On this basis, the addition of private enforcement on top of a continuously functioning regime of public enforcement has been criticised: J Kortmann and C Swaak, 'The EC White Paper on Antitrust Damage Actions: Why the Member States are (Right to be) Less Than Enthusiastic' [2009] *European Competition Law Review* 140.

and duration of the remaining litigation process, and—not least—the parties' views of the relative strengths of the underlying merits and defences.

Hence, considerable difficulties arise in estimating in advance how much will be paid by way of damages, and which parties may sue or otherwise make a claim. How can an appropriate level of fine be set if it is not known whether compensation will be paid, and to what extent? If the fine is set without knowledge of how much compensation is paid, how can it be said that a fine is just, proportionate, or produces under- or over- or optimal-deterrence? These are serious issues of justice and economics, with which debates over public and/or private enforcement during the past decade have failed to engage.

EU competition fines have hitherto been calculated on the assumption (which turns out to be incorrect) that compensation is rarely paid. So the fine can, it has been assumed, be calculated to reflect the level of deterrence that is theoretically appropriate. But if in future fines are imposed on the same basis, and compensation is (or is not) paid, the level of deterrence will by definition be too great or too high. If both systems are to co-exist, and to be decided by different procedures and decision makers at different times, with public enforcement preceding private enforcement, their inter-relation requires elucidation.[67] It is palpably inadequate for the Fining Guidelines merely to include a relatively obscure provision for mitigating circumstances to include, as one of a sequence of factors, that compensation given to third parties *may* be taken into account.[68]

What options exist to achieve greater coordination between the fine and damages? Let us examine six options.

The first option would be to adopt a system in which private damages were never paid. Hence, issues of coordination would not arise. If enforcement were all public, the authorities could ensure that compensation is paid and then an appropriate deterrent penalty could be calculated that is proportionate. If payment of full compensation were not achieved, the penalty could take that into account. That approach would encounter a series of major objections, such as the various points raised elsewhere in this chapter, not least the anti-competitive effect of not rectifying the market and the injustice of not repaying those harmed.

The second option would be to quantify the amount of harm at the time of imposing the fine, on the assumption that it would more or less equate to damages that would subsequently be paid or claimed. A variation of approach would be to try to estimate the amount of damages that would be claimed and paid. The naivety of those approaches, to say nothing of the extent of their technical difficulties and assumptions, place them quickly without need of further analysis.

The third option is more promising. Private claimants would be paid out of the fine recovered by the public authority. That approach would achieve all the theoretical objectives of 'perfect deterrence' and rectification of loss and of the market imbalance. Yet it would involve the authority in some administration, and hence would have resource implications. Claimants could either claim against the authority, or be paid a discretionary sum, whilst having no right to claim more against the infringers. The administration could perhaps be

---

[67] A further objection is that the separation of procedures for public and private enforcement produces two sets of costs.

[68] 2 cases: *Nintendo/Video Games* [2003] OJ L253/33, recitals 440 and 441, €300,000 reduction leaving fine of €168 million; *Pre-insulated Pipes* [1999] OJ L24/1, recital 172, €5 million reduction, leaving fine of €9.2 million.

outsourced by the authority. The costs of the claims and distribution could be billed to the infringers (but that would upset the 'perfect deterrence' figure that had already been paid). What would happen if the fine was less than the damages claimed? Would the public fund bear the shortfall? This occurs in the USA.[69]

The fourth option is the converse of the first. All enforcement would be private, and not public. If enforcement were all private, the payment by an infringer could be designed to impose both compensatory damages and a deterrent penalty at the same time. A simple (but in fact questionable) approach is that of the USA, where deterrence is said to be achieved by imposing at the same time as damages, a deterrent penalty equal to a multiple of the damages (traditionally double). But things become more challenging if multiple claimants and multiple infringers have to be considered. A mechanism would be needed such as a class action that would enable a single coordinated calculation to be made so as to coordinate deterrence for each infringer and complete restitution of each loser.

The fifth option is to achieve coordination between public and private enforcement by changing the current sequencing. This can be done if private damages are resolved before public sanctions. This is a perfect theoretical solution, which many might support, but is open to practical objections. As procedures currently stand, the discovery of cartels occurs because of the involvement of the public authorities, but their enforcement processes would have to be suspended pending completing any private litigation, after which the fine could be concluded. Given the uncertainties and long duration of private claiming and litigation processes, neither public nor private justice could be swiftly imposed under such a system.

However, a variation of the fifth option makes the sixth option appealing. If the payment of damages can be achieved through agreement swiftly and before conclusion of the public process, so as not to delay the public process, all goals would be achieved. Justice would be swift and comprehensive. This is the basis of the regulatory redress enforcement power, discussed in Part C below.

E. Confusions of the Objectives of Fines: Deterrence or Restoration?

The above issues reflect the confusion—inherent in the European competition enforcement system—over whether the purpose and/or function of fines is to deter and/or to compensate. Underlying this is a theoretical confusion over which of two enforcement theories noted above are being applied: The gain-deterrence theory or the harm-internalisation theory. Gain-deterrence focuses on the infringer and its behaviour, whereas harm-internalisation focuses on the damage caused to victims. Equating the two concepts has inherent problems. The amount of money involved under either approach may not be the same.

The European Commission has consistently emphasised that the purpose of competition fines is deterrence. According to European principles, public sanctions (fines) should be paid to the state and cannot be retained by private parties. Thus under the German skimming-off provisions, private parties may be authorised to make a claim for illicit profits but sums

---

[69] H First, 'The Case for Antitrust Civil Penalties' (2009) 76(1) *Antitrust Law Journal* 127 (the Federal Trade Commission has asserted power to seek disgorgement (deprive a wrongdoer of his unjust enrichment) and restitution (compensating victims), but in the 2000s decade it has only ordered restitution in three cases).

recovered must be paid to the state.[70] But restoration or skimming off of illicit profits are also consequences of fines, even if they are not formal purposes.[71]

From the viewpoint of restorative or societal justice, restoration of loss is an important goal. It is clear that the effect of fines is both to remove illicit profits from a firm (restitution) and to deter. Thus, different principles or viewpoints (achieving economic behaviour and justice) produce different results, which are hard to reconcile. The concept of optimal or perfect deterrence noted above, for example, may well be breached if considerations of fair justice are taken into account in imposing sanctions, as they are under the Commission's aggravating and mitigating circumstances that may be taken into account on a discretion- ary basis in setting competition fines.[72]

Are deterrence and compensation cumulative or not? If the removal of illicit gains can affect future behaviour, to what extent is the fine deterrent and to what extent is it restora- tive? It is impossible to predict what affects—adequately and sufficiently—individual and general behaviour. Inherent and unavoidable inconsistency arises between the goals of indi- vidual and general deterrence, and between setting principled penalties as between differ- ent individual infringers at any one time. The conclusion is that affecting future behaviour (deterrence) can only be an individualised, case-by-case exercise. It depends on what moti- vates the individual who broke the law.

F. The Enforcement Policy Imposes a Significant Amount of Unjustified Damage on the Wrong Targets

By imposing sanctions on 'the company' (irrespective of whether it may or may not be capable of having a *mens rea*), significant fines are imposed on the innocent. This is because the consequences of financial penalties on a business flow directly to its employees, suppli- ers, customers and shareholders.

The theory underlying current competition enforcement policy is that fines on compa- nies are specifically intended to diminish corporate assets, profitability and shareholder value. As Ginsburg and Wright state: 'The economic analysis of optimal sanctions and criminal punishments is built on the foundational insight that penalties should be suffi- cient to induce offenders to internalize the full social cost of their crimes.'[73] Hylton argues that when 'there are two general approaches a punishment authority can take under an optimal punishment regime. One is to *internalize consumer harm*. The other is to *deter com- pletely by eliminating the expected profits* from anticompetitive conduct. The internalization

---

[70] S Peyer, 'Private Antitrust Litigation in Germany from 2005 to 2007: Empirical Evidence' (2012) 8(2) *Journal of Competition Law and Economics* 331.

[71] It has been argued that facilitating the compensation of actual damages (lost profit) can increase consumer prices, increase the expected profits of cartelists and even decrease the expected profits of suppliers to cartelists: M Hunold, 'The Effects of Cartel Damage Compensations' Centre for European Economic Research Discussion Paper No 13-081 (2013).

[72] Guidelines on the method of setting fines imposed pursuant to Art 23(2)(a) of Reg N0 1/2003.

[73] DH Ginsburg and JD Wright, 'Antitrust Sanctions' *Competition Policy International* (2010) 6(2) 3–39. They cite the seminal analysis of GS Becker, 'Crime and Punishment: An Economic Approach' (1968) 76 *Journal of Political Economy* 169. See also WM Landes, 'Optimal Sanctions for Antitrust Violations' (1983) 50 *University of Chicago Law Review* 652.

approach is appropriate for conduct that is either efficient or has a significant chance of being efficient. The complete deterrence approach is appropriate for conduct that is unambiguously inefficient.'[74]

The adverse economic impact on shareholders, employees, creditors and customers is intended to induce them to exert pressure for compliance on directors and managers. What is the evidence that some of these groups may be able to influence the behaviour of the small circle of people involved in the cartel? What account is taken of the prevailing corporate culture? There has been a suggestion that some institutional investors deliberately invest in companies and managers who are risk-taking, and that behaviour displays widespread cynicism in the market that deserves a punitive response.[75] Yet, how widespread is that behaviour, can it be quantified, and what is the best way to change such a culture?

In any event, there are bound to be practical limitations to the effectiveness of such pressure. The outcome may be a limited effect on improved compliance but significantly adverse social and economic costs for those who have not committed any infringement and are unable to prevent occurrence or recurrence. The consequences would be adverse for the company's ability to sustain or create employment and investment. Limiting fines to a particular maximum percentage of corporate assets does not solve this problem, it merely limits its effects. The result, as Wils says, is unacceptable from a perspective of proportionality and retributive justice.[76]

The underlying claimed justification for sanctioning the company is punishment, that is, formal sanctioning by the state of an offender to indicate the seriousness of the crime, coupled with an attempt to prevent recurrence. But the essential justification for imposition of punishment by a democratic state has to be based on the morality of the action in protecting the state's order. In relation to competition sanctions imposed on a firm, however, this basis of morality is lacking, because of the absence of proximate causation of the harm. The wrongdoing was not instituted by the firm. The wrongdoing was instituted by a small number of humans who were conspirators in a cartel. The firm was, of course, a beneficiary of the wrong, but the firm only caused the harm if it actively contributed to it. There exists here a confusion of origins and consequences. The moral basis upon which a state is legitimately entitled to respond differs between those responsible for originating causes and those who may have benefitted from others' wrong.

It has been argued that 'it seems strange to penalise a company whose top management deliberately and systematically planned its cartel activities in the same fashion as a company whose vigorously-communicated compliance policy was ignored by several employees in one department of one wholly-owned subsidiary'.[77]

The problem lies with the rationale for imposing penalties. It is acceptable to remove illicit profits from a trader who has gained from wrongdoing, and thereby redistribute the wealth of those innocent employees and others who have gained from others' cartel. But it

---

[74] KN Hylton, 'Antitrust Enforcement Regimes: Fundamental Differences' *Boston University School of Law, Law and Economics Research Paper No 12-41* (original emphasis).

[75] WPJ Wils, 'Antitrust Compliance Programmes & Optimal Antitrust Enforcement' (2013) 1(1) *Journal of Antitrust Enforcement* 52.

[76] Wils (n 60) 54. The Charter of Fundamental Rights of the EU, art 49(3), states: 'the severity of penalties must not be disproportionate to the criminal offence'.

[77] Forrester (n 51) 817, 826.

is not justifiable to remove the property of the innocent stakeholders on the incorrect basis that they have done wrong in the past, that they could have prevented the wrongdoing by others when they could not have done so, or that their behaviour will be affected in future so as to achieve deterrence in wrongdoers with whom they work.

G. Constitutionalism and Fairness

The argument here is that the outcomes of current enforcement policy offend against constitutional principles of justice, fairness and proportionality. In doing so it cannot command democratic or moral support, and will not maximize compliance but generate condemnation. It was found in chapter one that compliance can be strongly enhanced where actors consider that the substance of the rules and the processes adopted by the regulator are regarded as conforming to the subject's internal moral values. The current competition enforcement regime gives rise to serious concerns over whether it satisfies these conditions. It contains several core features that can be criticised as constituting serious distortions of justice, and therefore deserving of moral condemnation and lack of democratic support, which tend to diminish the authorities' and the states' moral standing in the eyes of the regulated and the populace general.

To summarise the major concerns that have been noted in the paragraphs above. First, the system aims at the wrong targets, namely businesses rather than the humans who have committed the criminal conspiracy, largely ignoring whether the businesses could have taken steps to encourage or prevent the conspiracy. Second, it deliberately imposes adverse financial consequences on bystanders (employees, shareholders etc) on the assumption that they will be able to affect the behaviour of the business and of the conspirators. The basis on which this is done cannot be unjustified. The point becomes sharply focused when one considers the scale of the penalties applied. Imposing a very large fine where there is no moral guilt increases the offence against the principle that punishments should be proportionate, and the degree of moral offensiveness. Such fines are sometimes grossly disproportionate in value compared with sanctions imposed for other violations of regulatory or criminal law. Third, in many cases it lets those responsible for instigating and continuing the illegal behaviour escape without personal sanctions. Fourth, the leniency system is a distortion of justice, letting people who are guilty of serious wrongdoing off almost scot-free, and able to offend again. Fifth, the system fails to maximise identification of wrongdoing (seemingly only around 15 per cent are detected). Sixth, it takes such a long time to identify wrongdoing. The system is ineffective and inefficient in rectifying the consequences of the infringement, in restoring market balance, and in restoring losses to victims.

The major purposes of rules on fair procedures in criminal and similar sanctioning systems are to avoid hurting the morally innocent (Type I error; over-deterrence) and to avoid letting the morally guilty escape (Type II error; under-deterrence).[78] Competition enforcement, certainly at EU level, currently commits *both* types of errors.

---

[78] See RH Lande and JM Connor, 'Optimal Cartel Deterrence: An Empirical Comparison of Sanctions to Overcharges' (2012) 34 *Cardozo Law Review,* 427.

The current regulatory climate produces polarisation between enforcer and regulated, emphasising authoritarian punishment of wrongdoing, rather than positive achievement of shared desirable ends.

Calculations of the level of fines so as to provide optimal deterrence are based on the impact of penalties on the profitability of the business engaging in illicit activities.[79] The golden rule of the fine should be high enough to wipe out any expected profit from the infringement, given the probability of detection. Why is it just to base the calculation on the probability of detection? The economic argument for the policy is based on a theoretical calculation that the risk of getting caught will deter an individual, but there is a difference between affecting future behaviour and sanctioning past behaviour. Public sanctioning is usually based on moral culpability. Why should that not be the case for competition sanctions? If it is difficult to gauge the extent of moral culpability, or of the likelihood that a 'business will reoffend', should the basis of imposing sanctions not just be to wipe out any anticipated profit?

Overall, it is of considerable concern that the system as a whole cannot convincingly provide, in the majority of cases, early identification of serious and lengthy wrongdoing, reparation for loss, removal of illicit profits, and controls that are properly targeted at effectively affecting future behaviour. The level of injustice in this system, and failure to apply lessons that many other regulators have adopted, is little short of scandalous.

H. The Current Enforcement Policy is Ineffective

There is evidence that current antitrust enforcement policy is not working.[80] By definition, the ongoing occurrence of any infringements constitutes a failure of an enforcement policy, but that needs to be seen against the context of the background incidence of infringement, and whether it is rising, stable or falling. The evidence suggests that only perhaps 15 per cent of cartels are identified and prosecuted, and that many still operate. However, the actual incidence of cartels is unknown, and the speculative figure is merely a mathematical extrapolation from the numbers of cartels that are identified. There is clear evidence of recidivism by companies. There is evidence that cartels tend to last an unacceptably long time (an average of nine years), so the policy on the means of identifying them does not produce impressive results. The risk of being caught is low. Limited survey evidence indicates only a modest level of knowledge about competition rules or the existence of infringements.

None of these findings suggests that the perception by those who instigate cartels that their risk of being caught and sanctioned—which is believed to be critical for an enforcement

---

[79] M-L Allain, M Boyer, R Kotchoni and J-P Ponssard, 'The Determination of Optimal Fines in Cartel Cases—The Myth of Underdeterrence' *CIRANO Working Paper*, 2011.

[80] See OECD, Roundtable on Promoting Compliance with Competition Law—Issues Paper by the Secretariat, DAF/COMP(2011)4 (1 June 2011). M Orey, 'Price Fixing: the Perpetual sequel' *Business Week* Sept 28, 2009 (price fixing appears to be as pervasive as ever); ME Stucke, 'Am I a Price-Fixer? A Behavioral Economic Analysis of Cartels' in C Beaton-Wells and A Ezrachi (eds), *Criminalising Cartels: A Critical Interdisciplinary Study of an International Regulatory Movement* (Oxford, Hart Publishing, 2010) ('despite (i) escalating criminal and civil fines in the US (and abroad), (ii) treble private damages, (iii) longer jail sentences, and (iv) generous leniency program, the United States has not reached optimal deterrence').

policy to succeed—is anywhere near a level that is effective. Let us look at the evidence on how many cartels are detected, what the risk is of being caught and what business people think.

i. How Many Cartels are Detected?

It is widely asserted within the competition world that only between 10 per cent and 20 per cent of cartels are detected in Europe.[81] A view on whether that rate is or is not satisfactory will be subjective, but it would clearly not found a widely held perception that the risk of detection is inevitable or high. However, these figures are themselves unreliable since they are in fact estimates based on calculations made on numbers of cartels that have been detected.[82]

The extent of non-compliance is actually unknown and the assertions by the Directorate General for Competition (DG COMP) of the level of detriment are entirely speculative, since the empirical evidence for the extent of non-compliance is based on mathematical extrapolation from data on the number of people caught, rather than the number not caught. It may admittedly be difficult to measure the total number of cartels, particularly those undetected, but it would seem important to do so if major policy decisions are to be founded on the figure, and there is a significant element of risk in basing policy decisions on assumptions that are unsubstantiated and even significantly incorrect. For example, the figure is central to the calculation that produced the Commission's assertion that the annual direct cost to consumers and other victims of competition infringements in the EU ranges between €13 billion and €37 billion.[83]

Only two significant attempts have been made to estimate detection rates for cartels,[84] one in the USA on data now 25 years old, and the other on cases dealt with by the European

---

[81] These figures were taken as to benchmarks for calculations and policy in the 2008 White Paper: See Commission Staff Working Document accompanying the White Paper on damages actions for breach of the EC antitrust rules: Impact assessment, SEC(2008) 405, 2.4.2008. See also *Private Actions in Competition Law: Effective Redress for Consumers and Business*, Office of Fair Trading, 2007, para 5.7, at http://www.oft.gov.uk/shared_oft/reports/comp_policy/oft916resp.pdf.

[82] A report by a New Zealand commission asserted that deterrence requires the *damages* awarded to be 100% of the damage to all victims adjusted for such factors as the likelihood of detection and successful punishment: *Penalties, Remedies and Court Processes under The Commerce Act 1986: A Discussion Document*, Ministry of Commerce, 1998.

[83] Impact Assessment para 42 and Impact Study para 2.1.1 (n 81).

[84] The Impact Study para 2.1.1 lists a series of references prior to the Combe et al study that derive from the Bryant and Eckard study, except for a small data set of international cases reported. See *Report on the Nature and Impact of Hard Core Cartels and Sanctions against cartels under National Competition Laws*, OECD, DAFFE/COMP(2002)7, 9.4.2002. Significant theoretical papers with the percentages that they estimate for the level of probability of detection include: Landes (n 73) (33% assumption underlying the United States rule on treble damages); GJ Werden and MJ Simon, 'Why Price Fixers Should Go to Prison' (1987) 32 *Antitrust Bulletin*, 917–37 (a conservative estimate from road building cases of 10%); A Beckenstein and H Landis-Gabel, 'Antitrust Compliance: Results of a Survey of Legal Opinion' (1982) 52 *Antitrust Law Journal* 459 (50% of a survey of American Bar Association members in 1980); E Combe and C Monnier, 'Fines Against Hard Core Cartels in Europe: The Myth of Over Enforcement' Cahiers de Recherche PRISM-Sorbonne, June 2009, at http://ssrn.com/abstract=1431644http://ssrn.com/abstract=1431644 (15%).

Commission between 1969 and 2007.[85] Bryant and Eckard examined cases selected from those pursued by the US Department of Justice to a successful conclusion from 1961 to 1988.[86] They calculated that the annual probability of getting caught for the cartels in their data set that were eventually detected was between 13 per cent and 17 per cent.[87] The reliability of this data and relevance to contemporary European conditions, with its significantly different and evolving enforcement regime, is highly questionable. Combe and colleagues have recently reviewed the 86 cartel cases dealt with by the European Commission between 1969 and 2007.[88] Their calculations were that the probability of detection in a given year for this group, *conditional on being detected*, was between 12.9 per cent and 13.2 per cent. But, of course, none of these estimate the number or proportion of cartels that will in fact be detected. Combe noted after 1996, when the EU introduced its leniency programme, the detection rate increased from an average of 1.64 per annum to five per annum (again, of those actually detected).

Given that the only hard data that are available relate to enforcement activity, it is surprising that the number of case investigations of which the EC Network has been informed has fallen consistently since 2004, at both Commission and national level, until an increase in national cases in 2013 (Figure 5.4).[89] Given the increased powers and enforcement activism by the authorities generally in this period, this is counter-intuitive. It is clear that the Commission's policy in the Modernisation programme is to push cases down to Member State level, so that the Commission itself can concentrate on the larger cartels.[90] However, possible further explanations for the fall might be that the authorities' investigative capacity has significantly fallen, or that the authorities are uncovering larger cartels that need increased resources, or that there may be fewer significant cartels and other infringements worthy of investigation. There is a need for further inquiry into this position. It is asserted by industry that antitrust enforcement by European public authorities has been increasingly strong and effective.[91]

---

[85] An economic projection based on data from recent legal cases and a small number of case studies of cartels in specific industries concluded that a theoretical approach tended to underestimate the role of communication in cartel sustainability and that drawing conclusions was 'not straightforward': PA Grout and S Sonderegger, *Predicting cartels: Discussion paper 773* (OFT, 2005).

[86] PG Bryant and EW Eckard, 'Price Fixing: The Probability of Getting Caught' (1991) 73 *Review of Economics & Statistics* 531–36.

[87] Werden and Simon (n 84).

[88] E Combe, C Monnier and R Legal, 'Cartels: The Probability of Getting Caught in the European Union' BEER paper no 12, available at http://www.concurrences.com/article.php3?id_article=13955.

[89] In contrast, some commentators interpret the figures as showing overall a substantial increase in workload: AM Mateus, 'Ensuring a More Level Playing Field in Competition Enforcement Throughout the European Union' [2010] *European Competition Law Review* 514.

[90] See *Report on Competition Policy 2006*, COM(2007) 358, at http://ec.europa.eu/comm/competition/annual_reports/.

[91] *Private Enforcement in the European Union—Pitfalls and Opportunities* (Berlin, Bundesverband der Deutschen Industrie eV and Freshfields Bruckhaus Deringer, 2007).

	Total Year 2004	Total Year 2005	Total Year 2006	Total year 2007	Total year 2008	Total year 2009	Total Year 2010	Total Year 2011	Total Year 2012	Total Year 2013
Total number of case investigations of which the Network has been informed[a]	301	203	165	150	159	150	169	163	112	121
— of which EU Commission cases	101	22	21	10	10	21	11	26	6	5
— of which National Competent Authority (NCA) cases	200	181	144	140	149	129	158	137	106	116
Cases in which an envisaged decision has been submitted by NCAs during the period indicated[b]	32	76	64	72	60	70	94	88	91	60

Figure 5.4: EU Competition Case Investigations 2004–2013[92]

[a] Case investigations started whether by a National Competition Authority (NCA) or by the Commission.
[b] Cases having reached the envisaged decision stage; only submissions from the NCAs under Art 11(4) of Council Regulation (EC) No 1/2003 of 16 December 2002 on the implementation of the rules on competition laid down in Arts 81 and 82 of the Treaty.

[92] http://ec.europa.eu/comm/competition/ecn/statistics.html.

ii. Extent of Recidivism

A significant number of companies involved in cartels offend again. Connor and Helmers noted that the number of worldwide judgments against 11 multinational companies between 1990 and 2009 ranged from 28 to 10, and commented that 'Recidivism bedevils the international cartel scene'.[93] Harding and Gibbs found that out of 74 cases in which the Commission applied the 1998 Guidelines up to the end of 2006, 17 cases involved a finding of repeated infringement by at least one undertaking, making a total of 28 findings of repeat offending. They considered that these figures indicated an 'awesome level of recidivism on the part of major companies who appear as usual suspects in the world of business cartels. In short, this suggests a confirmed culture of delinquency'.[94] However, Wils' review of the decisions adopted by the European Commission during the following period 2006–2010 led him to conclude that there did not appear to be a continuing trend of increased recidivism. He found that 12 per cent (31 out of 255) of the undertakings found to have participated in cartels were recidivists.[95] To the extent there was a trend within this five year period, Wils found a declining one: 24 per cent in 2006 (11 out of 45), 11 per cent in 2007 (seven out of 64), 13.5 per cent in 2008 (five out of 37), 13 per cent in 2009 (five out of 38), and four per cent in 2010 (three out of 71).

Recidivism data are, of course, only part of the picture, and must be seen against the total number of infringements and the position in particular sectors or countries. If one views the wrongdoers as firms, then finding that a significant phenomenon of recidivism exists is both a conundrum for enforcers and an indictment of the failure of their enforcement and deterrence actions. However, if one adopts the viewpoint that humans in some markets tend to adopt certain behaviours, then different interpretations and approaches to enforcement suggest themselves, as will be discussed below.

Recidivism data by companies raises the question of whether the source of problems lies with the firms or lies elsewhere, for example with the structure of competition in the particular sector, with the culture of the sector or firm, with controls in business, or simply with individuals who cannot be controlled by the firm. There is little knowledge on recidivism data by the individuals involved.

iii. What is the Risk of being Caught?

Is the perceived risk of being caught sufficiently high? It would appear not. First, cartels typically last for several years before they come to light (and official investigations take

---

[93] JM Connor and G Helmers, 'Statistics on Modern Private International Cartels, 1990–2005' (American Antitrust Institute, Working Paper No 07-01, 2007); JM Connor and G Helmers, 'Statistics on Private International Cartels 1995–2005' (Working Paper, 2008). See also JM Connor, 'Recidivism Revealed: Private International Cartels 1990–2009' (Autumn 2010) *Competition Policy International* 101 at 116 but see GJ Werden, SD Hammond and BA Barnett, 'Recidivism Eliminated: Cartel Enforcement in the United States Since 1999' (October 2011) *CPI Antitrust Chronicle* 1.

[94] C Harding and A Gibbs, 'Why Go to Court in Europe? An Analysis of Cartel Appeals 1995–2004' (2005) 30 *European Law Review* 369. Further statistics for cartels discovered throughout the world 1990–2005, with rankings of top cartel recidivists (mostly European), can be found at JM Connor and CG Helmers, 'Statistics on Modern Private International Cartels 1990–2005' *Purdue University Dept of Agricultural Economics Working Paper 06-11* (November 2006) 23–25, at http://www.agecon.purdue.edu/working_papers/workingpaper.connor.11.10.06.pdf.

[95] WPJ Wils, 'Recidivism in EU Antitrust Enforcement: A Legal and Economic Analysis' (March 2012) *World Competition: Law and Economics Review*, at http://ssrn.com/abstract=1957088; Wils (n 75).

several more years). Combe and Monnier calculated that the lifetimes of the cartels identified between 1975 and 2009 had slightly *increased* over time, from an average of just over five years in 1975 to an average of around nine years in 2009 (overall average seven years), although the size of the annual affected market was not increasing.[96] The nine year average duration of cartels dealt with at EU level between 1990 and 2009 was stable over each segment of five years.[97] The median for those dealt with at European level has been calculated as five and a half years.[98] In those cartels sanctioned by the European Commission in 2011 and 2012 the average duration increased from 3.3 to 6.1 years.[99] Average duration appears to be nine years in the USA,[100] where the individuals who instigated the cartel will typically have moved firms *twice* before the cartel is discovered, and have no risk of adverse consequences from the infringing firm.[101]

Second, the European Commission took between two and seven years (average 4.3 years) in investigating these cartels.[102] Stephan has noted lengthy individual cases.[103] In the *Car Glass* cartel case, the €896 million fine imposed on French glass producer Saint-Gobain was imposed more than a decade after the anti-competitive behaviour was first instigated and some nine years after the infringement ceased.[104]

Third, the evidence (discussed below) is that cartels involve a very small number of individuals within each company, who take care to keep their conspiracy secret, both internally and publicly.

iv. British Business Survey Evidence

A survey comprising 30 interviews with British competition lawyers, economists and firms' managers responsible for competition compliance in 2006, with telephone surveys of 234 senior competition lawyers based in London and Brussels in 2006, and 202 British companies in 2007 sought reasons for the abandonment or modification of proposed mergers or potentially anti-competitive conduct following recent competition authority interventions.[105] The survey found that 'companies abandoned or significantly modified a large number of possible anti-competitive agreements and conduct because of the risk of

---

[96] Combe and Monnier (n 84).

[97] JK Ashton and AD Pressey, 'Who Manages Cartels? The Role of Sales and Marketing Managers within International Cartels: Evidence from the European Union 1990–2009' CCP Working Paper 12-11 (2012).

[98] JM Connor, 'Cartel Fine Severity and the European Commission: 2007–2011' (2013) 34 *European Competition Law Review* 58–77.

[99] C Veljanovski, *European Cartel Fines in 2012* (London, Case Associates, 2013).

[100] SJ Evenett and VY Suslow, 'Preconditions on Private Restraints on Market Access and International Cartels' (2000) 3(4) *Journal of International Economic Law* 593–631 reported that the mean for pre-WWII international cartels was 4 to 8 years, although an iodine cartel lasted 61 years: PL Eckbo, *The Future of World Oil* (Cambridge, Ballinger, 1976).

[101] DA Crane, *The Institutional Structure of Antitrust Enforcement* (Oxford, Oxford University Press, 2011).

[102] C Veljanovski, *European Cartel Fines Under the 2006 Penalty Guidelines—A Statistical Analysis* (London, Case Associates, 2010) available at http://ssrn.com/abstract=1723843.

[103] A Stephan, 'See No Evil: Cartels and the Limits of Antitrust Compliance Programmes' (2010) 31(8) *The Company Lawyer* 3.

[104] DG Competition Press Release, 'Antitrust: Commission Fines Car Glass Producers over €1.3 Billion for Market Sharing Cartel' (12 November 2008) IP/08/1685.

[105] *The Deterrent Effect of Competition Enforcement by the OFT: Discussion Paper 963* (Office of Fair Trading, 2007). The authors calculated a supposed cartel abandonment rate of 5:1 per actual OFT decision.

OFT investigation.' However, these conclusions have been criticised, Ginsburg and Wright saying they 'should be handled with some caution'.[106]

Further Office of Fair Trading (OFT) research into the construction industry reported that the 'risk of an OFT investigation had not made any impact on the majority of contractors surveyed'.[107] It found that there was a very low level of awareness of any of the OFT's activities directed at the construction sector, particularly the six cases completed between 2004 and 2006, and respondents did not consider 'that there was any clear message about bid rigging coming from the OFT during this period'.

A survey of 2,009 UK businesses in seven sectors interviewed in 2011[108] reported that:

— A minority (20 per cent) claimed to have directly come across *breaches* of competition law by others, and one in 10 was not sure.
— A very small proportion of businesses said they had *abandoned or changed* arrangements in the last two years (three per cent) because of the risk of infringing competition law.
— A sizable minority (23 per cent) claimed they either did *not take action* to ensure compliance with competition legislation, or simply did not know whether this happened.
— The survey found that 35 per cent of respondents *did not know* the sorts of things competition law was supposed to prevent, and 34 per cent had no awareness of any competition enforcement action; 41 per cent thought abuse of dominance was happening in their local region, and 22 per cent thought there was collusion.[109]

III. Conclusions on the Current Enforcement Policy

Crane has noted that 'Antitrust has become almost exclusively the concern of small groups of legal and economic specialists, who carry on their work without widespread public interest or support.'[110] The analysis above has set out a series of substantive criticisms with the current policy for enforcement of competition law as it exists at EU level. The basis of this policy is a theory of deterrence, applied solely of an ex post context, with a theory of internalisation of financial sanctions, on the assumption that firms are capable of controlling all their staff. It should not come as a surprise that the policy gives rise to problems at both the theoretical and practical levels: The following sections summarise why this is so.

---

[106] Ginsburg and Wright (n 73). These authors noted several methodological shortcomings (small sample; type of cartel; need to separate modified and abandoned cartels; exclusion of firms previously involved in infringements; did not probe impact of different types of sanctions; lawyers' tendency and interest to exaggerate the number averted).

[107] *Evaluation of the Impact of the OFT's Investigation into Bid Rigging in the Construction Industry* (OFT, 2010) OFT1240. This was undertaken before a Statement of Objections was issued to 112 construction companies in April 2008.

[108] *Competition Law Compliance Survey. Prepared for the Office of Fair Trading by Synovate (UK) Ltd* (Office of Fair Trading, 2011) at http://www.oft.gov.uk/shared_oft/ca-and-cartels/competition-awareness-compliance/oft1270.pdf.

[109] ibid.

[110] Crane (n 103). Crane cites R Hofstadter, 'What Happened to the Antitrust Movement?' in *The Paranoid Style in American Politics and Other Essays* (Cambridge MA, Harvard University Press, 1966) 188.

Importantly, the policy is based on deterrence *alone*, and not an enforcement policy that incorporates other elements, such as are found in almost all enforcement policies adopted in areas policed by other enforcement bodies, whether sectoral regulators, or those responsible for more horizontal subject-matter, such as consumer law, bribery or criminal law. The key elements that are found in other enforcement systems include a series of escalating sanctions, an ultimate deterrent sanction (competition law does not permit making a company insolvent or removing a licence to operate), a responsive approach to imposition of sanctions, and the existence of sanctions for individuals as well as firms.

A. Problems with Deterrence

An enforcement policy based on deterrence alone is inherently limited and does not produce satisfactory results. The conclusion of chapter two was that a system based on deterrence can only work if there is a high level of detection and enforcement, so that anyone who might consider breaking the rules perceives that the likelihood of being caught is high. Economic theory, applied in competition enforcement, is that the two relevant levers on behaviour are the likelihood of being caught and the severity of punishment imposed. However, the psychological evidence also showed that the severity of the penalty (which is such a notable feature of the competition enforcement system, highly emphasised by the authorities) is of little relevance to achieving actual deterrence.[111]

In competition enforcement, by contrast, the policy that is pursued is to maximise the severity of punishment by imposing high fines. If that policy were incorrect, therefore, the imposition of very high fines on companies is merely disguised taxation, and does little if anything in achieving its claimed objective of deterrence. Conversely, if the policy were effective, one would expect that the imposition of high fines, significantly increased in size over time, would have an effect on levels of infringement. If the level of infringement remains high, the main problems would seem to be either that the fines have no effect, perhaps because they are too low or because they are aimed at the wrong targets.

Determination of whether there has been any deterrent effect is a well-known problem of criminology and penology in relation to the deterrence of criminal behaviour.[112] A 2009 review of the literature noted that 'there are in fact very few studies that attempt to directly measure the impact of a particular penalty regime on the incidence of cartelisation.'[113] It noted two studies affording some broad international perspectives. First, Clarke and Evenett's data on vitamin imports from 1985 to 2000 across over 90 countries showed that vitamin prices tended to increase less in countries where cartels are prosecuted and where

---

[111] A recent indication was the survey of over 2300 Australian businesses, which concluded that higher sanctions alone are unlikely to lead to optimal compliance: C Parker and V Lehmann Nielsen, 'Deterrence and the Impact of Calculative Thinking on Business Compliance with Competition and Consumer Regulation' (2011) 56(2) *The Antitrust Bulletin* 377.

[112] TC Pratt, FT Cullen, KR Blevins, LE Daigle and TD Madensen, 'The Empirical Status of Deterrence Theory: A Meta-Analysis' in FT Cullen, JP Wright and KR Blevins (eds), *Taking Stock: The Status of Criminological Theory* (New Brunswick NJ, Transaction Publishers, 2009).

[113] *An Assessment of Discretionary Penalties Regimes. Final Report. A Report Prepared for the Office of Fair Trading by London Economics* (Office of Fair Trading, 2009) OFT1132, available at http://londoneconomics.co.uk/wp-content/uploads/2011/09/30-An-assessment-of-the-UK-Discretionary-Penalties-Regime.pdf.

fines and other forms of sanctions are imposed.[114] This evidence suggested that active anti-cartel regimes have some degree of effectiveness in deterring cartel activity. Second, Hylton and Deng's comparison of regimes found that the scope of a country's competition law (the types of conduct prohibited under competition laws, the types of penalties that might be adopted under the law and the procedures for enforcing those laws) was positively associated with a measure of the intensity of competition in the country's economy.[115] They also found that increasing the range of instruments available to enforcement authorities had a significant impact on the competition intensity of a country.

On the other hand, a 1994 empirical study into legal case histories in four significant international markets (diamonds, uranium, silver and gold) found an upsurge of cartel criminalisation.[116] Ginsburg and Wright's 2010 study of US stock price movements following indictments for price-fixing concluded that current American sanctions have no more than a transitory impact upon market outcomes and little, if any, deterrent value.[117] They concluded that 'The bulk of scholarly opinion is consistent with the view that despite ever-increasing levels of corporate fines and longer jail sentences, cartel activity is currently under-deterred'.[118] Harding's 2011 review of cartel deterrence concluded that regulators ought not to assume that their enforcement actions are well-known and convey menace.[119]

B. Limitations with Public Sanctioning Ex Post

The competition law system is based virtually exclusively on public enforcement by a public authority. This classic 'command and control' approach to regulation is bound to be limited in effectiveness. Effectiveness would be increased in firms' internal systems and personnel, and any external personnel and systems, were more closely engaged in the system. In other words, the system should adopt a more multi-level and meta approach to regulatory control of behaviour. Such an approach would involve enlisting internal compliance systems, supporting the behaviour of all staff as being based on ethical conduct, providing internal and external whistleblowing, and modifying the perverse motivations for individuals to break the law.

The competition regulatory system for cartels and abuse of dominance omits any ex ante controls, and relies solely on ex post imposition of sanctions. Adopting only an ex post approach is a driver towards adopting an enforcement theory based on deterrence. By definition, the offensive behaviour that has already occurred cannot now be prevented. Therefore, the imposition of sanctions can act only as a retrospective token of society's retribution, and as a means of signalling to the offender and to others that future offences will receive similar treatment. As a means of controlling future behaviour, restricting

---

[114] JL Clarke and SJ Evenett, 'The Deterrent Effects of National Anti-cartel Laws: Evidence from the International Vitamins Cartel' (2003) 48 *Antitrust Bulletin* 689.

[115] KN Hylton and F Deng, 'Antitrust Around the World: An Empirical Analysis of the Scope of Competition Laws and Their Effects' (2007) 74 *Antitrust Law Journal* 2.

[116] DL Spar, *The Cooperative Edge: The Internal Politics of International Cartels* (Ithaca, Cornell Studies in Political Economy, 1994).

[117] Ginsburg and Wright (n 73).

[118] See Y Bolotova, JM Connor and DJ Miller, 'Factors Influencing the Magnitude of Cartel Overcharges: An Empirical Analysis of the US Market' (2009) 5 *Journal of Competition Law and Economics* 361; Y Bolotova, 'Cartel Overcharges: An Empirical Analysis' (2009) 70 *Journal of Economic Behavior and Organization* 321.

[119] C Harding, 'Cartel Deterrence: The Search for Evidence and Argument' (2011) 56(2) *The Antitrust Bulletin* 345–76.

intervention aimed at controlling it only to the point after an offence has occurred has obvious limitations. Prevention is more likely to be effective if intervention can occur in advance of undesirable acts.

The problem is that it is difficult to design an effective ex ante control for the type of wrongdoing involved here, namely conspiracies such as cartels. The same problem occurs in other generic issues such as bribery. An ex ante licensing system based on an application for an approval to break the law would clearly not be relevant. The nature of the wrongdoing is binary: It is plain wrong, and unlike most regulatory systems the activity is not one that can be carried out in a way that is acceptable to society.

Examples of ex ante regulatory interventions that could be adopted include: Requiring individuals to seek permission for certain activities before they are taken; requiring certain actors to have undergone specified education or to hold professional qualifications, requiring firms to operate internal compliance systems, and requiring regular audit. The EU competition enforcement regime neither requires nor incentivises any of these techniques. Some of these techniques may at first sight seem difficult to apply to the competition context. But they are not impossible: Although a public licensing system for breaches of competition law is inappropriate, requiring certain management decisions to be referred to internal or external counsel for advice, or to a competition agency for advice, coupled with a revised sanctioning regime, is not impossible to contemplate. However, the EU positively rejects including incentives for firms to have compliance systems, even though they are tacitly understood to be relevant, as noted below.

C. Limitations with Focusing only on Firms: The Internalisation Fallacy

Competition enforcement policy assumes that firms are able to control the behaviour of all their personnel. Why should it be assumed that this is any more true than the proposition that a state is able to control the behaviour of all of its subjects? Both a state and a company are human constructs. No state is able to achieve complete adherence to its laws, whether by economic or repressive sanctions. Businesses possess far fewer means of control over their personnel than does a state: Imprisonment or fining are not usually options. Yet economists believe that business entities are able to achieve virtually complete control over staff actions. Posner holds that a 'corporation has effective methods of preventing its employees from committing acts that impose huge liabilities on it'.[120] Page believes that 'actions of employees are fully attributable to the corporation' and argues that the way that this can be achieved is because major firms have compliance programmes that identify the sorts of practices to avoid.[121] But Page agrees[122] agency costs may prevent the firm from controlling its managers in some instances, most likely criminal price fixing conspiracies.[123]

---

[120] RA Posner, *Antitrust Law* (Chicago, University of Chicago Press, 2001) 271.

[121] WH Page, 'Optimal Antitrust Remedies: A Synthesis' in RD Blair and DD Sokol (eds), *The Oxford Handbook of International Antitrust Economics, Volume 1* (Oxford, Oxford University Press, 2012) ch 11; citing AB Lipsky, 'Managing Antitrust Compliance through the Continuing Surge in Global Enforcement' (2009) 75 *Antitrust Law Journal* 965–95.

[122] Page was responding (and objecting) to Crane (n 101).

[123] RH Lande and JP Davis, 'Benefits from Private Antitrust Enforcement: An Analysis of Forty Cases' (2008) 42 *University of San Francisco Law Review* 879–918.

Arlen and Kraakman argue that companies should not be strictly vicariously liable for the wrongdoing of their employees, since it gives rise to a perverse incentive for companies not to monitor their employees if it gives rise to sanctions on the company.[124] Instead, they argue that corporate criminal liability should be duty-based, so that they could avoid criminal liability if they engage in optimal policing (monitoring, self-reporting and cooperating), and they should face 'residual' civil liability designed to ensure that they adopt optimal prevention measures[125]—unless market forces ensure the firm internalises the social cost of employees' wrongs.[126]

Wils, noting that Arlen and Kraakman's starting assumption is that employees 'commit crimes to benefit themselves',[127] accepts that this would appear to be an adequate assumption for certain types of wrongdoing by employees, such as embezzlement or harassment, which are committed by employees solely for their own benefit, without any benefit for the company, so that there is a natural alignment of the interests of the government and the company to prevent such wrongdoing. But Wils argues that it is legitimate to sanction only firms in the case of antitrust infringements since companies are generally best placed to prevent antitrust infringements, and to do so in the most cost-effective way. He suggests that such a policy avoids perverse incentives, avoids unfairness, and that parent company liability is appropriate. He bases his argument on the assertions that antitrust infringements have the following characteristics.[128] First, antitrust infringements involve employees that have been given substantial authority by their company. The empirical evidence from the population of antitrust infringements that have been detected and prosecuted by antitrust authorities is that most infringements involve senior management.[129] He suggests that the 'rogue employee' explanation, a classic defence in cartel cases, clearly does not fit the many cases where the highest levels of the company are involved. Second, antitrust infringements are financially beneficial to the company. Third, employees are primarily motivated by what they perceive to be their company's interest and/or by the incentives the company has set

---

[124] J Arlen, 'The Potentially Perverse Effects of Corporate Criminal Liability' (1994) 23 *Journal of Legal Studies* 833, and J Arlen and R Kraakman, 'Controlling Corporate Misconduct: An Analysis of Corporate Liability Regimes' (1997) 72 *New York University Law Review* 687; see also S Oded, 'Inducing Corporate Compliance: A Compound Corporate Liability Regime' (2011) 31 *International Review of Law & Economics* 272; S Oded, *Corporate Compliance: New Approaches to Regulatory Enforcement* (Cheltenham, Edward Elgar, 2013).

[125] Arlen and Kraakman, ibid.

[126] Arlen (n 27).

[127] Arlen (n 124) 834.

[128] Wils (n 75).

[129] See M Berzins and F Sofo, 'The Inability of Compliance Strategies to Prevent Collusive Conduct' (2008) 8 *Corporate Governance* 669 at 675 (finding that senior management were involved in 80% of 69 publicly available cases from Australia, Canada, Denmark, the European Commission, Ireland, Japan, Korea, The Netherlands, New Zealand, the UK and the USA between 2000 and 2006); A Stephan, 'Hear no Evil, See no Evil: Why Antitrust Compliance Programmes may be Ineffective at Preventing Cartels', University of East Anglia CCP Working paper 09-09 (July 2009), 8–10 (listing the positions of individuals involved in 40 international cartels and named in decisions of the European Commission or press releases of the US Department of Justice between 1998 and 2008); JC Gallo, K Dau-Schmidt, JL Craycraft and CJ Parker, 'Department of Justice Antitrust Enforcement, 1955–1997: An Empirical Study' (2000) 17 *Review of Industrial Organization* 75 (69% of all individual criminal defendants in cases brought by the US Department of Justice Antitrust Division between 1955 and 1997 were corporate officers); WJ Kolasky (US Department of Justice) 'Antitrust Compliance Programs: The Government Perspective', Speech given to Corporate Compliance 2002 Conference, Practicing Law Institute, July 12, 2002, San Francisco; and JM Connor, *Global Price Fixing: Our Customers are the Enemy* (Vienna, Kluwer, 2001) 11–12.

for them.[130] Fourth, performance targets and incentives are imposed by firms and exert important effects on individual behaviour.

However, Wils has also previously argued that competition law must impose sanctions on individuals because the level of fines imposed on employers that is required effectively to deter anti-competitive conduct by their employees far exceeds the employers' ability to pay, and because an employer may not in reality be capable of adequately controlling the behaviour of its agents.[131]

Wils notes that there are many examples of cases in which antitrust infringements were committed in (flagrant) disregard of compliance programmes.[132] However, he suggests that leniency programmes are a much better way to incentivise companies to detect and report cartel behaviour engaged in by their employees than granting fine reductions or immunity to all companies that have a compliance programme. Both Page and Wils therefore argue that compliance systems are capable of discovering internal conspiracies involving employees, and imply that such means are capable of discovering virtually *all* such conspiracies. There is no evidence for this. It is true that large companies typically control compliance with much regulatory law through compliance systems, but there is no evidence that that technique is effective in relation to hidden conspiracies involving a small number of individuals. Stephan argues that a problem with compliance systems is that the support of these individuals is considered important to the effectiveness of a compliance programme. In order to avoid detection, they may either underfund compliance efforts altogether, or create a façade of compliance without any serious mechanisms for detecting or preventing cartel behaviour.[133] Yet this is all assumption without empirical support.

There is a marked antipathy within the Commission's sentencing Guidelines towards compliance systems, with the result that they are clearly not incentivised (unlike under almost all other sophisticated regulatory systems, even including the bribery regime). A 2011 UK survey found that although most large companies already use some voluntary compliance measures, '[v]oluntary competition compliance could be strengthened as

---

[130] See J Sonnenfeld and PR Lawrence, 'Why do Companies Succumb to Price Fixing?' (July–August 1978) *Harvard Business Review* 145; J Sonnenfeld, 'Executive Apologies for Price Fixing: Role Biased Perceptions of Causality' (1981) 24 *Academy of Management Journal* 192; WE Baker and RR Faulkner, 'The Social Organization of Conspiracy: Illegal Networks in the Heavy Electrical Equipment Industry' (1993) 58 *American Sociological Review* 837; JM Conley and WM O'Barr, 'Crime and Custom in Corporate Society: A Cultural Perspective on Corporate Misconduct' (1997) 60 *Law and Contemporary Problems* 5; C Parker, P Ainsworth and N Stepanenko, *ACCC Enforcement and Compliance Project: The Impact of ACCC Enforcement Activity in Cartel Cases* (Canberra, Australian National University, Centre for Competition and Consumer Policy, May 2004); Interview of B Allison by M O'Kane, 'Does Prison Work for Cartelists?—The View from Behind the Bars' (2011) 56 *Antitrust Bulletin* 483, 498; and Kolasky (n 129) at 14; see also C Parker, 'Criminal Cartel Sanctions and Compliance: The Gap between Rhetoric and Reality' in C Beaton-Wells and A Ezrachi, *Criminalising Cartels: Critical Studies of an International Regulatory Movement* (Oxford, Hart Publishing, 2011) 239; and Stucke (n 80).
[131] WJ Wils, 'Is Criminalisation of EU Competition Law the Answer?' in KJ Cseres, MP Schinkel and FOW Vogelaar (eds), *Criminalisation of Competition Law Enforcement: Economic and Legal Implications* (Cheltenham, Edward Elgar, 2006) 81.
[132] See Berzins and Sofo (n 129) 675–78; Parker, Ainsworth and Stepanenko (n 130) at 34, 35 and 60; and Kolasky (n 131); see also the case of Intel, whose antitrust compliance programme was once heralded in the Harvard Business Review to have prevented antitrust infringements, but later turned out not to have: DB Yoffie and M Kwak, 'Playing by the Rules: How Intel Avoids Antitrust Litigation' (2001) 79 *Harvard Business Review* 119 and C Roquilly, 'Intel, dix ans après: Le mythe de la compliance revisité?' *Concurrences* N° 2-2010, 50.
[133] Stephan (n 103).

overall 58 per cent of small companies surveyed and 37 per cent of large companies have no compliance measures in place'.[134]

In contrast, Crane argues that the entire concept of relying on private antitrust damages to deter is flawed because the prospect of damages will not deter managers within firms.[135] Ginsburg and Wright urge that fines alone will not provide sufficient deterrence and alternative sanctions such as imprisonment, which is costly, and debarment, which is not costly, should also be used in antitrust enforcement.[136] They argue that viewing 'the corporation' as an entity is fallacious, since shareholders cannot prevent price-fixing by employees, directors and officers have an incentive to increase corporate value, and no incentive to prevent price-fixing.[137] Shareholders may choose to pursue derivative actions against the senior managers responsible, on behalf of the firm.[138] However, as Stephan points out, there are a number of reasons why such actions are unlikely. 'First, there is little evidence of antitrust audits successfully uncovering secretive hardcore cartels. Knowledge of the infringement will normally surface years after it was instigated and even ceased, meaning that many of the managers responsible may have moved on or retired. Secondly, shareholders may have little incentive to pursue derivative actions. Directors' and officers' liability insurance does not cover intentional breaches of duty by management, meaning that the funds which might be recovered will be relatively minimal.'[139]

A further problem is with the alignment between the intentions of the firm and its 'agents'. The purpose of businesses in a capitalist market system is to make profits, and the economic purpose of employees is to make profit for themselves. The interests of both are frequently aligned by the use of bonuses and share incentives. But this does not mean that every business, or every employee, will make all decisions based exclusively on maximisation of economic benefits. One of the *consequences* of individual employees being involved in illegal activity during the course of their employment may be that either or both of them and their firms gain economically. But does this mean that the firm has approved of their actions, whether in advance or subsequently, or adopted them? How often do company Boards or official management decisions adopt or sanction breaking the law? Did the breach occur because of the negligence or recklessness of 'the firm', through having an aggressive policy on profits or because of a lack of effective internal compliance and detection systems? Will a firm be guilty if an employee kills an employee of a competitor firm, which has a consequence that the former's firm gains economically? At what point can individual agents' actions be taken to 'be' actions of the principal, or to give rise to a liability of the principal?

---

[134] *Competition Law Compliance Survey* (n 108) paras 1.26 and 1.38.

[135] Crane (n 101) 175–82.

[136] Ginsburg and Wright (n 73): they cite Werden and Simon (n 84); AM Polinsky and S Shavell, 'Should Employees Be Subject to Fines and Imprisonment Given the Existence of Corporate Liability?' (1993) 13 *International Review of Law & Economics* 239.

[137] Ginsburg and Wright (n 73).

[138] In the UK under Companies Act 2006, ss 260–69; F Wagner-von Papp, 'Suing the Suits: Derivative Shareholder Actions to bring home the Message of Antitrust', speaking at UCL/IMEDIPA Santorini Workshop, 28 May 2009.

[139] Stephan (n 103).

6

Empirical Evidence

I. Empirical Evidence on Individual Deterrence

A recent summary of the evidence on deterrence in relation to criminal activity concluded that the results of the general body of research, involving different methodologies, are 'fairly consistent':[1]

(a) The mere existence of criminal law and the criminal justice system has some effect on preventing crime.[2]

(b) Increases in the severity or certainty of punishment alone result in only modest, if any, increases in deterrence.[3]

(c) Studies show statistically significant correlation between *certainty* of punishment and crime rates.[4] The key issue is not the objective risk of being caught, but the *perception* by a person of the severity of the risk that he will be caught, exposed to others

---

[1] A Bottoms and A von Hirsch, 'The Crime-Preventive Impact of Penal Sanctions' in P Cane and HM Kritzer, *The Oxford Handbook of Empirical Legal Research* (Oxford, Oxford University Press, 2010) 104. See developing realisation of the significance of the evidence a decade earlier in A von Hirsch, AE Bottoms, E Burney and P-O Wikström, *Criminal Deterrence and Sentence Severity. An Analysis of Recent Research* (Oxford, Hart Publishing, 1999).

[2] PH Robinson and JM Darley, 'Does Criminal Law Deter? A Behavioral Science Investigation' (2004) 24 *Oxford Journal of Legal Studies* 173 (citing von Hirsch, Bottoms, Burney and Wikstrom (n 1); A Blumstein, J Cohen and D Nagin (eds), *Deterrence and Incapacitation* (Washington DC, The National Academy of Sciences Panel, 1978) 47.

[3] LS Beres and TD Griffith, 'Habitual Offender Statutes and Criminal Deterrence' (2001) 34 *Connecticut Law Review* 55, 59; see I Ehrlich, 'Crime, Punishment, and the Market for Offenses' (1996) 10 *Journal of Economic Perspectives* 43, 55–63 (surveying the research on the question); PW Greenwood et al, *Three Strikes and You're Out: Estimated Benefit and Cost of California's Mandatory New Sentencing Laws* (Los Angeles, RAND Corporation, 1994) 16 (surveying recent research supporting that increases in sentencing does not provide additional deterrence). But see D Kessler and SD Levitt, 'Using Sentence Enhancements to Distinguish Between Deterrence and Incapacitation' (1999) 42 *Journal of Law & Economics* 343 (discriminating between deterrent and incapacitation effect and finding deterrent effect to be significant).

[4] DP Farrington, PA Langan and P-O Wikström, 'Changes in Crime and Punishment in America, England and Sweden between the 1980s and 1990s' (1994) 3 *Studies in Crime and Crime Prevention* 104–31; D Nagin, 'Criminal Deterrence Research at the Outset of the Twenty-first Century' in M Tonry (ed), *Crime and Justice: A Review of Research* (Chicago, University of Chicago Press, 1998); PA Langan and DP Farrington, *Crime and Justice in the United States and England and Wales, 1981–96* (Washington DC, Bureau of Justice Statistics, 1998); PH Robinson and JM Darley, 'The Role of Deterrence in the Formulation of Criminal Law Rules: At Its Worst when Doing Its Best' (2003) 91 *Georgetown Law Journal* 949, 953–56; A Blumstein, 'Prisons' in JQ Wilson and J Petersilia (eds), *Crime* (San Francisco, Institute for Contemporary Studies Press, 1995) 387, 408–09; FH Easterbrook, 'Criminal Procedure as a Market System' (1983) 12 *Journal of Legal Studies* 289, 295 and fn 7.

and punished, although this may have only a relatively minor influence on people's behaviour.[5]

(d)   The major association studies,[6] and meta-analysis,[7] tend *not* to disclose statistically significant correlations between levels of *severity* of sanctions and crime rates. Studies from the 1950s and 1960s had showed, first, that US States with and without the death penalty, that appeared otherwise comparable, had similar homicide rates and, second, that in both the USA and Europe, those jurisdictions that had abolished the death penalty showed no unusual increases in homicide rates.[8] So discouraging has the accumulated evidence now become that some experts have concluded that 'the null hypothesis' should be accepted, namely that variations in the severity of punishment have no effect on crime rates.[9] However, an effect might occur in certain conditions.[10] A sanction at the level of contract or tort compensatory damages is likely to be inadequate, whereas there is some evidence that punitive penalties have an effect.[11]

(e)   Deterrence decays over time.[12] This effect suggests a need to reverse the decay with continued high levels of education and visible enforcement.

Hence, social control strategies based exclusively on a rational choice and deterrence model of human behaviour have had at best limited success,[13] and leading criminologists stress the 'importance of linking the deterrence (or rational choice) perspective with theories that rely on other types of control mechanisms' in society (especially normative attachments).[14] Further, studies have found that 'Variables indicating the threat of non-legal sanctions were among the most robust of the deterrence theory predictors'.[15] In other words, the

---

[5] R MacCoun, 'Drugs and the Law: A Psychological Analysis of Drug Prohibition' (1993) 113 *Psychological Bulletin* 497–512; PH Robinson and J Darley, *Justice, Liability and Blame* (Colorado, Westview, 1995); PH Robinson and J Darley, 'The Utility of Desert' (1997) 91 *Northwestern University Law Review* 453–99; HL Ross, *Deterring the Drinking Driver* (Lexington MA, Lexington Books, 1982); Nagin (n 4).

[6] Farrington, Langan and Wikström (n 4); Nagin (n 4).

[7] TC Pratt, FT Cullen, KR Blevins, LE Daigle and TD Madensen, 'The Empirical Status of Deterrence Theory: a Meta-analysis' in FT Cullen, JP Wright and KR Blevins (eds), *Taking Stock: The Status of Criminological Theory* (New Brunswick NJ, Transaction Publishers, 2006).

[8] Quoted in von Hirsch, Bottoms, Burney and Wikström (n 1) 11.

[9] AN Doob and C Webster, 'Sentence Severity and Crime: Accepting the Null Hypothesis' (2003) 30 *Crime and Justice: A Review of Research* 143–95.

[10] Robinson and Darley (n 2); C Engel, 'Deterrence by Imperfect Sanctions: A Public Good Experiment' (2013) *MPI Collective Goods Preprint*, 2013/9 (finding that imperfectly deterrent sanctions may affect the behaviour of individuals who hold social preferences such as concern for the victim's loss).

[11] T Eisenberg and C Engel, 'Assuring Adequate Deterrence in Tort: A Public Good Experiment' (2014) 11(2) *Journal of Empirical Legal Studies* 301–49.

[12] J Henstridge, R Homel and P Mackay, *The Long-Term Effects of Random Breath Testing in Four Australian States: A Time-Series Analysis* (Canberra, Commonwealth Department of Transport and Regional Development, 1997).

[13] See generally T Brooks (ed), *Deterrence* (Farnham, Ashgate, 2014) (debates continue over whether it is even possible); DS Nagin, 'Criminal Deterrence Research at the Outset of the Twentieth Century' (1998) 23 *Crime and Justice* 1 (review of the literature); M Tonry, 'Learning from the Limitations of Deterrence Research' (2008) 37 *Crime & Justice* 279 (discussing the divergent results of empirical studies on the effect of sanctions on criminal behaviour).

[14] Pratt, Cullen, Blevins, Daigle and Madensen (n 7) 385. See further P-O Wikström, 'Deterrence and Deterrent Experiences: Preventing Crime Through the Threat of Punishment' in SG Shoham, O Beck and M Kett (eds), *International Handbook of Penology and Criminal Justice* (Boca Ration FL, CRC Press, 2008); M Tonry, 'Learning from the Limitations of Deterrence Research' (2009) 37 *Crime and Justice: A Review of Research* 279–311.

[15] Pratt, Cullen, Blevins, Daigle and Madensen (n 7) 385.

imposition of sanctions by the state may not be the most effective means of influencing future behaviour, if other less formal influences are available.

A significant blow to the rational cost calculation concept is dealt by the finding that individuals can be induced to change their behaviour in many cases even when no economic incentives are present.[16] Interventions such as feedback, peer education and social marketing campaigns have successfully reduced energy use among office employees, dormitory residents and individuals living on military bases, when they were not financially responsible for their energy consumption.[17] Other interventions, such as time-of-use information about usage and costs, have reduced energy use without changes in price.[18]

Empirical evidence from examination of rehabilitation of young offenders (borstal) found no appreciable effects on recidivism.[19] Some rehabilitative programmes work, and reduce recidivism by 10 to 20 per cent, where two conditions are fulfilled: (i) There is 'substantial, meaningful contact between the treatment personnel and the participant'; and (ii) the programmes focus on 'developing skills and use behavioural (including cognitive–behavioural) methods.[20] Bottoms and von Hirsch consider that desistance from further offending by those who have committed crimes, where it occurs, seems largely to be accomplished by the probationers themselves through their motivation, and from changes in the nature of the social context in which they live.[21] They note a surprising lack of research evaluating the effectiveness of special deterrence, fines and specially designed penalties, aimed at inducing convicted offenders to desist through 'shock treatments'.[22] Success in affecting the future behaviour of individuals can be influenced by the personal skill of an individual enforcement officer, rather than be a function of the sanction imposed and the theory underlying its imposition. 'Although deference to legal authorities is the norm, disobedience occurs with sufficient frequency that skill in handling the rebellious, the disgruntled, and the hard to manage—or those potentially so—has become the street officer's performance litmus test.'[23] Further, social, environmental and cultural factors can

[16] The following examples are noted by MP Vandenbergh, AR Carrico and LS Bressman, 'Regulation in the Behavioral Era' (2011) 95 *Minnesota Law Review* 715–81.

[17] JE Petersen et al, 'Dormitory Residents Reduce Electricity Consumption When Exposed to Real-Time Visual Feedback and Incentives' (2007) 8 *International J Sustainability Higher Education* 16, 29; AH McMakin et al, 'Motivating Residents to Conserve Energy Without Financial Incentives' (2002) 34 *Environmental Behaviour* 848, 856.

[18] See review in W Abrahamse et al, 'A Review of Intervention Studies Aimed at Household Energy Conservation' (2005) 25 *Journal of Environmental Psychology* 273, 278–79 (reductions in home energy use within a range of 5 to 15%).

[19] R Martinson, 'What Works? Questions and Answers About Prison Reform' (1974) 35 *The Public Interest* 22–54; D Lipton, R Martinson and J Wilks, *The Effectiveness of Correctional Treatment* (New York, Praeger, 1975); L Sechrest, LO White and ED Brown (eds), *The Rehabilitation of Criminal Offenders: Problems and Prospects* (Washington DC, National Academy of Sciences, 1979); SR Brody, *The Effectiveness of Sentencing*, Home Office Research Study No 35 (London, HMSO, 1976).

[20] LW Sherman, DP Farrington, BC Welsh and DL MacKenzie, *Evidence-Based Crime Prevention* (Abingdon, Routledge, 2006).

[21] S Farrall, *Rethinking What Works With Offenders: Probation, Social Context and Desistance From Crime* (Cullompton, Willan Publishing, 2002) 175. This conclusion has led to supporting attempt at self-help and identifying 'hooks for change'.

[22] Bottoms and von Hirsch (n 1).

[23] TR Tyler, 'Psychology and the Law' in *The Oxford Handbook of Law & Politics* (Oxford, Oxford University Press, 2008); SD Mastrofski, JB Snipes and AE Supina, 'Compliance on Demand: The Public's Responses to Specific Police Requests' (1996) 33 *Journal of Crime and Delinquency* 269–301, 272.

all affect success in future compliance: 'Many decades of research have demonstrated that community factors are powerful determinants of levels of crime.'[24] How a person responds to regulation appears to be influenced by personality traits and characteristics.[25]

In direct contradiction to the assumptions of the rational calculator theory, Anderson's interviews with 278 male US prisoners found that about 76 per cent of active criminals and 89 per cent of the most violent criminals either perceive no risk of arrest or give no thought to their possible punishment.[26]

Tyler considers that deterrence works reasonably well in relation to murder in the United States, where significant resource has been devoted and the objective risk of being caught and punished for murder is approximately 45 per cent.[27] Similarly, the USA altered its incarceration practices, increasing the prison population sevenfold, from 200,000 in 1973 to 2 million (7 per cent of the population) in 2000, a rate that is the highest prison population in the world,[28] far surpassing Europe,[29] but declined to 1.6 million in 2011.[30]

II. Empirical Evidence on Corporate Regulatory Deterrence

The empirical evidence of the existence of an effect of general deterrence is at best mixed. Some studies have found that 'deterrence, for all its faults, may impact more extensively on risk management and compliance activity' than applying remedial strategies after the event.[31] Perceptions of the certainty and severity of punishments for violations were found to have virtually no correlation with nursing homes' regulatory compliance rates in most cases.[32] Gunningham, Kagan and Thornton found that mega-penalties tend to penetrate corporate consciousness in a way that other penalties do not.[33] Yeung considered that

---

[24] W Skogan, 'Crime and Criminals' in P Cane and HM Kritzer, *The Oxford Handbook of Empirical Legal Research* (Oxford, Oxford University Press, 2010).

[25] G Pogarsky, 'Identifying "Deterrable" Offenders: Implications for Research on Deterrence' (2002) 19 *Justice Quarterly* 431–52.

[26] DA Anderson, 'The Deterrence Hypothesis and Picking Pockets at the Pickpocket's Hanging' (2002) 4(2) *American Law and Economics Review* 295.

[27] Robinson and Darley (n 5) 453–99.

[28] United States Department of Justice 2001 (approximately seven million Americans are either in prison, on probation or on parole, and nearly 60 million (almost 30% of the US adult population) have a criminal record; the costs of this punishment have increased 660% from $9 billion in 1982 to $69 billion in 2006); SN Durlauf and DS Nagin, 'Imprisonment and Crime: Can Both Be Reduced?' (2011) 10 *Criminology and Public Policy* 13; C Haney and P Zimbardo, 'The Past and Future of US Prison Policy: Twenty-five Years after the Stanford Prison Experiment' (1998) 53 *American Psychologist* 709–27; TR Clear, 'The Effects of High Imprisonment Rates on Communities' (2009) 37 *Crime and Justice: A Review of Research* 459–80.

[29] D Garland, *The Culture of Control* (Oxford, Clarendon Press, 2001).

[30] US Bureau of Justice Statistics, 2011, at http://bjs.gov/.

[31] R Baldwin, 'The New Punitive Regulation' (2004) 67 *Modern Law Review* 351–83, 373.

[32] J Braithwaite and T Makkai, 'Testing an Expected Utility Model of Corporate Deviance' (1991) 25 *Law and Society Review* 7–40, 35

[33] N Gunningham, R Kagan and D Thornton, *Shades of Green: Business, Regulation and Environment* (California, Stanford University Press, 2005).

criminal empirical studies have failed to provide reliable findings about the relative deterrent effects of various types and levels of penalty for various offences.[34]

Studies reveal that the profit-maximisation motive as a driver of corporate behaviour is not always present.[35] For example, in anti-competitive acts, only some (price fixing and monopoly, illegal tying and downstream pressures on suppliers) were linked to economic strain. Other types were associated with economic munificence (patent, warranty and advertising), and some defied economic modelling.[36] Longitudinal antitrust studies have found legal sanctions had only modest specific deterrent effects on recidivism.[37] Simpson and Rorie comment that one interpretation is that the objective risk of discovery and sanction in those studies was quite low.[38]

Gunningham, Kagan and Thornton found that hearing about legal sanctions against other firms in the mining sector prompted many of them to review, and often to take further action to strengthen, their own firm's compliance programme.[39] Thus, publicity about prosecution may have a general deterrent effect, especially in strongly regulated industries. Gunningham suggests that the spread of regulation and extensive publicity of prosecutions against reputation-sensitive companies has diminished the deterrent impact of tough enforcement.[40]

In relation to specific deterrence, Gunningham considers[41] that the evidence of a link between past penalty and improved future performance is stronger than it is for general deterrence, and suggests that a legal penalty against a company in the past influences the future level of compliance.[42] He relied on the finding by Baldwin and Anderson that 71 per cent of companies that had experienced a punitive sanction reported that 'such sanctioning had impacted very strongly on their approach to regulatory risks ... For many companies the imposition of a first sanction produced a sea change in attitudes.'[43] However, Gunningham noted that the literature also suggests that action falling short of prosecution (for example, inspection, followed by the issue of administrative notices or administrative penalties) can also achieve a 're-shuffling of managerial priorities'[44] even when those

[34] K Yeung, *Securing Compliance. A Principled Approach* (Oxford, Hart Publishing, 2004), quoting: A Ashworth, *Sentencing and Criminal Justice* (London, George Weidenfeld and Nicholson, 2000) 60–61; D Beyleveld, 'Deterrence Research as a Basis for Deterrence Policies' (1979) 18 *Howard Journal of Criminal Justice* 135; Bottoms, Burney, von Hirsch and Wikstrom (n 1) (capable of having deterrent effects).

[35] 'Studies are fairly inconsistent regarding economic characteristics and noncompliance' and 'The inhibitory value of formal legal sanctions is far weaker than we might expect': SS Simpson and M Rorie, 'Motivating Compliance: Economic and Material Motives for Compliance' in C Parker and VL Nielsen (eds), *Explaining Compliance. Business Responses to Regulation* (Cheltenham, Edward Elgar, 2012).

[36] SS Simpson, 'The Decomposition of Antitrust: Testing a Multi-level, Longitudinal Model of Profit-squeeze' (1986) 51 *American Sociological Review* 859–75.

[37] SS Simpson and C Koper, 'Deterring Corporate Crime' (1992) 30 *Criminology* 347–76.

[38] Simpson and Rorie (n 35).

[39] Gunningham, Kagan and Thornton (n 33).

[40] N Gunningham, 'Enforcement and Compliance Strategies' in M Cave, R Baldwin, M Lodge (eds), *The Oxford Handbook of Regulation* (Oxford, Oxford University Press, 2010).

[41] Gunningham, ibid.

[42] S Simpson, *Corporate Crime and Social Control* (Cambridge, Cambridge University Press, 2002).

[43] R Baldwin and J Anderson, *Rethinking Regulatory Risk* (London, DLA/LSE, 2002) 10.

[44] J Baggs, B Silverstein and M Foley, 'Workplace Health and Safety Regulations: Impact of Enforcement and Consultation on Workers' Compensation Claims Rates in Washington State' (2003) 43 *American Journal of Industrial Medicine* 483–94, 491.

penalties are insufficient as to justify action in pure cost–benefit terms.[45] However, routine inspections without any form of enforcement apparently have no beneficial impact.[46] Gunningham's conclusion is that 'the impact of deterrence is significant but uneven and that unless it is used widely and well, it may have negative consequences as well as positive ones.'[47]

Some consider that certain organisations are *predisposed* to break rules, and can be 'distinguished by structural, cultural, or procedural characteristics that increase the odds that their personnel will recognize and exploit lure [the attractions and opportunities for crime]'[48] That perspective leads to viewing certain companies as having a culture that is more or less 'moral'. Some studies report that price fixing tends to be viewed as standard operating procedure and is rarely seen as criminal.[49]

However, a different view would be that it is the culture of the individuals in the given organisation whose culture and behaviour is the cause of the problem rather than the culture of 'the firm'. The existence of predisposing factors within a particular firm would be a predictor but not a cause that could justify punishment of 'the company'. Certainly, the motivations of individual managers have been noted as relevant by some research. Managers have been noted to be more willing to break the law when they perceive individual 'career' benefits.[50] Equally, a strong inhibitory effect of morality on non-compliance has consistently been seen across studies, and not a classic cost–benefit calculus, although the threat of formal sanctions increased the perceived immorality of the behaviour.[51] Perceptions of the immorality of an action strongly inhibit manager intentions to offend.[52]

Whilst it is argued that since no one system of behaviour-control is satisfactory, and hence a pluralist approach should be adopted, problems of injustice and over-deterrence arise as a result of a lack of coordination between different sanctions. For example, a firm might suffer a criminal penalty, civil liabilities and reputational damage. There is little attempt to coordinate these sanctions, and to ensure that their combined impact is proportionate, just and effective.

Research has shown that corporations convicted of US federal crimes in 2006–2008 were fined in the range from $5.7 to $17.3 million, and faced significant additional civil sanctions

---

[45] WB Gray and JT Scholz, 'Does Regulatory Enforcement Work: A Panel Analysis of OSHA Enforcement Examining Regulatory Impact' (1993) 27 *Law and Society Review* 177–213.

[46] S Shapiro and R Rabinowitz, 'Punishment versus Cooperation in Regulatory Enforcement: A Case Study of OSHA' (1997) 14 *Administrative Law Review* 713–62, 713.

[47] Gunningham (n 40).

[48] N Shover and A Hochstetler, *Choosing White-Collar Crime* (New York, Cambridge University Press, 2006) 51.

[49] G Geis, 'The Heavy Electrical Equipment Antitrust Cases of 1961' in G Geis and R Meier (eds), *White-collar Crime: Offenses in Business, Politics, and the Professions* (New York, Free Press, 1977) 117–32; SS Simpson and N Leeper Piquero, 'The Archer Daniels Midland Antitrust Case of 1996: A Case Study' in H Pontell and D Shichor (eds), *Contemporary Issues in Crime and Criminal Justice: Essays in Honour of Gilbert Geis* (New Jersey, Prentice Hall, 2001) 175–94.

[50] SS Simpson and N Leeper Piquero, 'Low Self-control, Organizational Theory and Corporate Crime' (2002) 36 *Law & Society Review* 509–48; SS Simpson, C Gibbs, L Slocum, M Rorie, M Cohen and M Vandenbergh, 'An Empirical Assessment of Corporate Environmental Crime-Control Strategies' (2013) 103(1) *Journal of Criminal Law and Criminology* 231.

[51] Simpson and Rorie (n 35).

[52] R Paternoster and SS Simpson, 'Sanction Threats and Appeals to Morality: Testing a Rational Choice Model of Corporate Crime' (1996) 30 *Law & Society Review* 549–84; Simpson and Leeper Piquero (n 50); SS Simpson, J Garner and C Gibbs, *Why do Corporations Obey Environmental Law? Assessing Punitive and Cooperative Strategies of Corporate Crime Control*, National Criminal Justice Reference Service Report (2007) 2001-IJ-CX-0020.

in which the civil element exceeded the criminal fine by more than $30 million in 1996 dollars.[53] The stock price of convicted firms falls as a result of the market's anticipation that it will earn less revenue, have higher costs, and/or face a market that does not give full weight to any positive financial information.[54] However, whilst corporate market value declines sharply where fraud is alleged, and the decline exceeds the sanctions imposed and the loss of criminal profits,[55] firms do not suffer a market sanction when they are either sanctioned for regulatory violations involving non- contracting third parties[56] or convicted of an environmental violation.[57] Any analysis that does not incorporate these sanctions into the expected government-imposed penalty will obtain an artificially high measure of the reputational penalty.[58]

III. Studies on Liability Deterrence

There are significant challenges in undertaking empirical studies on whether, and the extent to which, law in general, or specific types of law (criminal, private, tort, etc) or features (differing types of severity or incidence of penalties, or caps on liability or many other features) might have an effect on future behaviour. However, it remains true that there is no single comprehensive study that looks broadly at the deterrent effect of tort law.[59] Instead, we have to draw conclusions from two types of research studies: Those that look at individual facts, and the few that attempt to take an overview of other studies. The most important are summarised below, starting with the large meta studies from around two decades ago, followed by the more significant of the recent individual studies.

Before proceeding, we can note a recent behavioural science study that found that although the threat of potential criminal sanctions on individuals had a large and statistically significant effect on subjects' stated willingness to engage in risky behaviour, the threat of potential tort liability did not.[60] This supports the 'incremental theory' above,

---

[53] C Alexander, J Arlen and MA Cohen, 'Regulating Corporate Criminal Sanctions: Federal Guidelines and the Sentencing of Public Firms' (1999) 42 *Journal of Law and Economics* 393, 410; J Arlen, 'Corporate Criminal Liability: Theory and Evidence' in A Harel and KN Hylton (eds), *Research Handbook on the Economics of Criminal Law* (Cheltenham, Edward Elgar, 2012).

[54] JM Karpoff and JR Lott, Jr, 'The Reputational Penalty Firms Bear from Committing Fraud' (1993) 36 *Journal of Law and Economics* 757.

[55] Karpoff and Lott, Jr, ibid; see JM Karpoff, DS Lee and GS Martin, 'Cost to Firms of Cooking the Books' (2008) 43 *Journal of Financial and Quantitative Analysis* 581.

[56] Karpoff and Lott, Jr, ibid.

[57] JM Karpoff, JR Lott, Jr and E Wehrly, 'The Reputational Penalties for Environmental Violations: Empirical Evidence' (2005) 68 *Journal of Law and Economics* 653.

[58] CR Alexander, 'On the Nature of the Reputational Penalty for Corporate Crime: Evidence' (1999) 42 *Journal of Law and Economics* 489.

[59] See MM Mello and TA Brennan, 'Deterrence of Medical Errors: Theory and Evidence for Malpractice Reform' (2002) 80 *Texas Law Review* 1595 at 1604 stating that 'empirical evidence of deterrence is indeed difficult to come by'.

[60] WJ Cardi, RD Penfield and AH Yoon, 'Does Tort Law Deter Individuals? A Behavioural Science Study' (2012) 9 *Journal of Empirical Legal Studies* 567. The study surveyed over 700 first-year US law students, presenting a series of vignettes, and asked subjects to rate the likelihood that they would engage in a variety of potentially tortious behaviours under different legal conditions. Students were randomly assigned one of four surveys, which differed only in the legal rules applicable to the vignettes.

while suggesting that there may be a threshold effect, and that tort liability deterrence might fall below the scale of effectiveness.

A. Meta Studies

Three studies are noted here. Schwartz undertook a 1994 survey of the evidence of deterrence in the areas of workers' compensation, no-fault automobile laws, medical malpractice, products liability, nonprofit and governmental agency liability, landowner liability, and New Zealand's replacement of its tort system with a national accident compensation fund.[61] He concluded that although tort law does not result in 'strong deterrence'—that is, tort law does not deter economically inefficient tortious behaviour comprehensively and systematically—there was some evidence that it serves as a 'weak' deterrent—that it deters in some situations.[62] The evidence underlying Schwartz's conclusions was not primarily quantitative, however, but largely anecdotal.[63]

Dewees, Duff and Trebilcock made a comprehensive overview of quantitative data from the United States and Canada on automobile, medical, product, environmental and workplace injuries, published in 1996.[64] They concluded that the common law torts system may have some deterrent effect, but it varies depending on context, and the effect is not sufficient to overcome the many significant defects in the tort system.[65] In relation to medical accidents, it was 'impossible to reach firm conclusions regarding the medical malpractice system as a mechanism for deterring accidents'.[66] A similar conclusion applied in relation to work accidents.[67] In relation to road accidents, the authors compared the data from tort-based systems and non-tort, first-party insurance systems, and concluded on the basis of the available evidence that both systems would have similar deterrent effects provided they contain similar incentives to take care in the form of risk-related insurance premiums.[68]

They found that the tort liability system is not achieving its goals at a reasonable cost, has expanded far beyond the areas in which it is cost effective, and should be substantially contracted and supplemented by administered compensation systems:

> [T]he empirical evidence has convinced us that a single instrument, the tort system, cannot successfully achieve all … of the major goals claimed for it, and attempting to use it in pursuit of objectives for which it is not well suited is both costly and damaging to its ability to perform well with respect to other goals that it is better able to realize.[69]

---

[61] GT Schwartz, 'Reality in the Economic Analysis of Tort Law: Does Tort Law Really Deter?' (1994) 42 *UCLA Law Review* 377, 381–87 (describing a number of realistic objections), at 377.

[62] ibid, 379.

[63] Mello and Brennan (n 59) 1604.

[64] DN Dewees, D Duff and M Trebilcock, *Exploring the Domain of Accident Law: Taking the Facts Seriously* (Oxford, Oxford University Press, 1996).

[65] ibid at 413; see also D Dewees and M Trebilcock, 'The Efficacy of the Tort System and its Alternatives: A Review of Empirical Evidence' (1992) 30 *Osgoode Hall Law Journal* 57, 131–34 (finding mixed evidence of deterrence after reviewing studies in automobile safety, malpractice, product liability, workplace injuries and environmental harm).

[66] Dewees, Duff and Trebilcock (n 64) 112.

[67] ibid, 355.

[68] ibid, 416.

[69] ibid, 412.

They endorsed no-fault compensation systems and proposed extensions of them, preserving tort to a residual role in cases of egregious behaviour causing serious harm.

Smith's 2005 study compared the data on motor vehicle and non-motor vehicle fatality rates reported from 113 countries to the World Health Organization's mortality database over a period of 50 years, on the basis that such events were causes whose likelihood of occurrence was affected by the degree of care.[70] He found that motor vehicle accident fatality rates in countries whose legal systems are based on English common law have fallen below those in civil law countries, especially French and Socialist civil code systems, and also German code jurisdictions. Motor vehicle accident rates do not differ significantly between common law and Scandinavian systems. Fatality rates for accidents other than motor vehicles were lowest (and had fallen faster) in common law countries, followed by French, German and then Scandinavian civil code countries, with the highest fatality rates occurring in former members of the Soviet Union and Eastern Bloc countries. Various major problems arise with this study, not least reliance on gross fatalities and variations in private liability law as measures of deterrence, variations in driving culture and circumstances, and criminal law (Germany has no upper speed limit). It should be noted that Scandinavian countries have long relied on no fault insurance compensation schemes.

B. Individual Studies

Studies often provide only indirect evidence on whether the general threat of tort liability deters risky conduct. Moore and Viscusi's celebrated study of the creation of workers' compensation systems, and the consequential imposition of premiums on all employers, found a decrease in worker fatality rates.[71] However, although this says something about compensation schemes compared with tort law, it says little about any underlying level of deterrence by tort law. Viscusi found no clear correlation or pattern between punitive damages and deterrence of risky behaviour.[72] Looking at jury verdicts in automobile accident cases, White found that drivers take less care in states that have comparative fault rules than in states employing contributory negligence.[73] Sloan et al found that both requiring drivers to purchase third-party insurance and higher alcohol prices discouraged binge drinking, whilst switching from contributory to comparative negligence increased it, and generally neither tort nor non-tort deterrents affected the fraction of bingeing episodes after which the individual drove.[74] Comparing various tort reform changes in different states between 1981 and 2000, Rubin and Shepherd found that various reforms (caps on non-economic damages, a higher evidence standard for punitive damages, product liability reform, and

[70] ML Smith, 'Deterrence and Origin of Legal System: Evidence from 1950–1999' (2005) 7 *American Law & Economics Review* 350.

[71] MJ Moore and WK Viscusi, *Compensation Mechanisms for Job Risks. Wages, Workers' Compensation, and Product Liability* (Princeton, Princeton University Press, 1990); see also JR Chelius, 'Liability for Industrial Accidents: A Comparison of Negligence and Strict Liability Systems' (1976) 5 *Journal of Legal Studies* 293, 303–06.

[72] WK Viscusi, 'The Social Costs of Punitive Damages Against Corporations in Environmental and Safety Torts' (1998) 87 *Georgetown Law Journal* 285, 296–98.

[73] MJ White, 'An Empirical Test of the Comparative and Contributory Negligence Rules in Accident Law' (1989) 20 *RAND Journal of Economics* 308.

[74] FA Sloan, BA Reilly and C Schenzler, 'Effects of Tort Liability and Insurance on Heavy Drinking and Drinking and Driving' (1995) 38 *Journal of Law & Economics* 49.

prejudgment interest reform) were associated with fewer non-motor vehicle accidental deaths, while reform of the collateral source rule (which bars evidence that the plaintiff has already been compensated by other sources) was associated with an increase in deaths.[75] On the other hand, in a separate study Shepherd found that some tort reforms in the medical malpractice area (caps on total damages and collateral source rules) were associated with increases in death rates, while others were not.[76]

More relevant are the studies that compare liability with non-liability. A number of studies have found that imposition of liability on commercial servers of alcoholic beverages consistently reduces fatalities from alcohol-related motor vehicle accidents.[77] Comparisons of states that rely on tort liability litigation as against states that have no-fault automobile compensation systems, which bar negligence suits for automobile accidents, has produced mixed results: Some studies finding a greater increase of fatalities,[78] and some not.[79]

C. Medical Malpractice

The United States has experienced three 'medical malpractice crises', triggered by spikes in liability insurance premiums in the mid-1970s, mid-1980s and around 2000.[80] There has been widespread tort reform aimed at restricting liability and limiting insurance costs, although it has been argued that each 'crisis' in liability insurance pricing was a by-product of insurance cycles.[81] At the same time, there has been a long-term decline in the volume of medical malpractice litigation.[82]

---

[75] PH Rubin and JM Shepherd, 'Tort Reform and Accidental Deaths' (2007) 50 *Journal of Law & Economics* 221. Overall, the tort reforms led to an estimated 14,222 fewer accidental deaths.

[76] J Shepherd, 'Tort Reforms' Winners and Losers: The Competing Effects of Care and Activity Levels' (2008) 55 *UCLA Law Review* 905; see also AH Yoon, 'Damage Caps and Civil Litigation: An Empirical Study of Medical Malpractice Litigation in the South' (2001) 3 *American Law & Economics Review* 199, 221–23 (finding that the enactment of damage caps reduced the average damage awards in medical malpractice litigation, while its later nullification increased the awards).

[77] FA Sloan, EM Stout, K Whetten-Goldstein and L Liang, *Drinkers, Drivers, and Bartenders: Balancing Private Choices and Public Accountability* (Chicago, University of Chicago Press, 2000).

[78] A Cohen and R Dehejia, 'The Effect of Automobile Insurance and Accident Liability Laws on Traffic Fatalities' (2004) 47 *Journal of Law & Economics* 357, 382 (an increase in fatalities of approximately 10% with the adoption of no-fault rules); JD Cummins, RD Phillips and MA Weiss, 'The Incentive Effects of No-Fault Automobile Insurance' (2001) 44 *Journal of Law and Economics* 427 (a significant positive association between no-fault and increased fatalities); ME Landes, 'Insurance Liability and Accidents: A Theoretical and Empirical Investigation of the Effect of No-Fault Accidents' (1982) 25 *Journal of Law & Economics* 49, 50 (an increase in fatalities); FA Sloan et al, 'Tort Liability Versus Other Approaches for Deterring Careless Driving' (1994) 14 *International Review of Law & Economics* 53, 66–67 (an 18% increase in fatalities with the adoption of no-fault rules).

[79] AR Derrig et al, 'The Effect of Population Safety Belt Usage Rates on Motor Vehicle-Related Fatalities' (2002) 34 *Accidents Analysis & Prevention* 101 (no significant effect); P Zador and A Lund, 'Re-analysis of the Effects of No-Fault Auto Insurance on Fatal Crashes' (1986) 53 *Journal of Risk & Insurance* 226, 235 (a decrease in fatalities with the adoption of no-fault rules); SP Kochanowski and MV Young, 'Deterrents Aspects of No-Fault Automobile Insurance: Some Empirical Findings' (1985) 52 *Journal of Risk & Insurance* 269 (finding no significant effect).

[80] Annual medical liability system costs are estimated to be $55.6 billion in 2008 dollars, or 2.4% of total health-care spending: M Mello, A Chandra, AA Gawande and DM Studdert, 'National Costs of the Medical Liability System' (2010) 29(9) *Health Affairs* 1569.

[81] F Sloan and L Chepke, *Medical Malpractice* (Cambridge MA, The MIT Press, 2008). Arguing that trends in premiums 'have been more moderate than much of the rhetoric asserts', rising from 0.91% of US healthcare spending in 1975 to 1.58% in 2002 [58–59].

[82] DA Hyman and C Silver, 'Double, Double, Toil and Trouble: Justice-Talk and the Future of Medical Malpractice Litigation' (2014) 63 *DePaul Law Review* 547.

Sloan and Chepke concluded that there is no statistical association between the sophistication of physicians' practices and the frequency of lawsuits against them.[83] They concluded: 'There is no convincing empirical evidence to indicate that the threat of a medical malpractice claim makes health care providers more careful. This lack of empirical support represents a serious indictment of medical malpractice as it currently exists.'[84] In 2002, Mello and Brennan, reviewing the literature in this area, had found only 'thin' evidence that medical malpractice liability deters malpractice.[85]

Kessler and McClellan examined the effect of tort reforms that directly reduce expected malpractice awards, such as caps on non-economic damages, on Medicare hospital spending for acute myocardial infarction and ischaemic heart disease from 1984 to 1990. The reforms lowered hospital spending by 5.3 per cent for myocardial infarction and 9.0 per cent for heart disease.[86] In subsequent work examining data through 1994, Kessler and McClellan found that such direct reforms reduced hospital spending by 8.3 per cent, but this estimate was based only on myocardial infarction.[87] In a further analysis incorporating information about levels of managed care through 1994, they estimated that direct reforms reduced hospital spending by 3.8 per cent for myocardial infarction and 7.1 per cent for heart disease.[88] These studies showed no difference in mortality rates between those groups of states that had and had not introduced tort reforms, suggesting that liability-restrictive reform reduced defensive medicine (in this case, diagnostic and therapeutic procedures in excess of what is called for solely by professional judgement) without harm to patients.[89]

Reviewing data from the 1979 to 2005 National Hospital Discharge Surveys and an extensive set of variations in various tort rules, Frakes found a small and statistically insignificant relationship between malpractice forces and avoidable hospitalisation rates (reflective of outpatient quality) and inpatient mortality rates for selected medical conditions.[90]

Paik, Black and Hyman found that the per-physician rate of paid medical malpractice claims has been dropping for 20 years, irrespective of whether states had a liability cap or not, and in 2012 was less than half the 1992 level.[91] Lawsuit rates, in the states with available

[83] Sloan and Chepke (n 81).

[84] ibid, 80–81.

[85] See Mello and Brennan (n 59) 1598.

[86] D Kessler and M McClellan, 'Do Doctors Practice Defensive Medicine?' (1996) 111(2) *Quarterly Journal of Economics* 353; D Kessler and M McClellan, 'The Effects of Malpractice Pressure and Liability Reforms on Physicians' Perceptions of Medical Care' (1997) 60 *Law & Contemporary Problems* 81.

[87] D Kessler and M McClellan, 'How Liability Law Affects Medical Productivity' (2002) 21(6) *Journal of Health Economy* 931.

[88] D Kessler and M McClellan, 'Malpractice Law and Health Care Reform: Optimal Liability Policy in an Era of Managed Care' (2002) 84(6) *Journal of Health Economy* 175.

[89] Sloane and Chepke (n 81) 77, suggest that the context of an argued reduction in the cost of care by 5 to 9% is that 'real spending on personal health services increases by about this much in a two-to-three-year period. These reforms are not a panacea for reducing the growth in [health care] expenditures.'

[90] M Frakes, 'Does Medical Malpractice Deter?' The Impact of Tort Reforms and Malpractice Standard Reforms on Healthcare Quality' *Cornell Legal Studies Research Paper No 12-29*. 'At most, the evidence implies an arguably modest degree of malpractice-induced deterrence. For instance, at one end of the 95% confidence interval, the lack of a non-economic damages cap (indicative of higher malpractice pressure) is associated with only a 4% decrease in avoidable hospitalizations.'

[91] M Paik, BS Black and DA Hyman, 'The Receding Tide of Medical Malpractice Litigation: Part 1—National Trends' (2013) 10 (4) *Journal of Empirical Legal Studies* 612. 'Small' paid claims (payout <$50,000 in 2011 dollars) have been dropping for the full period; 'large' paid claims (payout ≥$50,000) have been dropping since 2001. Payout per large paid claim was roughly flat. Payouts per physician have been dropping since 2003, and by 2012 were 48% below their 1992 level. The 'third wave' of damage cap adoptions over 2003–2006 contributed to this trend, but there were also large declines in no-cap states.

data, had also declined, at similar rates.[92] Allowing for the gradual phase-in of damages caps, strong evidence was found that damage caps reduce both claim rates and payout per claim, with a large combined impact on payout per physician.[93] Allowing for phase-in also found that tort reforms other than damage caps had no significant impact on either claim rates or payout per claim.[94] The same researchers also found that damage caps had no significant impact on Medicare[95] hospital spending, but led to four to five per cent higher Medicare physician spending.[96] They found no evidence of a post-adoption drop (or rise) in spending for these caps, and concluded that (i) there is no evidence that damage caps reduce overall Medicare spending, and (ii) third-wave caps induce a gradual increase in Medicare physician spending.[97]

A study of hospitals in North Carolina from January 2002 to December 2007 reports that there was no statistically significant decrease in medical errors during this period, in spite of efforts to reduce them.[98] On the other hand, Zabinski and Black's analysis of five states that had adopted caps on non-economic damages during 2003–2005 found consistent evidence that patient safety (measured by adverse events) generally falls after the reforms, compared to control states.[99]

Chen and Yang studied the impact of a series of court rulings in Taiwan that increased physicians' perceived liability exposure, and subsequent amendment to the law that reversed the courts' rulings, on physicians' test-ordering behaviour and choice of delivery method.[100] They found that obstetricians most at risk for liability increased laboratory tests in response to the ruling, but did not change the likelihood of delivery by Caesarean sections. They identified no consistent patterns of preventable complications, post-delivery emergency department visits, or hospital re-admissions associated with physician behavioural change. The overall pattern of results was highly suggestive of the practice of defensive medicine among physicians in Taiwan, but payment incentives and provider organisational forms may have mediated the impact of changing liability risks.

A study of a medical liability insurer's archive of death cases in North Carolina from 2002 to 2009 (156 cases involving 401 physician-defendants) found that men were significantly

---

[92] ibid.

[93] M Paik, BS Black and DA Hyman, 'The Receding Tide of Medical Malpractice Litigation: Part 2—Effect of Damage Caps' (2013) 10(4) *Journal of Empirical Legal Studies* 639. The drop in claim rates was concentrated in claims with larger payouts, which might be expected to be most affected by a damages cap. Stricter caps have larger effects.

[94] ibid.

[95] In the USA, there is free hospital care only for the elderly (Medicare) and poor (Medicaid), disability benefits only for persons (under 65) who suffer total and lasting disablement. Over 85% covered by private medical insurance (before the Patient Protection and Affordable Care Act of 2010): JG Fleming, *The American Tort Process* (Oxford, Clarendon Press, 1988).

[96] M Paik, B Black and DA Hyman, 'Do Doctors Practice Defensive Medicine, Revisited' draft 2014.

[97] ibid.

[98] C Landrigan, GJ Parry, CB Bones, DA Goldmann, AD Hackbarth, DA Goldman and PJ Sharek, 'Temporal Trends in Rates of Patient Harm Resulting from Medical Care' (2010) 363(22) *New England Journal of Medicine* 2124.

[99] Z Zabinski and BS Black, 'The Deterrent Effect of Tort Law: Evidence from Medical Malpractice Reform' (2014) Northwestern Law & Econ Research Paper No 13-09.

[100] BK Chen and C-Y Yang, 'Increased Perception of Malpractice Liability and the Practice of Defensive Medicine' (2014) 11(3) *Journal of Empirical Legal Studies* 446.

more at risk for diagnostic errors, and some evidence that age and number of defendants were predictive of treatment errors.[101]

Arlen's study of accidental medical error found that many, if not most, physicians who provided suboptimal care did not know they were doing so but instead misdiagnosed the patient, unintentionally selected the wrong treatment or erred in treatment provision.[102]

A 2006 Canadian review of patient safety and tort law concluded:[103]

> The debate about medical error and patient safety has been reframed to reflect a new understanding of how error and injury in health care occur. Rather than the traditional focus on the personal responsibility of health care providers, this new patient safety approach maintains that it is the institutional systems within which health care providers operate that cause harm more than individual practitioners. Reconfiguring the system and the way error is treated within it, it is contended, will result in safer care. Underlying systemic factors play a significant causal role in most adverse events and near misses in health care; it is thus inappropriate to blame individual health care providers when patients are injured. Analysis cannot be limited to occurrences at the 'sharp end', where practitioners interact with patients and each other in the process of delivering care, but must also include consideration of the role played by the 'blunt' or remote end of the system, ie regulators, administrators, policy makers and technology suppliers, who shape the environment in which practitioners work. However, the extent to which this approach to error reduction, and in particular, the de-emphasis on individual fault-finding, has been or can be incorporated into legal reasoning is not clear. It contrasts starkly with tort law, in which recovery of damages is largely premised on a finding of fault. The intersection of the two affects uptake of the patient safety approach, since law shapes the environment for the provision of health care, assessment of risks, and response to adverse events by all concerned. In important ways, law conditions the solutions that can be implemented, because people are guided in their conduct by the applicable legal frameworks and requirements.

Hyman, Rahmati, Black and Silver have recently analysed the database of the Illinois Department of Insurance for all claims from 1980 to 2010,[104] which covered three of four crises in medical malpractice premiums and resultant tort reform. They found that the total direct cost of Illinois' med mal system has never exceeded one per cent of health care spending, and that figure has declined steadily since 1992. Paid claim rates rose sharply from 1980–1985, roughly levelled off from 1986–1993, and then experienced a sustained decline. By 2010, paid claims rates were 75 per cent lower than in the peak year (1991). Mean and median payout per claim steadily increased since 1980, but these increases are largely attributable to the disappearance of smaller claims involving less severe injuries. In summary, of the three med mal insurance crises during the sample period, the researchers found that only the first coincided with a major change in med mal liability risk.

---

[101] CT Harris and RA Peeples, 'Medical Errors, Medical Malpractice and Death Cases in North Carolina: The Impact of Demographic and System Variables' (2014) Wake Forest University Legal Studies Paper No 2469959.

[102] J Arlen, 'Economic Analysis of Medical Malpractice Liability and Its Reform' NYU School of Law, Public Law Research Paper No 13-25 NYU Law and Economics Research Paper No 13-15.

[103] JM Gilmour, *Patient Safety, Medical Error and Tort Law: An International Comparison. Final Report* (Toronto, Osgoode Hall Law School, 2006).

[104] DA Hyman, MH Rahmati, BS Black and C Silver, 'Insurance Crisis or Liability Crisis? Medical Malpractice Claiming in Illinois, 1980–2010', Northwestern Law & Econ Research Paper No 13-29 U of Texas Law, Law and Econ Research Paper No 524 Illinois Program in Law, Behavior and Social Science Paper No LBSS 14-12.

7

Conclusions

Deterrence is a simple idea, that casts a massive shadow across legal theory and some—but not all—areas of enforcement policy. It plays a fundamental role in the theoretical justification and goals of the enforcement of competition law globally (whether by public or private means) and of the system of private enforcement that is at the heart of the US legal system. In contrast, despite repeated references in scholarly literature, deterrence has a much lower profile in both theory and practice in relation to English law, whether criminal enforcement or private liability. We will see in chapters 8 to 20 that deterrence plays little role in the enforcement of regulatory law in the UK.

The idea that a democratic society should attempt to influence its actors to abide by its legitimate rules is not controversial. However, any justification for deterrence as a policy of enforcement of law needs to be founded on the fact that it actually works—or, at least, works in a sufficient number of instances and works in ways that are fair and do not produce an unacceptable incidence of undesirable effects. In short, there needs to be robust evidence that deterrence affects future behaviour. The many historical assertions that enforcement of law deters future behaviour will no longer do: We need actual proof from empirical evidence. On the evidence assembled in this Part, such evidence is simply not convincing. Furthermore, as chapter one shows, there are far better explanations of what *does* affect human behaviour.

Individual deterrence comes up against the major problem that humans make decisions for many different reasons, as discussed in chapter one above. The rational actor of economic theory is an inaccurate model on which to predict human behaviour: We are *homo sapiens* not *homo economicus*. It should, therefore, be no surprise to note the evidence above of failings by criminal sanctions, liability law and competition enforcement policies to produce effective deterrence. A person who receives a sanction once might commit the same infringement again for all sorts of reasons.

A deterrence theory postulates that a sanction imposed *after* an infringement will affect the incidence of the same infringement in future, or maybe a related infringement. However, it would appear more likely that an ex ante control will be more effective in affecting future behaviour than an ex post sanction. That idea suggests that we should look at regulation, commitments and culture for mechanisms that might be more effective than ex post deterrent sanctions.

General deterrence seeks to affect everyone, whether or not they have committed an infringement. It comes up against a major problem in relation to affecting businesses. No convincing explanation has emerged as to *how* imposing a fine on a business affects the behaviour of any—let alone all—of the individuals who work in the business, or how the managers affect staff behaviour, or how it will affect the systems and culture of the organisation. There is surprisingly little empirical evidence on how firms take decisions, how often decisions are based on solely economic factors, and to what extent risks of future costs affect decisions. Much of the literature on the effects and origins of corporate infringements fails to distinguish adequately between the roles, motivations, behaviours and effects of sanctions on, on the one hand, the corporation and, on the other hand, the humans involved. Behaviour that is initiated by individual employees, or a small number of employees, is frequently attributed to the corporation that employs them without further analysis. Whilst (some of) the *consequences* of an infringement may be attributed to an employer (such as vicarious or strict liability to pay compensation for damage caused to a third party, or to remove profits that have been obtained illegally), an assumption that the *cause* of an infringement should be attributed to an inanimate corporate entity rather than to the humans involved raises a logical inconsistency. It might be productive to consider business organisational structures and how they work, make decisions, discipline staff and affect their behaviour. A convincing causative mechanism is lacking for deterrence. We start to address these questions in the rest of this book.

General deterrence in tort law is a theory about producing an optimal level of accidents and who should bear the costs of accidents, based on economic theory about how competitive markets work.[1] It is not a theory about who should be paid compensation, and is not convincing as a theory of affecting behaviour. Not only does the evidence suggest that tort law has limited potential to deter,[2] but tort law also does not distribute the cost of accidents in the way general deterrence theory would require.[3]

It cannot be said that an ex post sanction would never have any effect. Indeed, the empirical evidence from the psychology research finds that people will obey a rule where they perceive that the likelihood of being identified in breaking it, and subject to moral embarrassment (not necessarily significant punishment), is high. An everyday example can be seen in the behavior of drivers who can exceed the speed limit where they think that the likelihood of being identified by an official and fined a small sum is negligible, but take care not to exceed the limit where the risk is high (such as where average speed checks exist that are believed to be operational).

There is certainly evidence that the US liability system *does* affect some business decisions, for example in not marketing certain products or making changes in design, labelling and warnings. But it has not been shown whether those business decisions were the result of regulation or other reasons. Would the decisions have been made anyway, perhaps for ethical, commercial or regulatory reasons? Or could appropriate decisions be better induced by such alternative means? The development of liability enforcement as a means of regulation occurred at a time when little regulation existed. The interaction of regulation, reputation, ethics and liability constraints has never been satisfactorily elucidated. Assertions about the deterrent effect of tort liability on its own have continued to be made within a closed silo of tort academics and liability lawyers, without outward-looking illumination. The position on product warnings is almost a travesty: Lengthy information documents list every

---

[1] Based on G Calabresi, *The Costs of Accidents* (New Haven CT, Yale University Press, 1970). Enormous literature, including: R Bowles, *Law and Economy* (Oxford, Martin Robertson, 1982) ch 7; AM Polinsky, *An Introduction to Law and Economics* 2nd edn (Boston, WoltersKluwer, 1989) chs 6 and 7; RA Posner, *Economic Analysis of Law* 9th edn (New York, WoltersKluwer, 2014) ch 6.

[2] This was questioned some time ago even in the USA: GT Schwartz, 'Reality in Economic Analysis of Tort Law: Does Tort Law Really Deter?' (1994) 42 *UCLA Law Review* 377.

[3] G Calabresi, 'Does the Fault System Optimally Control Primary Accident Costs?' (1968) 33 *Law and Contemporary Problems* 429.

possible adverse consequence and thereby exempt the manufacturer from legal liability, whilst this does little for achieving safety in practice. Viscusi concluded that the safety-inducing potential of product liability fails to be realised, and that risks from new and innovative products are especially uncontrollable by liability.[4]

Corporate actions are now subject to very extensive regulatory systems and requirements, which have been extended over the past 50 years very extensively, covering almost every aspect of business economic practice and in considerable detail. It is these regulatory rules, and businesses' associated internal systems and rules, that drive and extensively control many granular decisions made within businesses. Such decisions are not made in a theoretical vacuum in which the only consideration is, for example, to balance the possible costs and benefits of the consequences of an individual decision. An indication of the extent of such systems for various sectors is given in the descriptions of the basic architecture of safety regulation in chapters 19 and 20 below.

Various adverse consequences of pursuing deterrence through the liability system have also been noted, such as it is very expensive, it results in unfair settlements and unjustly excessive penalties, sometimes imposes significant costs on the innocent, attracts certain types of case and ignores others, is significantly diluted and gamed as a result of insurance, and can produce resistance and reduced cooperation. The list is worrying, especially when clear positive evidence that future behaviour is *actually* affected is lacking. As Cane concludes, given the high administrative costs of the tort system, it may be that such deterrence as the tort system achieves is not worth the price paid for it.[5]

In both competition and liability systems, there is a tendency to believe that sanctions should be large and ever increasing in order to have effect. This appears to impose damage on a wide range of stakeholders and does not guarantee an absence of repetition of non-compliance or recidivism. Imposing a fine on a corporate group without sanctioning the one or two managers responsible for a cartel, who will usually be working in different businesses by the time both the firm and the authorities have identified their behaviour, achieves little. Of course the firm should adopt compliance and scrutiny procedures, and be incentivised to do so, but the underlying fault is that of the individuals concerned. As we will see in Part C, this means that there should be at least Ayers-Braithwaite pyramids that address both the individuals and the organisation—in different ways.

Kahan argues that deterrence plays a relatively small role in shaping individuals' policy preferences. He argues that public debate on issues such as capital punishment, gun control or hate crimes is captured by the hard and simplistic rhetoric of deterrence, so that although many people support social norms and liberal morality, they feel forced to avoid adopting such soft views publicly.[6] It may be said that the result is a policy schizophrenia in which deterrence is widely talked about, but the reality that it is ineffectual is ignored. Hence there is a social and political barrier to adoption of an approach to 'enforcement' that works more effectively. Deterrence is mere chimera: What matters is what we value and not whether deterrence plays some role.[7]

---

[4] WK Viscusi, 'Does Product Liability Make Us Safer?' (2012) 35(1) *Regulation* 24.

[5] P Cane, *The Anatomy of Tort Law* (Oxford, Hart Publishing, 1997); P Cane, *Atiyah's Accidents, Compensation and the Law* 8th edn (Cambridge, Cambridge University Press, 2013) 477.

[6] DN Kahan, 'The Secret Ambition of Deterrence' (1999) 113 *Harvard Law Review* 414.

[7] KM Carlsmith, JM Darley and PH Robinson, 'Why Do We Punish? Deterrence and Just Motives for Punishment' (2002) 83 *Journal of Personality and Social Psychology* 284.

The adherence to deterrence in the United States owes much to its Constitutional ideology (individualism, personal freedom and dislike of public regulation) and the political structures that this has entrenched (especially those involved in the litigation industry). In contrast, European jurisdictions, irrespective of whether they are traditionally based on common law or civil law foundations, place little credence in the idea that liability law has much effect on the future behaviour of either individual defendants or of others.

An important point of social policy also arises. Does a society wish to be based on an aggressive, accusatory and adversarial culture, in which individuals assert unlimited personal freedom until condemned, or does it prefer a culture of inter-relational support and cooperation? The US adversarial model tends to the former type and the EU (European Union) solidarity model tends towards the latter type. Is deterrence the right concept? The word carries connotations that are negative, repressive and authoritarian.[8] It is in fact antipathetic to personal freedom, rather than supportive.

If these concerns are correct, the justification of enforcement on grounds of deterrence fails, in which case the ongoing reliance on such a theory as a basis for upholding law is both unjustified and unethical. This has major implications for the whole basis of the American legal system, and for competition enforcement, with ever-increasing fines.

This idea has profound implications for law and legal theory in Europe. It is time to accept that liability law has little deterrent effect, and to examine the consequences for substantive law and for legal structures. If we start from the proposition that deterrence is basically not produced by legal rules, structures or procedures, how should we (re)design those legal rules, structures and procedures so as to achieve the twin underlying objectives of affecting future behaviour and delivering support to those who have suffered harm? For a start, if we jettison the idea of deterrence, the tort liability system looks even more inadequate, ineffective and costly than most scholars already know it to be. And we need to look for completely different means of affecting behaviour.

The idea of what sort of culture we wish to encourage is important for another reason. The purpose of legal rules is to set standards of behavior that the collective society wishes to adopt as universal rules. Given the pervasive nature of regulatory rules that cover so many aspects of behavior, noted above, it is important that the regulatory and compliance systems within which such rules exist operate so that compliance is maximised (and not merely optimal, as the economics standard would have). If compliance is to be maximised, many systems now function simply on the constant monitoring and circulation of information, as will be discussed in chapter 17 onwards below. The critical finding is that people are far more likely to share the information that is vitally needed in order to maintain performance standards if the culture of both their business environment and public space is ethical, positive and supportive, as opposed to being based on blame and repressive deterrence.

---

[8] Leader, 'Corporate Settlements in the United States: The Criminalisation of American Business' *The Economics* 30 August 2014, 10; arguing that the legal system has become 'an extortion racket' involving untransparent use of excessive power by public prosecutors. It has been noted above that Qui Tam claims under the False Claims Act have generated some 3,000 lawsuits and $20 billion in recoveries in the period 1999–2014. Although dwarfed by fines in securities, fraud and antitrust cases, fines imposed by, for example, the Consumer Product Safety Commission in 2014 for failure to report potential product defects reached a high of $12.2 million, including an agreed civil penalty of $4.3 million against Baja Inc and One World Technologies Inc involving minibikes and go-carts: *World Technologies Inc vs Baja Inc*, CPSC Docket 15-C0001, available at: www.cpsc.gov/PageFiles/17214 4/15012CivilPenaltyAgreement.pdf.

That finding emerges from both the psychology set out in chapter one and the empirical evidence in chapter 19. On this basis, the evidence suggests that it is important to have a positive and supportive culture, and that a repressive and sanctioning culture will be positively harmful. That is not to deny the psychology finding that where mistakes are made, and especially where rules are broken, they need to be identified, acknowledged and lead to a proportionate response. The nature of that response, however, should be punitive only where the actions have been the result of morally bad intentions. The response to mistakes should, of course, be to repair the damage and take steps to avoid the risk of repetition. These ideas will be expanded upon in the chapters that follow.

Part C

Regulation

8

Public Regulation

I. The Purposes of Regulation

Various definitions have been given for regulation.[1] Drawing on syntheses by Karen Yeung and Christine Parker, we can consider regulation for present purposes to be 'the sustained and focused attempt by the state to alter behaviour thought to be of value to the community'[2] in accordance with achieving behaviour that corresponds with defined standards.[3] There are two principal ideas here. First, the underlying activity involved is fundamentally thought to be of value to the community, in contrast with other activities that are essentially anti-social and labelled as criminal.[4] Indeed, the underlying activity is to be encouraged, since it contributes to economic or social welfare. However, the second idea is that the state sets standards for the performance of aspects of the desired fundamental activity, which it wishes to see observed. It is one aspect of the manner in which the essential activity is being pursued that gives rise to concern, since the actor is not complying with the particular standard in relation to that aspect. In response to that aspect of non-compliance, the state adopts a concerted attempt to modify the non-compliant behaviour, and to preserve the continuance of the economic and social benefits of the underlying enterprise. The primary aim of regulation is, therefore, to modify the particular behaviour rather than to punish or censure those engaging in the regulated activity.[5]

---

[1] A sociological definition is: 'the organized ways in which society responds to behaviour and people it regards as deviant, problematic, worrying, threatening, troublesome or undesirable in some way or another': S Cohen, *Visions of Social Control: Crime, Punishment and Classification* (Cambridge, Policy, 1985).

[2] K Yeung, *Securing Compliance. A Principled Approach* (Oxford, Hart Publishing, 2004), drawing on AI Ogus, *Regulation: Legal Form and Economic Theory* (Oxford, Oxford University Press, 1994), P Selznick, 'Focusing Organizational Research on Regulation' in R Noll (ed) *Regulatory Policy and the Social Sciences* (California, Berkeley, 1985), P Vincent-Jones, 'Values and Purposes in Government: Central-local Relations in Regulatory Perspective' (2002) 29 *Journal of Law and Society* 27 (emphasising 'systematic control'), J Black, 'Enrolling Actors in Regulatory Systems: Examples from the UK Financial Services Regulation' (2003) *Public Law* 63. Yeung considers that regulation involves intervention by the state, so excludes non-state actors. Her analysis occurred before the concepts of decentered and meta regulation were developed. As will appear at ch 17 and elsewhere below, I consider that regulation may be imposed by actors other than the state, in accordance with objectives that are fundamentally overseen by the state.

[3] J Black, *Critical Reflections on Regulation* CARR Discussion Paper, DP 4 (London School of Economics and Political Science, London, UK, 2002), (2002) 27 *Australian Journal of Legal Philosophy* 1–35, reprinted in F Haines (ed), *Crime and Regulation* (Farnham, Ashgate, 2007).

[4] Selznick (n 2) 363. See also A Sanders, 'Reconciling the Apparently Different Goals of Criminal Justice and Regulation: The "Freedom" Perspective' in H Quirk, T Seddon and G Smith (eds), *Regulation and Criminal Justice* (Cambridge, Cambridge University Press, 2013), arguing that there are many exceptions to the 'encouraged activity' idea, and defining 'criminal justice' as legal state coercion that is determinable in the criminal courts.

[5] Yeung (n 2).

The intervention is directed at one aspect in which the underlying activity is being carried out, not at the entirety of the activity. In simple terms, the message that the state is sending is 'we like what you are doing, but we don't want you to do it this way'. Thus, the intervention is purposive and interventionist but not necessarily directorial. Much regulatory intervention attempts to prohibit certain aspects of the way in which the fundamental activity is carried out, but does not attempt to prescribe a single particular way in which the activity should be carried out. For example, the objective here is not to inhibit a vibrant market, in which competition and innovation can flourish. Prescribing every aspect of how business should be carried out would stifle such vibrancy.

Regulation is also perceived as a means of managing unavoidable risk. Risk is inherent in human life and society,[6] and particularly in activities that are undertaken by concerted groups of individuals who are organised into groups, such as commercial firms. Further, many activities may benefit some individuals and groups but cause harm of loss to others. Regulation is not an attempt to eradicate risk, but an attempt to manage it, and so reduce it.[7] Accordingly, regulatory law is simultaneously constitutive and constraining.[8] Its function is to provide a *constitutive* framework for the particular market, through defining its structures and procedures, so as to empower participants to operate legally within it, *constrained* by specific rules that maintain order, backed by the coercive power of the state.[9] Fisher argues that since technology risks are inherently uncertain, the institutional context within which it is regulated is that of public administration, rather than science or democracy, and that a rational–instrumental paradigm has given way to a deliberative–constitutive paradigm.[10]

The archetypal form of regulation is known as 'command and control', under which the state may prescribe specific ways of doing, or not doing, something, and may authorise or prohibit certain activities, breach of which will render the infringer liable to a sanction or sanctions: This approach is examined further below. In contrast to that 'top down' view of control, the converse view of 'bottom up' gives rise to self-regulatory structures, especially those in which trade sectors aim to control aspects of their own behaviour without state intervention. As examined in chapter 17, hybrid forms of co- or meta regulation have evolved.

Galligan notes that the social and moral foundation of some regulatory rules is less deep than most criminal laws. For example, murder and even physical violence are generally held to be intrinsically more serious in terms of constituting a threat to society than misleading advertising of consumer goods that does not give rise to personal injury.

> Regulatory law requires compliance with standards that often (but not always) are contrary to the interests of those required to comply with them, and that often (but again not always) lack deep

---

[6] See A Giddens, *The Consequences of Modernity* (Cambridge, Cambridge University Press, 1990); A Giddens, 'Risk and Responsibility' (1999) 60(1) *Modern Law Review* 1–10; U Beck, *Risk Society: Towards a New Modernity* (New Delhi, Sage, 1992); C Hood, H Rothstein and R Baldwin, *The Government of Risk* (Oxford, Oxford University Press, 2001); J Steele, *Risks and Legal Theory* (Oxford, Hart Publishing, 2004); and many others.

[7] BM Hutter, *Regulation and Risk: Occupational Health and Safety on the Railways* (Oxford, Oxford University Press, 2001).

[8] PC Stenning, CD Shearing, SM Addario and MG Condon, 'Controlling Interests: Two Conceptions of Order in Regulating a Financial Market' in ML Friedland (ed), *Securing Compliance* (Toronto, University of Toronto Press, 1990).

[9] Hutter (n 7) 77.

[10] E Fisher, *Risk: Regulation and Administrative Constitutionalism* (Oxford, Hart Publishing, 2007).

social or moral foundations. The consequence is that those to whom the standards are addressed have no clear or strong reason to comply (beyond the fact that it is a legal standard), with the further consequence that enforcement or the threat of enforcement by coercion becomes a necessary feature of regulatory regimes.[11]

Nevertheless, some behaviour that is classified as 'regulatory' is highly damaging to society and the market. For example, selling dangerous products can cause serious and widespread injury. Cartels, involving artificial distortions of prices and free competition, are conspiracies that can have serious widespread effects on markets and prices, and hence affect the livelihoods of many people, in the same way as other insidious criminal conspiracies such as bribery of public officials.

II. Enforcement of Regulation

It is not sufficient for a state to promulgate laws without it being able also to take steps to enforce compliance with the standards set. The state must in fact do so in a sufficient number of cases of infringement, if it is to maintain its credibility and that of the relevant standards. If the law is to be effective in fulfilling its regulatory role, most citizens must obey most laws most of the time.[12] Hence, an essential feature of public law, being rules that are promulgated by a state, is that officials are empowered to take formal action against noncompliance, which is ultimately backed by coercive sanctions imposed by the authority of the state.[13] In a democratic state, the process by which laws are made, the substance of the laws, and the means by which enforcement is undertaken, should all be transparent and fair.

Traditionally, the response of a state to breach of its criminal (public) law is to impose criminal sanctions. Criminal law is invoked to censure the most serious instances of anti-social or morally reprehensible conduct. In other words, the conduct is of sufficient concern to maintenance of the social order that the state takes action against the conduct (as opposed to leaving the dispute to be decided between the parties under private civil law or some other means) and uses particular procedures and sanctions that signify the official seriousness of the offence to society. Criminal sanctions may be taken against either or both of individuals and corporate entities.

Whilst criminal prosecutions and sanctions such as fines and imprisonment continue to be regarded as the most serious formal sanctioning steps, they are not used frequently.[14] Indeed, criminal sanctions are criticised as being lenient and lacking deterrence. Monetary penalties have been described as 'derisory' and companies cannot be imprisoned.[15] A major function of criminal sentencing, therefore, at least in the regulatory context, is symbolic.

Instead of extensive use of criminal sanctioning, extensive administrative infringement procedures and sanctions have emerged during the second half of the twentieth century for

---

[11] DJ Galligan, *Law in Modern Society* (Oxford, Oxford University Press, 2007) 149.

[12] TR Tyler, *Why People Obey the Law* (Hartford CT, Yale University Press, 2006).

[13] HLA Hart, *The Concept of Law* (Oxford, Oxford University Press, 1961); Galligan (n 11) 151.

[14] K Hawkins, *Law as a Last Resort: Prosecution Decision-Making in a Regulatory Agency* (Oxford, Oxford University Press, 2002).

[15] H Croall, 'Combating Financial Crime: Regulatory Versus Crime Control Approaches' (2003) 11 *Journal of Financial Crime* 45–55, reprinted in Haines (n 3).

responding to infringements of what are seen as requirements of public administrative or regulatory law rather than of criminal law. These administrative sanctions are frequently regarded as less serious than criminal provisions, and are now widely used by regulatory enforcement authorities. They may be considered to be administrative penalties, or civil sanctions, and can sometimes be imposed by public authorities, sometimes by courts or tribunals. Although one reason why criminal machinery has given way to regulatory machinery may be a perceived difference in the extent of moral opprobrium of infringements, another is that specialist regulatory agencies are better equipped to investigate and respond to corporate activity, and criminal procedures have been bypassed.[16]

Public sanctions, whether criminal or regulatory/administrative in nature, can occur alongside, or in substitution one way or the other for, other forms of sanctions, such as responses by markets, customers, suppliers, commentators, rating agencies, peers, trade bodies and so on, affecting a firm's reputation. It may be incorrect to envisage such sanctions in a hierarchy such as that shown in Figure 8.1, since several types of sanctions may be imposed at the same time in response to the same behaviour. Indeed, the different types are not (fully) co-ordinatable, and will have differing force depending on the context. For example, market- or peer-imposed sanctions may be very powerful, even destroying a firm. But criminal or regulatory enforcers sometimes take the existence of effective market sanctions as justifying the imposition of lesser penalties under their systems.

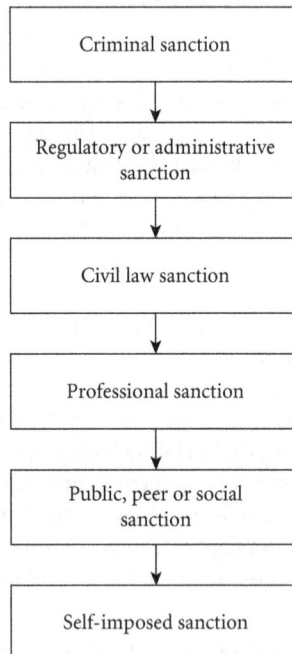

Figure 8.1: Sanctions Hierarchy

---

[16] C Wells, 'Corporate Crime: Opening the Eyes of the Sentry' (2010) 30(3) *Legal Studies* 370.

Hence, as noted in chapter 11, a hierarchy of sanctioning powers usually exists in a state, representing a pyramid with criminal law at the apex and a larger volume of administrative sanctions underneath. Both in the sphere of crimes committed by individuals and particularly in the sphere of regulatory infringements committed by corporations, formal sanctions are not imposed on every occasion on which an infringement is detected. Enforcement is an art, not a matter of automation, in which officials have considerable discretion that may be exercised in responding to particular infringements.[17] Enforcers frequently refer to having a toolbox of powers that they may wield, and that the greater the range of tools they have available in the toolbox, the more likely they are to be effective and efficient in responding to non-compliance and supporting future compliance. The most draconian powers are seen as ones to invoke as a matter of last resort,[18] yet their availability is not only symbolically important but also contributes to the effectiveness of other intrinsically less forceful powers.

Grabosky suggests that enforcers consider the following factors when evaluating whether or not to initiate prosecutions, notably:[19]

— The degree of harm to persons and property caused by the behaviour in question;
— the degree of criminal intent on the part of the alleged perpetrator (malice/recklessness/carelessness; ignorance);
— the prior record of the alleged perpetrator;
— the extent to which the accused cooperated with the investigation;
— the cost of prosecution;
— the probability of conviction;
— the likelihood of a significant sentence in the event of conviction;
— the public interest in prosecution: eg would a successful prosecution close down the city's major employer? Would it deter future wrongdoing? And media attention accorded to *both* the harm in question *and* the government's response.

In order to constitute a breach of criminal law, states usually require the offender to have a *mens rea* (guilty mind). A problem here is that since a corporation is a legal construct (virtual entity, legal fiction) and so has no human mind, it is debatable whether it can be considered to have a *mens rea*. This problem has been avoided in two main ways; first by arguing (not overly convincingly) that senior officers constitute the controlling mind of the virtual entity and, second, by basing many regulatory offences on strict liability, requiring proof only of the commission of the offending conduct.[20] Strict liability has, however, come under increasingly strong criticism.[21]

---

[17] K Hawkins, *The Uses of Discretion* (Oxford, Clarendon Press, 1995); K Hawkins, *Environment and Enforcement* (Oxford, Oxford University Press, 1984).

[18] Galligan (n 11) 149.

[19] P Grabosky, 'On the Interface of Criminal Justice and Regulation' in Quirk, Seddon and Smith (n 4); see also J Rowan-Robinson, P Wachtman and C Barker, *Crime and Regulation: A Study of the Enforcement of Regulatory Codes* (Edinburgh, T & T Clark, 1990).

[20] G Richardson, A Ogus and P Burrows, *Policing Pollution* (Oxford, Clarendon Press, 1984) 16 and 57; L Leigh, *Strict and Vicarious Liability* (London, Sweet & Maxwell, 1982) 14–16.

[21] N Lacey, 'In Search of the Responsible Subject: History, Philosophy and Social Sciences in Criminal Law Theory' (2001) 64 *Modern Law Review* 350, 354; P Cane, *Responsibility in Law and Morality* (Oxford, Hart Publishing, 2002) 109–10; AP Simester (ed), *Appraising Strict Liability* (Oxford, Oxford University Press, 2005). Note the move away from strict liability in USA: S Oded, PhD thesis: *Inducing Corporate Proactive Compliance: Liability Controls & Corporate Monitors* (Erasmus Universiteit Rotterdam, 2012) 129ff, citing various scholars as preferring a duty-based approach with a 'due diligence' defence: WS Laufer, 'Integrity, Diligence, and the Limits of Good

However, it is clear that individual directors or employees of companies can behave in such a way not only as to commit serious breach of their terms of employment but also to offend against the state's law. Such individuals' behaviour may place their employing company in breach of regulatory provisions but, more fundamentally, may constitute criminal activity by themselves. There is little difficulty in recognising that such individuals have the necessary *mens rea* and can be considered guilty of offences that can be defined as criminal.

We now turn to examining the various theories that are applied in enforcement.

A. The 'Command and Control' Approach

The 'command and control' model of regulation is built on the theoretical foundation of deterrence as the effective means of affecting future behaviour. Its roots lie in authoritarian concepts of the state's rule-making power (*imperium*) and property power (*dominium*).[22] In the corporate context, it assumes that both companies and employees are rational actors, who are concerned primarily with maximising their own outcomes in work settings.[23]

The 'command and control' concept has long dominated enforcement theory, and can be identified in the policies and approaches of many public enforcers. However, it has been significantly undermined by empirical observations of how enforcers operate on the ground (as is noted in this chapter; the significant reforms of regulatory policy in the United Kingdom are charted in chapter nine).

Tyler has summarised the evidence on the 'command and control' model as follows.[24] Studies do lend some support to the suggestion that instrumental strategies can shape people's behaviour,[25] with some studies supporting this argument in work settings.[26] However, the use of instrumental strategies requires constant monitoring and sanctioning of deviant behaviour, which requires significant resources.[27] Overall, the effectiveness of command and control strategies is 'unclear'. In legal settings, sanction-based deterrence strategies are

Corporate Citizenship' (1996) 34(2) *American Business Law Journal* 157–82; A Weismann, 'A New Approach to Corporate Criminal Liability' (2007) 44 *American Criminal Law Review* 1319–42; A Weismann and D Newman, 'Rethinking Criminal Corporate Liability' (2007) 82 *Indiana Law Journal (Bloomington)* 411–51.

[22] TC Daintith, 'The Techniques of Government' in J Jowell and D Oliver (eds), *The Changing Constitution* 3rd edn (Oxford, Oxford University Press, 1994).

[23] M Blair and L Stout, 'Trust, Trustworthiness and the Behavioural Foundations of Corporate Law' (2001) 149 *University of Pennsylvania Law Review* 1735–810.

[24] TR Tyler, 'The Psychology of Self-regulation: Normative Motivations for Compliance' in C Parker and VL Nielsen (eds), *Explaining Compliance. Business Responses to Regulation* (Cheltenham, Edward Elgar, 2012).

[25] D Nagin, 'Criminal Deterrence Research at the Outset of the Twenty-first Century' in M Tonry (ed), *Crime and Justice: A Review of Research, Volume 23* (Chicago, Chicago University Press, 1998) 1–42; D Nagin and R Paternoster, 'The Preventive Effects of the Perceived Risk of Arrest: Testing an Expanded Conception of Deterrence' (1991) 29 *Criminology* 561–87; R Paternoster, 'The Deterrent Effect of the Perceived Certainty and Severity of Punishment: A Review of the Evidence and Issues' (1987) 4 *Justice Quarterly* 173–217; R Paternoster, 'Decisions to Participate in and Desist from Four Types of Common Delinquency: Deterrence and the Rational Choice Perspective' (1989) 23 *Law & Society Review* 7–40.

[26] M Huselid, 'The Impact of Human Resource Management Practices on Turnover, Productivity, and Corporate Financial Performance' (1995) 38 *Academy of Management Journal* 635–72; JG Douglas, A Mitra, N Gupta and J Shaw, 'Are Financial Incentives Related to Performance? A Meta-analytic Review of Empirical Evidence' (1998) 83 *Journal of Applied Psychology* 777–87.

[27] D Langvoort, 'Monitoring: The Behavioural Economics of Corporate Compliance with Law' (2002) *Columbia Business Law Review* 71–118.

consistently found to have at best a minor influence on rule breaking behaviour.[28] Meta-analysis reaches a similar conclusion.[29] These results suggest that, while they are somewhat effective, such systems may only have a limited impact on employee behaviour. The limits of the command and control model have been noted with increasing frequency.[30] Thus, the managerial relevance of these critiques remains open to question.

III. The Institutional and Political Dominance of Regulation in Europe

In Part B above, the dominance of private enforcement over public enforcement was noted in the USA. There does, of course, exist an extensive regime of public administration and regulation in the USA,[31] but it attracts major criticism,[32] and private enforcement remains a dominant mode over public enforcement.[33] In contrast, EU (European Union) Member States, being secular capitalist democracies with some common deep-seated roots in commitment to fundamental human rights,[34] have developed strong models of social justice,[35] exemplified by the use of the term 'solidarity' in the French revolutionary constitution, the post-1945 welfare state, and ideas of constitutional pluralism.[36] The importance

---

[28] R MacCoun, 'Drugs and the Law: A Psychological Analysis of Drug Prohibition' (1993) 113 *Psychological Bulletin* 497–512 (a 5% variance in drug use was explained by deterrence factors); TR Tyler and SL Blader, *Cooperation in Groups: Procedural Justice, Social Identity, and Behavioral Engagement* (Philadelphia, Psychology Press, 2000) (10% variance in employee behaviour was shaped by incentives): Tyler (n 12).

[29] P Podsakoff, W Bommer, N Podsakoff and S MacKenzie, 'Relationships among Leader Reward and Punishment Behaviour and Subordinate Attitudes, Perceptions, and Behaviours: A Meta-analytic Review of Existing and New Research' (2006) 99 *Organizational Behaviour and Human Decision Processes* 113–42.

[30] B Fisse, 'Reconstructing Corporate Criminal Law: Deterrence, Retribution, Fault and Sanctions' (1983) 56 *Southern California Law Review* 1141–246; B Fisse and J Braithwaite, *Corporations, Crimes, and Accountability* (Cambridge, Cambridge University Press, 1993); N Katyal, 'Deterrence's Difficulty' (1997) 95 *Michigan Law Review* 2385–476; T Malloy, 'Regulation and the Compliance Norm' (unpublished manuscript, 2002); D Markell, 'The Role of Deterrence-based Enforcement in a "Reinvented" State/Federal Relationship: The Divide between Theory and Reality' (2000) 24 *Harvard Environmental Law Review* 1–114; J Sutinen and K Kuperan, 'A Socioeconomic Theory of Regulatory Compliance' (1999) 26 *International Journal of Social Economics* 174–93.

[31] R Rabin, 'Federal Regulation in Historical Perspective' (1986) 38 *Stanford Law Review* 1189; CR Sunstein, *After the Rights Revolution: Reconceiving the Regulatory State* (Boston MA, Harvard University Press, 1990).

[32] G Lawson, 'The Rise and Rise of the Administrative State' (1994) 107 *Harvard Law Review* 1231 (argument that the post-New Deal administrative state is unconstitutional).

[33] AM Polinsky and S Shavell, 'The Economic Theory of Public Enforcement of Law' [2000] XXXVIII *Journal of Economic Literature* 45; AJ Sebok and L Tragardh, 'Adversarial Legalism and the Emergence of a New European Legality: A Comparative Perspective' Cardozo Legal Studies Research Paper No 377.

[34] See European Convention on Human Rights, first introduced in 1970, and Charter of Fundamental Rights of the EU, proclaimed 2000 and binding from 2009.

[35] W Streek, 'Competitive Solidarity: Rethinking the "European Social Model"' MPIfG Working Paper 99/8, 1999; G Helleringer and K Purnhagen (eds), *Towards a European Legal Culture* (Baden-Baden/München/Oxford, CH Beck/Nomos/Hart, 2014); H-W Micklitz, 'Social Justice and Access Justice in Private Law', EUI Working Papers Law 2011/02; H-W Micklitz, 'Judicial Activism of the European Court of Justice and the Development of the European Social Model in Anti-Discrimination and Consumer Law' EUI Working Papers, Law 2009/19.

[36] A Stone Sweet, 'A Cosmopolitan Legal Order: Constitutional Pluralism and Rights Adjudication in Europe' (2012) 1 *Global Constitutionalism* 53.

of regulation in the structure and operation of the EU internal market is well known.[37] The United Kingdom has long been regarded as a leader[38] in regulation[39] and self- or co-regulation.[40] Prosser's study noted that an important reason for not adopting older or US models in the UK was a desire to avoid judicialisation of regulatory proceedings and to prevent the courts from having a major role as a means of challenge of regulatory decisions.[41] There is a notable absence in British literature of empirical evidence of capture of regulatory agencies. In a rare example, a study of 143 complaint files at the Financial Ombudsman Service found that the data did not support the expectation that complaints against larger and/or more experienced firms would be less successful.[42]

Coglianese and Kagan argue that the American pattern of legalistic, private and judicial enforcement does not appear as strong in nations, such as those of Europe, with parliamentary government, cohesive political parties, robust national bureaucracies, and strong national trade associations.[43] Armour's comparison of American and British corporate and securities law demonstrated that the latter system does not, to any significant extent, rely on formal private enforcement and, instead, more work is done by public enforcement agencies, with significant informal private enforcement through exercise of shareholders' governance entitlements.[44] The widespread adoption by British and other regulatory and

---

[37] G Majone, 'The Rise of the Regulatory State in Europe' (1974) 17 *West European Politics* 77; G Majone, *Regulating Europe* (London, Routledge, 1996); M Loughlin and C Scott, 'The Regulatory State' in P Dunleavy, R Heffernan, P Cowley and C Hay (eds), *Developments in British Politics* (London, Macmillan, 1997); M Moran, 'Review Article: Understanding the Regulatory State' (2002) 32 *British Journal of Political Science* 391; T Zwart and L Verhey (eds), *Agencies in European and Comparative Law* (Antwerp, Intersentia, 2003); B Eberlein and E Grande, 'Beyond Delegation: Transnational Regulatory Regimes and the EU Regulatory State' (2005) 12 *Journal of European Public Policy* 89; D Gerardin, R Muñoz and N Petit (eds), *Regulation through Agencies in the EU. A New Paradigm of European Governance* (Cheltenham, Edward Elgar, 2005). See also P Eleftheriadis, 'The Moral Distinctiveness of the European Union' (2011) 9 (3–4) *International Journal of Constitutional Law* 695–713.

[38] OECD, *Government Capacity to Assure High Quality Regulation: Regulatory Reform in the United Kingdom* (2002) 6.

[39] T Prosser, *Law and the Regulators* (Oxford, Clarendon Press, 1997); Loughlin and Scott (n 37); C McCrudden (ed), *Regulation and Deregulation. Policy and Practice in the Utilities and Financial Services Industries* (Oxford, Clarendon Press, 1999); D Coen and C Doyle 'Designing Economic Regulatory Institutions for the European Network Industries' (2000) 9 *Current Politics and Economics of Europe* 83; M Moran, *The British Regulatory State: High Modernism and Hyper-Innovation* (Oxford, Oxford University Press, 2003); Fisher (n 10); T Prosser, *The Regulatory Enterprise: Government, Regulation, and Legitimacy* (Oxford, Oxford University Press, 2010); D Oliver, T Prosser and R Rawlings (eds), *The Regulatory State: Constitutional Implications* (Oxford, Oxford University Press, 2010).

[40] R Baggott, 'Regulatory Reform in Britain: the Changing Face of Self-Regulation' (1989) 67(4) *Public Administration* 436–54, 436–38; T Porter and K Ronit, 'Self-Regulation as Policy Process: The Multiple and Criss-Crossing Stages of Private Rule-Making' (2006) 39 *Policy Sciences* 41–72; reprinted in Haines (n 3); DD Murphy, *The Structure of Regulatory Competition. Corporations and Public Policies in a Global Economy* (Oxford, Oxford University Press, 2004).

[41] Prosser, *Law and the Regulators* (n 39) 57.

[42] S Gilad, 'Why the "Haves" Do Not Necessarily Come Out Ahead in Informal Dispute Resolution' (2010) 32(2) *Law & Policy* 283.

[43] C Coglianese and RA Kagan, *Regulation and Regulatory Processes* (Farnham, Ashgate, 2007) xix, citing LA Scruggs, 'Institutions and Environmental Performance in Seventeen Western Democracies' (1999) 29 *British Journal of Political Science* 1–31; RA Kagan, *Adversarial Legalism. The American Way of Law* (Boston MA, Harvard University Press, 2001).

[44] J Armour, *Enforcement Strategies in UK Corporate Governance: A Roadmap and Empirical Assessment*, European Corporate Governance Institute, Law Working Paper No 106/2008; J Armour, B Black, B Cheffins and R Nolan, 'Private Enforcement of Corporate Law: An Empirical Comparison of the UK and US' (2009) 6 *Journal of Empirical Legal Studies* 701.

enforcement authorities of an enforcement policy of responsive regulation, examined in chapter 11 below, demonstrates that access to legal justice in the courts is not the normative ideal of the meta-regulatory perspective on law.[45] Prominent American academic analyses have rejected public enforcement in favour of private enforcement in financial markets.[46] However, Jackson and Roe's multi-jurisdiction comparison found that public enforcement is correlated significantly with financial market depth and performance, is overall as important as disclosure rules in explaining financial market outcomes, and substantially more strongly associated with robust capital markets than several other indices of private enforcement, including liability rules and anti-director rights.[47] There is no uniform model of liability regimes amongst Member States under the Prospectus Directive,[48] and instead a huge variation in national regimes for civil, administrative, criminal and governmental liability.[49]

A 2008 review of consumer protection enforcement revealed a patchwork of public and private approaches across Member States.[50] Member State opposition to the European Commission's moves to promote litigation as the primary mode of enforcement of environmental law led to a shift towards reliance on a network of public authorities[51] and criminal sanctions.[52] Similar political opposition to the introduction of a harmonised European regime of class actions has restricted the development of collective private enforcement as an EU model, and although a significant number of Member States have introduced domestic collective action mechanisms, general usage is remarkably low, especially when compared with that of the USA.[53] Litigation has not emerged as a major regulatory control of data protection in Europe, and a strong reliance on self-regulation persists.[54]

The EU's core rationale is the market, and this has led to a focus on harmonisation of regulatory rules and authorities. The regulatory and governance architecture that has emerged in the EU comprises multi-levels[55] and multi-actors. Typical examples of such

---

[45] J Braithwaite and C Parker, 'Conclusion' in C Parker, C Scott, N Lacey and J Braithwaite, *Regulating Law* (Oxford, Oxford University Press, 2004).

[46] *Institutional Foundations for Financial Markets* (World Bank, 2006), available at http://siteresources. worldbank.org/INTTOPACCFINSER/Resources/Institutional.pdf; S Djankov, R La Porta, F Lopez-de-Silanes and A Shleifer, 'The Law and Economics of Self–dealing' (2008) 88 *Journal of Financial Economics* 430; R La Porta, F Lopez-de-Silanes and A Shleifer, 'What Works in Securities Laws?' (2006) 61 *Journal of Finance* 1.

[47] HE Jackson and MJ Roe, 'Public and Private Enforcement in Securities Laws: Resource-Based Evidence' (2009) 93 *Journal of Financial Economics* 207.

[48] Dir 2010/73/EU amending Dir 2003/71/EU on then prospectus to be published when securities are offered to the public or admitted to trading.

[49] *Report: Comparison of Liability Regimes in Member States in Relation to the Prospectus Directive* (European Securities and Markets Authority, 2013).

[50] M Faure, A Ogus and N Philipsen, 'Enforcement Practices for Breaches of Consumer Protection Legislation' (2008) 20(4) *Loyola Consumer Law Review* 361.

[51] Dir 2004/35/EC, 2004 OJ L 143, 56.

[52] Dir 2008/99/EU, 2008 OJ L 328.

[53] C Hodges, 'Collective Redress: A Breakthrough or a Damp Sqibb?' (2014) 34 *Journal of Consumer Policy* 67; V Harsági and CH van Rhee (eds), *Multi-Party Redress Mechanisms in Europe: Squeaking Mice?* (Antwerp, Intersentia, 2014).

[54] F Bignami, 'Cooperative Legalism and the Non-Americanization of European Regulatory Styles: The Case of Data Privacy' (2011) 59 *The American Journal of Comparative Law* 411.

[55] RA Wessel and J Wouters, 'The Phenomenon of Multilevel Regulation' in RA Wessel and J Wouters (eds), *Multilevel Regulation and the EU: The Interplay between Global, European and National Normative Processes* (Leiden, Martinus Nijhoff Publishers, 2008) 9; N Chowdhury, *Pursuing Legal Certainty in Multilevel Regulation* (PhD, University of Twente, 2013).

multiplicity would include national political oversight, the European Commission, some European regulatory authorities, multiple national regulatory and enforcement authorities, traders, external monitors such as financial auditors and notified bodies, and professional and consumer users. Such a system requires a consensus-building process instead of a 'command and control' approach if it is to function.[56] Cooperation among supervisory authorities is a natural consequence of establishing common rules at the EU level.[57] There should be no surprise in identifying extensive self- and co-regulation models as alternatives to legislation in EU regulatory structures.[58] Many such features are noted in the analyses of different regulatory architectures discussed in chapters 19 and 20 below.[59] European models or regulation have evolved away from rigid command and control models to encompass various more open structures. A well-known example is the Open Method of Coordination (OMC).[60] Considerable scholarly analysis has been devoted to the development of open models, and their governance and constitutional aspects.[61] The development of open and flexible models owes much to the political environment of the EU, with the need to support a cohesive open market that knits together a range of individual regimes, each with individual political, cultural and regulatory distinctiveness—in other words, pluralism is unavoidable, and authoritarianism is not an option.

Political scientists note two points that are significant in this inquiry. First, the attempt to strike a balance between the state and the market reflects the struggle for delineation between public and private power and the actors in each field.[62] Second, there has occurred a significant transfer of power from politicians to regulators, expressed in the concepts of 'regulatory capitalism'[63] and a 'post-regulatory State'.[64] This transfer has emerged as a natural consequence of the political structures of the EU but also of the need for expertise in the complex multiple areas covered by regulatory regimes.[65] The implementation of regulatory

---

[56] G Bertezzolo, 'The European Union Facing the Global Arena: Standard-setting Bodies and Financial Regulation' (2009) 34 *European Law Review* 257; RiskMetrics Group, *Study on Monitoring and Enforcement Practices in Corporate Governance in the Member States* (2009).

[57] N Moloney, *EU Securities Regulation* (Oxford, Oxford University Press, 2002).

[58] Commission staff working document, 'Instruments for a modernised single market' SEC (2007) 1518.

[59] See an analysis of the enforcement approaches of public authorities in M Scholten and A Ottow, 'Institutional Design of Enforcement in the EU: The Case of Financial Markets' (2014) 10(5) *Utrecht Law Review* 80.

[60] A framework for cooperation between the Member States based on 'soft law' alignment of national policies, introduced first in employment law and subsequently in various fields and defined as an EU instrument in the Lisbon strategy: see http://europa.eu/legislation_summaries/glossary/open_method_coordination_en.htm.

[61] See S Hix, 'The Study of the European Union II: The "New Governance" Agenda and its Rival' (1998) 5(1) *Journal of European Public Policy* 38; G de Búrca and J Scott (eds), *Law and New Governance in the EU and the US* (Oxford, Hart Publishing, 2006).

[62] C Semmelmann, 'Theoretical Reflections on the Public-Private Distinction and Their Traces in European Union Law' (2012) 2(4) *Oñati Socio-Legal Series*.

[63] D Levi-Faur, 'The Global Diffusion of Regulatory Capitalism' (2005) 598 *The Annals of the American Academy of Political and Social Science* 12; J Braithwaite, *Regulatory Capitalism: How it Works, Ideas for Making it Work Better* (Cheltenham, Edward Elgar, 2008); J Jordana, 'Globalizing Regulatory Capitalism' (2005) 598 *The Annals of the American Academy of Political and Social Science* 184; D Halberstam, 'The Promise of Comparative Administrative Law; A Constitutional Perspective on Independent Agencies' in S Rose-Ackerman and P Lindseth (eds), *Comparative Administrative Law* (Cheltenham, Edward Elgar, 2010).

[64] C Scott, 'Regulation in the Age of Governance: The Rise of the Post-regulatory State' in J Jordana and D Levi-Faur (eds), *The Politics of Regulation: Institutions and Regulatory Reforms for the Age of Governance* (Cheltenham, Edward Elgar, 2004).

[65] S Turner, 'Expertise and the Process of Policy Making: The EU's New Model of Legitimacy' in S Eliason (ed), *Building Civil Society and Democracy in New Europe* (Newcastle, Cambridge Scholars Publishing, 2008).

policy has been gradually and significantly removed from direct political interference and controlled by expert bodies and committees.[66]

Subsequent chapters highlight the extensive British regime of public enforcement. In examining extensive policy documents issued by the government and regulatory bodies, it will be seen that there is an almost complete absence of references to private enforcement, and (save in relation to competition law) no suggestion that private enforcement could or should play a role in affecting the behaviour of firms or staff.

[66] R Baldwin and C McCrudden (eds), *Regulation and Public Law* (London, Weidenfeld and Nicolson, 1987).

9

The Structure of Regulation and Self-Regulation in the UK

I. Public Authorities, Self-Regulation and Co-Regulation

This chapter describes the key structural features of the British model of regulation, so that individual elements can be recognised as they occur amidst a large amount of detail. The model imposes regulatory controls on behaviour through combinations of public and private actors. The major historical driver that has produced this model may have been an economic one of saving public funds by pushing down responsibilities from public authorities to those regulated, or others in the private sector that could influence them. Thus, the resource-saving imperatives of governmental budget-saving and 'Better Regulation' policies can be seen. But an equally important driver has been the recognition that 'bottom up' influences can deliver effective controls for many responsible businesses through internal control systems. Such an approach has obvious recommendations in saving public expenditure on regulatory bodies. Recommendations to government by the Regulatory Policy Committee (RPC), established in 2009 as an independent review body of all regulatory proposals, highlighted rules of 'Don't presume regulation is the answer, take time and effort to consider all the options (including doing nothing and alternatives to regulation), make sure you have substantive evidence, and produce reliable estimates of costs and benefits'.[1]

Self-regulation is a notable feature of the UK's approach to regulation and enforcement.[2] The problem with self-regulatory systems is that they can inevitably tend to be self-serving, and fail to deliver acceptable behaviour or raise standards, even if they have wide coverage. But the key to the effectiveness of a self- or co-regulatory system is the realisation that standards and behaviour can be effectively delivered if the system is transparent and open to scrutiny by relevant stakeholders. Some external scrutiny, and imposition of required standards, may come vertically from above, so we often see regulatory bodies overseeing self-regulatory schemes (and for similar reasons Parliamentary committees and the National Audit Office oversee the performance of public bodies themselves). But we also see scrutiny and direction of both regulators and business schemes through arrangements on governance (boards and advisory committees) and transparency (publication of all

---

[1] *Reviewing Regulation. An Independent Report on the Analysis Supporting Regulatory Proposals, December 2009–May 2010* (Regulatory Policy Committee, 2010).

[2] *United Kingdom, Challenges at the Cutting Edge* (Paris, OECD, 2002). I Bartle and P Vass, *Self-Regulation and the Regulatory State—A Survey of Policy and Practice* (Bath, Centre for the Study of Regulated Industries, University of Bath School of Management, 2005). The government's Better Regulation Task Force published a sequence of reports pressing the advantages of self-regulation between 1999 and 2005.

information about activities, except for personal data restricted by law or national security, including consultation of proposed changes), which gives opportunities for scrutiny by all stakeholders and the media. These functions of governance and oversight are therefore performed by combinations of actors at different levels, comprising elected parliamentarians, various elements of the public executive and regulatory officials, corporate structures, shareholders, trade associations, customers, consumers and/or civil society organisations.

By these means, different combinations of incentives and levers can involve a multi-layered institutional structure, with several *tiers* of 'controllers', perhaps in a hierarchy of public officials at the top of a structure or pyramid (and perhaps both national and local officials), and underneath them trade associations, consumers associations, the media, individual consumers and individual market trading operators.

The policy is based on academic regulatory theory and experience that self-regulatory structures are particularly effective when subject to public oversight based on systems control, transparency and accountability.[3] The model has recently been called *meta regulation*. These theoretical aspects are discussed further at chapter 17.

It will be seen that the *meta* or tiered approach to regulation is similar to the emphasis on alternative dispute resolution (ADR) that is found in relation to resolution of private law claims, by avoiding the court system. ADR has essentially emerged within sophisticated self-regulatory structures, notably through the development of many ombudsmen,[4] and specialist tribunals linked with business codes of conduct.[5] Typical governance and transparency structures have been applied to ensure the accountability of ADR bodies.

II. The Landscape of Public Regulatory Bodies

The classic means of imposing regulation is through a public administrative structure, comprising of an official regulatory body created by the state and empowered to impose rules and sanctions for specific behaviour.

The United Kingdom has many such regulatory bodies, created in response to old or new markets. Privatisation of certain functions, such as utilities or railways, has usually been accompanied by creation of a regulatory body to control the new private market operators. New markets can also be created spontaneously, such as by commercialisation of new technology. The European Union's harmonisation of market sectors has been a major source of regulation and regulatory authorities.

---

[3] AI Ogus, 'Rethinking Self-Regulation' (1995) 15 *Oxford Journal of Legal Studies* 97–108; J Black, 'Constitution-alising Self-regulation' (1996) 59 *Modern Law Review* 24–55; Bartle and Vass, ibid.

[4] As at April 2013, there were 49 members of the Ombudsman Association, most of whom were public sector bodies: see at www.ombudsmanassociation.org/association-members-by-country.php?area=1. A recent list of public sector Ombudsmen included 24 UK Ombudsmen, 30 other public complaint handling bodies and 50 public sector tribunals.

[5] *United Kingdom, Challenges at the Cutting Edge* (Paris, OECD, 2002). J Stuyck and others, *Commission Study on Alternative Means of Consumer Redress other than Redress through Ordinary Judicial proceedings* (Catholic University of Leuven, January 17, 2007, issued April 2007).

Public regulation is regarded as essential in Britain. The consumer policy body, Consumer Focus, said in 2010:

> Effective regulation is critically important in protecting consumers from harm, ensuring fair access to essential services, stopping market abuses, establishing standards to enable competition, and removing barriers to entry.[6]

England and Wales has a number of national regulatory authorities and a network of local authorities. The major authorities (75 of them) are listed in Table 9.1.

Table 9.1: List of UK National Regulators[7]

Animal Health and Veterinary Laboratories Agency*
Animals in Science Regulation Unit*
Architects Registration Board
British Hallmarking Council+
Care Council for Wales+
Care Quality Commission+
Charity Commission for England and Wales+
Civil Aviation Authority+
Claims Management Regulation Unit+
Coal Authority+
Commission for Irish Lighthouses*
Commission for Equality and Human Rights+
Companies House+
Consumers and Markets Authority
Council for Healthcare Regulatory Excellence
Disclosure and Barring Service+
Drinking Water Inspectorate*
Driver and Vehicle Licensing Agency*
Driving Standards Agency*

(continued)

---

[6] *Regulating in the Consumer Interest: Fresh Thinking* (London, Consumer Focus, 2010) available at http://www.consumerfocus.org.uk/assets/1/files/2010/03/Fresch-thinking-Regulation.pdf (accessed 16 August 2010). Consumer Focus was created from the previous National Consumer Council in 2007.

[7] Updated from Lord Heseltine, *No Stone Unturned in Pursuit of Growth* (Department for Business, Innovation & Skills, 2012) 102, available at http://www.bis.gov.uk/assets/biscore/corporate/docs/n/12-1213-no-stone-unturned-in-pursuit-of-growth.pdf and *Regulators' Code: Summary of Regulators and Regulatory Functions Covered* (Department for Business, Innovation & Skills, Better Regulation Delivery Office, 2014). See also http://www.bis.gov.uk/policies/better-regulation/improving-regulatory-delivery/implementing-principles-of-better-regulation/reviewing-regulators/hampton-implementation-review-reports.

Table 9.1: *(Continued)*

Employment Agency Standards Directorate*
English Heritage+
Environment Agency+
Financial Conduct Authority+
Financial Reporting Council*
Fish Health Inspectorate (of which Centre for Environment, Fisheries and Aquaculture Science*)
Fire and Rescue Authorities in England+
Food and Environment Research Agency*
Food Standards Agency+
Forestry Commission+
Gambling Commission+
Gangmasters Licensing Authority+
Groceries Code Adjudicator+
Health and Safety Executive+
HM Revenue and Customs+
Highways Agency*
Homes & Communities Agency+
Human Fertilisation and Embryology Authority+
Human Tissue Authority+
Information Commissioner's Office+
Insolvency Service including Insolvency Practitioner Unit*
Intellectual Property Office*
Legal Services Board+
Marine Management Organisation+
Maritime and Coastguard Agency*
Medicines and Healthcare products Regulatory Agency*
Monitor+
National Counter Terrorism Security Office*
National Measurement Office*
Natural England+
Natural Resources Body for Wales+
Northern Lighthouses Board*
Office of Communications
Office for Fair Access*
Office for Nuclear Regulation*

(continued)

Table 9.1: *(Continued)*

Office for Standards in Education, Children's Services and Skills+
OFQUAL
Office of Rail Regulation
Office of the Regulator of Community Interest Companies+
OFGEM
Pensions Regulator+
Prudential Regulatory Authority+
Regulator of Social Housing+
Rural Payments Agency*
Security Industry Authority+
Senior Traffic Commissioner
Sports Grounds Safety Authority+
The Birmingham Assay Office+
The Edinburgh Assay Office+
The London Assay Office+
The Sheffield Assay Office+
Traffic Commissioners+
Trinity House Lighthouse Service*
Vehicle and Operator Services Agency*
Vehicle Certification Agency*
Veterinary Medicines Directorate*
Water Services Regulation Authority

Note: Agencies are subject to the Regulators' Code if marked * in relation to specified functions exercised by Ministers, and if marked + in relation to all regulatory functions.

Some more information is set out in chapter 13 below on some of the major entities whose activities have particular impact on consumers, and who may now be able to facilitate the delivery of compensation by traders to consumers.

In addition to national regulatory authorities, enforcement responsibilities are held by the police (organised on a county basis), and the Trading Standards departments that are part of the services of local councils.

It can be seen that numerous different authorities affect the relationships between traders/businesses and consumers, both vertically (in sectors such as healthcare, financial services, utilities, communications and so on) and horizontally (general consumer protection and law enforcement).

III. The Development of Policy on Regulation and Enforcement

This section outlines the current policy on public regulation in the United Kingdom, and the development of policy on enforcement used by public regulatory agencies.[8] What is highlighted is the emergence of a new approach towards enforcement generally, which has also incorporated restorative justice (ie redress, compensation and restoration of the status quo *ante*) as a key role for public enforcers. In this respect, the UK has internationally been probably the leading state in the development of policy in the regulatory field, as noted by the Organisation for Economic Co-operation and Development (OECD) and discussed in chapter 10 below.

The account set out here will largely adopt a historical approach and chart the main milestones in the development of practice and policy on regulation and enforcement.[9] Significant change has occurred since 2000. The development of the new policy proceeded with the sequential occurrence of a series of key steps that occurred in parallel in different fields, so it is something of a challenge to set out a narrative that is fully coherent. In order to see the full picture, one needs to note both the overall picture and the interplay of various different issues that were occurring in different areas at the same time, especially criminal law, regulatory reform, self-regulation and the judicial system. These subjects necessarily have to be set out topic by topic, but in reality their historical development occurred contemporaneously and in inter-connected tracks. The current position has been arrived at as a result of the influence of various different factors, involving politics, economic and budgetary issues, academic empirical and theoretical analyses, and the practical operations of enforcers. These separate tracks have not always been easy to bind together into a coherent whole. However, the general direction of evolutionary change is clear, even though it may still evolve further, and has resulted in fundamental reform of the approaches to regulation, enforcement and restitution. This chapter notes in passing some academic theories on regulation and enforcement, but they are analysed in greater detail at chapter 11.

The principal building blocks are the 'Better Regulation' agenda, reducing burdens on business and reducing public resource and expenditure, adopting responsive enforcement in addition to, and sometimes in place of, traditional punitive enforcement, expanding the range of available sanctions so as to enable flexible and targeted responses, and including outcomes for markets and consumers in the goals of regulators, thereby necessarily importing restorative justice as an integral function of enforcement functions.

An important historical strand is the adoption by government of 'Better Regulation' policy, which seeks to enhance competitiveness through reducing burdens on business, adopting a risk-based approach to enforcement, and simultaneously saving money on public regulation by making regulators more efficient. Reducing burdens on business, it was claimed,

---

[8] Some of this draws on various of the author's previous publications, notably C Hodges, *The Reform of Class and Representative Actions in European Legal Systems: A New Framework for Collective Redress in Europe* (Oxford, Hart Publishing, 2008).

[9] This chapter draws on previous accounts, notably Hodges, ibid; F Cafaggi and H-W Micklitz (eds), *New Frontiers of Consumer Protection. The Interplay between Private and Public Enforcement* (Antwerp, Intersentia, 2009); CJS Hodges, 'From Class Actions to Collective Redress' (2009) 28(1) *Civil Justice Quarterly* 41–66.

would improve profitability, innovation and competitiveness. 'Better Regulation' principles have been much in evidence in the development of UK policy in particular sectors, such as in UK review of consumer policy. Indeed, a strong link has been made between, on the one hand, enforcement of consumer protection and competition regulation, and, on the other hand, competitive markets.

Two crucial points should be noted in this narrative. First, we see the development of ideas and policy on how regulators and others should control corporate behaviour. Broadly speaking, the approach moved from a traditional, authoritative 'command and control' approach to one based on responsive approaches towards human behaviour, and how best to incentivise and regulate it within complex organisational structures and systems. References to controlling behaviour through deterrence or punishment have almost disappeared in the policy documents in which the new approach has been developed. Instead, there is considerable reliance on treating most businesses as responsible, and motivated to comply with the rules, and who can be expected to amend their behaviour through advice, guidance, assistance and support. In short, the approach is based on responsibility and compliance, rather than authoritarian repression.

Second, we see that instead of requiring private parties to seek redress through themselves initiating action in the courts for damages (or injunctions), public bodies can not only be involved in facilitating or delivering redress but can be highly effective in doing so. Indeed, such techniques may be more effective, fast and cheap than traditional civil pathways or other techniques. A regulatory approach can be especially useful when large numbers of people or widespread business behaviour is involved. Hence, regulators can be a particularly effective means of addressing mass or collective redress issues, without the cost, delay or abuse of private collective civil litigation.

A. Better Regulation and the Hampton Review

Better Regulation is a policy aimed at reducing two costs: First, the cost to the public purse of public administrative, regulatory and enforcement authorities and, second, the cost to business of inspection and compliance. The UK has led the way in Better Regulation,[10] and the policy has had a profound impact in making both public expenditure and business costs in relation to regulation and compliance more efficient and effective.[11] The expansion of

---

[10] The OECD's 2010 review of capacities for effective regulatory management in 15 EU Member States noted that the 'vigour, breadth and ambition of the United Kingdom's Better Regulation policies are impressive.... An effective balance, rare in Europe, has been achieved between policies to address both the stock and the flow of regulations': see *Better Regulation in Europe: United Kingdom* (Paris, OECD, 2010) 14; further national reports from the OECD's 'EU 15' project are at http://www.oecd.org. The UK inspired an EU policy that included 'smart regulation': Commission Communication on 'A Strategic Review of Better Regulation in the EU' COM (2006) 689, 14.11.2006. President Barroso's 2009 *Political Guidelines for the next Commission*, at http://ec.europa.eu/commission_barroso/president/pdf/press_20090903_EN.pdf.

[11] The evolution of policy can be traced through the following considerable—and incomplete—list of official documents: *Lifting the Burden* (HMSO, 1985) Cmnd 9571; *Building Businesses ... Not Barriers* (HMSO, 1986) Cmnd 9794; *Releasing Enterprise* (HMSO, 1988) Cmnd 512; *Checking the Cost to Business: A Guide to Compliance Cost Assessment* (Department of Trade and Industry, 1992); *Principles of Good Regulation* (Better Regulation Task Force, 1998); the Regulatory Reform Act 2001; *Imaginative Thinking for Better Regulation* (Better Regulation Task Force, 2003); *Better Policy Making: A Guide to Regulatory Impact Assessment* (Cabinet Office, 2003);

Better Regulation policy[12] developed at the start of the new century through a 'governance' structure for promoting Better Regulation, involving the establishment in 2005 of a Better Regulation Executive at the heart of government, to exercise strong influence on new or reformed delivery of regulation,[13] a Better Regulation Action Plan,[14] and a requirement for regulatory impact assessments for new legislation.[15] Scotland is producing its own similar Better Regulation programme, and Regulators' Code.[16]

A further key step was the influential 2005 Hampton Report on reducing unnecessary regulatory burdens on business.[17] Hampton's mission was to examine ways of 'reducing administrative burdens by promoting more efficient approaches to regulatory inspection and enforcement, without compromising regulatory standards or outcomes'.[18] He found that regulators lack effective tools to punish persistent offenders and to reward compliant behaviour by business. He advocated that regulators should adopt a risk-based approach towards securing compliance, and use advice and persuasion as the first step. Hampton included a specific reference to restorative justice.[19] Eliminating resource on unnecessary

---

Avoiding Regulatory Creep (Better Regulation Task Force, 2004); Sir P Gershon, *Releasing Resources for the Front-line: Independent Review of Public Sector Efficiency* (HM Treasury, 2004); *Reducing the Administrative Burdens—the Consumer and Trading Standards Agency: Consultation* (Department of Trade and Industry, 5 July 2005); Better Regulation Executive, *A Bill for Better Regulation: Consultation Document* (Cabinet Office, 2005); *Better Regulation: Draft Simplification Plan* (DTI, 2005); P Hampton, *Reducing Administrative Burdens: Effective Inspection and Enforcement* (HM Treasury, 2005); *Moving Towards The Local Better Regulation Office: The Way Ahead* (Department for Trade and Industry, 2005); *Review of the Regulatory Reform Act 2001* (Cabinet Office, 2005); *Routes to Better Regulation; A Guide to Alternatives to Classic Regulation* (Better Regulation Task Force, 2005); *Less is More: Reducing Burdens, Improving Outcomes* (Better Regulation Task Force, 2006); *The Tools to Deliver Better Regulation: Revising the Regulatory Impact Assessment: A Consultation* (Cabinet Office, Better Regulation Executive, July 2006); *Implementing Hampton: from enforcement to compliance* (HM Treasury, Better Regulation Executive, and Cabinet Office, 2006); *Risk, Responsibility, Regulation: Whose Risk Is It Anyway?* (Better Regulation Commission, 2006); the Legislative and Regulatory Reform Act 2006; *The Efficiency Programme: A Second Review of Progress. Report by the Comptroller and Auditor General* (National Audit Office, 2007) HC 156 I & II 2006–2007; *Government response to Better Regulation Commission report 'Risk, Responsibility, Regulation: Whose Risk Is It Anyway?'* (Cabinet Office, 2007); *Better Regulation, Better Benefits: Getting the Balance Right* (Department for Business, Innovation & Skills, 2009); *Better Regulation in the United Kingdom* (OECD, 2009); Better Regulation Executive, *Better Regulation Made Simple* (HMSO, 2010).

[12] For academic analysis see S Weatherill (ed), *Better Regulation* (Oxford, Hart Publishing, 2007); C Hodges, 'Encouraging Enterprise and Rebalancing Risk: Implications of Economic Policy for Regulation, Enforcement and Compensation' [2007] *European Business Law Review* 1231.

[13] The Better Regulation Executive aimed for a 25% reduction in administrative burdens by 2010, saving £3.3 billion: HM Government, *Summary of Simplification Plans 2009* (December 2009) 14: http://www.bis.gov.uk/files/file54013.pdf.

[14] See http://webarchive.nationalarchives.gov.uk/+/http://www.hmtreasury.gov.uk/better_regulation_action_plan.htm.

[15] See www.cabinetoffice.gov.uk/making-legislation-guide/impact_assessment.aspx.

[16] See the Regulatory Reform (Scotland) Act 2014, and http://www.scotland.gov.uk/Topics/Business-Industry/support/better-regulation/BetterRegulationBillConsultation.

[17] Hampton (n 11).

[18] ibid, Executive Summary. At that stage, regulatory inspection and enforcement was divided between 63 national regulators, 203 trading standards offices and 408 environmental health offices in 468 local authorities.

[19] Whilst 'restorative justice' is a term applied principally to techniques within criminal law enforcement, as discussed in chapter 11, the general concepts of restoration and reparation, and of improving compliance through advice and discussion rather than through confrontational enforcement, were invoked by Hampton.

and duplicative inspections by different agencies should enable them to divert energies to giving advice. In relation to penalties, he concluded:

> Businesses and regulators have an interest in proper sanctions against illegal activity in order to prevent businesses operating outside the law from gaining a competitive advantage. At present, regulatory penalties do not take the economic value of a breach into consideration and it is quite often in a business's interest to pay the fine rather than comply. This is especially true where a business feels able to shrug off the reputational risk of prosecution. If businesses face no effective deterrent for illegal activity, some will be tempted to break the law, and regulators will need to inspect more businesses.[20]

Hampton set out the following 'principles of inspection and enforcement', which were subsequently referred to as the Hampton Principles:

— Regulators, and the regulatory system as a whole, should use comprehensive risk assessment to concentrate resources on the areas that need them most;
— Regulators should be accountable for the efficiency and effectiveness of their activities, while remaining independent in the decisions they take;
— All regulations should be written so that they are easily understood, easily implemented, and easily enforced, and all interested parties should be consulted when they are being drafted;
— No inspection should take place without a reason;
— Businesses should not have to give unnecessary information, nor give the same piece of information twice;
— The few businesses that persistently break regulations should be identified quickly, and face proportionate and meaningful sanctions;
— Regulators should provide authoritative, accessible advice easily and cheaply;
— When new policies are being developed, explicit consideration should be given to how they can be enforced using existing systems and data to minimise the administrative burden imposed;
— Regulators should be of the right size and scope, and no new regulator should be created where an existing one can do the work; and
— Regulators should recognise that a key element of their activity will be to allow, or even encourage, economic progress and only to intervene when there is a clear case for protection.

In the 2005 Consumer White Paper, the government set out 'a strategy to empower consumers and support business success' for the next five to 10 years, which included a strong recapitulation of the 'responsive regulation', risk-based enforcement and Hampton approaches:

> We have rejected the old-fashioned idea that businesses need to be routinely regulated and inspected to keep them in line. The vast majority of businesses want to act responsibly. The pressure to attract and retain customers is a far more powerful and effective incentive on business to act with integrity and responsibility than anything Central or Local Government can do…[21]

---

[20] Hampton (n 11) para 16. The review encountered numerous examples where penalties fell far short of the commercial value of the regulatory breach.

[21] *A Fair Deal for All. Extending Competitive Markets: Empowered Consumers, Successful Business* (Department for Trade and Industry, 2005) para 1.2.

Our consumer regime will be based on the principle of proportionate, risk-assessed and evidence-based intervention. Instead of regulating and inspecting on a routine all-inclusive basis, we want to see more effort targeted on rogue traders, and a lighter touch for mainstream responsible businesses.[22]

The 2006 UK Treasury review on implementation of Hampton stated:

Globalisation increases competition and places a premium on a strong business environment. As markets become more competitive, it is important to do more to ensure the right conditions are in place to enable businesses and individuals to respond to new opportunities and incentives....

It is no longer true that most businesses, if unregulated, will act irresponsibly. Well-informed consumers, corporate social responsibility, organised labour, pressure and interest groups have all encouraged businesses to take measures to reduce risk to society. For example, the number of reported non-fatal injuries at work has fallen by 68 per cent between 1974 and 2006....

In this context it is clear that regulatory regimes need to adapt to the changing world of the 21st century. The Hampton principles outline a risk-based approach to regulation which sits in line with a world where competition is fierce, consumers are better informed, and resources are scarce....

Underpinning the review's recommendations on advice was the principle that regulators should also support economic progress by only intervening where there was a clear case for protection, as well as taking action to encourage economic growth where possible. Therefore it is important that regulators take responsibility for any costs that they bring to businesses and work to minimise them. Regulators should also be held accountable for their effectiveness.[23]

B. The Macrory Penalty Principles

An international comparison carried out by the UK had found that the UK consumer policy regime was amongst the best in several areas, but behind other countries in having a more fragmented enforcement framework that led to inconsistent enforcement.[24]

As noted in chapter 10 below, in 2003 the making of reparation by offenders to persons affected by their offences was explicitly included as one of the purposes of the criminal justice system.[25] In a parallel development in the area of regulatory enforcement, a revolution occurred in United Kingdom policy in the first decade of the twentieth century, when restoration became an integral part of regulatory enforcement rather than a separate activity undertaken always by separate persons and processes. The new approach forged a holistic linkage between public and private consequences of illicit behaviour.

In 2006 Professor Richard Macrory reported to the government on his review of regulatory enforcement penalties.[26] Macrory's initial aim was to ensure a level playing field for

---

[22] ibid, para 1.9.
[23] HM Treasury, Better Regulation Executive, and Cabinet Office, *Implementing Hampton: From Enforcement to Compliance*, November 2006, 32.
[24] *Comparative Report on Consumer Policy Regimes* (Department of Trade and Industry, 2003).
[25] Criminal Justice Act 2003, s 142.
[26] R Macrory, *Regulatory Justice: Making Sanctions Effective* (HM Treasury, 2006); reprinted in R Macrory, *Regulation, Enforcement and Governance in Environmental Law* (Oxford, Hart Publishing, 2010).

all businesses through removing any financial gain from failure to comply. Most breaches would face penalties that are quicker and easier to apply while there would be tougher penalties for rogue businesses that persistently break the rules. Greater flexibility would be introduced so as to provide regulators with better deterrence options and therefore encourage compliance from business. However, in order to reduce the risk that authorities might abuse their increased powers and discretion, the regime included significant governance controls on regulators, with access to the new powers requiring that the authority demonstrate that it has adopted a risk-based approach to enforcement.

Coming from a background of environmental law, Macrory identified a set of six Penalty Principles that should apply to all regulatory enforcement.[27] These Penalty Principles were:

1. Aim to change the behaviour of the offender;
2. aim to eliminate any financial gain or benefit from non-compliance;
3. be responsive and consider what is appropriate for the particular offender and regulatory issue, which can include punishment and the public stigma that should be associated with a criminal conviction;
4. be proportionate to the nature of the offence and the harm caused;
5. aim to restore the harm caused by regulatory non-compliance, where appropriate; and
6. aim to deter future non-compliance.

Strong similarity will be seen between these Penalty Principles and the purposes of enforcement of criminal law noted in chapter 10 below. The first focus is on *behaviour*—supporting ongoing compliance and changing behaviour that results in non-compliance. Such change in behaviour is not expressed solely—or principally—in terms of 'deterrence', although deterrence is mentioned (albeit last in the list). The second focus is on *justice*, but removing illicit gains of wrongdoing from the offender and restoring harm caused, whether to individuals, businesses or the environment. Thus the Macrory approach constitutes a revolutionary shift in the policy, justification and purposes of regulatory enforcement, away from a retributive or deterrent approach to an approach based on maximising compliance and justice. He later noted:

> Perhaps the two key principles were that first a sanctioning regime should not be designed to punish *per se* (though sometimes punishment was necessary) but to ensure that the offending business was brought back into compliance, and second, that an effective regime should ensure that no economic gains are made from non-compliance.[28]

It will be seen that Principles two and five are complimentary in approaching the consequences of the illegal activity from both of the opposing sides, in that the former is targeted at removing the infringer's illicit gains,[29] whereas the latter seeks restoration of the victim to the ex ante position. Principle five explicitly sets out a restorative justice goal, focusing on a holistic process that addresses the repercussions and obligations created by harm with a

---

[27] Macrory reviewed 61 national regulators, but not financial regulators or regulators of privatised utilities.

[28] Macrory, *Regulation, Enforcement and Governance in Environmental Law* (Oxford, Hart Publishing, 2010) 15.

[29] Macrory recommended wider use of Profit Orders to address the level of illicit gain by an offender, Confiscation Orders under the Proceeds of Crime Act 2002, and the introduction of Corporate Rehabilitation Orders, designed to address a company's poor practices and prevent future non-compliance, such as through commitment to a plan of action to remedy a matter.

view to putting things right.[30] Hence, the purpose of regulatory penalties expressly seeks to achieve the same objective as private compensation law and procedures. The emphasis is on a *process* 'whereby those most directly affected by a wrongdoing come together to determine what needs to be done to repair the harm and prevent a reoccurrence.'[31]

Macrory also set out seven 'characteristics' that regulators should adopt:

1. Publish an enforcement policy;
2. measure outcomes not just outputs;
3. justify their choice of enforcement actions year on year to stakeholders, Ministers and Parliament;
4. follow-up enforcement actions where appropriate;
5. enforce in a transparent manner;
6. be transparent in the way in which they apply and determine administrative penalties; and
7. avoid perverse incentives that might influence the choice of sanctioning response.

Macrory recommended that enforcers should have available a new range of administrative sanctions, to complement the traditional criminal provisions. The 'civil sanctions' were intended to complement existing criminal powers, and fill the gap between formal criminal actions and mere persuasion, thereby enhancing the power to persuade and also reducing swifter, more effective and proportionate responses in most cases of regulatory non-compliance. The civil sanctions comprised:

A. *Fixed Monetary Penalties*, which could only be imposed where the regulator is satisfied beyond reasonable doubt that the person has committed the relevant offence.
B. *Discretionary requirements*, which could only be imposed where the regulator is satisfied beyond reasonable doubt that the person has committed the relevant offence. These include:
   — *Variable monetary penalties*, requiring a person to pay a monetary penalty the value of which is determined by the regulator. A person may give a third party undertaking to compensate persons affected by an offence, and the regulator if it accepts the undertaking must take it into account in determining the variable monetary penalty.
   — *Compliance notices*, requiring a non-compliant business to undertake specified actions within a stated period to bring them back to compliance, and to secure that an offence does not continue or happen again.
   — *Restoration notices*, requiring a person to undertake specified actions within a stated period to restore the position to what it had been had the non-compliance not occurred.
C. *Stop notices*, requiring a person to cease an activity that is or is likely to cause serious harm and is or is likely to give rise to regulatory non-compliance. This would apply until the person has taken steps to come back into compliance. Stop notices are

---

[30] Macrory (n 28) para 4.32.
[31] *Restorative Justice and Practices*—presented at 'Restorative Justice in Action … into the Mainstream', The 3rd International Winchester Restorative Justice Group Conference, 29 and 30 March 2006, London: quoted in Macrory (n 28) para 4.33.

designed to prevent an activity or planned activity causing serious harm or a significant risk of serious harm to the environment or human health. As part of the power to serve a stop notice, there must be provision for the regulator to compensate the person for any loss suffered as a result of the service of the notice and for appeal against a decision by the regulator not to award compensation.

D.   *Enforcement undertakings*, an agreement offered by a person to a regulator to take specific corrective actions set out in the undertaking related to what the regulator suspects to be an offence. This enables a person to give an undertaking to do what a regulator would otherwise have to take formal action to specify.

C. Implementation of Hampton and Macrory: The RESA and Regulators' Compliance Code

The Labour government swiftly adopted all the recommendations in the Hampton Report[32] and Macrory Report and enshrined the new regime on administrative sanctions in the Regulatory Enforcement and Sanctions Act 2008 (RESA).[33] Hence, the Better Regulation initiative culminated in the government introducing legislation that provided a new enforcement framework and powers, involving a combination of components, notably a duty on many regulatory bodies[34] to observe statutory principles of good regulation, that 'regulatory activities should be carried out in a way which is transparent, accountable, proportionate, consistent, and that regulatory activities should be targeted only cases in which action is needed.'[35] The specified regulatory bodies are subject[36] to a Code of practice for the exercise of regulatory functions,[37] which is an expansion of the principles. It was issued

---

[32] See intermediate steps in *Implementing Hampton: From Enforcement to Compliance* (HM Treasury, Better Regulation Executive, Cabinet Office, 2006).

[33] See J Norris and J Philips, *The Law of Regulatory Enforcement and Sanctions. A Practical Guide* (Oxford, Oxford University Press, 2011).

[34] See The Legislative and Regulatory Reform (Regulatory Functions) Order 2007, SI 2007/3544 specified various bodies including 27 national regulatory agencies including the Civil Aviation Authority, the Environment Agency, the Financial Services Authority, the Food Standards Agency, the Health and Safety Commission, the Health and Safety Executive, the Office of Fair Trading (other than any regulatory function under competition or merger law), the Pensions Regulator. See subsequent amendments in The Legislative and Regulatory Reform (Regulatory Functions) (Amendment) Order 2009, SI 2009/2981, The Legislative and Regulatory Reform (Regulatory Functions) (Amendment) Order 2010, SI 2010/3028, The Legislative and Regulatory Reform (Regulatory Functions) (Amendment) Order 2014, SI 2014/860 (adding the Groceries Code Adjudicator, Monitor and the Regulator of Community Interest Companies, and omitting three others). An order may not specify *regulatory* functions in relation to the Gas and Markets Authority, the Office of Communications, the Office of Rail Regulation, the Postal Services Commission, and the Water Services regulatory Authority (since these are specified in primary legislation): LRRA, s 24(5).

[35] LLRA 2006, s 21. The government later claimed that the principles of Good Regulation were 'a widely accepted definition of best practice': S Vadera, *Government Response to the House of Lords Select Committee on Regulators-Report on UK Economic Regulators* (Department for Business Enterprise & Regulatory Reform, 2008) para 1.2.

[36] LLRA 2006, s 22(2) and (3). The Code is issued by a Minister. Any business that believes that a regulator is failing to have regard to the Code will be able to seek redress by complaining to the relevant regulator or the Parliamentary Ombudsman. It may also be possible to apply for judicial review of the regulator's actions.

[37] 'Regulatory function' means (a) a function under any enactment of imposing requirements, restrictions or conditions, or setting standards or giving guidance, in relation to any activity; or (b) a function which relates

as the Regulators' Compliance Code in 2007.[38] As discussed below, a revised Regulators' Code came into force on 6 April 2014.

Part 4 of RESA created a *duty on specified bodies not to impose or maintain unnecessary burdens in the exercise of regulatory functions.*[39] This duty applied to the Gas and Electricity Markets Authority, the Office of Fair Trading, the Office of Rail Regulation, the Postal Services Commission and the Water Services Regulation Authority, other than any function exercised under competition law.[40] A body to which this obligation applied was required to publish a statement setting out what they proposed to do pursuant to the duty. The statement must explain what has been done in respect of the duty since the previous statement, except if it is the first statement that has published. Where a burden that is unnecessary has not been removed, the statement must explain why its removal would be disproportionate or impracticable.[41]

The Regulators' Compliance Code applied to the exercise of specified functions by specified regulators. Any regulator whose functions are so specified must have regard to the Code (a) when determining any general policy or principles about the exercise of those specified functions;[42] or (b) when exercising a specified regulatory function which is itself a function of setting standards or giving general guidance about other regulatory functions (whether their own functions or someone else's functions).[43] Thus, the Code does not apply to the exercise of any specified regulatory function in individual cases.

The statutory principles of the Code were a restatement of the Hampton principles, and the Better Regulation Commission's Principles of Good Regulation.[44] The main text of the Code is set out in Box 9.1. The introduction to the Code stressed:

> the need for regulators to adopt a positive and proactive approach towards ensuring compliance by:
>
> —   helping and encouraging regulated entities to understand and meet regulatory requirements more easily; and
> —   responding proportionately to regulatory breaches.[45]

The 2007 Code included a number of important innovations. First, it made clear that regulators play an integral role in the economic system, and so their actions must be subject to assessment of the effect that they have on businesses, especially small and medium sized enterprises (SMEs). Second, their resources must be targeted where they can be most effective, and this must be done on the basis of assessing risks, so as to prioritise action accordingly. Third, regulators should provide general information, advice and guidance to

---

to the securing of compliance with, or the enforcement of, requirements, restrictions, conditions, standards or guidance which under or by virtue of any enactment relate to any activity: Legislative and Regulatory Reform Act 2006, s 32(2).

[38] *Regulators' Compliance Code: Statutory Code of Practice for Regulators* (Department for Business Enterprise and Regulatory Reform, 17 December 2007), at http://www.berr.gov.uk/files/file45019.pdf. The Code is made under the LRRA, s 22(1).

[39] RESA, s 72. Under s 73(3)–(6).

[40] ibid, s 73(2).

[41] ibid, s 72(3)–(6).

[42] LRRA, s 22(2).

[43] s 22(3).

[44] See *Explanatory Notes to Legislative and Regulatory Reform Act 2006.*

[45] Code (n 38) para 1.3.

businesses so as to support maximisation of compliance. This reflects a wide understanding of the role and functions of regulators, which is far from being solely about enforcement. Fourth, there was a specific requirement on regulators to comply with the Macrory principles (paragraph 8), thereby including the aims of changing offenders' behaviour, eliminating any financial gain or benefit from non-compliance, and restoring harm caused where appropriate.[46]

Box 9.1: Regulatory Compliance Code 2007

3. Economic progress[47]

3.1 Regulators should consider the impact that their regulatory interventions may have on economic progress, including through consideration of the costs, effectiveness and perceptions of fairness of regulation. They should only adopt a particular approach if the benefits justify the costs and it entails the minimum burden compatible with achieving their objectives.

3.2 Regulators should keep under review their regulatory activities and interventions with a view to considering the extent to which it would be appropriate to remove or reduce the regulatory burdens they impose.

3.3 Regulators should consider the impact that their regulatory interventions may have on small regulated entities, using reasonable endeavours to ensure that the burdens of their interventions fall fairly and proportionately on such entities, by giving consideration to the size of the regulated entities and the nature of their activities.

3.4 When regulators set standards or give guidance in relation to the exercise of their own or other regulatory functions (including the functions of local authorities), they should allow for reasonable variations to meet local government priorities, as well as those of the devolved administrations.

4. Risk Assessment

4.1 Regulators should ensure that the allocation of their regulatory efforts and resources is targeted where they would be most effective by assessing the risks to their regulatory outcomes. They should also ensure that risk assessment precedes and informs all aspects of their approaches to regulatory activity, including:
— data collection and other information requirements;
— inspection programmes;
— advice and support programmes; and
— enforcement and sanctions.

---

[46] Code (n 38) para 8.3. As mentioned above, the same approach was previously mandated under 'Purpose (e)' of the purposes of sentencing set out in s 142 of the Criminal Justice Act 2003: 'Any court dealing with an offender in respect of an offence must have regard to the following purposes of sentencing … (e) the making of reparation by offenders to persons affected by their offences.'

[47] The numbering of the original started at 3.

4.2   Risk assessment should be based on all available relevant and good-quality data. It should include explicit consideration of the combined effect of:
   —   the potential impact of non-compliance on regulatory outcomes; and
   —   the likelihood of non-compliance.

4.3   In evaluating the likelihood of non-compliance, regulators should give consideration to all relevant factors, including:
   —   past compliance records and potential future risks;
   —   the existence of good systems for managing risks, in particular within regulated entities or sites
   —   evidence of recognised external accreditation; and
   —   management competence and willingness to comply.

4.4   Regulators should consult and involve regulated entities and other interested parties in designing their risk methodologies, and publish details of the methodologies.

4.5   Regulators should regularly review and, where appropriate, improve their risk methodologies. In doing so, they should take into account feedback and other information from regulated entities and other interested parties.

5. Advice and Guidance

5.1   Regulators should ensure that all legal requirements relating to their regulatory activities, as well as changes to those legal requirements, are promptly communicated or otherwise made available to relevant regulated entities.

5.2   Regulators should provide general information, advice and guidance to make it easier for regulated entities to understand and meet their regulatory obligations. Such information, advice and guidance should be provided in clear, concise and accessible language, using a range of appropriate formats and media.

5.3   Regulators should involve regulated entities in developing both the content and style of regulatory guidance. They should assess the effectiveness of their information and support services by monitoring regulated entities' awareness and understanding of legal requirements, including the extent to which those entities incur additional costs obtaining external advice in order to understand and comply with legal requirements.

5.4   Regulators should provide targeted and practical advice that meets the needs of regulated entities. Such advice may be provided in a range of formats, such as through face-to-face interactions, telephone helpline and online guidance. In determining the appropriate formats, regulators should seek to maximise the reach, accessibility and effectiveness of advice while ensuring efficient use of resources. There may remain a need for regulated entities with particularly complex practices to use specialist or professional advisors as appropriate.

5.5   When offering compliance advice, regulators should distinguish between statutory requirements and advice or guidance aimed at improvements above minimum standards. Advice should be confirmed in writing, if requested.

5.6   Regulators should provide appropriate means to ensure that regulated entities can reasonably seek and access advice from the regulator without directly triggering an enforcement action. In responding to such an approach, the regulator should seek primarily to provide the advice and guidance necessary to help ensure compliance.

5.7 Advice services should generally be provided free of charge, but it may be appropriate for regulators to charge a reasonable fee for services beyond basic advice and guidance necessary to help ensure compliance. Regulators should, however, take account of the needs and circumstances of smaller regulated entities and others in need of help and support.

6. Inspections and other visits

6.1 Regulators should ensure that inspections and other visits, such as compliance or advice visits, to regulated entities only occur in accordance with a risk assessment methodology (see paragraphs 4.2. and 4.3), except where visits are requested by regulated entities, or where a regulator acts on relevant intelligence.

6.2 Regulators should use only a small element of random inspection in their programme to test their risk methodologies or the effectiveness of their interventions.

6.3 Regulators should focus their **greatest** inspection effort on regulated entities where risk assessment shows that both:
  — a compliance breach or breaches would pose a serious risk to a regulatory outcome; and
  — there is high likelihood of non-compliance by regulated entities.

6.4 Where regulators visit or carry out inspections of regulated entities, they should give positive feedback to the regulated entities to encourage and reinforce good practices. Regulators should also share amongst regulated entities, and with other regulators, information about good practice.

6.5 Where two or more inspectors, whether from the same or different regulators, undertake planned inspections of the same regulated entity, regulators should have arrangements for collaboration to minimise burdens on the regulated entity, for example, through joint or coordinated inspections and data sharing.

7. Information requirements

7.1 When determining which data they may require, regulators should undertake an analysis of the costs and benefits of data requests to regulated entities. Regulators should give explicit consideration to reducing costs to regulated entities through:
  — varying data requests according to risk, as set out in paragraph 6.3;
  — limiting collection to specific regulated entities sectors/sub-sectors;
  — reducing the frequency of data collection;
  — obtaining data from other sources;
  — allowing electronic submission; and
  — requesting only data which is justified by risk assessment.

7.2 If two or more regulators require the same information from the same regulated entities, they should share data to avoid duplication of collection where this is practicable, beneficial and cost effective. Regulators should note the content of the Information Commissioner's letter when applying the Data Protection Act 1998 in order to avoid unnecessarily restricting the sharing of data.

7.3   Regulators should involve regulated entities in vetting data requirements and form design for clarity and simplification. They should seek to collect data in a way that is compatible with the processes of regulated entities and those of other regulators who collect similar data.

8. Compliance and enforcement actions

8.1   Regulators should seek to reward those regulated entities that have consistently achieved good levels of compliance through positive incentives, such as lighter inspections and reporting requirements where risk assessment justifies this. Regulators should also take account of the circumstances of small regulated entities, including any difficulties they may have in achieving compliance.

8.2   When considering formal enforcement action, regulators should, where appropriate, discuss the circumstances with those suspected of a breach and take these into account when deciding on the best approach. This paragraph does not apply where immediate action is required to prevent or respond to a serious breach or where to do so is likely to defeat the purpose of the proposed enforcement action.

8.3   Regulators should ensure that their sanctions and penalties policies are consistent with the principles set out in the Macrory Review. This means that their sanctions and penalties policies should:
—   aim to change the behaviour of the offender;
—   aim to eliminate any financial gain or benefit from non-compliance;
—   be responsive and consider what is appropriate for the particular offender and regulatory issue, which can include punishment and the public stigma that should be associated with a criminal conviction;
—   be proportionate to the nature of the offence and the harm caused;
—   aim to restore the harm caused by regulatory non-compliance, where appropriate; and
—   aim to deter future non-compliance.

8.4   In accordance with the Macrory characteristics, regulators should also:
—   publish an enforcement policy;
—   measure outcomes not just outputs;
—   justify their choice of enforcement actions year on year to interested parties;
—   follow-up enforcement actions where appropriate;
—   enforce in a transparent manner;
—   be transparent in the way in which they apply and determine penalties; and
—   avoid perverse incentives that might influence the choice of sanctioning response.

8.5   Regulators should ensure that clear reasons for any formal enforcement action are given to the person or entity against whom any enforcement action is being taken at the time the action is taken. These reasons should be confirmed in writing at the earliest opportunity. Complaints and relevant appeals procedures for redress should also be explained at the same time.

8.6   Regulators should enable inspectors and enforcement officers to interpret and apply relevant legal requirements and enforcement policies fairly and consistently between like-regulated entities in similar situations. Regulators should also ensure that their own inspectors and enforcement staff interpret and apply their legal requirements and enforcement policies consistently and fairly.

9. Accountability

9.1   Regulators should create effective consultation and feedback opportunities to enable continuing cooperative relationships with regulated entities and other interested parties.

9.2   Regulators should identify and explain the principal risks against which they are acting. They should, in consultation with regulated entities and other interested parties, set and publish clear standards and targets for their service and performance. These standards should include:
   — regulatory outcomes (capturing the principal risks);
   — costs to regulated entities of regulatory interventions; and
   — perceptions of regulated entities and other interested parties about the proportionality and effectiveness of regulatory approach and costs.

9.3   Regulators should measure their performance against the standards in paragraph 9.2 and regularly publish the results. To aid understanding, regulators should also explain how they measure their performance.

9.4   Local authorities and fire and rescue authorities are exempt from the requirements of paragraphs 9.2 and 9.3.

9.5   Regulators should ensure that their employees provide courteous and efficient services to regulated entities and others. They should take account of comments from regulated entities and other interested parties regarding the behaviour and activity of inspectors and other enforcement staff.

9.6   Regulators should provide effective and timely complaints procedures (including for matters in this Code) that are easily accessible to regulated entities and other interested parties. They should publicise their complaints procedures, with details of the process and likely timescale for resolution.

9.7   Complaints procedures should include a final stage to an independent, external, person. Where there is a relevant Ombudsman or Tribunal with powers to decide on matters in this Code, the final stage should allow referral to that body. However, where no such person exists, a regulator should, in consultation with interested parties, provide for further complaint or appeal to another independent person, for example, an independent professional body.

In 2008 the government issued a Code of Practice on Guidance on Regulation[48] and, for civil servants, a Guide to Code of Practice on Guidance, which cover issuing good guidance on regulation. The policy enshrined in these documents rested on the premise that public regulation should only be introduced, or continued, where it is absolutely necessary. Alternatives to regulation should always be considered wherever appropriate.

D. The Relationship Between Criminal and Regulatory Enforcement

It is general practice for the enforcement powers of enforcement bodies to include criminal enforcement provisions,[49] in addition to sector-specific provisions for those bodies that are sectoral regulators, such as to make certain rules, orders and remove certain authorisations. A further consequence of the Macrory review was reconsideration by the Law Commission of when the criminal law should be used in relation to business enterprises, given that virtually every aspect of business conduct was governed by regulatory requirements.[50] The Law Commission recommended that criminal law should only be used for the most serious cases of non-compliance with the law. An academic paper on which the Commissioners relied indicated that criminal proceedings did not bring much benefit in terms of either individual retribution or general deterrence, so it seemed to them to be an expensive, uncertain and ineffective main strategy.[51] The Law Commission set out the following general principles:

1. The criminal law should only be employed to deal with wrongdoers who deserve the stigma associated with criminal conviction because they have engaged in seriously reprehensible conduct. It should not be used as the primary means of promoting regulatory objectives.
2. Harm done or risked should be regarded as serious enough to warrant criminalization only if:
    (a)   in some circumstances (not just extreme circumstances), and individual could justifiably be sent to prison for a first offence, or
    (b)   an unlimited fine is necessary to address the seriousness of the wrongdoing in issue, and its consequences.
3. Low-level criminal offences should be repealed in any instance where the introduction of a civil penalty (or equivalent measure) is likely to do as much to secure appropriate levels of punishment and deterrence.[52]

As noted in chapters 10 and 11, other relevant changes in restorative justice and criminal law were also pursued, including the extended use of compensation orders and deferred prosecution agreements.

---

[48]   Better Regulation Executive, 7 July 2008, at http://www.bis.gov.uk/files/file53268.pdf.
[49]   For example, trading standards authorities have prosecution powers under the Weights and Measures Act 1985, s 83; the Consumer Protection from Unfair Trading Regulations 2008/1277, s 19(1); the Public Bodies (The Office of Fair Trading Transfer of Consumer Advice Scheme Function and Modification of Enforcement Functions) Order 2013/783, s 13(4).
[50]   *Criminal Liability in Regulatory Contexts: A Consultation Paper* (The Law Commission, 2010), Consultation Paper No 195, note para 1.34.
[51]   ibid, paras 1.7 and 1.8, referring to J Black, 'A Review of Enforcement Techniques', Appendix A to the Consultation Paper.
[52]   ibid, paras 1.28–1.30.

E. Regulation Supporting Growth

The 2009 Anderson Review estimated that 'uncertainty' over regulations in general (with the under/over-compliance it brings) cost business over £880 million a year.[53] On assuming office in May 2010, the Coalition government adopted much of the previous government's policy and continued the trend to reform regulatory and enforcement policy, starting with establishing new principles to underpin its approach to regulation. It noted criticism of recurrent weaknesses in departments' assessments of costs and benefits when designing regulation.

Almost all government policies at this time were directed at delivering the central economic strategy set out in the 2011 Budget of a national plan for growth so as to recover from the financial crisis. The intention was that public sector expenditure would be cut significantly but the consequential rise in unemployment should be offset by a strong private sector recovery. Coalition government priorities included not only reducing regulation but also to 'strengthen consumer protections, especially for the most vulnerable, and promote more responsible corporate and consumer behaviour through greater transparency and by harnessing the insights from behavioural economics and social psychology'.[54]

The Coalition Government swiftly set out its policy on regulation in 2010, namely that 'reducing regulation is a key priority'.[55] It stated the 'strategic context' as follows:

> Reducing regulation matters. Through eliminating the avoidable burdens of regulation and bureaucracy, the Government aims to promote growth, innovation and social action.
>
> Freeing businesses and civil society groups from unnecessarily burdensome regulation, and simplifying the complex regulatory system, can free up the capacity they have to innovate, diversify and grow. Striking the right balance—'a level of regulation that promotes competition and stability without impinging on businesses' ability to operate'[56]—is therefore a core element of the Government's strategy for supporting economic growth.[57]

To eliminate the avoidable burdens of regulation and bureaucracy, the Government stated that it would:[58]

— Remove existing regulation that unnecessarily impedes growth;
— introduce new regulation only as a last resort;
— reduce the overall volume of new regulation;
— improve the quality of the design of new regulation;
— reduce the regulatory cost to business and civil society groups;
— move to a risk-based enforcement regime where inspections are minimised.

---

[53] S Anderson, *The Good Guidance Guide: Taking the Uncertainty out of Regulation* (Better Regulation Executive, 2009) www.bis.gov.uk/files/file49881.pdf.

[54] See *The Path to Strong, Sustainable and Balanced Growth* (HM Treasury and Department for Business, Innovation & Skills, 2010).

[55] *Reducing Regulation Made Simple: Less Regulation, Better Regulation and Regulation as a Last Resort* (HM Government, 2010).

[56] Citing: *From A Strategy for Sustainable Growth*, published by BIS 2010, available at https://www.gov.uk/government/uploads/system/uploads/attachment_data/file/31997/10-1058-strategy-for-sustainable-growth.pdf. The supporting economic annex is available at https://www.gov.uk/government/uploads/system/uploads/attachment_data/file/31998/10-1059-sustainable-growth-economic-annex.pdf.

[57] *Reducing Regulation Made Simple* (n 55) para 1.1 and 2.

[58] ibid, para 1.5.

The 'New Regulatory Framework' had four elements:

1. A different approach to thinking about and using regulation
2. A new decision-making structure for regulatory proposals
3. Tougher scrutiny of existing regulations
4. Streamlining and improving the system of enforcement, departing from 'tick-box' systems of inspection and audit

A vision was set out of how the new approach would apply to Parliament, ministers, civil servants, enforcers, businesses, civil society groups and citizens. In relation to enforcers of regulation, the vision was:[59]

—   Work with the grain of businesses' and other organisations' own incentives and processes, reducing oversight and inspection of organisations where effective self-regulatory systems and controls exist;
—   focus efforts on high risk businesses, particularly those who deliberately seek to get an advantage over their competitors by breaking the law.

The policy paper set out alternative approaches to introducing 'command and control' regulation, which are referred to in chapter 11. It announced a new decision-making structure for regulatory proposals, which included scrutiny by the Cabinet's Reducing Regulation Committee, a 'one-in, one-out' rule, independent scrutiny of impact assessments by a Regulatory Policy Committee, sunset clauses for new regulations, and rules for transposing EU Directives.[60] Under the policy of streamlining and improving the system of enforcement, the paper said:[61]

> 57. Where regulation is necessary, enforcement needs to be considered early in the policy-making process. Regulation that cannot be enforced is not just ineffective; it may actively harm businesses who do their best to comply, when their competitors fail to do so.

> 58. In addition, regulators' resources are often wasted on intrusive monitoring of the work of compliant businesses, and insufficient energy is given to dealing with those that choose to operate outside the system. The Government aims to move away from a culture of rigid 'tick-box' regulation to one founded on professional competence, pragmatism and trust where businesses are treated as partners in securing the right regulatory outcomes and play a role in the design and implementation of standards, as well as the inspection and enforcement models which are right for the job.

> 59. The Hampton Report set out a number of principles for effective inspection and enforcement. These remain valid. They emphasise good practice, including prioritisation of enforcement according to risk, and the provision of support in the form that is most useful for business.

> ...

> Developing Co-regulatory Approaches

> 63. One of the more challenging aspects of implementing truly risk-based enforcement of regulation is to give appropriate recognition to a business's own efforts to comply with regulation.

---

[59]   ibid, Diagram 1.
[60]   ibid, ss 3.2 and 3.3.
[61]   ibid, s 3.4.

64. More needs to be done to ensure that, where businesses have a good track record of compliance, this is taken into account by regulators, who will then reduce the inspection burden for them. A large number of businesses use independent certification and audit to monitor the quality of their systems as a routine part of their work and the scope of these audits often overlaps with government-instigated regulation and inspection. BRE will work with departments and regulators to reduce the scale of state-led inspection and monitoring where such recognised systems of independent audit and assurance exist.

65. In sectors where businesses' own measures are sufficiently robust, there may be scope to go beyond simply reducing the burden of state-led inspections and to consider the role of third parties and industry bodies as an explicit part of the regulatory regime. This could include third parties taking a leading role on standard setting, professional development, the operation of compliance regimes and independent professional audit. BRE will work with departments and regulators to identify opportunities to expand the role of third parties, and will review existing legislation to determine where there are legal obstacles to such an approach and to identify what can be done to overcome any such barriers.

The Coalition Government followed in 2011 with its *Principles for Economic Regulation*, which were intended to be applied principally to economic regulation, and hence to 'set the framework for delivering greater clarity about the respective roles of Government, regulators and producers'.[62] Six principles were enumerated: Accountability, predictability, coherence, adaptability, focus and efficiency.

Descriptions of the principles included the following expansions:

Accountability

— independent regulation needs to take place within a framework of duties and policies set by a democratically accountable Parliament and Government
— roles and responsibilities between Government and economic regulators should be allocated in such a way as to ensure that regulatory decisions are taken by the body that has the legitimacy, expertise and capability to arbitrate between the required trade-offs
— decision-making powers of regulators should be, within the constraints imposed by the need to preserve commercial confidentiality, exercised transparently and subject to appropriate scrutiny and challenge

Focus

— the role of economic regulators should be concentrated on protecting the interests of end users of infrastructure services by ensuring the operation of well-functioning and contestable markets where appropriate or by designing a system of incentives and penalties that replicate as far as possible the outcomes of competitive markets
— economic regulators should have clearly defined, articulated and prioritised statutory responsibilities focused on outcomes rather than specified inputs or tools
— economic regulators should have adequate discretion to choose the tools that best achieve these outcomes...

---

[62] *Principles for Economic Regulation* (Department for Business, Innovation & Skills, 2011) available at http://www.bis.gov.uk/assets/biscore/better-regulation/docs/p/11-795-principles-for-economic-regulation, see para 7.

Predictability

— the framework for economic regulation should provide a stable and objective environment enabling all those affected to anticipate the context for future decisions and to make long term investment decisions with confidence
— the framework of economic regulation should not unreasonably unravel past decisions, and should allow efficient and necessary investments to receive a reasonable return, subject to the normal risks inherent in markets

Efficiency

— policy interventions must be proportionate and cost-effective while decision making should be timely, and robust.

The government statement included a strong emphasis on regulating only where satisfactory outcomes cannot be achieved by alternative, co- or self-regulatory, or non-regulatory approaches. Its 2011 discussion paper *Transforming Regulatory Enforcement* expounded the policy that regulation should involve a 'more mature relationship' between regulators and business.[63] Enforcement strategy would be built around three basic principles: Greater accountability of enforcers, recognising and promoting best practice, and greater transparency of regulators and enforcement actions. It was said that a presumption would be introduced that regulators should *help businesses comply* with the law. Relevant aspects of the 2011 discussion paper are set out in Box 9.2. A key finding of an inquiry by the National Audit Office in 2011 was that businesses, in particular SMEs, often lack clarity about *how* to comply (see further chapters 2, 14 and 18).[64]

Box 9.2: Extracts from *Transforming Regulatory Enforcement: Discussion Paper* 2011

(ix) This paper sets out our plan for making a significant contribution to a business-led recovery by beginning a transformation in the way regulation is enforced. We need to move to a different and more mature relationship with business, working with—not against—the grain of all the good practice already out there. We need a transparent and light-touch system based on real risks. And we need to end the tick-box approach to inspection, freeing up useful time so that business can instead get on with the urgent work of helping return the economy to sustained growth.

A different and more mature relationship with business

(x) We will review all regulators, not just to examine the case for continued existence, but to make sure each one is making the fullest possible use of the range of alternatives to conventional enforcement models, working with business and others and reducing state

---

[63] *Transforming Regulatory Enforcement: Discussion Paper* (Department for Business, Innovation & Skills, 2011), at http://www.bis.gov.uk/assets/biscore/better-regulation/docs/t/11-989-transforming-regulatory-enforcement-consultation.pdf.
[64] *Delivering Regulatory Reform. Report by the Comptroller and Auditor General* (National Audit Office, 2011), available at http://www.nao.org.uk/idoc.ashx?docId=89f6cf32-eeeb-4f0a-b862-d5a9feec4388&version=-1.

activity wherever possible. We will expect to see a significant reduction in state-led enforcement activity each and every year throughout this Parliament. The reviews will also identify areas of good practice, and we will build on them.

(xi) There will be a presumption that co-regulation be introduced wherever this is practical—we recognise that co-regulation may sometimes be more expensive and burdensome for business.

(xii) We want to see existing regulatory regimes make much more use of 'earned recognition'. This means developing approaches that incentivise and reflect businesses' own efforts to comply with the law.

(xiv) We will establish a presumption that regulators should help businesses comply with the law. The aim of any interaction with business should be to support the business in achieving compliance. This presumption will be considered for inclusion in the Regulators' Compliance Code as part of a post-implementation review which will be launched in 2012.

(xv) We will also clarify that no business should face a sanction for simply having asked a regulatory authority for advice. This could also be achieved through extending the Regulators' Compliance Code. Exceptions will be defined and are likely to include where there is an emergency or imminent risk to health.

A transparent and light-touch risk-based system

(xvi) We will put a new partnership between government, regulators and businesses at the heart of the regulatory system, bringing the expertise of the Local Better Regulation Office into government.

....

9. We propose an enforcement strategy built around three basic principles:
— greater accountability;
— recognising and promoting good practice; and
— greater transparency.

10. We want to create a new relationship between regulators and businesses where the default setting is trust rather than distrust; where there is greater common sense; and where businesses have effective channels through which they can inform, hear and challenge regulators. We want businesses to get the recognition they deserve for the work they do to comply. Most importantly we want to free up business resources to support business growth, and to see regulators' resources targeted where they are most needed.

Principle 1: Greater accountability

11. Businesses need to be able to influence directly how enforcement operates and to use their knowledge and experience to help improve front line delivery. As a start, we want to use this consultation process to find new ways of allowing business to inform our thinking. We are particularly keen that businesses feel able to provide a frank account of their day-to-day experience of regulatory enforcement—what works well, and what needs fixing.
12. We envisage a number of routes for business to input to this process but we particularly want to work with trade associations and business organisations so that people feel free to express their views through trusted bodies, and so that common themes across particular sectors can be identified....

Principle 2: Recognising and promoting best practice

18. We want to give businesses the means to make a reality of 'earned recognition'. We will do this by requiring regulators to take account of businesses' efforts to comply with regulations and to adjust their enforcement plans accordingly. We want to create positive incentives to recognise and promote best practice; and we want to deter those who seek competitive advantage, or pose a real material risk, by flouting the rules....

Principle 3: Greater transparency

21. Although there have been some successes in improving the transparency of enforcement it is still patchy. Businesses tell us that they value clear advice and support from regulators, rather than fault finding and criticism which lowers trust. Without transparent standards businesses do not know what is expected and see enforcement as inconsistent. We think that this can be improved by regulators working jointly with trade associations, accreditation and professional bodies to design common sets of standards that everyone can sign up to. This will enable businesses to better understand what regulators expect of them and to design internal systems that regulators can trust and are prepared to accept.'

The government's conclusions[65] in response to the above consultation exercise, published in December 2011, stated that the local regulatory system was too often a burden, and led to business complaints of inconsistency and unpredictability. It was decided to simplify the landscape.

'Overall, what we heard was that while there is evidence of good practice of regulators and business working together on compliance, there are too many areas where the enforcement of regulation is heavy-handed, inefficient, overly prescriptive and culturally risk-averse, all of which combines to act as a drain on productive business time and resources.'[66]

The government announced the following policies:

(x) **We will review all regulators**, not just to examine the case for continued existence, but to make sure each one is making the fullest possible use of the range of alternatives to conventional enforcement models, working with business and others and reducing state activity wherever possible. We will expect to see a significant reduction in state-led enforcement activity each and every year throughout this Parliament. The reviews will also identify areas of good practice, and we will build on them.

(xi) There will be a **presumption that co-regulation be introduced** wherever this is practical—we recognise that co-regulation may sometimes be more expensive and burdensome for business.

(xii) We want to see existing regulatory regimes make **much more use of 'earned recognition'**. This means developing approaches that incentivise and reflect businesses' own efforts to comply with the law.

(xiv) **We will establish a presumption that regulators should help businesses comply with the law.** The aim of any interaction with business should be to support the business in

---

[65] *Transforming Regulatory Enforcement: Government Response to the Consultation on Transforming Regulatory Enforcement* 11/1408, 6 Dec 2011 http://www.bis.gov.uk/assets/biscore/better-regulation/docs/t/11-1408-transforming-regulatory-enforcement-government-response.

[66] ibid, Foreword, para (vi).

achieving compliance. This presumption will be considered for inclusion in the Regulators' Compliance Code as part of a post-implementation review which will be launched in 2012.

(xv) **We will also clarify that no business should face a sanction for simply having asked a regulatory authority for advice.** This could also be achieved through extending the Regulators' Compliance Code. Exceptions will be defined and are likely to include where there is an emergency or imminent risk to health.[67]

The principles for economic regulation noted above can be compared with five principles for modernisation of public sector services that were published by the Coalition government in 2011:[68]

Choice—Wherever possible we will increase choice.
Decentralisation—Power should be decentralised to the lowest appropriate level.
Diversity—Public services should be open to a range of providers.
Fairness—We will ensure fair access to public services.
Accountability—Public services should be accountable to users and taxpayers.

The government said that individual service providers should be licensed or regulated, and it was important that users have a form of redress if choice was not available or where standards were not good enough, through the availability of the most appropriate means of redress, such as Ombudsmen.[69]

Further, in 2012 the National Audit Office set out 10 principles for delivering value for money from public services markets, which focused on the importance of competition and the delivery of desired outcomes:[70]

— *Rules for ensuring a competitive market*
— Principle One: There are rules to ensure the effective operation of the market.
— Principle Two: The rules of the marketplace are enforced if necessary.
— *Enabling users to participate actively in the market*
— Principle Three: Users are empowered to make appropriate choices.
— Principle Four: Users have effective mechanisms for redress.
— *Promoting healthy competition between providers*
— Principle Five: There is a level playing field for all providers, whether public or private.
— Principle Six: Providers can easily enter the market, expand and exit.
— Principle Seven: There are arrangements to ensure service continuity where provider failure could result in harm to users.
— *Ensuring the market is delivering the public policy objectives*
— Principle Eight: Market oversight is based on good quality financial monitoring and market intelligence.

---

[67] ibid, Foreword.
[68] *Open Public Services. White Paper* (HM Government, July 2011) http://www.cabinetoffice.gov.uk/sites/default/files/resources/open-public-services-white-paper.pdf.
[69] ibid, ch 3.
[70] *Delivering Public Services through Markets: Principles for Achieving Value for Money* (NAO, 2012) http://www.nao.org.uk/publications/1213/delivering_public_services.aspx.

— Principle Nine: The oversight body has sufficient expertise to understand the market and will intervene, if appropriate, to remedy market failures.
— Principle Ten: The body responsible for delivery of public policy regularly reviews whether public service outcomes are being delivered.

In 2012 the government issued a series of proposals on policy in consumer and competition areas, in pursuit of the over-riding goal of stimulating economic growth. A 2012 BRDO (Better Regulation Delivery Office) paper had highlighted the role of regulation in supporting growth, calling on bodies to reduce business costs, improve confidence and control, and realise wider economic benefits.[71] Examples of good practice cited included a requirement in food hygiene legislation for food businesses to implement a food safety management system (FSMS) based on Hazard Analysis and Critical Control Points (HACCP) principles: A survey found that 87 per cent of SMEs thought that FSMS helped them manage their businesses, and it had made 45 per cent more profitable. Studies also criticised the imposition of various burdens on businesses by non-regulatory bodies[72] or through government-imposed voluntary requirements.[73] Many other related reforms were also proposed by government in other sectors, notably in the NHS[74] and financial services.[75]

The government set out to 'tackle red tape' by adopting a four-pronged policy. First, it would stem the flow of new regulation through the introduction of a 'One-In, One-Out' rule, under which any increase in the cost of regulation must be at least matched by reduction elsewhere. It was claimed that this saved businesses around £1 billion in regulatory costs by summer 2013.[76] From January 2013, the rule was tightened to be 'One-In, Two-Out', under which departments must find £2 of saving for every £1 of extra cost imposed, with the aim of making it harder for ministers to regulate. These arbitrary rules received considerable criticism as hampering substantial reforms that might incur transitional costs.[77] Second, the government tackled the existing stock of regulation through the Red Tape Challenge, which was a review whose starting point was that regulation should go unless there is good justification for the government being involved. It was claimed that over 3,500 regulations were identified for reform, and that by late 2013 650 changes were implemented, saving businesses over £215 million per year.[78] Third, an EU taskforce was established to identify and tackle European rules that inhibit growth.[79]

Fourth, the government committed to improve how regulation is enforced. In response to its 2011 *Transforming Regulatory Enforcement* consultation noted above, businesses told government, broadly, three things. What was needed was a more mature relationship

---

[71] *Regulation and Growth* (Better Regulation Delivery Office, 2012).

[72] *Business Experience of Regulatory-type Burdens Imposed by Non-regulatory Bodies* (ICF GHK, 2013).

[73] C Decker and C Hodges, *Government-imposed Voluntary Regulation* (British Retail Consortium, 2014).

[74] *White Paper Equity and Excellence: Liberating the NHS* (Department of Health, 2010) at http://www.dh.gov.uk/en/Healthcare/LiberatingtheNHS/index.htm.

[75] See ch 20.

[76] Michael Fallon MP, *Speech: Deregulation and Economic Growth: Priorities for Government Reform* 12 November 2013.

[77] The NAO found that 'almost all the economic impact of regulatory proposals derives from a small number of relatively high value proposals': *Better Regulation Executive. Submission of Evidence: Controls on Regulation* (National Audit Office, 2012).

[78] Fallon (n 76).

[79] See *Let's Get Down to Business. Smart Regulation, More Growth, Better Europe* (Department for Business, Innovation & Skills, 2011).

between business and regulators, a more transparent system of local regulation, and a simpler and more understandable regulatory landscape designed more around those who are regulated and protected, rather than Whitehall priorities. This resulted in a series of Focus on Enforcement reviews, which looked at the totality of regulator and enforcement action as it was experienced by an individual company in a series of sectors.[80] The picture showed excellent practice by some regulators, but also examples of overlapping, conflicting and duplicated regulatory requirements, delays, incomprehensible guidance and companies wanting to comply left frustrated and bewildered as to where to turn.[81] However, the response by regulators to identification of such issues was positive. One example of this was a 2013 *Concordat* reached between key government departments and regulators, such as the Marine Management Organisation (operating marine licences), the Environment Agency (water discharge permits) and Natural England (advise on impact on wildlife), along with the Special Interest Group of Coastal Authorities of the local government association, to coordinate applications by developers and others wanting to invest in projects along the English coast. The *Concordat* created a single point of entry, a single body to assist applicants in navigating the system, and a lead agency so as to cut overlap and duplication.

In a paper in March 2012, the government announced that it would reduce the regulatory burdens on businesses by consolidating and simplifying consumer law powers, scattered in around 60 pieces of consumer legislation, into a single generic set.[82] This became the Consumer Rights Act 2015, discussed at chapter 14. It also proposed to introduce some new safeguards in relation to the generic investigatory powers, such as a requirement for officers to give businesses reasonable notice of routine inspections, subject to a number of exemptions, and maintaining a number of existing safeguards, for example, the prohibition on officers requiring a person to produce or seizing from any person any document that they would be entitled to refuse to hand over on the grounds of legal professional privilege.[83] Further to the coalition's commitment to protecting civil liberties and to rolling back state intrusion,[84] it introduced the Protection of Freedoms Act 2012, which provides for a code of practice to cover enforcement officers' powers of entry, with the exercise of these powers being subject to review and repeal. In pursuance of 'Encouraging more proportionate enforcement by removing barriers to the use of civil enforcement', the government enabled Trading Standards officers to present civil cases in the civil County Courts, rather than just in the criminal courts, which was estimated to reduce their costs of bringing a simple case by as much as a third.[85]

[80] See http://discuss.bis.gov.uk/focusonenforcement/published-reviews-and-closed-focus-areas.
[81] Fallon (n 76).
[82] *Enhancing Consumer Confidence through Effective Enforcement: Consultation on Consolidating and Modernising Consumer Law Enforcement Powers* (DBIS, March 2012) available at http://www.bis.gov.uk/assets/biscore/consumer-issues/docs/e/12-543-enhancing-consumer-confidence-effective-enforcement-consultation.pdf. See also *Consultation on Enhancing Consumer Confidence by Clarifying Consumer Law: Consultation on the Supply of Goods, Services and Digital Content* (Department for Business, Innovation & Skills, July 2012) available at http://www.bis.gov.uk/assets/biscore/consumer-issues/docs/e/12-937-enhancing-consumer-consultation-supply-of-goods-services-digital.pdf.
[83] *Enhancing Consumer Confidence through Effective Enforcement*, ibid, para 12.
[84] *The Coalition: Our Programme for Government*, HM Government, May 2010, 11, at http://www.cabinetoffice.gov.uk/sites/default/files/resources/coalition_programme_for_government.pdf
[85] *Enhancing Consumer Confidence* (n 82) 40.

Particular attention was focused on small and medium-sized enterprises (SMEs) in view of their importance for generating innovation and economic growth.[86] There were an estimated 4.9 million private sector businesses in the UK at the start of 2013, of which 99.9 per cent were SMEs. SMEs accounted for 59.3 per cent of private sector employment and 48.1 per cent of private sector turnover. Thus, SMEs were said to make a disproportionate contribution to job creation and played a key role in growth by driving competition and stimulating innovation.[87] The government's review identified key enablers of business success, grouped into three clusters, that included 'tipping points' in the ability to expand or reduce business growth:

— internal capacity and capability, including skills and innovation
— external environment, including access to finance, exports and government procurement
— vision of the business owner, including growth ambitions and use of business support.

The paper noted the impact that external advice could have on improving performance. A review had found that businesses reported significant benefits from using business information and advice, and that the absorptive capacity of SMEs depends on the skills of business owner-managers and employees within the firm.[88] Advice on dealing with regulation, tax and compliance was said to produce somewhat or significant improvement in around 50 per cent of cases.[89] However, less than half of UK SME employers used business support, due primarily to difficulties in accessing information or advice; doubts about the benefits of business support, and concerns about the competence and trustworthiness of support providers.

Four case studies demonstrated that localised policy interventions that support and/or complement national provision can deliver benefits and economic growth.[90]

F. National Enforcement Priorities

A 2007 review of enforcement priorities across the country, as part of Hampton implementation, identified six national enforcement priorities, and a need to improve coordination between enforcement at national and local levels.[91] The six priorities were:

— Air quality, including regulation of pollution from factories and homes
— Alcohol, entertainment and late night refreshment licensing and its enforcement

---

[86] See also Lord Young, *Making Businesses Your Business. Supporting the Start-up and development of Small Business* (Cabinet Office, 2011).

[87] *SMEs: The Key Enablers of Business Success and the Economic Rationale for Government Intervention* (BIS, 7 December 2013) at https://www.gov.uk/government/uploads/system/uploads/attachment_data/file/263863/bis-13-1320-smes-key-enablers-of-business-success.pdf.

[88] BIS estimates from BIS Small Business Survey, 2010 and *Research to understand the barriers to take up and use of business support* (London, Centre for Enterprise and Economic Development Research, 2011).

[89] ibid, Fig 8.

[90] *Research on Understanding Localised Policy Interventions in Business Support and Skills* (BIS, 7 December 2013), https://www.gov.uk/government/uploads/system/uploads/attachment_data/file/263716/bis-13-1316-understanding-localised-policy-interventions-in-business-support-and-skills.pdf. The cases were: Greater Manchester Business Growth Hub, Plymouth Growth Acceleration and Investment Network, New Anglia Business Information Portal, and West of England Employability Charter Mark.

[91] P Rogers, *National Enforcement Priorities for Local Authority Regulatory Services* (Cabinet Office, 2007) at http://www.bis.gov.uk/files/file45168.pdf.

— Hygiene of businesses selling, distributing and manufacturing food and the safety and fitness of food in the premises
— Improving health in the workplace
— Fair trading (trade description, trade marking, mis-description, doorstep selling)
— Animal and public health, animal movements and identification.[92]

The six areas were selected on the basis of the criteria that each:

— Aims to prevent high levels of risk distributed through society, and local authority controls are capable of being effective in doing so, and/or
— Requires a national control system where all parts of the enforcement regime are in place to prevent harm, and/or
— Is a nationally important political priority.[93]

In selecting the above six areas as national priorities, the Rogers review considered over 60 policy areas, as shown in Figure 9.1.

The Rogers review noted that the Trading Standards and Environmental Health services of local authorities together comprise the largest enforcement operation in England, with

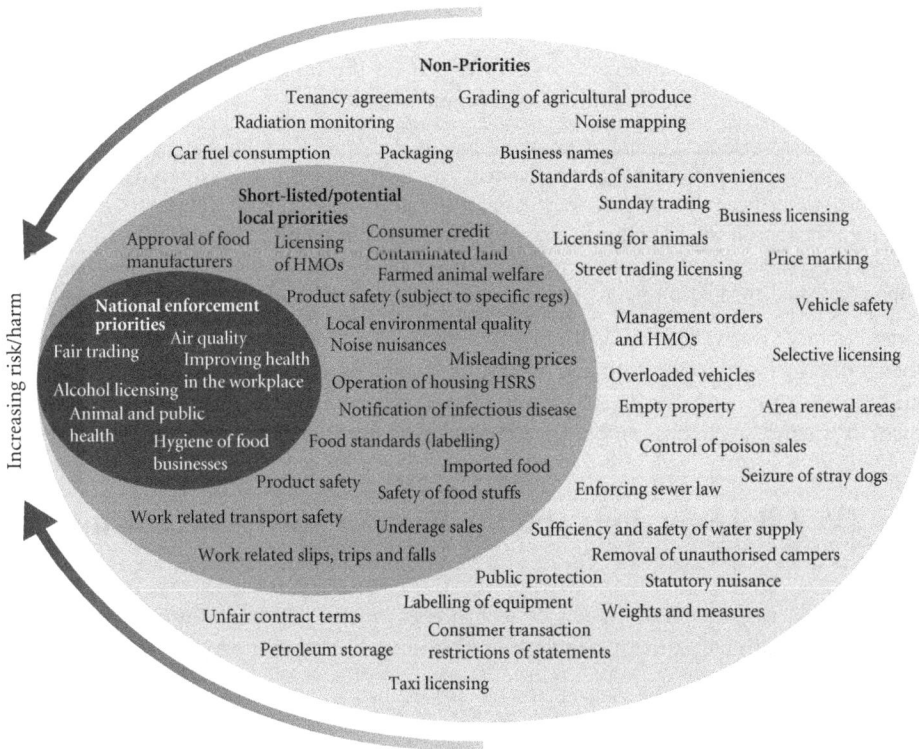

Figure 9.1: The Rogers Review's Map of National Enforcement Priorities

[92] Responsibility for this sixth area rested with local rather than national authorities, whereas the other five are all shared.
[93] Rogers (n 91) para 6.

expenditure that dwarfs that of the Environment Agency or Health and Safety Executive. It noted:

> Local authority regulatory services play a crucial role in their local communities. In terms of impacting on business, and in delivering regulatory objectives for government, the importance of these services cannot be underestimated. As the Hampton Review recognised, they serve as a key source of advice to business, especially small businesses. They deliver both national and local regulatory objectives, supporting the delivery of a wide range of policy areas in the process. But they are hindered, as Hampton argued, by the diffuse structure of local authority regulation, not least difficulties arising from the lack of both effective priority-setting from the centre and the lack of effective central and local coordination. Hampton also identified problems with consistency of local authority enforcement that related in large part to lack of planning across policy areas and services. The key aim of this Review is to help solve these difficulties.[94]

In 2009 the paradox was examined that local enforcement authorities may deal with issues of national importance, but at disproportionate cost to the local taxpayers, and this may chill local expenditure. A case study of checks on imported goods at Felixstowe docks estimated that absent any regulation the level of detriment to UK citizens and economy would be £160 nationally.[95] In contrast, then the current level of regulation benefited the UK economy as a whole of approximately £35 for every £1 spent on local regulation of goods entering ports of entry.

In its response to the Anderson review's report on the importance of providing good guidance to business,[96] the Coalition Government noted that

> the LBRO was working to promote the establishment of a World Class Regulatory Services System to 'simplify the complex local regulatory system and enable all local authority regulatory services to work more efficiently and effectively'. As part of this drive, the LBRO will work with national regulators and professional bodies to establish a common framework for competence to ensure the professional skills of local authority regulatory services staff meet the increasing challenges placed upon them and are able to respond to the demands of their stakeholders, including businesses.[97]

Initiatives taken forward included a Competence Project, to develop a common competence framework for application across trading standards, environmental health, licensing and fire regulation, and Trading Places, an exchange scheme between regulators and businesses to enhance awareness and understanding, which was commenced in 2009.[98]

IV. Civil Sanctions and the Purposes of Enforcement

Under the Macrory-inspired aspects of RESA, regulators could be authorised to exercise a new category of civil sanctions, including imposing discretionary requirements that the

---

[94] ibid, para 2.
[95] *Addressing National Threats Through Local Service Delivery* (Local Better Regulation Office, 2009).
[96] *The Good Guidance Guide* (n 53)
[97] *Government Response to the Anderson Review* (Department for Business, Enterprise and Regulatory Reform, 2009) available at http://www.bis.gov.uk/files/file50352.pdf, 17.
[98] *Progress Report on Commitments Made in Response to the Anderson Review* (Department for Business, Enterprise and Regulatory Reform, 2009) available at http://www.bis.gov.uk/assets/biscore/better-regulation/docs/10-823-progress-reports-response-anderson-review.pdf, 18–19.

offender must take steps specified by the regulator, within a stated period, designed to secure (a) that the offence does not continue to recur (a 'compliance requirement') and (b) that the position is restored, so far as possible, to what it would have been if no offence had been committed (a 'restoration requirement').[99] If a person refused to comply with a discretionary requirement or undertaking, the enforcer could decide to bring a prosecution for the original offence.[100]

The new administrative sanctions were intended to be available to 62 of the regulators identified by Hampton and 56 identified by Macrory, and over 400 local authorities.[101] A two year pilot was announced under which the OFT (Office of Fair Trading) and selected Trading Standards Services would test the new civil sanctions powers under the RESA as alternatives to criminal offences.[102] The consultation emphasised:

> Alongside promoting compliance with the law, the provision of voluntary restoration to consumers who suffer detriment as a result of unsafe products or unfair or misleading business practices is a key policy objective.

> Enforcers will engage with traders to seek voluntary compliance and voluntary restoration for consumers affected by their actions where this is appropriate. The formal Pilot powers are only likely to be used if an informal approach fails to secure compliance or appropriate restoration for consumers, consistent with the enforcer's expectations.[103]

Practical problems had arisen for enforcers being able to apply for civil sanctions in the civil courts, since they were more familiar with the criminal courts. The civil and criminal cases taken by the Local Authority Trading Standards Service (LATSS) strongly emphasised

Table 9.2: Local Authority Enforcement Data 2007–08 to 2011–12

Financial year	Criminal prosecutions	Enforcement Orders	Enforcement Undertakings
2011/12	1866	7	99
2010/11	1695	5	125
2009/10	2450	8	175
2008/09	1872	4	144
2007/08	1887	3	131

[99] Regulatory Enforcement and Sanctions Act 2008, s 42. See *Regulatory Enforcement and Sanctions Act 2008: Guidance to the Act* (Department for Business Enterprise and Regulatory Reform, July 2008) at http://www.berr.gov.uk/file47135.pdf.

[100] *Regulatory Enforcement and Sanctions Act 2008: Guidance to the Act*, ibid, para 50. The coercive background is, therefore, strongly similar to the powers of Nordic Consumer Ombudsmen explained at ch 14.

[101] Hansard, HL Deb, vol 701, col 26 (28 April 2008).

[102] This was later scheduled to being in April 2011, after confirmation of the policy by the subsequent government: *Civil Sanctions Pilot. Joint Consultation by the OFT and LBRO on the Operation of the BIS Civil Sanctions Pilot* (Local Better Regulation Office and Office of Fair Trading, 2010) OFT1296, available at http://www.oft.gov.uk/OFTwork/consultations/current/civil-sanctions.

[103] ibid, paras 2.7 and 2.8. The Pilot powers were: Enforcement undertakings, fixed monetary penalties, discretionary requirements (variable monetary penalties, a compliance requirement, and a restoration requirement), and stop notices. For all except enforcement undertakings, appeals by traders may be made to the First Tier Tribunal. Enforcers can recover their investigation and enforcement costs.

criminal prosecutions, with a far smaller number of enforcement undertakings and very few enforcement orders, as shown in Table 9.2.[104]

However, civil sanctions were not made freely available to enforcers. A major objection to them that arose in political approval of the 2008 Act was that giving enforcers enhanced powers to threaten imposing civil sanctions themselves without involvement of a court might lead to abuse and injustice. The regime provided that traders could appeal to the General Regulatory Chamber of the First-tier Tribunal.[105] A number of authorities, such as the Environment Agency and Information Commissioner, were designated as able to use the civil sanctions,[106] but other authorities were required to apply to be awarded the powers, on the basis that they satisfied certain conditions, such as they were and remained in compliance with the 'Principles of Good Regulation' (colloquially known as being 'Hampton compliant'), that they were transparent, accountable, proportionate, consistent and targeted only at cases where action is required.[107]

Thus, a safeguard against abuse was that the relevant minister awards the civil sanctioning powers on the basis that the minister is satisfied that the applicant authority satisfies and will observe the criteria. The minister has responsibility to review how the powers are used, and to suspend use of the powers in the event that the minister is satisfied that the authority is repeatedly misusing them.[108] Hence, as discussed further in chapter 13 below, many regulators reviewed their enforcement policies, whether as a result of pressure from Better Regulation oversight and in order to demonstrate Hampton compliance, or specifically in order to consider whether to apply for award of civil sanction powers.

The resultant enforcement policies thereby demonstrated two transformative characteristics. First, new governance requirements and transparency were put in place in relation to enforcement policies, procedures and imposition of sanctions. Regulators who use civil sanctions are obliged to issue guidance on their sanctions policies, which explain how they will use civil sanctions after non-compliance has been found, and to have regard to that guidance when issuing penalties.[109] Second, this approach represented a major move away from 'old fashioned command and control' approaches that relied almost exclusively on deterrence, to applying a risk-based approach, and including, usually for the first time, a formal objective of focusing on achieving good outcomes for customers and restorative actions.

However, this was not the end of the story, since the Coalition government announced a revised policy in November 2012.[110] The Coalition government was opposed to giving enforcers unfettered power, partly as a constitutional matter based on ideological considerations of personal liberty, partly so as not to give authorities too much power and to avoid abuse, and partly to avoid imposing excessive burdens on business. The environmental

---

[104] Data notified to the OFT or recorded on the OFT's Consumer Regulations Website (CRW).

[105] Regulatory Enforcement and Sanctions Act 2008, s 54(1)(a). Administrative Tribunals were reorganised under the tribunals, Courts and Enforcement Act 2007. See also the Tribunal Procedure (First-tier Tribunal) (General Regulatory Chamber) Rules 2009/1976.

[106] Regulatory Enforcement and Sanctions Act 2008, Sch 5.

[107] The process is described at Norris and Philips (n 33) ch 4.

[108] Regulatory Enforcement and Sanctions Act 2008, ss 67 and 68. The authority is subject to a three-yearly review.

[109] Regulatory Enforcement and Sanctions Act 2008, s 63(2)(e).

[110] *Civil Enforcement Remedies: Consultation on Extending the Range of Remedies Available to Public Enforcers of Consumer Law* (Department for Business, Innovation & Skills, 5 November 2012) at http://www.bis.gov.uk/assets/biscore/consumer-issues/docs/c/12-1193-civil-enforcement-remedies-consultation-on-extending. The Impact assessment is at http://bis.gov.uk/assets/biscore/consumer-issues/docs/c/12-1194-civil-enforcement-remedies-impact-assessment.pdf.

enforcement authorities had been given civil sanctions powers,[111] but a different approach would now apply. Enforcers may be given wider powers but, in the area of consumer enforcement at least, the enforcers will be required to seek court approval for orders against traders, rather than be empowered to impose sanctions themselves subject to appeal to a tribunal. The Government stated that it was 'not convinced' that RESA powers would be effective in consumer law, for the following reasons:

> Firstly, much of the focus of the RES Act is on the use of penalties as an ultimate sanction, which, while effective, do not in themselves secure remedies for individual consumers. Secondly, the Government has concerns that a purely administrative approach does not guarantee sufficient right to respond for businesses who are innocent. Under the RES Act, the business must appeal against a decision of the enforcer, and the Government believes that in disputed cases it should be for the enforcer rather than the business to bring the first legal challenge.[112]

In accordance with a wider policy of reducing burdens of small businesses, the government also announced on 8 November 2012 that, when considering whether to make Orders under RESA to provide a regulator with powers to impose certain civil sanctions as an alternative to prosecution, it would, in general, observe the following principles:[113]

— Powers to impose Fixed Monetary Penalties, Variable Monetary Penalties and Restoration Notices would, as a general rule, only be granted where their use is restricted to undertakings with more than 250 employees;[114] and
— Powers to impose Enforcement Undertakings, Stop Notices and Compliance Notices may be granted without restriction as to the size of undertaking against whom they might be used.

Rather than expand civil sanctions, the Coalition Government adopted a modified approach to enforcement powers, which it codified in the Consumer Rights Act 2015, discussed in chapter 14.

V. The 2014 Regulators' Code

The Coalition government's consultations found consistent examples of cross-cutting or systemic problems. It was felt that regulators failed to see businesses as stakeholders; regulators lacked knowledge of the businesses they regulate; enforcement decisions were inconsistent and disproportionate; there was a lack of clear, consistent advice; regulators' failure to consider the impact of their decisions in terms of growth; a lack of effective appeals

---

[111] The Environmental Civil Sanctions (England) Order 2010/1157 and The Environmental Civil Sanctions (Miscellaneous Amendments) (England) Order 2010/1159.

[112] *Civil Enforcement Remedies: Consultation* (n 110) Executive Summary, para 5.

[113] *Written Ministerial Statement—Department for Business, Innovation & Skills: Use of Civil Sanctions Powers Contained in the Regulatory Enforcement and Sanctions Act 2008* (Department for Business, Innovation & Skills, November 2012) available at http://www.parliament.uk/documents/commons-vote-office/November_2012/08-11-12/1.BIS-Use-of-Civil-Sanctions-Powers.pdf.

[114] Small and medium sized enterprises (SMEs) are defined as having under 250 employees: *The Good Guidance Guide* (n 53).

processes; and that regulator fees and charges regimes created perverse incentives.[115] In 2012 the government announced its Better Enforcement Programme, containing five elements:[116] Introduction of a new Regulators' Code; introduction of a legal 'growth duty' to ensure that economic growth forms a part of regulators' decision making;[117] an Accountability for Regulator Impact initiative; a review of regulators' appeals processes; and removal of perverse financial incentives from regulators.

The 2007 Regulators' Compliance Code was superseded by the Regulators' Code, which came into force on 6 April 2014[118] (Box 9.3) and had significantly different objectives, structure and content.[119] The 2014 Code reflected the government's intention to shape the behaviour of regulators in a different way, by expecting more businesses to shape regulators through mutual engagement, feedback and challenge. The 2014 Regulators' Code was a step change. It effectively signalled that rules only exist in so far as they can be enforced. Recognising that almost all rules are in fact enforced internally by businesses, the Code adopted the stance that it would itself be enforced by business alone, and not by some superior governmental or external authority. Therefore, government would not overly internally police the Code, and it was written to be self-policing, with a built-in capacity for business to challenge enforcers.

Box 9.3: The Regulators' Code 2014

This Code was laid before Parliament in accordance with section 23 of the Legislative and Regulatory Reform Act 2006 ('the Act'). Regulators whose functions are specified by order under section 24(2) of the Act **must** have regard to the Code when developing policies and operational procedures that guide their regulatory activities. Regulators must equally have regard to the Code when setting standards or giving guidance which will guide the regulatory activities of other regulators. If a regulator concludes, on the basis of material evidence, that a specific provision of the Code is either not applicable or is outweighed by another relevant consideration, the regulator is not bound to follow that provision, but should record that decision and the reasons for it.

---

[115] Fallon (n 76).

[116] See also *Better Regulation Framework Manual. Practical Guidance for UK Government Officials* (Department for Business, Innovation & Skills, 2013).

[117] The government pursued 'a new approach to how government and industry work together' through eleven sector strategies and an overall strategy: see *Industrial Strategy: Government and Industry in Partnership. Progress Report* (HM Government, 2014).

[118] By The Legislative and Regulatory Reform Code of Practice (Appointed Day) Order 2014 No 929. The public bodies that are subject to the Code are marked in Table 9.1 above; various other private bodies or persons are also subject to the Code: see *Regulators' Code: Summary of Regulators and Regulatory Functions Covered* (Department for Business, Innovation & Skills, Better Regulation Delivery Office, 2014).

[119] *Regulators' Code* (Department for Business, Innovation & Skills, 2013). The following Orders, made under s 24(2) of the Legislative and Regulatory Reform Act 2006, specify the scope of the Code: Legislative and Regulatory Reform (Regulatory Functions) Order 2007; Legislative and Regulatory Reform (Regulatory Functions) (Amendment) Order 2009; Legislative and Regulatory Reform (Regulatory Functions) (Amendment) Order 2010; Legislative and Regulatory Reform (Regulatory Functions) (Amendment) Order 2014.

Regulators should carry out their activities in a way that supports those they regulate to comply and grow

Regulators should avoid imposing unnecessary regulatory burdens through their regulatory activities[120] and should assess whether similar social, environmental and economic outcomes could be achieved by less burdensome means. Regulators should choose proportionate approaches to those they regulate, based on relevant factors including, for example, business size and capacity.

1.2 When designing and reviewing policies, operational procedures and practices, regulators should consider how they might support or enable economic growth for compliant businesses and other regulated entities,[121] for example, by considering how they can best:

understand and minimise negative economic impacts of their regulatory activities;
minimising the costs of compliance for those they regulate;
improve confidence in compliance for those they regulate, by providing greater certainty; and encourage and promote compliance.

1.3 Regulators should ensure that their officers have the necessary knowledge and skills to support those they regulate, including having an understanding of those they regulate that enables them to choose proportionate and effective approaches.

1.4 Regulators should ensure that their officers understand the statutory principles of good regulation[122] and of this Code, and how the regulator delivers its activities in accordance with them.

Regulators should provide simple and straightforward ways to engage with those they regulate and hear their views

2.1 Regulators should have mechanisms in place to engage those they regulate, citizens and others to offer views and contribute to the development of their policies and service standards. Before changing policies, practices or service standards, regulators should consider the impact on business and engage with business representatives.

2.2 In responding to non-compliance that they identify, regulators should clearly explain what the non-compliant item or activity is, the advice being given, actions required or decisions taken, and the reasons for these. Regulators should provide an opportunity for dialogue in relation to the advice, requirements or decisions, with a view to ensuring that they are acting in a way that is proportionate and consistent.

This paragraph does not apply where the regulator can demonstrate that immediate enforcement action is required to prevent or respond to a serious breach or where providing such an opportunity would be likely to defeat the purpose of the proposed enforcement action.

2.3 Regulators should provide an impartial and clearly explained route to appeal against a regulatory decision or a failure to act in accordance with this Code. Individual officers of

[120] The term 'regulatory activities' refers to the whole range of regulatory options and interventions available to regulators.
[121] The terms 'business or businesses' is used throughout this document to refer to businesses and other regulated entities.
[122] The statutory principles of good regulation can be viewed in Pt 2 (21) on p 12: http://www.legislation.gov.uk/ukpga/2006/51/pdfs/ukpga_20060051_en.pdf.

the regulator who took the decision or action against which the appeal is being made should not be involved in considering the appeal. This route to appeal should be publicised to those who are regulated.

2.4 Regulators should provide a timely explanation in writing of any right to representation or right to appeal. This explanation should be in plain language and include practical information on the process involved.

2.5 Regulators should make available to those they regulate, clearly explained complaints procedures, allowing them to easily make a complaint about the conduct of the regulator.

2.6 Regulators should have a range of mechanisms to enable and regularly invite, receive and take on board customer feedback, including, for example, through customer satisfaction surveys of those they regulate.[123]

Regulators should base their regulatory activities on risk

3.1 Regulators should take an evidence based approach to determining the priority risks in their area of responsibility, and should allocate resources where they would be most effective in addressing those priority risks.

3.2 Regulators should consider risk at every stage of their decision-making processes, including choosing the most appropriate type of intervention or way of working with those regulated; targeting checks on compliance; and when taking enforcement action.

3.3 Regulators designing a risk assessment framework,[124] for their own use or for use by others, should have mechanisms in place to consult on the design with those affected, and to review it regularly.

3.4 Regulators, in making their assessment of risk, should recognise the compliance record of those they regulate, including using earned recognition approaches and should consider all available and relevant data on compliance, including evidence of relevant external verification.

3.5 Regulators should review the effectiveness of their chosen regulatory activities in delivering the desired outcomes and make any necessary adjustments accordingly.

4. Regulators should share information about compliance and risk

4.1 Regulators should collectively follow the principle of 'collect once, use many times' when requesting information from those they regulate.

4.2 When the law allows, regulators should agree secure mechanisms to share information with each other about businesses and other bodies they regulate, to help target resources and activities and minimise duplication.

---

[123] The Government will discuss with national regulators a common approach to surveys to support benchmarking of their performance.

[124] The term 'risk assessment framework' encompasses any model, scheme, methodology or risk rating approach that is used to inform risk-based targeting of regulatory activities in relation to individual businesses or other regulated entities.

5. Regulators should ensure clear information, guidance and advice is available to help those they regulate meet their responsibilities to comply

5.1 Regulators should provide advice and guidance that is focused on assisting those they regulate to understand and meet their responsibilities. When providing advice and guidance, legal requirements should be distinguished from suggested good practice and the impact of the advice or guidance should be considered so that it does not impose unnecessary burdens in itself.

5.2 Regulators should publish guidance, and information in a clear, accessible, concise format, using media appropriate to the target audience and written in plain language for the audience.

5.3 Regulators should have mechanisms in place to consult those they regulate in relation to the guidance they produce to ensure that it meets their needs.

5.4 Regulators should seek to create an environment in which those they regulate have confidence in the advice they receive and feel able to seek advice without fear of triggering enforcement action.

5.5 In responding to requests for advice, a regulator's primary concerns should be to provide the advice necessary to support compliance, and to ensure that the advice can be relied on.

5.6 Regulators should have mechanisms to work collaboratively to assist those regulated by more than one regulator. Regulators should consider advice provided by other regulators and, where there is disagreement about the advice provided, this should be discussed with the other regulator to reach agreement.

6. Regulators should ensure that their approach to their regulatory activities is transparent

6.1 Regulators should publish a set of clear service standards, setting out what those they regulate should expect from them.

6.2 Regulators' published service standards should include clear information on:
   a) how they communicate with those they regulate and how they can be contacted;
   b) their approach to providing information, guidance and advice;
   c) their approach to checks on compliance[125], including details of the risk assessment framework used to target those checks as well as protocols for their conduct, clearly setting out what those they regulate should expect;
   d) their enforcement policy, explaining how they respond to non-compliance;
   e) their fees and charges, if any. This information should clearly explain the basis on which these are calculated, and should include an explanation of whether compliance will affect fees and charges; and
   f) how to comment or complain about the service provided and routes to appeal.

---

[125] Including inspections, audit, monitoring and sampling visits and test purchases.

6.3 Information published to meet the provisions of this Code should be easily accessible, including being available at a single point[126] on the regulator's website that is clearly signposted, and it should be kept up to date.

6.4 Regulators should have mechanisms in place to ensure that their officers act in accordance with their published service standards, including their enforcement policy.

6.5 Regulators should publish, on a regular basis, details of their performance against their service standards, including feedback received from those they regulate, such as customer satisfaction surveys, and data relating to complaints about them and appeals against their decisions.

Reviews have been undertaken of enforcement practices, but on a sector-by-sector basis.[127] The review on the pharmaceutical manufacturing and production sector noted 'considerable positive feedback on the operation of the regulatory regime' and the high reputation of the Medicines and Healthcare products Regulatory Agency (MHRA), specifically in relation to being open and risk-based, and 'trying to do the right thing', whilst noting some areas for attention.[128] The review on public houses found that the sector was often afforded little trust by regulators, that much enforcement activity did not feel risk-based, and that the approach to under-age sales could feel disproportionate and confrontational, with heavy-handed enforcement of minor rules, requirements and breaches with formal measures.[129]

---

[126] This requirement may be satisfied by providing a single web page that includes links to information published elsewhere.

[127] See http://discuss.bis.gov.uk/focusonenforcement/published-reviews-and-closed-focus-areas. For example, *Focus on Enforcement (FoE) Review of Adult Care Homes* (Care Quality Commission, 2014) http://www.cqc.org.uk/sites/default/files/media/documents/20140508_foe_final_reponse.pdf.

[128] *Focus on Enforcement Regulatory Reviews: Review of the Pharmaceutical Manufacturing and Production Sector* (Department for Business, Innovation & Skills, 2014). See also *MHRA Response to the Findings of the Focus on Enforcement (FoE) Regulatory Review of the Pharmaceutical Manufacturing and Production Sector* (MHRA, 2014).

[129] *Focus on Enforcement Pubs Review* (Department for Business, Innovation & Skills, May 2014) https://www.gov.uk/government/uploads/system/uploads/attachment_data/file/311537/bis-14-840-focus-on-enforcement-pubs-review.pdf.

10

Developments in Criminal Enforcement in the United Kingdom

This chapter outlines developments in criminal enforcement in the United Kingdom that are of particular significance for enforcement of regulatory law and incentivisation of corporate compliance. The account set out here does not seek to give a complete account of criminal or sentencing law or practice, or of all developments in those fields.

Criminal law enforcement is relevant to the narrative of this book for three reasons. First, ultimate enforcement of administrative law is through criminal sanctions imposed by the criminal courts. Second, in 2010 an explicit link was made between criminal and regulatory enforcement policy in the light of the Macrory Sentencing Review and Law Commission report, and the relationship between criminal and regulatory enforcement was rebalanced. Third, trends have occurred in both criminal and regulatory enforcement policy and practice that are strikingly similar, and constitute a move towards intermingling or even fusion of what were previously the separate areas of criminal/regulatory and private enforcement.

The specific developments are as follows. First, the goals of criminal sentencing have been reformed from punishment and deterrence to encompass a wide range of purposes, including affecting future behaviour and the making of reparation by offenders to victims. Second, a technique known as 'restorative justice' has spread from some areas of conflict resolution into the criminal justice system, since it has proven to be more effective in reducing reoffending by certain recidivists than traditional punitive techniques. Restorative justice brings the offender and victim together, with a dual aim. First, it aims to affect the offender's future behaviour by confronting him with the effects of his crime. The approach moves them away from sole reliance on traditional deterrence-based approaches. Second, it aims to restore the victim's sense of injury by giving an opportunity to express her feelings. Where this technique is successful, it achieves a social and behavioural rebalancing. It can also lead to reparative actions by the offender, not least saying sorry. Third, the legal mechanisms by which reparative compensation may be paid to victims of crime have been developed. Several mechanisms exist, and from 2012 criminal courts are required to consider making a compensation order after every conviction.

Thus, the public criminal enforcement system now includes delivery of reparation to victims of crime as an inherent function. This avoids victims then having to take their own individual actions for compensation after or separate from criminal proceedings. The overall process can, at least in some circumstances, therefore achieve greater efficiency, since two sets of proceedings are avoided.

There appears to have been no deliberate link between these developments. They have not occurred as a result of any overriding policy. The fact that they have occurred spontaneously in different contexts with such force and clarity increases the sense that an important general move has occurred not just in the legal system but also in society. Together, these developments indicate a concern to ensure the delivery of redress to victims and a concern for efficiency in the legal system as a whole, by combining what were previously public and private enforcement systems.

The chapter begins by examining the purposes of criminal sanctions, and then the relationship between criminal and regulatory law. It then considers the interlinked issues of the rise of restorative justice in criminal contexts, and various reforms in three mechanisms of the criminal system that have extended removal of illicit gains from offenders and payment of compensation to victims, namely the 'proceeds of crime' regime, the rules on compensation to victims of violent crime, and the extension of general compensation orders to all crime victims, coupled with the recent expansion in policy on victims and reparation. The use and expansion of Sentencing Guidelines is then considered, noting some Guidelines that are relevant to businesses, before reviewing the introduction from 2013 of Deferred Prosecution Agreements.

I. The Purposes of Criminal Sanctions

A traditional view of the functions of criminal sentencing would focus on punishment and deterrence. However, a far wider view was mandated for criminal sentencing in the Criminal Justice Act 2003, which specified that the purposes of all criminal sentencing are:[1]

(a)   the punishment of offenders,
(b)   the reduction of crime (including its reduction by deterrence),
(c)   the reform and rehabilitation of offenders,
(d)   the protection of the public, and
(e)   the making of reparation by offenders to persons affected by their offences.

Thus, neither punishment nor deterrence are the sole focus of sentencing, but each are (only) one aspect of an integrated package of five purposes.[2] This policy focuses not just on imposing punishment on the offender, but also on *future prevention* of crime and on *restoring victims*. The crime reduction goal focuses not just on the offender, or other offenders, through a deterrent approach, but also hints that the imposition of punitive sanctions might not be effective in affecting future behaviour of actual or potential offenders, since reformative, rehabilitative and other approaches may be needed. Further, the making of reparation by offenders to persons affected by their offences is one of the purposes of *all* criminal sentencing. This formulation, therefore, explicitly links the public and private

---

[1] Criminal Justice Act 2003, s 142. This followed 'widespread agreement' that sentencing serves the goals of contributing to good order in society, through visibly upholding society's norms and standards and achieving a satisfactory level of public confidence, as well as punishment, crime reduction *and reparation*: *Making Punishments Work: Report of a Review of the Sentencing Framework for England and Wales* (Home Office, 2001) para 1.3.

[2] It can be noted here that current enforcement of competition law by the OFT (Office of Fair Trading) is non-compliant with this policy, since it omits requirement (e), leaving that entirely to private actors, and requirement (c).

consequences of illicit behaviour, and also the supposedly separate public (criminal) and private systems of law enforcement, by including 'private' compensation as an objective of the 'public' sentencing machinery.

Further, the factors that are to be taken into account in sentencing include 'the seriousness of the offence', any previous convictions and any failure to respond to previous sentences. In determining what sentence to pass on an offender, a court shall take into account the fact that an offender has pleaded guilty and the stage in the proceedings at which that indication was given.

Academic typological analysis has contributed to a shift in the framing and terminology of profit-driven crimes from 'criminal', motivational or sociological viewpoints towards recognising the importance of restitution, forfeiture and compensation.[3]

Tentative developments have occurred recently at EU (European Union) level in moving towards an EU policy on criminal law and enforcement. This is constrained by the fact that EU competence is limited, not least by the principles of necessity, proportionality and subsidiarity, so that enforcement mechanisms and sanctions for breach of EU law are generally within the competence of Member States.[4] General EU law goes only as far as requiring that national measures conform to the principles of effectiveness, proportionality and dissuasiveness.[5]

The European Commission initiated examination in 2011 of whether to include types of sanctions other than imprisonment and fines to ensure a maximum level of effectiveness, proportionality and dissuasiveness, as well as the need for additional measures, such as confiscation; and whether to impose criminal or non-criminal liability on legal persons, in particular with regard to crime areas where legal entities play a particularly important role as perpetrators.[6] The Commission expanded on the three principles as follows:

> Effectiveness requires that the sanction is suitable to achieve the desired goal, i.e. observance of the rules; proportionality requires that the sanction must be commensurate with the gravity of the conduct and its effects and must not exceed what is necessary to achieve the aim; and dissuasiveness requires that the sanctions constitute an adequate deterrent for potential future perpetrators.[7]

Only in a limited number of sectors has it been established that criminal law measures at EU level are *required*, namely measures to fight serious damaging practices and illegal profits in some economic sectors in order to protect activities of legitimate businesses and safeguard the interest of taxpayers, such as the financial sector concerning market manipulation or insider trading,[8] the fight against fraud, the protection of the euro against counterfeiting. A move towards involvement of criminal law is, however, gathering momentum in relation

---

[3] RT Naylor, 'Towards a General Theory of Profit-Driven Crimes' (2003) 43 *British Journal of Criminology* 81–101: Suggesting a tripartite typology of predatory, market-driven and commercial crimes.

[4] See ch 4.

[5] That phrase is used in many EU measures, based on case law, notably: Case 68/88 *Commission v Greece* [1989] ECR 2965 paras 22–27; Case C-326/88 *Anklagemyndighedem v Hansen & Sons I/S* [1990] I ECR 2911; Case C-36/94 *Siesse v Director da Alfandega de Alcantara* [1995] ECR I-3573 paras 19–21; Case C-83/94 *Leifer* [1995] ECR I-3231 paras 32–41; Case C-341/94 *Allain* [1996] ECR I-4631 para 24; Case C-29/95 *Pastoors v Belgium* [1997] ECR I-285 paras 24–26.

[6] Communication from the Commission. 'Towards an EU criminal policy: Ensuring the effective implementation of EU policies through criminal law', COM(2011) 573 final, 20.9.2011.

[7] ibid, 9.

[8] See Communication on reinforcing sanctioning regimes in the financial sector, COM (2010) 716 final, 8.12. 2010, 14.

to serious breaches in a range of other areas, including road transport, data protection, customs and environmental protection.[9] The Commission noted:

> The seriousness and character of the breach of law must be taken into account. For certain unlawful acts considered particularly grave, an administrative sanction may not be a sufficiently strong response. On the same line, criminal law sanctions may be chosen when it is considered important to stress strong disapproval in order to ensure deterrence. The entering of convictions in criminal records can have a particular deterrent character. At the same time, criminal proceedings provide often for stronger protection of the rights of the accused, reflecting the seriousness of the charge. The efficiency of the sanction system must be considered, as well as the extent to which and the reasons why existing sanctions do not achieve the desired enforcement level. The type of sanction that is considered to be the most appropriate to reach the global objective of being effective, proportionate and dissuasive should be chosen. An administrative sanction can often be decided and executed without delay, and lengthy and resource demanding procedures can thereby be avoided. Administrative sanctions may for this reason be considered in areas where, for example the offence is not particularly severe or occurs in large numbers as well as in areas where administrative sanctions and procedures are suitable and effective for other reasons (eg complex economic assessments). In many cases, administrative law also provides for a broader range of possible sanctions, from fines and suspension of licenses to exclusion from entitlement to public benefits, which can be tailored to the specific situation. In many cases, administrative sanctions may therefore be sufficient or even more effective than criminal sanctions.[10]

In summary, statements at both UK and EU levels reserve criminal sanctions for more serious behaviour. The next section notes that the same conclusion was reached by the Law Commission in reviewing the relationship between criminal and regulatory systems.

A. The Relationship Between Regulatory and Criminal Law

The Macrory Report on regulatory enforcement, discussed in the preceding chapter, triggered a linked review of the criminal liability regime by The Law Commission, which issued an important consultation in September 2010 dealing with the use of the criminal law in regulatory contexts, and with some aspects of corporate criminal liability. The Law Commission closely aligned their approach with that of Macrory, and set out the case for reducing the scope for criminal law to be used in regulated fields. The Law Commission's proposals included the following:

a.   The criminal law should only be employed to deal with wrongdoers who deserve the stigma associated with criminal conviction because they have engaged in seriously reprehensible conduct. It should not be used as the primary means of promoting regulatory objectives.

---

[9] Commission Staff Working Paper SEC (2011) 391, 28.3.2011, accompanying the White Paper 'Roadmap to a Single European Transport Area—Towards a competitive and resource efficient transport system', COM (2011) 144, 28.3.2011, para 176; Communication 'A comprehensive approach on personal data protection in the European Union', COM (2010) 609, 4.11.2010, 9; Communication 'Delivering an area of freedom, security and justice for Europe's citizens—Action Plan implementing the Stockholm Programme', COM (2010) 171, 20.4.2010, 22; Dir 2008/99/EC on the protection of the environment through criminal law, OJ L 328/28, 6.12.2008; and Dir 2009/123/EC on ship-source pollution and on the introduction of penalties for infringements, OJ L 280/52, 27.10.2009.

[10] Communication from the Commission (n 6) 11.

b.   Low-level criminal offences should be repealed in any instance where the introduction of a civil penalty is likely to do as much to secure appropriate levels of punishment and deterrence.

c.   Criminal and civil measures should form a hierarchy of seriousness.

d.   More use should be made of process fairness to increase confidence in the criminal justice system. Duties on regulators formally to warn potential offenders that they are subject to liability should be supplemented by granting the courts power to stay proceedings until non-criminal regulatory steps have been taken first, in appropriate cases.

e.   A regulatory scheme that makes provision for the imposition of any civil penalty, or equivalent measure, must also provide for unfettered recourse to the courts to challenge the imposition of that measure, by way of rehearing or appeal on a point of law.

f.   The courts should be given a power to apply a due diligence defence to any statutory offence that does not require proof that the defendant was at fault in engaging in the wrongful conduct. The burden of proof should be on the defendant to establish the defence.

g.   When it is appropriate to provide that individual directors (or equivalent officers) can themselves be liable for an offence committed by their company, on the basis that they consented or connived at the company's commission of that offence, the provision in question should not be extended to include instances in which the company's offence is attributable to neglect on the part of an individual director or equivalent person.

The consultation also proposed that regulatory authorities should make more use of cost-effective, efficient and fairer civil measures to govern standards of enforcement, such as 'stop' notices, enforcement undertakings and fixed penalties; and a set of common principles be established to help agencies consider when and how to use the criminal law to tackle serious wrongdoing.

   Scholars have noted that most financial crime control is conducted by 'forward looking compliance orientation' with 'arrest, prosecution and imprisonment viewed as subordinate methods'.[11] In other words, an ex ante approach is preferred to an ex post approach.

II. Restorative Justice in Criminal Law

A. Restorative Justice: Theory and Application in Dispute Resolution

Restorative justice is an approach that has ancient origins in customary societies, notably North American and Australasian indigenous peoples. When what was later christened as restorative justice was rediscovered in the late twentieth century, it was first applied initially in addressing situations in which other more authoritative approaches were not achieving

---

[11] M Levy, 'What Works in Combating White-Collar Crime: Some Reflections' in S Lindgren (ed), *White-Collar Crime Research. Old Views and Future Potentials* (National Council for Crime Prevention, Sweden Bar Report, 2001) 1; H Croall, 'Combating Financial Crime: Regulatory Versus Crime Control Approaches' (2003) 11 *Journal of Financial Crime* 45–55, reprinted in F Haines (ed), *Crime and Regulation* (Farnham, Ashgate, 2007).

success, such as in controlling anti-social behaviour by youths, and then extended to many other situations.[12]

Many manifestations of restorative justice involve two forms of cultural involvement. First, the injured party and offender may be brought directly together so that the former may express feelings of injury and what is desired by way of restoration and contrition by the latter, and the latter may be forced to confront the fact and extent of the damage he has caused, and agree steps to restore the position and modify future behaviour as well as express contrition. Victims are, therefore, involved in the process of sanctioning and of formal attempts to affect the future behaviour of offenders. These aspects have echoes in the addition of mediation, and other alternative dispute resolution (ADR) techniques, to traditional civil procedure of law suits, affording restorative opportunities to be added to adversarial procedures, as well as being a means of negotiating settlement of the civil dispute. Very high levels of satisfaction with the restorative justice process are reported by victims who have participated, and professionals report effective reductions in re-offending.[13]

The second technique of cultural influencing that is found within restorative justice is to identify one or more individuals who can exert influence over the offender, and create opportunities for them to do so. In the case of an anti-social youth, the effective influencer might be his grandmother or his peers. This technique has clear application in criminal law settings. But it also has echoes in contemporary regulatory schemes that enlist not only external scrutiny of corporate behaviour by consumer bodies and the media through requiring transparency of activities, governance and information, but also self-regulatory influence by trade associations and competitors. Those aspects are examined further in chapter 17.

In 2012 the UK government announced a rapid expansion of restorative justice, giving victims of crime the opportunity to engage with their offender, under a nationwide action plan for the criminal justice system.[14] An associated report adopted a definition of restorative justice as:

> … processes which bring those harmed by crime or conflict, and those responsible for the harm, into communication, enabling everyone affected by a particular incident to play a part in repairing the harm and finding a positive way forward.[15]

A considerable scholarly literature has emerged on restorative justice in its application in regulatory situations.[16] For present purposes, a restorative justice approach is relevant since

---

[12] See D Sullivan and L Tifft (eds), *Handbook of Restorative Justice* (Abingdon and New York, Routledge, 2006); D Miers and J Willemsens (eds), *Mapping Restorative Justice: Developments in 25 European Countries* (Leuven, European Forum for Victim-Offender Mediation and Restorative Justice, 2004); I Aertsen, R Mackay, C Pelikan, M Wright and J Willemsens, *Rebuilding Community Connections—Mediation and Restorative Justice* (Council of Europe, Strasbourg, 2004). In the United Kingdom, restorative justice was first extensively used in relation to juvenile crime: see Home Office, *Restorative Justice: the Government's Strategy* (Home Office, 2003).

[13] *Facing Up To Offending: Use of Restorative Justice in the Criminal Justice System* (Criminal Justice Joint Inspection, September 2012) available at http://www.hmic.gov.uk/media/facing-up-to-offending-20120918.pdf.

[14] *Restorative Justice Action Plan for the Criminal Justice System* (Ministry of Justice, 2012) http://www.justice.gov.uk/downloads/publications/policy/moj/restorative-justice-action-plan.pdf.

[15] *Facing Up To Offending: Use of Restorative Justice in the Criminal Justice System* (n 13) quoting a definition from the Restorative Justice Council website, www.restorativejustice.org.uk.

[16] Just some examples are I Ayres and J Braithwaite, *Responsive Regulation: Transcending the Deregulation Debate* (Oxford, Oxford University Press, 1992); J Braithwaite, *Restorative Justice and Responsive Regulation* (Oxford, Oxford University Press, 2002). CJS Hodges, 'Encouraging Enterprise and Rebalancing Risk: Implications of Economic Policy for Regulation, Enforcement and Compensation' [2007] *European Business Law Review* 1231.

it offers, in some circumstances, opportunities to achieve resolution of *both* behaviour control (regulatory) *and* compensatory aspects of a problem in a single holistic fashion. The approach can therefore deliver integrated solutions that combine what were frequently formerly viewed as separate remedies available under public law and private law, which had to be achieved through separate procedures. It should, of course, be emphasised that a restorative justice approach is not intended to apply or to be successful in every situation: But it does offer a number of advantages in various situations.

There are obvious attractions in the possibility, after damage has been caused illegally in breach of both public (or administrative) and private rules, of achieving, first, restoration of the *status quo* ante, second, of bringing about future change in behaviour by the offender and others, and third, of imposing any appropriate sanction on the offender all in a single procedure. Above all, such a solution may be quicker and cheaper than other approaches. If so, it would satisfy a 'better regulation' policy of achieving efficiency, and imposing low cost on the enforcement budget of public regulatory authorities, and be cheaper than many private enforcement techniques, notably American-style class actions. Such a holistic approach may also demonstrate the force of justice and the law more effectively than a bifurcated (or worse) series of steps, especially if the end result is otherwise slow, expensive and results in unsatisfactory outcomes.

Restorative justice also has the attraction of being a more principled enforcement policy than traditional 'command and control' approaches. The latter rest significantly on deterrence as a theory of achieving conformity, whereas the former rests on a wider moral basis since it combines restoration as well as behaviour control aspects. The widening out of an enforcement policy from a heavily punitive approach to one that rests more on application of positive values may assist in achieving a culture of compliance, which research has identified as being important in securing compliance with regulatory rules.

Research in a number of organisational control trials of restorative justice with serious offences (robbery, burglary and violent offences) by adult offenders found that 85 per cent of victims that participated in the conferencing method of restorative justice were satisfied with the experience.[17] The majority of victims chose to participate in face-to-face meetings with the offender, when offered by a trained facilitator. It also found the process was associated with an estimated 14 per cent reduction in the frequency of re-offending,[18] with calculated savings of £9 for every £1 spent on restorative justice.

The Ministry of Justice expanded restorative justice under an Action Plan issued in 2012,[19] and by empowering the courts to defer sentence after conviction to allow for restorative activities to take place.[20]

A revised Victims Code was applied from December 2013 that included for the first time, information on restorative justice for victims of adult offenders as well as victims of young offenders. The new Code also made it clear that restorative justice activities must be conducted in a safe, secure environment with an appropriately trained facilitator according to recognised quality standards. In 2013, the Ministry announced that at least £29 million

---

[17] J Shapland, G Robinson and A Sorsby, *Restorative Justice in Practice* (London, Routledge, 2011).
[18] *Restorative Justice Action Plan for the Criminal Justice System* (n 14) 3.
[19] ibid.
[20] The Crime and Courts Act 2013, s 44 and Sch 16.

recovered from offenders would be allocated to police and crime commissioners and charities to help deliver restorative justice for victims over the following three years.[21] Ministers created a Victims' Panel to represent victims in advising them on how the criminal justice system could better serve victims.[22]

One of the reasons for the rise in interest in restorative justice has been a waning of belief in traditional deterrent punishment as a means of affecting behaviour. Reoffending rates have continued to be unacceptably high.[23] A series of individual or social factors are understood to be associated with an increased risk of reoffending, including static factors (criminal history, age and gender) and dynamic factors (such as education, employment and drug misuse), the latter being amenable to change.[24]

Provision of information to victims on accessing compensation and on available restorative justice services is a requirement under EU legislation applicable from 2015.[25]

B. Reparation: Payment of Compensation Through the Criminal Enforcement System

Compensation can be paid to victims of crime through various different mechanisms. First, proceeds of crime can be removed from offenders, such as disgorgement of profits from scammers or drug dealers. In the regulatory context, this may be referred to as 'skimming off' illicit profits, such as those obtained by cartel members through their having charged illegally inflated prices. Second, compensation can be paid by the state to victims of violent crime. Third, compensation can be paid by offenders to anyone who has been harmed by the offence, which has been widened significantly as of 2012. Fourth, compensation can be paid by the state for miscarriage of justice to persons wrongly convicted.[26] The first three of these mechanisms will now be examined further.

i. Proceeds of Crime

The Proceeds of Crime Act 2002 (PoCA) increased previously wide-ranging powers available to the courts in relation to the confiscation and asset forfeiture regimes provided under

---

[21] Press release: *New Victims' Funding for Restorative Justice* (Ministry of Justice, 19 November 2013).

[22] Press release: *Criminals Paying More than Ever to Help Victims* (Ministry of Justice, 7 April 2014).

[23] *Transforming Rehabilitation: A Summary of Evidence on Reducing Reoffending (second edition)* (Ministry of Justice, 2014): The reoffending rates to January 2014 showed that the proportion of adults reoffending within 12 months was: (a) 58% of prisoners released between April 2011 and March 2012 after serving custodial sentences of less than 12 months; (b) 34% of prisoners released between April 2011 and March 2012 after serving custodial sentences of 12 months or more (excluding prisoners given life sentences or indeterminate sentences for public protection); and (c) 34% of those starting a court order (Community Order or Suspended Sentence Order) between April 2011 and March 2012.

[24] See DA Andrews and J Bonta, *The Psychology of Criminal Conduct* 5th edn (Cincinatti OH, Anderson Publishing, 2010).

[25] Dir 2012/39/EU on establishing minimum standards on the rights, support and protection of victims of crime, and replacing Council Framework Decision 2001/220/JHA, art 4.1(e) and (j).

[26] Criminal Justice Act 1988, s 133; The Victims of Violent Intentional Crime (Arrangements for Compensation) (European Communities) Regs 2005/3396, implementing Dir 2004/80/EC. For a useful summary see *Miscarriages of Justice: Compensation Schemes* (House of Commons Library, SN/HA/2131, August 2012) available at http://www.parliament.uk/briefing-papers/SN02131.pdf.

the Criminal Justice Act 1988 and the Drug Trafficking Act 1994.[27] It extended the benefit provisions, introduced 'lifestyle offences' and enhanced and strengthened the 'cash seizure and forfeiture' provisions. An investigating authority[28] can seek a 'civil recovery' order, without the triggering conviction, that specified property is recoverable (liable to forfeit) on the basis that it is or represents the proceeds of criminal conduct. The action is against property, not the person of the offender. The 2002 PoCA established the Assets Recovery Agency, to recover in civil proceedings property obtained through conduct that is unlawful under the criminal law.[29] In 2008, the functions were transferred to the Serious Organised Crime Agency[30] and in 2013 to the National Crime Agency (NCA).[31] Law enforcement agencies or prosecution authorities can refer cases to the NCA for consideration for civil recovery or tax action if they meet specified criteria. EU legislation is following a similar path to that discussed here at national level.[32]

The NCA is principally directed at serious criminal activity. In addition to criminal powers, it has a series of powers aimed at making it more difficult for criminals to get their hands on their money and launder the profits of their crimes. The principal civil orders are:[33]

— Confiscation Order.[34] Where a person has been convicted of an offence in the Crown Court, and the court decides that the defendant has benefited either from the particular criminal conduct or from his conduct in a general criminal lifestyle, it must make a confiscation order for a 'recoverable amount', being the defendant's benefit from the conduct.[35]
— Recovery Order. Civil proceedings in the High Court by an enforcement authority for recovery of property that is obtained through unlawful criminal conduct.[36] No criminal conviction is needed.
— Recovery Order for property, transferring it to the Trustee for Civil Recovery.[37]
— Forfeiture Order for cash seized under section 295, available in magistrates courts.[38]

The government has commented on this regime somewhat critically.

Under the PoCA, civil recovery can be used to recover the proceeds of unlawful conduct, ensuring that commercial organisations and individuals do not profit from wrongdoing.

---

[27] See *Recovering the Proceeds of Crime. A Performance and Innovation Unit Report* (Cabinet Office, 2000). Revised guidance is *National Best Practice Guide to Confiscation Order Enforcement* (Home Office, September 2012), available at http://www.homeoffice.gov.uk/publications/crime/confiscation-order-enforcement?view=Binary.

[28] The Serious Fraud Office, the Crown Prosecution Service, and the Serious Organised Crime Agency; formerly also the Revenue and Customs Prosecutions Office, which merged with the Crown Prosecution Service on 1 January 2010.

[29] PoCA 2002, s 240.

[30] See http://www.soca.gov.uk/about-soca/how-we-work/asset-recovery.

[31] Crime and Courts Act 2013.

[32] Dir 2014/42/EU on the freezing and confiscation of instrumentalities and proceeds of crime in the European Union.

[33] Jurisdictional amendments were made in the Crime and Courts Act 2013, s 48 to the PoCA.

[34] ibid, ss 6–13.

[35] ibid, s 7.

[36] ibid, s 240–43.

[37] ibid, s 266.

[38] ibid, s 298(2).

In general, criminal investigation and recovery takes priority over civil recovery, and to date this has only been considered where criminal prosecution and confiscation has no, or limited, prospects of success.

Civil recovery is solely a mechanism to recover the proceeds of 'unlawful conduct' and does not enable punishment of wrongdoing, or compensation of victims of the unlawful conduct. Victims must therefore seek a declaration that they own property which is subject to a pending civil recovery order, and then initiate their own proceedings to recover such property.

Civil Recovery Orders (CROs) cannot include conditions to cater for issues such as monitoring and compliance training unless there is agreement between the parties or a Serious Crime Prevention Order in place. However, of the five CROs made by the Serious Fraud Office (SFO) by mid-2014, four included monitoring arrangements.[39] Under the Crime and Courts Act 2013, a civil recovery investigation can be taken to identify property valued at over £10,000 which is, or represents, the proceeds of unlawful conduct.[40]

A successful example of disgorgement of profits was that effected by the medicines regulator (MHRA).[41] Some criticism is directed at PoCA on the basis of a low recovery rate of confiscation orders.[42]

ii. Compensation for Victims of Violent Crime

The Criminal Injuries Compensation Scheme was made by the Secretary of State under the Criminal Injuries Compensation Act 1995 and is operated by the Criminal Injuries Compensation Authority.[43] It pays money to people who have been physically or mentally injured on or after 1 August 1964, because they were the blameless victim of a violent crime.[44] The 1995 Act established a statutory tariff, and two agencies: The Criminal Injuries Compensation Authority and an Appeals Panel. Reforms in 2001 provide for payment of a lump sum consisting of (a) a standard amount fixed by tariff with descriptions of over 400 different types of injury, each corresponding to one of 25 levels of compensation, (b) compensation for loss of earnings, including future loss of earnings, except for the first 28 weeks of loss, limited to one and a half times gross average industrial earnings, and (c) compensation for special expenses, including reasonable private health treatment.

---

[39] *Consultation on a New Enforcement Tool to Deal with Economic Crime Committed by Commercial Organisations: Deferred Prosecution Agreements* (Ministry of Justice, CP9/2012, May 2012) available at https://consult. justice.gov.uk/digital-communications/deferred-prosecution-agreements/supporting_documents/deferredprosecutionagreementsconsultation.pdf.

[40] Crime and Courts Act 2013, s 48. Such orders under Ch 2 of Pt 5 of the PoCA may be made in relation to property outside the United Kingdom: ibid, ss 48 and 49 and Schs 18, 19 and 25, reversing *Perry v SOCA* [2012] UKSC 35.

[41] The purveyor of an unlicensed medicine that had been illegally marketed (as 'Flabjab') with a claim that it would lead to slimming was fined £5,000 in a criminal prosecution by MHRA. MHRA then brought a civil application under s 243 of the Proceeds of Crime Act 2002, and obtained a court order for disgorgement of £800,000 profits. See http://www.mhra.gov.uk/PrintPreview/PressReleaseSP/CON043922, 8 April 2009.

[42] R Sahota, 'Orders need to suit the facts' *Law Gazette* 2 September 2013, 10 (in 2011/12 60% of confiscation orders were unpaid, being £780m of £1.3bn).

[43] See http://www.justice.gov.uk/victims-and-witnesses/cica. The first Criminal Injuries Compensation Scheme was established in 1964, and placed on a statutory footing by the Criminal Justice Act 1988.

[44] The history and an overview of operations is: K Oliphant, 'Landmarks of No-Fault in the Common Law' in WH van Boom and M Faure (eds), *Shifts in Compensation between Private and Public Systems* (Vienna, Springer, 2007).

The current Scheme was introduced on 27 November 2012 and applies to any application made on or after that date.[45] The Scheme links with similar national arrangements for victims of a violent intentional crime committed in a Member State other than where the applicant is habitually resident, who may apply to an authority for payment of compensation by the Member State on whose territory the crime was committed.[46]

iii. Compensation Orders in Criminal Courts

Public authorities have power to seek a compensation order from the courts as part of the criminal enforcement process.[47] Criminal courts possess a general power to order a person convicted of an offence to pay compensation for any personal injury, loss or damage resulting from that offence, or any other offence that is taken into consideration by the court in determining sentence. Such compensation shall be such amount as the court considers appropriate, having regard to any evidence and representations made. If a person in whose favour such a compensation order is made also claims damages in civil proceedings, such damages shall be assessed without regard to the compensation order, but the claimant may only recover an amount equal to the aggregate of any amount by which the award of damages exceeds the compensation order, or a sum equal to any portion of the compensation which he fails to recover. The court also has power to order anyone who has possession of stolen goods to restore them to the person entitled to them (a restoration order).

Since 2013, criminal courts have a duty to consider making a compensation order in *every case*.[48] Anecdotal reports suggest that criminal courts were in fact making compensation orders as a matter of course, so this statutory duty made little difference in practice, but, as will be seen below, this legislative confirmation was part of general policy towards victims, and shifting the financial burden of compensation away from state funds and on to offenders.

C. Reparative Justice for Victims of Crime

In December 2010 the government published a consultation document, *Breaking the Cycle*, which proposed wide-ranging reforms to the way in which offenders are sentenced by the courts and are subsequently dealt with in custody and in the community. The intention

[45] *The Criminal Injuries Compensation Scheme 2012*, Ministry of Justice 2012, available at http://www.justice.gov.uk/downloads/victims-and-witnesses/cic-a/am-i-eligible/criminal-injuries-comp-scheme-2012.pdf.

[46] Dir 2004/80/EC of 29 April relating to compensation to crime victims, OJ L 261/15, 6.8.2004, arts 1 and 2. See also Dir 2012/39/EU on establishing minimum standards on the rights, support and protection of victims of crime, and replacing Council Framework Decision 2001/220/JHA. See also Council of Europe Recommendation No R(85) 11 on the position of the victim in the framework of criminal law and procedure; Recommendation No R(87) 21 on assistance to victims and the prevention of victimization; Recommendation No R(2000) 19 on the role of the public prosecution in the criminal justice system; and the European Convention on the compensation of victims of violent crimes (1983). In UK see the Victims of Violent Intentional Crime (Arrangements for Compensation) (European Communities) Regs 2005/3396.

[47] Powers of Criminal Courts (Sentencing) Act 2000, s 130. Originally introduced by the Criminal Justice Report 1972, s 1, after the Widgery Report 1970. Re-enacted as from 1974 by Powers of Criminal Courts Act 1973, s 35, amended by Magistrates Court Act 1980, s 40 and Criminal Justice Act 1982, s 67.

[48] The Legal Aid, Sentencing and Punishment of Offenders Act 2012, s 63.

was to make offenders take greater responsibility for their crimes and do more to repair the damage they had caused, based on three principles:

—   Offenders should bear a greater proportion of the costs incurred by the state in supporting victims to cope and recover following crime.
—   Offenders paying compensation direct to victims should be the norm, and any compensation awarded should be received by the victim in full.
—   There should be greater opportunities for victims and offenders to participate in restorative justice.

The Government response to the consultation was published in July 2012 and a package of measures was enacted in the Legal Aid, Sentencing and Punishment of Offenders Act 2012, Part three, including the duty noted above that criminal courts must consider making a compensation order in every case where a conviction is made.

In January 2012 the government published proposals to further support victims and witnesses, including dealing with offenders in a way that reduces the likelihood of their re-offending and creating more victims.[49] The proposal again included the principle that 'offenders should make reparation for the impact of their crimes', but the underlying policy of shifting 'to a situation in which more offenders take personal responsibility for the harm they have caused by offering an apology or by making the appropriate financial or practical reparation'[50] was influenced by shifting away from compensation funded by the taxpayer, so as to save public expenditure.

The policy drew a distinction between restorative justice and reparation, whilst seeking to expand the delivery of both concepts. Under restorative justice, 'offenders should be made to face up to the impact of their offending and the harm they have done to victims'.[51] On the other hand, there should be a shift away from compensation to victims of crime being paid by the state and towards reparation being paid to them by offenders, under a 'Victim Surcharge'.[52] The Criminal Injuries Compensation Scheme cost over £200 million a year, whereas only £30 million was paid by offenders in court-ordered compensation in 2010/11. The Victim Surcharge then raised about £10 million annually,[53] but the government proposed to increase the rate ordered on fines and extend it to the full range of sentences ordered in court, and also use increased revenue from Penalty Notices for Disorder and motoring Fixed Penalty Notices, the aim was to raise up to an additional £50 million each year.

---

[49]   *Getting it Right for Victims and Witnesses, Consultation Paper CP3/2012*, Ministry of Justice, January 2012, at https://consult.justice.gov.uk/digital-communications/victims-witnesses.
[50]   ibid, para 8.
[51]   ibid, para 19.
[52]   The surcharge was introduced under the Criminal Justice Act 2003 s 161A, and set at £15. Under the Criminal Justice Act 2003 (Surcharge) Order 2012/1696 it was set at 10% of a fine, with a minimum of £20 and maximum of £120, mostly applying even if no financial penalty is imposed. For criticism see J Rosenberg, 'A chance to look tough' *Law Gazette* 1 July 2013, 8.
[53]   From 2010 to August 2014 it raised £51 million: Press release 'Offenders to pay more towards victim support services' (Ministry of Justice, 8 August 2014). When the surcharge was introduced, offenders sentenced in magistrates' courts could opt for extra days in prison instead of paying the surcharge, but payment was made mandatory under the Anti-Social Behaviour, Crime and Policing Act 2014, s 179, amending the Criminal Justice Act 2003, s 161A.

The above policies were adopted in the government's Response to the Consultation, its 'Victims Strategy', issued in July 2012.[54] It was said that 'We do not believe that compensation is the most effective way of helping victims recover but in some circumstances it is plainly right to provide financial assistance'[55] and 'Restorative Justice is not a panacea but a recent Ministry of Justice/Home Office evaluation of restorative justice pilots found that 85% of victims who participated in a trial scheme were satisfied with the experience.'[56] A 'Restorative Justice Action Plan for the Criminal Justice System' was published in September 2012.[57]

Also in July 2012,[58] a different Ministry of Justice White Paper noted:

It is a basic principle of justice that it should be delivered without delay....

The public has a right to expect the justice system to be swift and sure:

— swift: so that the low-level, straightforward and uncontested cases, where a quick response is appropriate, are dealt with promptly and efficiently; and
— sure: so that the system can be relied upon to deliver punishment and redress fairly and in accordance with the law and public expectation.[59]

A revised Code of Practice for Victims of Crime was issued in 2013,[60] which listed a series of victims' entitlements, including making a Victim Personal Statement (VPS) to explain how the crime affected the victim, applying for compensation under the Criminal Injuries Compensation Scheme, receiving information about Restorative Justice and how the victim can take part.

A 2013 study found that victims 'are crucial in ensuring the delivery of justice.'[61] There was a high level of awareness of the organisation Victim Support for both victims of crime and non-victims (84 per cent and 81 per cent respectively). However, this did vary, with those living in higher-income households, those from a white ethnic background, those aged 25 and over, and those who had a long-standing illness or disability being more likely to be aware of Victim Support. For non-victims, the most common method of hearing about Victim Support was through the media, such as newspapers and television (50 per cent), or from a friend or family member (12 per cent). Overall in the 2008/09 Crime Survey of England and Wales, victims said they wanted some form of support, information or advice in 19 per cent of incidents and they received some form of support, information or advice in nine per cent of incidents. The types of support wanted most often were information from the police (10 per cent of all incidents), protection from further victimisation (six per cent of all incidents) or someone to talk to or moral support (five per cent of all incidents).

---

[54] *Getting it Right for Victims and Witnesses, the Government Response* (n 49).
[55] ibid, para 4.
[56] ibid, para 105.
[57] *Restorative Justice Action Plan for the Criminal Justice System* (n 14). See also *Facing Up To Offending: Use of Restorative Justice in the Criminal Justice System* (n 13).
[58] *Swift and Sure Justice: The Government's Plans for Reform of the Criminal Justice System* (Ministry of Justice, July 2012), Cm838, available at http://www.justice.gov.uk/downloads/publications/policy/moj/swift-and-sure-justice.pdf.
[59] ibid, Foreword by the minister, and Executive Summary.
[60] Pursuant to the Domestic Violence, Crime and Victims Act 2004, s 33.
[61] L Freeman, *Support for Victims: Findings from the Crime Survey for England and Wales* (Ministry of Justice, 2013).

The types of support that were most received were information from the police (three per cent of all incidents), someone to talk to or moral support (three per cent of all incidents) and information about security or crime prevention (two per cent of all incidents).

The amounts paid for financial impositions ordered by criminal courts (including fines, prosecutors' costs, compensation orders and victim surcharge) increased significantly from late 2012, from around £120 million annually to around £28 million in 2014.[62]

III. Sentencing Guidelines

In order to promote consistent sentencing by judges and magistrates, when sentencing an offender for an offence committed on or after 6 April 2010, a court must follow any relevant Sentencing Guidelines.[63] Sentencing Guidelines have been used for some years, and set out a decision-making process that specify the factors that should be taken into account in deciding on sentencing. The regime under the Coroners and Justice Act 2009 is that they are made by the Sentencing Council,[64] after public consultation.[65] The governing Act specifies, as quoted in Box 10.1, a format for Sentencing Guidelines that requires certain factors to be included, ranges of sentences to be specified and aggravating or mitigating factors to be listed.

Box 10.1. Sentencing Ranges: Coroners and Justice Act 2009, s 121

Sentencing ranges

(1) When exercising functions under section 120, the Council is to have regard to the desirability of sentencing guidelines which relate to a particular offence being structured in the way described in subsections (2) to (9).

(2) The guidelines should, if reasonably practicable given the nature of the offence, describe, by reference to one or more of the factors mentioned in subsection (3), different categories of case involving the commission of the offence which illustrate in general terms the varying degrees of seriousness with which the offence may be committed.

(3) Those factors are—
  (a) the offender's culpability in committing the offence;
  (b) the harm caused, or intended to be caused or which might foreseeably have been caused, by the offence;

---

[62] *Court Statistics Quarterly*, 2014.

[63] Coroners and Justice Act 2009, s 120. See A Ashworth and JV Roberts (eds), *Sentencing Guidelines: Exploring the English Model* (Oxford, Oxford University Press, 2013).

[64] Created under the Coroners and Justice Act 2009, s 118; see Sch 15.

[65] See eg *Fraud, Bribery and Money Laundering Offences Guideline. Consultation* (Sentencing Council, 2013) at https://consult.justice.gov.uk/sentencing-council/fraud-bribery-money-laundering-offences-guideline/supporting_documents/Fraud%20Consultation.pdf.

(c)   such other factors as the Council considers to be particularly relevant to the seriousness of the offence in question.

(4)   The guidelines should—

(a)   specify the range of sentences ('the offence range') which, in the opinion of the Council, it may be appropriate for a court to impose on an offender convicted of that offence, and

(b)   if the guidelines describe different categories of case in accordance with subsection (2), specify for each category the range of sentences ('the category range') within the offence range which, in the opinion of the Council, it may be appropriate for a court to impose on an offender in a case which falls within the category.

(5)   The guidelines should also—

(a) specify the sentencing starting point in the offence range, or

(b)   if the guidelines describe different categories of case in accordance with subsection (2), specify the sentencing starting point in the offence range for each of those categories.

(6)   The guidelines should—

(a)   (to the extent not already taken into account by categories of case described in accordance with subsection (2)) list any aggravating or mitigating factors which, by virtue of any enactment or other rule of law, the court is required to take into account when considering the seriousness of the offence and any other aggravating or mitigating factors which the Council considers are relevant to such a consideration,

(b)   list any other mitigating factors which the Council considers are relevant in mitigation of sentence for the offence, and

(c)   include criteria, and provide guidance, for determining the weight to be given to previous convictions of the offender and such of the other factors within paragraph (a) or (b) as the Council considers to be of particular significance in relation to the offence or the offender.

(7)   For the purposes of subsection (6)(b) the following are to be disregarded—

(a)   the requirements of section 144 of the Criminal Justice Act 2003 (c 44) (reduction in sentences for guilty pleas);

(b)   sections 73 and 74 of the Serious Organised Crime and Police Act 2005 (assistance by defendants: reduction or review of sentence) and any other rule of law by virtue of which an offender may receive a discounted sentence in consequence of assistance given (or offered to be given) by the offender to the prosecutor or investigator of an offence;

(c)   any rule of law as to the totality of sentences.

(8)   The provision made in accordance with subsection (6)(c) should be framed in such manner as the Council considers most appropriate for the purpose of assisting the court, when sentencing an offender for the offence, to determine the appropriate sentence within the offence range.

(9)   The provision made in accordance with subsections (2) to (8) may be different for different circumstances or cases involving the offence.

> (10)   The sentencing starting point in the offence range—
>
>   (a)   for a category of case described in the guidelines in accordance with subsection (2), is the sentence within that range which the Council considers to be the appropriate starting point for cases within that category—
>
>   (i)   before taking account of the factors mentioned in subsection (6), and
>
>   (ii)   assuming the offender has pleaded not guilty, and
>
>   (b)   where the guidelines do not describe categories of case in accordance with subsection (2), is the sentence within that range which the Council considers to be the appropriate starting point for the offence—
>
>   (i)   before taking account of the factors mentioned in subsection (6), and
>
>   (ii)   assuming the offender has pleaded not guilty.

By mid-2014 26 Guidelines had been produced.[66] For present purposes, the Guidelines on Reduction in Sentence for a Guilty Plea, Corporate Manslaughter & Health and Safety Offences Causing Death, and Fraud, Bribery and Money Laundering: Corporate Offenders, are particularly instructive.

The Guideline on Reduction in Sentence for a Guilty Plea, first introduced in 2004 and revised in 2007, expands on the statutory requirement that, in determining what sentence to pass, a court must take into account the stage in the proceedings at which the offender indicated his intention to plead guilty, and the circumstances in which this indication was given.[67] The Guideline notes that a custodial sentence and a community order must be commensurate with the seriousness of the offence but, once that decision is made, a court is required to give consideration to the reduction for any guilty plea. 'As a result, the final sentence after the reduction for a guilty plea will be less than the seriousness of the offence requires.'[68] The rationale for reduction stated is primarily concerned with saving public costs and then reducing pressure on witnesses, rather than on the basis of an ethical principle of remorse, apology or redress, although remorse is to be taken into account in quantifying any reduction:

> 2.2 A reduction in sentence is appropriate because a guilty plea avoids the need for a trial (thus enabling other cases to be disposed of more expeditiously), shortens the gap between charge and sentence, saves considerable cost, and, in the case of an early plea, saves victims and witnesses from the concern about having to give evidence. The reduction principle derives from the need for the effective administration of justice and not as an aspect of mitigation....

> 2.4 When deciding the most appropriate length of sentence, the sentence should address separately the issue of remorse, together with any other mitigating features, before calculating the reduction for the guilty plea. Similarly, assistance to the prosecuting or enforcement authorities is a separate

---

[66]   See http://sentencingcouncil.judiciary.gov.uk/guidelines/guidelines-to-download.htm.

[67]   Criminal Justice Act 2003, s 144.

[68]   Guideline on *Reduction in Sentence for a Guilty Plea*, at http://sentencingcouncil.judiciary.gov.uk/docs/Reduction_in_Sentence_for_a_Guilty_Plea_-Revised_2007.pdf, para 2.1.

issue which may attract a reduction in sentence under other procedures; care will need to be taken to ensure that there is no 'double counting'....

2.6 A reduction in sentence should only be applied to the punitive elements of a penalty. The guilty plea reduction has no impact on sentencing decisions in relation to ancillary orders, including orders of disqualification from driving.

The Guideline on Corporate Manslaughter & Health and Safety Offences Causing Death,[69] published in 2010, is directed at sentencing of organisations rather than individuals. The Guideline applies where it is proved that the offence was a 'significant cause of death, not simply that death occurred.'[70] The factors likely to affect seriousness include:

(a) How foreseeable was the injury?
(b) How far short of the applicable standard did the [organisation] fall?
     I How common is this kind of breach in this organisation?
(d) How far up the organisation does the breach go?[71]

It is relevant to take into account the size of the organization, but a fixed correlation between the fine and either turnover or profit is not appropriate.[72] In assessing the financial consequences of a fine, the court should consider (inter alia) the following factors:[73]

(i)   the effect on the employment of the innocent may be relevant;
(ii)   any effect upon shareholders will, however, not normally be relevant; those who invest in and finance a company take the risk that its management will result in financial loss;
(iii) the effect on directors will not, likewise, normally be relevant;
(iv)   nor would it ordinarily be relevant that the prices charged by the defendant might in consequence be raised, at least unless the defendant is a monopoly supplier of public services;
(v)   the effect upon the provision of services to the public will be relevant; although a public organisation such as a local authority, hospital trust or police force must be treated the same as a commercial company where the standards of behaviour to be expected are concerned, and must suffer a punitive fine for breach of them, a different approach to determining the level of fine may well be justified;
       'The Judge has to consider how any financial penalty will be paid. If a very substantial financial penalty will inhibit the proper performance by a statutory body of the public function that it has been set up to perform, that is not something to be disregarded.'[74]
       The same considerations will be likely to apply to non-statutory bodies or charities if providing public services.
(vi)   the liability to pay civil compensation will ordinarily not be relevant; normally this will be provided by insurance or the resources of the defendant will be large enough to meet it from its own resources (for compensation generally see paragraphs 27–28 below);

---

[69] *Corporate Manslaughter & Health and Safety Offences Causing Death. Definitive Guideline* (Sentencing Guidelines Council, 2010), at http://sentencingcouncil.judiciary.gov.uk/docs/web__guideline_on_corporate_manslaughter_accessible.pdf. The offence of corporate manslaughter was created by the Corporate Manslaughter and Corporate Homicide Act 2007. The health and safety offences typically arise under the Health and Safety at Work Act 1974, ss 2 and 3.
[70] ibid, para 4 (c).
[71] ibid, para 6.
[72] ibid, paras 12–17.
[73] ibid, para 19.
[74] *Milford Haven Port Authority* [2000] 2 Cr App R(S) 423 per Lord Bingham CJ at 433–34.

(vii)   the cost of meeting any remedial order will not ordinarily be relevant, except to the overall financial position of the defendant; such an order requires no more than should already have been done;

(viii) whether the fine will have the effect of putting the defendant out of business will be relevant; in some bad cases this may be an acceptable consequence.

In relation to compensation, the Guideline states:

27.   The assessment of compensation in cases of death will usually be complex, will involve payment of sums well beyond the powers of a criminal court, and will ordinarily be covered by insurance.

28.   In the great majority of cases the court should conclude that compensation should be dealt with in a civil court, and should say that no order is made for that reason.[75] There may be occasional cases, for example if the defendant is uninsured and payment may not otherwise be made, when consideration should be given to a compensation order in respect of bereavement and/or funeral expenses.[76]

The Guideline states that a defendant ought by the time of sentencing to have remedied any specific failings involved in the offence and if it has not will be deprived of significant mitigation.[77] However, if appropriate, a remedial order can be made.

The Guideline on Fraud, Bribery and Money Laundering in relation to corporate offenders was made in 2014 and applies to a range of offences committed by corporations.[78] The factors listed that reduce seriousness or reflect mitigation are:

No previous relevant convictions or relevant civil or regulatory enforcement action;
Victims voluntarily reimbursed/compensated;
No actual loss to victims;
Corporation co-operated with investigation, made early admissions and/or voluntarily reported offending;
Offending committed under previous director(s)/manager(s);
Little or no actual gain to corporation from offending.

The overall effect of the sentence should be that

[t]he combination of orders made, compensation, confiscation and fine ought to achieve:

— the removal of all gain
— appropriate additional punishment, and
— deterrence.[79]

The court should also identify whether any combination of the following additional factors, or other relevant factors, should result in a proportionate increase or reduction in the level of fine:

Fine fulfils the objectives of punishment, deterrence and removal of gain
The value, worth or available means of the offender

---

[75] Powers of Criminal Courts Act 2000, s 130(3)

[76] Made under Powers of Criminal Courts Act 2000, s 130(9) and (10).

[77] Guideline, para 34.

[78] *Fraud, Bribery and Money Laundering Offences Definitive Guideline* (Sentencing Council, 2014) 50, see https://www.sentencingcouncil.org.uk/wp-content/uploads/Fraud_bribery_and_money_laundering_offences_-_Definitive_guideline.pdf; See https://www.sentencingcouncil.org.uk/wp-content/uploads/Fraud_Response_to_Consultation_web1.pdf.

[79] ibid, 52.

Fine impairs offender's ability to make restitution to victims

Impact of fine on offender's ability to implement effective compliance programmes

Impact of fine on employment of staff, service users, customers and local economy (but not shareholders)

Impact of fine on performance of public or charitable function.[80]

It can be seen that there has been an advance in thinking in the Guidelines from the 2007 Guilty Plea guideline, through the 2010 guideline on *Corporate Manslaughter*, and to that for 2014 on *Fraud*. The approach has become more consistent with underlying principles on expecting corporations to behave well both before and after the criminal process. In the latter stage, the expectation is that they will own up to the offence at an early stage, take full remedial action in terms of making full redress and taking actions to avoid repetition of the offence. The incentives set by the Sentencing Guidelines should be set to support such behaviour: The more recent Guidelines largely achieve such ends, but could be clearer about spelling out the motivational objectives, and the older Guidelines could be updated. The principle of incentivisation through offering a reduced sentence is long-established, and has recently been taken a step further through deferred prosecution agreements, to which we now turn.

IV. Deferred Prosecution Agreements

A. Development of Policy

One of the objectives outlined in the 2012 White Paper was to secure guilty pleas earlier in the prosecution process, improving efficiency, reducing paperwork and process times, and alleviating the burden on witnesses and victims of crime. Accordingly, in October 2012, the Ministry of Justice announced a highly significant change away from 'command and control', deterrence-based enforcement policy, and the introduction of deferred prosecution agreements (DPAs) for cases of major economic crime.[81] Use of DPAs and non-prosecution agreements (NPAs) had increased strikingly in USA since 2004 (126 publicly-held firms were subject to DPAs and NPAs) in contrast to a major fall in convictions of corporations.[82] The case for change in the UK was made on three grounds: The behaviour of commercial organisations involved in serious crime; problems in effective co-operation with prosecutors in other jurisdictions; and the length and cost of proceedings. The earlier consultation had stated:

1. Corporate economic crime causes serious harm to its direct victims and grave damage to our economy. In 2012, the National Fraud Authority estimated that fraud committed by all types of offenders costs the UK £73 billion per year....

---

[80] ibid.

[81] *Deferred Prosecution Agreements Government Response to the Consultation on a New Enforcement Tool to Deal with Economic Crime Committed by Commercial Organisations* (Cm 8463: Ministry of Justice, October 2012) available at https://consult.justice.gov.uk/digital-communications/deferred-prosecution-agreements/results/deferred-prosecution-agreements-response.pdf.

[82] JM Anderson and I Waggoner, *The Changing Role of Criminal Law in Controlling Corporate Behaviour* (Los Angeles CA, RAND Corporation, 2014); J Arlen and M Kahan, 'Corporate Regulation Through Non-Prosecution' (2012) working paper.

5. ... We believe that deferred prosecution agreements (DPA), ... can make a valuable contribution to efforts to identify and address corporate economic crime. A DPA would sit alongside existing means of tackling crime, criminal prosecution and civil proceedings. Under its terms, a prosecutor would lay but would not immediately proceed with criminal charges against a company pending successful compliance with tough requirements such as financial penalties, restitution for victims, confiscation of the profits of wrongdoing and measures to prevent future offending.

6. DPAs would be a fair and pragmatic approach to tackling a serious problem and would need to be used judiciously. Where the alleged wrongdoing is most serious, or the public interest would otherwise require it, a criminal prosecution would continue to be the most appropriate course of action. As DPAs would be sanctioned by judges, the judiciary would be able to block DPAs which they do not think would serve the interests of justice, for example where prosecution would be the appropriate response. Entering into a DPA will be voluntary both for companies accused of wrongdoing and for prosecutors.

7. DPAs would contribute to a just outcome, enabling prosecutors to secure penalties for and the surrendering of the proceeds of wrongdoing, and providing benefits for victims in a way that is sanctioned by a judge, without the uncertainty, expense, complexity or length of a full criminal trial. They also enable commercial organisations to be held to account—but without unfairly affecting employees, customers, pensioners, suppliers and investors who were not involved in the behaviour that is being penalised. The process will be transparent; as DPAs will be public, the public will always know what wrongdoing has taken place, and the penalty that has been paid.

8. Our ambition is to ensure that a higher proportion of economic crime is identified, investigated and dealt with....[83]

The May 2012 consultation DPAs set out the following case for change and need for new enforcement approaches:

22. Treating economic crime as seriously as other crime and taking steps to combat it effectively are key commitments in the Coalition Agreement. Economic crime is increasingly sophisticated. As the size of commercial organisations and the reach of their interests grow, so too do the difficulties of identifying criminal activity and of prosecution at national level for what can often be wrongdoing across a number of jurisdictions.

23. The present justice system in England and Wales is inadequate for dealing effectively with criminal enforcement against commercial organisations in the field of complex and serious economic crime.

27. While criminal prosecution can effectively punish a commercial organization using existing criminal penalties, it can also end up having unintended detrimental consequences, such as adverse share price movements and failure of organisations, which in turn can impact on blameless employees, customers, pensioners, suppliers and investors. A criminal conviction can also mean the organization is unable to bid for EU and US public procurement tenders, which may be disproportionate and particularly damaging.

29. The alternative civil recovery route can be effective in relation to recovery of proceeds of unlawful conduct (which go to the Government)...

---

[83] *Consultation on a New Enforcement Tool to Deal with Economic Crime Committed by Commercial Organisations: Deferred Prosecution Agreements* (n 39).

The consultation also noted a number of factors in relation to seeking to influence commercial organisations' behaviour:

31. There are currently insufficient incentives for commercial organisations to engage and cooperate with UK authorities at earlier stages to achieve better outcomes.

32. Restitution and punishment will only occur where commercial organisations are prepared to engage and plead guilty to a criminal charge or against whom the legal and evidential difficulties of proving corporate liability can be overcome. From the perspective of victims, no order can be made for restitution until the offender has been convicted, and there are limited opportunities to pursue civil remedies against a commercial organization.[84]

34. Commercial organisations are therefore likely to be deterred from engaging with prosecution authorities to deal with wrongdoing within the organization and to conclude investigations quickly.

35. ... Ultimately, commercial organisations wish to survive and flourish and thus minimise investor disquiet or share-price impacts. Removing uncertainty from business operations is a vital factor influencing behaviour.

36. Another factor weighing against engagement by commercial organisations is the uncertainty of any penalty that may be imposed. While there is some guidance on calculation of fines for corporate offenders, there is not at present a framework for doing so set out in sentencing guidelines as there is for individual offenders.

37. Taking all of these circumstances together, the prosecutor at present has little to offer the commercial organization by way of encouragement to engage, cooperate or plead. The organization has no real incentive of its own to resolve issues with the prosecutor, particularly as there will be significant uncertainty over where the process will lead...

41. A late guilty plea costs the SFO around £1.6 million and takes around eight years to conclude, including any monitoring and reporting requirements.

US prosecutors are not restricted in the same way as their UK counterparts. The consultation contrasted the problems that arose through the separation of civil and criminal pathways with the more integrated approach in the United States:

US authorities have placed an increasing focus on crime committed by commercial organisations and the enforcement of the Foreign Corrupt Practices Act (FCPA), through a deliberate policy of giving organizations meaningful credit for voluntarily disclosing their conduct and cooperating with Department of Justice (DOJ) investigations by self reporting.

In return for prosecutors either deferring their decision to prosecute or deciding not to prosecute, NPAs and DPAs require commercial organisations to comply with a set of terms that may include significant monetary penalties (which averaged over $100 million in 2011, across 29 NPAs and DPAs), requirements to improve governance structures and internal compliance, make reparations, and the appointment of independent monitors (at the organization's expense) to review the effectiveness of any compliance programme. Commercial organisations may also agree to act as whistleblowers for other commercial organizations which have committed offences in their sector. Commercial organizations also agree not to appeal, or to appeal only specified aspects, of a

---

[84] Claimants may seek to rely upon s 11 of the Civil Evidence Act 1968, which provides that a criminal conviction is admissible as evidence in civil proceedings.

DPA. If at the end of the deferral period for a DPA, the prosecutor is satisfied that the commercial organization has fulfilled its obligations, then the prosecutor will make an application to dismiss or withdraw the charges.

Neither NPAs nor DPAs have a statutory basis, relying instead on the United States Attorney's manual, Principles of Federal Prosecution of Business Organisations, which sets out the circumstances in which they are appropriate and the factors to consider when investigating, charging, and discussing an agreement.

It was stated that a DPA would not be a sentence upon conviction for an offence, but should fulfil some or all of the statutory purposes of a sentence, referred to above. For example, the 'reduction of crime' purpose might be fulfilled by conditions to deter future offending, including changes to organisational governance or disciplinary procedures within a commercial organisation that enters into a DPA. The 'reparation to victims' purpose might lead to a condition including compensatory payments to those affected by a commercial organisation's offending organisation, or an organisation's staff meeting with those affected to discuss the impact of the wrongdoing, be held directly to account and to apologise.

Two key principles were said to be required and effective in commanding public confidence and tackling economic crime committed by commercial organisations:[85]

— Transparency: To provide a process which encourages potential defendants to discuss 'without prejudice' and to ensure that the operation of justice is transparent to the public; and
— Consistency: To ensure both prosecutor and commercial organisation are working from common principles when entering into the DPA process, and to give both an indication of the likely package of terms, including a penalty, which a court would approve.

B. DPA Rules

DPAs were given a statutory basis in 2013,[86] supported by a Code of Practice.[87] A Code for Crown Prosecutors issued in 2013 sets out general principles to be applied when making decisions about prosecutions.[88] This is divided into applications at different stages: The Full Code Test (under which Prosecutors must be satisfied that there is sufficient evidence to provide a realistic prospect of conviction against each suspect on the particular charge),

---

[85] (n 39) para 78.
[86] Crime and Courts Act 2013, s 45 and Sch 17. See *Deferred Prosecution Agreements Government Response to the Consultation on a New Enforcement Tool to Deal with Economic Crime Committed by Commercial Organisations* (n 81).
[87] *Deferred Prosecution Agreements Code of Practice* (SFO and CPS, 2014), available at http://www.sfo.gov.uk/media/264623/deferred%20prosecution%20agreements%20cop.pdf. Issued under Crime and Courts Act 2013, Sch 17, para 6. See *Crime and Courts Act 2013: Deferred Prosecution Agreement Code of Practice. Consultation on Draft Code* (SFO, 27 June 2013), http://www.sfo.gov.uk/press-room/latest-press-releases/press-releases-2013/deferred-prosecution-agreements-consultation-on-draft-code-of-practice.aspx.
[88] *The Code for Crown Prosecutors*, available at http://www.cps.gov.uk/publications/code_for_crown_prosecutors. See earlier *The Code for Crown Prosecutors: Consultation Document* (Director of Public Prosecutions, 2012), available at http://www.cps.gov.uk/consultations/code_2012_consultation.html.

the Evidential Stage, and a Public Interest Stage, the latter specifying that amongst the questions that prosecutors should consider is: 'How serious is the offence committed? The more serious the offence, the more likely it is that a prosecution is required.'[89]

DPAs are restricted to listed offences.[90] They apply to organisations, not individuals. During the negotiation stage, the prosecutor must apply to the Crown Court for a declaration that entering into a DPA with a defendant (P) is likely to be in the interests of justice, and the proposed terms of the DPA are fair, reasonable and proportionate.[91] The DPA must subsequently be approved by the Crown Court in a declaration that the DPA is in the interests of justice, and the terms of the DPA are fair, reasonable and proportionate.[92]

Terms and conditions of DPAs are specific to individual cases and to the purposes to be addressed, but requirements that a DPA may impose include, but are not limited to, the following:[93]

(a)   To pay to the prosecutor a financial penalty;[94]
(b)   to compensate victims of the alleged offence;
(c)   to donate money to a charity or other third party;
(d)   to disgorge any profits made by the person from the alleged offence;
(e)   to implement a compliance programme or make changes to an existing compliance programme relating to the person's policies or to the training of the person's employees or both;
(f)   to co-operate in any investigation related to the alleged offence;
(g)   to pay any reasonable costs of the prosecutor in relation to the alleged offence or the DPA.

The prosecutor is required to apply a two stage test, and be satisfied (and record) that both the evidential stage and public interest stage are satisfied.[95] The evidential stage test is either that the Full Code test in the Code for Crown Prosecutors is satisfied or, if it is not, that there is at least a reasonable suspicion based upon some admissible evidence that the business (P) has committed the offence, and there are reasonable grounds for believing that a continued investigation would provide further admissible evidence within a reasonable period of time, so that all evidence together would be capable of establishing a realistic prospect of conviction in accordance with the Full Code test. The public interest stage is that the public interest would be properly served by the prosecutor not prosecuting but instead entering into a DPA with the business in accordance with the evidential stage tests.

---

[89] ibid, para 4.12(a).
[90] Crime and Courts Act 2013, Sch 17 Part 2. The list includes conspiracy to defraud, theft, forgery, and various contraventions under the Financial Services and Markets Act 2000, the Proceeds of Crime Act 2002, the Companies Act 2006, the Bribery Act 2010 and the Money Laundering Regs 2007.
[91] Crime and Courts Act 2013, Sch 17 para 7.
[92] ibid, Sch 17 para 8.
[93] ibid, Sch 17 para 5(3).
[94] The amount of any financial penalty agreed between the prosecutor and P must be broadly comparable to the fine that a court would have imposed on P on conviction for the alleged offence following a guilty plea: ibid, para 5(4).
[95] *Deferred Prosecution Agreement Code of Practice* (n 87).

A specific procedure is mandated for concluding a DPA, which starts with the prosecutor issuing an invitation to the business to enter negotiations. The prosecutor has complete discretion over whether to issue an invitation, and must be satisfied, inter alia, that the full extent of the alleged offending has been identified.[96]

The Code of Practice specifies the following factors in favour of, or against, prosecution:[97]

2.8.1 Additional public interest factors in favour of prosecution:

    i. A history of similar conduct (including prior criminal, civil and regulatory enforcement actions against P and/or its directors/partners and/or majority shareholders). Failing to prosecute in circumstances where there have been repeated or serious breaches of the law may not be a proportionate response and may not provide adequate deterrent effects.

    ii. The conduct alleged is part of the established business practices of P.

    iii. The offence was committed at a time when P had no or an ineffective corporate compliance programme and it has not been able to demonstrate a significant improvement in its compliance programme since then.

    iv. P had been previously subject to warning, sanctions or criminal charges and had nonetheless failed to take adequate action to prevent future unlawful conduct, or had continued to engage in the conduct.

    v. Failure to notify the within reasonable time of the offending conduct coming to light.

    vi. Reporting the wrongdoing but failing to verify it, or reporting it knowing or believing it to be inaccurate, misleading or incomplete.

    vii. Significant level of harm caused directly or indirectly to the victims of the wrongdoing or a substantial adverse impact to the integrity or confidence of markets, local or national governments.

2.8.2 Additional public interest factors against prosecution

    i. Co-operation: Considerable weight may be given to a genuinely proactive approach adopted by P's management team when the offending is brought to their notice, involving within a reasonable time of the offending coming to light reporting P's offending otherwise unknown to the prosecutor and taking remedial actions including, where appropriate, compensating victims. In applying this factor the prosecutor needs to establish whether sufficient information about the operation and conduct of P has been supplied in order to assess whether P has been co-operative. Co-operation will include identifying relevant witnesses, disclosing their accounts and the documents shown to them. Where practicable it will involve making the witnesses available for interview when requested. It will further include providing a report in respect of any internal investigation including source documents.

    ii. A lack of a history of similar conduct involving prior criminal, civil and regulatory enforcement actions against P and/or its directors/partners and/or majority shareholders; The prosecutor should contact relevant regulatory departments (including where applicable those overseas) to ascertain whether there are existing investigations in relation to P and/or its directors/partners and/or majority shareholders;

    iii. The existence of a proactive corporate compliance programme[98] both at the time of offending and at the time of reporting but which failed to be effective in this instance;

---

[96] Code, paras 2.1 and 2.2.

[97] *Deferred Prosecution Agreements Code of Practice* (n 87) para 2.8.1.

[98] The prosecutor may choose to bring in external resource to assist in the assessment of P's compliance culture and programme for example as described in any self-report.

iv.   The offending represents isolated actions by individuals, for example by a rogue director;

v.   The offending is not recent and P in its current form is effectively a different entity from that which committed the offences—for example it has been taken over by another organisation, it no longer operates in the relevant industry or market, P's management team has completely changed, disciplinary action has been taken against all of the culpable individuals, including dismissal where appropriate, or corporate structures or processes have been changed to minimise the risk of a repetition of offending;

vi.   A conviction is likely to have disproportionate consequences for P, under domestic law, the law of another jurisdiction including but not limited to that of the European Union, always bearing in mind the seriousness of the offence and any other relevant public interest factors;[99]

vii.   A conviction is likely to have collateral effects on the public, P's employees and shareholders or P's and/or institutional pension holders.

A DPA must be approved by the court, on the basis of an application by the prosecutor accompanied by a statement of facts, which must give particulars relating to each alleged offence and include details where possible of any financial gain or loss, which reference to key documents that must be attached.[100] If a DPA is approved, the court must make a declaration to that effect along with reasons in an open hearing.[101] The DPA may include a broad range of terms, including over future behaviour, and will normally include a financial order, payment of the prosecutor's reasonable costs, cooperation with an investigation. Financial terms are suggested to include compensating victims, payment of a financial penalty, donations to charities which support the victims of the offending and disgorgement of profits.[102] A monitor may be appointed for a specified time, to oversee compliance and change, and to report thereon. The Code states:

> 7.11 An important consideration for entering into a DPA is whether P already has a genuinely proactive and effective corporate compliance programme. The use of monitors should therefore be approached with care. The appointment of a monitor will depend upon the factual circumstances of each case and must always be fair, reasonable and proportionate.
>
> 7.12 A monitor's primary responsibility is to assess and monitor P's internal controls,
>
> advise of necessary compliance improvements that will reduce the risk of future recurrence of the conduct subject to the DPA and report specified misconduct to the prosecutor.
>
> 7.13 Where the terms require a monitor to be appointed it is the responsibility of P to pay all the costs of the selection, appointment, remuneration of the monitor, and reasonable costs of the prosecutor associated with the monitorship during the monitoring period. In assessing whether a term of monitoring may satisfy the statutory test the prosecutor should give consideration to the costs of such a term as these may be relevant.
>
> 7.14 P shall afford to the monitor complete access to all relevant aspects of its business during the course of the monitoring period as requested by the monitor. Any legal professional privilege that may exist in respect of investigating compliance issues that arise during the monitorship is unaffected by the Act, this DPA Code or a DPA.

---

[99] Any candidate or tenderer (including company directors and any person having powers of representation, decision or control) who has been convicted of fraud relating to the protection of the financial interests of the European Communities, corruption, or a money laundering offence is mandatorily excluded from participation in public contracts within the EU. Discretionary exclusion may follow in respect of a conviction for a criminal offence.

[100] *Deferred Prosecution Agreement Code of Practice* (n 87) para 6.1.

[101] ibid, para 11.1.

[102] ibid, para 7.9.

Any financial penalty is to be broadly comparable to a fine that the court would have imposed upon P following a guilty plea.[103] To be considered as voluntary and therefore mitigating, cooperation should be over and above mere compliance with any coercive measures.[104]

Plea bargaining offers various benefits, mainly in terms of swift resolution of proceedings and cost savings.[105] However, academic criticism has been directed at 'plea bargaining' in the criminal process, principally over concerns that constitutional values such as due process and fairness may produce injustice.[106] It will be seen that significant attempts have been made to guard against the risks of potential corruption and of pressuring companies into entering into DPAs for commercial reasons, as being a cheaper option than disputing ongoing proceedings.[107] Principal safeguards include the separation of prosecution and judicial functions, and the detailed procedural requirements, including requirements to satisfy criteria and publicly document such satisfaction.

V. Conclusions

The goals and practices of criminal law have undergone a significant major reform in the past decade. The traditional and popular view of criminal sentencing as delivering retributive punishment as a means of deterring future behaviour has significantly broadened to adopt a wider range of techniques but deployed within a narrower view of the function of criminal law and its purposes. In relation to the arena of business activities, the Law Commission firmly focused the use of criminal law *only* on individuals or companies that deserve the *stigma* of public approbation for seriously reprehensible conduct. It said that criminal law should not be used as the primary means of promoting regulatory objectives. Nevertheless, criminal law and sanctions should form a hierarchy with regulatory or compliance systems.

Accompanying this narrowing of focus for criminal law in the business world has been, at the same time, a broadening of the *goals* of sentencing and a widening of *techniques* used in responding to criminal activity. Underlying these developments lies concern that traditional punishment techniques (imprisonment, fines) do not respond to reducing the incidence of offences committed by recidivist criminals and do not address the circumstances of criminal conduct in the commercial and business world. Equally, concern with the position of victims has driven a desire to ensure that victims receive redress.

---

[103] ibid, para 8.3.

[104] ibid, para 8.5.

[105] *Negotiated Justice: A Closer Look at the Implications of Plea Bargains* (Justice, London, 1993).

[106] A Ashworth, *The Criminal Process: An Evaluative Study* 2nd edn (Oxford, Oxford University Press, 1998); K Mack and S Anleu, *Pleading Guilty: Issues and Practices* (Carlton South VIC, Australian Institute of Judicial Administration, 1995); *Negotiated Justice: A Closer Look at the Implications of Plea Bargains*, ibid; P Curran, 'Discussions in the Judge's Private Room' [1991] *The Criminal Law Review* 79–86; K Yeung, 'Better Regulation, Administrative Sanctions and Constitutional Values' (2013) 33(2) *Legal Studies* 312.

[107] *Deferred Prosecution Agreements Code of Practice. The Directors' response to the public consultation* (Serious Fraud Office, 2013) at http://www.sfo.gov.uk/media/264627/dpa%20code%20of%20practice%20response.pdf, para 12.

Thus, a holistic approach has emerged, which combines and balances formerly separate focuses on offenders and victims. Requiring offenders to make their victims whole again necessarily balances the victims' desire to be made whole, and society's goal in maintaining just relationships. Thus, we see development of mechanisms to remove offenders' illicit proceeds of crime, and to compensate victims of crime—initially violent crime but now any crime, through making compensation orders standard practice.

Similarly, we also see widespread interest in restorative justice, with its techniques based on affecting behaviour through human interaction between offender and victim, and the rise of a focus on assisting the plight of victims through a Victims' Charter or Code. The restorative justice movement is based on a pragmatic concern for what works in reducing crime but also a philosophical concern for human healing, and strengthening individuals and communities.

This philosophical concern can be seen in the latest versions of Sentencing Guidelines. Offering offenders a reduction in sentence for pleading guilty, and doing so at an early stage, can be viewed mechanistically as a means of saving public resource in operating the full investigative and criminal process. But it can also be viewed as providing positive encouragement to offenders to 'do the right thing' by acknowledging their conduct and putting it right as early as possible. Hence, the latest Sentencing Guidelines develop the restorative and redress elements found in section 142 of the Criminal Justice Act, the Macrory Principles and the DPA scheme. Whilst this ethical approach, based on acknowledgement and redress, can clearly be seen to have emerged in all of the various policy documents and legal provisions analysed above, it could now be made more explicit. If the system and its documents made even more clear that the central principle was expecting (and incentivising) people to 'do the right thing', the system would be more coherent and it is possible that behaviour might improve, both in relation to general compliance with the rules and in putting things right after infringements.

Incentivising people to enter into agreements that they have broken the law by bargaining for a lower sentence raises the concern of abuse by the officials involved. This risk is manifest in the context of a business defendant, where the consequences may apply only indirectly to the managers who take the decisions, but may have greater effect on shareholders and employees who are not involved in the negotiation. A range of safeguards have been consciously put in place in the DPA regime in order to guard against that risk of abuse. For example, the process is regulated, criteria require the prosecutor to be satisfied that the offence has been committed or that there is sufficient evidence to provide a realistic prospect of conviction, the full terms of the agreement are generally public and must be approved independently by a judge.

If it is correct that the developments that have been highlighted here in relation to the goals and operation of criminal law and sentencing are manifestations of a wider philosophical or social movement, we should expect to see these themes repeated when we look further at regulation.

11

Responsive, Meta and Compliance Theories

I. Responsive Regulation

While the origin of deterrence theory lies in history and legal philosophy, and that of rational choice theory lies in economic theory, compliance theory emanated from empirical observational research into how regulatory enforcers actually operate in practice. The findings of this research formed the basis of a series of theories that were developed about how to explain what was going on in practice. A principal finding is that much regulatory craft[1] is gentle, with the basic tools of regulators being negotiation, persuasion and the provision of information.[2]

The seminal theory was 'responsive regulation', developed by Ayres and Braithwaite.[3] Two key behaviours were observed from the operation of enforcers in a wide range of sectors and situations. First, almost all enforcers operated on the basis of a range of sanctions, rather than just one technique. Indeed, the sanctions could not only be ranked into a sequence of hard and soft techniques, illustrated by an 'enforcement pyramid', a developed version of which is shown in Figure 11.1. The vertical dimension of the pyramid represents the variability of coercion: As one progresses up the pyramid, the techniques become successively 'harder'. The pyramid has at its apex a sanction of removal from society (removal of liberty, or license to operate, or disqualification as a director), which functions as a deterrent that has maximal impact but is in practice rarely invoked. At the base of the pyramid is the opposite of a 'hard' deterrent sanction, namely a soft and informal approach based on simple, low key discussions and suggestions.

The second observation was that much of the time the enforcers were operating through the soft techniques at the bottom of the pyramid, rather than invoking the hard deterrent technique at the top. This statistical observation explains why the theory was illustrated as a pyramid rather than a column.

The theory advocates that a regulator should have a range of powers (a big stick), which would rarely be used in relation to genuine businesses, who would usually prefer to comply

---

[1] M Sparro, *The Regulatory Craft: Controlling Risks, Solving Problems, and Managing Compliance* (Washington DC, Brookings Institution Press, 2000).

[2] P Grabosky, 'On the Interface of Criminal Justice and Regulation' in H Quirk, T Seddon and G Smith (eds), *Regulation and Criminal Justice* (Cambridge, Cambridge University Press, 2013).

[3] I Ayres and J Braithwaite, *Responsive Regulation: Transcending the Deregulation Debate* (Oxford, Oxford University Press, 1992).

with clear requirements, guidance and persuasion. Instead, enforcement resources could be targeted on rogues, involving increasingly serious penalties. Ayres and Braithwaite argued that in many situations regulatory compliance directed at the well-intentioned is best secured by persuasion in the first instance, with inspection, enforcement notices and penalties being used for more risky or less compliant businesses further up the pyramid.

Ayres and Braithwaite initially proposed that enforcers would primarily adopt an enforcement approach at the bottom of the pyramid and 'respond' to individual organisations' behaviour. If the organisation was responsive, the enforcement approach would remain low key, but if the regulate was non-compliant and resistant the enforcement response would ratchet up to a higher level on the pyramid. Similarly, the approach could ratchet down in response to cooperative and compliant behaviour. However, such a 'tit for tat' and ratcheting response up and down a hierarchy of sanctions was observed in practice only for some enforcement contexts but not for many. It also acts as a constraint on the discretion of officers to respond in a proportionate way to either major or minor issues. Thus, the 'tit for tat' aspect has not been regarded as an essential part of the general theory.[4]

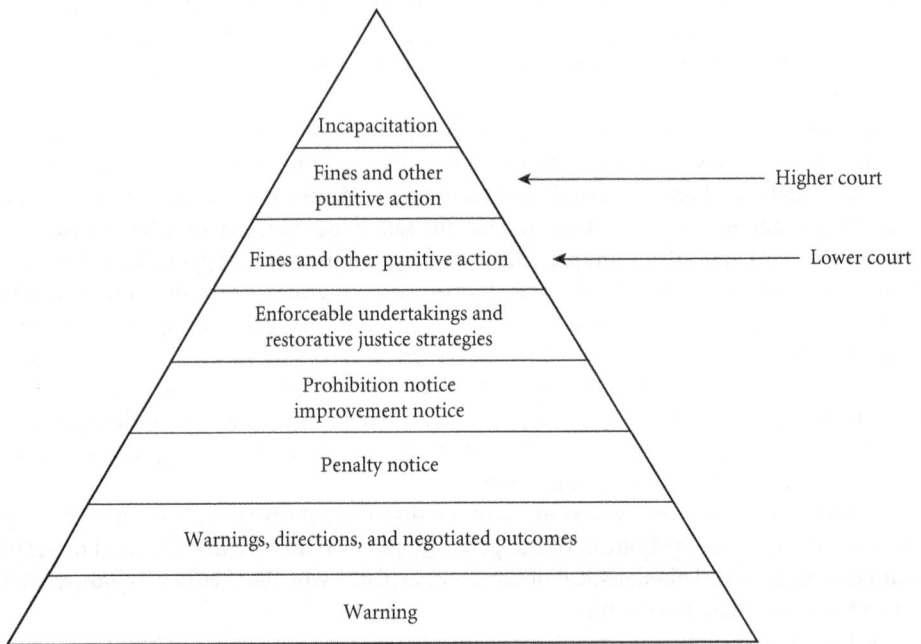

Figure 11.1: Enforcement Pyramid[5]

[4] K Yeung, *Securing Compliance. A Principled Approach* (Oxford, Hart Publishing, 2004); WPJ Wils, *Principles of European Antitrust Enforcement* (Oxford, Hart Publishing, 2005); B Morgan and K Yeung, *An Introduction to Law and Regulation* (Cambridge, Cambridge University Press, 2007).
[5] N Gunningham, 'Enforcement and Compliance Strategies' in M Cave, R Baldwin, M Lodge (eds), *The Oxford Handbook of Regulation* (Oxford, Oxford University Press, 2010) Fig 7.1.

But the hierarchy of techniques, forming an enforcement 'toolbox', and their statistical incidence, remained valid in a wide range of differing regulatory contexts. Another approach might be that the enforcer would select a sanction at a high point on the pyramid in response to organisations' behaviour that was intrinsically more serious than normal, in accordance with a proportionality principle.

The enforcement pyramid illustrated in Figure 11.1 is illustrative and not of universal application or exclusive of other approaches. In differing contexts it may contain a different series or combination of carrots and sticks that an agency might wish to invoke as part of an escalating strategy of enforcement.

II. Examples of Regulatory Practice

Responsive regulation and enforcement theory grew out of a series of socio-legal studies of how enforcement officials actually operate 'in real life'. This produced the revolutionary observation that deterrence might play a part in how they operate, but it is often a small part, and far removed from how legal theorists image the world to be. Studies accumulated on different regulatory contexts, especially from Australia and the United Kingdom, which supported similar conclusions about how regulatory and enforcement systems operate, and could be designed to provide optimal outcomes. Braithwaite's observations were based on research in a range of situations including care homes for the elderly, aboriginal disputes. A number of other leading studies were undertaken by others.[6] Hutter studied occupational health and safety and environmental control by inspectors from the Factory Inspectorate, the Industrial Air Pollution Inspectorate and the Railway Inspectorate,[7] and later systemic controls on railway safety. Grabosky and Gunningham have looked at environmental protection.[8] Haines has studied deaths in the Australian mining industry[9] and Thai manufacturing context.[10] Hutter and Jones have studied food businesses.[11]

Black studied the relationship between law and social systems in America, identifying four main styles of law: Penal, compensatory, therapeutic and conciliatory.[12] Grabosky and

[6] K Hawkins, *Environment and Enforcement: Regulation and the Social Definition of Pollution* (Oxford, Clarendon Press, 1984); K Hawkins, *Law as Last Resort* (Oxford, Oxford University Press, 2002); B Hutter, *The Reasonable Arm of the Law?* (Oxford, Oxford University Press, 1988); R Baldwin, 'Why Rules Don't Work' (1990) 54 *Modern Law Review* 321; J Braithwaite and P Grabosky, *Of Manners Gentle: Enforcement Strategies of Australian Business Regulatory Agencies* (Melbourne, Oxford University Press, 1987); H Genn, 'Business Responses to the Regulation of Health and Safety in England' (1993) 15 *Law and Policy* 219.

[7] BM Hutter, *Compliance: Regulation and Environment* (Oxford, Clarendon Press, 1997).

[8] P Grabosky, 'Beyond the Regulatory State' (1994) 27(2) *Australian and New Zealand Journal of Criminology* 192–97; P Grabosky, 'Green Markets: Environmental Regulation by the Private Sector' (1994) 16(4) *Law and Policy* 419–48; N Gunningham and P Grabosky, *Smart Regulation. Designing Environmental Policy* (Oxford, Oxford University Press, 1998).

[9] F Haines, *Corporate Regulation. Beyond 'Punish or Persuade'* (Oxford, Clarendon Press, 1997).

[10] F Haines, 'Regulatory Reform in Light of Regulatory Character: Assessing Industrial Safety Change in the Aftermath of the Kader Toy Factory Fire in Bangkok, Thailand' (2003) 12 *Social and Legal Studies* 461–87; reprinted in F Haines (ed), *Crime and Regulation* (Farnham, Ashgate, 2007).

[11] BM Hutter and C Jones, 'From Government to Governance: External Influences on Business Risk Management' (2007) 1 *Regulation & Governance* 27–45.

[12] DJ Black, *The Behaviour of Law* (New York, Academic Press, 1976); DJ Black, *The Manners and Customs of the Police* (New York, Academic Press, 1980); DJ Black, *Sociological Justice* (New York, Oxford University Press, 1989).

Braithwaite tested Black's theory in a study of 96 Australian regulatory agencies.[13] Their data strongly supported hypotheses that:

— The agencies which regulated companies drawn from a single industry would resort to less formal means of achieving compliance than those which regulated a relatively large number of companies from diverse industries;

— agencies whose inspectors had frequent contact with the same firms would use less formal sanctions than those characterised by more impersonal contact.

But they did not support a hypothesis that agencies which regulated a relatively small number of companies would use legal action less often than those regulating a large number of companies.

We now proceed to illustrate responsive regulation theory in a number of different business contexts, with leading studies in water pollution, railways safety, fisheries protection and food production.

A. Water Pollution Enforcement

In his ground-breaking socio-legal study, Hawkins describes how pollution control officers operated around 1984.[14] The picture is of officers constantly visiting significant businesses, rivers and sites across their geographical areas and checking what is going on. Samples may be taken to check on pollution levels in water, and findings of concern then often require detective work to establish the source. What might be described as 'enforcement' should be seen not as rare formal acts but as a constant activity of monitoring, surveillance and particularly conversations. Conversations are undertaken constantly with firms' employees, at all levels of firms, to 'get a feel' for the extent to which a firm and its staff are controlling pollution and are 'on top of' their ability to control pollution. The activities are what would in later decades be described as outcome-focused: The field officer's 'instincts are to stop the pollution, identify its source, and negotiate for preventive or remedial measures.'[15]

Statutory limits are set for the release or presence of particular chemicals. The extent to which these levels are exceeded or not varies constantly. '[T]he issue is not whether to allow pollution, but how much pollution to allow.'[16] Since this is regulation rather than repression, every officer necessarily has discretion over 'enforcement' decisions. What occurs is a constant 'enforcement game' usually involving a mixture of advice and bargaining against a background of official coercive and sanctioning powers. Bargaining is possible only because the law need not be formally enforced in every instance of possible infringement,[17] and officers have a high degree of flexible discretion that is wielded fairly. 'Compliance is an elaborate concept, one better seen as a process, rather than a condition.... Compliance is

---

[13] Braithwaite and Grabosky (n 6).
[14] Hawkins, *Environment and Enforcement* (n 6).
[15] ibid, 7.
[16] ibid, 10.
[17] ibid, 123.

negotiable and embraces action, time, and symbol.'[18] 'The object is to produce change, not to repress it.'[19] 'Flexible control is made possible by time, bargaining, and privacy.'[20]

> All enforcement work is adaptive. [Officers] have to develop various systems of intelligence to facilitate discovery and prevention of deviance, much of which, of course, is intended to defy discovery.

> Some forms of pollution are difficult to discover. Some are intended to escape discovery; some cannot be recognized as pollution; and some are events which are impossible to predict. ... Proactive strategies are most useful in discovering the invisible, persistent, or episodic pollutions.[21] Reactive strategies, dependent on complaints and tip-offs, are generally animated by the more conspicuous—hence the more serious—cases, many (perhaps most of which are isolated incidents ('one-offs').[22]

Most serious pollutions are 'one-offs'—spot discharges, rather than persistent failures to comply. The one-off usually comes to agency attention as a result of a complaint from a third party. Enforcement activity with one-offs is directed towards correcting damage done, preventing its recurrence and deterring others. A compliance strategy[23] will often be elastic, and depends on the apparent 'progress' made by the polluter and other exigencies affecting his relationship with the field officer. Compliance has a symbolic significance.

Negotiating tactics[24] involve a logical sequence of decisions, for example setting targets and dates for achieving them.[25] 'Failure to meet a date is a breach of the implied bargain and gives the officer grounds to be less forbearing towards the polluter....'[26] 'The approach to enforcement reflects the complexity of the problem; the technical and economic capacity of the polluter to conform; and his willingness to comply—his 'cooperativeness'.[27] Officers also intrinsically evaluate whether it is technically in the discharger's power to do something about the 'problem', and whether there is economic capacity to comply.[28] 'The officer has in practice an array of moves at his disposal in seeking compliance. The tactics are employed serially, the sequence moving from a more conciliatory to a more coercive approach, if conciliation fails.'[29] This approach is therefore clearly consonant with the pyramid theory of Ayres and Braithwaite.

Officers develop images of polluters: The socially responsible, unfortunate, careless, and malicious.[30] 'Most are regarded as "socially responsible" ... "Large industries" said an area supervisor, "have a policy of 'We conform with the law—however much it costs".[31] Those dischargers who cause serious difficulties are a small minority.[32] Farmers feature regularly as more difficult.

---

[18] ibid, 126, 127.
[19] EM Lemert, *Human Deviance, Social Problems and Social Control* 2nd edn (Englewood Cliffs NJ, Prentice-Hall, 1972) 55.
[20] Hawkins, *Environment and Enforcement* (n 6) 196.
[21] AJ Reiss, 'Discretionary Justice' in D Glaser (ed), *Handbook of Criminology* (Chicago, Rand McNally, 1974).
[22] Hawkins, *Environment and Enforcement* (n 6) 90.
[23] ibid, ch 6.
[24] ibid, ch 7.
[25] ibid, 124.
[26] ibid, 125.
[27] ibid, 129.
[28] ibid, 73.
[29] ibid, 130.
[30] ibid, 110–18.
[31] ibid, 110.
[32] ibid, 111.

For an officer to be too eager or abrasive in enforcement is to risk encouraging in polluters an uncooperative attitude or even downright hostility. 'Deterrence resides in the threats which precede use of the formal law, or in the informal sanctions which accompany it.'[33]

> Compliance is more complex where organizations are involved. It is more than remedial action performed by some individual. It demands an exercise of corporate will, a collective determination to make expenditures on plant, equipment, or manpower. Senior executives must be prepared to devote resources to pollution control, and manual workers to do the often time-consuming and unpleasant job of maintaining treatment plant.[34]

Resort to criminal process is a rather rare event. Prosecution takes time and resource, and is generally only undertaken where there is a strong likelihood of conviction. Instituting formal enforcement steps will often antagonise the relationship between official and firm, and reduce a polluter's willingness to take further steps to improve. A criminal trial stigmatises. Regulatory enforcement is a symbolic matter. Prosecution brings regulatory deviance to public view.

A judgement of the polluter's cooperativeness is highly important. 'Blameworthy conduct is punishable conduct.'[35] 'What is really being sanctioned is not pollution, but deliberate or negligent law-breaking and its symbolic assault on the legitimacy of the regulatory authority.'[36] Hawkins' central thesis is that law enforcement demands a moral as well as a legislative mandate.[37]

> What is sanctionable is not rule-breaking as such, but rule-breaking which is deliberately or negligently done, or rule-breaking accompanied by an unco-operativeness which amounts to a symbolic assault upon the enforcer's and the agency's authority and legitimacy.... it is possible to conceive of the law being enforced even though the formal apparatus of prosecution is hardly ever used.... The common theme in all of this is human judgment.[38]

He concluded that law may be enforced by compulsion and coercion, or by conciliation and compromise.

> Compliance strategy seeks to prevent a harm rather than punish an evil. ... Recourse to the legal process here is rare, a matter of last resort, since compliance strategy is concerned with repair and results, not retribution.
>
> ... A penal style is accusatory and adversarial.... In a compliance strategy, on the other hand, the style is conciliatory, and relies on bargaining to attain conformity.[39]

'Regulation and its enforcement are treated as social processes.'[40] 'Control, in short, is regarded as a reciprocal relationship.'[41] Hawkins notes American capture theory[42] but found that 'there is little evidence from the present research to support this argument.'[43]

---

[33] ibid, 116.
[34] ibid, 146.
[35] ibid, 197.
[36] ibid, 205.
[37] ibid, xiii.
[38] ibid, xiv.
[39] ibid, 4.
[40] ibid, 15.
[41] ibid, 16.
[42] R Nader, 'Foreword', in JC Esposito, *Vanishing Air: The Ralph Nader Study Group Report on Air Pollution* (New York, Grossman, 1970), viii.
[43] Hawkins, *Environment and Enforcement* (n 6) 192.

B. Railways Health and Safety

Hutter carried out extensive research on the British railway system in the late 1980s and early 1990s. At that stage the railways employed 100,000 waged staff, over 30,000 salaried staff, operated 23,000 miles of track, and had an annual turnover in 1988 of £3.3 billion. The railway system was privatised in 1993, which heightened the tensions between, on the one hand, risk and regulation and, on the other hand, productivity and safety. A series of major disasters in the railway system[44] or elsewhere[45] placed safety issues firmly in the public consciousness. Under the Health and Safety at Work etc Act 1974, workplace health and safety law in Britain had been revised to embody a radical new approach, emphasising self-regulation and employees as participatory rather than passive agents in the workplace.[46] The policy was enforced self-regulation.

Hutter grouped the formal sanctions available under the law into a sanctions hierarchy that closely resembled that of Ayres and Braithwaite (Figure 11.2).

Hutter noted that the state of theoretical analysis described competing enforcement styles: Accommodative[47] or compliance[48]; sanctioning[49] and deterrent models.[50] She found

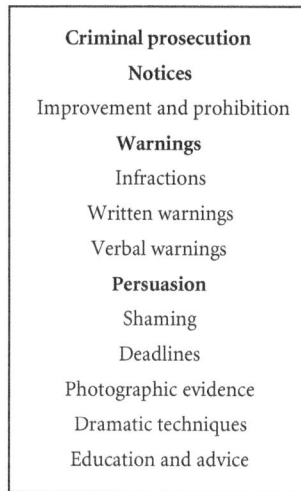

Criminal prosecution

Notices

Improvement and prohibition

Warnings

Infractions

Written warnings

Verbal warnings

Persuasion

Shaming

Deadlines

Photographic evidence

Dramatic techniques

Education and advice

Figure 11.2: Health and Safety Enforcement Powers

[44] Kings Cross 1987 underground fire (30 deaths), Clapham Junction 1988 rail crash (35 dead, 500 injured), Southall 1997 rail crash (7 dead), Ladbrook Grove 1999 rail crash (31 dead), Hatfield 2000 rail crash (4 dead).

[45] Herald of Free Enterprise 1987 ferry sinking, Piper Alpha 1988 oil rig fire, 1984-91 failure of 1,400 United States savings and loans banks: see GJ Caprio and D Klingebiel, *Bank Insolvencies: Cross Country Experience* (Washington, DC, World Bank, 1996).

[46] Based on A Robens, *Safety and Health at Work-Report of the Committee 1970–72* (HM Government, 1972).

[47] GM Richardson, with AI Ogus and P Burrows, *Policing Pollution: A Study of Regulation and Enforcement* (Oxford, Clarendon Press, 1983).

[48] Hawkins, *Environment and Enforcement* (n 6); J Reiss, *Reforming the Workplace: a Study of Self-Regulation in Occupational Safety* (Philadelphia PA, University of Pennsylvania Press, 1984).

[49] Hawkins, ibid.

[50] Reiss (n 48).

that in reality all enforcement agencies would use all styles. Hutter's extended observations were able to describe how organisational structures and individuals evolved over time, in the context of changing legal and social contexts.

> British Railways ... had instituted risk management systems and procedures. There were elaborate systems for the promotion of health and safety in the workplace, comprised of policy documents, specialist staff, a committee structure, training programs and monitoring procedures. These emanated from the Board at a regional level and at a departmental level. Yet everyday awareness and understanding of both legal and corporate risk management systems was sketchy. Many employees found the written documentation too detailed, difficult to understand and uninteresting. There were no centralized corporate understandings of risk. For example, accident data were collected according to the reporting regulations, but beyond this there were no centrally held understandings of what could be learned from them about compliance.[51]

Her findings included:[52]

— There were no centralised corporate understandings of risk;
— at the individual level employees did have a broad understanding of the risks associated with their work;
— most of the time employees complied, but situational and structural imperatives did lead to non-compliance;
— the empowerment of employees was variable and the communitarian objectives of regulation remained largely unfulfilled in this period;
— respondents saw the control aspects of regulation as necessary, but there was no evidence of fear of the criminal sanction;
— legal action was judged on its merits on a case-by-case level, and where it was regarded as 'unfair' it had less impact on the corporation;
— the research period saw an increasing inclination to challenge regulatory agency decisions.

She concluded that where regulatory ambitions were not being met the main obstacles emerged as:

— The fragmentation of the company, both organisationally and geographically;
— serious communication difficulties;
— inequalities in knowledge of regulation and risk;
— difficulties in the perceived legitimacy of state regulation and corporate risk management efforts.

Hutter concluded in her 1997 study that compliance is a continually creative process. And in many important respects full compliance may be elusive.[53] She also found further evidence of a growth of conciliatory and accommodative legal methods is the increasing popularity of mediation and negotiation as methods of dispute resolution.[54] In her 2001

---

[51] BM Hutter, 'Negotiating Social, Economic and Political Environments: Compliance with Regulation within and beyond the State' in C Parker and V Lehmann Nielsen (eds), *Explaining Compliance. Business Responses to Regulation* (Cheltenham, Edward Elgar, 2012) 314.
[52] BM Hutter, *Regulation and Risk: Occupational Health and Safety on the Railways* (Oxford, Oxford University Press, 2001) 301 ff.
[53] Hutter (n 7).
[54] ibid, 243.

study she found that non-compliance may be the result of incompetence or a lack of communication. Indeed large organisations may be extremely difficult to control precisely because of their size; thus communication emerges as a key factor in the ability of companies to self-regulate and manage risk.[55] The complexity of large companies lends itself to conflicting goals, misunderstood messages and unintended consequences.[56] There is considerable variability between companies and also within companies.[57] Corporate risk management parallels regulation.[58]

Hutter concluded that the key task is to make bureaucracies think like responsible individuals. The law penetrated deep into the organisation in an attempt to make individuals within organisation act responsibly. It did this by attempting to constitute regulation as part of organisational life, and getting the organisation and those within it to take responsibility for regulation. Regulation is not an attempt to eradicate risk, but an attempt to manage it. She found that corporate culture is significant in the extent to which rules are observed.

Writing in 2012, Hutter summarised an overview of regulation as 'typically involv[ing] long term organizational compliance rather than transitory temporary encounters with individuals.'[59] Legal design is an important factor in variations between different agencies and areas or work. 'Most relevant here is the specificity of legal rules. Where there are detailed rules enforcement officials tend to "go by the book", but where there are broad standards they are much more flexible, even lenient.'[60] Hutter noted Hawkins' suggestion that a division may exist between the preferences of policy makers (for principles) and those of enforcers (for rules).[61]

C. Fisheries Protection

Baldwin and Black considered enforcement challenges of fish protection laws.[62] Geographical areas to monitor are extensive, regulates are highly mobile, there is a large number of landing sites, inspection at sea is very resource intensive, there are many ways to avoid detection, enforcement funding is limited. The number of undetected infringements is 'impossible to determine.'[63] Officers had to rely on tip-offs from the public and hot-lines and whistleblowing by those involved. They proposed that enforcement should be broken down into five elements: *Detecting* undesirable or non-compliant behaviour, developing tools and strategies for *responding* to that behaviour, *enforcing* those tools and strategies on the ground, *assessing* their success or failure and *modifying* approaches accordingly.[64]

---

[55] Hutter (n 52) 307.
[56] ibid, 308.
[57] ibid, 315.
[58] ibid, 319.
[59] Hutter (n 51) 305.
[60] Hutter, ibid 307.
[61] Hawkins, *Law as Last Resort* (n 6).
[62] J Black and R Baldwin, 'Really Responsive Regulation' (2008) 71(1) *Modern Law Review* 59.
[63] National Audit Office, *Fisheries Enforcement in England* HC 563 Session 2002–2003 (April 2003).
[64] The 'DREAM' framework: see further R Baldwin and J Black, *A Review of Enforcement Measures* (Defra, 2005).

D. Food

Small and medium sized enterprises (SMEs), especially micro-businesses, account for 99.8 per cent of all food businesses within the catering, hotel and retail sectors.[65] Interviews with food businesses, the Food Standards Agency (FSA), trade associations and consumer groups around 2001–2002 found consistent themes.[66] Small businesses believed that they were fully compliant with the law and that their operations were not capable of harming the public. They believed they were fully compliant if they had done what the enforcer had requested following an inspection, rather than because they were aware of the legislative requirements that applied to them. The majority of small businesses were striving to be fully compliant, but the enforcement and stakeholder community believed that compliance was merely, and consistently, partial.[67] The main motivator to comply with food safety *legislation* was fear of being prosecuted and the adverse publicity that it would bring.[68] But the main reason to comply with requests from the *enforcer* was to reduce the latter's attention to the business. The focus of the legislation on Hazard Analysis Critical Control Point (HACCP) procedures was too complex for small businesses to adequately comprehend, in view of its theoretical approach, requirement for technical knowledge in identifying hazards, pressures on time, the burdensomeness of record keeping required in many risk management systems like HACCP, and lack of motivation to change.[69] Fairman and Yapp noted that trade associations may be a useful food safety information intermediary but many food SMEs are not members.[70]

An interesting study in improving compliance arose in relation to inspectors' observations of restaurants in London's Chinatown.[71] Food safety inspectors regularly found non-compliance and serious hygiene issues, which were repeated even after issuing warnings and sometimes sanctions. After deeper investigation of the situation, they concluded that the essential problem lay in communication problems: Chefs did not understand the regulations as they were formulated, frequent turnover with new chefs coming from China meant that the warnings issued in previous inspections were not taken into account, and the way inspectors were addressing remarks to chefs was seen as a 'loss of face' and provoked adverse reactions. The solution was found in developing a 'Safer Food, Better Business' toolkit, including very clear guidance, translated into all key languages used by the large number of chefs and cooks (including both Mandarin and Cantonese), and in organising seminars for chefs and restaurant operators in Chinatown. This strategy resulted in a dramatic increase

---

[65] *Small and Medium Enterprise (SME) Statistics for the UK 2000* (Department of Trade and Industry, 2001).

[66] R Fairman and C Yapp, 'Compliance with Food Safety Legislation in Small and Micro-businesses: Enforcement as an External Motivator' (2004) 3(2) *Journal of Environmental Health Research* 44.

[67] In 2002 45% of all businesses inspected were 'found to have breached some food regulations in some way': *Task Force on the Burdens of Food Regulations on Small Food Businesses* (FSA, 2002) 11.

[68] It may be wondered if that conclusion was one that framed the expectation and questions of the researchers in 2001, and whether a different result might be found if the study were to be repeated on a different basis.

[69] E Taylor, 'HACCP in Small Companies: Benefit or Burden?' (2001) 12 *Food Control* 217; H Rakel, S Gerrard, G Piggott and G Crick, 'Evaluating Contact Techniques: Assessing the Impact of a Regulator's Intervention on the Health and Safety Performance of Small to Medium Sized Businesses' (1998) 29(4) *Journal of Safety Research* 235.

[70] Fairman and Yapp (n 66).

[71] Summarised in J Monk, *Reform of Regulatory Enforcement and Inspections in OECD Countries* (Paris, OECD, 2013) http://www.oecd.org/gov/regulatory-policy/Reform%20of%20inspections%20-%20Web%20-%20Julie%20Monk.pdf, para 53.

in levels of compliance, hygiene and safety. It also led to better commercial results, and enabled inspectors to transform an ineffective confrontational situation into an effective constructive relationship.

E. Danish Farmers

May and Winter undertook a survey in 1998 of 216 of the 258 municipalities in Denmark in relation to enforcement of agro-environmental laws that applied to the country's 45,000 farmers.[72] They found that enforcement effectiveness was affected more by choices made by enforcement agencies (on issues such as tools, priorities and effort) than by the enforcement styles of individual inspectors.[73] Compliance was increased by farms that used third party agricultural consultants, more frequent inspection, and setting priorities for inspection of major items. In relation to enforcement styles, they found that it was necessary for inspectors to get tough up to a point, but beyond that the threat of coercion could be counterproductive. Overall, they concluded that overly legalistic enforcement styles were questionable, at least in the cooperative culture of Denmark.

F. Low Risks

A potential risk with a risk-based regulatory policy is that attention will be focused on high risks and low risks will be ignored. Yet low risks can still give rise to major harm, especially if aggregated or cumulative. Baldwin, Black and O'Leary have devised an organised method for addressing low risks,[74] after work with environmental regulators. The recommendation was that attention should be paid to five key factors: The need to apply combinations of tools to different risks while taking on board interactions between these tools; the ways in which the motivations and capacities of different regulatees affect the efficacy of different tools; the organisational and political factors that affect regulatory tool use; the need to assess regulatory performance in an ongoing manner; and the value of being adaptable to changes in regulatory challenges and contexts.[75] The 22 potential tools identified were grouped as screening and rule-based strategies, inspection/monitoring and proxy strategies (whether by an agency, proxy, firm, or third-party monitor), and engagement and incentive strategies.[76]

---

[72] PJ May and S Winter, 'Regulatory Enforcement and Compliance: Examining Danish Agro-Environmental Policy' (1999) 18(4) *Journal of Policy Analysis and Management* 625–51; PJ May and S Winter, 'Reconsidering Styles of Regulatory Enforcement: Patterns in Danish Agro-Environmental Inspection' (2000) 22 *Law and Policy* 143–73.

[73] There was a general pattern that inspectors who used coercion perceived farmers to be recalcitrant and believed that coercion was effective.

[74] Good Regulatory Intervention Design (GRID).

[75] SNIFFER (Scotland and Northern Ireland Forum for Environmental Research) (2011), *Assessing the Effectiveness of Regulatory Activities at 'Low Risk' Sites and Proposed Good Practice Framework—Final Report on Project ER13*. Edinburgh.

[76] R Baldwin, J Black and G O'Leary, 'Regulating Low Risks: Innovative Strategies and Implementation', LSE Legal Studies Working Paper No 9/2013.

III. Evolving Responsive Regulation

The 'Ayres–Braithwaite pyramid' also inherently includes a 'risk-based' approach to regulation, which has evolved from both regulatory practice and governmental instruction.[77] A risk-based policy is essentially a response to two elements: First, a regulatory context in which there may be a large number of regulates, activities or sites, which may present practical challenges for the regulator to exercise full control and, second, limitations on the resource available to public regulators. The policy therefore targets public resources on enforcement by prioritising areas where a risk analysis of the evidence base indicates that there is greatest risk.

The 'responsive regulation' model inherently combines *both* compliance and deterrence. Indeed, the ability of an enforcer to operate for much of the time at the bottom of the pyramid, and for such a sift approach to be successful (both in relation to spreading compliance and in saving enforcement resources) itself depends on the presence of the superior hierarchy of alternative and more serious sanctions that can be invoked and, indeed, on the presence of an ultimate sanction that is of the greatest weight. The approach was described by its authors as 'talking softly but carrying a big stick'. It is precisely the presence of the (deterrent) big stick that makes the soft enforcement effective in many cases. The ultimate deterrent is, therefore, rarely used, but its mere presence has a major function.

The accuracy of 'responsive regulation' in describing how many regulators in fact operate, and in theorising how they should operate, has now been tested in many contexts and is supported by a mass of research evidence from Europe, the USA and Australia.[78] The model therefore integrates deterrence into a more sophisticated theory, and affords it a significant function, whilst transforming the whole approach to regulation into what has been found to be an optimal regulatory strategy in many contexts.

More recently, Baldwin and Black have expounded a further approach, namely that to be 'really responsive' regulators have to be responsive not only to the compliance performance of the regulate but also in five further ways: To the undertakings' own operating and cognitive frameworks (their 'attitudinal settings'); to the broader institutional environment of the regulatory regime; to the different logics of regulatory tools and strategies; to the regime's own performance; and finally to changes in each of these elements.[79] Baldwin and Black assert that a 'really responsive' approach is holistic in combining the other approaches within a rational framework in differing ways depending on the circumstances, so as to deliver the five functions of enforcement (namely detecting undesirable or non-compliant behaviour, developing tools for responding to that behaviour, enforcing those tolls and strategies on the ground, assessing their success or failure and modifying approaches accordingly). This approach highlights the need to assess performance not only on a continuing basis, but also in a manner that responds to shifts in objectives and regulatory environments, if the regime is to cover previously uncontrolled behaviour and respond to changing circumstances.

---

[77] The development of risk-based policy in the United Kingdom is noted in ch 9.

[78] Ayres and Braithwaite (n 3); RA Kagan, 'Regulatory Enforcement' in D Rosenbloom and R Schwartz (eds), *Handbook of Regulation and Administrative Law* (New York, Dekker, 1994): M Wright, S Marsden and A Antonelli, *Building an Evidence Base for the Health and Safety Commission Strategy to 2010 and beyond: A Literature Review of Interventions to Improve Health and Safety Compliance* (Norwich, HSE Books, 2004).

[79] Black and Baldwin (n 62) 181.

Chenoweth and colleagues have examined the role of violence in nations' regime change. The success rate of 323 resistance movements between 1900 and 2006 was 26 per cent for a violent strategy and 53 per cent for resistance that was predominantly non-violent.[80] Participation levels are important: Every one the campaigns studied that achieved active and sustained participation of more than 3.5 per cent of the population succeeded, and every campaign that passed the 3.5 per cent threshold was non-violent. Where non-violent campaigns achieve change, it is more likely that the successor regime will be democratic and peaceful.[81]

IV. Smart and Meta Regulation

Ayres and Braithwaite had identified regulatory tripartism, involving regulator, regulated and third parties.[82] Gunningham and Grabosky developed this with the concept of 'Smart Regulation', referring to a form of regulatory pluralism that seeks to harness not just governmental bodies but also business structures and third parties in controlling business activities.[83] In this viewpoint, behaviour is 'in the hands not of governmental officials but of the myriad individuals employed in the private sector' and that, often, more can be achieved by harnessing the enlightened self-interest of the private sector than through command and control regulation.[84] It is based on a wider vision of commercial activity than the concept of a binary vertical relationship between regulator and regulatee, and embraces emerging forms of social control that involve the influence that a wider group of stakeholders can exert on corporate decisions and activity. The concept of Smart Regulation can be both wide and flexible, encompassing as many influences are relevant to the particular context. In effect, it enlists other parties to act as quasi-regulators, supplementing the enforcement role of the state.

In relation to enforcement, in contrast to the single instrumental approach (state regulation) of Braithwaite's pyramid, Smart Regulation utilises a range of parties, creating a range of different instruments. It also conceives of each party operating on a different face of the pyramid, each with its own series of instruments and operational level of coerciveness. On individual faces, there may be greater or lesser opportunity to operate at different levels of escalation, and controlled escalation is only possible where the instruments in question lend themselves to a graduated, responsive and interactive enforcement strategy.

> The two instruments which are most amenable to such a strategy (because they are readily manipulated) are command and control and self-regulation. Thus, it is no coincidence that the first example of how to shift from one face of the pyramid to another as one escalates and of how to invoke the dynamic peak was taken from precisely this instrument combination. However, there are other instruments which are at least partially amenable to such a response, the most obvious being insurance and banking.[85]

---

[80] E Chenoweth and MJ Stephan, *Why Civil Resistance Works: The Strategic Logic of Nonviolent Conflict* (New York, Columbia University Press, 2011). See also K Shock and E Chenoweth, *Radical Flank Effects and the Outcomes of Civil Resistance Movements* (Washington DC, Fletcher Summer Institute, 2012) at http://www.slideshare.net/NonviolentConflict/fsi2012-radical-flank-effects.

[81] Chenoweth and Stephan (n 80) 11.

[82] Ayres and Braithwaite (n 3).

[83] Gunningham and Grabosky (n 8); see also Gunningham (n 5).

[84] Gunningham and Grabosky (n 8).

[85] Gunningham (n 5).

One problem with Smart Regulation is that formal cooperation between the different actors and faces may not be possible, even though overall coordination may be achieved in relation to outcomes.

The key insight of legal pluralism is that regulating activity can be influenced by the myriad of individuals employed by the private sector in various positions of authority or influence, both within and outside a firm, including trade associations, professional advisers and auditors, standards and certification bodies, banks requiring certification with ISO standards, insurers imposing pre-contractual requirements and policy conditions,[86] investors, commentators, rating agencies, and customer or consumer bodies,[87] as well as employees, even acting as whistle-blowers.[88] In terms of political and constitutional theorising, 'power comes from everywhere'.[89]

Recognising this, Parker proposed the concept of 'decentered regulation'.[90] Grabosky and others also described 'regulation of regulation', in which regulators oversee sector or firm level regulatory schemes, also known as meta-regulation.[91] Rather than conceptualising regulatory systems as involving the privatising of public sector activity, some are in reality the governmentalising of activity which to date has been largely private.[92] The functioning of such schemes, and hence features that may be included in their design, has been described as constituting multiple polycentric nodal points.[93] It has been argued that nodally thick environments tend to be more effective and legitimate than nodally thin ones.[94]

Haines' study of three major differing disasters suggests that the success of a regulatory regime is highly context-specific, and needs to address not only the technical and actuarial

---

[86] BJ Richardson, 'Mandating Environmental Liability Insurance' (2001) 12 *Duke Environmental Law and Policy Forum* 293–329.

[87] RH Kraakman, 'Gatekeepers: The Anatomy of a Third-Party Enforcement Strategy' (1986) 2 *Journal of Law, Economics and Organization* 53–104.

[88] DJ Ventry, 'Whistleblowers and Qui Tam for Tax' (2008) 61(2) *Tax Lawyer* 357–406.

[89] M Foucault, *The History of Sexuality: An Introduction* vol 1 (New York, Random House, 1990) 93.

[90] J Black, 'Critical Reflections on Regulation' CARR Discussion Paper, DP 4 (London, London School of Economics and Political Science, 2002). J Black, 'Critical Reflections on Regulation' (2002) 27 *Australian Journal of Legal Philosophy* 1–35, reprinted in F Haines (ed), *Crime and Regulation* (Farnham, Ashgate, 2007).

[91] P Grabosky, 'Using Non-Governmental Resources to Foster Regulatory Compliance' (1995) 8(4) *Governance: An International Journal of Policy and Administration* 527–50; C Parker and J Braithwaite, 'Conclusion' in C Parker, C Scott, N Lacey and J Braithwaite (eds), *Regulating Law* (Oxford, Oxford University Press, 2004); C Parker, 'Meta-regulation: Legal Accountability for Corporate Social Responsibility' in D McBarnet, A Voiculescu and T Campbell (eds), *The New Corporate Accountability: Corporate Social Responsibility and the Law* (Cambridge, Cambridge University Press, 2007) 207–40; C Coglianese and E Mendelson, 'Meta-Regulation and Self-Regulation' in Cave, Baldwin and Lodge (n 5); J Bomhoff and A Meuwese, 'The Meta-regulation of Transnational Private Regulation' (2011) 38(1) *Journal of Law and Society* 138–62.

[92] D Kettl, *Sharing Power: Public Governance and Private Markets* (Washington DC, Brookings Institution, 1993) 14.

[93] C Shearing, J Wood, with J Cartwright and M Jenneker, 'Nodal Governance, Democracy and the New "Denizens": Challenging the Westphalian Ideal' (2003) 30(3) *Journal of Law and Society* 400; S Burris, P Drahos and C Shearing, 'Nodal Governance' (2005) 30 *Australian Journal of Legal Philosophy* 30–58; C Shearing and J Froestad, 'Nodal governance and the Zwelethemba Model' in Quirk, Seddon and Smith (n 2) 103–33. Application of nodal approaches to security concerns in communities of South Africa has led to the establishment of 'trust networks': C Tilly, *Trust and Rule* (Cambridge, Cambridge University Press, 2005).

[94] C Shearing and P Stenning, 'From the Panopticon to Disney World: The Development of Discipline' in AN Doob and EL Greenspan (eds), *Perspectives in Criminal Law: Essays in Honour of John Ll J Edwards* (Toronto, Canada Law Book, 1985) 335–49.

aspects of risk but also the socio-cultural and political dimensions.[95] She suggests that the political dimension is the most powerful and that a regime must have political support if it is to provide effective outcomes. This approach ties in with the idea of firms' multiple licences discussed below.

These conceptions of regulatory systems and how best to achieve optimal compliance can be seen to support self- or co-regulatory systems, cooperative enforcement approaches and firms' internal compliance systems. Each of these approaches adopts a constitutive regulatory model,[96] in which the enforcement task is preventative and restorative.[97] It presumes that many companies can and will sincerely and creatively seek to advance regulatory goals. There has been an increase in 'management-based regulation', whereby agencies require companies to formulate and implement their own plans and procedures for reducing hazards (and to report on progress), perhaps overseeing or approving plans, or inspecting systems, premises, records or reports.[98]

Cooperative enforcement[99] fosters regulatory compliance through cooperative governance, bargaining and persuasion methods.[100] Hutter argues that the growth of trust systems has replaced the function of surveillance that a 'command and control' regulatory system would require.[101] Cooperative enforcement is argued to have advantages of being able efficiently to overcome deficiencies in ambiguous or inefficient regulations,[102] and to facilitate information sharing, especially on risks and how to avoid them. Its disadvantages can include an internal laxity or complacency in observance of standards, a tendency to delay or avoid beyond compliance so as to avoid incurring costs, and in involving insufficiently strong incentives or forces to induce compliance.[103] In worst cases, it may involve too close a relationship between regulator and regulated that may involve 'capture' of the former[104] or even corruption. The informality of individual relationships may provide little externalised general deterrence.

---

[95] F Haines, *The Paradox of Regulation: What Regulation Can Achieve and What it Cannot* (Cheltenham, Edward Elgar, 2011), analysing the 1998 Longford Gas Plant explosion in Australia, the terrorist attacks of 11 September 2001 in USA and the collapse of HIH Insurance in Australia.

[96] 'Constitutive rules define a form of conduct in such a way that the distinction between the rule and the ruled activity disappears': RM Unger, *Knowledge and Politics* (New York and London, Free Press/Collier Macmillan, 1975) 68–69.

[97] See ch 17 below on self-regulation.

[98] C Coglianese and D Lazer, 'Management-based Regulation: Prescribing Private Management to Achieve Public Goals' (2003) 37 *Law & Society Review* 691–730.

[99] Summarized in S Oded, PhD thesis: *Inducing Corporate Proactive Compliance: Liability Controls & Corporate Monitors* (Erasmus Universiteit Rotterdam, 2012).

[100] N Shover, D Clelland and J Lynxwiler, *Enforcement Or Negotiation: Constructing a Regulatory Bureaucracy.* SUNY Series in Critical Issues.(Albany NY, State University of New York Press, 1986).

[101] Hutter (n 7).

[102] JT Scholz, 'Cooperation, Deterrence, and the Ecology of Regulatory Enforcement' (1984) 18 *Law and Society Review* 179–224; EA Bardach and RA Kagan, *Going by the Book: The Problem of Regulatory Unreasonableness* (Philadelphia PA, Temple University Press, 1982).

[103] J Baggs, B Silverstein and M Foley, 'Workplace Health and Safety Regulations: Impact of Enforcement and Consultation on Workers' Compensation Claims Rates in Washington State' (2003) 43(5) *American Journal of Industrial Medicine* 483–94.

[104] R Baldwin and M Cave, *Understanding Regulation: Theory, Strategy, and Practice* (New York NY, Oxford University Press, 1999); SP Huntington, 'The Marasmus of the ICC: The Commission, the Railroads, and the Public Interest' (1952) 61(4) *The Yale Law Journal* 467–509; GJ Stigler, 'The Theory of Economic Regulation' (1971) 3 *Bell Journal of Economics and Management Science* 3–18; ME Levine and JL Forrence, 'Regulatory Capture, Public Interest, and the Public Agenda: Toward a Synthesis' (1990) 6(1) *Journal of Law, Economics, & Organization* 167–98; J-J Laffont and J Tirole, 'The Politics of Government Decision-Making: A Theory of Regulatory Capture' (1991) 106(4) *The Quarterly Journal of Economics* 1089–127; May and Winter, 'Regulatory Enforcement and Compliance' (n 72).

Major cooperative enforcement regimes include 'negotiated compliance' (agreeing to avoid prosecution of past violations in return for commitment for future compliance)[105] and 'regulatory dealing' (where interaction exists in more than one context or domain, trade can occur between action taken in different domains).[106]

However, Doreen McBarnet and colleagues have identified a phenomenon of 'creative compliance' in which firms comply (or make it seem that they comply) with the rules in letter but not in spirit, thereby defeating the purpose of the rules and of regulation and enforcement.[107] This process of resistant non-compliance may be deliberate or accidental. Indeed, the process of constructing the meaning of the regulatory rules may be two-way. A 'New Institutional *legal endogeneity* model' model posits that although organisations are affected by legal pressures, so equally does the state's legal system gradually assimilate business constructions of what the law entails.[108] Sharon Gilad's study of the construction of the FSA's 'Treating Customers Fairly' initiative shows how the requirements were framed by the agency in a particular way, but re-framed by the banks in 'managerialising' the meaning and compliance: See chapter 20 below. When coupled with a belief that the banks were already compliant with the requirements, and all that was being requested was a call for evidence (which led to massive investment in information management systems), the substance of the programme was completely frustrated until evidence of ongoing outcomes from customer complaints showed that a serious problem had continued and therefore escalated.

Simpson and Rorie's review of internal compliance systems suggests that those that maximise the risk of intra-organisational discovery and salient (but not necessarily harsh) punishments are more likely to yield compliance.[109] They conclude that the studies imply that the structure of the system (eg audits, hotlines, ethics codes and mandatory ethics training) may be less important than how non-compliance is treated when it is discovered. For instance, internal reprimands appear to have a greater deterrent effect than do more punitive firm interventions (eg being fired). However, both of these outcomes yield greater results than doing nothing at all. That conclusion chimes with Braithwaite's 'reintegrative shaming' concept.[110]

---

[105] P Fenn and CG Veljanovski, 'A Positive Economic Theory of Regulatory Enforcement' (1998) 98 *The Economic Journal* 1055–70.

[106] AG Heyes and N Rickman, 'Regulatory Dealing—Revisiting the Harrington Paradox' (1999) 72(3) *Journal of Public Economics* 361–78.

[107] D McBarnet and C Whelan, 'The Elusive Spirit of the Law: Formalism and the Struggle for Legal Control' (1991) 54 *MLR* 848; D McBarnet and C Whelan, 'Challenging the Regulators; Strategies for resisting Control' in C McCrudden (ed), *Regulation and Deregulation. Policy and Practice in the Utilities and Financial Services Industries* (Oxford, Clarendon Press, 1999); see also McBarnet, Voiculescu and Campbell (n 91).

[108] LB Edelman, LH Krieger, SR Eliason, CR Albiston and V Mellema, 'When Organizations Rule: Judicial Deference to Institutionalized Employment Structures' (2011) 117 *American Journal of Sociology* 888–954; LB Edelman and SA Talesh, 'To Comply or Not to Comply—That Isn't the Question: How Organizations Construct the Meaning of Compliance' in C Parker and V Nielsen, *Explaining Compliance: Business Responses to Regulation* (Cheltenham, Edward Elgar, 2011) 103–22.

[109] SS Simpson and M Rorie, 'Motivating Compliance: Economic and Material Motives for Compliance' in C Parker and VL Nielsen (eds), *Explaining Compliance: Business Responses to Regulation* (Cheltenham, Edward Elgar, 2012).

[110] J Braithwaite, *Crime, Shame and Reintegration* (Sydney, Cambridge University Press, 1989).

12

OECD Policy on Regulation and Enforcement

I. OECD's Recommendations of Regulatory Policy and Risk Management

The Organisation for Economic Co-operation and Development (OECD) has issued occasional but important papers on regulation since 1993.[1] In these, it has strongly championed the adoption of responsive regulation by Member States. In 2000, it issued a paper written by Professor Christine Parker, a leading expert in responsive and open regulation, which explained those concepts, and examined the importance of the subjects of regulation being aware of and comprehending the rules, and being willing and able to comply with them.[2] It noted that governments have a clear long-term aim in maintaining positive attitudes toward the regulatory system among citizens and businesses, since these attitudes largely determine the level of 'voluntary compliance'. It also pointed out that enforcement cannot substitute for low levels of voluntary compliance. It recommended monitoring compliance trends as a key part of ex post evaluation of regulatory programmes, and shifting towards output measures and behavioural outcomes. It concluded that awareness of compliance problems is growing but action to improve compliance was uncoordinated and unsystematic.

An economics-based analysis of enforcement regimes in 2006, which adopted a theoretical framework of deterrence, compared leading examples of four approaches from leading jurisdictions: Enforcement based on criminal, administrative, private and self-regulatory approaches. The authors concluded that it was highly unlikely that any single model of practices and procedures would provide cost-effective means of achieving a high degree of compliance across OECD countries.[3] The example taken of a criminal justice system imposing financial penalties, the United Kingdom, reported enforcement procedures in general to be effective, but to provide inadequate deterrence for serious cases because the penalties imposed by the criminal courts were too low and no adverse financial consequences were attached to enforcement orders obtained in civil proceedings. It recommended the introduction of a suitable system of administrative financial penalties to enhance compliance. The example of where administrative agencies had themselves power to impose

---

[1] *Improving Regulatory Compliance: Strategies and Practical Applications in OECD Countries* (Paris, OECD, 1993).

[2] *Reducing the Risk of Policy Failure: Challenges for Regulatory Compliance* (Paris, OECD, 2000).

[3] *Best Practices for Consumer Policy: Report on the Effectiveness of Enforcement Regimes* (Paris, OECD, 2006); this was written by Professors Anthony Ogus and Michael Faure, and Dr Niels Philipsen.

financial penalties, Belgium, had low transactional costs but was hampered by inadequate resources in the prosecution service and by the fact that some of the cases referred to that service could more appropriately be resolved in the civil courts. A system relying on private enforcement, Australia, appeared to the reviewers to be an effective way of stopping illegal conduct by recalcitrant traders and achieving timely redress for consumers, but the civil regime did not then allow the courts to impose financial penalties. Use of 'probation orders' and adverse publicity were regarded as important devices for inducing compliance. Finally, reliance primarily on self-regulatory arrangements, exemplified by the Netherlands, was dependent to a large extent on consumer activism, self-regulation and the informal resolution of disputes. It worked well where contraventions were easily detected and where traders were 'benevolent'. Industry self-regulatory compliance schemes were thought to be capable of playing an important complementary and cost-effective role to consumer policy enforcement regimes. Nevertheless, there was perceived to be inadequate deterrence for 'mala fide' traders. It was noted that a new administrative agency with powers to impose financial penalties was due to be implemented.

The economic and financial crisis from 2008 catapulted regulation into a high profile, with many arguments over whether regulation as a technique had failed or could ever be sufficiently reliable. In 2010, the OECD published a lengthy and thoughtful compilation of articles written by a group of regulatory experts from around the world.[4] The thrust of the compilation was to explain that regulation was necessary for governments and societies but could not remove all risks, and hence could not avoid the occurrence of harmful and unexpected events. Amongst the recommendations were adopting advanced risk management systems, good governance arrangements, management-based regulation, conceptual frameworks of decision making under uncertainty, and guidelines for risk assessment and management. Evidence of adoption of best practices in risk regulation within OECD governments was said to be limited.[5]

It was noted that risk management is typically divided into three sequential phases (assessment, management and review) that are operated continuously and permanently.[6] However, the system should not be regarded as fail-safe. Nor should the state be regarded as being able to control, or having responsibility for controlling, every risk: A UK policy paper was quoted to support the latter proposition.

> The state should not intervene and assume that responsibility for risks that are better managed by individuals, families, businesses, organizations or local communities ... We can think about the management of risk in terms of a Risk Management Hierarchy. At the top is the individual, at the bottom the EU and other international organisations. The policy-making task should be unequivocal—to push as far up the hierarchy as prudence permits on each and every single occasion.[7]

In 2012 the OECD issued a Council Recommendation on regulatory policy and governance, specifically in response to the financial and economic crisis.[8] It recommended that

---

[4] *Risk and Regulatory Policy: Improving the Governance of Risk* (Paris, OECD, 2010).

[5] G Bounds, 'Challenges to Designing Regulatory Policy Frameworks to Manage Risks' in *Risk and Regulatory Policy: Improving the Governance of Risk* (Paris, OECD, 2010) 33.

[6] O Renn and P Graham, *Risk Governance—Towards an Integrative Approach* (International Risk Governance Council, 2006); *Risk and Regulation: Issues for Discussion* (Paris, OECD, 2006) GOV/PGC/REG(2006)1.

[7] *Risk Responsibility and Regulation—Whose Risk is it Anyway?* (Better Regulation Council, 2006) 31.

[8] *Recommendation of the Council on Regulatory and Policy Governance* (Paris, OECD, 2012). See earlier D Rodrigo, L Allio and P Andres-Amo, 'Multi-Level Regulatory Governance: Policies, Institutions and Tools for

states review and strengthen their regulatory capacity and quality, with measures that include whole-of-government policy for regulatory quality; adhering to principles of open government (including transparency and participation in the regulatory process); establish mechanisms to provide oversight of regulatory policy procedures and goals, support and implement regulatory policy; integrate impact assessment into the policy process; review stocks of significant regulation; publish regular reports on performance of regulatory policy; develop a consistent policy covering the role and functions of regulatory agencies in order to provide greater confidence that regulatory decisions are made on an objective, impartial and consistent basis, without conflict of interest, bias or improper influence; ensure the effectiveness of systems for the review of the legality and procedural fairness of regulations and of decisions made by bodies empowered to issue regulatory sanctions; and apply risk assessment, risk management and risk communication strategies to the design and implementation of regulations to ensure that regulation is targeted and effective. 'Regulators should assess how regulations will be given effect and should design responsive implementation and enforcement strategies.'[9] It also said that '[i]n an increasingly globalised economy, international regulatory co-operation must become integral to risk management and long-term policy planning.'[10]

II. OECD's Best Practice Principles for Improving on Enforcement and Inspections

The OECD issued in 2014 its important *Best Practice Principles for Regulatory Policy: Regulatory Enforcement and Inspections*,[11] which presented a range of core principles on which effective and efficient regulatory enforcement and inspections should be based in pursuit of the best *compliance outcomes* and highest regulatory quality.[12] It asserted:

> A well-formulated enforcement strategy is one that provides correct incentives for regulated subjects as well as appropriate guidelines for enforcement staff, and minimises both the monitoring effort and the costs for the regulated subjects and the public sector. To achieve this, any strategy needs to rely on a clear and sound vision of what the drivers of compliance are—both in terms of the effect of activities of the regulatory bodies, but also in terms of characteristics of the regulated businesses and of external factors (in particular market characteristics).[13]

Regulatory Quality and Policy Coherence' *OECD Working Papers on Public Governance*, No 13 (2009): This noted that regulatory policies in a multi-level context can only be effective if they reflect the diversity of needs and interests and encourage co-ordination (horizontal and vertical) and cooperation mechanisms across levels of government.

[9] *Recommendation of the Council on Regulatory and Policy Governance*, ibid, Recommendation 9.

[10] ibid, Appendix 1, s 12.

[11] *OECD Best Practice Principles for Regulatory Policy: Regulatory Enforcement and Inspections* (Paris, OECD, 2014). See earlier *Consultation on Public Consultation Best Practice Principles for Improving on Enforcement and Inspections* (OECD, June 2013) para 2, available at http://www.oecd.org/regreform/regulatory-policy/enforcement-inspections.htm. This was published shortly after *Consultation on the Principles for the Governance of Regulators* (Paris, OECD, 2012), which specified such principles as role clarity, preventing undue influence and maintaining trust, decision making and governing body structure for independent regulators, accountability and transparency, engagement, funding and performance evaluation.

[12] The UK Better Regulation Development Office (BRDO) and the Dutch government had contributed a major input into the development of the final Recommendation.

[13] *OECD Best Practice Principles for Regulatory Policy* (n 11) 12.

The 11 principles addressing the design of the policies, institutions and tools for promoting effective compliance and the process of reforming inspection services to achieve results are shown in Box 12.1.

Box 12.1: OECD *International Best Practice Principles: Improving Regulatory Enforcement and Inspections*

Evidence-based enforcement. Regulatory enforcement and inspections should be evidence-based and measurement-based: deciding what to inspect and how should be grounded on data and evidence, and results should be evaluated regularly.

Selectivity. Promoting compliance and enforcing rules should be left to market forces, private sector and civil society actions wherever possible: inspections and enforcement cannot be everywhere and address everything, and there are many other ways to achieve regulatory objectives.

Risk focus and proportionality. Enforcement needs to be risk-based and proportionate: the frequency of inspections and the resources employed should be proportional to the level of risk and enforcement actions should be aiming at reducing the actual risk posed by infractions.

Responsive regulation. Enforcement should be based on 'responsive regulation' principles: inspection enforcement actions should be modulated depending on the profile and behaviour of specific businesses.

Long term vision. Governments should adopt policies and institutional mechanisms on regulatory enforcement and inspections with clear objectives and a long-term road-map.

Co-ordination and consolidation. Inspection functions should be co-ordinated and, where needed, consolidated: less duplication and overlaps will ensure better use of public resources, minimise burden on regulated subjects, and maximise effectiveness.

Transparent governance. Governance structures and human resources policies for regulatory enforcement should support transparency, professionalism, and results-oriented management. Execution of regulatory enforcement should be independent from political influence, and compliance promotion efforts should be rewarded.

Information integration. Information and communication technologies should be used to maximise risk-focus, co-ordination and information-sharing—as well as optimal use of resources.

Clear and fair process. Governments should ensure clarity of rules and process for enforcement and inspections: coherent legislation to organise inspections and enforcement needs to be adopted and published, and clearly articulate rights and obligations of officials and of businesses.

Compliance promotion. Transparency and compliance should be promoted through the use of appropriate instruments such as guidance, toolkits and checklists.

Professionalism. Inspectors should be trained and managed to ensure professionalism, integrity, consistency and transparency: this requires substantial training focusing not only on technical but also on generic inspection skills, and official guidelines for inspectors to help ensure consistency and fairness.

It will be seen that the principles are firmly grounded on an approach to inspection and enforcement that is evidence-based, risk-based, outcome-producing, proportionate, coordinated, fair, transparent and uses 'responsive regulation'. The previous consultation had included references to both responsive regulation and deterrence, but the final Recommendation omitted any reference to deterrence—the word was not used. The Consultation had said:

Experience and research suggest that optimal results in terms of compliance and burden can best be achieved by combining broad compliance-promotion efforts with well-targeted controls, and the availability of deterrent sanctions for serious violations. Effective compliance can only be achieved if regulations are realistic and adequate for a given country—and no amount of enforcement will make unrealistic rules work. At the same time, in order for enforcement activities to deliver their expected results, they need to be properly resourced—which means that risk-based strategic planning must be conducted to ensure that sufficient resources are available to address key risks, and that over-ambitious aims at not ascribed to enforcement agencies. Prioritisation is essential to ensure that results are achieved where they are most needed.[14]

In contrast, the OECD's 2014 policy document switched from significant reliance on deterrence and suggested the following approach to enforcement, based on 'responsive regulation':

— Businesses that show a pattern of systematic and repeated violations of regulations are assigned a higher risk level, and accordingly checked more frequently;
— Businesses which commit repeated and systematic violations are also showed no leniency when significant violations are found, and enforcement may immediately escalate to sanctions, and possibly suspension of operations, rather than just giving an improvement notice. Inspectors should also take into account the response of the business operator to the inspection and the identification of violations (eg whether the operator attempts to hide problems or is transparent about them, whether immediate corrective action is taken or on the contrary the operator seeks every possible way to hinder the inspection or challenge even the most obvious findings etc);
— On the contrary, businesses which have a history of compliance should be gradually checked less often (their risk level being rated lower) inspectors should also generally start with improvement notices or (in the case of lesser violations) verbal warnings, except in cases of major, imminent hazard;

---

[14] Public Consultation on Best Practice Principles for Improving Regulatory Enforcement and Inspections: Draft Report Submitted to the Public for Comments (Paris, OECD, 2013) para 9.

— Recently created businesses should be similarly first given a chance to improve, rather than immediately resorting to sanctions, so as to promote a culture of openness on their side (except, once again, if violations are seen to be particularly dangerous and/or were clearly committed on purpose—in which case the regulatory enforcement agency should use sanctions as appropriate);

— Proportionality and risk-responsiveness mean that, even if a violation is found in a business which is usually compliant (or is a new business), but this violation is particularly egregious and poses very serious threats to life, health or other essential public goods or rights, the enforcement response should be stronger and more coercive than in cases where violations are relatively less grievous or do not create an imminent hazard;

— In order to be effective, the 'responsive regulation' approach also requires that the range of potential penalties available to regulatory enforcement agencies be sufficiently broad and differentiated to really treat different behaviours in a proportionate manner, but also to exert real deterrence when needed—with penalties that clearly will impose higher cost than the violation may have brought in undue profits to the business operator, and a process for imposing sanctions that uses administrative penalties (and not prosecutions in courts) for at least a significant share of violations so as to ensure more rapid and predictable enforcement. If sanctions are insufficiently deterrent, there is a high likelihood that 'rogue operators' will continue to commit major violations even after having been caught once (or repeatedly)....[15]

In relation to Principle 1 on system design, the OECD said:

Comparative research has shown that a high number of inspections do not guarantee greater levels of compliance, and many sanctions do not necessarily safeguard the public. On the other hand a small number of checks or prosecutions do not mean that compliance is high, as it may just reflect a lack of inspection resources, or lax enforcement. It is acknowledged that properly assessing the effectiveness of enforcement and inspection agencies is difficult, because improvements or worsening outcomes (health, safety etc) cannot directly be attributed to their activities because of the vast number of other, often more important, factors. Nonetheless, it remains crucial to monitor such outcomes in order to judge whether enforcement is having any positive contribution.[16]

In relation to Principle 2 on selecting the right approach in order to achieve the desired outcomes, a number of factors were listed to be taken into account in evaluating ex ante and ex post, regulatory or litigation, market-based, formal state or informal civil society, approaches. There was a strong statement that responsibility for compliance rests with businesses.

It should be made clear, both in law and in practice that the primary responsibly for compliance and with safety lies with the regulated subjects. Inspectors and regulators are here to assist and promote compliance, but not to actually implement regulations—and they cannot be the ones ensuring safety, as they are not the business operators. Where appropriate and if this does not create disproportionate burden, this may also mean that requirements for self-monitoring and, in some cases, reporting can be introduced for certain operators which present a significant level of risk, so as to allow for less frequent inspection visits. These inspections can then focus on verifying how effective the self-monitoring and risk-management systems implemented by the business operator are, and whether they seem to work in practice and not only on paper. It is important to remember

---

[15] *OECD Best Practice Principles for Regulatory Policy* (n 11) 33–34.
[16] ibid, 18.

that such 'system inspections' need to incorporate effective 'reality checks' and not trust that systems always work as designed.[17]

The OECD noted various possible structures for public bodies, in order to respond to the problem of diversity and coverage. One possible model would be that local inspectors could form a 'front line', with a broad mandate and a specific training allowing them to spot issues pertaining to a number of different regulatory fields, collecting information with 'eyes and ears' for specialist agencies.

III. The OECD Studies

The draft of the Best Practice Principles discussed above were published in 2013 with two study reports into the status of enforcement and inspection by public regulatory bodies in OECD countries by Monk[18] and by Blanc.[19] These indicated that much of the ground-breaking development on policy and practice had occurred in the UK and the Netherlands, and that the 'organisation, design and delivery of inspection and enforcement is an under studied area of regulatory policy'.[20]

Much of the OECD's focus was on how to reduce costs of enforcement and inspection, for both public and business budgets, following Better Regulation principles, whilst maintaining desired outcomes of compliance. Monk's review noted:

> Ensuring effective compliance with rules and regulations is an important factor to create trust in a functioning society and in government. The challenge is to develop an enforcement strategy that induces the highest possible compliance while keeping the costs as low as possible. A well-formulated enforcement strategy, providing correct incentives for regulated subjects, can reduce the monitoring effort and the costs for both the businesses and the public sector....[21]

Monk found that although there is some good practice, it varies between sectors. This is an area where there was large scope for reform because practice is very complex, inconsistent between countries, not very transparent, and varies between sectors. She set out 17 recommendations, which were developed into the 11 2014 Principles. Monk's list was based on the UK's Hampton risk-based prioritised inspection principles, which she regarded as having been 'widely accepted'.[22] She also noted adoption in Australia of the responsive regulation enforcement pyramid developed from that by Ayres and Braithwaite.[23] Relying on the

---

[17] ibid, 25.

[18] J Monk, *Reform of Regulatory Enforcement and Inspections in OECD Countries* (Paris, OECD, 2013) http://www.oecd.org/gov/regulatory-policy/Reform%20of%20inspections%20-%20Web%20-%20Julie%20Monk.pdf. This focused on inspections especially in the fields of tax, environment and occupational health and safety through the analysis of current practice within the 25 member states who responded to the OECD questionnaire commissioned in February 2012.

[19] F Blanc, *Inspections Reforms: Why, How and With What Results* (Paris, OECD, 2013) http://www.oecd.org/gov/regulatory-policy/Inspection%20reforms%20-%20web%20-F.%20Blanc.pdf.

[20] Monk (n 18) para 12.

[21] ibid, para 16.

[22] ibid, para 114.

[23] See ch 11 above.

Hampton report[24] and two other British studies,[25] Monk concluded that providing advice should be a central regulatory function (Recommendation 17) and that the selection of the choice of intervention that would be most effective should be based on considering two variables, one showing the businesses' ability to comply (or its state of knowledge) and the other showing its willingness to comply (or attitude), a quadrant is produced, which she illustrated in Figure 12.1. She considered that it is therefore important for regulators and inspection authorities to segment their markets in selecting the appropriate intervention that would be most effective.

> ... Those with a high ability and high state of willingness to comply are likely to be fully compliant and do not need regulatory intervention or an inspection. Those with a high ability but a low willingness are non-compliant and the only intervention likely to work is enforcement. However the other two quadrants show a low ability to comply. In these businesses it is important to provide advice and guidance to help increase their understanding and knowledge.
>
> For the willing companies they can quickly be provided with support to help them become compliant and move into the fully compliant category requiring little or no intervention by the regulator.

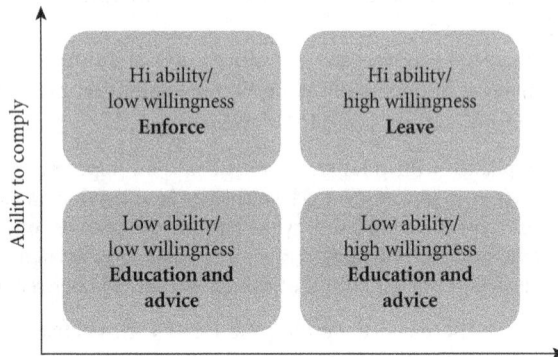

Figure 12.1: Vectors of Ability and Willingness to Comply

[24] P Hampton, *Reducing Administrative Burdens: Effective Inspection & Enforcement* (HM Treasury, 2005): Hampton found that 92% of businesses in his review said that they wanted more advice from regulators. He recommended that regulators should provide authoritative, accessible advice easily and cheaply; that regulators should monitor business awareness and understanding of regulations and make on-site and tailored advice available to businesses; and that businesses should be able to find out quickly what regulations apply to them, what they require, and how they can improve compliance beyond minimum standards. Advice was particularly important for small businesses who often do not have access to the experts that larger businesses can afford to employ and it produces a more open and productive relationship.

[25] C Jackson, A Furnham and K Willen, 'Employer Willingness to Comply with the Disability Discrimination Act regarding Staff Selection in the United Kingdom'(2000) 73 *Journal of Occupational and Organisational Psychology* 119–29 (employer willingness to comply with the Disability Discrimination Act was predicted by *attitude* towards disabled people and *knowledge* of the legislation); *Research Report: Individuals Prioritisation—An Investigation into the Segmentation of the Individuals Customer Base* (HM Revenue and Customs, 2009) available at: http://www.hmrc.gov.uk/research/individuals-prioritisation-publication.pdf (increased compliance and reduced the cost of non-compliance with tax legislation was assisted by segmenting non-compliers into four dimensions: awareness of one's obligations, motivation to comply, ability to comply and opportunity not to comply. They found that 8% of their regulated subjects were unaware, 12% were reluctant conformists, 4% were 'dodgers', 18% needed help and 58% were willing conformists); see Monk (n 18) paras 152–58.

For the unwilling category of business, advice may help them understand their duties and responsibilities, which will shift them into the bottom right quadrant, with more advice they can then move into the full compliant top right quadrant. It can therefore be demonstrated that in the majority of cases it is important for businesses to receive advice to improve regulatory outcomes and compliance.[26]

Blanc began his study by noting:

> In spite of the increasing focus on improving regulations for businesses (and citizens), enforcement and delivery of these regulations, and in particular inspections, have been the object of considerably less attention. Studies and reform programmes often 'assume' delivery, effectiveness, compliance and tend to pay too little attention to how third parties, but also the state administration, are actually supposed to work with rules in practice.[27]

Blanc concluded that the picture presented by business inspections around the world is often unsatisfactory, that outcomes are disappointing in terms of securing public goods, and/or cost-effectiveness is low, and that agencies lack uniform guidelines and approaches, and frequently focus on finding violations rather than improving compliance and outcomes.[28] He noted the spread of a broader understanding of 'enforcement' based on Ayres and Braithwaite's enforcement pyramid, and the UK's concentration on 'regulatory delivery' through the Better Regulation Delivery Office. However, he also noted the limited number of studies on 'regulatory effectiveness', which had most often been done on occupational safety and health, environment, tax and food,[29] but which leave a number of issues and gaps.[30] Blanc noted:

> Regulations as such, how they are designed and developed, how to improve them and make them 'smarter', have been considerably more studied than delivery mechanisms such as inspections and other enforcement tools. There is however ample evidence that enforcement and inspections are in fact crucial to how the regulatory sphere affects businesses and the economy. First, inspections and enforcement actions are generally the primary way through which businesses, in particular SMEs, 'experience' regulations and regulators. Second, inadequate approaches or lack of changes in enforcement and inspections can mean that changes in regulations fail to deliver their full benefits. Third, evolutions in inspections and regulatory delivery to make them more compliance-focused, more supportive and risk-based can all lead to real and significant improvements for economic actors, even within the framework of existing regulations (which may, for different reasons, be very difficult to change 'on the books'—so the ability to change the way they are enforced in practice matters). Finally, enforcement and inspections are as much about methods and culture as institutions, and as much about organizational mechanisms as legislation.[31]

Blanc concluded that inspections were fundamentally important to achieving compliance, that there were many differing practices in relation to inspections, with no model and little coherence, and that there were relatively rare examples of good practices based on risk-based planning, of which he singled out the UK's Health and Safety Executive as

---

[26] Monk (n 18) paras 157, 158.
[27] Blanc (n 19) para 1.
[28] ibid, para 2.
[29] Blanc noted the valuable collection of studies in the Netherlands' inspections portal library of effectiveness studies at: www.inspectieloket.nl/vernieuwing_toezicht/toezichtmeteffect/bibliotheek.
[30] Blanc (n 19) paras 17–27.
[31] ibid, para 24.

an example.[32] As examples of good practice in inspections generally, he noted the use of 'delegated' inspections or 'second-level control' (such as the EU's (European Union) New Framework, discussed in chapter 19 below), the need to reduce overlaps and duplication so as to improve efficiency, the importance of risk-based targeting, and of sharing information.[33] In discussing how to make regulatory enforcement more effective, Blanc referred to the role of adequate sanctions and liability provisions, saying:

— Excessively heavy sanctions for relatively minor violations can create problems in several ways—very high direct costs for affected businesses, important opportunities for abuses of powers by inspectors, confrontational relation between state authorities and private sector, etc.
— Insufficient liability provisions may mean that businesses feel "off the hook" in case of problems, and/or that potential victims of serious violations/crimes are not adequately compensated if problems happen.
— Inadequate sanctions, not commensurate to the potential size of undue profits and/or of damages, may be insufficient to deter violations. The same applies if potential sanctions are severe, but the probability of them being inflicted is low because of the complexity of the procedure (criminal prosecution and trial in all cases, for instance).[34]

Blanc noted that the mechanisms of compliance may be more complex than Hampton and Macrory suggested, and referred to work of Henk Elffers and Dick Hessing that suggests that:

— Statutory sanctions are ineffective for 'conformist compliers', ie those who comply with rules only because they fear punishment. There is only an effect if—and this is generally not feasible, and perhaps not desirable either—the punishment threatened is certain, quick and severe.
— Statutory sanctions have an indirect effect on the identifiers, those who comply with rules because they want to belong to a social group for which compliance is the norm; imposing sanctions on the others, those who break the rules, is necessary and useful for the identifiers, because this serves to maintain the social norm for them, the norm that keeps them on the straight and narrow.
— Statutory sanctions are superfluous for the internalisers, those who comply with rules because they have made these rules part of their own world view.[35]

Blanc went on to conclude:[36]

In this perspective, sanctions are not, in fact, effective to deter the 'real criminals', those that in UK parlance are often called 'rogue traders'. These are, simply, not to be deterred. … even in countries with potentially crippling civil damage awards, such as the USA, reckless behaviour can very well happen. In short, there is a percentage of actors for whom no rules, sanctions, enforcement measures etc. will be effective. There is also, on the opposite end of the spectrum, a share of people who will comply and try and work properly even when there is no real credible threat of any sanction.

---

[32] ibid, ch 2.

[33] ibid, ch 4.

[34] ibid, para 256.

[35] ibid, para 261, citing H Elffers, *De ratione leregelovertreder* (inaugural lecture for Antwerp University, 26 October 2004) Boom Juridische Uitgevers, Den Haag, the summary above courtesy of unpublished work by Professor W Voermans, Leiden University.

[36] Blanc (n 19) paras 262–64.

The focus of the sanctioning system is much more the mass of those 'in between'—they might cut corners if they think cutting corners 'is OK', but not if they see it as being strongly socially reprehensible, and punished. Sanctions are signals for this majority.

The importance of 'signaling' is also underlined by both Hampton and Macrory, who both insist on the importance of 'reputational' sanctions—the 'stigma of criminal prosecution' (Hampton) and specific actions by regulators to 'name and shame' non-compliant businesses. Indeed, the most effective sanction scheme in many cases may indeed be the one that deters consumers from using this particular business—such as the display of inspection results through schemes such as 'Scores on the Door'.[37]

IV. OECD Recommendations on Redress

Providing mechanisms for consumer redress has been OECD policy since 2007.[38] It called for cost-effective and proportionate mechanisms, including ADR (alternative dispute resolution), small claims procedures, collective means and regulatory authorities obtaining or facilitating redress on behalf of consumers.

A 2014 Council Recommendation was made on consumer policy decision making that states should define problems and determine which consumer authority would be best placed to address it, and then assess the nature and magnitude of consumer detriment before determining what action is warranted.[39]

V. Conclusions

The extent to which governments around Europe or beyond adopt enforcement policies, and the nature of those enforcement policies, is currently difficult to verify. Little exists in English on such issues. It may well be that many EU Member States have not adopted any written enforcement policies, and they may be unfamiliar with concepts of responsive regulation and enforcement. In any event, the OECD has strongly championed responsive regulation as its recommended policy for regulatory systems. In relation to enforcement and inspections by public bodies, the OECD has so far—and only in 2014—issued a Best Practice statement. However, that statement sets out a familiar Better Regulation approach, firmly based on evidence-based enforcement, risk-based and proportionate enforcement, and responsive regulation. The OECD views the UK, followed by the Netherlands, as the leading exponents of the recommended approaches, probably by some margin over many other states.

---

[37] See study on the original scheme in Los Angeles (started 1998)—P Simon, P Leslie, G Run, G Zhe Jin, R Reporter, A Aguirre and JE Fielding, 'Impact of Restaurant Hygiene Grade Cards on Foodborne-Disease Hospitalizations in Los Angeles County' (2005) 67(7) *Journal of Environmental Health* 32–36.

[38] *OECD Recommendation on Consumer Dispute Resolution and Redress* (Paris, OECD, 2007). See also *Dispute Resolution and Redress. Review of the 2007 Council Recommendation* (Paris, OECD, 22–23 April 2013).

[39] *Recommendation of the Council on Consumer Policy Decision Making* (Paris, OECD, 2014).

It is suggested that future work should focus on mapping the regulatory structures and hence enforcement practices and policies in states. Only then can an overview be taken of whether responsive regulation and responsive enforcement would be possible.

In the EU context, the impediment created by the principles of subsidiarity and domestic autonomy have prevented the European Commission from researching or attempting to harmonise national regulatory and enforcement structures or practices. This lack of harmonisation constitutes a major barrier to effective control of the single market. It also constitutes a wasted opportunity to engage in comparing best practices. Such international comparative work is urgently needed.

13

The Enforcement Policies
of Individual Agencies

Chapter 11 identified national policy on enforcement and the requirement for most regulatory authorities to publish an individual enforcement policy, under the Legal and Regulatory Reform Act 2006, the 2007 first version of the Regulators' Code, the Regulatory Enforcement and Sanctions Act 2008 (RESA) or a specific sectoral duty (such as for gas). This chapter reviews the revised enforcement *policies* issued by selected leading regulators, in order to illuminate an examination of their nature and goals. It is not directed at describing the *powers* that the selected enforcers have at their disposal, but instead focuses on how they state that they *intend to use* such powers. What policies do the individual authorities state that they are pursuing when they take enforcement action? Are there variations in approach between different authorities and sectors? If so, what are the reasons for this and can they be justified?

The sectors that have been selected for inclusion in this survey are environmental protection, financial services, communications, energy, water, railways, civil aviation, legal services, and health and safety in the workplace. Two further enforcement policies are set out separately and should be considered along with those set out here. Those are for general consumer protection and competition (chapters 14 and 15 respectively), which it is more appropriate to consider in the context of particular arrangements in those sectors and of a series of behavioural studies undertaken by the relevant regulators, that are also summarised there. One important omission from this survey is an enforcement policy of Trading Standards officers of local authorities, which is included in chapter 14. Overlaps between agencies sometimes arise, and are addressed by Memoranda of Understanding that are agreed between them.[1]

The analysis here is necessarily detailed. Conclusions on this chapter are held over to chapter 16, since it is necessary first to consider the information in the next two chapters before drawing conclusions. However, two broad themes should be noted in considering what follows. First is the fact that every public authority *has* issued an official enforcement policy. Second, the enforcement policies generally correspond to the principles of Better Regulation, including risk-based approaches. Several specifically adopt Ayres-Braithwaite pyramids to use and prioritisation of sanctions. In this chapter, the Civil Aviation Authority is a classic example of such a pyramid. The approach in that sector should be read together

---

[1] For example, *Memorandum of Understanding Between the Office of Fair Trading and the Financial Conduct Authority* (OFT & FCA, April 2013) available at http://www.fca.org.uk/static/fca/documents/mou/mou-oft.pdf, which sets out how the FCA will access in financial services the powers under the Unfair Terms in Consumer Contracts Regs that OFT uses elsewhere.

with the important analysis in chapter 19. Many, but not all, of them firmly adopt responsive enforcement approaches and a Macrory approach to sanctions. The area of workplace health and safety has a longer history than many areas in which public regulation has only emerged in the past decade or two, so is particularly interesting as it illustrates an evolution in approach from a more authoritarian style to one that is clearly risk-based and involves providing advice and guidance in many situations. Third, the wider focus can be seen on outcomes, especially for consumers, and redress. Railways now focus on consumer satisfaction. The leading example here is in financial services, and the same approach has spread to energy and utilities.

I. Environment

The Environment Agency's purpose is 'to protect or enhance the environment, taken as a whole' so as to promote 'the objective of achieving sustainable development'.[2] The Environment Agency has extensive functions, encompassing pollution control, waste regulation, management of water resources, flood and coastal risk-management, fisheries, conservation and navigation. It impacts on activities ranging from recreational pursuits to highly complex industrial processes. English Nature is the statutory adviser on the natural environment in England. Its role comprises two main elements: Wildlife and landscapes.[3]

A. Restorative Powers

The logic of using public restorative remedies in relation to environmental damage is clear, especially since private rights of action are restricted. The EU Environment Directive establishes a 'polluter pays' liability regime but it is enforced by public rather than private action.[4] Accordingly, the Environment Agency and English Nature were the first to be awarded the Regulatory Enforcement and Sanctions Act (RESA) Part 3 power to impose civil sanctions, as of 6 April 2010.[5] Civil sanctions were intended to provide new ways to protect the environment, supplementing the normal criminal-law based enforcement tools, and focusing on investment in environmental clean-up rather than paying fines.

The two authorities were granted the full range of powers, including not only the ability to impose financial penalties,[6] but also the ability to issue a Compliance Notice, requiring specified steps within a stated period to secure that an offence does not continue or happen again;[7] issue a Restoration Notice requiring specified steps within a stated period to secure

---

[2] Environment Act 1995, s 4.
[3] It was established in 2006, merging English Nature and the Countryside Agency.
[4] Dir 2004/35/EC on environmental liability with regard to the prevention and remedying of environmental damage.
[5] The Environmental Civil Sanctions (England) Order 2010/1157 and The Environmental Civil Sanctions (Miscellaneous Amendments) (England) Order 2010/1159.
[6] An upper limit of £250,000 has been imposed on variable monetary penalties for 'either way' offences.
[7] Sch 2 of the Order.

that the position is restored, so far as possible, to what it would have been if no offence had been committed;[8] issue a Stop Notice, which will prevent a person from carrying on an activity described in the notice until it has taken steps to come back into compliance;[9] accept Enforcement Undertakings, which will enable a person, who a regulator reasonably suspects of having committed an offence, to give an undertaking to a regulator to take one or more corrective actions set out in the undertaking;[10] a person may give a Third Party Undertaking to compensate persons affected by an offence, and the regulator if it accepts the undertaking must take it into account in determining the variable monetary penalty.

The Explanatory Memorandum that accompanied the Order stated:

> a non-compliance penalty will be based on the cost being avoided, in restoration of harm for example. This will ensure a proportionate penalty that will level the playing field for businesses who do comply with sanctions. It will also give priority to compliance and restoration ahead of taking monetary penalties. The non-compliance penalty will not be payable if the original requirement is complied with in the time set for the penalty to be paid. The regulator will also have the flexibility to reduce the penalty to reflect part compliance. The provision avoids the likely rigidity and potential lack of proportionality of a daily fine which most responses to the consultation preferred.[11]

The authorities stated that they would still prosecute serious offenders, but would

> be able to use alternative sanctions with legitimate businesses who are trying to do the right thing. They will be able to put right the damage they have done and local communities will see a direct improvement in the environment as a result. A business who wishes to repair any environmental damage they may have caused can set out how they propose to do this in an Enforcement Undertaking. If we accept their proposals, this becomes a legally binding voluntary agreement.[12]

The guidance stated that the total amount of a 'variable monetary penalty' would be reduced by £1 for every £1 spent on a Third Party Undertaking. They would not normally apply a financial civil sanction to a person who is part of the cross compliance scheme unless there is evidence of significant financial gain.

The first civil sanction was imposed on 22 July 2011, comprising an undertaking imposed on Invensys PLC to pay £21,000 following the self-reporting of packaging waste offences between 1998 and 2010.

B. Enforcement Policy

The 2010 review of the Environment Agency for Hampton-compliance found significant evidence of cultural change, that it was increasingly driven by outcomes rather than processes, and that relationships both internally and externally with businesses had improved.[13]

---

[8] ibid.
[9] Sch 3 of the Order.
[10] Sch 4 of the Order.
[11] See Guidance *Enforcement and Civil Sanctions* at http://www.environment-agency.gov.uk/business/regulation/116844.aspx?style=print.
[12] ibid.
[13] *The Environment Agency: A Review of its Progress since its Hampton Implementation Review* (Department for Business, Innovation & Skills, 2010).

The Environment Agency's *Enforcement and Sanctions—Guidance* was issued in 2014[14] and displayed full alignment with Hampton, Macrory, RESA and regulators' Code ideals, emphasising that the essential focus was on achieving the best *outcomes* and utilising all possible tools to that effect.

> We will use the full range of enforcement and sanctioning tools that are available to us, in combination if necessary, to achieve the best outcomes for the environment and for people. This may range, for example, from providing advice and guidance through to prosecution. Within this overall approach, where an offence has been committed we will consider issuing some form of sanction as well as any other preventative or remedial action taken to protect the environment and people.[15]

'Outcome focused-enforcement' was the sole basis of the policy and was divided into four general types:[16]

A.   To stop offending—aim to stop an illegal activity from continuing/occurring.
B.   To restore and/or remediate—aim to put right environmental harm or damage.
C.   To bring under regulatory control—aim to bring an illegal activity into compliance with the law.
D.   Punish and/or deter—to punish an offender and/or deter future offending.

The Guidance listed the multiple tools that were available in relation to each of the above outcomes, as summarised in Table 13.1.

Table 13.1: Outcomes and Tools of the Environment Agency

Outcome	Tools
A. Stop offending	Injunctions; Court Order under the Environmental Permitting (England and Wales) Regulations 2010 [EP Regulations]; Stop Notice; Suspension notice; groundwater prohibition notice; Anti-pollution works notice
B. Restore or remediate	Restoration notice; Enforcement notice; Notice to remove waste; Anti-pollution works notice; Power to seek a regulation 44 remediation order under the EP Regulations
C. Bring under regulatory control	Compliance notice; Enforcement notice; Suspension notice; Anti-pollution works notice; Revocation of an environmental permit; Variation of permit conditions; Acceptance of an Enforcement Undertaking
D. Deter and/or punish	Criminal sanctions; Variable Monetary penalties; Fixed Monetary penalties; Additional civil penalties for the EU Emissions Trading Scheme and the Carbon Reduction Commitment Energy Efficiency Scheme

---

[14] *Enforcement and Sanctions—Guidance. Operational Instruction 1356_10, version 3* (Environment Agency, 2014).

[15] ibid, para 1.

[16] ibid, para 2.

In relation to choosing the appropriate response in any given situation, the Guidance stated that there will normally be a range of possible sanctioning responses available.[17] Some sanctions had statutory limitations on availability.

> First we will consider the outcome that we are seeking to achieve in accordance with our commitment to outcome-focused regulation. We will consider what immediate action is needed as a response to protect the environment, such as the need to immediately serve a notice, and whether further action is then required to secure the desired outcomes....
>
> Where we consider that advice and guidance has not or will not achieve the necessary outcome, and that some form of sanction (either criminal or civil) is required to secure that outcome, then we will consider the facts against public interest factors ... in order to decide what type of sanction to impose.
>
> Where the circumstances leading to the offence could reasonably have been foreseen, and adequate avoiding and/or preventative measures were not taken, the response will normally give rise to a sanction beyond advice and guidance or issuing a warning.[18]

The 'public interest factors' that the Agency will consider are listed: Intent, foreseeability, environmental effect, nature of the offence, financial implications, deterrent effect, previous history, attitude of the offender, personal circumstances. 'Other public interest considerations' were listed as: Serious offences; minor breaches; repeat offending; failure to comply with a notice; operating without a permit, licence or other authority; multiple site operations; offences by bodies corporate; and combining sanctions. All of these factors were elaborated, such as follows:

4.1.6 Deterrent effect

When choosing a sanction we will consider the deterrent effect, both on the offender and others. Prosecutions, because of their greater stigma if a conviction is secured, may be appropriate even for minor non-compliances where they might contribute to a greater level of overall deterrence.

Where the use of a sanction is likely to reduce future self-reporting of offences or noncompliance, a different sanction may be appropriate.[19]

4.1.8 Attitude of the offender

Where the offender has a poor attitude towards the offence and/or is uncooperative with the investigation or remediation, this will normally mean that we consider a prosecution or a Variable Monetary Penalty. Conversely, where the offender provides us with the details of an offence voluntarily or through a self-reporting mechanism, we will take this into account when deciding on a sanction or whether advice and guidance will suffice.[20]

4.2.7 Offences by bodies corporate

We will take enforcement action against those persons responsible for the offence. Where a company is involved, it will be usual practice to enforce against the company where the offence resulted from the company's activities. However, where an offence has been committed by a body corporate and is attributable to the consent, connivance or neglect of any director, manager, secretary or

---

[17] ibid, para 4.
[18] ibid, para 4.
[19] ibid, para 4.1.6.
[20] ibid, para 4.1.8.

other officer, that person can be guilty of an offence and is liable to be the subject of enforcement action for that offence. In such circumstances we will take action against the most appropriate body (corporate and/or individual) or in combination, using the full range of the enforcement tools at our disposal. In appropriate cases, we will consider seeking disqualification of directors under the Companies Act.[21]

Also in 2014 Sentencing Guidelines came into force in relation to environmental offences, which increased levels of fines.[22]

II. Financial Services

Prior to 2013 the primary authority for financial services was the Financial Services Authority (FSA).[23] The regulatory system was also designed (formally from 2000) to include the specific sectoral dispute resolution mechanism of the Financial Ombudsman Service (FOS) and the Financial Services Compensation Scheme.[24] A private dispute resolution scheme that has also continued to be operated by business for its members is the Finance & Leasing Association's Arbitration Service.[25]

From April 2013, the FSA was replaced by the Prudential Regulation Authority (PRA) and the Financial Conduct Authority (FCA).[26] Regulation in the sector developed over several decades, gradually firming up requirements on banks[27] and public regulation,[28] as

[21] ibid, para 4.2.7.
[22] *Environmental Offences. Definitive Guideline* (Sentencing Council, 2014), at http://sentencingcouncil. judiciary.gov.uk/docs/Final_Environmental_Offences_Definitive_Guideline_(web).pdf. For the background to Sentencing Guidelines, see ch 10. Companies with a turnover of over £50 million might be fined £3 million per offence.
[23] The FSA regulated most UK financial services markets, exchanges and 29,000 firms in 2011. For an overview see R Sullivan, *Quality in Other Regulated Professions* (Legal Services Board, November 2011), available at http:// www.legalservicesboard.org.uk/news_publications/latest_news/pdf/quality_in_other_regulated_professions.pdf.
[24] On its creation under the Financial Services and Markets Act 2000 ('FSMA'), the Financial Services Authority inherited conduct-of-business regulation in respect of investments (including intermediaries) from those previously charged with this under the Financial Services Act 1986. This included investment sales by banks, notably sales of mortgage endowments. Conduct-of-business regulation of mortgages (including intermediation) was introduced in 2004 and insurance (including intermediation) in 2005, which included mortgages and insurance sales by banks (notably, sales of payment protection insurance (PPI)).
[25] See C Hodges, I Benöhr and N Creutzfeldt-Banda, *Consumer ADR in Europe* (Oxford, Hart Publishing, 2012) 282–84.
[26] Financial Services Act 2012. For the background see: *A New Approach to Financial Regulation* (HM Treasury, 2010) at http://www.parliament.uk/deposits/depositedpapers/2010/DEP2010-2070.pdf. The FCA was initially named the Consumer Protection and Markets Authority. For the organisational plan and management structure, see *Transition to New Regulatory Structure. Letter from H Sants* (Financial Services Agency, 7 February 2011) available at http://www.fsa.gov.uk/pubs/international/dceo_transition.pdf. See also *Journey to the Financial Conduct Authority* (Financial Services Agency, October 2012) available at http://www.fca.org.uk/static/documents/ fsa-journey-to-the-fca.pdf.
[27] Principle 3 of the FSA's Principles for Businesses states that 'a firm must take reasonable care to organise and control its affairs responsibly and effectively, with adequate risk management systems'.
[28] For recent changes see HM Treasury's June 2011 *White Paper: A New Approach to Financial Regulation: The Blueprint for Reform* (HM Treasury, 2011), at http://www.hm-treasury.gov.uk/d/consult_finreg__new_approach_ blueprint.pdf and *Independent Commission on Banking: Final Report Recommendations* (Independent Commission on Banking, September 2011), available at http://bankingcommission.s3.amazonaws.com/wp-content/ uploads/2010/07/ICB-Final-Report.pdf. The latter recommended a series of measures to improve stability and

discussed in chapter 20. In March 2013 the government announced proposals to transfer responsibility for regulating consumer credit from the Office of Fair Trading (OFT) to the FCA.[29]

The pensions sector is overseen by The Pensions Regulator and disputes may be resolved by The Pensions Ombudsman, and The Pensions Advisory Service.

The FCA has power to impose a financial penalty or to publish a public censure against an approved person or firm.[30] It can prosecute a range of criminal offences.[31] It also has power to vary or cancel an authorised person's permission,[32] and to prohibit individuals who are not fit and proper from carrying out functions in relation to regulated activities.[33] It may apply to the court for an order for a trader to stop an activity,[34] or to issue a Warning Notice and a Decision Notice.[35]

From 1 April 2013, financial penalties imposed by the Bank of England, the FCA or PRA under the Financial Services and Markets Act 2000 (FSMA) or the Banking Act 2009 from prosecution of criminal offences and from stand-alone regulatory regimes such as the Money Laundering Regulations 2007, and winding-up of firms that have carried on a regulated activity without authorisation, are to be paid to the Treasury after deduction of the agency's enforcement costs and expenses.[36] This also applies to sums recovered from the winding-up of firms that have carried on a regulated activity without authorisation.

An example of the new approach was a financial penalty of £28,038,800 imposed on Lloyds TSB Bank plc and Bank of Scotland plc in December 2013 for breaches in selling over 630,000 protection and investment products to over 399,000 UK retail customers from January 2010 to March 2012. The breaches were viewed as particularly serious but a 20 per cent discount was given since the firms agreed to settle at an early stage, agreeing to carry out a review of sales and provide redress to customers.[37]

Both the FSA and FCA have issued fines regularly. The FSA found that bringing regulatory action for market abuse was not having much effect, so introduced a 'credible deterrence' policy in 2005 and started to bring criminal cases for insider dealing. The total number of fines imposed increased from 2006 to a peak of 80 fines in 2010, after which it decreased somewhat, whilst the total value of fines imposed increased sharply in 2012 to

competition in UK banking, including structural reform and enhanced loss-absorbing capacity for UK banks. To improve competition, the Commission recommended structural change in UK banking markets; improving switching and consumer choice; and pro-competitive regulation of financial services.

[29] The move was instigated to provide a 'more responsive and dynamic regime': *A New Approach to Financial Regulation: Transferring Consumer Credit to the Financial Conduct Authority* (HM Treasury and Department for Business, Innovation & Skills, March 2013) available at http://www.hm-treasury.gov.uk/d/consult_transferring_consumer_credit_regulation_to_fca.pdf.

[30] FSMA, ss 63, 66, 123, 131, 205 and 206.
[31] FSMA, ss 401 and 402.
[32] FSMA, s 45.
[33] FSMA, s 56.
[34] An example of where the FSA issued 'strong advice' under the shadow of this power related to mortgage exit fees. After the banks raised exit fees from around £50 or £100 to £200, they were asked where this was permitted under the terms and conditions. The result was that the practice stopped.
[35] FSMA, ss 387 and 388.
[36] The Payment to Treasury of Penalties (Enforcement Costs) Order 2013/418.
[37] *Final Notice* (FCA, 10 December 2013) at http://www.fca.org.uk/static/documents/final-notices/lloyds-tsb-bank-and-bank-of-scotland.pdf.

£312 million, and to £472 million in 2013.[38] From 1 April 2012 to 30 September 2014, fines rose substantially to exceeding £1 billion, largely driven by a handful of very large fines in connection with manipulation of LIBOR and other benchmark lending rates.[39]

This section will continue by looking first at the role of the FOS before examining the arrangements put in place in 2011 between the various authorities and the FOS to monitor new and emerging issues. It will then note the FCA's enforcement powers and, in particular, the 2010 powers in relation to delivering redress. It is important to note how various powers are combined in practice, especially the power to require firms to undertake self-reviews and make voluntary payments, powers to make compensation orders, powers to impose consumer redress schemes, and the ability for consumers to complain to the Financial Ombudsman Service, whose determinations are binding on firms if accepted by the consumer. Only at that stage can the enforcement policies of the two new regulators, issued from 2012, be seen in proper context.

A. The Financial Ombudsman Service

As noted above, the FOS was established in 2000 as the principal mechanism for handling consumer complaints.[40] Its powers and modes of operation in relation to delivering redress have been described elsewhere.[41] Its statutory remit is to decide individual complaints against financial service providers on the basis of what appears fair and reasonable in the circumstances of the individual case.[42] However, one of the primary functions of the FOS, implicit in its original design in the 2000 legislation, is to perform a regulatory function by identifying information on market behaviour both by individual financial institutions and in general trends.

The FOS has a power to require a business to provide information, and requests information regularly but has not so far had to take a firm to court under this power.[43] It can take a business to the High Court, and has threatened to do so. It may make an award for pain and suffering, distress or inconvenience.[44]

The FOS has no specific collective claim mechanisms, but has developed a number of procedures to deal with multiple horizontal issues, notably a lead case process, a test case

---

[38]   Report by the Comptroller and Auditor General. *The Financial Conduct Authority and the Prudential Regulation Authority. Regulating Financial Services* (National Audit Office) HC 1072, Session 2013–14, 25 March 2014.
[39]   R Patton, *Trends in Regulatory Enforcement in UK Financial Markets. 2014/15 Mid-Year Report* (NERA Economic Consulting, 2014).
[40]   FSMA, Pt XVI.
[41]   C Hodges, *The Reform of Class and Representative Actions in European Legal Systems: A New Framework for Collective Redress in Europe* (Oxford, Hart Publishing, 2008) Appendix I: Some aspects have now been updated, as noted here.
[42]   FSMA, s 228(2). Further, firms are required to treat customers fairly, under the FSA's Principles for Businesses, Principle 6.
[43]   FSMA, s 231. An example of where the FSA made a stop order was tracker mortgages, in which clauses enabled banks to alter the margin. The FSA required the banks to identify where this was permitted in their Key Facts documents, and since those documents contained no such reference, the practice was banned.
[44]   *Technical Note: Compensation for Distress, Inconvenience or Other Non-financial Loss* (Financial Ombudsman, May 2012) available at http://www.financial-ombudsman.org.uk/publications/technical_notes/distress-and-inconvenience.htm#1.

procedure,[45] and collaboration mechanism under the FSA/OFT/FOS Coordination Committee, discussed below. The last of these (called the Wider Implications procedure until 2012) applies where there is a new or emerging issue that raises significant implications for consumers in general, or for industry, or even for one business, and it may involve more than one of the FCA, FOS and OFT. Most issues have been identified by FSA or FOS; the consumers' association has raised one, and industry none.

B. Complaints Handling and Transparency

The authorities considered that consumer detriment from inadequate complaint handling and systemic problems remained a major issue. They increased pressure on firms to operate effective systems to handle consumer complaints fairly and promptly, so that consumers with products or services that have gone wrong receive swift and effective redress, to identify and remedy any recurring or systemic problems brought to light by complaints; and to consider whether they should act on their own initiative to review the position of consumers in a similar position, but who have not yet complained.[46] The FSA identified poor quality complaints handling as a key conduct risk and said it would be maintaining complaints handling as a key area of focus, to increase compliance with the complaint handling standards set out in Chapter 1 of the FSA's *Dispute Resolution: Complaints (DISP) Sourcebook*.[47] It noted research that customer satisfaction rates were almost as high among customers who had complained about a problem and had it satisfactorily resolved, as they were among customers who had not experienced a problem at all. Further, actual insurance renewal rates were higher (85 per cent for customers who complained and were satisfied with the outcome of their complaint, compared to an average renewal rate of 68 per cent for customers who experienced no problem).[48]

From September 2009, the FOS has published half-yearly figures on the complaints it has handled about individual, named, firms that had at least 30 new and 30 resolved cases during the period.[49] The figures show the number of new cases and the percentage of closed cases in which the ombudsman service changed the outcome in favour of the consumer. From the same date, the FSA has published regular reports of the overall number of complaints reported by all firms,[50] broken down by type of firm, the products and services complained about and the cause of the complaints, as well as overall figures on the number of complaints closed within eight weeks and the proportion of complaints upheld or rejected

---

[45] The test case procedure has not been applied, although one insurance firm did seek to invoke the test case procedure over the impact of the Icelandic volcano on travel insurance claims, but the ombudsman said it was inappropriate in the circumstances of the particular case.

[46] *Discussion Paper 10/1. Consumer Complaints (Emerging Risks and Mass Claims)* Financial Ombudsman Service, Financial Services Authority and Office of Fair Trading, March 2010) at http://www.fsa.gov.uk/pages/library/policy/DP/2010/10_01.shtml. In 2009, firms were recording around 3 million consumer complaints per year. This number excluded complaints resolved by the close of the next business day, which the FSA did not require firms to report. The FOS upheld 56% of complaints in favour of the consumer it resolved during 2009, which it concluded indicated that some firms might not be handling consumer complaints fairly.

[47] *Financial Risk Outlook 2010*, FSA, March 2010, 69.

[48] The Leadership Factor, Association of British Insurers Complaint Management Seminar, 1 December 2009.

[49] www.ombudsman-complaints-data.org.uk.

[50] The figures which firms report do not include the complaints which have been resolved to the satisfaction of the complainant by the close of the next business day.

by firms.[51] From 2010, the FSA required firms receiving 500 or more reportable complaints in any six-month period to publish details of the complaints received in the period as well as details of all the complaints closed in the same period. The FSA/FCA then aggregates the data and publishes it by firm.[52]

As part of the adoption of delivering more intensive and intrusive supervision coupled with credible deterrence, the FSA considered that complaint data was able to provide a highly valuable overview of firms' activities, and it made arrangements to ensure that complaint handling data consistently informs its supervision of firms' conduct.[53]

> The FSA considers that complaints data does not, by itself, necessarily provide evidence that an individual firm is treating complainants unfairly. But it does provide a basis for the FSA to challenge and make judgements about individual firms. For example, patterns of high ombudsman service uphold rates could be evidence that there might be problems with the complaint handling procedures in some firms. This can lead to further work, including in-depth assessments of firms' complaint handling.[54]

C. New and Emerging Issues

Recognising that trends in complaints data can help reveal common failings in firms' conduct, and that where these are identified early the regulators have an opportunity to head-off issues before they become widespread, a revised system was put in place for identifying emerging risks.[55] The Co-ordination Committee[56] considers:

— Whether new and emerging risks that have been identified are likely to result in mass claims if mitigation is not put in place; and
— the relative merits of dealing with particular issues by regulatory action or by means of individual complaints.

The committee comprises the FCA,[57] the OFT, the FOS. The FCA also liaises with the Claims Management Regulator, which includes the sharing of intelligence.[58] The committee may

---

[51] www.fsa.gov.uk/Pages/Library/Other_publications/complaints_data/index.shtml.

[52] FSA originally proposed to publish the complaints returns submitted to it by firms. The industry argued that this would be unlawful, as this was confidential information collected for another purpose. FSA's solution was to require the firms to publish, which meant the data were no longer confidential, so FSA could then republish them itself.

[53] *Consumer Complaints (Emerging Risks and Mass Claims): Feedback on DP10/1* (FOS, FSA, OFT, March 2011) at http://www.fsa.gov.uk/pubs/discussion/fs11_02.pdf.

[54] *Discussion Paper 10/1. Consumer Complaints (Emerging Risks and Mass Claims)* (n 46) para 3.37.

[55] The first case study related to precipice bonds, which involve a lump sum with a guaranteed high income level but the small print says that if the stock market falls below a certain level the investor's 'guaranteed' income would come out of capital. There were a number of cases against one bank, mostly involving older customers, located right across the country, who were targeted through a phone call, hence indicating a formal policy rather than local practice. FOS informed the FSA, and the bank was fined £1.7m, and the FSA also indicated that consumers in a defined group should automatically be compensated, with others being entitled to go to FOS.

[56] The minutes of the Coordination Committee are published at http://www.fsa.gov.uk/Pages/Library/Other_publications/coordination/index.shtml.

[57] The FCA's role includes undertaking comprehensive risk analysis and research to identify, at an earlier stage, the sources and nature of risks to retail customers: *A New Approach to Financial Regulation: Building a Stronger System*, HM Treasury, February 2011, at www.hm-treasury.gov.uk/d/consult_newfinancial_regulation170211.pdf.

[58] See *Memorandum of Understanding between the FSA and the CMR*, at http://www.fsa.gov.uk/pubs/mou/fsa_cmr.pdf.

decide to seek information from the industry or consumer bodies. If the regulator sets a clear timetable for regulatory action, the FOS can decide whether or not it would be appropriate to put cases on hold. Once the regulator has taken regulatory action, the FOS can decide whether or not it would be appropriate to dismiss complaints. The consultation stated that:

> A useful guide to whether an issue should be treated as being potentially widespread is whether it involves (or is likely to involve):
>
> — a number of firms;
> — 5,000 or more complaints referred (or likely to be referred) to the ombudsman service; and
> — the underlying cause of complaints is very similar.[59]

The authorities noted that in some instances, only the courts can provide an authoritative answer on the legal effect of a contractual term underlying a mass claim, for example when the law is unclear.[60] An example occurred in relation to a lengthy dispute over the level of bank charges.[61] Determination of the law can then be implemented by all concerned, although since regulators do not have the facilities to consider individual cases, such individual determinations that are not resolved between firms and customers would continue to fall to the ombudsman service or the courts.

D. Development of Consumer Redress Policy and Powers

The development of consumer redress preceded the 2013 enforcement policies, so it is helpful to review the issues in that order. The FCA may apply to the court for a Restitution Order,[62] or may make such an Order itself where it is satisfied that an authorised person has contravened a relevant requirement, or been knowingly concerned in the contravention of such a requirement, and either that profits have accrued to him as a result of the contravention, or that one or more persons have suffered loss or been otherwise adversely affected as a result of the contravention.[63] A potential impediment when deciding whether or not to use restitutionary powers is that a regulator might be affected by other statutory responsibilities, such as maintaining confidence in the system or the financial viability of regulated institutions.

The FSMA 2000 introduced a provision for the Treasury to order the regulator to establish and operate a multi-firm scheme for reviewing past business.[64] Such a scheme could be made if the Treasury are satisfied that there is evidence suggesting that (a) that there has been a widespread or regular failure on the part of authorised persons to comply with rules relating to a particular kind of activity, and (b) that, as a result, private persons have suffered (or will suffer) loss in respect of which authorised persons are (or will be) liable to make compensation payments. The scheme would (a) determine the nature and extent

---

[59] *Discussion Paper 10/1. Consumer Complaints (Emerging Risks and Mass Claims)* (n 46) para 5.22.
[60] ibid, para 5.29.
[61] *Office of Fair Trading v Abbey National plc & Others* [2009] UKSC 6.
[62] FSMA, s 383. An example is *Financial Services Authority v Anderson* [2010] EWHC 1547 (Civ), para 74, in which £115 million was recovered by the FSA.
[63] FSMA, s 384.
[64] FSMA, s 404.

of the failure, (b) establish the liability of authorised persons to make compensation payments, and (c) determine the amounts payable by way of compensation payments.

This scheme was cumbersome,[65] and not formally used in the subsequent decade. However, as noted in examples given below, an overwhelming number, if not all, of the cases where it might have been used were resolved through settlements that resulted in agreed payment of redress. Regrettably, little publicity was given to such redress payments at that stage.

During this period, 'the FSA waited for clear evidence that a product had been mis-sold and consumers harmed before it took action'.[66] Financial regulators that had an overarching statutory responsibility of maintaining confidence in the system or the financial viability of regulated institutions, and were not historically mandated to go into details of individual products, might be understandably inhibited in deciding whether or not to use restitutionary powers in individual instances. However, that restrictive approach changed.

The FSA issued a consultation on its new enforcement policy of 2009, which firmly adopted 'restorative justice' principles: It lists disgorgement (removing the benefit of any breach), discipline (penalties for offenders) and deterrence (of the offender from committing further breaches and of others from committing similar breaches in future), in that order.[67]

At this time, many claims had emerged against financial institutions as a result of their extended previous and inadequately supervised conduct. The two largest examples were mortgage endowments (over 400,000 such cases brought to the FOS), and mis-selling of payment protection insurance (PPI)[68] (over 500,000 cases brought to the FOS, many more to banks).[69] PPI claims became the largest category of claims made to the FOS, and mushroomed hugely in numbers. The total paid out for mis-sold PPI between January 2011 and January 2013 exceeded £8 billion, and in 2011/2012 there were 157,716 PPI cases (60 per cent of new cases), making a total of 355,059 since 2007.[70] By July 2014 the total cost of PPI redress was estimated to be £22 billion.[71]

---

[65] For example, s 404(1)(b) required consumers to have a private law remedy, and the FSA was required to implement detailed rules. The restitutionary powers under ss 382–84 are less unwieldy and were invoked on occasion by the FSA. However, voluntary arrangements were not impeded by such barriers.

[66] Sullivan (n 23) para 117.

[67] *FSA Consultation Paper [CP09/19] on Enforcement of Financial Penalties* at http://www.fsa.gov.uk/pubs/cp/cp09_19.pdf, para 2.10; Final rules in *FSA Policy Paper PS10/4: Enforcement Financial Penalties—Feedback on CP09/19* (FSA, 26 February 2010), http://www.fsa.gov.uk/pages/Library/Policy/Policy/2010/10_04.shtml. The order in which the three objectives appeared, as listed here, is interesting but not intended to prioritise any one over the others: Personal communication with FCA. In practice, in a case where consumers suffer loss, the FCA will normally agree a redress scheme, in which case the disgorgement element of the penalty will not be applied. If a disgorgement penalty is applied, normally where there is no clearly defined class of consumers who have suffered loss, the penalty is paid to the FCA, and ultimately to HM Treasury less enforcement costs. Personal communication with FCA, April 2014.

[68] 'PPI was a major retail market, with sales of over 5 million policies a year during 2000 to 2005, with premiums in the region of £7 billion a year. It was very profitable for firms. Often the underlying loan served as a loss leader on which to sell PPI. It was targeted at consumers taking on debt, many of whom were financially vulnerable, as their focus was typically on securing the loan with the insurance incidental to the transaction.' *The Financial Conduct Authority: Approach to Regulation* (Financial Services Authority, June 2011) para 5.12.

[69] See *Finalised Guidance. Payment Protection Products. FSA/OFT Joint Guidance* (Office of Fair Trading and FSA, 2013).

[70] *Annual Review, Fnancial Year 2011/2012 of Consumer Complaints about Insurance, Credit, Banking, Savings, Investments* (Financial Ombudsman Service, 2013) at www.financial-ombudsman.org.uk/publications/ar12/ar12.pdf.

[71] J Cusick, 'Banks under threat from £22bn mis-selling scandal' *Independent* (London, 19 July 2014).

Historically, the FSA had not wanted to get involved in such mass redress issues.[72] Neither did the Labour government wish the FSA to get involved: Prime Minister Blair publicly criticised the FSA for being too heavy handed. The FOS wrote formally to the FSA requesting the FSA to resolve this conundrum. Eventually, in September 2009, the FSA set out a proposal for guidance on the fair assessment and redress of complaints related to sales of PPI, and *rules requiring firms to re-assess*, against the proposed new guidance, complaints about PPI sales.[73] The banks then challenged the Guidance through judicial review, but lost.[74]

It was also observed that potentially conflicting legal objectives apply to the regulator and ombudsman. On the one hand, the regulator seeks a result which is broadly fair across the market as a whole. On the other hand, the Ombudsman is required by law to decide what is fair in the circumstances in the individual case for those who complain, as noted above. This situation might result in inconsistent decisions between the two institutions. The solution was to provide for the regulator to accept responsibility for imposing a solution that the FOS would then be bound to apply.

The 2009 consultation on *Consumer Complaints (Emerging Risks and Mass Claims)* summarised the FSA's strategy at that stage as being based on 'more intensive and intrusive supervision coupled with credible deterrence'. It defined the last concept as:

> Credible deterrence involves the FSA taking a more proactive approach to enforcement and using all of its powers to deliver its mandate. During 2009 the FSA:
>
> — took enforcement action against four firms, which led them to proactively contact around 400,000 consumers and offer full redress (with the redress payable by one firm alone exceeding £7.7 million);
> — imposed fines of nearly £3.6 million on three firms for failing to treat their customers fairly and for inadequate complaint handling; and
> — withdrew approval of two persons for complaint handling failures.[75]

The Treasury's 2009 White Paper *Reforming Financial Markets* asked the Retail Financial Services Forum to consider processes that would incentivise firms to close down new and emerging issues proactively, with little or no need for regulatory action, so that fewer risks go on to become mass claims.[76] In 2010, the statutory bodies noted:

> Mass claims typically hinge on widespread or common sales practices or contracts that are alleged to amount to mis-selling or an unfair contract term. It is primarily the responsibility of regulators to resolve these. In this context:
>
> 1. the FSA and the OFT can consider action to address the underlying issues (whether or not affected customers have made an individual complaint); but

---

[72] The effort involved was minimal compared with that required for private litigation: The FSA estimated in 2012 that a typical section 404 case required 0.4FTE of legal work and 0.1 FTE of policy work for a period of around three months. *Impact Assessment. Private Actions in Competition Law: A Consultation on Options for Reform* (Department for Business, Innovation & Skills, 2012) at http://www.bis.gov.uk/assets/biscore/consumer-issues/docs/p/12-743-private-actions-in-competition-law-impact-assessment.

[73] http://www.fsa.gov.uk/pages/Library/Corporate/Annual/ar09_10.shtml.

[74] *R (on the application of the British Bankers' Association) v Financial Services Authority* [2011] EWHC 999 (Admin).

[75] *Discussion Paper 10/1. Consumer Complaints (Emerging Risks and Mass Claims)* (n 46) para 3.16.

[76] The Retail Financial Services Forum is a high-level group, sponsored by HM Treasury, where representatives of industry, consumers, regulators and the ombudsman service can discuss strategic issues concerning retail financial services.

2. the ombudsman service can only consider the cases of affected consumers who have complained to the firm and then gone on to refer their complaint to the ombudsman.[77]

A judicial representative claim was tabled by the Labour government in 2009 to be a last resort[78] but was unacceptable to the Conservative opposition[79] and was dropped in the swift 'wash up' of Parliamentary business when the general election was called in early 2010. However, a proposal to expand the regulator's power to impose a redress solution (see below) survived.

E. The Consumer Redress Scheme Powers

In 2010, the consumer redress scheme was invented to address the issues.[80] The text of the amended section 404 is at Appendix 1 below. In short, the regulator considers whether a widespread problem exists and a court would award redress to consumers.[81] The regulator can make rules requiring a relevant firm to establish and operate a consumer redress scheme, which may include requirements for the firm to investigate whether it has failed to comply with the law, to determine whether the failure has caused or may cause loss to consumers, to determine what the redress should be, and to make the redress to the consumers.[82] Where a consumer makes a complaint to the Ombudsman in relation to an act or omission of a firm that is covered by a consumer redress scheme, the Ombudsman is required to determine the complaint by reference to what, in the Ombudsman's opinion, the determination under the consumer redress scheme should be or should have been, and may make an appropriate payment award.[83] In effect, therefore, the Ombudsman applies the solution mandated by the regulator, and decides if the business has done what the regulator required.

---

[77] *Discussion Paper 10/1. Consumer Complaints (Emerging Risks and Mass Claims)* (n 46) para 5.7.

[78] Financial Services Bill, clauses 18–25, which proposed that an individual may bring representative proceedings on behalf of others who are entitled to bring proceedings of the same, similar or related issues of fact or law, subject to the court approval of a collective proceedings order. The court would decide on whether an opt-in or opt-out model would apply. Extensive subsidiary regulations and rules are envisaged: See Draft court rules for collective proceedings by the Civil Justice Council at http://www.civiljusticecouncil.gov.uk/files/CJC_Draft_Rules_for_Collective_Actions_Feb_2010.pdf.

[79] The Labour government was also greatly concerned about introducing a collective action procedure, since it would at that stage have exposed every local government authority to equal pay collective actions. In the subsequent Equality Act, a proposed collective action procedure was dropped, and instead the mechanism that was passed imposed a duty on local authorities to have a stated policy on equal pay, which would equalise pay over time and could be policed through judicial review.

[80] Financial Services Act 2010, ss 14 and 26(3), significantly extending s 404 of the FSMA. The new rules were brought into force from 12 October 2010 by The Financial Services Act 2010 (Commencement No 1 and Transitional Provision) Order 2010/2480. The FSA decided not to apply for civil sanction powers under RESA since it concluded that having them would not make a material difference to the effectiveness of its enforcement action.

[81] FSMA s 404, as amended by Financial Services Act 2010, s 14: The power for the Authority to make rules requiring each relevant firm (or each relevant firm of a specified description) to establish and operate a consumer redress scheme arises where it appears to the Authority that there has been a widespread failure to comply with applicable requirements and as a result, consumers have suffered loss or damage in respect of which, if they brought legal proceedings, a remedy or relief would be available.

[82] FSMA s 404 (4)–(7). A firm may apply to the Tribunal for a review of any rules made by the Authority: s 404D.

[83] FSMA s 404B. The award is subject to the Ombudsman's upper limit, but he may recommend that the firm pay a larger amount: s 404B(5) and (6).

In addition, the regulator was given a power under section 404F(7) to apply a redress scheme to a single firm. This is not a 'consumer redress scheme'[84] but the similar result is achieved by the Authority altering a firm's permissions or authorisation to operate,[85] and can be done either at the request of the firm or on the Authority's initiative. The Authority may include the same requirements on the individual firm as under section 404, and apply the Ombudsman's jurisdiction as under section 404B. In effect, therefore, the regulator's decision on a scheme alters the basis on which the Ombudsman considers cases that fall under the scheme (the question being whether the relevant company has followed the requirements of the scheme in compensation decisions affecting its customers, rather than whether the matter complained about was fair).

The result is that, both under a 'consumer redress scheme' under section 404(1) or a single firm scheme under section 404F(7), a procedure for handling mass claims is put in place. Under this procedure, the initial complaint handling and spontaneous repayment is to be undertaken by the relevant firm(s), and consumers may then apply to the Ombudsman. In either case, the Ombudsman's basis of decision has been amended by the regulator to that of applying the terms of the scheme. The Ombudsman may, of course, consider cases which fall outside the scope of the scheme or variation of permission, on the normal basis (applying the criterion of fairness). Public accountability for a redress scheme exists through the regulator, who has to consult before imposing the scheme, and through firms' right of appeal to the Tribunal. Guidance expands on the statute, and states that a consumer redress scheme is a set of rules under which a firm is required to take one or more of the following steps:

(a)   Investigate whether, on or after a specific date, it has failed to comply with particular requirements that are applicable to an activity it has been carrying on;
(b)   determine whether the failure has caused (or may cause) loss or damage to consumers;
(c)   determine what the redress should be in respect of the failure; and make the redress to the consumers.[86]

F. Powers on Pro-Active Review by Traders

In 2011, the FSA introduced four linked measures to require firms to take pro-active steps to deliver collective redress:[87]

1.   New obligation on firms to carry out proactive reviews of their complaints and sales: This was first introduced in guidance in November 2007,[88] but that left it to firms to decide when proactive redress would be appropriate; the FSA subsequently made it clear that it expects firms to carry out customer contact exercises in most cases where a systemic problem is identified; consultation paper CP11/10 introduces new guidance as of September 2011, providing further details of when proactive reviews are required.

---

[84]   It is referred to as 'a scheme which corresponds to, or is similar to, a consumer redress scheme'.
[85]   The FCA Register states firm's permissions.
[86]   Guidance note No 10 (FSA, 2010). See Consumer Redress Schemes sourcebook, at http://fshandbook.info/FS/html/FCA/CONRED.
[87]   See Consultation Paper CP11/10.
[88]   DISP 1.3.5G.

2. A requirement that in doing so they take account of decisions of the FOS; FSMA section 225 states that the purpose of the FOS is to provide a scheme under which certain disputes may be resolved 'quickly and with minimum formality'. FSA expects firms to take account also of FOS' published online decisions, as well as decisions that they receive directly:[89] By November 2010, published contents covered more than 90 per cent of FOS' caseload, so firms should be able to judge what complaints FOS is likely to uphold.
3. New rules requiring firms to provide the FSA with complaints handling data.
4. A requirement from September 2011 for a firm to appoint an 'approved person' individual with official responsibility for oversight of the firm's compliance with complaints handling rules.[90]

G. Examples of Redress Cases

In the decade in which the original powers under FSMA 2000 applied, redress was paid in a number of significant cases that resulted from action by the FSA,[91] although usually as a result of agreed settlements and any redress element was given little publicity, so little information is identifiable.[92] Cases often involved a voluntary agreement to pay redress rather than being agreed as part of the settlement of official action (such as in the Abbey case). Over time, the FSA became more keen to publicise the redress element of a settlement.[93] In 2011–12 a total in excess of £150 million was secured by the FSA in redress for consumers.[94]

In the first two years of the new regime from 2010 described above, a number of cases were resolved through the intervention of the regulator with firms, in different ways. The amount of redress the firm has to pay can be well in excess of the fine.[95] First, a series of cases was dealt with under section 404F(7):

—   One case involving Bank of Scotland related to interest rate variation on Halifax tracker mortgages. The interest rate was Bank of England base rate plus a percentage, which varied. The issue was that the variations were applied in a questionable way.

---

[89] Under the guidance in DISP 1.4.2 G 'factors that may be relevant in the assessment of a complaint ... include ... appropriate analysis of decisions by [FOS] concerning similar complaints received by the respondent...' This refers back to the more general guidance in DISP 1.3.2A G.

[90] DISP 1.3.7R.

[91] See Egg Banking (PPI mis-selling, Dec 08), see para 2.6(5), at http://www.fsa.gov.uk/pubs/final/egg.pdf; AWD Chase de Vere (unsuitable advice regarding its pension transfer, pension annuity and income withdrawal business, Nov 08), see para 2.5(4), at http://www.fsa.gov.uk/pubs/final/awd.pdf; Alliance and Leicester (PPI mis-selling, Oct 08), see para 2.7(5), at http://www.fsa.gov.uk/pubs/final/alliance_leicester.pdf; GE Capital Bank (PPI mis-selling, Jan 07), see paras 2.4 and 2.6, at http://www.fsa.gov.uk/pubs/final/gecb.pdf;

Abbey National (complaints mishandling, May 05), see para 2.9(1), at http://www.fsa.gov.uk/pubs/final/abbey_25may05.pdf; Capita Trust Company (precipice bonds mis-selling, October 04), see para 2.9(3), at http://www.fsa.gov.uk/pubs/final/capita_20oct04.pdf.

[92] Personal communications between the author and members of the Enforcement and Financial Crime Division of the FCA, noted in the Acknowledgements to this book.

[93] See recently *Enforcement Annual Performance Account 2010/11* (FSA, 2011) para 21, at http://www.fsa.gov.uk/pubs/annual/ar10_11/enforcement_report.pdf.

[94] *Enforcement Annual Performance Account 2011/12* (FSA, 2012) para 19, at http://www.fsa.gov.uk/static/pubs/annual/ar11-12/enforcement-report.pdf.

[95] See eg the CPP press release: http://www.fsa.gov.uk/library/communication/pr/2012/102.shtml. In 2012 the FCA secured over £150 million in redress for consumers.

The regulator ruled that letters were to be sent to all customers, and reached agreement with the bank that the latter would automatically compensate some borrowers. £30 million was paid in compensation fairly quickly and without having to complain. Significantly, the FSA agreed that other borrowers were *not* entitled to compensation. That formal agreement therefore pre-empted other litigation.

— Welcome Financial Services Ltd got into severe financial difficulties after mis-selling PPI. It reached an agreement with the Financial Services Compensation Scheme and the FSA.

— Three arrangements related to the manager and two depositaries involved in Arch Cru funds, which promised high returns and were in fact speculative investments made through Guernsey. The facts were complicated and there was no proof that the managers, Capita, had done anything wrong. However, the following variations in permissions providing compensation arrangements were agreed:
   a. Capita, the managers.
   b. HSBC, depositary of one of the funds.
   c. BNY Mellon, depositary of another of the funds.

Second, a 'consumer redress scheme' was made under section 404 in relation to intermediaries involved in Arch Cru funds.[96]

Third, various other arrangements were agreed 'in the shadow' of the rules, without the formal powers being invoked. One arrangement concerned interest rate hedging products (IRHPs), which were sold to small and medium sized firms. An FSA review in 2012 found serious failings in the sale of IRHPs by four banks. After discussions, those four banks, followed by nine others, had agreed to review their sales. A pilot review of sales to 'non-sophisticated' customers from the first four banks found that over 90 per cent did not comply with one or more regulatory requirements, and that the involvement of independent reviewers plays a vital role in ensuring that outcomes for customers are fair and reasonable. The banks undertook to continue their internal reviews and to achieve fair and reasonable redress in each non-compliant case, according to a set of principles about outcomes, depending on whether the customer would have purchased the same product in any event, or would not have done so, or would have purchased a different product.[97]

A further voluntary arrangement was applied by banks to cash-machine (ATM) withdrawals covering a certain period from 2009 and the date of new rules, where a customer walked away from the ATM leaving the money behind, after which the machine swallowed it and the customer's account remained debited. It appears that the retail banks instituted voluntary action to credit relevant customers after regulators approached the banks against the background of the regulator's powers to go further.

In 2014, the FCA fined Credit Suisse International £2,398,100 and Yorkshire Building Society £1,429,000 (both at Stage 1, therefore including a 30 per cent discount) for failing to ensure that promotions of a structured product (Cliquet product, designed to

[96] *Consumer Redress Scheme in Respect of Unsuitable Advice to Invest in Arch Cru Funds: Consultation Paper* (FSA, CP12/9, April 2012) available at http://www.fsa.gov.uk/static/pubs/cp/cp12-09.pdf.
[97] *Interest Rate Hedging Products. Pilot Findings* (FSA, 31 January 2013), http://www.fsa.gov.uk/static/pubs/other/interest-rate-swaps-2013.pdf.

provide capital protection and a guaranteed minimum return with potential for significantly greater return if the FTSE 100 performed consistently well), were clear, fair and not
misleading, since the promotions highlighted the maximum return whilst the chances of
investors receiving it were 'close to zero'. Both companies agreed to contact customers who
bought the Cliquet product between 1 November 2009 and 17 June 2012 to offer them the
chance to exit the product without penalty and with interest paid up to the date of exit.[98]

H. Enforcement Policies of the Agencies

In May 2010, the FSA had issued its policy document on future regulation to protect investors and the global primacy of the UK market.[99] This noted the FSA's statutory obligations,
derived from the FSMA 2000, to ensure that markets are efficient, orderly, fair, internationally attractive and sustainable. The FSA's policy was to pursue appropriate regulatory
standards and resist regulatory arbitrage. They considered it important to maintain market confidence. The document avoided mentioning compensation or rectification issues: It
stated that default arrangements should allow transactions with a defaulting market participant to be handled in a timely and efficient manner, and the outcome be consistent
with the contracting parties' reasonable expectations.[100] In combating insider dealing and
market manipulation, the FSA stated that it would continue to pursue a policy of credible
deterrence, which entails devoting substantial resources to surveillance, investigating suspi-
cious transactions and applying the full range of civil and criminal prosecution tools, so
that those caught are punished.[101]

As described in chapter 20, under the new model of regulation from 2013, the Financial Policy Committee (FPC), within the Bank of England, is responsible for protecting
the stability of the financial system as a whole and macro-prudential regulation. The PRA
is a subsidiary of the Bank of England, supervising deposit takers, insurers and a small
number of significant investment firms at a more granular level than the FCA. The FCA
is then responsible for regulating conduct in retail and wholesale markets (including both
exchange-operated markets and over-the-counter (OTC) dealing); supervising the trading
infrastructure that supports those markets; and for the prudential regulation of firms not
prudentially regulated by the PRA.

Documents setting out the approach to supervision and to enforcement were issued for
the Bank of England, the PRA and the FCA from 2013, and are considered below. In May
2014 the Treasury launched a review of the fairness, transparency, speed and efficiency of
the institutional arrangements and processes for enforcement decision making at the FCA
and PRA.[102]

[98] FCA Press release at http://www.fca.org.uk/news/fca-fines-credit-suisse-and-yorkshire-building-society-
for-financial-promotions-failures.
[99] *The FSA's Market Regulatory Agenda* (Financial Services Authority, 2010).
[100] ibid, para 4.16.
[101] ibid, para 4.41.
[102] *Review of Enforcement Decision-making at the Financial Services Regulators: Call for Evidence* (HM Treasury,
2014).

i. Enforcement Policy of the Bank of England

The Bank's approach to the supervision of securities settlement systems, central counter-parties and recognised payment systems stated in relation to enforcement:[103]

> The Bank, where practicable, seeks to supervise with the support of FMIs and their participants, having clearly explained the risk rationale for its supervisory priorities and actions. The Bank's supervision is, however, conducted in the shadow of the powers granted by Parliament, and these powers will be used where necessary to effect change.

> The Bank hopes that it will not need to make regular use of powers to direct, and that it will not face cases where an institution fails to act in accordance with a direction. Should this occur, how-ever, public censure and financial penalties may be applied to supervised FMIs, qualifying parent undertakings or, in certain circumstances, action may be taken against individuals employed by the supervised FMIs. Where the Bank imposes a financial penalty, proceeds will be transferred by the Bank to the Treasury so that it can benefit the taxpaying public.[104,105]

ii. Enforcement Policy of the PRA

The PRA's approach to enforcement in banking supervision was stated to be a preference to 'use its powers to secure *ex ante*, remedial action, given its approach of intervening early to address emerging risks,' but it does have 'a set of disciplinary powers, including the power to impose financial penalties or publish public censures, for cases where such a sanction is an appropriate response to the firm failing to meet the PRA's regulatory requirements.'[106]

> The intention in deploying disciplinary powers might include: reinforcing the PRA's objective and priorities; changing, and promoting high standards of, regulatory behaviour; the need to send a clear signal to a firm, and to the regulated community more widely, about the circumstances in which the PRA considers a firm's behaviour to be unacceptable; and deterring future misconduct.[107]

It also holds powers against individuals (Approved Persons).

The PRA's statutory statements of policy[108] on enforcement cover (in some detail) its enforcement decision-making procedures, issue of statutory notices, imposition and

---

[103] *The Bank of England's Approach to the Supervision of Financial Market Infrastructures* (Bank of England, April 2013), available at http://www.bankofengland.co.uk/financialstability/Documents/fmi/fmisupervision.pdf.

[104] Footnote from original source: In some cases a part of the penalty may be used to meet costs incurred by the Bank in enforcement.

[105] See www.hm-treasury.gov.uk/press_90_12.htm.

[106] *The Prudential Regulation Authority's Approach to Banking Supervision* (PRA, April 2013) paras 199 and 200, available at http://www.bankofengland.co.uk/publications/Documents/praapproach/bankingappr1304.pdf. See also *The Prudential Regulation Authority's Approach to Insurance Supervision* (PRA, April 2013) available at http://www.bankofengland.co.uk/publications/Documents/praapproach/insuranceappr1304.pdf. The prior con-sultation contained a number of differences: *The PRA's Approach to Enforcement: Consultation on Proposed Statu-tory Statements of Policy and Procedure* (The Bank of England, Prudential Regulation Authority, December 2012) CP12/39, at http://www.fsa.gov.uk/static/pubs/cp/cp12-39.pdf. The consultation draft stated that it 'will always aim for a focused, proportionate and fair outcome in each case' (para 1.6) and that a key element of the PRA's regulatory approach is the personal responsibility of a PRA-authorised firm's board of directors and senior man-agement to ensure that the firm is run prudently (para 3.2). It also referred to the possibility of imposing a punitive sanction.

[107] *The Prudential Regulation Authority's Approach to Banking Supervision* (PRA, April 2013) para 201.

[108] The PRA is required to give a statement of its proposed procedures regarding decisions that create an obli-gation to give a statutory notice under FSMA (required by s 395(5)); a statement of the PRA's proposed policy on the imposition and amount of penalties under FSMA (required by ss 63C(1), 69(1), 192N(1) and 210(1)); a

amount of financial penalties, imposition of suspensions and restrictions, settlement procedure, policy for the determination of the amount of penalties, approach to publicity of regulatory action, and the conduct of investigative interviews.[109] The PRA operates through a number of internal committees and decision-making procedures in relation to taking regulatory and sanctioning decisions, depending on their severity.

In determining whether to impose a financial penalty, the PRA will consider the individual features of each case, including factors such as:[110]

(a) The impact or potential impact of the misconduct on the stability of the financial system.
(b) The seriousness of the breach.
(c) The extent of the person's responsibility for the breach.
(d) The conduct of the person after the breach was committed.
(e) Any previous disciplinary and/or supervisory record of the person.
(f) Relevant guidance provided by the PRA, FCA and/or any predecessor regulators, which existed and was in force at the time of the behaviour in question.
(g) Any relevant action by other domestic and/or international regulatory authorities or law enforcement agencies (including whether, if such agencies are taking or propose to take relevant action regarding the behaviour in question, it is necessary or desirable for the PRA also to take its own separate action).

Steps may be taken to publish a statement of the person's misconduct (public censure).[111] Particular provisions apply to approved persons, persons who perform a controlled function without approval, and parent undertakings.[112] In determining the amount of the financial penalty, a five-step approach will be applied:[113]

(1) Step 1: Where relevant, the disgorgement of any economic benefits derived from the breach.
(2) Step 2: The determination of a 'starting point' figure for a financial penalty having regard to the seriousness of the breach and the size and financial position of the firm or the income of the individual that committed the breach.
(3) Step 3: Where appropriate, an adjustment to the figure determined at Step 2 to take account of any aggravating, mitigating or other relevant circumstances.

statement of the PRA's proposed policy on the imposition and period of suspensions or restrictions under FSMA (required by ss 69(1) and 210(1)).4; a statement of how a potential PRA policy on the settlement of cases involving the imposition of financial penalties, suspensions or restrictions may look if implemented; a statement of the PRA's proposed policy on the publication of disciplinary and other enforcement actions (in part required by section 395); and a statement of the PRA's proposed policy regarding the conduct of certain interviews at the request of overseas regulators (required by s 169(9)).

[109] *The Prudential Regulation Authority's Approach to Enforcement: Statutory Statements of Policy and Procedure* (PRA, April 2013) available at http://www.bankofengland.co.uk/publications/Documents/other/pra/approach-enforcement.pdf.
[110] ibid, Annex: Statement of the PRA's Policy on the Imposition and Amount of Financial Penalties under the Act, para 3.
[111] ibid, para 4.
[112] ibid, paras 7–11.
[113] ibid, para 3.8.

(4)   Step 4: Where appropriate, an upwards adjustment to the figure determined following Steps 2 and 3, to ensure that the penalty has an appropriate and effective deterrent effect.

(5)   Step 5: if applicable, one or both of the following factors may be applied to the figure determined following Steps 2, 3 and 4:

  a.   a settlement discount;[114]

  b.   an adjustment based on any serious financial hardship which the PRA considers payment of the penalty would cause the firm or individual.

The overall penalty arrived at must be 'appropriate and proportionate to the relevant breach'.[115] Each of the above considerations is expanded in the Statement, listing a series of factors. For example, in relation to Step 4:

> 27. If the PRA considers the penalty determined following steps 2 and 3 is insufficient effectively to deter the person who committed the breach and/or others who are subject to the PRA's regulatory requirements from committing similar or other breaches, it may increase the penalty at step 4 by making an appropriate deterrence adjustment to it.
>
> 28. The circumstances in which the PRA may make a deterrence adjustment to the penalty include:
>
> (a)   Where the PRA considers the value of the penalty is too small in relation to the breach to achieve effective deterrence.
>
> (b)   Where previous action by the PRA, FCA and/or any predecessor regulators in respect of the same or a similar breach has failed to improve or sufficiently improve the relevant standards of the subject of the PRA's action and/or relevant industry standards.
>
> (c)   Where the PRA considers it likely that, in the absence of a deterrence adjustment, the same or a similar breach will be committed in the future by the relevant firm or individual or by other members of the regulated community more widely.[116]

The PRA's policy on supervision of insurance companies, issued in June 2014, was based on the twin complementary objectives of promoting the safety and soundness of all firms and contributing to the securing of an appropriate degree of protection for those who are or may become policyholders, given that insurers' liabilities involve an inherent uncertainty that does not apply to banks.[117] It noted that contributing to an appropriate degree of policyholder protection and promoting resilience against failure 'does not mean protecting all policyholders in full in all circumstances, not does it mean preventing all instances of failure'.[118] The approach relies significantly on the judgement of supervisors, based on evidence and analysis, and is forward-looking.[119] The PRA aims to engage in dialogue with boards and senior management of insurance companies.[120] In enforcement, its 'preference is to use its powers to secure *ex ante* remedial action' but would use its disciplinary powers

---

[114] See *Statement of the PRA's Settlement Decision-making Procedure and Policy for the Determination and Amount of Penalties and the Period of Suspensions or Restrictions in Settled Cases.*

[115] *The Prudential Regulation Authority's Approach to Enforcement: Statutory Statements of Policy and Procedure* (n 109) para 13.

[116] ibid, paras 27 and 28.

[117] *The Prudential Regulation Authority's Approach to Insurance Supervision* (PRA, 2014).

[118] ibid, 6.

[119] ibid, 6–7.

[120] ibid, 7.

of financial penalties, publishing public censure, instituting criminal proceedings and prohibiting certain individuals, thereby

> changing, and promoting high standards of behavior among firms; sending a clear signal to the insurer, and to the regulated community more widely, about the circumstances in which the PRA considers an insurer's behavior to be unacceptable; and in deterring future misconduct.[121]

iii. Enforcement Policy of the FCA

The FCA stated that it would deliver its responsibility for protecting consumers and markets' regulation from the end of 2012 by adopting 'a new approach to conduct regulation' in the light of a low level of confidence in the financial services sector,[122] after 'the significant instances of widespread mis-selling of financial products to retail consumers' since 1990.[123]

The government stressed the importance of the FCA adopting a distinctive organisational culture and behaviour, but internally and transparently so as to command the respect of consumers and of the firms it regulates. The FCA has the single strategic objective of ensuring that the relevant markets function well and three operational objectives:

— Securing an appropriate degree of protection for consumers;
— promoting effective competition in the interests of consumers in the markets for regulated financial services; and
— protecting a nd enhancing the integrity of the UK financial system.[124]

The government endowed the FCA with new powers in product intervention; to direct firms to withdraw or amend mis-leading financial promotions with immediate effect; and to publish the fact that a warning notice in relation to a disciplinary matter has been issued. A key task is

> to ensure that the conduct of participants is compatible with fair and safe markets. The FCA will, therefore, focus more closely on wholesale conduct than the FSA. It will adopt a more issues and sector-based supervisory approach across the 24,500 firms which it will regulate for conduct and prudential purposes. A considerable investment in resources will be needed to deal with these significant supervisory responsibilities.[125]

---

[121] ibid, paras 223–28.

[122] Consumer research commissioned by the Financial Services Consumer Panel (2008) showed that consumers were confused about the type of advice they receive, unable to distinguish between the different types of advisers. Many people were 'resigned to not getting the best advice when they talk to a financial adviser' (Consumer Panel Website). The Consumer Panel called for a need to distinguish between 'truly independent advice… and mere sales.' Quoted in Sullivan (n 23).

[123] *The Financial Conduct Authority: Approach to Regulation* (n 68) para 1.1. The instances cited included personal pensions, mortgage endowment policies, split capital investment trusts and payment protection insurance (PPI). 'Millions of consumers have suffered detriment on a large-scale and, together, the industry has had to make compensation payments of approximately £15 billion, with most PPI redress still to come. Such outcomes would be regarded as unacceptable in other sectors of the economy.'

[124] ibid, para 1.5. See now ss 1B–1E of FSMA.

[125] ibid, para 1.10. An intermediate step was that the FSA proposed in 2011 that it should seek to identify emerging consumer detriment problems at a far earlier stage, and use new tools of intervention to prevent consumer detriment emerging: revised *Conduct Risk Strategy and the Product Intervention Discussion Paper* (FSA, January 2011).

The government's intention was to establish the FCA as an organisation which will:

promote good outcomes for consumers, through a differentiated and proportionate approach which takes into consideration the knowledge and financial sophistication of the various types of consumer and which promotes competition, so far as is compatible with its objectives;

be more outward-looking and engaged with consumers than the FSA has been, (providing more consumer-oriented and more effective communications) and better informed about their concerns and behaviour where this is relevant to regulatory action;

set clear expectations for firms and be clear about what firms can expect from the FCA;

intervene earlier to tackle potential risks to consumers and market integrity before they crystallise; and

be tougher and bolder, building on and enhancing the FSA's credible deterrence strategy, using its new powers of intervention and enforcement.[126]

The FCA must also have regard to eight regulatory principles, which are now set out in section 3B of FSMA:

1.1 the need to use the resources of each regulator in the most efficient and economic way;

1.2 the principle that a burden or restriction which is imposed on a person, or on the carrying on of an activity, should be proportionate to the benefits, considered in general terms, which are expected to result from the imposition of that burden or restriction;

1.3 the desirability of sustainable growth in the economy of the United Kingdom in the medium or long term;

1.4 the general principle that consumers should take responsibility for their decisions;

1.5 the responsibilities of the senior management of persons subject to requirements imposed by or under this Act, including those affecting consumers, in relation to compliance with those requirements;

1.6 the desirability where appropriate of each regulator exercising its functions in a way that recognises differences in the nature of, and objectives of, businesses carried on by different persons subject to requirements imposed by or under this Act;

1.7 the desirability in appropriate cases of each regulator publishing information relating to persons on whom requirements are imposed by or under this Act, or requiring such persons to publish information, as a means of contributing to the advancement by each regulator of its objectives;

1.8 the principle that the regulators should exercise their functions as transparently as possible.

The FCA will aim to intervene earlier in retail markets to protect consumers before they suffer direct effects as a result of failures in these markets.[127] This duty to protect retail consumers necessitates a focus not only on firms' conduct towards them directly, but also

---

[126] *The Financial Conduct Authority: Approach to Regulation* (n 68) para 1.11.
[127] ibid, para 3.9.

on the knock-on effects and adverse implications that may result from activities in retail-related wholesale markets. This approach entails the following main elements:

Preventative action

The FCA will be ready to intervene in relation to the operation of markets for financial products and services where there is evidence that these are not operating in the interests of retail consumers or the wider economy. The FCA will also be more ready to intervene, making full use of its powers, to tackle potential and emerging risks to consumer protection and market integrity before they materialise, and in order to prevent large-scale detriment.

The FCA will also intervene where the product may be well known and of utility to consumers but the sales and distribution process of a firm does not meet regulatory standards and consumer detriment is occurring.

Causes and symptoms

The FCA will aim to shift the balance towards tackling the root causes of problems, not just the symptoms. The traditional focus on firm conduct at the point of sale has limitations. In particular, when poor conduct is discovered, detriment has already occurred. If this is on a significant scale, market confidence can be damaged.

If the FCA can address the root causes, at least some of the poor outcomes for consumers should be prevented.

Differentiated approach

The FCA will tailor its approach and the use of its regulatory tools, to the particular risks in the sectors, firms and products which it regulates. The emphasis will be more on thematic work, targeting product services and practices which have the potential to cause consumer or market detriment, than on firm-specific risk. The emphasis, however, will continue to be on intensive, institution-specific supervision for those institutions that individually can cause significant consumer or market detriment.

Fair and safe markets

The FCA will intervene proactively to make markets more efficient and resilient, enhancing integrity and choice, taking into account the duty to promote competition.

Engaging with retail consumers

The FCA will focus on reducing and preventing consumer detriment in the retail sector.[128]

A more interventionist stance and lower tolerance for consumer detriment was said to require strong activity in enforcement, and to strengthen a credible deterrence strategy by a penalty framework that provides a stronger link between the benefit a firm receives from its misconduct and the size of the fine.[129] The concept of 'Credible Deterrence' was explained as:

The FSA's credible deterrence strategy is a deliberate strengthening of the enforcement function to achieve better outcomes for consumers and across markets. Under the strategy, the FSA has made

---

[128] ibid, paras 4.3–4.10.
[129] ibid, para 4.13.

full use of its enforcement powers, bringing tough, targeted, public action in areas of risk to its objectives. This has ensured that those who break the law or who do not meet the standards that are rightly expected of them are subject to tough sanctions.

The strategy includes:

1. higher penalties;
2. bringing criminal prosecutions;
3. focusing closely on the responsibility of individuals—especially Significant Influence Function holders…; and
4. in the area of consumer protection, holding firms to account for misconduct and requiring them to make good on the losses they cause consumers.…[130]

A risk-based approach was said to support the FCA's key activities, namely: Supervision, policy, enforcement and authorisation.[131] The FCA would 'require firms to provide prompt and effective redress' and 'ensure that firms are not benefiting from exploitation of market failures'.[132]

The FCA will have additional tools to facilitate consumer redress. It is the government's intention that the new FSA power to establish consumer redress schemes will be given to the FCA. The FCA will be willing to establish such schemes, working with the ombudsman service and other stakeholders, in order to put right consumer detriment where there have been widespread or regular failings in firms' conduct. These schemes should prove a powerful tool which the FCA can use to secure good outcomes for a large number of consumers.

The government has also put forward a proposal that, if and when there may be a need for large-scale consumer redress, there is a clear process in place to ensure that the issue is tackled by the FCA thoroughly and promptly. As indicated in HM Treasury's June 2011 White Paper: *A new approach to financial regulation: the blueprint for reform*, this would provide for a range of organisations, including the ombudsman service and consumer groups, to make a referral where they think that there may be mass consumer detriment. The FCA would be required to respond within a certain time period and, where appropriate, set out the action it intends to take. The government has invited responses to this proposal and, if appropriate, will bring forward legislative provisions when the Bill is introduced.[133]

In July 2013 the FCA issued a statement on how it proposed to approach its three statutory operational objectives of protecting consumers, maintaining market integrity and promoting effective competition.[134] It confirmed that it would operate on a risk-based approach, by identifying, assessing, prioritising, managing and mitigating risks. In relation to protecting consumers, it aimed to:

— Ensure customers are treated in a way that is appropriate for their level of financial knowledge and understanding;

---

[130] ibid.

[131] ibid, para 5.6.

[132] ibid, para 5.40.

[133] ibid, paras 5.41 and 5.42.

[134] *The FCA's Approach to Advancing its Objectives* (FCA, July 2013) available at http://www.fca.org.uk/static/documents/fca-approach-advancing-objectives.pdf. The statement was issued under the category of the guidance, pursuant to the requirement in FSMA s1K that general guidance given by the FCA under s 139A must include guidance about how it intends to advance its operational objectives in discharging its general functions in relation to different categories of authorised person or regulated activity.

— be more outward looking, by engaging more with consumers and understanding more about their concerns and behaviour;
— set clear expectations for firms and be clear about what firms can expect from us;
— intervene early to tackle potential risks to consumers before they take shape;
— be tougher and bolder, following a strategy of credible deterrence, using new powers of intervention and enforcement.

The FCA noted that the six retail outcomes set out in the FSA's earlier Treating Customers Fairly (TCF) initiative[135] remained central to its consumer protection objective, guiding general policy and principles by which it makes rules, prepares and issues codes, and gives general guidance. 'Getting a fair deal for consumers is at the heart of our approach.'

The six outcomes to treating customers fairly

— Outcome 1: Consumers can be confident that they are dealing with firms where the fair treatment of customers is central to the corporate culture.
— Outcome 2: Products and services marketed and sold in the retail market are designed to meet the needs of identified consumer groups and are targeted accordingly.
— Outcome 3: Consumers are provided with clear information and are kept appropriately informed before, during and after the point of sale.
— Outcome 4: Where consumers receive advice, the advice is suitable and takes account of their circumstances.
— Outcome 5: Consumers are provided with products that perform as firms have led them to expect, and the associated service is of an acceptable standard and as they have been led to expect.
— Outcome 6: Consumers do not face unreasonable post-sale barriers imposed by firms to change product, switch provider, submit a claim or make a complaint.

The FCA stated that it would aim to respond to emerging issues quickly, put in place interventions that deal effectively with the underlying problems and anticipate market responses to what it does.

In relation to enforcement, the FCA said that it would follow a strategy of 'credible deterrence, taking tough and meaningful action against the firms and individuals who break our rules as well as those who carry out illegal unauthorised business', supported by a range of regulatory powers, including both civil and criminal prosecution.[136] It would continue to publish case details, 'which can be an effective way of raising awareness of our regulatory standards and deterring future rule-breaking'.[137] Its approach to meeting the consumer protection objective through credible deterrence would be by:

— Bringing more enforcement cases and pressing for tough penalties for infringements of rules;
— removing firms or individuals who do not meet our standards from the industry;

---

[135] www.fca.org.uk/fair-treatment.

[136] The selection method for cases, a description of main information gathering and investigation powers, and the conduct of investigations are set out in the Enforcement Guide, http://fshandbook.info/FS/html/FCA/EG.

[137] Our approach to publicising enforcement action is set out in the Enforcement Guide (see above link) and does not distinguish between different types of authorised firm or regulated activity.

— taking more cases against individuals and holding members of senior management accountable for their actions;
— prioritising compensation for consumers.

It would aim to take action early, including where it considered that 'part of a firm's business model or culture—such as its product selection, training and recruitment, or remuneration practices—are likely to harm consumers'. It also intended to resolve many enforcement cases by early settlement, which would have 'many potential advantages', including that consumers could obtain compensation earlier than would otherwise be the case.[138] It also signalled that it would seek to sanction firms and senior managers.

The FCA's Decision Procedure and Penalties (DEPP) Manual sets out its decision-making procedure for giving statutory notices.[139] It includes a formal early settlement procedure.[140] In deciding whether to take action, the FCA's Handbook lists the following non-exclusive factors:

(1) The nature, seriousness and impact of the suspected breach, including:
    (a) whether the breach was deliberate or reckless;
    (b) the duration and frequency of the breach;
    (c) the amount of any benefit gained or loss avoided as a result of the breach;
    (d) whether the breach reveals serious or systemic weaknesses of the management systems or internal controls relating to all or part of a person's business;
    (e) the impact or potential impact of the breach on the orderliness of markets including whether confidence in those markets has been damaged or put at risk;
    (f) the loss or risk of loss caused to consumers or other market users;
    (g) the nature and extent of any financial crime facilitated, occasioned or otherwise attributable to the breach; and
    (h) whether there are a number of smaller issues, which individually may not justify disciplinary action, but which do so when taken collectively.

(2) The conduct of the person after the breach, including the following:
    (a) how quickly, effectively and completely the person brought the breach to the attention of the FCA or another relevant regulatory authority;
    (b) the degree of co-operation the person showed during the investigation of the breach;
    (c) any remedial steps the person has taken in respect of the breach;
    (d) the likelihood that the same type of breach (whether on the part of the person under investigation or others) will recur if no action is taken;
    (e) whether the person concerned has complied with any requirements or rulings of another regulatory authority relating to his behaviour (for example, where relevant, those of the Takeover Panel or an RIE); and
    (f) the nature and extent of any false or inaccurate information given by the person and whether the information appears to have been given in an attempt to knowingly mislead the FCA.

---

[138] Details of our settlement decision procedure and a description of our approach to settlement can be found in the *Decisions, Procedures and Penalties Manual*, http://fshandbook.info/FS/html/FCA/DEPP and *Enforcement Guide*.

[139] At http://fshandbook.info/FS/html/FCA/DEPP.

[140] DEPP 5.

(3)   The previous disciplinary record and compliance history of the person including:

    (a)   whether the FCA (or any previous regulator) has taken any previous disciplinary action resulting in adverse findings against the person;

    (b)   whether the person has previously undertaken not to do a particular act or engage in particular behaviour;

    (c)   whether the FCA (or any previous regulator) has previously taken protective action in respect of a firm, using its own initiative powers, by means of a variation of a Part 4A permission1 or otherwise, or has previously requested the firm to take remedial action, and the extent to which such action has been taken; and

    (d)   the general compliance history of the person, including whether the FCA (or any previous regulator) has previously issued the person with a private warning.[141]

In determining the appropriate level of financial penalty, the following principles are specified:

(1)   Disgorgement—a firm or individual should not benefit from any breach;

(2)   Discipline—a firm or individual should be penalised for wrongdoing; and

(3)   Deterrence—any penalty imposed should deter the firm or individual who committed the breach, and others, from committing further or similar breaches.[142]

The fine payable is said to be made up of two elements:

  (i)   disgorgement of the benefit received as a result of the breach; and

 (ii)   a financial penalty reflecting the seriousness of the breach.[143]

These elements are incorporated in a five-step framework:

(a)   Step 1: the removal of any financial benefit derived directly from the breach;

(b)   Step 2: the determination of a figure which reflects the seriousness of the breach;

(c)   Step 3: an adjustment made to the Step 2 figure to take account of any aggravating and mitigating circumstances;

(d)   Step 4: an upwards adjustment made to the amount arrived at after Steps 2 and 3, where appropriate, to ensure that the penalty has an appropriate deterrent effect; and

(e)   Step 5: if applicable, a settlement discount will be applied. This discount does not apply to disgorgement of any financial benefit derived directly from the breach.[144]

The Parliamentary Commission on Banking Standards had recommended that regulators be given additional powers to address 'failure of standards at the most senior levels of a bank'. The FCA responded that its existing powers enabled it to address such failings, especially by invoking its Enhanced Supervision regime.[145]

In response to a review of enforcement decision making by the financial service regulators in 2014, the British Bankers Association (BBA) supported the current 'relatively

[141] DEPP 6.
[142] DEPP 6.5.1.
[143] DEPP 6.5.2.
[144] DEPP 6.5.2.
[145] *Tackling Serious Failings in Firms. A Response to the Special Measures Proposal of the Parliamentary Commission on Banking Standards* (FCA, 2014).

informal nature in terms of its relative speed and efficiency'.[146] BBA included the following comments:

> We recognise that regulators frequently come under significant public and political pressure to take strong enforcement action against firms or individuals. It is important, if the enforcement process is to remain fair and credible, for regulators to reserve enforcement action for the most egregious cases, to ensure that penalties imposed are proportionate and to pursue alternative, less draconian and more constructive, avenues in appropriate cases. Enforcement is of course only one of the factors driving a firm's or individual's behaviour and in a sense can be regarded as the negative reasons for compliance (or 'the stick'). Firms will also be driven positively to demonstrate improved conduct standards because it is simply the 'right thing to do' and an important part of rebuilding the trust of customers and shareholders across the industry. Other initiatives, both on the part of regulators and the industry—whether early intervention, the introduction of the senior managers and certification regimes or work relating to professionalism and values— are positive in nature and seek to reduce the need for enforcement action in the first place. The extent to which these positive drivers (or 'carrots') are a factor must also be weighed up alongside the 'stick' of the enforcement processes when considering the effectiveness of enforcement as a deterrent.

> As regards what is meant by 'credible deterrence', we believe this is a complex concept. From both an industry and consumer perspective it is important that regulators are clear and consistent in confirming the objective measures they will rely upon to demonstrate that credible deterrence is actually being achieved. Deterrence cannot, for instance, be proven simply by pointing to the scale of financial penalties imposed on the industry or on individuals over comparative periods. Rather, it must be based on a far deeper analysis of the role of enforcement processes, inter alia, in changing the types of organisational and individual behaviours that have, in the past, led to regulatory breaches.

> By way of example of the dangers of taking too simplistic an approach on this issue, it is important to remember that a significant proportion of recent enforcements relate to historic behaviour— in some cases behaviour pre-dating the 2008 financial crisis. If, however, one were simply to look at the rising trend in number of enforcements and scale of fines in isolation, one might form the misleading impression that the underlying culture in financial services has not changed since 2008 despite repeated, significant enforcement and other regulatory interventions.

> Enforcement action often takes place after a lengthy period of investigation and in these instances the deterrent effect can be limited ... In any event, prevention is clearly preferable to cure and so we would venture that it should be seen as a positive outcome if regulatory and industry-based initiatives aimed at improving behaviour resulted in a reduction in enforcement actions.[147]

iv. Enforcement by the Financial Reporting Council

The Financial Reporting Council amended its disciplinary schemes procedure to enable cases to be concluded by agreement, without the need for a full tribunal hearing; to refine

---

[146] Letter from British Bankers Association to HM Treasury, 4 July 2014, available at https://www.bba.org.uk/policy/financial-and-risk-policy/bank-reform/resolution-planning/bba-response-to-hmt-review-of-enforcement-decision-making-at-the-financial-regulators/.

[147] ibid, 2–3.

the criteria for the commencement of an investigation; and to introduce a power to impose interim orders.[148] It also adopted a new procedure for imposing regulatory sanctions on auditors, effective from November 2013.[149]

v. 2014 Review of Enforcement

HM Treasury undertook a review of the enforcement decision making by the FCA and PRA in 2014.[150] This included consultation with financial service providers, who expressed a reasonable level of satisfaction with existing decision-making processes and arrangements.[151] The review stated that the objectives of enforcement are to make fair, transparent, timely, and efficient enforcement decisions. It noted that in the year 2013–14 the FCA had imposed fines totalling £425 million.[152] By October 2014, £450 million had been paid under an FCA redress scheme to consumers who were mis-sold card and identity protection policies.[153] In November, the FCA took action in response to attempted manipulation of the FX market, so far fining five banks £1.1 billion, with potentially criminal misconduct by individuals being investigated by the Serious Fraud Office.[154] In 2014 payday lender Wonga agreed to pay £2.6 million in redress and write off over £200 million of loans, following intervention by the FCA.[155] The FCA and PRA had also imposed combined fines of £56 million following an investigation into IT system failings at RBS, Natwest and Ulster Bank which left customers without access to their funds.[156]

The primary theme of the review was said to be to take the right action to 'change culture'. The document's summary of this policy mixed references to deterrence and to responsive regulatory approaches, with no reference to culture:

> When firms break the rules, the regulators must act to make sure that they change the way they do business. Holding firms to account by taking tough enforcement action, and so sending a strong deterrent to others, will often be the only appropriate response. But sometimes, prompt, robust supervisory action—stopping firms doing business while they fix problems, or requiring them to quickly pay redress to consumers—will be the better immediate course.

> The government's recommendations will ensure senior consideration of the full range of regulatory options, a focus on identifying and implementing the right regulatory response and consistency of referral decision-making. Increased reporting of the regulators' supervisory interventions will help to change behaviour right across the industry.[157]

---

[148] *Disciplinary Schemes Proposed Changes: A Consultation Paper* (Financial Reporting Council, June 2012) available at http://www.frc.org.uk/images/uploaded/documents/Disciplinary%20Schemes%20Proposed%20 Changes%20-%20June%202012%20final1.pdf.

[149] *Auditor Regulatory Sanctions Procedure* (FRC, November 2013) available at http://www.frc.org.uk/ Our-Work/Publications/Audit-Quality-Review/Auditor-Regulatory-Sanctions-Procedure-Feedback-St.pdf.

[150] *Review of Enforcement Decision-making at the Financial Services Regulators: Final Report* (HM Treasury, 2014).

[151] ibid, para 1.7.

[152] In the financial year 2008/2009, the Financial Services Authority ('FSA') imposed what was then a record £27 million in financial penalties.

[153] http://www.fca.org.uk/news/compensation-for-card-and-identity-protection-policyholders.

[154] http://www.fca.org.uk/news/fca-fines-five-banks-for-fx-failings, http://www.sfo.gov.uk/press-room/latest-press-releases/press-releases-2014/forex-investigation.aspx.

[155] http://www.fca.org.uk/news/wonga-major-changes-to-affordability-criteria.

[156] http://www.fca.org.uk/news/fca-fines-rbs-natwest-and-ulster-bank-ltd-42m-for-it-failures, http://www. bankofengland.co.uk/publications/Pages/news/2014/152.aspx.

[157] *Review of Enforcement Decision-making* (n 150) paras 1.9 and 1.10.

The review noted that the success of the FCA's 'credible deterrence' approach depended on it 'showing that meaningful, proportionate enforcement action will be taken across a wide range of markets, firms and individuals.'[158] That approach contrasted with the PRA's policy of focusing on 'ex ante remedial action' as its primary regulatory tool, which was said—without further analysis—to be important in the context of prudential supervision, and led to the scope for enforcement being 'more limited, consistent with the number of firms it supervises and its statutory objectives.'[159] There was a clear statement that enforcement investigations are expensive and resource intensive.[160]

In expanding on 'the purposes of enforcement', the review took a wider view of deterrence and 'an alternative regulatory response':

> The purposes of enforcement action are numerous. Where misconduct has occurred, those responsible should be held to account, and meaningful, proportionate penalties should be applied. Wrongdoers should also be deterred from repeating their behaviour, and in some circumstances, prevented from doing so by removal from the industry. Where misconduct has resulted in losses to consumers, enforcement action may be an important step towards securing redress.

> But, more widely, enforcement has a general deterrence value. Unlike most supervisory interventions, enforcement usually results in a public outcome. And so another purpose of enforcement action is to serve a strong reminder to firms and individuals of what will happen if they break the rules.

> From a subject's perspective, this is challenging; that action should be taken against them not only because of their misconduct and its consequences, but also because of the potential for that action to promote compliance among the wider market or industry. Yet in circumstances where there are more than 70,000 firms within the FCA's regulatory perimeter and finite regulatory resources, a strategic approach to enforcement is essential.[161]

The government recommended that the FCA and PRA should each publish referral criteria which explicitly consider whether an enforcement investigation, rather than an alternative regulatory response, is the right course in all of the circumstances. The FCA and PRA should also ensure that their respective referral criteria reflect the various objectives of their enforcement action, including its strategic purpose in publicly reinforcing the regulatory requirements in priority areas.[162]

The review noted that 'in many cases, identifying the right regulatory response is a hugely complex decision'.[163] A supervisory response might typically include obtaining a firm's agreement to take particular steps to address an issue. The range of options on the supervision-enforcement spectrum was illustrated by a previous review on financial crime controls:

> The FCA needed to assess the right regulatory response for each of the firms involved. In addition to advising individual firms to make specific changes, the FCA used a range of more formal supervisory and enforcement tools to address failings. That resulted in 4 firms agreeing to restrict their

---

[158] ibid, para 2.1.
[159] ibid, para 2.2.
[160] The 2013/14 FCA Enforcement Annual Performance Account noted that the cost of regulatory cases 'can range from around £250 to over £5m': http://www.fca.org.uk/your-fca/documents/corporate/enforcement-annual-performance-account-13-14.
[161] ibid, paras 2.6 to 2.8.
[162] *Review of Enforcement Decision-making* (n 150), Recommendation 1.
[163] ibid, para 2.16.

business to mitigate the risks posed by the failings, pending the problems being fixed. However, 3 banks were required to commission independent reviews of their systems and controls to ensure that the full extent of issues are understood, and an adequate remediation programme identified and implemented. Most seriously, 2 firms were referred for enforcement investigation. The FCA is also proposing further industry-wide guidance. By publicly describing the action it is taking in respect of these firms, the FCA intends to ensure wider adherence to the regulatory requirements.[164]

The review expanded on the importance of identifying the appropriate regulatory response. Importantly in relation to a preventive approach, the powers of the FCA and PRA to appoint investigators are not triggered by a breach but by 'circumstances suggesting' a breach,[165] and for powers to conduct a 'general investigation' there must be 'good reason for doing so'.[166] Frameworks should promote: Consideration of appropriate alternative regulatory responses; referral to enforcement only where that is considered to be the appropriate regulatory response; and consistency of approach to referral decision making by each regulator.[167]

The review also addressed improving operational coordination between the FCA and PRA, providing more information to the subjects of investigation, supporting fairness of process and supporting early settlement.[168] Regulators should aim to notify subjects 28 days before formal enforcement begins; the 30 per cent discount regime should be continued for subjects who settle within 28 days of formal commencement, but reduced discounts should not apply at later stages, since the evidence indicated that cases either settled quickly or did not.[169] Regulators should hold scoping meetings with subjects once they were in a position to share their indicative plans on the direction of an investigation and timetabling of key milestones.[170] Subjects should be expressly invited at scoping meetings or at an early stage to indicate whether they accept the suspected misconduct, or specific aspects of it.[171] The review noted:

> There is scope for more consistent constructive interaction between the regulators and the subjects of enforcement investigations. Many of the actions recommended—more information at referral, improved scoping meetings, periodic updates and preliminary meetings prior to settlement—are intended to foster more constructive communication, and so promote efficient investigations and outcomes. Effecting behavioural change—on the part of the regulators and the firms and individuals they regulate—is likely to be more difficult.[172]

Further recommendations were made as to the composition of decision-making committees, bearing in mind the need for independent oversight and senior involvement but not involving excessive resource, and access to judicial review of decisions through the Upper Tribunal.

---

[164] ibid, Box 2.B. The review had looked at the controls in place at 10 commercial insurance intermediaries and 21 banks, some of which had been included in similar, prior reviews. Improvements and good practice were discovered, but so were a range of weaknesses, some of which were significant. See http://www.fca.org.uk/news/fca-finds-small-firms-need-to-manage-financial-crime-risks-more-effectively.

[165] FSMA, ss 97 and 168.

[166] FSMA, s 167.

[167] *Review of Enforcement Decision-making* (n 150) Recommendation 3.

[168] Of 106 cases closed in the previous year, 50 were concluded by executive settlement. Many of the cases settled involved firms, whereas individuals were less likely to settle. ibid, para 5.1.

[169] ibid, ch 5.

[170] ibid, Recommendation 17.

[171] ibid, Recommendation 18.

[172] ibid, para 4.19.

Some subsequent developments are illuminating. The US and UK financial authorities continued to impose large fines on financial institutions as a series of misdeeds came to light. Some issues related to failure to implement repayment of customers where that had been required, and others to manipulation of markets.[173] However, the efficacy of the FCA's policy of 'credible deterrence' was questioned when it became clear that some fines related to actions that had occurred *after* a bank had been investigated and fined for similar misconduct.[174] The President of the German Federal Financial Supervisory Authority (*Bundesanstalt für Finanzdienstleistungsaufsicht*, or BaFin) also noted that the financial supervisors in jurisdictions where large fines had been imposed (notably the US and UK) were not notably operating more successfully, or financial institutions in such jurisdictions behaving more legally, than in jurisdictions where fines were significantly lower (such as in Germany).[175]

III. Communications

The Office of Communications, Ofcom,[176] is the regulatory authority set up under the Communications Act 2003 to oversee the working of broadcasters and telecoms providers and to protect consumers. Ofcom describes its responsibilities as falling into six main areas: Ensuring the optimal use of the electro-magnetic spectrum, ensuring that a wide range of electronic communications services—including high speed data services—is available throughout the UK, ensuring a wide range of TV and radio services of high quality and wide appeal, maintaining plurality in the provision of broadcasting, applying adequate protection for audiences against offensive or harmful material and applying adequate protection for audiences against unfairness or the infringement of privacy.

Ofcom has responsibility for setting policy and enforcing any regulatory obligations that policy gives rise to, as well as enforcing the law. Enforcement is described as an ongoing programme of work undertaken to promote, monitor and investigate compliance with existing

---

[173] Failures in processes for handling 126,000 PPI complaints between May 2011 and July 2013 by Clydesdale Bank, in which 42,200 may have been rejected unfairly and 50,900 resulted in inadequate redress, drew a fine of £20,678,300 (after a 30% discount for early settlement) on 15 April 2015; a fine of £117 million for Lloyds Banking Group for mishandling thousands of PPI complaints between March 2012 and May 2013, and an agreement by the bank to review 1.2 million complaints, for which a further £710 million was added to the £12 billion already set aside to cover repayments; the conspiracy to fix the LIBOR rate led to fines on various banks, of which the largest was £227 million (part of a total imposed by US and other regulators of $2.5 billion) on Deutsche Bank, in which the FCA increased the penalty to reflect 'the seriousness and duration of the breaches committed' and because the bank had been involved in 'repeatedly misleading us'; a total of $5.6 billion in penalties was imposed by US and UK authorities on six banks in relation to manipulation of currency markets, including £284,432,000 on Barclays Plc for failing to control its business practices, in which it 'allowed a culture to develop which put the firm's interests ahead of those of its clients and which undermined the reputation and integrity of the UK financial system'.

[174] Such as the Barclays fine for foreign exchange noted in n 163, for which the events overlapped with and followed fines for the LIBOR and Gold benchmarks: see M Bonnell, 'Is Credible Deterrence really Working? And Other Questions Arising from a Mixed Week for the FCA' RPC blog, at http://www.rpc.co.uk/index.php?option=com_easyblog&view=entry&id=1518&Itemid=108.

[175] S Afhüppe, Y Osman and D Schäfer, 'Small Lenders, Big Problems' *Handelsblatt* March 24, 2015, No 142. The President, Mr F Hufeld, confirmed this view to the author in a meeting on 3 June 2015.

[176] See http://www.ofcom.org.uk/. Ofcom was created in 2004 by merging five authorities: The Broadcasting Standards Commission, the Radio Communications Agency (covering spectrum management), the Independent Television Commission, Oftel (telecoms regulation) and the Radio Authority.

regulation across television, radio, telecommunications and wireless communication service providers, as well as other regulation relating to the protection and management of the radio spectrum.[177] Ofcom takes enforcement action across a number of industry sectors and is able to use a range of statutory powers granted by, amongst others, the Broadcasting Act 1990, the Communications Act 2003, the Wireless Telegraphy Act 2006, the Enterprise Act 2002, the Broadcasting Acts 1990 and 1996, the Postal Services Act 2011 and EU Regulations.

Ofcom operates under statutory duties, principal amongst which are:

(a) to further the interests of citizens in relation to communications matters; and
(b) to further the interests of consumers in relevant markets, where appropriate, by promoting competition.[178]

Ofcom must act in accordance with the six Community requirements which give effect, amongst other things, to the requirements of Article 8 of the Framework Directive. In summary, those requirements are:

— To promote competition in communications markets;
— to secure that Ofcom contributes to the development of the European internal market;
— to promote the interests of all European Union citizens;
— to act in a manner which, so far as practicable, is technology-neutral;
— to encourage, to the extent Ofcom considers it appropriate, the provision of network access and service interoperability for the purposes of securing efficiency and sustainable competition in communications markets and the maximum benefit for the customers of providers of communications networks and services; and
— to encourage such compliance with certain international standards as is necessary for facilitating service interoperability and securing freedom of choice for the customers of communications providers.

In addition to annual reports, it publishes annual Consumer Policy Statements, which review the state and trend of consumer problems and how it has impacted on them.[179] A 2010 Report by the National Audit Office concluded:

> Ofcom's consumer research shows that levels of customer satisfaction are generally high. For consumers of communications products and services, outcomes such as availability and choice, falling prices and good quality products and services have been largely positive. For example, since 2004 a representative basket of mobile phone services has fallen in price from £36 per month to £15 per month in 2009…

---

[177] In some instances, Ofcom determines disputes between providers. In 2012 Ofcom consulted on recovering its own costs and expenses incurred when making a determination for resolving a dispute pursuant to ss 185–91 of the Communications Act 2003, and requiring payment of another party's costs and expenses incurred in connection with a dispute: *Payment of Costs and Expenses in Regulatory Disputes: Guidance on Ofcom's Approach* (OFCOM, October 2012) available at http://stakeholders.ofcom.org.uk/binaries/consultations/payment-costs/summary/main.pdf.

[178] Communications Act, s 3.

[179] For example, *The Consumer Experience of 2012* (Ofcom, January 2013), available at http://stakeholders.ofcom.org.uk/binaries/research/consumer-experience/tce-12/Consumer_Experience_Researc1.pdf. That report considered the changing use of communications, the availability of services and providers, the take-up of services and devices, consumer choice and value, consumer interest and activity (including switching) and consumer protection issues.

There is still scope for improvement in some areas. Two of the top ten areas in which complaints were made to the consumer helpline Consumer Direct in 2009 were in the communications market. Ofcom's data demonstrates some specific areas where improvements are needed, for example: switching ... broadband speed ... and silent calls.[180]

Ofcom publishes a set of overarching regulatory principles to guide how it operates.[181] These principles are consistent with Ofcom's duty under the Communications Act, and the Postal Services Act, to have regard to regulatory principles of transparency, accountability, proportionality, consistency and the targeting of regulation only at cases where action is needed, and to other principles Ofcom considers represent best regulatory practice. Ofcom's regulatory principles[182] are that it will:

— Regulate with a clearly articulated and publicly reviewed annual plan, with stated policy objectives;
— intervene where there is a specific statutory duty to work towards a public policy goal which markets alone cannot achieve;
— operate with a bias against intervention, but with a willingness to intervene firmly, promptly and effectively where required;
— strive to ensure its interventions will be evidence-based, proportionate, consistent, accountable and transparent in both deliberation and outcome;
— always seek the least intrusive regulatory mechanisms to achieve its policy objectives;
— research markets constantly and will aim to remain at the forefront of technological understanding; and
— consult widely with all relevant stakeholders and assess the impact of regulatory action before imposing regulation upon a market.

The regulatory system is strongly based on 'regulatory oversight' of providers' systems and activities by Ofcom, rather than on extensive direct intervention. Extensive rules and guidance are published, after public consultation, and amended regularly. A notable feature of the architecture is the involvement of providers' internal complaint handling systems and (two) external ADR schemes.[183] Ofcom has limited resources and cannot investigate every complaint that it receives. Its guidelines explain how it decides what to investigate, and sets out the prioritisation framework that it uses to decide whether or not to open (or continue) an investigation.[184] It regularly reviews evolving threats to citizens and consumers, and responds accordingly. In 2008, for example, after issuing a record number of broadcasting statutory sanctions, Ofcom introduced new consumer protection programmes and investigations, and identified a range of enforcement priorities to ensure the protection of consumers in the future in the areas of broadcasting. Particularly close attention was paid to participation television and the use of premium rate phone services, in competition and consumer investigations to ensure the market provides clear, honest and transparent value,

---

[180] *Ofcom: The Effectiveness of Converged Regulation* (Report by the Comptroller and Auditor General, HC 490, Session 2010–2011, November 2010) paras 10 and 11.
[181] http://www.ofcom.org.uk/about/sdrp/.
[182] ibid.
[183] Ombudsmen Services: Communications and CISAS; see Hodges, Benöhr and Creutzfeldt-Banda (n 25).
[184] *Enforcement Guidelines: Ofcom's Guidelines for the Handling of Competition Complaints and Complaints Concerning Regulatory Rules* (Ofcom, July 2012) available at http://stakeholders.ofcom.org.uk/binaries/consultations/draft-enforcement-guidelines/annexes/Enforcement_guidelines.pdf.

and in spectrum enforcement. The objective was to target the most persistent and harmful illegal equipment manufacturers and retailers and illegal users of the radio spectrum including illegal (pirate) broadcasters.[185]

Ofcom issues the following advice to consumer complainants:

> If you are thinking of making a complaint to Ofcom, we recommend that you read these guidelines thoroughly and consider the following advice:
>
> — speak to us first: We are always prepared to discuss emerging issues. We cannot give a view on the merits of a complaint but may be able to refer you to previous policy decisions or investigations that have dealt with similar issues.
>
> — try and resolve matters through commercial discussions: Not every matter of disagreement between communications providers and postal operators is suitable for resolution through an investigation. If it is appropriate, there may be benefits in trying to resolve problems directly with the target of your complaint before asking Ofcom to intervene.
>
> — read and apply the rules: We may not accept complaints that do not comply with the submission criteria set out in these guidelines.
>
> — consider any relevant decisions: The issue you want to complain about may have been the subject of previous investigations or policy decisions. Details of investigations are published in the Competition and Consumer Enforcement Bulletin (CCEB) section of Ofcom's website. The CCEB gives details of any appeals against Ofcom decisions, which may help you in considering how to submit your case.
>
> — gather as much evidence and information as possible: We often decide not to pursue complaints where the complainant does not provide any evidence to support an allegation. We realise that, in some cases, complainants will not have access to all relevant information (for example competitors' cost data). However, you should provide as much evidence as you can, rather than gathering the minimum requirement for submission. We do not apply this rule where issues have been raised by a 'whistleblower'....
>
> — be prepared: We commit to a demanding timetable in handling investigations and expect large and well-resourced organisations to do the same in supporting an investigation, for example, in meeting deadlines for information requests. If you submit a complaint, we will assume that you have considered and are prepared to meet this commitment.[186]

Differing sanctioning provisions apply for breaches of the rules for broadcasting (issuing a direction, making a broadcasting correction, imposing a fine or revocation of licence),[187] and radio spectrum or illegal broadcasting (seizure of equipment, issuing suspension notices against manufacturers and marketers of illegal apparatus, issuing fixed penalties, and instituting criminal proceedings),[188] and consumer law. Under the regulatory system for communications, licences are issued to providers of services of radiocommunications, and radio and television broadcasting, which include General Conditions of entitlement.[189]

---

[185] See *Enforcement Report. A Report on Ofcom's Approach to Enforcement and Recent Activity* (Ofcom, 2009) at http://stakeholders.ofcom.org.uk/enforcement/enforcement-report/enforcement_report.pdf.

[186] *Enforcement Guidelines* (n 184) para 1.21.

[187] Communications Act 2003, ss 344–56, 392, 403, Sch 13. See *Procedures for the Consideration of Statutory sanctions in breaches of broadcast licences* (Ofcom, 2013) at http://stakeholders.ofcom.org.uk/broadcasting/guidance/complaints-sanctions/procedures--sanctions.

[188] Wireless Telegraphy Act 2006. A fixed penalty regime was introduced under the Wireless Telegraphy (Fixed Penalty) Regulation 2011. Illegal use of the radio spectrum will automatically result in a notification of breach, and if no action is taken a fixed penalty of £100 will be incurred. If no action ensues after a reasonable opportunity, revocation of licence or criminal proceedings will follow.

[189] See http://stakeholders.ofcom.org.uk/telecoms/ga-scheme/general-conditions.

A. Enforcement and Consumer Redress

Ofcom is required to publish a statement containing the guidelines it proposes to follow in determining the amount of penalties imposed by it apart from under the Competition Act 1998.[190] Penalty guidelines revising those of 2003 were published in June 2011.[191] These included the following statements:

3. Ofcom will consider all the circumstances of the case in the round in order to determine the appropriate and proportionate amount of any penalty. The central objective of imposing a penalty is deterrence. The amount of any penalty must be sufficient to ensure that it will act as an effective incentive to compliance, having regard to the seriousness of the infringement.
4. The factors taken into account in each case will vary, depending on what is relevant. Some examples of potentially relevant factors are:
    (i)   The degree of harm, whether actual or potential, caused by the contravention, including any increased cost incurred by consumers or other market participants;
    (ii) The duration of the contravention;
    (iii) Any gain (financial or otherwise) made by the regulated body in breach (or any connected body) as a result of the contravention;
    (iv) Any steps taken for remedying the consequences of the contravention;
    (v)   Whether the regulated body in breach has a history of contraventions (repeated contraventions may lead to significantly increased penalties);
    (vi) Whether in all the circumstances appropriate steps had been taken by the regulated body to prevent the contravention;
    (vii) The extent to which the contravention occurred intentionally or recklessly, including the extent to which senior management knew, or ought to have known, that a contravention was occurring or would occur;
    (viii) Whether the contravention in question continued, or timely and effective steps were taken to end it, once the regulated body became aware of it; and
    (ix) The extent to which the level of penalty is proportionate, taking into account the size and turnover of the regulated body.

...

8. Ofcom may increase the penalty where the regulated body in breach has failed to cooperate fully with our investigation.
9. Ofcom will ensure that the overall amount does not exceed the maximum penalty for the particular type of contravention.
10. Ofcom will have regard to any representations made to us by the regulated body in breach.[192]

Ofcom has powers to facilitate consumer redress through giving notification to a provider of electronic communications networks or services of contravention of the conditions. The notification sets out the determination made by Ofcom, specifies the condition and contravention in respect of which that determination has been made, and specifies the period during which the person notified has an opportunity of making representations about the matters notified, complying within one month with notified conditions of which he remains in contravention, and remedying the consequences of notified contraventions.[193]

---

[190] Communications Act 2003, s 392.
[191] *Penalty Guidelines* (Ofcom, 2011) at http://www.ofcom.org.uk/files/2010/06/penguid.pdf.
[192] ibid.
[193] Communications Act 2003, s 94. The conditions are set under s 45.

If such a notification has not been remedied, Ofcom may serve an enforcement notification which imposes on the provider either a requirement to take such steps for complying with the notified condition as may be specified in the notification, and/or a requirement to take such steps for remedying the consequences of the notified contravention as may be so specified.[194] The provider is under a statutory duty to comply with an enforcement notification, which is enforceable by Ofcom in civil proceedings for an injunction, for specific performance of a statutory duty,[195] or for any other appropriate remedy or relief.[196] In urgent cases, the provider's entitlement to provide a network or services may be suspended.[197]

Ofcom may also impose a penalty on the provider.[198] Any fixed penalty may not exceed 10 per cent of turnover of the provider's relevant business for the relevant period. The level of any daily penalty may not exceed £20,000 per day. Consumer complaints may be referred to one of two approved consumer alternative dispute resolution (ADR) bodies.[199]

These powers form the backdrop for regular regulatory conversations between Ofcom and service providers. In one case relating to the billing by a telephone company of customers for services that had been cancelled, Ofcom required the company to repay customers and to pay compensation where it was appropriate. As a result, some 62,000 customers received a total of around £2.5 million in refunds and goodwill payments. Ofcom also imposed a fine of over £3 million.[200]

A 2013 policy speech by Ofcom's Chief Executive confirmed:

> Consumers are at the heart of everything Ofcom does … all our activities are focussed on good consumer and citizen outcomes. More than just a statutory duty—we have tried to ensure that this focus is deeply embedded in the culture of the organisation.

Demand side issues that require regulation

Broadly speaking, this work is targeted in three areas:

— Firstly, when consumers are unable to make effective choices because they don't have access to the right information or find it difficult to switch. The regulator has a role to ensure that consumers are empowered and have the skills, confidence, and tools to engage with the market, and that barriers to switching are removed.

— Second, consumers must be protected from scams and unfair practices. And they must be able to get effective redress when things go wrong.

— Third, we have a role to help citizens and consumers who are unable to participate or face barriers to participation—for example as a result of low income or disability.

Consumer Protection

A vital function of our work for consumers is to protect them from scams and unfair practices. [Examples are prohibited rollover contracts, nuisance calls, and bill shock.]

---

[194] ibid, s 95.
[195] Under s 45 of the Court of Session Act 1988 (c 36).
[196] Communications Act 2003, s 95.
[197] ibid, s 98(4).
[198] ibid, s 96.
[199] Ombudsman Services: Communications and CISAS: see Hodges, Benöhr and Creutzfeldt-Banda (n 25) 291–306.
[200] *Consultation on a Proposed New Power for Ofgem to Compel Regulated Energy Businesses to Provide Redress to Consumers* (Department of Energy and Climate Change, April 2012) para 13.

Redress

When things go wrong for consumers, it is important that they can get effective redress, and if they don't get it from their provider, they need to have recourse to an alternative dispute resolution (ADR) mechanism…

Ofcom has been active in ensuring that consumers can access fair, transparent and effective complaints handling processes, and we have implemented obligations on CPs to ensure that consumers can have their complaints resolved quickly and effectively.

All CPs are required to provide ADR facilities for their customers, and we approve two ADR schemes for electronic communications and one for post.[201]

In 2013 Ofcom reviewed a range of information remedies, including branded purchasing information on products/services price; features; and performance.[202] The recommended characteristics of information provision were stated in Table 13.2. The importance was noted of leveraging transparency and exposure of firms to reputational risk.

Table 13.2: Ofcom: Characteristics of Information Provision

AWARENESS	Are consumers aware of the information?
ACCESSIBLE	Is the information easy to access, find and use? Is it clearly identifiable?
TRUSTWORTHY	Is the source of the information trustworthy and totally impartial? Has the information been endorsed by multiple stakeholders?
ACCURATE	Is it true to a sufficient level of resolution, and can it be checked for correctness? Is it up-to-date and pertains to consumers' current situation?
COMPARABLE	Is it presented in such a way by different providers to allow for easy and sensible comparisons?
CLEAR AND UNDERSTANDABLE	Is the information expressed in units, concepts, or terminology that is unambiguous and easy to understand? Do consumers have the technical competence to understand it?
TIMELY	Is the information readily available at the point of making decisions?

IV. Electricity and Gas Services

EU legislation requires that national regulatory authorities for electricity[203] should pursue a number of stated objectives, including secure, reliable and efficient non-discriminatory systems that are consumer oriented, promoting effective competition and helping to ensure

---

[201]   Speech by Ed Richards, Chief Executive, Ofcom, 16 September 2013.

[202]   *A Review of Consumer Information Remedies* (Ofcom, March 2013) available at http://stakeholders.ofcom. org.uk/binaries/research/research-publications/information-remedies.pdf.

[203]   Similar provisions apply to gas under Dir 2009/73/EC concerning common rules for the internal market in natural gas.

consumer protection.[204] National authorities are to have a series of specified supervisory, investigative and enforcement powers, including issuing binding decisions and imposing effective, proportionate and dissuasive penalties.[205] Against this coercive background, Member States shall ensure that an independent mechanism such as an energy ombudsman or a consumer body is in place in order to ensure efficient treatment of complaints and out-of-court dispute settlements.[206]

The Gas and Electricity Markets Authority (GEMA), through its Office of Gas and Electricity Markets (Ofgem),[207] has the principal objective of protecting the interests of consumers by promoting competition, wherever appropriate, and regulating the monopoly companies which run the gas and electricity networks. The interests of gas and electricity consumers are their interests taken as a whole, including their interests in the reduction of greenhouse gases and in the security of the supply of gas and electricity to them.

Ofgem acts by administering the gas and electricity licensing regime and enforcing other relevant obligations[208] with which businesses operating in these sectors are required to comply. It has powers under the Gas Act 1986 and the Electricity Act 1989 to take enforcement action including imposing financial penalties for breaches of requirements imposed under or pursuant to those Acts, and to make consumer redress orders. Under the Competition Act 1998, Ofgem has concurrent powers with the Competition and Markets Authority to bring an end to anti-competitive behaviour as well as impose financial penalties. The Authority may apply to the court for an order to stop breaches of certain consumer legislation.[209] Ofgem was for some time the only regulator to issue an overarching strategic Social Action Plan.[210]

Ofgem may conduct investigations into companies that it considers may be in breach of this legislation. Investigations can be undertaken on Ofgem's own initiative or on the receipt of complaints or on referrals from other regulatory bodies. Monitoring and reporting form a key part of Ofgem's work to protect the interests of vulnerable customers. Standard Licence Condition (SLC) 32 requires energy suppliers to provide information to Ofgem relevant to their dealings with domestic gas and electricity customers. Under SLC 32, suppliers are required to submit quarterly and annual data to Ofgem on a variety of areas of their operation, including debt levels, disconnection rates, prepayment meters, payment methods used by customers and help for vulnerable customers (referred to as the social obligations monitoring). The information is used to review suppliers' performance in relation to

---

[204] Dir 2009/72/EC concerning common rules for the internal market in electricity, art 36.

[205] ibid, art 37.

[206] ibid, art 3.13.

[207] See http://www.ofgem.gov.uk.

[208] The relevant legislation is the Electricity Act 1989 and the Gas Act 1986. A business's relevant obligations depend on what function it performs (eg electricity generator or gas transporter) and whether or not it holds a licence under the Electricity Act 1989 or the Gas Act 1986 to do so. A licensed business's relevant obligations are made up of its licence conditions and other statutory obligations for the type of business it is in Sch 6 of the Electricity Act 1989 or Sch 4B of the Gas Act 1986; those of non-licence holding businesses ('exempt' operators) are simply as specified in the Schedules.

[209] Under the Enterprise Act 2002, the Unfair Terms in Consumer Contracts Regs 1999 and the Business Protection from Misleading Marketing Regs 2008.

[210] This was commended by Consumer Focus, *Regulating in the Consumer Interest* (2010) http://www. consumerfocus.org.uk/files/2010/10/Fresh-thinking-Regulation.pdf.

specific social obligations, including areas of operation where vulnerable customers may be affected. By monitoring these statistics, Ofgem can identify areas of suppliers' policies and practices where improvements are needed. The information is published on Ofgem's website on a quarterly and annual basis.[211]

Ofgem publishes reviews of its effectiveness for consumers, and is reviewed by the National Audit Office,[212] to brief Parliament's briefing for the Environment and Climate Change Committee. It undertakes Better Regulation reviews to consider whether any regulatory requirements will be effective in achieving objectives and to find the best ways of achieving the right outcomes.[213] A focus in 2012 was to secure that British Gas, EDF, E.ON, npower, Scottish Power and SSE publish improved and more accessible information on how many complaints they each get and how quickly these are handled.[214]

Ofgem's enforcement powers include the ability to impose fines of up to 10 per cent of turnover for regulatory breaches.[215] The 2003 *Statement of Policy with Respect to Financial Penalties* (which is somewhat outdated, since it did not mention taking reparation into account) stated:

4.3 Factors tending to make the imposition of a financial penalty more likely than not include:

— the contravention or the failure has damaged the interests of consumers or other market participants;
— to do so would be likely to create an incentive to compliance and deter future breaches.

4.4 Factors tending to make the imposition of a financial penalty less likely than not include:

— if the contraventions were of a trivial nature;
— that the principal objective and duties of the Authority preclude the imposition of a penalty;
— that the breach or possibility of a breach would not have been apparent to a diligent licensee.

...

5.3 Factors tending to lead to an increase in the level of any penalty may include, but would not necessarily be limited to:

— repeated contravention or failure;
— continuation of contravention or failure after either becoming aware of the contravention or failure or becoming aware of the start of Ofgem's investigation.
— the involvement of senior management in any contravention or failure;
— the absence of any evidence of internal mechanisms or procedures intended to prevent contravention or failure; and
— the extent of any attempt to conceal the contravention or failure from Ofgem.

[211] See *Guidance on Monitoring Suppliers' Performance in Relation to Domestic Customers* (OFGEM, April 2012) available at http://www.ofgem.gov.uk/Sustainability/SocAction/Monitoring/SoObMonitor/Documents1/SOR%20guidance_27-03-12.pdf.

[212] *Overview of Ofgem 2011–12* (National Audit Office, November 2012) available at http://www.nao.org.uk/publications/1213/departmental_overview_ofgem.aspx?utm_source=Feed&utm_medium=rss&utm_campaign=naoorguk.

[213] *Ofgem Simplification Plan 2012–13* (Ofgem, July 2012) available at http://www.ofgem.gov.uk/About%20us/BetterReg/SimpPlan/Documents1/Ofgem%20Simplification%20plan_WEB.pdf.

[214] *Ofgem Review Delivers Improved Supplier Complaints Data* (OFGEM, 11/02/2013) available at http://www.ofgem.gov.uk/Media/PressRel/Documents1/Complaint%20Data%20Review%20Press%20Release.pdf.

[215] Electricity Act 1989, s 27A(3) and Gas Act 1986, s 30A(3).

5.4 Factors tending to decrease the level of any penalty would include, but would not necessarily be limited to:

— the extent to which the licensee had taken steps to secure compliance either specifically or by maintaining an appropriate compliance policy, with suitable management supervision;
— appropriate action by the licensee to remedy the contravention or failure;
— evidence that the contravention or failure was genuinely accidental or inadvertent;
— reporting the contravention or failure to Ofgem; and
— co-operation with Ofgem's investigation.[216]

All fines imposed flow directly to the HM Treasury Consolidated Fund, with the result that customers directly affected by any such failure to comply remain uncompensated. The regime, under which undertakings are subject to licence conditions, and hence the threat that a licence may be revoked or that conditions may be imposed, enables Ofgem to exert strong influence on operators' market behaviour without recourse to formal sanctioning procedures, although the ability is only to negotiate voluntary redress using the threat of financial penalties as a bargaining tool. However, Ofgem did not have power either to compel businesses to offer redress or to distribute the fines it levies to consumers.

It is important to note the role that consumer ADR plays in incentivising energy suppliers to respond to customer complaints. All electricity[217] and gas[218] suppliers to consumers in the EU are subject to national ombudsman or similar redress schemes. In the UK, all licensed energy providers (gas and electricity suppliers, and gas transmission and electricity distribution companies) who provide a supply to domestic and micro-business customers are required to join a redress scheme which has been approved by GEMA.[219] In UK, a single Energy Ombudsman is approved by Ofgem, to avoid creation of multiple redress schemes. Customer complaints are required to be handled by companies under strict complaints handling standards[220] within eight weeks and may then be referred to the Energy Ombudsman.[221] From 2013, suppliers were required to release consistent quarterly data on complaints. Ofgem described the figures as high and 'damning',[222] and it instituted various responses to improve suppliers' market behaviour, such as specific enforcement action and

---

[216] *Utilities Act. Statement of Policy with Respect to Financial Penalties* (Ofgem, 2003) available at http://www. ofgem.gov.uk/About%20us/Documents1/Utilities%20Act%20-%20Statement%20of%20policy%20with%20 respect%20to%20financial%20penalties.pdf.

[217] Dir 2009/72/EC concerning common rules for the internal market in electricity and repealing Dir 2003/54/ EC, art 3.13 (Member States shall ensure that an independent mechanism such as an energy ombudsman or a consumer body is in place in order to ensure efficient treatment of complaints and out-of-court dispute settlements).

[218] Dir 2009/73/EC concerning common rules for the internal market in electricity and repealing Dir 2003/55/ EC, art 3.9 (Member States shall ensure the provision of single points of contact to provide consumers with all necessary information concerning their rights, current legislation and the means of dispute settlement available to them in the event of a dispute. Such contact points may be part of general consumer information points. Member States shall ensure that an independent mechanism such as an energy ombudsman or a consumer body is in place in order to ensure efficient treatment of complaints and out-of-court dispute settlements.)

[219] The Gas and Electricity Regulated Providers (Redress Scheme) Order 2008/2268; Consumers, Estate Agents and Redress Act 2007, ss 42–52.

[220] The Gas and Electricity (Consumer Complaints Handling Standards) Regs 2008, SI 2008/1898.

[221] Contactable at http://www.ombudsman-services.org/energy.html. The Energy Ombudsman has operated since 2008, replacing a 2005 voluntary scheme. See Hodges, Benöhr and Creutzfeldt-Banda (n 25) 269–72 and 307–11.

[222] *Annual Report and Accounts 2013–14* (Office of Gas and Electricity Markets, 2014) 11.

testing new approaches to improving customer engagement. In 2014 the complaint scheme was extended to benefit around 150,000 micro businesses by raising the upper consumption limits.[223]

A. Enforcement Policy

Ofgem issued guidelines on its processes and policies for enforcing the legislation for which it is responsible in 2007.[224] The guidance was revised after consultation[225] in 2012.[226] The 2012 revision included expanded or new coverage on early resolution, consumer protection and provisional orders. Instead of completing the procedures to impose a formal sanction, Ofgem may accept undertakings from a company, or impose a lower penalty under the Settlement Procedure.[227] It stated:

> The aim of settlement is to reach agreement on the nature and extent of breaches, an appropriate level of penalty and, where appropriate, proposals for reparation. Ofgem may agree other terms with the company as part of settlement…[228]

A further consultation on enforcement was issued in March 2013, which proposed the 'vision for enforcement: To achieve a culture where businesses put energy consumers first and act in line with their obligations'.[229] An in-depth review was concluded in March 2014, after which draft revised Guidelines were published for consultation,[230] and the final Enforcement Guidelines were issued in September 2014.[231] Similar consultation led to policy on financial penalties and consumer redress being issued in November 2014.[232]

The 2014 Enforcement Guidelines cover GEMA's enforcement of regulatory conditions and requirements, anti-competitive behaviour, and non-compliance with consumer

---

[223] For electricity to 100,000 k Wh per year, and for gas to 293,000 k Wh per year. See Ofgem Standard Licence Condition 7A, effective from 31 March 2014, and *The Gas and Electricity Regulated Providers (Redress Scheme) Order 2008 Consultation: Government Response* (Department of Energy and Climate Change, December 2013).

[224] *Ofgem Enforcement Guidelines on Complaints and Investigations* (Ofgem, 28 September 2007) available at: http://www.ofgem.gov.uk/About%20us/enforcement/Documents1/Enforcement%20Guidelines%20post%20 consultation.pdf.

[225] Draft Enforcement Guidelines on Complaints and Investigations (for consultation) (Ofgem, December 2011) available at http://www.ofgem.gov.uk/About%20us/enforcement/Documents1/Enforcement%20guidelines.pdf. Ofgem's response to the key points made by stakeholders in relation to the six main areas of the Enforcement Guidelines was: *Consultation on Draft Enforcement Guidelines on Complaints and Investigations—Outcome* (OFGEM, June 2012) available at http://www.ofgem.gov.uk/Pages/MoreInformation.aspx?docid=38&refer=About%20us/ enforcement.

[226] *Enforcement Guidelines on Complaints and Investigations* (OFGEM, June 2012) available at http://www. ofgem.gov.uk/About%20us/enforcement/Documents1/Enforcement%20guidelines%202012.pdf.

[227] ibid, paras 4.22 and 4.26.

[228] ibid, para 4.30.

[229] M Forbes, *Review of Ofgem's Enforcement Activities—Consultation on Strategic Vision, Objectives and Decision Makers* (Ofgem, March 2013).

[230] https://www.ofgem.gov.uk/publications-and-updates/consultation-and-decision-ofgems-enforcement-guidelines.

[231] *Enforcement Guidelines* (Ofgem, 2014) at https://www.ofgem.gov.uk/ofgem-publications/89753/enforce-mentguidelines12september2014publishedversion.pdf. For the response to consultation see *Decision: Ofgem's Enforcement Guidelines* (Ofgem, 2014).

[232] The Gas and Electricity Markets Authority's Statement of Policy with respect to Financial Penalties and Consumer Redress under the Gas Act 1986 and the Electricity Act 1989 (Ofgem, 2014) at https://www.ofgem.gov. uk/ofgem-publications/91201/financialpenaltiesandconsumerredresspolicystatement6november2014.pdf.

protection, unfair terms and misleading marketing regulations noted above.[233] The following objectives and regulatory principles are stated:

> 1.9 The Authority's principal objective in carrying out its functions is to protect the interests of existing and future gas and electricity consumers. The interests of consumers include their interests in the reduction of gas and electricity supply emissions of greenhouse gases and the security of their supply of gas and electricity.[234] The Authority must carry out its functions in the manner best calculated to further that objective, wherever appropriate by promoting effective competition.[235] Before exercising its functions to promote competition, it must consider whether the interests of consumers would be better protected by exercising its functions in other ways.[236]

> 1.10 We will have regard to better regulation principles of transparency, accountability, proportionality, consistency and targeting regulatory activities only at cases in which action is needed, and to other principles that we consider represent best regulatory practice.[237]

> 1.11 Our vision for our enforcement work is to achieve a culture where businesses put energy consumers first and act in line with their obligations.

> 1.12 Our strategic objectives are to:

> — deliver credible deterrence across the range of our functions
> — ensure visible and meaningful consequences for businesses who fail consumers and who do not comply
> — achieve the greatest positive impact by targeting enforcement resources and powers.

> 1.13 We aim to achieve these objectives by:

> — using a range of enforcement tools
> — identifying poor behaviour early and taking action
> — being transparent and fair in the enforcement process and visible in the actions that we take
> — learning from everything we do.

> 1.14 The Authority sets annual priorities for enforcement to enable us to respond to changes in the regulatory landscape and market environment and to target issues causing consumer detriment as they arise.

Non-compliance with statutory conditions and requirements, and other obligations such as the Standards of Conduct,[238] may be dealt with by a provisional order to do or not do something to prevent loss or damage,[239] a final order[240] and a financial penalty.[241] If a regulated person fails to comply with a final order, confirmed provisional order or does

---

[233] When dealing with criminal prosecutions for offences, the Code for Crown Prosecutors is followed. The following analysis covers the general provisions and omits in particular the competition provisions.

[234] S 4AA of the Gas Act and s 3A of the Electricity Act.

[235] The Authority's principal objective does not apply when it is exercising functions under the Competition Act, consumer protection legislation and REMIT.

[236] S 4AA(1C) of the Gas Act and s 3A(1C) of the Electricity Act.

[237] S 4AA(5A) of the Gas Act and s 3A(5A) of the Electricity Act.

[238] See https://www.ofgem.gov.uk/ofgem-publications/84946/implementation-domestic-standards-conduct-decision-make-licence-modifications.pdf. The SOC has been implemented by amending SLC 1 and inserting the new licence conditions SLC 25C and SLC 7B.

[239] S 28(2) of the Gas Act and s 25(2) of the Electricity Act.

[240] Ss 28(1) and 29 of the Gas Act and ss 25(1) and 26 of the Electricity Act.

[241] S 30A of the Gas Act or 27A of the Electricity Act. It may not impose a financial penalty for a contravention that is likely to occur.

not pay any financial penalty, Ofgem may decide to revoke a licence.[242] The Authority can enforce a final order, provisional order or consumer redress order by civil proceedings.[243] Any outstanding financial penalty (and interest) may be recovered by the Authority as a civil debt.[244]

Companies may self-report cases, and this tends to decrease any financial penalty imposed.[245] Ofgem will consider alternatives to formal enforcement before deciding to open a case, and may do one or more of the following:[246]

— enter into dialogue or correspondence with a company and warn them about potentially harmful or unlawful conduct
— agree a period of reporting by the company, either to ensure that behaviour is not repeated or to show that they have taken certain action to address the issue
— request that the company engages independent auditors or other appropriately skilled persons to conduct a review focused on a particular area of concern
— agree other voluntary action, such as the company implementing certain remedial or improvement actions, issuing a press notice and/or making voluntary payments to affected consumers
— accept non-statutory undertakings or assurances from a company to comply with a particular obligation.[247]

When deciding whether an issue can properly be resolved without the need to seek a finding of breach or infringement or other use of statutory enforcement powers, Ofgem will have regard to its prioritisation criteria. It will have regard to its Enforcement Vision and Strategic Objectives when deciding whether alternative action is sufficient to deal with the conduct, and will have regard to:

— whether the relevant concerns can be appropriately addressed by the alternative action being considered
— what alternative action best achieves this and
— whether the alternative action being considered can be implemented effectively.[248]

In considering priorities, a range of factors will be considered, including:

1) the harm or potential harm:
   — to consumers (including business consumers)
   — to our ability to regulate effectively
   — to competition
   — that resulted or could have resulted from the alleged breach
2) whether the company has derived or is deriving a financial gain or other benefit from the alleged breach
3) the strength of the evidence and what other evidence is or may be available[249]

---

[242] See the list of revocation conditions at https://www.ofgem.gov.uk/licences-codes-and-standards/licences/revoking-licence.
[243] Ss 30(8) and 30L of the Gas Act and ss 27(7) and 27L of the Electricity Act.
[244] S 30F of the Gas Act and s 27F of the Electricity Act.
[245] *Enforcement Guidelines* (n 231) s 3.
[246] ibid, para 3.25.
[247] ibid.
[248] ibid, paras 3.27 and 3.28.
[249] The assessment takes account of the different thresholds for opening different types of cases and the corresponding difference in the amount of evidence likely to have been gathered at the time we consider whether to open a case.

4) whether the alleged breach is ongoing and/or whether the company is taking action to address the situation

5) whether the allegation concerns conduct that is, or appears to be, an intentional or reckless breach

6) whether there has been a failure to comply with a previous undertaking or assurances made to us (see paragraph 3.29)

7) whether the company has a history of similar breaches, or a demonstrated record of poor compliance

8) whether there have been a series of concerns raised over time (including issues brought to the attention of the Ombudsman, the Citizens Advice consumer service or Citizens Advice's Extra Help Unit), none of which in isolation might be considered serious enough to warrant opening a case

9) whether the type of breach is a widespread problem across the industry

10) the likely impact of enforcement action and whether action would be likely to discourage similar behaviour in the future, either by the same company or by others

11) the annual priorities for enforcement set by the Authority

12) any action already taken, or to be taken, by another body to remedy the situation (see paragraphs 3.43 to 3.47)

13) the resources required to open (or continue) a case and those available.[250]

The procedure for conducting investigations[251] commences generally with notification to the company, accompanied by an outline of the allegations and a provisional timeline. The opening and closing of cases is usually made public. Issues resolved by alternative action where no case has been opened will not usually be published. Meetings may be held as part of an information or evidence-gathering exercise or be used for updates on the progress of the investigation. In most cases, a Summary Statement of Initial Findings is served, after which the company may make representations in response, normally for 21 days, and if the case is contested a Panel will be selected to hear it from the Enforcement Decision Panel,[252] after disclosure of all documents, and an opportunity for the company to make written and oral representations.

A case may be settled where a company voluntarily signs an agreement admitting the breach(es).[253] Three settlement windows are prescribed (the first normally 28 days), within which settlement will attract decreasing levels of penalty discount. Early settlement is adopted since it resolves cases more quickly and saves resources for both the company and Ofgem.[254] The case team has to obtain a settlement mandate from a Settlement Committee.[255]

Ofgem responded to objections that it would otherwise constitute prosecutor, judge and jury by providing for independent personnel to deal with case investigation, settlement

---

[250] *Enforcement Guidelines* (n 231) para 3.37.

[251] ibid, s 4.

[252] Three Ofgem staff independent of the case team.

[253] *Enforcement Guidelines* (n 231) s 5.

[254] ibid, para 5.15. Note that this rationale does not mention issues of ethics or culture. See also *Decision on Ofgem's Enforcement Guidelines* (Ofgem, 2014) para 3.10: 'We do not consider that a system of partial settlements, which would still require us to go through a contest on some issues, would realise the resource savings that we are seeking to achieve to justify the discounts being offered'. Penalties below £100,000 or issues unlikely to attract significant industry or media interest may be dealt with by a senior Ofgem official.

[255] *Enforcement Guidelines* (n 231) s 6.

decisions and enforcement decisions, and the Enforcement Oversight Board.[256] Appeals may be made to the High Court, although on limited grounds, such as breach of procedure, and not by way of rehearing on the merits.

Power to make a consumer redress order had been created in 2013.[257] The policy on financial penalties and consumer redress stated that the central objectives of imposing financial penalties and making consumer redress orders, and of determining their amount and type, are to:

— obtain fair outcomes for consumers when they have been adversely affected by a regulated person's actions (or inactions)
— deter future non-compliance not only by the regulated person concerned but also by any other regulated person.[258]

The Authority will seek to calculate the gain to the regulated person, whether in the form of additional profits, avoided costs or some other undue advantage, 'as accurately as it can'.[259] It expects regulated persons will not seek to recover the costs of financial penalties or consumer redress from their customers.[260]

> The Authority is clear that regulated persons should not benefit financially from any contravention or failure. Indeed, the Authority considers that non-compliance should normally cost significantly more than compliance and that financial penalties should act as a significant deterrent to future non-compliance. The Authority will, therefore, normally seek to ensure that any financial penalty, and compensation or other payment under a consumer redress order, or any combination of them, significantly exceeds:
>
> — the gain to the regulated person, where this can reasonably be calculated or estimated, and
> — the detriment caused to consumers, whether individually or as a group, affected by the contravention or failure.
>
> When determining the amount of a financial penalty and/or consumer redress payment, the Authority will consider any remedial measures that have been taken by a regulated person. However, the Authority may impose a financial penalty significantly in excess of the gain or detriment even where the gain or detriment has been mitigated in full. The Authority considers that this may be necessary in order to deter non-compliance and provide appropriate encouragement for all regulated persons to comply with their obligations.[261]

Penalties and redress are determined through the following steps: Calculation of detriment and gain, assessment of seriousness, adjustment for aggravating or mitigating factors, adjustment for deterrence of the regulated person, or others, from committing further or similar contraventions or failures, and applying a discount in settled cases (30 per cent in the early settlement window, 20 per cent in the middle settlement window, and 10 per cent in the late settlement window).

---

[256] See *Decision on Ofgem's Enforcement Guidelines* (Ofgem, 2014).

[257] S 30G of the Gas Act and s 27G of the Electricity Act as inserted by s 144 of, and Sch 14 to, the Energy Act 2013.

[258] *The Gas and Electricity Markets Authority's Statement of Policy with respect to Financial Penalties and Consumer Redress under the Gas Act 1986 and the Electricity Act 1989* (Ofgem, 2014) para 2.3, at https://www.ofgem.gov.uk/ofgem-publications/91201/financialpenaltiesandconsumerredresspolicystatement6november2014.pdf.

[259] ibid, para 5.7.

[260] ibid, para 1.7.

[261] ibid, paras 2.4 and 2.5.

B. Consumer Outcomes

Between April 2010 and March 2013, Ofgem imposed fines on licensees totalling over £35 million and was instrumental in achieving redress payments to customers of around £6 million.[262] This included not meeting relevant obligations in relation to providing connections, failing to meet reporting requirements and mis-selling.

The influence that Ofgem is able to wield, given its ability to amend or remove licences and to attract publicity to energy issues, means that redress can often be achieved through negotiation. The following outcomes occurred even before the formal redress power was available. On 9 March 2012 Ofgem accepted an offer from EDF Energy to invest £4.5 million to help vulnerable customers and consequently reduced a penalty for breach of marketing rules to £1.[263] In November 2012, Ofgem secured a commitment from E.ON to pay back around £1.4 million (an average rebate of £14.83, including eight per cent interest) to approximately 94,000 consumers who were incorrectly charged exit fees or overcharged following price rises that were incorrectly implemented too early.[264] In addition, E.ON agreed to make an additional payment of around £300,000 as a goodwill gesture to a consumer fund which they run in partnership with Age UK.[265] In August 2013 E.ON paid a £500,000 penalty and £2.5 million to benefit customers in fuel poverty after incorrect claims under the Carbon Emissions Reduction Target.[266] In October 2013, ScottishPower agreed with Ofgem that it had misled customers in sales approaches, and agreed to pay £7.5 million to around 140,000 vulnerable consumers (identified under the Warm Home Discount Scheme) estimated to be £50 each and establish a £1 million compensation fund for customers to access.[267] In December 2013, Npower agreed to pay £3.5 million under a similar arrangement after breaches on telesales and face-to-face marketing,[268] and separately apologised to customers and agreed a £1 million payment.[269] In February 2013, Ofgem called on the energy companies to return credit balances retained after customers had switched suppliers.[270] It estimated 3.5 million domestic and 300,000 business accounts were affected, involving £202 million and £204 million respectively. It issued advice to customers to contact

---

[262] Forbes (n 229).

[263] Details of Ofgem's decision are available at: http://www.ofgem.gov.uk/Media/PressRel/Documents1/EDF%20press%20notice%20March%209%202012.pdf.

[264] Press release, 'Ofgem secures £1.7 million for consumers following E.ON error' (Ofgem, 27 November 2012) at http://www.ofgem.gov.uk/Media/PressRel/Documents1/20121127_EON_Press_Release.pdf.

[265] The Engage Fund is run in partnership with Age UK Group to help fund services to maximise incomes of older people by providing benefits advice and financial help through benefits health checks carried out either face to face or by telephone in local Age UK offices enabling some to be lifted out of fuel poverty.

[266] *Annual Report and Accounts 2013–14* (n 222) 11.

[267] Press release, 'ScottishPower agrees to pay customers £8.5 million following Ofgem sales investigation' (Ofgem, 22 October 2013).

[268] Press release, 'Npower agrees to pay customers £3.5 million to help vulnerable customers following Ofgem energy sales investigation' (Ofgem, 20 December 2013).

[269] Press release, 'Npower publishes apology and promises to pay £1m to vulnerable consumers after Ofgem intervened on poor service' (Ofgem, 3 December 2013).

[270] Press release, 'Ofgem calls on suppliers to take action on over £400 million they hold from customers' closed accounts' (Ofgem, 28 February 2014) at https://www.ofgem.gov.uk/press-releases/ofgem-calls-suppliers-take-action-over-%C2%A3400-million-they-hold-customers-closed-accounts.

their suppliers, which was given wide publicity.[271] In July 2014 British Gas repaid £130 to around 4,300 customers (totaling £566,000) and paid £434,000 to the British Gas Energy Trust in relation to a further 1,300 customers it had been unable to trace, following misleading statements that customers would save money by switching.[272]

The watchdog Consumer Futures can investigate complaints from consumers if they are of wider public interest. It has no legal powers to secure redress on their behalf,[273] but it has successfully negotiated with energy companies to secure redress for consumers, for example, securing payments of £70 million for Npower customers in 2010 when the company made changes to its tariff structure without giving adequate notification to its customers.[274]

Redress may arguably be taken into account under the requirement on Ofgem to issue a final compliance order where it is satisfied that a licence holder is, or is likely to be, in contravention of a condition or requirement so as to secure compliance.[275]

In order to improve both payment of redress to consumers, and the regulator's leverage in bringing redress about, the Energy Act 2013 copied the Ofcom regime and included powers to secure direct redress for customers, whether domestic or businesses, pursuant to breaches of regulatory requirements that are principally set out in the Electricity Acts 1989 and the Gas Act 1986.[276] Under these provisions, Ofgem is required to give notice to the company and any other affected party at least 21 days before making the order for redress. When giving notice, Ofgem is required to set out which condition has been breached, how in its view the licensee has breached it, and the remedy it deems appropriate. The licence holder has a minimum of 21 days to make representations to Ofgem regarding the proposed order for redress. The White Paper expanded on the way in which the powers were intended to work:

> Although Ofgem would hold a significant degree of discretion, the theory behind the measures is not that the regulator use such powers as a matter of course, instead, that the very existence of the power of redress will be enough to simultaneously act as a deterrent and an incentive to gas and electricity companies: a deterrent from breaching obligations in the first instance and an incentive to put in place policies of compensation for any customers that do suffer loss following a breach.[277]

> In certain circumstances, Ofgem can and does impose substantial fines on businesses for breach of their regulatory obligations. But the Government believes that where individual consumers have suffered a direct loss as a result of such breaches the ideal remedy should be compensation. When

---

[271] Press release, 'Closed account balances—advice for consumers' (Ofgem, 28 February 2014) at https://www.ofgem.gov.uk/news/closed-account-balances-%E2%80%93-advice-consumers; 'Energy firms told to return £400m from closed accounts', BBC News, 28 February 2014.

[272] Press release, 'British Gas to compensate customers over mis-selling' (Ofgem, 4 July 2014), at https://www.ofgem.gov.uk/news/british-gas-compensate-customers-over-mis-selling.

[273] See http://www.consumerfutures.org.uk.

[274] *Consultation on a Proposed New Power for Ofgem to Compel Regulated Energy Businesses to Provide Redress to Consumers* (Department of Energy and Climate Change, April 2012) para 11.

[275] Gas Act 1986, s 28 and Electricity Act 1989, s 25.

[276] Energy Act 2013, s 144 and Sch 14, inserting Gas Act 1986 s30G-O and Electricity Act 1989 s 27G-O. See the *Consultation on a Proposed New Power for Ofgem to Compel Regulated Energy Businesses to Provide Redress to Consumers* (Department of Energy and Climate Change, April 2012) 12D/060, available at http://www.decc.gov.uk/assets/decc/11/consultation/4975-consultation-on-a-proposed-new-power-for-ofgem-to-.pdf.

[277] Press release, Department of Energy and Climate Change, April 2012.

Ofgem investigates an alleged breach it is well-placed to establish whether any consumers have suffered a loss and whether compensation is appropriate. It regularly negotiates with businesses to obtain compensation for consumers but there is currently no obligation on businesses to provide redress and no formal mechanism by which Ofgem can make them do so…

4. When Ofgem investigates an alleged breach of a relevant obligation, it will often assess the impact on consumers in order to determine the extent of the harm the breach may have caused and the level of the appropriate penalty. Any financial losses that consumers have suffered as a result of being overcharged for their energy, for example, will be factors for consideration. Where Ofgem is able to determine the financial loss suffered by consumers it will be in a good position to identify the appropriate level of redress, including monetary compensation, but it has no powers which it can use to compel compensation to be paid…

23. We do not propose any changes to Ofgem's fining powers. Fines and redress serve different purposes. A fine is punitive whereas redress seeks to address the harm caused to those affected by the breach and we see no justification for reducing the existing cap on financial penalties of 10% of the company's annual turnover. There will be occasions where redress is ordered as an alternative to the imposition of a fine, and there will sometimes be wrong doing that does not affect consumers or other market participants directly so it does not necessitate the making of an order for redress. Where appropriate Ofgem would be able to fine a company alongside making an order for redress…

27. … we anticipate that Orders for redress may include provisions on 'pound for pound' compensation for consumers who suffer a measurable loss, good will payments where it is difficult or impractical to determine the individual loss and requirements relating to information and publicity.[278]

C. Redress in Wholesale Transactions (REMIT)

Specific regimes apply to some commercial relationships, disputes and enforcement. One example of encouragement of restitution arises under the wholesale market regime. Ofgem included a clear incentive for companies to agree restitution in implementation of the EU 'REMIT' Regulation,[279] which includes requirements on market participants to notify the national Authority without delay if they reasonably suspect that a wholesale energy market transaction might breach the prohibitions on insider trading or market manipulation, and to publicly disclose inside information in an effective and timely manner.[280] Ofgem's 2013 Statement of Policy set out the following objectives:

 — maintaining confidence in the integrity of wholesale energy markets;
 — ensuring that wholesale energy market prices are set in an efficient manner;
 — discouraging failures to comply with REMIT requirements;
 — ensuring that no profits can be drawn from market abuse;
 — fostering competition in wholesale energy markets for the benefit of final consumers of energy; and

---

[278] ibid.
[279] Reg (EU) No 1227/2011 of 25 October 2011 on wholesale energy market integrity and transparency.
[280] ibid, arts 15 and 4.

— protecting the interests of consumers in wholesale energy markets and of final consumers of energy, including vulnerable consumers.[281]

The Authority proposed to 'take full account of the particular facts and circumstances of each case when determining whether to impose a financial penalty and/or issue a statement of noncompliance.'[282] Included in the factors relevant to determining the level of penalty were 'the amount of any benefit gained or loss avoided as a result of the breach (financial or otherwise, potential or actual)' and 'the degree of harm or increased cost incurred or potentially incurred by consumers or other market participants after *taking account of any restitution paid to those affected*' (emphasis added).[283] One of the resolution options open to the Authority would be its early resolution Settlement Procedure:

> The aim of settlement is to reach agreement on the nature and extent of breaches, an appropriate level of penalty and, where appropriate, proposals for restitution. Ofgem may agree other terms with the person as part of settlement. Where agreement is reached on the breaches, Ofgem will seek to agree the amount of the financial penalty and/or restitution to those adversely affected.[284]

Another example of a dispute resolution regime is the process for determining disputes between National Grid Electricity Transmission plc (NGNET) and participants in the Capacity Market and Contracts for Difference mechanisms.[285]

V. Water and Sewerage Services

The Water Services Regulation Authority (Ofwat)[286] was established in 1989 when the water and sewerage industry in England and Wales was privatised. Their statutory role and duties are primarily laid out in the Water Industry Act 1991. Ofwat is responsible for making sure that the regulated water and sewerage companies in England and Wales give the consumer a good-quality, efficient service at a fair price. Ofwat is a non-ministerial government department.

Ofwat is subject to statutory duties under section 2 of the Water Industry Act 1991. Its overarching duties are to:

— Protect the interests of consumers; having regard to the interests of vulnerable groups, and to do so wherever appropriate by promoting effective competition;

---

[281] *Consultation Decision—REMIT Penalties Statement and Procedural Guidelines* (Ofgem, 2013) available at https://www.ofgem.gov.uk/publications-and-updates/consultation-decision-remit-penalties-statement-and-procedural-guidelines. *The Authority's Statement of Policy with Respect to Financial Penalties under REMIT* (Ofgem, 2013). See earlier *Consultation on our Proposed REMIT Penalties Statement and Procedural Guidelines* (Ofgem, June 2013).

[282] *The Authority's Statement of Policy with Respect to Financial Penalties under REMIT* (Ofgem, 2013) para 3.2. See also *REMIT Penalties Statement and Procedural Guidelines* (Ofgem, November 2013) available at https://www.ofgem.gov.uk/ofgem-publications/84345/remitdecisionletter8november2013.pdf.

[283] ibid, para 4.2.

[284] *Proposed Procedural Guidelines on the Authority's use of its Investigatory and Enforcement Powers under REMIT* (Ofgem, 2013) para 8.6.

[285] *Electricity Market Reform Dispute Resolution Guidance* (Ofgem, 2014).

[286] See http://www.ofwat.gov.uk.

— secure that the functions of each undertaker (ie water company) are properly carried out;
— secure that companies are able to finance their functions by securing reasonable returns on their capital;
— secure that companies with water supply licences (ie those selling water to large business customers, known as licensees) properly carry out their functions; and
— secure long-term resilience.[287]

Subject to these, Ofwat has duties to:

— Contribute to the achievement of sustainable development;
— promote economy and efficiency by companies in their work;
— secure that no undue preference or discrimination is shown by companies in fixing charges;
— secure that consumers' interests are protected where companies sell land;
— ensure that consumers' interests are protected in relation to any unregulated activities of companies;
— have regard to the principles of best regulatory practice; and
— consider the effect on the environment when exercising their powers.

Ofwat is subject to policy for the sector established by the government.[288]

Ofwat published a strategic report in 2008[289] that included a statement that it would enforce standards and compliance using a transparent enforcement policy and that it would use its judgement about whether, and how far, to take specific cases. Its expectation was that each company will comply with its obligations. Where this did not happen, appropriate action would be taken to secure that companies comply with their obligations. The protection of consumers' interests was said to be paramount.

Companies hold appointments under the Water Industry Act 1991 and are subject to conditions of appointment.[290] Ofwat must impose an enforcement order where it believes there has been, or is going to be, a breach of obligations, except where the breach is trivial.[291] A procedure applies to the making of an enforcement order, which gives the opportunity for Ofwat to specify what should be remedied so that the undertaking may remedy the issue.[292] Ofwat may also impose a financial penalty of such amount as is reasonable where it is satisfied, inter alia, that an undertaking has contravened or is contravening any condition of the appointment.[293]

---

[287] This last was added by the Water Act 2014.

[288] *Defra's Strategic Policy Statement to Ofwat. Incorporating Social and Environmental Guidance* (Defra, 2013) available at http://www.defra.gov.uk/publications/files/pb13884-sps-seg-ofwat-201303.pdf.

[289] A policy was established to meet a challenge of increased water scarcity due to climate change and demographic trends and highlighted an increased emphasis on resilience, long term planning and customer choice: see the Water White Paper *Water for Life* (Department for Environment Food and Rural Affairs, 2011). See also *Ofwat Strategy: Taking a Forward Look* (Ofwat, 2008) available at http://www.ofwat.gov.uk/aboutofwat/reports/forward-programmes/rpt_fwd_ofwatstrategy.pdf.

[290] Water Industry Act 1991, Pt 2.

[291] Water Industry Act 1991, s 18.

[292] ibid, s 20.

[293] ibid, s 22A.

A. Enforcement Policy

Having taken into account the better regulation principles[294] and the Macrory principles, Ofwat's 2009 enforcement policy stated that 'The aims of our approach to enforcement are to secure companies' compliance and to change their behaviour. This is so that consumers' interests are protected.'[295] A stepped approach was specified to enforcement, with escalating steps in order to secure compliance. It was noted that since April 2005 Ofcom had imposed eight financial penalties in total on five different companies.[296] Under the objective of 'protecting consumers', Ofcom said:

> When we consider the appropriate action to take, we will also consider the effect of the contravention or failure on the customers of the company, consumers in general and the regulatory regime. We will also consider whether the company has wrongfully benefited from the incident. This may include financial benefits, reputational benefits or benefits arising from access to or provision of information or services. Companies may have benefited financially through price limits or through incentive mechanisms, such as the overall performance assessment (OPA). If this occurs, we expect companies to provide full redress to their customers.[297]

> If breaches are identified, we will make an assessment of the position the company would have been in had the failure or contravention not occurred, and of the benefit it has gained. We will review this and take it into account, along with any action the company has taken to provide redress and/ or compensation, when pursuing enforcement action. As part of any sanction we will aim to restore the harm that regulatory non-compliance has caused.[298]

> If a company has benefited and customers have suffered, we expect the company to provide redress as soon as possible to restore customers to the position they would have been in. In some circumstances, we would expect companies to provide compensation to their customers to reflect the harm and inconvenience they have suffered. In addition, we expect companies to act swiftly to put right the contravention or failure and to make sure that it does not happen again. We expect companies to provide us with an informal undertaking to secure this.[299]

The 2009 policy placed considerable weight on data collection and monitoring as a way of ensuring the companies complied with their regulatory obligations. However, Ofwat subsequently considered that that approach did not necessarily get the best results for customers, was costly in terms of regulatory resources, could mean the companies responded to the regulator rather than to their customers, and did not incentivise better performance.[300]

Accordingly, in 2011 Ofwat set out two significant shifts in the way it approached regulatory compliance, aimed at underpinning a revised approach to the delivery of its

---

[294] That regulatory activities should be transparent, accountable, proportionate, consistent and targeted.

[295] *Ofwat's Approach to Enforcement* (Ofwat, 2009) at http://www.ofwat.gov.uk/regulating/enforcement/ pap_pos_enforcementapproach.pdf. This was focused on formal enforcement action framed around its statutory powers under the Water Industry Act 1991 but not powers under the Competition Act 1998 and Arts 81 and 82 of the EC Treaty.

[296] ibid, para 8.

[297] ibid, para 23.

[298] ibid, para 25.

[299] ibid, para 26.

[300] *Regulatory Compliance—A Proportionate and Targeted Approach A Consultation* (Ofwat, October 2011) available at http://www.ofwat.gov.uk/consultations/pap_con111006regcompliance.pdf?download=Download.

strategy—sustainable water—and to regulation generally,[301] and in line with the recommendations set out in an independent review of Ofwat[302] and consumer representation in the water sector. First, the system of regulatory reporting was changed so that companies were no longer required to submit annual returns but were required to develop their own systems and assurance processes to enable their Boards to sign off a risk and compliance statement, verifying that the company is in compliance with its regulatory obligations. The statement would be published annually. This put the companies in charge of managing their risks, and moved Ofwat away from detailed regulatory monitoring of compliance, and instead had the role of holding them to account for the results, not the processes they adopt to ensure compliance. Second, Ofwat itself adopted a risk-based framework. This included a systematic assessment of risk and opportunity, and was designed to allow it to focus the allocation of its own resources. These proposed changes were adopted in 2012.[303]

Under the Water Act 2014, Regulations may provide that if a water licensee fails to meet a prescribed standard the licensee must pay such amount as may be prescribed to any person who is affected by the failure and is of a prescribed description.[304] This provision strengthens the regulator's oversight of licensees and avoids or simplifies users' needs to make claims.

In 2013 Ofwat published a statement setting out its revised approach to empowering water and sewerage customers through information.[305] Its new approach placed the onus on water companies to ensure that their approach to information provision complies with six broad principles (accuracy, transparency, clarity, accessibility, timeliness and customer-led). The water companies must provide assurance that the information provision required under their licences is consistent with these principles. Ofwat announced that it would be conducting risk-based reviews of companies' compliance.

VI. Railways

The Office of Rail Regulation (ORR)[306] is the independent safety and economic regulator for Britain's railways. ORR aims to enable the railway to be safe, well maintained and efficient, and to ensure that it provides value for money for users and for its funders. Its principal powers as economic regulator lie in the Railways Act 1993 (as amended), and, as a competition authority for rail, the Competition Act 1998, the Enterprise Act 2002 and

---

[301] ibid.

[302] D Gray, *Review of Ofwat and Consumer Representation in the Water Sector* (Department for Environment Food and Rural Affairs and Llywodraeth Cymru, 2011) available at http://www.defra.gov.uk/publications/files/ofwat-review-2011.pdf. This recommended that government should provide greater clarity on its objectives for the sector and on the respective roles of Government, Ofwat and other regulators; and recommended that Ofwat engage more constructively and effectively with the full range of stakeholders in the sector, and be more transparent in its decision making.

[303] *Delivering Proportionate and Targeted Regulation: Ofwat's Risk-based Approach* (Ofwat, March 2012) available at http://www.ofwat.gov.uk/regulating/compliance/pap_pos1203regcomp.pdf. See also *Ofwat Forward Programme 2012–13 to 2014–15* (Ofwat, 2012).

[304] Water Act 2014, s 29 inserting s 38ZA(3) into the Water Industry Act 1991.

[305] *Empowering Water and Sewerage Customers through Information—Ofwat's Approach* (Ofwat, May 2013) available at http://www.ofwat.gov.uk/regulating/tools/consumerpolicy/pap_tec201305infoprovision.pdf.

[306] See http://www.rail-reg.gov.uk.

under Articles 81 and 82 of the European Treaty.[307] ORR adopts independently reviewed industry risk models,[308] and in 2012 assessed its capability against functions and against a potentially expanded role.[309]

Where it is satisfied that a licence holder is contravening a condition of its licence, ORR must issue an enforcement order unless a specified exception applies.[310] The order shall require the operator to do, or not to do, such things as are specified in the order and may include a 'reasonable sum'.[311]

ORR is required to issue a penalties statement in relation to the *economic* enforcement of licence obligations.[312] Enforcement orders can include a requirement that an operator pay a reasonable sum if it fails to meet the target.[313] The revision of 2012 incorporated the Hampton principles and was expressly based on the Macrory principles.[314] In calculating the amount of a penalty, adjustment would be based on mitigating or aggravating factors, including any steps that had been taken to rectify the breach, and 'any actions which have been or will be taken to make worthwhile restoration to those who suffered the consequences of the breach, where any committed expenditure is verifiably additional'.[315]

In relation to its *safety* aims, ORR's 2008 strategy has been 'for all parts of the railways to have excellent health and safety culture and risk control processes by 2014.'[316] Its 2012 enforcement strategy for safety and health incorporates principles of proportionality, consistency, targeted enforcement action, and transparency and accountability.[317] ORR publishes an enforcement policy statement setting out how it will use its powers under the Health and Safety at Work etc Act 1974, to enforce compliance with both health and safety

[307] *Promoting Safety and Value in Britain's Railways. Our Strategy for 2009–14* (ORR, 2008) at http://www.rail-reg.gov.uk/upload/pdf/388.pdf.

[308] T Taig and M Hunt, *Review of LU and RSSB Safety Risk Models: A Report produced for the Office of Rail Regulation* (TTAC Limited, 2012) available at http://www.rail-reg.gov.uk/upload/pdf/ttac-safety-risk-models-review.pdf.

[309] *Capability Review of the Office of Rail Regulation* (ORR, April 2012) available at http://www.rail-reg.gov.uk/upload/pdf/orr-capability-review.pdf. This followed a review recommendation in Sir R McNulty, *Realising the Potential of GB Rail. Report of the Rail Value for Money Study* (Department for Transport, May 2011) available at http://www.rail-reg.gov.uk/upload/pdf/rail-vfm-detailed-report-may11.pdf.

[310] Railways Act 1993, s 55.

[311] ibid, s 55(7) and (7A). The sum may not exceed 10% of the turnover of the relevant operator: s 55(7B).

[312] Railways Act 1993 (as amended), s 57B.

[313] See Letter, 'ORR Decision on Network Rail Breach of Licence' 29 May 2012, in relation to a proposed enforcement order against Network Rail for its failure to meet operational performance requirements in the long distance sector in 2012–13 and 2013–14, in breach of condition 1 of Network Rail's network licence. That was followed by Network Rail Monitor report of 13 June 2012, proposing that if the company failed to deliver its 2013–14 end of year punctuality target of 92%, it would face a financial penalty of £1.5m for every 0.1 percentage point it falls short of the target: http://www.rail-reg.gov.uk/upload/pdf/network_rail_monitor_1112q4.pdf.

[314] *Economic Enforcement Policy and Penalties Statement* (ORR, 2012) paras 1.9 and 4.6.

[315] ibid, para 4.19(a) and (c).

[316] *Promoting Safety and Value in Britain's Railways: Our Strategy for 2009–14* (Office of Rail Regulation, 2008) available at http://www.rail-reg.gov.uk/upload/pdf/388.pdf. The Health and Safety (Enforcing Authority For Railways and Other Guided Transport Systems) Regs 2006, amended in 2008, set out the enforcement responsibilities of ORR. Activities or premises not allocated to ORR for enforcement under EARR Activities are subject to enforcement by either the Health & Safety Executive (HSE) or Local Authorities according to the Health and Safety (Enforcing Authority) Regs 1998.

[317] *ORR's Strategy for Regulation of Health and Safety Risks* (Office of Rail Regulation, 2012) available at http://www.rail-reg.gov.uk/upload/pdf/orr-safety-risk-strategy.pdf. The strategy is deliberately similar to other industries so that enforcement across industrial sectors is approached in a consistent manner.

law and the following specific legislation ('relevant non-H&S legislation') for which ORR is the enforcing authority.[318] Fines for safety issues can be significant, especially where death and personal injury occur.[319]

The 2013 edition of the enforcement policy statement[320] sets out a classic 'Braithwaite escalation' approach to enforcement, on the basis that 'Many deficiencies can be dealt with before formal enforcement becomes necessary':

Several levels of enforcement action are available:

— *Information and advice*: This could be given verbally, or a written warning of non-compliance.
— *Improvement notices*: Whereby there has to be an improvement in activity within a set timescale.
— *Prohibition notices*: Whereby work must stop completely until an issue has been addressed.
— *Issue cautions*: A formal caution is a statement by an inspector and accepted in writing by the dutyholder, that the dutyholder has committed an offence for which there is a realistic prospect of conviction. It will be very unusual for a caution to be issued.
— *Prosecution*: The final stage where we take action under health and safety legislation. Cases can be prepared against both companies and individuals. They can be heard in either magistrates or crown courts. Those being prosecuted can be fined, although breaches of enforcement notices can result in prison sentences.

A public register gives details of the issue of improvement notices, prohibition notices and prosecutions.[321]

From 2010 ORR also adopted a new approach to enforcement of breaches of licences,[322] using a 'recovery board', which includes the relevant licence holder and the parties most significantly and directly affected by the licence breach. The aim of the board is to give the affected parties direct influence over the actions to be taken by the licence holder to remedy the breach and mitigate its consequences. The aim of this was to encourage decentralisation of decisions closer to users of the railways and to promote an environment in which the industry takes greater responsibility for its own problems. ORR noted that use of the recovery board would depend on the nature of the breach and the remedy required (in particular whether quick action is required). It also recognised that the design of the recovery board would be important and it would be designed to meet the circumstances of the case. For example, ORR's role on the recovery board would need to be decided on a case by case basis.

---

[318] The Railways (Interoperability) Regs 2006, the Rail Vehicle Accessibility (Non-Interoperable Rail System) Regs 2010, and the Train Driving Licences and Certificates Regs 2010.

[319] Network Rail was fined £4 million and ordered to pay costs of £118,052 for a breach of health and safety law which caused a train to derail near Grayrigg in 2007, causing the death of one passenger and injuring 86 people: *Network Rail Fined £4 million for Grayrigg Train Derailment* (ORR, 4 April 2012) available at http://www.rail-reg. gov.uk/server/show/ConWebDoc.10897.

[320] *ORR's HSWA Enforcement Policy Statement*, April 2013, available at http://www.rail-reg.gov.uk/server/show/ nav.1849. Previous editions were August 2010, updated 25 January 2012 to reflect publication of the Railway (Interoperability) Regs 2011.

[321] http://www.rail-reg.gov.uk/server/show/nav.1283.

[322] ORR letter, 'Office of Rail Regulation: Empowering Stakeholders through Enforcement' 4 June 2010, available at http://www.rail-reg.gov.uk/upload/pdf/empowering_through_enforcement_040610.pdf.

A new enforcement policy issued in 2012 allows ORR to take account of reparations made when setting a penalty but only if the reparations are made unconditionally (so, for example, without knowing how they will be treated). The prior consultation proposed a policy of accepting 'reparations' where there had been a breach, to encourage rail operators to spend money within the industry to 'make good' the harm brought about by a breach of licence instead of paying a financial penalty.[323] This approach received widespread industry support, and would 'incentivise operators to think about the impact problems have on their customers and could bring more immediate, tangible benefits than a financial penalty alone would'. Two main changes were proposed to the policy statement. Firstly, the requirement that reparations must be offered unconditionally was removed. Secondly, ORR would be prepared in principle to reduce a penalty '£ for £' to reflect reparations offered where appropriate. These changes were also to bring ORR more into line with the approach adopted by other regulators, such as Ofgem's acceptance of 'alternative reparation'.[324] ORR expected that these changes would give it more flexibility to accept reparations in lieu of a financial penalty than it had previously, and that it would be more likely an operator would offer to make good the harm brought about by a breach of its licence obligations as an alternative to paying a financial penalty. 'The reform should incentivise compliance and change future behaviour no less than a penalty without reparations would, but with the added advantage that operators will be actively encouraged to think directly about the impact they have had on their customers and their customers' needs.'[325] ORR cited that the change would be compliant with the Macrory principle that penalties should aim to restore the harm done by non-compliance.

After responsibility for approval and monitoring of train and station operators' complaint handling procedures (CHPs) was transferred from the Department for Transport to ORR in 2013, ORR issued its regulatory policy on how CHPs should operate.[326] This included a notable extension from the traditional focus on economic and safety regulation noted above to encompass the passenger *experience*:

> we see complaint handling as a core part of the passenger experience and vital to building and maintaining confidence in rail … it is … important that passengers—as customers—are able to have trust in their operators and feel that they will be taken seriously if they make a complaint.

> Effective complaints handling demonstrates that operators have customers at the heart of their approach as well as genuine commitment to meeting their needs. The information provided by complaints, as well as customer feedback more generally, enables operators to identify root causes of dissatisfaction and take action to improve the experience of customers…

> Our overall policy objective for complaints handling role is:

> To promote continuous improvement in passengers' experience of rail through operators proactively acting on feedback and complaints.[327]

---

[323] *Rail Operator Penalties to Benefit Customers, Proposes Regulator* (ORR, 14 May 2012) available at http://www. rail-reg.gov.uk/server/show/ConWebDoc.10919.

[324] ORR had previously said that it was not minded to reduce a penalty '£ for £':

[325] ORR letter, 14 May 2012 (n 322).

[326] *Complaints Handling Procedures—A Regulatory Statement* (ORR, 2014).

[327] ibid, paras 3, 5, 6.

The ORR wanted operators to resolve individual complaints promptly and fairly and also continuously to improve, so that 'complaints and feedback are acted on by the operator so that in the medium term the root causes of complaints are addressed.'[328] The ORR issued guidance that operators should develop a comprehensive data set that would enable monitoring of operators' performance in complaint handling procedures:

> An important way in which we plan to monitor operators' performance is through establishing a 'core data' set. This data will be published. This will improve the transparency of passengers' experience. It will also strengthen reputational incentives, allowing operators' progress over time to be tracked, but would not report against any specific or minimum targets.[329]

The Delay Repay scheme within rail paid £9,549,000 compensation to consumers in 2011–12.[330]

VII. Civil Aviation

The UK's specialist aviation regulator, the Civil Aviation Authority (CAA) has the sole purpose of protecting the interests of the consumers and the public.[331] It has a strong emphasis on safety issues, as noted in chapter 19, and also consumer trading issues. The CAA has operated a Passenger Advice and Complaints Service.[332] Complaints against airlines score highest in those made to European Consumer Centres, comprising 22 per cent of all complaints in 2012.[333] Regulation EC 261/2004 lays down statutory compensation levels of €250–€600 per person for flight delays over three hours and cancellations if within the airline's control, in addition to refund/re-route for cancellation and refreshments/hotel for delay.

After consultation on a Consumer Enforcement Strategy,[334] the CAA issued its Regulatory Enforcement Policy in 2012, to secure compliance with the Better Regulation Agenda and citing the Macrory principles.[335] The consultation included the following statements:

> In order to achieve this, we expect the following from industry:
>
> We expect industry to develop internal management systems that ensure senior managers are able to both secure (and provide assurance of) compliance with legal responsibilities. We do not regard time for internal escalation as a reason to delay action to ensure compliance…

---

[328] ibid, para 7.

[329] Letter from A Eggington, 'Developing Minimum Core Data for Monitoring Operators' CHP and DPPP performance' (ORR, 17 July 2014). This noted example data including the following categories: Proportion of cases successfully closed within a specified number of days; average response times; satisfaction with complaint handling; proportion of cases appealed; total customer contacts' and proportion of complaints; and improvement actions taken to resolve complaints.

[330] M Corry and G Mather, *Fine Outcomes. Making Better Use of Regulatory Fines* (European Policy Forum, 2013) para 8.

[331] The CAA is a public corporation whose core responsibilities are outlined in primary legislation, (principally the Civil Aviation Act 1982, the Transport Act 2000 and the Civil Aviation Act 2012), European legislation, and in secondary legislation (notably the Air Navigation Order 2009).

[332] See http://www.caa.co.uk/default.aspx?catid=2226.

[333] *Help and Advice on your Purchases Abroad. The European Consumer Centres Network 2012 Annual Report*, available at http://ec.europa.eu/consumers/ecc/docs/report_ecc-net_2012_en.pdf.

[334] *Civil Aviation Authority: Interim Consumer Enforcement Strategy* (CAA, September 2011) available at <http://www.caa.co.uk/docs/2107/Interim_Consumer_Enforcement_Strategy.pdf.

[335] *Civil Aviation Authority Regulatory Enforcement Policy* (Civil Aviation Authority, October 2012) available at http://www.caa.co.uk/docs/2516/Regulatory_Enforcement_Policy.pdf.

The purpose of enforcement is to protect consumers from unfair practices and from businesses who do not comply with the law. We are committed to taking action where we have identified serious harm to consumers and/or where businesses are disregarding their legal obligations.

As described in more detail below, a range of enforcement sanctions are available to us to secure compliance. These include regulatory sanctions including: providing advice to businesses; publishing industry guidance; developing self- and co-regulation schemes; issuing warning letters; and securing legal undertakings.

For the most serious breaches, we can seek an Enforcement Order from the Court under Part 8 of the Enterprise Act 2002 or could pursue criminal sanctions again through the Courts. Consistent with our Prioritisation Principles, in choosing where to take action and which sanctions to use to secure compliance, our approach will be risk-based and proportionate and our actions will be prioritised to ensure that resources are used to the greatest effect. We will also consider the impact on businesses to ensure that our actions do not place an unnecessary burden on them. Our preference is for action that changes individual behaviour and has a general impact on the sector…

The diagram below shows the flexibility of our approach to securing compliance and the enforcement sanctions that we have available to us:[336]

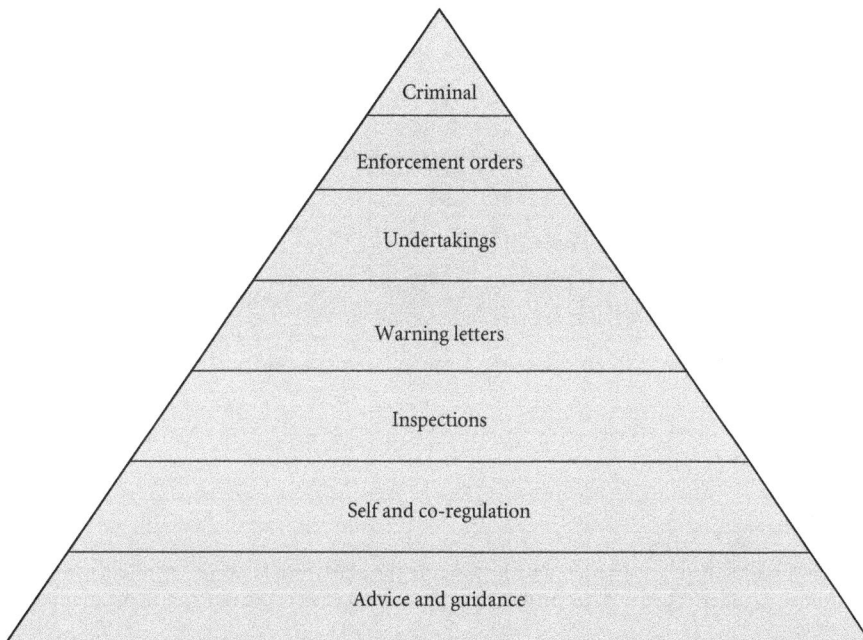

The 2012 Regulatory Enforcement Policy included the following:

Our ambition is that routine compliance with civil aviation rules and regulations is the norm … Establishing a transparent and consistent approach to enforcement reinforces a 'just culture' …

---

[336] *Civil Aviation Authority: Interim Consumer Enforcement Strategy* (n 334) 2–3.

As our policy makes clear, enforcement activity forms an important part of our regulatory toolkit, sitting alongside our other activities such as continuing oversight.

We will continue to work with those we regulate to encourage and support compliance, but we will become much more visible and proactive in dealing with those who do not, or choose not, to comply with the rules. We will use all of the enforcement tools available to us in a proportionate, transparent and consistent manner to ensure a return to compliance and deter future noncompliance.

...

We will work collaboratively with those we regulate to ensure there is clarity about how to comply...

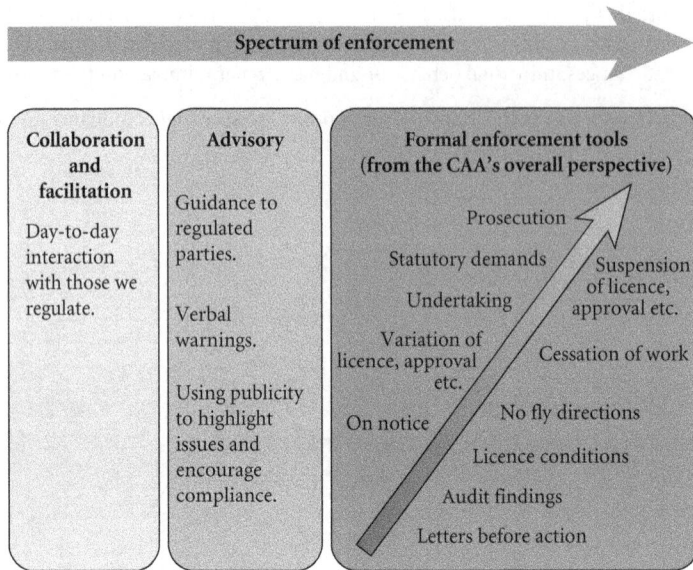

Our policy

Our policy is designed to use enforcement to secure the behaviours that we want to encourage and monitor, in a cost effective way. Its primary purpose is to protect consumers and the public by:

— encouraging compliance with the rules, both by the aviation community generally and in individual cases; and
— deterring non-compliance.

... The policy is complementary to our commitment to a 'just culture' approach to safety regulation but will ensure that we proactively take action where necessary to address noncompliance with the regulations....

Three principles characterise our approach to enforcement:

— we will use a proportionate and risk-based approach;

— we will take independent, evidence-based decisions;
— we will publicise our enforcement action where publication is in the interests of the consumer or the public.[337]

This policy did not mention redress, in view of the existence of the statutory payment schedules for delayed flights under Regulation EC 261/2004 noted above. However, the CAA has operated a complaints section for over 40 years, latterly as the Passenger Advice and Complaints Team, much of whose work has been in effect to provide a means of enforcement of those compensation provisions. The CAA has used the momentum in consumer redress provided by the Consumer ADR Directive[338] to support the industry to establish its own ADR arrangements.[339]

VIII. Legal Services

Major reform of legal services took place under the Legal Services Act 2007,[340] which imposed a statutory framework to replace the previous self-regulation by professional associations, the Bar Council and the Law Society.[341] The Legal Services Board was established as an oversight regulator to challenge and support the approved regulators.[342] A Legal Ombudsman (the Office of Legal Complaints) was created to handle complaints.[343] The Legal Services Board and Office for Legal Complaints are subject to triennial reviews by the Ministry of Justice,[344] particularly examining the control and governance arrangements in place to ensure that the public bodies comply with recognised principles of good corporate governance.

---

[337] *Civil Aviation Authority Regulatory Enforcement Policy* (n 335) 2–4.

[338] Dir 2013/11/EU.

[339] *Reforming Consumer Complaints Handling: Consultation on the CAA's Draft Policy* (Civil Aviation Authority, 2014) CAP 1257.

[340] The economic rationale for legal regulation: www.legalservicesboard.org.uk/news_publications/latest_news/pdf/economic_rationale_for_Legal_Services_Regulation_Final.pdf.

[341] This established the objectives of (a) protecting and promoting the public interest; (b) supporting the constitutional principle of the rule of law; (c) improving access to justice; (d) protecting and promoting the interests of consumers; (e) promoting competition in the provision of specified services; (f) encouraging an independent, strong, diverse and effective legal profession; (g) increasing public understanding of the citizen's legal rights and duties; and (h) promoting and maintaining adherence to the professional principles: Legal Services Act 2007, s 1.

[342] Legal Services Act 2007, Pt 4. The regulators are: Association of Chartered Certified Accountants (for reserved probate activities); Association of Costs Lawyers, through the Costs Lawyer Standards Board; Bar Council, through the Bar Standards Board (for barristers); Chartered Institute of Patent Attorneys, through the Intellectual Property Regulation Board; Council for Licensed Conveyancers; Institute of Chartered Accountants in Scotland (for reserved probate activities); Chartered Institute of Legal Executives; Institute of Trade Mark Attorneys, through the Intellectual Property Regulation Board; Law Society, through the Solicitors Regulation Authority; and Master of the Faculties (for notaries).

[343] Legal Services Act 2007, Pt 6. See *The Office for Legal Complaints: Annual Report and Accounts For the Year ending 31 March 2012: Legal Ombudsman* (Office for Legal Complaints, July 2012) available at http://www.legalombudsman.org.uk/downloads/documents/publications/Annual_report_2011_2012_Final_v1.pdf.

[344] *Legal Services Board and Office for Legal Complaints Triennial Reviews* (Ministry of Justice, January 2012) available at http://www.justice.gov.uk/consultations/review-lsb-olc.htm.

In introducing the new regime, an extensive series of discussion papers on regulatory standards was issued,[345] with considerable external scrutiny by consumer bodies.[346] At the same time, government supported the development of promoting the UK's legal services sector abroad,[347] whilst domestically significantly cutting the legal aid budget once again and dealing with a constriction on the supply of domestic services.

The regulatory policy that was introduced was based on 'outcomes-focused regulation'.[348] In 2012, the Legal Services Board consulted on options for regulators to consider when deciding how best to prevent risks to, and improve, the quality of legal services consumers receive.[349] It described risks to quality and offered suggestions on how best to prevent them, as well as how to incentivise improvement of quality. It noted that 'Opinion Leader' described seven consumer outcomes which, in essence, are broad principles of quality service delivery: Transparency, communication (initial choice and active ongoing engagement), professionalism and integrity (good quality advice), timeliness, an alignment with the consumer's best interests (utility), and fair and efficient complaint handling. The quality consultation document also included the analysis of suggested best regulatory practice in relation to quality assurance shown in Table 13.3.

The Legal Services Board identified three categories of regulatory intervention:[350]

— Before the event assurance—entry hurdles, training and accreditation, and assurance of competency.
— Increased consumer empowerment—transparent/published data and tools to support choice (based upon after the event information).
— Targeted supervision—proportionate and risk-based by regulators or on behalf of regulators, but touching all who deliver a legal service (ie not reserved to lawyers).

---

[345] *Response to Legal Services Board Consultation: Developing Regulatory Standards* (Legal Ombudsman, June 2011) available at http://www.legalombudsman.org.uk/downloads/documents/consultations/Legal%20Ombudsman's%20consultaton%20response%20to%20LSB%20regulatory%20standards%20discussion%20paper.pdf; *A Framework to Monitor the Legal Services Sector* (Oxera, August, 2011) available at http://www.legalservicesboard.org.uk/news_publications/latest_news/pdf/a_framework_to_monitor_the_legal_services_sector.pdf; *Benchmarking the Supply of Legal Services by City Law Firms* (Charles River Associates, prepared for the Legal Services Board, August 2011); Sullivan (n 23); *Approaches to Quality: A Consultation Paper* (Legal Services Board, March 2012) available at http://www.legalservicesboard.org.uk/what_we_do/consultations/open/pdf/20120311_approaches_to_quality_consultation.pdf; *Legal Services Benchmarking* (Legal Services Board and BDRC Continental, July 2012) available at http://www.legalservicesboard.org.uk/what_we_do/Research/Publications/pdf/individual_consumers_use_of_legal_services_lsb_report_17_07_12_ii.pdf; Investigation into Individual Consumer Engagement (Legal Service Board, September 2012) available at http://www.legalservicesconsumerpanel.org.uk/ourwork/Choosing%20Using/20120924%20Letter%20Chris%20to%20Elisabeth%20Davies.pdf.
[346] *Legal Services Consumer Panel Consumer Impact Report 2012* (LSCP, July 2012) available at http://www.legalservicesconsumerpanel.org.uk/publications/research_and_reports/documents/CIR_final_full%202012%2007%2025.pdf; *Risk and the Role of Regulation* (Legal Services Consumer Panel, February 2013) available at http://www.legalservicesconsumerpanel.org.uk/publications/research_and_reports/documents/Vanilla%20Research%20Risk%20and%20Regulation%20final.pdf.
[347] *Plan for Growth: Promoting the UK's Legal Services Sector* (Ministry of Justice, September 2011) available at http://www.justice.gov.uk/downloads/publications/corporate-reports/MoJ/legal-services-action-plan.pdf.
[348] *Outcomes-focused Regulation: Overview* (Law Society, September 2011) available at http://www.lawsociety.org.uk/productsandservices/practicenotes/ofroverview/4988.article.
[349] *Approaches to Quality: A Consultation Paper* (Legal Services Board, March 2012) available at http://www.legalservicesboard.org.uk/what_we_do/consultations/open/pdf/20120311_approaches_to_quality_consultation.pdf.
[350] ibid, para 38.

Table 13.3: Legal Services Board Proposals on Best Regulatory Practice in Relation to Quality Assurance

Better regulation principle	Purpose
Proportionate	Reducing the burden, ensuring effective functioning in the market whilst protecting the consumer
Accountable	Cost benefit justification and a robust and compelling case to introduce, achieving the objective at the least cost and with the least coercion and with clear, transparent, time-bound evaluation.
Consistent	Enabling a firm basis for decisions by consumers to choose suppliers confidently and suppliers to invest and innovate with a proper degree of certainty
Targeted	Remove existing regulation that unnecessarily impedes growth whilst seeking to modernise and improve compliance methods
Transparent	Consulting with those affected and being clear about how effectiveness will be monitored

In April 2012 the Legal Services Board concluded that a 'risk based' approach was required, segmenting the market where common risks are identified.[351]

The Claims Management Regulator has accepted undertakings from Real Time Claims Ltd to refund clients that have paid an upfront fee for regulated claims management activities.[352] The undertaking was provided after the regulator expressed concern that the business was using agents for regulated claims management activity, some of which had charged clients an upfront fee, that were not complying with the conduct rules.

IX. Health and Safety in the Workplace

Legislation on workplace health and safety has a lengthy history[353] and is subject to EU minimum requirements.[354] There is an EU Agency, which has no executive powers and

---

[351] *Enhancing Consumer Protection, Reducing Regulatory Restrictions: Summary of Responses to the Discussion Paper and Decision Document* (Legal Services Board, April 2012) available at http://www.legalservicesboard.org.uk/what_we_do/consultations/closed/pdf/6.pdf.

[352] *Claims Management Regulator—Undertaking—Real Time Claims Ltd* (MoJ, April 2013) available at http://www.justice.gov.uk/downloads/claims-regulation/real-time-claims-undertaking.pdf.

[353] In UK with roots in the 19th century. After the Robens Report (Lord Robens, *Safety and Health at Work. Report of the Committee 1970–72*, 1972 HMSO Cmnd 5034) the Health and Safety at Work etc Act 1974 introduced general duties on employers to protect the health and safety of employees and others who interact with the workplace. It established the principle that those who create risks from work activities are best placed to protect employees and the public from the consequences. Employers, the self-employed, employees, designers, manufacturers, importers, suppliers and those in charge of premises all have specific responsibilities.

[354] See the Framework Dir 89/391/EEC on the introduction of measures to encourage improvements in the safety and health of workers at work. http://eur-lex.europa.eu/LexUriServ/LexUriServ.do?uri=CELEX:31989L039

acts as an information secretariat,[355] and Member States are responsible for enforcement, and the picture is a patchwork of different approaches and effectiveness. In the UK,[356] the Health and Safety Executive (HSE) is the national regulatory body responsible for promoting better health and safety at work in Great Britain,[357] sharing enforcement of the majority of workplaces with local authorities.[358] The HSE also has duties to conduct research and provide information and advice. The role of local authorities has increased over time because of growth of the service sector and decline of industrial sectors,[359] and nowadays they inspect the majority (over 1 million)[360] of workplaces.[361] HSE's 2014 independent review noted its high reputation for professionalism and impartiality, although recommended that an absence of data against which performance could be assessed should be remedied.[362]

HSE has not applied for the civil sanction powers since it considers that its current toolkit is effective and sufficiently flexible. The law places duties on employers, the self-employed, employees and others.

> Sometimes the law is prescriptive—spelling out in detail what must be done. However, much of modern health and safety law is goal setting—setting out what must be achieved, but not how it must be done. Advice on how to achieve the goals is often set out in Approved Codes of Practice (ACOPs). These give practical advice on compliance and have a special legal status. If someone is prosecuted for a breach of health and safety law and did not follow the relevant provisions of an ACOP, then the onus is on them to show that they complied with the law in another way. Advice is also contained in other HSE guidance material describing good practice. Following this guidance

1:en:HTML. This Directive and numerous others enacted under its provisions are implemented in the UK by Regs such as the Management of Health and Safety at Work Regs, Manual Handling Operations Regs, Display Screen Equipment Regs, Workplace (Health, Safety and Welfare) Regs, the Provision and Use of Work Equipment Regs and Personal Protective Equipment Regs. www.hse.gov.uk/research/crr_pdf/1998/crr98177.pdf. For a history of the introduction of new regulations in response to incidents such as the 1988 Piper Alpha disaster and emerging risks and occupational health issues see: Health and Safety Executive, *Thirty Years on and Looking Forward* (HSE Books, 2004). www.hse.gov.uk/aboutus/reports/30years.pdf.

[355] See https://osha.europa.eu/en/about.

[356] In Scotland, HSE presents findings of investigations to the Crown Office Procurator Fiscal Service for a decision about prosecutions under health and safety laws.

[357] The 1974 Act established the Health and Safety Commission and Health and Safety Executive, which were merged in 2008 to form a single Health and Safety Executive. The 1974 Act gave the HSE the five functions of standard-setting and making regulations; enforcement; research; guidance and advice; and Ministerial advice.

[358] Health and Safety (Enforcing Authority) Regs 1998.

[359] *Improving Outcomes from Health and Safety, 2008, A Report to Government* (Better Regulation Executive, 2008) at www.bis.gov.uk/files/file47324.pdf.

[360] House of Commons Work and Pensions Select Committee, *The Role of the Health and Safety Commission and the Health and Safety Executive in Regulating Workplace Health and Safety: Third Report of the Session*, 2008. www.publications.parliament.uk/pa/cm200708/cmselect/cmworpen/246/246i.pdf.

[361] R Löfstedt, *Reclaiming Health and Safety for All: An Independent Review of Health and Safety Legislation* (London, Department for Work and Pensions, 2011) 8.7.

[362] M Temple, *Triennial Review Report: Health and Safety Executive. An Independent Review of the Function, Form and Governance of the Health and Safety Executive (HSE)* (Department for Work & Pensions, January 2014) https://www.gov.uk/government/uploads/system/uploads/attachment_data/file/270015/hse-function-form-governance-triennial-review.pdf.

is not compulsory, but doing so is normally enough to comply with the law. Neither ACOPs nor guidance material are in terms which necessarily fit every case.[363]

A. Historical Enforcement Policy

HSE has issued an Enforcement Policy Statement for many years, the latest such Statement in 2009 expressly to be in accordance with the Regulators' Compliance Code and the regulatory principles required under the Legislative and Regulatory Reform Act 2006, which all local and national health and safety enforcing authorities are required to follow.[364] The 'ultimate purpose' of the enforcing authorities is 'to ensure that dutyholders manage and control risks effectively, thus preventing harm'.[365] The 'purpose of enforcement' is to:

A.   ensure that dutyholders take action to deal immediately with serious risks;
B.   promote and achieve sustained compliance with the law;
C.   ensure that dutyholders who breach health and safety requirements, and directors or managers who fail in their responsibilities, may be held to account, which may include bringing alleged offenders before the courts in England and Wales, or recommending prosecution in Scotland…[366]

The authorities have a wide range of enforcement tools at their disposal, and considerable discretion, which they are to exercise subject to the (Hampton) principles of proportionality in applying the law and securing compliance; consistency of approach; targeting of enforcement action; transparency about how the regulator operates and what those regulated may expect; and accountability for the regulator's actions.[367] These principles should apply both to enforcement in particular cases and to the health and safety enforcing authorities' management of enforcement activities as a whole.[368] HSE intends enforcement to be 'firm but fair'.[369] Its Enforcement Guidelines for Inspectors set out extensive details on the investigation process and on considerations to be considered in decisions on whether to prosecute.[370] Enforcement is meant to be guided and calibrated proportionately by the Enforcement Manual Model (EMM).[371]

---

[363] *Enforcement Policy Statement* (HSE, 2009) 02/09 http://www.hse.gov.uk/pubns/hse41.pdf, para 8. A review of approximately 200 sets of regulations and 53 ACOPs was undertaken in 2012–2013 to cull or simplify some, recommended by Löfstedt (n 361), which concluded that there is no case for radically altering current health and safety legislation. See *Progress Report on Health & Safety Reforms* (Department for Work & Pensions, 2013). For an explanation of the circumstances in which ACOPs are used see *Reducing Risks, Protecting People—HSE's Decision Making Process* (HSE, 2001) www.hse.gov.uk/risk/theory/r2p2.pdf.
[364] *Enforcement Policy Statement*, ibid.
[365] ibid, para 1.
[366] ibid, para 2.
[367] ibid, para 10.
[368] ibid, para 10.
[369] ibid, para 10. See http://www.hse.gov.uk/enforce/prosecutions.htm, which is a database of past HSE prosecutions and enforcement notices (not covering local authorities' actions), which is colloquially known as the 'name and shame' website.
[370] http://www.hse.gov.uk/enforce/enforcementguide/index.htm.
[371] http://www.hse.gov.uk/enforce/emm.pdf.

The enforcement tools are expected to be selected in an ascending sequence (that corresponds exactly to the Braithwaite approach) in the following order:

A.   Offering dutyholders information, and advice, both face to face and in writing. This may include warning a dutyholder that in the opinion of the inspector, they are failing to comply with the law.
B.   Where appropriate, inspectors may also serve improvement and prohibition notices,[372] withdraw approvals, vary licence conditions or exemptions, issue simple cautions[373] (England and Wales only), and
C.   They may prosecute (or report to the Procurator Fiscal with a view to prosecution in Scotland).

Giving information and advice, issuing improvement or prohibition notices, and withdrawal or variation of licences or other authorisations are stated to be the main means that inspectors use to achieve the broad aim of dealing with serious risks, securing compliance with health and safety law and preventing harm.[374] Enforcing authorities in England and Wales should make arrangements for the publication annually of the names of all the companies and individuals who have been convicted in the previous 12 months of breaking health and safety law.[375] They should also have arrangements for making publicly available information on these convictions and on improvement and prohibition notices which they have issued.[376]

In accordance with the principle of targeting, action is to be directed 'primarily on those whose activities give rise to the most serious risks or where the hazards are least well controlled; and that action is focused on the dutyholders who are responsible for the risk and who are best placed to control it—whether employers, manufacturers, suppliers, or others.'[377]

> HSE expects enforcing authorities to have systems for deciding which inspections, investigations or other regulatory contacts should take priority according to the nature and extent of risks posed by a dutyholder's operations. The dutyholder's management competence is important, because a relatively low hazard site poorly managed can entail greater risk to workers or the public than a higher hazard site where proper and adequate risk control measures are in place. Certain very high hazard sites will receive regular inspections so that enforcing authorities can give public assurance that such risks are properly controlled.
>
> Any enforcement action will be directed against dutyholders responsible for a breach. This may be employers in relation to workers or others exposed to risks; the self-employed; owners of premises;

---

[372] Every improvement notice contains a statement that in the opinion of an inspector an offence has been committed. Information about Notices is available at http://www.hse.gov.uk/enforce/enforcementguide/notices/notices-intro.htm. Improvement and prohibition notices, and written advice, may be used in court proceedings. A prohibition notice stops work in order to prevent serious personal injury. HSE may use these powers even when the duty holder has voluntarily undertaken to do, or is already doing, what the Notice specifies as HSE's requirements: See *Smallwood v Railtrack* [2001] All ER (D) 103 (Jan).
[373] A simple caution is a statement by an inspector, which is accepted in writing by the duty holder, that the duty holder has committed an offence for which there is a realistic prospect of conviction. A simple caution may only be used where a prosecution could be properly brought. 'Simple cautions' are entirely distinct from a caution given under the Police and Criminal Evidence Act 1984 by an inspector before questioning a suspect about an alleged offence. Enforcing authorities should take account of current Home Office guidelines when considering whether to offer a simple caution. Use of simple cautions appears to be very rare.
[374] *Enforcement Policy Statement* (n 363) para 4.
[375] ibid, para 44.
[376] ibid, paras 4 and 44.
[377] ibid, para 17.

suppliers of equipment; designers or clients of projects; or employees themselves. Where several dutyholders have responsibilities, enforcing authorities may take action against more than one when it is appropriate to do so in accordance with this policy.[378]

Indicative targets related to levels of investigation by HSE are normally specified in HSE's Business Plan, which is approved by the Government. Investigations are undertaken in order to determine:

— causes;
— whether action has been taken or needs to be taken to prevent a recurrence and to secure compliance with the law;
— lessons to be learnt and to influence the law and guidance;
— what response is appropriate to a breach of the law.[379]

HSE expects that, in the public interest, enforcing authorities should normally prosecute, or recommend prosecution, where, following an investigation or other regulatory contact, one or more of the following circumstances apply:

— death was a result of a breach of the legislation;
— the gravity of an alleged offence, taken together with the seriousness of any actual or potential harm, or the general record and approach of the offender warrants it;
— there has been reckless disregard of health and safety requirements;
— there have been repeated breaches which give rise to significant risk, or persistent and significant poor compliance;
— work has been carried out without or in serious non-compliance with an appropriate licence or safety case;
— a dutyholder's standard of managing health and safety is found to be far below what is required by health and safety law and to be giving rise to significant risk;
— there has been a failure to comply with an improvement or prohibition notice; or there has been a repetition of a breach that was subject to a simple caution;
— false information has been supplied wilfully, or there has been an intent to deceive, in relation to a matter which gives rise to significant risk;
— inspectors have been intentionally obstructed in the lawful course of their duties.[380]

HSE also expects that, in the public interest, enforcing authorities will consider prosecution, or consider recommending prosecution, where following an investigation or other regulatory contact, one or more of the following circumstances apply:

— it is appropriate in the circumstances as a way to draw general attention to the need for compliance with the law and the maintenance of standards required by law, and conviction may deter others from similar failures to comply with the law;
— a breach which gives rise to significant risk has continued despite relevant warnings from employees, or their representatives, or from others affected by a work activity.[381]

Subject to the above, enforcing authorities should identify and prosecute or recommend prosecution of individuals

if they consider that a prosecution is warranted. In particular, they should consider the management chain and the role played by individual directors and managers, and should take action

---

[378] ibid, paras 18 and 19.
[379] ibid, para 31.
[380] ibid, para 40.
[381] ibid, para 42.

against them where the inspection or investigation reveals that the offence was committed with their consent or connivance or to have been attributable to neglect on their part and where it would be appropriate to do so in accordance with this policy. Where appropriate, enforcing authorities should seek disqualification of directors under the Company Directors Disqualification Act 1986.[382]

Enforcement is distinct from civil claims for compensation and is not undertaken in all circumstances where civil claims may be pursued, nor to assist such claims.[383] As one of many reforms intended to reduce burdens on business and stimulate economic growth, civil liability for breach of statutory health and safety duties was removed in 2013, and can in future only apply where specifically designated by Regulations.[384]

From April 2012, HSE must recover its costs from those against whom it takes enforcement action, in accordance with the 'polluter pays' principle.[385] The 'fee for intervention' (FFI) has been applied previously in some sectors that have special safety regimes, such as rail, oil and gas chemical plants, although it is not applied by Local Authorities, and does not price any remediation of breaches, so is not true 'polluter pays'. The 2012 rules extended FFI to all HSE work where in their opinion they find a 'material' breach. HSE then issues a bill based on fixed hourly rates, recoverable as a civil debt. An appeal mechanism exists. FFI has been strongly criticised by stakeholders as potentially damaging the perception of HSE's impartiality, and inappropriate for where rules are not black and white rather than goal-setting, and HSE's 2013 independent reviewer recommended that it be phased out.[386]

In 2013 the government tabled the Social Action, Responsibility and Heroism Bill 2014, which would provide that when a court, in considering a claim that a person was negligent or in breach of statutory duty, is determining the steps that the person was required to take to meet a standard of care, must have regard to whether the alleged negligence or breach of statutory duty occurred when the person was acting for the benefit of society or any of its members, and must also have regard to whether the person, in carrying out the activity in the course of which the alleged negligence or breach of statutory duty occurred, demonstrated a generally responsible approach towards protecting the safety or other interests of others. The rationale for this was explained by the Lord Chancellor and Secretary of State for Justice as follows:

> All too often people who are doing the right thing in our society feel constrained by the fear that they are the ones who will end up facing a lawsuit for negligence.

> Take the responsible employer who puts in place proper training for staff, who has sensible safety procedures, and tries to do the right thing. And then someone injures themselves doing something stupid or something that no reasonable person would ever have expected to be a risk. Common sense says that the law should not simply penalise the employer for what has gone wrong.[387]

---

[382] ibid, para 43.

[383] ibid, para 2.

[384] Enterprise and Regulatory Reform Act 2013, s 69.

[385] See http://www.hse.gov.uk/fee-for-intervention/index.htm. See *Guidance on the Application of Fee for Intervention (FFI)* (HSE, 2012), and *HSE Proposal for Extending Cost Recovery* (HSE, 2011). Fee for Intervention Receipts for the period 1 October 2012 to 30 November 2012, involving 1491 bills issued totaled £727,644.81; only 10% were over £1000, and 70% were less than £500.

[386] Temple (n 362).

[387] C Grayling MP, 'Our Bill to Curb the Elf and Safety Culture' June 2 2014, at http://www.conservativehome.com/platform/2014/06/chris-grayling-mp-our-bill-to-curb-the-elf-and-safety-culture.html.

B. Current Enforcement Policy

An Enforcement Code binding on all Local Authorities (LAs) was issued in 2013,[388] following a recommendation in the Löfstedt review for HSE to be given a stronger role in directing LA health and safety inspection activity to ensure a more consistent and proportionate approach to enforcement.[389] The Code clarifies the roles and responsibilities of business, regulators and professional bodies to ensure a shared understanding on the management of risk; outlines the risk-based regulatory approach that LAs should adopt with reference to the Regulator's Compliance Code, HSE's Enforcement Policy Statement and the need to target relevant and effective interventions that focus on influencing behaviours and improving the management of risk; sets out the need for the training and competence of LA Health & Safety regulators linked to the authorisation and use of Health and Safety at Work etc Act 1974 (HSWA) powers; and explains the arrangements for collection and publication of LA data and peer review to give an assurance on meeting the requirements of the Code.[390] In relation to roles and responsibilities, it said:

> 8. Businesses, regulators, and professional bodies all have a role and responsibility to help prevent work place death, injury and ill health and to apply health and safety at work in a proportionate way.

> *Business*

> 9. Health and Safety law in Great Britain clearly sets out that the primary responsibility for managing risks to workers and the public who might be affected by work activity lies with the business or organisation that creates the risks in the first place. This applies whether the organisation is an employer, self-employed, service provider or a manufacturer or supplier of articles or substances for use at work. Whilst the primary responsibility sits with the business, workers also have a responsibility to care for their own health and safety and others who may be affected by their actions. Workers should accordingly be engaged by their employers on health and safety issues...

> *Regulators*

> 11. The role of the regulator is to support, encourage, advise and where necessary hold to account business to ensure that businesses effectively manage the occupational health and safety risks they create.

> 12. Regulators should ensure they make best use of their resource and help improve the effective management of health and safety risks in a proportionate way. This is achieved through choosing the most appropriate way of influencing risk creators and by targeting their interventions, including inspection, investigation and enforcement activity, on those businesses and sectors that represent a higher level of risk to the health and safety of workers and the public...[391]

---

[388] *National Local Authority Enforcement Code. Health and Safety at Work. England, Scotland & Wales* (Health and Safety Executive, 2013) http://www.hse.gov.uk/lau/national-la-code.pdf. The Code is given legal effect as HSE guidance to LAs under s 18(4) (b) of the HSW Act 1974 and applies to England, Wales and Scotland. It replaces the previous S18 Standard. Enforcement of health and safety is split between HSE and approximately 382 LAs in accordance with the Enforcing Authority (Health & Safety) Regs 1998.

[389] Löfstedt (n 361).

[390] *National Local Authority Enforcement Code* (n 388) para 4.

[391] ibid, paras 8–9 and 11–12.

With its central health and safety policy role HSE is to provide:

— Authoritative health and safety advice and guidance for business;
— Stakeholder engagement through involvement in industry liaison forums and other appropriate national forums;
— Specialist health and safety support and advice to LAs;
— Specific sector strategies with associated national planning priorities to inform LA regulatory interventions;
— A list of those high risk sectors/activities appropriate to be targeted for proactive inspection by LAs;
— Support for Primary Authorities and their inspection plans;
— Support LA peer review of their enforcement decisions, intervention plans and professional competence; and
— Monitor and publish LA intervention data for benchmarking purposes via the LAE1 return.[392]

In relation to risk-based interventions, the Code said that LA regulators should use a range of interventions, utilising all available methods and techniques, 'to influence behavioural change in the way business manages or undertakes its work.'[393] Interventions should be targeted on 'those activities that give rise to the most serious risks or where the hazards are least well controlled.'[394]

26. Proactive inspection must only be used to target the high risk activities in those sectors specified by HSE or where intelligence suggests risks are not being effectively managed. For this purpose HSE will publish a list of high risk sectors (and the key activities that make them such) that are to be subject to proactive inspections by LAs.[395]

Interventions and enforcement should be proportionate, 'related to the relative level of health and safety risks, including the potential or actual harm, or to the seriousness of any breach of the law', and

can achieve this by having trained and competent officers who can exercise professional judgement to:

— Differentiate between different levels of risk or harm;
— Decide how far short a business has fallen from managing the risks it creates effectively; and
— Apply proportionate decision making in accordance with the LA's Enforcement Policy, HSE's Enforcement Policy Statement and Enforcement Management Model…

LAs should maintain a strong deterrent against those businesses who fail to meet their health and safety obligations and put their employees at material risk thereby also deriving an unfair competitive advantage. LAs achieve this by continuing to take proportionate enforcement action in accordance with the Enforcement Management Model. LAs should publicise successful enforcement action to maintain a strong deterrent effect.[396]

LAs have a statutory duty to 'make adequate arrangements for enforcement' and to legally appoint suitably qualified inspectors to carry out the range of regulatory duties they have

---

[392] ibid, para 16.
[393] ibid, para 20.
[394] ibid, para 22.
[395] ibid, para 26.
[396] ibid, paras 30 and 34.

been appointed for.[397] The Code mandates data collection activities and peer review, which was said to have the advantages that it:

a) Provides an opportunity to discuss, refresh and share best working practices through seeing the work of others, and hearing different views and approaches;
b) Offers a means to instigate improvement in working practices. Ideas for improvement can be discussed, moderated, and developed during the peer review process;
c) Can verify that key messages have been understood and necessary change properly embedded;
d) Raises confidence and competence (eg confirming good practice and providing reassurance).[398]

The 2014 Triennial Independent Review of HSE recorded 'nearly universal praise and support for HSE' from stakeholders who responded to the consultation, but also that there had been a significant reduction in proactive inspections caused by budget cuts.[399] The review noted the importance of HSE's vital role in providing high level advice on compliance, clarifying and promoting health and safety.[400] However, organisations with a mature health and safety management system were concerned that they did not get enough HSE time or support in stimulating and assisting them deliver continuous improvement in their performance and that of their supply chain, which they saw as integral to their business philosophy and sustainability.[401] Some said they were more than willing to pay HSE for this service. The Review urged HSE to adopt innovative forms of delivering advice to sectors, through all modern forms such as Apps, Facebook and Twitter.[402]

X. Serious Fraud

Fraud was estimated to cost the UK economy £52 billion in 2012–13.[403] The lead agency is the Serious Fraud Office (SFO), which is an independent government department established in April 1988,[404] whose aim is 'to protect society from extensive, deliberate criminal deception which could threaten public confidence in the financial system. We investigate fraud and corruption that requires our investigative expertise and special powers to obtain and assess evidence to successfully prosecute fraudsters, freeze assets and compensate victims'.[405] It has separate divisions that handle fraud and bribery cases.

---

[397] See HSW Act 1974, s 18 (Authorities responsible for enforcement of the relevant statutory provisions); section 19 (Appointment of Inspectors) and s 20 (Powers of Inspectors).

[398] ibid, paras 45–57.

[399] Temple (n 362).

[400] ibid, para 2.31.

[401] ibid, Summary para 53. An 88% drop in inspections by HSE occurred from 2009–10 to 2012–13 (118,000 to 14,400): ibid, para 2.33.

[402] ibid, para 3.53–3.55.

[403] *Annual Fraud Indicator* (National Fraud Authority, 2013) https://www.gov.uk/government/uploads/system/uploads/attachment_data/file/206552/nfa-annual-fraud-indicator-2013.pdf. The previous year the figure was £73 billion.

[404] Criminal Justice Act 1987, following The Fraud Trials Committee Report (1986), 'Roskill Report'.

[405] See http://www.sfo.gov.uk/. The SFO was established in April 1988 under the Criminal Justice Act 1987 (as amended).

The SFO has extensive powers, notably to search property and compel persons to answer questions and produce documents.[406] It is subject to a number of codes that apply to prosecutors.[407] It aims to take on a small number of large cases. The SFO is unique amongst UK criminal enforcement agencies in both investigating and prosecuting cases. For this reason, it is not an educator or adviser,[408] and so has not adopted a more supportive approach towards business that is seen by other agencies.

Many victims of fraud and corruption suffer detriment, and face significant difficulties in recovering their losses. When considering enforcement, the SFO believes that the position of victims is a principal consideration. Accordingly, restorative justice constitutes a major enforcement objective, in addition to seeking criminal sanctions. The SFO states that it is 'focused on supporting victims and getting justice for them'.[409] The SFO has power to seek a confiscation order and has used this regularly,[410] although there has been some resistance from criminal judges.[411] The civil recovery powers under Part V of the Proceeds of Crime Act 2002 are available to the Director of the SFO for where property derived from crime can be identified, whether it is held by an individual or body corporate. In exercising these powers, the Director of the SFO will follow the Attorney General's guidance to prosecuting bodies on their asset recovery powers.[412] These relate to where it is not feasible to secure a conviction, or a conviction has been secured but no confiscation order made.

---

[406] Criminal Justice Act 1987, s 2.

[407] The Code for Crown Prosecutors, Joint prosecution guidance on the Bribery Act 2010, Guidance on Corporate Prosecutions, Attorney General's guidance on Asset Recovery Powers under 2A of the POCA 2002, Attorney General's guidance on Plea Discussions.

[408] S Alford QC, 'Enforcing the UK Bribery Act-The UK Serious Fraud Office's Perspective' speech at the Anti-Corruption in Oil & Gas Conference 2014, 17 November 2014, at http://www.sfo.gov.uk/about-us/our-views/other-speeches/speeches-2014/stuart-alford-qc-enforcing-the-uk-bribery-act---the-uk-serious-fraud-office's-perspective.aspx.

[409] 'Common Misconceptions' at http://www.sfo.gov.uk/about-us/common-misconceptions.aspx.

[410] See ch 10 above. In one case, confiscation orders were made amounting to £24 million: See Carlton Cushnie, at http://www.sfo.gov.uk/our-work/our-cases/historic-cases/versailles-plc---a-trade-finance-fraud.aspx. In the Alta Gas case, Peter Brain Bradley was jailed for an extra five years for failing to pay a £1 million confiscation order, which was to be paid as compensation to victims of the fraud: At http://www.sfo.gov.uk/our-work/our-cases/historic-cases/alta-gas-plc.aspx. In the Operation Anderson case, Philip Anthony Bates was ordered to pay a confiscation order of £1,479,404 by 26 November 2010, or serve a default sentence of five years imprisonment. Bates was originally sentenced in December 2008 for defrauding major insurance companies into paying over £1M in up-front commissions on fake policies.

The confiscation included an order for compensation in the sum of £1,022,523 to be paid out of the confiscation funds with a separate compensation order of £123,799 made in respect of one victim. See http://www.sfo.gov.uk/our-work/our-cases/historic-cases/operation-anderson.aspx. In the Practical Property Portfolio Ltd case, around 4,000 residential properties in the north of England were sold to over 1,750 investors as a buy-to-let scheme. Confiscation orders were made against five defendants totalling approximately £1.7 million. See http://www.sfo.gov.uk/our-work/our-cases/historic-cases/practical-property-portfolio-ltd-.aspx.

[411] In prosecution of directors of Innospec Limited, the proposed restorative sum was added to the fine: see https://www.sfo.gov.uk/press-room/latest-press-releases/press-releases-2014/four-sentenced-for-role-in-innospec-corruption.aspx.

[412] *Asset Recovery Powers for Prosecutors: Guidance and Background Note 2009* (Attorney General's Office, 2009) at https://www.gov.uk/asset-recovery-powers-for-prosecutors-guidance-and-background-note-2009, issued under the Proceeds of Crime Act 2002, s 2A.

XI. Bribery

A strong international consensus has moved against corruption and bribery in recent years.[413] The UK Bribery Act 2010 introduced the ability to impose deterrent criminal sanctions on both individuals and commercial organisations. The Act contains an express defence for a corporation where it can show that it had in place 'adequate procedures' designed to prevent bribery on its behalf.[414] This has resulted in all companies of any size adopting sophisticated internal compliance regimes.[415] Bribery is regarded as a serious issue by the government.[416] Globally, bribery is concentrated in certain sectors.[417]

The Ministry of Justice's guidance sets out how the offences should apply, in particular with respect to corporate hospitality, facilitation payments, joint ventures, subsidiaries and supply chains.[418] It refers to being outcome-focused and flexible. The guidance explains the policy behind the corporate offence (section 7) and its defence where 'adequate procedures designed to prevent persons associated with [the firm] from undertaking' the prescribed conduct as

> not to bring the full force of criminal law to bear upon well-run commercial organisations that experience an isolated incident of bribery on their behalf. So in order to achieve an appropriate balance, section 7 provides a full defence. This is in recognition of the fact that no bribery prevention programme will be capable of preventing bribery at all times. However, the defence is also included in order to encourage commercial organisations to put procedures in place to prevent bribery by persons associated with them.[419]

---

[413] OECD Declaration on International Investment and Multinational Enterprises 1976, revised 1979, 1984 and 1991; OECD Convention on Combating Bribery of Foreign Public Officials in International Business Transactions, adopted by the Negotiating Conference on 21 November 1997; Council of Europe, Civil Law Convention on Corruption, 4 November 1999 and Council of Europe, Criminal Law Convention on Corruption, 27 January 1999; see in respect of the former also Civil Law Convention on Corruption (ETS No 174) 4 XI 1999, Council of Europe, Explanatory Report, http://conventions.coe.int/treaty/en/treaties/html/174.htm.

UN Convention against Corruption 2003: http://www.unodc.org/unodc/en/treaties/CAC/index.html; UN Convention against Corruption 2003; *OECD Guidelines for Multinational Enterprises, Recommendations for Responsible Business Conduct in a Global Context,* OECD Ministerial Meeting 25 May 2011, available at: http://www.oecd.org/dataoecd/43/29/48004323.pdf; in USA, the Foreign Corrupt Practices Act of 1977, as amended, 15 USC §§ 78dd-1 ff.

[414] Bribery Act 2010, s 7(2).

[415] It was reported that the number of businesses self-reporting white collar crime to the Serious Fraud Office almost doubled from seven reports in 2010–2011 to 12 in 2011–2012, attributable to introduction of the Act: *Corporate Confessions to Serious Fraud Office almost Double in Last Year* (Pinsent Masons, 2013) available at http://www.pinsentmasons.com/en/media/press-releases/2013/corporate-confessions-to-serious-fraud-office-almost-double-in-last-year/.

[416] *UK Anti-Corruption Plan* (HM Government, 2014).

[417] *OECD Foreign Bribery Report. An Analysis of the Crime of Bribery of Foreign Public Officials* (OECD, 2014): Finding that two-thirds of foreign bribery cases occurred in four sectors: Extractive (19%), construction (15%), transportation and storage (15%), and information and communication (10%). 57% of cases involved obtaining public procurement contracts. 41% of cases involved payments or authorisations by management-level employees. One in three cases were self-reported by companies. Companies that self-reported became aware mainly through internal audit (31%) and merger and acquisition due diligence procedures (28%); only 2% involved whistleblowers.

[418] *The Bribery Act 2010. Guidance about Procedures which Relevant Commercial Organisations can put into Place to Prevent Persons Associated with them from Bribing (Section 9 of the Bribery Act 2010)* (Ministry of Justice, 2011) available at http://www.justice.gov.uk/downloads/legislation/bribery-act-2010-guidance.pdf.

[419] ibid, para 11.

The guidance suggests that[420] commercial organisations, in setting up procedures designed to prevent bribery,[421] should consider six broad principles when designing their procedures, which are not prescriptive and are not intended to be 'one-size-fits-all':

— Proportionate Procedures—'The action you take should be proportionate to the risks you face and the size of your business'.
— Top-level commitment—'Those at the top of an organisation are in the best position to ensure their organisation conducts business without bribery'.
— Risk Assessment—'Think about the bribery risks you might face. For example, do some research into the markets you operate in and the people you do business with…'
— Due diligence—'Knowing exactly who you are dealing with can help to protect your organisation from taking on people who might be less than trustworthy'.
— Communication (including training)—'Communicating your policies and procedures to staff and to others who will perform services for you…'
— Monitoring and review—'The risks you face and the effectiveness of your procedures may change over time'.

Specialist lawyer commentators have noted:

> The key element is proportionality. What procedures will be 'adequate' for any particular corporate will vary, according to considerations such as the organisation's size, sector and the countries in which it operates. So, for example, a small firm in a low-risk sector may be doing enough simply to have a clear set of relevant anti-corruption principles in place that it has communicated to its workforce. However, for bigger organisations operating in high-risk jurisdictions or high-risk industries, far more will be expected.[422]

The Bribery Act was followed in 2014 by related Sentencing Council Guidance, which applied to a range of conduct: Fraud; possessing, making or supplying articles for use in frauds; revenue fraud; benefit fraud; money laundering; bribery; and corporate offenders.[423] The British Bankers' Association (BBA) also published updated anti-bribery and corruption guidance intended to advise the banking sector about taking the necessary actions that are relevant and proportionate to their individual circumstances and risk profile to meet the legal and regulatory requirements arising from the Bribery Act 2010 and subsequent FCA guidance.[424] The revised guidance gave greater weighting to regulatory considerations and recognised the importance of recent FCA thematic reviews, enforcement actions and policy statements. The BBA guidance recommended that meeting the 'adequate procedures' standard would need to include aspects listed in Box 13.1.

---

[420] The following commentary is taken from O Quereshi and J Smith, *The UK Bribery Act 2010: What You Need to Know* (London, CMS Cameron McKenna, 2011).
[421] A model compliance system that has been favourably commented on by the UK authorities is the Anti-Corruption Training Manual (GIACC and Transparency International (UK)) available at http://www.giaccentre.org/anti_corruption_training.php.
[422] Quereshi and Smith (n 420).
[423] *Fraud, Bribery and Money Laundering Offences Guideline. Definitive Guidance* (Sentencing Council, 2014) at http://sentencingcouncil.judiciary.gov.uk/docs/Fraud_bribery_and_money_laundering_offences_-_Definitive_guideline.pdf. See further ch 10 above.
[424] *Anti-Bribery and Corruption Guidance* (BBA, May 2014) available at https://www.bba.org.uk/wp-content/uploads/2014/05/ABC_guidelines_designed-final.pdf.

Box 13.1: BBA Anti-Bribery and Corruption Guidance: Meeting the Standard[425]

It is not possible to be entirely prescriptive regarding the characteristics of systems and controls that meet the requisite 'adequate' standard, but they may include some or all of the following:

— the active and ongoing sponsorship by senior managers
— adequate resourcing of anti-bribery work
— standardisation and consistency across the entire business
— risk assessment procedures and bribery prevention policies for different project or business areas
— budgetary, authorisation and audit controls in relation to all financial transactions, with a review of such requirements on a periodic basis and regular 'stress testing', including a procedure to govern the response to changes in both the internal and external environment
— a new business approvals process that incorporates anti-bribery and corruption considerations
— a clear, consistent and practical gifts and corporate hospitality controls system
— controls and processes for the authorisation and tracking of non-'business as usual', gratuitous or 'non-core business' payments such as sponsorships, corporate hospitality and expenses, and charitable and political donations
— due diligence on associated persons and controls over outsourcing with standard procurement and tendering processes
— governance over associates' relationships including pre- and post-contractual agreements
— enforcement and incident management policies and procedures
— whistle-blowing policies and procedures
— enhanced controls where 'cross border' activity is undertaken, with particular consideration to the risks arising from facilitation payments
— staff code of conduct and incorporation of standards into employment terms and remuneration policies that embed a zero tolerance policy
— staff training for all employees within an organisation, with enhanced training provided for those staff who have been assessed as holding higher-risk positions
— recruitment processes that screen staff based on a risk assessment of the role in question
— communication of policies and procedures
— monitoring, review and evaluation.

XII. The Care Quality Commission

The Care Quality Commission (CQC) is the independent regulator of health and adult social care in England. It regulates a wide range of large and small organisations providing

---

[425] ibid, 16.

treatment, care and support services, services under the Mental Health Act.[426] The CQC's purpose is to make sure health and social care services provide people with safe, effective, compassionate, high-quality care and to encourage care services to improve.[427] Its role is to monitor, inspect and regulate services to make sure they meet fundamental standards of quality and safety, and to publish what it finds, including performance ratings to help people choose care. It publishes regular reports on the state of healthcare in the country.[428] Registered persons 'must have regard' to guidance issued by the CQC,[429] and it is itself required to take guidance into account in making its regulatory decisions.[430]

The background to a sequence of serious failings, amidst much safe and effective care, in the NHS are given in chapter 19 below, and explain the main drivers for a major change in approach initiated in 2014.[431]

The regulatory system specifies fundamental standards, below which care must never fall. Facilities must be registered, and the CQC inspects facilities and entities, with inspectors specialised in a particular care sector and accompanied by specialist inspectors and experts, and rates them based on professional and clinical judgement not compliance. It operates a new intelligence driven model to assess the ongoing risks to the quality of care in providers, and to guide its inspection activity.[432]

The fundamental standards are:[433]

1. Care and treatment must be appropriate and reflect service users' needs and preferences.
2. Service users must be treated with dignity and respect.
3. Care and treatment must only be provided with consent.
4. Care and treatment must be provided in a safe way.
5. Service users must be protected from abuse and improper treatment.
6. Service users' nutritional and hydration needs must be met.
7. All premises and equipment used must be clean, secure, suitable and used properly.
8. Complaints must be appropriately investigated and appropriate action taken in response.
9. Systems and processes must be established to ensure compliance with the fundamental standards.
10. Sufficient numbers of suitably qualified, competent, skilled and experienced staff must be deployed.

---

[426] There are three categories: (1) Hospitals, mental health and community services, including: 276 independent acute hospitals, 47 independent treatment centres, 162 NHS trusts, 58 mental health trusts and Mental Health Act functions, 11 ambulance services, and 353 community health care services; (2) Adult social care, including: 52 specialist college services, 64 community-based services for people with a learning disability, 109 Shared Lives, 17,350 residential social care homes with and without nursing, 202 hospices, 8,110 home care services, 105 Extra Care housing services, and 271 supported living services; (3) Primary medical services and integrated care, including: 8,592 GP practices, out-of-hours services and mobile doctors, 10,102 dental care locations, 146 prison health-care services, 9 remote clinical advice services, and 35 urgent care services.

[427] See *About us, What we Do and How we Do it* (Care Quality Commission, 2013); *Raising Standards, Putting People First. Our Strategy for 2013 to 2016* (Care Quality Commission, 2013).

[428] *The State of Health Care and Adult Social Care in England 2013/14* (Care Quality Commission, 2014).

[429] Health and Social Care Act 2008 (Regulated Activity) Regs 2014 (as amended), reg 21.

[430] Health and Social Care Act 2008, s 25(1).

[431] Extended powers were granted in the Care Act 2014.

[432] *Annual Report 2013/14* (Care Quality Commission, 2014).

[433] The Health and Social Care Act 2008 (Regulated Activities) Regs 2014/2936.

11. Persons employed must be of good character, have the necessary qualifications, skills and experience, and be able to perform the work for which they are employed (fit and proper persons requirement).
12. Registered persons must be open and transparent with service users about their care and treatment (the duty of candour).

The CQC adopted language from the aviation sector in aiming to create a 'just and open culture in CQC, one that is open about what people think and believe, where we learn from mistakes to get better, and are encouraged to raise concerns that will be listened to'.[434]

The CQC took 1,523 enforcement actions in 2013/14, compared with 1,029 in 2012/13, a rise of 50 per cent. Most of these were warning notices: 1,456 compared with 910 in 2012/13. Overall, 4,679 locations cancelled their registration in the year; of these 567 (12 per cent) cancelled while not meeting one or more standards.[435] In its Quarter 3 post-inspection survey, 83 per cent of adult social care services agreed or strongly agreed that the inspection visit helped them reflect how they could improve their service, and 73 per cent of services agreed or strongly agreed that the inspection report provided information that will help them to take action to improve their service. The figure was 90 per cent and 86 per cent respectively for NHS respondents.

A new Enforcement Policy came into force from April 2015,[436] concerning enforcement of the Health and Social Care Act 2008, the Health and Social Care Act 2008 (Regulated Activities) Regulations 2014,[437] and the Care Quality Commission (Registration) Regulations 2009.[438] The approach sets out a backstop of criminal or civil enforcement actions but clearly prioritises softer actions to support and improve the performance of entities.

The CQC states that there are two primary purposes when using its enforcement powers:

1. To protect people who use regulated services from harm and the risk of harm, and to ensure they receive health and social care services of an appropriate standard.
    — We may work with a provider without using enforcement powers to improve standards where the quality or safety of a service is below the required standards but we assess the risk of harm is not immediate and we consider the provider should be able to improve standards on their own
    — We may take enforcement action to compel improvement where the quality or safety of a service has fallen to unacceptable levels, especially where there is a risk of harm to service users. In such cases we may intervene directly (for example, to restrict a service) or trigger others to intervene.
2. To hold providers and individuals to account for failures in how the service is provided.
    — We have powers to pursue criminal sanctions when there has been a breach of the fundamental standards of quality and safety or some other criminal offence.

---

[434] *Annual Report 2013/14* (n 432).

[435] ibid.

[436] *Enforcement Policy* (Care Quality Commission, 2015). See also *Enforcement Decision Tree* (Care Quality Commission, 2015).

[437] As amended by a) Health and Social Care Act 2008 (Registration and Regulated Activities (Amendment) Regs 2015 and b) The Health and Social Care Act 2008 (Regulated Activities) (Amendment) Regs 2012.

[438] As amended by a) The Care Quality Commission (Registration) and (Additional Functions) and Health and Social Care Act 2008 (Regulated Activities) (Amendment) Regs 2012 and b) The Care Quality Commission (Registration and Membership) (Amendment) Regs 2012.

— Using the full range of our enforcement powers, including criminal sanctions, should ensure that providers are focused on the need to provide services that meet Parliament's regulatory requirements.[439]

It states five principles to guide the use of decision making in relation to its enforcement powers:

1. Being on the side of people who use regulated services
2. Integrating enforcement into our regulatory model
3. Proportionality
4. Consistency
5. Transparency.

The CQC includes the following statements:

— The starting point for considering the use of all enforcement powers is to assess the harm or the risk of harm to people using a service.
— We will only take action that we judge to be proportionate. This means that our response, including the use of enforcement powers, must be assessed by us to be proportionate to the circumstances of an individual case. Where appropriate, if the provider is able to improve the service on their own and the risks to people who use services are not immediate, we will generally work with them to improve standards rather than taking enforcement action. We generally intervene if people are at an unacceptable risk of harm or providers are repeatedly or seriously failing to comply with their legal obligations.[440]

The rating that a facility receives drives the type of action that is taken, as shown in Table 13.4.

— Our inspections first assess if the care provided is good. Where it is not, we will explore if care requires improvement or is inadequate. At that stage, we will consider whether any of the regulations are being breached. For care to be rated as requires improvement, it does not necessarily mean there is a breach of a regulation. Where care falls below the standard required by the regulations, it will at best be rated as requires improvement. Care rated as inadequate will normally be in breach of regulations.
— While we publish ratings for most providers registered with us, the regulations apply to everyone, including those registered providers for whom we do not publish ratings. We will apply this policy to consider whether we should take enforcement action against providers and others where we find breaches of the regulations.[441]

Where breaches of regulations do not constitute a criminal offence, standards may be enforced by using civil powers to impose conditions, suspend a registration or cancel a registration. Failure to comply with the steps required under our civil powers is a criminal offence and so may result in a prosecution.

---

[439] *Enforcement Policy* (n 436) ch 1.
[440] ibid, 7–8.
[441] ibid, 9.

Table 13.4: Relationship between the CQC's Ratings and the Regulations[442]

Overall rating	Level of meeting the regulations	High-level characteristics of each rating level
Inadequate	Providers rated as inadequate are generally likely to be not meeting the standards set in the regulations (with the possible exception of the well-led rating, which is not completely covered by the regulations).	Significant harm has occurred or is likely to occur. There are shortfalls in practice and ineffective action or no action has been taken to put things right or improve standards.
Requires improvement	Providers rated as requires improvement may or may not be meeting the standards set out in the regulations.	Providers may have elements of good practice, but provide inconsistent standards of care. This gives rise to potential or actual risk to people using services and/or the provider gives inadequate or inconsistent responses when things go wrong.
Good	Providers rated as good are meeting the standards set out in the regulations and display the characteristics of good care (that is, to be rated good means more than just meeting the standards set out in the regulations).	Providers demonstrate a consistent level of service that meets or exceeds the regulatory standards. The provider has robust arrangements in place for when things go wrong.
Outstanding	Providers rated as outstanding are meeting the regulations and display the characteristics of outstanding care.	Providers are innovative and creative, and are constantly striving to improve standards. They are open and transparent.

Decisions on what action to take are guided by the two basic purposes:

1. To protect people who use regulated services from harm and the risk of harm, and to ensure they receive health and social care services of an appropriate standard. We can do this by either requiring or forcing improvement.
2. To hold providers and individuals to account for failures in how a service is provided.[443]

Thus, particular purposes are likely to be linked to use of specific enforcement tools:

Purpose: Requiring improvement to protect people from harm or the risk of harm:

— Requirement Notices (formerly known as 'compliance actions')
— Warning Notices
— Section 29A Warning Notices[444,445]

---

[442] ibid, 9.
[443] ibid, 18.
[444] S 29A only relates to NHS trusts (including foundation trusts).
[445] *Enforcement Policy* (n 436) 18.

Purpose: Using civil powers to protect people from harm or the risk of harm and to improve care standards:
Civil enforcement powers

— Imposing, varying or removing conditions of registration
— Suspending registration
— Cancelling registration
— Urgent procedures

Special measures

— Time-limited approach ensures inadequate care is not allowed to continue
— Coordination with other oversight bodies[446]

Purpose: Holding providers and individuals to account for failure
Criminal powers

— Simple cautions
— Penalty notices
— Prosecution

Holding individuals to account

— Fit and proper person requirement
— Prosecution of individuals[447]

The CQC uses a four-stage decision-making process to reach enforcement decisions (enforcement decision tree).

1. Initial assessment;
2. Legal and evidential review;
3. Selection of the appropriate enforcement action: out criteria that are used to assist in this decision-making process are:
   — Seriousness of the concerns.
   — Evidence of multiple and/or persistent breaches.
4. Final review.[448]

XIII. Conclusions

This chapter has examined the enforcement policies that have been issued by a range of public regulatory authorities from 2010 to date, mostly pursuant to requirements imposed by central government to issue such policies. Most of the authorities, but not all, had previously published enforcement policies. It can be seen that the enforcement policies are not identical in approach, although there are various important similarities. The general approach has shifted from an historical approach based firmly on sanctioning, punishment

---

[446] ibid, 20.
[447] ibid, 26.
[448] *Enforcement Decision Tree* (n 436).

and deterrence to a wider and softer approach that generally displays firm roots in responsive regulation policy, with elements of supporting responsible businesses to maintain or improve compliance with requirements by means of providing advice and support. Firmer approaches do, of course, remain to respond to instances where deliberately illegal or criminal actions occur, or serious harm is caused. Regulators now have considerable flexibility in responding to particular situations as a result of having a wide toolbox that encompasses not just criminal powers but also civil sanctions and the wider abilities, such as to accept undertakings, give advice. It can also be seen that the enforcement policies include an evolution in focus that has been spurred by the better regulation focus that has developed on markets and outcomes. Accordingly, various regulators have widened their conceptions of their role and how they should use their powers, as can be seen by the strong focus of some of them on ensuring that redress is made by those whose illegal acts have resulted in harm to others. These points are considered further in the general conclusions to Part C in chapter 16.

14

Consumer Trading and Protection

Enforcement of general consumer protection law has always had a complex history. This chapter begins by noting the evidence of significant consumer detriment as a result of non-compliance with trading law. It then sets out the complexities of the landscape of consumer enforcement, advisory and advocacy bodies, which has undergone significant recent reform, spurred by the need to reduce public expenditure but also with the aim of simplifying the landscape and making the system more effective. The consumer trading area is unusual in that it has been the subject of a number of research studies carried out by the national body, Competition and Markets Authority (formerly the Office of Fair Trading (OFT)), and various other bodies. The studies have examined what drives compliance and non-compliance by businesses, large and small. Many of the studies are of limited scientific value, being based on surveys, but together they constitute an important corpus, not least because they have been used as the foundation for the OFT's published enforcement policies. We then review the development of governmental enforcement policies in relation to consumer trading and protection law, before drawing conclusions. Although the topics and materials have been grouped (of necessity, in order to form a coherent narrative) into the subject headings noted above (need, landscape, powers, studies, policy) in reality multiple strands were developing contemporaneously, so a different viewpoint can be obtained by taking an integrated overview of developments: To facilitate this, dates have been included throughout.

I. Evidence of Need

Research into levels of consumer detriment caused by unfair trading has been carried out in the UK by the OFT in 2008[1] and updated by Consumer Focus in 2012.[2] This mirrors research on the EU (European Union) position by the European Commission.[3] Studies have

---

[1] *Consumer Detriment: Assessing the Frequency and Impact of Consumer Problems with Goods and Services* (Office of Fair Trading, 2008) OFT992, available at http://www.oft.gov.uk/shared_oft/reports/consumer_protection/oft992.pdf.

[2] TNS BMRM, *Consumer Detriment 2012* (Consumer Focus, 2012) at http://www.consumerfocus.org.uk/publications/consumer-detriment-2012.

[3] Evidence on EU consumer detriment and complaints is summarised at C Hodges, 'Consumer Redress: Ideology and Empiricism' in K Purnhagen and P Rott (eds), *Varieties of European Economic Law and Regulation. Festschrift for Hans Micklitz* (Vienna, Springer, 2014).

been consistent over some years in revealing significant levels of consumer detriment,[4] at national level and EU level.[5] The estimated annual consumer detriment from unfair trading in the UK was estimated in 2011 at £6.6 billion, and the estimated minimum annual cost of detriment occurring across local authority boundaries at £4.8 billion.[6] However, 78 per cent of consumers in the UK felt adequately protected by consumer protection arrangements.[7]

The 2012 study by Consumer Focus, based on a corpus of interviews,[8] estimated that a total of 15.7 million problems had been experienced with goods and services purchased in the previous 12 months. The number was a significantly lower number than in 2008 (25.5 million), which was attributed to a combination of a reduction in GDP,[9] lower consumer spending power and strengthening of consumer protection and safeguards with consequent improvements in the quality of goods and services supplied.[10] Consumers were most likely to have experienced problems with household fittings and appliances and other household requirements such as food and drink, utilities, DIY materials, gardening and cleaning services. A fifth of consumers (22 per cent) experienced one or more problems with goods or services purchased in the previous 12 months. This was significantly lower than the 2008 survey (down 12 percentage points). In terms of the more detailed (tier two) categories of problems, consumers most frequently reported having experienced problems with home improvements (two per cent), personal banking (two per cent), internet facilities (two per cent) domestic fuel (two per cent) and telecommunications (two per cent).

The problems consumers most frequently reported related to the quality of the service or the product. Three in 10 (31 per cent) problems were with the quality of service; being either poor service quality (20 per cent) or the service not being provided or up to standard

[4] For the difficulties of measuring consumer detriment, and a view that some form of cost-benefit analysis is the best approach, see *Consumer Detriment under Conditions of Imperfect Information* (Office of Fair Trading, 1997) Research Paper 11, available at: http://www.oft.gov.uk/shared_oft/reports/consumer_protection/oft194.pdf.

[5] *Communication from the Commission: Monitoring Consumer Outcomes in the Single Market. The Consumer Markets Scoreboard* (European Commission, 1998) http://eur-lex.europa/LexUriServ/LexUriServ.do?uri-COM:2008:0031:FIN:EN:PDF ('Policies need to be more evidence-based and outcome-oriented'. '... political currents driving the growth of consumer policy [being] part of a wider political trend for policies that deliver effective solutions to the problems faced by the general public'.). For a recent summary see Hodges (n 3).

[6] Department for Business, Innovation & Skills, the Office of Fair Trading and Local Authority Trading Standards Services. *Protecting Consumers—The System for Enforcing Consumer Law*. Report by the Comptroller and Auditor General (National Audit Office, 15 June 2011) http://www.official-documents.gov.uk/document/hc1012/hc10/1087/1087.pdf.

[7] ibid.

[8] 10,036 interviews were conducted. All respondents were asked to identify any problems (up to six) they had experienced with various goods and services within the last year. A total of 1,314 respondents were then asked more detailed questions about 1,726 problems encountered in the last 12 months.

[9] Decrease in GDP and consequent spend on goods and services over the last four years. The Family Spending Survey [ONS Family Spending survey: Report on the 2010 Living Costs and Food Survey Edition 2011] indicates that average weekly expenditure per person fell from £207.40 in 2008 to £201.30 in 2010. Further, gross average weekly household income peaked in 2008 at £742 per week as did average household disposable income at £606 per week. In 2010 average household income had fallen to £700 and £578 per week respectively. However, average weekly household expenditure has remained about the same (£474 per week in 2010 compared with £471 per week in 2008).

[10] The potential improvement in quality of goods and services supplied was evidenced by the fall in the number of cases reported to Consumer Direct over the period. Consumer Direct received over 1.05 million cases between April 2010 and March 2011, which was an 8% decrease from the 1.14 million cases reported in 2007: See http://www.oft.gov.uk/shared_oft/annual_report/2007/hc836f.pdf.

(13 per cent). 78 per cent of consumers experienced no problems in the previous 12 months (68 per cent in 2008).

Half of all problems were connected with purchasing household fittings and appliances and other household requirements. Just over a third of problems are with regulated services (37 per cent).[11] Table 14.1 shows the total number of problems in each sector in the previous 12 months.[12] Just over four million problems were experienced with house fittings and appliances and a similar number (3.8 million) with other household requirements. Almost six million (5.8 million) problems were experienced in the previous 12 months with regulated services.

Table 14.1: Estimate of Total Number of Problems Experienced by Consumers per Sector in Previous 12 Months

Household fittings and appliances	4.1m
Other household requirements	3.8m
Leisure	2.4m
Professional and financial services	2.4m
Transport	1.6m
Personal goods and services	1.4m
Any regulated service (NET)	5.8m

Looking at the more detailed categorisation of goods and services, the most frequently occurring problems were with fixed and mobile telecommunications (8 per cent), personal banking (7 per cent), domestic fuel (6 per cent) and internet services (6 per cent). Within house fittings and appliances, the most frequent problems were with home maintenance and improvements (5 per cent), large domestic appliances (4 per cent) and PCs (3 per cent) (see Figure 14.1).

The most frequent problems consumers encountered with these goods and services include poor service quality (31 per cent) or the service not being up to standard (20 per cent) and the goods being defective (24 per cent) or faulty, damaged or lacking durability (19 per cent) (see Table 14.2). This is very similar to the kinds of problems encountered by consumers in 2008. The only problem consumers mention significantly less frequently than in 2008 is problems with the price of goods and services (three per cent compared with seven per cent in 2008).

---

[11] Regulated goods and services included: Gas and electricity, water, postal services, communications (covering fixed landline telephones, mobile telephone, broadband, internet service providers and broadcast services), public transport (covering rail, bus, tram, underground/metro) and UK airports.
[12] Department for Business, Innovation & Skills, the Office of Fair Trading and Local Authority Trading Standards Services (n 6) Table 4.3.

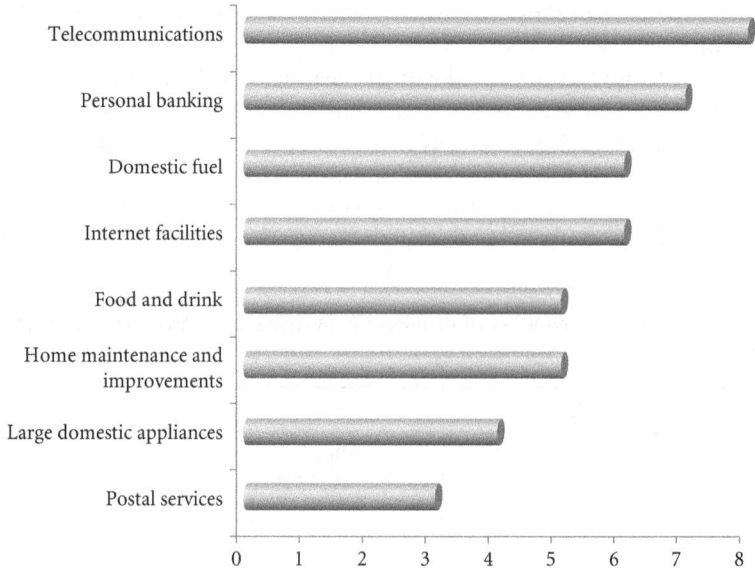

Figure 14.1: Goods and Services-sectors (Second Tier Categories) with the Highest Proportion of Problems[13]

Table 14.2: Types of Consumer Problem[14]

Problem	
Poor service quality	31%
Defective goods	24%
Service not provided	20%
Faulty/Damaged goods/wear out quickly	19%
Being overcharged	10%
Wrong/Unsuitable product	8%
Delivery/Collection/Repair problems	8%
Goods/Service incorrectly described/misleading advertisement	6%
Goods/Service delivered late/not at all	6%
Price too high for quality	6%
Failure/Delay in promised repair	5%
Difficulty sorting out problems with retailer	5%
Base: All problems identified at Q1	3,085

---

[13] ibid, Chart 4.6.
[14] ibid, Table 4.2.

The overall level of consumer detriment, as reported by consumers, in 2012 was estimated to be £3.08 billion. This excluded detriment of which consumers were not yet aware, for instance mis-selling of financial products that comes to light much later. This was lower than in 2008, reflecting the lower number of problems and higher proportion incurring no financial detriment. In both cases the overall figures are dominated by a very small number of high cost events. Problems that cost a consumer more than £1,000 make up only 2 per cent of consumer problems in 2012, but they comprise 75 per cent of the total financial detriment.

Most problems incurred little or no financial detriment; 65 per cent of all consumers' problems led to financial detriment of less than £5, including 46 per cent incurring no financial detriment. But detriment of £5 or less only comprised 0.3 per cent of the total financial detriment (£9 million). Problems that incurred more than £20 of financial detriment accounted for a quarter of all consumer problems (24 per cent), but comprise 99 per cent of all financial detriment.

Average financial loss consumers incurred from a problem was £196 (down from £249 in 2008). Excluding problems with no financial detriment the mean average was £376 of financial detriment, which shows no real change from 2008 (£368). Problems with the highest levels of financial detriment were for professional and financial services (mean average £464) and transport (mean average £413). Problems with regulated services incurred lower levels of financial detriment (£48 on average). Non-financial impacts including personal time spent rectifying the problem, welfare effects and social effects increase with financial detriment levels.

Table 14.3: Total Consumer Detriment by Sector[15]

	Total GB
Professional and financial services	£1.22 billion
Transport	£695 billion
Household fittings and appliances	£477 million
Leisure	£324 million
Personal goods and services	£194 million
Other household requirements	£167 million
Any regulated service (NET)	£178 million

Half of problems (50 per cent) were considered resolved, while over a third (36 per cent) were considered not to be resolved at all (similar pattern in 2008). For consumers where the problem has been completely resolved, more than three quarters are satisfied with the final outcome of the problem (80 per cent). Companies and firms took varied action to resolve the problems with goods and services that consumers experience. Companies and firms had taken some action to resolve 61 per cent of problems. This was a significant decline in the number of companies taking action (to date) to resolve the problem compared with

[15] ibid, Table 5.1.

the previous study in 2008 (72 per cent). The main actions taken (at the date of preparation of the study) were to acknowledge the problem (20 per cent), to solve or investigate the problem (22 per cent) and to apologise (20 per cent). In just over a quarter of cases consumers were given/offered a replacement or alternative (13 per cent) or full or partial refund (14 per cent) or credit note (two per cent). For over a third (35 per cent) of problems companies had not done anything, but not all consumers who have cause to complain about a problem actually do. In a quarter of problems that are not fully resolved, the consumer has not and is not intending to pursue the matter with the company/firm involved.

A study by the European Commission showed that the paradigm of the informed rational consumer is far from the truth in making investment choices, and decisions can be influenced by many choices, some of which can appear trivial to others.[16] Of five investment choices presented to participants in the study, less than two per cent of participants made the right choice every time.[17] A Commission 'mystery shopping' trawl found that independent investment advice to consumers was in many cases more in the provider's interest than the consumer's.[18]

The Commission emphasised a need for public regulatory bodies in 1998, and also an increased need for cooperation:

> Whilst consumers have a responsibility to promote their own interests, they heavily depend on public authorities to promote their health and safety on their behalf, by ensuring that products and services on the market meet high standards. Public bodies will always be best placed to independently monitor the complicated processes by which products and services reach the market and give consumers confidence. Again, while consumers can defend themselves to a certain extent, they will look to public authorities to establish a fair regulatory framework for the business consumer relationship, before, during and after each transaction. The need for intervention varies depending on the nature of the consumer, with a greater need for more vulnerable consumers.

> It is not, therefore, the fundamental purpose of consumer policy or the rights of consumers that are changing but, rather, the interaction between consumer interests and the interests of other stakeholders. More specifically, as interests become more inter-linked, interactions need to be characterised by increased cooperation. Sometimes the respective interests of consumers and other groups will be mutually reinforcing, sometimes they will not and tradeoffs will have to be found. Consumers themselves can recognise and accept such trade-offs because they are not only consumers but taxpayers, employees and beneficiaries of public policies too. They can also accept that they have responsibilities and that their immediate interests as consumers have to be reconciled with longer-term concerns for the environment and society. EU consumer policy should therefore ensure that consumer interests are equitably reconciled with those of other stakeholders. This reconciliation of interests will usually be a positive-sum game.[19]

---

[16] European Commission, *Consumer Decision-Making in Retail Investment Services: A Behavioural Economics Perspective* (2010) at http://ec.europa.eu/consumers/strategy/docs/final_report_en.pdf.

[17] ibid.

[18] European Commission, *Consumer Market Study on Advice within the Area of Retail Investment Services* (2011) at http://ec.europa.eu/consumers/rights/docs/investment_advice_study_en.pdf.

[19] European Commission, *Consumer Policy Action Plan 1999–2001* (1998) available at http://ec.europa.eu/consumers/cons_int/serv_gen/links/action_plan/ap01_en.pdf.

A pan-EU network of national public regulatory bodies overseeing consumer protection is at the heart of the EU's policy for the internal market.[20]

II. The Consumer Enforcement Landscape

Enforcement of consumer protection law is split in various ways. The first split is between local and national levels, and the second is between different agencies that are focused on particular aspects.

Primary enforcement of consumer protection law is the responsibility of 197 Trading Standards Services (TSSs) that are part of every upper tier local authority. In 2014 there were 163 trading standards services across England and Wales, employing the full time equivalent of just under 890 staff.[21] The TSSs carry out the majority of consumer law enforcement, and received 86 per cent (£213 million) of the overall funding of £247 million for enforcement bodies in 2009–10. TSS' budgets range from £240,000 to £6 million. Each TS officer serves an average of 45,200 people. The potential cost of a large and complex cross-border enforcement case is £200,000. The annual benefit to consumers from TSS fair trading work is estimated at £42 million, with a benefit-cost ration of £6:£1. There are eight Regional Intelligence Officers.

TSS officers are expert in core skills of fair trading, product safety and age restricted sales, and more dispersed specialist skills are intellectual property, metrology, food standards, credit, animal health, e-crime and general consumer advice. However, budgets were significantly cut as a result of public expenditure austerity from 2008, and the average budget for trading standards fell by 21.7 per cent between 2010–11 and 2013–14, to slightly over £800,000.[22]

At national level, there is an authority that covers both competition law and market aspects of consumer trading. Until 2013 this was the Office of Fair Trading (OFT).[23] The OFT's mission was 'to make markets work for consumers'.[24] It exercised a range of statutory functions including: Enforcement of competition and consumer law;[25] researching and publishing market studies;[26] making market investigation references to the Competition

---

[20] Reg (EC) No 2006/2004 on Consumer Protection Cooperation (CPC).

[21] *Trading Standards Workforce Survey* (Trading Standards Institute, 2014).

[22] ibid.

[23] The OFT was established by statute in 1973 as a non-ministerial government department, its powers latterly arising under the Enterprise Act 2002. It would generally only take enforcement action in cases where the unlawful practice(s) causes or risks significant consumer detriment nationally, or in at least two UK nations or regions, or where the case has an international dimension: *Criminal Enforcement of the Consumer Protection from Unfair Trading Regulations 2008. OFT Policy* (Office of Fair Trading, September 2010) OFT1273, http://www.oft.gov.uk/shared_oft/policy/OFT1273.pdf.

[24] Enterprise Act 2002, s 8(1).

[25] Including strategic issues such as in *Protecting Consumers Online: A Strategy for the UK* (Office of Fair Trading, 2010) OFT1252, available at http://oft.gov.uk/shared_oft/consultations/eprotection/OFT1252.pdf.

[26] Such as *Market Study Report: Consumer Contracts* (Office of Fair Trading, 2011) OFT1312, http://www.oft.gov.uk/OFTwork/markets-work/completed/consumer-contracts.

Commission; advising government;[27] encouraging industry codes and self-regulation; promoting business and consumer education; and supporting the provision of advice to individual consumers via Consumer Direct.[28] Its enforcement function stretched across a wide range of business sectors and it had a number of enforcement duties and a range of enforcement powers derived from consumer protection legislation.[29]

In 2014 a series of reforms were made in order to simplify the UK's consumer landscape.[30] They were driven by government policy to save public expenditure. First, consumers would be empowered through enhanced information, ability to choose and switch between traders, and ability to complain and resolve disputes more quickly.[31] Some relevant points were 'opening up regulatory data' by making ombudsmen's complaints data transparent so as to enhance 'the power of the crowd' through the ability of markets to exert pressure on traders to be competitive and observe high standards.[32] Alternative dispute resolution (ADR) redress schemes were extended from electronic communications, financial services, electricity, gas, and postal services to the water, and transport sectors. Consumer credit law was also reformed so as to improve access to credit.[33]

Second, the consumer protection institutions were rationalised,[34] and revisions were made to the Local Better Regulation Office (LBRO) and the Primary Authority scheme (discussed further at section V.F below).[35] The National Audit Office (NAO) had issued a report

---

[27] An example of many published replies to consultation is: *Enhancing Consumer Confidence by Clarifying Consumer Law: Consultation on the Supply of Goods, Services and Digital Content: The OFT's Response to the Government's Consultation* (Office of Fair Trading, 2012) OFT1453resp, available at http://www.oft.gov.uk/shared_oft/reports/oft_response_to_consultations/OFT1453resp.pdf.

[28] The OFT itself does not have the role of providing advice to the public on consumer problems in general, and is unable directly to take up complaints on behalf of individual consumers.

[29] Notably: The Consumer Credit Act 1974 as amended by The Consumer Credit Act 2006; The Estate Agents Act 1979 as amended by The Consumers, Estate Agents and Redress Act 2007; The Unfair Terms in Consumer Contracts Regs 1999; The Consumer Protection (Distance Selling) Regs 2000 as amended by the 2005 Regs; The Consumer Protection from Unfair Trading Regs 2008; The Business Protection from Misleading Marketing Regs 2008; The Enterprise Act 2002 (pt 8), which gives OFT the power to enforce a wide range of existing consumer protection legislation, including provisions derived from European Dirs and purely domestic legislation. The OFT also has enforcement duties under the Money Laundering Regs 2007 (it is the supervisory authority for estate agents and consumer credit financial institutions).

[30] For a review, see *Update on Consumer Protection Landscape Reforms* (National Audit Office, April 2014) available at http://www.nao.org.uk/wp-content/uploads/2014/04/Update-on-consumer-protection-landscape-reforms.pdf.

[31] *Better Choices: Better Deals. Consumers Powering Growth.* (Department for Business, Innovation & Skills and Cabinet Office Behavioural Insights Team, 2011) at http://www.bis.gov.uk/assets/biscore/consumer-issues/docs/b/11-749-better-choices-better-deals-consumers-powering-growth.

[32] ibid, 33.

[33] *A New Approach to Financial Regulation: Consultation on Reforming the Consumer Credit Regime*, 2011, at http://bis.gov.uk/Consultations/consultation-reforming-consumer-credit?utm_source=feedburner&utm_medium=feed&utm_campaign=Feed%3A+bis-consultations+%28BIS+Consultations%29&utm_content=FeedBurner.

[34] *Empowering and Protecting Consumers. Consultation on Institutional Changes for Provision of Consumer Information, Advice, Education, Advocacy and Enforcement* (Department for Business Enterprise and Skills, 2011); *Empowering and Protecting Consumers: Government Response to the Consultation on Institutional Reform* (Department for Business, Innovation & Skills, 2012).

[35] *The Future of the LBRO and the Primary Authority Scheme: A Consultation* (Department for Business, Innovation & Skills, 2011) at http://www.bis.gov.uk/assets/biscore/better-regulation/docs/f/11-985-future-local-better-regulation-office-consultation.pdf. The LBRO was established in 2007 and was subsequently given a range of statutory duties and powers under the Regulatory Enforcement and Sanctions Act 2008. Its status was switched from a non-departmental public body to being a constituent part of BIS (the Better Regulation Delivery Organisation (BRDO)), carrying out specified functions.

in June 2011 that considered the effectiveness of the arrangements to enforce consumer law by examining whether system resources were used efficiently and targeted towards high risk areas where consumers are more likely to suffer greater detriment.[36] It identified the costs to consumers, and hence the economy, of unfair trading, ranging from pressure selling to systematic scams by criminals, as £6.6 billion—but the system for enforcing consumer law was not delivering value for money. The NAO drew attention to the uncoordinated structure between national and multiple local authorities, and their need to work collaboratively and to strengthen cross-border working. It concluded that 'The system for enforcing consumer law is not delivering value for money because the architecture in place to bring together what is a very fragmented delivery landscape is not functioning properly, and the Department has few levers to directly influence policy delivery.'[37] Recommendations included the need to provide a national intelligence network and ensure sources of data on the prevalence and nature of consumer detriment.

The idea behind rationalisation of the consumer protection institutions[38] was that there would be a 'front line' of education, advice and advocacy for consumers[39] through an enhanced Citizens Advice service and Citizens Advice Scotland,[40] and a 'front line' of enforcement remaining at local level with TSS.[41] It was intended to strengthen the relationship between the Citizens Advice service and Trading Standards in supporting local consumers. Almost all government spending on consumer policy was focused on those two groups.

Earlier reform had enhanced the regulatory effect of the consumer 'voice' in a competitive marketplace[42] by amalgamating seven pre-existing official consumer watchdog bodies into a single body, Consumer Voice.[43] The Citizens Advice bodies became responsible for

---

[36] *Department for Business, Innovation & Skills, the Office of Fair Trading and Local Authority Trading Standards Services: Protecting Consumers—The System for Enforcing Consumer Law* (HC Paper No 1087: National Audit Office/TSO, June 2011).

[37] ibid, para 17.

[38] *Empowering and Protecting Consumers: Government Response to the Consultation on Institutional Reform* (n 34). Amendments were made under the Enterprise Act 2002, the Consumers, Estate Agents and Redress Act 2007, by Orders under the Public Bodies Act 2011 and the Enterprise and Regulatory Reform Act 2012. See The Public Bodies (The Office of Fair Trading Transfer of Consumer Advice Scheme Function and Modification of Enforcement Functions) Order 2013 No 783.

[39] This reform by the Coalition Government followed quickly behind a 2009 reform by the previous New Labour Government, which had created a national first point of contact for consumers, called Consumer Direct, which referred consumers to high quality specialist advice and redress services.

[40] Citizens Advice is an independent charity that, together with Citizens Advice Scotland and Citizens Advice Northern Ireland, provides financial, legal and consumer advice across the UK.

[41] In 2014, the Public Bodies (The Office of Fair Trading Transfer of Consumer Advice Scheme Function and Modification of Enforcement Functions) Order 2013, 2013/783 amended the Enterprise Act 2002 s24 so that enforcers were no longer required to consult with the OFT before making an application for an enforcement order in relation to the enforcement of consumer infringements; instead they were required to notify the CMA that they are making an application (art 9); and the OFT no longer has a duty but a power to enforce the unfair contracts, distance selling, misleading advertising and unfair trading Reg (arts 10–13).

[42] AO Hirschmann, *Exit, Voice and Loyalty: Responses to Decline on Firms, Organizations, and States* (President and Fellows of Harvard College, 1970).

[43] *Strengthen and Streamline Consumer Advocacy: Consultation on Consumer Representation and Redress* (Department of Trade and Industry, 2006). This estimated that expenditure of £29.9 million on the seven bodies could be reduced by £18.0 million. An earlier example of such advocacy was a report that identified wide variations in accessibility, standards and performance of dispute resolution mechanisms: *Seeking Resolution* (National Consumer Council, 2004).

consumer-facing education and advice from April 2014,[44] and also assumed consumer advocacy (in place of Consumer Focus and various other bodies),[45] undertaking research and horizon-scanning about consumer issues. Emphasis has long been placed on the value of consumer education, to inform intelligent purchasing, to enlist market forces in achieving regulatory outcomes, and to prevent problems from arising.[46] A consumer education strategy and framework, particularly access to information on rights, responsibilities and options on redress, were set out in 2004,[47] following the award of new powers in the Enterprise Act 2002 to use consumer education to support the goal of making markets work well for consumers, and the setting up of a Consumer Education Strategy Group in October 2003.[48]

The relationship between local TSS and national enforcers was revised,[49] transferring the primary duty to enforce key consumer protection legislation from the OFT to TSS, apart from the Unfair Terms in Consumer Contract Regulations. The TSS was intended to be protected from local government expenditure cuts by allocation of ring-fenced national funds. TSS activities on a national level would be coordinated through a new body, the Trading Standards Policy Board (TSPB), run by Chief Trading Standards Officers. The National Trading Standards Board (NTSB) prioritises national and cross-local authority boundary enforcement in England and Wales across local TSSs.[50] The Trading Standards Institute (TSI)[51] is responsible for most business-facing education activities from April 2013 under the authority of the NTSB.[52] In addition, a small Regulated Industries Unit (RIU) was created, initially with responsibility for postal services and energy across England, Scotland and Wales with additional responsibility for water in Scotland. In a widely criticised move,

---

[44] The Public Bodies Order (The Office of Fair Trading Transfer of Consumer Advice Scheme Function and Modification of Enforcement Functions) Order 2013, 2013/783 authorised the transfer of the OFT's statutory consumer advice scheme function to Citizens Advice and Citizens Advice Scotland.

[45] Which were temporarily rebranded Consumer Focus, thereby rationalising a plethora of other sectoral consumer bodies, notably Consumer Focus, the Consumer Council for Water, Waterwatch Scotland, Passenger Focus, the Public Transport Committee in Wales, the Legal Service Consumer Panel, and the Communications Consumer Panel. Power to support a consumer advice scheme was transferred from the OFT to the National Association of Citizens Advice Bureaux and the Scottish Association of Citizens Advice Bureaux: The Public Bodies (The Office of Fair Trading Transfer of Consumer Advice Scheme Function and Modification of Enforcement Functions) Order 2013, 2013/783.

[46] See *Modern Markets: Confident Consumers, The Government's Consumer White Paper* (Department of Trade and Industry, 1999). This included initiatives on increasing consumer self-reliance through better education, information and advice. It also presaged a new regime for codes of practice based on a set of core principles against which the OFT would hallmark schemes that complied with the principles. Targeted enforcement was maintained against rogue traders (including powers to ban continual offenders from trading) while reducing burdens on honest businesses to allow them to focus on giving good customer care.

[47] *Consumer Education: A Strategy and Framework* (Office of Fair Trading, 2004); see also *Strategy and Framework for Consumer Education, a Consultation Paper* (Office of Fair Trading, 2004) http://www.oft.gov.uk/shared_oft/653849/consumer_education/oft735.pdf.

[48] See also *Empowering Consumers of Public Services through Choice-tools* (Office of Fair Trading, 2011) OFT1321.

[49] Under the Public Bodies (The Office of Fair Trading Transfer of Consumer Advice Scheme Function and Modification of Enforcement Functions) Order 2013, SI 2013/783).

[50] *The Future of the LBRO and the Primary Authority Scheme* (n 35).

[51] The Trading Standards Institute is an association that represents UK trading standards professionals working in local authorities, business and consumer sectors and central government.

[52] The NTSB was created in April 2012. It comprises senior TS officers from across England and Wales. Equivalent functions are performed in Scotland by the Convention of Scottish Local Authorities (COSLA) and in Northern Ireland by the Department of Enterprise, Trade and Investment (DETI).

responsibility for overseeing the Consumer Code Approval Scheme (CCAS) was transferred from the OFT to the TSI.[53] The TSI subsequently transferred management of CCAS to its Consumer Codes Approval Board (CCAB).

A Consumer Protection Partnership (CPP) of the leading enforcement bodies[54] was created to better identify current and emerging areas where there is, or is likely to be, greatest consumer detriment, and to prioritise and coordinate collective action. The CPP's initial work included agreeing a common definition of 'consumer detriment', developing communications and intelligence sharing strategies, and implementing an action plan for tackling mass marketing scams.[55]

The third major landscape reform took place in relation to enforcement of competition law, by merging the OFT and the Competition Commission, to create the Competition and Markets Authority (CMA).[56] The CMA had a primary objective of promoting competition for the benefit of consumers. Although it was originally proposed that the OFT's national consumer functions would be transferred to the NTSB, the CMA ultimately retained consumer enforcement powers as remedies for use in markets where competition is not working appropriately due to practices and market conditions that make it difficult for consumers to exercise choice. Linked to this, it retained primary expertise in the enforcement of unfair contract terms legislation. A Strategic Intelligence, Prevention and Enforcement Partnership (SIPEP) was established, comprising the NTSA, CMA, RIU and the Citizens Advice service, which reports regularly to the Minister for Consumer Affairs to provide joint accountability on how the system as a whole is operating. Information flows would also take place between the SIPEP and sectoral regulators.

The fourth relevant reform was further to transform regulatory enforcement of consumer law, with a change in approach from the RESA: This was discussed in chapter nine.[57]

A coalition of leading consumer organisations put forward a Consumer Charter for Regulators in late 2012, which asserted that the main purpose of regulation is to promote and protect the interests of consumers in sectors where market forces alone would not deliver the best outcome.[58] It called for governance arrangements that included a Board with a lay Chair and a lay majority including consumer expertise. It also stressed that regulators should understand what a good *outcome* looks like for all consumers and deliver it.

---

[53] See *Consultation on Consumer Codes Approval Scheme* (Trading Standards Institute, 2012).

[54] The CPP includes BIS, the CMA, the NTSB, the TSI, Trading Standards Scotland, Citizens Advice and Citizens Advice Scotland, the Financial Conduct Authority, the Consumer Council for Northern Ireland and DETI.

[55] See *Consumer Protection Partnership: Priorities Report 2013–14. Report on the Partnership's Work to Date and Future Priorities* (2013). 'Consumer detriment' was defined as 'the harm (loss of welfare) caused to individuals as a result of a problem with a commercial practice or the behaviour of a business or trader. Possible causes of detriment include problems with traders, consumers' inability to exercise choice—for example because of the complexity of products and services—and failure of markets': ibid para 2.2. Priorities for 2013–14 were mobile phones and mobile technology, second hand cars sector, home building sector, unfair terms, scams, doorstep crime and the Green Deal. See also *Consumer Protection Partnership: Priorities Report 2015. Second Report on the Partnership's Work to Date and Future Priorities* (2015), which set priorities for 2015 as online markets, unfair terms and conditions, travel, and quality of services.

[56] *A Competition Regime for Growth: A Consultation on Options for Reform*, 2011, at http://www.bis.gov.uk/ Consultations/competition-regime-for-growth?cat=open. The CMA was created under the Enterprise and Regulatory Reform Act 2013, s 5.

[57] *Transforming Regulatory Enforcement: Discussion Paper* (Department for Business, Innovation & Skills, 2011) at http://www.bis.gov.uk/assets/biscore/better-regulation/docs/t/11-989-transforming-regulatory-enforcement-consultation.pdf.

[58] *Consumer Charter for Regulators* (Consumer Focus, 27/11/2012) available at http://www.consumerfocus.org.uk/feature/consumer-charter-for-regulators.

III. Codified Enforcement Powers

Certain tools are diagnostic (such as the CMA's research and market studies). Preventative self-regulatory tools are strongly encouraged (such as the Consumer Codes Approval Scheme, although that is now administered by TSI).[59] Enforcement tools include investigative and prosecution powers under a wide range of consumer protection legislation.[60] Part 8 of the Enterprise Act 2002 introduced a framework for new powers for regulators, to introduce greater choice in how they enforce, ensuring that the action taken is proportionate to the offence and the harm caused to consumers. That Act empowers enforcement of a wide range of existing consumer protection legislation, including provisions derived from European Directives and purely domestic legislation.

Enforcement powers were updated in codified form in the Consumer Rights Act 2015. The basic enforcement powers available to domestic enforcers[61] are as follows. First, there is power to require the production of information specified in a notice,[62] for the purpose of ascertaining whether there has been a breach of the enforcer's legislation,[63] either where the enforcer is a market surveillance authority, or where the an officer reasonably suspects a breach.[64] Second, the toolbox of general powers, which may be exercised subject to specific purposes and in specified circumstances, comprises powers to purchase products, to observe carrying on of business, to enter premises without a warrant, to inspect products and take copies of records or evidence, to test equipment, to require the production of documents, to seize and detain goods, to decommission or switch off fixed installations, to break open containers or access electronic devices, to enter premises with warrants, and to require assistance from persons on premises.[65] Supplementary provisions include an offence of obstruction or of purporting to act as an officer, a right of persons to access seized goods and documents, a requirement for notice to be given of the testing of goods, a right to appeal against detention of goods and documents, and a requirement on officers to pay compensation to any person with an interest in goods seized for loss or damage caused by the seizure or detention if the goods have not disclosed breach and the power was not exercised as a result of any neglect or default of the person seeking compensation.[66]

---

[59] See http://www.tradingstandards.gov.uk/advice/ConsumerCodes.cfm.

[60] Notably: The Consumer Credit Act 1974, as amended by The Consumer Credit Act 2006; The Estate Agents Act 1979, as amended by The Consumers, Estate Agents and Redress Act 2007; The Unfair Terms in Consumer Contracts Regs 1999 (UTCCR); The Consumer Protection (Distance Selling) Regs 2000, as amended by the 2005 Regs; The Money Laundering Regs 2007; The Consumer Protection from Unfair Trading Regs 2008; and The Business Protection from Misleading Marketing Regs 2008. See *Consumer Protection: Guidance on the CMA's Approach to Use of its Consumer Powers* (CMA, 2014) CMA7, Annex; *Statement of Enforcement Principles* (Office of Fair Trading, 2010) OFT 1221.

[61] Domestic enforcers are contrasted with EU enforcers, as defined in Sch 5 arts 3 and 4 respectively.

[62] Consumer Rights Act 2015, Sch 5, art 14.

[63] ibid, Sch 5, art 13(4).

[64] ibid, Sch 5, art 13(5) and (6).

[65] ibid, Sch 5, arts 19–35.

[66] ibid, Sch 5, arts 36–42.

The prior consultation on consolidation and simplification of consumer law powers into a generic set, which became the Consumer Rights Act 2015, began by noting that trust was central:[67]

> Markets work best when consumers have trust in the businesses with which they contract. High levels of consumer confidence encourage experimentation, which helps market entry, boosts competition and drives innovation … Consumer confidence is also rapidly eroded by rogue traders.[68]

> An effective enforcement regime requires several elements: law which is clearly understood by businesses and consumers; resources to promote compliance and appropriate enforcement tools to investigate and tackle non-compliance wherever it occurs; and organisation of such resources around the country so that rogue traders have nowhere to hide.[69]

The Government supported both flexible, non-regulatory approaches to ensuring consumers are empowered and protected and law-abiding businesses are not hindered by excessive regulation, and also a framework of law needs to be in place and enforcement of that law needs to be simple and transparent and also more efficient.[70] It proposed reforms to the consumer law enforcement regime guided by the following objectives:

— *Reducing the regulatory burdens on businesses*—by simplifying and consolidating enforcers' investigatory powers so that they are clear and transparent for businesses and enforcers alike.
— *Rolling back state intrusion and protecting civil liberties*—by applying stronger safeguards to the more intrusive investigatory powers before they can be exercised.
— *Improving the effectiveness and efficiency of enforcement*—by removing bureaucratic legislative restrictions which prevent Trading Standards Services from operating in an efficient, cost effective way.[71]

Accordingly, the proposals had focused on simplification of enforcement officers' investigatory powers, the removal of barriers to trading standards operating efficiently, and improving cross-boundary cooperation and authorisation by enabling individual Trading Standards professionals to present cases in County Courts[72] using an existing Approved Regulator[73] to accredit them and thereby encourage the use of civil enforcement. New safeguards would be introduced in relation to the generic investigatory powers, such as a requirement for officers to give businesses reasonable notice of routine inspections, subject to a number of exemptions. A number of safeguards would be maintained, for example, the prohibition on officers requiring a person to produce or seizing from any person any document that they would be entitled to refuse to hand over on the grounds of legal professional privilege. In accordance with a commitment to protecting civil liberties and to rolling back state intrusion,[74] the use of covert investigative techniques under the

---

[67] *Enhancing Consumer Confidence through Effective Enforcement: Consultation on Consolidating and Modernising Consumer Law Enforcement Powers* (Department for Business, Innovation & Skills, March 2012) available at http://www.bis.gov.uk/assets/biscore/consumer-issues/docs/e/12-543-enhancing-consumer-confidence-effective-enforcement-consultation.pdf.

[68] ibid, Foreword by Norman Lamb MP, Minister for Employment Relations, Consumer and Postal Affairs.

[69] ibid, para 4.

[70] ibid, para 5.

[71] ibid, para 6.

[72] Under Pt 3 of Sch 4 to Legal Service Act 2007.

[73] Approved Regulators are designated under the Legal Services Act 2007 and governed by the Legal Services Board (LSB).

[74] *The Coalition: Our Programme for Government* (HM Government, 2010), http://www.cabinetoffice.gov.uk/sites/default/files/resources/coalition_programme_for_government.pdf.

Regulation of Investigatory Powers Act 2000 (RIPA) by councils, unless they are signed off by a magistrate and required for stopping serious crime, would be reduced.[75]

Further additions to enforcement were made in the Small Business, Enterprise and Employment Act 2015. Directors convicted abroad of an offence related to the running of a company would be disqualified in the UK.[76] The Secretary of State may apply to the court for a compensation order in favour of creditors of a company against a director who has been disqualified where the conduct for which that person has been disqualified has caused loss to one or more creditors of an insolvent company of which they have at any time been a director.[77] The Secretary of State may accept a compensation undertaking from a director where the conditions for the making of a compensation order are met, instead of applying or proceeding with an application to court for a compensation order.[78]

IV. Research on Compliance with Consumer Trading Law

The OFT has undertaken a series of studies into what drives business compliance with consumer law. As noted in chapter 15 on competition law, the two series of research papers should be read and compared together, since the OFT's approach to consumer markets was heavily influenced by its approach to enforcement of competition law, which was based firmly on economic deterrence theory.

An academic analysis of 2008 set out a classic view about the role of consumers, markets and regulation:

> Consumers play a key role in activating competition and making markets work well. Without their active participation in a market, firms may not have incentives to deliver what consumers want and consumers will not get the full benefits of competition. Consumers may at times not play a very proactive role in the competitive process and there are a number of reasons why this may occur. For example, searching the market for the best deal and switching between suppliers can be a costly and/or confusing business; and suppliers may be able to exacerbate the problem by making consumers' tasks more difficult.
>
> When markets fail to work well because of poor consumer decisions, policymakers can intervene to facilitate and encourage consumers to take a more informed and active role.[79]

That paper considered the effectiveness of three interventions that were intended to help consumers to play a more active role in markets by doing three things: Obtain information and make comparisons, make informed choices at the point of sale and switch suppliers. In

---

[75] A code of practice under the Protection of Freedoms Bill to cover enforcement officers' powers of entry, with the exercise of these powers being subject to review and repeal.

[76] Small Business, Enterprise and Employment Act 2015, cl 92.

[77] ibid, cl 98. The compensation order must be made within two years. Any person against whom a compensation order has been made, or who has had a compensation undertaking accepted by the Secretary of State, must pay the amount specified in the order or undertaking to the person or persons specified: Company Directors Disqualification Act 1986 (CDDA), s 15B. The factors that the court or Secretary of State must have particular regard to when deciding on the amount of compensation to award or seek are in CDDA, s 15B(3).

[78] CDDA, s 15A(2).

[79] L Garrod, M Hviid, G Loomes and C Waddams Price of the ESRC Centre for Competition Policy, *Assessing the Effectiveness of Potential Remedies in Consumer Markets* (Office of Fair Trading, 2008) OFT994 available at http://www.oft.gov.uk/shared_oft/economic_research/oft994.pdf, paras 1.1 and 1.2.

relation to helping consumers obtain information and make comparisons, the appropriate measures would include providing information about quality, standardisation of pricing structures (to facilitate comparisons) and encouraging price comparison sites. In relation to helping consumers make informed choices at the point of sale, relevant interventions to reduce a firm's advantage were written quotations that last for a fixed period, in-store price comparisons and cooling-off periods. Switching suppliers would be assisted by establishing cancellation rights, enhancing product attribute portability and customer information portability, and intervening in potentially collusive consumer markets.[80]

In 2010 the OFT presented its 'Statement of consumer protection enforcement principles',[81] which were informed by a series of studies that it had commissioned in the preceding couple of years, and which will now be examined in turn.

A. London Economics' Study of Six Enforcement Interventions

In the first study, London Economics reviewed the effectiveness of a sample of six case studies of consumer enforcement interventions, summarised at Table 14.4, to assess and discuss the implications of the approaches adopted and to consider how to monitor and enhance performance in future interventions.[82] The six cases involved interventions relating to

1) airline pricing;
2) MB Designs: The trading activities of a double glazing company;
3) Book Club Associates: Misleading advertising;
4) Dabs.com: Unfair terms and conditions of an online IT retailer, and inhibition by customers to pursue because of costly and slow process;
5) Ryanair terms and conditions after flight cancellation: Consumers received inadequate compensation (for cancellations, delays, denied boarding, and problems with lost or delayed baggage); consumers faced excessive costs when seeking redress (time spent, repeated contact required, restrictive procedures); consumers were deterred from complaining and seeking redress;
6) Consumer Credit Act 1974, section 75: Protection of customers who buy goods worth over £100 and up to £30,000, by making the credit card company jointly and severally liable with the supplier of the goods; litigation by OFT to clarify the law.

---

[80] However, for criticism of consumers' ability to make rational, informed choices, especially in financial services, and a need to adopt greater differentiation between individual consumers, see V Mak, 'The Myth of the Empowered Consumer—Lessons from Financial Literacy Studies' TISCO Working Paper Series on Banking, Finance and Services No 03/2012.

[81] *Statement of Consumer Protection Enforcement Principles* (Office of Fair Trading, 2010) OFT1221. The statement was revised in 2012: *Statement of Consumer Protection Enforcement Principles* (Office of Fair Trading, February 2012) available at http://www.oft.gov.uk/shared_oft/reports/consumer_protection/OFT1221. See also *OFT Prioritisation Principles* (Office of Fair Trading, 2008) OFT953; *Criminal Enforcement of the Consumer Protection from Unfair Trading Regulations 2008* (n 23).

[82] London Economics, *Evaluation of a Sample of Consumer Enforcement Cases* (Office of Fair Trading, 2009) OFT1139 available at http://www.oft.gov.uk/OFTwork/publications/publication-categories/reports/Evaluating/oft1139.

Table 14.4: OFT Case Study on Interventions: Summary of the Six Cases[83]

Case study	OFT contentions	Relevant legislation	Sources of ACD		Intervention tools
Airline pricing	Advertised prices and first prices shown on websites did not include all compulsory charges	Control of Misleading Advertising Regulations 1988 (CMARs)	—	Sub-optimal purchases — Time cost — Associated frustration	Dialogue and settlement
MB Designs Double Glazing	Inadequate quality of products and fitting of windows and similar	Sale of goods and services Regulations Unfair Terms in Consumer Contract Regulations 1999 (UTCCRs)	—	Goods not fit for purpose — Installation of goods not of satisfactory quality — Redress lacking	Court order and undertakings to the Court
BCA Book club	Advertising did not clearly set out membership obligations	CMARs	—	Consumers unclear about membership obligations — Costs associated with making complaints returning unwanted books	Dialogue and accepted undertakings
Dabs e-retailer of computers and accessories	Unfavourable terms regarding returns and refunds	UTCCRs Distance Selling Regulations	—	High cost of making returns — Deterred from seeking redress	Dialogue and accepted undertakings
Ryanair Terms and conditions	Unfavourable for passengers: not reflecting consumers' full rights under the relevant legislation	UTCCRs	—	Insufficient compensation (for cancellations, delays, denied boarding, and delayed baggage) — Cost of seeking redress — Deterred from seeking redress	Dialogue and settlement
Section 75	Lack of recognition of right of UK credit card holders to get compensation from the issuer in relation to purchases abroad	Consumer Credit Act	—	Reduced use of credit cards abroad — Loss of protection for purchases made abroad — Deterred from seeking redress	OFT launched test case and obtained favourable Court clarification

[83] ibid, Fig 2.1.

It was found that the interventions in all of the cases had delivered positive benefits for consumers, albeit in widely differing amounts, as shown in Table 14.5 (p 368) and Figure 14.2 (p 370). The estimated total overall yearly benefit figure of £243 million compared very favourably with estimated costs to OFT of £2.4 million, and included:

— An estimated saving of £131 million a year delivered by cross-industry action in respect of airline pricing (the size of the online flight ticket booking market was estimated at £7.4 billion) through the inclusion of fixed non-optional costs in advertised prices;
— an estimated saving of £99 million a year delivered by the OFT clarifying the applicability of section 75 to overseas credit card transactions;
— a saving of £10.7 million due to an intervention against the unfavourable trading activities of MB Designs (a double glazing supplier);
— smaller savings in other markets, such as book clubs and electronic goods, as well as an intervention that resulted in Ryanair amending their terms and conditions.

The study found that benefits to consumers are delivered in a variety of ways. Whilst a precondition for success was that businesses change their prior conduct, for the six cases examined, the impacts found differed significantly in magnitude. By far the greatest benefits were delivered in these cases where interventions resulted in consumers incurring lower costs and making better choices in transactions (accounting for 76 per cent of overall yearly benefits).[84] The next highest benefit came from a reduction in deterred complaints (19 per cent of overall yearly benefits).[85] The six cases had a smaller impact (less than four per cent of yearly benefits) in terms of deterring similar actions by non-targeted business, where this was thought to be particularly likely for precedent setting cases that receive media attention and also cases with high visibility amongst competitors (the MB Designs and Ryanair cases).[86] In this sample, interventions targeting unfavourable terms and conditions had relatively less impact than those targeting advertising that was considered to be misleading or Sales of Goods Act cases.

London Economics concluded that there were two main ways in which results from these case studies may inform future thinking. First, it should improve measurement of the success of consumer interventions, in terms of calculating the achieved reduction in 'assumed consumer detriment' (ACD),[87] in which aggregated information from consumer complaints can play a significant role.[88] Second, better targeting of enforcement could be achieved through focusing on particular businesses. The enforcer should note the mechanism through which the intervention is expected to operate in changing the behaviour of the particular business, and the ways in which such operation might be frustrated.[89] The

---

[84] ibid, para 1.7.

[85] ibid, para 1.8. 'The study of the six interventions highlighted a number of reasons why consumers may be deterred from seeking redress when problematic situations occur. When an intervention succeeds in improving consumer awareness of their rights and confidence in the process of seeking redress, the consumer benefit achieved is significant. However, to fully maximise this benefit requires the targeted company to have in place a satisfactory approach to complaint handling.'

[86] ibid, para 1.9.

[87] ibid, para 1.14. However, the authors noted that the evidence did not prove that any individual experienced any harm: para 2.1.

[88] See the assessment of consumer complaining behaviour at *Consumer Detriment: Assessing the Frequency and Impact of Consumer Problems with Goods and Services* (n 1).

[89] ibid, paras 1.18–1.12 and 4.8.

Table 14.5: OFT Case Study on Interventions: Quantification of Impacts

Case	Estimated size of affected market	Relevant legislation	Estimated OFT costs	Estimated yearly reduction in ACD	How the reduction in ACD is broken down			
					Consumers have lower costs/make better choices	Improved consumer confidence: Fewer deterred complaints	Deterrent effect on other businesses	Other benefits from better business conduct
Airline pricing	£7.4 billion	CMARs	£310 million	£131 million	100%			
Section 75	£11 billion	Consmer Credit Act	£1 million	£99 million	54%	46%		
MB Designs	£3 million	Sale of Goods Act Supply of Goods and Services Act UTCCRs	£520,000	£10.7 million			78%	22%
Ryanair	£950 million	UTCCRs	£360,000	£1.4 million		39%	48%	14%
BCA	£100 million	CMARs	£210,000	£876,000	100%			
Dabs	£200 million	UTCCRs Distance Selling Regulations	£13,000	£78,000		46%		54%
Total (£ 000s)			£2.4 million	£243 million	£185,336	£46,110	£9,004	£2,588

authors noted that interventions targeting problems that potentially occur more frequently or that potentially affect a very large share of all transactions are likely to have a larger impact on consumers.[90] They asserted that the enforcer should consider the way in which an intervention would deter similar problems 'through adverse reputational effects and through anticipation of [high] financial penalties which remove/reduce the gains from infringements and also through criminalisation, for instance when dealing with rogue traders such as scammers'.[91] It was thought to be a problem that the OFT did not have the power at the time of imposing financial penalties on infringing businesses, and it was argued that '[h]eavy financial sanctions are likely only ever to be available where there are serious and undoubted breaches of law. But in appropriate cases, the anticipation of high financial costs can be an effective deterrent to potential infringers.'[92] No references were cited for these assertions. The authors suggested that deterrence 'is generally associated with interventions that are highly publicised and cause embarrassment to targeted businesses. It is more likely to occur in markets where firms' reputation is important and where consumers actively choose which firms to deal with.'[93] However, the authors accepted that the above points were based on their expectations and in most of the cases they 'lacked information to make a detailed assessment of the deterrent effect' on any other businesses operating in the market.[94] They noted that in these interventions, the OFT focused on stopping what was considered to be sub-optimal practices but did not (because it could not) either impose fines or secure compensation for those (if any) who might have been legally entitled to it.[95]

B. Ipsos MORI's Interviews with Businesses on Drivers of Compliance

In the second 2010 study, Ipsos MORI conducted 44 in-depth interviews with traders across a number of business sectors.[96] Self-reported non-compliance by interviewees was very low with no reports of ongoing non-compliance.[97] Noting that the sample should not be taken as representative of traders generally, on the basis of interview evidence, it was Ipsos MORI's view that three main drivers of compliance with consumer protection law emerged, listed in descending order of relative priority:

— Consumer pressure
— relationship with or pressure from external organisations
— traders' understanding of consumer protection obligations and risks.[98]

---

[90] ibid, para 1.20.
[91] ibid, para 1.22.
[92] ibid, para 1.22.
[93] ibid, para 5.14.
[94] ibid, para 4.25. The only two interventions cases in which they found some evidence of deterrent effects were the MB Designs and Ryanair cases. The Dabs and BCA cases had 'minimal impact' on deterrence, since the reputational cost of unfavourable terms is low compared to a reputation of selling goods of inadequate quality, and, in the BCA case, there are very few companies applying the business 'book club' business model, in which the market was contracting: paras 4.26 and 4.27.
[95] ibid, para 4.31.
[96] *Drivers of Compliance and Non-compliance with Consumer Protection Law: A Report by Ipsos MORI Commissioned by the OFT* (Office of Fair Trading, 2010) OFT1225a, at http://www.oft.gov.uk/shared_oft/reports/Evaluating-OFTs-work/OFT1225a.pdf.
[97] ibid, para 1.4.
[98] ibid, paras 1.5 and 1.6.

Case study (relevant legislation)	Changes in business conduct (LE assessment)	Absolute reduction in ACD37	Relative reduction in ACD38	Improved consumer confidence: Reduction of deterred complaints	Countervailing actions by firms	Deterrence for other businesses	Positive impact on competition in the market
Airline pricing (Control of Misleading Advertisement)	high	very large	moderate	n.a.	possibly significant	important	moderate
MB Designs (Sale of Goods Act; Supply of Goods and Services Act; UTCCRs)	high	large	very large	not effective	none	important	moderate
BCA (Control of Misleading Advertisements)	high	small	moderate	unlikely to have been effective	none	minimal	minimal
Dabs (UTCCRs; Consumer Protection DSRs)	medium high	small	large	effective	unlikely to have been significant	minimal	Minimal
Ryanair terms and conditions (UTCCRs)	adequate	moderate	moderate	effective	possibly significant	moderate	moderate
Section 75 (Consumer Credit Act applicability)	no behavioural change	very large	moderate	effective	none	n.a.	n.a.

Figure 14.2: Typology of Cases: Effectiveness[99]

99 ibid, fig 4.1.

Consumer pressure came from two primary sources: The traders' own desire to satisfy the needs of customers and maintain a good reputation, and consumers' awareness of their rights and traders' obligation towards them.[100]

> For the majority of respondents, compliance with the law is assumed to be part of being a customer-focused business. Failure to comply, and to be the recipient of enforcement action, has the potential to damage their reputation. This is a major concern for many traders as it risks alienating current and potential customers.
>
> Reputational risk is a concern for both large and small businesses interviewed. The former feel they are vulnerable to media attention, while many of the latter are operating in localised markets where word of mouth is a key driver of new business.
>
> Although many respondents say that consumers' own understanding of their rights is poor, the majority see customers becoming more demanding. Traders have to respond to this, though many say they seek to avoid any argument and try to avoid any recourse to consumer law. Most will try to resolve any disputes before the consumer refers to their legal rights or tries to enforce them in court. Media activity is widely seen as the driver of changing attitudes among customers.[101]

A number of relationships with third-parties were found to be important in supporting compliance with consumer protection law. First, membership of trade associations or other collective bodies provided accurate, up-to-date and sector-specific information and support (such as standard terms and conditions) to traders on their obligations.[102] They appeared to offer to smaller businesses some of the advantages available to larger businesses—such as access to expert legal advice and helplines—that they could not otherwise afford. Trade associations were also seen as a way of pushing rogue or illegal traders out of a sector by allowing members to distinguish themselves from other businesses. Second, a relationship with local authority TSS was generally regarded in a positive light where it existed, since TSS were able to offer authoritative advice (though some concerns do exist for a minority in this area), impartial adjudication and (for larger businesses with networks of outlets) a coordinated way of dealing with multiple TSS contacts.[103] Third, larger businesses were able to utilise external legal advice, which was perceived as a high quality and reliable resource of expert opinion.[104] Fourth, in some sectors, companies monitored the behaviour of competitors and initiated complaints or action against each other.[105] Larger businesses were also able to build processes for addressing consumer protection law issues in their organisation, for example through training, guidance and escalation procedures. These processes did exist in smaller businesses but tended to be less formal.[106]

The responses indicated that:

> About half the sample indicates that compliance with consumer protection law is a priority, either ahead of or on a par with other legal or regulatory obligations. Prioritisation appears to be associated with role specialisation, customer focus, and a desire to minimise the risks of noncompliance.

---

[100] ibid, para 1.7.
[101] ibid, paras 1.18–1.10.
[102] ibid, para 1.12.
[103] ibid, para 1.13.
[104] ibid, para 1.14.
[105] ibid, para 1.15.
[106] ibid, para 1.17.

The deterrent effect of enforcement action can be a significant driver of compliance. However, the impact of this driver may be minimal where there is limited awareness of the consequences of breaching consumer protection legislation. Negative experiences, for example dealing with the Small Claims Court, appear to have a particularly strong impact.[107]

However, somewhat at odds with the above assertion of 'the deterrent effect of enforcement', for which little substantiation was apparent in the study, the researchers concluded that three major drivers of non-compliant behaviour could be inferred:[108]

a) *Limited understanding of consumer protection law.* Poor understanding of the detail of consumer protection law was widespread. Larger businesses and those in specialised roles were generally better informed.[109] Where there was an absence of detailed knowledge, many argued that they followed the principles of consumer protection law rather than the letter of it (sometimes expressed as following the 'spirit of the law'). Alternatively it was thought that a focus on customer service and common sense is sufficient.[110] Traders who were not members of a trade association and who lacked a relationship with TSS referred to the internet, showed poor understanding.[111]

b) *Limited deterrent effect from consumer protection law and its enforcement.* 'The deterrent effect from consumer protection law and its enforcement via enforcement bodies such as TSS is not widely felt.'[112] 'We found little evidence that traders have detailed knowledge about the penalties for breaches of consumer protection law. These are generally assumed to be fines but there is not much understanding as to how big these fines can be or in what circumstances they can be imposed. Similarly there is little awareness of the enforcement activity taken by TSS or the OFT.'[113] 'The consequences of this lack of knowledge is a perception among several that action is not likely and companies will not be penalized heavily. This is reinforced by perceptions of patchy or variable enforcement.'[114]

c) *Economic and market pressures.* Additional factors that increased the pressures on respondents to behave in ways that might lead to non-compliance were relationships with suppliers (even felt by relatively large retailers) and economic pressures, such as on revenues and margins.[115]

In considering the implications of the findings in relation to helping business to comply with the law, the authors noted that almost all businesses had expressed some need for additional support or help.[116] Traders were looking for information and support that was authoritative and timely (providing them with definitive up-to-date answers that they could rely upon), and relevant and easy to understand (tailored to their needs so easy to absorb and implement).[117] Official bodies such as the OFT and TSS had an important role to play,

---

[107]   ibid, paras 1.18 and 1.19.
[108]   ibid, para 1.20.
[109]   ibid, para 1.21.
[110]   ibid, para 1.22.
[111]   ibid, para 1.23.
[112]   ibid, para 1.26.
[113]   ibid, para 1.27.
[114]   ibid, para 1.28.
[115]   ibid, para 1.31.
[116]   ibid, para 1.34.
[117]   ibid, para 1.35.

especially in providing guidance and raising awareness of what information is available to businesses, and where. Trade associations were highly respected for their ability to produce material relevant to the needs of particular industries.[118] No one channel would meet the needs of all traders, and online sources were widely used.[119] A large proportion of traders valued personal contact with an expert advisor via telephone or visits, as it would enable traders to review and clarify problems.[120] Techniques that were appreciated by some were certification (for example of terms and conditions), because it bolstered their reputation, and especially training courses, because they drove up levels of knowledge among traders (though many of the smaller traders say they would struggle to find the time for this).[121]

Ipsos MORI found three significant barriers to communication with traders: Fear of enforcement agencies, clarification of the existence and role of TSS and the OFT, and the sheer volume of regulation.[122]

C. IFF Research's Study of Compliance with Codes

In the third OFT 2010 study, IFF Research conducted a telephone survey of 482 personnel in businesses with 25 or more employees who were responsible for ensuring that their business complied with consumer law.[123] The business sectors were chosen to enable comparisons between sectors where the OFT had previously intervened (the 'Target' group, comprising businesses in the home improvement, furniture, clothing and holiday retail sectors) and sectors where it had not (the 'Comparison' group, in the entertainment and food retail sectors).

In response to questions on awareness of consumer protection law and cases, 20 per cent claimed to be very familiar and 59 per cent claim to be fairly familiar with consumer protection law and cases.[124] However, familiarity with specific consumer protection laws was lower (large businesses scored higher than small), and although 44 per cent claimed familiarity with OFT enforced cases, unprompted awareness of specific OFT decisions or cases was low, with just one per cent of respondents able to mention any specific cases of relevance.[125]

Sixty-one per cent of businesses saw organisational benefits as a result of the enforcement of consumer protection law (more likely among larger businesses), with the most commonly cited benefit of enforcement being that it created a level playing field, followed by its positive impact on customers (in terms of more satisfied customers and greater confidence in the sector).[126] When asked to name their 'top three' regulatory priorities, 71 per cent did not mention consumer protection law.[127] Only four per cent of respondents considered

---

[118] ibid, para 1.36.
[119] ibid, paras 1.37 and 1.38.
[120] ibid, para 1.39.
[121] ibid, para 1.40.
[122] ibid, para 1.41.
[123] *Factors Affecting Compliance with Consumer Law and the Deterrent Effect of Consumer Enforcement Prepared for the Office of Fair Trading By IFF Research* (Office of Fair Trading, 2010), OFT1228, at http://www.oft.gov.uk/shared_oft/reports/Evaluating-OFTs-work/OFT1228.pdf.
[124] ibid, para 1.6.
[125] ibid, paras 1.7–1.9.
[126] ibid, para 1.10.
[127] ibid, para 1.11.

that there was a very high risk of businesses in their sector breaching consumer protection law,[128] although 31 per cent believed that they had been disadvantaged by competitors breaching consumer law.[129] Businesses in the 'Target' group were more likely than those in the 'Comparison' group to cite consumer law as their top regulatory priority and to claim to have been disadvantaged by competitors having breached consumer protection law.[130]

The overwhelming majority (95 per cent) of respondents claimed that they had policies and practices in place to ensure that they comply with consumer protection law.[131] Over 80 per cent of businesses claimed to have taken at least one of the following actions in the last 12 months to raise staff awareness of their obligations regarding consumer protection law: Conducted an internal review of compliance; have a written policy or code of conduct; provided ongoing training in compliance to update existing staff; or provided induction training in compliance to new staff.[132] Smaller businesses and single-site businesses were less likely to have undertaken these actions. Only six per cent of businesses reported having done nothing in the previous 12 months to ensure compliance with consumer protection law. The most commonly cited means of ensuring compliance with consumer law were having a system for handling customer complaints (87 per cent) and having a system for handling compliance failures (64 per cent): Small businesses were more likely than average to have done nothing (11 per cent).[133]

The authors suggested that senior management attitudes, risk of damage to reputation amongst customers, fear of criminal prosecution and risk of damage to reputation within the industry were perceived to be the main factors encouraging businesses to comply with the law.[134] The risk of action by TSS had the greatest impact (6.2 out of a scale of one to 10), followed by the OFT (5.8) and the Advertising Standards Agency (5.3).[135] Responses suggested that building positive customer relationships and the threat of adverse publicity were crucial in motivating compliance: 92 per cent of respondents agreed that 'knowing we are doing the right thing for customers encourages us to comply with consumer protection laws' and 89 per cent of respondents agreed that 'the threat of adverse publicity associated with breaching consumer law is as important as any financial penalty'.[136] Over-complex and unfair regulations were perceived to be the most powerful barriers to compliance with consumer law.[137]

A further study reviewed customer satisfaction levels in three sectors where there were trade association codes of practice, noting two primary roles associated with

---

[128]   ibid, para 1.12.
[129]   ibid, para 1.13. Businesses perceived they had been disadvantaged by competitors breaching regulations inhibiting a level playing field (29%), acting dishonestly with customers (22%), and using misleading advertising (19%).
[130]   ibid, para 1.14.
[131]   ibid, para 1.15.
[132]   ibid, para 1.16.
[133]   ibid, para 1.17.
[134]   ibid, para 1.19.
[135]   ibid, para 1.20.
[136]   ibid, para 1.21.
[137]   ibid, para 1.22.

codes: Signalling quality and raising standards across an entire sector.[138] In relation to the first aspect, evidence was not consistent across the three codes, which was related to the different stages of development and differences between the sectors studied.[139]

D. OFT's 2010 Policy on Compliance with Consumer Law

The OFT issued three documents on the 'drivers of compliance and non-compliance' based on the research summarised above, the first reporting on the OFT's findings from the above research on compliance with *consumer* law,[140] the second a related statement on behaviour in compliance with *competition* law,[141] and the third setting out advice to business.[142] In the summary paper, the OFT identified four key findings, grouped under four broad themes:

Theme 1: The importance of reputation and the influence of consumers

Key finding 1. A desire to win and then retain customers means that many businesses are naturally focused on protecting their customer relationships and reputation for the quality of product they supply and/or the service they provide.

Key finding 2. Informed consumers asserting their rights can have a significant impact on business behaviour and appear to be a key driver of compliance. The desire to satisfy consumers can therefore sometimes act as an incentive for businesses to meet or exceed the requirements of consumer protection laws.

Theme 2: Business awareness of, and attitudes towards, consumer protection laws

Key finding 3. In general businesses seek to treat consumers fairly although they may have a limited understanding of the law. SMEs in particular are likely to have less awareness of the detail of consumer protection laws, and how they can access relevant information to assist compliance. Larger businesses are more likely to understand the detail of the laws but may have different drivers for not complying.

Key finding 4. Fear of enforcement action acts as a driver for compliance even though there is, across all business, evidence of low levels of awareness of the details of enforcement activity and the potential consequences of non-compliance.

Key finding 5. Compliance with consumer protection laws is low on the list of priorities for some businesses.

---

[138] *Consumer Codes Approval Scheme: Evaluating Consumer Experiences. Report by IFF Research* (Office of Fair Trading, 2010) OFT1247, available at http://www.oft.gov.uk/shared_oft/reports/Evaluating-OFTs-work/oft1247.pdf.

[139] The codes were: The Carpet Foundation Code, which had achieved OFT Approval in March 2007, before the period covered by the research; the British Healthcare Trades Association Code, which had completed Stage One before the period covered by the research and has since achieved OFT approval; and the Motor Industry Service and Repair Code, operated by Motor Codes Ltd, which had businesses joining in and completed Stage One during the period covered by the research.

[140] *Consumer Law and Business Practice. Drivers of Compliance and Non-compliance* (Office of Fair Trading, 2010) OFT1225, available at http://www.oft.gov.uk/shared_oft/reports/Evaluating-OFTs-work/OFT1225.pdf.

[141] *Drivers of Compliance and Non-compliance with Competition Law. An OFT Report* (Office of Fair Trading, 2010) OFT1227, available at http://www.oft.gov.uk/shared_oft/reports/comp_policy/oft1227.pdf.

[142] *How Your Business Can Achieve Compliance. Guidance* (Office of Fair Trading, 2010) OFT1278, October 2010.

Theme 3: Guidance and support

Key finding 6. Some businesses rely heavily on their relationships with local authority Trading Standards Services (TSS) and/or trade associations while others rely increasingly on the internet for the information they need.

Theme 4: The influence of competitor behaviour

Key finding 7. Competitor behaviour, and practices which become the norm in a market, can impact on compliance levels and may act as a driver for both compliance and non-compliance.

In considering the implications of these findings, the OFT noted its engagement in a wide range of work aimed at improving compliance, such as engaging with business to increase its understanding of consumer protection laws, promoting self-regulation, delivering consumer awareness and education programmes, and where necessary taking enforcement action in respect of consumer protection laws.[143] It committed itself to exploring how it could deliver better messages to consumers about their rights; support stakeholders to deliver messages to businesses, especially SMEs (small and medium sized enterprises); assist businesses (especially SMEs) access information and raising awareness of the consequences of breaching consumer laws; harness the business desire to build and maintain reputation, and their intuitive approach to fairness, in order to raise the awareness and priority of consumer protection laws; identify which tools could best address non-compliance where it has become an accepted market practice; and enhance the deterrent effect of enforcement actions.[144]

In referring to the research by London Economics and IFF Research, the OFT concentrated on the (admittedly small) deterrence effect,[145] and referred to Deloitte's 2007 analysis of deterrence in competition enforcement,[146] which claimed a significant effect on corporate behaviour because of the risk of OFT investigation, and to a report by London Economics[147] assessing how the UK penalty regime compares to an 'optimal' regime concluding that '[t]hese reports note the importance of financial penalties, damage to reputation, criminal sanctions, director disqualification and private actions'.[148]

Noting findings that compliance with consumer law was afforded lower priority than compliance with other laws,[149] and research on compliance and enforcement in fisheries regulation[150] and food safety law,[151] and that intensifying enforcement pressure is not

---

[143] ibid, para 1.10.

[144] ibid, para 1.12.

[145] ibid, para 2.15.

[146] *The Deterrent Effect of Competition Enforcement by OFT. A Report Prepared for the OFT by Deloitte* (Office of Fair Trading, 2007) OFT962, www.oft.gov.uk/shared_oft/reports/Evaluating-OFTswork/oft962.pdf; see ch 15.

[147] *An Assessment of Discretionary Penalty Regimes. A Report Prepared for the OFT by London Economics* (Office of Fair Trading, 2009) OFT 1132, www.oft.gov.uk/shared_oft/economic_research/oft1132.pdf.

[148] ibid, para 2.18.

[149] S Anderson, *Anderson Review of Government Guidance on Regulation* (Department for Business, Enterprise and Regulatory Reform, 2009) at www.bis.gov.uk/policies/better-regulation/reviewing-regulation/anderson-review-of-guidanceprovision.

[150] Robert Baldwin and Julia Black, *Really Responsive Regulation* LSE Law, Society and Economy Working Papers 15/2007 London School of Economics and Political Science Law Department at http://eprints.lse.ac.uk/23105/1/WPS2007-17BlackandBaldwin.pdf.

[151] R Fairman and C Yapp, 'Compliance with Food Safety Legislation in Small and Micro-businesses: Enforcement as an External Motivator' (2004) 3(2) *Journal of Environmental Health Research* 40.

always commensurate with enhanced compliance,[152] the OFT noted the importance of reputation and fear of bad publicity as extremely important as drivers for compliance.

In a separate 2010 paper on enforcement of the Regulations on unfair trading, the OFT noted '[i]n many instances we encourage businesses to comply with the regulations through the provision of advice and guidance and we foster self-regulation and the resolution of issues through compliance partnerships.'[153] However, it maintained that enforcement action was a key part of its toolkit, and it would use the civil injunctive powers contained in Part 8 of the Enterprise Act 2002,[154] or carry out a criminal investigation with a view to prosecuting those responsible.[155] The OFT noted that prosecutions may be brought against individuals responsible for the offences, corporate bodies, or officers of corporate bodies who have consented or connived in the commission of the offence.[156] It also noted the intention in future cases to request courts to make a confiscation order under the Proceeds of Crime Act 2002.[157]

In 2010 the OFT also published its long-term strategy to protect consumers shopping online,[158] which involved 'strategic enforcement to tackle new and complex forms of unfair trading that harm both consumers and markets'. The strategy set out key priorities to help prevent misleading selling, deceptive online advertising and malicious practices. The OFT intended to provide clarity on consumer law in relation to online shopping; more effective enforcement; business compliance; and better consumer understanding of their rights. It noted high levels of trust and comparatively substantial online spend in the UK internet economy, with a declining level of fraudulent use of credit cards online.[159] The strategy to help empower consumers would involve:

— Educating consumers about their online rights and working with consumer bodies to ensure consistent messages
— working on initiatives that improve the transparency of the transactions, and the security of payment mechanisms
— improving the access and quality of consumer redress, and consumer learning (for example, consumer feedback and rating sites).[160]

The OFT identified a need to improve consumer redress, since consumers were often unclear where to go to seek help, firms are often unclear of their responsibilities and the legal framework could also be made more effective.[161] A survey had shown that a quarter of

---

[152] *A Research Report on the Determinants of Compliance with Laws and Regulations with Special Reference to Health and Safety A Literature Review* by Dr Tola Amodu for the Health and Safety Executive www.hse.gov.uk/research/rrpdf/rr638.pdf.

[153] *Criminal Enforcement of the Consumer Protection from Unfair Trading Regulations 2008* (n 23) para 1.7.

[154] www.oft.gov.uk/shared_oft/business_leaflets/enterprise_act/oft512.pdf.

[155] At that time, the OFT expected to participate in a BIS Pilot of Civil Sanctions powers for the CPRs.

[156] *Criminal Enforcement of the Consumer Protection from Unfair Trading Regulations 2008* (n 23) para 4.2. See Reg 15.

[157] ibid, para 4.5.

[158] *Protecting Consumers Online: A Strategy for the UK* (n 25).

[159] *Fraud the Facts 2010* (UK Cards Association, 2010), www.theukcardsassociation.org.uk/files/ukca/fraud_the_facts_2010.pdf.

[160] *Protecting Consumers Online* (n 25) para 2.10.

[161] ibid, para 4.69.

consumers who bought goods on the internet (26 per cent, based on 735 responses) stated that either they did not know who to turn to or they would not turn to anyone else in the event of a dispute with an online seller.[162] Most would turn to TSS (20 per cent) or their credit card company (19 per cent), followed by Citizens Advice (nine per cent).[163] Problems were noted with litigation remedies and Group Litigation Orders,[164] whereas a forthcoming pilot of new civil sanctions under the RESA was noted.

In its 2010 advice to business on how to achieve compliance, the OFT repeated the four-step process that it had published for creating a culture of *competition* law compliance in a business (see chapter 15), acknowledging that 'the majority of businesses wish to comply with competition law'.[165] It referred to the importance of culture and focused on the role of senior management:

> 2.1 The core of an effective compliance culture is for a business to have an unambiguous commitment to competition law compliance, throughout the organisation. Senior management commitment is the essential ingredient for an effective compliance culture. Indeed, the board and senior management are ultimately accountable for ensuring a business's commitment to compliance. Though as suggested below, one senior person may have the *role* of driving compliance within the business, *overall accountability* for ensuring a commitment to compliance cannot simply be passed on to one person.

> 2.2 … Means by which this commitment at all levels can be communicated and demonstrated include:

> — Expressly including competition compliance in the business's code of conduct and making clear that activity that risks causing an infringement of competition law attracts disciplinary sanctions
> — Ensuring that one board member or other suitably senior manager has the role of driving compliance within the business …[166]

E. The Anderson Review

Contemporaneously with the above research and statements by the OFT, various documents were issued by parts of government. The 2009 Anderson review of guidance on regulation focused on the need for government to give businesses greater certainty over finding, following and interpreting guidance.[167] It encouraged regulators to increase certainty over outcomes, make guidance more accessible, provide clearer guidance, achieve consistent guidance across government, and to achieve the Hampton vision of a fundamental change

---

[162] *Attitudes to Online Markets* (Office of Fair Trading, 2010) OFT1253, at www.oft.gov.uk/shared_oft/consultations/eprotection/oft1253.

[163] ibid. The remedy of claiming against a credit card company for any breach of contract or misrepresentation by the trader where the purchase price of a single item is more than £100 and does not exceed £30,000, under the Consumer Credit Act, s 75, was particularly effective in supplying trust and redress. The potential gap in trust between consumer and trader was bridged by the relationship between credit company and trader.

[164] *Protecting Consumers Online* (n 25) para 7.18.

[165] *How Your Business Can Achieve Compliance. Guidance* (n 142).

[166] ibid.

[167] See recommendations on providing good guidance in *The Good Guidance Guide: Taking the Uncertainty out of Regulation* (Better Regulation Executive, 2009) available at http://www.bis.gov.uk/files/file49881.pdf.

in the culture of the relationship between regulators and businesses 'from one of inspection and punishment to one of advice and guidance.'[168]

The Anderson review conducted two studies. The first was a series of interviews with 90 SMEs.[169] This found that businesses had positive views of some areas of government guidance, especially from regulators websites. Businesses had concerns that the volume of, and regular changes to, regulation and guidance made it more difficult for them to run their business effectively. Respondents highlighted employment and health and safety regulations as areas where they found compliance most difficult. They found that even when guidance was available it was difficult to be certain that following it would mean they were complying with the law. They had concerns about where and how to access guidance, that guidance was often not written clearly, in plain English, and that this complexity made compliance problematic. They said regulatory change was not communicated to them effectively and that inspectors focused on enforcement rather than on helping SMEs comply.

The second survey was interviews with 759 senior managers from SMEs.[170] This found that the majority of SMEs (58 per cent) treated complying with regulation as a crucial or very important business responsibility. One in ten considered it not very important (10 per cent) and a similar proportion said it was not at all important (9 per cent). Health and safety was regarded as the most time-consuming (31 per cent of SMEs highlighted this area) and costly (33 per cent) aspect of regulation.[171] A significant proportion of SMEs reported that they did not seek guidance on issues of employment (37 per cent do not) or health and safety (48 per cent). SMEs generally recognised and accepted the importance of and their responsibility in complying with regulation. However, one in ten (9 per cent) believed complying with regulation was 'not at all important' and a significant proportion realised they could do more to be compliant, with smaller SMEs doing less than their larger counterparts. This was thought to be partly because of smaller businesses' lower awareness and use of government-provided sources of advice. There was, however, an appetite for receiving this guidance; only 15 per cent said they did not want it and two-thirds (65 per cent) would have been interested in using such a support mechanism. The researchers identified a typology of five clusters: Prepared and Established; Guilty Procrastinators; Capable but unconcerned; Conscientious but challenged; and Blind-eye turners.

The government's response to the Anderson review committed to take actions that included piloting a telephone advice service providing tailored, insured advice to help businesses comply with employment and health and safety law; removing the disclaimers which

---

[168] ibid, 5.

[169] *The Anderson Review. Summary of Views from Meetings with Small and Medium Sized Enterprises (SMEs)* (Department for Business, Enterprise and Regulatory Reform, 2009) available at http://www.berr.gov.uk/files/file49882.pdf.

[170] *The Anderson Review of Government Guidance on Regulation. Business Perspectives of Government Guidance. Research Study Conducted for Department for Business, Enterprise and Regulatory Reform. Final Report* (Ipsos MORI, 2008) available at http://www.berr.gov.uk/files/file49883.pdf.

[171] However, treating 'employing' SMEs as a subgroup, discounting those without staff, employment was considered the second most time-consuming (26%) and *the most* expensive (40%). SMEs felt much better placed to deal with health and safety regulation than employment (87% and 53% respectively said they were very or fairly well equipped to comply). A quarter (25%) said they were not well equipped for employment regulation compared to one in eight (13%) for health and safety.

create uncertainty when relying on government guidance; giving inspectors greater discretion about the prosecution of businesses that reasonably believe they are following guidance; and setting out when it will update the most frequently used guidance to comply with the 'Code of Practice on Guidance'.[172]

F. NAO Surveys

The National Audit Office's (NAO) survey of businesses in 2009 suggested that businesses found regulation a burden. NAO found that only 1 per cent said that complying with regulation had become easier or less time consuming, with 37 per cent of businesses saying it had become more time consuming in the preceding year.[173]

Following the change of Government in May 2010, the National Audit Office advised that although government understood which areas of regulation concerned business most, it did not know what the total impact of regulation was on business.[174] Businesses, in particular SMEs, often lacked clarity about how to comply. There were recurrent weaknesses in departments' assessments of costs and benefits when designing regulation. There was no routine evaluation of the realised impact on business of regulation once it has come into effect. Good information and coordination was essential for effective management of the use of resources. Evaluation and feedback remained a weak element of regulatory management.

G. BRE Survey of Micro-Businesses

A 2010 Better Regulation Executive (BRE) report surveyed the experience of 500 micro businesses (under 10 employees) and summarised the experiences they reported in dealing with the overall regulatory burden.[175] Its findings included: The cumulative burden on micro businesses of regulations, licences and fees was considerable and hampered their ability to stay profitable, grow, invest, hire staff and even pay themselves a wage; policy-makers were still not 'thinking small first' when designing and implementing

---

[172] *Government Response to the Anderson Review* (Department for Business, Enterprise and Regulatory Reform, 2009) available at http://www.bis.gov.uk/files/file50352.pdf. See also *Progress Report on Commitments made in Response to the Anderson Review* (Department for Business, Enterprise and Regulatory Reform, 2009), available at http://www.bis.gov.uk/assets/biscore/better-regulation/docs/10-823-progress-reports-response-anderson-review.pdf.

[173] *Complying with Regulation—Business Perceptions Survey* (National Audit Office, 2009).

[174] *Delivering Regulatory Reform* Report by the Comptroller and Auditor General (National Audit Office, 2011). 2006 BRE research estimated that just the administrative cost of regulation to UK businesses was £13 billion a year. UK annual spend on competition regime totals £27 million.

[175] *Lightening the Load: The Regulatory Impact on UK's Smallest Businesses* (Department for Business, Innovation & Skills, 2010) available at http://www.bis.gov.uk/assets/biscore/better-regulation/docs/l/10-1251-lightening-the-load-regulatory-impact-smallest-businesses.pdf.

regulations; and principles-based regulations could be difficult to interpret for micro businesses.

> Most frequently we were told that they try to do the right thing, but felt that they were not supported and were unreasonably expected to cope with the same levels of paperwork and regulatory obligations as larger companies.[176]

Three key themes emerged from what the surveyed businesses said. First, there were significant levels of frustration with the extent of regulation, the pace of regulatory flow and the expectation by government that a single business owner could cope with the cumulative array of regulations. Second, the range and complexity of regulation placed a huge cumulative burden on micro businesses, and produced misunderstanding. Examples cited were employment law, health and safety regulations (widely misunderstood and interpreted to cover a range of regulatory areas from environment to food safety. Third, the tax system was perceived to be problematic 'regulation' by most micro businesses.

BRE noted that micro businesses, which are often owner-operated, have limited ability to understand and interpret regulations across the regulatory field, leaving them feeling confused and 'on their own' when trying to cope with regulation. As a result they often unknowingly either under or over comply with regulations. Many businesses simply do not understand why certain regulations are introduced or why they are asked to provide information to government, for example data protection requirements; keeping written records of refused sales or statistics. The level of managerial capability in micro businesses is a key constraint. BRE concluded that the move towards more targeted inspection and enforcement meant that fewer businesses were inspected and they had limited if any contact with other local and central government officials.[177] They lacked a connection to an official source. Our consultations found that in a majority of cases face-to-face contact was desired and many businesses see (the good) inspectors as a valuable source of advice and guidance. Micro businesses would prefer a twin-track regulatory solution, namely that businesses could choose to adopt the principles based approach, interpreting and embedding regulatory principles in their business practice or, simple prescriptive rules about what is legal and illegal tailored to a micro business.[178]

H. OFT Study of Consumers with Contract Problems

An OFT market study of 2011 found that 20 per cent of people said they had experienced a problem with a consumer contract in the previous year.[179] This study set out a systematic approach for assessing the overall effects of consumer contract terms. The OFT would be likely to intervene against breaches of the Unfair Terms in Consumer Contracts Regulations

---

[176] ibid, 1.
[177] ibid, para 2.16.
[178] ibid, para 2.20.
[179] *Market Study Report: Consumer Contracts* (n 26).

(UTCCRs)[180] and the Consumer Protection from Unfair Trading Regulations (CPRs)[181] such as the following:

— *Unexpected restrictions to contract scope.* For example, restrictions of service or quality detailed only in small print or not clearly presented to consumers. The OFT has intervened against football season tickets not guaranteeing seats, and extended warranties offering limited cover.
— *Terms that impose unexpected risks on consumers.* For example, terms excluding a firm's liability for failure or external disruption, or imposing liabilities on consumers. The OFT intervened on Sale and Rentback deals in part on the basis that the tenancy offered was much less secure than many people realised.
— *Complex, deferred or contingent charges exceeding efficient costs.* Consumers expect firms to make money on the main elements of the deal and not to profit from small print charges. Recently, the OFT brought a successful case against a letting agent over small print charges that did not correspond to any service provided.
— *Obstructions to consumer switching.* These include onerous cancellation requirements, excessive cancellation fees, and rollover terms that are unclear or difficult to opt out of. Recently, the OFT has intervened against cancellation terms used by gyms.

I. IFF Research Business Perceptions Survey 2012

The 2012 Business Perceptions Survey found that fewer businesses felt that the overall level of regulation in the UK was an obstacle to their business success when compared to three years previously.[182] It was stated that 'Compliance matters to businesses as it gives a positive message to customers'.[183] 'Most businesses do not employ anyone specifically to deal with their compliance issues. Businesses are generally positive, however, that the time they need to put in to ensure they are compliant will either stay the same or decrease in the next 12 months.'[184]

> The perceived burden of regulation was placed into context relative to the other challenges that businesses may face … Attracting and retaining customers continued to be most often considered as the greatest challenge; the proportion citing this increased from 41% in 2010 to 45% in 2012. Only 14% of respondents felt that complying with regulation was the greatest challenge to their business, which is consistent with 2010 (although it has decreased since 2009). The proportion of businesses stating that the level of regulation is 'about right' remained unchanged from 2010 (39%) to 2012 (41%).[185]

> Businesses regard compliance with regulation as very important to their brand image: 80% agreed that 'If my business was found to be non-compliant, I would be concerned that it would affect our

---

[180] The Unfair Terms in Consumer Contracts Regs 1999/2083.
[181] The Consumer Protection from Unfair Trading Regs 2008/1277.
[182] *Business Perceptions Survey 2012* (IFF Research, 2012). This comprised 2,294 15-minute telephone interviews with senior business decision-makers covering four areas of regulation: Company law, employment law, health and safety law and planning law.
[183] ibid, para 1.7.
[184] ibid, para 1.8.
[185] ibid, para 1.13.

relationships with customers' and 69% agreed that 'It matters to our business that our customers know that we invest in compliance.'[186]

The sources of information and advice used by businesses in complying with regulation are varied. Around half of businesses had used trade associations, government department websites, insurance companies and accountants to help them comply with regulation. Four in ten mentioned the Businesslink website in relation to advice on regulatory requirements, whilst one in three mentioned their local council and around a quarter mentioned direct contact with a government department.[187] Many businesses (70 per cent) used external agents as a source of information and advice in complying with regulation.[188]

J. ORC Interviews with Mid-Sized Businesses

Interviews carried out in the first half of 2012 with a range of mid-sized businesses (MSBs[189]) investigating business growth identified, amongst other factors, the importance of max-imising long-term, trust-based relationships with customers; product quality, uniqueness and/or innovation and—particularly in the prevailing economic conditions—efficiency and cost-effectiveness in order to be more attractive to procurers.[190] A related survey of SMEs found that 77 per cent considered that they were part of a supply chain, and large businesses could be highly important to stimulating SME growth.[191] Being an accredited supplier could lead to more exposure and work, and large organisations assisted in up-skilling SMEs and improving their work processes. Large organisations also trained future entrepreneurs who in turn set up their own SMEs, driving innovation in the economy. However, large businesses can also hamper SME growth through late payments, pressure to drive costs down, and the burdensome, administrative compliance with procurement and audit procedures, especially since these are different for each customer.

A research summary by BIS concluded that key enablers affecting business success by SMEs could be grouped into the following three clusters, within each of which business could face barriers:[192]

— Internal capacity and capability—including skills and innovation
— external environment—including access to finance, exports and government procurement

---

[186] ibid, para 1.15.

[187] ibid, para 1.26.

[188] ibid, para 1.27. This was up from 64% in the 2010 survey. Businesses were more likely to use external agents as a source of information in cases of Employment Law (86%) and Company Law (81%), and less likely to use agents for Food Safety (44%) and Fire Safety (55%).

[189] MSBs were defined as businesses with a turnover of between £25m and £500m.

[190] *Large Businesses and SMEs: Exploring how SMEs Interact with Large Businesses* (ORC International, 2012) http://www.bis.gov.uk/assets/biscore/enterprise/docs/e/12-1196-exploring-how-smes-interact-with-large-businesses. The research was based on 21 in-depth interviews.

[191] ibid. A telephone survey of 506 SMEs (10–249 employees) was conducted alongside a further 49 in depth interviews with SMEs to explore issues around supply chains and other types of relationships with large businesses and how they impact on SME growth.

[192] *SMEs: The Key Enablers of Business Success and the Economic Rationale for Government Intervention* (Department for Business, Innovation & Skills, 2013), https://www.gov.uk/government/uploads/system/uploads/attachment_data/file/263863/bis-13-1320-smes-key-enablers-of-business-success.pdf.

— vision of the business owner—including growth ambitions and use of business support.

It noted that there were an estimated 4.9 million private sector businesses in the UK at the start of 2013, of which 99.9 per cent were SMEs, accounting for 59.3 per cent of private sector employment and 48.1 per cent of private sector turnover at the start of 2013. As well as making a disproportionate contribution to job creation they play a key role in growth by driving competition and stimulating innovation. SMEs drive economic growth by stimulating innovation, acting as a competitive spur to existing businesses and making a disproportionately large contribution to job creation.

K. IFF Research on Consumer Business Practices

A 2013 report examined business approaches towards consumer rights and complaints.[193] It found that an estimated total of 454,470 UK businesses sell goods to consumers: 127,505 selling goods, 1,782 selling digital content and 325,483 selling services. Looking at the profile of UK businesses selling goods, services or digital content to consumers by size, 390,601 were micro businesses, 54,504 were small, 7,811 were medium-sized and 1,553 were large businesses.[194] More than half of all businesses (54 per cent) reported they had pre-drafted standard terms and conditions for sales to, supply to, or contracts with, consumers, rising in line with business size: 52 per cent of micro businesses did so, compared to 81 per cent of large businesses.[195]

Just over one-quarter (27 per cent) of all businesses reported that existing consumer rights legislation was 'not very' or 'not at all easy' to understand; medium and large businesses were more likely to report this (37 per cent and 38 per cent respectively).[196] Just over one-quarter (27 per cent) of businesses employing staff provided some training on existing consumer rights legislation in the last 12 months. Propensity to train increased in line with business size and businesses in the services sector were most likely to have provided training.[197] Just over one-third of businesses (37 per cent) employed staff to deal with legal compliance (including staff for whom dealing with legal compliance only formed part of their role), although the majority only employed one member of staff with this responsibility.[198] One-fifth of businesses (20 per cent) reported that they had ever used

---

[193] *Consumer Rights and Business Practices* (IFF Research, March 2013, https://www.gov.uk/government/uploads/system/uploads/attachment_data/file/274801/bis-13-914-iff-report-consumer-rights-and-business-practices.pdf. It was based on 1,000 20-minute telephone interviews with senior decision-makers of businesses which sell goods, services or digital content to consumers; and 60 completed 'cost sheets' from businesses, between September 2012 and January 2013.

[194] ibid, para 1.3.

[195] ibid, para 1.4.

[196] ibid, para 1.8.

[197] ibid, para 1.9.

[198] ibid, para 1.11.

the services of private law firms to provide advice on complying with consumer rights. Just over half (55 per cent) of large businesses had done so, compared to under one-fifth (17 per cent) of micro businesses. Larger businesses and businesses in the digital content sector were also more likely to be more frequent users of such advice.[199]

One-third of businesses (31 per cent) reported that they had ever sought advice on complying with consumer rights from other organisations, such as trade bodies. Again, larger businesses were more likely to have done so, and to have done so more frequently. Only around a quarter of businesses that had used such advice reported that they had paid for it (27 per cent), although large businesses were more likely to have paid.[200]

Overall, 53 per cent of businesses reported that they handled at least some dissatisfied customers each year. Just under half (46 per cent) of these businesses reported that 90 per cent or more of complaints were resolved by providing explanations or advice, although there was considerable variation by business size: almost half of micro businesses reported resolving 90 per cent or more of complaints in this way, compared with one-fifth of large businesses.[201] Businesses operating in the services sector were also more likely to resolve issues informally: Half reported that 90 per cent or more of complaints were resolved by providing explanations or advice compared with around a third of digital content and goods businesses. Only three per cent of businesses which had experienced complaints or issues with customers reported that these had led to legal proceedings, but this varied considerably by size: 36 per cent of large businesses had experienced legal proceedings compared with only three per cent of micro businesses.[202] The average annual cost to business of handling consumer complaints was £10,407.[203] Overall, 14 per cent of businesses had a dedicated department for dealing with customer complaints, such as a customer services department, on which they spent on average £15,474 per year on running costs.[204]

Among both goods and digital content businesses, by far the most common approach taken to consumer redress—in the event that a customer reported that a purchase product was faulty or did not meet its description, or a purchased service had not been delivered with reasonable care and skill—was to offer a replacement item (94 per cent and 90 per cent respectively).[205] Businesses where this was not the most common approach generally offered a full refund as their most common approach (goods: 25 per cent; digital content: 21 per cent). In the services sector there was more variation in the approach that businesses most commonly took. Around half (48 per cent) most commonly offered to repair/remedy the service provided, while another one in five (20 per cent) would most commonly offer a partial refund and just under one in five (17 per cent) offer a full refund.[206]

---

[199] ibid, para 1.12.
[200] ibid, para 1.13.
[201] ibid, para 1.15.
[202] ibid, para 1.16.
[203] ibid, para 1.17.
[204] ibid, paras 1.18 and 1.19.
[205] ibid, para 1.20.
[206] ibid.

V. Enforcement Policy

A. Development of Hampton Compliance by the OFT

The OFT issued a considerable number of consultation and discussion papers over several years, covering issues such as implementing the government's Better Regulation agenda, and simplifying the rules and procedures;[207] measuring the extent of consumer detriment;[208] education of consumers; the encouragement of reliable self-regulatory mechanisms;[209] encouragement of compliance; as well as enforcement policies. Those papers that impact on business behaviour are referred to in chapter nine.

The OFT was subject to external review in 2008 to assess its compliance with the Hampton principles,[210] but the review contained no evaluation of compliance with the Macrory Penalties Principles. This omission was curious in view of the formal target that OFT delivers direct financial benefits to consumers of at least five times that of its cost to the taxpayer,[211] and adoption of a restorative justice approach could deliver considerably in excess of a multiple of five. The review recorded that

> OFT is moving to a more risk-based approach to resource allocation across its activities and also adopting such an approach to its revised consumer credit responsibilities and new anti-money laundering responsibilities.

> There is a strong focus on outcomes and their evaluation amongst OFT's senior management. OFT has agreed a new performance framework with Treasury which will be much more outcome-focused, and includes new reporting requirements which should improve accountability and transparency.[212]

---

[207] The 2008 Simplification Plan, for example, noted that areas in which the OFT was applying better regulation principles can be grouped under six headings: Overall approach to targeting and organising work; intervention to secure compliance with competition and consumer law; approach to consumer credit licensing; working in partnership with others; encouraging compliance and self-regulation; and work to reduce burdens on business through market study recommendations, competition advocacy and reviews of previous competition remedies: *Simplification Plan,* Office of Fair Trading, 2008, OFT984, available at http://www.oft.gov.uk/shared_oft/529862/oft984.pdf.

[208] *Consumer Detriment. Assessing the Frequency and Impact of Consumer Problems with Goods and Services* (n 1); London Economics, *Evaluation of a Sample of Consumer Enforcement Cases* (n 82).

[209] *Policy Statement. The Role of Self-regulation in the OFT's Consumer Protection Work* (Office of Fair Trading, 2009) OFT 1115 available at http://www.oft.gov.uk/shared_oft/reports/consumer-policy/oft1115.pdf; *The Economics of Self-regulation in Solving Consumer Quality Issues* (Office of Fair Trading, 2009) OFT 1059 available at http://www.oft.gov.uk/shared_oft/economic_research/oft1059.pdf; *Business Leadership in Consumer Protection. A Discussion Document on Self Regulation and Industry-led Compliance,* (Office of Fair Trading, 2010) OFT1058 available at http://www.oft.gov.uk/shared_oft/reports/consumer-policy/oft1058.pdf.

[210] *Effective Inspection and Enforcement: Implementing the Hampton Vision in the Office of Fair Trading. A Review supported by the Better Regulation Executive and National Audit Office* (Better Regulation Executive, Department for Business Enterprise & Regulatory Reform and National Audit Office, 2008) available at http://www.bis.gov.uk/files/file45359.pdf.

[211] *Approach to Calculating Direct Benefits to Consumers* (Office of Fair Trading, 2008) OFT955, available at http://www.osservatorioair.it/wp-content/uploads/2009/08/approach_to_calculating_direct_benefits.pdf.

[212] *Effective Inspection and Enforcement: Implementing the Hampton Vision in the Office of Fair Trading. A Review supported by the Better Regulation Executive and National Audit Office* (Better Regulation Executive, Department for Business Enterprise & Regulatory Reform and National Audit Office, 2008) available at http://www.bis.gov.uk/files/file45359.pdf.

The OFT then responded to its Hampton Implementation Review, setting out how it proposed to meet the obligations under the RESA, to comply with the statutory principles of good regulation, and the Regulators' Compliance Code—but again making no mention of the Macrory principles.[213] Indeed, it argued that was not primarily a regulator, and the majority of its functions were outside the scope of Part 4 of the RESA and the better regulation agenda, although it accepted that it did have functions within the scope of the regulatory reform agenda, namely consumer enforcement, licensing and market supervision, which conferred powers to take individually targeted enforcement action.[214] The response stated:

Developing alternatives to enforcement

A.17 Preventing harm in the first place is better for consumers than taking enforcement action afterwards. It is also less burdensome for business, provided it is achieved by cooperation rather than compulsion. Alongside our statutory consumer enforcement powers, we also employ a number of tools which promote self-regulation and stronger consumer confidence and empowerment. We provide incentives to improve trading practice: we rely, where appropriate on 'established means'[215] as a way of dealing with consumer complaints about, for example, misleading advertising and have consulted about how to extend our network of 'Compliance Partnerships'. We target enforcement activity in line with our Prioritisation Principles towards cases of high detriment. Under the prioritisation framework we have first to consider whether the OFT is the most appropriate body to deal with the issue. Implicitly, this requires us to think about what else might be done to address the issue and this includes consideration of what other body might be able to take speedy, effective action to stop the harm to consumers.[216]

The 2009 Plan also referred to promoting the voluntary adoption of good trading practice through the Consumer Code Approval Scheme (CCAS),[217] and undertaking awareness programmes with businesses and consumers and coordinating an alliance of consumer education partners. A series of surveys and advice documents to business followed.[218] The OFT also set out the desire that its enforcement interventions would be seen by all stakeholders as proportionate and consistent.[219]

The OFT has taken care to make the case that its work has produced significant benefit for consumers and markets. As part of the Comprehensive Spending Review settlement

[213] *Simplification Plan* (Office of Fair Trading, 2009) OFT1067 available at http://www.oft.gov.uk/shared_oft/529862/oft1067.pdf.
[214] ibid, paras 1.6 and 2.2.
[215] Established means are bodies able to act in place of OFT in encouraging compliance with the consumer protection Regs. We are consulting on ways in which we can extend the reach of established means to aid compliance with the CPRs see www.oft.gov.uk/shared_oft/consultations/oft1043con.pdf.
[216] ibid, para A.17.
[217] The CCAS set out criteria for official approval of codes of practice, especially including consumer alternative dispute resolution (ADR) schemes: see C Hodges, I Benöhr and N Creutzfeldt-Banda, *Consumer ADR in Europe* (Oxford, Hart Publishing, 2012) ch 11.
[218] Including *Consumer Law and Business Practice. Drivers of Compliance and Non-compliance* (n 141); *Consumer Law and Business Practice. Drivers of Compliance and Non-compliance* (n 140); *How Your Business Can Achieve Compliance. Guidance* (n 142); *Mapping UK Consumer Redress. A Summary Guide to Dispute Resolution Systems* (Office of Fair Trading, May 2010) available at http://www.oft.gov.uk/shared_oft/general_policy/OFT1267.pdf; *The OFT's Approach to Promoting Business Compliance with Consumer Protection Law* (Office of Fair Trading, April 2011) OFT1292, http://www.oft.gov.uk/shared_oft/policy/OFT1292.pdf.
[219] *Flexibility for Changing Markets. Annual Plan 2009–10* (Office of Fair Trading, 2009).

2007, the OFT agreed with HM Treasury a performance framework which included the following two high-level targets:[220]

— Target A: In each annual report provide quantitative evidence of how the OFT delivers direct financial benefits[221] to consumers of at least five times that of its cost to the taxpayer across the spending review period.
— Target B: In each annual report estimate the additional wider benefits of OFT's work, eg increasing consumer and business confidence in markets and deterring future anti-competitive behaviour.[222]

It estimated in 2010 that OFT's work had saved consumers at least £359 million per year on average over the period April 2007 to March 2010, against the average annual OFT spend of £50 million, giving a benefit to cost ratio of around 7:1.[223] The breakdown of the figures is given in Table 14.6.

The OFT set out principles for prioritising its work under four headings: Impact on consumer welfare and also economic efficiency; Strategic Significance for the OFT's objectives; Risks (including the likelihood of a successful outcome); and Resources, noting:

> 1.2 Markets usually work well for consumers and the economy without any need for intervention. The OFT only intervenes when it can improve the way in which markets work. The OFT's

Table 14.6: Estimated Consumer Savings and OFT Costs for 2007–10

	Estimated average annual consumer savings 2007–2010
Competition enforcement	£84m
Merger control	£125m
Market studies, reviews of orders and undertaking, and market investigation references	£107m
Consumer protection enforcement	£42m
Total benefits	**£359m**
Total OFT costs (averaged over 2007–10)	**£50m**
Partial OFT costs (averaged over 2007–10)	£37m
Benefit/ Total OFT costs	**7**
Benefit / Partial costs	10

---

[220] *Approach to Calculating Direct Benefits to Consumers* (n 211).
[221] Financial benefits to consumers include: Decrease in price, monetised improvements in quality range or service, monetised time savings, and the benefits that consumers gain from making better informed choices about what goods to purchase. Calculations do not include redress benefits from private actions. See *Approach to Calculating Direct Benefits to Consumers* (n 211) para 2.8ff.
[222] ibid.
[223] *Positive Impact 09/10. Consumer Benefits from the OFT's Work* (Office of Fair Trading, 2010) OFT1251 available at http://www.oft.gov.uk/shared_oft/reports/Evaluating-OFTs-work/oft1251.pdf.

interventions therefore seek to promote open competition, and to encourage the unrestricted availability of products and services and the provision of accurate, non-deceptive information between businesses and consumers.

1.3 We therefore focus our efforts and resources on deterring and influencing behaviour that poses the greatest threat to consumer welfare, and intervene in order to protect consumer welfare and, in the process, drive higher productivity growth. We also recognise the need to avoid imposing unnecessary burdens on business…

1.5 In seeking to target both our resources and enforcement strategy, the OFT needs to consider a range of factors including impact on consumers, strategic significance, risks and resources.[224]

A sequence of policy papers issued by the OFT itself took forward aspects of implementation of the above policies. The OFT promised, in its March 2009 Annual Plan, to adopt a responsive approach that included continuing to focus on high-profile enforcement action, and reported the first ever criminal convictions against individuals for price-fixing offences.[225] However, it may be wondered whether such an approach in fact continued a command and control or US-style deterrent policy, rather than truly responsive policy, although the top of Ayres' and Braithwaite's enforcement pyramid does provide for effective deprivatory sanctions. In responding to the Law Commission review of criminal liability in regulatory contexts, pursuant to the Macrory review,[226] the OFT clung to use of criminal enforcement and deterrence:

Making prosecution possible only as the final stage in a rigid procedural hierarchy to be in place under *all* circumstances is undesirable. Such a change would result in the loss of a deterrent which we consider has a very real effect on the level of detriment that may be experienced by consumers.[227]

However, a different approach was signalled by the Government in its 2009 consumer policy White Paper, which presaged an innovative enforcement regime for consumer protection law, aiming to

develop an enforcement culture that focuses first on compliance, second on restoring any damage done to consumers by breaches of the law, and only third on punitive prosecution. [The government] does not want to see a surge in monetary penalties as the new powers are used more and more. Rather it wants companies who have infringed legal provisions to take the opportunity to put things right before any formal public enforcement takes place. Many good businesses do this already…

Enforcement authorities should take into account any compensation awards by the business in their decision making. They should use the new powers to help persuade businesses to do the right thing, reserving formal action only for those who refuse to do so. But if businesses break the law and refuse to compensate, they should not be allowed to gain from this refusal.[228]

---

[224] *OFT Prioritisation Principles* (n 81).

[225] *Annual Plan 2009* (Office of Fair Trading, 2009) at http://nds.coi.gov.uk/content/detail.asp?ReleaseID=396663&NewsAreaID=2&NavigatedFromSearch=True (OFT, 26/03/2009).

[226] See ch 9 above.

[227] *Criminal Liability in Regulatory Contexts. Response to the Law Commission Consultation* (Office of Fair Trading, 2010) OFT1285.

[228] Consumer White Paper, *A Better Deal for Consumers. Delivering Real Help Now and Change for the Future,* 2009, Cm 2669, available at http://www.bis.gov.uk/files/file52072.pdf, 49.

This change of direction was supported by OFT research published in 2010 that reputation and the influence of consumers were the most important drivers of business compliance or non-compliance: The details are given above and in chapter 15.

B. OFT Enforcement Policy

The 2010 'Statement of consumer protection enforcement principles'[229] was issued in order to take account of the Macrory principles. Here, which the OFT asserted:

> We believe that most businesses aim to treat their customers fairly and comply with consumer protection law and that OFT aims to enable and encourage them to do so, and to take enforcement action only where there is no better route to securing compliance…[230]

> When it is necessary to use enforcement action to achieve compliance, we aim to ensure that such interventions deliver high impact results, for example, by changing market behaviour, clarifying laws or providing the necessary level of deterrence to those who would deliberately flout their legal obligations. We take a risk-based approach, prioritising our actions to ensure resources are used to maximum effect and to avoid burdening business with the costs of unnecessary interventions…[231]

> We seek to ensure that our choice of enforcement sanctions is consistent with the principles set out in the Macrory report, namely to:

> — aim to change the behaviour of the business and others in the sector
> — aim (where our powers allow this) to eliminate any financial gain or benefit from non-compliance
> — be responsive and consider what is appropriate for the particular breach and particular offender which may, or may not, include punishment and a criminal conviction.[232]

Significantly, however, although this reference to the Macrory principles refers to eliminating any financial gain, it omitted reference to the principles of restoration and reparation to victims. The OFT illustrated the range of compliance options available to it in relation to enforcement of consumer protection legislation (but not competition legislation) by the pyramid shown in Figure 14.3, which is a typical example of the Ayres and Braithwaite format.[233] This records an enforcement policy in which different sanctions are imposed on different infringers, for different infringements of consumer law. The OFT commented: 'It shows the flexibility of our approach in using education, guidance and advice to secure compliance and enforcement options including civil and criminal powers.'[234]

---

[229] *Statement of Consumer Protection Enforcement Principles* (n 81). See also *OFT Prioritisation Principles* (n 81); *Criminal Enforcement of the Consumer Protection from Unfair Trading Regulations 2008* (n 23).

[230] ibid, para 2.3.

[231] ibid, para 2.7.

[232] ibid, para 2.8.

[233] ibid, para 2.14. See ch 9.

[234] ibid, para 2.14. The Statement comments: 'The diagram does not replicate the order in which options are considered. For example, informal dialogue could take place before formal guidance is issued and formal advice is provided.… Similarly, the diagram does not reflect the specifics of the licensing regime, where requirements can be imposed and licences refused or revoked. However, the principle of formal action at the top of the enforcement triangle still applies.'

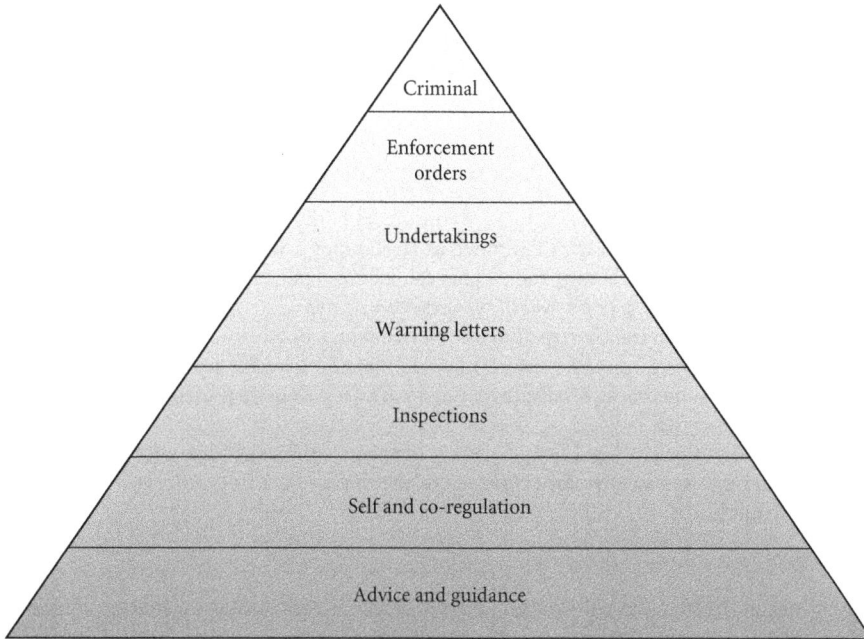

Figure 14.3: OFT's 2010 Enforcement Pyramid

The OFT also expressed a 'commitment to supporting and working with self-regulation', although this was removed in the 2012 revision after the OFT lost the function of supervision of the CCAS, noting

> 1.7 In many instances we encourage businesses to comply with the regulations through the provision of advice and guidance and we foster self-regulation and the resolution of issues through compliance partnerships. However, enforcement action is a key part of our toolkit…[235]

There was also an explanation that in enforcing the unfair trading Regulations, the OFT would either use the civil injunctive powers contained in Part 8 of the Enterprise Act 2002,[236] or carry out a criminal investigation with a view to prosecuting those responsible, whether individuals responsible for the offences, corporate bodies or officers of corporate bodies who have consented or connived in the commission of the offence.[237] In qualifying cases the OFT said it would usually ask the sentencing court to proceed with a view to making a confiscation order under the Proceeds of Crime Act 2002 unless it would be unjust to do so.[238]

Research into case studies had found that two important lessons for consumer enforcement were to measure the success of consumer interventions and to target enforcement

---

[235] *Criminal Enforcement of the Consumer Protection from Unfair Trading Regulations 2008* (n 23).
[236] www.oft.gov.uk/shared_oft/business_leaflets/enterprise_act/oft512.pdf.
[237] Reg 15.
[238] *Criminal Enforcement of the Consumer Protection from Unfair Trading Regulations 2008* (n 23).

work.[239] In April 2011 the OFT published a policy statement of how it intended, by its own interventions and through partnerships with others, to promote and motivate business compliance with consumer protection law to secure better outcomes for consumers.[240] Noting its limited resources, it stated its intention to utilise the full range of its powers and functions relating to its role in protecting consumers, including promoting good practice and enforcement. It stated that it built on research findings on compliance, which included:

— in general most businesses seek to treat consumers fairly although they may have a limited understanding of the law, and this limited understanding can act to reduce compliance levels;
— informed consumers asserting their rights can have a significant impact on business behaviour and appear to be a key driver of business compliance;
— there is a lack of awareness regarding the consequences of a breach of consumer protection law and the types of possible enforcement action. Some businesses have a general understanding, but sometimes perceive there to be a greater risk of inspection, fines and sanctions than perhaps exists;
— concerns about negative publicity are likely to enhance the deterrence effect of enforcement actions, and businesses are concerned about the impact breaches of the law might have on their reputation.[241]

The approach focused on two themes:

1. How we can influence business and consumers to bring about greater compliance with consumer protection law without the need for enforcement action, and
2. How we can secure compliance through effective tough action against deliberate non-compliant behaviour.

In relation to the first theme, the approaches would include influencing business by:

— improving guidance material to business to increase understanding of complex legislation, and delivering it in forms which business finds most useful (for example the development of the Sale of Goods Act Hub)
— working closely with business, trade associations and others when developing guidance to ensure effective promotion of and availability of guidance
— working with others to ensure information is available and consistent on websites used by business, for example Business Link
— working to encourage the development of simplified legislation.[242]

In relation to the second, enforcement, theme, the OFT said it would

take tough action for deliberate non-compliant behaviour. In particular, we believe there are opportunities to use our existing enforcement powers more effectively and innovatively to increase the compliance effect of our cases. Examples of this include:

— focusing on market problems, rather than individual traders, and more closely linking enforcement activity to our market study work, aiming to tackle problems across whole markets or by theme;

[239] London Economics, *Evaluation of a Sample of Consumer Enforcement Cases* (n 82).
[240] *The OFT's Approach to Promoting Business Compliance with Consumer Protection Law* (n 218). See also *How Your Business Can Achieve Compliance: Summary of Responses to the OFT's Consultation and OFT's Conclusions and Decision Document* (Office of Fair Trading, 2011) OFT1278resp, available at http://www.oft.gov.uk/shared_oft/ca-and-cartels/competition-awareness-compliance/oft1278resp.pdf.
[241] ibid, para 1.4.
[242] ibid, para 1.7.

— using communications to support enforcement and other OFT activity (such as market studies) to draw out learning points for businesses/consumers, and maximise the deterrent effect of enforcement action;
— publishing case information at an earlier date where there is a compelling need to do so and it is possible to do so within the law;
— where appropriate, increasingly asking businesses to make corrective statements to remedy a misleading impression given to consumers regarding a good or service;
— using existing powers to empower consumers to take action for themselves, such as by ensuring they can secure redress, have ready access to information about traders and are not inhibited from taking what steps they can to tackle malpractice;
— linking non-compliant behaviour and the harm caused to actual individuals in the business who are responsible, for example seeking enforcement orders or undertakings from company directors as well as the company concerned;
— providing guidance to other enforcers to avoid inconsistencies of enforcement and advice.[243]

Finally, 'To help inform the OFT's decisions on the most appropriate way of addressing non-compliant behaviour in the future we will evaluate the impact that interventions have had on raising compliance levels by creating a deterrence effect.'[244] The OFT set 'high impact enforcement' and 'influencing' as strategic objectives for 2012–13: As in Table 14.7.[245]

In November 2011, 'High Impact Enforcement' and 'Influencing' were stated to be two of the three annual targets, both of which were explained as 'Changing behaviour', with 'Influencing' described as 'Changing behaviour in markets through advocacy and guidance, and taking action using non-enforcement tools.'[246] The backdrop was a 25 per cent budget cut imposed in the 2010 Spending Review settlement.

A stepped approach to enforcement of the marketing of products was stated in December 2011:

The UK has a preference for a preventive route towards enforcement …

General Approach when Products are found to present a Risk:

All [Market Surveillance Authorities (MSAs)] will have an extensive range of statutory powers to deal with contraventions. MSA will always seek a voluntary compliance from an economic operator

Table 14.7: OFT's Strategic Enforcement Objectives 2012–2013

High Impact Enforcement	Influencing	Organisational delivery and capability
Changing behaviour in forms through our enforcement work—doing so faster and achieving greater impact, and taking greater risks where potential outcomes justify doing so	Changing behaviour in markets through advocacy and guidance, and taking action using non-enforcement tools	Driving forward improvements to the consumer, competition and credit regimes—while not being distracted from our focus of delivering improvements in markets today; ensuring the OFT is in shape to meet tighter constraints in future years

[243] ibid, para 1.8.
[244] ibid, para 1.9.
[245] *Annual Plan Consultation Document 2012–13* (Office of Fair Trading, 2011) OFT1382con, available at http://www.oft.gov.uk/shared_oft/consultations/annual-plan-cons/OFT1382con.pdf.
[246] *Annual Plan Consultation document 2012–13*, ibid.

when a product is found to contravene legislation. MSA, however, can issue formal notices to require duty holders to bring about such compliance in the products that they supply. Where the significance of non-compliances makes it appropriate, MSA can take more rigorous action, including preventing duty holders from supplying the goods until the non-compliances have been rectified or judgements in the courts. Successful prosecutions can result in monetary penalties or, in the most extreme cases, imprisonment.[247]

In June 2012, the OFT's response to government consultation on modernising consumer law enforcement powers[248] agreed that simplification and consolidation of enforcers' investigatory powers was necessary and supports consolidating enforcers' investigatory powers.[249]

1.2 Our work is strategic, driven by market analysis and evidence—particularly complaint evidence—and targeted on the basis of published prioritisation principles. It is not based on inspections or routine information returns…

1.3 The OFT supports the three objectives of the proposals; reducing burdens by simplifying and consolidating enforcers' investigatory powers so they are clear and transparent, protecting civil liberties by applying strong safeguards to more intrusive investigatory powers, and improving the effectiveness and efficiency of enforcement…

1.6 We wish to stress the importance of constructive engagement between enforcers and traders in promoting compliance. Many businesses value advice and guidance on compliance offered by trading standards officers. Small businesses may find an informal visit of a trading standards officer more helpful in achieving compliance than a formal visit based on 'suspicion' of a breach…

1.7 Already a large number of safeguards: Regulators' Compliance Code, judicial review, required to publish enforcement policies, Ombudsmen.

Potential model for aligning powers, levels of intrusion and safeguards

1.10 OFT supports creating a generic set of consumer enforcement powers which aligns safeguards with the levels of intrusion/burdens on business potentially caused…

1.11 To be effective, we think the generic set of powers should include powers for enforcers to observe the carrying on of a business, and to search premises with a warrant in order to obtain evidence.[250]

The OFT has not sought the civil sanction powers. A consultation on a civil sanctions pilot was mooted in 2010 but was overtaken by the government proposal on consumer redress in November 2012, which in effect adopted the Macrory approach of prioritising delivery of redress through regulatory rather than litigatory means.[251]

---

[247] *New Legislative Framework. The General National Market Surveillance Programme for the United Kingdom* (Department for Business, Innovation & Skills, 2011).

[248] *Enhancing Consumer Confidence through Effective Enforcement: Consultation on Consolidating and Modernising Consumer Law Enforcement Powers* (n 67).

[249] *Consumer Law Enforcement Powers: A Consultation Response by the Office of Fair Trading* (Office of Fair Trading, 2012) OFT1427, available at http://oft.gov.uk/shared_oft/consultations/OFT1427resp_Consumer_Law_En1.pdf.

[250] ibid.

[251] *Civil Sanctions Pilot. Joint Consultation by the OFT and LBRO on the Operation of the BIS Civil Sanctions Pilot* (Local Better Regulation Office and Office of Fair Trading, 2010) OFT1296, at http://www.oft.gov.uk/shared_oft/consultations/OFT1296.pdf.

Meanwhile, the Government developed ideas on improved regulation inspired by 'better regulation' policy in adopting an 'outcomes based' approach to regulation[252] and utilising the power of market reputation on affecting companies' behaviour, such as 'the power of information' through increased transparency and 'the power of the crowd' by opening up regulatory data.[253] Coalition government priorities included not only reducing regulation but also to 'strengthen consumer protection, especially for the most vulnerable, and promote more responsible corporate and consumer behaviour through greater transparency and *by harnessing the insights from behavioural economics and social psychology*' (emphasis added).[254] The government noted the value of redress schemes, including ombudsmen and consumer ADR schemes, in delivering compensation to consumers often at no cost to consumers, as well as being able to influence business behaviour, and they were to be extended.[255]

C. The CMA's 2014 Consumer Enforcement Powers Guidance

It was only in 2014, after the CMA had been created but also after most other regulatory authorities had issued their enforcement policies (see chapters nine and 13), that the CMA issued its *Guidance* on how it intended to use its consumer protection powers, as from 1 April 2014.[256] The policy objectives were drafted in the context of Government's aim

to increase consumer empowerment by:

— reducing the complexity of the consumer landscape—the publicly funded
— institutions that exist to help consumers
— strengthening the effectiveness of enforcement of consumer rights, and
— ensuring that activities which help consumers to be empowered are delivered more cost-effectively and in a way that links national and local intelligence about the problems consumers face.[257]

Against this background, the CMA stated its role in relation to its 'consumer powers' (rather than to the interests of consumers or markets) as follows:

3.8 The CMA will seek to target consumer enforcement action where it can secure wide-ranging changes to markets and tackle significant consumer detriment, particularly in emerging trends.

---

[252] *Transforming Regulatory Enforcement: Discussion Paper* (n 57); *Transforming Regulatory Enforcement: Government Response to the Consultation on Transforming Regulatory Enforcement* (Department for Business, Innovation & Skills, 2011). See Department for Business, Innovation & Skills, the Office of Fair Trading and Local Authority Trading Standards Services (n 6).

[253] *Better Choices: Better Deals. Consumers Powering Growth* (n 31); *Midata; Government Response to 2012 Consultation* (Department for Business, Innovation & Skills, 2012).

[254] *Business Plan 2011–2015* (Department for Business, Innovation & Skills, 2011) 4. http://www.number10. gov.uk/wp-content/uploads/BIS-Business-Plan1.pdf.

[255] *Empowering and Protecting Consumers. Consultation on Institutional Changes for Provision of Consumer Information, Advice, Education, Advocacy and Enforcement* (Department for Business, Innovation & Skills, 2011) 4.50–4.60, at http://www.bis.gov.uk/Consultations/empowering-and-protecting-consumers;http://www.bis. gov.uk/assets/biscore/consumer-issues/docs/e/11-970-empowering-protecting-consumers-consultation-on-institutional-changes.pdf.

[256] *Consumer Protection: Guidance on the Use of its Consumer Powers* (Competition and Markets Authority, 2014) CMA7.

[257] ibid, para 3.3, quoting *Empowering and Protecting Consumers. Government Response to the Consultation on Institutional Reform* (Department for Business, Innovation & Skills, 2012).

The CMA will place its interventions in the context of broader market analysis with cases informed by clear theories of harm which take account of dynamic economic analysis where necessary. This helps ensure that interventions are proportionate to need and do not impose unnecessary burdens on business but, on the contrary, help create a framework in which competitive business can thrive and consumers are protected.

3.9 For the CMA, enforcement action may be appropriate where it has determined that breaches of law point to systemic failures in a market (sector or geographic), where changing the behaviour of one business would set a precedent or have other market-wide implications, where there is an opportunity to set an important legal precedent or where there is a strong need for deterrence or to secure compensation for consumers. The CMA will make strategic choices about the cases it takes and apply its prioritisation principles. It is not the role of the CMA to take a case against a single national company purely because it is a large company and/or the case requires significant resource. Under the new arrangements in the consumer landscape most single trader national cases are likely to be taken by TSS. For the CMA to take a case there would often need to be an additional factor to demonstrate why the case is justified in wider market terms. However, where cases relate to breaches of the UTCCRs, it is possible that the CMA, as lead authority, would take cases without a wider market justification, to uphold the effectiveness of the regime.

3.10 The CMA will work with partners through the CPP to assess and provide coordinated responses to economic threats to consumers. It will work with trade bodies and firms to develop market-wide solutions and, where necessary, pursue multiparty enforcement and litigation, generally in the higher courts. The CMA will take largely civil cases, often relying on legislation such as the UTCCRs which can only be used in the civil courts. It acts mainly in the High Court and above, supported by the specialist advisory and litigation resources that are needed for such cases. Where a business, which is party to CMA action, has a primary authority relationship with a TSS office, the CMA will, where appropriate, liaise in the first instance with the relevant TSS department before approaching the business.[258]

Partnerships were noted with The Consumer Protection Partnership;[259] TSS; the TSI; concurrent consumer enforcers;[260] the Consumer Protection Cooperation Forum;[261] Citizens

---

[258] ibid, paras 3.8–3.10.

[259] Members and their functions are: Department for Business, Innovation & Skills (BIS) as Government lead for consumer policy in the UK; Trading Standards in England and Wales, represented by the National Trading Standards Board (NTSB), with responsibility for enforcement and threat assessment—local, regional and national in England and Wales; Trading Standards Scotland, overseen by the Convention of Scottish Local Authorities (CoSLA) and with co-ordination and action via Trading Standards Scotland (TSScot), in relation to local, regional and national enforcement in Scotland; Trading Standards in Northern Ireland—Department of Enterprise, Trade and Investment (DETI), in relation to local, regional and national enforcement in Northern Ireland; Trading Standards Institute (TSI), in relation to business education and Consumer Codes Approval Scheme; the CMA, in relation to enforcement to address systemic failures in a market, where changing the behaviour of one business would set a precedent or have other market-wide implications, where there is an opportunity to set an important legal precedent or where there is a strong need for deterrence or to secure compensation for consumers. UTCCRs enforcement leadership, enforcement and business education; Citizens advice (England and Wales), in relation to consumer advocacy, education and provision of consumer advice including the Citizens Advice consumer helpline; and Citizens Advice Scotland and Consumer Council for Northern Ireland, in relation to consumer advocacy, education and advice in their respective territories.

[260] The Consumer Concurrencies Group (CCG), comprising Advertising Standards Authority, Civil Aviation Authority, CMA, Financial Conduct Authority, Ofcom, Office of the Rail Regulator, Ofgem, Ofwat, PayphonePlus, TSS and Which?.

[261] This comprises all UK designated CPC authorities and BIS.

Advice and other consumer bodies; and self-regulation, 'established means'[262] and compliance partnerships. In relation to 'established means', the CMA said:

4.26 The CMA understands that these regulations are intended to encourage the control of unfair commercial practices/misleading marketing activities through the use of alternative sets of arrangements where it is appropriate to do so. The primary concern is to gain compliance. If an alternative process is well placed to achieve this in place of the CMA, then this expands the reach of compliance processes in the UK.

4.27 In working with established means/compliance partnerships the CMA will have regard to the following principles.

PRINCIPLE 1

4.28 In circumstances where the CMA is aware of, or suspects, non-compliance with the Regulations, it may deal with the matter itself, or seek to refer the matter to compliance partner(s), in line with its prioritisation principles…

4.29 The CMA targets its enforcement activity towards cases that are likely to deliver high impact results for consumers, in line with its prioritisation principles. The CMA will intervene in those cases where it is appropriate for it to do so, but, using appropriate 'established means' as a first port of call for resolving compliance issues will expand the reach of the Regulations and bring benefits to consumers, business and enforcers alike.

PRINCIPLE 2

4.30 The CMA will seek to refer a matter to the compliance partner best placed to resolve the problem. The CMA may consider it appropriate in some circumstances for different partners to tackle different elements of an issue. Where appropriate, the CMA will seek to nominate a 'lead partner' which may in turn seek to liaise with other interested parties. In making this assessment we will have regard to the principles of better regulation, any protocols that are in place between the OFT and its partners and the principle of who is best placed to act.

4.31 When assessing which partner may be best placed to deal with the issue the CMA will satisfy ourselves that the chosen partner has an effective way of bringing about the control of unfair commercial practices. The CMA will therefore not pass on an issue to a body that has shown itself unwilling or incapable of controlling unfair commercial practices. The CMA will consider and engage with those partners that are relevant to the circumstances of the particular case. So what is appropriate in one case may not necessarily be appropriate in another.

4.32 Factors the CMA will take into account in referring to a compliance partner or partners may include:

— degree of detriment
— geographical location of detriment
— sector in which the detriment is arising
— nature and seriousness of the unfair commercial practice
— complexity of the issue
— history of the trader in dealing with compliance requests, and
— degree of compliance partner's alignment with the public interest.

---

[262] Under the Consumer Protection Regs the CMA is required to 'have regard to the desirability of encouraging control of unfair commercial practices by such established means as it considers appropriate having regard to all the circumstances of the particular case.' (Reg 19.4). The Business Protection from Misleading Marketing Regs 2008 (BPRs) contains similar provisions.

4.33 The CMA will use its discretion to decide who is best placed to meet the circumstances of each particular case. The CMA may approach a different body or use a different set of arrangements from those used on a previous occasion. This is not to say the CMA will be inconsistent in its referrals and in most cases it will be clear who is best placed to act.

PRINCIPLE 3

4.34 In considering whether compliance partners are an effective means of addressing non-compliance the CMA will look for the following essential and desirable qualities.

Essential qualities/systems

4.35 A body, or set of arrangements, will be able to demonstrate the following:

— it has adequate resources to address instances of non-compliance within its community
— it is law abiding in its own operation
— it is recognised by its community
— it is properly incentivised to act
— it has systems to place requirements on its community
— it has systems to enforce those requirements within its community
— there is an appropriate degree of independence in governance
— there is an appropriate degree of objectivity in governance
— it has regard for principles of better regulation and the Human Rights Act with regard to the rights of consumers and traders/businesses
— it has adequate controls in place for the safeguarding of confidential information, and
— it is willing to report to the CMA on its compliance partnership activity.

Desirable qualities/systems

4.36 Compliance partners will also be able to display some or all of the following:

— systems for providing information/communication within markets
— a public facing element that may incorporate a complaint handling facility, and
— systems for staying abreast of developments in the law

PRINCIPLE 4

4.37 Ultimately, the CMA is empowered to enforce the Regulations

4.38 The CMA wishes to foster trust with its compliance partners. However, the CMA will only consider making referrals to compliance partners that appear to it to meet the qualities described above to a sufficient degree. If a body fails to address an unfair commercial practice in a market speedily and successfully, the CMA may refer a matter to another compliance partner or take action itself to prevent continued harm to consumers. The CMA expects action taken by a compliance partner will be successful in the vast majority of cases. However, it will always retain its discretion to refer or not to refer to a compliance partner and whether to intervene in any case following referral.[263]

The CMA also referred to wider international working with other EU authorities, the International Consumer Protection and Enforcement network (ICPAN), the OECD, and the London Action Plan agreed by 19 bodies from 15 countries to communicate and cooperate on enforcement action to tackle economic threats to consumers online and malware.

---

[263] ibid, paras 4.26–4.38.

The *Guidance* then set out the CMA's approach to compliance and enforcement of consumer protection law, which developed that stated previously by the OFT. The key paragraphs were:

5.2 The law sets minimum standards for behaviour in markets and the CMA has a range of enforcement options to ensure compliance with them.

5.3 The diagram[264] below illustrates the range of enforcement and compliance options available to the CMA. It shows enforcement options including civil and criminal powers but also the flexibility of the CMA approach in using clear, targeted and timely information, advice and education to secure compliance. Further detail on the CMA's approach to compliance and enforcement is set out below.

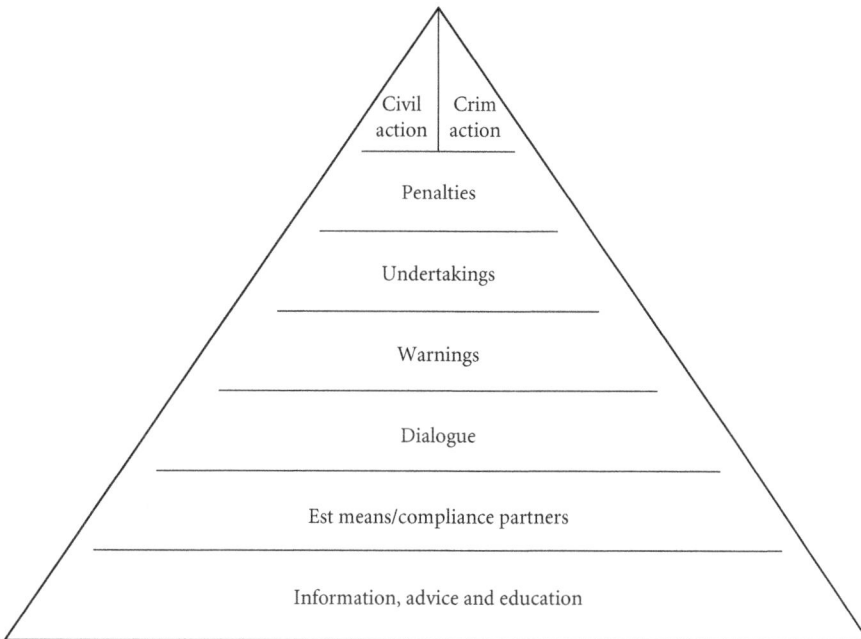

The CMA's Approach to Compliance

5.4 As set out in Chapter 4, the CMA encourages higher standards using tools other than enforcement either itself or through working with compliance partners.

5.5 For example, the CMA supports the provision of clear, targeted and timely information and guidance to businesses, to educate, enable and encourage their compliance with consumer protection legislation, and to consumers, to educate and empower them and so reduce the need for enforcement action.

---

[264] The diagram does not replicate the order in which options are considered.

5.6 The CMA may issue specific guidance to businesses in a sector where, for example, it has published a market study, or to businesses in relation to the application of the UTCCRs.

5.7 The CMA relies, where appropriate, on its compliance partners to educate consumers,[265] to encourage compliance and also to deal with consumer complaints.[266]

5.8 Further detail on the CMA's relationship and division of work as between compliance partners is set out in chapter 4.

The CMA's Approach to Enforcement

5.9 When it is necessary to use enforcement action to achieve compliance, the CMA aims to ensure that such interventions deliver high impact results, for example, by changing market behaviour, clarifying laws or providing the necessary level of deterrence to those who would deliberately flout their legal obligations. The CMA takes a risk-based approach, prioritising its actions to ensure resources are used to maximum effect and to avoid burdening business with the costs of unnecessary interventions. The CMA aims to be as robust as necessary to gain compliance while allowing maximum freedom for effective competition within the law.

5.10 The CMA is committed to the principles of good regulation in relation to its enforcement action as set out in statute and aims to ensure when carrying out such activity that its action is:

— proportionate and consistent
— targeted
— clear, and
— accountable.

Further detail was given on how those principles would be applied. The *Guidance* also expanded on use of civil and criminal enforcement powers. In relation to the former, it noted its powers of investigation, to gain access to premises without or under a warrant, and various additional powers, and included the statement:

6.3 For the CMA, enforcement action may be appropriate where it has determined that breaches of law point to systemic failures in a market, where changing the behaviour of one business would set a precedent or have other market-wide implications, where there is an opportunity to set an important legal precedent or where there is a strong need for deterrence or to secure compensation for consumers. The CMA will make strategic choices about the cases it takes and apply its prioritisation principles.

In relation to use of criminal powers, it particularly highlighted situations where a trader 'misleads, behaves aggressively or otherwise acts unfairly towards consumers' which is likely to constitute breach of the law.[267] Action may be appropriate where

breaches of law point to systemic failures in a market, where changing the behaviour of one business would set a precedent or have other market-wide implications, where there is an opportunity to set an important legal precedent or where there is a strong need for deterrence or to secure

---

[265] In relation to consumer guidance on consumer law, the role in educating consumers is provided by Citizens Advice services.
[266] While the CMA has powers under the CPRs to take enforcement action in response to a complaint concerning misleading advertising, in practice the CMA will give existing organisations, in this case the Advertising Standards Authority (a self-regulatory body which as a compliance partner acts as 'established means' for this purpose) the opportunity to deal with complaints in the first instance.
[267] *Guidance* (n 256) para 7.3.

compensation for consumers. The CMA will make strategic choices about the cases it takes and apply its prioritisation principles.[268]

The CMA said that it will generally use its criminal powers when:

— civil enforcement is unlikely to be effective in achieving a change in behaviour, and/or
— the breach is sufficiently serious that the conviction and punishment of offenders ought to be pursued, for example to protect the public and to provide wider deterrence.[269]

A decision by the CMA to prosecute a case criminally will be taken in accordance with the two stage test set out in the 'Code for Crown Prosecutors', that is, the 'evidential sufficiency test' and the 'public interest' test.[270] Prosecutions may be brought against: Individuals responsible for the offences; corporate bodies; or officers of corporate bodies who have consented or connived in the commission of the offence or where the commission of the offence by the relevant corporate body is proved to be attributable to the officer's neglect.[271]

D. Enforcers and Consumer Redress

Before considering the coordinated enforcement policy on consumer issues that was introduced in 2014 by the Coalition Government, it is instructive to note how thinking had already evolved on the topic of consumer redress. The issue of collective redress for consumers was highly debated during much of the 2000s, both nationally and at EU level.[272] Strong calls for the extension of collective judicial procedures gradually diminished as it became realised that other techniques were more effective, notably ADR, ombudsmen,[273] and—of particular relevance to the current analysis—enabling regulators to oversee delivery of redress.

The Labour Government strongly supported a restorative justice approach in its 2009 White Paper on a framework for consumer policy[274] and paper on collective redress.[275] The latter rejected a proposal by the Civil Justice Council that a new collective litigation procedure was needed to deliver collective redress. The government's response was based on an assessment of whether there was empirical need on a sectoral basis (which it held was not established for consumer redress), and the policy that regulatory and ADR solutions offered greater advantages and fewer disadvantages than a litigation-based approach. Similarly, in addressing inequality in women's pay, a judicial approach was dropped from the Equality Act, and instead a new duty applies to public authorities, which is collectively monitorable through judicial review.[276]

[268] ibid, para 7.4.
[269] ibid, para 7.7.
[270] ibid, para 7.16. See www.cps.gov.uk/publications/code_for_crown_prosecutors.
[271] CPRs, Reg 15.
[272] See C Hodges, 'Collective Redress: A Breakthrough or a Damp Sqibb?' (2014) 34 *Journal of Consumer Policy* 67.
[273] The development of consumer ADR was later given significant impetus under Dir 2013/11/EU, which created a pan-European framework of consumer ADR bodies. For a review of such bodies in ten Member States, including the UK, see Hodges, Benöhr and Creutzfeldt-Banda (n 217).
[274] Consumer White Paper (n 228).
[275] *UK Government's Response to the Civil Justice Council's Report: 'Improving Access to Justice through Collective Actions'* (Ministry of Justice, 2009).
[276] Equality Act 2010, ss 1–3.

The Consumer White Paper viewed a judicial compensation technique to be a matter of last resort in the consumer sector. In enhancing consumer redress, the government concluded that there was a lack of clear evidence for introducing representative actions, but that there was a gap between successful enforcement action and adequate consumer compensation and that representative actions by an independent publicly-funded figure could be a way to meet this gap alongside attempts to deliver compensation though public enforcement.[277] In order to position such an approach as a last resort and to control its operation, to avoid abuse by private actors, the Labour government proposed that a collective judicial process should be controlled by a new quasi-ombudsman, the Consumer Advocate.[278] The Consumer Advocate, which was modelled on the Danish Consumer Ombudsman, would have monitored cases where a large number of consumers have been affected in a similar way by a business found guilty of breaking the law, to liaise with relevant enforcers and seek to help the business in question to propose a satisfactory compensation package on a voluntary basis. The Advocate would have had powers:

— to take legal actions on behalf of a group of consumers following a breach of consumer protection law if other routes for obtaining compensation have been tried or judged inappropriate;
— to distribute compensation to UK consumers from ill-gotten gains seized by overseas enforcement agencies;
— to tackle unfairness in consumer credit agreements.

The Consumer Advocate would have been expected to use a third party to carry out the detailed work to identify and distribute the compensation to consumers and would need to be able to recover costs. In some cases the Advocate might conclude that the administrative costs of identifying relevant consumers and distributing the compensation to them would be disproportionate to the amount of compensation available. In these circumstances the Advocate would need to have the power instead to use the compensation to finance, for example, relevant consumer awareness and education activities. A consultation was issued on the Consumer Advocate proposal by the coalition government,[279] but the mechanism was subsequently not pursued.

In relation to redress, the Coalition Government pursued the policy described below of including in regulatory enforcement policy the mechanism of empowering enforcement bodies to incentivising businesses to make voluntary redress, or forcing them to do so. The developments in use of restorative justice by public authorities occurred against the background of governmental disquiet about litigation generally. A Report to the Prime Minister published on 15 October 2010 by Lord Young of Graffham, which primarily concerned reducing burdens on business of health and safety law, contained a strong attack on

---

[277] J Peysner and A Nurse, *Representative Actions and Restorative Justice: A Report for the Department for Business, Enterprise and Regulatory Reform (BERR)* (Lincoln Law School, University of Lincoln, 2008) at http://www.berr.gov.uk/whatwedo/consumers/enforcement/index.html.
[278] Consumer White Paper (n 228).
[279] *Consultation: The Role and Powers of the Consumer Advocate* (Department for Business, Innovation & Skills, 2009) at http://www.berr.gov.uk/consultations/page53813.htm.

a perceived 'compensation culture'.[280] It supported implementation of the recommendations of the Jackson Review of Civil Litigation Costs[281] on reform of civil procedure costs and funding systems, which included a series of measures aimed at reducing lawyer-funded litigation by undermining the conditional fee arrangements (CFA) regime through removal of a successful claimant's right to recover the premium of an after-the-event insurance policy.[282] Lord Justice Jackson stated that his numerous recommendations achieved reforms that were balanced overall, and that no individual items should be seen in isolation. However, against the backdrop of significant cuts in legal aid,[283] some elements facilitated litigation, such as a 10 per cent increase in general damages and the introduction of a 'qualified one-way cost shift' (QOCS) for personal injury claims.[284]

In relation to mass or collective redress, the Coalition government in November 2012, rejected a litigation approach to redress and favoured voluntary redress schemes, ADR, encouraged and backed by new powers for regulators.[285] Although collective litigation was a theoretical option, the government was 'concerned about the scope for such mechanisms to create incentives for intermediaries, the economic cost of such intermediation and the very heavy burden which a proliferation of such cases may impose on businesses.'[286] Only in enforcement of competition law were all three approaches to delivering redress favoured (regulatory, ADR and litigation).[287]

E. A Combined Approach: Compliance, Redress and Empowerment

The government's June 2011 consultation on consumer empowerment strategy set out four key policies:[288]

1.   The Power of Information.
2.   The Power of the Crowd.

---

[280] *Common Sense, Common Safety. A Report by Lord Young of Graffham to the Prime Minister following a Whitehall–wide Review of the Operation of Health and Safety Laws and the Growth of the Compensation Culture* (HM Government, 2010) available at http://www.number10.gov.uk/wp-content/uploads/402906_Common-Sense_acc.pdf.

[281] R Jackson, *Review of Civil Litigation Costs: Preliminary Report* (London, TSO, 2009); R Jackson, *Review of Civil Litigation Costs: Final Report* (London, TSO, 2010), at http://www.judiciary.gov.uk/NR/rdonlyres/8EB9F3F3-9C4A-4139-8A9356F09672EB6A/0/jacksonfinalreport140110.pdf.

[282] Legal Aid, Sentencing and Punishment of Offenders Act 2012. See *Proposals for Reform of Civil Litigation Funding and Costs in England and Wales. Implementation of Lord Justice Jackson's Recommendations* (Ministry of Justice, 2010) Consultation Paper CP 13/10, available at http://www.justice.gov.uk/consultations/docs/jackson-consultation-paper.pdf.

[283] *Consultation Paper, Proposals for Reform of Legal Aid in England and Wales* (Ministry of Justice, 2010) available at: http://www.justice.gov.uk/consultations/legal-aid-reform-151110.htm.

[284] For the policy on which the revised Civil Procedure Rules are based see *Written Ministerial Statement: Implementation of Part 2 of the Legal Aid, Sentencing and Punishment of Offenders Act 2012: Civil Litigation Funding and Costs* (Ministry of Justice, 2012) amended 17 July, available at http://www.parliament.uk/documents/commons-vote-office/July_2012/10-07-12/11-MOJ-Civil-Litigation-Funding.pdf.

[285] *Civil Enforcement Remedies: Consultation on Extending the Range of Remedies available to Public Enforcers of Consumer Law* (Department for Business, Innovation & Skills, 2012) at http://www.bis.gov.uk/assets/biscore/consumer-issues/docs/c/12-1193-civil-enforcement-remedies-consultation-on-extending.

[286] ibid, para 3.10. The exception it made related to competition law, which lead to specific provisions in the Consumer Rights Act 2015.

[287] Consumer Rights Act 2015, Sch 8.

[288] *Better Choices: Better Deals. Consumers Powering Growth* (n 31).

3.   More Support for the Vulnerable.
4.   A New Role for Business and Government.

In 2012, the Coalition Government set out its objective that any remedies should be aimed at achieving one or more of the following outcomes:

A.   increased business compliance with the law;
B.   improved redress for consumers affected by the breach; and
C.   more confident consumers who are empowered to exercise greater consumer choice.[289]

Separate proposals were made under each of the above three headings, which are summarised below. However, the three goals, and action taken under them, are in practice strongly inter-related. They are reviewed below.

i.   *Increased Business Compliance with the Law*

Enforcers (primarily Local Authority Trading Standards Services (LATSS) and the Office of Fair Trading (OFT)) would usually, in the first instance, seek to work informally with the trader to secure remedial actions to amend its behaviour. But they had no powers to do this. They tended to categorise businesses into two types: Rogues and serious businesses. The preferred response to the former should involve speedy injunctions and criminal actions. The former may disappear swiftly, and money removed from victims may no longer be recoverable, so slower private actions are usually almost pointless. Responsible businesses are likely to continue in business and to have committed technical breaches, to which the appropriate response would tend to rely on behavioural levers and providing redress. Private enforcement by victims will theoretically produce compensation but may take too long and be too costly. However, it was realised that public authorities may use powers effectively so as to induce both modified behaviour and redress for individuals.

The government noted that

> If goods or services are not up to standard, or if the trader has otherwise broken the law, the consumer will expect some sort of remedial action, be that a replacement, refund, or some other form of remedy ...

> The best traders will be keen to help consumers in this situation. They will ensure that the consumer's own position is not adversely affected by the problem, and that obligations under consumer law are fully met thereby safeguarding their own reputation as lawful traders. This will encourage the individual consumer, and others, to continue to trade with them rather than switching to a competitor.[290]

Yet 'when a criminal prosecution takes place, the courts tend to issue a fine punishing past behaviour and/or a prison sentence. There was no scope to secure commitments from the business not to break the law again and compensation is rarely awarded.'[291] So a key issue to be addressed was the lack of remedies available under the current public enforcement regime.

---

[289]   *Consultation. Civil Enforcement Remedies* (n 285).
[290]   ibid, paras 1.2 and 1.3.
[291]   ibid, para 1.6.

At the time, a court could only make an Enforcement Order where it found that the business has engaged, or, in some cases, is likely to engage, in conduct that constituted an infringement.[292] In an Enforcement Order a court will require the business to stop the infringing action. It can also order that the business publish the order as well as a corrective statement. Alternatively the court can accept undertakings from the business. As part of the undertaking to the court the business may be required to publish the terms of the undertaking and a corrective statement. Finally, the court may pass the case back to the enforcer to attempt further action to seek an undertaking.

The Government amended Part 8 of the Enterprise Act 2002 to allow specified enforcers[293] to attach remedies focused on behavioural undertakings ('enhanced consumer measures') to Enforcement Orders and undertakings.[294] Where an enforcer accepts an undertaking from a business, the remedies to be attached are to be agreed between the parties. Where there is a dispute over remedies, the case would proceed to court. Use of these expanded Enforcement Orders and undertakings is limited to designated public enforcers under the Enterprise Act 2002, that is the CMA, LATSS, the Department for Enterprise, Trade and Investment in Northern Ireland and designated sectoral regulators.

The Government intended that possible remedies to secure greater business compliance with the law could include one or more of:[295]

— Signing up to a Primary Authority scheme (see below);
— Appointing a compliance officer;
— Providing training/preparing guidance to staff;
— Undertaking internal spot checks (and maintaining records of these);
— Improving record-keeping;
— Collecting (and acting on) customer feedback;
— Introducing a robust customer complaints-handling scheme; or
— Signing up to an ADR scheme for future complaints and committing to be bound by decisions of an independent ADR provider.

Enhanced consumer measures can fall within three categories: The redress category, the compliance category and the choice category.[296] Measures in the redress category are measures that offer compensation or other redress to consumers who have suffered a loss as

---

[292] Enforcement Orders and undertakings under Part 8 of the Enterprise Act 2002, ss 215, 217 and 219. An enforcement order that the infringer stops engaging in the conduct in question is issued by a court, and either a court or an enforcer may accept an undertaking from the business that it will not engage in conduct that involves an infringement.

[293] The Enterprise Act 2002, s 213 provides for categories of enforcer: General (the Competition and Markets Authority, Trading Standards Services in Great Britain; Department of Enterprise, Trade and Investment in Northern Ireland); designated (see SI 2003/1399 as amended SI 2005/917 and SI 2013/478: The Civil Aviation Authority, Director General of Electricity Supply for Northern Ireland, Director General of Gas for Northern Ireland, Ofcom, The Water Services Regulation Authority, The Gas and Electricity Markets Authority, the Information Commissioner, ORR, the Consumers' Association and the Financial Conduct Authority); community (a qualified entity for the purposes of the Injunctions Dir EC 98/27); and CPC (various bodies designated as national contract points under Reg (EC) No 2006/2004 on Consumer Protection Cooperation).

[294] Consumer Rights Act 2015, s 79 and Sch 7.

[295] *Civil Enforcement Remedies: Consultation* (n 285) para 3.3.

[296] Enterprise Act 2008, s 219A, inserted by the Consumer Rights Act 2015, Sch 7, art 8.

a result of the underlying conduct, or measures offering such consumers the option of terminating[297] (but not varying) a contract, or, where such consumers cannot be identified, or cannot be identified without disproportionate cost to the business, measures intended to be in the collective interests of consumers. Such measures are subject to a cost proportionality requirement[298] and certain safeguards.[299] Measures in the compliance category are measures intended to prevent or reduce the risk of the occurrence or repetition of the conduct to which the enforcement order or undertaking relates. Measures in the choice category are measures intended to enable consumers to choose more effectively between persons supplying or seeking to supply goods or services.

It will be noted that these definitions of enhanced consumer measures are deliberately wide and purposive, and allow flexibility for businesses and enforcers in deciding, and negotiating, what actions and undertakings are appropriate in the circumstances in responding to the underlying and future behaviour and in providing redress. However, any enforcement order or undertaking may include only enhanced consumer measures as the court or enforcer considers to be just and reasonable.[300] Strong similarities will also be seen between, on the one hand, the consumer regime of resolving consumer protection law issues by negotiation and undertakings between enforcers and traders and, on the other hand, the deferred prosecution agreement regime in criminal law, discussed in chapter 10.

ii. Improved Redress for Consumers Affected by the Breach

The Coalition Government noted that private enforcement, whether individual or collective redress mechanisms, are slow, expensive and frequently ineffective in delivering compensation to consumer victims. It planned to develop collective mechanisms to allow private enforcement, alongside ADR and regulatory powers, in cases where competition law has been broken.[301] In other cases, however:

> [T]he Government is concerned about the scope for such mechanisms to create incentives for intermediaries, the economic cost of such intermediation and the very heavy burden which a proliferation of such cases may impose on businesses. In particular, in the consumer law area, much of the law is based on general principles rather than detailed provisions, and private collective redress could lead to abundant litigation on fine points of law, creating high costs for business, which would then raise prices for consumers as a whole. By contrast, public enforcers would only

---

[297] Further guidance is given, including case study examples of how the approach is intended to work, in *Enhanced Consumer Measures: Guidance for Enforcers of Consumer Law* (Department for Business, Innovation & Skills, 2015). This highly important document is set out at Appendix 2.

[298] An enforcement order or undertaking in the redress category may only include redress measures in a loss case and if the court or enforcer is satisfied that the cost of such measures to the subject (excluding administrative costs) is unlikely to be more than the sum of the losses suffered by consumers as a result of the underlying conduct: Enterprise Act 2008, s 219B (2), (4) and (5).

[299] Enterprise Act 2008, s 219C.

[300] Enterprise Act 2008, s 219B(1).

[301] *Private Actions in Competition Law: A Consultation on Options for Reform—Government Response* (Department for Business, Innovation & Skills, 2013) available at https://www.gov.uk/government/uploads/system/uploads/attachment_data/file/69123/13-501-private-actions-in-competition-law-a-consultation-on-options-for-reform-government-response.pdf.

take action under the Enterprise Act 2002 in the public interest and would only generally prioritise action if the breach were both significant and clear. Businesses would be given the opportunity to resolve any complaint informally, before court action would be considered.[302]

The Government's preferred approach sought to encourage businesses to put in place schemes aimed at providing redress to collective consumers when a breach of consumer law arises and causes consumers significant losses. The Government cited three examples:

— *Where a trader has access to a list of all customers,* the trader could write to all customers informing them of their right to a sum of money if they send back tear-off slip within a set time-period. Terms and conditions should not be complex. The trader would reimburse every consumer who responds within 30 days. *Enforcers would check that letters had been sent out and all claims answered within 30 days.*

— *Where a trader has no list of customers but there is likely to be take-up if advertised,* the trader could take out adverts in national, regional or specialist press. Advertising would be proportionate, targeted and effective. The advert would operate in a similar way as product recall where if people showed they were affected by the issue they would receive a sum of money. Additionally, the availability of redress could be flagged to consumers complaining to the Citizens Advice consumer helpline. *Enforcers would monitor that adverts had been placed and compensation paid to claimants.*

— *Where individual consumers cannot be identified,* however, alternative measures may be effective, such as advertising that consumers (who can prove they were affected by the issue) can claim an agreed sum of money from the company or from an appointed ADR provider or offering discounts to all future consumers for a fixed period of time to mitigate against any financial gain arising from the breach.

The Government's aim was that the business would propose a scheme which they would agree with the enforcer (with failure to comply with the terms of the scheme being a matter for consideration by a court choosing to apply an Enforcement Order and ultimately a factor to be taken into account if an Enforcement Order is not followed).[303]

Where a business is unwilling to propose a scheme, the Government believed there should be a power for a court to impose one on application by an enforcer (subject to the correct

---

[302] *Consultation. Civil Enforcement Remedies* (n 285) para 3.10. In relation to the reference to 'incentives for intermediaries', there has been considerable disquiet about the activities of claims intermediaries in relation to the largest current compensation challenge, namely mis-selling of payment protection insurance (PPI) products by financial institutions. Many PPI claims are being brought through the courts and especially the Financial Ombudsman Service. Claims intermediaries have marketed their services heavily. However, a significant number of claims have been brought by intermediaries that are unsubstantiated, and some fraudulent, necessitating regulatory action. See recently *Claims-management Regulation. Proposals for Amendment to the Conduct of Authorised Persons Rules* (Ministry of Justice, August 2012); *CAB Evidence Briefing: The Claims Pests—CAB Evidence on PPI and Claims-management Companies* (Citizens Advice Bureau, 2012), available at http://www.citizensadvice.org.uk/index/policy/policy_publications/er_legal/the_claims_pests.htm; *Claims Management Regulation: Approach and Enforcement of the Referral Fee Ban* (Ministry of Justice, November 2012) available at http://www.justice.gov.uk/downloads/claims-regulation/cmr-referral-fee-ban.pdf; *Payday Lending Compliance Review. Interim Report* (Office of Fair Trading, 2012) OFT1466 http://www.oft.gov.uk/shared_oft/business_leaflets/consumer_credit/OFT1466.pdf; *The PPI Claims Market: Dealing with Malpractice* (Ministry of Justice, 2013) available at http://www.justice.gov.uk/downloads/claims-regulation/ppi-claims-market-malpractice.pdf.

[303] *Consultation* (n 301) para 3.16.

judicial process). This was stated to be necessary both to increase the possibility of redress and to ensure an effective sanctions regime by providing greater incentives to encourage businesses to propose agreements. However, it should be seen as the last resort.[304]

Powers for sectoral regulators to obtain court orders for consumer redress schemes were extended from the financial services sector to the energy sector, as discussed in chapter 13. An example of where the OFT has used its authority to effect significant repayments occurred in 2014 over repayment of charges and interest by banks and building societies to large numbers of customers over failure to comply with legal requirements in credit agreements.[305]

iii. More Confident Consumers who are Empowered to Exercise Greater Consumer Choice

The Government believed there was a gap in consumer information about where companies have broken the law or failed to offer a good service. If consumers keep using the same businesses, the incentive to improve is lower. Accordingly, it aimed to encourage greater consumer empowerment, enabling enhanced consumer choice, through remedies such as:

— Businesses signing up to an established customer review/feedback site;
— Breaches being flagged on some sort of publicly accessible 'naming and shaming' database of non-compliant businesses;
— Businesses being required to provide greater consumer information, including linking up with 'midata';[306]
— Businesses being required to inform existing customers (either directly or through publicity) of the breach and any remedial action taken—this would be particularly appropriate for long-term or repeat contracts where the consumer and supplier are in some form of ongoing relationship (for example, utilities, telecommunications, gym contracts);
— Allowing consumers to terminate ongoing contracts without penalty—for example, a consumer who has been mis-sold a mobile phone contract which would normally be for a certain amount of time, could be allowed (but under no obligation) to terminate the contract early and seek out a tariff more appropriate for their needs; or

---

[304] ibid, para 3.17.

[305] In March 2014 OFT announced that 17 banks and building societies would repay over £149 million in charges and interest to around 497,000 customers because they had failed to provide customers with certain post-contractual information under the Consumer Credit Act (CCA): Press release 'Over £149 million to be repaid to bank and building society customers following OFT action' (Office of Fair Trading, 2014), 18/14 20 March, http://www.oft.gov.uk/news-and-updates/press/2014/18-14. The OFT accepted that the failings were not deliberate but non-compliance with the statutory requirements and wording rendered the charges illegal under the CCA 1974 ss 77A and 68B. After similar issues had come to light involving other banks, which resulted in redress of over £370 million, the OFT had written to 50 banks and building societies in November 2013 (http://www.oft.gov.uk/shared_oft/CreditEnforcement/banks-letter.pdf) asking them to confirm that they had fully discharged their obligations to provide post contract information under the CCA.

[306] Midata is a programme of work which will allow individuals to view access and use their personal consumption and transaction data in a way that is portable and safe: *Introductory Briefing on Midata* (Department for Business, Innovation & Skills, 2013).

— Businesses in an ongoing relationship with consumers being required to provide details about other suppliers' products and offers, to more actively promote switching—it would be unlikely this last option would be imposed by a court given the difficulty in proving benefit to consumers but could potentially be offered as an undertaking which would affect the enforcer's decision over whether to prosecute.

Research supported the hypothesis that simplification of consumer law has a positive impact on wider economic outcomes and growth.[307] It also noted findings that the behaviour and rationality of consumers is highly uncertain and fragmented.

F. Coordinating Local Enforcement: Primary Authority

In 2008, the RESA had provided for the coordination of enforcement across boundaries by local authorities, intended to provide national coverage in relation to pursuing rogues and consistency for businesses that operated nationally.[308] This 'primary authority scheme' built on a previous voluntary arrangement, the 'home authority principle',[309] breaches of which had been a source of irritation to national businesses for some time. A business that operated nationally or in the area of more than one local authority could be prosecuted, or subject to the views, of any local authority, and this led to complaints of inconsistency between different Trading Standards officers in different parts of the country. Under the non-binding home authority principle, before instituting any action, a local authority should liaise with the local authority in whose area the business has its headquarters. The business and its home authority were thereby encouraged to develop a relationship of communication and understanding on what constitutes relevant trading standards and practice.

The situation was developed with introduction of the Primary Authority scheme, which enabled businesses to enter into constructive, legally-recognised partnerships with a nominated single local authority, which includes the provision of reliable advice to business and arrangements for coordinated and consistent enforcement, through oversight and handling notifications of proposed enforcement actions.[310] Such partnerships formed the basis for robust and reliable advice for other councils to take into account when carrying out inspections or dealing with non-compliance. Under Primary Authority, inspection plans are developed by the primary authority, which is required to consult the business, and the plan takes effect after it is approved by the BRDO.[311] Guidance advising local authorities

---

[307] *Consumer Rights and Economic Growth* (ICF GHK, 2013).

[308] Regulatory Enforcement and Sanctions Act 2008, Pt 2, brought into force on 6 April 2009 under The Regulatory Enforcement and Sanctions Act 2008 (Commencement No 1) Order 2008/2371.

[309] The 'Home Authority' scheme existed in practice on a voluntary basis between local authorities for some decades. Before instituting enforcement action a local authority was supposed to liaise with the authority in whose area the business had its principal office.

[310] See *Primary Authority Guidance* (Local Better Regulation Office, 2009); now the Primary Authority page of the Better Regulation Delivery Office at http://www.bis.gov.uk/brdo/primary-authority. The Guidance is issued under the Regulatory Enforcement and Sanctions Act 2008, s 33, amended by the Enterprise and Regulatory Reform Act 2013, s 67.

[311] Enterprise and Regulatory Reform Act 2013, ss 67, 68.

on the operation of the Primary Authority Scheme[312] was issued in April 2009 by the Local Better Regulation Office.[313]

The principles of Primary Authority are set out in the Regulatory Enforcement and Sanctions Act 2008,[314] and amended by the Enterprise and Regulatory Reform Act 2013 (ERR Act),[315] which broadened the eligibility criteria for participation in Primary Authority, and strengthened inspection plans. An objective was to enable businesses to access assured advice from regulators on regulatory compliance, and deliver earned recognition for businesses with recognised compliance capability.[316] Supported by new statutory guidance, the scheme is now accessible to more small businesses and covers more regulations.

The scheme is administered by the Better Regulation Delivery Office (BRDO). The Primary Authority User Group, including local authority and business representatives, supports BRDO in its operation and development of the scheme. The BRDO have aimed to build on the Anderson report on provision of guidance and support, especially to SMEs.[317]

A framework[318] setting out how Home Authority operates alongside Primary Authority aims to ensure no overlap or duplication between the two schemes, improving coherence between them whilst recognising that there are differences in the objectives of the two schemes. It supports an agreement, *Towards a Unified Vision for Primary Authority and Home Authority* (an annex included in the framework), made between the BRDO, the Trading Standards Institute (TSI) and the Chartered Institute of Environmental Health (CIEH) in September 2011.

The policy constitutes a major shift in the approach to influencing behaviour by adopting a relationship-based approach. There was some early concern over the possibility of regulatory capture but no evidence indicating this has been seen.[319]

The fundamentally different vision for the Primary Authority system was introduced from October 2013 under the ERR Act, aiming to establish a new relationship between business and officials. It was recognised that many businesses aim to comply but can struggle to do so, for a variety of reasons. The ERR Act introduced two changes. First, it provided a change in status of inspection plans and, second, change in the eligibility criteria of admission to the Primary Authority scheme, under which groups of businesses that share

---

[312] The Primary Authority Scheme co-ordinates enforcement action by different local authorities, such as local council Trading Standards Departments and local authority delivery of health & safety: see The Co-ordination of Regulatory Enforcement (Enforcement Action) Order 2009 No 665, The Co-ordination of Regulatory Enforcement (Procedure for References to LBRO) Order 2009 No 670, and The Co-ordination of Regulatory Enforcement (Regulatory Functions in Scotland and Northern Ireland) Order 2009. It was extended in 2013 under the Enterprise and Regulatory Reform Act 2013, s 67: *Press Release: Thousands More Firms to Benefit from Enterprise-friendly Regulation Scheme* (Department for Business, Innovation & Skills, 2013).

[313] The Local Better Regulation Office was a national independent, expert on local regulation with the statutory powers to drive progress in reducing red tape for law-abiding businesses to allow greater focus on targeting the rogue traders who harm vulnerable people and damage our communities. It acted as a catalyst, drawing on its unique relationships with business, local authorities and national regulators to deliver better local regulation. It was dissolved in 2012 and its functions taken over by the Better Regulation Delivery Office.

[314] The primary authority scheme commenced on 6 April 2009 under the Regulatory Enforcement and Sanctions Act 2008 (Commencement No 1) Order 2008, SI 2371/2008.

[315] s 67.

[316] *Enterprise and Regulatory Reform Bill. Policy Paper* (Department for Business, Innovation & Skills, 2012).

[317] http://www.bis.gov.uk/file49881.pdf.

[318] https://primaryauthorityregister.info/par/images/documents/home-authority-framework.pdf.

[319] Personal communications with BRDO, 2014.

a common focus are permitted to make a joint application. It is the second reform that was fundamental. It enables not just group companies but trade associations and franchisors to be the main points of contract with the Local Authority, and able to disseminate the agreed practice to members or franchisees.[320] This intentionally builds on the research finding (see chapter 14) that the behaviour of many businesses, particularly smaller firms, can be influenced by receiving information on how to improve compliance from any outsider with authority, such as a trade association or franchisor, and not necessarily an official. The Local Authority still has a formal, legal relationship with the individual businesses but can communicate and discuss common issues with the coordinating representative body.

The BRDO and enforcers had found that businesses ask for challenge. The 2013 policy is to build a relationship of trust. It has since been found that businesses are now sharing more information with the officials, and relationships are becoming stronger, more collaborative in raising problem issues that benefit from discussion and more effective in achieving good outcomes.[321] There was initially some Local Authority resistance to the scheme but by mid-2014 this was evaporating. Local Authorities are also building their expertise through having better understanding of particular businesses, how they operate, and the problems they face. The key is to have coordinated partnerships. Trading Standards Departments have established expert panels that share information, so support consistency and peer review.

Local Authorities may charge to recover some or all of their costs through these partnerships. Cost recovery is not considered to be charging for enforcement.[322] Businesses agree to pay for the level of compliance support service that they ask for and agree. Cost levels are set by Local Authorities individually, and some do not seek cost recovery, whilst others vary in their approaches, such as with exempting charities or capping costs up to a certain number of hours. The BRDO has neither come across evidence of pushback from businesses on cost, nor evidence of forum shopping between authorities. The Primary Authority scheme may have reduced previous business expenditure on compliance advice from other sources, such as in-house, external lawyer, and so on. Membership of the scheme might reduce insurance premiums.

As at 1 January 2015, 146 Local Authorities were offering Primary Authority partnerships (of which 17 were fire and rescue authorities), and the Primary Authority scheme

---

[320] In introducing the change, reference was made to members of trade associations such as the British Frozen Food Federation, or franchises such as Pizza Hut: *Press Release* (n 312). The British Frozen Food Federation was quoted as welcoming a significant reduction in duplication of effort between businesses and local authorities, whilst ensuring improved levels of consistent compliance and consumer protection. The National Federation of Meat & Food Traders, which has 13,000 members and for which the Primary Authority is Horsham District Council, was quoted as supporting consistency for its 1,000 craft butchers, 'who are very skilled practically but not necessarily comfortable dealing with paperwork.' The Trading Standards Lead Officer for Cambridgeshire Trading Standards was quoted saying: 'From both a service and professional standpoint we can see huge benefits to both regulators and businesses in actively supporting these working partnerships. In receiving assured advice, businesses have greater confidence and certainty when making decisions in complex areas of trading law. The extension of the scheme to organisations with a shared approach to compliance now enables us to share these benefits with many more businesses and promote good practice across trade sectors. The net effect of this not only helps business but also consumers and the wider economy.'

[321] Personal communications with BRDO, 2014.

[322] In licensing regimes covered by the Provision of Services Regs 2009, the costs of enforcement against unlicensed operators cannot be recovered from licensed operators, and thus cross-subsidy is not considered to arise: *R (Hemmings and others) v Westminster City Council* (2012). http://www.localgovernmentlawyer. co.uk/index.php?option=com_content&view=article&id=14421%3Alocal-authorities-licensing-fees-and-the-hemming-case&catid=61%3Alicensing-articles&Itemid=29.

included 2,147 businesses, of which 33 per cent were large, 13 per cent medium-sized and 54 per cent were small.[323] 134 businesses were in fire safety partnerships. The number of 'co-ordinators' (such as trade associations,[324] franchisors[325] or company groups) that had taken on responsibility for facilitating the relationship between the primary authority and a group of businesses in offer primary authority partnerships to a group of businesses that 'share an approach to compliance' was 41.

In January 2013, a review of Primary Authority commissioned by the BRDO[326] concluded that businesses were deriving a wide range of benefits from Primary Authority, including: A reduction in the amount of time businesses spend on regulatory activities; improvements in relationships with regulators; improved intelligence about regulatory matters; improvements in the consistency of regulatory advice and guidance; access to advice, both Primary Authority Advice and other informal (non-statutory) advice; support for staff development; advice on planned or future developments; support for addressing incoming regulatory issues from enforcing authorities; advice on standardising policies, procedures, systems and documentation; and that Primary Authority had had an impact on enforcement activity.

There is some scepticism by consumer representatives whether isolated and under-resourced Trading Standards officers have enough power to get redress. Will TSS be subject to a barrier in seeking redress because of the requirement that costs and redress must be proportionate, and they must support business growth, not just take it into account?

Analysis was undertaken through case studies of localised policy interventions relating to business and skills support, and the enablers for achieving intended outcomes, through contrasting business support structures: The Greater Manchester Business Growth Hub, the Plymouth Growth Acceleration and Investment Network, the New Anglia Business Information Portal, and the West of England Employability Charter Mark.[327]

A Retail Enforcement Pilot carried out by some 30 local authorities coordinated by the Local Better Regulation Office found significant advantages where authorities worked together in a more collaborative basis in sharing information and over inspections.[328] Authorities were able to highlight premises where urgent intervention was required by other agencies, and to perceive a more cohesive view on overall compliance. Changing to a collaborative approach involved a change in culture, and saved resources for some authorities but increased burdens on others.

---

[323] Information kindly supplied by BRDO. See https://primaryauthorityregister.info/par/index.php/public register.

[324] Including Association of Convenience Stores, British Association of Removers, British Frozen Food Federation, Construction Products Association, Food Storage and Distribution Federation, National Federation of Meat and Food Traders, National Federation of Property Professionals, Ornamental Aquatic Trade Association Ltd, Proprietary Association of Great Britain, and Specialist Cheesemakers Association.

[325] They include Dominos Pizza and Kentucky Fried Chicken.

[326] *Interim Evaluation of Primary Authority. Final Report* (ACL Consulting, 2013) at https://primaryauthorityregister.info/par/index.php/background/evaluation.

[327] *Research on Understanding Localised Policy Interventions in Business Support and Skills* (BIS, 2013) https://www.gov.uk/government/uploads/system/uploads/attachment_data/file/263716/bis-13-1316-understanding-localised-policy-interventions-in-business-support-and-skills.pdf.

[328] A Page, M Hewitt and S Lundy, *Lessons Learnt: Retail Enforcement Pilot* (Local Better Regulation Office, 2010) at https://www.gov.uk/government/uploads/system/uploads/attachment_data/file/262040/10-1407-rep-lessons-learned.pdf.

Where activities are well targeted, in accordance with risk, resources can be focused on the rogue traders, persistent offenders and high risk sites that present the greatest hazard to consumers, communities and other businesses.

Listening to businesses across the UK economy tells us that they respond in different ways to regulatory requirements. Many businesses value visits from regulators, using the opportunity to seek guidance and advice from professional officers or to receive validation of their efforts in achieving compliance.[329]

VI. Conclusions

A. Enforcement Policy

Supporting and ensuring consumer protection is a hugely diverse task, in view of the range of issues, traders, consumers, transactions and risks that arise. This analysis has, first, identified the involvement of multiple public bodies at both local and national levels, and resultant difficulties of coordination between them. Second, it has shown that 'enforcement' is a multi-faceted phenomenon. At one level, a distinction is sometimes drawn between 'rogues' and 'responsible businesses', and this categorisation of stereotypes leads to a differentiation of responses, using criminal or hard enforcement in relation to the former and a range of less formal administrative or civil procedures, or even 'mere' advice and negotiation in relation to the latter. The rogue–respectable juxtaposition probably has some justification, but another framework is that of risk. It is true that fraudulent internet scams can cause major detriment, and are categorised as criminal, but it is also true that more innocent trading activity can cause widespread harm. A risk-based enforcement policy has clearly been adopted by regulators and enforcers, although in selecting which powers to deploy in individual situations, officials have a wide range of options, encompassing a toolbox of criminal, regulatory, civil and informal powers. However, Government has made clear statements that the majority of businesses intend to comply with the law, and should not usually be subject to harsh sanctions when they fail but instead supported to make changes, so as to comply in future, and to put right harm caused.

In other words, there has been a manifest shift from 'command and control' enforcement to 'enforcement' that is better characterised as responsive compliance. However, the extensive official statements on enforcement policy noted above come exclusively from central government and the national consumer market authority (the OFT, now CMA), and there are no statements from local authorities or their national bodies the NTSB and TSI. This is a curious omission, which is only partly diminished by the existence of a national Regulators' Code, codified enforcement powers in the Consumer Rights Act 2015, and a level of coordination by the BRDO. A large question that remains is to what extent cuts in funding for TSSs will diminish the effectiveness of local enforcement, just at a time when the TSS community has been placed in the front line of local enforcement.

---

[329] ibid, Foreword by C Grace and G Russell.

In supporting compliance, a starting point is the role of consumers themselves. There is a string emphasis on consumer education and advice, so as to support intelligent and appropriate purchasing, switching between providers, and avoiding inappropriate providers. However, a question remains over how well the Citizens Advice community will deliver against their objectives. Potential new actors are emerging in the form of ombudsmen, who provide expert sources of consumer advice as well as dispute resolution and also sources of aggregated data on market activities, which can be used by enforcers, the media and consumers.

There has been a distinct shift in the enforcement policy of what was the OFT. That body was dominated by personnel expert in competition thinking, and it is unsurprising to find that enforcement policy documents from 2010 referred to deterrence.[330] There was initial resistance by the OFT to embracing Hampton, the RESA and Macrory—in stark contrast to the attitudes of the other sectoral regulators whose revised enforcement policies are reviewed in this book. However, a Macrory approach was adopted in 2010, when the revised enforcement policy took a noticeably different stance, adopting a classic 'responsive regulation' Ayres and Braithwaite-type enforcement pyramid. Nevertheless, a dualistic approach continued in the OFT's 2011 policy statement. One the one hand it would 'work to influence business behaviour to increase compliance levels without the need for enforcement action' but on the other hand it would 'take tough action for deliberate non-compliant behaviour' and 'evaluate the impact that interventions have had on raising compliance levels by creating a deterrence effect'.[331] It can be said that these two approaches are not inconsistent, in that the deterrent approach is intended to apply to 'deliberate' non-compliance whereas the soft, influential approach applies elsewhere. But is the deliberate–unintentional distinction appropriate, and based on reliable evidence? The OFT did not seek civil sanction powers, but will have the option of being granted Consumer Rights Act enhanced consumer measures. The impression remains, however, that the CMA has not shifted its thinking from competition-induced deterrence to the responsive approach set out in the 2011 *Transforming Regulatory Enforcement* and 2012 *Civil enforcement remedies* policy papers.

Dramatic change has occurred in national policy in relation to redress. There has been a rejection of private collective litigation as a principal means of seeking or delivering redress, and instead redress has been included firmly not only as a matter to be expected from business but also as a mainstream issue within the remit of consumer enforcers. Voluntary payment of redress is encouraged, where necessary through schemes, assisted by the new DPA-style powers for enforcers to agree undertakings by businesses instead of pursuing aggressive enforcement actions. Providing redress is now part of expected business behaviour, and overseeing it is a core function of consumer enforcers.

B. The Implications of the Research

Surveys are of limited scientific validity, but the sequence of interviews and surveys undertaken for the OFT, and by BIS and the NAO, are significant for a number of reasons. First,

---

[330] *OFT Prioritisation Principles* (n 81); and *Criminal Liability in Regulatory Contexts. Response to the Law Commission Consultation* (Office of Fair Trading, 2010) OFT1285.

[331] *The OFT's Approach to Promoting Business Compliance with Consumer Protection Law* (n 218). See also *How Your Business Can Achieve Compliance: Summary of Responses to the OFT's Consultation and OFT's Conclusions and Decision Document* (n 240).

the findings are reasonably consistent, not only with each other but also with the findings of the more weighty socio-legal studies on enforcement discussed at chapter 11. Second, the findings were relied on by the OFT in setting its policy on enforcement and its general activities. It is, therefore, important to ask various questions. What evidence is the enforcement policy based on? Is the policy supported by the available evidence, and by sufficiently adequate and comprehensive evidence?

The findings of the evidence summarised above point to some clear conclusions when compliance is looked at from the viewpoint of businesses, rather than enforcers or other external commentators. Businesses generally intend to comply with the rules. They also think that they comply overall with the rules. But many businesses find the volume, complexity and speed of change of the overall regulatory burden to be barriers to knowledge, comprehension, clarity and compliance. These adverse effects increase as firm size decreases, and decrease to some extent as firm size increases. Smaller firms have less resource, time, access to reliable advice and sometimes internal beliefs that they are complying that are unjustified. SMEs—defined as businesses with fewer than 250 employees—account for the vast majority of all firms in the UK and around 60 per cent of overall private sector employment.[332] An estimated 4.7 million of them employ about 10.5 million people. Larger firms have greater resource to devote to internalised systems aimed at knowledge and compliance, and obtaining external advice from consultants and lawyers, but can sometimes fail to comply because of the inflexibility of internal systems and objectives.

It may be expected that the profit motive might override a desire for compliance in firms large and small, but this issue curiously did not emerge from any of the study findings: Perhaps it was not looked for, but one might have expected it to be commented on by some. Rather than the profit motive 'at any cost' driving breaking the rules, a consistent finding is that firms are driven by their desire to maintain a good reputation, since that drives commercial success. Thus, the principal motivators for compliance lie in internal culture and the need to maintain reputation. Reputation is adversely affected by knowledge held by actual and potential customers. Thus, it is not the fact of a (rare) criminal conviction or of some enforcement action that in itself 'deters' future compliance, but when such knowledge comes to the attention of customers and is viewed by them as being a significant matter that affects their trust in, and desire to buy from, the firm.

Thus, contrary to the traditional assertions of enforcement bodies, formal enforcement action itself has little effect on the desire to comply in future by most businesses—or, in other words, such action has little 'deterrent' effect on the firm enforced against, and certainly on other firms, since they usually tend to believe that they are in compliance and that the risk to their reputation is slight.

That analysis, if correct, fully supports the conclusion of Hampton that the most important needs for businesses—and the strategy that should be pursued by public regulatory systems—are not punishment and deterrence but advice and guidance. The principal need is for access to reliable information, coupled with a form of independent checking that is less formal than authoritative inspection but as thorough whilst being more supportive. The purpose of inspection and audit is to identify and apply improvements, rather than to identify infringements that will then be sanctioned.

---

[332] Pre-Budget Report, Treasury, November 2008.

Adopting this 'positive compliance' strategy may present a challenge for some enforcement authorities. A strong reason for this is that the work of many agencies is dealing with those who fail to comply, including those who positively intend not to comply. In such circumstances, more traditional 'enforcement' towards the top of the Ayres-Braithwaite pyramid of sanctions does appear entirely justified. But in dealing with too many 'rogues', there is a risk that some enforcers may lose sight of the more positive, supportive agenda that is needed for most businesses.

The need to ensure that a comprehensive and balanced overall approach is taken is primarily a matter for government. In this respect, developing the function of a body such as the BRDO (with the NAO) is important. It should be the function of a national coordinating and oversight body to ensure that all appropriate regulatory, enforcement and compliance activities are adequately undertaken, and to ensure proper coordination.

In 2011 Consumer Focus reviewed the consumer interest in regulation.[333] It referred to a perception that the extensive regulatory state had 'too many silos and not enough joined-up strategy' and an inconsistency between regulators. Only Ofcom had an explicit duty to further the interests of citizens, and only Ofgem had an overarching strategy.[334] It called for increased clarity of objectives and who does what; a more integrated way of undertaking policy work within and across economic sectors, which harnesses the expertise that each actor has to offer; and greater transparency and accountability for all actors.

It is admirable that the OFT commissioned such extensive research on drivers of compliance and non-compliance, but somewhat concerning that the statements of enforcement policy that subsequently emerged appear to have to some extent failed to grasp the research findings. This may be more of a structural issue of the role of the OFT within the national architecture of public bodies, rather than a criticism of the OFT itself, but there does appear to be a problem. The OFT is right to highlight its work on supporting compliance through the CCAS (since moved to TSI), in providing consumer information generally, and in targeting its enforcement activities where they can have greatest impact. But the 2010 statement of enforcement policy is distinctive when compared with other similar statements made by other regulatory enforcement bodies (summarised in chapter 13) in being obviously less compliant with the Hampton-Macrory philosophy, and emphasising 'strong' enforcement and deterrence. However, the enforcement policy for consumer markets is markedly less extreme from this perspective than that for competition enforcement, as will be seen in chapter 15. It is interesting that the 2009 London Economics' case studies review noted that a precondition for the success of OFT intervention is that *businesses change their prior conduct*,[335] but the 2010 enforcement policy says little about how such change will in fact be achieved. The OFT's summary of the 2010 research highlighted the importance of reputation,[336] and it appears that the purpose of the 'high impact enforcement' that it intends to pursue remains based on the assumption that change of behaviour will be through 'deterrence'.[337] That assertion is ambiguous. If it means that enforcement

---

[333] *Regulating in the Consumer Interest* (Consumer Focus, 2010) at http://www.consumerfocus.org.uk/files/2010/10/Fresh-thinking-Regulation.pdf.

[334] See *Social Action Plan: Improving Social Obligations Proposals Document* (Ofgem, 2000); *Social Action Plan Annual Review 2005* (Ofgem, 2005).

[335] London Economics, *Evaluation of a Sample of Consumer Enforcement Cases* (n 82).

[336] *Consumer Law and Business Practice. Drivers of Compliance and Non-compliance* (n 140).

[337] *Statement of Consumer Protection Enforcement Principles* (n 81).

will be targeted at situations where consumer detriment is widespread and a clarification in practice can produce widespread change and benefit, then that is supported by the evidence. Such change might be by clarifying the law and obtaining widespread publicity, for example through a sector's trade press and with the active support of its trade associations. But if it means that high penalties will be imposed on one or two individual firms, then the effect may not produce entirely positive consequences.

The finding from Ipsos MORI's study that 'The deterrent effect from consumer protection law and its enforcement via enforcement bodies such as TSS is not widely felt'[338] may need interpretation. It may mean that TSS are ineffective in changing the behaviour of many businesses. But it may equally mean that it is inherent in the localised nature of TSS' work that wider effects are more difficult to achieve. Given that TSSs spend much effort on advising consumers, advising local businesses on improving their standards, and dealing with local rogues through criminal law, there may be not so much of concern here. The real issues are whether the functions of advice to consumers and businesses, and of hard enforcement, should be performed by a different array of organisations. Much advice could be delivered through web-based or ombudsmen systems. Business support and inspection could be assisted by local chambers of commerce or trade associations.

A strong finding of the research surveys is that firms crave sources of reliable, accurate, up-to-date advice. The finding is highly relevant here that people think they are doing the right thing until it is pointed out to them—in an authoritative but non-threatening way—that they are not, and they could or should be doing something differently. Further than just a source of information, the advice should have practical application to the particular business. In other words, people need to be told how to do, and how to improve what they are doing. Such advice might traditionally be from an inspector, but it could be from consultants, auditors, lawyers, or trade associations.

The Primary Authority scheme has huge significance. Its formal partnerships between public and private bodies are designed to provide support and advice to businesses, especially SMEs. The latest extension of the scheme recognises the crucial role that trade associations can play in providing reliable advice, tailored to the needs of companies in the particular sector, in supporting compliance and reputation, and thereby maintaining standards and identifying unacceptable practice.

---

[338] *Drivers of Compliance and Non-compliance with Consumer Protection Law: A Report by Ipsos MORI Commissioned by the OFT* (n 96) para 1.26.

15

Competition

This chapter notes UK policy on public enforcement of competition law. It should be read together with chapter four on EU competition enforcement policy, since the general approach is very similar.

It is instructive to compare the Competition and Markets Authority (CMA)'s approach to enforcement of competition law with its approach to enforcement on consumer market issues. The Office of Fair Trading (OFT) carried out significant quantities of theoretical analyses and market research in both the competition and consumer areas, and it appears not to have been fully recognised that they showed somewhat different things. The consumer research has been set out in chapter 14 and the competition research is set out below.

It will be seen that the approach of the CMA, and of its predecessor the OFT, towards enforcement of competition law is firmly based on theories of deterrence and economics. In these respects, comparisons with the enforcement policies of virtually every other public authority considered in chapter 13 show that the approach to competition enforcement is an outlier. There does not appear to have been any thought given to why a different approach is justified, and why the competition approach effectively differs fundamentally from the responsive regulation and compliance approaches that are national enforcement policy.

I. Evidence of Need

EU (European Union)-level evidence on this issue has been discussed at chapter four. Anti-competitive activity is viewed seriously. The UK annual spend on its competition regime totals £27 million.[1]

II. Background to Competition Enforcement

From April 2013 the national competition authority is the CMA. Prior to that, there was the OFT, with the Competition Commission at a superior level. The OFT's functions included[2]

---

[1] *Review of the UK's Competition Landscape. A Review by the Comptroller and Auditor General* (National Audit Office, 2010) http://www.nao.org.uk/publications/0910/competition_landscape.aspx.

[2] For an overview of the functions of competition law and a summary of the institutional arrangements for enforcing it see R Whish and D Bailey, *Competition Law* 7th edn (Oxford, Oxford University Press, 2012) 2–3, and *The UK Competition Regime* (House of Commons SN04814, October 2012), available at http://www.parliament.uk/briefing-papers/SN04814.pdf.

merger control; making 'Market Investigation References' to the Competition Commission; prohibition of agreements preventing, restricting or distorting competition, including prosecution for cartel offences; and prohibition of abuse of a dominant position. Responsibility for enforcing the Competition Act 1998 is shared concurrently between the CMA and the sectoral regulators for communications and postal matters, gas, electricity, water and sewerage, railway and air traffic services.[3] Appeals from the CMA may be made to the Competition Appeal Tribunal (CAT).[4]

In addition to responsibility for enforcement of competition law, the CMA has retained the OFT's responsibility for national consumer markets oversight. The historical approach of the OFT to enforcement of consumer protection law developed in parallel to its development of enforcement of competition law, but with some distinct differences. The former, and the CMA's 2014 policy, which are discussed at chapter 14, have some fundamental differences from the competition approach that is discussed here.

The CMA has extensive enforcement powers under the Competition Act 1998[5] and the Enterprise Act 2002. The policy is to ensure the full independence of competition enforcement. Accordingly, functions under competition law are excluded from the scope of the Regulatory Enforcement and Sanctions Act 2008 (RESA) Part 4 and related legislation. However, the OFT/CMA does have legal powers, which fall with the statutory definition of regulatory functions and as such are subject to the better regulation provisions referred to in the introduction.[6] In relation to any function exercised under competition law, the OFT was exempted from the duty under RESA not to impose or maintain unnecessary burdens in the exercise of regulatory functions.[7]

Thus, competition enforcement is the one area that has resisted adopting a reformed approach. The policy papers contain virtually no references to better regulation, risk-based regulation, responsive regulation, restorative justice or redress. The 2013 consultation on the new authority's enforcement policy, and its subsequent 'vision statement', therefore made no mention of Macrory, or a regulatory objective of ensuring that victims were paid back.[8]

The dominant policy in enforcement of competition law is driven by the US-inspired theory of deterrence, through high ex post fines being imposed on firms by the public

---

[3] Under the Competition Act 1998, s 54 and sch 10, as at 1 September 2012 the regulators were the Office of Communications (Ofcom), the Gas and Electricity Markets Authority (Ofgem), the Utility Regulator (Northern Ireland), the Water Services Regulation Authority (Ofwat), the Office of Rail Regulation (ORR) and the Civil Aviation Authority (CAA).

[4] *The Competition Appeal Tribunal and the Competition Service. Triennial Review* (Department for Business, Innovation & Skills, 2014) recommending retention of the CAT as a specialist NDPB Tribunal.

[5] See *A Guide to the OFT's Investigation Procedures in Competition Cases* (OFT, October 2012) OFT1263rev.

[6] The OFT's competition and markets functions were outside the remit of the Hampton Review and are excluded from the scope of related legislation in particular the Legislative and Regulatory Reform Act and the Regulatory Enforcement and Sanctions Act.

[7] RESA, s 72.

[8] *Vision, Values and Strategy for the CMA. Consultation Document* (Competition & Markets Authority, October 1st, 2013). Surprisingly, for example, the OFT's 2007 consultation on encouraging more private actions did not mention the Macrory Review or its conclusions, but repeated the importance of deterrence and removal of illicit profit as being a justification for private collective actions, but does not address how the wider payment of damages is to be coordinated, in terms of the resulting levels of deterrence, rectification of market balance and behaviour control, with a regime that has hitherto seemingly operated solely with fines: Office of Fair Trading Discussion Paper, *Private Actions in Competition Law: Effective Redress for Consumers and Business*, April 2007.

enforcement authorities.[9] This approach focuses on markets at macro level, treating companies as individual entities, which internalise the cost of fines and hence are capable of completely controlling the actions of all staff.[10] That theory was significantly undermined by a unanimous ruling of the Court of Appeal in 2010 that a corporate undertaking upon which the OFT had imposed a penalty for breaches of competition law could not sue its former directors or employees for damages equivalent to that penalty or the costs of the OFT investigation.[11]

References to UK competition enforcement being solely based on deterrence have appeared consistently in all official literature.[12] Identification of cartels has been almost exclusively through the operation of an EU-style leniency policy, which produces the curious and unjust result that the first company to own up to involvement in a cartel can totally avoid any penalty.[13]

References to risk-based enforcement are distinguished by their rarity in an extensive sequence of official publications:

> The OFT seeks to minimise unnecessary costs for business arising from its competition work, by ensuring through application of our Prioritisation Principles that it is risk-based, targeted and proportionate. When enforcement puts undue burdens on business, the costs are passed on to consumers. We believe that an approach that is properly focused on consumer welfare, such as the OFT's, will necessarily tend to ensure proportionality for that reason. The general purpose and effect of competition enforcement and advocacy is, in any case, to complement the regulatory reform agenda, not to cut across it, because it is focused on the objective of ensuring markets remain open and well-functioning.[14]

However, the OFT was forced to ignore primacy of deterrence and apply pragmatism in resolving a high profile case in 2006. After a large number of private schools were found to have exchanged information on prices, if fines had been imposed at normal levels, the national education system would have collapsed. Fines would also have been funded by parents of current and future pupils, rather than borne by those who had earlier benefitted

---

[9] G Becker, 'Crime and Punishment: An Economic Approach' (1968) 76 *Journal of Political Economy* 169–217; GJ Stigler, 'The Theory of Economic Regulation' (1971) 2 *Bell Journal of Economics and Management Science* 3–21; WM Landes, 'Optimal Sanctions for Antitrust Violations' (1983) 50 *The University of Chicago Law Review* 652; RA Posner, *Antitrust Law* 2nd edn (Chicago, University of Chicago Press, 2001) vii–ix; M Faure, A Ogus and N Philipsen, 'Curbing Consumer Financial Losses: The Economics of Regulatory Enforcement' (2009) 31 *Law & Policy* 161–91.

[10] Among much literature, see WPJ Wils, *Efficiency and Justice in European Antitrust Enforcement* (Oxford, Hart Publishing, 2008); P Buccirossi, L Ciari, T Duso, G Spagnolo and C Vitale, 'Deterrence in Competition law' Paper of Wissenschaftszentrum Berlin für Sozialforschung, 2009, ISSN 0722-6748.

[11] *Safeway Ltd & Others v Simon Twigger & Others* [2010] EWCA Civ 1472.

[12] *Productivity and Enterprise: A World Class Competition Regime* (HMSO, 2001) Cm 5233 (this UK Competition White Paper announced a 'strong deterrent effect' in attacking anti-competitive behaviour); *The Deterrent Effect of Competition Enforcement by the OFT. Discussion Document.* (Office of Fair Trading, 2007) OFT963, available at http://www.oft.gov.uk/shared_oft/reports/Evaluating-OFTs-work/oft963.pdf. See L Garrod, M Hviid, G Loomes and C Waddams Price of the ESRC Centre for Competition Policy, *Assessing the Effectiveness of Potential Remedies in Consumer Markets* (Office of Fair Trading, 2008) OFT994 available at http://www.oft.gov.uk/shared_oft/economic_research/oft994.pdf.

[13] *Leniency and No-action. OFT's Guidance Note on the Handling of Applications* (Office of Fair Trading, 2008) OFT803, available at http://www.oft.gov.uk/shared_oft/reports/comp_policy/oft803.pdf.

[14] *Simplification Plan* (Office of Fair Trading, 2009) OFT1067, para 1.12, available at http://www.oft.gov.uk/shared_oft/529862/oft1067.pdf.

from the lower fees. The solution found was based on restitution. The schools each paid a nominal penalty of £10,000 and together made *ex gratia* payments totalling £3 million to a charitable fund to benefit the future education of those pupils who had attended the schools during the period of the cartel.[15]

Private enforcement, through payment of damages, is not intended to have a deterrent effect and is seen as secondary—and subsequent—to public enforcement. In other words, delivery of redress is desirable but not a priority, and not a function of the public authority but can be left to private actors.

The Enterprise and Regulatory Reform Act 2013 enabled the CMA, amongst other enforcers, to use civil enforcement of investigation powers.[16] These include a power to impose a penalty for failure to comply with requirements, of such amount as CMA considers appropriate, not exceeding £30,000, or daily rate of £15,000. The CMA must publish a statement of policy on such use of its powers.[17] Another important power is that of issuing an enforcement order that appoints an independent person to (a) monitor compliance with such terms of the order as are so specified or described or terms of any directions given under the order; or (b) determine any dispute between persons who are subject to the order about what is required by any such terms and determination of disputes.[18]

A. Sanctions on Individuals

Until recently there was no differentiation between the acts and culpability of a firm and of its individual employees. British enforcement policy, however, has added to the strict paradigm described above and in chapter nine, and as espoused by the European Commission. First, a criminal offence applies to individuals who engage in cartel arrangements that fix prices, limit supply or production, share markets or rig bids in the UK. The criminal cartel offence only applies to relevant agreements in respect of arrangements between undertakings operating at the same level of the supply chain, known as horizontal agreements.[19] Vertical agreements which are intended to operate between undertakings at different levels in the supply chain, for example between a manufacturer and a distributor, or between a distributor and a retailer, are not covered by the offence.

Second, the Company Directors Disqualification Act 1986 provides that, where a company breaches UK or EU competition law, the OFT or sectoral regulators may apply to the court for a Competition Disqualification Order (CDO).[20] Under such an order, a director can be disqualified from acting as a director for up to 15 years if the court deems them unfit to be involved in the management of a company. Citing the need to ensure effective

---

[15] Decision of the OFT No CA98/05/2006 *Exchange of Information on Future Fees by Certain Independent Fee-paying Schools* (20 Nov 2006; Case CE/2890-03).

[16] Enterprise and Regulatory Reform Act 2013, s 40, inserting s 40A into the 1998 Act.

[17] ibid, s 40B.

[18] ibid, s 49, inserting para 20C into Sch 8 of the Enterprise Act 2002.

[19] Enterprise Act 2002, s 188. See guidance documents *Powers for Investigating Criminal Cartels* (Office of Fair Trading, 2004) OFT515, and *Applications for Leniency and No-action in Cartel Cases* (n 13) referring to applications for immunity from prosecution for the criminal cartel offence under s 190(4) of the Enterprise Act 2002.

[20] Company Directors Disqualification Act 1986, s 9A.

deterrence, the OFT announced in 2010 that it would take a tougher stance with directors through applying for more CDOs, targeting not only directors who were directly involved in an infringement, but also those directors who should have known or suspected competition law breaches at a company.[21] The 2010 policy changes included that directors who fail to co-operate with any leniency process in an OFT investigation will not be offered immunity from CDOs whereas those that do cooperate and whose company benefits from leniency will be immune.

The implications of the revised guidance on CDOs illustrated the importance of implementing a rigorous compliance policy throughout a company and of encouraging a culture of compliance. Directors were advised to implement clear reporting requirements for commercial arrangements that may involve competition issues, check on a regular basis the level of compliance in a company by using compliance training and audits and take action immediately where any breach is discovered.[22]

In order to make the criminal cartel offence easier to prosecute, the requirement to prove dishonesty as an element of the cartel offence was removed in 2013, and statutory exclusions and defences added in its place.[23]

B. Guidance on Financial Penalties

The OFT was required[24] to issue guidance as to the appropriate amount of a penalty, including guidance as to the circumstances in which, in determining a penalty, the OFT may take into account the effects of an infringement in another Member State. Revised guidance was issued in September 2012.[25] The OFT was required to have regard to the guidance for the time being in force when setting the amount of any penalty to be imposed.[26] The predominance of deterrence, and its exclusivity as an enforcement policy, will be seen throughout the official approach.

The 2012 guidance stated the twin policy objectives of policy on financial penalties as:

— to impose penalties on infringing undertakings which reflect the *seriousness of the infringement*, and
— to ensure that the threat of penalties will *deter* both the infringing undertakings and other undertakings that may be considering anti-competitive activities from engaging in them.[27]

---

[21] *Director Disqualification Orders in Competition Cases. Revised Guidance* (Office of Fair Trading, 2010) at http://www.oft.gov.uk/shared_oft/business_leaflets/enterprise_act/oft510.pdf.
[22] ibid.
[23] Enterprise and Regulatory Reform Act 2013 s 47, which amended the Enterprise Act 2002 s 188, and provided for the notification exclusion (s 188A(1)(a)) and the publication exclusion (s 188A(1)(c)).
[24] Competition Act 1998, ss 38(1), 38(1A) and 38(3).
[25] *OFT's Guidance as to the Appropriate Amount of a Penalty* (Office of Fair Trading, 2012) OFT423, at http://www.oft.gov.uk/shared_oft/business_leaflets/ca98_guidelines/oft423.pdf. This revised Guidance first issued in 2004.
[26] Although there is no equivalent statutory obligation on the other regulators to publish guidance as to the appropriate amount of a penalty, those regulators are required to have regard to the OFT's published guidance for the time being in force when setting the amount of any penalty to be imposed under the Competition Act 1998.
[27] *Guidance* (n 25) para 1.4.

Noting that the OFT has a discretion to impose financial penalties, the guidance said that the OFT

> intends, where appropriate, to impose financial penalties which are severe, in particular in respect of agreements between undertakings which fix prices or share markets, other cartel activities and serious abuses of a dominant position. The OFT considers that these are among the most serious infringements of competition law.[28]

It set out two aspects to the deterrence objective:

> First, there is a need to deter the undertakings which are subject to the decision from engaging in future anti-competitive activity (often referred to as 'specific deterrence'). Second, there is a need to deter undertakings at large which might be considering activities contrary to any of Article 101, Article 102, the Chapter I or Chapter II prohibitions from breaching the law (often referred to as 'general deterrence').[29]

The guidance noted the importance of ensuring that penalties imposed on individual undertakings are proportionate and not excessive,[30] and of encouraging undertakings to come forward with information relating to any cartel activity in which they are involved.[31] The OFT therefore sets out in part three of this guidance when lenient treatment will be given to such undertakings.

Extracts from the guidance are set out at Figure 15.1. Broadly, the approach involves a six-step approach having regard to factors such as the seriousness of the infringement and its duration, applying a rate of up to 30 per cent of the undertaking's annual turnover, then adjusting the figure to take account of certain aggravating or mitigating circumstances. Fines are intended to be large sums, in accordance with the deterrence principle. However, in order to detect infringements, a leniency policy is operated, under which the first applicant may be completely excused imposition of any fine, and the second applicant may have half the fine remitted.

In 2012 the government stated its intention

> to legislate that financial penalties should reflect the seriousness of the infringement and the need to reduce the incidence of infringement through specific and general deterrence; and that the CAT should have regard to the statutory guidance (as updated) on the appropriate amount of a penalty.[32]

In its 2012 review of how competition could be strengthened so as to contribute to economic growth,[33] the government decided that:

— The CMA should be able to require parties to appoint an independent third party to monitor and/or arbitrate on the implementation of remedies, and enabling the CMA to require parties to publish certain non-price information.[34]

[28] ibid.
[29] ibid, para 1.5.
[30] ibid, para 1.6.
[31] ibid, para 1.7.
[32] *Growth, Competition and the Competition Regime. Government Response to Consultation* (Department for Business, Innovation & Skills, 2012) at http://www.bis.gov.uk/assets/biscore/consumer-issues/docs/g/12-512-growth-and-competition-regime-government-response.pdf, para 6.27.
[33] ibid.
[34] Consumer Rights Act 2015, amending Sch 8 of the Employment Act 2002.

2 STEPS FOR DETERMINING THE LEVEL OF A PENALTY

Method of calculation

2.1   A financial penalty imposed by the OFT under section 36 of the CA98 will be calculated following a six-step approach:
— calculation of the starting point having regard to the seriousness of the infringement and the relevant turnover of the undertaking
— adjustment for duration
— adjustment for aggravating or mitigating factors
— adjustment for specific deterrence and proportionality
— adjustment if the maximum penalty of 10 per cent of the worldwide turnover of the undertaking is exceeded and to avoid double jeopardy
— adjustment for leniency and/or settlement discounts.

Step 1—starting point

2.3   The starting point for determining the level of financial penalty which will be imposed on an undertaking is calculated having regard to:
— the seriousness of the infringement, and
— the relevant turnover of the undertaking.

The starting point will be calculated as described below.

Assessment of seriousness—application of percentage rate to relevant turnover

2.5   The OFT will apply a rate of up to 30 per cent to an undertaking's relevant turnover in order to reflect adequately the seriousness of the particular infringement and, in so doing, to deter the infringing undertaking and other undertakings generally from engaging in that particular practice or type of practice in the future. The OFT will use a starting point towards the upper end of the range for the most serious infringements of competition law, including hardcore cartel activity and the most serious abuses of a dominant position.

2.6   It is the OFT's assessment of the seriousness of the infringement which will be taken into account in determining the percentage rate for the starting point. When making its assessment, the OFT will consider a number of factors, including the nature of the product, the structure of the market, the market share(s) of the undertaking(s) involved in the infringement, entry conditions and the effect on competitors and third parties. The seriousness assessment will also take into account the need to deter other undertakings from engaging in such infringements in the future. The damage caused to consumers whether directly or indirectly will also be an important consideration. The assessment will be made on a case-by-case basis for all types of infringement, taking account of all the circumstances of the case.

Figure 15.1: Extracts from OFT's Guidance as to the Appropriate Amount of a Penalty (OFT, September 2012) OFT423

Step 3—adjustment for aggravating and mitigating factors

2.13   The basic amount of the financial penalty, adjusted as appropriate at step 2, may be increased where there are aggravating factors, or decreased where there are mitigating factors.

2.14   Aggravating factors include:
— persistent and repeated unreasonable behaviour that delays the OFT's enforcement action
— role of the undertaking as a leader in, or an instigator of, the infringement
— involvement of directors or senior management (notwithstanding paragraph 1.16 above)
— retaliatory or other coercive measures taken against other undertakings aimed at ensuring the continuation of the infringement
— continuing the infringement after the start of the investigation
— repeated infringements by the same undertaking or other undertakings in the same group (recidivism)
— infringements which are committed intentionally rather than negligently
— retaliatory measures taken or commercial reprisal sought by the undertaking against a leniency applicant.

2.15   Mitigating factors include:
— role of the undertaking, for example, where the undertaking is acting under severe duress or pressure
— genuine uncertainty on the part of the undertaking as to whether the agreement or conduct constituted an infringement
— adequate steps having been taken with a view to ensuring compliance with Articles 101 and 102 and the Chapter I and Chapter II prohibitions
— termination of the infringement as soon as the OFT intervenes
— cooperation which enables the enforcement process to be concluded more effectively and/or speedily.

Step 4—adjustment for specific deterrence and proportionality

2.16   In considering whether any adjustments should be made at this step for specific deterrence or proportionality, the OFT will have regard to appropriate indicators of the size and financial position of the undertaking—including, where they are available, total turnover, profits, cash flow and industry margins—as well as any other relevant circumstances of the case. For these purposes, the OFT will consider the relevant indicators of the undertaking's size and financial position as at the time the penalty is being imposed. The OFT may also consider indicators of size and financial position from the time of the infringement.

2.17   The penalty figure reached after steps 1 to 3 may be increased to ensure that the penalty to be imposed on the undertaking will deter it from breaching competition law in the future, given its specific size and financial position and any other relevant circumstances of the case....

Figure 15.1: *(Continued)*

Step 5—adjustment to prevent maximum penalty being exceeded and to avoid double jeopardy
Step 6—application of reductions under the OFT's leniency programme and for settlement agreements

2.25 The OFT will reduce an undertaking's penalty where the undertaking has a leniency agreement with the OFT, entered into as a result of an application pursuant to section 3 below and in accordance with the OFT's published guidance on leniency, provided always that the undertaking meets the conditions of the leniency agreement.

2.26 The OFT will also apply a penalty reduction where an undertaking agrees to settle with the OFT, which will involve, among other things, the undertaking admitting its participation in the infringement.

3 LENIENT TREATMENT FOR UNDERTAKINGS COMING FORWARD WITH INFORMATION IN CARTEL ACTIVITY CASES

Immunity from or reduction in financial penalty for undertakings coming forward with information in cartel activity cases

3.2 Undertakings participating in cartel activities might wish to terminate their involvement and inform the OFT of the existence of the cartel activity, but be deterred from doing so by the risk of incurring large financial penalties.

3.3 The OFT considers that it is in the interest of the economy of the UK, and the European Union more generally, to have a policy of granting lenient treatment to undertakings which inform it of cartel activities and which then cooperate with it in the circumstances set out below. It is the often secret nature of cartel activities which justifies such a policy. The interests of customers and consumers in ensuring that such activities are detected and prohibited outweigh the policy objectives of imposing financial penalties on those undertakings which participate in cartel activities but which cooperate to a significant degree with the OFT as set out below.

3.4 In order to encourage undertakings participating in cartel activities to come forward, the OFT **will** grant total immunity from financial penalties for an infringement of Article 101 and/or the Chapter I prohibition to a participant in cartel activity who is the first to come forward before the OFT has commenced an investigation and who satisfies the requirements set out in paragraphs 3.13 and 3.14. Alternatively, the OFT **may** offer total immunity or a reduction of up to 100 per cent from financial penalties to a participant who is the first to come forward and who satisfies the requirements set out in paragraphs 3.16 and 3.17. An undertaking which is not the first to come forward, or does not satisfy these requirements may benefit from a reduction of up to 50 per cent in the amount of the financial penalty imposed if it satisfies the requirements set out in paragraphs 3.18 to 3.20.

Figure 15.1: *(Continued)*

— Enforcement of competition law should be 'embedded as an enhanced administrative approach', separating those responsible for final decisions from those who carry out investigations, but *not* adopting a prosecutorial approach.
— Financial penalties should reflect the seriousness of the infringement and 'the need to reduce the incidence of infringement through specific and general deterrence'. The CAT should have regard to the statutory guidance (as updated) on the appropriate amount of a penalty.[35]
— The competition authorities should have power to impose civil financial penalties on parties who do not comply with certain formal requirements during investigations. Applications for warrants to enter premises will be made to the CAT.
— Cost recovery would *not* be introduced in antitrust investigations.

C. The Effect of 'Private Enforcement'

Extensive discussion occurred over many years of the extent to which mechanisms should be enhanced to facilitate payment of damages for loss by private parties from competition infringements, especially cartels. The dominant policy debate occurred at EU level.[36] The issues of relevance to the current analysis were the policy determinations that deterrence remained paramount in competition enforcement and that private enforcement and redress remained subservient to deterrence administered by public enforcement. Research revealed that redress was paid, at least by 2013, more frequently than had been thought a few years previously.[37]

In 2013 the British Coalition government issued its proposals to deliver increased competition damages by means of three techniques: Encouraging ADR, a regulatory redress

---

[35] *Growth, Competition and the Competition Regime. Government Response to Consultation* (n 32) para 6.27.

[36] See Case C-453/99 *Courage and Crehan* [2001] ECR I-6297; J Stuyck, E Terryn, V Colaert, T Van Dyck, N Peretz, N Hoekx and P Tereszkiewicz, *Study on Alternative Means of Consumer Redress other than Redress through Ordinary Judicial Proceedings* (Leuven, Catholic University of Leuven, 17 January 2007); White Paper on Damages Actions for Breach of the EC Antitrust Rules, COM(2008) 165, 2.4.2008; C Hodges, *The Reform of Class and Representative Actions in European Legal Systems: A New Framework for Collective Redress in Europe* (Oxford, Hart Publishing, 2008); DA Crane, *The Institutional Structure of Antitrust Enforcement* (New York, Oxford University Press, 2010); European Parliament resolution of 2 February 2012 on 'Towards a Coherent European Approach to Collective Redress' 2011/2089(INI); Communication from the Commission, Towards a European Horizontal Framework for collective Redress, COM(2013) 401/2, 11.6.2013; Commission Recommendation of 11 June 2013 on common principles for collective redress mechanisms in the Member States for injunctions against and claims on damages caused by violations of EU rights, COM(2013) 3539/3, 11.6.2013; Proposal for a Directive of the European Parliament and of the Council on certain rules governing actions for damages under national law for infringements of the competition law provisions of the Member States and of the European Union, COM(2013) 404, 11.6.2013.

[37] BJ Rodger, 'Private Enforcement of Competition law, the Hidden Story: Competition Litigation in the United Kingdom, 2000–2005' [2008] *European Competition Law Review* 96 (a survey of UK lawyers recording 43 settlements between 2000–2005, increasing to 14 in 2005); BJ Rodger, 'Competition Litigation in the UK Courts; A Study of all Cases 2005–2008—Part I' [2009] *Global Competition Litigation Review* 92; BJ Rodger, 'Competition Litigation in the UK Courts; A study of all cases 2005–2008—Part II' [2009] *Global Competition Law Review* 136; B Rodger (ed), *Competition Law: Comparative Private Enforcement and Collective Redress Across the EU* (London, Kluwer, 2014).

power,[38] and a private class action.[39] The 'limited' opt-out class action in the CAT for damages 'with strong safeguards' to prevent against a US regime was based on the 'reality that some traders need a threat to encourage settlement'.[40] In its consultation, the government anticipated that the majority of cases in which a regulatory power for competition damages could be used would in fact primarily benefit consumers,[41] noting that:

> Some cases would be much more appropriate for the use of such a power than others: in particular, this procedure would likely be most appropriate for cartel cases involving large numbers of undifferentiated products bought by many consumers, such as milk or football shirts. As it happens, these are cases where there is often most consumer detriment in aggregate, and where bringing cases before the UK courts can be most difficult.[42]

In response, both Citizens Advice and Which? called for the authorities to have the power to require businesses to compensate affected consumers as part of the standard enforcement process.[43] Neither the government nor the OFT (as it then was) was particularly keen on a redress power, but the Government recognised that[44]

> there are some situations where it may be appropriate for the public enforcement body to consider mechanisms for redress, as part of its administrative settlement of cases. For example, in its case against certain independent schools, the OFT decided to impose a fine on the schools found to be price-fixing but also agreed that they would establish a series of trust funds to benefit the pupils who attended the schools during the academic years in which the infringement took place.[45]

The government implemented 'enhanced consumer measures' for the competition regulator under the Consumer Rights Act 2015. The proposals authorise either an enforcement order or an undertaking that a trader will, inter alia, offer compensation or redress to consumers who have suffered loss, or take measures intended to be in the collective interests of consumers where individual consumers cannot be identified or could not be identified without disproportionate cost, or will take compliance measures, or take measures intended to enable consumers to choose more effectively between persons supplying or seeking to supply goods or services.[46]

---

[38] Encouraged by a reduction in fines of up to 10% in relation to companies offering to make redress and arranging settlement schemes. There will also be a collective settlement procedure, based on the Dutch model.

[39] *Private Actions in Competition Law: A Consultation on Options for Reform—Government Response* (Department for Business, Innovation & Skills, January 2013) ('Consultation').

[40] Business immediately objected to the proposals, saying that the opt-out proposal fails the 'growth test' for the economy and 'crosses the Rubicon' of unacceptability: CBI Press Release. Safeguards would include certification that the case is suitable for opt-out; no treble or exemplary damages; loser pays costs; and claimants must be representative bodies, not special purpose vehicles.

[41] Consultation, para 6.34.

[42] Consultation, para 6.36. The Response to the Consultation by R Mulheron and V Smith agreed that power 5 would apply 'typically in those cases where a cartel has substantially affected individual end-consumers' and that an opt-out class action would not work in such a situation.

[43] Responses to Consultation, available at https://www.gov.uk/government/consultations/private-actions-in-competition-law-a-consultation-on-options-for-reform.

[44] Consultation, para. 6.27, available at https://www.gov.uk/government/uploads/system/uploads/attachment_data/file/69123/13-501-private-actions-in-competition-law-a-consultation-on-options-for-reform-government-response.pdf.

[45] See OFT press release 166/06, 23 November 2006. It should be noted that this was a settlement in lieu of a higher fine being imposed; it was not a settlement that would have protected the school against subsequent private actions.

[46] Consumer Rights Act 2015, s 81 and Sch 6, amending Enterprise Act 2002, ss 217–19.

III. Research on Enforcement and Compliance

From 2000 the OFT sponsored a series of studies into what drives compliance, with both competition and consumer law, and relied on the findings to illuminate its policy documents on enforcement. Those relating to consumer law are summarised in chapter 13, and should be read together with those on competition law summarised below. The studies were mostly surveys of attitudes to regulation by businesses, rather than academically rigorous behavioural research. It might appear that the results were interpreted in the light of pre-existing understanding of deterrence theory.

Before publishing its consumer enforcement policy in 2010, the OFT reviewed previous research, and found that a number of firms mentioned the importance of individual sanctions, such as the risk of criminal proceedings, director disqualification, personal reputational damage or internal disciplinary sanctions, in encouraging individuals to focus on competition law compliance.[47] It published a related policy paper on its proposed actions.[48]

In 2007 it published the results of 30 interviews with competition lawyers, economists and firms' managers responsible for competition compliance in 2006; and telephone surveys of 234 senior competition lawyers based in London and Brussels in 2006, and 202 British companies in 2007.[49] The questioning probed the reasons for abandonment or modification of proposed mergers or potentially anti-competitive conduct following recent competition authority interventions, and made the following findings:

> In regard to individual decisions, it appears that the deterrent effect arising from competition law enforcement operates in a different way from merger control. In the interviews we were provided with several examples of proposed *mergers* which had been abandoned or modified specifically as a result of an earlier individual OFT or CC merger decision. By contrast, in the context of competition law, while there were many examples of *agreements and initiatives* that were abandoned or modified because of the risk of OFT enforcement action, none were said to have been abandoned or modified specifically as a result of an earlier individual decision. (emphasis added: note that this analysis did not refer to cartels).[50]

The authors noted various official statements asserting the effectiveness of deterrence, and the limited empirical evidence on the subject, together with the fact that difficulties of measuring deterrence effects had been widely recognised.[51] Despite these limitations,

---

[47] *Consumer Law and Business Practice. Drivers of Compliance and Non-compliance* (Office of Fair Trading, 2010) OFT1225, available at http://webarchive.nationalarchives.gov.uk/20140402142426/http:/www.oft.gov.uk/shared_oft/reports/Evaluating-OFTs-work/OFT1225.pdf.

[48] *Consumer Law and Business Practice. Drivers of Compliance and Non-compliance* (Office of Fair Trading, 2010) OFT1227, available at https://www.gov.uk/government/uploads/system/uploads/attachment_data/file/284405/oft1227.pdf.

[49] *The Deterrent Effect of Competition Enforcement by the OFT. A Report Prepared for the OFT by Deloitte* (Office of Fair Trading, 2007) OFT962, available at http://www.oft.gov.uk/shared_oft/reports/Evaluating-OFTs-work/oft962.pdf.

[50] ibid, paras 1.20, 5.60 and 5.61.

[51] The authors cited: 'One of the joys of deterrence effects … is that they are very hard to measure with any confidence', P Geroski 'Measuring and quantifying the influence that competition authorities have on the economy is difficult, with some outcomes, such as deterrence effects, virtually impossible to measure' (National Audit Office, 2005). PA Geroski (2004), 'Is Competition Policy Worth it?', speech on the opening of the Centre for Competition Policy at the University of East Anglia, available at www.competition-commission.org.uk.

the authors proceeded to calculate estimates of the 'deterrence ratios' from OFT activity. In discussing the Deloitte study, the OFT asserted that[52]

> The report suggests that the deterrent effect is significantly greater than the direct effect of enforcement in all areas of merger control and enforcement of competition law against both anti-competitive agreements and conduct.

And that

> The research confirms that the OFT's merger control and competition law enforcement work plays an important role in preventing other anticompetitive behaviour from taking place and that the benefits of OFT work go well beyond the direct financial benefits in terms of lower prices that consumers get as a direct result of our merger and infringement decisions. Activity that deters cartels or abuse of dominance leads to major benefits: lower prices, wider choice, higher productivity and higher innovation. To put a price on all of this is difficult, but as the direct effect of competition enforcement in 2006/7 was £116m, OFT estimates that, given the scale of the deterrence effect, the benefits to consumers from OFT work may be at least a further £600m per year. This compares to an OFT total annual budget of about £70m.

Little focus was directed to the finding that the most important sanctions that motivated compliance were sanctions on individuals, such as criminal penalties and disqualification of directors. By comparison with the figures estimated, for 2010–2011 the OFT estimated that its activities in competition enforcement saved consumers around £83 million,[53] and the government estimated the total annual consumer benefits of the regime at £689 million.[54]

Further research in the construction industry produced less optimistic findings regarding a deterrent effect, and reported that the 'risk of an OFT investigation had not made any impact on the majority of contractors surveyed'.[55] The overall conclusion was that there was a very low level of awareness of any of the OFT's activities directed at the construction sector, particularly the six cases completed between 2004 and 2006, and respondents did not consider 'that there was any clear message about bid rigging coming from the OFT during this period'. Admittedly, these results were before a Statement of Objections was made to 112 construction companies in April 2008.[56]

A study published in 2009 commissioned by the OFT to assess the deterrent power of its penalties regime asserted that that 'high fines are a crucially important element of deterrence'[57] but that 'additional deterrence' was needed in the form of individual sanctions,[58] since the levels of fines imposed on firms might not deter individual managers.[59]

---

[52] *The Deterrent Effect of Competition Enforcement by the OFT: Discussion Paper 963* (n 12).

[53] *Positive Impact 10/11—Consumer Benefits from the OFT's Work OFT1354*, July 2011, 27. The figures relate just to the OFT's work, not the regime as a whole.

[54] *The Value of the Consumer Benefits of the Competition Regime* (Department for Business, Innovation & Skills, 2011).

[55] ibid, para 4.59.

[56] *Evaluation of the Impact of the OFT's Investigation into Bid Rigging in the Construction Industry* (Office of Fair Trading, 2010) OFT1240.

[57] *An Assessment of Discretionary Penalties Regimes. Final Report. A Report Prepared for the Office of Fair Trading by London Economics* (Office of Fair Trading, 2009) OFT1132, available at http://www.oft.gov.uk/shared_oft/economic_research/oft1132.pdf, para 1.15.

[58] ibid, para 1.27.

[59] ibid, para 1.4.

The London Economics Report suggested that, if anything, OFT financial penalties were relatively low by international standards. OFT financial penalties were found to be around 65 to 75 per cent lower than financial penalties imposed by the other competition authorities considered in the report. The consultants' review of the literature concluded that an optimal regime should comprise both monetary and non-monetary sanctions, and that the UK's non-monetary sanctions regime compared well to international comparators, by providing for competition disqualification orders for anti-competitive practices, up to five years imprisonment and no limit on personal fines for cartel offences.[60]

A. OFT's Understanding on Compliance with Competition Law

In 2010 the OFT issued its report on drivers of compliance and non-compliance with competition law,[61] contemporaneously with its similar document on consumer law, discussed at chapter 13 above.[62] It began by stating:

> 1.2 We recognise that the majority of businesses want to comply with competition law. Whilst we will take enforcement action where necessary, we also wish to support businesses seeking to achieve a competition law compliance culture, so that breaches of competition law are avoided in the first place.

It referred to the previous research by Deloitte on the perceived importance of sanctions in deterring infringements of competition law[63] and London Economics' thoughts on an 'optimal' penalty regime.[64] The OFT summarised the Deloitte findings of the 'ranking' of the views of business and lawyers interviewed as shown in Table 15.1.

The OFT's report gave its findings from 22 interviews with in-house counsel from larger companies and other in-house competition law compliance specialists from a cross-section of businesses either based in, or trading in, the UK. The majority of businesses interviewed adopted a risk-based approach to competition law compliance, focusing efforts on the areas

Table 15.1: Ranking of Sanctions by Businesses and Lawyers

Ranking by Business	Ranking by Lawyers
1. Criminal Penalties	1. Criminal Penalties
2. Disqualification of Directors	2. Fines
3. Adverse publicity	3. Disqualification of Directors
4. Fines	4. Adverse publicity
5. Private damages actions	5. Private damages actions

---

[60] ibid, paras 1.6 and 1.10. It noted that Germany and the USA have similar sanctions with jail sentences of up to five years and 10 years, and personal fines of up to $1 million and €1.8 million respectively.

[61] *Drivers of Compliance and Non-compliance with Competition Law. An OFT Report* (n 48)

[62] *Consumer Law and Business Practice. Drivers of Compliance and Non-compliance* (n 47).

[63] *The Deterrent Effect of Competition Enforcement by the OFT. A Report Prepared for the OFT by Deloitte* (n 49).

[64] *An Assessment of Discretionary Penalties Regimes. Final Report. A Report Prepared for the Office of Fair Trading by London Economics* (n 57) para 1.15.

of greatest risk within the business. Businesses gave examples of activities they had under-taken to promote compliance with competition law. These included obtaining the commit-ment of senior management to competition law compliance, tailoring training to the areas and employees most likely to be dealing with compliance issues, ensuring that employees can access guidance and legal advice, and appointing a 'compliance champion' to promote compliance issues.[65] The OFT recognised that one size will not fit all in competition law compliance and that the appropriate actions to achieve a compliance culture will vary by size of business and also by the nature of the risks identified.[66]

The conclusions on drivers of compliance and non-compliance were summarised as follows:

1.9 A number of the businesses we interviewed emphasised that, whilst important for their organi-sation, competition law compliance was part of a *broader compliance agenda*. Competition law com-pliance often stands alongside other compliance requirements in areas such as health and safety, environmental protection or anti-bribery and corruption. Some businesses sought to emphasise their commitment to competition law compliance through including it in their business's overall corporate responsibility or ethical trading statement.

1.10 The key drivers for competition law compliance mentioned by respondents were the fear of *reputational damage* and *financial penalties*. A number of respondents mentioned the importance of *individual sanctions*, such as the risk of criminal proceedings, director disqualification, personal reputational damage or internal disciplinary sanctions, in encouraging individuals to focus on competition law compliance. A *commitment* to competition law compliance from the top of the organisation down was a key driver of compliance in the organisation as a whole. Certain respond-ents specifically mentioned that they viewed competition law compliance as helping them to win business through being able to position themselves as *ethical* businesses. One respondent thought that competition law compliance activities resulted in *confident employees* who knew the rules of the game and who could compete for business without fear of breaching competition law.

1.11 We explored with respondents the competition law challenges that might arise despite their compliance efforts. Any apparent *ambiguity or lack of management commitment* to competi-tion law compliance was mentioned by the majority of respondents as creating the risk of non-compliance. Other possible reasons for non-compliance mentioned include *rogue employees*, confusion or *uncertainty* about the law, *employee error* or naivety, *loss of trust* in legal advice, a '*box-ticking*' approach to compliance and competition law compliance having to compete for attention with other compliance activities.[67]

In considering what more OFT could do to drive compliance, the focus was on financial penalties, especially a business's request that the OFT change its policy in relation to setting fines and applying discounts where a party had undertaken appropriate competition law compliance prior to an infringement.[68] The OFT rejected the suggestions, the main reason being that it considered that the avoidance of a breach in the first place is the product of an effective competition law compliance programme.[69] The OFT recognised that if it were to treat an ineffective compliance programme as an aggravating factor, this could act as

---

[65] *An Assessment of Discretionary Penalties Regimes. Final Report. A Report Prepared for the Office of Fair Trading by London Economics* (n 57) para 1.5.

[66] ibid, para 1.7.

[67] ibid, paras 1.9–1.11.

[68] ibid, ch 5.

[69] ibid, para 6.7.

a disincentive to businesses engaging in compliance activities. The OFT also considered whether its penalties policy should take account of breaches caused by a rogue employee in an otherwise compliant business. It concluded that this would not be appropriate for a number of reasons, including the possible risk of incentivising businesses to find a scape-goat to present as a rogue employee in order to obtain a penalty discount instead of dealing with the actual compliance issues.

In conclusion, the OFT proposed to update its guidance that businesses should adopt a four-step approach to effective competition law compliance culture:

— Risk identification
— Risk assessment
— Risk mitigation
— Review

B. Further Research

A 2010 survey of 2009 UK businessmen[70] included the findings that 35 per cent of respondents did not know the sorts of things competition law was supposed to prevent, and 34 per cent had no awareness of any competition enforcement action; 41 per cent thought abuse of dominance was happening in their local region, and 22 per cent thought there was collusion.

A 2011 survey by London Economics of 501 responses from large firms and 308 from small firms, with responses from two business organisations and 27 telephone interviews with professionals concluded:[71]

> The results of the business survey clearly indicate that, while other sanctions and enforcement tools also have significant deterrence effects, the three most important factors deterring potentially anti-competitive behaviour are, in order of importance:
>
> — the risk of reputational damage for the company
> — criminal sanctions for individuals, and
> — financial penalties for the company.[72]

This study concluded that it had identified three key 'pillars of compliance': Knowledge and awareness of competition law, sanctions and enforcement (aimed at increasing the cost of non-compliance to a business), and firms' internal voluntary compliance measures.[73] However, the views of businesses revealed serious shortcomings in each of these areas. Only 57 per cent of large businesses and 35 per cent of small businesses reported that they felt very or fairly knowledgeable about competition law.[74] Very few businesses reported behavioural change due to specific cases overall.[75]

---

[70] *Competition Law Compliance Survey. Prepared for the Office of Fair Trading by Synovate (UK) Ltd* (Office of Fair Trading, 2011) at http://www.oft.gov.uk/shared_oft/ca-and-cartels/competition-awareness-compliance/oft1270.pdf.

[71] *The Impact of Competition Interventions on Compliance and Deterrence* (Office of Fair Trading, 2011) OFT1391, available at http://www.oft.gov.uk/shared_oft/reports/Evaluating-OFTs-work/oft1391.pdf.

[72] ibid, paras 6.5 and 6.6.

[73] ibid, para 1.10.

[74] ibid, para 1.15.

[75] ibid, para 1.16.

London Economics noted academic suggestions that reputational damage from competition enforcement is an important deterrent for businesses.[76] It also noted that, contrary to the predictions of the literature,[77] private damages were ranked relatively low by respondents in terms of being an effective deterrent.[78] However, it contrasted this with an earlier finding that sanctions at the individual level are the most important.[79]

This study claimed that 'There is also clear evidence that businesses perceive OFT enforcement tools and sanctions as important drivers of compliance. Most important are fines to the company, reputational damage to the company and criminal sanctions.'[80] Although most large companies used some voluntary compliance measures, most commonly seeking external advice, smaller companies face many other compliance issues (for example, occupational health and safety) and their compliance measures were typically ad hoc, often with no compliance officers, so compliance with competition law 'may be put on the back burner'.[81]

The consultants confidently estimated the number of cases deterred due to the risk of OFT intervention for every case it undertook (deterrence ratios).[82] They reiterated the general view that the deterrent effect of enforcement tools depends on both the probability of detection and the severity of the sanction if detected.[83]

C. Comments

Both the estimates from the 2011 and 2007 studies were entirely spurious. The methodology, findings and credibility of these calculations were subsequently strongly criticised.[84] Further, all of the studies and subsequent official policy papers attempted to shoe-horn the findings into an assumed framework, namely that deterrence was the sole relevant theory driving both enforcement by public authorities and compliance by both firms and their entire staff.

It is alarming how thin the research base is on which rests a significant edifice of policy. There is almost no solid empirical research into the motivations of managers and 'firms' in compliance or infringement of competition law, or of the validity of deterrence as a, let alone

---

[76] JC Bosch and EW Eckard, 'The Profit of Price Fixing: Evidence From Stock Market Reaction to Federal Indictments' (1991) 73(2) *The Review of Economics and Statistics* 309–17; A Gunster and MA van Dijk, 'The Impact of European Antitrust Policy: Evidence from the Stock Market' Working Paper (2011) http://ssrn.com/abstract=1598387.

[77] For example *A World Class Competition Regime* (Department of Trade and Industry, 2001) and S Calkin, 'Corporate Compliance and the Antitrust Agencies' Bi-modal Penalties' (2007) 60(3) *Law and Contemporary Problems* 127–67.

[78] *The Deterrent Effect of Competition Enforcement by the OFT* (n 49) para 6.10: 'Our survey suggests that at present the threat of private actions is not seen as a serious deterrent in comparison to the possibility of public enforcement action.'

[79] ibid, para 6.14, referring to Deloitte and Touche, *The Deterrent Effect of Competition Enforcement by the OFT* (Office of Fair Trading, 2007).

[80] ibid, para 1.19.

[81] ibid, paras 1.26 and 7.5.

[82] ibid, para 1.17.

[83] ibid, para 3.28.

[84] C Harding, 'Cartel Deterrence: The Search for Evidence and Argument' (2011) 56(2) *The Antitrust Bulletin* 345–76; C Veljanovski, *The Deterrent Effects of the UK Competition Act 1998* (2014). https://www.researchgate.net/publication/256045539_The_Deterrent_Effects_of_the_UK_Competition_Act_1998. Some criticisms include the questions that were put to interviewees, their 'leading' nature, the logical basis on which the conclusions made were drawn, and various statistical issues.

the, basis for enforcement policy. There are indications that the three areas of competition law (mergers, cartels, abuse of dominance) may need to be considered separately in these respects. There are clear indications that a distinction needs to be made between how to affect the behaviour of firms and the behaviour of those humans within firms who take decisions or affect 'corporate behaviour'. But further illumination of these aspects is primitive.

The studies fail to show a deterrent effect of public enforcement, at least as practiced by the OFT in the last decade. Instead, they show a clear lack of awareness by individuals of both competition law and its enforcement. Those findings could not support an argument for the effectiveness of deterrence as a theory or practice. There are indications (and not more strong than that) that reputational risk for a company and sanctions on individuals may be significant motivators in relation to preventing decisions that lead to infringement (as opposed to compliance per se). The basis for concluding that three 'key pillars of compliance' have been identified is wholly unsubstantiated.

The result is that the enforcement of competition law is unsupported by adequate evidence, and based on theory (deterrence) that is not only unsupported by the limited available empirical evidence but also contradicted by it. Current enforcement policy is at best confused in its schizophrenic focus on both deterring firms and some individuals within them, in a wholly uncoordinated fashion.

IV. CMA's 2014 Enforcement Policy

In January 2014, the government issued five strategic goals for the CMA: To deliver effective enforcement, extend competition frontiers, refocus consumer protection, achieve professional excellence and develop integrated performance.[85] In relation to outcomes, the government merely said that success with the strategic goals would increase the CMA's impact and make it respected and influential abroad and a great place to work. There was no mention of consumer outcomes.

Contemporaneously, the CMA issued its 'vision, values and strategy', which confirmed its policy on enforcement.[86] The key provisions are set out in Figure 15.2. Emphasis was placed on deterrence, and there was no mention whatever of providing redress or rectifying markets that had been unbalanced by illegal activity. The CMA also stated that it would prioritise enforcement cases on the basis of impact, strategic significance, risk of an unsuccessful outcome and resources.[87]

A policy statement issued in January 2014 set out the CMA's approach to imposing administrative penalties for failure to comply with certain investigatory and interim

---

[85] *Competition and Markets Authority. Performance Management Framework* (Department for Business, Innovation & Skills, 2014).

[86] *Vision, Values and Strategy for the CMA* (Competition & Markets Authority, 2014). See earlier *Vision, Values and Strategy for the CMA. Consultation Document* (n 8).

[87] *Prioritisation Principles for the CMA. Consultation Document* (Competition & Markets Authority, 2014).

Primary Duty

The CMA must seek to promote competition, both within and outside the United Kingdom, for the benefit of consumers.
Enterprise and Regulatory Reform Act 2013 s25(3)

CMA Mission

The CMA makes markets work well in the interests of consumers, businesses and the economy.

CMA Overall ambition

Consistently be one of the leading competition and consumer agencies in the world. To achieve this, it has set itself five goals. It will:

1 Deliver effective enforcement

— Deter wrongdoing and prevent consumers losing out from anticompetitive mergers or practices
— Ensure that businesses and individuals understand the law and know that effective sanctions follow if they break it
— Pursue the right cases and manage them well so it makes good, timely decisions that stand up to appeal

2 Extend competition frontiers

— Use the markets regime to improve the way competition works where evidence shows it can most benefit consumers
— Ensure the application of competition law and policy in regulated sectors, working alongside and supporting sector regulators
— Act to encourage effective competition where markets and business models are evolving

3 Refocus consumer protection

— Empower consumers to exercise informed choice, using both competition and consumer powers to help markets work well
— Lead policy development and identify and pursue complex, precedent-setting cases where it is best placed to intervene and can have the greatest impact on markets
— Support and work effectively alongside other UK consumer agencies

4 Achieve professional excellence

— Conduct legal, economic and financial analysis to the highest international standards while avoiding unnecessary burdens on business
— Manage all its cases efficiently, transparently and fairly to meet demanding deadlines and external expectations of pace, rigour and fairness
— Lead the development of legal, economic and business thinking on competition

Figure 15.2: The CMA's 2014 Vision

---

5 Develop integrated performance

— Combine staff from different professional and organisational backgrounds into effective multi-disciplinary teams
— Use all the competition and consumer measures at its disposal where they can have most impact and apply lessons and experience from each to improve its performance
— Complement and support the work of other consumer, regulatory and enforcement authorities, and act as a trusted competition adviser across government

Success with these five goals will make the CMA:

— An agency that has a beneficial impact on consumers, on business behaviour and on productivity and growth in the economy;
— A respected and influential independent authority in the UK and abroad; and
— A great place to work

Figure 15.2: *(Continued)*

measures powers under the Enterprise Act 2002 and Competition Act 1998.[88] This gave the policy objectives of the use of the CMA's investigatory and interim measures powers as being intended to:

— Ensure that the CMA can expediently gather information to carry out its functions with the best available evidence in compliance with relevant investigation timetables (in particular but not limited to statutory timetables in mergers and markets cases)
— prevent action which might prejudice any reference, impede the taking of action following a reference, or cause detrimental and irreversible changes to market dynamics, and
— ensure that the threat of penalties will deter future non-compliance with relevant CMA powers, by those on whom penalties have been imposed and other persons who may be considering future non-compliance.

Where the CMA has a choice as to the type of penalty that may be imposed, it said that it would consider a number of factors, in the round, on a case-by-case basis, including: The factual circumstances in which a penalty is being considered; the deterrent effect of the penalty on both the person sanctioned and more generally on others, and whether the failure to comply has been remedied.[89]

---

[88] *Administrative Penalties: Statement of Policy on the CMA's Approach* (Competition & Markets Authority, 2014) CMA4, available at https://www.gov.uk/government/uploads/system/uploads/attachment_data/file/270245/CMA4_-_Admin_Penalties_Statement_of_Policy.pdf. See earlier *Administrative Penalties: Statement of Policy on the CMA's Approach: Consultation Document* (Department for Business, Innovation & Skills, July 2013) available at https://www.gov.uk/government/uploads/system/uploads/attachment_data/file/212288/CMA4con_-_Administrative_penalties.pdf.
[89] *Administrative Penalties: Statement of Policy on the CMA's Approach*, ibid, para 4.10.

Also in 2014 the CMA published its policy on aiming to operate transparently, while seeking to maintain (as appropriate) the confidentiality of information it obtains in the exercise of its functions. It also aims to be reasonable when requesting and handling information, and to protect confidential information in a manner that is appropriate in the circumstances of the case.[90] It noted that transparency is a means of achieving due process and ensuring that parties directly involved in a case are treated fairly. But providing clear information about its cases also enhances the visibility of the CMA's work, thereby increasing its impact, predictability and accountability.[91]

Finally, a comparison should be made between the CMA's approach to enforcing competition law and its *Guidance* on use of its consumer protection powers:[92] The latter are discussed at chapter 13.

It is noteworthy that the OECD (Organisation for Economic Co-operation and Development) has identified the importance of evaluating the long term outcomes of enforcement activity. A survey evaluating competition enforcement and advocacy activities of 46 competition agencies published in 2013 by the OECD reviewed three methodologies of evaluation exercises undertaken: evaluation for accountability, ex post evaluation of specific interventions and of their impact on the affected market(s) and evaluation of the broader impact of competition policy.[93]

V. Criticisms of a Lack of Effectiveness of Competition Enforcement

Deterrence theory rests on maintenance of perceptions of a high risk of detection and imposition of significant sanctions.[94] However, concerns have been expressed that official enforcement activities fall short of the desired level of enforcement.

In 2005 the National Audit Office (NAO)[95] and House of Commons' Public Affairs Committee[96] found major failings in the way cases were handled by the OFT and recommended that it clear a large backlog of unresolved cases. The NAO's 2009 progress report concluded that things had improved considerably but there remained concerns.[97] In 2011 the Government expressed concern that 'antitrust cases take too long, and result in

---

[90] *Transparency and Disclosure: Statement of the CMA's Policy and Approach* (Competition & Markets Authority, 2014) at https://www.gov.uk/government/publications/transparency-and-disclosure-statement-of-the-cmas-policy-and-approach. See earlier *Transparency and Disclosure: Statement of the CMA's policy and Approach—Consultation Document* (Department for Business, Innovation & Skills, July 2013) available at https://www.gov.uk/government/uploads/system/uploads/attachment_data/file/212290/CMA6con_-_Transparency.pdf.
[91] *Transparency and Disclosure: Statement of the CMA's Policy and Approach* (2014), ibid, para 2.4.
[92] *Consumer Protection: Guidance on the Use of its Consumer Powers* (Competition & Markets Authority, 2014) CMA7.
[93] *Evaluation of Competition Enforcement and Advocacy Activities: The Results of an OECD Survey* (Paris, OECD, April 2013) available at http://search.oecd.org/officialdocuments/displaydocumentpdf/?cote=DAF/COMP/WP2(2012)7/FINAL&docLanguage=En.
[94] See ch 2.
[95] Report by the Comptroller and Auditor General, *Enforcing Competition in Markets*, HC 593, Session 2005–06.
[96] Committee of Public Accounts (PAC), *Enforcing Competition in Markets*, HC 841, Session 2005–06.
[97] Report by the Comptroller and Auditor General, *The Office Of Fair Trading—Progress Report on Maintaining Competition in Markets*, HC 127 Session 2008–2009, 5 March 2009.

too few decisions, thus having less deterrent effect on anti-competitive activity than they should'.[98] International comparisons indicated that the OFT was under-enforcing the law in comparison with other EU competition agencies: Data on new investigations and decisions made by European competition authorities placed France top and UK bottom of the list, as shown in Table 15.2.[99]

Table 15.2: Aggregate Figures on Antitrust Cases for Selected Member States 1 May 2004–1 September 2010

Member State	New case investigations	Decisions notified to the European Commission
France	189	70
Germany	128	58
Italy	81	58
Netherlands	76	32
Denmark	62	32
Spain	75	30
Greece	31	22
Hungary	79	20
Sweden	36	16
Slovenia	24	12
UK	52	11
European Commission	195	N/A

In an important review in 2013, Veljanovski, a respected academic and practitioner, concluded that the performance of the OFT fell short of its image as a highly rated enforcer.[100] He concludes that the OFT's survey research resting on the 'three pillars of competition compliance' (knowledge of competition law, voluntary compliance and sanctions and enforcement) lacked a theory and credibility, and that the survey finding of 'significant deterrent effects' is questionable, if not implausible. He pointed out that those interviewed in the surveys had little knowledge of competition law, and the sanctions and enforcement levels were very low. He proceeded to analyse the statistics on the OFT's enforcement activities undertaken between 2002 and 2012 from its online Public Register[101] and list of ongoing investigations.[102] After clearing the backlog of cases in around 2007, he identified

---

[98] *A Competition Regime for Growth: A Consultation on Options for Reform* (Department for Business, Innovation & Skills, 2011) 45, available at http://www.bis.gov.uk/assets/biscore/consumer-issues/docs/c/11-657-competition-regime-for-growth-consultation.pdf. Challenged at *The OFT's Response to the Government's Consultation* (Office of Fair Trading, 2001) OFT 1335, 57.

[99] *A Competition Regime for Growth*, ibid, 47 and Table 5.1.

[100] Veljanovski (n 84).

[101] Available at http://www.oft.gov.uk/OFTwork/competition-act-andcartels/ca98/decisions/?Order=Date#. UK9tjYcifiw.

[102] Available at http://www.oft.gov.uk/OFTwork/competition-act-and-cartels/ca98current/#.UK9uRYcifiw.

that the OFT began operating at a much lower level of enforcement activity, presumably also affected by the global financial crisis. Veljanovski's findings are shown in Table 15.3.

Table 15.3: OFT Decisions by Type of Offence, 2001–2012[103]

	Cartel	Anti-competitive agreements	Abuse of dominance	Total
Investigations	28	15	17	60
Decisions	26	7	14	47
Infringements found	20	5	5	30
Leniency applicants	10	—	—	—
Fines (£ '000)	302,841	274,510	17,000	594,351
Firms fined	211	19	2	232

Over the period the OFT found an infringement in 30 of the 47 (64 per cent) decided cases, but if 26 'missing decisions' were included the decision rate fell to 72 per cent. The average duration for an investigation of an anti-competitive agreement was 37 months, for cartels 33 months, and an abuse of dominance 25 months. In 16 (35 per cent) investigations the OFT failed to find an infringement, and cases took an average of 21 months to conclude. Ten of the 28 cartel cases were initiated by a whistleblower or leniency applicant. Surprisingly the OFT took 38 months on average to conclude leniency-based investigations compared to 29 months for those without a leniency applicant.

Fines were imposed in 21 of 46 decisions on 232 offending firms. Fines after leniency but before appeal were £594 million—about £303 million was imposed on firms participating in cartels (51 per cent); £274 million (46 per cent) on firms engaged in anti-competitive agreements; and £17 million (three per cent) on those abusing their dominant position. In nine of the 30 infringement decisions no penalty was imposed. Appeals against the OFT's decisions on grounds of liability and/or the level of fines imposed were relatively common. One or more firms appealed in 16 of the 30 (53 per cent) infringement decisions.

Since 2010, it is notable that the CMA has been more focused in enforcement, and has employed a wider and more integrated range of powers and sanctions. A fine of £58.5 million was imposed on British Airways in 2012 in a civil case on airline passenger fuel surcharges,[104] and in 2011 a £28.59 million fine was imposed on the Royal Bank of Scotland in a case on loans for professional services firms.[105] Almost half of the CMA's new cartel investigations opened since 2010 have been intelligence led.[106] In the *Marine Hose* case, three individuals were given significant custodial sentences (20 to 30 months), disqualified

---

[103] Veljanovski (n 84).
[104] Case reference CE/7691-06.
[105] Case reference CE/8950/08. A follow-on damages action brought by the UK Ministry of Defence against British Airways was settled.
[106] S Branch, 'Competition, the Revised Cartel Offence and the CMA—A New Landscape' speech to the Business Crime–2014 Conference, at https://www.gov.uk/government/speeches/sonya-branch-speaks-about-the-cartel-offence-and-the-cma.

as directors (five to seven years) and made subject to confiscation orders (totalling over £1 million).[107] A programme to educate industry on key lessons drawn from completed casework has been implemented, such as speaking at trade conferences, publishing articles in trade magazines, social media and sending an open letter to the industry, which was distributed by the National Franchise Dealer Association to approximately 80 per cent of the 200,000 people working in franchised car and commercial vehicle dealers in the UK, highlighting lessons from a cartel case involving Mercedes-Benz commercial vehicles.[108] The CAT stated a policy of affording the CMA a large margin of appreciation in its decisions to accept commitments, since it held that overly-intrusive judicial oversight would but be appropriate in relation to the exercise of judgement by the CMA.[109]

VI. Conclusions

The enforcement policies issued successively by the OFT and CMA are distinctive when compared with those of the other public authorities examined in chapters 13 and 14. The approach in competition law has stuck firmly to deterrence as being the central objective, in its classic form discussed—and rejected—in chapters two and four above, of aiming to ensure compliance by creating fear of the imposition of large penalties. The OFT and CMA have stated the classic formulation of the importance of both the severity and likelihood of sanctions, with no reference to the findings of behavioural psychology that any effect of sanction severity is at best limited and the major driver of a policy that is based on repression is the perceived likelihood of being found out and perhaps publicly ridiculed and losing reputation (chapter one). It is noteworthy that there are references to risk of exposure and loss of reputation, which were in fact found in the surveys carried out, but the impact of that information appears to have been lost and ignored. There must be a strong suspicion that the studies were all mis-framed: They were carried out largely by economic consultants who were well aware of the orthodoxy on deterrence espoused by the authorities, and so the questions asked and certainly the answers found, were framed in terms of the anticipated framework of deterrence. As appears from the review of enforcement policies of various other authorities in chapter 13, and other analyses, such as the no blame reporting culture in civil aviation discussed at chapter 19, the enforcement policy in relation to competition law is a curious outlier, notably in its central reliance on deterrence.

---

[107]   *Competition Law Risk. A Short Guide* (CMA and Institute of Risk Management, 2014). Case COMP/39406—*Marine Hoses.*

[108]   See *Commercial Vehicles Case Cartel Enforcement Lessons* (CMA, 2014) at https://www.gov.uk/government/publications/letter-from-the-cma-to-the-motor-industry-about-cartel-enforcement, and the tweets from the CMA:

— Where's the line between chatting and forming a cartel?
— A single meeting can be enough to find yourself part of a cartel
— Smaller businesses don't get a free pass on competition law

[109]   *Skyscanner Limited v Competition and Markets Authority* [2014] CAT 16.

Similarly, the OFT/CMA statements make little reference to policies that have been adopted by so many other sectors, and constitute government policy (see chapters eight and nine), in relation to better regulation, cooperation with and support of businesses, reduction in burdens and redress. The OFT was at best lukewarm in relation to being given a regulatory redress power in the Consumer Rights Act 2015, and far preferred to rely on the private enforcement and class action mechanism—again, in stark contrast to the focus on outcomes adopted by other agencies, and hence their assumption of responsibility for ensuring that redress was made. These points are discussed further in chapter 16. The current position calls for a reasoned explanation of why enforcement of competition law should differ from any other sector or approach.

The OFT has been called on by business to take into account in setting fines the extent to which adequate steps had been taken to comply with competition law, and situations where infringements were committed by 'rogue employees', but has recently rejected this approach. Its reasons were that:

> [A]n effective competition law compliance culture will tend to deter 'rogue employees' by increasing the perception that their activities will be detected and unacceptable, with serious consequences for the employee involved. Furthermore the OFT is concerned to avoid creating any incentives for businesses to identify an employee responsible for the breach, since the employee concerned may be a 'scapegoat' rather than a rogue employee. It therefore does not consider that it is appropriate to address the rogue employee issue in a publication intended to help businesses to take practical steps to comply with competition law. Far from encouraging compliance, doing so could create the impression that businesses did not necessarily need to take responsibility for the actions of their employees.[110]

Those reasons are entirely unconvincing and produce injustice. They fail to separate the responsibilities and roles of companies and of employees and the effects of enforcement on each. It is clear that rogue employees should be deterred by stiff penalties (imposed by a company, a professional body and by the state) but it is not clear how imposing fines that primarily affect shareholders, innocent employees and ability to compete would deter rogue employees. Further, the competition 10 per cent discount for leniency is lukewarm compared with 33 per cent offered under the bribery regime. The policy demonstrates negligible understanding of the incentives that affect the behaviour of companies and individuals, and how they can be affected by regulatory action.

In the case of the OFT/CMA, in contrast to many other enforcement agencies, enforcement policy is influenced by several stimuli. First, there is the doctrine of economic theory, which is highly influential. Second, there is the research sponsored by the OFT itself. Third, there is general government policy. Considering the totality of evidence, one is left with the impression that the influences rank in that order of priority.

At a more mundane level, the policy conclusions of the OFT on both competition and consumer enforcement have been based on what appears at first sight to be an extensive series of research reports but, on closer analysis, turns out to be a somewhat numerically limited base of surveys, with little substantial, reliable empirical and objective research

---

[110] *How Your Business Can Achieve Compliance. Summary of Responses to the OFT's Consultation and OFT's Conclusions and Decision Document* (Office of Fair Trading, 2011) para 2.40.

into the drivers for compliance or non-compliance. References in those surveys or policy documents to behavioural economics are almost non-existent, and there are no references to academic sources on responsive regulation or cognitive or behavioural psychology.

Some differences can be observed, however, between the approaches to consumer and competition enforcement, the former being examined in the previous chapter. The former is somewhat more 'responsive' in approach, and refers to advice and support, being closer to the approach in other sectors, even if not going as far as the other sectors usually do. This somewhat schizophrenic difference in approach between two parts of the same authority call for an explanation, and strengthen the call for an explanation of why competition enforcement should be different.

On a more positive note, UK competition enforcement adopts a more rational approach than many other jurisdictions in focusing on wrongdoing by individuals as well as companies. The classic macro-economic approach is to treat companies as the sole wrongdoer and source of wrongdoing, and to leave them to sanction and control all employees, as discussed in chapter two. It is, of course, true that individuals are sometimes subject to sanctions in USA, but this does not apply under the EU regime, although individuals could be prosecuted under some national regimes. There are several references in the surveys to the fact that it is the behaviour of *individuals* and their fear of loss of reputation that is the critical issue. The UK director disqualification regime constitutes a sanction that is the apex of the Ayres and Braithwaite pyramid, but a range of lesser sanctions, such as warnings, are not used.

From 2015, competition enforcement will be expanded by the new mechanisms for damages, especially collective damages. The argument that restoration of market balance, and hence compensation, is not the function of a public authority is looking thin and outdated. It has been pointed out that the current enforcement policies of many European competition authorities fail to identify whether the combination of public and private enforcement has achieved restoration of market balance or competitive conditions, or are even capable of identifying the extent to which infringers' anti-competitive activities have distorted the market.[111] Thus, it should be the duty of a competition regulator to ensure not just that compensation is paid, but to establish how much is paid. That proposition was supported by Which?[112] Ezrachi and Ioannidou have noted that the black line distinction between the functions of public and private actors has started to crumble. It is no longer appropriate that public actors just deal with findings of infringement in those cases that they choose to deal with and only then impose fines, but do not look at the restorative functions and the market effects.[113] Scholars have called for the inclusion of agreements on damages in any settlement procedure on economic grounds.[114]

---

[111] C Hodges, 'A Market Based Competition Enforcement Policy' [2011] *European Business Law Review* 261; C Hodges, 'European Competition Enforcement Policy: Integrating Restitution and Behaviour Control' (2011) 34(3) *World Competition* 383.

[112] *Response by Which? to Consultation* (Which?, 2012), available at https://www.gov.uk/government/consultations/private-actions-in-competition-law-a-consultation-on-options-for-reform.

[113] A Ezrachi and M Ioannidou, 'Public Compensation as a Complementary Mechanism to Damages Actions: from Policy Justifications to Formal Implementation' (2012) 3 (6) *Journal of European Competition Law & Practice* 536.

[114] Response by a group from the ESRC Centre for Competition Policy to Consultation, para 4.4, available at https://www.gov.uk/government/consultations/private-actions-in-competition-law-a-consultation-on-options-for-reform: 'This would be a better, more cost effective, alternative to running the case again as a follow-on litigation ... Pure follow-on cases would add nothing positive to deterrence but mean duplication of enforcement efforts.'

The move by other agencies away from 'command and control' enforcement towards risk-based, responsive, restorative enforcement complies with national policies on reducing regulatory burden, and relying on most businesses to comply through controlled self-regulation. Different means of identifying non-compliance would operate than a discredited leniency policy. It is strongly suggested that these more modern enforcement policies can be expected to encourage satisfactory compliance at far more acceptable cost—both to agencies' budgets and to the private sector economy as a whole—than a 'deterrence only' policy.

The creation of a new CMA is a golden opportunity to review competition enforcement policy, to instil a new culture aimed at compliance, and to bring the OFT into compliance with criminal law and government policy on regulatory enforcement. If its current policy is not illegal, there is a clear case that it is ineffective and disproportionate.

16

Conclusions on Current Enforcement Policy

This chapter summarises the conclusions from all of the chapters in Part C. It will be clear from the above account of the development of regulatory policy over the past decade that the area is complex and that there has been extensive evolution in policy. Various strands of thought intertwine. The purpose of this section is to summarise the main strands and the current position.

I. General Description

The regulatory system in the United Kingdom is sophisticated and complex. It relies on meta-regulation, involving tiers comprising parliamentary and governmental oversight, public authorities, co-regulatory arrangements with sectoral trade associations, and undertakings' internal compliance systems. Principles of full transparency and the involvement of all stakeholders in governance are observed at all levels so as to build trust and guard against abuse.

Regulation is organised vertically for many specialist sectors, but more horizontally for general consumer trading, bribery and corruption, and both vertically and horizontally for competition law. Notable features of regulation in the United Kingdom are: The existence of many public regulatory agencies, a strong history of reliance on self- and co-regulation, increased trust in both public and private regulation through strengthening of governance and compliance of relevant bodies, transparency, and recognition that all bodies and structures can be mutually inter-dependent.

National policies have been established by government on regulation and regulatory penalties, based on Better Regulation and risk-based principles. These principles and requirements have been imposed on most regulatory agencies. The public authorities have extensive formal enforcement powers under criminal law, to which have recently been added civil law enforcement powers. Almost all public authorities' enforcement powers and policies have been reformed in the past four years, to focus on delivering *outcomes* of compliance, restitution of market balance and redress for those harmed. These reforms mirror parallel changes in criminal law enforcement. The enforcement policies now emphasise supporting traders' compliance through advice, guidance and internal compliance mechanisms. Redress and restoration have also been included as objectives of public enforcers, instead of leaving such outcomes to private litigation by those harmed. New regulatory goals, powers and approaches have been developed to support enforcers' activities in ensuring that redress occurs.

Affecting future conduct is a clear goal of public authorities' actions, but rarely through imposition of deterrent sanctions. The area in which deterrence alone is used is competition law, but that approach is looking insufficiently effective and highly wasteful of resources for both public and private actors.

II. Regulatory Policy

Perhaps the most striking development is a consistent trend, supported by successive governments and enforcement bodies, away from understanding regulation and enforcement in terms of 'command and control' and towards collaborative partnerships between most businesses and enforcers, based on two-way communication and advice. This approach accords with academic theories on 'new governance' and 'open corporations' discussed in chapter 11, although almost no policy documents refer to such theories or, indeed, any academic analysis. The approach reflects a political view of the role of government as not involving top-down management of 'delivery chains' but of creating a system and a set of incentives within which local actors then operate, creating the conditions in which performance will improve.[1] Such a policy supported a level of devolution of power to local people whilst balancing central oversight and coordination.

Responsive regulation had its origins at least as far back as the 1960s, as indicated by the research noted in chapter 11. In those enforcement bodies who were not dominated by economic thinking, the question of how to maximise compliance by companies received a very practical answer: Monitor, inspect, suggest, persuade, and only rarely threaten and pillory. A whole range of authorities found that that approach works in many different situations, and is the central approach.

The origins of the revolution in enforcement through the Better Regulation approach clearly lie in a drive for increased efficiency, by reducing burdens on both public finances and the 'regulatory burden' on business. Such policies pre-dated the economic crisis by some years, but assumed high profile as a means of recovering from that crisis. The development of these ideas led directly to grounding the design and operation of regulation on the concept of risk. Two features underpin risk-based regulation. First, both regulators and businesses have to prioritise their resources in addressing hazards, and analysing and ranking hazards in terms of relative risks provides a rational tool for achieving this. Risk-based regulation involves a grading and prioritisation of risks. Second, given the difficulty in comparing hazards across a wide range of different sectors, each with differing regulatory landscapes, systems and priorities, a risk analysis tool provides a matrix for rational generalisation. This is so even though there remains a difference in 'colour' between serious risks in different sectors, such as nuclear power accidents, flooding, a virulent virus, food contamination or an air crash, not least in their differing actual and potential levels

---

[1] D Cameron, speech to Civil Service Live, 8 July 2010; see M Hallsworth, *System Stewardship* (London, Institute for Government, 2011).

of incidence and damage. Future work should attempt to increase coordination between individual sectors in comparative risk analysis: The 2014 Regulators' Code encourages regulators to share data and the revised consumer enforcement bodies' landscape encourages increased coordination between bodies.

A fundamental feature is the publication by central government of high level policy on regulation, in the form of principles of regulation and of enforcement. The Regulators' Codes also shifted from the 2007 to 2014 versions from a longer rule-based statement towards a shorter more principles-based statement.

A further fundamental feature has been the requirement for bodies to create and publish enforcement policies. This has resulted in the proliferation in the period from roughly 2011 to 2014 of multiple enforcement policies by regulatory agencies, that are somewhat uncoordinated, despite the existence of broad principles such as those on the function of criminal law in enforcement and the Macrory penalties guidelines. A detailed analysis of a number of statements of enforcement policy is set out at chapter 13. At this stage, it appears that there has been no official coordination or systemic review of them, and no standardisation or best practice in enforcement policy or techniques. Such work could usefully be undertaken.

A consequence of the publication of the purposes of a regulatory body and of its enforcement policy is that its performance and enforcement record can be measured against the relevant regulatory principles such as proportionality, efficiency and so on, and that challenge can occur. Indeed, the opportunity for challenge is now a striking feature of the 2014 Regulators' Code and the Primary Authority scheme. The idea here is to go so far as to enlist businesses as regulators of enforcers. This approach turns regulation on its head. It is a logical progression from the viewpoint that one of the functions of regulators is to support, rather than hinder, valid economic activity, and to support growth. Out of that position grew the imposition of requirements on regulators and enforcers through a Code, and the later recognition that supervision or 'enforcement' of the Code could not be done by government itself but by challenge from businesses.

III. Enforcement Policy

The position in relation to the substance of enforcement policy is particularly striking. Instead of general policy statements that offenders should be treated severely, and that deterrence is either the primary goal of enforcement or at least one of the major goals, we find statements by successive governments that most businesses aim to comply with the law and that compliance is to be assisted by 'soft' means, notably providing information and advice so that either large or small businesses (who will have differing abilities to respond to regulatory systems and to adopt compliance systems and enlist expert internal or external resource) can be expected to react without punitive approaches. The depiction of business as not to be trusted but to be constantly challenged and deterred is largely absent from the UK or European landscape.

There are essential milestones of the revolution in British enforcement policy in the past decade. A number of key policy statements in different contexts together not only adopt similar philosophies and approaches but also add up collectively to a coherent approach to enforcement. First, the scene was set by statutory statement of the purposes of all criminal sentencing[2] as not only encompassing the punishment of offenders, the reduction of crime (including its reduction by deterrence), and the protection of the public, but also the reform and rehabilitation of offenders, and the making of reparation by offenders to persons affected by their offences. Second, there were the Law Commission's principles that criminal law should only be employed to deal with wrongdoers who deserve the stigma associated with criminal conviction because they have engaged in seriously reprehensible conduct. It should not be used as the primary means of promoting regulatory objectives.[3] Third, Macrory's statement of six Penalty Principles that should apply to all regulatory enforcement:[4]

1. Aim to change the behaviour of the offender;
2. Aim to eliminate any financial gain or benefit from non-compliance;
3. Be responsive and consider what is appropriate for the particular offender and regulatory issue, which can include punishment and the public stigma that should be associated with a criminal conviction;
4. Be proportionate to the nature of the offence and the harm caused;
5. Aim to restore the harm caused by regulatory non-compliance, where appropriate; and
6. Aim to deter future non-compliance.

Fourth, the enshrining of the Better Regulation, Hampton and Macrory philosophies into a policy that was binding on enforcers under the 2007 Regulators' Compliance Code and Regulators' Code from 2014.[5] Fifth, the reform and codification of civil sanctions under the Consumer Rights Act 2015.

The espousal of responsive regulation has not been limited in impact to the UK. The OECD (Organisation for Economic Co-operation and Development) has adopted the same language, concepts and policies. It has specifically recommended a risk-based approach, and has clearly been adopted in the UK, in relation to both regulation and enforcement. As a consequence of this, categorisation of business risks and enforcement are now undertaken on the basis of risk, in other words, the potential for and magnitude of harm that might occur through an absence of compliance.

Purnhagen has recently said that whenever the EU (European Union) failed to regulate responsively, it was forced to remedy this lack of taking into account 'the social' reactively.[6] He cited three examples of where this occurred: Cheese from raw milk, consumer product safety standards and GMO authorisation. He recommends that the EU should avoid looking only at the proper function of the democratic legitimacy chain (legality) and the output of an efficient internal market (output-legality), since this runs the risk of the people of Europe not subscribing to the actions of EU institutions any longer (input-legitimacy). Instead, he firmly asserts that regulating responsively and systematically has the potential to ensure trust in the European Institutions.[7]

---

[2] Criminal Justice Act 2003, s 142.

[3] *Criminal Liability in Regulatory Contexts: A Consultation Paper* (The Law Commission, 2010) Consultation Paper No 195, paras 1.28–1.30.

[4] Macrory reviewed 61 national regulators, but not financial regulators or regulators of privatised utilities.

[5] *Regulators' Code* (Department for Business, Innovation & Skills, 2013).

[6] K Purnhagen, 'Why do we need Responsive Regulation and Behavioural Research in EU Internal Market Law?' in K Mathis (ed), *European Perspectives on Behavioural Law and Economics* (Cham, Springer, 2014), ch 4.

[7] K Lenaerts, '"In the Union we Trust": Trust-enhancing Principles of Community Law' (2004) 41 *Common Market Law Review* 317–43.

Yeung has noted the shift from 'hard' to 'soft' enforcement in negotiated penalty settlements, bargaining and negotiation in law enforcement, enforcement undertakings and firm-specific advice by regulators.[8] I suggest that things have gone further, and the essence of 'enforcement' has moved beyond 'compliance' and is now on cooperation and culture. The image of a regulator or enforcer as the most powerful actor in a binary relationship with a regulatee has given way in many cases to a matrix of inter-connected relationships between multiple actors (regulators, ombudsmen, courts, notified bodies, trade associations, many companies, insurers, reinsurers and consumers) and can only work as a pluralistic system on the basis of collaboration. But further evidence for those developments is set out in subsequent chapters.

It is clear that the toolbox of enforcement powers has been significantly widened. The empirical research noted in chapter 11, such as that by Hawkins, describes both a range and a hierarchy of responses by inspectors, regulators and authorities. Ayres and Braithwaite graphically described these in pyramidal form, representing the fact that the most serious sanctions (death penalty, removal of licence to operate, disqualification as a director) were rarely used, but still had potential as perhaps a deterrent but also as providing the ultimate boundary of a framework under which more cooperative approaches could operate effectively.

At various points, the preferences of different governments have had significant impact, such as on whether regulators should be granted power to impose civil sanctions, acting as investigatory, prosecutor, judge and jury, or whether the functions of challenge and sentencing should be the responsibility of separate entities, with the latter function being that of the courts or some other tribunal. However, this ideological split over civil sanctions should not obscure the fact that such formal sanctions play a relatively limited role in the practice of enforcement.

The recent change is about more than adding civil sanctions to criminal sanctions. Whether the sanctions and penalties are classified as criminal, administrative or civil, the toolbox now comprises a wide range of levers, that can be viewed in a hierarchy of severity, with removal from the market at the top, and public sanctioning such as prosecution for serious transgressions, down to far greater informal, negotiated or volunteered agreements such as formal undertakings (future breach of which may trigger formal action) or informal agreements to change behaviour. It also includes market and reputational responses and sanctions—strongly noted in the OFT (Office of Fair Trading)'s surveys of businesses. As a result, enforcers have a considerable range of tools to support compliance, but at the same time the increased flexibility gives considerable discretion. The parallel development of rehabilitative, responsive or compliance goals in both criminal and business 'enforcement' is striking. However, there has been criticism that enforcement powers have been developed in regulatory statutes in the absence of an overarching cross-sectoral framework, and especially that the use of fines differs between enforcers.[9]

---

[8] K Yeung, 'Better Regulation, Administrative Sanctions and Constitutional Values' (2013) 33(2) *Legal Studies* 312–99.

[9] M Corry and G Mather, *Fine Outcomes. Making Better Use of Regulatory Fines* (London, European Policy Forum, 2013) para 8.

What is lacking here is a coherent or unified understanding of which tool(s) might be used in what circumstances, and whether there should be some consistency between different enforcers. One possible way of addressing this potential disparity or conflict of approach between regulators is that the new opportunities for collaboration within the regulatory communities and for challenge by regulates might produce some harmonisation. However, some more organised approaches may be required.

Nevertheless, the purposes of enforcement have also widened, in two ways. First, enforcement is aimed at *behaviour* and producing or supporting future compliance (but not, or not just, deterrence) and, second, the focus has broadened to include producing *holistic outcomes*, which encompass restoration and redress of harm and rebalancing of markets, rather than just sanctioning of infringers.

An expansion of the purposes of regulatory activity (enforcement is hardly the correct word any more in many circumstances) into supporting ongoing compliance has produced the logical development that regulators and enforcers need to be concerned with *outcomes*. Merely imposing a penalty and expecting that an offender will behave in future, is simply not credible as enforcement behaviour and more. Achievement of compliance may involve many tools and approaches, and vary depending on the circumstances, but it is about supporting an ongoing high level of compliance with the rules, so that risk is reduced. In short, as Gill and Frankel have recently commented in a global review of regulation, the formal system of 'policing' regulatory regimes is built around 'alarms going off' rather than 'regular routine patrols'.[10]

Less than 10 years ago, a continuum in enforcement approaches was described between a *cops and robbers* climate and a *service for clients* climate.[11] The former is characterised by mutual distrust and enmity, with a focus on enforcing through audits and fines, persecution and prosecution, and attempts to detect 'tax ghosts'. The latter is characterised by mutual trust, based on cooperation supported by perceptions of fair treatment, personal and social norms.[12] In the past decade, the balance has clearly swung towards the more open, collaborative end in terms of policy. In a striking example of New Public Management, tax authorities have turned towards considering taxpayers as customers.[13] More detailed examples of this will be examined in succeeding chapters. It does not mean that strenuous enforcement responses do not occur—actions against banks are clear evidence to the contrary—but it does mean that the objectives are not solely punitive but include major elements of ensuring ongoing compliance, beyond merely putting faith in the belief that imposition of a punitive penalty will induce respect and compliance.

---

[10] D Gill and S Frankel, 'Learning the Way Forward? The Role of Monitoring, Evaluation and Review' in S Frankel and J Yeabsley (eds), *Framing the Commons: Cross-Cutting Issues in Regulation* (Wellington, New Zealand, Victoria University Press, 2014) 60.

[11] E Kirchler and E Hoelzl, 'Modelling Taxpayers' Behaviour as a Function of Interaction between Tax Authorities and Taxpayers' in H Elffers, P Verboon and W Huisman (eds), *Managing and Maintaining Compliance* (The Hague, Boom Legal Publishers, 2006).

[12] I Ramsay, *Consumer Law and Policy. Text and Materials on Regulating Consumer Markets* (Oxford, Hart Publishing, 2012).

[13] M Andrews, 'New Public Management and Democratic Participation: Complementary or Competing Reforms? A South African Study' (2003) 26(8–9) *International Journal of Public Administration* 991; G Gruening, 'Origin and Theoretical Basis of New Public Management (2001) 4(1) *International New Public Management Journal* 1; S Horton, 'Guest Editorial: Participation and Involvement—The Democratisation of New Public Management?' (2003) 16(6) *International Journal of Public Sector Management* 403.

The new approach is not intended to be light on serious wrongdoing. There is a difference between 'light regulation' and 'light enforcement'. The former may be applied to many types of activity but that does not imply that enforcement responses will be 'weak'. Explicit statements have been made that most breaches will face penalties that are quicker and easier to apply while there will be tougher penalties for rogue businesses that persistently break the rules. However, what has changed is that responses to non-compliance have changed from traditional punishment-based sanctions to a broader range of techniques, based on empirical evidence that there may be better ways to bring about future compliance than mere punishment. The approach is focused firmly on outcomes rather than on moral retribution.

IV. A Comparison of Sectoral Approaches

All the above developments and features can be illustrated by a brief summary of the enforcement policies of the various authorities noted in chapters 13 to 15. All of the agencies have issued enforcement policies since 2010, some for the first time. They display significant similarities in largely conforming to the government's risk-based and responsive approach—with the notable exception of the Competition and Markets Authority (CMA) in relation to competition law, as noted in chapter 15, which sticks rigidly to deterrence as its central approach. A comparison here between CMA in relation to competition and consumer enforcement, and with the Serious Fraud Office (SFO)'s approach to serious fraud and bribery, shows the differences in approach. Whilst the competition and fraud policies treat the non-compliance as serious crimes, the core of the CMA's policy is to impose large fines on the firms involved (and to try, albeit without much success until recently) to prosecute a few individuals, and to leave payment of damages to other means, whereas the SFO's central approach is to prosecute the individuals and remove their illegal gains, which the SFO sees as a clear part of its duty to ensure are returned to victims.

Omitting the competition side of the CMA and the SFO, all the other authorities in our survey adopt responsive regulatory approaches, emphasising working with firms to achieve compliance through support and advice as essential functions. Indeed, the enforcement policies of the CMA's consumer side and the Civil Aviation Authority (CAA) include classic examples of Ayres-Braithwaite pyramids.

A recent independent policy review of the practice of different regulators in relation to use of financial penalties was critical that enforcement powers have been developed in regulatory statutes in the absence of an overarching cross-sectoral framework and they should be standardised.[14] It concluded that some authorities used to achieve different end goals:

— The Financial Conduct Authority (FCA) sees financial penalties as a means of punishment and deterrence, not a substitute for consumer compensation.
— In contrast, Ofgem accepts other measures in lieu of a penalty, with consumer redress packages and restitution.

---

[14] Corry and Mather (n 9) para 8.

— The ORR financial penalty framework focuses primarily on compliance, threat to change behaviour. But redress is taken into account as a mitigating factor.
— Ofwat has a broad approach encompassing redress and restitution as well as punishment through disgorgement of any gain and deterrence. Unlike the FCA, penalties are applied as an alternative to other sanctions, not in parallel.
— Ofcom liked punish, but use of daily penalties highlights a greater emphasis on deterrence.

The study authors concluded that the transformation of fines into customer benefits means that a newer form of penalty, one which is seen to give some behaviour redress to customers, is more likely to be used as a regular feature of the regulators' tool kits.[15]

The Enforcement Management Model (EMM) approach of the Health and Safety Executive (HSE) is in practice a rather unwieldy tool, and although it seeks to promote objectivity and consistency it leaves considerable scope for subjective interpretation. The heart of the matter lies in the statistics on enforcement, which suggest that other policy and resource factors are more decisive than the EMM.

The OFT's studies include several consistent findings about the problems of SMEs and the best means of supporting them to comply with regulation. The studies reveal a picture of SMEs struggling with regulatory burdens and compliance, needing but finding difficulty in accessing reliable support, believing that they are largely compliant and perhaps oblivious to whether this is the case, and being perfectly willing to change things when a person whom they respect suggests that they should do things differently. There are several references to the fact that large or small businesses rely on trade associations for advice and practical information about how to comply with regulation. The extension of the Primary Authority scheme has imaginatively seized on this point, and the indications are that the ability for groups of companies and especially trade associations to sign up to the scheme are working very well in terms of disseminating information, advice and change. Could local Chambers of Commerce similarly assist here?

Local authorities have a significant but under-appreciated role in shaping the economic and social well-being of an area across a wide range of matters, including food safety, health and safety in workplaces, licensing, housing and fire safety.

Almost every enforcement policy surveyed includes an incentivised approach for firms to put things right before sentencing in order to bargain or qualify for a reduction in sanction. Many of the provisions are extensive. These are sensible incentivisers. The approach is exemplified by Ofgem's 'culture of customers first' policy. Several of the authorities refer to considering formal enforcement measures as a last resort, and prefer to resolve issues of ongoing behaviour by agreement, especially voluntary proposals from traders.

It would be good to see the adoption of a unified national approach to this sort of plea bargaining, encompassing Deferred Prosecution Agreements, so that a unified message is communicated nationally across all sectors. It would be even better to see the point stated not just in negative terms (if you put things right you will earn a reprieve) but also as a simple positive message (we do things right, and expect everyone to do that, and putting things right after they have gone wrong is just part of this).

---

[15] ibid, para 138.

The last point reflects a general issue. The language of enforcement has evolved from repression and deterrence towards compliance and expecting compliance as the norm.[16] Basing enforcement on encouraging compliance, rather than only on imposing deterrence, has moral, behavioural, political and economic aspects. It is essentially positive, rather than negative. The FCA and Ofgem still refer to 'credible deterrence' but other authorities hardly mention deterrence. Those two agencies, as do others, in effect have an ultimate deterrent at the top of the pyramid through control over ongoing licence to operate. Is it necessary to say more, if a punitive approach is in fact not desired or desirable in most cases? Of course, activity that is classified as criminal deserves serious proportionate response. But is it time, given frequent statements that 'we believe that most businesses try to comply, and we want to help them to do so', which also includes enlisting the assistance of businesses in identifying instances where things have gone wrong, either internally or with other firms, that the next step should be a national statement based in positive language? Might the business community step up, adopt a positive ethical statement on intention to ensure compliance, and thus, bargain for a Primary Authority-like partnership and sympathetic consideration in the event that things go wrong, on the basis that members who subscribe will actively seek to do the right thing before and after any problems might be encountered?

The term 'credible deterrence' has limited meaning as a policy statement. It could be valid if *empirically* breaches of the rules were identified by the particular regulatory authority with very high frequency, and offenders exposed to public censure. But there is no way of knowing what the frequency of identification and exposure is: Wrongdoers who are not identified will merely scoff and continue to believe that they will escape exposure. It is true that the term 'credible deterrence' carries some value in the political and media arenas, since it carries the implication of tough and successful identification and sanctioning of wrongdoers that are required in those arenas. But it is a hostage to fortune if major scandals in fact occur that are not identified by the authority's activities—for which the risk must currently be high.

V. Redress

As noted above, the addition of a focus on *outcomes* to the responsibilities of enforcers has logically led to a widening of their remit, which is seen most strikingly in relation to their assuming responsibility for overseeing *redress* or *rectification*. Redress is specifically listed as an objective under both the criminal and regulatory sanctioning regimes. Redress was included in the Macrory principles, and in the first statement of the regulatory principles in 2007, although it was omitted from the simplified recast in 2014.

The focus on outcomes and redress brings a holistic approach to responding to setting matters right, by combining behavioural and redress outcomes. It addresses the problem noted in Part A above of inconsistency if public and private enforcement mechanisms are pursued separately and not coordinated. It is felt in the consumer world that recompense packages can have a much greater deterrence effect than fines.[17]

---

[16] CAA's enforcement policy: Routine compliance is the norm.
[17] Corry and Mather (n 9) para 125.

The oversight of public bodies in payment of redress by businesses can clearly replace the need for private individuals to do so in at least some circumstances. Instead of abandoning private parties to seek redress themselves by initiating action in the courts for damages (or injunctions), public bodies can not only be involved in facilitating or delivering redress but (as evidence noted in chapter 13 above shows) can be highly effective in doing so. Indeed, such techniques may be more effective, fast and cheap than traditional civil pathways or other techniques. A regulatory approach can be especially useful when large numbers of people or widespread business behaviour is involved. Hence, regulators can be effective in addressing mass or collective redress issues, without the cost, delay or abuse of private collective civil litigation.

Similarly in criminal enforcement, greater effectiveness can be anticipated through widening of techniques to give better outcomes (lower repeat offending), and adopting a restorative justice technique in place of punitive approach for many offenders, but also involving making reparation as an outcome.

The extent to which the UK authorities—with the unacceptable exception of the OFT/ CMA—have adopted a new approach is striking. Traditions that enforcers and regulators are aiming solely at prosecutions have given way with remarkable speed to a major broadening of approach to encompass ensuring that fair outcomes are achieved and redress is paid or harm otherwise rectified. The success of cases brought by the FCA, SFO and Ofgem noted above is impressive. Not only have illicit gains been removed, but compensation has been paid swiftly and effectively. The availability of regulatory redress powers working together with ombudsmen (now commonplace for financial services, communications, energy and in the process of expanding to all other sectors) is particularly striking. Ofgem and Ofwat (expecting firms to institute redress immediately) have shown that they do not need formal court-backed redress powers to achieve swift payments. On the pyramid approach, however, it should assist if the authority were to have a generic redress power, and evidence from the FCA and Danish Consumer Ombudsman shows that such a power is rarely needed to be activated as cases are resolved informally, but ideally subject to court or independent approval.

The empowerment of public authorities is complemented by an expansion of ombudsmen or related 'alternative dispute resolution' (ADR) bodies (ombudsmen and ADR schemes linked to business sector codes of conduct), which will increasingly work together in delivering both increased behaviour control for traders and redress for consumers. 'Private enforcement' of individual rights has moved away from courts and lawyers to ombudsmen and other ADR mechanisms,[18] and this trend is set to be cemented by EU legislation.[19] Collective private enforcement will not be encouraged through collective actions (class actions) but will take place through the ADR schemes and otherwise be nudged, or overseen by the public authorities, backed by wider restorative justice powers available through

---

[18]   C Hodges, I Benöhr and N Creutzfeldt-Banda, *Consumer ADR in Europe* (Oxford, Hart Publishing, 2012).

[19]   Proposal for a Directive of the European Parliament and of the Council on alternative dispute resolution for consumer disputes and amending Reg (EC) No 2006/2004 and Dir 2009/22/EC (Dir on consumer ADR), COM (2011) 793/2; and Proposal for a Regulation of the European Parliament and of the Council on online dispute resolution for consumer disputes (Reg on consumer ODR), COM(2011) 793/3.

courts.[20] These provisions are welcome for consumers.[21] There is likely to be increased—and swifter—payment of compensation, and rectification of poor trading, that will drive trading standards upwards and hence, as the Government intends, contribute to economic recovery and vibrancy.[22]

A very large number of policy papers have been reviewed in this Part. Two points are striking by their absence. First, nowhere apart from in relation to competition enforcement is it argued that litigation or private enforcement is a potential means of affecting business behaviour. Second, there is no reference to a risk that any regulatory body is concerned about a risk of capture by its regulate businesses or is at risk of such capture. There are, not surprisingly, some references to regulators needing sufficient resource, but no suggestion that they cannot succeed.

VI. Governance and Capture

It may be objected at this point that the relationship between businesses and enforcers may be at risk of becoming too cosy, and that enforcers would be 'captured' by businesses. Such an objection would certainly be made in the USA. The UK policy response is that various arrangements are designed to minimise this risk, and to be successful in doing so, as OECD mandates.[23] First, regulatory agencies are established to be operationally independent of government: They may be supervised by ministers but are run by CEOs and independent boards that include consumers and others, and feedback mechanisms from stakeholders.[24] Second, governance and transparency requirements apply to public bodies, with periodic inspection by the National Audit Office. Authorities publish remits, modes of operation, objectives, policies, performance, information on remuneration and conflicts, in accordance with standard Nolan principles that apply across the civil service. Third, the professional ethos of officials is strong in the UK, and arrangements are in place for peer coordination and support, both horizontally and coordinated through the Better Regulation Delivery Office (BRDO), which holds regular meetings. Fourth, transparency enables meta- oversight by elected legislators, the regulated community, and the general public and media commentators. The UK model of regulatory architecture employs tiers of regulation and self-regulation (chapter 17), which operate on a coordinated basis. Regulatory systems frequently adopt multiple governance and oversight features. These can be horizontal or

---

[20] A parallel can be seen with use of more sophisticated regulatory powers in fighting fraud and major crime: *Deferred Prosecution Agreements Government Response to the Consultation on a New Enforcement Tool to Deal with Economic Crime Committed by Commercial Organisations* (Cm 8463: Ministry of Justice, October 2012) available at https://consult.justice.gov.uk/digital-communications/deferred-prosecution-agreements/results/deferred-prosecution-agreements-response.pdf.

[21] *BIS Consultation on New Powers to Protect Consumers* (Consumer Focus, 05/11/2012) at http://www.consumerfocus.org.uk/news/bis-consultation-on-new-powers-to-protect-consumers.

[22] Contemporaneous with the enforcement proposals, see Lord Heseltine, *No Stone Unturned in Pursuit of Growth* (Department for Business, Innovation & Skills, 2013) http://www.bis.gov.uk/assets/biscore/corporate/docs/n/12-1213-no-stone-unturned-in-pursuit-of-growth.pdf.

[23] See *Recommendation of the Council on Regulatory Policy and Governance* (Paris, OECD, 2012); Draft *Principles for Governance of Regulators* (Paris, OECD, 2013).

[24] J Black, 'Tensions in the Regulatory State' (2007) Spring *Public Law* 58.

vertical (tiers of oversight are evolving). Such governance is intended to afford transparency, and hence provide voice and scrutiny. In order to give greater focus and impact to the consumer voice, bodies such as Consumers Direct and Consumer Focus have been formed, and effort put into consumer education, particularly access to information on rights, responsibilities and options on redress. Fifth, enforcement decisions are subject to either imposition by courts or review by tribunals. Sixth, a recent technique adopted within the EU is peer review of agencies and notified bodies through carrying out joint inspections, for example in competition law,[25] medical devices[26] and the new structure of financial services.[27] This has been reported to enable both horizontal and vertical learning by all involved.

The US phenomenon of capture involves several aspects: Capture of the CEO by appointment by the President of a political collaborator; economic capture by voting of finance by Congress; and capture by regulates, or through 'revolving doors'. In the UK, by contrast, the first aspect is far diminished, the resource issue is influenced by parliamentary scrutiny of government as the source of funds, and the third is an issue of culture and distance.

The UK academic literature reveals a dearth of scholarly empirical evidence on capture. There are statements that capture is rare, and that the approach to governance and transparency are generally adequate to address the risk.[28] The debate is largely theoretical.[29] Benefits of independent regulators rest on the claims to expertise, flexibility, relative independence from political influence, and consistency over time.[30] Attacks that may have greater substance than capture are based on an account that agencies lack democratic legitimacy and accountability for their decisions.[31]

VII. Review

It is suggested that a next step should be a concerted overarching review of the enforcement policies and practices of enforcement authorities, involving a significant element of dialogue in which authorities can debate which approaches are more appropriate than others,

---

[25] Communication from the Commission: Ten Years of Antitrust Enforcement under Reg 1/2003: Achievements and Future Perspectives, COM(2014) 453.

[26] *Restoring Confidence in Medical Devices. Reporting on the Success of the PIP Action Plan, European Commission* (European Commission, 2014) at http://ec.europa.eu/health/medical-devices/regulatory-framework/pip-action-plan/index_en.htm.

[27] Report from the Commission to the European Parliament and the Council on the operation of the European Supervisory Authorities (ESAs) and the European System of Financial Supervision (ESFS), European Commission COM(2014) 509.

[28] K Hawkins, *Environment and Enforcement: Regulation and the Social Definition of Pollution* (Oxford, Clarendon Press, 1984) 192; G Trumbull, 'Consumer Policy' in D Coen, W Grant and G Wilson (eds), *The Oxford Handbook on Business and Government* (Oxford, Oxford University Press, 2010); Ramsay (n 12).

[29] K Yeung, 'Design for Regulation' in J van den Hoven, I van de Poel and PE Vermaas (eds), *Handbook of Ethics, Values and Technological Design* (Vienna, Springer, 2014).

[30] D Levi-Faur, 'The Global Diffusion of Regulatory Capitalism' (2005) 598 *Annals of the American Acdemy of Political and Social Sciences* 12; B Levy and PT Spiller, *Regulations, Institutions and Commitment* (Cambridge, Cambridge University Press 1996).

[31] See eg C Graham, 'Is There a Crisis in Regulatory Accountability?' in R Baldwin, C Scott and C Hood (eds), *A Reader on Regulation* (Oxford, Oxford University Press, 1998); R Baldwin, *Rules and Government* (Oxford, Clarendon Press 1996); K Yeung, 'The Regulatory State' in R Baldwin, M Cave and M Lodge (eds), *Oxford Handbook on Regulation* (Oxford, Oxford University Press, 2011); C Scott, 'Accountability in the Regulatory State' (2000) 27 *Journal of Law and Society* 38.

and why deviations from general policy are justified, and they can also have the opportunity learning from a peer review process and from the conclusions that flow from behavioural psychology that are set out in chapter one above.

This chapter has focused on the traditional regulator–regulatee relationship, in which the former is a public body and the latter is a private body. However, references appear throughout the above examination to wider ideas of collaboration and open governance and open corporations. These ideas can be taken further by noting the important place of self- and co-regulation within the regulatory structure, in which separate private sector bodies play roles as regulators. To that issue we now turn in chapter 17.

Part D

Regulation and Compliance by Business

17

Standards, Accreditation, Self-Regulation and Co-Regulation

I. Introduction

This chapter examines how businesses 'self regulate' their activities in a concerted fashion. It covers a number of different techniques, in which groups of businesses adopt a concerted arrangement to observe a particular standard of business practice, based on mutual agreement. There may, or may not, also be arrangements to monitor compliance by those who have agreed to the arrangement, and to be subject to some sanction in the event of non-compliance. But the essential elements are agreement, rules and a particular standard, usually related to an aspect of the quality of trading, and publication of the arrangements.[1] The arrangements are usually established, and sometimes administered, by trade associations, usually on a sectoral basis.

The inquiry into self-regulation is relevant for three reasons. First, self-regulation forms an important place in how businesses apply law—or other external norms of society—to themselves. It will be clear from previous chapters that a conception of legal obedience and enforcement that only considers public forms (regulators or courts) is far from a complete conception of what happens on the ground. In a subsequent chapter we will continue this approach by considering how business structures apply internal systems to achieve compliance with rules. For the present, we need to focus on compliance mechanisms that are created by groups of businesses, usually through a trade association or some other body or structure.

Second, many public regulatory regimes work together with self-regulatory structures or as part of co-regulatory schemes, so it is necessary to understand how the individual components and combinations operate. Third, the issue of how to design regulatory systems that are effective, and also reduce expenditure from public funds on public enforcement authorities, has become highly relevant for contemporary public policy. The cost of public regulation and of private law instruments in times of reducing regulatory burdens, and the ability of appropriately-designed self-regulation to provide a better (cheaper) method of solving problems of market failure and information asymmetries than conventional public

---

[1] Self-regulatory schemes have different ways of achieving their aims. All create rules and some sort of operational activity designed to encourage the modification of behaviour, including persuasion, pre-entry checks, complaint based disciplinary action, proactive monitoring and disciplinary action, and intervention initiative: *Business Leadership in Consumer Protection. A Discussion Document on Self Regulation and Industry-led Compliance* (Office of Fair Trading, 2010) OFT1058, para 2.34.

regulation, have supported the case for self-regulation, and the desirability of maximum feasible self-regulation.[2]

A number of different approaches can be identified under a broad heading of 'self-compliance'. The general use of standards, accreditation, self-regulation and co-regulation are outlined below, but these modes are illustrative and not comprehensive. Also relevant are certification, registration, licensing, industry guidelines, consumer signposting, public commitments, approval, advice and training, complaint handling and dispute resolution, redress schemes, monitoring and a range of possible sanctions.[3] It will be seen that the individual elements frequently operate together. As examples of leading arrangements, the Consumer Codes Approval Scheme, the Advertising Standards Authority (ASA) and the two contrasting arrangements for the advertising of medicines will be outlined at the end of the chapter.

The UK has a well-established policy of encouraging self-regulation, which has strong cultural roots stretching back to nineteenth century origins,[4] is a notable feature of the UK's approach to regulation and enforcement, and has led this approach amongst European states.[5] Codes developed within trades and professions as a means by which professionals regulated their relationship with one another, developing later to include their relationships with their clients—and in some cases subsequently being underpinned by statute. Many trade associations developed codes in the twentieth century, partly as a means of self-regulation of appropriate standards and to police against unacceptable quality, and partly as a defence against imposition of public regulation. A 2005 study concluded that the new wave of ADR (alternative dispute resolution) procedures should be seen not so much as part of a deregulatory agenda, but as a more efficient and effective mode of operation for the regulatory state—consistent with the 'better regulation' agenda.[6]

The prevalence of pre-existing self-regulatory arrangements was given statutory backing in 1988 when the OFT (Office of Fair Trading) was permitted to require a person making a complaint about misleading advertising to show that 'established means' had had a reasonable opportunity to deal with it and had not done so, and the OFT was required to have regard to 'the desirability of encouraging control, by self-regulatory bodies, of advertisements'.[7] In practice this meant that the OFT and the pre-existing relevant bodies (notably the ASA) were able to refer complaints between each other according to which was the more appropriate to take action in each case. The ASA is recognised as the first port of call (or 'established means') for resolving complaints about advertisements across all media and tackling non-compliance.

---

[2] P Selznick, 'Self-regulation and the Theory of Institutions' in G Teubner, L Farmer and D Murphy (eds), *Environmental Law and Ecological Responsibility: The Concept and Practice of Ecological Self-organization* (Chichester, John Wiley & Sons, 1994).

[3] See *Business Leadership in Consumer Protection. A Discussion Document on Self Regulation and Industry-led Compliance* (n 1).

[4] *Regulating in the Consumer Interest* (Consumer Focus, 2010).

[5] *United Kingdom, Challenges at the Cutting Edge* (Paris, OECD, 2002). I Bartle and P Vass, *Self-Regulation and the Regulatory State—A Survey of Policy and Practice* (Centre for the Study of Regulated Industries, University of Bath School of Management, 2005). The government's Better Regulation Task Force published a sequence of reports pressing the advantages of self-regulation between 1999 and 2005.

[6] Bartle and Vass, ibid. The government's Better Regulation Task Force published a sequence of reports pressing the advantages of self-regulation between 1999 and 2005: See ch 9 above.

[7] The Control of Misleading Advertising Regulations 1988 (CMARs).

The place of self- and co-regulatory arrangements has been firmly entrenched in British lawmaking within the past decade, as a technique that has to be considered before legislative regulation is proposed. The entire Better Regulation policy is based on that premise that public regulation should only be introduced, or continued, where it is absolutely necessary. Accordingly, alternatives to regulation should always be considered wherever appropriate. Process rules require consideration of all options (including 'do nothing' and self- or co-regulation) and detailed comparative evaluation of their advantages and disadvantages, and of their costs, including the impact assessment process and scrutiny by the Regulatory Policy Committee.[8] Details are discussed in chapter nine.

The structure of the chapter is as follows. We begin by defining the major types of arrangements: Standards and accreditation, earned recognition, self-regulation and co-regulation. Some of the major examples are then examined: The Consumer Codes Approval Scheme and the ABTA Code of Conduct system. This is followed by examination of the extensive self-regulatory system that governs advertising, exemplified by the Codes and roles of the Advertising Standards Authority, the Prescription Medicines Code of Practice Authority and the Proprietary Association of Great Britain (PAGB). These examples illustrate both ex ante vetting systems and ex post complaint-based systems. The German self-regulatory system for unfair commercial practices is then noted, again showing how private sector bodies operate almost to the exclusion of public enforcement, in this case by some ex ante vetting and strong ex post power to seek court injunctions. Academic analysis of the area of self-regulation is then reviewed before conclusions are suggested.

II. Government Policy

The Coalition Government set out a firm policy on coming to office in 2010 that 'command and control' regulation was appropriate in some circumstances, but all alternatives should first be evaluated before deciding to introduce regulation.[9] Details of that policy have been discussed in chapter nine. In relation to alternatives, the Government said:

> At the core of the new framework is a focus on helping policy-makers to identify the most effective approach to achieving a desired policy outcome by ensuring alternative approaches to regulation are thoroughly explored, and that traditional 'command and control' regulation is seen as the last, not first, resort.[10]

It set out an illustrative 'map of options' which included all of the main types discussed above, plus information and education, and a 'do nothing' option: See Figure 17.1. Consideration of means other than regulation was also recommended by the OECD (Organisation for Economic Co-operation and Development) Regulatory Policy Committee.[11]

---

[8] See also *Code of Practice on Guidance on Regulation* (Better Regulation Executive, 2008) at http://www.bis. gov.uk/files/file53268.pdf. Similarly, specified bodies are under a duty not to impose or maintain unnecessary burdens in the exercise of regulatory functions: Regulatory Enforcement and Sanctions Act 2008, ss 72, 73(3)–(6).

[9] *Reducing Regulation Made Simple: Less Regulation, Better Regulation and Regulation as a Last Resort* (HM Government, 2010).

[10] ibid, para 23.

[11] *Recommendation of the Council on Regulatory and Policy Governance* (Paris, OECD, 2012) Recommendation 4.

Self-regulation: An approach initiated and undertaken by those whose behaviour is to be regulated. For example, an industry or profession might choose to develop and adopt its own code of practice promoting ethical conduct.

Examples
— Unilateral codes of conduct
— Customer charter
— Unilateral sector codes
— Negotiated codes

Co-regulation: Similar to self-regulation but involves some degree of explicit government involvement. For example, an industry might work with government to develop a code of practice. The code would usually be enforced by the industry itself, or a professional organisation, rather than by the government.

Examples
— Recognised codes
— Statutory codes
— Approved codes
— Voluntary agreements
— Trade association codes approved by the office of fair trading
— Accreditation and standards

Information and education: Can be used to empower consumers to take their own informed decisions.

Examples
— Inform, enhance consumer choice
— Independent recommendation schemes
— Ratings systems
— Labelling, disclosure

Economic instruments: Can be used to modify behaviour by adjusting the economic incentives facing businesses and citizens. This approach allows individuals to make their own decisions, based on their estimates of whether the benefits of acting in a certain way justify the costs.

Examples
— Taxes
— Subsidies
— Quotas and permits
— Vouchers
— Auctions
— Competition

No new intervention: In many instances, it might not be necessary for government to initiate new action at all. Regulation and its alternatives will almost always impose costs as well as generating benefits, so policy makers should think carefully about whether action by government is required at all.

Examples
— Using existing regulation
— Simplify or clarify existing regulation
— Improved enforcement of existing regulation
— Make legal remedies more accessible or cheaper
— Do nothing at all

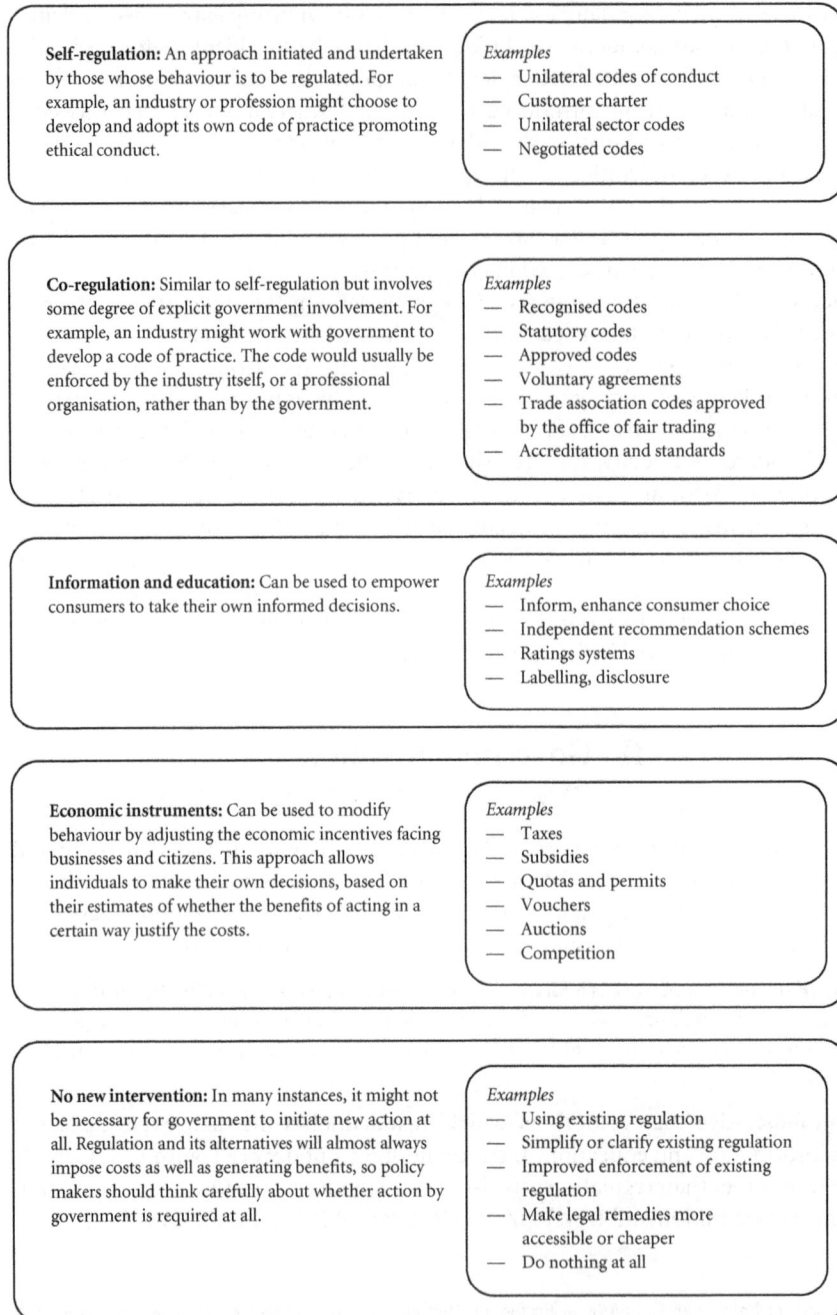

Note: The list above is not intended to be exhaustive.

Figure 17.1: Examples of Alternatives to 'Command and Control' Regulation[12]

[12] ibid, Diagram 2.

III. Typology

A. Standards and Accreditation

Standards are defined, in a broad sense, as 'an agreed way of doing something'. They may define the characteristics of a particular outcome, such as the physical or chemical composition of a good, substance or service,[13] or a process by which something is done. The substance of the standard may be agreed by a particular group, such as the qualifications of a professional body, or given formal legal recognition. Compliance with standards is voluntary, but affords benefits that flow from external recognition of their achievement. Many industry and professional bodies publish standards,[14] compliance with which may be a qualification of membership or of the achievement of higher or specialist achievement. Compliance with some standards affords commercial or legal benefits, as discussed below. Compliance with a standard may be demonstrated by an internal procedure or by external assessment and certification. Standards exist at national (British Standards: BS), European (EN) and international (ISO/IEC) levels. Publicly Available Specifications (PAS) are also used.

Accreditation is a process which determines the technical competence and integrity of an organisation that offers conformity assessment services such as testing, certification, inspection and calibration.[15]

B. Earned Recognition

Companies that demonstrate compliance with standards may earn recognition from regulators, by showing that they have achieved a desired level of control over legal requirements, and hence deserve a level of trust in compliance. There would be no legal assumption that compliance has been achieved, but a regulator's risk-based policy would justify ranking those that comply at a lower level, enabling a reduction in oversight and inspection visits.[16]

An example applies in environmental management. Businesses may choose to adopt the business management tool, and be certified by an accreditation body, of complying with the environmental management system standard ISO 14001. The Environment Agency gives credit to such businesses under the Integrated Prevention and Control legislation, resulting in reduced environmental levies and reduced inspection requirements.

---

[13] The British Pharmacopoeia, established in 1864 and run by the British Pharmacopoeia Commission, provides authoritative official standards for pharmaceutical substances and medicinal products: See https://www.pharmacopoeia.gov.uk.

[14] Notably the British Standards Institute, founded in 1901 as the world's first national standards body, now a non-profit distributing Royal Charter Company, recognised by the government as the national body under a Memorandum of Understanding, and as the UK member of the international and European standards organisations, ISO/IEC and CEN/CENECLEC respectively.

[15] The UK national accreditation body is the UK Accreditation Service (UKAS), a non-profit distributing company limited by guarantee, which operates under a Memorandum of Understanding with the Department for Business, Innovation & Skills.

[16] See *Standards and Accreditation. Tools for Delivering Better Regulation* (BSI and UKAS, undated).

C. Self-Regulation

Many self-regulatory schemes exist, usually operated by a trade association, such as through a code of practice, customer charter or other voluntary agreement. A code of practice can be given formal recognition or approval by a regulator. An example of this is the Health and Safety Executive's approved code of practice on the control of Legionella, which requires employers and landlords to carry out a risk assessment undertaken by a 'competent person'. The standard BS 8580: 2010 specifies a Legionella risk assessment, and inspection organisations may be assessed against this by UK Accreditation Service (UKAS), resulting in an increased level of confidence by businesses and the HSE in compliance and the existence of an acceptable level of risk.

A study for the Better Regulation Delivery Office in 2013 noted that there is a lack of literature relating to business awareness of regulatory-type requirements, perhaps because businesses may struggle to differentiate between core regulation and regulatory-type requirements with which they comply.[17] The quasi-regulatory bodies interviewed indicated that business awareness of regulatory-type requirements comes largely from requirements via their supply chains. In addition, trade associations often make businesses aware of both their own and other industry-specific requirements. Experiences of regulatory-type requirements therefore seem to vary by sector, for example high industry standards in construction and manufacturing may mean that there are an increased number of regulatory type requirements or more stringent requirements which can lead to high costs for businesses. The research suggested two broad areas for policy makers to focus on: Best practice and data sharing so as to reduce the number of times businesses have to provide the same information to different bodies, and addressing inconsistencies and reducing burdens.[18]

D. Co-Regulation

Co-regulation operates through a tiered approach. At the top level, government sets legal requirements, usually in general terms, expressed as essential requirements, principles or outcomes, but without mandating the mechanisms or details by which the legal requirements are to be satisfied. Below this, the market or standards may develop that fill out particular options for achieving the essential requirements. Compliance with some officially-recognised standards may trigger a legal presumption of compliance with the essential requirements.

Numerous examples of the co-regulatory model exist. In 2011 the government cited the following leading examples:[19]

— The OFT's Consumer Codes Approval Scheme (CCAS), described below. The model establishes benchmarks for redress schemes that are approved by the OFT, including a

---

[17] *Business Experience of Regulatory-type Burdens Imposed by Non-regulatory Bodies. Report by ICF GHK* (Better Regulation Delivery Office, 2013) BIS/13/591.

[18] Organisations identified during this study which were said to set requirements that lead to high perceived benefits include the International Standards Organisation (ISO), Trustmark, the Marine Stewardship Council (MSC), Investors in People (IiP) and the British Frozen Food Federation (BFFF).

[19] *Better Choices: Better Deals. Consumers Powering Growth* (Department for Business, Innovation & Skills and Cabinet Office Behavioural Insights Team, 2011).

template and requirements that provide for oversight and governance aspects in both horizontal and vertical dimensions.

— The supervision by Ofcom of two private sector ADR bodies in the communications sector.[20]
— The Estate Agents Redress Scheme: This was superceded by a legislative framework in 2013.[21]
— Government endorsement of *Trustmark*, an accreditation scheme to give consumers the opportunity to identify tradespersons in the domestic building/home repair sector who agree to abide by minimum standards for trade competency and practice.
— Local authorities' *Buy with Confidence* scheme,[22] put together by a partnership of Local Authority Trading Standards Services to help consumers avoid rip-offs and cowboys by providing a list of reputable local businesses in a wide range of different trades.
— The Local Authority Assured Trader Scheme Network (LAATSN), set up in 2006 to assist the development of assured trader schemes that are operated by Local Authority Trading Standards Services.[23] LAATSN aims to bring greater consistency to such schemes through its underpinning framework of minimum standards, and to develop schemes by providing best practice guidance. LAATSN is supported by the Local Authorities Coordinators of Regulatory Services (LACORS), the Trading Standards Institute, and the CMA (Competition and Markets Authority).
— The Advertising Standards Authority (ASA, see below), the independent body responsible for resolving complaints about advertisements across all media and tacking non-compliance. Its Advertising Codes supplement legislation and fill gaps where the law does not reach, for instance, they ensure that advertisements are tasteful, decent and contain measures which display a social responsibility.
— Gas Safe Register, the official gas registration body for the UK appointed by the Health and Safety Executive who make sure all 120,000 gas engineers on the register are gas safe and qualified to work with gas.
— The Bar Council, the Law Society, the General Medical Council: examples of arrangements for the self-regulation of professions which are largely industry-led but under the supervision of a statutory regulator.

A further example of co-regulation is the UK Green Deal programme, which aims to improve the energy efficiency of properties. The general requirements for Green Deal installers are specified in the Energy Act 2011, and detailed requirements are set out in PAS 2030, developed by BSI with input from stakeholders. Installers' compliance with PAS 2030 is assessed by certification bodies accredited by UKAS.

The longest running code is that operated by the travel agents' trade association, ABTA.[24] This has been operated to a high standard for many years, although it does not have approval under CCAS since there was a difference of view between ABTA and the OFT over the relevance of a consumer insurance aspect. Many businesses and their trade associations would historically have been most reluctant for the trade association to act as a regulator

[20] Ombudsman Services: Communications and CISAS; see C Hodges, I Benöhr and N Creutzfeldt-Banda, *Consumer ADR in Europe* (Oxford, Hart Publishing, 2012) ch 11.
[21] Under the Enterprise and Regulatory Reform Act 2013, ss 83–88; The Redress Schemes for Lettings Agency Work and Property Management Work (Approval and Designation of Schemes) (England) Order 2013/3192.
[22] http://www.buywithconfidence.gov.uk/sitepages/bwchome.aspx.
[23] http://www.ukecc-services.net/LocalAuthorityAssuredTraderSchemeNetwork.cfm.
[24] The scheme is described in Hodges, Benöhr and Creutzfeldt-Banda (n 20).

of the sector, and impose sanctions on their own members. In contrast, the attitude of the travel sector has changed significantly in this respect over time. It is notable that ABTA regards itself as the sector's guardian of good practice, for the good of all operators, and exerts significant influence on behaviour, including imposing fines and other sanctions on non-compliant members. This situation contrasts with traditional criticism of codes that the only sanction available is the ultimate one of expulsion from membership of the trade association, and that this is ineffective, inflexible and unlikely to be applied. Clearly, practice is developing.

The largest structural example of co-regulation is possibly the EU's New Framework for products, which is underpinned by over 4000 harmonised European standards.[25]

The European Commission approved incorporating self-regulatory codes within a legislative framework in its 2001 Green Paper on EU consumer protection.[26] The general duty on traders to act fairly in the Directive on Unfair Commercial Practices[27] recognises the role of codes of conduct, if individual Member States so decide, in controlling unfair commercial practices, and as being alternative to recourse for remedies to judicial or administrative proceedings, although not deemed equivalent to such judicial or administrative proceedings.[28]

IV. The Consumer Codes Approval Scheme

A. Development of the CCAS

It is interesting to see how codes of practice have been supported through the development of mandatory requirements for official recognition. Business codes have a lengthy history, and have developed since the 1960s alongside the growth of consumer protection and regulatory law generally.[29] Motivations for introducing self-regulation have evolved as markets have matured. From the 1960s, self-regulation was presented by business as a way for consumers to identify better traders who subscribe to codes of practice. In reality, however, those business sectors that established codes of conduct were primarily concerned to enhance the image of the trade or sector and to forestall the possible or threatened

---

[25] The system is described in ch 19 below. See also C Hodges, *European Regulation of Consumer Product Safety* (Oxford, Oxford University Press, 2005). Regulation (EU) No 1025/2012 on European standardisation.

[26] *Green Paper on EU Consumer Protection* 2001, COM(2001) 531 final.

[27] Dir 2005/29/EC of the European Parliament and of the Council of 11 May 2005 concerning unfair business-to-consumer commercial practices in the internal market and amending Council Dir 84/450/EEC, Dirs 97/7/EC, 98/27/EC and 2002/65/EC of the European Parliament and of the Council and Reg (EC) No 2006/2004 of the European Parliament and of the Council ('Unfair Commercial Practices Directive'), OJ L 149, 11.6.2005, 22.

[28] ibid, art 10.

[29] An early evaluation was G Borrie and A Diamond, *The Consumer, Society and the Law* (London, Penguin Books, 1964). See also *Government and Consumers: A Consultation Document* (National Consumer Council, 1997). In 2000, the Secretary of State for Trade and Industry (and consumers) stated that consumer markets had changed out of all recognition since the 1960s: Speech by S Byers, 'New Economy: New Consumerism' at the Social Market Foundation, 21 September 2000. More recently see S Weatherill, 'Consumer Policy' in P Craig and G de Búrca, *The Evolution of EU Law* 2nd edn (Oxford, Oxford University Press, 2011).

imposition of statutory regulation by government.[30] The threat of possible regulation grew from the 1970s, but self-regulation also matured into a viable alternative to regulation by government.[31] Soft law was also seen by consumer representatives as a means of controlling behaviour that crosses national boundaries, but self-regulation alone would be unacceptable to consumers where the risks involved fraud, risk to life and/or health, where unfair advantage is taken of vulnerable people, where competition alone cannot deliver essential services to consumers who are not of commercial interest to suppliers, and where regulation is needed to make competition work.[32]

When the OFT was established in 1973, although principally concerned with introducing criminal sanctions, the Director General of Fair Trading was required to encourage trade associations to prepare, and to disseminate to their members, codes of practice for guidance in safeguarding and promoting the interests of consumers.[33] The initial focus of the early codes was on unfair contract terms, as was noted by Lord Borrie, writing in 1984:

> Between 1973 and 1984, 20 codes were launched, covering a wide variety of industries—electrical servicing, shoes, the motor industry and travel are among them. One important aspect of several codes of practice is that certain types of contractual terms that have given rise to consumer complaint in the past are banned and other terms are required to be inserted in contracts. The codes therefore help to rewrite standard form contracts so that they are less one-sided than before.[34]

The OFT initially assessed the detailed wording of individual codes, but found this to be resource intensive and took too long to get through the approval process. There were also problems of signposting for consumers, since there were too many different badges and logos of different codes: This was too confusing for consumers. From 1991, it endorsed codes that met a series of 'best practice' criteria.[35] By 1995, Britain was described as 'something of a haven for self-regulation', being the principal controlling device for a wide range of activities including, notably, advertising, financial services, and the practice of a large variety of professional occupations.[36]

A major concern was how to avoid the inherent problem that the business sponsors and members of a self-regulatory regime would design and operate it to their advantage without outcomes that adequately observed the principles of consumer requirements[37] in producing balanced markets, not least in restricting competition.[38] This phenomenon of bias is a manifestation of the regulatory theory of 'capture' of a system by those who should be subject to its controls.[39] As information technology expanded, there was also concern that

---

[30] I Ramsay, *Consumer Protection. Text and Materials* (London, Weidenfeld and Nicolson, 1989) 135.

[31] *Better Business Practice. How to Make Self-regulation Work for Consumers and Business* (National Consumer Council, January 2001) PD 54/P/00.

[32] *Soft Law in the European Union, A Discussion Paper by the National Consumer Council* (National Consumer Council, 2001) PD 027/2001. See also *Self Regulation. The National Consumer Council's Position* (National Consumer Council, March 2003) PD 26/03.

[33] See G Borrie, *The Development of Consumer Law and Policy—Bold Spirits and Timorous Souls* (London, The Hamlyn Lectures, 1984) 36th series.

[34] Borrie, ibid.

[35] G Howells and S Weatherill, *Consumer Protection Law* 2nd edn (Farnham, Ashgate, 2005) 72–77 and 580–85.

[36] A Ogus, 'Rethinking Self-Regulation' (1995) 15(1) *Oxford Journal of Legal Studies* 97–108.

[37] The key consumer principles were stated in 1997 to be access, choice, safety, information, fairness, redress and representation: see *Government and Consumers: A Consultation Document* (n 29).

[38] N Philipsen, 'Regulation of Professions: A European Perspective' in M Faure and F Stephen (eds), *Essays in the Law and Economics of Regulation In Honour of Anthony Ogus* (Antwerp, Intersentia, 2008).

[39] AI Ogus, *Regulation: Legal Form and Economic Theory* (Oxford, Oxford University Press, 1994).

the key consumer requirement of having adequate information on price, quality and terms of trade to enable full and fair purchasing choices to be made was not being fulfilled. The OFT felt that consumer ignorance was so high that a significant level of consumer detriment was occurring.[40]

In 1998 the European Commission's Consumer Policy Action Plan[41] referred to the 'political currents driving the growth of consumer policy [being] part of a wider political trend for policies that deliver effective solutions to the problems faced by the general public'. The emphasis on solutions is interesting, and rare in policy documents of that time, which were primarily focused on consumer rights and not on results.[42] The Commission emphasised a need for cooperation between consumers and business, and a balancing of interests.

In an important consumer policy White Paper in 1999, the UK government repeated the policy of driving vigorous competition in markets and well informed, empowered consumers.[43] In addition to strengthening public powers and sanctions for enforcement of competition law under the Competition Act 1998, and initiatives on increasing consumer self-reliance through better education, information and advice, a new regime was proposed for codes of practice. The White Paper set out targeted enforcement against rogue traders (including powers to ban continual offenders from trading) while reducing burdens on honest businesses to allow them to focus on giving good customer care.

The new UK regime for codes was based on establishing a strong consumer brand for codes that were endorsed by the OFT, effectively marketed.[44] The new approach introduced a two-stage approach which aimed to encourage trade associations to re-assess their existing codes of practice or introduce new codes of practice that address consumer detriment within their sectors. The first stage (establishing core criteria) could be delivered within OFT's existing powers, and the second stage (an approval power) was mandated under the Enterprise Act 2002. The core criteria for the new OFT CCAS were published in July 2001[45] and core criteria and guidance notes were issued in 2008. The Enterprise Act also empowered the OFT to take steps to promote consumer education.[46] Similar developments took place in other sectors. For example, the Communications Act 2003 specified a duty on the communications regulator, Ofcom, to promote self-regulation. The regulatory architecture of the financial services sector does not use codes,[47] but does rely on principles that encourage self-regulation, such as transparency and extensive rules. An international review in 2010 focused on four aspects of transparency: Disclosure of complaints data, disclosure

---

[40] *Consumer Detriment under Conditions of Imperfect Information* (Office of Fair Trading, 1997) Research Paper 11.

[41] *Consumer Policy Action Plan 1999–2001* (European Commission, 1998).

[42] In 2008, the Commission stated that 'Policies need to be more evidence-based and outcome-oriented': Communication from the Commission: Monitoring Consumer Outcomes in the Single Market. The Consumer Markets Scoreboard, http://eur-lex.europa/LexUriServ/LexUriServ.do?uri-COM:2008:0031:FIN:EN:PDF.

[43] *Modern Markets: Confident Consumers, The Government's Consumer White Paper* (Department of Trade and Industry, 1999).

[44] *The OFT's New Approach to Consumer Codes of Practice, A Consultation Paper* (Office of Fair Trading, 2001).

[45] Available at: http://www.oft.gov.uk/shared_oft/Approvedcodesofpractice/oft344.pdf. An earlier version was *Consumer Codes Approval Scheme: Core Criteria and Guidance* (Office of Fair Trading, 2004).

[46] See *A Strategy and Framework for Consumer Education, a Consultation Paper* (Office of Fair Trading, 2004); *Consumer Education: A Strategy and Framework* (Office of Fair Trading, 2004).

[47] See ch 20 below. A Report by the Regulatory Policy Committee in 2010 urged that regulators should not presume that regulation is the answer to every problem, and that all options should be considered, including the 'do nothing' option: *Reviewing Regulation: An Independent Report on the Analysis Supporting Regulatory Proposals, December 2009–May 2010* (Regulatory Policy Committee, 2010)

of firms entering an enforcement process, the transparency of regulators' governance procedures, and disclosure of complaints data about financial promotions.[48] These factors paralleled the OFT's CCAS approach.

A business survey in 2001 found that businesses viewed the purpose of corporate self-regulation through a code of conduct as being the promotion of high standards of integrity in business transactions. Codes represented what was by then regarded as good commercial practice. The common factor influencing the development of business ethics in general was found to be the desire to protect or improve reputation. This was found to be more common in heavily branded companies than in SMEs (small and medium sized enterprises).[49] A detailed comparative review by the UK government in 2003 of consumer policy regimes in various countries noted:[50]

> A common incentive for businesses is the need to keep customers happy and in most markets this will act as a deterrent against behaviour which causes consumers major problems. Most consumer problems are dealt with bilaterally and retailers often compete in terms of the ease with which they are willing to accept returns and correct faults. Building a reputation for high levels of service is seen as a key variable in brand building and growing profitable companies.

Maintaining balance and fairness as between consumers and business was emphasised. Further expansion of the OFT CCAS was mooted amongst a long list of reforms in 2005.[51] A scholarly review found:

> The impact, and potential, of the 'new wave' of self-regulation has surprised us, and one tentative conclusion is that current trends reflect a move towards a new regulatory 'paradigm' or exemplar. The policy and practice implications are quite profound—reconciling an extensive role for the regulatory state with light-touch regulation based on securing industry led, self-regulatory solutions. Self-regulation has for all intents and purposes become 'embedded' within the regulatory state—and our survey shows that it reflects various forms of public–private 'partnership', perhaps best reflected in the general term 'co-regulation'. It is clear to us that such a regulatory model has to be founded on transparency and accountability for it to inspire confidence and be sustained; transparency and accountability which applies equally to both the regulators and the regulated. Effective compliance regimes are an integral part of this process. Through this, roles and responsibilities are better understood, control can be effectively exercised through the provision of information, and trust can be developed.[52]

In 2009–2010 the OFT published a series of research and policy papers on regulatory issues, which strongly confirmed the place and utility of self-regulation, business codes and their dispute resolution functions. It noted the wide range of self-regulatory arrangements, which defied categorisation, but involved different aspects of the following components:[53]

a. Structure (ranging from an umbrella scheme, to complex governance arrangements, distinct self-regulatory arrangements, an industry body, or a working party);

---

[48] J Leston, *Transparency as a Regulatory Tool. An International Literature Review* (The Financial Services Consumer Panel, 2010).

[49] See *The Anderson Review of Government Guidance on Regulation. Business Perspectives of Government Guidance. Research Study Conducted for Department for Business, Enterprise and Regulatory Reform. Final Report* (Ipsos MORI, 2008).

[50] *Comparative Report on Consumer Policy Regimes* (Department of Trade and Industry, 2003).

[51] *A Fair Deal For All: Extending Competitive Markets: Empowered Consumers, Successful Business* (Department of Trade and Industry, 2005).

[52] Bartle and Vass (n 5).

[53] *Business Leadership in Consumer Protection. A Discussion Document on Self Regulation and Industry-led Compliance* (n 1).

b.   Coverage (entire industry, industry partnerships, all members of a single industry body, voluntary scheme within an industry body);
c.   Toolkit (codes of practice, standards, accreditation/certification/licensing, industry guidelines, registration, consumer signposting, public commitments, approval, advice and training, compliant handling and dispute resolution, redress schemes, and monitoring and a range of sanctions);
d.   Operational activity (persuasion, pre-entry checks, compliant-based disciplinary action, proactive monitoring and disciplinary action, intervention initiative);
e.   Legislative backing or government involvement (significant, low, none);
f.   Quality level (raise standards above legal minimum, legal compliance, non-legal standard).

The OFT stated the benefits and risks of self-regulation,[54] the benefits being:

a.   Helps to build a good reputation;
b.   The industry takes control (an example being the Car Servicing and Repair Code);
c.   provides speed and flexibility (an example being The Payments Council, established in 2007);
d.   utilising industry knowledge (the Renewable Industry Association consumer code);
e.   raising standards above the law (an example being the Direct Selling Association);
f.   providing consumer redress (the Ombudsman for Estate Agents Company Ltd's complaints procedure);
g.   affording better regulation for regulators.

Whereas the risks were stated as:

a.   Partial coverage;
b.   rules are ineffective;
c.   ineffective monitoring and limited sanctions;
d.   anti-competitive practices; and
e.   self-regulation being seen as a solution, whereas in practice there are no neat solutions.

An economic analysis recognised the utility of self-regulation in solving quality issues, and in contributing to overcoming situations in which consumers found it hard to judge quality in advance of making purchasing decisions (the asymmetric information issue).[55] This linked with research that found that reputation and the influence of consumers was the most important driver of business compliance or non-compliance.[56] In its overall policy statement of 2010, the OFT reaffirmed its commitment to supporting self-regulation as a central part of its regulatory armoury, based on its belief that self-regulation 'offers benefits for consumer protection and adds real value to the functioning of efficient markets'.[57] It considered that self-regulation cannot remove a credible and effective statutory backstop

---

[54]   ibid. See also the similar list in *Policy Statement. The Role of Self-regulation in the OFT's Consumer Protection Work* (Office of Fair Trading, 2009) OFT 1115.
[55]   *The Economics of Self-regulation in Solving Consumer Quality Issues* (Office of Fair Trading, 2009) OFT 1059.
[56]   *Consumer Law and Business Practice. Drivers of Compliance and Non-compliance* (Office of Fair Trading, 2010).
[57]   *Policy Statement. The Role of Self-regulation in the OFT's Consumer Protection Work* (n 54). See also *Statement of Consumer Protection Enforcement Principles* (Office of Fair Trading, 2010) OFT1221.

or 'safety net', with powers of enforcement by statutory authorities, to ensure mandatory adherence, by all businesses, to minimum acceptable standards.[58]

Noting that there is no perfect formula for successful self-regulatory approaches, the OFT identified the following situations in which it would consider such an approach:[59]

— Where quality of a product or service is not readily discernible so that consumers cannot judge exactly what they are getting;
— where there is a relatively large proportion of small suppliers in the market, as small businesses may struggle to build reputation without a collective means of doing so;
— where market players have concern that the reputation of the whole industry could be harmed by the bad behaviour of a few and want to change the incentives for, and police their behaviour of, those who have less to lose;[60]
— where harm to consumers would be high without the introduction of some form of regulation (or further regulation) in the market concerned; and
— where there are sufficient checks and balances in place to mitigate against risks, so that self-regulatory promises are met.

B. Operation of the CCAS

Businesses operating to a code approved under the CCAS qualify to use and display the OFT Approved code logo. The OFT approves a consumer code in two stages. In Stage One, code sponsors promise that their code meets the core criteria in principle. A code sponsor is defined as any body that administers voluntary business to consumer codes (as opposed to statutory codes) and can influence and raise standards within its sector.[61] The Enterprise Act 2002[62] allows the OFT to consider applications from a wider range of organisations than previously. In Stage Two they demonstrate with evidence that their codes are working in practice. This process, which is intentionally diligent usually takes at least six months. It includes auditing, consumer satisfaction surveys and a final review of the code by the OFT. There is a fundamental code-review every three years where the code sponsors must consult with other bodies that are committed to the scheme, such as Which?, Age Concern, Consumer Focus and Trading Standards. In April 2012, the Department for Business, Innovation & Skills (BIS) invited the Trading Standards Institute (TSI) to establish a successor to the OFT CCAS on a self-funding basis from April 2013. The management of the CCAS transferred to the Consumer Codes Approval Board (CCAB) operated by TSI.[63]

Core criteria are specified that need to be achieved for a code to be approved.[64] The core criteria are summarised at Table 17.1, and may be summarised as:

— A commitment to provide customers with adequate information about goods and services
— the use of clear and fair contracts

---

[58] *Policy Statement*, ibid, para 3.11.
[59] *Policy Statement*, ibid.
[60] Likely to be a collection of businesses in a market and may include larger businesses often concerned over the behaviour of smaller firms.
[61] Consumer Codes Approval Scheme: Core Criteria and guidance.
[62] For more information: http://www.oft.gov.uk/about-the-oft/legal-powers/legal/enterprise-act/#.
[63] See http://www.tradingstandards.gov.uk/advice/ConsumerCodes.cfm.
[64] *Consumer Codes Approval Scheme. Core Criteria and Guidance* (Office of Fair Trading, 2008) OFT 390.

— the protection of deposits or prepayments
— low cost, independent dispute resolution if a complaint is not dealt with satisfactorily.[65]

The aims for establishing the core criteria for the scheme are summarised as follows:

1. Organisational criteria
2. Preparation of the code criteria
3. Content of the code criteria
4. Complaints handling criteria
5. Monitoring criteria
6. Enforcement criteria[66]
7. Publicity criteria

The CCAS criterion states that 'Code sponsors shall have adequate resources and funding to ensure the objectives of the code are not compromised'.[67] A written statement is required from the code sponsor to confirm adequate resource and funding. The CCAB does not hold cost information about code sponsors or individual businesses relating to the administration of the codes scheme in its entirety or the ADR/independent redress mechanism specifically. In 2014, code sponsors are:[68]

— British Association of Removers[69]
— British Healthcare Trades Association[70]
— The Carpet Foundation[71]
— Debt Managers Standards Association[72]
— Institute of Professional Willwriters[73]
— Motor Codes (service and repair)[74]
— Motor Codes (new cars) [75]
— The Property Ombudsman[76]
— Renewable Energy Association
— Robert Bosch Ltd[77]
— Vehicle Builders Repairers Association Ltd[78]

---

[65] www.oft.gov.uk.

[66] These set of criteria are aimed at making sure that any breach of a code of practice is dealt with as effectively, impartially and quickly as possible. This includes making sure that consumers and code members are clear about the escalating sanctions that code members will face for any breaches of a code practice.

[67] Consumer Codes Approval Scheme: Core Criteria and Guidance [2008]; now see *Trading Standards Institute, Consumer Codes Approval Scheme. Core Criteria and Guidance* (Trading Standards Institute, 2013) A3.

[68] The Direct Selling Association's code used to be recognised. Other codes that were under consideration in 2010 were those of Motor Codes Ltd (Vehicle Warranty Products), the Renewable Energy Association and SafeBuy.

[69] http://www.bar.co.uk/Default.aspx.

[70] http://www.bhta.net.

[71] http://www.carpetfoundation.com/.

[72] http://www.demsa.co.uk/.

[73] http://www.ipw.org.uk/.

[74] http://www.motorcodes.co.uk/motorist/the-codes/service-and-repair-code.html.

[75] http://www.motorcodes.co.uk.

[76] http://www.tpos.co.uk/.

[77] http://www.boschcarservice.co.uk/.

[78] http://www.vbra.co.uk/.

Table 17.1: CCAS: Overview of the Core Criteria 2008

<table>
<tr><td>

1. Organizational criteria
   a. Code sponsors should have a significant influence on the sector.
   b. Codes shall include a provision that compliance with the code is mandatory. Code sponsors must be able to demonstrate that members are prepared to observe the code's provisions.
   c. Code sponsors shall have adequate resources and funding to ensure the objectives of the code are not compromised.
</td></tr>
<tr><td>

2. Preparation of the code criteria
   a. Code sponsors shall be able to demonstrate that organizations representing consumers, enforcement bodies and advisory services have been adequately consulted throughout the preparation of the code.
   b. Code sponsors shall be able to demonstrate that organizations representing consumers, enforcement bodies and advisory services have been adequately consulted throughout the operation and monitoring of the code.
</td></tr>
<tr><td>

3. Content of the code criteria
   a. The code shall include measures directed at the removal or erasing of consumer concerns and undesirable trade practices arising within the particular sector.
   b. The code shall require that code members ensure that their relevant staff know about and meet the terms of the code as well as their legal responsibilities. Appropriate training is to be provided.
   c. The code shall address clear and truthful marketing and advertising as appropriate to the sector.
   d. The code shall address clear and accessible pre-contractual information as appropriate to the sector.
   e. The code shall address high-pressure selling as appropriate to the sector.
   f. The code shall address clear terms and conditions of supply and fair contracts as appropriate to the sector.
   g. The code shall address delivery and completion dates as appropriate to the sector.
   h. The code shall address cancellation rights as appropriate to the sector.
   i. The code shall address guarantees and warranties as appropriate to the sector.
   j. The code shall address protection of deposit or prepayments as appropriate to the sector.
   k. The code shall address customer service provisions as appropriate to the sector.
   l. The code shall address the additional effort/help to be provided to vulnerable consumers as appropriate to the sector.
</td></tr>
<tr><td>

4. Complaints handling criteria
   a. the code shall include a requirement that code members shall have in place speedy, responsive, accessible and used friendly procedures for dealing with consumer complaints. A specific reasonable time limit for responding to complaints shall be prescribed.
   b. The code shall include a requirement that code members will offer the same level of co-operation with local consumer advisers or any other intermediary acting on behalf of a consumer when making a complaint as they would to the complaint.
   c. The code shall include procedures for dealing with complaints including the availability of conciliation services directed at arranging a decision acceptable to both parties.
   d. The code shall include the availability of a low-cost, speedy, responsive, accessible and user-friendly independent redress scheme to act as an alternative to seeking court action in the first instance.
</td></tr>
</table>

(continued)

Table 17.1: *(Continued)*

The scheme shall be binding in respect of code members who shall not be able to refuse to allow a complaint to go before the scheme if a customer so chooses.
The code member shall be bound to accept a decision made under the scheme. Any such scheme shall be able to take into account possible breaches of the code where relevant to the complaint.

5. Monitoring criteria
   a. The code sponsor shall develop performance indicators, e.g. mystery shopping exercises and independent compliance audits, to measure the effectiveness of the code.
   b. The code sponsor shall implement the performance indicators and make available the results of their monitoring procedures and satisfaction surveys to demonstrate the effectiveness of the code.
   c. The code sponsor shall provide a written report annually to the OFT on the operation of the code to include:
      — Changes to the code agreed with the OFT and implemented
      — Numbers and types of complaints including information on outcomes from the conciliation process and the independent redress scheme
      — Results from monitoring, satisfaction surveys and the disciplinary process
      It would be preferable if the report were compiled by an independent person or body with powers to recommend actions.
   d. The code sponsor shall provide copies of the annual reports to the OFT.
   e. The code sponsor shall regularly review the code and update its provisions in the light of changing circumstances and expectations.
   f. Consumer satisfaction shall be regularly assessed.

6. Enforcement criteria
   a. code sponsors shall establish a procedure for handling on-compliance by members with the code. The procedure shall include independent disciplinary procedure and reasonable timescales for action.
   b. The code sponsor shall also set out a range of sanctions, eg warning letters, fines, terminations of membership, for dealing with non-compliance.

7. Publicity criteria
   a. codes sponsors and members shall ensure that their customers are aware of the code.
   b. Code members are to make clear, eg in advertising, point of sale, their adherence to a code of practice.
   c. Copies of codes shall be available without charge to customers, to members, to local consumer advisers and to others with a legitimate interest.
   d. Copies of any code related publicity generated by the code sponsor shall be provided to the OFT in advance of publication.
   e. Code sponsors and members shall publicise the fact that OFT has approved the code by using the CCAS logo in the prescribed manner.
   f. Code sponsors shall comply with the terms of the standard copyright licence, disseminate the terms to their members and monitor their members' use of CCAS logo. Appropriate action shall be taken by the code sponsors against a member for non-compliance with the copyright licence.

V. ABTA: The Travel Association

The Travel Association (formerly the Association of British Travel Agents, ABTA) is the largest trade association in the travel industry with a wide ranging membership including high street travel agents, small specialist independents, large travel companies and tour operators, all of whom operate under the ABTA logo.[79] ABTA aims to maintain high standards of trading practice for the industry at large, its members and the consumers they serve.

ABTA was originally formed in 1950 to give the industry a stronger voice in negotiations with government. As a trade association, it continues to represent the industry nationally and internationally but its evolution over time has added other practical benefits to membership through, for example, clarity and standardisation within the supply chain and the protection of moneys between booking agents and holiday providers/operators. Such benefits have allowed The Travel Association to build up a substantial membership but, importantly, it also focuses on the reputation of the industry, aiming to ensure a healthy future for its members through enhanced consumer confidence. Its major tool is the ABTA logo, backed up by the code of conduct which was first introduced in 1960. The ABTA logo enjoys high consumer recognition.[80]

The Association's Code of Conduct plays a central role in supporting good practice by members. It contains all relevant requirements under UK and European law, and in some instances sets expanded standards. The Code lays down practical and general conduct requirements for travel providers right through the travel booking process from advertising and pre-contractual information through to after sales service. For example, rules cover: Accurate information provision (including prices), advertising, fair dealing over cancellations or alterations, provision of compensation where appropriate and complying with all statutory requirements. The Code aims to provide high standards of customer service and covers issues such as ensuring the travel sold is appropriate to customer requirements, clearly informing customers of booking conditions or other requirements, providing clarity over financial protection and dealing with disputes fairly.

The Code is policed by a Code of Conduct Committee, which reviews the content of the Code and decides disciplinary cases, supported by the Association's secretariat. The Committee may impose a range of sanctions on members, including accepting an undertaking as to future conduct, issuing a reprimand, imposing an unlimited fine, or terminating membership.

Members view the Code and its associated dispute resolution and conduct functions as being essential in being an accessible, visible, effective and fair means of swiftly identifying and resolving customer complaints, placating unhappy customers and maintaining industry standards. Representatives of both the Association and of members strongly support the need for the Code to function well, and remark on how the Association has

---

[79] For further details of what follows see Hodges, Benöhr and Creutzfeldt-Banda (n 20) 328–34.

[80] An Ipsos MORI survey in 2008 found that 74% of the public recognised the ABTA brand: *Business Leadership in Consumer Protection. A Discussion Document on Self Regulation and Industry-led Compliance* (n 1).

in effect become self-policing, and constantly vigilant to maintain high standards across the industry. The media are not slow to pick up stories of dissatisfied holidaymakers or stranded passengers, so there is a clear driver for firms to maintain the reputation of the sector and of individual firms.

VI. British Franchise Association

The British Franchise Association (BFA) is the trade association that represents the UK franchise industry, including franchisors, franchisees and expert professional advisors, including bankers and lawyers. Of the national permanent base of around 600 firms, the BFA has 270 firms in membership, which is large by international standards, and the BFA attributes to a national commercial focus on outsourcing. BFA members have a total turnover of £14 billion, and 500,000 employees.

The BFA presents itself as the voice of *ethical* franchising. There is a European Code of Ethics for Franchising of the European Franchising Federation. The BFA requires members to pass quality standards accreditation, which it administers through its own team of trained assessors. It regards this ex ante technique as essential to maintain quality in the sector and to educate potential individuals and businesses that consider franchising. It turns down nine out of 10 applicants at first application, although is eventually able to accept perhaps eight of them after further discussions and education about their approaches to quality and ethics. It audits members on a random basis, roughly once every three years, but also based on intelligence from other franchisees or professionals, and its professional advisory committee. It has power to terminate membership of businesses that do not satisfy its standards, and does so.

In recent years, the BFA has developed awareness campaigns to consumers, has launched industry recognised qualifications,[81] has developed nationally recognised educational franchise seminars and has launched the first UK Franchising Trust.

The strong self-regulatory structure is partly a function of the structure of this sector. It contains a large number of small businesses that do not attract media or reputational interest, unlike large businesses with major brands. Accordingly, adverse news about individual businesses does not easily reach potential customers or business partners. Franchisees have usually borrowed significantly (often two-thirds of the business capital) and have secured it on their houses. Therefore, the BFA believes that pre-accreditation is essential in order to support quality and avoid problems arising. The sector has a commercial dependency on being seen to comprise businesses of high standard. The churn rate of businesses involved in franchising in UK is four per cent or five per cent, which contrasts with a rate of 30 per cent in the USA.

The BFA has a complaints procedure, which is not anonymous, with formal mediation and arbitration schemes. However, it finds these are not particularly popular and in recent years have become more litigious.

---

[81] The Qualified Franchise Professional (QFP), see http://www.thebfa.org/qfp.

VII. Lending Standards Board

There are numerous trade bodies covering the consumer credit market, many with their own code of practice or equivalent principles. Leading bodies are the British Bankers Association, the Building Societies Association, the UK Cards Association, the Finance and Leasing Association, the British Cheque and Credit Association, the Consumer Credit Trade Association, the Consumer Finance Association, the National Association of Pawnbrokers, the Credit Services Association, the Debt Managers Standards Association, the Debt Resolution Forum, and the Peer-to-Peer Finance Association.

The Lending Standards Board (LSB) is a not-for-profit private company whose registered firms are drawn from members of the British Bankers' Association (BBA), the Building Societies Association (BSA), the Credit Services Association and the UK Cards Association. Its Board consists of eight directors; three public interest directors, an independent chairman, the executive directors of the three sponsoring trade bodies, the BBA, BSA and the UK Cards Association and the chief executive of the LSB. The LSB began work on 2 November 2009 as the successor organisation to the Banking Code Standards Board following the transfer of responsibilities for the conduct of business regulation for deposit and payment products to the (then) Financial Standards Authority on 1 November 2009.

The LSB monitors a Lending Code, owned by the three sponsoring trade bodies, which is a voluntary code of practice which sets standards for financial institutions including debt collection and debt purchase firms to follow when they are dealing with their personal and small business customers in the United Kingdom. The Lending Code is complementary to the extensive relevant legal provisions and requirements issued by regulatory bodies. It aims to protect three categories of borrowing customers: Consumers, micro-enterprises (businesses that employ fewer than 10 persons and have a turnover or annual balance sheet that does not exceed £2 million), and charities that have an annual income of less than £1 million. It sets standards of good lending practice in relation to loans, credit cards, current account overdrafts, and lending to micro-enterprises and charities. It does not apply to non-business borrowing secured on land or to sales finance. The Code contains key commitments and detailed notes on how customers should be dealt with through the whole product life cycle, from marketing and account opening, maintenance and the provision of information on changes to terms and conditions and interest rates. Important protection is also included to help when something goes wrong, including when someone is experiencing financial difficulties.

The LSB has a number of key objectives:

— To assist firms to interpret and meet the requirements of the Lending Code;
— to monitor and enforce compliance with the Code and take enforcement action for material breaches; and
— to identify any gaps and deficiencies in the Code that could lead to consumer detriment and to advocate change.

The Lending Code is independently reviewed every three years. The last full review was undertaken in 2010 and led to a new Code being issued in March 2011.

Subscribers to the Lending Code fall into two categories, full and associate subscriber. Full subscribers are lenders who are required to follow all sections of the Lending Code, whilst associate subscribers are debt collection and debt purchase firms, where activities are primarily covered by section 9 of the Code (Financial Difficulties). In early 2015 the LSB had 39 subscribers, covering an estimated 70 per cent of the consumer credit market by outstandings.

The LSB aims to work in harness with other bodies who are involved in consumer protection and credit regulation. It has Memoranda of Understandings on cooperation with the Financial Conduct Authority, which provides a framework for the relationship between them, and Financial Ombudsman Service. The aim of the cooperation is to prevent either gaps in regulatory coverage or unnecessary duplication. It also has regular contact with consumer bodies and the money advice sector, and seeks to respond to information based on their experiences and research.

The LSB's monitoring takes a number of different forms including pre-registration reviews, themed reviews, investigations, and review of annual statements of compliance completed by firms. A Compliance Monitoring Team visits subscribers and their agents checking their systems and activities, including documentation, interviewing, and listening to calls. The monitoring activities are not intended to be a 'tick box' approach but to ensure that there is substantial evidence of good practice. The aims are to define and spread best practice, and to support firms' performance of compliance. It will inform subscribers of examples of best practice that it identifies anywhere, through such means as seminars and communications to compliance officers. It maintains an enforcement mechanism as a last resort, which are considered by its independently-chaired Adjudication Committee and can lead to formal warnings in serious cases. The LCB does not publicise all Code breaches, on the basis that most are minor and technical, and swiftly corrected.[82]

Overall, the LSB aims to self-regulate its subscribers effectively and complement the work of the statutory regulators.

VIII. Advertising

A. The ASA

i. Overview

The UK operates the largest self-regulatory system in the world in relation to control of advertising.[83] It comprises public regulatory bodies (the CMA and Ofcom)[84] overseeing

---

[82] In 2013–14 a total of 145 breaches were identified, around 60% of which were reported by subscribers themselves through their own internal monitoring; for all significant breaches an action plan was agreed. One formal warning notice was issued, in relation to failure to monitor a debt collection firm acting on the subscriber's behalf. One Executive Warning and 13 less material breaches were dealt with under the 'remedial Action agreed by Executive' procedure and reported to the Board. *Annual report 2013–2014* (Lending Standards Board, 2014).

[83] The ASA deals with the following types of marketing communications: Print and press ads, posters, television commercials, radio ads, internet ads (banners, pop-ups, sponsored search but not company websites), e-mail and text messages, direct mail, competitions, special offers, sales promotions, cinema commercials and teleshopping.

[84] The Office of Communications, established as regulator for all telecommunications under the Communications Act 2003.

a large self-regulatory agency (the ASA), which enforces Codes made by the advertising and broadcasting sector bodies (CAP (Committee of Advertising Practice) and BCAP (Broadcasting Committee on Advertising Practice)). The law is enforced by the regulatory bodies,[85] and the ASA enforces the Code. For non-broadcasting issues, the ASA is the 'established means' of regulation, and resolves the overwhelming majority of issues that arise, being able to refer breaches of the law to the CMA, but this has occurred only around 30 times in the last 10 years. The ASA can refer broadcasters who have broken the law in any way to Ofcom: Between 2005 and 2010 this was done three times.

Given the previous success of CAP and the regulation of print advertisements, Ofcom decided to contract out the regulation of broadcast advertising to the ASA, and the co-regulatory Broadcast Committee of Advertising Practice was formed. The ASA has also been designated by Ofcom[86] to regulate advertising in On Demand Programme Services. The statutory background rests on the Audiovisual Media Services (AVMS) Directive,[87] implemented through the ATVOD[88] Rules,[89] which set out the statutory requirements with regard to content with which providers of VOD (Vision on Demand) Services must comply, addressing issues as to material likely to incite racial hatred, protection of the under-18s, sponsorship and product placement. ATVOD has a Procedure of Complaints[90] about Editorial Content on VOD services, which outlines the procedure that it will normally follow in the handling of complaints concerning editorial content on VOD services. The ASA adjudicated on four VOD adverts between 19 May 2010 and 22 September 2010. In addition to the usual ASA sanctions for adverts found in breach of the CAP code, Ofcom has backstop powers to intervene if advertising continues to appear on VOD services despite an ASA adjudication against it.

The ASA's Advertising Codes are amongst the strictest in the world and UK advertisers are considered to have a good track record of communicating responsibly. The industry has made commitments to adhering to the Codes and the ASA considers that the vast majority of ads that appear in the UK can be trusted: ASAs' regular surveys show that over 90 per cent of advertisements are compliant with the rules.

ii. Organisation of the ASA

The ASA is the UK's independent self-regulatory body responsible for maintaining high standards in advertising for the benefit of consumers, advertisers and society at large. The ASA considers complaints about advertising and makes decisions on compliance with the

---

[85] Such as The Consumer Protection from Unfair Trading Regs 2008/1277, and the Business Protection from Misleading Marketing Regs 2008/1276.

[86] Under s 368B of the Communications Act 2003. See OFCOM statement of 20 September 2010, referring complainants to ATVOD or the ASA as appropriate and providing further information to VOD service providers at http://stakeholders.ofcom.org.uk/broadcasting/tv/video-on-demand/vod-regulation.

[87] Dir 2010/13/EU on the coordination of certain provisions laid down by law, regulation or administrative action in Member States concerning the provision of audiovisual media services (Audiovisual Media Services Directive).

[88] The Authority for Television On Demand (ATVOD) is the co-regulator, delegated by OFCOM, for the editorial content of UK video on demand services that fall within the statutory definition of On Demand Programme Services, see http://atvod.co.uk. The statutory duties and powers derive from the Communications Act 2003, as amended by the Audiovisual Media Services Regs 2009 and the Audiovisual Media Services Regs 2010.

[89] http://atvod.co.uk/uploads/files/ATVOD_Rules_and_Guidance_Ed1.1_Mar_2011.pdf.

[90] http://atvod.co.uk/complaints.

Codes. The ASA is designed to be independent of both the Government and the advertising industry, and operates according to published standards of service.[91]

The ASA has been responsible for policing non-broadcast advertising standards since it was established in 1962, when the industry created it to administer the CAP Code for non-broadcast advertising.[92] The success of the system led to the delegation by Ofcom to ASA of the responsibility for regulating broadcast (TV and radio) advertising in 2004. This move was approved by Parliament and created a 'one-stop shop' for all advertising complaints.[93] This means that a 'one-stop shop' has been responsible for regulating advertisements across all media since 2004.

The ASA deals with complaints relating to:

— Misleading, harmful or offensive advertisements
— difficulty getting goods or a refund for items bought by mail order or through television shopping channels
— promotions that are unfairly run or special offers that have left you disappointed
— unwanted mail from companies sent either by post, e-mail, text message or fax
— data capture and protection of privacy.

The CAP, BCAP and ASA share the same secretariat, but operate independently. The ASA views advertisements from the perspective of the audience, very often the general public, and demand that advertisers only make claims they can substantiate with evidence. It works closely with statutory regulatory partners, such as Trading Standards, the OFT and Ofcom. Its authority is recognised by the Government, the courts and regulators as the established means of consumer protection from misleading advertising.

The adjudication body of the ASA is its Council, on which two-thirds of members are independent of the advertising industry and one-third are industry experts. The independent Chairman is appointed after an open competition: The Council observes the Nolan Principles for public appointments.

The ASA's work includes acting on and investigating complaints as well as proactively monitoring and taking action against misleading, harmful or offensive advertisements, sales promotions and direct marketing. It is not just concerned with formal compliance, but with maintaining a high standard of compliance. It offers confidential advice to members, and guidance, such as advice notes on the website (for example, on sunbeds), including free pre-vetting of non-broadcasting advertisements. Pre-vetting is compulsory for broadcasting advertisements, under the Communications Act, but it would be too great a task for the non-broadcasting sector. Pre-vetting is carried out by Clearcut, a separate body originally established by ITV, which applies the ASA Codes and is funded by broadcasters. However,

---

[91] http://asa.org.uk/About-ASA/Our-Mission.aspx.

[92] Control of advertisements was introduced in legislation when commercial TV began in 1955. In 1961, the Advertising Association and other industry bodies agreed that it was important that advertisements were welcomed and trusted by consumers in non-broadcast media. As a result, the CAP was formed and produced the first edition of the British Code of Advertising Practice. In the same year, the Report on Consumer Protection by the Molony Committee concluded that a voluntary approach would be preferable to statutory regulation by an American-style Federal Trade Commission. ASBOF was created in 1974 to provide finance for the ASA, assuring its independence. The self-regulatory system was affirmed in 1988 with the introduction of the Control of Misleading Advertisements Reg, which strengthened backing from the OFT.

[93] *A History of the Advertising Regulatory System*, available at: http://asa.org.uk/Regulation-Explained/History-of-Ad-Regulation.aspx.

all advertisements, whether pre-vetted or not, are subject to the ASA as final arbitrators under the Codes.

The ASA is funded by a levy on industry members, of 0.1 per cent on advertising spend and 0.2 per cent on mail shots. The levy is voluntary (firms may untick a box on annual membership forms). The levy is collected at arms-length by separate industry bodies, rather than by the ASA, to maintain its independence: The Advertising Standards Board of Finance (ASBOF) and the Broadcasting Advertising Standards Board of Finance (BASBOF). The result is that the ASA is unaware who has paid and who may not have paid. All firms operating in the sector are subject to the Code, whether or not they have paid the levy.

iii. The Codes and the Bodies that Write them

The self-regulatory rules contained in the Codes[94] are made by committees representing the advertising and broadcasting industries, respectively the CAP and the BCAP. The membership of those committees is entirely industry personnel, from the three segments of the industry, namely advertisers, media owners and agencies (including individual broadcasters).

— BCAP is responsible for writing and maintaining the TV and Radio Advertising Standards Codes.
— CAP is responsible for the rulebook for non-broadcast advertisements, sales promotions and direct marketing. Non-broadcast means advertisements in media such as cinema, press, posters and online.

The Codes contain wide-ranging rules designed to ensure that advertising does not mislead, harm or offend. The Codes are based on over-arching principles that advertisements, wherever they appear, remain legal, decent, honest and truthful. Advertisements must also be socially responsible and prepared in line with the principles of fair competition. These broad principles apply regardless of the product being advertised. The Codes are extensive but not an overly-prescriptive series of rules. The ASA states that it administers the rules in the spirit as well as the letter, making it almost impossible for advertisers to find loopholes or 'get off on a technicality'. This common sense approach takes into account the nature of the product being advertised, the media used and the audience being targeted.

In addition, the Codes contain specific rules for certain products and marketing techniques. These include rules for alcoholic drinks, health and beauty claims, children, medicines, financial products, environmental claims, gambling, direct marketing and prize promotions. These rules add an extra layer of consumer protection on top of consumer protection law and aim to ensure that UK advertising is responsible.

Codes have evolved to reflect the standards of taste and decency as they evolve in society. The secretariats of the committees work extensively with consumers to obtain their opinions, so that prevailing opinion can be reflected in the content of the two Codes. Important routes for feedback include annual conferences and periodic satisfaction surveys. In September 2010 new Codes were introduced that included many small changes, some of some significance, such as advertisements must be socially responsible.

---

[94] http://bcap.org.uk/The-Codes.aspx.

The twelfth edition of *The UK Code of Non-Broadcast Advertising, Sales Promotion and Direct Marketing* (the CAP Code)[95] came into force on 1 September 2010. Its chapter headings are listed in Table 17.2. From 2011, the rules in the CAP Code apply in full to marketing communications online, including the rules relating to misleading advertising, social responsibility and the protection of children. The remit[96] will apply to all sectors and all businesses and organisations regardless of size.[97]

The current *UK Code of Broadcast Advertising* (BCAP Code) came into force on 1 September 2010, replacing four previous separate BCAP Codes for broadcast advertising.[98] The Code applies to all advertisements (including teleshopping, content on self-promotional television channels, television text and interactive television

Table 17.2: The CAP Code

— Preface
— Scope of the Code—Introduction
— Section 1—Compliance
— Section 2—Recognition of marketing communications
— Section 3—Misleading advertising
— Section 4—Harm and offence
— Section 5—Children
— Section 6—Privacy
— Section 7—Political advertisements
— Section 8—Sales promotions
— Section 9—Distance selling
— Section 10—Database practice
— Section 11—Environmental claims
— Section 12—Medicines, medical devices, health-related products and beauty products
— Section 13—Weight control and slimming
— Section 14—Financial products
— Section 15—Food, food supplements and associated health or nutrition claims
— Section 16—Gambling
— Section 17—Lotteries
— Section 18—Alcohol
— Section 19—Motoring
— Section 20—Employment, homework schemes and business opportunities
— Section 21—Tobacco, rolling papers and filters
— How the system works
— History of self-regulation
— Appendix 1: The CPRs and BRPs
— Appendix 2: Advertising rules for on-demand services regulated by statute
— Index

[95] http://www.cap.org.uk/The-Codes/CAP-Code.aspx.
[96] The new remit will ensure the same high standards as in other media and will cover: Advertisers' own marketing communications on their own websites and; marketing communications in other non-paid-for space under their control, such as social networking sites like Facebook and Twitter.
[97] Landmark Agreement extends ASA's digital remit, ASA PR 1 September 2010.
[98] http://www.cap.org.uk/The-Codes/BCAP-Code.aspx.

advertisements) and programme sponsorship credits on radio and television services licensed by Ofcom. The chapter headings of the BCAP Code are given at Table 17.3.

CAP and BCAP do a lot of work in training the industry in the Codes, and publish guidance to industry that contains precedents from adjudications and informal views of the ASA. In 2009, advice and training was given to advertising industry practitioners on 47,933 occasions.[99]

Table 17.3: BCAP Code Chapter Headings

— Introduction
— Section 1—Compliance
— Section 2—Recognition of advertising
— Section 3—Misleading advertising
— Section 4—Harm and offence
— Section 5—Children
— Section 6—Privacy
— Section 7—Political and controversial matters
— Section 8—Distance selling
— Section 9—Environmental claims
— Section 10—Prohibited categories
— Section 11—Medicines, medical devices, treatments and health
— Section 12—Weight control and slimming
— Section 13—Food, food supplements and associated health or nutrition claims
— Section 14—Financial products, services and investments
— Section 15—Faith, religion and equivalent systems of belief
— Section 16—Charities
— Section 17—Gambling
— Section 18—Lotteries
— Section 19—Alcohol
— Section 20—Motoring
— Section 21—Betting tipsters
— Section 22—Premium-rate telephone services
— Section 23—Telecommunications-based sexual entertainment services
— Section 24—Homeworking schemes
— Section 25—Instructional courses
— Section 26—Services offering individual advice on consumer or personal problems
— Section 27—Introduction and dating services
— Section 28—Competitions
— Section 29—Private investigation agencies
— Section 30—Pornography
— Section 31—Other categories of radio advertisements that require central copy clearance
— Section 32—Scheduling
— Appendix 1: Statutory framework for the regulation of broadcast advertising
— Appendix 2: Extracts from directive 89/552/EEC as amended (audiovisual media services directive
— Appendix 3: The Consumer Protection from Unfair Trading Regulations 2008 (the CPRs) and the Business Protection from Misleading Marketing Regulations 2008 (the BPRs)
— Index

---

[99] Annual Report 2009.

iv. Complaints Procedures

Anyone can complain to the ASA. The vast majority of complaints are received from consumers. Any consumer may make a complaint, which is free and confidential. Complaints are also received from competitors, in which case the complainant is named, but making the complaint is still free.

The easiest way to complain is to complete the online complaints form,[100] but complaints can also be made in writing by post or fax. Complaints over the phone are only accepted if it's about a TV, radio or cinema commercial, or a poster or national press advertisement. Complaints are investigated free of charge but the ASA requests that they are submitted within a reasonable time of the appearance of an advertisement, usually within three months of the advertisement appearing. When making a complaint, a copy (web-link, scan, photo, photocopy etc) of the advertisement in question is required alongside as much detail as possible outlining the concerns and where and when the ad was seen to help the ASA to assess the complaint.

Every individual complaint is investigated: Numbers of complaints are irrelevant for initiating an investigation. Multiple complaints are regularly received,[101] and all are acknowledged and processed.

Complaints are first assessed by the Complaints Reception Team to confirm that they fall within the ASA's jurisdiction. Every complainant is contacted to acknowledge the complaint, given a unique reference number to quote for future reference, and given information on the process (including the name of the case handler and contact details) and progress. Some complaints are referred at that stage to the OFT, Trading Standards Service or Press Complaints Commission. Some complaints fall out of ASA's remit because the Advertising Codes do not cover the type of activity or communication complained about. On those occasions ASA will always try to direct the consumer to the right people who may be able to help. For instance, TS (Trading Standards) departments regulate shop window displays and point of sale material. The FSA regulates financial aspects of advertisements, like the use of APRs (annual percentage rates) and disclaimers.

A complaint that falls within the ASA's jurisdiction is then passed to the Complaints Team, which contacts the advertiser and asks for comments. A complaint will always be the responsibility of a named individual who will write to the complainant. A complaint will be dealt with as quickly as possible and in line with the ASA's standards of service.[102] All complaints are anonymous unless the complainant asks the ASA to get their name taken off a mailing list or is complaining on behalf of a company or organisation.

The ASA has a power to initiate investigations itself, subject to different formalities. This self-starting power is invoked in circumstances such as consistent breach, or a problem in the sector. The Compliance and Marketing Team takes action and meets trade associations.

The Codes provide that advertisers must hold satisfactory evidence to justify any claim. Accordingly, when an advertiser is contacted in relation to a complaint, the advertiser will be expected to produce such evidence without delay. The consumer or other complainant

---

[100] http://asa.org.uk/Complaints/How-to-complain/Online-Form/Step1.aspx.
[101] An example in 2010 concerned the advertising of a post-conception advice service.
[102] http://asa.org.uk/About-ASA/Our-Mission.aspx.

does not have the burden of proving or establishing any complaint. A number of cases drop out at that stage. Files are then passed to the Investigations Team, which compiles all the relevant evidence before a file is submitted to the ASA Council for decision. The Investigations Team makes a recommendation based on its extensive expertise. The substantiation for advertisements may comprise complex scientific or technical information, in which case the Team may obtain external independent advice from academics to help assess the evidence. Assessment is made of the advertisement, not the product that is being advertised.

Complaints may be resolved informally, if the advertiser accepts the complaint and/or offers to amend or remove it. The ASA will still publish an adjudication, but say that the matter has been resolved informally, and will tell the consumer. Complainants and advertisers may request a review of an adjudication through the Independent Review procedure.

The policy is to be open and transparent. Adjudications are published every Wednesday, and available on the ASA website as a precedent bank. The Compliance and Marketing Team will follow up advertisers after a breach and monitor output. More formal investigation powers to enter premises and access files are unnecessary, since all advertisements are publicly available. A 2011 project enabled the ASA to be compliant with the Freedom of Information regime: This was complex in view of the large amount of confidential commercial information that is held.

The Compliance and Marketing Team carries out five surveys each year on different sectors, and targets sectors that have low compliance rations or are sensitive areas. Examples are those involving finance, advertisements to children, and alcohol, in each of which there is potential for consumer detriment. The survey looks at every single advertisement issued, and identifies issues. The ASA published a series of Research Reports and background Briefings.

In 2012 ASA/CAP received 31,298 complaints about 18,990 advertisements, and its action led to 3,700 advertisement campaigns being changed or withdrawn.[103] Complaints from the public represented 96 per cent of the complaints received and those from industry accounted for four per cent of the total. It provided advice and training to industry on 101,442 occasions that year.

B. Medicines

Two self-regulatory systems are operated in relation to promotion of medicines, one by each of the two principal trade associations, respectively covering the research-based sector and its relations with doctors and the NHS and the other covering over-the-counter products. Both European and national law specify regulatory requirements for the promotion of medicinal products, and criminal offences exist under national law that are invoked regularly against illegal activity, but almost never against established companies. In respect of the latter, the authorities have always regarded the Codes as providing satisfactory controls. There therefore exists a division of labour: The public authorities prosecute rogues whilst industry polices itself.

---

[103] Advertising Standards Authority and the Committee of Advertising Practice Annual Report 2012, available at: http://www.asa.org.uk/About-ASA/Annual-Report.aspx.

i. The Prescription Medicines Code of Practice Authority (PMCPA)

The Association of the British Pharmaceutical Industry (ABPI) established a Code of Practice for the Pharmaceutical Industry in 1958. All ABPI member companies are obliged to comply with the Code and about 50 non-member companies have voluntarily agreed to comply with it. The aim of the Code is to ensure that the promotion of medicines to health professionals and to administrative staff is carried out in a responsible, ethical and professional manner, within a robust framework to support high quality patient care. The Code also sets standards relating to the provision of information to patients and the public and relationships with patient groups. The Code has been regularly updated over the last 50 years and has always included requirements that go beyond UK (and therefore also EU) law, as well as the World Health Organisation (WHO) ethical criteria for medicinal drug promotion and the Code of Practice of all European national members of the European Federation of Pharmaceutical Industries and Associations (EFPIA).[104]

Companies are expected to respect the spirit, as well as the detail, of the Code.[105] In particular, material must be accurate, balanced, fair, objective and unambiguous, be based on an up-to-date evaluation of all the evidence, and must not mislead (Clause 7.2). Material must be capable of substantiation and substantiation must be provided on request (Clauses 7.4 and 7.5). Companies should not make disparaging remarks about other companies and products or of health professionals and their opinions (Clause 8). High standards are expected at all times (Clause 9.1). A ruling that an activity has brought discredit upon or reduced confidence in the pharmaceutical industry is a sign of particular censure (Clause 2).

Since 1993 the ABPI Code of Practice has been administered by the Prescription Medicines Code of Practice Authority (PMCPA), independently of the ABPI.[106] The Authority has its own staff and although it reports directly to the ABPI Board of Management it is not part of the operation of the trade association which is the ABPI and does not report to the ABPI Director-General. The ABPI and the PMCPA exist in parallel, and regard themselves as operationally independent.[107]

The PMCPA is responsible for the provision of advice, guidance and training on the Code of Practice as well as for the complaints procedure. It is also responsible for arranging for conciliation between companies when requested to do so and for scrutinising advertising and meetings on a regular basis.

The Authority is not an investigatory body as such. It asks the respondent company for a complete response and may ask the parties to a case for further information in order to clarify the issues. It is essentially an adversarial process in which the evidence to be taken into account comes from the complainant and the respondent company. A complainant has the

---

[104] Available at: http://www.codeinpractice.co.uk/images/EFPIA%20CODE%20UPDATED_222.pdf.

[105] http://www.abpi.org.uk/%2Fpublications%2Fpdfs%2Fquick_guide_to_the_code_for_health_professionals_final.pdf.

[106] available at: http://www.pmcpa.org.uk/files/The%20First%20Fifty%20Years%20-%20A%20history%20of%20the%20ABPI%20Code.pdf.

[107] In 1997, in order to re-affirm the independence of the operation of the PMCPA from that of the ABPI itself, the PMCPA and the ABPI settled a 'Protocol of Agreement', which sets out the respective roles of the PMCPA, its Director, the Code of Practice Panel, the Code of Practice Appeal Board, the ABPI and the ABPI Board of Management, and provides for arbitration between the PMCPA and the ABPI in the event of difference arising between the parties which affects the ability of the PMCPA to carry out its work in an impartial manner.

burden of proving their complaint on the balance of probabilities. Anonymous complaints are accepted and like all complaints are judged on the evidence provided by the parties. The weight to be attached to any evidence may be adversely affected if the source is anonymous and thus in some instances it will not be possible for such a complaint to proceed.

Complaints made under the Code about promotional material or the promotional activities of companies are considered by the Code of Practice Panel. Complaints are ruled upon in the first instance by the Code of Practice Panel which is made up of the Director, Secretary and Deputy Secretary of the PMCPA, with the benefit of independent medical and/or other expert advice as appropriate. The largest number of complaints usually come from health professionals.[108]

A complainant whose complaint has been rejected or a company ruled to be in breach of the Code may appeal the Panel's ruling to the Code of Practice Appeal Board. In serious cases a company may be required by the Panel to suspend the material or activity at issue pending the outcome of an appeal. The Appeal Board has an independent chairman and eight other independent members. There are also 12 senior executives from pharmaceutical companies on the Appeal Board. In addition to its role in relation to appeals, the Appeal Board receives reports on all cases considered by the Panel and oversees the work of the PMCPA.

In each case where a breach of the Code is ruled, the company concerned must give an undertaking that the practice in question has ceased forthwith and that all possible steps have been taken to avoid a similar breach in the future. An undertaking must be accompanied by details of the action taken to implement the ruling.

The PMCPA publishes reports of all completed cases on its website at www.pmcpa.org.uk and in its quarterly Code of Practice Review. It advertises in the medical, pharmaceutical and nursing press brief details of all cases where companies are ruled in breach of Clause 2 of the Code, are required to issue a corrective statement or are the subject of a public reprimand. The website also carries brief details of complaints which are under consideration or, if resolved, details of those cases not yet published.

Additional sanctions can also be imposed, including:

— An audit by the PMCPA of a company's procedures to comply with the Code; the principal elements of an audit are an examination of documentation and the questioning of appropriate members of staff; following an audit, a company can be required to submit its promotional material to the PMCPA for pre-vetting for a specified period;
— requiring the company to take steps to recover material from those to whom it has been given;
— the publication of a corrective statement;
— a public reprimand; or
— suspension or expulsion from membership of the ABPI for ABPI members.[109] In the case of a non-member company, the Medicines and Healthcare products Regulatory Agency (MHRA) can be advised that responsibility for that company under the Code can no longer be accepted.

---

[108] See PMCPA Annual Reports.
[109] Two companies have been suspended from ABPI membership and only readmitted after satisfactory audit: Abbott Laboratories in 2006 (http://www.abpi.org.uk/press/press_releases_06/060210.asp case information: http://www.pmcpa.org.uk/files/August_2006.pdf#page=17) and Roche Pharma in 2008 (http://www.abpi.org.uk/press/press_releases_08/140708.asp (accessed on 21 July 2010) case information: http://www.pmcpa.org.uk/?q=node/583).

ii. OTC Medicines: The PAGB

The Proprietary Association of Great Britain (PAGB) represents the manufacturers of over-the-counter (OTC) medicines[110] that are subject to a marketing authorisation, registered traditional herbal medicines, and food supplements in the United Kingdom. PAGB was founded in 1919 with the aim of promoting responsible consumer healthcare. The organisation was set up by a group of pharmaceutical manufacturers who wanted to protect the public from misleading medicines advertising. They devised a system of self-regulation to ensure that their advertising was balanced and responsible. The system required member companies to submit all of their advertising to the association for checking, before publication, and to abide by the rulings made. This self-regulatory system has remained the primary mechanism of regulating OTC medicines' advertising and promotion for almost 100 years. It has repeatedly been endorsed as effective by the government and professional associations. Recognition of its success by the European Commission led to self-regulation of advertising for medicines being built into European law when regulation was introduced in the 1980s.

PAGB drafts and publishes two principal codes of practice,[111] a Consumer Code and a Professional Code. The Consumer Code applies to advertising materials aimed at consumers and those persons who may legitimately purchase medicines on behalf of another consumer (for example parents who purchase medicines on behalf of their children). The Professional Code covers all advertising of OTC medicines aimed at persons qualified to prescribe or supply, and those who work for such persons.[112] Compliance is required with both the letter and the spirit of each Code.

The system of control under the Consumer Code is a pre-publication approval system for advertising: Under the Professional Code it is a post-event complaints system. For the former, it is a condition of membership that all advertising aimed at consumers must be submitted to PAGB for screening and PAGB approval must have been given prior to its release into the public domain. It is the responsibility of each member company to seek fresh approvals when this is necessary. Whilst member companies are legally responsible for their advertising, the prepublication approval system aims to help members ensure that their consumer advertising complies with the legal and self-regulatory requirements and that the messages portrayed are legal, balanced, truthful and responsible.

Draft advertising is checked by PAGB for compliance with the provisions of the PAGB Consumer Code. Where an advertisement complies with all of the requirements, PAGB will return a copy of the advertisement marked with the PAGB stamp of approval. Where an advertisement does not comply with requirements, PAGB will provide comments to assist

---

[110] The law divides medicines into three categories, depending on inherent risk: Those that are available on prescription only, or supplied under the supervision of a pharmacist, or in pharmacies over-the-counter. See http://www.pagb.co.uk/.

[111] http://www.pagb.co.uk/advertising/PDFs/advertisingcode.pdf. See also the PAGB Medicines Advertising Codes for Traditional Herbal Medicines, which applies to advertising for over-the-counter medicines that are registered under the Traditional Herbal Medicines Registration Scheme; and the PAGB Code of Practice for Pack Design for Over-the-Counter Medicines.

[112] This includes professionals at hospitals and health centres, doctors, dentists, nurses, pharmacists, optometrists, chiropodists, midwives and ancillary health workers and assistants of all the above, including buyers.

member companies in making the required amendments. To enable PAGB to carry out this process, a copy of both the Marketing Authorisation and the Summary of Product Characteristics (SmPC) must be submitted.

It is a condition of PAGB membership that all members comply with the PAGB medicines advertising Codes in both the letter and the spirit. PAGB requires members to uphold the reputation of the over-the-counter medicines industry and to maintain recipients' confidence in the advertisements they receive.

The PAGB medicines advertising Codes reflect the law and provide an interpretation of the law. In some areas they go beyond the law and consider other aspects of advertising, such as taste and decency and sponsorship. Advertising complaints under the code are published.[113]

IX. Some International Comparisons

Although the national architectures for enforcement of public and private law differ between European states, and also differ in how they split functions between public and private structures, the self-regulatory model is virtually the same across Europe in relation to control of advertising.[114]

Enforcement of the law (the UWG)[115] regulating any kind of unfair commercial practice[116] in Germany[117] has, since legal controls on unfair competition were introduced in 1909, been undertaken almost exclusively[118] by private sector bodies. The UWG grants those whose rights have been infringed the right to apply to a court in civil proceedings for an injunction against others' unfair competition.[119] However, such rights are also exercisable by a private sector body, the Wettbewerbszentrale (WBZ)[120] and, since 1965,[121] by consumer associations. Almost all enforcement is done by these bodies, and seemingly little by the public authorities. The system has been operating effectively, swiftly and cheaply for 100 years. The enforcement system is free to consumers: Losers pay under the court costs rules. The establishment costs of the consumer associations are paid by the state, and those of the WBZ are paid for by businesses.

---

[113] http://www.pagb.co.uk/advertising/PDFs/NiQuitinMinisComplaintReport.pdf.

[114] F Weber, *The Law and Economics of Enforcing European Consumer Law. A Comparative Analysis of Package Travel and Misleading Advertising* (Farnham, Ashgate, 2014); F Weber, 'The Law and Economics of Self-regulation in Advertising' (2014) 1 *Journal of European Consumer and Market Law* 5.

[115] The Act against Unfair Competition (*Gesetz gegen den unlauteren Wettbewerb*: UWG).

[116] ie misleading practices, unfair business terms, distance selling contracts, guarantees, e-commerce.

[117] This section is edited from I Benöhr, C Hodges and N Creutzfeldt-Banda, 'Germany' in Hodges, Benöhr and Creutzfeldt-Banda (n 20) ch 4.

[118] Some codes exist covering questions of taste and decency. Specific types of advertising, such as concerning alcohol and cars, discrimination and the role of women in advertising, are dealt with by the German Advertising Council (Deutscher Werberat).

[119] UWG, s 8.

[120] See UWG, para 8.3 and the German Law on injunctions *(Unterlassungsklagengesetz (UklaG))*. See also, s 33 of the German Act Against Restraints on Competition *(Gesetzes gegen Wettbewerbsbeschränkungen*: GWB), para 33 regarding cartel damages. The ABZ was founded in 1912 specifically in order to self-enforce the UWG.

[121] In order to implement Regulation (EC) 2006/2004 on consumer protection cooperation, in the *Verbraucherschutzdurchsetzungsgesetz* (the Law on Consumer Protection Enforcement).

The WBZ comprises all chambers of commerce, most trade and craft corporations, about 750 other industrial or commercial associations and approximately 1,300 companies. It deals with over 15,000 complaints a year at its head office in Bad Homburg and five regional branch offices (Berlin, Dortmund, Hamburg, Munich and Stuttgart). Its total annual budget is not published. Infringement cases are handled by a team of in-house lawyers. Where court proceedings are instituted, cases are outsourced to a member of a panel of external law firms. The annual budget for such external work is €750,000, although the court-specified level of costs is recovered in those cases that are won.

An important function of the WBZ is to provide information and advice to its members concerning advertising and marketing practices in the planning stage (copy advice), so as to prevent infringements from occurring. This ex ante function is effective and widely used by companies, preventing litigation.

Consumer associations (*Verbraucherzentralen*) operate at national and *Länder* levels. Two large consumer organisations operate throughout Germany and receive funding from the federal budget, the Federation of German Consumer Organisations (*Verbraucherzentrale Bundesverband eV*: VZBV))[122] and *Stiftung Warentest*, the premier consumer testing organisation. 42 other consumer organisations or consumer-policy oriented associations operate and are members of VZBV. Other consumers organisations also exist, such as the German Consumer Initiative (*Verbraucherinitiative eV*).

The VZBV[123] is a non-governmental, independent organisation that represents the political, economic and social interests of consumers, vis-a-vis policy-makers and the private sector.[124] The federation was established in 2000 as a result of the merger of three consumer-interest organisations[125] and has approximately 100 staff members working in the Berlin offices.[126] Registered as a non-profit association, it acts as an umbrella organisation for the 16 consumer advice centres in the federal states and for 26 other consumer-policy oriented associations. These consumer bodies form an integrated system of advice, information, law enforcement and representation of political interests promoting consumer interests which has more than eight million individual members.[127] Consumers receive advice from a network of 190 advice centres dealing with around four million individual contacts with consumers per year. All advice centres have recourse to a database of 'advisory stances' (ie model answers for typical problems). The formulation of advisory stances is coordinated by the federal association and is subject to a uniform quality management. The individual advisory activities are stored in a central computer database. This constitutes the basis for, on the one hand, being able to systematically take action against recurring violations and, on the other hand, for obtaining a precise empirical picture of existing consumer problems.

The €8.7 million annual budget of VZBV is 90 per cent funded from annual institutional grants provided by the federal government,[128] together with contributions from public authorities, businesses, economic operators and civil society at national, European and

---

[122] www.vzbv.de/go.
[123] ibid.
[124] www.verbraucherzentrale.de/en/wir.php.
[125] The AgV, the VSV and the *Stiftung Verbraucherinstitut*.
[126] www.vzbv.de/go/wir/wir_ueber_uns/index.html.
[127] www.vzbv.de/go, see the note on Germany on the EU Commission website: http://ec.europa.eu/consumers/index_en.htm.
[128] The Federal Ministry of Food, Agriculture and Consumer Protection (BMELV).

international level.[129] At the federal state level, the consumer advice centres receive both institutional and project financing. The centres also contribute to this funding with consultation fees and the sale of consumer advice guides.

VZBV deals with a wide range of consumer topics such as sustainable consumption, financial services, health care and food law. Its tasks include enforcement through lawsuits, the development of standards and providing professional training for the staff of member organisations. VZBV is particularly active on three levels:

— Consumer-policy lobbying and advising politicians and policy-makers to achieve rules that guarantee a transparent market;
— legal implementation, by highlighting irregularities and enforcing consumer rights in courts;
— promoting consumer advice services.[130]

Consumer complaints that involve breaches of consumer law may be made to the WBZ or any consumer association. Those bodies are empowered to bring injunction proceedings to end the infringement, but do not have power to seek damages. Complaints are received from any source, including competitors, consumers, trade associations and public authorities such as the police, trade and health authorities. Business organisations and authorities provide 80 per cent of complaints to the WBZ.

In practice, enforcement cases are frequently resolved at an early stage. The body will usually first write to the trader asking him to sign an undertaking (*Abmahnung*) to amend or discontinue the advertising or commercial practice.[131] This declaration contains a penalty clause, so breach of which will give rise to a fine.[132] Legal action is threatened in the case of non-compliance. The threat of an injunction to protect the collective interests of consumers can be sufficiently powerful to result in swift settlement, although some cases are taken to the courts for wider market reasons, including setting a precedent.

In urgent cases, the body can seek a preliminary court injunction prohibiting the unfair commercial practice. Cases that involve unfair competition law usually satisfy the requirement for urgency. Therefore, many such cases are dealt with this way. The court will normally issue the preliminary injunction within a day by immediate order. In the case of contravention, the court can charge the opponent with an administrative fee of up to €250,000.

In non-urgent cases, before taking court action, the WBZ will—in appropriate cases—try to reach an amicable agreement, which may involve the complaint being brought before the Board of Conciliation of the regional Chamber of Commerce.[133] Court proceedings may be instituted in the *Landgericht*, and are subject to the normal loser pays rules. A claimant has to prove all details and facts in his claim, but the burden of proof rests on the

---

[129] The Federal Ministry funds also individual projects run by different consumer organizations, such as the German Nutrition Society and the Information Service for Consumer Protection, Food and Agriculture.

[130] www.verbraucherzentrale.de/en/wir.php.

[131] The WZB is authorised by s 13 *Unterlassungsklagengesetz* (Law on injunctions, implementing Dir 98/27 EG on Injunctions for the Protection of Consumers' Interests) to request information from postal and telephone authorities and companies on a customer's personal data. Thus, the WZB has the power to disclose the identity of the owner of a German PO Box or telecommunication service.

[132] See: http://www.vzbv.de/cps/rde/xbcr/vzbv/rechtsdurchsetzung_broschuere_vzbv_2011.pdf, 7.

[133] http://www.wettbewerbszentrale.de/de/home.

defendant to produce the evidence that his advertising complies with the law, so firms usually can either produce such evidence or not, and that result determines the outcome of a challenge. If a case proceeds to the trial stage, the judge will often be faced with complex technical evidence.

The consumers associations and the WBZ liaise regularly, and sometimes institute cases against the same infringers. The WBZ's approach is to respond to individual complaints by instituting individual cases, finding solutions and stopping unfair advertising. Consumer associations can, in addition, sometimes raise issues that have more political aspects, and seek media coverage aimed at highlighting issues. The WBZ considers that the Federal competition authority (*Bundeskartellamt*) is better equipped to obtain facts and market information in relation to competition law issues: The private bodies do not have power to inspect companies, and civil procedure law contains no general right to discovery of documents.

X. Theoretical Analysis of Self-Regulation

In 1990, Rowan-Robinson, Wachtman and Barker studied self-regulation in a number of different sectors, and identified a series of advantages and disadvantages of the technique,[134] having identified around 20 codes, whose scope was to provide consumer information, set out detailed performance standards, prohibit unfair practices and establish redress procedures.[135] Rowan-Robinson and colleagues considered the advantages of self-regulatory codes to be:

a.   They were more flexible and can adjust readily to changing circumstances;
b.   enforcement was the responsibility of those who had specialised knowledge of the sector;
c.   they relied upon cooperation and consent rather than upon the force of law;[136]
d.   they may offer consumer benefits over and above their rights under the general law;
e.   dispute resolution may be simpler; and
f.   they reduced public enforcement costs.[137]

The disadvantages identified were:

a.   Their status may be unclear;[138]
b.   they were not enforceable against non-trade association members;

---

[134] J Rowan-Robinson, P Wachtman and C Barker, *Crime and Regulation. A Study of the Enforcement of Regulatory Codes* (Edinburgh, T & T Clark, 1990).
[135] I Ramsay, 'The Office of Fair Trading: Policing the Consumer Market Place' in R Baldwin and C McCrudden (eds), *Regulation and Public Law* (London, Weidenfeld and Nicolson, 1987).
[136] G Ganz, *Quasi-Legislation: Recent Developments in Secondary Legislation* (London, Sweet & Maxwell, 1987).
[137] *A General Duty to Trade Fairly. A Discussion Paper* (Office of Fair Trading, 1986).
[138] R Baldwin and J Houghton, 'Circular Arguments: The Status and Legitimacy of Administrative Rules' [1986] *Public Law* 239; Ganz (n 136).

c.   enforcement against members depends on the willingness and ability of associations to exert discipline; and

d.   the ultimate sanction of expulsion from the association may be counter-productive as it frees the offender from the constraint of the code.[139]

The authors commented that '[a]lthough trade associations can conciliate between member firms and dissatisfied customers it has usually proved unrealistic to expect them to act as effective enforcement agents. Their primary role is to represent their members' interests.'[140]

  The above list can be contrasted with those noted above by the OFT in 2008.[141] Official use of self-regulation has mushroomed rather than been restricted, so there must be some confidence that means of unlocking the advantages of 'greater flexibility and speed than Government regulation' have been found.[142] The central challenge is to overcome the issue that 'with self-regulation, regulatory capture is there from the outset'[143] and that those with authority may be unwilling to address deficiencies amongst their own members. In essence, developments in the design of self-regulatory systems in the past 30 years have attempted to address the potential disadvantages, particularly through improved understandings of compliance and an enhanced constitutional mode of operation for self-regulatory structures.[144] Providing acceptable solutions to those two issues can unlock the advantages that business codes can deliver of flexibility, speed of updating, enlisting business ownership of trading standards, and saving public costs by avoiding full-blown regulatory structures.

  Key features that emerge from the more successful models outlined above are having a Code structure that is transparent and in which outsiders play key functions (in other words, appropriate design of governance, discussed further below), so that a sufficient degree of independent action can be maintained. This is easier to achieve in sectors where strong consumer and media pressure can be brought to bear if customers are dissatisfied, such as for retailers, travel agents. In other words, fear of diminution in *reputation* can drive not only compliance by individual firms but also effective functioning of self-regulatory bodies. In sectors that are more distant from consumers, such as trade suppliers, reputational effects can still exist, but be weaker. In such areas, self-regulation is likely to be less effective and state regulation may be required.

A. Enhancing Compliance Through Reputation and Transparency

The crucial step is to view self-regulation, in the same way as any other mode of regulation, as potentially comprising multi-stakeholder involvement or meta-regulation, as discussed in chapter 11 above, rather than a simple 'vertical command and control' system. Ramsay

---

[139] *A General Duty to Trade Fairly. A Discussion Paper* (n 137).

[140] ibid. See also DA Garvin, 'Can Industry Self-Regulation Work?' (1983) 25(4) *California Management Review* 37–52; A De Jong et al, 'The Role of Self-Regulation in Corporate Governance: Evidence and Implications from the Netherlands' (2004) 11(3) *Journal of Corporate Finance* 473–503.

[141] *Consumer Codes Approval Scheme. Core Criteria and Guidance* (n 63).

[142] *The OFT's New Approach to Consumer Codes of Practice, A Consultation Paper* (Office of Fair Trading, 2001).

[143] J Kay, 'The Forms of Regulation' in A Seldon (ed), *Financial Regulation—Or Over Regulation* (London, Institute for Economic Affairs, 1988) 34.

[144] J Black, 'Constitutionalising Self-Regulation' (1996) 59(1) *The Modern Law Review* 24–55.

points out that it is a mistake to regard self-regulation as an imperfect substitute for government regulation, and that a pluralistic model of law would not necessarily assume its hierarchical inferiority.[145] Indeed, he notes that it is not necessarily seen as an alternative to state regulation but as one of a number of governance options,[146] where the central issues become expertise, efficiency, accountability and legitimacy.

Where sufficient external forces can be brought to bear on behaviour, a need for 'downward' sanctions and enforcement of the classical type by a public body may be diminished or unnecessary. The policy is based on academic regulatory theory and experience that self-regulatory structures are particularly effective when subject to public oversight based on systems control, transparency and accountability.[147]

The design features are, therefore, to provide for adequate pressure on behaviour to be applied by competitors, customers and markets. That is done by ensuring full transparency of the nature and operation of a self-regulatory system, and of the extent to which all of those subject to it comply. Sanctions may therefore be 'applied' by market pressure on the reputations and brands of individual traders and of the group, which incentivise the likelihood of compliance and rectification by individual traders and policing activity by those responsible for group compliance. But in many self-regulatory schemes, as in formal state enforcement, sanctions are rarely applied, since education, advice and warnings are frequently judged sufficient to encourage businesses to modify their behaviour.[148]

Clearly, these forces cannot be expected to work in circumstances where there is inadequate transparency, competition or reliance on individual and collective reputations. As the European Commission recognised in its 2001 Green Paper on EU consumer protection:[149]

> Many problems may not be suitable for regulatory action. Self-regulation can achieve some consumer protection goals, especially in industries that recognise they have a strong common interest in retaining consumer confidence and where free riders or rogue traders can harm this confidence...

> For codes to work they must be recognised as a valuable signal of quality and trustworthiness by consumers and business at a level which is high enough to create both brand recognition and brand value. In order for this to happen codes need teeth and there must be significant commercial detriments for traders who cannot meet the requirements of strong codes and commercial value for those who can.

There should be little surprise that current self-regulatory systems exhibit a multitude of different models, since the elements of competition, reputation and forces acting on compliance and identification of non-compliance differ significantly between business sectors. Transparency and openness to scrutiny can emanate from different sources, and variations in 'control' or 'enforcement' by external stakeholders, trade associations, code controllers or public enforcers will differ depending on the circumstances. Significant forces may be applied through a number of means.

---

[145] I Ramsay, *Consumer Law and Policy. Text and Materials on Regulating Consumer Markets* 3rd edn (Oxford, Hart Publishing, 2012) 93.

[146] H Schepel, *The Constitution of Private Governance: Product Standards in the Regulation of Integrating Markets* (Oxford, Hart Publishing, 2005) 31.

[147] Ogus (n 36); Black (n 144); Bartle and Vass (n 5).

[148] P Grabosky and J Braithwaite, *Of Manners Gentle: Enforcement Strategies of Australian Business Regulatory Agencies* (Melbourne, Oxford University Press, 1988).

[149] *Green Paper on EU Consumer Protection* 2001, COM(2001) 531 final, para 4.4.

First, the power of market reputation, for those businesses that rely for commercial success on maintaining high reputations, is an essential and powerful force. The commercial impact of reputation and brand value can be focused through ensuring accountability of a self-regulatory system through transparency of the quality data—and complaint and claim data—that it generates. A business survey in 2001 found that business viewed the purpose of corporate self-regulation through a code of conduct as being the promotion of high standards of integrity in business transactions. Codes represented what was by then regarded as good commercial practice. The common factor influencing the development of business ethics in general was found to be the desire to protect or improve reputation. This was found to be more common in heavily branded companies than in SMEs.

Second, a regulatory structure is required in which code sponsors (usually trade associations) oversee enforcement of codes on their members, but are themselves subject to formal supervision by a public body, such as the OFT, which operates with sufficiently strong background powers, and is itself subject to governmental and public, Parliamentary scrutiny and accountability. A 2005 scholarly review noted the extent to which co-regulatory schemes had become embedded within the regulatory state, and stated that such a regulatory model 'has to be founded on transparency and accountability for it to inspire confidence and be sustained', and that 'effective compliance regimes are an integral part of this process'.[150]

Hence, some of the best examples adopt a tiered structure: The top tier will comprise oversight by Parliament against a threat by government of introducing more extensive formal regulation; the second tier is a public regulatory authority, which oversees the self-regulatory activities by business, and possesses wide enforcement powers, which it can use as a threat of last resort but may rarely be used in practice is the system is effective; the third tier comprises the self-regulatory scheme, usually operated by the trade association for a sector, or a specially-created trade association, and the fourth tier comprises the regulated firms, who are subject to internal and external incentives to adopt the code values of best practice in order to maximise reputation and hence commercial success. This structure also means that the scope and cost of the formal regulatory structure can be contained.

The operation and performance of all tiers are subject to public transparency, with a view to countering the inherent phenomenon of self-interest bias (known in regulatory theory as 'capture' of a system by those who should be subject to its controls). The objective should be to ensure that the structure, rules, operation, personnel and decisions taken by the private sector body are fully available for external scrutiny by the population, the media, the regulator and the legislature. This can be achieved through making regular reports, and having all information on the website. The objective is to ensure that the key consumer requirements are met: Having adequate information on price, quality and terms of trade, to enable full and fair purchasing choices to be made, and to ensure democratic accountability through transparent governance systems that involve adequate external personnel.

One possible approach is for an official model to be created by the government or the regulator of the parameters of how the business' self-regulatory system will be designed or will operate. The CCAS model mandates the essential requirements in the form of principles, but only grants the valued brand denoting compliance with the principles on the basis of a strenuous evaluation process and subsequent auditing.

---

[150] Bartle and Vass (n 5).

A further possible feature is for supervisory functions over the code, and decisions on disputes, that are taken at trade association level to be outsourced to independent committees, somewhat akin to a 'separation of powers' approach under constitutional theory. Thus, both the substance of business codes, and decisions on their interpretation and enforcement, are often dealt with by decision-making and sanction-imposing committees that are administered by the trade association but whose members are independent of the business sector. Thus, the separate committee will have a chair and majority of the members are independent of the sector (professors of law, consumer representatives, other outsiders).

B. Enhancing Constitutionality Through Governance

Criticisms of pure self-regulatory schemes can be founded on constitutional grounds: A closed group of people make their own rules, and apply them, and are not publicly accountable. In theoretical terms, it is a closed, autopoietic model.[151] Thus, the superimposition of state oversight, or providing governance from other sources, may address the classic deficits of lack of accountability or transparency, failure to act in the public interest (and even continuation of anti-competitive rents), and lack of performance or inefficiency.[152] Similarly, decentered regulatory legitimacy, beyond and above the state, can be provided,[153] involving a significant amount of horizontal decentering, with private parties deeply embedded in the regulatory landscape.[154] Hence, the British model now involves involvement of not only business bodies, providing the supportive and controlling functions intended in 'responsive regulation theory,[155] but also consumer scrutiny through transparency of the operation of codes and the opportunity for public democratic evaluation and criticism by consumer bodies and the media.

A frequent feature is for there to be independence of functions, somewhat akin to a 'separation of powers' approach under constitutional theory. Thus, some code violation issues are dealt with by independent decision-making and sanction-imposing bodies (such as the ABPI's Prescription Medicines Code of Practice Authority), or overseen by boards that include independent representation (such as ABTA's Code of Conduct Committee, which includes consumer and regulatory representatives as well as industry personnel). A third approach is to incorporate elements of competition between self-regulatory agencies, which enables consumers to choose between competing self-regulatory regimes.[156] A regime based on Coasian consensual bargaining is appropriate only where there are no significant externalities or information asymmetries.[157]

---

[151] G Teubner, *Law as an Autopoietic System* (Oxford, Blackwells, 1993); G Di Minico, 'A Hard Look at Self-Regulation in the UK' (2006) 17(1) *European Business Law Review* 183–211.

[152] Such a system is entirely consistent with the 'responsive regulation' system. There are parallels with state regulation of notified bodies under the Community's New Approach system.

[153] B Morgan and K Yeung, *An Introduction to Law and Regulation* (Cambridge, Cambridge University Press, 2007).

[154] J Freeman, 'Private Parties, Public Function and the Real Democracy Problem in the New Administrative Law' in D Dyzenhaus (ed), *Recrafting the Rule of Law* (Oxford, Hart Publishing, 1999) 331–70; J Freeman, 'The Private Role in Public Governance' (2000) 75 *New York University Law Review* 543.

[155] Discussed in ch 11 above.

[156] Ogus (n 36).

[157] ibid.

By these means, different combinations of incentives and levers can involve multi-layered institutional structure, with several tiers of 'controllers', perhaps in a hierarchy of public officials at the top of a structure or pyramid (and perhaps both national and local officials), and underneath them—or horizontally, in a 'meta/open governance' structure—trade associations, consumers associations, the media, individual consumers and individual market trading operators. Thus, accountability of private sector bodies that have regulatory functions can be through 'diffuse constitutionalism'.[158]

The involvement of both public and private actors contributes to development of common values across public and private law. The development of mechanisms and norms through which private actors are enrolled in the delivery of public functions has been referred to as the 'publicization of private law'.[159] The emergent principles call for transparency and participation in decision making, reasoned decisions, compliance with principles of legality and provision for review.[160] Harlow suggests Global Administrative Law may extend beyond procedural principles to encompass values of the rule of law, good governance and human rights, lending a substantive dimension resonant as much with constitutional as with administrative law.[161] As Scott notes,[162] from this perspective, it is the excessive concentration of power, rather than its diffusion, that is a problem. A broader approach seeks a *wider* range of institutionalised mechanisms equivalent to constitutional controls.

Reflexive law theory also suggests that the oversight of the self-regulatory body should be procedural, on the basis of controlling systems and transparency rather than intervening in individual outcomes.[163] Accordingly, British self-regulatory regimes are often associated with governing legislation. Indeed, both theoretical and practical experience supports the view that self-regulation will be most effective when subject to public oversight based on systems control, transparency and accountability.[164] Accordingly, provided there are adequate governance controls, the state may, therefore, set standards but leave it to the industry itself to police compliance. Alternatively, the state may require that standards be set by the industry, then check the adequacy of those standards.[165]

Provided the wider control strategies are present of institutionalisation and the concomitant creation of a corporate culture, involving openness and the creation of internal moralities, with an ideal of responsive regulation, self-regulatory models can function satisfactorily. In reaching an appropriate policy balance, it should be recalled that arguments for the advantages of self-regulation have increased over recent decades.

---

[158] C Scott, 'Regulatory Governance and the Challenge of Constitutionalism' in D Oliver, T Prosser and R Rawlings (eds), *The Regulatory State: Constitutional Implications* (Oxford, Oxford University Press, 2010).

[159] J Freeman, 'Extending Public Law Norms Through Privatization' (2003) 116 *Harvard Law Review* 1285.

[160] B Kingsbury, N Krisch and RB Stewart, 'The Emergence of Global Administrative Law' (2005) 8 *Law & Contemporary Problems* 17.

[161] C Harlow, 'Global Administrative Law: The Quest for Principles and Values' (2006) 17 *European Journal of International Law* 187.

[162] Scott (n 158).

[163] Black (n 144); Bartle and Vass (n 5).

[164] Ogus (n 36); Black (n 144); Bartle and Vass, ibid.

[165] Howells and Weatherill (n 35) 72–77 and 580–85.

XI. Conclusions

The UK operates extensive self- or co-regulatory systems, especially in relation to advertising and consumer-promotion generally. Stable and responsible trade associations must exist in order to establish and support such systems, and to sponsor Codes of Practice,[166] but the norm is now for separate entities to administer the self-regulatory functions in order to provide and demonstrate sufficient independence. In some sectors, where business has a strong need to maintain reputation, self-regulatory systems have operated strikingly well in the UK—and many other European countries—for many decades. In stable and appropriate circumstances, business can both fund and be controlled by private sector regulation. It is preferable for funding and operational regulatory decisions to be controlled by entities that are independent of trade associations, and for them to have governance structures that involve sufficient independent representation and full transparency. In some circumstances, self-regulation is backed by public regulation, and the potential backstop of criminal sanctions thereby provides an ultimate sanction or deterrent, at the top of the Ayres-Braithwaite pyramid of enforcement.

Effective self-regulatory entities operate in functionally similar ways to public enforcement authorities, namely by investigating complaints, making decisions, requiring changed behaviour, imposing sanctions and publishing decisions. Private regulators do not usually operate pro-actively by undertaking inspections or instituting inquiries. However, some can operate effective ex ante vetting functions. Many bodies also provide important advisory and educational functions.

The major advantage of a self-regulatory system lies in the fact that funding comes exclusively (in the UK, although not always in Germany) from business. This saves public expenditure on public authorities, and also allows public enforcers to concentrate on 'rogues' who would only respond to speedy and formal state enforcement, backed by criminal sanctions.

---

[166] Trade associations have a long pedigree in the UK: P Atiyah, *The Rise and Fall of Freedom of Contract* (Oxford, Clarendon Press, 1979) 597–98; DC Cousins and JF Pickering, 'Codes of Practice as an Element in Consumer Policy Research into the British Experience' in MJ Baker and D Tixier (eds), *Consumerism, Public Policy and Consumer Protection* (Cergy, ESSEC, 1981).

18

Compliance within Business Organisations

I. Looking Inside: Why Internal Compliance is Relevant

It is apparent from previous chapters that much theorising about regulation and enforcement assumes that the imposition of traditional techniques of public or private enforcement on businesses will produce desired outcomes. Almost no attention has been devoted to *how* external legal techniques might bring about compliance, or *how* business structures operate and can be influenced, or *how* the behaviour of individuals working within businesses can be affected. One is compelled to a conclusion that most law on enforcement, and legal scholars, focus on *external* issues but are far less familiar with the *internal* issues of how business structures work, and why people who work in them obey, infringe or flout rules.

The arguments that businesses are able to internalise all external legal sanctions, to control the behaviour of all staff, and to control all of the businesses' impacts on the external world, are fundamental to theories of deterrence and rational economic action.

If the goal is to maximise compliance with rules by corporations, then it would be logical to examine how business organisations operate internally, and how their systems and cultures can contribute to or impede such compliance. It should also be asked whether internal or external levers are more effective in supporting compliance, and how such internal and external elements might sensibly be combined. Such an approach is strikingly lacking from much legal theory and literature, which is restricted to the external dimension, and based on the assumption that only external enforcement is necessary. This chapter examines the evidence on these issues.

II. Multiple Modes of Corporate Organisation

Cooperation between all those involved in an enterprise is a requirement in order to achieve a shared, or certain, end.[1] A mode of organisation is needed to enable coordinated collective

---

[1] CI Barnard, *The Functions of the Executive* (Cambridge MA, Harvard University Press, 1938) 4.

action by multiple actors.[2] Small businesses may have little formal structure, other than little more than an authoritative core, and few other organs or centres of decision making. Most complex organisations have at their disposal a host of financial, technical and administrative means that natural individuals do not have.[3]

Businesses exist in all shapes and sizes, and have multiple variations in modes of internal organisation. Mintzberg structured organisations into five types:[4] Simple; machine bureaucracy (achieves coordination through standardisation of work processes); professional bureaucracy (standardisation of skills); divisionalised form (quasi autonomous entities coupled together by a central administrative structure, with coordination achieved by a performance control system) and adhocracy (designed for innovation, aiming to fuse experts).

Complexity stems from the number of parts and the number of different kinds of parts found within an organisation.[5] Business architecture is founded on a categorisation of multiple functions that may (or may not) be needed in order that the commercial purpose of the organisation can be fulfilled, for example:[6] Vision, strategies and tactics; customers, suppliers and competitors; initiatives and projects; organisation units; assets; products and services; capabilities; information and vocabulary; business processes; policies, rules and regulations.

It is not proposed to attempt to give here a comprehensive account of business organisation structures or modes of operation. But some important points can be drawn out that illuminate the focus on modes of 'enforcement' or compliance. We can start by contrasting two opposing models for the structure of organisations: A vertical bureaucracy and a horizontal dispersed model.

In a vertical bureaucracy, power is supposedly concentrated at the top, although elements of power are possibly delegated in decreasing amounts to lower tiers. Crozier set out a classic vertical organisational analysis of the structure of French work organisations (a clerical agency and an industrial monopoly) as at the early 1960s.[7] He noted the existence of four basic characteristics.[8] First, the creation of a vast body of detailed written and impersonal rules and procedures prescribing what is to be done in all conceivable situations. Second, decision making was centralised, creating great distance between those who had to decide and those who had the relevant information decisions. This situation led to the adoption of an impersonal decision-making style based on abstract principles of equity, equality and

---

[2] D Black, *The Behaviour of Law* (Bingley, Emerald Group Publishing Limited, 1976, special edition 2010) (organisation is the capacity for collective action); W Ulrich and N McWhorter, *Business Architecture. The Art and Practice of Business Transformation* (Tampa FL, Meghan-Kiffer Press, 2011) (organisations might be best thought of as a hive of individuals all generally working toward a common goal) 63; A Cohen, *Two Dimensional Man* (London, Routledge and Kegan Paul, 1974) 66 (A 'collectivity of people without organisation is not a group').

[3] JK Galbraith, *The New Industrial State* (New York, Princeton University Press, 1976) 85–88; JS Coleman, *The Asymmetric Society* (Syracuse NY, Syracuse University Press, 1982) 21.

[4] H Mintzberg, *The Structuring of Organisations* (Englewood Cliffs NJ, Prentice-Hall, 1979).

[5] J Whelan and G Meaden, *Business Architecture. A Practical Guide* (Farnham, Gower, 2012) 30.

[6] N McWhorter and W Ulrich, 'Defining Requirements for a Business Architecture Standard' (2009) at http://bawg.omg.org/Bus_Arch_Ecosystem_White_Paper_Draft.pdf.

[7] M Crozier, *The Bureaucratic Phenomenon* (The University of Chicago Press, 1964, revised New Brunswick, Transaction Press, 2010).

[8] This summary draws on the Introduction to the 2010 edition by E Friedberg.

precedent, and was often ill-adjusted to the problem that the decision was supposed to solve. Third, the existence of hierarchical strata insulated from each other and exerting great pressure for conformity on its members. Fourth, the 'creation of parallel informal power relations around the groups or individuals capable of coping with residual and unanticipated contingencies and uncertainties affecting the organization's capacity to function in a satisfactory way.'[9] Together, these characteristics created 'vicious circles' of self-reinforcing behavioural patterns. Crozier argued that bureaucracy is a mode of organisation that is incapable of correcting its behaviour in the face of its results. It created self-reinforcing behavioural patterns that reinforced impersonality and centralisation. Change would not be piecemeal or incremental, but occur after crises.

In contrast to the ultimately sclerotic bureaucratic culture described above, a diametrically opposed mode of business organisation would reflect a flatter structure, in which power is devolved to multiple local groups. This would concentrate elements of information and authority in multiple discrete groups, so that informed, intelligent and swifter decisions could be facilitated, with innovation. Rapid extension of new technology into all sectors of the economy in the twentieth century has meant much greater devolution of responsibility inside organisations, accompanied by an enormous increase in self-employment.[10] Globalisation of labour markets and economies has introduced a raft of culturally related complexities and challenges,[11] and challenges for management.[12]

Weber described large scale, bureaucratic organisations as having an oligarchical distribution of power, formally determined spheres of competency, an impersonal character, and a rational and impartial management on the basis and with the help of regulations.[13] He developed principles for designing a hierarchy that effectively allocates decision-making authority and control over resources.[14] Problems arise of external adaptation and internal integration.[15] In this context, Teubner's ideas of the autopoietic character of different social sub-systems are illuminating.[16] He argues that the 'legal discourse is closed ... and produces its own construction of reality'.[17] Also relevant is Luhmann's idea of law as a system of communication, with own meanings not directly mapped onto the real world.[18]

---

[9] ibid.

[10] P Sedgwick, *The Enterprise Culture* (London, SPCK, 1992) 4.

[11] AS Bachmann, 'Melting Pot or Tossed Salad? Implications for Designing Effective Multicultural Workgroups' (2006) 26(6) *Management International Review* 721, 722.

[12] JE McLean and RD Lewis, 'Communicating Across Cultures: Management Matters' (2010) Summer *British Journal of Administrative Management* 30.

[13] M Weber, *Wirtschaft und Gesellschaft: Grundriss der verstahende Soziologie* 5th edn (Tübingen, Mohr, 1920, 5th edn 1980) 551–56.

[14] HH Gerth and CW Mills (eds), *From Max Weber: Essays in Sociology* (New York, Oxford University Press, 1946); M Weber, *Economy and Society* G Roth and C Wittich (eds) (Berkeley, University of California Press, 1978).

[15] E Schein, 'The Role of the Founder in Creating Organizational Culture' (1983) *Organizational Dynamics* 13, 14.

[16] Autopoiesis is defined as a system which, though complete in its structural elements, can be defined in its regulatory contents on the basis of its continuous interaction with outward reality: G Teubner, 'Substantive and Reflexive Elements in Modern Law' (1983) 17 *Law and Society Review* 239; G Teubner and A Febbraio (eds), *State, Law and Economy as Autopoietic Systems* (Milano, Giuffrè, 1992).

[17] G Teubner, 'How the Law Thinks' (1989) 23 *Law and Society Review* 727–57, 745.

[18] N Luhmann, *Law as a Social System* (K Ziegert trans, Oxford, Oxford University Press, 2004) 70–74.

Peters and Waterman's influential 1982 management text prescribed three key features of a successful organisation:[19]

1. An emphasis on methods to communicate key values and objectives and to ensure that action is directed towards these.
2. Delegation of identifiable areas of responsibility to relatively small units, which are encouraged to carry out their responsibilities with considerable autonomy and scope for initiative, but are subject to performance assessments which manifest a preservation of tight central control.
3. Use of a simple lean structure of management to avoid rigidities of bureaucracy, the complexities of the matrix, and the overheads of both.

Whatever the business structure, contemporary descriptions of business architectures form a consensus that business structures of any size are complex and contain multiple diverse organisational, and hence social, groups, each with their own purpose and social culture. The complexity of organisations is revealed in the multiple differing images that they present,[20] such as a machine bureaucracy, organisms, cultures, political systems and various other images.

> Organizations have grown so complex in recent years that it is difficult to visualize or understand how all of the parts fit together. Every business unit has its own set of funded initiatives and it is difficult to see how or even if these initiatives align to a common business strategy.[21]

It would follow that controlling the behaviour and performance of a large multi-functional organisation would be a challenge.

> The complex structure of the organisations involved means that it does not always appear possible for controlling organs, both within the organisations themselves and outside them, to become aware of potential problems sufficiently in good time. As a consequence, after the event it is often particularly difficult to determine whether or to what extent certain individuals can be held responsible for the course of events.[22]

III. The Multiplicity of Cultures

Irrespective of the level of complexity or dispersal in a business, both sociological studies of organisations and recommendations by leading business consultants have focused on the fact that a business is comprised of multiple *individuals* operating within multiple localised

---

[19] T Peters and RH Waterman Jr, *In Search of Excellence: Lessons from America's Best-Run Companies* (New York, Harper & Row, 1982); this summary is from M Parker, *Organizational Culture and Identity* (London, SAGE Publications, 2000).

[20] For an overview see G Morgan, *Images of Organization* (Beverley Hills, Sage, 1986); discussed B Fisse and J Braithwaite, *Corporations, Crime and Accountability* (Cambridge, Cambridge University Press, 1993) 118–23.

[21] Ulrich and McWhorter (n 2).

[22] M Bovens, *The Quest for Responsibility: Accountability and Citizenship in Complex Organisations* (Cambridge, Cambridge University Press, 1998) 4.

cultures.[23] The importance to business of culture and of recognising the existence of a diversity of cultures has been recognised at least since the 1950s:

> The culture of the factory is its customary and traditional way of thinking and of doing things, which is shared to a greater or lesser extent by all its members, and which new members must learn, and at least partially accept, in order to be accepted into service in the firm. Culture in this sense covers a wide range of behaviour: the methods of production; job skills and technical knowledge; attitudes towards discipline and punishment; the customs and habits of managerial behaviour; the objectives of the concern; its way of doing business; the methods of payment; the values placed on different types of work; beliefs in democratic living and joint consultation; and the less conscious interventions and taboos.[24]

Hofstede has demonstrated the diversity of people and cultures, and dismissed the idea that people are basically alike and will react similarly in similar situations.[25] Parker's study of a series of different organisations concluded that each had common notions about management as a response to a turbulent environment, and had a particular combination of people and circumstances that made each unique, with a series of internal localised cultures.[26] He identified three divisions between business units, and their connections with sponsoring or hindering change within an organisation: First, spatial/functional (geographic and/or departmental divides: 'Them over there, us over here'); second, generational (age and/or historical divides: 'Them from that time, is from this time'); and third, occupational/professional (vocational and/or professional divides: 'Them who do that, us who do this'). Parker concluded that all organised cultures are unique, yet they share some similar features, and some locations were more connected to others, which led to increased features of similarity in their local cultures.

Parker noted that to participate in organisation is to accept limits on individual freedom,[27] so as to gain the personal benefits of employment and remuneration, in return for assisting in the concerted benefits achieved by the organisation. However, the assumption that consensus is (and should be) the normal property of organisations, has not been found by research to exist in large organisations. Instead, many possible 'cultures of' exist within an organisation, and managerial intervention can never totally control outcomes.[28] Clans exist, allowing mutual socialisation of discrete units, as noted in Japanese companies.[29]

> Organizational culture is ... a continuing process of articulating contested versions of what the organization should be doing, who it should be responsible to and who does what for reward.[30]

Given the existence of multiple sub-units within businesses, each with individual functions, groups of individuals, and sub-cultures, an idea that the behaviour of every internal group can be absolutely controlled so as to conform to every required norm, whether

---

[23] Parker (n 19) 231.

[24] E Jacques, *The Changing Culture of a Factory* (London, Tavistock, 1951) 251.

[25] G Hofstede and GJ Hofstede, *Cultures and Organizations: Software of the Mind* 3rd edn (New York, McGraw-Hill, 2010).

[26] Parker (n 19) ch 8.

[27] ibid, 232.

[28] ibid, 220, 231.

[29] W Ouchi, *Z Theory* (New York, Avon Books, 1981).

[30] Parker (n 19) 226.

the source of control emanates from an internal or—even less—external position, appears highly unlikely.[31] Thus, theories that behaviour is controlled through deterrence or rational action appear to be questionable, and will certainly differ in force both between different organisations and within organisations.

Instead, a socio-legal approach would focus not on a single theory of how to 'control' the behaviour of organisations, but on the considerable variation in the types of organisations (and therefore in their different behaviours and responses to levers), and on the extent to which there exists within any given single 'business' a number—perhaps a multiplicity—of discrete individual socio-technical systems,[32] each of whose behaviour has to be 'controlled' by particular individual means. Fisse and Braithwaite noted:

> We find no single theory of how organisations make decisions to break the law, and how they hold actors accountable for them, of sufficient generality and explanatory power to be a practical guide to the design of a corporate criminal law appropriate to all types of organisations. It is not a matter of empirical evidence on organisations showing that the theories provide an overly simplified account of organisational diversity; the theories themselves posit a diversity which renders impossible a single model of legal responsibility consonant with organisational life.[33]

It seems such an obvious and uncontroversial aspiration to define legal principles of responsibility for corporate crime consistently with the way organisations actually make decisions. Yet we have seen that organisation theory posits such diversity in the way organisations make decisions, in the way they are structured, in their cultures, and in the way they define responsibility, that positivist organisation theory can never give clear guidance to the law on this question.[34]

IV. The Ideal of Unified Core Values

Given the existence of diversity within organisations, how do the multiple internal operational organs need to function cooperatively so as to enable the business to succeed? Establishing the function, goals and targets for each unit or individual may not be enough. Habermas assumes that an 'ideal speech situation' is needed, in which there is an equality of power and absence of deceit, as an implied possibility within all human communication.[35]

Studies on the causes of sustained long-term business success have concluded that it is critical to establish clear *core values*, which are shared by all members of the workforce, form an ideology that is enduring and able to be applied consistently in different trading and geographical circumstances, whilst operational goals are constantly examined and develop.[36]

> A global visionary company separates operating practices and business strategies (which should vary from country to country) from core values and purpose (which should be universal and enduring within the company, no matter where it does business).[37]

---

[31] Whelan and Meaden (n 5) (There are many scenarios of communication failure).

[32] FE Emery (ed), *Systems Thinking* (Harmondsworth, Penguin, 1969).

[33] Fisse and Braithwaite (n 20) 122.

[34] ibid, 131.

[35] J Habermas, *The Philosophical Discourse of Modernity* (Oxford, Polity, 1987).

[36] J Collins and JI Porras, *Built to Last: Successful Habits of Visionary Companies* 12th edn (London, HarperCollins, 1994, 2005).

[37] ibid, xxii.

The idea is that companies should set a high standard of values and performance that its people feel compelled to try to live up to.[38] This affords a way of unifying disparate internal functions and groups. Indeed, it was found that visionary companies focus primarily not on beating their competitors but on beating *themselves*.[39] Ideological control preserves the core while operational autonomy simulates progress. They develop a relentless, creative drive, constantly experimenting and innovating, Darwinianly discarding what does not work, but firmly retaining their core values.[40] Further, the existence of a charismatic visionary leader is absolutely *not required* for a visionary company:[41] Indeed, it has been said that the qualities needed are a paradoxical blend of personal humility and professional will.[42] However, similarity has been noted between highly successful companies and cults: Fervently-held ideology, indoctrination, tightness of fit and elitism.[43] They do not tend not to have much room for people unwilling or unsuited to their demanding standards.

V. Management Systems

An organisation cannot function operationally to achieve its goals without management systems and processes. If the management structure does not operate then nothing happens as intended.[44] The principal purpose of organisational structure is to control the way *people* coordinate their actions so as to achieve organisational goals and the means used to motivate them to achieve the goals.[45] The design and operation of organisational design has to achieve a balancing between three opposites: Differentiation and integration, centralisation and decentralisation, and standardisation and mutual adjustment.[46]

International Standard IS9000 series defines the key business processes that should be included in a management system.[47] These and similar standards provide general guidance and requirements on management practices, covering many business aspects, for instance, social responsibility (ISO 26000), risk management (ISO 31000:2009), quality management (ISO 9001:2008) and environmental management (ISO 14001:2004). Some ISO standards are industry specific, aiming at increasing safety and environmental protection, improving governance and decision making, minimising losses in such fields as, for example, energy, food safety, healthcare and others. The ISO standards are global in their character, and they are designed for different types of organisations. Therefore, they do not specify certain

---

[38] ibid, xix.

[39] ibid.

[40] ibid.

[41] ibid.

[42] J Collins, *Good to Great* (New York, Harper Business, 2001). This was a review of 11 companies with average cumulative stock returns 6.9 times the general market in the 15 years following their transition point, compared with 11 direct comparisons and six unsustained comparisons.

[43] ibid, 122.

[44] D Boehme and JE Murphy, 'Fear No Evil: A Compliance and Ethics Professional's Response to Dr Stephan' (2012) available at http://papers.ssrn.com/sol3/papers.cfm?abstract_id=1965733.

[45] GR Jones, *Organizational Theory, Design, and Change* (Harlow, Pearson, 2013) 30–31.

[46] ibid, ch 4.

[47] This was first introduced in 1979 as BS5750. See C Hodges, M Tyler and H Abbott, *Product Safety* (London, Sweet & Maxwell, 1996) ch 14.

organisational designs, but rather provide general recommendations, codify best practices and advise the application of certain management systems.[48]

The processual model produces the result that each organisation constructs for itself the meaning of compliance and law through managerial logic.[49]

VI. Modes of Internal Compliance

By what means do businesses achieve internal compliance? This section will note four approaches: Authoritarianism, compliance systems, whistleblowing and culture.[50]

A. Contractual and Disciplinary Systems

It can first be observed that, mirroring the traditional existence of 'command and control' modes for enforcement of criminal and public law, authoritarian approaches to internal discipline exist within private organisations, at least to some extent. The importance of contractual arrangements and terms in regulating the behaviour of actors in supply chains and employment arrangements has been noted in chapter two above.[51] Virtually every organisation and employment contract provides for disciplinary proceedings, and the possibility of imposition of sanctions ultimately including dismissal from employment. Disciplinary techniques form a backdrop, but how much they are used is a different question.

B. Compliance Systems

Many companies have compliance and risk departments as integral parts of their internal management systems. This is always found within firms of any size that operate in regulated sectors, and compliance activities are strongly related to firm size.[52] Most prevailing corporate governance regimes require extensive risk management and control systems.[53]

---

[48] K Grabovets, *Organizational Design and Tort Law: A Synthesis of Organizational Studies and the Economic Analysis of Tort Law*, PhD thesis, Erasmus University, Rotterdam, 2014.

[49] LB Edelman and SA Talesh, 'To Comply or Not to Comply—That isn't the Question: How Organizations Construct the Meaning of Compliance' in C Parker and V Lehmann Nielsen (eds), *Explaining Compliance. Business Responses to Regulation* (Cheltenham, Edward Elgar, 2012) ch 5.

[50] For a management analysis of achieving change, see Jones (n 45) chs 10–14.

[51] F Cafaggi and H Muir Watt (eds), *The Regulatory Function of European Private Law* (Cheltenham, Edward Elgar, 2009).

[52] Although 2012 interviews with UK business people found that only one-quarter of businesses reported that they employed somebody specifically to deal with compliance: *Business Perceptions Survey 2012* (London, IFF Research, 2012) para 1.22. A survey of companies found that some compliance action related to competition law had been taken in the previous year by over 92% of companies with over 50000 employees, falling to 26% for those with 200–499 staff: *The Deterrent Effect of Competition Enforcement by the OFT. A Report Prepared for the OFT by Deloitte* (Office of Fair Trading, 2007) OFT962, para 5.99.

[53] BJ Schoordijk, 'Risk Management Alshoeksteen Van Corporate Governance' in SHA Dumoulinea (ed), *Tussen Themis en Mercurius*, BedrijfsjuridischebijdragenaaneenEuropesebeleidsconcurrentie, LustrumuitgaveNederlandsGenootschap van Bedrijfsjuristen (Deventer, Kluwer, 2005) 309–29; DAMHW Strik, Deel II— Aansprakelijkheidvoorfalendrisicomanagement, in *Ondernemingsbestuur en risicobeheersing op de drempel van*

A formal compliance system is only one aspect of the management structure of an organisation: The allocation of tasks, authority and means of coordination and control within organisations.[54] It does not stand alone sending unambiguous messages and instructions.[55]

From an internal perspective, a compliance system is a vital function, since compliance with regulatory requirements is essential in order for the firm to continue to market products or services, and to support a reputation for quality as shown in high and consistent levels of performance.[56] From an external perspective, reliance on an internal compliance system recognises that non-compliance can usually be identified more swiftly, frequently and cheaply than by external observers and authorities.

Corporate compliance programmes have attracted criticism that their existence is to improve their corporate image and that they do not have any actual effect.[57] Nevertheless, their use is widespread, and has been increasingly encouraged or mandated by law and regarded as both acceptable and effective.[58] They are now high profile in certain sectors, notably financial services, environment,[59] competition,[60] health and safety, food safety and various aspects of healthcare.[61] Miller has described the compliance function as a form of internalised law enforcement which, if it functions effectively, can substitute for much of the enforcement activities of the state.[62] He has also noted the transformation in importance and authority of internal risk and compliance functions.[63] In many businesses,

---

eennieuw decennium: eenondernemingsrechtelijkeanalyse, Preadvies van de Vereeniging 'Handelsrecht' 2009 (Deventer, Kluwer, 2009); J Eijsbouts, *Corporate Responsibility, Beyond Voluntarism. Regulatory Options to Reinforce the Licence to Operate* (Inaugural lecture, Maastricht University, 2011).

[54] H Mintzberg, *Structure in Fives: Designing Effective Organizations* (Englewood Cliffs, Prentice-Hall, 1983).

[55] C Parker and S Gilad, 'Internal Corporate Compliance Management Systems: Structure, Culture and Agency' in C Parker and V Lehmann Nielsen (eds), *Explaining Compliance. Business Responses to Regulation* (Cheltenham, Edward Elgar, 2012).

[56] 15 minute telephone interviews with 2,294 UK business people in 2012 found a strong link between a reputation for compliance and business success: *Business Perceptions Survey 2012* (London, IFF Research, 2012). 80% agreed that 'If my business was found to be non-compliant, I would be concerned that it would affect our relationships with customers' and 69% agreed that 'It matters to our business that our customers know that we invest in compliance.' A similar survey was undertaken in 2010.

[57] KD Krawiec, 'Cosmetic Compliance and the Failure of Negotiated Governance' (2003) 81 *Washington University Law Quarterly* 487, 491; Parker and Gilad (n 55).

[58] F Cafaggi and A Renda, 'Public and Private Regulation: Mapping the Labyrinth' CEPS Working Document No 370, 2012.

[59] For USA: Environmental Protection Agency, 'Incentives for Self-Policing: Discovery, Disclosure, Correction, and Prevention of Violations', *Fed Reg* 60 (1995), 66706; revised Environmental Protection Agency, 'Incentives for Self-Policing: Discovery, Disclosure, Correction, and Prevention of Violations', *Fed Reg* 65 (2000), 19618.

[60] For USA, see ABA Section of Antitrust Law, *Antitrust Compliance: Perspectives and Resources for Corporate Counselors* (Chicago, ABA Publishing, 2005). In UK see *How your Business can Achieve Compliance with Competition Law: Guidance* (Office of Fair Trading, 2011) at http://www.oft.gov.uk/shared_oft/ca-and-cartels/competition-awarenesscompliance/oft1341.pdf. Discussions at A Stephan, 'See No Evil: Cartels and the Limits of Antitrust Compliance Programmes' (2010) 31(8) *The Company Lawyer* 3; K Voss, 'Preventing the Cure: Corporate Compliance Programmes in EU Competition Law Enforcement' (2013) 16(1) *EuroparättsligTidskrift* 28.

[61] For USA: Department of Health and Human Services (HHS), Office of Inspector General (OIG), 'Publication of OIG Compliance Program Guidance for Clinical Laboratories' *Fed. Reg.* 63, no 163 (1998): 45076–87; Department of Health and Human Services (HHS), Office of Inspector General (OIG), 'Publication of OIG Compliance Program Guidance for Hospitals' *Fed Reg.* 63, no 35 (1998): 8987–98; Department of Health and Human Services (HHS), Office of Inspector General (OIG), 'Publication of OIG Compliance Program Guidance for Third-Party Medical Billing Companies' *Fed Reg.* 63, no 243 (1998): 70138–52.

[62] GP Miller, 'The Compliance Function: An Overview' New York University School of Law, Law & Economics Research Paper Series, Working Paper No 14-36.

[63] GP Miller, 'The Role of Risk Management and Compliance in Banking Integration New York University School of Law, Law & Economics Research Paper Series, Working Paper No 14-34.

compliance management has been elevated from 'box ticking' so as to provide a paper trail as a defence mechanism against external interference to a very senior function, capable of shutting down non-compliant operations on their own authority.[64]

Compliance monitoring programmes have assumed particular importance in the USA,[65] as a mitigating factor under sentencing guidelines[66] or as a shield from criminal liability.[67] Despite their importance in the American legal system, and the fact that many companies have strengthened their compliance programmes, there is mounting concern at the ongoing incidence of workplace misconduct and fraud.[68] By contrast, in the UK, the Bribery Act 2010 section 7(2) provides a defence for a commercial organisation to prove that it had in place adequate procedures designed to prevent persons associated with it from undertaking such conduct. Sigler and Murphy argued in 1988 that immunity should be granted for firms that implement corporate compliance programmes beyond a certain standard.[69] However, some ambivalence has been noted in official attitudes towards compliance systems.

US and EU competition enforcers, for example, have been resistant to giving credit for companies who operate such systems, and who regard them as failures if a single violation occurs,[70] as contrasted with more positive encouragement for programmes given by others such as the Canadian Competition Bureau[71] and the Competition Commission of Singapore.[72]

---

[64] An example is an Australian mining firm: GA Smith and D Feldman, *Newmont Mining Corporation: Community Relationships Review: Global Summary Report* (Foley Hoag LLP, 2009).

[65] For an overview see GP Miller, 'An Economic Analysis of Effective Compliance Programs' (2014) New York University School of Law, Law & Economics Research Paper Series, Working Paper No 14-39. Miller concludes that there is no universally accepted definition of an effective compliance programme, and that various official models differ somewhat.

[66] See chs 4 and 10 above. Such as the Environmental Protection Agency, 'Incentives for Self-Policing: Discovery, Disclosure, Correction, and Prevention of Violations', *Fed Reg* 60 (1995), 66706; revised Environmental Protection Agency, 'Incentives for Self-Policing: Discovery, Disclosure, Correction, and Prevention of Violations', *Fed Reg* 65 (2000), 19618. The audit policy offers a complete elimination of the gravity-based penalties for corporations that satisfy all nine conditions. If they meet all conditions except the first, 75% mitigation is given. The conditions are:

    i.   Systematic discovery; discovered through an environmental audit or a compliance management system
    ii. Voluntary discovery
    iii. Prompt disclosure
    iv. Independent discovery and disclosure
    v.   Correction and remediation
    vi. Prevent recurrence
    vii. No repeat violations
    viii. Excluded types of violations
    ix. Cooperation.

[67] S Oded, *Corporate Compliance: New Approaches to Regulatory Enforcement* (Cheltenham, Edward Elgar, 2013). See the US Federal Department of Justice, Antitrust Division, *Corporate Leniency Policy* (August 10, 1993), which aims at encouraging offenders to step forward and report their own violations.

[68] MD Greenberg, *Transforming Compliance: Emerging Paradigms for Boards, Management, Compliance Officers, and Government* (Los Angeles CA, RAND Corporation, 2014).

[69] JA Sigler and JE Murphy, *Interactive Corporate Compliance: An Alternative to Regulatory Compulsion* (New York, Quorum Books, 1988).

[70] Boehme and Murphy (n 44).

[71] See Competition Bureau Canada, 'Corporate Compliance Programs' (2010), http://www.competitionbureau.gc.ca/eic/site/cb-bc.nsf/vwapj/CorporateCompliancePrograms-sept-2010-e.pdf/$FILE/CorporateCompliancePrograms-sept-2010-e.

[72] See http://www.ccs.gov.sg/content/ccs/en.html. In addition, in the US at least one court has accepted evidence of a compliance programme to prove that a company effectively withdrew from a cartel. *United States v Stolt-Nielsen SA* No 06-cr-466 (ED Pa, November 29, 2007).

Three particular challenges to the effectiveness of compliance systems may be noted. First, the particular forms of compliance that come to be understood as legal and rational may vary across social contexts and legal jurisdictions.[73] Second, the imposition of ever more and detailed legal rules produces an internal response within organisations of creating new offices and developing written rules, procedures and policies in an attempt to achieve legal legitimacy, while simultaneously limiting law's impact on managerial power and unfettered discretion over employment decisions.[74] Law becomes 'managerialised', misunderstood and diluted.[75] Third, employees have been shown to develop a 'culture of regulatory resistance' within firms, with managers and staff refraining from doing anything more than minimally comply with existing regulations (rather than seeking to go beyond compliance) and frequently to resist agency enforcement efforts.[76] The strategy of 'creative compliance' is also identified, involving finding ways of behaving in ways that can be claimed to comply with the letter of rules but not their spirit.[77] These tendencies will be enhanced where deterrent enforcement is applied excessively, indiscriminately or in ways that are perceived to be morally illegitimate. Shapiro and Rabinowitz concluded that 'if the government punishes companies in circumstances where managers believe that there has been good faith compliance, corporate officers may react by being less cooperative with regulatory agencies'.[78] The same applies to internal compliance, discipline and managerial systems.

Key elements for the success of compliance systems are widely agreed to be:[79] The support of senior management[80] and status within the organisation,[81] the existence of 'an internal

---

[73] S Talesh, 'The Privatization of Public Legal Rights: How Manufacturers Construct the Meaning of Consumer Law' (2009) 43 *Law & Society Review* 527–62.

[74] PJ DiMaggio and W Powell, 'The Iron Cage Revisited: Institutional Isomorphism and Collective Rationality in Organizational Fields' (1983) 48 *American Sociological Review* 147–60; LB Edelman, 'Legal Environments and Organizational Governance: The Expansion of Due Process in the American Workplace' (1990) 95 *American Journal of Sociology* 1401–40; LB Edelman, 'Legal Ambiguity and Symbolic Structures: Organizational Mediation of Civil Rights Law' (1992) 97 *American Journal of Sociology* 1531–76.

[75] Edelman and Talesh (n 49) ch 5.

[76] E Bardach and R Kagan, *Going by the Book: The Problem of Regulatory Unreasonableness* (Philadelphia, Temple University Press, 1982).

[77] D McBarnet, 'Law, Policy, and Legal Avoidance: Can Law Effectively Implement Egalitarian Policies?' (1988) 15 *Journal of Law and Society* 113–21; D McBarnet and C Whelan, 'Challenging the Regulators; Strategies for Resisting Control' in C McCrudden (ed), *Regulation and Deregulation* (Oxford, Clarendon Press, 1999); D McBarnet and C Whelan, 'The Elusive Spirit of the Law: Formalism and the Struggle for Legal Control' (1991) 54 *MLR* 848; and other essays collected in D McBarnet, *Crime, Compliance and Control* (Aldershot, Ashgate, 2004).

[78] S Shapiro and R Rabinowitz, 'Punishment versus Cooperation in Regulatory Enforcement: A Case Study of OSHA' (1997) 14 *Administrative Law Review* 713–62, 718.

[79] See Parker and Gilad (n 55) ch 8.

[80] Many studies and official statements support this. J Braithwaite, *To Punish or Persuade: Enforcement of Coal Mine Safety* (Albany, State University of New York Press, 1985) 61; DP McCaffrey and DW Hart, *Wall Street Polices Itself: How Securities Firms Manage the Legal Hazards of Competitive Pressures* (New York, Oxford University Press, 1998) 174; J Rees, *Hostages of Each Other: The Transformation of Nuclear Safety Since Three Mile Island* (Chicago, University of Chicago Press, 1994); *How your Business can Achieve Compliance* (Office of Fair Trading, 2005) OFT 424, 10; KS Desai, 'Antitrust Compliance Programmes' *The European Antitrust Review 2006* (Global Competition Review, 2006) Nov Supp 15–21; J Joshua, 'Antitrust compliance programmes for multinational companies [2001] *International Financial Law Review Supplement* (Competition and Antitrust, 2001); ABA, *Antitrust Compliance*, 2005, 81.

[81] M Weait, 'The Role of the Compliance Officer in Firms Carrying on Investment Business' (1994) 9(8) *Butterworth's Journal of International Banking and Financial Law* 381–83.

constituency advocating and working for compliance',[82] communication of the policy and practical implications to all staff, including by training and regular refreshers, auditing, and employees' internalisation of the values and practical actions involved in carrying out daily procedures, operations, reward and performance review systems.[83]

Parker and Nielsen found that each of six central elements of formal compliance systems is associated with the organisation managing compliance better in practice: (1) A written compliance policy; (2) a dedicated compliance function; (3) a clearly defined system for handling complaints from customers or clients; (4) a clearly defined system for handling compliance failures; (5) induction for new employees that includes compliance training; and (6) external review of the compliance system.[84]

A good compliance programme will use the full range of management techniques to support understanding and compliance, and prevent and detect misconduct.[85] The Canadian Competition Bureau's Bulletin on compliance programmes includes the following techniques:[86]

— Compliance controls;
— an executive-level chief ethics and compliance officer directly responsible to the board of directors;
— active board oversight;
— background checks and disqualification of those who would undercut the compliance programme;
— ongoing communications and training;
— a system that encourages reporting without fear of retaliation;
— audits, monitoring and other forms of checking;
— periodic evaluation of the programme;
— discipline (including for failure to take steps to prevent violations);
— use of incentives to promote the programme;
— system to investigate and resolve allegations of misconduct; and
— a benchmarking to keep up with industry practice.

The US Sentencing Commission's Federal Sentencing Guidelines Manual has established a detailed definition of compliance management systems, operation of which will be taken into account by courts and prosecutors in the imposition of fines and jail sentences for violations of criminal laws, such as the antitrust laws and the anti-bribery laws.[87] These

---

[82] J Braithwaite, *Corporate Crime in the Pharmaceutical Industry* (London, Routledge and Kegan Paul, 1984) 359; V Braithwaite, 'The Australian Government's Affirmative Action Legislation: Achieving Social Change through Human Resource Management' (1993) 15 *Law & Policy* 327–54; J Rees (n 80) 92, 98–99, 108; S Taylor, *Making Bureaucracies Think: The Environmental Impact Statement Strategy of Administrative Reform,* (Stanford, Stanford University Press, 1984).

[83] A Newton, *The Handbook of Compliance: Making Ethics Work in Financial Services* (London, Financial Times Prentice Hall, 1998) 74.

[84] C Parker and VL Nielsen, 'Corporate Compliance Systems: Could They Make Any Difference?' (2009) 41 (1) *Administration & Society* 3.

[85] Boehme and Murphy (n 44).

[86] *Bulletin: Corporate Compliance Programs,* Competition Bureau of Canada, 2010, http://www.competitionbureau.gc.ca/eic/site/cb-bc.nsf/vwapj/CorporateCompliancePrograms-sept-2010-e.pdf/$FILE/Corporate CompliancePrograms-sept-2010-e.pdf.

[87] The US Federal Sentencing Guidelines, Compliance Program Requirements http://www.ussc.gov/Guidelines/2010_guidelines/Manual_HTML/8b2_1.htm.

guidelines, therefore, are an example of inducement of companies to adequate self-regulation in the fields of substantive legislation. There are two major modules:[88]

A. *A Compliance and Ethics Programme*, which involves self-policing activities undertaken by corporations to prevent, detect, and investigate employees' violations. Seven criteria are stated for the establishment of an 'effective' compliance and ethics programme:
   i.   Establishment of standards and procedures
   ii. Oversight by high-level personnel
   iii. Due care in delegating substantial discretionary authority
   iv. Effective communication for employees at all levels
   v.   Active monitoring
   vi. Incentivising and disciplinary mechanisms
   vii. Preventing recurrence.

B. *A Self-Reporting Mechanism*, containing seven criteria for the establishment of an 'effective compliance and ethics program':
   i.   Establishment of standards and procedures
   ii. Oversight by high-level personnel
   iii. Due care in delegating substantial discretionary authority
   iv. Effective communication for employees at all levels
   v.   Active monitoring
   vi. Incentivising and disciplinary mechanisms
   vii. Preventing recurrence:
        a. self-reporting,
        b. cooperating with the investigation, and
        c. affirmative acceptance of responsibility for the misconduct.

C. External Information and Advice

Compliance—or enforcement—can be supported by a range of third parties, in addition to the classic bilateral relationship between regulator/enforcer and business. The options include standardisation organisations, accreditation agencies, ranking institutions, credit rating agencies, auditors, in-house counsel, external lawyers. These are usually repeat players that serve many clients by acting as 'reputational intermediaries'.[89]

---

[88] US Sentencing Commission, *Federal Sentencing Guidelines Manual: Chapter Eight—Sentencing of Organizations* (2009) 495. JM Kaplan, 'Corporate Sentencing Guidelines: Overview' in JM Kaplan and JE Murphy (eds), *Compliance Programs and the Corporate Sentencing Guidelines: Preventing Criminal and Civil Liability* (St Paul MN, Thomson/West, rev 2009); RJ Maurer, 'The Federal Sentencing Guidelines for Organizations: How Do They Work and What Are They Supposed to Do? (1993) 18 *Dayton Law Review* 799–833; NE Clark, 'Corporate Sentencing Guidelines: Drafting History' in Kaplan and Murphy (n 88); JC Coffee, Jr, 'The Attorney as Gatekeeper: An Agenda for the SEC' (2003) 103 *Columbia Law Review* 1293–316; JR Steer, 'Sentencing Guidelines: In General' in Kaplan and Murphy (n 88); IH Nagel and WM Swenson, 'The Federal Sentencing Guidelines for Corporations: Their Development, Theoretical Underpinnings, and some Thoughts about their Future' (1993) 71 *Washington University Law Quarterly* 205–59; JS Parker, 'Rules without…: Some Critical Reflections in the Federal Corporate Sentencing Guidelines' (1993) 71 *Washington University Law Quarterly* 397–442.

[89] Oded (n 67).

UK government research in 2012 found that many businesses use external agents as a source of information and advice in complying with regulation (70 per cent, up from 64 per cent in 2010).[90] Around half of businesses had used trade associations, government department websites, insurance companies and accountants to help them comply with regulation. Four in ten mentioned the Businesslink website in relation to advice on regulatory requirements, whilst one in three mentioned their local council and around a quarter mentioned direct contact with a government department.[91] Businesses were more likely to use external agents as a source of information in cases of employment law (86 per cent) and company law (81 per cent), and less likely to use agents for food safety (44 per cent) and fire safety (55 per cent).[92]

Most businesses expected regulators to provide some help and guidance rather than simply enforcing rules and regulations only. Four-fifths thought that the role of regulators was to enforce regulations and to provide advice rather than only to enforce rules and regulations, but only two-fifths agreed that 'Regulators help my business to address regulatory risks and prevent non-compliance from happening' and 'Regulators provide clarity about what regulatory requirements apply to my business.'[93]

In a 2007 survey in relation to competition law, the commonest compliance measure was taking external legal advice (40 per cent of companies).[94] Other relatively common measures were a policy code (34 per cent), seminars on competition law (26 per cent), employing a dedicated competition compliance officer (20 per cent), taking economic advice (16 per cent) and requiring employees to take an online training programme (nine per cent).[95]

Engagement by a firm of third party monitors, appointed to oversee internal compliance management system, to disrupt misconduct, has become a typical condition in the USA of Deferred Prosecution Agreements.[96]

VII. Corporate Social Responsibility

Strengthening of the relationship between businesses and social values can be seen in the development of corporate social responsibility (CSR). CSR has been defined by the European Commission as 'a concept whereby companies integrate social and environmental concerns

---

[90] *Business Perceptions Survey 2012* (London, IFF Research, 2012) para 1.27. The survey comprised 15 minute telephone interviews with 2,294 business people.
[91] ibid.
[92] ibid, para 1.27.
[93] *Business Perceptions Survey 2012* (London, IFF Research, 2012) paras 1.16 and 1.17.
[94] *The Deterrent Effect of Competition Enforcement by the OFT. A Report Prepared for the OFT by Deloitte* (n 52).
[95] ibid.
[96] See LD Thompson, Deputy Attorney General, *Memorandum for Heads of Department Components United States Attorneys: Principles of Federal Prosecution of Business Organizations* (US Department of Justice, Office of the Deputy Attorney General, January 20, 2003) available at: http://www.justice.gov/dag/cftf/corporate_guidelines.htm; GG Grindler, Acting Deputy Attorney General. *Memorandum for Heads of Department Components United States Attorneys: Additional Guidance on the use of Monitors in Deferred Prosecution Agreements and Non-Prosecution Agreements with Corporations* (US Department of Justice, Office of the Deputy Attorney General, May 25, 2010), available at: http://www.justice.gov/PrintOut2.jsp. Discussed in Oded (n 67). See statistics at: *2014 Corporate Deferred Prosecution and Non-Prosecution Agreements* (Los Angeles, Gibson Dunn, 2014) at http://www.gibsondunn.com/publications/default.aspx.

in their business operations and in their interactions with stakeholders on a voluntary basis' and as concerning 'actions by companies over and above their legal obligations towards society and the environment.'[97] The relationship between basic economic conditions and corporate behaviour is mediated by several institutional conditions, such as: Private and public regulation; the presence of other organisations that monitor corporate behaviour; institutionalised norms regarding appropriate corporate conduct; associative behaviour among corporations, and organised dialogue between corporations and stakeholders.[98]

The Commission stated that because CSR 'requires engagement with internal and external stakeholders, it enables enterprises to better anticipate and take advantage of fast changing societal expectations and operating conditions', and that building trust is critical: 'By addressing their social responsibility enterprises can build long-term employee, consumer and citizen trust as a basis for sustainable business models. Higher levels of trust in turn help to create an environment in which enterprises can innovate and grow.'[99] The Commission noted the increasing importance of a strategic approach for the competitiveness of enterprises. 'CSR in its core is nothing more than decent business, perceived as such by society'.[100]

CSR is in reality the alignment of business operations with social values.[101] The assumption underlying CSR is that the ethical substance of a norm remains constant, so if it is strongly valued in the community in which a firm operates, it can also be applied by the firm in its internal behaviours and especially in its interaction with the relevant external community (internalisation or management of externalities).[102] One theoretical approach seeks to balance or reciprocate the receipt by businesses of privileges from society, as part of a social licence to operate.[103] This draws historically on Rousseau's social contract theory, revived in terms of corporate citizenship under the influence of John Rawls[104] and Amartya Sen.[105] The licence to operate theory has been noted above as expounded by Gunningham

---

[97] Communication *A Renewed EU Strategy 2011–14 for Corporate Social Responsibility* COM(2011) 681, 25.10.2011, http://ec.europa.eu/enterprise/newsroom/cf/_getdocument.cfm?doc_id=7010. See also definition at International Standard guidelines for social responsibility (SR) ISO 26000 released on 1 November 2010.

[98] JL Campbell, 'Why would Corporations Behave in Socially Responsible Ways? An Institutional Theory of Corporate Social Responsibility' (2007) 32(2) *Academy of Management Review* 946.

[99] ibid.

[100] Rapport van de CommissieBurgmans over de verhouding MVO en corporate governance, uitgebracht op 6 november 2008 aan de Staatssecretaris van EconomischeZaken (*www.ez.nl*).

[101] AV Joseph, 'Successful Examples of Corporate Social Responsibility' (2009) 44(3) *The Indian Journal of Industrial Relations* 402, 403.

[102] Eijsbouts (n 53). Eijsbouts' normative description of CSR is the responsibility of corporations to meet the legitimate expectations of society for the firm to conduct its businesses in ways that produce economic, social and ecological benefits to relevant stakeholders and society at large.

His operational or process description is: CSR as a process is the structured and systematic approach by which firms are embedding all aspects of the applicable CSR- norms in their daily operations at all relevant levels, monitoring compliance and results and reporting to relevant stakeholders and society at large.

[103] T Donaldson, *Corporations and Morality* (Englewood Cliffs NJ, Prentice Hall, 1982). See also SC de Hoo, *In Pursuit of Corporate Sustainability and Responsibility: Past Cracking Perceptions and Creating Codes* Inaugural Lecture Maastricht University, 2011, 11, referring to the principle of reciprocity, also a corporate social contracts based approach.

[104] The presumption of justice as fairness: J Rawls, *A Theory of Justice* (Boston MA, Harvard University Press, 1971).

[105] A Sen, *The Idea of Justice* (London, Allen Lane, 2009) 361–64 on human rights.

in relation to corporate environmental responsibility,[106] it chimes with the concept of meta-regulation and Parker's Open Corporation.[107]

CSR has been subject to criticism that it has no teeth and is therefore ineffective.[108] Whether that is true or not, the phenomenon of CSR, which is now fairly widely found, constitutes some attempt by business to be open to the values expressed by local communities or more general populations. Doing the 'right thing' has been recognised as having commercial value in at least some circumstances, producing financial or reputational benefit.[109]

Authoritative guidance on CSR is provided by internationally recognised principles and guidelines, in particular the recently updated OECD (Organisation for Economic Co-operation and Development) Guidelines for Multinational Enterprises, the 10 principles of the United Nations Global Compact,[110] the OECD Guidelines for Multinational Enterprises,[111] the ISO 26000 Guidance Standard on Social Responsibility,[112] the ILO (International Labour Organization) Tri-partite Declaration of Principles Concerning Multinational Enterprises and Social Policy,[113] and the United Nations Guiding Principles on Business and Human Rights.[114]

The UN Human Rights Guiding Principles on Business and Human Rights are based on a 'Protect, Respect and Remedy' Framework proposed by Professor John Ruggie.[115] Ruggie clearly distinguished and specified the state *duty to protect* and the corporate *responsibility to respect* human rights. This corporate responsibility to respect human rights is not a legal responsibility, but a 'universal baseline expectation' from society, so an uncodified social norm.[116] The third pillar of his framework relates to adequate remedies, both judicial and non-judicial. The 2011 Guiding Principles specify how corporations should live up to their responsibility to respect human rights. Under a 'risk based due diligence' approach, corporations should on a continuous basis assess whether and in what ways their actual or

---

[106] N Gunningham and P Grabosky, *Smart Regulation. Designing Environmental Policy* (Oxford, Oxford University Press, 1998).

[107] C Parker, 'Meta-regulation: Legal Accountability for Corporate Social Responsibility' in D McBarnet, A Voiculescu and T Campbell (eds), *The New Corporate Accountability: Corporate Social Responsibility and the Law* (Milton Keynes, The Open University, 2007) ('it is possible, in principle at least, to imagine (and even to see partial examples) of meta-regulation that holds business organisations accountable for putting in place corporate conscience processes that are aimed at substantive social values') 207ff.

[108] C Mayer, *Firm Commitment: Why the Corporation is Failing us and How to Restore Trust in it* (Oxford, Oxford University Press, 2013) 241; SJ Padfield, 'Corporate Social Responsibility & Concession Theory' (2015) 6 *William & Mary Business Law Review* 1.

[109] T Gillis and N Spring, 'Doing Good is Good for Business' (2001) 18(6) *Communication World* 23–26.

[110] https://www.unglobalcompact.org.

[111] http://www.oecd.org/daf/inv/mne.

[112] http://www.iso.org/iso/home/standards/iso26000.htm.

[113] http://www.ilo.org/empent/Publications/WCMS_094386/lang--en/index.htm.

[114] J Ruggie, *The Special Representative of the Secretary-General, Report of the Special Representative of the Secretary-General on the Issue of Human Rights and Transnational Business Corporations and other Business Enterprises, Guiding Principles on Business and Human Rights: Implementing the United Nations 'Protect, Respect and Remedy' Framework*, A/HRC/17/31, 21 March 2011.

[115] J Ruggie, *The Special Representative of the Secretary-General, Report of the Special Representative of the Secretary-General on the Issue of Human Rights and Transnational Corporations and Other Business Enterprises: Protect, Respect and Remedy: a Framework for Business and Human Rights*, delivered to the Human Rights Council, A/HRC/8/5, 7 April 2008.

[116] Eijsbouts (n 53).

intended operations run the risk to impact on the human rights of others and take preventive or remedial steps. This assessment of the relevant substantive CSR norms is a process of contextualisation: Each company will have to analyse its position based on its specific industrial characteristics and the given societal context and this in a continuing dialogue with the relevant stakeholders in that same context.

VIII. Corporate Responsibility

Various initiatives have taken a broader approach to corporate responsibility. The UK government built on the established foundations of corporate *social* responsibility as part of its response to the 2008–2012 financial crisis,[117] by launching a generalised initiative on *corporate responsibility* (CR) in 2013. It defined CR as the voluntary action businesses take over and above legal requirements to manage and enhance economic, environmental and societal impacts.[118] The government expressed several aims: To align approaches to responsibility in the UK with various global approaches; to encourage increased reporting and disclosure against consistent, comparable and voluntary metrics; to strengthen supply chain management;[119] to encourage more small and medium-sized enterprises to adopt responsible business activities; to strengthen the relationship between business and society; to strengthen business observance of human rights; to determine the scope to expand professional development in corporate responsibility and in the role of consumers.[120] The policy issued in 2014 noted that CSR had evolved from philanthrophy to a core activity for an increasing number of businesses, and 'from how businesses spread their money to how they earn it'.[121] This transformation had been supported by wider realisation of the economic benefits to businesses, such as: Staff recruitment and retention; managing risk in supply chains; driving innovation and productivity; and opening up new markets and new business models.[122] Respondents to the debate noted the fact that variations in business size, sector, complexity and communities in which they operated, led to differences in how CR was practised. They also called for the need to support forms of collaboration, and to bridge a disconnection between business and society.

In 2013, the European Commission has also adopted a broad approach in seeking to define the core propositions that frame effective voluntary multi-stakeholder action, in the context of a wide range of voluntary and self- and co-regulation processes, and 'profound

---

[117] This is discussed in detail in ch 20.

[118] *Corporate Responsibility. Good for Business and Society: Government Response to Call for Views on Corporate Responsibility* (Department for Business, Innovation & Skills, 2014) https://www.gov.uk/government/uploads/system/uploads/attachment_data/file/300265/bis-14-651-good-for-business-and-society-government-response-to-call-for-views-on-corporate-responsibility.pdf.

[119] This issue was highlighted by a scandal over use of horsemeat in food, in which the ingredients appeared to have been correctly identified at source (eg in Romania) but to have become wrongly passed on at some stage in a lengthy supply chain.

[120] *Corporate Responsibility: A Call for Views* (Department for Business, Innovation & Skills, 2013) available at https://www.gov.uk/government/uploads/system/uploads/attachment_data/file/209219/bis-13-964-corporate-responsibility-call.pdf.

[121] *Corporate Responsibility. Good for Business and Society: Government Response to Call for Views on Corporate Responsibility* (n 118) para 2.1.

[122] ibid, para 1.2.

world-wide patterns of change'.[123] The initiative was launched by the Commission's Directorate-General Connect, in the context of its expanding digital agenda. The Commission adopted the description 'Effective Open Voluntarism', defined as good design principles for self- and co-regulation and other multi-stakeholder actions, and invited bodies and organisations to sign a code that would commit to mutual sharing of their overall experience of the application of the code and undertake to seek the broader application by other parties of the approach set out in it. The Commission aimed to establish a principle of open governance for activities, open for ownership and participation at various levels by all public or private actors. The Code stated the following principles: Clear objectives; representativeness; legal compliance; good faith; learning through an iterative process; accountability for participants' roles, monitoring of performance against each actor's performance; reporting of performance monitoring results by each actor for discussion; a compliance system allowing complaints by non-participants and participants to be evaluated by independent assessors; with any panel comprising a majority of independent individuals, and publication of evaluation results; non-compliance shall be subject to a graduated scale of penalties, with exclusion included, and without prejudice to any consequences of non-compliance under the terms of the Unfair Commercial Practices Directive. The Commission also stated:

> Success requires without exception that an initiative:
>
> — Secures broad support among, and participation from, interested parties;
> — Defines effective rules for rapid collective and individual action;
> — Sets clear performance indicators, agreed with interested parties;
> — Mandates regular and open reporting on performance and provides a mechanism to take account of feedback in adapting the approach and improving delivery;
> — Makes available the resulting body of knowledge to drive better policy making.[124]

IX. Whistleblowing

A. Reporting, Barriers and Inertia

As noted above and in chapter 19, business systems operate on the basis of continual circulation and evaluation of information. '[T]he first people to know of any risk will usually be those who work in or for the organisation.'[125] However, in some circumstances, notification may not occur. At one extreme is a situation in which data is generally circulated but one or more individual items are omitted, and, at the other extreme, there may be a general failure to circulate relevant information at all, and even to conceal the true picture. The latter

---

[123] *Consultation about a Code for Effective Open Voluntarism* (European Commission DG INFSO, 2012).
[124] ibid.
[125] *Code of Practice on Whistleblowing Arrangements* (British Standards Institution), para 1.2. This states that the main reason enlightened organisations implement whistleblowing arrangements is that they recognise that it makes good business sense, as able to deter wrongdoing; pick up problems early; enable critical information to get to the people who need to know and can address the issue; demonstrate to stakeholders, regulators and the courts that they are accountable and well managed; reduce the risk of anonymous and malicious leaks; minimise costs and compensation from accidents, investigations, litigation and regulatory inspections; and maintain and enhance its reputation.

situation can occur where the business culture itself is poor, failing or fraudulent. In such situations, channels for reporting major issues, internally and perhaps externally,[126] may be important. This 'unusual' reporting arrangement is generally known as whistleblowing. Whistleblowing has been defined as the raising of a concern, either within the workplace or externally, about a danger, risk, malpractice or wrongdoing which affects others.[127] A key element is that the communication is usually about an issue that the communicator feels cannot be raised through normal internal management channels so is raised by some external or other route, which the corporation may regard as a breach of internal procedures, duties of employment or discipline.

Examples of the relevance of whistleblowing exist from diverse sectors.[128] A prominent example of is Edward Snowden's leaking of United States documents to Wikileaks. Whistleblowing has been formally recognised by numerous international bodies as an effective instrument against corruption.[129] In its 2012 Report, the Association of Certified Fraud Examiners found that 50.9 per cent of reported fraud within organisations is identified by tip-offs from employees or contractors.[130] In 2014 the Association calculated that three times as many frauds are discovered by tip-offs than by any other method.[131] Disclosure may be the first means by which wrongdoing comes to the attention of an external authority, although meta-sharing and analysis may be required. The Francis Inquiry into the Mid Staffordshire NHS Foundation Trust concluded that

> communication of intelligence between regulators needs to go further than sharing existing concerns identified as risks, and it should extend to all intelligence which when pieced together with that possessed by partner organisations may raise the level of concern.[132]

However, there are frequent references to the problem that individuals may not report concerns because of the fear of adverse personal consequences. This is especially so in relation

---

[126] 'Whistleblowers are a vital source of information for regulators as they can provide a perspective that is not readily available in other ways. Collating management information on whistleblowing cases can provide valuable intelligence on areas that need further examination or controls.': *Making a Whistleblowing Policy Work* (London, National Audit Office, March 2014) para 3.14.

[127] *The Whistleblowing Commission: Report on the Effectiveness of Existing Arranges for Workplace Whistleblowing in the UK* (London, Whistleblowing Commission, November 2013), available at http://www.pcaw.org.uk/files/WBC%20Report%20Final.pdf, para 2.

[128] Feldman and Lobel cite important examples of information being provided by whistleblowers in WorldCom and Enron, Wigand in relation to tobacco, Moore at HBOS, and Adams at Hoffman-LaRoche: Y Feldman and O Lobel, 'Individuals as Enforcers: The Design of Employee Reporting Systems' in C Parker and V Lehmann Nielsen (eds), *Explaining Compliance. Business Responses to Regulation* (Cheltenham, Edward Elgar, 2012).

[129] The G20 Anti-corruption Action Plan 2013–2014 (http://dialogues.civil20.org/file/301363/download/326897); the OECD whistleblowing toolkit (http://www.oecd.org/cleangovbiz/toolkit/whistleblowerprotection.htm); United Nations Convention Against Corruption (art 33), and the Council of Europe (Parliamentary Assembly of the Council of Europe resolution for the protection of whistleblowers, 2010, (http://assembly.coe.int/main.asp?link=/documents/adoptedtext/ta10/eres1729.htm). Parliamentary Commission on Banking Standards, 'Changing Banking for Good' June 2013, para 142.

[130] *Report to the Nation on Occupational Fraud Abuse: 2012 Global Fraud Study* (Association of Certified Fraud Examiners, 2012) at http://www.acfe.com/uploadedFiles/ACFE_Website/Content/rttn/2012-report-to-nations.pdf.

[131] Schumpeter, 'The Enemy Within. Fraud Within Companies is a Risk that can Never be Eliminated, just Managed' *The Economist* (London, 1 March 2014) 73.

[132] *Report of the Mid Staffordshire NHS Foundation Trust Public Inquiry*, HC 947, Public Inquiry, Chaired by Robert Francis QC, February 2013, para 3.15. Following this, the regulators Monitor and the Care Quality Commission have committed to share information between them: Comptroller and Auditor General, *Monitor, Regulating NHS Foundation Trusts*, Session 2013–14, HC 1071, National Audit Office, February 2014.

to reporting practices that are systemic or undertaken by more senior staff. There are three aspects here: Not only is prevailing practice illegal or unethical, but a significant number of individuals either condone or ignore this, and the firm's management appears to the informer to be incapable of changing the situation for the better. Accordingly, the informer feels unable to report through normal managerial channels, and often seeks to blow the whistle through an external route.

The Francis report exposed unacceptable levels of patient care and a staff culture that deterred whistleblowers from raising concerns.[133] Many staff felt that if they raised concerns about poor care they would not be listened to,[134] or would be victimised. Similarly, the Parliamentary Commission on Banking Standards stated:

> [T]he Commission was shocked by the evidence it heard that so many people turned a blind eye to misbehaviour and failed to report it. Institutions must ensure that their staff have a clear understanding of their duty to report an instance of wrongdoing, or 'whistleblow', within the firm. This should include clear information for staff on what to do. Employee contracts and codes of conduct should include clear references to the duty to whistleblow and the circumstances in which they would be expected to do so.[135]

Research for the Institute of Business Ethics has shown that while one in four workers are aware of misconduct at work, more than half (52 per cent) of those stay silent.[136] A 2008 study of 333 participants found that the likelihood and the manner of reporting varied depending on the type of illegality, and is strongly correlated to perceptions of legitimacy of organisational rules, job security and voice within the workplace.[137] Comparing illegalities, employees preferred to report clear violations by rank and file employees, rather than violations by managers. At the same time, external reporting to government or media entities was most likely when violations involved the organisation as a whole, or implicated top management.

Feldman and Lobel's research also found that workers are most likely to report their co-workers when they witnessed localised employee theft, than environmental illegality, sexual harassment, corporate financial fraud and safety issues.[138] People believe that they themselves will report more frequently than other people, and that others are motivated by different rationales than themselves. Women are more likely to report corporate misconduct, and are motivated to report by different factors than men. Generally people prefer to confront illegal behaviour from within their organisation, rather than reporting it externally, as long as they believe that internal reporting will be effective. The existence of a duty to report can make a huge difference.

---

[133] *Report of the Mid Staffordshire NHS Foundation Trust Public Inquiry*, HC 947, Public Inquiry, Chaired by Robert Francis QC, February 2013.

[134] A review of 150 NHS complaints found failings in the handling of over one third, and that 28 should have been investigated as a Serious Untoward Incident: *Press Release, Ombudsman finds Variation in Quality of NHS Investigations into Complaints of Avoidable Death and Avoidable Harm* (Parliamentary and Health Service Ombudsman, 7 February 2015).

[135] Parliamentary Commission on Banking Standards, 'Changing Banking for Good' (June 2013), para 142.

[136] British Standards Institution, *Whistleblowing Arrangements Code of Practice*, PAS 1998: 2008, July 2008.

[137] Y Feldman and O Lobel, 'Behavioral Versus Institutional Antecedents of Decentralized Enforcement: An Experimental Approach' (2008) 2 *Regulation and Governance* 165–92; Y Feldman and O Lobel, 'The Incentives Matrix: The Comparative Effectiveness of Rewards, Liabilities, Duties and Protections for Reporting Illegality' (2010) 87 *Texas Law Review* 1151–212.

[138] ibid. See summary at: Feldman and Lobel (n 128).

B. The Relevance of Culture

Whistleblowing carries a connotation of exposing extensive unethical practices within an organisation that the majority of employees, relevant managers or firm's culture condone or to which they turn a blind eye. A series of official reports have highlighted that the underlying problem lies with the *culture* of the firm or relevant group of employees.

Thus the Committee on Standards in Public Life has highlighted the role which whistleblowing plays 'both as an instrument in support of good governance and a manifestation of a more open culture.'[139] The Whistleblowing Commission, a charity, considers:

> Effective whistleblowing arrangements are a key part of good governance. A healthy and open culture is one where people are encouraged to speak out, confident that they can do so without adverse repercussions, confident that they will be listened to, and confident that appropriate action will be taken. This is to the benefit of organisations, individuals and society as a whole.[140]

Dame Janet Smith commented in her report on the inquiry which followed the conviction of Harold Shipman, a GP who had killed at least 215 of his patients over a period of 24 years:

> To modern eyes, it seems obvious that a culture in all healthcare organisations that encourages the reporting of concerns would carry with it great benefits. The readiness of staff to draw attention to errors or 'near misses' by doctors and nurses, and the facility for them to do so, could have a major impact upon patient safety and upon the quality of care provided.[141]

> I believe that the willingness of one healthcare professional to take responsibility for raising concerns about the conduct, performance or health of another could make a greater contribution to patient safety than any other single factor.[142]

C. Official Statements on Whistleblowing

Whistleblowing arrangements are recommended by various official bodies, or required by law, especially since the 2008 financial crisis.[143] The legal framework typically requires a firm to have a reporting structure for reporting outside normal channels, and provides some protection for whistleblowers against recrimination or discrimination.

Thus, the UK Financial Conduct Authority encourages organisations to have whistleblowing arrangements in place.[144] The UK Financial Reporting Council's Corporate

---

[139] Committee on Standards of Public Life, 'Getting the Balance Right: Implementing Standards in Public Life', Tenth Report of the Committee on Standards in Public Life, 2005, para 4.31, at http://www.official-documents. gov.uk/document/cm64/6407/6407.pdf.

[140] *The Whistleblowing Commission: Report on the Effectiveness of Existing Arranges for Workplace Whistleblowing in the UK* (Whistleblowing Commission, November 2013), available at http://www.pcaw.org.uk/files/ WBC%20Report%20Final.pdf.

[141] Fifth Report of the Shipman Inquiry, 'Safeguarding Patients: Lessons from the Past—Proposals for the Future' (9 December 2004) para 11.50.

[142] ibid, para 81.

[143] M Schmidt, '"Whistle-blowing" Regulation and Accounting Standards Enforcement in Germany and Europe: An Economic Perspective' (2005) 25 *International Review of Law and Economies* 153–61.

[144] Financial Conduct Authority Handbook, at http://fshandbook.info/FS/html/FCA.

Governance Code 2012 recommends that listed companies should have whistleblowing policies in place, or explain why they do not have them.[145]

In the USA, significant financial incentives can apply for people to inform. The US False Claims Act allows private citizens to recover a percentage of the amount of a procurement fraud. A 1986 amendment to prohibits retaliation against employees who sue. The Sarbanes-Oxley Act of 2002 strengthened the protections offered to whistleblowers in publicly traded corporations. Reporting is encouraged by offering a financial incentive, which was significantly expanded under the Dodd Frank Act of 2010. An employee who related key facts to the US Department of Justice concerning employer JP Morgan's issue of mortgages, in relation which the involvement of guarantees by state entities brought the issue under the False Claims Act, was paid $63,870,000 after JP Morgan settled the case by paying $614 million.[146]

Following that approach, the European Union Market Abuse Regulation requires financial service organisations and their regulators to have whistleblowing arrangements in place, and permit Member States to provide financial incentives to whistleblowers.[147] However, the UK government firmly rejected making payments to incentivise whistleblowing, saying that there is no empirical evidence that such incentives lead to an increase in the number or quality of disclosures received by regulators, and that the culture should be that speaking up should become normal business practice.[148]

The UK created a new offence in 2010 of failing to prevent bribery. Commercial organisations commit the offence if employees or other associated persons commit offences of bribery.[149] It is a defence if the organisation proves that it had adequate procedures in place. In the government guidance accompanying the Bribery Act 2010 whistleblowing or 'Speak Up' policies are recommended[150] as part of the adequate procedures to prevent bribery. The British Standards Institution's standard for Anti-Bribery Management Systems includes whistleblowing arrangements and sectoral guidance exists.[151]

Given that revealing internal information to the public may breach employment or public laws, a line has to be drawn between disclosure that is legitimate or not. The essential criterion that has emerged is whether disclosure is in the public interest,[152] and thus

---

[145] The UK Corporate Governance Code (C.3.5) states for companies listed on the London Stock Exchange it is a matter for the Board, and specifically the Audit Committee, to ensure that arrangements are in place for staff to raise concerns in confidence about possible financial and other improprieties, and for such concerns to be proportionately and independently investigated and followed up. Available at: http://www.frc.org.uk/Our-Work/Codes-Standards/Corporate-governance/UK-Corporate-Governance-Code.aspx.

[146] 'Whistleblowers. A $64m Question' *The Economist* (London, March 15th 2014) 73.

[147] Reg (EU) No 596/2014 on market abuse (market abuse regulation) and repealing Dir 2003/6/EC of the European Parliament and of the Council and Commission Dirs 2003/124/EC, 2003/125/EC and 2004/72/EC, art 29. See H Fleischer and KU Schmolke, 'Financial Incentives for Whistleblowers in European Capital Markets Law? Legal Policy Considerations on the Reform of the Market Abuse Regime'. ECGI—Law Working Paper No 189/2012.

[148] *Financial Incentives for Whistleblowers* (Prudential Regulation Authority and Financial Conduct Authority, 2014).

[149] Bribery Act 2010, s 7.

[150] *Bribery Act 2010: Guidance about Commercial Organisations Preventing Bribery* https://www.justice.gov.uk/downloads/legislation/bribery-act-2010-guidance.pdf.

[151] *Anti-Bribery and Corruption Guidance* (BBA, May 2014), available at https://www.bba.org.uk/wp-content/uploads/2014/05/ABC_guidelines_designed-final.pdf.

[152] In relation to disclosure by public officials: *Making a Whistleblowing Policy Work* (National Audit Office, March 2014). In general, the Law Society said 'There is widespread support for the notion that

overrides other obligations of confidentiality.[153] The problem in practice is that a public interest test can only be validated after an individual disclosure has taken place. Accordingly, some systems provide a process solution, which encourages confidential disclosure to particular internal or external officers. Research has found that raising a concern with a regulator decreases the chance of dismissal.[154] In 2013 the UK government published a list of prescribed people and bodies to whom malpractice can be reported other than to an employer, updated in 2015.[155]

In order to attempt to shield whistleblowers from recognised behaviour of adverse consequences, some legislative protections have been enacted. In the UK, employees who report wrongdoing have been provided a remedy since 1988 should they suffer any detriment or be dismissed as a result of blowing the whistle.[156] Various reforms were made in 2013–2015.[157] First, an individual who has suffered a detriment from a co-worker as a result of blowing the whistle, such as bullying or harassment, may bring a claim against that individual and the employer may be vicariously liable for the actions of the co-worker.[158] Second, individuals who bring a claim at the Employment Tribunal must show a reasonable belief that their disclosure was made in the public interest.[159] Third, it is no longer a requirement for a disclosure to be made in good faith.[160] If made in bad faith, it may reduce any compensation awarded to the worker by up to 25 per cent.[161] Nevertheless, The Whistleblowing Commission called in 2013 for making whistleblowing policies mandatory, introducing rewards, extending protection to a wider category of workers, and an exemption from tribunal fees for whistleblowing claims.[162] In 2015, workers have the right not to

---

encouraging those who witness wrongdoing to report what they have seen is right as a matter of principle and is in the public interest.': *The Whistleblowing Framework: Response to the BIS call for evidence* (Law Society, November 2013) available at http://www.lawsociety.org.uk/representation/policy-discussion/documents/whistleblowing-call-for-evidence---law-society-response/.

[153] It has been argued that whistleblowing is constitutionally a form of free speech and expression of citizenship: Bovens (n 22) 195. Bovens gives examples of justification as identification of: Knowledge of penal offences; a substantial and specific danger to public health, safety, or the environment; a gross waste or unauthorised use of public funds; the misleading of controlling or supervising bodies.

[154] *Whistleblowing: The Inside Story—A Study of the Experiences of 1,000 Whistleblowers* (Public Concern at Work and the University of Greenwich, 2013).

[155] *Blowing the Whistle to a Prescribed Person: List of Prescribed People and Bodies* (Department for Business, Innovation & Skills, February, 2013); *Blowing the Whistle to a Prescribed Person: List of Prescribed People and Bodies* (Department for Business, Innovation & Skills, January, 2015).

[156] The Public Interest Disclosure Act 1998 inserted Part IVA into the Employment Rights Act 1996. Only the UK, Hungary and Slovenia operate comprehensive legislative frameworks, while a number of others have implemented legislation which addresses whistleblowing in certain sectors and industries only.

[157] In addition to points mentioned, the definition of 'worker' in s 43K of the Employment Rights Act 1996 (ERA) was amended to include certain new contractual arrangements within the NHS so that individuals working under such contracts are covered by the whistleblowing protections. Alongside this, a power was introduced to enable the Secretary of State to make any further changes to the definition of 'worker' by secondary legislation.

[158] Enterprise and Regulatory Reform Act 2013, s 19, referring to the Employment Rights Act 1996, s 47B. Detrimental acts of one co-worker towards another who has blown the whistle are treated as being done by the employer, therefore making the employer responsible; subject to a defence for an employer who is able to show that they took all reasonable steps to prevent the detrimental treatment of a co-worker towards another who blew the whistle.

[159] Enterprise and Regulatory Reform Act 2013, s 17, amending the Employment Rights Act 1996, s 43B.

[160] ibid, s 18(1).

[161] ibid, s 1894) and (5).

[162] *Whistleblowing Commission: Strengthening Law and Policy* (London, Whistleblowing Commission, April 2013) available at http://www.pcaw.org.uk/whistleblowing-commission-public-consultation.

be unfairly dismissed or suffer a detriment as a result of making a 'protected disclosure', as defined, made either internally to their employer or another responsible person or to various specified external bodies.[163]

D. Theoretical Insights

Whistleblowing has been said to involve a triangular relationship between the reporting individual, the detected organisational misconduct at a particular institutional setting, and the regulatory regime that defines the contours of legality.[164] I would suggest that the role of co-workers is also important, and the external context is not merely a regulatory regime but the social culture and norms.

Whistleblowing has been viewed as functioning within concepts of 'new governance' and wider accountability for organisational compliance at a time in which the role of the state in regulation is changing.[165] It alters the balance between 'voice' and 'exit'.[166] Feldman and Lobel have summarised the position thus:[167]

> The tension—promoting internal compliance as a matter of corporate culture, while at the same time ensuring the ability of individuals to speak out against their organization's noncompliance— is at the root of the puzzle. How do organizations effectively promote compliance? From Aristotle to Rawls, political philosophers have recognized that individual good citizenry includes multiple obligations, which can be classified into three categories: obedience, loyalty and participation.[168] Obedience involves recognition of rational authority and compliance with its rules and processes. Loyalty involves respect for and service to the community as a whole. Participation includes civic engagement which entails voicing orderly dissent and reporting noncompliance. Much like polity citizenship, individuals within organizations frequently voluntarily behave in ways that are beneficial to the organization, quite absent direct or explicit commands or reward systems. Organizational citizenship behaviour (OCB) is the social science term used to describe the range of behaviours that individuals engage in within their institution beyond explicit acts of following orders. These behaviours include compliance with organizational norms, altruistic behavior toward others and participation in one's institution.

It has been noted above that the ultimate cause of the perceived need by an individual to raise what are believed to be serious concerns is deficiency in the culture of the

---

[163] The Small Business, Enterprise and Employment Act 2015, s 148, inserting s 43FA into the ERA.

[164] MP Miceli and J Near, *Blowing the Whistle: The Organizational and Legal Complications for Companies and Employees* (New York, Lexington Books, 1992); Feldman and Lobel (n 137), 'Behavioral Versus Institutional Antecedents of Decentralized Enforcement: An Experimental Approach' (n 137).

[165] O Lobel, 'Interlocking Regulatory and Industrial Relations: The Governance of Worker Safety' (2005) 57 *Administrative Law Review* 1071–152; Feldman and Lobel, 'Behavioral Versus Institutional Antecedents of Decentralized Enforcement: An Experimental Approach' (n 137); Y Feldman and O Lobel, 'The Incentives Matrix: The Comparative Effectiveness of Rewards, Liabilities, Duties and Protections for Reporting Illegality' (n 137).

[166] A Hirschman, *Exit, Voice and Loyalty: Responses to Decline in Firms, Organizations and States* (Cambridge, Harvard University Press, 1970) 78.

[167] Feldman and Lobel (n 128) 267.

[168] Footnote from original source: BS Turner, *Citizenship and Social Theory* (Thousand Oaks CA, Sage Publications, 1993); J Carens, *Culture, Citizenship, and Community: A Contextual Exploration of Justice as Evenhandedness* (Oxford, Oxford University Press, 2000); D Heater, *A Brief History of Citizenship* (Edinburgh, Edinburgh University Press, 2004); W Maas, *Creating European Citizen* (Lanham MD, Rowman and Littlefield, 2007).

organisation.[169] The situation will give rise to a serious imbalance between the norms and behaviour inside the organisation and those that apply in the outside society. There may well be a belief that reporting internally will produce no significant improvement, and may lead to recrimination, and the absence of internal observance of norms and fair procedures is so serious that only an external disclosure will satisfy the conscience of a reporter who acts in good faith and/or produce normalisation. Accordingly, official recommendations stress the need for best practice in policies, accountability, governance, multiple routes for information (including line management, leapfrogging, human resources, audit, audit committees, directors, external routes), feedback and publication after reporting, providing reassurance,[170] briefing managers, checking awareness of staff.[171] In short, the conclusion is that the diagnosis and prescription in relation to 'whistleblowing' are the same as for best practice under 'normal' business practices. Arrangements and requirements might support desired practice, but only motivational culture can inspire the best behaviour.

X. Conclusions

This chapter has noted that a focus exclusively on external public 'regulatory' or 'enforcement' systems fails to note the existence of even more extensive management and compliance systems that operate within every business. Firms of any size have substantial management and compliance systems with extensive technical, information technology and human resources. The ability of firms to influence the behaviour of some other firms and of employees is significant but not absolute. Forms and their relevant personnel face the same problems of control, access to information, and effecting change that are faced by external public authorities.

Tallberg argued a decade ago that what used to be seen as alternative and conflicting perspectives on compliance—public enforcement and internal management—are in fact most effective when combined.[172] Further, he asserted that the architecture of many EU regulatory systems inherently consists of the combination of both, first, centralised, active and direct 'police-patrol' supervision conducted by the EU's supranational institutions and, second, decentralised, reactive and indirect 'fire-alarm' supervision, where national courts and societal watchdogs are engaged to induce state compliance.

The analysis in chapter 19 finds that many EU regulatory systems inherently rely on both internal and external elements, which are designed to operate collectively as part of a coherent holistic system.

---

[169] *Whistleblowing and Corporate Governance, the Role of Internal Audit in Whistleblowing* (London, Chartered Institute of Internal Auditors, 2014): 'There is a symbiotic relationship between whistleblowing and an organisation's culture. Effective internal whistleblowing arrangements are an important part of a healthy corporate culture. But it is also crucial to have the right organisational culture which encourages people to speak out without fear.'

[170] Of 1,000 whistleblowers who contacted the PCaW advice line between 20 August 2009 and 30 December 2010, 56% raised a concern more than once, and 60% received no response from management either negative or positive: *Whistleblowing: The Inside Story—A Study of the Experiences of 1,000 Whistleblowers* (Public Concern at Work and the University of Greenwich, 2013) para 1.3.

[171] *Making a Whistleblowing Policy Work* (National Audit Office, March 2014).

[172] J Tallberg, 'Paths to Compliance: Enforcement, Management, and the European Union' (2002) 56(3) *International Organization* 609.

It has been found by experience that issues of culture are significant in affecting the behaviour of employees. The larger the organisation, the more the sub-cultures that exist. Various studies have noted that when organisational structures or rules change, behaviour stays rigid.[173] Accordingly other means are required to affect institutionalised and localised culture.

A notable corporate movement has occurred under the title of Corporate Social Responsibility in which some firms engage with external stakeholders in relation to achieving wider social goals that temper classic economic goals of business. The CSR movement originated in the environmental field but has widened to any social aspect. Whilst some have criticised CSR arrangements as lacking effective sanctions, it is the widening of goals that is relevant to the analysis of this book. CSR has now widened to general issues of corporate responsibility, encouraged by the European Commission in its Effective Open Voluntarism initiative in the communications sector. That approach chimes with the Open Corporation concept noted in chapter 11 above.

Allied to these issues, and certainly spurred by problems in the financial services sector noted below in chapter 20 and in healthcare and national secrecy and security, has been a resurgence of interest in encouraging whistleblowing. However, it will be seen in chapter 20 below, especially from the civil aviation sector, that whistleblowing is essentially irrelevant if a firm has an open and culture of sharing information, supported by a general 'no blame' environment and enforcement policy.

---

[173] For a management analysis of achieving change, see Jones (n 45) chs 10–14.

Part E

Regulatory Architectures

19

Regulating Safety

This chapter considers the ways in which regulatory regimes control the *safety* of selected types of consumer products and services. All of the relevant law is based on EU (European Union) measures, and in almost every case the rules are now exclusively EU rather than national, although applied nationally. There are differences between the regimes for different products and services, which can broadly be related to the particular characteristics of the subject product or service and to variations in levels of risk between them, so that more extensive regimes apply to more serious risks and hazards. The current status of individual sectoral regimes is, of course, also affected by political and other external factors, but those aspects are outside the scope of this study.

The systems for controlling safety and risk are outlined in general terms in a number of sectors, so as to provide an opportunity for comparisons to be made. The sectors are medicinal products, engineered products, general consumer products, health and safety in the workplace, and the aviation sector. It is not intended to undertake a complete analysis of the regulatory systems in any of these sectors. The purpose is to gain an overview of the *systems and techniques* that are adopted in the legally binding regulatory systems.

A series of points should be noted. First, every such regime is based on a quality management system, operated within every firm. Quality management is a concept that is universally recognised within both the business and regulatory communities, and is harmonised through international standards.

Second, every regulatory regime has evolved over time, as more sophisticated and extensive requirements have been added. There are striking similarities in the developments that have occurred in different sectors. Many regimes began by covering ex ante rules, such as on pre-market testing, approval and advertising, and it was only later that ex post systems were put in place for monitoring safety in use and implementing relevant action, such as changes in design, production, information or advertising, or suspension of marketing, withdrawal, modification or recall. Currently, however, post-marketing safety vigilance systems have developed into highly important features in ensuring ongoing safety in use. Both the pre-marketing approval stage and the continuous post-marketing vigilance and surveillance aspects are regarded as important and necessary for almost every regulatory system. Safe use of products or systems cannot be supported without either or both mechanisms, so regulatory systems involve both parts as integral requirements in all the systems considered here.

Third, some systems place critical functional reliance on the expertise and judgements of experts. A notable example is the regime for medicinal products, which relies on individuals' medical or pharmacy qualifications.

Fourth, vigilance systems that rely on occurrence reporting by individuals can only be effective, and generate reports that deliver the crucial information, if potential reporters are convinced that they will not attract personal blame or peer criticism. The aviation sector has therefore developed a reporting system based on a no blame 'Just Culture', which guarantees anonymity and feedback of actions taken, and an intra-organisation Open Culture, which encompasses constant focus on improvement in safety performance and outcomes.

I. The Need for Product Safety Regulation

The European Commission administers a pan-EU Rapid Alert System for non-food product safety (RAPEX)[1] In 2013, a total of 2,364 notifications on dangerous products were submitted through the RAPEX system by Member States, of which 1,981 notifications concerned products which posed a serious risk to consumers.[2] The most frequently notified products were clothing, textiles and fashion items (25 per cent), toys (25 per cent), electrical appliances and equipment (nine per cent), motor vehicles (seven per cent), and cosmetics (four per cent): See Figure 19.1.[3] Figure 19.2 shows that the five most frequently notified risk categories were injuries (23 per cent), chemical (20 per cent), choking (14 per cent), electric shock (12 per cent) and strangulation (nine per cent).

The number of notifications of dangerous products by country of origin has risen steadily since 2003, albeit with a slight fall in 2011, as Figure 19.3 shows.

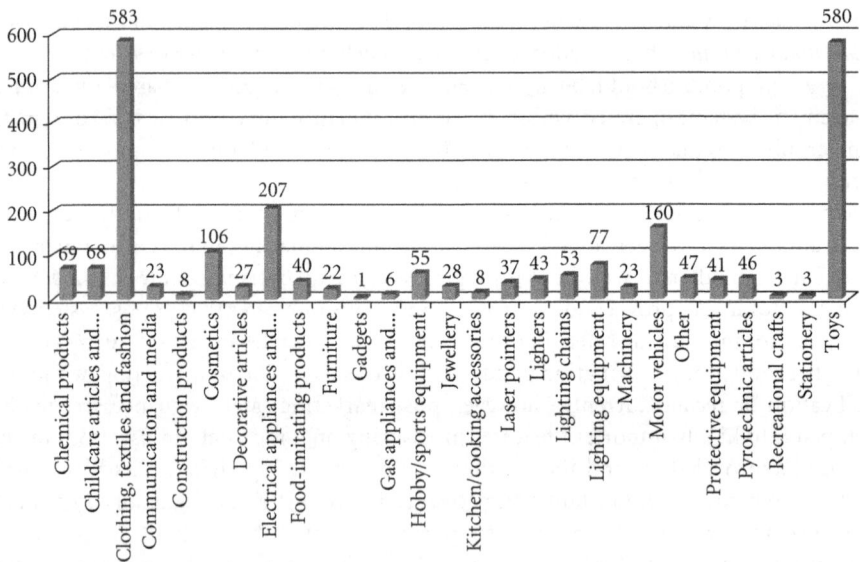

Figure 19.1: Number of Notifications by Product Category (Absolute Values)[4]

[1] Also excluding medicinal products, but including workplace, home and leisure accidents.
[2] *2013 Annual Report on the Operation of the Rapid Alert System for Non-food Dangerous Products RAPEX* (European Commission, 2014).
[3] ibid.
[4] ibid, Fig 6.

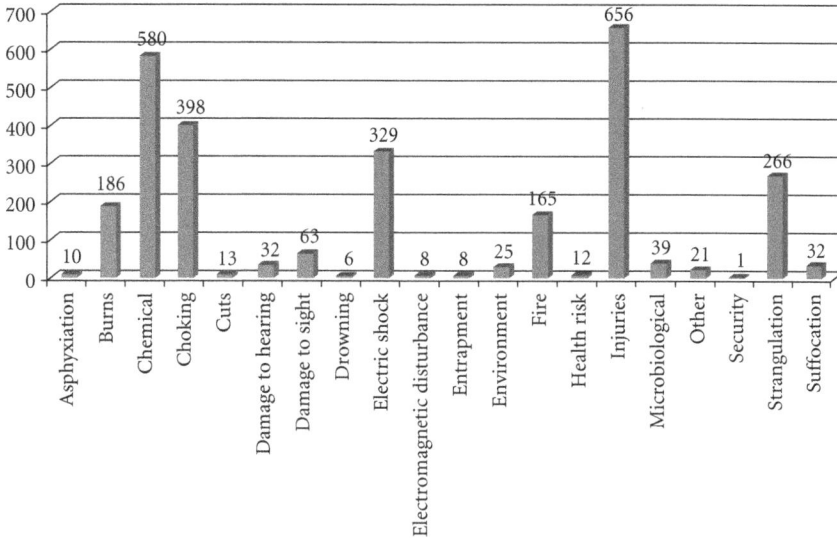

Figure 19.2: **Number of Notifications by Type of Risk (Absolute Values)**[5]

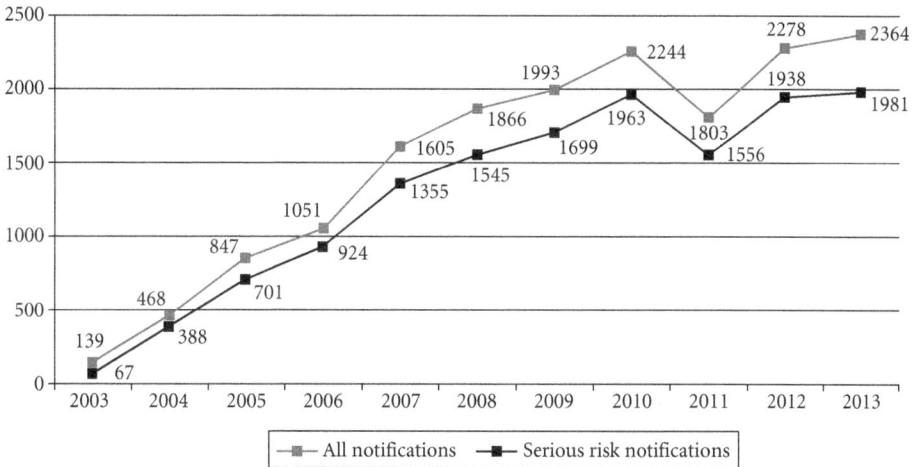

Figure 19.3: **Notifications of Dangerous Products through the EU RAPEX System 2003–2013**[6]

Table 19.1 shows the 2013 EU data in relation to deaths (238,122), hospital admissions (5,382,000), hospital outpatient cases (35,700,000) in 31 European states for road traffic, workplace, school, sports, home and leisure, homicide, suicide and self-harm causes.[7] The

---

[5] ibid, Fig 13.
[6] RAPEX Facts and Figures 2013. Complete Statistics, European Commission, 2014. For RAPEX see http://ec.europa.eu/consumers/consumers_safety/safety_products/rapex/index_en.htm.
[7] ibid.

Table 19.1: Injuries in RAPEX for EU-28 in 2013

	Road traffic	Work-place	School	Sports	Home, leisure	Total of unintentional injuries	Homicide, assault	Suicide, self-harm	Total of all injuries
Fatalities	39 895 15%	4 616 2%	1 154 0.5%	7 000 3%	104 381 44%	154 064 65%	4 568 2%	59 920 25%	238 122 100%
Hospital admissions	665 000 12%	241 000 4%	38 000 1%	402 000 7%	3 633 000 67%	4 968 000 92%	202 000 4%	212 000 4%	5 382 000 100%
Hospital outpatients	3 792 000 11%	3 260 000 9%	740 000 2%	5 750 000 16%	20 801 000 58%	34 342 000 96%	1 167 000 3%	190 000 1%	35 700 000 100%
All hospital patients	4 494 000 11%	3 360 000 8%	737 000 2%	5 890 000 14%	24 712 000 60%	39 193 000 95%	1 384 000 3%	500 000 1%	41 081 000 100%

classification of fatal injuries for 2013 is at Figure 19.4, the number of notifications by product category and by type of risk are at Table 19.1 and Figure 19.4 respectively. The notifications by country of origin at Figures 19.5 and 19.6 indicate that the overwhelming safety problem arises from products imported into the EU from China, and that by comparison EU-manufactured products appear to have a high level of safety.

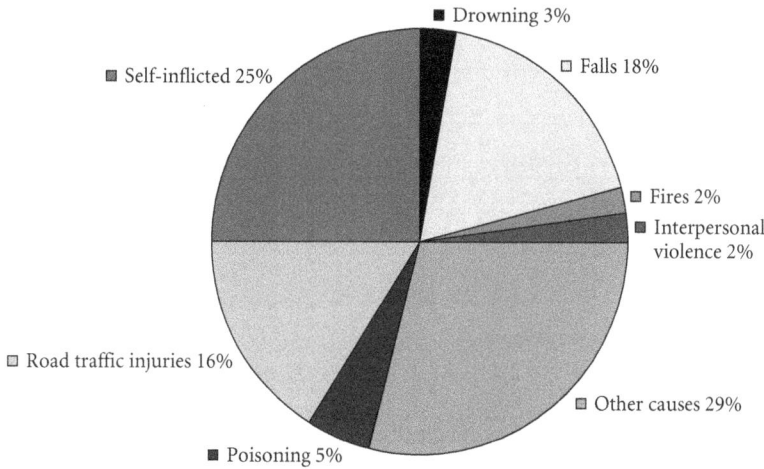

Figure 19.4: Fatal Injuries by Causes of Death in RAPEX EU-28 States in 2013

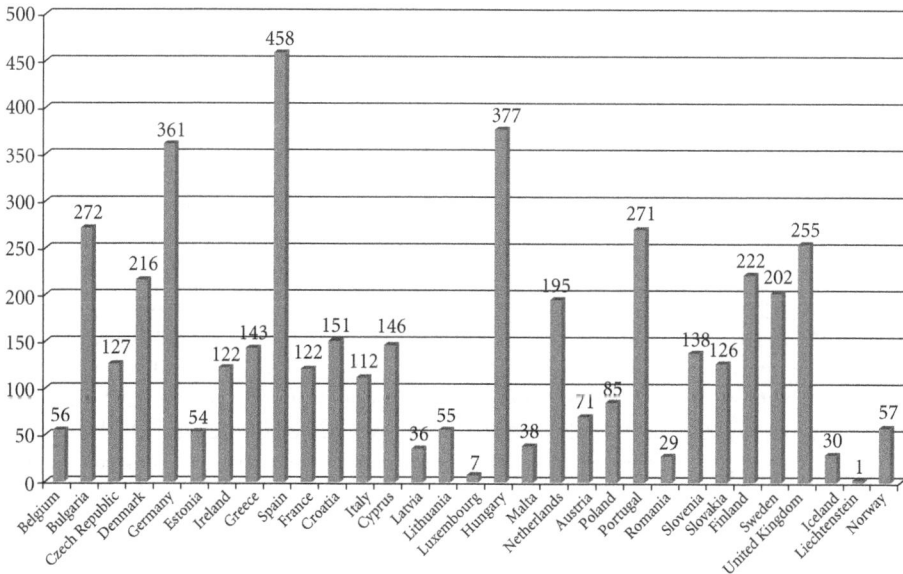

Figure 19.5: Overall RAPEX Alerts per Country in 2013

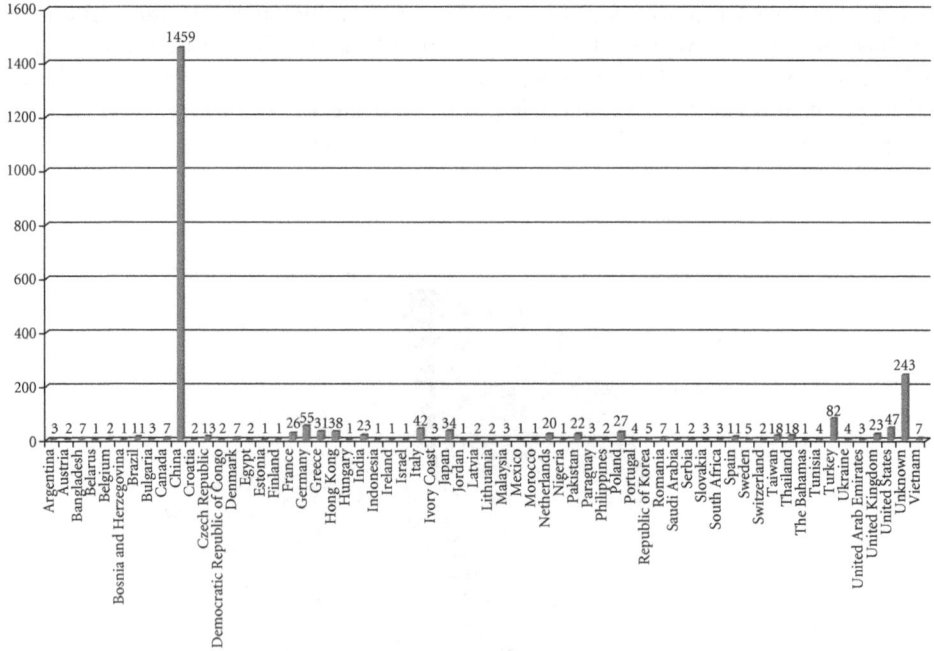

Figure 19.6: Number of RAPEX Notifications in 2013 by Country of Origin of the Notified Product

II. Quality Systems

It is important to realise that many regulatory systems—and, more importantly, corporate systems—are based on a quality system framework. This involves processes that comprise a cycle of continuous evaluation and improvement. This was illustrated in the 2013 report by the European Commission on the RAPEX system, as shown in Figure 19.7.

An international family of standards, ISO 9000, establishes the fundamentals of quality management systems (QMSs).[8] Standard ISO 9001:2008 defines a QMS as the organisational structure, accountabilities, corporate resources, processes and procedures necessary to establish and promote a system of continual improvement while delivering a product or service. Six procedures are specified, each of which must be documented: Control of documents, control of records, internal audits, control of nonconforming product/service, corrective action and preventive action. The standard also requires the organisation to issue and communicate a documented quality policy, a quality manual and numerous records. Numerous standards apply customised approaches of the general QMS approach in relation to specific sectors or families of products or services. External certification

---

[8] YC Tsim, VWS Yeung and ETC Leung, 'An Adaptation to ISO 9001:2000 for Certified Organisations' (2002) 17(5) *Managerial Auditing Journal* 245; KR Beattie, 'Implementing ISO 9000: A Study of its Benefits among Australian Organizations' (1999) 10 *Total Quality Management* 95.

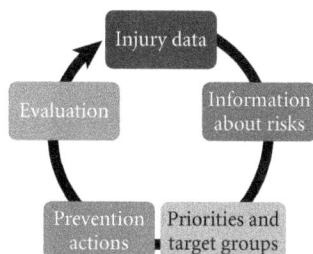

Figure 19.7: The Cycle of Action for Injury Prevention

bodies certify and audit compliance with relevant standards. Standards have been described as expert knowledge stored in the form of rules.[9] In effect, they are the internal laws of business organisation.

Systems are, therefore, essential to how business organisations of any size operate, and—thus inevitably—necessarily embedded in almost every regulatory system. Further, in 2014, the UK Government Chief Scientific Adviser recommended that a systems approach needs to be taken to regulatory mechanisms in order to support innovation.[10]

III. Medicinal Products

A. The Need for Regulation

The ingestion of biomedical compounds carries inherent risk. It is recognised that the evaluation of whether a medicine is sufficiently safe to be publicly available involves the exercise of judgement, based on an evaluation of risks and benefits:

> [T]here is no absolute standard of safety. Very few drugs are entirely free from the risk of inducing adverse side effects in some patients. The question must always be whether the degree of risk is sufficiently low to be acceptable, and this cannot be addressed without an appreciation of the benefits to be gained from taking a risk of that degree.[11]

Over one million adverse events reports were recorded by the European Medicines Agency (EMA) in 2013 in relation to human medicinal products, of which some 40,000 were for investigational products in the European Economic Area.[12] From these, 2,449 potential safety signals were reviewed by the EMA, resulting in 43 signals being validated and analysed. Member States also detected and validated 57 signals. Among the 43 signals raised by the EMA, two had been under monitoring by the signal-validation team at the Agency in

---

[9] See N Brunsson, B Jacobsson et al, *A World of Standards* (Oxford, Oxford University Press, 2000) 41.

[10] *Innovation: Managing Risk, Not Avoiding it. Annual Report of the Government Chief Scientific Adviser 2014* (Government Office for Science, 2014).

[11] *Organon Laboratories Limited v Department of Health and Social Security* [1990] 2 CMLR 49 CA, at 78 per Mustill LJ.

[12] Annual Report 2013 (n 2).

2012, eight were prompted by the scientific literature and five by information received from other regulatory authorities.

Of the 43 signals validated by the EMA, 21 led to a recommendation for changes to the product information, either directly (seven) or following a cumulative review (14), providing information to patients and healthcare professionals on the safe use of these products. For four signals, this also included the distribution of direct healthcare professional communications (DHPCs) to increase awareness about the new safety information.

Of the 43 referral procedures, 25 were initiated to address either efficacy or quality (rather than safety) concerns, or a need for EU-wide harmonisation of product information, or were triggered by differences between the Member States in the mutual recognition and decentralised procedures.[13]

The labelling information for medicinal products is, however, constantly monitored and regularly updated.

B. Pre-Marketing Authorisations

The Thalidomide tragedy in the early 1960s spurred European states to introduce extensive ex ante controls on the safety of medicinal products.[14] The initial model has been regularly revised and extended but its framework remains.[15] Various measures were collected into a Community Code in 2001.[16] Particular rules apply for certain types of products that are not discussed here, such as human blood products,[17] homeopathic medicinal products,[18] and herbal medicinal products[19] and 'advanced therapy' products.[20]

No medicinal product may be placed on the market unless it has a marketing authorisation.[21] Marketing authorisations were initially granted by national competent authorities, and the system has evolved towards a centralised procedure,[22] focused on the EMA,[23] although a decentralised (mutual recognition) procedure remains available.[24] All decisions

---

[13] Annual Report 2013 (n 2) 44.

[14] The first statutory measures were Dir 65/65/EEC, and in the UK the Medicines Act 1968.

[15] Extensive guidance is published at http://ec.europa.eu/enterprise/pharmaceuticals/eudralex/vol2_en.htm.

[16] Dir 2001/83/EC of the European Parliament and of the Council of 6 November 2001 on the Community code relating to medicinal products for human use. For detailed examinations of the regulatory provisions see C Hodges, 'The Regulation of Medicines and Medical Devices' in A Grubb, J Laing, J McHale and I Kennedy (eds), *Principles of Medical Law* 3rd edn (Oxford, Oxford University Press, 2011); R Goldberg, *Medicinal Product Liability and Regulation* (Oxford, Hart Publishing, 2013); E Jackson, *Law and the Regulation of Medicines* (Oxford, Hart Publishing, 2012).

[17] Dir 2002/98/EC of the European Parliament and of the Council of 27 January 2003 setting standards of quality and safety for the collection, testing, processing, storage and distribution of human blood and blood components and amending Dir 2001/83/EC.

[18] Reg (EC) 1901/2006/EC (for which no therapeutic indication appears on the labelling or any information relating to the product and there is a sufficient degree of dilution).

[19] Dir 2004/24/EC of the European Parliament and of the Council of 31 March 2004 amending, as regards traditional herbal medicinal products, Dir 2001/83/EC on the Community code relating to medicinal products for human use (notably those that have at least 30 years' traditional use).

[20] Reg (EC) 1394/2007.

[21] Reg (EEC) 726/2004, art 3; Dir (EC) 2001/83, art 6(1).

[22] Council Reg (EC) 726/2004.

[23] Established as of 1995 under Reg (EC) 726/2004, art 5. The EMA has the power to impose financial penalties for infringement of the centralised system: Commission Reg (EC) 658/2007.

[24] Dir 2001/83/EC as amended. This procedure is not examined in detail here.

to grant, refuse, vary, suspend, withdraw or revoke a marketing authorisation shall state in detail the reasons on which they are based and be notified to the party concerned.[25] A marketing authorisation shall not be refused, varied, suspended, withdrawn or revoked except on the grounds set out in the legislation.[26]

In order to be granted a marketing authorisation, new compounds[27] must be evaluated in a sequence of animal toxicology tests,[28] followed by trials in healthy human volunteers and then clinical trials,[29] ideally double-blind prospective studies in which a new product is compared with the current best treatment.[30] From 2011, certain adverse events must be reported by investigators to trial sponsors and by sponsors to competent authorities and ethics committees.[31] The resulting data[32] is evaluated by experts, within or external to the manufacturer, and by the competent authority, against criteria of safety, efficacy and quality.[33] The criterion of safety is evaluated through applying a risk–benefit test: An application for a marketing authorisation shall be refused if, inter alia, the risk–benefit balance is not considered favourable.[34] Under the centralised procedure, the authorisation shall be refused if, after verification of the required information and particulars submitted, 'it appears that the applicant has not properly or sufficiently demonstrated the quality, safety or efficacy of the medicinal product'.[35] Authorisation shall likewise be refused if the particulars and documents provided by the applicant are incorrect or if the labelling and package leaflets proposed by the applicant are not in accordance with the requirements.[36]

The competent authority publishes, and is required to update, its assessment report on the product.[37] It also has to approve the wording of a 'summary of product characteristics' (SmPC)

---

[25] Reg (EEC) 726/2004, art 81 and Dir 2001/83/EC, art 125. A relevant authority or advisory committee must be allowed a broad discretion by the courts in judicial review cases in considering how best to approach scientific evidence (such as evidence of a lack of safety in overdose by the elderly) and what weight to give to it: *In the matter of Organon Laboratories Ltd* (CA transcript CO/1738/88, 17 February 1989).

[26] Reg (EEC) 726/2004, art 81.2 and Dir 2001/83/EC, art 126.

[27] The procedure for compounds for which tests and trail data already exists is shortened to require instead the relevant published data.

[28] The individuals, facilities and performance of animal experiments are regulated under Dir 86/609/EEC, and experiments must be carried out in accordance with the standard of good laboratory practice (GLP) under Dirs 2004/10/EC and 2004/9/EC.

[29] Clinical trials of medicinal products for human use are governed by Dir 2001/20/EC, and must observe the principles and guidelines on good clinical practice (GCP) under Commission Dir 2005/28/EC, which applies the Declaration of Helsinki: *Recommendations Guiding Physicians in Biomedical Research Involving Human Subjects* (World Medical Association, 1957 as amended), available at www.wma.net/e/policy/17-c_e.html.

[30] Dir 2001/83/EC, art 8(3) and Annex I.

[31] Communication from the Commission—detailed guidance on the collection, verification and presentation of adverse event/reaction reports arising from clinical trials on medicinal products for human use ('CT-3'), OJ C 172/1, 11.6.2011.

[32] Satisfying the extensive list of requirements at art 8(3) and Annex I of Dir 2001/83/EC. Limited exceptions exist such as under Reg (EC) 141/2000 on orphan medicinal products.

[33] See Reg (EC) 726/2004, recital 13.

[34] Dir 2001/83/EC, Art 26 as amended. 'Risk–benefit balance' is defined as an evaluation of the positive therapeutic effects of the medicinal product in relation to the risks. 'Risks related to use of the medicinal product' are defined as (a) any risk relating to the quality, safety or efficacy of the medicinal product as regards patients' health or public health, and (b) and risk of undesirable effects on the environment. See Dir 2001/83/EC, art 1 points 28 and 28a, inserted by Dir 2004/27/EC.

[35] Reg (EC) 726/2004, art 12.

[36] ibid.

[37] Dir 2001/83/EC, art 21, as amended by Dir 2004/27/EC.

proposed by the manufacturer.[38] The SmPC must contain the information specified,[39] and all labelling,[40] package leaflets and advertising[41] must conform to its contents.

Manufacturing quality and consistency are controlled by the grant by the competent authority of a manufacturer's authorisation.[42] Wholesale distribution[43] and retail supply[44] activities are also subject to licensing. Manufacturing and distribution activities are subject to checks on the authorisation holder and their establishments and inspection of premises.

C. Pharmacovigilance

By the time that a medicinal product is marketed, it has only been tested in perhaps 1,000–2,000 human subjects and that cohort will not identify some significant potential hazards.[45] It was recognised by around 1990 that the safe use of medicinal products is not simply a matter to be assessed at the time of marketing, but that there is a need for the continuous collection and re-evaluation of data relating to a product, throughout the time that its product type is marketed and/or remains on the market.[46] The legislation implicitly recognises the limitations on the understanding of the level of safety which is possible at the time of authorising its marketing that use of a product will present in normal, 'practical conditions of use'.[47]

From 1993 extensive ex post controls have been imposed, which have been built into an extensive and sophisticated post-marketing vigilance system known as the pharmacovigilance system.[48] The pharmacovigilance system integrates spontaneous reporting by health care professionals and others, and imposes (i) recording and reporting obligations on the commercial enterprises involved, and (ii) surveillance and other regulatory obligations on Member States, the Commission, the EMA and the Committee on Human Medicinal Products (CHMP). Different post-marketing obligations for medicinal products apply to the holders of marketing authorisations, the holders of manufacturing authorisations and the

---

[38] ibid, art 8(2)(j).

[39] Reg (EC) 469/2009.

[40] Labelling requirements are set by Dir 2001/83/EC, art 54.

[41] Dir 2001/83/EC, arts 86 and 87.

[42] Dir 2001/83/EC, art 40; certain exemptions exist. Principles and guidelines of good manufacturing practice set out in Commission Dir 2003/94 must be observed.

[43] Dir 2001/83/EC, art 77. See also Dir 2011/62/EU of the European Parliament and of the Council of 8 June 2011 amending Dir 2001/83/EC on the Community code relating to medicinal products for human use, as regards the prevention of the entry into the legal supply chain of falsified medicinal products.

[44] Imposed under national law.

[45] AP Fletcher and S Shaw, 'The Safety of Medicines' in JP Griffin and J O'Grady (eds), *The Textbook of Pharmaceutical Medicine* 4th edn (Oxford, Wiley Blackwell, 2002).

[46] See SM Roden, 'An Introduction to Drug Safety Surveillance' in Glaxo Group Research, *Drug Safety: A Shared Responsibility* (London, Churchill Livingstone, 1991).

[47] This phrase appeared in Dir 93/39/EEC recital 7 which justified the initial introduction into Community legislation of the pharmacovigilance system but was not repeated in recital 54 to Dir 2001/83/EC. Recital 15 to Reg (EEC) No 2309/93, only referred to the mechanistic 'intensive monitoring of adverse reactions' though it reappears at art 57(1)(c) of Reg (EC) 726/2004 in connection with the designation of the EMEA's tasks.

[48] Dir 2001/83/EC on the Community code relating to medicinal products for human use. Extensive guidelines see are at Vol 9A of the Rules Governing Medicinal Products in the European Union: Guidelines on Pharmacovigilance for Medicinal Products for Human Use, which includes guidelines for competent authorities and the EMEA at Part II.

holders of wholesale distribution authorisations. A centralised database (the Eudravigilance database) was introduced from 2004.[49] Reforms strengthening and further centralising the pharmacovigilance system were made in 2010[50] and 2012.[51] Pharmacovigilance is now clearly based on quality system principles[52] over the whole life-cycle management of the product.[53]

The pharmacovigilance system is based on identifying *signals*[54] that need to be evaluated from reports in medical literature[55] and reports of adverse reactions that are collected within as large a database as possible,[56] and evaluated by an expert committee, the Pharmacovigilance Risk Assessment Committee, based on internationally agreed terminology and formats.[57] The following categories of adverse reactions are specified:[58]

(i) 'adverse reaction' means a response to a medicinal product which is noxious and unintended and which occurs at doses normally used in man for the prophylaxis, diagnosis or therapy of disease or for the restoration, correction or modification of physiological function,

(ii) 'serious adverse reaction' means an adverse reaction which results in death, is life-threatening, requires inpatient hospitalisation or prolongation of existing hospitalisation, results in persistent or significant disability or incapacity, or is a congenital anomaly/birth defect;

(iii) 'unexpected adverse reaction' means an adverse reaction, the nature, severity or outcome of which is not consistent with the summary of product characteristics.

Commission Guidance covers the collection, verification and presentation of adverse reaction reports, including technical requirements for electronic exchange of pharmacovigilance information.[59] Particular reporting requirements apply to different categories of adverse reactions.

---

[49] Reg (EC) No 726/2004, amended by Commission Implementing Reg (EU) No 520/2012 of 19 June 2012 on the performance of pharmacovigilance activities provided for in Reg (EC) No 726/2004 of the European Parliament and of the Council and Dir 2001/83/EC of the European Parliament and of the Council, ch III.

[50] Reg (EU) No 1235/2010 of the European Parliament and of the Council amending, as regards pharmacovigilance of medicinal products for human use, Reg (EC) No 726/2004 laying down Community procedures for the authorisation and supervision of medicinal products for human and veterinary use and establishing a European Medicines Agency, and Reg (EC) No 1394/2007 on advanced therapy medicinal products; Dir 2010/84/EU of the European Parliament and of the Council of 15 December 2010 amending, as regards pharmacovigilance, Dir 2001/83/EC on the Community code relating to medicinal products for human use. See earlier *Strategy to Better Protect Public Health by Strengthening and Rationalising EU Pharmacovigilance*, European Commission, 2007.

[51] Reg (EU) No 1027/2012 of the European Parliament and of the Council of 25 October 2012 amending Reg (EC) No 726/2004 as regards pharmacovigilance; Dir 2012/26/EU of the European Parliament and of the Council of 25 October 2012 amending Dir 2001/83/E as regards pharmacovigilance.

[52] Commission Implementing Reg (EU) No 520/2012, ch II.

[53] ibid, recital 2.

[54] ibid, arts 20–24.

[55] Reg (EU) No 726/2004, art 27.

[56] Commission Implementing Reg (EU) No 520/2012, recital 9.

[57] ibid, ch IV.

[58] Directive 2001/83/EC, art 1: also adopted in Reg (EC) No 726/2004, art 21.

[59] Dir 2001/83/EC, art 106 and Reg (EC) 726/2004, Art 26. The suspension or revocation of a marketing authorisation may only be decided on the grounds laid down in the Community provisions: Case C-83/92 *Pierrel SpA v Ministerio della Sanita* [1993] ECRI-06419.

i. Obligations on Authorisation Holders

All *suspected serious* adverse reactions occurring within the Community to a medicinal product which are brought to the attention of the marketing authorisation holder by a health care professional must be recorded and reported immediately to the Member States in whose territory the incident occurred, and in no case later than 15 days following the receipt of the information.[60] They must also notify the Eudravigilance database of any suspected serious adverse effect coming to light in the Union with 90 days of becoming aware of the occurrence. There are further obligations in relation to maintaining detailed records of all *suspected* adverse reactions occurring within or outside the Community that are reported by a health care professional.[61] If a *suspected serious unexpected* adverse reaction to a centrally licensed product occurs in a non-Community country, a report must be made both to all Member States and to the Agency/Eudravigilance database.

Under the centralised system, arrangements for the reporting of suspected *adverse reactions* within or outside the Community which are reported by a health care professional to the marketing authorisation holder on the following basis. Unless other requirements have been laid down as a condition for the granting of the marketing authorisation by the Community, the detailed records of such suspected adverse reactions, which the marketing authorisation holder is required to maintain, must be submitted by the marketing authorisation holder to the Agency and Member States immediately upon request or at least every six months after authorisation until placing on the market. Periodic safety update reports (PSURs) must also be submitted immediately upon request or at least every six months during the first two years following the initial placing on the Community market and once a year for the following two years. Thereafter, the reports shall be submitted at three-yearly intervals together with the application of renewal of the authorisation, or immediately upon request. These records shall be accompanied by a scientific evaluation particularly of the risk–benefit balance of the product. From 2012 risk-management systems are required for all newly authorised medicines, and PSURs are not required for products with low risk or for old established products unless concerns arise.[62] Authorities may require marketing authorisation holders to undertake post-authorisation safety and efficacy reports.[63] The Code sets out broadly equivalent requirements for products authorised nationally or under the decentralised/mutual recognition procedure.[64]

ii. Obligations on Authorities

Each Member State shall ensure that all *suspected serious* adverse reactions occurring within their territory to a medicinal product authorised under the centralised system which are brought to their attention are recorded and reported promptly to the Agency

---

[60] Under the centralised procedure, Reg (EC) No 726/2004, art 24: Under the Code, Dir 2001/83/EC, art 104; both provisions add that this applies to reactions brought to his attention by a healthcare professional and that separate guidance applies to the reporting and recording of other suspected serious adverse reactions.

[61] ibid, and Reg (EC) No 726/2004, Art 24.

[62] Reg (EC) 726/2004, arts 14a and 21.

[63] Reg (EC) 726/2004, art 10a. Commission Implementing Reg (EU) No 520/2012, art 36.

[64] Reg (EC) 726/2004, art 24.3; Dir 2001/83/EC, art 104. The suspension or revocation of a marketing authorisation may only be decided on the grounds laid down in the Community provisions: Case C-83/92 *Pierrel SpA v Ministerio della Sanita* (n 59).

and the marketing authorisation holder, and in no case later than 15 days following the receipt of the information.[65] This provision is followed, under the centralised system but not the mutual recognition system, by an obligation on the Agency to inform the national pharmacovigilance systems of reports which it receives. Implicitly in this context such reports are received only from Member States—the legislation seemingly does not contemplate that the Agency will receive reports from any source other than Member States or marketing authorisation holders, and it does not explicitly require the Agency to inform Member States of any reports which it receives other than those of suspected serious adverse reactions received from Member State authorities. Nevertheless, the legislation specifies a mechanism for the Commission in consultation with the Agency, Member States and interested parties, to draw up guidance on the collection, verification and presentation of adverse reaction reports.[66]

The legislation on the centralised system, but not on the decentralised/mutual recognition system, states that the Agency, in consultation with the Member States and the Commission, shall set up a data-processing network for the rapid transmission of data between the competent Community authorities in the event of an alert relating to faulty manufacture, serious adverse reactions and other pharmacovigilance data regarding medicinal products marketed in the Community.[67] Further, the Agency shall collaborate with the World Health Organisation on international pharmacovigilance and shall take the necessary steps to submit promptly to the World Health Organisation appropriate and adequate information regarding the measures taken in the Community which may have a bearing on public health protection in third countries and shall send a copy thereof to the Commission and the Member States.[68]

Central coordination of pharmacovigilance in the Community is a key feature:

> The Agency, acting in close co-operation with the national pharmacovigilance systems established in accordance with Article 102 of Directive 2001/83/EC, shall receive all relevant information about suspected adverse reactions to medicinal products which have been authorised by the Community in accordance with the centralised system. Where appropriate the CHMP may, in accordance with Article 5 of Regulation 726/2004, formulate publicly accessible opinions on the measures necessary. These measures shall be adopted in accordance with the procedure laid down in Article 87(3) of the Regulation.

> The marketing authorisation holder and the competent authorities of the Member States shall ensure that all relevant information about suspected adverse reactions to medicinal products authorised in accordance with the Regulation are brought to the attention of the EMEA in accordance with the provisions of the Regulation. Patients shall be encouraged to communicate any adverse reaction to health care professionals.[69]

The pharmacovigilance system has certain strengths and weaknesses. Its strengths lie in the expertise available to review and assess the data compiled by the system (in leading regulators and companies, both calling on leading clinicians where appropriate), and the ability to amass extensive data. Weaknesses occur in the ability to capture sufficiently comprehensive

---

[65] Reg (EC) 726/2004, art 25.
[66] ibid, art 26; Dir 2001/83/EC, art 106.
[67] Reg (EC) No 726/2004, art 26.
[68] ibid, arts 27 and 28c.
[69] ibid, art 22.

data quickly: Adverse reaction input reporting at the 'front line' by patients (whose input may be scientifically unreliable), nurses, pharmacists and doctors has been known to be less than completely comprehensive, so signals may not be generated early enough.[70]

iii. Supervision

National competent authorities are required to ensure that the legal requirements governing medicinal products are complied with by means of repeated inspections.[71] They are empowered to inspect manufacturing or commercial establishments and laboratories, to take samples, and to examine any documents.[72] Member States are required to take 'all appropriate steps' to ensure that manufacturing processes of immunological products maintain batch-to-batch consistency.[73] They are required to ensure that holders of marketing and manufacturing authorisations furnish proof of all controls carried out.[74] They shall suspend an authorisation, and prohibit supply and require withdrawal, where a product proves to be harmful in the normal conditions of use, or where its therapeutic efficacy is lacking, or where its qualitative and quantitative composition is not as declared.[75]

D. Discussion

The EU regulatory system for medicinal products comprises a system with a number of notable features. First, the same harmonised rules apply throughout the system. Second, safety is based on the evaluation of data by experts. Third, data is required both before marketing and subsequently throughout the approved life of a product. Fourth, data is shared vertically between authorisation holders and authorities, and horizontally between authorities (at both national and EU levels). Fifth, both the framework and substance of the rules are similar across the developed world,[76] and there are strong links between leading agencies that facilitate sharing of issues. A 2014 review of the enforcement system for the UK regulatory system found that 'the need for regulation in the sector is very clearly understood, accepted and valued by industry.'[77]

i. Involvement of Expert Personnel

One of the striking features of the regulatory regime for medicinal products is the embedded functional reliance on the expertise and judgement of expert individuals at all critical

---

[70] See C Hodges, *European Regulation of Consumer Product Safety* (Oxford, Oxford University Press, 2005) 51.

[71] Dir 2001/83/EC, art 111.1.

[72] ibid.

[73] ibid, art 111.2.

[74] ibid, art 112.

[75] ibid, arts 116 and 117.

[76] See D Carpenter, *Reputation and Power. Organizational Image and Pharmaceutical regulation at the FDA* (Princeton NJ, Princeton University Press, 2010). The EU system was inspired by ideas proposed by the US Food and Drug Administration (which had existed since 1938). Extensive alignment has been achieved through the International Conference on Harmonisation of Technical Requirements for Registration of Pharmaceuticals for Human Use (ICH), which since 1990 has brought together the regulatory authorities of Europe, Japan and the US and experts from the pharmaceutical industry: see http://www.ich.org.

[77] Review of enforcement in the pharmaceutical manufacturing and production sector, Department for Business, Innovation & Skills website summary, at http://discuss.bis.gov.uk/focusonenforcement/review-findings/review-of-the-pharmaceutical-manufacturing-and-production-sector.

stages. In commercial enterprises, such experts are known as 'qualified persons'. The following is a summary of the nodal points in the system where such individuals are required.

a) *Product evaluation.* An application for a marketing assessment must be drawn up and signed by experts with the necessary technical or professional qualifications. Signed reports from experts in each of three disciplines for which documents are required (analysis, pharmacology and similar experimental sciences, and clinical trials) are to be submitted with the particulars and documents of the application.[78] The experts are specified to fulfil two functions: First, verification that the experts have carried out the relevant scientific research tasks and have described the results objectively; second, to describe their observations in accordance with the requirements of Annex I of Directive 2003/63/EC. In addition, the experts fulfil the further function of regulatory verification and assessment of the application prior to that of the competent authority. The competent authority may use its power of assessment to ascertain whether or not the applicant, and consequently the expert who prepared the documentation supporting the application, took account of current technical developments and scientific progress and whether or not he or she was satisfied that the scientific publications were up to date.[79] An expert need not be independent of the applicant, but must satisfy the technical or professional qualifications.

b) *Evaluation at EU level.* A centralised application is considered by the Committee for Medicinal Products for Human Use (CHMP), which is responsible for formulating the opinions of the EMA on any question concerning the admissibility of the files submitted, the granting, variation, suspension or withdrawal of a marketing authorisation and pharmacovigilance. The CHMP consists of representatives of the Member States and of the Commission and the EMA and draws up its own rules of procedure.[80] A centralised marketing authorisation is issued by the Commission. The Commission issues a draft of the decision and has power to make a decision that is not in accordance with the opinion of the EMA, in which case its draft decision shall annex a detailed explanation of the reasons for the differences.[81] The Commission's draft decision is forwarded to the Member States and the applicant. It is also forwarded to the Standing Committee on Medicinal Products for Human Use, whose function is to 'assist' the Commission. This Committee delivers its opinion on the draft decision, based on weighted majority voting. The Commission shall adopt the measures envisaged if they are in accordance with the opinion of the Committee. If the measures envisaged are not in accordance with the opinion of the Committee, or if no opinion is delivered, the Commission shall, without delay, submit a proposal to the Council, which shall act by a qualified majority. If, on the expiry of three months from the date of referral to the Council, the Council has not acted, the Commission shall adopt the proposed measures, save where the Council has decided against the measures by a simple majority.[82] Each Member State may forward written observations to the Commission and where,

---

[78] Dir 2001/83/EC, art 12 (first introduced by Dir 75/319/EEC, art 2); Reg (EC) 726/2004, art 6.
[79] Case C-440/93 *R v Licensing Authority of the Department of Health and Norgine Ltd, ex p Scotia Pharmaceuticals Ltd* [1995] ECR I-2851.
[80] Reg (EC) 726/2004, art 61.
[81] ibid, art 10.
[82] ibid, art 87.

in the opinion of the Commission, these observations raise important new questions of a scientific or technical nature that have not been addressed in the opinion of the EMA, the matter is referred back to the EMA for further consideration.

c)   *Manufacturing.* The holder of the manufacturing authorisation must have permanently and continuously at his disposal the services of at least one qualified person who is responsible for securing[83] that the manufacturer or importer is able to carry out manufacture in accordance with the particulars supplied pursuant to the application for marketing authorisation[84] and/or to carry out controls according to the methods described in the particulars accompanying the application.[85] The qualified person must fulfil specified minimum conditions of qualification, including a four year university course, or its equivalent, in one of the scientific disciplines of pharmacy, medicine, veterinary medicine, chemistry, pharmaceutical chemistry and technology or biology, plus at least two years practical experience, in one or more undertakings which are authorised to manufacture medicines, in qualitative and quantitative analysis of and quality testing and checking of medicinal products.[86]

d)   *Distribution.* The holder of a wholesale distribution authorisation must have staff, and in particular a qualified person designated as responsible, meeting the conditions.[87]

e)   *Approving advertising.* In the United Kingdom, the legal scheme and requirements[88] exist as a backdrop but are very rarely invoked, since two self-regulatory schemes are operated in practice. Manufacturers of prescription products who are members of the Association of the British Pharmaceutical Industry observe its *Code of Practice for the Pharmaceutical Industry*, which is administered by the Prescription Medicines Code of Practice Authority. Manufacturers of over-the-counter products who are members of the Proprietary Association of Great Britain observe its *Code of Standards of Advertising Practice for Over-the-Counter Medicines*.

f)   *Scientific information service.* A marketing authorisation holder is required to establish within his undertaking a scientific service in charge of information about the medicinal products that he places on the market.[89]

g)   *Promotion.* Medical sales representatives must have adequate training and scientific knowledge to be able to provide precise and complete information about the medicinal products they promote to health professionals.[90] They must give the persons visited, or have available to them, summaries of the product characteristics of each medicinal product they present.[91] There are restrictions on promotional activities.[92]

h)   *Pharmacovigilance.* At EU level, expert evaluation is coordinated by the Pharmacovigilance Risk Assessment Committee. A marketing authorisation holder is required to

---

[83] Dir 2001/83/EC, art 20, which empowers an authority to permit certain variations.

[84] ibid, art 8(3)(d).

[85] ibid, art 8(3)(h).

[86] ibid, art 49.

[87] Dir 2001/83/EC, art 79(b).

[88] The Medicines (Advertising) Requirements 1994, SI 1994 No 1932; the Medicines (Monitoring of Advertising) Regs 1994, SI 1994 No 1933; the Control of Misleading Advertisement Regs 1988, SI 1988 No 915.

[89] Dir 2001/83/EC, art 98.1.

[90] Dir 2001/83/EC, art 93.1.

[91] ibid, art 93.2.

[92] ibid, arts 94 to 96.

have permanently and continuously at his disposal a 'qualified person' responsible for pharmacovigilance, who has the following obligations:

(a) the establishment and maintenance of a system which ensures that information about all suspected adverse reactions which are reported to the personnel of the company, and to medical representatives, is collected and collated in order to be accessible at least at one point within the Community;

(b) the preparation for the competent authorities of reports on specified adverse reactions;

(c) ensuring that any request from the competent authorities for the provision of additional information necessary for the evaluation of the benefits and risks afforded by a medicinal product is answered fully and promptly, including the provision of information about the volume of sales or prescriptions for the medicinal product concerned.[93]

Qualified Persons have, however, reported significant irritation at what they perceive to be lack of sufficient discretion when releasing product to market, which leads to an increasingly bureaucratic workload and complaint by some that they are 'highly qualified box tickers'.[94]

Feedback in the 2014 enforcement review was that MHRA (Medicines and Healthcare products Regulatory Agency) was widely perceived as a highly respected regulator, a generally open organisation, which made considerable effort to be risk-based and was willing to engage with industry and tried to 'do the right thing', although there was some concern about inconsistency in advice.[95] Its inspectors were felt to have very good knowledge and be highly professional.[96]

ii. Evidence of Safe Operation

Are medicines safe? Research in 2006 found that the general public has a confidence in the safety of medicines and medical devices that seems to stem from overall confidence in doctors, and in their ability to weigh up the risks and benefits.[97]

It is difficult to compare data on the overall incidence of usage, withdrawals and adverse events.[98] In 2013 the EMA issued 436 recommendations based on PSURs of reviews of active substances (not medicinal products), which led to 76 CHMP variations, and no suspensions or revocations.

However, medicines safety is a prime example of the observation that risk and safety have become politicised terms.[99] The system continues to operate on a daily basis, but if an event

---

[93] Dir 2001/83/EC, art 103; for the centralised procedure see Reg (EC) No 726/2004, art 23, which is almost identical. These provisions are supplemented by guidance in Vol 9A of the Rules Governing Medicinal Products in the European Union.

[94] *Focus on Enforcement Regulatory Reviews. Review of the Pharmaceutical Manufacturing and Production Sector* (Department for Business, Innovation & Skills, 2014) Finding 5.

[95] ibid.

[96] ibid.

[97] *Risks and Benefits of Medicines and Medical Devices—Perceptions, Communication & Regulation* (Ipsos MORI, 2006).

[98] Hodges (n 70) App 3.

[99] R Baldwin, C Scott and C Hood, *A Reader on Regulation* (Oxford, Oxford University Press, 1998) 35.

captures media and then political attention, the decisions that are taken owe more to fear and a desire to be seen to be tough than to objective scientific logic.[100]

E. Balancing Safety and Market Access

One complaint is that the network of EU medicines authorities is too cumbersome and slow. A decade ago, the cost of developing a new drug was put at over $800 million, and rising at an annual rate of 7.4 per cent above general price inflation.[101] A 2009 European Commission Report noted industry figures of between $800 million and $1 billion, whilst non-industry sources suggested $450 million.[102] Industry reported that as few as one in 5,000 to 10,000 compounds tested were subsequently successfully launched as products.[103] The Commission concluded that the network 'requires optimisation to improve its efficiency, minimise the regulatory burden it generates and thus speed up market access for medicines'.[104]

There are indications that further integration would be beneficial.[105] The vestiges of relying on national licences alone prevent peer review by other agencies, and may give rise to opportunities for local corruption. The availability of peer review might have prevented the French scandals of isomeride and fenfluramine in the late 1990s,[106] and of the drug Mediator in 2011.[107]

A further topical issue is whether all data is made available to regulators or publicly, especially clinical trial data if it is not positive.[108]

F. Adaptive Licensing

A revolutionary new approach has recently emerged in relation to medicines licensing. In the classic model, a great deal of data would be amassed leading to a binary decision by a regulator on approval or rejection of a compound. However, a trial of a compound in

---

[100] See C Hodges, 'Regulating Risk or Advancing Therapies? Regulation and Sustainability of Medicines in a Cash-limited Economy' [2008] *European Business Law Review* 389.

[101] Boston Consulting Group, *A Revolution in R&D: How Genomics and Genetics are Transforming the Biopharmaceutical Industry* (Boston Consulting Group, 2001); J DiMasi, RW Hanson and HG Grabowski, 'The Price of Innovation: New Estimates of Drug Development Costs' (2003) 22 *Journal of Health Economics* 151–85; DW Light and RN Warburton, 'Extraordinary Claims Require Extraordinary Evidence' (2005) 24(5) *Journal of Health Economics* 1030–33.

[102] *Pharmaceutical Sector Inquiry. Final Report* (European Commission, 2009) para 149. No sources were stated for the figures.

[103] EFPIA Submission to the European Commission in relation to the pharmaceutical sector inquiry, 13 June 2009, 20.

[104] *Pharmaceutical Sector Inquiry. Final Report* (European Commission, 2009) para 1585.

[105] Hodges (n 70).

[106] See *Current Problems* (MHRA), articles June 1992, Feb 1997, Dec 1997.

[107] A Morelle, AC Bensadon and E Marie, *Enquête sur le Mediator* (Paris. Inspection Générale des affaires sociales, 2011) see www.igas.gouv.fr/spip.php?article162.

[108] B Goldacre, *Bad Pharma* (London, Fourth Estate, 2012); B Rawal and BR Deane, 'Clinical Trial Transparency: An Assessment of the Disclosure of Results of Company-sponsored Trials Associated with New Medicines Approved Recently in Europe' (2013) *Current Medical Research & Opinion* 1–11; House of Commons Committee of Public Accounts, *Access to Clinical Trial Information and the Stockpiling of Tamiflu*, 35th Report of Session 2013–14, Report, together with formal minutes, oral and written evidence, 18 December 2013.

1,000 carefully selected patients does *not* show efficacy. A complete change in mindset has occurred, towards a life-span assessment of compounds. Several key issues have converged to drive change: Growing patient demand for timely access to promising therapies, emerging science leading to fragmentation of treatment populations and away from 'blockbuster' drugs, rising payer influence on product accessibility, and pressure on pharmaceutical companies and investors in research to ensure sustainability of drug development, leading to a different 'value concept'.[109] The outstanding example of an early assessment of efficacy is a product for multiple myeloma, Velcade, using a bio marker in plasma, NKFB p65, presence of which indicates a greater likelihood of success. Hence, the benefit–risk balance can be estimated, and, if it is found to be positive, the funder will pay the manufacturer, but if not, would not.

Assessment of safety is undertaken continuously, because of the existence of permanent monitoring systems. A switch has occurred from looking at causality of harm to showing co-relation. Safety monitoring is likely to be transformed by access to 'big data'.

Importantly, patients are now involved in discussions with regulators and developers on access of products to market, assessing those in which they would be prepared to accept the risk of serious side effects. The risk–benefit evaluation is, therefore, influenced on an individual condition or product basis by those who accept the risks and benefits, rather than solely by third parties. This model therefore involves a wide range of stakeholders in making safety and economic decisions.

IV. Engineered Products

A. Pre-Marketing Controls

European rules regulate the safety of many types of products that are used for professional and consumer use. The regimes that apply are designed to be appropriate to the safety issues that arise with the particular product type, and can have significant differences between themselves.[110] Broadly speaking, that for medicinal products is the most complex and onerous amongst products used by consumers.

The regulatory systems for engineered products generally fall within a broad matrix now known as 'the New Framework'.[111] All New Framework product regulatory systems place strong emphasis on pre-marketing controls to establish the safety and performance of products. Proof of conformity with mandatory essential requirements authorises the manufacturer to affix CE marking to a product.[112] Some product types may comprise a

---

[109] H-G Eichler and others, 'From Adaptive Licensing to Adaptive Pathways: Delivering a Flexible Life-Span Approach to bring New Drugs to Patients' (2015) 97(3) *State of the Art* 234.

[110] This section draws significantly on Hodges (n 70).

[111] Known as the New Approach when first introduced in 1993. See *State of the Implementation of the New Legislative Framework (NLF)* (European Commission, 2010), at http://ec.europa.eu/enterprise/policies/single-market-goods/files/new-legislative-framework/nlf_implementation_reports/nlf_implementation_report_en.pdf.

[112] Decision No 768/2008/EC of the European Parliament and of the Council of 9 July 2008 on a common framework for the marketing of products, and repealing Council Decision 93/465/EEC, recital 29 and arts 3 and 5. Also Reg (EC) No 765/2008, art 30.

range of sub-types that give rise to a variation in safety issues. Some products may present limited risks, whereas others may present numerous risks or significant particular hazards. These variations in product risks have been accounted for through classification of product types, and the availability of a range of modules for conformity assessment procedures.[113] Products in higher risk classes may, for example, be subject to initial and/or ongoing type inspection or assessment of the quality system for their design and manufacture by independent notified bodies.[114] The sectoral product types that are included within the New Framework are at Table 19.2. The model framework provisions in Decision 768/2008/EC are implemented into the specific legislation covering each product type.

The philosophy that underpins the New Approach framework is that 'The manufacturer, having detailed knowledge of the design and production process, is best placed to carry out the complete conformity assessment procedure. Conformity assessment should therefore remain the obligation of the manufacturer alone.'[115] Pre-marketing approval by a public authority is, therefore, not required. Manufacturers are obliged to:[116]

— Draw up the required technical documentation;
— carry out the conformity assessment procedure applicable or have it carried out;
— where compliance of a product with the applicable requirements has been demonstrated by that procedure, draw up an EC declaration of conformity and affix the conformity marking;
— keep the technical documentation and the EC declaration of conformity;
— when deemed appropriate with regard to the risks presented by a product, manufacturers shall, to protect the health and safety of consumers, carry out sample testing of marketed products, investigate, and, if necessary, keep a register of complaints, of nonconforming products and product recalls, and shall keep distributors informed of any such monitoring;
— ensure that their products bear a type, batch or serial number or other element allowing their identification, or, where the size or nature of the product does not allow it, that the required information is provided on the packaging or in a document accompanying the product.
— indicate their name, registered trade name or registered trade mark and the address at which they can be contacted on the product or, where that is not possible, on its packaging or in a document accompanying the product. The address must indicate a single point at which the manufacturer can be contacted;
— ensure that the product is accompanied by instructions and safety information in a language which can be easily understood by consumers and other end-users, as determined by the Member State concerned.

[113] Decision No 768/2008/EC, art 4: the modules are set out in Annexes.
[114] Criteria for designation of notified bodies by competent authorities is at Decision No 768/2008/EC, Annex I ch R4.
[115] Decision No 768/2008/EC, recital 21 and art 1.
[116] Decision No 768/2008/EC, Annex I, ch R2.

Table 19.2: New Framework Sectors that are subject to collective alignment with the New Legislative Framework (NLF) Decision

— *Civil Explosives*: Directive 93/15/EEC on the harmonisation of the provisions relating to the placing on the market and supervision of explosives for civil use — *ATEX Directive*: Directive 94/9/EC on the approximation of the laws of the Member States concerning equipment and protective systems intended for use in potentially explosive atmospheres — *Lifts*: Directive 95/16/EC of 29 June 1995 on the approximation of the laws of the Member States relating to lifts — *Pressure Equipment*: Directive 97/23/EC on the approximation of the laws of the Member States concerning pressure equipment — *Measuring Instruments*: Directive 2004/22/EC on measuring instruments — *Electromagnetic Compatibility (EMC)*: Directive 2004/108/EC on the approximation of the laws of the Member States relating to electromagnetic compatibility and repealing Directive 89/336/EEC — *Low Voltage*: Directive 2006/95/EEC on the harmonisation of the laws of Member States relating to electrical equipment designed for use within certain voltage limits — *Pyrotechnic Articles*: Directive 2007/23/EC on the placing on the market of pyrotechnic articles — *Non-automatic Weighing Instruments (NAWI)*: Directive 2009/23/EC on non-automatic weighing instruments — *Simple Pressure Vessels*: Directive 2009/105/EC relating to simple pressure vessels — *Hazardous substances in electrical and electronic equipment*: Directive 2011/65/EU of the European Parliament and of the Council (OJ L 174/88, 1/7/2011) of 8 June 2011 on the restriction of the use of certain hazardous substances in electrical and electronic equipment (recast) — *Ecodesign*: Directive 2009/125/EC of the European Parliament and of the Council of 21 October 2009 (OJ L 285/10 of 31/10/2009) of 21 October 2009 establishing a framework for the setting of ecodesign requirements for energy-related products (recast)
New Framework Sectors that have been, or are being, individually aligned with the NLF Decision
— *Recreational Craft*: Directive 94/25/EC of the European Parliament and of the Council of 16 June 1994 on the approximation of the laws, regulations and administrative provisions of the Member States relating to recreational craft (consolidated version) — *R&TTE Directive*: Directive 1999/5/EC of the European Parliament and of the Council of 9 March 1999 on radio equipment and telecommunications terminal equipment and the mutual recognition of their conformity[117] — *Medical Devices*: Directive 93/42/EEC on medical devices[118] — *Active Implantable Medical Devices*: Directive 90/385/EEC on active implantable medical devices (AIMDD)[119]

(continued)

---

[117] See Proposal for a Dir of the European Parliament and of the Council on the harmonisation of the laws of the Member States relating to the making available on the market of radio equipment, COM (2012) 584 final, 17.10.2012.

[118] See Proposal for a Reg of the European Parliament and of the Council on medical devices, and amending Dir 2001/83/EC, Reg (EC) No 178/2002 and Reg (EC) No 1223/2009, COM (2012) 542 final, 26.9.2012.

[119] See ibid.

Table 19.2: *(Continued)*

— *In Vitro Diagnostic Medical Devices*: Directive 98/79/EC of the European Parliament and of the Council of 27 October 1998 on in vitro diagnostic medical devices (IVDMD)[120] — *Construction Products*: Regulation (EU) No 305/2011 of the European Parliament and of the Council of 9 March 2011 laying down harmonised conditions for the marketing of construction products and repealing Council Directive 89/106/EEC; originally Directive 93/68/EEC

Other Sectors Based on the New Approach
— *Appliances Burning Gaseous Fuels*: Directive 2009/142/EC of the European Parliament and of the Council of 30 November 2009 relating to appliances burning gaseous fuels (codified version); originally Directive 90/396/EEC — *Machinery*: Directive 98/37/EC of the European Parliament and of the Council of 17 May 2006 on machinery, and amending Directive 95/16/EC (recast); originally Directive 98/37/EC — *Personal Protective Equipment*: Directive 89/686/EEC of 21 December 1989 on the approximation of the laws of the Member States relating to personal protective equipment — *Toys*: Directive 2009/48/EC of the European Parliament and of the Council of 18 June 2009 on the safety of toys; originally Directive 88/378/EEC — *Cableways*: Directive 2000/9/EC of the European Parliament and of the Council (OJ L 106 of 3/5/2000) of 20 March 2000 relating to cableway installations designed to carry persons — *Boilers*: Council Directive 93/42/EEC (OJ L 169 of 12/7/93) of 14 June 1993 concerning medical devices (amended by Directive 98/79/EC of the European Parliament and of the Council (OJ L 331 of 7/12/98), Directive 2000/70/EC (OJ L 313 of 13/12/2000), Directive 2001/104/EC of the European Parliament and of the Council (OJ L 6 of 10/01/2002), Directive 2007/47/EC of the European Parliament and of the Council (OJ L 247 of 21/9/2007) and Regulation (EC) No 1882/2003 of the European Parliament and of the Council (OJ L 284 of 31/10/2003))

B. Post-Marketing Controls

Over the past two decades, post-marketing vigilance systems and requirements have been added to the pre-marketing rules, broadly following the trail blazed by the pharmacovigilance regime described above.

Member States are responsible for ensuring strong and efficient market surveillance on their territories and should allocate sufficient powers and resources to their market surveillance authorities.[121] If marketed products are found to present a risk to the health or safety of persons, market surveillance authorities (MSAs) are required without delay to evaluate the position and, if a product is not in conformity, require the relevant economic operator to take all appropriate corrective action to bring the product into compliance with those requirements, to withdraw the product from the market, or to recall it within

---

[120] See Proposal for a Reg of the European Parliament and of the Council on *in vitro* diagnostic medical devices, COM(2012) 541 final, 26.9.2012.

[121] Decision No 768/2008/EC, recital 34.

a reasonable period, commensurate with the nature of the risk, as they may prescribe.[122] MSAs are required to inform the relevant notified bodies, the Commission and the other Member States without delay. The economic operator shall ensure that all appropriate corrective action is taken throughout the Community market.[123] Similar actions apply where a product is in compliance but nevertheless presents a risk to the health or safety of persons or to other aspects of public interest protection.[124]

Under what is known as the 'safeguard procedure',[125] where objections are raised against a national measure, or where the Commission considers a national measure to be contrary to Community legislation, the Commission shall without delay enter into consultation with the Member States and the relevant economic operator or operators and shall evaluate the national measure. On the basis of the results of that evaluation, the Commission shall decide whether the national measure is justified or not. If the national measure is considered justified, all Member States shall take the measures necessary to ensure that the non-compliant product is withdrawn from their market, and shall inform the Commission accordingly. If the national measure is considered unjustified, the Member State concerned shall withdraw the measure.

The related obligations on manufacturers are:

8. Manufacturers who consider or have reason to believe that a product which they have placed on the market is not in conformity with the applicable Community harmonisation legislation shall immediately take the necessary corrective measures to bring that product into conformity, to withdraw it or recall it, if appropriate. Furthermore, where the product presents a risk, manufacturers shall immediately inform the competent national authorities of the Member States in which they made the product available to that effect, giving details, in particular, of the noncompliance and of any corrective measures taken.

9. Manufacturers shall, further to a reasoned request from a competent national authority, provide it with all the information and documentation necessary to demonstrate the conformity of the product, in a language which can be easily understood by that authority. They shall cooperate with that authority, at its request, on any action taken to eliminate the risks posed by products which they have placed on the market.[126]

Similar obligations apply to distributors and importers who 'being close to the market place, should be involved in market surveillance tasks carried out by national authorities, and should be prepared to participate actively, providing the competent authorities with all necessary information relating to the product concerned.'[127]

C. Discussion

The New Framework system places primary responsibility for compliance with safety and performance issues on manufacturers. Manufacturers of products that inherently have

---

[122] Decision No 768/2008/EC, Annex I, art R31.1.
[123] ibid, art R31.3.
[124] ibid, art R33.
[125] Decision No 768/2008/EC, Annex I, art R32.
[126] ibid, Annex I, art R2 8.
[127] ibid, recital 27. For obligations on importers see Annex I, art R4, and on distributors, art R5.

higher risks are required to obtain assessment and certification by notified bodies, which are non-governmental organisations who exercise quasi-public functions. Marketing or manufacturing authorisation is not required from public authorities. If safety issues arise post-marketing, the system mandates an integrated approach by all relevant public and private actors. One notable feature of the system is the extent of cooperation and collaboration that is expected and mandated between the various actors (authorities, notified bodies, manufacturers, importers, distributors). Indeed, the words 'cooperation' and 'collaboration' occur throughout the EU legislation.[128]

The post-marketing system has been integrated with that for general consumer products, so is discussed further below.

A series of inter-related issues have arisen with:

— Variations in the quality of notified bodies.[129]
— Vigilance procedures, such as exchanges of experience and information between notified bodies and notifying authorities and between notified bodies, should be consolidated.[130]
— Variations in the surveillance and enforcement capabilities of national competent authorities.[131]
— A lack of understanding of what CE marking means amongst economic operators, in particular SMEs (small and medium sized entities).[132]

In 2010 accreditation of notified bodies was introduced so as to provide an authoritative statement of the technical competence of notified bodies.[133] Every Member State is required to have a single national accreditation body,[134] and national accreditation bodies shall subject themselves to peer evaluation organised by a body recognised by the Commission.[135] The requirements for national accreditation bodies are in line with globally accepted

---

[128] In addition to various references noted above and below, see also Reg (EC) No 765/2008, recitals 24, 28 and 40.

[129] An early instance was criticism in AH Powell, *Study on the Implementation of the Low Voltage Directive* (European Commission, 1999) paras 5.5.8 and 9.2.7.

[130] Decision No 768/2008/EC, recital 46.

[131] Decision No 768/2008/EC: Recitals stated '(37) Experience has shown that the criteria set out in sectoral legislation which conformity assessment bodies have to fulfil to be notified to the Commission are not sufficient to ensure a uniformly high level of performance of notified bodies throughout the Community. It is, however, essential that all notified bodies perform their functions to the same level and under conditions of fair competition. That requires the setting of obligatory requirements for conformity assessment bodies wishing to be notified in order to provide conformity assessment services. (38) In order to ensure a consistent level of quality in the performance of conformity assessment it is necessary not only to consolidate the requirements that conformity assessment bodies wishing to be notified must fulfil, but also, in parallel, to set requirements that notifying authorities and other bodies involved in the assessment, notification and monitoring of notified bodies must fulfil.'

[132] Report from the Commission to the European Parliament, the Council and the European Economic and Social Committee on the implementation of Reg (EC) No 765/2008 of the European Parliament and of the Council of 9 July 2008 setting out the requirements for accreditation and market surveillance relating to the marketing of products and repealing Reg (EEC) No 339/93, COM(2013) 77, 13.2.2013, para 5.1.

[133] Reg (EC) No 765/2008 of the European Parliament and of the Council of 9 July 2008 setting out the requirements for accreditation and market surveillance relating to the marketing of products and repealing Reg (EEC) No 339/93, recital 9 and ch II.

[134] ibid, art 4.

[135] ibid, arts 10 and 14.

requirements in ISO/IEC international standards.[136] Peer evaluation is 'possibly the most essential tool' and must be 'rigorous': The next stage is for it to be further strengthened.[137] The European Cooperation for Accreditation operates as the accreditation infrastructure.[138]

Particular concern arose with notified bodies in the medical devices sector after a number of incidents, notably the PIP breast implants scandal, in which a manufacturer used silicone of lower quality than that approved, and concealed this from the notified body.[139] Particular reforms were introduced in that sector before the legislation was amended,[140] by setting benchmark general guidelines for audits and assessments by notified bodies, including audit of critical subcontractors and suppliers, and requiring them to perform unannounced audits.[141] The procedures for designation and supervision of notified bodies by authorities were clarified, notably by the introduction of joint assessments by designating authorities of three Member States, and allowing the Commission to investigate notified bodies.[142] This element of collaboration and peer support was intended to increase transparency and mutual trust, as well as further align practice.[143] The changes had effect, and by late 2014 the number of notified bodies designated for medical devices had reduced from 80 to 67, and many continuing bodies reduced their field of application. The joint inspections were reported to have succeeded in spreading best practice through a two-way peer review process between competent authorities and notified bodies.[144]

V. General Consumer Products

A. The GPS Regime

The marketing of consumer products that are not subject to specific vertical regulatory regimes is subject to general pre-marketing requirements. However, once again, post-marketing systems have been extended for such products.

---

[136] See Report from the Commission to the European Parliament, the Council and the European Economic and Social Committee on the implementation of Reg (EC) No 765/2008 of the European Parliament and of the Council of 9 July 2008 setting out the requirements for accreditation and market surveillance relating to the marketing of products and repealing Reg (EEC) No 339/93, COM(2013) 77, 13.2.2013, para 2.1.

[137] Report from the Commission to the European Parliament, the Council and the European Economic and Social Committee on the implementation of Reg (EC) No 765/2008 of the European Parliament and of the Council of 9 July 2008 setting out the requirements for accreditation and market surveillance relating to the marketing of products and repealing Reg (EEC) No 339/93, COM(2013) 77, 13.2.2013, para 2.3.

[138] See General guidelines for the cooperation between the European Cooperation for Accreditation and the European Commission, the European Free Trade Association and the competent national authorities. OJ 2009/C 116/04: http://eurlex.europa.eu/LexUriServ/LexUriServ.do?uri=OJ:C:2009:116:0006:0011:EN:PDF.

[139] Proposal for a Reg of the European Parliament and of the Council on medical devices, and amending Dir 2001/83/EC, Reg (EC) No 178/2002 and Reg (EC) No 1223/2009, COM(2012) 542 final, 26.9.2012.

[140] See Commission Staff Working Document Implementation of the Joint Plan for Immediate Actions under the existing Medical Devices legislation, SWD(2014) 195 final, 13.6.2014.

[141] Commission Recommendation of 24 September 2013 on the audits and assessments performed by notified bodies in the field of medical devices, OJ L 253/27, 25.6.2013.

[142] Commission Implementing Reg (EU) No 920/2013 of 24 September 2013 on the designation and the supervision of notified bodies under Council Dir 90/385/EEC on active implantable medical devices and Council Dir 93/42/EEC on medical devices, OJ L 253/8, 25.9.2013.

[143] ibid, recital 8.

[144] Presentation by J Wilkinson of MHRA at the ABHI Annual Regulatory Conference, London, 25 November 2014.

General safety requirements were introduced in 1992,[145] and revised and extended in 2001.[146] The purpose is to ensure that products placed on the market are safe,[147] and producers are obliged to place only safe products on the market.[148] Safety requirements imposed by other Community legislation take precedence,[149] and conformity with a residual 'general safety obligation' is assessed by taking into account in particular the following elements where they exist:[150]

(a)   Voluntary national standards transposing relevant European standards other than those transposing harmonised European standards that have been published by the Commission;
(b)   the standards drawn up in the Member State in which the product is marketed;
(c)   Commission recommendations setting guidelines on product safety assessment;
(d)   product safety codes of good practice in force in the sector concerned;
(e)   the state of the art and technology;
(f)   reasonable consumer expectations concerning safety.

Producers shall provide consumers with the relevant information to enable them to assess the risks inherent in a product throughout the normal or reasonably foreseeable period of its use, where such risks are not immediately obvious without adequate warnings, and to take precautions against those risks.[151] Distributors

> shall be required to act with due care to help to ensure compliance with the applicable safety requirements, in particular by not supplying products which they know or should have presumed, on the basis of the information in their possession and as professionals, do not comply with those requirements. Moreover, within the limits of their respective activities, they shall participate in monitoring the safety of products placed on the market, especially by passing on information on product risks, keeping and providing the documentation necessary for tracing the origin of products, and cooperating in the action taken by producers and competent authorities to avoid the risks. Within the limits of their respective activities they shall take measures enabling them to cooperate efficiently.[152]

Producers and distributors shall, within the limits of their respective activities, cooperate with the competent authorities, at the request of the latter, on action taken to avoid the risks posed by products which they supply or have supplied.[153] The procedures for such cooperation, including procedures for dialogue with the producers and distributors concerned on issues related to product safety, shall be established by the competent authorities.[154] Member States shall ensure that producers and distributors comply with their obligations under this Directive in such a way that products placed on the market are safe.[155] They

---

[145] Dir 92/59/EEC on general product safety.
[146] Dir 2001/95/EC on general product safety.
[147] ibid, art 1.1. 'Safe product' is defined in art 2(b).
[148] ibid, art 3.1.
[149] ibid, art 3.2 and 3.3.
[150] ibid, art 3.3.
[151] ibid, art 5.1.
[152] ibid, art 5.2.
[153] ibid, art 5.4.
[154] ibid.
[155] ibid, art 6.1.

shall establish or nominate authorities competent to monitor the compliance of products with the general safety requirements and arrange for such authorities to have and use the necessary powers to take specified surveillance and enforcement measures.[156] Administrative cooperation is provided through a network of national authorities coordinated by the Commission, which includes the RAPEX system.[157]

B. The Market Surveillance Regime

From 2010, in response to concern 'to achieve a higher level of safety' for consumer products,[158] the Community Market Surveillance Framework was created for the market surveillance of products 'to ensure that those products fulfil requirements providing a high level of protection of public interests, such as health and safety in general, health and safety at the workplace, the protection of consumers, protection of the environment and security'.[159] Member States are required to organise and carry out market surveillance so as to withdraw, prohibit or restrict the availability of products which, when used in accordance with their intended purpose or under conditions which can be reasonably foreseen and when properly installed and maintained, are liable to compromise the health or safety of users, or which otherwise do not conform to applicable requirements set out in Community harmonisation legislation.[160] Member States are required to establish appropriate communication and coordination mechanisms between their market surveillance authorities.[161] They must establish adequate procedures in order to:

(a) Follow up complaints or reports on issues relating to risks arising in connection with products subject to Community harmonisation legislation;
(b) monitor accidents and harm to health which are suspected to have been caused by those products;
(c) verify that corrective action has been taken; and
(d) follow up scientific and technical knowledge concerning safety issues.[162]

Member States shall entrust market surveillance authorities with the powers, resources and knowledge necessary for the proper performance of their tasks.[163] They shall ensure that market surveillance authorities exercise their powers in accordance with the principle of proportionality.[164] Member States shall perform appropriate checks on the characteristics of products on an adequate scale.[165] Member States shall ensure efficient cooperation and exchange of information between their market surveillance authorities and those of the

---

[156] ibid, arts 6.2, 7, 8 and 9.
[157] ibid, arts 10, 11 and 12.
[158] Reg (EC) No 765/2008 of the European Parliament and of the Council of 9 July 2008 setting out the requirements for accreditation and market surveillance relating to the marketing of products and repealing Reg (EEC) No 339/93, recital 6.
[159] ibid, art 1.2 and ch III.
[160] ibid, art 16.1. See also art 21. Rapid intervention in respect of serious risks is required under art 20, and immediate notification to the Commission through the Community Rapid Information System (RAPEX): art 22.
[161] ibid, art 18.1.
[162] ibid, art 18.2.
[163] ibid, art 18.3.
[164] ibid, art 18.4.
[165] ibid, art 18.6.

other Member States and between their own authorities and the Commission and the relevant Community agencies regarding their market surveillance programmes and all issues relating to products presenting risks.[166] They shall provide mutual assistance and may share resources and expertise.[167]

Also in 2010, a harmonised methodology was established for classifying and reporting consumer complaints and enquiries.[168] This was partly to assist in working towards the establishment of a Union-wide database of consumer complaints.

Notwithstanding the establishment of the surveillance frameworks noted above, dissatisfaction continued with practical operation of the system. A 2011 report identified a series of shortcomings providing 'clear indications that the present system is no longer "fit for purpose"':[169]

— Lack of resources clearly affected the impact of market surveillance in many Member States;
— the need for co-ordination was recognised but no solutions had been universally adopted;
— joint enforcement programmes were not normal custom and practice;
— good practice was being followed in many Member States but not being universally applied;
— there was very little performance information available regarding the market surveillance activities of Member States and accurate benchmarking is impossible.

Based upon the results of its questionnaire, the Review Team identified some clear routes to improvement of service delivery including:

— The advantages of scale can be a benefit when utilised within Member States and increasingly so when resulting from coordinated programmes between Member States;
— the main requirements will always be sufficient assured funding and numbers of qualified Inspectors working within a framework that incorporates as many aspects of best practice as possible with reasonable access to accredited testing facilities;
— a wider range of information sources would allow for better targeting;
— RAPEX notifications need to be transferred quicker and greater efforts should be made to provide more actionable information;
— information and advice to economic operators (SME) is a legitimate Member State function that needs to be given a greater priority.

The review of best practice equally gave clear examples of procedures that would improve the effectiveness and increase the efficiency of current practice, including:

— Best practice should become the basic operating procedures of all MSAs;
— a balance between reactive and proactive approaches;
— better use of consumer complaint and accident and injury data;

---

[166] ibid, art 24.
[167] ibid, arts 24, 25 and 26.
[168] Commission Recommendation of 12 May 2010 on the use of a harmonised methodology was established for classifying and reporting consumer complaints and enquiries, OJ L 136/1, 2.6.2010.
[169] *Final Report. The Future of Market Surveillance in the Area of Non-food Consumer Product Safety under the General Product Safety Directive* (BSI Development Solutions, 2011), SANCO/2009/B3/012, http://ec.europa.eu/consumers/safety/projects/docs/final_report_the_future_of_market_surveillance.pdf.

— databases of risk-assessed economic entities;
— risk-based inspection programmes;
— intelligence-led safety initiatives with precautionary principle in mind;
— published enforcement policies;
— national Market Surveillance Co-ordination Committees.

The report noted:

> Administrative fines appear to have little deterrent effect when used against large national or international economic operators and can be totally disproportional when levied against single and medium sized enterprises (SMEs).[170]

In 2013 the Commission tabled proposals to reform the consumer product safety legislation as a Regulation[171] and to reform an integrated market surveillance system.[172] The key elements of the Consumer Product Safety Regulation proposal included:

— Retention of the requirement that all consumer products must be safe when placed on the market, which was described as 'a fundamental pillar, although the rules were simplified to provide a clear link with sector-specific legislation and through simplifying rules on standards;[173]
— broadening the scope to subsume food-imitating products (products that resemble food but which instead have another purpose) and an extension to products that are made available to consumers via a service provider;
— greater traceability of products through the supply chain (for example distributors and manufacturers will need to include an indication of the country of origin of a product or, where that is not possible due to the size or nature of the product an indication that is included in the documentation or packaging of the product);
— clearer and more detailed obligations on businesses;
— adoption of common definitions used in EU product legislation (following the New Legislative Framework Model);
— simplified rules for the development of supporting standards, and;
— the use of delegated and implementing acts to support some aspects of the Regulation.

The Commission described market surveillance as 'our main tool' in combating unsafe products and rogue traders.[174] However, the confusing fragmentation of market surveillance

---

[170] ibid, para 12.

[171] Proposal for a Reg of the European Parliament and of the Council on market surveillance of products and amending Council Dirs 89/686/EEC and 93/15/EEC, and Dirs 94/9/EC, 94/25/EC, 95/16/EC, 97/23/EC, 1999/5/EC, 2000/9/EC, 2000/14/EC, 2001/95/EC, 2004/108/EC, 2006/42/EC, 2006/95/EC, 2007/23/EC, 2008/57/EC, 2009/48/EC, 2009/105/EC, 2009/142/EC, 2011/65/EU, Reg (EU) No 305/2011, Reg (EC) No 764/2008 and Reg (EC) No 765/2008 of the European Parliament and of the Council, COM(2013) 75, 13.2.2103.

[172] Proposal for a Reg of the European Parliament and of the Council on consumer product safety and repealing Council Dir 87/357/EEC and Dir 2001/95/EC, COM(2013) 78, 13.2.2103.

[173] Proposal for a Reg of the European Parliament and of the Council on consumer product safety and repealing Council Dir 87/357/EEC and Dir 2001/95/EC, COM(2013) 78, 13.2.2103, Explanatory memorandum, para 3.

[174] Communication from the Commission to the European Parliament, the Council and the European Economic and Social Committee: More Product Safety and better Market Surveillance in the Single Market for Products, COM(2013) 74, 13.2.2013, para 3; Explanatory Memorandum to Proposal for a Reg of the European Parliament and of the Council on market surveillance of products and amending Council Dirs 89/686/EEC and 93/15/EEC, and Dirs 94/9/EC, 94/25/EC, 95/16/EC, 97/23/EC, 1999/5/EC, 2000/9/EC, 2000/14/EC, 2001/95/EC, 2004/108/EC, 2006/42/EC, 2006/95/EC, 2007/23/EC, 2008/57/EC, 2009/48/EC, 2009/105/EC, 2009/142/EC, 2011/65/EU, Reg (EU) No 305/2011, Reg (EC) No 764/2008 and Reg (EC) No 765/2008 of the European Parliament and of the Council, COM(2013) 75, 13.2.2103, para 1.

rules and systems for consumer and product harmonising legislation was 'seriously hampering the efforts of market surveillance officers in the field' and justified creating a single integrated regime, coupled with strengthening controls at external borders.[175] Accordingly, the new single tier market surveillance regime was proposed that would merge the systems applying under the General Product Safety Directive (GPSD), Regulation (EC) 765/2008 and many sector-specific items of legislation, extending to non-harmonised consumer products, with certain exceptions including food products, medicines and medical devices that had their own systems. The key elements of the proposal included provisions on:

— Obligations for the organisation and conduct of market surveillance activity in Member States;
— rules on the controls and checks on products entering the European Union from 3rd countries and;
— the organisation and co-ordination of information on market surveillance activity between Member States and their Market Surveillance Authorities; and the control of products which present a risk.

VI. Health and Safety in the Workplace

A. The Need for Safety

Across the EU, the figures available in 2013[176] showed that 8.6 per cent of workers in the 27 Member States (20 million people) experienced a work-related health problem in the past 12 months. A further 3.2 per cent of workers in the EU-27 reported having an accident at work during a one year period, almost seven million workers. Bone, joint or muscle problems, and stress, anxiety and depression, were the most prevalent health problems. Estimates of fatalities attributable to work range between 5,000 and 7,000 for occupational accidents, depending on the source,[177] with 167,000 deaths in total attributed to work-related diseases and accidents.

Safety performance in Great Britain[178] has clearly steadily improved over the four decades since comprehensive modern regulation was introduced in 1974. The number of workplace fatalities has fallen (651 in 1974, around 300 in 1993/94 to 148 in 2012/13), as has the rate per 100,000 workers (1.2 in 1993/94 to 0.5 in 2012/13): See Figure 19.8.[179] The number of reported non-fatal injuries to employees fell by 70 per cent between 1974 and

[175] Communication from the Commission to the European Parliament, the Council and the European Economic and Social Committee: More Product Safety and better Market Surveillance in the Single Market for Products, COM(2013) 74, 13.2.2013, para 3.1.
[176] *EU-OSHA Multi-annual Strategic Programme 2014–2020* (European Agency for Safety and Health at Work, 2013), at https://osha.europa.eu/en/publications/corporate/eu-osha-multi-annual-strategic-programme-2014-2020.
[177] Eurostat, *Statistics in Focus, 40/2012, Population and Social Statistics*; figures cited by OSHA from the International Labour Organisation.
[178] ie excluding Northern Ireland.
[179] www.hse.gov.uk/statistics/history/histfatals.xls. The rate of fatal injuries to workers fell by 38 per cent between 1999/2000 and 2009/10: *Progress in Health and Safety Outcomes since 2000* (Health and Safety Executive, 2010) www.hse.gov.uk/statistics/history/progress-since-2000.pdf.

2007 to 78,222 in 2012/13, a rate of 311.6 per 100,000 employees (which represented a fall since 1974 of 76 per cent).[180] Of these, 19,707 were reported major injuries, with a rate of 78.5 per 100 000. The most common kinds of accident involved slips or trips (43 per cent), and falls from a height (13 per cent).[181] The number and rate of employer-reported non-fatal injuries to employees from 1996/97 to 2012/12 is shown in Figure 19.9. A certain number of high-profile incidents occur, such as the explosions at Buncefield Oil Storage Depot[182] and ICL Plastics in Glasgow.[183] The rates for fatalities, work-related accidents and sick leave in Great Britain compare well to other large economies such as Germany, Spain, Italy and France.[184]

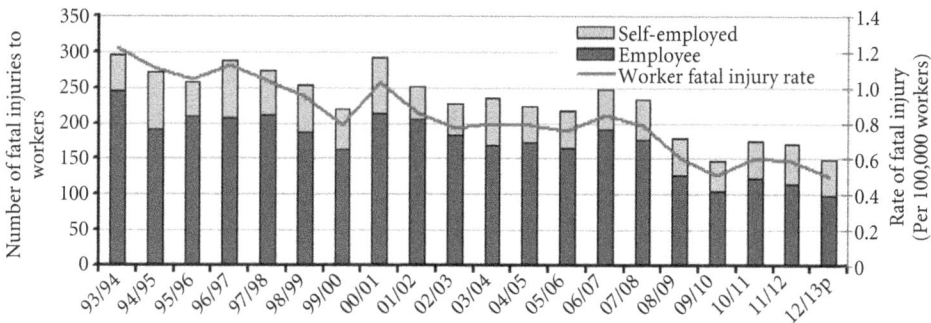

Figure 19.8: Number and Rate of Fatal Injury to Workers 1993/94–2012/13 (provisional)[185]

In 2012/13 the principal statistics were 148 workers killed, 78,000 other injuries reported under RIDDOR,[186] 175,000 over seven day absence injuries (LFS).[187] In 2011–12, 1.1 million working people were reported as suffering from a work-related illness, 27 million working days were lost due to work-related illness and workplace injury, and workplace injuries and ill health (excluding cancer) cost society an estimated £13.8 billion.[188] These figures do not take account of fatal injuries to non-employees, road-related deaths or those associated with work-related diseases due to past working conditions, including an estimated 8,000 cancer deaths in Britain each year that are attributable to past exposure to occupational

---

[180] Comments by Lord Grocott in Parliament in 2007, www.publications.parliament.uk/pa/ld200708/ ldhansrd/text/80704-0001.htm#08070478000003, quoted in R Löfstedt, *Reclaiming Health and Safety for All: An Independent Review of Health and Safety Legislation* (Health and Safety Executive, 2011).

[181] *Annual Statistics Report for Great Britain 2012/13* (Health and Safety Executive, 2013) at http://www.hse.gov. uk/statistics/overall/hssh1213.pdf.

[182] On 11 December 2005, a number of explosions occurred at Buncefield Oil Storage Depot, Hemel Hempstead, Hertfordshire: See www.buncefieldinvestigation.gov.uk/index.htm.

[183] On 11 May 2004, an explosion demolished much of the Stockline Plastics building in Grovepark Street, west of Glasgow city centre: See www.theiclinquiry.org/.

[184] *Annual Statistics Report for Great Britain 2012/13* (Health and Safety Executive, 2013) at http://www.hse.gov. uk/statistics/overall/hssh1213.pdf.

[185] *Statistics on Fatal Injuries in the Workplace in Great Britain 2013. Full-year Details and Technical Notes* (HSE, 2013) at www.hse.gov.uk/statistics/pdf/fatalinjuries.pdf

[186] The Reporting of Injuries Diseases and Dangerous Occurrences Regs 2013, SI 2013/1471, replacing SI 1995/3163.

[187] *Annual Statistics Report for Great Britain 2012/13* (Health and Safety Executive, 2013) at http://www.hse.gov. uk/statistics/overall/hssh1213.pdf.

[188] ibid.

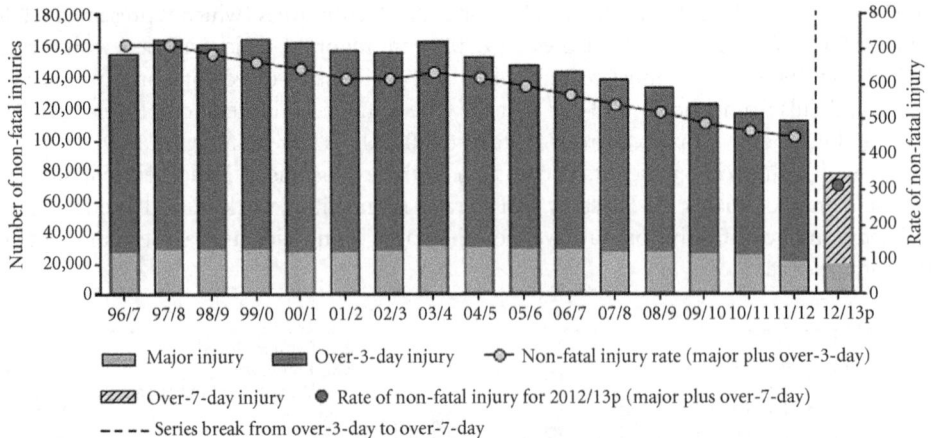

Figure 19.9: Employer-reported Non-fatal Injuries to Employees 1996/97 to 2012/13 (provisional) (n 187)

carcinogens.[189] Other estimates suggest that the cost to UK business of workplace accidents and ill health is just over £3 billion,[190] and the overall cost up to £20 billion a year.[191]

In relation to enforcement, in 2012/13[192] the Health and Safety Executive (HSE) prosecuted 574 cases, with a conviction secured in 547 cases, a conviction rate of 87 per cent. Local authorities prosecuted 105 cases, with a conviction secured in 100 cases (95 per cent rate). The Procurator Fiscal in Scotland heard 27 cases, and secured 25 convictions. In the total of 672 convictions, fines totalling £15 million were imposed, an average penalty of around £14,000 per offence. The number of notices issued by both HSE and local authorities in 2012/13 was 13,503, of which 8,810 were issued by HSE and 4,693 by local authorities. The level of enforcement activity has remained reasonably standard over several years, but there has been a shift in emphasis. From about 2000 to 2010 the numbers of prosecutions virtually halved while use of enforcement notices markedly increased.[193]

B. The Regulatory System

EU laws, principally the EU Framework Directive 89/391/EEC,[194] impose a requirement for businesses to adopt a management system, appointing designated staff or external advisors to assist them with compliance measures.[195] Figure 19.10 illustrates a successful health and safety management system.

---

[189] Löfstedt (n 180).

[190] M Pathak, *The Costs to Employers in Britain of Workplace Injuries and Work-related Ill Health in 2005/06*, HSE Discussion Paper Series No 002, 2008.

[191] *The Health and Safety of Great Britain: Be Part of the Solution* (Health and Safety Executive, 2009) at www.hse.gov.uk/strategy/strategy09.pdf.

[192] *Prosecutions in Great Britain (2012/13p). Enforcement Action taken by HSE, Local Authorities and, in Scotland, the Crown Office and Procurator Fiscal Service (2012/13p)* (Health and Safety Executive, 2013) http://www.hse.gov.uk/statistics/prosecutions.pdf.

[193] http://www.hse.gov.uk/aboutus/meetings/hseboard/2010/300610/pjunb1054.pdf.

[194] Dir 89/391/EEC on the introduction of measures to encourage improvements in the safety and health of workers at work.

[195] ibid, art 7.

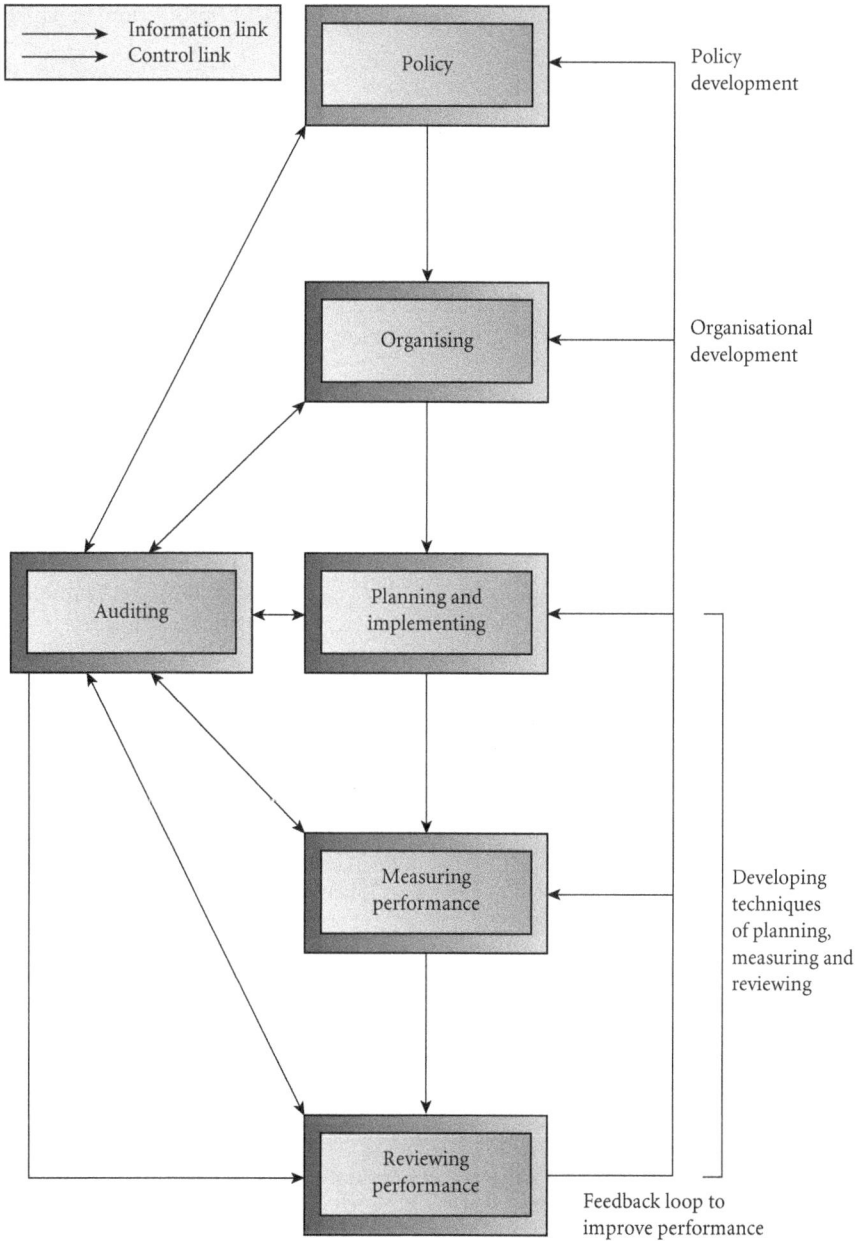

Figure 19.10: A Successful Health and Safety Management System[196]

---

[196] *Successful Health and Safety Management* (Health and Safety Executive, 1997) HSG65.

The management system must apply the following 'principles of protection', of which the key elements are:[197]

— Avoiding risks;
— evaluating the risks which cannot be avoided;
— combating the risks at source;
— developing a coherent overall prevention policy;
— giving appropriate instructions and training to staff.

Risk assessment is a central concept, and requires processes and documentation, including reports of occupational accidents.[198] Employers must ensure that workers receive all necessary information and adequate training, whilst employees are responsible to take care as far as possible for their own safety.[199]

Sites containing large quantities of dangerous substances are subject to other layers of control under the Seveso Directive,[200] for which a regulator must approve plans. A hybrid model is evolving, with a regulator imposing a duty to self-regulate. An operator must take all necessary measures to prevent major accidents, send prescribed information to the competent authority, draw up its major accident prevention policy (MAPP), produce safety reports if the establishment is high risk (upper tier), share emergency plans between upper-tier operators and the competent authority, provide certain information to the public, and take required action after a major accident.[201] Competent authorities are required to organise a system of inspection, and to exchange information on experience acquired.[202]

In the UK, the 'RIDDOR' legislation[203] places duties on employers, the self-employed and people in control of work premises to report serious accidents in the workplace, occupational diseases and specific dangerous occurrences. Reporting assists regulatory bodies in three respects: Establishing when further investigation is required, providing regulators with statistics which assist in identifying trends, and subsequently providing the most appropriate forms of guidance on prevention and need for regulatory interventions. The HSE said in 2012:

> Compliance with the current RIDDOR requirements is known to be low. Stakeholder engagement suggests that this is attributable to:
>
> — The complexity of the requirements, that results in inconsistencies both between regulators and duty holders, and between different duty holders (and even between departments within large organisations);
> — Perceived fears of over-zealous enforcement action; and

---

[197] ibid, art 6.2.
[198] ibid, art 9. D Walters et al, *Regulating Workplace Risks* (Cheltenham, Edward Elgar, 2011); DJ Ball and L Ball-King, *Public Safety and Risk Assessment—Improving Decision Making* (London, Earthscan, 2011).
[199] ibid, arts 6.3(d), 10, 11 and 12.
[200] From 2015, Dir 2012/18/EU on the control of major-accident hazards involving dangerous substances, amending and subsequently repealing Council Dir 96/82/EC. Dir 82/501/EC, known as the Seveso Dir after the Seveso disaster, aimed at improving the safety of sites containing large quantities of dangerous substances. Council Dir 96/82/EC of 9 December 1996 on the control of major-accident hazards involving dangerous substances (as amended, known as the Seveso II Dir). It was modified by Dir 2012/18/EU (the Seveso III Dir). It introduces a major change in use of the Globally Harmonised System (GHS) for classification of chemicals to determine whether they are within the scope of the Dir. The Seveso II Dir is implemented in the UK as the Control of Major Accident Hazards Regs 1999/743 (COMAH).
[201] Dir 2012/18/EU, arts 5, 7, 8, 10, 12, 14, 16–18.
[202] ibid, arts 20 and 21.
[203] The Reporting of Injuries, Diseases and Dangerous Occurrences Regs 2013, SI 2013/1471.

Confusion over whether reports through other systems satisfy the requirement to report under RIDDOR (eg systems in place for the protection of vulnerable children.)[204]

As a result, the data received is incomplete, unreliable and too late. The 2011 Löfstedt review concluded that

[R]egulation has a role to play in preventing injury and ill health in the workplace. Indeed, there is evidence to suggest that proportionate risk management can make good business sense.

Nonetheless, there are a number of factors that drive businesses to go beyond what the regulations require and beyond what is proportionate and I have made recommendations to tackle those which relate to regulations. These will enable businesses to reclaim ownership of the management of health and safety and see it as a vital part of their operation rather than an unnecessary and bureaucratic paperwork exercise.[205]

Löfstedt firmly supported regulation should be risk-based rather than hazard-based.[206] He noted:[207]

When taking a risk-based approach there are limits to what can be measured quantitatively and reliance on expert judgements rather than pure scientific evidence sometimes causes challenges. However, one of the main problems with basing regulation on hazard classification is that it is only one initial part of the risk analysis process, and without an assessment of actual risk it can inhibit activities which are not in fact risky and which may be beneficial to individuals and society.[208]

In the process it can ignore the opportunity cost of diverting scarce resources away from addressing activities or items which pose a greater risk to workers and the public and may lead to unintended consequences, including risk-risk trade-offs.[209]

A classic example of the risk-risk trade-off followed the Hatfield Rail Crash, when speed restrictions were imposed to avoid the risk of further accidents, leading to more commuters travelling by car, where the risk of fatality is greater.[210]

A key principle of the UK legislation is that employers should ensure the health, safety and welfare at work of their employees so far as is reasonably practicable (SFAIRP).[211] The SFAIRP principle provides flexibility and proportionality in managing risks. A variety of guidance exists for particular industries.[212] Löfstedt concluded

The 'so far as is reasonably practicable' qualification in much of health and safety legislation was overwhelmingly supported by those who responded to the call for evidence on the grounds that it allows risks to be managed in a proportionate manner. However, there is general confusion over what it means in practice and many small businesses find it difficult to interpret.[213]

---

[204] *Consultation: Proposals to Revise the Reporting of Injuries, Diseases and Dangerous Occurrences Regulations 1995 (as amended) (RIDDOR '95)* (Health and Safety Executive, 2012) para 16.

[205] Löfstedt (n 180).

[206] ibid, ch 2, para 12.

[207] ibid, ch 2, paras 14 and 15.

[208] Footnote from original source: R Löfstedt, 'Risk versus Hazard—How to regulate in the 21st Century' (2011) 2(2) *European Journal of Risk Regulation* 149–68.

[209] Footnote from original source: JD Graham and JB Wiener, *Risk vs Risk: Tradeoffs in Protecting Health and the Environment* (Cambridge MA, Harvard University Press, 1995).

[210] Better Regulation Commission, *Risk, Responsibility and Regulation –Whose Risk is it Anyway?* 2006, www.gov.uk/government/uploads/system/uploads/attachment_data/file/66790/lofstedt-report.pdf.

[211] See s 2(1) and s 3(1) of the Health and Safety at Work etc Act 1974. www.legislation.gov.uk/ukpga/1974/37/contents.

[212] See Internal HSE guides for staff at http://www.hse.gov.uk/risk/theory/alarp.htm, and for nuclear at http://www.hse.gov.uk/nuclear/operational/tech_asst_guides/ns-tast-gd-005.pdf.

[213] Löfstedt (n 180) para 5.

C. Critical Reviews

The burden of health and safety regulation has, however, been consistently criticised, especially by small and medium-sized enterprises (SMEs). Small businesses spend around one working day a month on compliance,[214] two-thirds of SMEs feel that the implementation of health and safety law is too time consuming,[215] and over a third of small businesses believe that health and safety regulations are an obstacle to growing their business.[216] A 2003 study found that the average annual expenditure by a large firm on health and safety was £420,000.[217] Total administration costs for all UK businesses, including tax/customs and financial services, were calculated in 2005 as £31.1 billion, and administrative burdens were £19.8 billion.[218] Of 21 principal government ministries, those imposing the highest burdens were trade and industry and HM Revenue and Customs. The annual cost of administrative burdens stemming from health and safety legislation was calculated at over £2 billion.[219] A 2009 business survey found that the annual value of time and expenditure by SMEs on health and safety guidelines was over £2 million, which was the second largest of seven different types of regulation on businesses.[220]

At EU level, the High Level Group of Independent Stakeholders on Administrative Burdens (the Stoiber Group)[221] recommended in 2009 that whilst very small firms involved in certain low-risk activities should still be required to carry out a risk assessment, it need not be in writing.[222]

A series of reviews of the health and safety system have been undertaken in the UK, notably by the Better Regulation Executive,[223] the House of Commons Work and Pensions Select Committee,[224] Lord Young of Graffham for the Coalition government,[225] and Professor

[214] C Taylor, *Health and Safety: Reducing the Burden* (London, Policy Exchange, 2010)www.policyexchange.org.uk/images/publications/pdfs/Health_and_Safety_-_Reducing_the_burden_-_March__10.pdf.

[215] British Chambers of Commerce, *Health and Safety—a Risky Business?* 2011 www.britishchambers.org.uk/zones/policy/press-releases_1/bcc-half-of-businesses-tied-up-in-health-and-safety-yellow-tape.html.

[216] ibid.

[217] R Lancaster, R Ward, P Talbot and A Brazier, *Costs of Compliance with Health and Safety Regulations in SMEs*, Health and Safety Executive Research Report 174, 2003. www.hse.gov.uk/research/rrpdf/rr174.pdf.

[218] See departmental reports eg *Administrative Burdens Measurement Exercise. Final Report* (Department of Trade and Industry, 2005), at www.bis.gov.uk/files/file35841.pdf, and summary K Hill, *Regulatory Reform in the UK Measuring Administrative Burdens* (Better Regulation Executive, 2008) at http://www.oecd.org/gov/regulatory-policy/41888214.pdf.

[219] Lancaster, Ward, Talbot and Brazier (n 217).

[220] *The Cost of Compliance on Micro, Small and Medium-sized Business Employers* (Forum of Private Business, 2009) at www.fpb.org/images/PDFs/referendum/FPB%20Referendum%20188%20report.pdf; *Health and Safety—a Risky Business?* (British Chambers of Commerce, 2011) www.britishchambers.org.uk/zones/policy/press-releases_1/bcc-half-of-businesses-tied-up-in-health-and-safety-yellow-tape.html (cumulative cost of health and safety regulation introduced in the UK since 1998 amounted to over £4 billion).

[221] http://ec.europa.eu/enterprise/policies/smart-regulation/administrative-burdens/high-level-group/index_en.htm.

[222] http://ec.europa.eu/enterprise/policies/smartregulation/files/hlg_opinion_working_environment_09052009_en.pdf. The Commission then undertook a cost–benefit analysis of the risk assessment obligation.

[223] *Improving Outcomes from Health and Safety* (Better Regulation Executive, 2008) www.bis.gov.uk/files/file47324.pdf.

[224] House of Commons Work and Pensions Select Committee, *The Role of the Health and Safety Commission and the Health and Safety Executive in Regulating Workplace Health and Safety: Third Report of the Session, 2008*, www.publications.parliament.uk/pa/cm200708/cmselect/cmworpen/246/246i.pdf.

[225] Lord Young of Graffham, *Common Sense, Common Safety* (HM Government, 2010) at www.number10.gov.uk/wp-content/uploads/402906_CommonSense_acc.pdf.

Ragnar Löfstedt.[226] Lord Young recommended a 'Shift from a system of risk assessment to a system of risk-benefit assessment and consider reviewing the Health and Safety at Work etc Act to separate out play and leisure from workplace contexts.'[227] In the subsequent review, Löfstedt noted:

6.   Meanwhile, there are instances where regulations designed to address real risks are being extended to cover trivial ones, whilst the requirement to carry out a risk assessment has turned into a bureaucratic nightmare for some businesses. The legal requirement to carry out a risk assessment is an important part of a risk management process but instead businesses are producing or paying for lengthy documents covering every conceivable risk, sometimes at the expense of controlling the significant risks in their workplace…

13.   Perhaps more than any particular regulatory requirement, the sheer mass of regulation is a key concern for many businesses. Although there is considerably less regulation than 35 years ago, businesses still feel that they have to work through too many regulations or use health and safety consultants…[228]

12.   There are complaints of an overly-complex and bureaucratic system which drives SMEs to seek out the services of consultants,[229] who, in turn, can provide advice that is not required by law and provides little or no benefit to workplace health and safety, adding further burdens to business.[230]

13.   'Health and safety' has become increasingly ridiculed, particularly in the media. There is a constant stream of stories in the press blaming health and safety and associated excessive bureaucracy for preventing individuals from engaging in socially beneficial activity, overriding common sense and eroding personal responsibility. Almond's 2009 paper provides a helpful discussion of this issue and its implications.[231] Furthermore, the media can amplify health and safety incidents beyond what is warranted. Previous studies have shown this on issues ranging from nuclear power accidents to the positioning of waste incinerators.[232, 233]

Löfstedt's recommendations to simplify the regulatory framework and undertake sector-specific consolidations, to reduce the number of regulations by about 35 per cent by April 2015, were accepted by the government.[234] One consequence was simplification of the RIDDOR requirements by removing the duty to report in those areas where the information can be better obtained from other sources or where the data is of little use to regulators or is unreliable.[235] A second consequence was removal of the duty on the self-employed to

---

[226] Löfstedt (n 180).

[227] ibid. See *Common Sense, Common Safety—Progress Report*, July 2011, www.dwp.gov.uk/docs/cscs-progress-july-11.pdf.

[228] Löfstedt (n 180) Executive Summary, paras 6 and 13.

[229] Footnote from original source: *Perceptions of the Health and Safety Regime* (Vanilla Research, 2008) at www.bis.gov.uk/files/file47058.pdf.

[230] Footnote from original source: *Improving Outcomes from Health and Safety* (n 223).

[231] Footnote from original source: P Almond, 'The Dangers of Hanging Baskets: "Regulatory Myths" and Media Representations of Health and Safety Regulations' (2009) 36 *Journal of Law and Society* 352–75.

[232] Footnote from original source: RE Kasperson et al, 'The Social Amplification of Risk: A Conceptual Framework' (1988) 8 *Risk Analysis* 177–87; N Pidgeon, RE Kasperson and P Slovic, *The Social Amplification of Risk* (Cambridge, Cambridge University Press, 2003).

[233] Löfstedt (n 180) ch 1, paras 12 and 13.

[234] *The Government Response to the Löfstedt Report* (Department for Work and Pensions, 2011); *A Progress Report on Implementation of Health and Safety Reforms* (Department for Work and Pensions, June 2012) available at http://www.dwp.gov.uk/docs/progress-report-health-safety-reforms-june-12.pdf.

[235] The Reporting of Injuries Diseases and Dangerous Occurrences Regs 2013, SI 2013/1471, replacing SI 1995/3163. See *Consultation Launched to Simplify RIDDOR August 2012* http://consultations.hse.gov.uk/gf2.ti/f/16770/442917.1/PDF/-/CD243.pdf.

report injuries and illnesses to themselves,[236] the requirement for employers to report dangerous occurrences outside of high-risk sectors, and the requirement to report most occupational diseases. The need to report all fatal injuries as a result of a work activity remains, as does the duty to report major injuries to workers. A further objective was to simplify the language of the reporting requirements by reviewing words, terms and phrases in the current regulations, to make compliance easier.

D. Evidence on How Regulation and Enforcement Works

HSE set out in 2001 its philosophy for securing health, safety and welfare of people at work and those affected by work activities and the procedures, protocols and criteria that underpins it.[237] This gave an overview of risk and risk management, and considered issues such as the tolerability of risk, how society views risk and the precautionary principle.

The literature has suggested at least a distinction between large and small businesses in relation to the ability to assimilate risk information and manage safe modes of working. A great deal more research exists for large organisations. 99 per cent of businesses employ under 50 people. Löfstedt summarised the position thus:

> 2.   The evidence suggests that businesses can benefit from and value inspections, with SMEs welcoming the constructive, reasonable advice and guidance that it can provide to help them improve health and safety in the workplace.[238] Nearly nine out of ten employers who have had contact with HSE see it as a 'helpful' organisation.[239] The evidence also suggests enforcement action can be particularly helpful when the regulations themselves are broadly defined and allow for discretion,[240] as is the case with health and safety regulation, and that inspection is an effective means of securing employer compliance and, if targeted at key groups, can bring about significant improvements in health and safety performance.[241, 242]

Many experts have identified a need to improve the public understanding of risk, and the facts that hazards cannot be removed and that the occurrence of an accident or injury does not by itself mean that the system of safety and risk regulation has failed.[243]

---

[236] The Health and Safety at Work etc Act 1974 places duties upon self-employed people to ensure that they and others affected by their activities are not exposed to harm. In addition, over 50 regulations exist which apply to self-employed workers either expressly or through a broader category of 'person'. Löfsted suggested that the exemption of self-employed workers be exempt from health and safety law if their work activities pose no potential risk to others would apply to approximately 1 million people. See *HSE Consultation on Proposals to Exempt Self-employed Workers from Health and Safety Laws* (Health and Safety Executive, 2013) http://consultations.hse.gov.uk/gf2.ti/f/16802/442789.1/PDF/-/CD242%20Complete.pdf.

[237] *Reducing Risks, Protecting People—HSE's Decision Making Process* (Health and Safety Executive, 2001) at www.hse.gov.uk/risk/theory/r2p2.pdf.

[238] *Perceptions of the Health and Safety Regime, Summary Report to the Better Regulation Executive* (n 229).

[239] www.hse.gov.uk/risk/attitudes.htm.

[240] T Amodu, *The Dof Compliance with Laws and Regulations with Special Reference to Health and Safety*, Health and Safety Executive Research Report 638, 2008, www.hse.gov.uk/research/rrpdf/rr638.pdf.

[241] J Hillage, C Tyers, S Davis and A Guppy, *The Impact of the HSC/E: A Review* (Institute of Employment Studies for Health and Safety Executive, 2001), www.hse.gov.uk/research/crr_pdf/2001/crr01385.pdf.

[242] Löfstedt (n 180) ch 8.

[243] F Bouder and R Löfstedt, *Improving Health and Safety—An Analysis of HSE's Risk Communication in the 21st century* (Health and Safety Executive, 2010) Health and Safety Executive Research Report 785, www.hse.gov.uk/research/rrhtm/rr785.htm.

A strong example of 'supply chain pressure' arose from construction of the London Olympic Park. The Olympic Delivery Authority (ODA) was committed to ensuring this was the 'safest and healthiest build on record'.[244] A number of elements contributed to the development of an effective safety culture on the Olympic Park site, including:

— The strategic role of the ODA across the Park, with safety being set as a priority and integrated into the companies from the outset through standards and requirements.
— Clarity throughout the supply chain of the organisational standards and requirements, including the desire for cultural alignment (ie consistent commitment to the same Health Safety and Environment standard).
— The empowerment of Tier 1 contractors to develop their own processes and systems to deliver the ODA's objectives. The ODA focused on engaging contractors, enabling them to develop their own good practice and drive their own performance. This allowed contractors to use and develop their own company processes.
— Recognition of the prestige of working on the Olympic Park and striving for excellence in all activities, including health and safety.
— The scale of the project and the length of the construction phase meant that there was sufficient time for initiatives to become embedded, and could be tailored to ensure their efficacy and success.
— Belief by workers in the genuine commitment within organisations, as the message was consistent and reiterated across the Olympic Park over time.

Authorities in different sectors have sponsored work to clarify what supports compliance and safety in different sizes of companies. A significant amount of this work comes from the health and safety field, but some other sectoral authorities have also contributed, and the major studies are summarised below.

i. Compliance in SMEs

Fairman and Yapp researched the impact of interventions on compliance with food safety law in SMEs.[245] Previous studies had supported the contention that SMEs want to be told exactly what to do and how to comply though face-to-face interventions with an inspector. Findings showed that SMEs have major difficulties identifying hazards and find the concept of self-assessment alien. This view is accepted in government, and has been highlighted in previous HSE funded research.

In those businesses overseen by local authority enforcement, various approaches are used to secure compliance with the requirements of health and safety legislation. These include inspection, educational activities including promotional campaigns and provision of training, and accident investigation. The type of approach adopted by local authorities is dependent upon the resources available to undertake inspections and follow-up activity; the views of those managing the health and safety function; and the field staff enforcing the legislation.

---

[244] See *RR942—Safety Culture on the Olympic Park* (Health and Safety Executive, 2012) http://www.hse.gov.uk/research/rrhtm/rr942.htm.

[245] R Fairman and C Yapp, *Making an Impact on SME Compliance Behaviour: An Evaluation of the Effect of Interventions upon Compliance with Health and Safety Legislation in Small and Medium Sized Enterprises* (Health and Safety Executive, 2005) Research Report 366.

Fairman and Yapp's project studied six to seven small hairdressers within the area of six local authorities in England, where the latter adopted levels of intervention varying from very low to high. Hairdressers were selected because the sector has similar influences and motivating factors, presents relatively high health risks, and were present in sufficient numbers in authorities to enable sampling to occur. The researchers noted that SMEs are not a homogenous group, and care has to be exercised extrapolating conclusions about one industry to another or from the micro (one to nine employees) to the medium (50–249). 85 per cent of the businesses within this study employed less than 10 people.

The main findings of this research were as follows. First, the small hairdressers all believed they complied with the law even though formal compliance levels (judged by independent assessment) ranged from 19.5 per cent (for COSHH), through 46.3 per cent (for risk assessment) to 61 per cent (for electrical safety). They believed that they were compliant until it was made known to them that they were not. In other words they viewed compliance reactively and not as a process in which they should be continually engaged. Compliance was not, as an enforcer would define it, complying with the requirements of the law. Non-compliance was related to harm, and many SMEs could not conceive non-compliance with self-assessment or risk assessment type requirements as these are proactive. Non-compliance was also related to things they perceived that might be prosecutable.

Second, compliance was not a decision or part of a decision-making process. None of the SMEs identified the range of options possibly available, weighed up the costs and benefits, and chose the most optimal course of action. Instead compliance was more a process of how the SME owner 'made sense' of what they were being required to do. The clear 'gap' between how things operated and how they should have operated should have been identified through the high levels of occupational ill-health prevalent in the businesses. 54 per cent of the hairdressing businesses in this study employed staff with dermatitis, 68 per cent of businesses had staff with back pain related to the job. These were both accepted hazards of the job. When asked (without prompting) what the hazards of the salon were, SME owners identified hazards that might affect their clients, and general safety issues such as slips, trips and falls. 54 per cent of SMEs stated that slips, trips and falls was a hazard they actively managed but only two per cent (one SME) had ever had experienced such an accident.

Third, improvements in compliance for the SMEs in this study were reactive. Firms relied on external influence to motivate change. The most effective way of the 'gap' between how things operated and how they were meant to operate being identified was through face-to-face intervention of someone with power over the business. In this research, this was either the local authority inspector or the representative of local training colleges who inspected salons to ensure that standards are satisfactory for trainee placements. Both of those categories of inspectors possessed power and were granted respect. These inspectors would define the action needed by the SME, and generally, without argument, these recommendations would be implemented. This was not a decision taken by the SME. There was an overriding belief in a duty to comply. The SME would do all they were told to as a result of an external intervention at an inspection, or advisory visit or other intervention. Local authority inspections had a statistically significant impact on compliance with electrical safety requirements (prescriptive requirements), whilst training college inspections were statistically significant in improving compliance with risk assessment legislation (risk assessment requirements).

Fourth, the main motivators for complying, or trying to comply, with the law were:

— A general fear of the law (the enforcement action believed to follow from the identification of non-compliance);
— liability (being sued by clients); and
— the threat from local colleges in removing students from the workplace if non-compliance was not remedied.

The reasons for non-compliance related to:

— A lack of 'awareness' of legislative requirements, or
— inadequate knowledge about how to comply with requirements.

Time, money and poor management structures were not seen to affect the level of compliance achieved within an SME. The researchers suggested that lack of awareness meant not being able to relate legislative requirements to individual business operations, and hence being unable to recognise non-compliance. Providing more information would not improve the situation, and might even make it worse by producing an information overload. What was needed is for the SME to recognise there is a difference in how they are operating and the levels of illness in their businesses, with how it ought to be. In this study, face-to-face intervention by a respected outsider was the most effective way of making businesses recognise the existence of a 'gap'.

ii. Larger Businesses

In larger enterprises, the evidence for deterrence is weak. Discussion papers from OECD (Organisation for Economic Co-operation and Development) focus on risk-based and responsive regulatory approaches, and omit reference to deterrence.[246] It has been noted in chapter 13 above that the 2014 OECD recommendations on regulation have quietly dropped reliance on deterrence in favour of a responsive regulation approach.[247]

Some conclusions on deterrence in enforcement have been reached in reports in the aviation sector:

> Enforcement does not work by a simple deterrence effect; neither do organisations apply a simple profit oriented or economic optimisation approach to compliance.[248]

and workplace health and safety:

> Prosecution and resultant fines can be argued as an incentive for improving safety, but significant fines are rare, and the deterrents to prosecution tend to be reputational (the shame of appearing in court, the concern to avoid moral condemnation, the fear of bad publicity) rather than financial.[249]

---

[246] *Risk and Regulatory Policy: Improving the Governance of Risk* (Paris, OECD, 2010).

[247] The shift was noted from *Consultation on Public Consultation Best Practice Principles for Improving on Enforcement and Inspections* (Paris, OECD, 2013) to *OECD Best Practice Principles for Regulatory Policy: Regulatory Enforcement and Inspections* (Paris, OECD, 2014).

[248] W Wright and J Marsden, *A Response to the CCA Report 'Making Companies Safe: What Works?'* (Reading, HSE, 2005) 19, see http://www.hse.gov.uk/research/rrpdf/rr332.pdf.

[249] *Director Leadership of Health and Safety, Report No HSL/2005/21* (Health & Safety Laboratory, 2005) 14, referencing A Hopkins, *Making Safety Work: Getting Management Committed to Occupational Health and Safety* (Sydney, Allen & Unwin Pty Ltd, 1995). See http://www.hse.gov.uk/research/hsl_pdf/2005/hsl0521.pdf.

Some studies suggest that 'showcase' actions, which are very focused and well-publicised, may have some targeted deterrent effect.[250] The HSE maintains a name and shame website, from which names are never removed.[251]

A series of HSE research studies has focused on management systems, and on leadership by senior managers.[252] A 2005 review of literature on the motivating factors for directors to engage with health and safety found the following indicators:[253]

— Compliance with legislation;
— Fear of loss of reputation is closely related to compliance with legislation, as fear of prosecution and the bad publicity it would bring is recognised by directors as being detrimental to business success.
— There are also more direct financial considerations for many companies; effective health and safety management is perceived as being good for business, with benefits ranging from increased profit and turnover, to increased staff morale and retention.
— For many smaller businesses health and safety management is also a necessary part of winning contracts when larger companies specify the health and safety standards they expect from their suppliers.
— Moral responsibility for protecting workers is another reason cited for director leadership of health and safety. This is particularly the case in small and medium sized businesses where directors are more likely to know their workforce and interact with them more frequently than in large organisations.

In 2011 the Institute of Directors and HSE published advice that the basic principles were:[254]

— Strong and active leadership from the top:
    — visible, active commitment from the board;
    — establishing effective 'downward' communication systems and management structures;
    — integration of good health and safety management with business decisions.
— Worker involvement:
    — engaging the workforce in the promotion and achievement of safe and healthy conditions;

---

[250] P May, 'Regulation and Compliance Motivations: Marine Facilities and Water Quality' in *Corporate Environmental Behaviour and the Effectiveness of Government Interventions: Proceedings of a Workshop Sponsored by the US EPA*, 26–27 April 2004, available at http://yosemite.epa.gov/ee/epa/eerm.nsf/vwGA/8f26f78fe81cc7d685256ee800 6be614!OpenDocument&ExpandSection=2.

[251] See http://www.hse.gov.uk/enforce/prosecutions.htm.

[252] MS Wright, *Factors Motivating Proactive Health and Safety Management* (Health & Safety Executive, 1998) Contract Research Report 179/1998; M Wright, S Marsden and J Holmes, *Health and Safety Responsibilities of Company Directors and Management Board Members* (Health & Safety Executive, 2003) Research Report 135; C Davis, *Making Companies Safe: What Works?* (Centre for Corporate Accountability, 2004); Wright and Marsden (n 248); FB Wright, *Directors' Responsibilities for Health and Safety: The Findings of Two Peer Reviews of Published Research* (Health & Safety Executive, 2006) Research Report 451; *Director Leadership Behaviour Research* (Health & Safety Executive, 2007) Research Report 816; K King, S Lunn and C Michaelis, *Director Leadership Behaviour Research* (Health & Safety Executive, 2010) Research Report 816; *Leading Health and Safety at Work. Leadership Actions for Directors and Board Members* (Institute of Directors and HSE, 2011); C Lekka, *A Review of the Literature on Effective Leadership Behaviours for Safety* (Health & Safety Executive, 2012) Research Report 952.

[253] M Miller, *Director Leadership of Health and Safety* (Health & Safety Laboratory, 2005) iv.

[254] *Leading Health and Safety at Work. Leadership Actions for Directors and Board Members* (Institute of Directors and Health & Safety Executive, 2011) http://www.hse.gov.uk/pubns/indg417.pdf.

— effective 'upward' communication;
— providing high-quality training.
— Assessment and review:
  — identifying and managing health and safety risks;
  — accessing (and following) competent advice;
  — monitoring, reporting and reviewing performance.

The advice stated that the requirements are: Competent advice, training and supervision; monitoring; risk assessment.

A 2012 meta-review of 40 papers, of which 35 were quantitative studies and five were qualitative studies, found the following consistent associations between specific leadership styles and safety outcomes:

— **Transformational leadership** (eg acting as a role model, inspiring and motivating employees to work safely and showing concern for employees' welfare) enhances a number of safety outcomes including fostering perceptions of a positive safety climate, promoting higher levels of employee participation in safety activities, compliance with safety rules and procedures and safety citizenship behaviours (eg participation in safety committees, looking out for workmates' safety).
— **Transactional (contingent reward) leadership** (eg clarifying performance expectations, monitoring and rewarding performance) is associated with perceptions of a positive safety climate, positive safety behaviours and reduced accident rates.
— **Passive leadership** (ie turning a blind eye to safety) is associated with lower levels of safety consciousness, negative perceptions of safety climate and an increase in safety-related events and injuries.
— The effects of transformational and transactional leadership are both direct and indirect. In the latter case, positive effects are achieved through the promotion of a positive safety climate. In addition, transformational leaders can influence safety by enhancing employees' levels safety consciousness (ie knowledge).
— The benefits of transactional leadership are enhanced when safety is valued across different levels of management. Transformational leadership styles combined with trusting relationships between management and employees enhance employee safety performance such as safety citizenship behaviours.
— **Trust in management** influences perceptions of safety climate as well as accident involvement. Behavioural consistency, honesty and integrity, sharing and delegation of control, openness and accuracy of communication, and demonstration of concern are qualities that influence the development of trust in leaders.
— The quality of relationships between employees and management, particularly supervisors, impacts on safety. **High quality leader-member exchanges, characterised by mutual trust, and openness** are associated with higher levels of upward safety communications, safety citizenship behaviours and reduced levels of safety-related events. Safety citizenship behaviours in particular, are pronounced when, in addition to high quality leader-member exchanges, leaders emphasise the value of safety and promote a positive safety climate.[255]

The review noted that those studies that focused on specific safety management attitudes, behaviours and practices have consistently shown that:

— *Management commitment to safety* is associated with a reduction in risk-taking behaviours and violations, lower levels of self-report incidents and higher levels of learning from safety events.

---

[255] Lekka (n 251).

— *Perceptions that safety policies and procedures are enforced* and consistently implemented are associated with lower levels of incident under-reporting, self-report injury incident and higher levels of satisfaction with the organisation.

— *Leader support for safety and openness to safety suggestions* is associated with higher levels of employee willingness to raise safety issues, lower levels of self-report injuries, higher levels of satisfaction with the organisation and can lead to a long-term improvement in safe working practices.

— *Safety communication* between management and the workforce is associated with a reduction in the levels of risk-taking behaviours, promotion of positive safety behaviours and reduced levels of self-report work-related pain.

— *Active involvement in safety* helps promote perceptions of a positive safety climate and fosters increased levels of employee accountability and responsibility for safety.

The review's analysis of 16 major incidents identified nine overarching themes as contributing factors to these incidents:

— *Commitment to safety* (including priority given to safety and resources dedicated to ensuring safety operations) and *complacency and lack of oversight* (eg the extent to which organisations tolerate unsafe working practices or failing to act promptly on safety concerns) were implicated in 12/16 and 11/16 incidents reviewed respectively.

— *Training and competence*, relating to inadequate training in dealing with unexpected events and emergencies, and inadequate knowledge of hazards, was implicated in 11/16 incidents reviewed.

— *Learning from previous incidents* (including an organisation's attentiveness to potential precursor events and carrying out incident investigations to identify root causes) was implicated in 10/16 incidents.

— *Adequacy of procedures* (including violation and/or poor enforcement, poor usability and/or absence of procedures) was a contributory factor in 9/16 incidents.

— *Safety communication* (including open and trusting channels for sharing safety-related information), and *hazard awareness and management* (including an organisations' use of audits and risk assessments to identify problems and put the necessary control measures in place) were identified as contributory factors in 8/16 and 9/16 incidents respectively.

— *Clarity of roles and responsibilities regarding safety* (such as accountability for safety at different levels of management) was implicated in 5/16 incidents.

— *Management of change* (the extent to which changes equipment or staffing resources are carried out by taking into consideration any potential consequences for the management of major hazards) was identified as a contributory factor in 5/16 incidents reviewed.

The review stated that although a complex interplay of factors at different organisational levels was involved in the causation of major incidents, leadership failings were a common contributory factor across the different incidents. Taken together, the findings from the empirical literature and the review of major incidents suggested that managers can positively influence safety by adopting active forms of leadership (as exemplified by transformational and transactional leadership styles) and promoting a positive safety culture and trusting employee–management relationships. The authors drew the following implications for practice:

— Managers can have a positive influence on safety by embracing transformational and transactional (contingent reward) leadership styles. These have been shown to have several safety benefits and are also crucial for the development of a positive safety culture. Training interventions may be an effective way of helping managers to develop these leadership skills.
— Management needs to actively demonstrate a visible commitment to safety. This may be done through prioritising safety and allocating the required resources, becoming involved in health and safety activities, encouraging staff to voice their safety concerns and make suggestions to improve safety in their workplace.
— Leaders should pay attention to the importance of open and trusting safety communications with the workforce. Developing good working relationships characterised by openness, support and mutual respect, behavioural consistency, sharing and delegation of control as well as demonstration of concern are some factors that help promote trust.

iii. Debate on Corporate Homicide

The effectiveness and relevance of deterrence versus compliance was debated during the 2000s when the then Health and Safety Commission (HSC) was under some pressure to consider recommending legally enforceable personal health and safety obligations on directors and over introduction of an offence of corporate manslaughter, following a tortuous history of consideration by the Law Commission.[256] The HSC proposed imposing punitive duties, because the evidence in favour was not sufficiently strong and it was felt that guidance for senior executives would be more effective.[257] The corporate homicide panel's recommendation[258] for fines to be imposed in the range 2.5%–10 per cent of turnover was criticised because for being too blunt and arbitrary for the range of potential offences and a departure from normal sentencing principles. The sentencing guidelines when published recommended a starting point for corporate manslaughter offences of £500,000, potentially going up to many millions, varying with ability to pay, and for health and safety convictions relating to fatalities a starting point of £100,000 going up to hundreds of thousands of pounds.[259]

The offence of corporate manslaughter as a result of serious management failures amount to a gross breach of a duty of care was introduced by the Corporate Manslaughter and Corporate Homicide Act 2007.[260] Three convictions were entered in the first

---

[256] *Legislating the Criminal Code: Involuntary Manslaughter* (Law Commission, 1996) Law Com No 237; *Reforming the Law on Involuntary Manslaughter: The Government's Proposals* (Home Office, 2000).

[257] Health and Safety Commission, Minutes HSC/06/M05, 9 May 2006, see http://www.hse.gov.uk/aboutus/meetings/hscarchive/2006/040706/cm05.pdf.

[258] *Advice To The Sentencing Guidelines Council—Sentencing for Corporate Manslaughter and Health and Safety Offences Involving Death* (Sentencing Advisory Panel, 2009).

[259] *Corporate Manslaughter & Health and Safety Offences Causing Death—Definitive Guideline* (Sentencing Guidelines Council, 2010).

[260] See *A Guide to the Corporate Manslaughter and Corporate Homicide Act 2007* (Ministry of Justice, 2007).

five years,[261] so some way below the 10 to 13 additional corporate manslaughter prosecutions per year on which the government's impact assessment was based. The legislation was expected to have a deterrent effect and save lives but the Act seems to have had little impact, and to date no large company has been convicted, only SMEs.

E. Conclusions

Successful reduction in workplace fatalities and injuries has been achieved through a combination of public regulation, management systems, and increased awareness of managers and especially workers. The evidence for deterrence is weak.

> The possibility of fines, sanctions, and inspections acts less as a deterrent threat than as a way to focus management attention on institutionalised expectations that may affect the legitimacy and operation of their enterprises.[262]

A regulatory model can impose management systems requirements on organisations, which are flexible and proportionate, and which can be aligned with motivations for socially responsible behaviour. Public regulation cannot hope to control the workplace system or activities of every business. Localised and constant operation is required, within a system supervised by managers at relevant levels and with the personal responsibility of every individual worker.

VII. Air Safety

A. The Need for Safety

Those responsible for the operation of air services share a common interest in maintaining public perception that services are safe. A perception that any operator, air traffic controller, maintenance service or other critical component is not to be trusted would risk undermining public confidence in the industry as a whole, and certainly lead to switching between airline providers. Hence, there is an inherent shared interest in maintaining safety.[263] It has been said that

> the aviation industry has methodically focused on improving safety performance since the first accident of the Wright brothers.[264]

---

[261] These include: Cotswold Geotechnical Holdings Ltd (which had entered voluntary liquidation shortly after judgment) and JMW Farms Ltd received fines of £385,000 and £187,500 respectively. In 2012 Lion Steel Limited pleaded guilty in connection with the death of Steven Berry who sustained fatal injuries after falling through a fragile roof panel at the firm's site in May 2008, was fined £480,000 and ordered to pay prosecution costs of £84,000.

[262] *Reducing the Risk of Policy Failure: Challenges for Regulatory Compliance* (Paris, OECD, 2000).

[263] 'Setting the Framework for Safe Transport is Essential for the European Citizen' per *White Paper. Roadmap to a Single European Transport Area—Towards a Competitive and Resource Efficient Transport System*, COM(2011) 144, 28.3.2011, para 39.

[264] B Yantis, 'SMS Implementation' in AJ Stolzer, CD Halford and JJ Goglia (eds), *Implementing Safety Management Systems in Aviation* (Farnham, Ashgate, 2011).

Air transport is widely considered to be one of the safest forms of travel.[265] In its 2011 White Paper on Transport the European Commission stated the clear aim that the European Union should be the safest region for aviation.[266] In 2012 there were 10.5 million flights in the EU, involving 925 million passengers and 14.5 million tonnes of cargo.[267] Data on accidents involving commercial aviation is at Table 19.3.[268] Data on accidents involving general aviation is at Table 19.4.[269]

B. Evolution of Regulation

The origins of international safety lie in the Convention on International Civil Aviation (the Chicago Convention) of 1944, which established rules of airspace, aircraft registration and safety, created the International Civil Aviation Organization (ICAO) to provide guidance and oversight of State civil aviation authorities, and requires Contracting States to implement a State Safety Programme (SSP) to identify hazards. The ICAO provides a global framework of Standards and Recommended Practices (SARPs), establishing a regulatory floor as a basis for mutual acceptance of flights amongst the over 190 signatory States.[270] An SSP is a system for the management of safety by the State, and is normally described in a single document which sets down a State's policy and objectives, risk management, safety assurance and safety promotion activities.[271] The Department for Transport, Civil Aviation Authority and other members of the State safety committee are responsible for issuing and updating the UK's Safety Plan.[272] For the EU, the European Aviation Safety Agency (EASA) now draws up the European Aviation Safety Plan (EASP), which sets out its view to the Commission on the best course of action to mitigate the risks, on the timescales for such actions, and the measurement of success, drawing on inputs from all stakeholders.[273] Safety performance indicators (SPI) are to be used, such as EASA's measurement of safety based on the annual rate of fatal accidents per million flights.

In Europe, milestones occurred with mutual acceptance of personnel licences in 1991,[274] investigation of aviation accidents and incidents in 1994,[275] the 'single European sky' framework in 2004, to improve the performance of air traffic management and air navigation

---

[265] *EASA Annual Safety Review 2012* (European Aviation Safety Agency, 2013) 9.

[266] *White Paper: Roadmap to a Single European Transport Area—Towards a Competitive and Resource Efficient Transport System*, COM(2011) 144, Annex I, para 17.

[267] ibid, 5.

[268] See *EASA Annual Safety Reviews* for 2012–2013.

[269] ibid. General aviation is all civil aviation operations other than scheduled air services and non-scheduled air transport operations for remuneration or hire. It includes flights in gliders, powered parachutes and corporate jets.

[270] *Safety Plan 2014–2016* (Civil Aviation Authority, updated 2014) http://www.caa.co.uk/docs/33/CAP%20 1100%20Safety%20Plan%20May%202014.pdf.

[271] *Communication from the Commission to the Council and the European Parliament. Setting up an Aviation Safety Management System for Europe*, COM(2011) 670, 25.10.2011, http://eur-lex.europa.eu/LexUriServ/Lex-UriServ.do?uri=COM:2011:0670:FIN:EN:PDF, 9.

[272] *Safety Plan 2014–2016* (n 269).

[273] *Report. European Aviation Safety Plan 2012–2015* (European Aviation Safety Agency, 2011) http://easa. europa.eu/sms.

[274] Council Dir 91/670/EEC of 16 December 1991 on mutual acceptance of personnel licences for the exercise of functions in civil aviation.

[275] Council Dir 94/56/EC of 21 November 1994 establishing the fundamental principles governing the investigation of civil aviation accidents and incidents.

Table 19.3: Overview of the Number of Commercial Air Transport Accidents, Fatal Accidents and Fatalities for EASA
MS Operated Aircraft above 2,250 kg MTOM, 2001–2013

Period	Aeroplanes				Helicopters			
	Number of accidents	Fatal accidents	Fatalities on Board	Ground Fatalities	Number of accidents	Fatal accidents	Fatalities on Board	Ground Fatalities
2001–2010 (Average per Year)	25.2	3.4	77.8	0.8	13.2	3.3	17.6	0.1
2011 (Total)	30	1	6	0	9	3	19	0
2012 (Total)	33	1	0	1	12	2	8	0
2013 (Total)	18	0	0	0	7	3	10	1

Table 19.4: Overview of the Number of Accidents, Fatal Accidents and Fatalities by Aircraft Category and Operation Type: All EASA MS Registered General Aviation Aircraft below 2,250 kg MTOM, 2007–2013

Aircraft Category	Period	Total number of accidents	Number of fatal accidents	Number of fatalities on board	Number of ground fatalities
	2007–2011 (average per year)	11.0	0.4	0.6	0
Balloons	2012	12	1	3	0
	2013	16	1	1	0
	2007–2011 (average per year)	0	0	0	0
Dirigibles	2012	0	0	0	0
	2013	0	0	0	0
	2007–2011 (average per year)	486.2	61.8	121.0	1.2
Aeroplanes	2012	397	51	108	0
	2013	378	42	82	0
	2007–2011 (average per year)	238.8	28.6	36	0.2
Gliders	2012	215	30	33	0
	2013	219	20	27	0
	2007–2011 (average per year)	15.4	4.2	5.0	0.2
Gyroplanes	2012	19	4	6	0
	2013	17	6	8	0
	2007–2011 (average per year)	56.2	8.2	18.0	0.6
Helicopters	2012	37	6	15	1
	2013	52	9	16	0
	2007–2011 (average per year)	222.2	38.0	55.4	0.2
Microlights	2012	219	39	59	0
	2013	219	40	57	0
	2007–2011 (average per year)	4.8	2.6	3.0	0
Other	2012	14	1	1	0
	2013	30	9	10	0
	2007–2011 (average per year)	1.0	0	0	0
Motorgliders	2012	5	1	1	0
	2013	17	1	1	0
Average total	2007–2011	**1035.6**	**143.8**	**239.0**	**2.4**
Total	2012	**918**	**133**	**226**	**1**
Total	2013	**948**	**128**	**202**	**0**
Change (%)	2012 over previous	**−11%**	**−8%**	**−5%**	**−58%**
	2013 over previous	**−10%**	**−16%**	**−21%**	**−100%**

services so as to enhance prevailing air traffic safety standards,[276] accident investigation in 1994 and 2010,[277] occurrence reporting in 2003,[278] establishment of EASA and airworthiness certification in 2003,[279] and increasingly strong developments from 2011 towards safety management systems (SMS) and supporting a 'just culture'. The system continues to evolve.[280] The main aspects will be considered below.

The air sector has extensive regulatory measures covering both ex ante and ex post situations, harmonised by EU legislation, but is still developing. The system and rules are overseen by EASA and National Aviation Authorities (NAAs). The approach to ex post reporting and evaluation is particularly notable. The aspects looked at more closely below are a brief outline of some licensing provisions, SMS, accident investigation and then occurrence reporting.

There are two important features to be noted in the aviation safety system. First, it has evolved from regulation based solely on *compliance* with prescriptive rules to encouragement of, and auditing against, operators' and regulators' *performance*. Second, the most striking feature of aviation safety is not the regulatory system but the *cultural approach*. The formal regulatory system has features familiar to safety systems in most other sectors noted above in this chapter, such as licensing regimes, safety management systems and reporting requirements for certain information. But these arrangements are external to companies, and it is the internal arrangements that affect safety in operation to a far greater extent. In this respect, a *safety culture* has developed that pervades the sector, and has spread *outwards* from leading airlines to be enshrined in the regulatory system itself. Before examining these issues, however, we outline the more conventional regulatory system.

C. Accident Investigation

A key component of safety information is the lessons to be learned from expeditious investigation of civil aviation accidents and incidents.[281] 'Reporting, analysis, and dissemination of findings of safety related incidents are fundamentally important to improving air safety.'[282]

Since 1994 Member States have been under an obligation to investigate every civil aviation accident and serious incident which has occurred in the territory of the Community.[283]

---

[276] Reg (EC) No 549/2004 of the European Parliament and of the Council of 10 March 2004 laying down the framework for the creation of the single European sky.

[277] Dir 94/56/EC; Commission Reg (EU) No 996/2010.

[278] Dir 2003/42/EC on occurrence reporting in civil aviation;

[279] Council Reg (EC) No 1592/2002 of the European Parliament and of the Council of 15 July 2002; Reg (EC) No 216/2008. The Commission publishes a list of banned aircraft, eg http://ec.europa.eu/transport/modes/air/safety/air-ban/doc/list_en.pdf. This also repealed Council Dir 80/51/EEC of 20 December 1979 on the limitation of noise emissions from subsonic aircraft.

[280] *A Policy Initiative on Aviation Safety and a Possible Revision of Regulation (EC) No 216/2008 on Common Rules in the Field of Civil Aviation and Establishing a European Aviation Safety Agency* (European Commission, May 2014) available at http://ec.europa.eu/transport/modes/air/consultations/2014-aviation-safety_en.htm; *General Aviation Unit: Let There be Flight: Regulating General Aviation in the UK: Consultation on the CAA's Draft GA Policy Framework* (Civil Aviation Authority, May 2014) available at http://www.caa.co.uk/docs/2836/CAP%20 1188%20GA%20policy%20consultation.pdf.

[281] Reg (EC) No 996/2010, recital 2.

[282] Reg (EC) No 996/2010, recital 3.

[283] Dir 94/56/EC establishing the fundamental principles governing the investigation of civil aviation.

The rules were updated in 2010. Responsibility for investigation by a permanent independent safety investigation authority rests with national air safety authorities,[284] with such assistance as may be requested from such authorities in other Member States,[285] and with the integral involvement of EASA and coordinated through the European Network of Civil Aviation Safety Investigation Authorities.[286] Investigating authorities are to be granted immediate access to accident sites, preservation of all important evidence.[287] The extent of investigations and the procedure to be followed in carrying out such investigations shall be determined by the investigating body, taking into account the principles and the objective of this Directive and depending on the lessons it expects to draw from the accident or serious incident for the improvement of safety.[288] An investigation report must be produced in a form appropriate to the type and seriousness of the accident or serious incident, protecting the anonymity of any individual involved, and without apportioning blame or liability, which are circulated amongst the authorities.[289] Safety recommendations may be made at any stage, and addressees must respond with actions taken.[290]

D. Licensing

Regulatory requirements apply to the design, production, maintenance and operation of aeronautical products, parts and appliances and personnel involved in such operations and in the operation of aircraft.[291] Detailed essential requirements apply to aircraft airworthiness licences, pilots, air operations, oversight and enforcement, and certification by qualified entities.[292] The EASA assists the Commission in certification, conducting standardisation inspections on national competent authorities,[293] and carries out functions concerning essential requirements and guidance, with power to issue fines and periodic penalty payments.[294] Licensing rules apply to aerodromes, which are highly prescriptive in approach.[295]

The 2004 framework for the 'single European sky',[296] set out requirements for the performance of air traffic management and air navigation services so as to enhance prevailing air traffic safety standards. A performance scheme applies to air navigation services and network functions, including monitoring of performance plans, and inspections and surveys.[297] The performance scheme aims, inter alia, at providing indicators and binding

[284] Reg (EU) No 996/2010, art 4.
[285] Reg (EU) No 996/2010, art 6.
[286] Reg (EU) No 996/2010, arts 1 and 7.
[287] Reg (EU) No 996/2010, arts 12–14.
[288] Reg (EU) No 996/2010, art 5.
[289] Reg (EU) No 996/2010, art 16.
[290] Reg (EU) No 996/2010, arts 17 and 18.
[291] Reg (EC) No 216/2008, art 1. See earlier Council Reg (EC) No 1592/2002.
[292] Reg (EC) No 216/2008, arts 4–16.
[293] Reg (EC) No 216/2008, art 54.
[294] Reg (EC) No 216/2008, arts 17–51.
[295] Commission Reg (EU) No 139/2014; the EASA rules are mostly based on ICAO Annex 14. EASA's Acceptable Means of Compliance (AMC), Certification Specifications (CS) and supporting Guidance Material (GM came into effect on 6 March 2014.
[296] Reg (EC) No 549/2004 of the European Parliament and of the Council of 10 March 2004 laying down the framework for the creation of the single European sky, art 11.
[297] Commission Reg (EU) No 691/2010 of 29 July 2010 laying down a performance scheme for air navigation services and network functions and amending Reg (EC) No 2096/2005 laying down common requirements for the provision of air navigation services.

targets in key performance areas to enable safety levels to be achieved and maintained. Whilst the first steps have therefore been taken in setting up a safety performance scheme it is currently restricted to European Air Traffic Management (ATM) and does not include other domains within the aviation safety arena.

E. Occurrence Reporting

The EU legislation still requires the reporting of specified information. (Whether this remains a sensible approach, and so a permanent or transition technique is discussed below.) The objective is the reporting and careful analysis of even the smallest incidents, failures and other occurrences in daily operations which may indicate the existence of potentially serious safety hazards which if not corrected may lead to accidents. In 2003 the EU legislator said that

> The rate of accidents in civil aviation has remained fairly constant in the last decade; nevertheless there is concern that the forecasted traffic increase could lead to an increase in the number of accidents in the near future…
>
> Experience has shown that often before an accident occurs, a number of incidents and numerous other deficiencies have shown the existence of safety hazards.
>
> The improvement of the safety of civil aviation requires a better knowledge of these occurrences to facilitate analysis and trend monitoring in order to initiate corrective action.[298]

Accordingly, a new approach was instituted with the objective of moving towards mandatory occurrence reporting by a wide range of individuals[299] to a single competent authority in each Member State and exchanged between them.[300] In addition to the system of mandatory reporting, Member States may put in place an optional system of voluntary reporting[301] 'to collect and analyse information on observed deficiencies in aviation which do not have to be reported under the system of mandatory reporting, but which are perceived by the reporter as an actual or potential hazard.'[302] The current rules on occurrence reporting date from 2010,[303] and include the following obligations:

> Any person involved who has knowledge of the occurrence of an accident or serious incident shall notify without delay the competent safety investigation authority of the State of Occurrence thereof.[304]

---

[298] Dir 2003/42/EC on occurrence reporting in civil aviation, recitals 1, 3 and 4.

[299] ibid, art 4. The list includes the operator or commander of an aircraft; a person who carries on the business of designing, manufacturing, maintaining or modifying aircraft or any equipment; a person who signs a certificate of maintenance review or the release to service of aircraft or equipment; an air traffic controller or flight information officer; an airport manager; a person who performs a function connected with the installation, modification, maintenance, repair, overhaul, flight-checking or inspection of air navigation facilities; a person who performs a function connected with the ground-handling of aircraft, including fuelling, servicing, loadsheet preparation, loading, de-icing and towing at an airport. The implementing rules are in Commission Reg (EU) No 1330/2007 of 24 September 2007 and Commission Reg (EU) No 1321/2007 of 12 November 2007.

[300] ibid, arts 5 and 6.

[301] ibid, art 9.

[302] Description taken from http://europa.eu/legislation_summaries/transport/air_transport/l24250_en.htm.

[303] Reg (EU) No 996/2010, art 19.

[304] Reg (EU) No 996/2010, art 9.1.

The safety investigation authority shall notify without delay the Commission, EASA, the International Civil Aviation Organisation (ICAO), the Member States and third countries concerned in accordance with the international standards and recommended practices of the occurrence of all accidents and serious incidents of which it has been notified.[305]

Reporting requirements also apply to air traffic controls. The Eurocontrol Safety and Regulatory Requirement (ESARR 2) instructs air traffic controllers and their organisations that 'all safety occurrences need to be reported and assessed, all relevant data collected and lessons disseminated.' In the UK the CAA (Civil Aviation Authority) operates a Mandatory Occurrence Reporting system and the voluntary scheme is the UK Confidential Human Factors Incident Reporting Programme for Aviation and Maritime (CHIRP), which is a charitable trust, has operated since 1982, and also covers maritime reporting worldwide.[306] It is linked with the International Confidential Aviation Safety Systems (ICASS) Group.

The European Commission tabled proposals to amend the occurrence reporting system in 2012,[307] in order to:

1. Ensure that all occurrences which endanger or would endanger aviation safety are collected and are providing a complete and clear picture of safety risks in the European Union and its Member States;
2. ensure that data issued from reported occurrences and stored in the national databases and in the European Central Repository (ECR) are complete and of high quality;
3. ensure that all safety information stored in the ECR is accessed adequately by appropriate authorities and that they are used strictly for safety enhancement purposes;
4. ensure that reported occurrences are effectively analysed, that safety hazards are identified and addressed where relevant and that the safety effectiveness of actions taken is monitored.

The proposals were also built around enshrining the principle of Just Culture, which needs to be examined next.

F. The Introduction of a Safety Management System Approach

It was recognised that compliance with licence requirements represented only a minimum foundation for operational safety but did not necessarily achieve the desired level of safety *performance*.[308] The UK Civil Aviation Authority summarised the new approach:

> To achieve our strategic objective and to improve what are already very high levels of safety, we need to do something different. Further regulation and just doing more of what we currently do will not have the greatest effect. We know that reacting after an incident or near miss is not the best way to prevent it happening again. We need to examine the causal factors more closely and transform our regulatory activities to follow a more risk and performance-based approach.[309]

---

[305] Reg (EU) No 996/2010, art 9.2.
[306] http://www.chirp.co.uk.
[307] Proposal for a Reg of the European Parliament and of the Council on occurrence reporting in civil aviation amending Reg (EU) No 996/2010 and repealing Dir No 2003/42/EC, Commission Reg (EC) No 1321/2007 and Commission Reg (EC) No 1330/2007, COM(2012) 776, 18.12.2012.
[308] 'Simply stated, a regulatory 'compliant' airline is not necessarily a safe airline.' Yantis (n 264).
[309] *The Transformation to Performance-based Regulation* (Civil Aviation Authority, 2014) 1.

There was considerable variation between operators' operational and safety standards and the expectations of different regulatory authorities. Regulatory compliance as the mainstay of safety was perceived to be reaching its limit as the aviation system grows ever more complex, and more is understood about the limitations of human performance and the impact of organisational processes.[310]

Accordingly moves were made to introduce 'structured operational management systems, operational procedures based on human factor considerations and implementation of vigorous accident prevention programs.'[311] A number of carriers approached the International Air Transport Association (IATA) to sponsor development of an international safety standard, as a result of which the voluntary IATA Operational Safety Audit (IOSA) Programme was developed and manuals were published containing best practices and an Organization and Management System.[312] The SMS standards were subsequently incorporated into regulatory requirements. This led to the mandatory approach of ICAO,[313] and was a significant enabler of the performance based regulation (PBR) approach.

Concern increased in international and European circles to improve air safety further. Although the aviation accident rate has declined in recent years, the rate of decline has slowed in Europe since 2004.[314] In 2010, it was predicted that the number of flights would almost double by 2030.[315] The Report of the High Level Group on Aviation Research stated a goal for 2050 of reducing the accident rate of commercial aircraft flights to less than one per 10 million flights, ie half the current level.[316] A move from 'regulation' to safety management was widely supported. Further movement towards a pro-active, evidence based management of aviation safety was agreed at the 2010 International Civil Aviation Organisation's (ICAO) High Level Safety Conference.[317]

In 2011 the European Commission announced the creation of a global safety management system (AVMS), stating:

> It is therefore clear that, in order to continue to make progress, the European Union must move beyond concentrating on rulemaking, important though this activity is, and place greater emphasis on addressing the risks to aviation safety in a systematic fashion. We must move from a primarily reactive system where regulations are changed as a result of experience towards a system which is pro-active and attempts to anticipate potential safety risks in order to further reduce the likelihood of an accident.[318]

> ..., it is particularly in the area of occurrence reporting that a significant fault line exists.... occurrence reporting in the EU and the use of the ECR are still affected by a number of shortcomings

---

[310] ICAO Document 9859 AN/474, 2nd edn, 2009.

[311] ibid, 161.

[312] The first *IOSA Standards Manual* was published 2002; see *ICAO Safety Management Manual* 2nd edn (International Civil Aviation Organization, 2009). See also *Safety Management Manual* (International Business Aircraft Council, 2006).

[313] ICAO Annex 19.

[314] EASA Annual Safety Reviews.

[315] *Long-Term Forecast–Flight Movements 2010–2030*, EUROCONTROL CND/STATFOR Doc415 of 17 December 2010.

[316] *Flightpath 2050—Europe's Vision for Aviation* (European Commission, 2011).

[317] ICAO Doc 9935, HLSC 2010.

[318] *Communication from the Commission to the Council and the European Parliament* (n 271) 3.

which limit the usefulness of the occurrence reporting system for accident prevention purposes. These problems are, notably, low quality of information, incomplete data, insufficient clarity in reporting obligations and in the flow of information, and legal and organisational obstacles to ensuring adequate access to the ECR information to enable information sharing. In addition there is considerable fragmentation within the current system. As well as the EU repository, Eurocontrol has its own safety repository and EASA is building its own internal database. It would be beneficial to combine this information on occurrences.[319]

The introduction of safety management principles into the EU aviation system will change the way we approach aviation safety, and will lead to a significant improvement in the way in which safety risks are controlled. However, the use of such principles should not be confined to the development of the Safety Plan alone but should encompass the whole system. The work by EASA in conducting standardisation inspections, required under Regulation (EC) No 216/2008 to monitor the application of that Regulation, should evolve beyond compliance monitoring towards an approach that is driven more by safety risks identified by the safety management system. This risk based approach would add benefit by focusing on those issues where mitigation action would have a clear benefit to safety.[320]

The move to system management necessitated fundamental changes for the institutional actors: For businesses by integrating safety management into the enterprise management system by involving all employee groups and partner organisations as stakeholders (an integrated management system) by making safety management an integral part of the business model; and for authorities from being inspectors to systems auditors.[321] The change meant that both businesses and regulators were collectively responsible, but for different aspects and in different ways. The stakeholder retains responsibility for management and ownership, and the regulator is responsible for accountability and assurance. Interestingly, implementation of an SMS was found to have significant cost savings.[322]

G. The Basis of a Safety Management System

A safety management system is defined by the Commission as:

> [A] pro-active system that identifies the hazards to the activity, assesses the risks those hazards present, and takes action to reduce those risks to an acceptable level. It then checks to confirm the effectiveness of the actions. The system works continuously to ensure any new hazards or risks are rapidly identified and that mitigation actions are suitable and where found ineffective are revised.[323]

In contrast to a quality system, which focuses on output and continuous improvement, a process-based approach focuses on monitoring performance (quality assurance activities) to ensure that the system is capable of reliably producing an acceptable level of output.[324]

---

[319] ibid, 5.
[320] ibid, 10.
[321] Yantis (n 264) 165, 166.
[322] 'For example, implementation of several elements of an SMS for a major operator's ground-handling program reduced lost time injury (LTI) costs by 13 per cent and ground damage costs by 41 per cent (slightly less than US$10 million).': ibid, 167.
[323] *Communication from the Commission to the Council and the European Parliament* (n 271) 3.
[324] AJ Stolzer, CD Halford and JJ Goglia, 'Introduction' in Stolzer, Halford and Goglia (n 264) xlviii.

An SMS requires the documented, repeatable processes of a quality management system. The classic tasks of risk management are involved: Hazard identification, analysis of data and risk, and risk reduction activity. An SMS comprises four components: *Safety policy, safety risk management, safety assurance* and *safety promotion*.

The major components of the ICAO's SMS are summarised in Table 19.5. They seek to balance the twin goals of production and protection. The objectives of system and task analysis within SMS, include:[325]

— Initial design of processes (describing workflows, attributes, etc)
— Task and procedure development (including documentation, job aids, etc)
— Hazard identification (what if things go wrong?)
— Training development (assessment, design, development, implementation and evaluation)
— Shaping *safety assurance* processes (what needs to be monitored, measured and evaluated?)
— Performance assessment (how are we doing?)

Training is a keystone requirement:

> Training provides the means for organizations to prepare their people to practice SRM and safety programs, and it is an integral part of safety promotion.[326]

Table 19.5: Components of ICAO's Safety Management System

Component 1: Safety policy and objectives
   Element 1.1 Management commitment and responsibility
   Element 1.2 Safety accountabilities
   Element 1.3 Appointment of key safety personnel
   Element 1.4 Coordination of emergency response planning
   Element 1.5 SMS documentation
Component 2: Safety risk management
   Element 2.1 Hazard identification
   Element 2.2 Risk assessment and mitigation
Component 3: Safety assurance
   Element 3.1 Safety performance monitoring and measurement
   Element 3.2 The management of change
   Element 3.3 Continual improvement of the SMS
Component 4: Safety promotion
   Element 4.1 Training and education
   Element 4.2 Safety communication

---

[325] D Arendt and A Adamski, 'System and Task Analysis' in Stolzer, Halford and Goglia (n 264) 1.

[326] *Safety Management System Framework: Safety Management System (SMS); Pilot Project Participants and Voluntary Implementation of Organization SMS Programs (rev 2)* (Washington, DC, US Department of Transportation, Federal Aviation Administration, Flight Standards Service-SMS Program Office, 2009).

H. The Need to Share Information

Information that is important for hazard and risk identification can come from a diversity of sources, so the system needs to be designed so as to enable such information to be contributed, and to encourage full and timely reporting.

> A variety of information sources are currently available, such as accident reports, ramp inspection reports from the Safety of Foreign Aircraft Programme (SAFA), the investigation and follow-up of incidents, data from occurrence reports integrated into the European Central Repository (ECR), oversight audits including EASA Standardisation Inspections, and information exchange. No one source provides all the required information, and an EU hazard identification process must make use of a combination of all sources, both reactive, proactive and predictive, and by sharing this information it can provide decision makers with comprehensive air safety 'intelligence'. [327]

A diversified system based on national authorities is no longer sustainable or permissible. A competent safety system has to be based on international coordination, and on the sharing of safety signals.

> … with the increasing sharing of the regulatory competencies for aviation safety between national and European authorities, it is no longer practical or desirable for the Member States or the Commission or EASA to be acting in isolation when seeking pro-active solutions to common problems. All the aviation safety 'players' in the EU must work together to ensure that the whole system is greater than the sum of its parts. [328]

> It is not about shifting the responsibility for taking action but about the need for increased cooperation to achieve better results. It should add value to the safety initiatives of the Member States by drawing together European wide information to aid the identification of risks to aviation safety across Europe. It should share information and act as a facilitator to enable concerted action to be taken. For this to happen it is clear that it will depend upon the assistance and contributions of the Member States and the aviation industry. It is by drawing together in a collaborative approach the work of safety management systems at Member State and industry level that European benefits are to be obtained. [329]

EASA and the competent authorities of the Member States are required to collaborate in the regular exchange and analysis of information. [330] However, the framework and tools required to realise this are still being developed. The Commission is assisted by the EASA Committee, [331] which facilitates evaluation, discussion and agreement between the Member States and the Commission. Information exchange was facilitated by the creation in 2007 of a European Central Repository. [332] Agreements have been put in place on international coordination. [333]

---

[327] *Communication from the Commission to the Council and the European Parliament* (n 270) 4.

[328] ibid, 3.

[329] ibid, 4.

[330] Commission Reg (EU) No 996/2010, art 19.

[331] Reg (EC) No 216/2008 of the European Parliament and of the Council of 20 February 2008 on common rules in the field of civil aviation and establishing a European Aviation Safety Agency, and repealing Council Dir 91/670/EEC, Reg (EC) No 1592/2002 and Dir 2004/36/EC.

[332] Commission Reg (EC) No 1321/2007 laying down implementing rules for the integration into a central repository of information on civil aviation occurrences exchanged in accordance with Dir 2003/42/EC of the European Parliament and of the Council. It is managed by the Joint Research Centre of the European Commission. In 2013, over 600,000 occurrences were stored in the European Central Repository.

[333] Memorandum of Understanding on a Global Safety Information Exchange (GSIE) between the Commission, ICAO, the FAA and IATA.

I. Enhancement of Performance

The move from a prescriptive compliance-based to a performance-based approach to aviation safety in Europe has been developed by leading national authorities and airlines working together. The UK Civil Aviation Authority aims to have completed the roll-out of performance-based regulation by April 2016, enabling the capability areas to begin providing assurance against performance.[334] The essence of this approach is to build on the integrated safety risk reporting and management system by identifying a total aviation risk picture and a series of prioritised risk mitigation activities, which will drive performance-based oversight and targeted improvements.[335] The intention is to quantify the importance of potential threats that will drive a systematic series of action plans directed at three types of actions: Actions to improve the capabilities of people and organisations in safety critical roles,[336] actions to improve technology and infrastructure that support safe operation, and actions to reduce risks from international issues and global new technologies.[337] This builds on analysis undertaken some years ago to identify the top 20 main aviation risks that could cause fatalities. The CAA illustrated how a series of root causes could lead to undesirable events, and one of the major high-risk outcomes that became known as the 'Significant 7': see Figures 19.11 and 19.12.[338]

Accidents			
Loss of control in flight	Runway excursion	Controlled flight into terrain	Aircraft fire
Incidents			
Runway incursion	Airborne conflict		Ground handling

Figure 19.11: The Significant 7 Aviation Safety

J. The Concept of Just Culture

A crucial component of managing aviation safety is the independent review of reports of actual or potential problems which may contribute to organisational learning in making things safer if lessons can be applied by everyone involved.[339] The approach is based on the recognition that human error, as well as system error, is unavoidable,[340] and also that

---

[334] *The Transformation to Performance-based Regulation* (Civil Aviation Authority, 2014) 1.

[335] ibid.

[336] Data from 250 fatal accidents involving large public transport aircraft showed that 66% of fatal accidents included pilot flight handling issues and 28% inappropriate action by crew. CAA data showed that in 29% of fatal accidents and 26% of UK high-risk events, technical failure was present, suggesting issues with maintenance and engineer performance. *Safety Plan 2014–2016* (n 270).

[337] *Safety Plan 2014–2016* (n 270).

[338] A widely used risk model was the 'bowtie' model, in which the two wings were threats and consequences respectively, connected at the centre by the critical 'top event'.

[339] Yantis (n 264) ch 6.

[340] D McCune, C Lewis and D Arendt, 'Safety Culture in Your Safety Management System' in Stolzer, Halford and Goglia (n 264) 138.

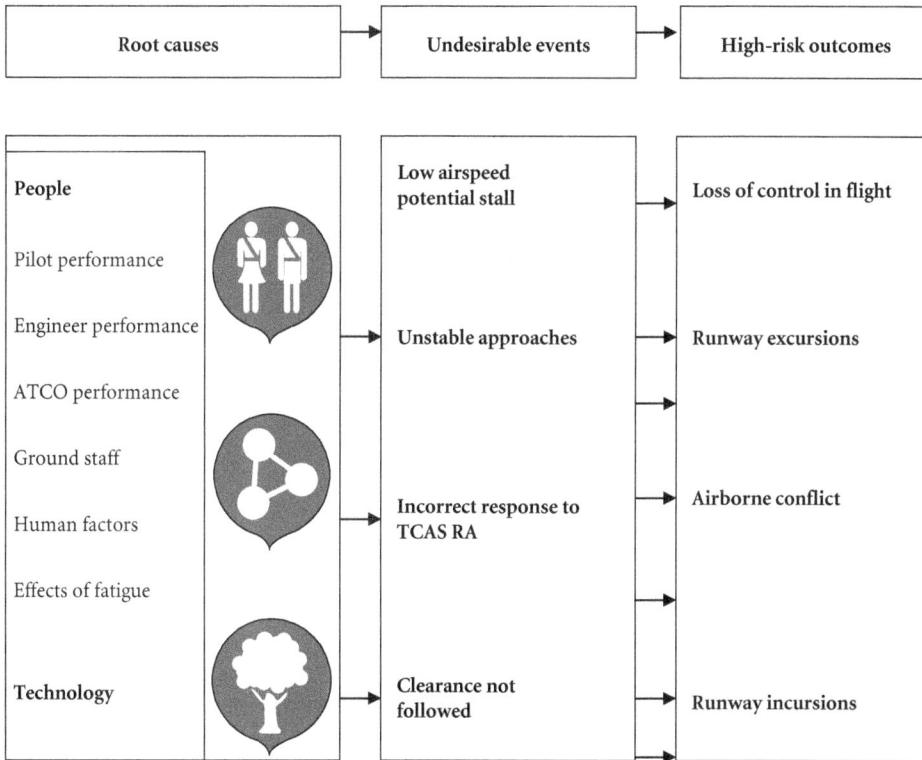

Figure 19.12: CAA Depiction of how Root Causes may Lead to High-risk Outcomes

multiple descriptions of events are plausible, so that finding truth in relation to making changes in how things are done requires multiple inputs.[341]

Thus, systems have been put in place that are accessible, encourage reports, assess them by independent experts, and feedback lessons widely. However, an equally crucial feature of encouraging spontaneous reports was the realisation that individuals will not do so if they fear potential adverse consequences, whether personal criticism, official investigations, criminal action, employment disciplinary action, social censure, embarrassment, or simply uncertainty over what will happen.[342] People rely on the evidence of what has happened when others have complained or blown whistles.[343]

Two alternative viewpoints were contrasted for viewing adverse events. On one approach adverse events are the product of human behaviour that falls into simplistic categories, such as 'human error', 'at-risk behaviour' or 'recklessness'. The assumption is that these labels

---

[341] S Dekker, *Just Culture. Balancing Safety and Accountability* (Aldershot, Ashgate Publishing, 2007) ix.

[342] *Report on Legal and Cultural Issues in Relation to ATM Safety Occurrence Reporting in Europe: Outcome of a Survey Conducted by the Performance Review Unit in 2005–2006* (Brussels, Eurocontrol Performance Review Commission, 2006). 'The sheer threat of judicial involvement is enough to make people think twice about coming forward with information about an incident that they were involved in.': Dekker, ibid 103.

[343] Dekker, ibid 55.

are stable categories of human performance, but they can be criticised as in fact being the observer's imposing a personal judgement of individual moral accountability rather than applying immutable categorisations. Another viewpoint is that consequences are products of circumstances and systems rather than human behaviour.[344]

Actions judged after the event focus on an adverse outcome that happened to occur, and this framing expands its significance.[345] This approach chimes with that taken in the report into the Clapham Junction rail crash: 'There is almost no human action or decision that cannot be made to look flawed and less sensible in the misleading light of hindsight. It is essential that the critic should keep himself constantly aware of that fact.'[346]

Thinking in the aviation sector has concluded that if safety systems are aimed at using information about risk, it is not enough for them to be based on the maxim 'if you have done nothing wrong you have nothing to fear'. That approach does not overcome anxiety about a wide range of potential consequences. Instead, the approach has to be based on a 'no blame' culture if sufficient core data is to be made available. The aviation industry has, therefore, developed the principle of a 'just culture' and an 'open culture', adopting particular approaches to safety and accountability.[347]

> Backward-looking accountability tries to find a scapegoat, to blame and shame an individual for messing up. Forward-looking accountability acknowledges the mistake and the harm resulting from it, should lay out the opportunities (and responsibilities!) for making changes so that the probability of such harm happening again goes down.[348]

The tension is 'between wanting everything in the open, while not tolerating everything' and this has to be based on relationships of trust, so that people will share their mistakes with others.[349] The culture is blame-free but not accountability-free. Accountability comes through sharing information about failures and improvements, and a mutual desire to learn lessons. The European Commission's 2012 proposals highlighted the following rationale:

> [W]hilst data is vital to identify safety hazards, there is not sufficient awareness of all safety occurrences. This situation is partly due to the discrepancy in the scope of reportable occurrences between the Member States. It also comes from the fact that individuals are afraid to report (the 'Just Culture' issue). Indeed to reach the goal of full reporting, individuals must have full confidence in the system because they are notably asked to report mistakes they may have made or contributed to. However, individuals are not equally protected among the Member States and they fear being punished by their hierarchy or being prosecuted. In addition, the lack of EU obligation to establish voluntary reporting scheme to complete the mandatory schemes and the insufficient clarity in occurrence reporting obligations and in the flow of information are also contributing to the insufficient collection of occurrences.[350]

---

[344] HS Becker, *Outsiders: Studies in the Sociology of Deviance* (London, Free Press of Glencoe, 1963); Dekker, ibid 73.

[345] Dekker, ibid.

[346] A Hidden, *Clapham Junction Accident Investigation Report* (London, HMSO, 1989).

[347] RL Helmreich, 'Building Safety on the Three Cultures of Aviation' in *Proceedings of the IATA Human Factors Seminar* (Bangkok, 1999) 39–43; McCune, Lewis and Arendt (n 339).

[348] Dekker (n 341) 9.

[349] ibid, 10, 53.

[350] Explanatory Memorandum, para 1.2, Proposal for a Reg of the European Parliament and of the Council on occurrence reporting in civil aviation amending Reg (EU) No 996/2010 and repealing Dir No 2003/42/EC, Commission Reg (EC) No 1321/2007 and Commission Reg (EC) No 1330/2007, COM(2012) 776, 18.12.2012.

K. Research Basis for Just Culture

The development of no blame reporting systems was underpinned by research, some of which is noted here. The background is that in a high-hazard industry, decision makers are limited by the prohibitively high costs of ordinary trial and error experimentation[351] and by a sparse history of accidents from which to draw conclusions.[352]

One theory of how to operate in such circumstances, named 'high reliability theory' postulated that organisational learning coexists with a strong emphasis on enforcement and accountability.[353] Such organisations usually operate according to complex and detailed collections of standard operating procedures (SOPs) and regulations. The threat of punishment could be used to discipline and deter. That theory was optimistic about possibilities of organisational learning from accidents, to a greater extent than normal accident theory.[354] However, these ideas were challenged.

An alternative approach posited that when an organisation emphasises rule enforcement and maintaining accountability, it will tend to hinder the organisation's efforts not only to gather hazard-related information from individuals directly operating the technology, but also to interpret and analyse the data collected.[355] The need was to expand and enrich the base of experience by collecting information about 'near accidents'.[356] It was noted that a nuclear plant manager had undermined efforts to promote incident reporting by punishing an employee for his involvement in a near miss.[357] It was argued that the use of incentives designed to discipline employee behaviour can inadvertently hinder information-gathering efforts. Stiff penalties give individuals incentives to withhold information that may reflect poorly on their performance. The effects of this process are intensified in high-hazard industries.[358] It was argued that the punitive measures designed to discipline employee behaviour not only stifle individuals' reporting of hazard-related information but also leave organisational decision makers with an incomplete database on the extent of possible dangers.[359] Thus, if the organisation depends on error reports from first-line employees to learn what went wrong, it will limit the organisational capacity for learning.

In a 1987 study, Tamuz observed the consequences of the introduction of computerised surveillance by air traffic controllers of particular parameters of the performance of

---

[351] TR La Porte, 'On the Design and Management of Nearly Error-free Organizational Control Systems' in DL Sills, CP Wolf and VB Shelanski (eds), *Accident at Three Mile Island: The Human Dimensions* (Boulder CO, P Westview, 1982).

[352] JG March, LS Sproull and M Tamuz, 'Learning from Samples of One or Fewer' (1991) 2(1) *Organizational Science* 1.

[353] TR La Porte and PM Consolini, 'Working in Practice but not in Theory: Theoretical Challenges of High Reliability Organizations' (1991) 1(1) *Journal of Public Administration and Theory* 19; study of navy air carriers and other high reliability organisations.

[354] SD Sagan, *The Limits of Safety: Organizations, Accidents and Nuclear Weapons* (Princeton NJ, Princeton University Press, 1993).

[355] M Tamuz, 'Learning Disabilities for Regulators. The Perils of Organizational Learning in the Air Transportation Industry' (2001) 33(3) *Administration & Society* 276.

[356] March, Sproull and Tamuz (n 352).

[357] DA Lucas, 'Organisational Aspects of Near Miss Reporting' in TW van der Schaaf, DA Lucas and AR Hale (eds), *Near Miss Reporting as a Safety Tool* (Oxford, Butterworths-Heinemann, 1991).

[358] EE Lawler and JG Rhode, *Information and Control in Organizations* (Pacific Palisades CA, Goodyear, 1976).

[359] Tamuz (n 355).

pilots.[360] It was found that when performance was measured precisely (through installation of computerised surveillance), individual performers shifted their attention towards those activities being measured. The number of reports of easily-measured air traffic violations increased dramatically. Further, when individuals focused much of their attention on precisely-measured activities, it did not distract them from also noticing those situations which were not being measured. Instead, the heightened awareness of the precisely-measured events seems to have generalised to other similar situations.[361] Pilots also substantially increased the number of reports they filed about potentially dangerous situations which the new computer system could not detect.

Tamuz followed with two studies reported in 2001. The first compared three aviation safety monitoring systems.[362] One system first introduced an offer of immunity from prosecution for pilots reporting, after which reporting increased dramatically (from 559 in 1965 to 2,230 in 1968), and later retracted immunity in 1972, after which reporting dropped (to 231 in 1987) and remained low (see Figures 19.13 and 19.14).[363]

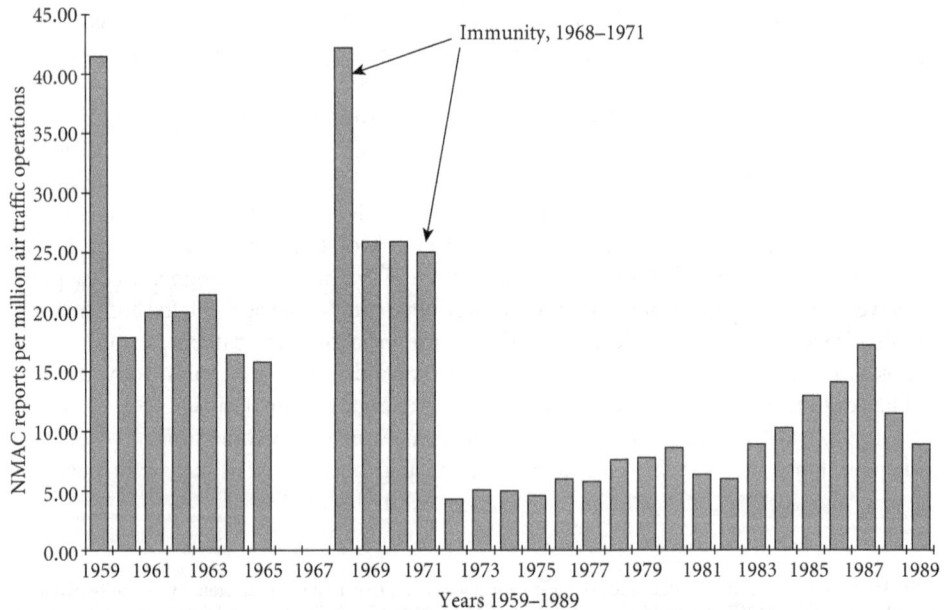

Figure 19.13: Pilot Reports of Near Midair Collisions (NMACs) 1959 to 1989 and under Federal Aviation Administration Grant of Immunity (1968–1971)[364]

---

[360] M Tamuz, 'The Impact of Computer Surveillance on Air Safety Reporting' (1987) 22(1) *Columbia Journal of World Business* 69.

[361] A possible interpretation of this is that the more analytical 'slow' brain was being forced to engage.

[362] Two US Federal Aviation Authority (FAA) systems had a dual mission (enforce and learn). The other system (Aviation Safety Reporting System (ASRS)), operated by NASA, focused solely on learning and could not enforce: It was voluntary and confidential.

[363] US FAA, Office of Aviation Safety, *Near Midair Collisions in the US* (unpublished statistics, 1987).

[364] Tamuz (n 355) Fig 2, citing original source as adaptation from U.S. Federal Aviation Administration, Office of Aviation Policy and Planning (1999) and US Federal Aviation Administration Office of Aviation Safety (1987). Data was missing for 1966 to 1967.

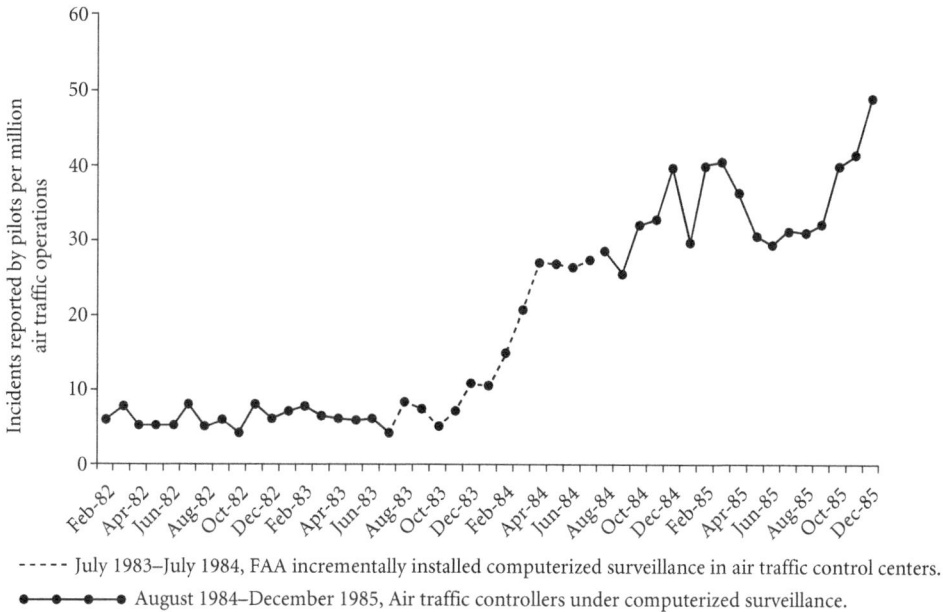

----- July 1983–July 1984, FAA incrementally installed computerized surveillance in air traffic control centers.

●—●—●—● August 1984–December 1985, Air traffic controllers under computerized surveillance.

Figure 19.14: Pilot Reports of Computer-detected Events to the Aviation Safety Reporting System (1982–1985)[365]

It was concluded that when the authority increased scrutiny on air traffic controllers, pilots also perceived that they were more likely to be caught, so there was a dramatic increase in the volume of pilot incident reporting following implementation of computerised surveillance.[366] But they reported throughout to the voluntary system (ASRS), which did not engage in disciplinary action. The ASAP (as soon as possible) system was established by the US pilots' association and management of American Airlines to operate as a learning-based, non-punitive safety reporting system. The ASAP safety committee, with members from the pilots' association, airline management and the Federal Aviation Agency (FAA), review and respond to each report, recommending corrective action if necessary.[367] They did not attempt to determine who was to blame, or initiate enforcement action. The FAA was prohibited from prosecuting air traffic violations based on confidential reports gathered by ASAP. It rigorously enforces the law if it discovered a potential violation from another source, such as from computerised surveillance. The FAA did not grant immunity to pilots for reporting air traffic violations to the ASAP, but it substantially reduced

---

[365] Tamuz (n 355) Fig 3, adapted from Tamuz (n 359) 66.
   US Federal Aviation Administration, Office of Aviation Policy and Planning (1999) and US Federal Aviation Administration Office of Aviation Safety (1987). Data was missing for 1966 to 1967.
[366] Tamuz (n 360) 69.
[367] S Griffith, *American Airlines ASAP*. Paper presented at the Global Analysis and Information network (GAIN) Workshop, Cambridge MA, (1996).

the punitive measures to those who had inadvertently violated a federal regulation and voluntarily reported it.

L. Just Culture in EU Legislation

In 2010 a 'no blame' and 'just culture' approach has been included in EU regulatory legislation:

> The sole objective of safety investigations should be the prevention of future accidents and incidents without apportioning blame or liability.[368]

> The civil aviation system is based on feedback and lessons learned from accidents and incidents which require the strict application of rules of confidentiality in order to ensure the future availability of valuable sources of information. In this context sensitive safety information should be protected in an appropriate way.[369]

> The civil aviation should equally promote a non-punitive environment facilitating the spontaneous reporting of occurrences and thereby advancing the principle of 'just culture'.[370]

> The information provided by a person in the framework of a safety investigation should not be used against that person, in full respect of constitutional principles and national law.[371]

> ... the difficulty in capturing all occurrences ... raises the need for action in the area of the implementation of a 'just culture'.[372]

> Further work is required to encourage a culture of open reporting within the aviation industry and to support the development of an environment where individuals feel able to report safety significant events without the fear of reprisal.[373]

The legislation defines 'Just culture' as meaning

> a culture in which front line operators or others are not punished for actions, omissions or decisions taken by them that are commensurate with their experience and training, but where gross negligence, wilful violations and destructive acts are not tolerated.[374]

However, just culture draws a line between acceptable and unacceptable behaviour. 'A wilful violation is not acceptable. An honest mistake is.'[375] Standards of behaviour require professional competence, openness, sharing, and taking responsibility for one's mistakes by correcting them and improving.[376]

---

[368]   Reg (EU) No 996/2010, recital 4. Even in 1994, it was provided that a safety recommendation shall in no case create a presumption of blame or liability for an accident or incident: Dir 94/56/EC, art 10.

[369]   Reg (EU) No 996/2010, recital 22.

[370]   Reg (EU) No 996/2010, recital 24.

[371]   Reg (EU) No 996/2010, recital 25.

[372]   Defined in Commission Reg (EU) No 691/2010 of 29 July 2010 laying down a performance scheme for air navigation services and network functions and amending Reg (EC) No 2096/2005 laying down common requirements for the provision of air navigation services, art 2(k).

[373]   *Communication from the Commission to the Council and the European Parliament* (n 271) 5.

[374]   Commission Reg (EU) No 691/2010 of 29 July 2010 laying down a performance scheme for air navigation services and network functions and amending Reg (EC) No 2096/2005 laying down common requirements for the provision of air navigation services, art 2(k).

[375]   Dekker (n 341) 15.

[376]   McCune, Lewis and Arendt (n 340) 195.

In 2008, the EU legislation was significantly reformed to institutionalise a 'no blame' culture:

> The promotion of a 'culture of safety' and the proper functioning of a regulatory system in the fields covered by this Regulation require that incidents and occurrences be spontaneously reported by the witnesses thereto. Such reporting would be facilitated by the establishment of a non-punitive environment, and appropriate measures should be taken by Member States to provide for the protection of such information and of those who report it.[377, 378]

Reports are made to independent committees, who can revert to reporters to seek further information. Reporters' names are not passed on, for example to line managers. Trust is supported by feeding back to reporters and openly the results of the expert evaluations. A major feature of EU occurrence reporting since the 2003 legislation has been that confidentiality is central:

> The sensitive nature of safety information is such that the way to ensure its collection is by guaranteeing its confidentiality, the protection of its source and the confidence of the personnel working in civil aviation.

> The public should be provided with general information on the level of aviation safety.[379]

When the provisions on dissemination and public access to information were widened in 2009, appropriate confidentiality was still preserved.[380] However, the 'just culture' approach is still relatively young and has not been fully implemented into operational cultures, so revisions to encourage improvements were proposed in 2012[381] to

— ensure full awareness of actual and potential risks in aviation safety by improving the collection of safety occurrences. The new rules aim to establish a system where people feel confident in reporting information;
— ensure that the information collected is analysed and that actions necessary for maintaining or enhancing the level of aviation safety are taken and their effectiveness monitored;
— ensure that the information collected is appropriately shared among Member States and that it is used only for the purpose of improving safety.

The 2012 proposal strengthened the rules on collection of occurrences, flow of information to the ECR, exchange of information, protection against inappropriate use of information (data confidentiality), protection of a reporter (not to be subject to prejudice from an employer except in cases of gross negligence), and introduced requirements on information

---

[377] Reg (EC) No 216/2008, recital 16.

[378] Reg (EC) No 216/2008 of the European Parliament and of the Council of 20 February 2008 on common rules in the field of civil aviation and establishing a European Aviation Safety Agency, and repealing Council Dir 91/670/EEC, Reg (EC) No 1592/2002 and Dir 2004/36/EC.

[379] Commission Reg (EC) No 1321/2007, above, recitals 11 and 12. The public are informed through Annual Safety Reviews.

[380] Reg (EC) No 596/2009 adapting a number of instruments to the procedure referred to in Art 251 of the Treaty to Council Decision 1999/468/EC with regard to the regulatory procedure with scrutiny, art 6.3.

[381] Proposal for a Reg on occurrence reporting in civil aviation amending Reg (EU) No 996/2010 and repealing Dir No 2003/42/EC, Commission Reg (EC) No 1321/2007 and Commission Reg (EC) No 1330/2007, see http://ec.europa.eu/transport/modes/air/safety/reporting_en.htm.

analysis and adoption of follow up actions at national level, with stronger analysis at EU level, and improved transparency towards the general public.[382] It noted that

> Individuals may be refrained to report occurrences by the fear of self-incrimination and their potential consequences in terms of prosecution before judicial authorities. In this context Member States should not institute proceeding against a reporter on the basis of its report, except in case of gross negligence. In addition, the cooperation between safety and judicial authorities should be enhanced and formalised by the means of advance arrangements which should respect the balance between the various public interests at stake and notably cover the access and use of occurrence reports contained in the national databases.[383]

Accordingly, the civil aviation system should promote a non-punitive environment facilitating spontaneous reporting of occurrences, advancing the principle of 'Just Culture'.[384] The insertion of a Just Culture approach into EU legislation is still relatively recent, and differences in its observance continue to exist.

The existence of Just Culture within airline regulation has not affected national criminal or regulatory systems or cultures. Tension can occur where the employees of an airline who are in the habit of openly sharing information come into contact with external regulators or enforcement officials whose goals are to determine whether there has been blame or the commission of criminal offences, the two cultures will clash and the requirement of trust that is crucial to the success of the former approach will quickly be destroyed. Such cultural clashes can occur not just within European jurisdictions but certainly where European airline staff come into contact with enforcement agencies in other parts of the world. A difference can be identified in terms of the intensity of legal scrutiny and consequences between the approaches of the EU and the USA. The latter remains essentially punitive. Individuals are required in the USA to file an ASAP report, which is reviewed by both groups of peers that include pilots and the Federal Aviation Authority, and part of the determination is whether actions were 'reckless', in which case anonymity is removed and individuals are prosecuted.

M. An Open Culture

Just Culture primarily describes an approach by the *public* regulatory system, under which reporting of certain events will lead to immunity from formal consequences. It can and should, of course, also apply *within* an organisation. This aspect is not highlighted within the legislative system. However, if all individuals are to perform well in prioritising safety, it is the *complete* internal cultural environment within an airline company that is of primary importance. The internal culture requires not just sharing of information but also training, listening, prompts, reminders, and the constant mutual support of all staff and managers. This is an Open Culture. It rests on the following main premises.[385]

---

[382] Proposal for a Reg of the European Parliament and of the Council on occurrence reporting in civil aviation amending Reg (EU) No 996/2010 and repealing Dir No 2003/42/EC, Commission Reg (EC) No 1321/2007 and Commission Reg (EC) No 1330/2007, COM(2012) 776, 18.12.2012.

[383] ibid, recital 35.

[384] ibid, recitals 29–31.

[385] The following points are taken from the *Safety Management Manual* of British Airways.

The core Safety Policy is that every employee accepts responsibility and accountability for occupational and operational safety. Everyone must be responsible for and consider the impact on safety of everything that they do. Selection, recruitment, development and training of staff should be aligned with the core policy. Responsibility for implementing the safety management system is delegated to the appropriate level in the organisation. The positive safety culture must be generated from the 'top down' and relies on a high degree of trust, respect and communication. All staff must believe without doubt that they will be supported in any decisions made in the interests of safety and they must also believe that breaches of safety standards will not be tolerated. Documented procedures should ensure that staff communicate significant safety concerns to the appropriate level of management for resolution, and receive feedback. There should be drives for continuous improvement in safety performance.

In adhering to a Just Safety culture, staff are clear about where the line must be drawn between acceptable and unacceptable behaviour. In assessing behaviour the following tests are applied:

— *Substitution test*: Would another ordinary person with the same competence (education, training and experience) behave in the same way in the same circumstances (time, goal, demands and organisational context)?
— *Routine test*: Has this event happened before to the individual or the organisation?
— *Proportionality test*: What safety vale will disciplinary action have? How supportive was the individual in terms of (a) reporting the event, (b) cooperating with the investigation, and (c) accepting of investigation findings?
— *Intervention*: What needs to happen to reduce the likelihood of recurrence at individual and organisational level?

Where behaviours optimised rule-breaking for personal gain, recklessness and sabotage, management response should be through administrative and disciplinary action. All other behaviours should be managed through improving performance-influencing factors.[386]

The workforce should have safety competence, which is a balance of the attributes of knowledge, skill and behaviours. Knowledge applies to an individual and to the organisation. The organisation has to have a memory, a means of identifying information, remembering, and applying it. Skills can be developed by education, training, practice and refreshment. Behaviours relate to how people manage performance. Individuals need to have a strong sense of responsibility and be instinctively predisposed to act accordingly in sharing information and reacting positively to incoming observations. Peer to peer observations[387] are more powerful in affecting behaviour than authoritarian orders. Superiors should exercise oversight, rather than supervision. The prime function of oversight is not to challenge whether a decision was right or wrong, but to challenge the basis on which the decision was made.

N. Conclusions on Aviation Safety

Aviation safety provides a series of important lessons. First, the system has evolved, and is continuing to do so. Second, it has evolved through distinct stages, such as investigational,

---

[386] Termination of employment or other punitive approaches have no value to an individual or to the organisation in encouraging learning or improving performance.
[387] The most junior pilot may raise a query about a decision or action of the most senior pilot without it being taken as criticism, but as a necessary and welcomed check.

safety reporting, classic 'regulatory' licensing to 'behavioural'. Third, the control of high risk activities requires constant capture of information and its expert evaluation and feedback to operators of systems and individual actors. Fourth, organisational contexts require a Safety Management System approach that coordinates both officials and commercial operators—and operates on a global basis. Fifth, the need for open sharing of information can only be achieved within a mutually supportive, non-punitive environment: This has led to a largely no-blame Just Culture, and also to a more extensive concept of an Open Culture within leading airlines. Accountability remains within an Open Culture, but in a different sense from that found in traditional legal contexts. Instead of blame-based accountability, accountability of individuals is permanent and full within a culture that is directed at constant sharing, learning and striving to achieve performance.

Nevertheless, both Just Culture and Open Culture are relatively new concepts and not fully operational. Tensions currently remain between anonymity and confidentiality, and between fully open cultures in certain airlines and the more punitive regimes operated by public enforcement systems in some countries.

The Just and Open Culture approaches support, and are integrally linked with, the development in regulatory style away from a prescriptive compliance basis to a performance basis. The latter approach constantly manages risk, and spurs constant monitoring and improvement in safety performance.

VIII. Health and Social Care

A. Basic Structure and Size

The National Health Service (NHS) comprises a wide range of organisations, each specialising in different types of services for patients. In simple terms, primary care is provided by general medical practitioners (GPs), dentists, opticians and pharmacists, and specialist, surgical and emergency care is provided at hospitals by NHS Trusts or NHS Foundation Trusts.[388] Services are commissioned either locally by a Clinical Commissioning Group or at national level by the NHS Commissioning Board (known in England as NHS England). Joint Strategic Needs assessments are issued by the Health and Wellbeing Boards of relevant local authorities. Public Health England provides central support to local authorities.

Various regulatory bodies exist: the Care Quality Commission (CQC), the Human Fertilisation and Embryology Authority, the Health Research Council, the Medicines and Healthcare products Regulatory Agency, Monitor,[389] and the Human Tissue Authority. Regulation

---

[388] See *Guide to the Healthcare System in England. Including the Statement of NHS Accountability* (NHS, 2013).

[389] Monitor is an overarching regulator, with responsibilities to ensure that (a) independent NHS foundation trusts are well-led so that they can provide quality care on a sustainable basis, (b) essential services are maintained if a provider gets into serious difficulties, (c) the NHS payment system promotes quality and efficiency, and (d) procurement, choice and competition operate in the best interests of patients. From 2015 to 2016 Monitor's priorities will be to: Provide *support*, alongside partner organisations as appropriate, to NHS foundation trusts to improve their institutional and individual capabilities; reduce the risk that failings go uncorrected for any significant period; make sure rules operate in the best interests of patients; and work closely with partner organisations, nationally and locally (emphasis added): see *Monitor's Strategy 2014 to 2017: Helping to Redesign Healthcare Provision in England* (Monitor, 2013).

of individuals by their professional bodies is an integral aspect of the structure. There are the following professional regulatory bodies: The General Medical Council (GMC: 252,431 doctors), Nursing and Midwifery Council (NMC: 675,148 nurses and midwives), General Dental Council (101,901 dental practitioners), General Optical Council, General Pharmaceutical Council (pharmacists), General Chiropractic Council, General Osteopathic Council, Health and Care Professions Council (310,942 health, psychological and social work professionals).[390]

B. Background: A Huge Operation but a Series of Serious Failures

The NHS treats more than a million people safely and successfully every day.[391] Of the more than one million patient safety incidents reported to the National Patient Safety Agency's National Reporting and Learning System (NRLS) every year, almost 764,000 (70 per cent) resulted in no harm to the patient, 260,000 (24 per cent) resulted in low harm; 65,000 (six per cent) resulted in moderate harm; and 8,200 (0.7 per cent) resulted in death or severe harm.[392]

The NHS has for many years been subject to a series of pressures, including increasing and seasonal demand, budgetary constraints, resource problems and a series of structural reorganisations imposed by different governments. The have been concerns over the quality of care, long waiting lists, people left abandoned on hospital trolleys, unresponsiveness to complaints, and major scandals and breakdowns. Governments have focused on delivery of care at controllable cost, but in this process focus at policymaking and operational levels have thus been diverted from aspects of care quality for patients. Successive serious scandals have occurred, after which official investigations have consistently noted the fundamental importance of culture in the NHS.

In response to the Inquiry into the management of the care of children receiving complex cardiac surgery at the Bristol Royal Infirmary (BRI) between 1984 and 1995,[393] the government accepted the findings on 'the flaws and failures of the organisation and culture, not only at the BRI in the years in question, but of the wider NHS at that time.'[394] The Chair of the Inquiry, Professor Sir Ian Kennedy, set out a wide ambition:

> to build a new culture, of trust not blame, within the NHS—a health service where there is greater partnership between patients and professionals; where lines of accountability are clear and where there is openness about mistakes; where services are designed from the patient's point of view and where safety for patients always comes first.[395]

---

[390] See *Guide to the Healthcare System in England* (n 388).

[391] *Implementing a 'Duty of Candour'; a New Contractual Requirement on Providers. Proposals for Consultation* (Department of Health, October 2011) para 2.1.

[392] National Patient Safety Agency (NPSA), *Organisation Patient Safety Incident Reports Covering Incidents that Occurred between October 2009 and September 2010 and Reported to the NPSA's National Reporting and Learning System (NRLS) by the December 2010*, published May 2011, http://www.nrls.npsa.nhs.uk/.

[393] *The Report of the Public Inquiry into Children's Heart Surgery at the Bristol Royal Infirmary 1984–1995: Learning from Bristol*, 2001, http://www.bristol-inquiry.org.uk/final_report/report/index.htm, https://www.gov.uk/government/uploads/system/uploads/attachment_data/file/273320/5363.pdf.

[394] *Learning from Bristol: The Department of Health's Response to the Report of the Public Inquiry into Children's Heart Surgery at the Bristol Royal Infirmary 1984–1995*, (2002) Cm 5363, https://www.gov.uk/government/uploads/system/uploads/attachment_data/file/273320/5363.pdf.

[395] ibid, i.

A major scandal erupted concerning Harold Shipman, a general medical practitioner who committed serious criminal acts throughout his professional career, and from 1974 until 1998 killed around 215 patients. A major inquiry subsequently issued a sequence of six reports from 2002 to 2005 on different aspects of concern.[396]

Concern at the rising cost of compensating clinical negligence claims led to a consultation by the Chief Medical Officer for England (CMO) in 2001,[397] a Report in 2003,[398] and enactment of a statutory compensation scheme for less serious cases under the NHS Redress Act 2006—which were never implemented after objections from lawyers. A survey of patients found that they want apologies (34 per cent), explanations (23 per cent), support with the consequences (17 per cent), financial compensation (11 per cent) or disciplinary action (six per cent).[399] The objectives of the NHS Redress scheme were to provide for 'a more consistent and open response to patients when things go wrong.'[400] A link was noted between data collected in claims and pro-active prevention:

> The reforms will help create a cultural shift within the NHS, moving the emphasis away—where appropriate—from attributing blame towards preventing harm, reducing risks and learning from mistakes. It will provide not only benefits for patients, but an impetus for wider NHS improvements.[401]

A 2005 Report by the Health Service Ombudsman highlighted the problems faced by people using NHS services in getting a satisfactory response to a complaint and the failure of the NHS to learn lessons from complaints.[402] There followed a survey that found that most people using adult care services saw 'no point' in making a complaint,[403] a National Audit Office Report on health and care services that asserted that people found making a complaint too complex and that many complaints took too long to resolve,[404] and a Healthcare Commission review that found that many NHS complaints related to the fundamentals of good healthcare, such as effective communication with patients, the attitude of staff, record-keeping, privacy and dignity, plus in 19 per cent of cases a problem with the way in which a complaint was handled.[405]

---

[396] See http://webarchive.nationalarchives.gov.uk/20090808154959/http://www.the-shipman-inquiry.org.uk/firstreport.asp, starting with The Shipman Inquiry; Chairman: Dame Janet Smith DBE, *First Report. Volume One. Death Disguised* (2002).

[397] Sir Liam Donaldson, *Call for Ideas* (Department of Health, 2001).

[398] *Making Amends: A Consultation Paper Setting out Proposals for Reforming the Approach to Clinical Negligence in the NHS* (Department of Health, 2003).

[399] L Fleck, [Department of Health] Paper 'NHS Redress Scheme for Severely Neurologically Impaired Babies' at the 'No-fault Compensation Scheme Conference', 16 March 2005, Centre for Socio Legal Studies, University Oxford.

[400] *NHS Redress: Improving the Response to Patients* (Department of Health, 2005) at http://www.dh.gov.uk/en/Publicationsandstatistics/Publications/PublicationsLegislation/DH_4123288. *NHS Redress: Statement of Policy* (Department of Health, 2005) at http://www.dh.gov.uk/en/Publicationsandstatistics/Publications/PublicationsLegislation/DH_4123281.

[401] ibid.

[402] *Report: Making Things Better? A Report on Reform of the NHS Complaints Procedure in England* 10 March 2005 available at: http://www.ombudsman.org.uk/hdc/document/nhscomp05/comp.pdf (accessed on 18 August 2010). See earlier H Wallace and L Mulcahy, *Cause for Complaint: An Evaluation of the Effectiveness of the NHS Complaints Procedure* (The Public Law Project, 1999).

[403] Department of Health commissioned survey, 2005, referred to in *Listening, Responding, Improving: A Guide to Better Customer Car* e (Department of Health, 26 February 2009).

[404] *Making Experiences Count: A New Approach to Responding to Complaints* (Department of Health, 2007).

[405] *Feeding Back? Learning from Complaints Handling in Health and Social Care* (National Audit Office, 2008).

The *NHS Constitution for England*[406] embeds the principles of a policy known as *Being open* as a pledge to patients in relation to complaints and redress:

The NHS also commits when mistakes happen to acknowledge them, apologise, explain what went wrong and put things right quickly and effectively.[407]

The 2009 revision of *Being open*,[408] stated that *Being open* involves:

— Acknowledging, apologising and explaining when things go wrong;
— conducting a thorough investigation into the incident and reassuring patients, their families and carers that lessons learned will help prevent the incident recurring;
— providing support for those involved to cope with the physical and psychological consequences of what happened.

A common approach to handling complaints in the NHS and adult social care services was introduced in 2009, based on the Health Service Ombudsman's six Principles of Good Complaint Handling,[409] and all organisations were requested to review their systems 'so as to be able to respond flexibly to complaints, concerns and complements and feed the resulting lessons into their work on learning from patients' feedback to improve services'.[410] The policy was to 'encourage a culture that seeks and then uses people's experiences to make services more effective, personal and safe'.[411] NHS organisations are subject to legal,[412] contractual[413] and professional[414] obligations to provide an accessible and suitably responsive complaints procedure for service users.

At this point, legislative and guidance registration of NHS entities supervised by the Care Quality Commission[415] required compliance with essential standards of quality and

---

[406] The Health Act 2009 places a duty on NHS organisations (including contractors) to 'have regard to the NHS Constitution'.

[407] *The NHS Constitution for England* (London, Department of Health, 2009).

[408] *Being Open Safer Practice Notice* (National Patient Safety Agency, 2005); *Being Open—Communicating Patient Safety Incidents with Patients and their Carers* (National Patient Safety Agency, 2009).

[409] *Spotlight on Complaints: A Report on Second-stage Complaints about the NHS in England* (Healthcare Commission, 2009). See earlier, *Principles of Good Administration* (March 2007) and *Principles for Remedy* (October 2007). The six principles are: Getting it right; being customer focused; being open and accountable; acting fairly and proportionately; putting things right; and seeking continuous improvement.

[410] *Listening, Improving, Responding: A Guide to Better Customer Care*, Letter from J Saddler, National Director of Patient and Public Affairs (Department of Health, 2009).

[411] ibid.

[412] The Local Authority Social Services and National Health Service Complaints (England) Regs 2009/308.

[413] From April 2009, all Primary Care Trusts (PCTs) are required to be registered with the Care Quality Commission, under the Health and Social Care Act 2008. As a condition of registration, a PCT is required to ensure that 'there are systems in place to ensure that patients, their relatives and carers:

— have suitable and accessible information about, and clear access to, procedures to register formal complaints and feedback on the quality of services
— are not discriminated against when complaints are made
— are assured that organizations act appropriately on any concerns and, where appropriate, make changes to ensure improvements in service delivery.' (Core standard C14, Standards for Better Health).

[414] For doctors: 'Patients who complain about the care or treatment they have received have a right to expect a prompt, open, constructive and honest response including an explanation and, if appropriate, an apology. You must not allow a patient's complaint to affect adversely the care or treatment you provide or arrange.' *Good Medical Practice* (General Medical Council).

[415] The Health & Social Care Act 2008 (Regulated Activities) Regs 2010 available at http://www.legislation.gov.uk/ukdsi/2010/9780111491942/contents.

safety,[416] and placed a number of requirements on providers to be open with service users about the care they received, including requiring providers to analyse incidents that could have caused harm; to involve service users in making decisions about their care; to have an effective complaints procedure; to notify CQC of a range of incidents resulting in harm to service users or with the potential to harm service users; and to reflect, where appropriate, published research evidence and guidance issued by the appropriate professional and expert bodies as to good practice in relation to such care and treatment.

Widespread systemic failure occurred at the Mid Staffordshire Hospital Trust. An investigation led by Robert Francis QC published a scathing Report on systemic failure in a hospital leading to patients' 'appalling experiences', which sparked further significant reforms in approach.[417] Francis found that 'the culture of the Trust was not conducive to providing good care for patients or providing a supportive working environment for staff.'[418] The factors that contributed to this were: Attitudes of patients and staff,[419] bullying (an atmosphere of fear of adverse repercussions in relation to a variety of events was described by a number of staff witnesses), target-driven priorities,[420] disengagement from management, low staff morale, isolation, lack of openness, acceptance of poor standards of conduct, reliance on external assessments, and denial. The accident and emergency department, which was a centre of problems, was also chronically understaffed. Incident reporting systems were inadequate. Complaints were poorly investigated, remedial action was often not applied, appraisal and professional development were accorded a low priority, the focus of the Board was on processes not outcomes, and its reaction to criticism was individually and collectively one of denial instead of searching self-criticism.

Among the themes the Inquiry identified were:

— A corporate focus on process at the expense of outcomes;
— a failure to listen to those who have received care through proper consideration of their complaints;
— staff disengaged from the process of management;
— insufficient attention to the maintenance of professional standards;
— lack of support for staff through appraisal, supervision and professional development;
— a weak professional voice in management decisions;
— a failure to meet the challenge of the care of the elderly through provision of an adequate professional resource. Some of the treatment of elderly patients could properly be characterised as abuse of vulnerable persons;
— a lack of external and internal transparency;
— false reassurance taken from external assessments; and
— a disregard of the significance of the mortality statistics.[421]

---

[416] Care Quality Commission, *Guidance about Compliance: Essential Standards of Quality and Safety*, March 2010, http://www.cqc.org.uk/_db/_documents/Essential_standards_of_quality_and_safety_FINAL_081209.pdf.

[417] *Independent Inquiry into Care provided by Mid Staffordshire NHS Foundation Trust January 2005—March 2009. Volume I. Chaired by Robert Francis QC*, HC375-I.

[418] *Francis Report*, ibid para 43.

[419] 'Patients' attitudes were characterised by a reluctance to insist on receiving basic care or medication for fear of upsetting staff. Although some members of staff were singled out for praise by patients, concerns were expressed about the lack of compassion and uncaring attitude exhibited by others towards vulnerable patients and the marked indifference they showed to visitors.': ibid.

[420] A high priority was placed on the achievement of targets, and in particular the A&E waiting time target. The pressure to meet this generated a fear, whether justified or not, that failure to meet targets could lead to the sack: ibid.

[421] *Francis Report* (n 418) para 80.

In relation to managers responding to criticism, Francis said:

> A common response to concerns has been to refer to generic data or benchmarks such as star rat-
> ings, rather than the experiences of actual patients. While benchmarks and data-based assessments
> are important tools, these should not be allowed to detract attention from the needs and experiences
> of patients. Benchmarks, ratings and status may not always bring to light serious systemic failings.[422]

Francis summarised what went wrong as:

> A long-term failure; problems identified but not addressed effectively; confused view of responsi-
> bilities; a lack of urgency; figures preferred to people; a lack of risk and impact assessment; a focus
> on systems not outcomes; those who received care were not listened to; staff disengaged from the
> process of management; insufficient attention to professional standards; lack of support for staff;
> a weak professional voice in management decisions; a failure to meet the challenge of caring for
> the elderly and the vulnerable; a lack of external and internal transparency; false reassurance taken
> from external assessments; and a disregard for the significance of mortality statistics.[423]

Concerns about the hospital were initially raised externally, including to the Health Service
Ombudsman,[424] but realised officially only after an inspection by the Healthcare Commis-
sion in 2009,[425] followed by two reviews commissioned by the Department of Health.[426]
Concerns were also raised internally, but either ignored or repressed by authoritarian staff.

> The few instances of reports by whistleblowers of which the Inquiry was made aware suggest that
> the Trust has not offered the support and respect due to those brave enough to take this step. The
> handling of these cases is unlikely to encourage others to come forward, and the responses to the
> investigation of the concerns raised have been ineffective.[427]

A later investigation into the quality of care and treatment provided by 14 hospital trusts
with persistently high mortality rates found in every one of them pockets of excellent practice but significant scope for improvement, with each needing to address an urgent set of
actions in order to raise standards of care.[428] The National Medical Director for the NHS in
England, Professor Sir Bruce Keogh, concluded that

> These organisations have been trapped in mediocrity, which I am confident can be replaced by a
> sense of ambition if we give staff the confidence to achieve excellence.[429]

He noted that all 14 trusts faced a different set of circumstances, pressures and challenges,
which included:

— The limited understanding of how important and how simple it can be to genuinely
   listen to the views of patients and staff and engage them in how to improve services;
— the capability of hospital boards and leadership to use data to drive quality improvement;

---

[422] ibid, para 79.

[423] ibid, 396–402.

[424] Baroness Fritchie, DBE, *Review of the Health Service Ombudsman's Approach to Complaints that NHS Service Failure led to Avoidable Death* (Parliamentary and Health Service Ombudsman, 2012).

[425] *Investigation into Mid Staffordshire Foundation Trust*, Healthcare Commission (2009).

[426] *Mid Staffordshire Foundation Trust: A Review of the Procedures for Emergency Admissions and Treatment, and Progress Against the Recommendation of the March Healthcare Commission Report*, Professor Sir George Alberti (2009); *A Review of Lessons Learnt for Commissioners and Performance Managers following the Healthcare Commission Investigation*, Dr David Colin-Thomé (2009).

[427] *Francis Report* (n 418) para 62.

[428] *Review into the Quality of Care and Treatment Provided by 14 Hospital Trusts in England: Overview Report* (NHS, 2013).

[429] ibid.

— the fact that some hospital trusts are operating in geographical, professional or academic isolation, which can lead to difficulties in recruiting enough high quality staff, and an over-reliance on locums and agency staff;
— the lack of value and support being given to frontline clinicians, particularly junior nurses and doctors; and
— imbalance around the use of transparency for the purpose of accountability and blame rather than support and improvement. 'Unless there is a change in mind set then the transparency agenda will fail to fulfil its full potential. Some boards use data simply for reassurance, rather than the forensic, sometimes uncomfortable, pursuit of improvement.

Sir Bruce warned against an authoritarian reaction to the findings, as opposed to a focus on improvement:

> However, this is not a time for hasty reactions and recriminations. Any immediate safety issues we uncovered have been dealt with. It is a time for considered debate, a concerted improvement effort and a focus on clear accountability. So, I expect the carefully considered and agreed action plans to be enacted with serious consequences for failure to do so.[430]

C. Reforms

In response to the Francis Report, the government initiated a series of fundamental reforms in regulation, of which the 2013 policy statement was central.[431] The then Secretary of State for Health, Jeremy Hunt MP, said bluntly:

> The report of the Mid Staffordshire NHS Foundation Trust Public Inquiry makes horrifying reading. At every level, individuals and organisations let down the patients and families that they were there to care for and protect. A toxic culture was allowed to develop unchecked which fostered the normalisation of cruelty and the victimisation of those brave enough to speak up. For far too long, warning signs were not seen, ignored or dismissed. Regulators, commissioners, the Strategic Health Authority, the professional bodies and the Department of Health did not identify problems early enough, or, when they were clear, take swift action to tackle poor care. They failed to act together in the interests of patients. This was a systemic failure of the most shocking kind, and a betrayal of the core values of the health service as set out in the NHS Constitution.[432]

The government noted that action was required by *every part* of the system, namely the four groups of patients and service users, frontline staff, leadership teams, and external bodies such as commissioners, regulators, professional bodies, local scrutiny bodies and Government. It set out a five point plan to 'revolutionise the care people receive':

1. Preventing problems;
2. Detecting problems quickly;
3. Taking action promptly;
4. Ensuring robust accountability, and
5. Ensuring staff are trained and motivated.

[430] ibid.
[431] *Patients First and Foremost. The Initial Government Response to the Report of The Mid Staffordshire NHS Foundation Trust Public Inquiry* (Department of Health, 2013).
[432] ibid, Foreword.

In relation to preventing problems, the policy paper emphasised deliverers of care having *time* to care. Detecting problems quickly would be achieved by appointing a Chief Inspector of Hospitals, and a Chief Inspector of Social Care. Hospitals were to be given clear ratings to assist in declaring and upholding the required standards of care provision: 'Outstanding', 'good', 'requiring improvement' or 'poor'. The CQC would, with the support of local Quality Surveillance Groups, work to ensure there are effective arrangements in place to identify rapidly those hospitals where there is a risk or reality of poor patient care. The CQC would adopt a 'comply or explain' approach, whereby when good practice is identified following inspections, other hospitals which do not follow that practice will be expected to introduce it or explain their non-compliance. This review of best practice will also extend to complaints procedures, to ensure that issues, when raised, are heard, addressed and seen as vital information for improvement as opposed to managerial annoyances. There would be a possibility of legal sanctions at a corporate level, where organisations massage figures or conceal the truth; and the imposition of a statutory duty of candour on providers to inform people if they believe that treatment has caused death or serious injury.[433] Clauses intended to prevent public interest disclosures on issues such as patient safety and death rates would be banned. Further, from 2013 the Parliamentary and Health Service Ombudsman planned to investigate more complaints and share more information with government organisations and the NHS, so as to have more impact for more people.[434]

In relation to taking action promptly, the CQC, working with the National Institute for Health and Care Excellence (NICE), commissioners, professionals, patients and the public, would first draw up simpler fundamental standards[435] which would make explicit the basic standards below which care should never fall. Where the Chief Inspector identifies poor care, a time limited failure regime will apply for both quality and finance. In the first stage, the Chief Inspector will require the hospital board to work with its commissioners to improve within a fixed time. In the second stage, if the hospital is unable to resolve its own problems, the CQC will call in Monitor or the NHS Trust Development Authority to take action. In the final stage, where fundamental problems have not been resolved, the Chief Inspector would initiate a failure regime in which the Board could be suspended or the hospital put into administration. In furtherance of the Chief Inspector's investigations, the CQC, the NHS Commissioning Board, Monitor and the NHS Trust Development Authority would be required to agree the data and methodology to be used for assessing hospitals. Providers will also be expected to publish annual Quality Accounts to demonstrate how well they are meeting these expectations.

In relation to ensuring robust accountability, where the Chief Inspector identifies criminally negligent practice, the CQC would refer the matter to the HSE to consider criminal prosecution of providers or individuals. The regulatory framework of the professional regulatory Councils will be modernised to enable them to be swifter and reactive in tackling

---

[433] Care Act 2014, s 81.

[434] See *More Investigations for More People* (PHSO, 2013); *Regulation 5: Fit and Proper Persons: Directors and Regulation 20: Duty of Candour: Guidance for NHS Bodies November 2014* (Care Quality Commission, November 2014).

[435] Contained in the Health and Social Care Act 2008 (Regulated Activities) Regs 2014, as amended by the Health and Social Care Act 2008 (Regulated Activities (Amendment) Regs 2015 and the Health and Social Care Act 2008 (Regulated Activities) (Amendment) Regs 2012.

poor care by individual professionals. Individual managers may be banned. The roles and responsibilities for tackling failure will be clear.

In relation to ensuring that staff are trained and motivated, every student who seeks NHS funding for a nursing degree would have to first serve as a healthcare assistant for a year to promote frontline expertise. Healthcare assistants would be regulated by a code of conduct and subject to minimum training, with a barring system for any who by virtue of their conduct prove unsuitable for the role. The NHS Leadership Academy is to initiate a programme of encouraging clinical professionals and those outside the NHS to take up managerial positions, with an elite fast-track programme for outsiders and MBA-style programmes for existing clinicians. To improve life-long care skills the NMC is to follow the GMC in introducing a programme of revalidation to ensure its members are up to date and fit to practice. The Department of Health, Ministers and Civil Servants are to have, over the next four years, 'sustained and meaningful experience' with frontline healthcare provision to help the Department reconnect with the patients it serves.

The government's 2013 policy also included a Statement of Common Purpose signed by the Chairs of 14 regulatory bodies, which committed their organisations to the values of the NHS, set out in its Constitution, namely: Working together for patients, respect and dignity, commitment to quality of care, compassion, improving lives, and everyone counts.[436]

A Report by Professor Norman Williams, President of the Royal College of Surgeons, and Sir David Dalton, Chief Executive of Salford Royal Hospital, into aspects of the 'duty of candour' recommended the importance of training and supporting staff, improving the levels and accuracy of reporting of patient safety incidents and spreading and applying lessons learned into practice.[437] It commented:

> While there can be a degree of individual responsibility when something goes wrong (and that is certainly how it feels to the practitioners concerned) it is vital for investigations of harm to consider the human factors in the context of team, organisation and system factors. This is not only because it is a fair and balanced way of understanding individual responsibility, but also because it provides a far firmer basis for understanding why harm has occurred and therefore of preventing future harm. Individual cases of harm, rightly considered, can provide insights into wider organisational issues that can contribute to harm, such as loss of notes, the poor management of resource pressures, and shortcomings in discharge processes.[438]

> A compliance-focused approach will fail. If organisations do not start from the simple recognition that candour is the right thing to do, systems and processes can only serve to structure a regulatory conversation about compliance. The commitment to candour has to be about values and it has to be rooted in genuine engagement of staff, building on their own professional duties and their personal commitment to their patients.[439, 440]

---

[436] *Patients First and Foremost* (n 429); see also *Integrated Care and Support: Our Shared Commitment* (Department of Health, 2013).

[437] *Building a Culture of Candour: A Review of the Threshold for the Duty of Candour and of the Incentives for Care Organisations to be Candid* (Royal College of Surgeons of London, 2014).

[438] ibid, para 1.29.

[439] For the impact of a lack of an enabling environment for candour /open disclosure, see K Mazor et al, 'Communicating with Patients about Medical Errors' (2004) 164(15) *Archives of Internal Medicine* 1690; C Vincent, 'Understanding and Responding to Adverse Events' (2003) 348(11) *New England Journal of Medicine* 1051.

[440] *Building a Culture of Candour* (n 437) para 1.32.

Further details of changes in the enforcement policy of the CQC are given in chapter 13. Although there is a strong backdrop of criminal, civil and administrative 'enforcement' powers, the primary focus is on supporting improvement through advice, encouragement and transparency.

IX. General Conclusions

EU product safety regulation has developed at different speeds for particular product types. The inherent nature of both particular products and particular risks and how they might be controlled will probably always require differentiated approaches. However, a series of general features will be noted here in relation to the various sectoral systems examined above.

First, all models have set *safety as an uncompromising goal*. It is accepted in every sector that safety is a relative concept, that absolute safety is unachievable, so sustained and constant efforts are needed to achieve a prevailingly acceptable level of safety.

Second, the focus of the approach to safety across almost all systems is on *preventive* mechanisms. The achievement of safety depends to a significant extent on the application of accumulated knowledge and of common sense.[441] It is inherent in the nature of human operations in the environment of this world that risk cannot be eliminated, that accidents will happen, and that harm will occur when unintended or undesired.

Third, each model has adopted essentially the same techniques in achieving safety, which can be categorised at the most general level as pre-marketing controls (including provision of information) and post-marketing surveillance. The similarities between these two broad mechanisms as they occur in different sectoral regimes are striking.

The fourth point to note is the important trend, which has developed over time, that every regime has been fleshed out. Regulation has deepened in the detail of its requirements and in the width of its scope. This has occurred in both pre-and—especially—post-marketing systems.

Fifth, the strengthening of post-marketing surveillance systems constitutes a major shift in emphasis from the approach to safety as it existed when virtually every safety regime was introduced. In other words, safety has been recognised to be an ongoing issue that cannot be controlled simply before or at the time of marketing, and required sophisticated and constant post-marketing vigilance and surveillance. Indeed, strong moves to strengthen market surveillance systems have been taken only recently, after recognition that effective control requires the effective, speedy and efficient means of collecting the broadest possible data set. Achieving such collection requires collaboration between all relevant actors—not just professional manufacturers, component or raw material suppliers, distributors, retailers and operators, but also NGOs, officials and even users. However, the growing regulatory burden has led to some interesting reforms: Various drivers have produced 'adaptive licensing' of medicines, based on a life-span approach and with the strong involvement of patients affected in safety decisions.

---

[441] For the impact of a lack of an enabling environment for candour /open disclosure, see K Mazor et al, 'Communicating with Patients about Medical Errors' (2004) 164(15) *Archiv.*

Sixth, every regime is based on a requirement for market operators to have a *safety management system*. The management system is, indeed, at the core of the control mechanisms that firms are expected to operate. There are three reasons for this. First, systems are the means by which companies operate. Accordingly, a successful externally imposed regulatory system is most likely to succeed if it can adopt the same pre-existing operational approach that is at the heart of how businesses manage their operations. Second, a management system approach has widespread acceptance as being the appropriate means to control risk. Risk is both a generic concept that can be applied to every safety system, and is also a concept that recognises that absolute safety is unattainable, so a risk-based system identifies individual hazards that are more or less risky and assists in prioritising them. Third, both pre- and post-marketing management systems rely on assessing sufficient quantities of relevant *information*. The regulatory systems therefore specify the constant collection, aggregation, and evaluation of relevant data, so as to monitor performance and trends, and feedback conclusions for further investigation or action. Quality management systems and data collection are critical to safety monitoring and so sustaining and improving an acceptable level of safety performance. In several situations, especially as medicines and aviation, only the collection and aggregation of a sufficient quantity of data from individual occurrences might reveal a signal that something might be amiss and deserves further attention. The size of a pool of data certainly affects the likely speed of detection: The larger the pool, the quicker the signal should achieve visibility.

Seventh, it follows from the reliance on safety management systems that the true *focus* of regulatory systems has to be on those to whom they are addressed. In considering regulatory systems, a focus on regulators or enforcement misses reality. It is economic operators, the addressees of regulatory requirements, who are the true focus of regulatory requirements. If we wish to understand *how* the rules are applied, the *extent to which* they are applied, the circumstances in which they are *not* applied, and how to *improve compliance*, the focus needs to be on the internal arrangements of firms, and the behaviour of relevant individuals who operate the systems, rather than on external activities such as rare examples of enforcement.

But solely to focus on firms, to the exclusion of regulators and others, also misses the point. Eighth, therefore, a complete picture of a regulatory system, and the maximisation of its effectiveness, can only be gained by seeing firms and regulators as forming *complementary elements of a single integral system*. Both limbs—and indeed other actors—need to operate together if the system is to function. For example, a post-marketing safety vigilance system requires information to be reported by users, collated by firms and reviewed by firms, experts and regulators, before the lessons are disseminated to all of them. The development of peer review in the medical devices sector has assisted competent authorities, notified bodies and manufacturers, horizontally across Member States and vertically in both upward and downward directions: It was not found that competent authorities possessed a monopoly on knowledge, but the peer review process brought gains for all parties.

Ninth, risks and actors are now both so extensive and complex that a regulatory model of regulators commanding and controlling what economic operators do is hopelessly inadequate. The trend in regulation has moved far beyond ideas of downward enforcement, and even of compliance/non-compliance, towards performance and increasing outcomes of safety. Having established a control system, the next stage is to operate it so as to achieve *performance-based regulation*. This approach uses the system to monitor and maintain performance, and strive to continually improve. The *relationship* between regulators and regulatees here shifts to one of mutual inter-dependence and collaboration. As noted in relation to the shift to system management in civil aviation, both businesses and regulators are *collectively responsible*, but for different aspects and in different ways. The operator retains responsibility for management and ownership, and the regulator is responsible for accountability and assurance. The regulator here provides assurance that the management *system* is operating as it should. The regulatory system, therefore, imposes a level of assurance that the system is functioning well at a 'higher' level than at that of the 'operational' level of individual decisions that are taken by the professionals, managers, officials and experts involved.

Tenth, these developments run parallel to and inherently encompass evolutions in how accidents are caused. Instead of viewing the cause of accidents as the result of wrongdoing by firms or individuals (as are inherent in deterrence and rational economic actor models), it is recognised that humans and systems may make incorrect choices that are behaviourally explicable and not driven by malicious intent or conduct that should be blamed, and that, if sufficient information and analysis are applied, modifications in both behaviour and systems can reduce future risk. On this approach, accessing and analysing information is vital in order to learn how to improve, and avoid mistakes. Both the wider view of the causes of accidents and the imperative to encourage humans to freely share information, especially if it might be embarrassing, has driven a shift away from a blame culture towards an open culture. Humans will not share information if either the external regulatory or enforcement culture or the internal managerial and local workforce cultures are unfair or people fear being blamed for being honest.

Hence, the *culture* of an organisation is a critical factor. It is striking when comparing the various safety systems described above that the aviation sector has found through experience two crucial facts. First, reports are necessary not just of accidents but also of near-misses, potential accidents, unsafe practices, or even ways that things can be done better. Second, if reports are to be received, then the motivations and concerns of potential reporters need to be taken into account in a fundamental way. People will not volunteer information if the culture of their group is unconducive to providing support, or is one in which they fear attracting blame or embarrassment. It is not enough just to incentivise reporters by removing the threat of punitive action through a leniency programme. Instead, reporters need to know that they need not fear criticism by providing information that might embarrass them or others, since everyone will freely contribute in a no blame, open culture.

Finally, lessons are available on how organisations learn. The workplace health and safety system highlights the danger of 'information overload' and excessive bureaucracy. Sometimes, what appears to be less control achieves' more safety. The evidence on how SMEs learn shows that imparting simple incremental lessons and changes can be highly productive. In larger companies, systematic means of learning can be deployed, including training, continuous professional development, professional qualification, technological support and nudges, and peer review and feedback mechanisms.

20

Financial Services

This chapter examines the changes to the regulatory system for financial services that have occurred since the crisis that began in 2008. The effects of the succession of crises that occurred were of huge significance for many economies and people. But from the point of view of the inquiry in this book, there have been many serious reports, reforms and academic comments, which highlight aspects of regulatory systems, enforcement and behaviour that are of considerable intrinsic interest and do not appear with such force from considering other sectors. Particularly important aspects that arise are: The extent and nature of regulatory systems; the need for regulation to operate globally, and for local systems to be compatible and work together; the extent to which pursuit of the profit goal can be regulated, whether by the threat or imposition of criminal sanctions, by controlling remuneration, by concentration on customer outcomes, and/or by culture and ethics.

I. The Need for Control

A. Significance of the Sector

Financial services are relied on by almost every individual, and certainly every business and government. This universality means that safety and reliability in banking is vital for almost everyone on the planet, and certainly for economies, governments, businesses, employees and receivers of state benefits. However, the 'trick' of banking is to 'trade in debt' by lending out money deposited whilst maintaining sufficient liquidity to repay the anticipated level of withdrawals.[1] Maintaining the right balance between short and long term debt on both sides depends on stability and the *perception* of liquidity. Public regulation seeks to provide a framework for supporting safe practices in banking and public confidence.[2]

The scale and diversity of the products and services offered by the financial services sector in the UK is considerable. The anatomy of the retail financial services sector in the UK in 2011 was as follows.[3] Each year about 30 million home insurance and 25 million motor insurance policies were bought in the country. Similarly, nearly 25 million travel insurance policies are bought every year, with annual gross written premia of over £700 million.

---

[1] HP Minsky, *Stabilizing the Unstable Economy* (New York, McGraw-Hill, 1986, reprint 2008) 279.

[2] AM Pacces, 'The Future in Law and Finance' *Erasmus Law Lectures 32* (Rotterdam, Eleven International Publishing and Erasmus Universiteit Rotterdam, 2013).

[3] *The Financial Conduct Authority: Approach to Regulation* (Financial Services Authority, June 2011) para 2.40.

Seven of the most significant insurance firms (including life, general and composite insurers) were responsible for over 60 million UK insurance policies. The seven largest deposit takers were estimated to have 125 million UK customer accounts. In 2008/09 around eight million households in England owned their property with a mortgage. In 2010 over 500,000 loans for house purchases were issued, with a value of £77.1 billion. In the period April 2009 to March 2010 over 2.7 million retail investment products (including pensions, investment bonds, endowment policies and ISAs) were sold in the UK.

As at 2013 the estimated value of the UK financial services industry was £234.2 billion.[4] In 2011, financial and insurance services contributed £125.4 billion in gross value added (GVA) to the UK economy, 9.4 per cent of the UK's total GVA.[5] The sector's contribution to UK jobs was around 3.6 per cent. Trade in financial services made up a substantial proportion of the UK's trade surplus in services. In 2010–11 the banking sector contributed £21.0 billion to UK tax receipts in corporation tax, income tax and national insurance.

By the end of 2012, banking sector assets in the euro area (on a consolidated basis, excluding very small entities) were €29.5 trillion, having dropped by almost 12 per cent since 2008.[6] This was accompanied by a decrease of 10 per cent in the number of credit institutions, from 2,909 to 2,645. Between 2008 and 2012, European governments provided state aid to financial institutions totalling €1.5 trillion, over 12 per cent of 2012 EU (European Union) GDP (Gross Domestic Product).[7] The cumulative EU losses in output were estimated to be between €6 and €12.5 trillion, between 50–100 per cent of annual pre-crisis EU GDP.[8]

B. Multiple Serious Failures

It is trite that the financial services sector produced a succession of major problems in recent years. The most dramatic was near-collapse of the global banking system, necessitating emergency state injection of public funds as equity and takeover of failed institutions, exceptional liquidity support arrangements and materially tougher capital requirements.[9] The sequence of events at global level was precipitated by inappropriate securitisation of US subprime mortgages and the collapse of this mortgage-backed securities market in August 2007,[10] the run on Northern Rock in September 2007,[11] bail out of Bear Stearns in March 2008, bankruptcy of Lehman Brothers in September 2008, the international financial crisis and the Euro area sovereign debt crisis. It is important to note that the crisis was global,

[4] Report by the Comptroller and Auditor General. *The Financial Conduct Authority and the Prudential Regulation Authority. Regulating Financial Services* (National Audit Office) HC 1072, Session 2013–14, 25 March 2014.
[5] *Financial Services: Contribution to the UK Economy* (House of Commons Library, SN/EP/06193, August 2012) available at http://www.parliament.uk/briefing-papers/SN06193.pdf.
[6] *Banking Structures Report. November 2013* (ECB, 04/11/2013) www.ecb.europa.eu/pub/pdf/other/bankingstructuresreport201311en.pdf.
[7] Commission Staff Working Document. Economic Review of the Financial Regulation Agenda SWD(2014) 158, 15.5.2014.
[8] ibid.
[9] See D Walker, *A Review of Corporate Governance in UK Banks and other Financial Industry Entities. Final Recommendations* (HM Treasury, 2009).
[10] M Hellwig, 'Systemic Risk in the Financial Sector: An Analysis of the Subprime-Mortgage Financial Crisis' (2009) 157(2) *De Economist* 129–207; GB Gorton, 'Questions and Answers about the Financial Crisis' National Bureau of Economic Research, Working Paper No 1578 (2010).
[11] *The Nationalisation of Northern Rock* (National Audit Office, 2009). *Review of HM Treasury's Management Response to the Financial Crisis* (HM Treasury, March 2012).

because the banking and economic market and system is global, so the solutions required need to be globally integrated.

A considerable literature has emerged on the causes of the various financial crises.[12] The Turner Review identified seven proximate causes of the financial crisis: (1) Large, global macroeconomic imbalances; (2) an increase in commercial banks' involvement in risky trading activities; (3) growth in securitised credit; (4) increased leverage; (5) failure of banks to manage financial risks; (6) inadequate capital buffers; and (7) a misplaced reliance on complex math and credit ratings in assessing risk.[13] Various scholars consider that the global financial crisis was a crisis of unregulated 'shadow banking',[14] and that innovative financiers will continue to create externalities of which they and/or regulators will be unaware until damage has already been done.[15] The Basel Committee on Banking Supervision of the Bank for International Settlements found that a significant cause of systemic instability was the inability of many banks to aggregate risk exposures and concentrations quickly and accurately at the bank group level, across business lines and between legal entities, as a result of weak risk data aggregation capabilities and risk reporting practices, which led to their inability to manage their risks.[16] Professor John Kay's report into the effect of UK equity markets on the competitiveness of UK business concluded that short-termism was a problem in UK equity markets, due to the decline of trust and the misalignment of incentives throughout the equity investment chain.[17]

Apart from the global financial crisis noted above, a series of domestic crises occurred, the following in the UK:

a)   Collapse of significant institutions, such as in the 1970s secondary banking crisis, BCCI in 1991,[18] Barings in 1995[19] and Equitable Life.[20]
b)   Repeated cycles of mis-selling consumer products, and persistent failures to comply with suitability rules,[21] such as pension transfers and opt-outs,[22] payment protection

[12] See Commission Staff Working Document. Economic Review of the Financial Regulation Agenda SWD(2014) 158, 15.5.2014.

[13] A Turner, *The Turner Review: Regulatory Response to the Global Banking Crisis* (Financial Services Authority, 2009).

[14] N Gennaioli, A Shleifer and RW Vishny, 'A Model of Shadow Banking' (2013) 68(4) *Journal of Finance* 1331–63; GB Gorton and A Metrick, 'Securitized Banking and the Run on Repo' (2012) 104(3) *Journal of Financial Economics* 425–51.

[15] Pacces (n 2).

[16] *Consultative Document: Principles for Effective Risk Data Aggregation and Risk Reporting* (Basel Committee on Banking Supervision, Bank for International Settlements, June 2012).

[17] *The Kay Review of UK Equity Markets and Long-term Decision Making: Final Report* (Department for Business, Innovation & Skills, 2012).

[18] *Report of the Inquiry into the Supervision of the Bank of Credit and Commerce International* 1991) HC 192.

[19] Strong criticism of the Bank of England was made in *A New Approach to Regulating and Developing Singapore's Financial Sector* (Singapore, Monetary Authority of Singapore, 1997); Board of Banking Supervision, *Report of the Board of Banking Supervision Inquiry into the Circumstances of the Collapse of Barings* (London, Bank of England, 1995).

[20] The Equitable Life Payments Scheme, and various progress reports, information at https://www.gov.uk/government/collections/equitable-life-payment-scheme-documents; *Administering the Equitable Life Payment Scheme* (NAO, April 2013).

[21] N Moloney, 'The Legacy Effects of the Financial Crisis on Regulatory Design in the EU' in E Ferran, N Moloney, JG Hill and JC Coffee, Jr, *The Regulatory Aftermath of the Global Financial Crisis* (Cambridge, Cambridge University Press, 2012). See *Guidance Consultation. Assessing Suitability* (FSA, 2011), outlining failures to assess the risks that consumers are prepared to sustain.

[22] J Black and R Nobles, 'Personal Pensions Misselling: The Causes and Lessons of Regulatory Failure' (1998) 61(6) *MLR* 789.

insurance (PPI)[23] and endowment mortgages with interest-only loans.[24] A 2011 trawl of 1,200 mystery shopping conducted across 27 EU Member States found that only 43 per cent of retail investment products were deemed to be broadly 'suitable' under a relatively simple rubric (ie basically fulfils shoppers' needs in terms of investment liquidity and risk level) while the remaining 57 per cent were assessed as broadly 'unsuitable'.[25]

c)   Mis-selling of interest rate hedging products, especially to businesses and particularly SMEs (small and medium sized entities).[26]

d)   Systemic manipulation by banks of the London Inter-Bank Offered Rate (LIBOR).[27]

e)   General business practices (various banks, including Barclays),[28] such as allegations of intentionally putting business customers into default so as to reap increased fees (RBS).[29]

f)   Payment of excessive remuneration to employees, especially through bonuses or selling incentives.[30]

One striking feature of this long series of serious failures is why lessons were not learned and changes made earlier. As a result of the emergence of this succession of failures, general

---

[23] P McConnell and K Blacker, 'Systemic Operational Risk: The UK Payment Protection Insurance Scandal' (2012) 7 *Journal of Operational Risk* 79; E Ferran, 'Regulatory Lessons from the Payment Protection Insurance Mis-selling Scandal on the UK' (2012) 13 *European Business Organization Law Review* 247. See recently *Finalised guidance. Payment Protection Products. FSA/OFT Joint Guidance* (FSA/OFT, 2013) FG13/02/OFT1474; *Press Release: Commitment to Help Consumers Agreed at PPI Summit* (BBA, 23/04/2012); *Treasury Committee Publishes Correspondence with FSA and FOS on Mis-selling* (House of Commons Select Committees, 23/05/2012); *Payment Protection Insurance Customer Contact Letters (PPI CCLs)—fairness, clarity and potential consequences* (FG12/17: FSA, July 2012); *PPI Complaint Handling—FSA Fine*, 4 January 2013; *Assessing the Quality of Investment Advice in the Retail Banking Sector. A Mystery Shopping Review* (FSA, February 2013); *TR13/7—Payment Protection Insurance Complaints: Report on the Fairness of Medium-sized Firms' Decisions and Redress* (FCA, August 2013); *Rogue PPI Claim Companies Targeted by Fines and Toughened Regulations* (Ministry of Justice, 21 November 2013).

[24] J Gray, 'The Legislative Basis of Systematic Review and Compensation for the Mis-Selling of retail Financial Services and Products' (2004) 25 *Statute Law Review* 196; *Dealing Fairly with Interest-only Mortgage Customers who Risk being Unable to Repay their Loan* (Financial Conduct Authority, May 2013).

[25] *Consumer Market Study on Advice within the Area of Retail Investment Services-Final Report* (London, Synovate Ltd, 2011) http://ec.europa.eu/consumers/rights/docs/investment_advice_study_en.pdf.

[26] *Interest Rate Hedging Products. Pilot Findings* (FSA, 31 January 2013); Letter from Clive Adamson to anonymous banks on Interest Rate Hedging Products Review, and associated Agreements, 29 January 2013, available at http://www.parliament.uk/business/committees/committees-a-z/commons-select/treasury-committee/news/treasury-committee-publishes-agreement-between-fca-and-banks-on-irhp-review/.

[27] S Miller, 'The Libor Scandal: Culture, Corruption and Collective Action Problems in the Global Banking Sector' in J O'Brien and G Gilligan (eds), *Integrity, Risk and Accountability in Capital Markets. Regulating Culture* (Oxford, Hart Publishing, 2013) (referring to institutional corruption). See *LIBOR, Public Inquiries and FSA Disciplinary Powers* (House of Commons Library, SN/BT/6376, July 2012); *The Wheatley Review of LIBOR: Initial Discussion Paper* (HM Treasury, August 2012); *Fixing LIBOR: Some Preliminary Findings* (House of Commons Treasury Select Committee—HC 481–I, August 2012), Volume I: Report, together with formal minutes and Volume II: Oral evidence; *The Wheatley Review of LIBOR: Final Report* (Martin Wheatley, September 2012); *Wheatley Review of LIBOR—Written Ministerial Statement* (HM Treasury, October 2012); *LIBOR, Public Inquiries and FSA Disciplinary Powers—Commons Library Note* (SN/BT/6376: House of Commons Library, November 2012); *Internal Audit report: A Review of the Extent of Awareness within the FSA of Inappropriate LIBOR Submissions* (FSA, March 2013); Press release, *LIBOR Becomes a Regulated Activity* (BBA, 02/04/2013).

[28] *The Salz Review of Barclays' Business Practices Report to the Board of Barclays PLC* (2013).

[29] *Independent Lending Review. Terms of Reference* (RBS, 2013); Sir A Large and Oliver Wyman, *Independent Lending Review* (25 November 2013); *Press Release: RBS to Act on SME Lending Review Findings*, 1 November 2013; L Tomlinson, *Banks' Lending Practices: Treatment of Businesses in Distress* (2013).

[30] *Final Notice to Lloyds TSB Bank plc and Bank of Scotland plc, 10 December 2013* (FCA), at http://www.fca.org.uk/static/documents/final-notices/lloyds-tsb-bank-and-bank-of-scotland.pdf.

confidence in this vital industry fell to an extremely low level, and remained so,[31] fuelled by popular perception that bankers continued to fail to grasp the public's lack of trust in them as evidenced by the continuing award and receipt of large bonuses, often against loss-making overall results.

C. Multiple Reforms

These issues have provoked extensive discussion at international, EU and national levels, and a raft of major regulatory reforms. In simple terms, the financial regulatory system as previously operated suffered from several severe problems: It did not operate sufficiently globally to enable essentially national regulators to control global institutions, and the ability of regulators to influence banks' prudential, structural and conduct activities was inadequate. This unprecedented period of reform has given rise to a large number of official and academic papers that analyse the issues, and in particular the underlying behaviour, and set out policy responses to reform systems and attempt to control future behaviour.

Before considering the reforms, a brief overview will be given of how the financial services regulatory system had developed and was operated before the crisis.[32]

II. Development of the Regulatory System

For much of the twentieth century the City of London operated as a largely self-contained market in which the self-regulation of 'club government' operated, based on maintaining reputations for trustworthiness, but oligarchic, informal and secretive.[33] After World War II the financial sector was highly fragmented, with participants being vetted to ensure they were 'fit and proper'.[34] Banking supervision in the 1950s was informal,[35] and 'distinctly low-key—to the point of invisibility'.[36]

Over time, demand increased, overseas banks arrived in London, consolidations produced sizeable financial institutions capable of operating in dispersed global markets to support the globalisation of trade. Competition and market growth were also encouraged so as to increase tax revenue. Business models were changed, and incentives for risk taking increased.[37] Economists argued that monetary incentives should be used to motivate people, on the theory that the measure of a company's success would be the extent to which it

---

[31] *Eurobarometer 74, Autumn 2010, Europeans, the EU and the Crisis* (European Commission, 2010).

[32] For detailed coverage, see J Armour, D Awrey, P Davies, J Gordon, C Mayer and J Payne, *Principles of Financial Regulation* (Oxford, Oxford University Press, 2015).

[33] M Moran, *The British Regulatory State: High Modernism and Hyper-Innovation* (Oxford, Oxford University Press, 2003).

[34] S Jaffer, N Morris, E Sawbridge and D Vines, 'How Changes to the Financial Services Industry Eroded Trust' in N Morris and D Vines (eds), *Capital Failure; Rebuilding Trust in Financial Services* (Oxford, Oxford University Press, 2014).

[35] D Kynaston, *The City of London, Volume IV: A Club No More 1945–2000* (London, Pimlico, 2002).

[36] F Capie, *The Bank of England: 1950s to 1979* (Cambridge, Cambridge University Press, 2010).

[37] AG Haldane, 'Control Rights (and Wrongs)', Wincott Annual Memorial Lecture, 24 October 2011.

enriched shareholders. The mantra of maximisation of shareholder value ruled (discussed in chapter 21).

In order to regulate the vibrant, (over-confident) financial services market, a new approach was put in place. The Banking Act 1979 mandated an assessment of credit quality and integrity by the Bank of England based on whether others would do business with a bank, providing a risk-based approach based on information supplied by the bank, with the assumption that banks would act with integrity.[38] A duty to supervise deposit takers was introduced in the Banking Act 1986, and a power to revoke authorisation was included in the first EC Banking Directive of 1977. However, all bank authorisation and supervisory functions were removed from the Bank of England on 1 June 1988,[39] leaving 'a yawning gap' in leadership of regulation and a focus on individual institutions rather than on the financial system as a whole.[40]

The 1986 deregulation of financial markets (known as the Big Bang) introduced reregulation,[41] but regulators saw their role as the expansion of the volume of financial trading in order to increase the profitability of, and therefore the taxable revenue of, the financial sector.[42]

> The form of financial services regulation that, in the UK, was introduced by the Big Bang was an excessively detailed attempt to provide rules and codes which … emptied financial services regulation of moral content…. [and had no] regard for the legitimate interests of the client…. It is *in principle* impossible to *ex ante* specify the rules because such specification must create the possibility of gaming those rules, as the process of rule-following is reflexive.[43]

Before the 2008 crisis, the FSA (Financial Services Authority) regulated 29,000 firms. It operated on a risk basis, namely addressing issues that had the potential to cause harm to one or more of the FSA's statutory objectives of maintaining confidence in the UK financial system, contributing to the protection and enhancement of stability of the UK financial system, securing the appropriate degree of protection for consumers, and the reduction of financial crime.

In addition to EU rules on 'passporting', whereby financial service firms authorised in other Member States are able to operate in the UK without being authorised by the Prudential Regulatory Authority (PRA) or Financial Conduct Authority (FCA) and being subject to a lesser extent of regulatory control,[44] two tiers of approval existed before the crisis.[45] Most firms and individuals were required to be 'authorised' to conduct regulated financial

---

[38] For the information in this paragraph see A Campbell and J Dahlgreen, 'The Future Role and Power of the Bank of England' in J O'Brien and G Gilligan (eds), *Integrity, Risk and Accountability in Capital Markets. Regulating Culture* (Oxford, Hart Publishing, 2013).

[39] Bank of England Act 1998, Part III.

[40] Campbell and Dahlgreen (n 38).

[41] D Gowland, *The Regulation of Financial Markets in the 1990s* (Cheltenham, Edward Elgar, 1990).

[42] S Vogel, *Freer Markets, More Rules* (Ithaca NY, Cornell University Press, 1996) ch 5.

[43] J O'Brien, 'Back to the Future: James M Landis, Regulatory Purpose and the Rationale for Intervention in Capital Markets' in J O'Brien and G Gilligan (eds), *Integrity, Risk and Accountability in Capital Markets. Regulating Culture* (Oxford, Hart Publishing, 2013) 68–69.

[44] See http://www.fca.org.uk/firms/being-regulated/passporting.

[45] The following description is taken from R Sullivan, *Quality in Other Regulated Professions* (Legal Services Board, November 2011) at http://www.legalservicesboard.org.uk/news_publications/latest_news/pdf/quality_in_ other_regulated_professions.pdf.

activities in the UK, whilst some only needed to be registered to do so. Both authorised and registered firms were required to meet standards and provide the regulator with information so it could monitor the business. The requirements were more onerous for those who were authorised, for example in the amount of information to be provided to the regulator or safeguards that applied to funds. Some payment services providers and electronic money institutions could be registered instead of authorised. A payment services firm could choose to be registered instead of authorised, where it had transferred an average of less than €3 million a month to people or businesses in the preceding 12 months.

A firm was required to employ personnel with the necessary skills, knowledge and expertise to discharge the responsibilities allocated to them (the 'competent employees rule'). The FSA expected firms to assess such individuals as competent. Firms were required to appoint an internal supervisor, whose function was 'paramount in ensuring good quality competence assessments within firms'. While the FSA allowed firms to decide on the most appropriate arrangements, they expected firms to have suitably qualified and experienced staff.[46]

The nature and extent of supervision of firms by the regulator was dependent on how much of a risk the regulator considered them to be. Firms' risk was assessed against a framework called the Advanced Risk-Responsive Operating framework (ARROW), which applied both to individual firms and to risks that involve several firms or the market generally (themes).[47]

If a firm was assessed as high or medium impact, the FSA coordinated its work through a relationship manager, who carried out a risk assessment on a cycle of one to four years, determining a risk mitigation programme proportionate to the risks identified. Planned ARROW visits to the firms were also undertaken throughout the regulatory period. The FSA also applies baseline monitoring activities, undertaken for all firms regardless of their impact scores, involving analysing a firm's financial and other returns.

If a firm was assessed as low impact it did not have a specific risk assessment or risk mitigation programme. They were usually required to send regulatory reports twice a year. Small firms are given the Firm Contact Centre as a primary contact, instead of a relationship manager. To regulate over 20,000 small firms, the FSA collected information, analysed the data to identify collective risks and investigated matters further, where necessary. The results were communicated through the website and press.

A. A Corpus of International Actors

A significant number of bodies have been involved in global aspects of regulation and setting global standards. These include the Basel Committee for Banking Supervision (BCBS), the G20 and its Financial Stability Board (FSB), the Organisation for Economic Cooperation and Development (OECD), the International Monetary Fund (IMF), the World Bank,

---

[46] For an explanation of the competent employees rules see http://www.fca.org.uk/firms/being-regulated/meeting-your-obligations/Training-and-Competence.

[47] For an explanation of how the FCA 'ranks' firms for supervision in terms of possible impact on the FCA's objectives see the guidance at: http://www.fca.org.uk/static/documents/fca-approach-advancing-objectives.pdf, 18 onwards.

the International Organisation of Securities Commissions (IOSCO), the International Association of Insurance Supervisors (IAIS), and the World Trade Organisation (WTO).

In Europe organisations include the European Commission, the European Banking Authority (EBA), European Insurance and Occupational Pensions Authority (EIOPA), Financial Action Task Force (FATF), the European Securities and Markets Authority (ESMA), the European Systemic Risk Board (ESRB) and the Joint Forum. The EU was proceeding with its normal policy of harmonising rules so as to facilitate a single market for financial services, including disclosure in the primary and secondary markets,[48] control of abusive practices,[49] and markets in financial instruments.[50] Before the crisis, the priority for the period to 2010 was thought to be further consolidation.[51]

III. The Structure of Reform

In the wake of the global financial crisis agreement was reached at global level on a package of reforms aimed at strengthening the regulation, supervision and risk management of the banking sector. Political leadership was taken by the G20, which produced a series of key policy papers that have driven national reforms.[52] The G20 swiftly reformed the Financial Stability Forum, which was created after that Asian financial crisis 1997–98, as the Financial Stability Board (FSB), with an expanded membership including the European Commission.[53]

The Bank for International Settlements, through its Basel Committee on Banking Supervision (BCBS), set out the minimum standard for sound prudential regulation and supervision of banks and banking systems in 1997. The significant Basel III revisions of 2012 required banks to hold more and better quality capital and higher levels of liquidity and also aimed to strengthen the requirements for supervisors, the approaches to supervision and supervisors' expectations of banks.[54] The 29 core principles for effective Banking Supervision are quoted at Box 20.2.

The European Commission set out a programme for reforming the regulatory and supervisory framework for EU financial markets[55] to implement, inter alia, the Basel III requirements, based on the conclusions of the de Larosière Report.[56] The general thrust of the

---

[48] Dir 2003/71/EC on the prospectus to be published when securities are offered to the public or admitted to trading and amending Dir 2001/34/EC; Dir 2004/109/EC on the harmonisation of transparency requirements in relation to information about issuers whose securities are admitted to trading on a regulated market and amending Dir 2001/34/EC.

[49] Dir 2003/6/EC on insider dealing and market manipulation.

[50] Dir 2004/39/EC on Markets in Financial Instruments (MiFID).

[51] *White Paper on Financial Services Policy 2005–2010*, COM(2005) 629.

[52] G Brown, *Beyond the Crash: Overcoming the First Crisis of Globalisation* (New York, Simon & Schuster, 2010) 117–18.

[53] G20, *Leaders' Statement: The Pittsburgh Summit*, September 24/25, 2009.

[54] Basel Committee on Banking Supervision, *Core Principles for Effective Banking Supervision* (Bank for International Settlements, September 2012). See also *Progress Report on Implementation of the Basel Regulatory Framework* (Basel Committee on Banking Supervision, 2014).

[55] *Communication: Driving European Recovery* COM(2009) 114, 4.3.2009.

[56] *Report of the High-Level Group on Financial Supervision in the EU* (European Commission, 2009). Mr Jacques de Larosière was chairman of the group.

EU reforms[57] was endorsed by the EU's Liikanen High-Level Expert Group on reforming the structure of the EU banking sector.[58] The Liikanen Group concluded that no particular business model had fared particularly well, or particularly poorly, in the financial crisis; and that the response needed was to address weaknesses that endanger financial system stability through a number of regulatory reforms.[59]

The European Commission admitted:[60]

3.6. The role of supervisory authorities

Generally speaking, the recent financial crisis revealed the limits of the existing supervision system: in spite of the availability of certain tools enabling them to intervene in the internal governance of financial institutions, not all supervisory authorities, either at national or European level, were able to carry out effective supervision in an environment of financial innovation and rapid change in the business model of financial institutions.

Furthermore, the supervisory authorities also failed to establish best practices for corporate governance in financial institutions. In many cases, supervisory authorities did not ensure that financial institutions' risk management systems and internal organisation were adapted to changes in their business model and financial innovation. Supervisory authorities also sometimes failed to adequately enforce strict eligibility criteria for members of boards of directors of financial institutions ('fit and proper test').[61]

The following analysis summarises the most important points in relation to how controls on behaviour are expected to apply. It does not attempt to be a complete analysis of either the financial regulatory system or of the various reforms that have been made. The purpose is to highlight some of the most important ways in which it has been thought to be relevant for public regulation to intervene in controlling the behaviour of a free market in financial services. The reforms will be considered under the following headings:

A.   Regulation, supervision and enforcement.
B.   Structural stability and recovery.

---

[57] Initiatives included a Bank Resolution and Recovery Directive (additional separation of activities conditional on the recovery and resolution plan; use of bail-in as a resolution tool) and Capital Requirements Dir/Reg (CRD IV, replacing Dirs 2006/48 and 2006/49 and including corporate governance requirements); Proposal on structural measures improving the resilience of EU credit institutions, COM(2014) 43, 29.1.2014. See *Bank Structural Reform—Position of the Eurosystem on the Commission's Consultation Document* (European Central Bank, January 2013); *Reforming the Structure of the EU Banking Sector* (European Commission, May 2013); *Consultation by the Commission on the Structural Reform of the Banking Sector* (MARKT/H2: European Commission, June 2013); *Memo. A Comprehensive EU Response to the Financial Crisis: A Strong Financial Framework for Europe and a Banking Union for the Eurozone* (European Commission, 10 July 2013) MEMO/13/679; *Proposal for a Regulation of the European Parliament and the Council Establishing Uniform Rules and a Uniform Procedure for the Resolution of Credit Institutions and Certain Investment Firms in the Framework for a Single Resolution Mechanism and a Single Bank Resolution Fund* (European Commission, July 2013); Press release. *Council Approves Single Supervisory Mechanism for Banking* (European Council, 15 October 2013). See LM Levi, 'The European Banking Authority: Legal Framework, Operations and Challenges Ahead' (2013) 28 *Tulane European & Civil Law Forum* 51. See also *Overview of the Potential Implications of Regulatory Measures for Banks' Business Models* (European Banking Authority, 2015).

[58] *High-level Expert Group on Reforming the Structure of the EU Banking Sector* (EC, October 2012).

[59] ibid.

[60] *Green Paper, Corporate Governance in Financial Institutions and Remuneration Policies*, European Commission COM(2010) 284 (footnotes omitted).

[61] See, for example, *Corporate Governance and the Financial Crisis, Recommendations* (Paris, OECD, 2009) 27.

C.   Corporate governance.
D.   Transparency.
E.   Increasing consumer protection and facilitating redress.
F.   Controls on Remuneration.
G.   Culture.

A. Regulation, Supervision and Enforcement

The near universal consensus was that regulation had failed.[62] Two competing narratives have been, first, that dynamic financial markets have outpaced static regulation, which was then overwhelmed by a 'perfect storm' and, second, that the regulatory system was captured by feckless regulators.[63] However, a more accurate analysis would be that it was the *type* and *extent* of regulation that had previously existed that had failed. The universal response was to reform and strengthen regulatory controls, not to remove them or replace them with other approaches such as private enforcement. A study of the credit crisis as it evolved until 2008 in Germany, Ireland and the UK found that different manifestations of financial distress occurred but all evoked similar reactions by regulators and national governments.[64] Professor Jack Coffee has noted that the 'regulatory sine curve'[65] leads to a regulatory boom after a financial market bust, followed by relaxation.

i. European Union Reforms

In the EU, G20-inspired regulatory reform has not only provoked a speeding up in measures to integrate the market in financial services, with reform of various measures and extension of regulation into new areas, but the EU area sovereign debt crisis drove a major relocation of regulatory control over financial markets, with centralisation of control in the euro area and indeed beyond.[66] The sheer volume of EU legislative initiatives in financial services is considerable—over 40 pieces of legislation.[67] As noted, the de Larosière Report gave the European Commission a platform to initiate reforms on improving regulation and supervision[68] and strengthening the institutional architecture of EU-level financial services supervision.[69]

---

[62] S Emmenegger, 'Procedural Consumer Protection and Financial Market Supervision' Bern University Law School, Working Papers Law No 2010/05 at http://papers.ssrn.com/sol3/papers.cfm?abstract_id=1616322.

[63] See AJ Levitin, 'The Politics of Financial Regulation and the Regulation of Financial Politics' (2014) 127(7) *Harvard Law Review* 1991, reviewing six books on the international financial crisis by Bernanke, Blinder, Bair, Barofsky, Connaughton and Admati & Hellwig.

[64] W Forbes, SF O'Donohoe and J Prokop, 'Financial Regulation and Nation State Crisis Management: Evidence from Germany, Ireland and the UK' ZenTra Working Paper in Transnational Studies No 18/2013.

[65] J Coffee, 'The Political Economy of Dodd-Frank: Why Financial Reform tends to be Frustrated and Systemic Risk Perpetuated' (2012) 97 *Cornell Law Review* 101.

[66] A review of securities markets and not the banking reforms see N Moloney, 'Resetting the Location of Regulatory and Supervisory Control over EU Financial Markets: Lessons from Five Years On' (2013) 62 *International and Comparative Law Quarterly* 955–65. For banking systems see Ferran, Moloney, Hill and Coffee, Jr (n 21).

[67] See summary at *Communication from the Commission. A Reformed Financial Sector for Europe* COM(2014) 279, 15.5.2014.

[68] *Driving European Recovery* COM(2009) 114.

[69] *European Financial Supervision* COM(2009) 252.

The Basel III 'more capital, more liquidity' requirements were introduced via the Capital Requirements Directive IV and the Capital Requirement Regulations.[70] Revisions were made to the Markets in Financial Instruments legislation, especially on authorisation, transparency and reporting,[71] and to the Market Abuse Directive[72] and the Transparency Directive.[73] Controls were extended to include the hedge fund sector, with OTC (over the counter) derivative markets and credit rating agencies,[74] OTC derivatives and trade repositories,[75] and credit rating agencies.[76] The EU also exerted control over national sanctioning regimes.[77]

The boldest step, taken in response to the Euro area sovereign debt crisis,[78] was the creation of banking union and Single Supervisory Mechanism (SSM), proposed in 2012. This introduced direct supervision of banks and in scope investment firms and national regulators by EU bodies, with mechanisms for intensive rule-making leading to a (massive) Single Supervisory Handbook produced by the European Banking Authority (EBA), and empowering the EBA and European Securities and Markets Authority (ESMA) to propose technical standards for adoption by the Commission.[79] The system also includes common deposit protection and single bank resolution mechanisms, to ensure coherence in banking supervision for all 27 EU countries.[80]

From 2011, the EBA, comprising the bank supervisors of the Member States, is at the centre of the European financial regulatory system, sharing responsibilities with the ECB.[81] The EBA's powers include:[82] To develop binding technical standards; to ensure compliance with EU law; to take certain action in the event of an emergency situation; and to

[70] Dir 2013/36/EU and Reg (EU) No 575/2013.
[71] Reg (EU) No 648/2012 2014 on markets in financial instruments; Dir 2014/65/EU of the European Parliament and of the Council of 15 May 2014 on markets in financial instruments and amending Dir 2002/92/EC and Dir 2011/61/EU (recast); Reg (EU) No 600/2014 of the European Parliament and of the Council of 15 May 2014 on markets in financial instruments and amending Reg (EU) No 648/2012.
[72] COM(2011) 656/4; Reg (EU) No 596/2014 of the European Parliament and of the Council of 16 April 2014 on market abuse (market abuse regulation) and repealing Dir 2003/6/EC of the European Parliament and of the Council and Commission Dirs 2003/124/EC, 2003/125/EC and 2004/72/EC (1).
[73] COM(2011) 683.
[74] Dir 2011/61/EU on Alternative Investment Fund Managers and amending Dirs 2003/41/EC and 2009/65/EC and Regs (EC) No 1060/2009 and (EU) No 1095/2010. See J Payne, 'Private Equity and its Regulation in Europe' (2012) 12 *European Business Organization Law Review* 559–85; E Ferran, 'After the Crisis: The Regulation of Hedge Funds and Private Equity in the EU' (2012) 12 *European Business Organization Law Review* 379–413; and D Awrey, 'The Limits of EU Hedge Fun Regulation' (2011) 5 *Law and Financial Markets Review* 119–28.
[75] Reg (EU) No 648/2012 on OTC Derivative Transactions, Central Counterparties and Trade Repositories.
[76] Reg (EU) No 1060/2009 on Credit Rating Agencies, Reg (EU) No 513/2011, Proposal COM(2011) 747/2.
[77] *Reinforcing Sanctioning Regimes in the Financial Services sector* COM(2010) 716; Dir 2014/57/EU on Criminal Sanctions for Insider Dealing and Market Manipulation COM(2011) 654.
[78] E Ferran, 'Crisis-driven Regulatory Reform: Where in the World is the EU Going?' in Ferran, Moloney, Hill and Coffee, Jr (n 21).
[79] Reg (EU) No 1095/2010 establishing a European Supervisory Authority (European Securities and markets Authority) (ESMA Reg) [2010] OJ L331/84. The same core content is also in Reg (EU) No 1093/2010 [on European Banking Authority] and Reg (EU) No 1094/2010 [on European Insurance and Occupational Pensions Authority].
[80] *Press Release. Towards a Banking Union* (CEC, 10/09/2012); *A Roadmap towards a Banking Union*, COM(2012) 510 final, September 2012; *Communication: A New Eurozone Banking Supervision System to Help Protect Taxpayers across Europe* (European Commission, September 2012); *Proposal for a Council Regulation Conferring Specific Tasks on the European Central Bank Concerning Policies Relating to the Prudential Supervision of Credit Institutions* COM(2012) 511 final, September 2012; *Towards a Genuine Economic and Monetary Union: Interim Report* (European Council, October 2012).
[81] E Ferran and V Babis, 'The European Single Supervisory Mechanism' Cambridge Research Paper No 10/2013.
[82] Reg (EU) 1093/2010, art 8.

settle cross-border disputes between supervisors by imposing a binding decision. It also has responsibilities that include writing non-binding guidelines and recommendations, conducting peer reviews, mediating disputes between supervisors on a non-binding basis, promoting supervisory cooperation, convergence and coordination, facilitating home/host Member State relations and providing opinions to the Union Institutions. The role of a national regulator will primarily be one of supervision and enforcement.[83] The Treaty on Stability, Coordination and Governance in the Economic and Monetary Union of 2 March 2012 was signed by 25 of the 27 Member States (excluding the UK[84] and Czech Republic), and initiated a new 'fiscal compact', with oversight of national budgets by the Commission, automatic consequences for breaches of agreed limits, verification of national transposition of the balanced budget rule and penalties by the Court of Justice, and significantly stronger coordination of economic policies in areas of common interest.[85] The legislation establishing the SSM was passed in 2013, and became effective in November 2014.[86] The ECB stated its supervisory principles as: Use of best practices; integrity and decentralisation; homogeneity within the SSM; consistency with the Single Market; independence and accountability; risk-based approach; proportionality; adequate levels of supervisory activity for all credit institutions; and effective and timely corrective measures.[87] It noted that it is empowered to require significant credit institutions in participating Member States to take steps *at an early stage* to address problems regarding compliance with prudential requirements, the soundness of management, and sufficiency of the coverage of risks.[88] In relation to enforcement and sanctions for breach of regulatory requirements, the ECB may impose administrative pecuniary penalties on credit institutions of up to twice the amount of the profits gained or losses avoided, or up to 10 per cent of the total turnover in the preceding business year.[89]

2014 reviews of the EU system noted that the institutions had been quickly established and were functioning.[90] However, a global review found that many banks had made

---

[83] H Sants, 'Delivering "Twin Peaks" within the FSA', speech February 2, 2012.

[84] Two reasons were cited: The political necessity of containing considerable national Euroscepticism, and a need to safeguard the City of London: The former may have been expedient but the latter had little logic.

[85] Treaty on Stability, Coordination and Governance in the Economic and Monetary Union, 2 March 2012. See European Commission, *A Roadmap to Stability and Growth* (COM (2011) 669); European Commission, *Proposal for a Regulation on Common Provisions for Monitoring and Assessing Draft Budgetary Plans and Ensuring the Correction of Excessive Deficit of the Member States in the Euro Area* (COM (2011) 821); European Commission, *Proposal for a Regulation on the Strengthening of Economic and Budgetary Surveillance of Member States Experiencing or Threatened with Serious Difficulties with Respect to their Financial Stability in the Euro Area* (COM/2011/819); European Council Statement of EU Heads of State or Government (26 October 2011); European Commission, *Green Paper on the Feasibility of Introducing Stability Bonds* (COM/2011/818); A Merkel and N Sarkozy, 'Letter to President van Rompuy' (7 December 2011, online: www.elysee.fr/president/root/bank_objects/111207Lettre_adressee_a_M_Herman_Van_Rompuy.pdf); European Council, *Statement by the Euro Area Heads of State or Government* (9 December 2011).

[86] Reg (EU) No 1024/2013 conferring specific tasks on the European central Bank concerning policies relating to the prudential supervision of credit institutions. See also Public Consultation on a Fraft Regulation of the European Central Bank (Draft Framework Regulation), February 2014. E Wymeersch, 'The Single Supervisory Mechanism or "SSM", Part One of the Banking Union' *Gent University Financial Law Institute, Working paper WP 2014-01*.

[87] *Guide to Banking Supervision* (European Central Bank, 2014).

[88] ibid, para 4.2.8.

[89] ibid, para 4.2.9.

[90] Report from the Commission to the European Parliament and the Council on the mission and organisation of the European Systemic Risk Board (ESRB), European Commission COM(2014) 508; Report from the

insufficient progress in implementing the Basel Committee's 2003 and 2011 Principles.[91] Peer review of the United Kingdom in September 2013 found that good progress had been made in addressing three areas of macro-prudential policy framework, micro-prudential supervisory approach, and supervision and oversight of central counterparties (CCPs), although reforms were ongoing.[92]

ii. United Kingdom Reforms

In 2013, the UK government claimed to have acted since 2010 to transform the banking industry through four key areas of reform:[93]

— *Supervision*: Putting the Bank of England back at the centre of the supervisory regime, with new powers to identify and address systemic risks as they emerge, ensuring safe banks that will not bring down the economy in the future.
— *Structure*: Separating the branch on the high street from the trading floor in the City to protect taxpayers when mistakes are made.
— *Culture*: Imposing higher standards of conduct on the banking industry by introducing a criminal sanction for reckless misconduct that leads to bank failure, and a more stringent approval regime for senior bankers.
— *Competition*: Empowering consumers by giving them greater choice, which should incentivise innovation and competition within the banking sector.

Two aspects that deserve particular mention are the re-ordering of regulatory bodies, in relation both to their roles and also their relationships with each other and with firms, and the introduction of new responsibilities and sanctions for senior managers.

Some political criticism was directed at the FSA for exposing consumers to scandalous detriment through a 'box-ticking' culture that failed to detect or predict failures.[94] However, it could equally be said that the root causes lay in more fundamental political choices over the design and restrictions of the regulatory system.

The UK government divided regulatory functions between different authorities, in order to strengthen supervision of the conduct of firms, which had previously deliberately been

---

Commission to the European Parliament and the Council on the operation of the European Supervisory Authorities (ESAs) and the European System of Financial Supervision (ESFS), European Commission COM(2014) 509; *Banking Structures Report* (European Central Bank, 2014).

[91] *Review of the Principles for the Sound Management of Operational Risk* (Basel Committee on Banking Supervision, 2014).

[92] *Peer Review of the United Kingdom. Review Report* (Financial Stability Board, 10 September 2013). This was carried out under the International Monetary Fund's Financial Sector Assessment Program (FSAP), established in 1999. See also *The Bank of England's Supervision of Financial Market Infrastructures—Annual Report* (Bank of England, 2014).

[93] Press release *Banking Reform Act Becomes Law* (HM Treasury, 18/12/2013), available at https://www.gov.uk/government/news/banking-reform-act-becomes-law. An alternative view of the last bullet point might be that regulators were given a remit to increase competition; the FCA through the FS Act 2012 and the PRA in the Banking Reform Act 2014. Reform proposals by the previous government were made in *Reforming Financial Markets* (HM Treasury, 2009) Cm 7667.

[94] In relation to that test, see *Treasury Select Committee (TSC) Report* on the appointment of John Griffith-Jones as Chair-designate of the Financial Conduct Authority, 18 January 2013.

'light touch'.[95] The Financial Policy Committee (FPC), within the Bank of England, was made responsible for protecting the stability of the financial system as a whole and macro-prudential regulation. In April 2013 the FSA was effectively split into two agencies. The Prudential Regulation Authority (PRA), a subsidiary of the Bank of England, supervises deposit takers, insurers and a small number of significant investment firms. The Financial Conduct Authority (FCA) is responsible for regulating conduct in retail and wholesale markets (including both exchange-operated markets and over-the-counter (OTC) dealing); supervising the trading infrastructure that supports those markets; and for the prudential regulation of firms not prudentially regulated by the PRA. The FCA has the single strategic objective 'to ensure that the relevant markets function well' and three statutory operational objectives:[96]

— To secure an appropriate degree of protection for consumers;
— to protect and enhance the integrity of the UK financial system; and
— to promote effective competition in the interests of consumers.

The FCA was given various new powers: In product intervention; to direct firms to withdraw or amend misleading financial promotions with immediate effect; and to publish the fact that a warning notice in relation to a disciplinary matter has been issued.[97] Primary functions are to promote good outcomes for consumers, to intervene earlier to tackle potential risks to consumers and market integrity before they crystallise and to use new tools of intervention to prevent consumer detriment emerging.[98] The regulation of consumer credit was transferred from the Office of Fair Trading to the FCA in April 2014.[99] The functions and enforcement policies of the Bank of England, PRA and FCA are described in greater detail in chapter 13.[100]

In 2014, the FCA regulated the conduct of 26,000 firms and the prudential aspects of 23,000 of them, and 1,700 firms were prudentially regulated by the PRA.[101] From 1 April 2014 the FCA took over responsibility for the regulation of around a further 50,000 consumer credit firms from the Office of Fair Trading. The FCA now issues an annual strategic

---

[95] Financial Services Act 2012, s 6. *A New Approach to Financial Regulation: Securing Stability, Protecting Consumers* (TSO, 2012) Cm8268; *Journey to the Financial Conduct Authority* (Financial Services Authority, 2012); *Sound Banking: Delivering Reform* (HM Treasury, 2012); *Banking Reform: A New Structure for Stability and Growth* (HM Treasury and Department for Business, Innovation & Skills, 2013).

[96] FSMA amended by the Financial Services Act 2012 and supporting legislation http://www.fca.org.uk/static/documents/fca-approach-advancing-objectives.pdf.

[97] See *The Financial Conduct Authority: Approach to Regulation* (Financial Services Authority, 2011).

[98] *The Financial Conduct Authority: Approach to Regulation* (Financial Services Authority, 2011) para 1.11.

[99] *A New Approach to Financial Regulation: Transferring Consumer Credit Regulation to the Financial Conduct Authority* (HM Treasury and Department for Business, Innovation & Skills, 2013); *High-level Proposals for an FCA Regime for Consumer Credit* (Financial Services Authority, 2013) CP13/7.

[100] A 2014 review of the new regulators concluded that it is premature to evaluate their performance: Report by the Comptroller and Auditor General. *The Financial Conduct Authority and the Prudential Regulation Authority. Regulating Financial Services* (National Audit Office) HC 1072, Session 2013–14, 25 March 2014.

[101] Report by the Comptroller and Auditor General. *The Financial Conduct Authority and the Prudential Regulation Authority. Regulating Financial Services* (National Audit Office) HC 1072, Session 2013–14, 25 March 2014. For conduct only: Banks, building societies, investment banks, credit unions, friendly societies, life insurers, general insurers, wholesale and commercial insurers and reinsurers, and Lloyd's and Lloyd's Agents. For conduct and prudential: Personal investment firms, insurance intermediaries, mortgage intermediaries, investment managers, non-deposit taking lenders, corporate finance firms, wholesale firms, custodians, professional firms, markets (exchanges and infrastructure providers), collective investment schemes, travel insurance firms, media firms, other brokers, managing agents and investment firms.

overview of its views on the risks to the sector and firms.[102] This has considerable potential in providing feedback on the system as a whole.

iii. Sanctions on Individuals

The report by the High-Level Group on Financial Supervision in the EU[103] recommended that a 'sound prudential and conduct of business framework for the financial sector must rest on strong supervisory and sanctioning regimes' but that Member States' competent authorities lacked adequate resources, powers or willingness to detect and investigate abuses. The Group recommended that supervisory authorities must be equipped with sufficient powers to act and should be able to rely on 'equal, strong and deterrent sanctions regimes against all financial crimes, sanctions which should be enforced effectively'.[104] Accordingly, pre-existing sanctions for insider dealing and market manipulation practices, jointly referred to as 'market abuse', were strengthened by requiring minimum standards for criminal offences and criminal sanctions for intentional insider dealing and market manipulation.[105] The Commission's policy was based on the view that sanctions in national regimes lacked impact and were insufficiently dissuasive, and that criminal sanctions, in particular imprisonment, are generally considered to send a strong message of disapproval that could increase the dissuasiveness of sanctions, provided that they are appropriately applied by the criminal justice system.[106] Effects of reputation were consciously intended:

> Criminal convictions for market abuse offences, which often result in widespread media coverage, help to improve deterrence as they demonstrate to potential offenders that the authorities take serious enforcement action which can result in imprisonment or other criminal sanctions and a criminal record.[107]

In the UK, three new offences were introduced in 2013: Making false or misleading statements; creating false or misleading impressions; and making false or misleading statements or creating a false or misleading impression in relation to specified benchmarks.[108] These offences originated from strong political pressure from the Parliamentary Commission on Banking Standards, responding to public concern, rather than from academic or research-based foundations.

---

[102] See *FCA Risk Outlook 2014* (FCA, 2014).

[103] Report of the High-Level Group on Financial Supervision in the EU, Brussels, 25.2.2009, 23. See also report of the Committee of European Securities Regulators (CESR) on administrative measures and sanctions, CESR/08-099, February 2008.

[104] Report of the High-Level Group on Financial Supervision in the EU, ibid, para 83.

[105] Dir on insider dealing and market manipulation (market abuse), 2003/6/EC. See Proposal for a Dir on criminal sanctions for insider dealing and market manipulation, COM(2011) 654, 20.10.2011 and Proposal for a Reg on insider dealing and market manipulation (market abuse), COM(2011) 651, 20.10.2011. The proposals were designed to be consistent with the emerging EU policy on the role of criminal law: see *Towards an EU Criminal Policy—Ensuring the Effective Implementation of EU Policies through Criminal Law* COM(2011) 573. Note that the UK opted out of the Regulation.

[106] European Commission, Communication on Reinforcing sanctioning regimes in the financial sector, COM(2010) 716, 8 December 2010. Five Member States did not provide for criminal sanctions for disclosure of inside information by primary insiders, eight Member States did not do so for secondary insiders, one Member State did not impose criminal sanctions for insider dealing by a primary insider, and four did not do so for market manipulation.

[107] ibid.

[108] Financial Services Act 2012, ss 89–95; see *Financial Services Act 2012: Summary of Consultation Responses on Draft Secondary Legislation and Government Response* (HM Treasury, 2013).

The UK's Parliamentary Commission on Banking Standards considered that a key problem lay with a lack of individual responsibility of bankers, and that the answer lay in punitive accountability:

The problem

Too many bankers, especially at the most senior levels, have operated in an environment with insufficient personal responsibility. Top bankers dodged accountability for failings on their watch by claiming ignorance or hiding behind collective decision-making. They then faced little realistic prospect of financial penalties or more serious sanctions commensurate with the severity of the failures with which they were associated. Individual incentives have not been consistent with high collective standards, often the opposite.[109]

In order to improve standards across the banking sector, the Parliamentary Commission recommended a package of reforms that were adopted by Parliament: Regulators needed further powers in relation to individual conduct, so the most important responsibilities within banks should be assigned to specific, senior individuals[110] so they could be held accountable; a certification regime underpinned by Banking Standards Rules; a new criminal offence for Senior Managers of reckless misconduct in the management of a bank;[111] a new remuneration code; and a power for the regulator to cancel all outstanding deferred remuneration for senior staff in the event of their banks needing taxpayer support. The Parliamentary Commission's approach was supported by the PRA and FCA.[112] However, practitioner lawyers criticised the notion of sanctioning senior managers of failed banks, on the basis that it failed to address two key problems: A lack of clarity about who was responsible for failure; and the absence of an agreed standard to which key roles should be

---

[109] *Changing Banking for Good: Report of the Parliamentary Commission on Banking Standards: Volume I: Summary, and Conclusions and Recommendations HC Paper No.27-I, II* Parliamentary Commission on Banking Standards, 2013; *Government Response to Parliamentary Commission on Banking Standards* (HM Treasury and Department for Business, Innovation & Skills, 2013) Cm 8661; *Banking Reform: A New Structure for Stability and Growth* (HM Treasury and Department for Business, Innovation & Skills, 2013); *Bank of England Response to the Final Report of the Parliamentary Commission on Banking Standards* (Bank of England, 2013); *The FCA's response to the Parliamentary Commission on Banking Standards* (FCA, 2013).

[110] Senior Persons are required to formally accept a written Statement of Responsibilities which sets out their role. This will allow deposit-taking institutions and regulators to ensure that a named individual is accountable for each key risk in their businesses, and will help regulators hold these individuals to account in the event of failure. Senior Persons are pre-approved by regulators before taking up a new post. Approvals may be subject to conditions, for example, where it is felt that individuals need to acquire a specific skill to carry out the job well. The Senior Persons Regime only includes the most senior individuals within deposit-taking institutions. The previously existing Approved Persons Regime continues to apply to all non-deposit-taking entities. Individuals holding posts that oversee both deposit-taking and non-deposit-taking institutions within a banking group may be subject to both the new Senior Persons Regime and the Approved Persons Regime. FSMA ss 59 (functions for which approval is required), 59ZA (senior management functions), 60 (statements of responsibilities) and 60A (vetting of relevant authorised persons), introduced by the Financial Services (Banking Reform) Act 2013. New 'threshold conditions' for persons: The Financial Services and Markets Act (Threshold Conditions) Order 2013/555. See *Regulatory Reform: The PRA and FCA Regimes for Approved Persons* (FSA, 2012) CP12/2.

[111] Introduced in the Financial Services (Banking Reform) Act 2013, s 36 as taking, or agreeing to the taking of, a decision as the way in which the business is to be carried on, or failing to take steps that could prevent such a decision, while being aware of a risk that the implementation of the decision may cause the failure of the group institution, such conduct falling far below what could reasonably be expected of a person in that position, and implementation of the decision causes the failure of the institution.

[112] *The FCA's Approach to Advancing its Objectives* (FCA, 2013); *The FCA's Response to the Parliamentary Commission on Banking Standards* (FCA, 2013). The latter referred to enforcement against individuals as 'cutting through the 'accountability firewall' and imposing tough penalties': para 6.

performed.[113] They criticised the criminalisation of individual conduct when key decisions are usually taken on a collective basis (board responsibility) and it was unjust to reverse the burden of proof, if a regulator could not satisfy a court that an individual had broken the rules, by making an individual prove the opposite.

In 2014 the PRA and FCA consulted on measures to strengthen *accountability* of individuals by regulatory means.[114] Citing the behaviour and culture of individuals within banks as having played a major role in the financial crisis, misspelling of insurance and manipulation of LIBOR, the proposals were 'intended to create a new framework to encourage individuals to take greater responsibility for their actions, and [would] make it easier for both firms and regulators to hold individuals to account'.[115] Three changes were introduced. First, a new 'Senior Managers Regime' (SMR) for individuals who are subject to regulatory approval requires firms to allocate a range of responsibilities to these individuals and to regularly vet their fitness and propriety. It focuses accountability on a narrower number of senior individuals in a firm than the previous Approved Persons Regime (APR). Second, a 'Certification Regime' requires relevant firms to assess the fitness and propriety of all employees who could pose a risk of significant harm to the firm or any of its customers. Third, a new set of 'Conduct Rules', with far wider application than previously, sets expectations about standards of behaviour, so as to provide a framework for regulators to make judgements. The proposed key new rules are four and five in Table 20.1. For the more detailed rules on Approved Persons and Senior Management see the FCA Handbook.[116]

The government also introduced general powers in relation to any directors of public companies, citing that 'some senior management individuals' behaviour in looking after the long-term interests of their company has been seriously deficient'.[117] First, sectoral regulators, such as the Pensions Regulator, FCA and PRA, were given additional powers to disqualify directors, either by taking court action or by accepting an undertaking from directors. Second, in order to assist in providing compensation to creditors, 'culpable directors' could be pursued where they were responsible for allowing companies to trade wrongfully or fraudulently by allowing a liquidator to sell or assign a civil action to a third party, and could be subject to compensatory awards made by the court at the time a disqualification order was made.

One consequence of an increase in risk of imposition of sanctions on firms and individuals was the publication of industry guidance stressing the need for firms to undertake risk assessment in relation to the potential for sanctions to be imposed on an international basis.[118]

---

[113] *Sanctioning the Directors of Failed Banks. Response to Consultation* (Law Society, 2012).

[114] *Consultation Paper. Strengthening Accountability in Banking: A New Regulatory Framework for Individuals* (PRA and FCA, 2014) FCA CP14/13 PRA CP 14/14.

[115] ibid, para 1.3.

[116] https://fshandbook.info/FS/html/FCA/.

[117] *Transparency & Trust: Enhancing the Transparency of UK Company Ownership and Increasing Trust in UK Business. Discussion Paper* (Department for Business, Innovation & Skills, 2013) para 9.3.

[118] eg *Lloyd's International Sanctions Guidance: Compliance, Delegated Authorities and Claims* (London, Lloyd's, 2015) Y4861.

Table 20.1: FCA Conduct Rules

First tier—Individual Conduct Rules	
Rule 1	You must act with integrity
Rule 2	You must act with due skill, care and diligence.
Rule 3	You must be open and cooperative with the FCA, the PRA and other regulators.
Rule 4	You must pay due regard to the interests of customers and treat them fairly.
Rule 5	You must observe proper standards of market conduct.
Second tier—Senior Manager Conduct Rules	
SM1	You must take reasonable steps to ensure that the business of the firm for which you are responsible is controlled effectively.
SM2	You must take reasonable steps to ensure that the business of the firm for which you are responsible complies with the relevant requirements and standards of the regulatory system.
SM3	You must take reasonable steps to ensure that any delegation of your responsibilities is to an appropriate person and that you oversee the discharge of the delegated responsibility effectively.
SM4	You must disclose appropriately any information of which the FCA or PRA would reasonably expect notice.

B. Structural Stability and Recovery

A key goal was to improve the banking sector's ability to absorb shocks arising from financial and economic stress, whatever the source, improving risk management and governance, and strengthen banks' transparency and disclosures. The G20 addressed these issues in Basel III.[119] A precipitate increase in demand by creditors of a bank (a run) can trigger systemic collapse since banks' liquidity is limited given that their asset base consists of limited liquidity reserves, together with short- and long-term investments.[120] In 1988 Basel I had established basic standards for computing a measure of bank capital adequacy called a risk-based capital ratio (RBCR), based on the amount of credit risk that a bank was exposed to. Basel II in 2004 embodied a more comprehensive view of capital regulation, establishing minimum risk-based capital requirements intended to cover not only credit risk, but also market and operational risk (Pillar I), guidelines for supervising banks' internal risk management processes and encouraging regulators to require that banks hold capital buffers above Pillar I minimums (Pillar II), and imposing public disclosure requirements on banks (Pillar III). Basel III set out a Global Regulatory Framework for More Resilient Banks and Banking Systems, requiring banks to hold more capital and liquidity, making improvements

---

[119] The series of documents can be found at http://www.bis.org/bcbs/basel3.htm. See GP Miller and F Cafaggi, *The Governance and Regulation of International Finance* (Cheltenham, Edward Elgar, 2013) ch 6.

[120] Some academic analysis tends to support a solution of insuring the value of long-term assets and deposit insurance: See respectively P Davies, 'Liquidity Safety Nets for Banks' (2013) 13 *Journal of Corporate Law Studies* 285 and JN Gordon and W-R Ringe, 'Banking Union Resolution without Deposit Guarantee: A Transatlantic Perspective on What It Would Take' at http://papers.ssrn.com/sol3/papers.cfm?abstract_id=2361347.

in frequency of reporting, monitoring and supervision of the internal management model. It also established stress testing. The EU will increase bank capital moderately, eventually capping risk-weighted leverage at around 22 times the equity.[121]

In enabling insolvent financial institutions to recover stability without calling on public funding, the problem experienced was that some institutions were 'too big to fail' and hence required urgent injections of public capital to stave off insolvency, rather than losses being assumed by equity and debt investors as an acceptable aspect of risk. UK reform to improve stability so as to enhance banks' loss-absorbing capacity and promote competition in the banking system was based on the 2011 recommendations of the Independent Commission on Banking to remove the implicit guarantee of taxpayer funding for banks, so that investors would pay before taxpayers,[122] thereby overcome the moral hazard and 'too big to fail' situation, and to separate retail and investment banking through a 'ring-fence'. The 'ring fence' element was to mandate separation of banking activities on which households and small and medium-sized enterprises depend ('core activities') from wholesale or investment banking activities that may involve a greater degree of risk and expose an entity undertaking them to financial problems arising elsewhere in the global financial system. Certain banks carrying on core activities will be required to be ring-fenced: That is, they have to comply with restrictions on the other activities they can undertake, and with rules made by the regulator intended to ensure that they are capable of carrying on the business of providing the core services related to the acceptance of deposits independently, should one of the other members in their group fail.[123] Statutory instruments detail the location of the ring-fence, including the scope of the ring-fence, the *de minimis* exemption from ring-fencing, the prohibitions on ring-fenced banks, and the precise conditions for exemptions.[124]

At EU level, a single resolution board (SRB) and single resolution fund (SRF) are required to be established by the Banking Recovery and Resolution Directive (BRRD).[125] The BRRD will require banks and '730K' investment firms to produce recovery plans from perhaps 2015.[126] All banks must by 2025 join a deposit guarantee scheme to be established in each

---

[121] Reg (EU) No 575/2013 on prudential requirements for credit institutions and investment firms and amending Reg (EU) No 648/2012, arts 81–88. See also the 'CRD IV' package.

[122] White Paper: *A New Approach to Financial Regulation: The Blueprint for Reform* (HM Treasury, 2011); *Independent Commission on Banking: Final Report Recommendations* (Independent Commission on Banking, 2011); *The Government Response to the Independent Commission on Banking* [Cm 8252] 19 Dec 2011.

[123] Financial Services (Banking Reform) Act 2013, ss 1–12. Rules may be brought into effect over several years from 2014 on: A timetable up to 2019 was envisaged during Parliamentary discussion, see http://www.publications.parliament.uk/pa/jt201213/jtselect/jtpcbs/98/9811.htm.

[124] *Banking Reform: Draft Secondary Legislation* (HMT/BIS, July 2013). See also *The Implementation of Ring-fencing: Consultation on Legal Structure, Governance and the Continuity of Services and Facilities* (Prudential Regulation Authority, 2014) CP19/14.

[125] Dir 2014/59/EU establishing a framework for the recovery and resolution of credit institutions and investment firms and amending Council Dir 82/891/EEC, and Dirs 2001/24/EC, 2002/47/EC, 2004/25/EC, 2005/56/EC, 2007/36/EC, 2011/35/EU, 2012/30/EU and 2013/36/EU, and Regs (EU) No 1093/2010 and (EU) No 648/2012. In UK see The Bank Recovery and Resolution Order 2014/3329; the Banks and Building Societies (Depositor Preference and Priorities) Order 2014/3486; *Recovery and Resolution Directive: Feedback on CP14/15 and Final Rules* (Financial Conduct Authority, 2015).

[126] *An EU Framework for Crisis Management in the Financial Sector* COM(2010) 579; Directive 2014/59/EU establishing a framework for the recovery and resolution of credit institutions and financial firms. The bail-in system will apply from 1 January 2016.

Member State, which must amount to one per cent of covered deposits in that country.[127] Eligible deposits of up to €100,000 would be protected, with the intention of protecting individuals and small companies.[128] The likely effect of use of the bail-in tool by a resolution authority in preference to other tools envisaged, including temporary public ownership, would be that share- and bond-holders should bear part of the cost of bank failure, with the minimum bail-in being eight per cent of liabilities or 20 per cent of risk weighted assets.[129] Thus, public money could only be used after eight per cent of the bank's assets had been bailed in. UK policy on resolution was published in 2014.[130]

Reforms to investor compensation schemes in the EU[131] and UK[132] simplify the rules, especially to make the claiming process simpler and faster, not least where the value of investments may be uncertain. Related reforms were made to the law[133] on insolvency, reorganisation and winding-up,[134] with a view to improving preparation and prevention, early intervention, resolution, cross-border cooperation and financing. Deposits should be repaid before investors.

Stress tests in 2014 at European[135] and national levels reviewed credit soundness, sovereign holdings and funding costs.[136] In parallel the ECB is undertaking an Asset Quality Review (AQR) examining the quality of the loan books of the 129 euro zone banks that it will become responsible for supervising in November 2014. The ECB noted that 'Market

---

[127] Amending Dir 94/19/EC on deposit-guarantee schemes.

[128] Dir 2014/59/EU establishing a framework for the recovery and resolution of credit institutions and investment firms; see also Dir 2014/49/EU of the European Parliament and of the Council of 16 April 2014 on deposit guarantee schemes (recast), art 6.

[129] ibid, art 44.5.

[130] *The Bank of England's Approach to Resolution* (Bank of England, 2014); *Supervisory Statement SS18/13: Recovery Planning* (Prudential Regulatory Authority, 2015).

[131] Dir 97/9/EC on investor-compensation schemes. Reforms were mooted in 2005, before the crisis, and the minimum compensation limit was raised to €50,000 by June 2009. See also *Evaluation of the Investment Compensation Scheme Directive. Executive Report and Recommendations* (DG Internal Market and Services, 2005) and *Description and Assessment of the National Investor Compensation Schemes Established in Accordance with Directive 97/9/EC Report Prepared for European Commission (Internal Market DG)* (Oxera, 2005); Proposal for a Dir amending Dir 97/9/EC of the European Parliament and of the Council on investor-compensation schemes, COM(2010) 371, 12.7.2010.

[132] See Financial Services Act 2010, ss 16, 17; *Financial Services Compensation Scheme: Changes to the Compensation Sourcebook* (FSA, March 2012) CP12/7; The Financial Services Compensation Scheme (FSCS) paid out £347 million in compensation to more than 86,000 claimants in 2011/12. It received almost 97,000 new claims during the year, an increase of 145% on 2010/11: *Financial Services Compensation Scheme Annual Report and Accounts 2011/12* (FSCS, July 2012); Financial Services (Banking Reform) Act 2013, ss 13–16 (deposits which are eligible for protection under the financial services compensation scheme are to be preferential debts, thereby ranking ahead of other unsecured claims in insolvency).

[133] Reg No 1346/2000/EC on Insolvency Proceedings; Dir 2001/17/EC on the reorganisation and winding-up of insurance undertakings; Dir 2001/24/EC on the reorganisation and winding-up of credit institutions.

[134] *Harmonisation of Insolvency Law at EU Level: Avoidance Actions and Rules on Contracts. Briefing Note* (European Parliament, Directorate General for Internal Policies, Policy Department C: Citizens' Rights and Constitutional Affairs, Legal Affairs, 2011); *Proposal for a Regulation of the European Parliament and of the Council Amending Council Regulation (EC) No 1346/2000 on Insolvency Proceedings* COM (2012) 744, 12.12.2012; *Proposal for a Directive establishing a Framework for the Recovery and Resolution of Credit Institutions and Investment Forms* SWD (2012) 167, 6.6.2012-07-07.

[135] Basel III: A Global Framework for More Resilient Banks and Banking Systems; Basel III: International Framework for Liquidity Risk Measurement, Standards and Monitoring; Basel III leverage ratio framework and disclosure requirements, January 2014.

[136] Recapitalisation Recommendation to strengthening of participating banks' capital bases (to 9% core tier 1) (EBA, December 2011).

participants and rating agencies continue to see banks and sovereigns as inextricably inter-linked, leading to acute pressure on funding costs and the stress tests and AQR are designed to break this perceived link.'[137]

Deposit insurance for investors has, however, been criticised as inducing blindness to risk-taking and diminishing vigilance.[138]

C. Corporate Governance

All of the major reviews of financial institutions in the past five years have focused on the need to improve corporate governance. Corporate governance was defined by the OECD as involving

> a set of relationships between a company's management, its board, its shareholders and other stake-holders. Corporate governance also provides the structure through which the objectives of the company are set, and the means of attaining those objectives and monitoring performance are determined.[139]

The 2008 meltdown in the United States was attributed to

> a combination of 'light touch' supervision, which relied too heavily on self-governance in finan-cial firms, and weak corporate governance and risk management at many systemically important financial institutions ... In several key markets, deregulation and market-based supervision were the political order of the day as countries vied for global capital flows, corporate headquarters, and exchange listings. Regulators also missed the potential systemic impact of entire classes of financial products, such as subprime mortgages, and in general failed to spot the large systemic risks that had been growing during the previous two decades.[140]

At international level, the Group of Thirty (G30)[141] issued detailed recommendations on improving governance. The Basel Committee issued Guidelines in 2010 and a draft revision in 2014.[142] The latter noted that sound corporate governance may permit the supervisor to place more reliance on the bank's internal processes.[143] Its revisions had four main aims. First, to explicitly reinforce the collective oversight and risk governance responsi-bilities of the board. Second, to emphasise key components of risk governance such as risk culture, risk appetite and their relationship to a bank's risk capacity.[144] Third, to delineate the specific roles of the board, board risk committees, senior management and the control functions including the chief risk officer (CRO) and internal audit. Fourth, to strengthen banks' overall checks and balances.

---

[137] *Report on Risks and Vulnerabilities of the European Banking System* (European Banking Authority, July 2012).

[138] Leader, 'Leviathan of Last Resort. State Subsidies and Guarantees are Once Again Corroding the Financial Sector and Creating New Dangers.' *The Economist* (London, 12 April 2014).

[139] *Principles of Corporate Governance* (Paris, OECD, 2004)11, at http://www.oecd.org/dataoecd/32/18/31557724.pdf.

[140] *Toward Effective Governance of Financial Institutions* (Group of 30, 2012) at http://www.group30.org/images/PDF/Corporate%20Governance%20050913.pdf.

[141] http://www.group30.org/images/PDF/TowardEffGov.pdf.

[142] Basel Committee on Banking Supervision, *Principles for Enhancing Corporate Governance– Final Document* (Basel, Bank for International Settlements, 2010); Basel Committee on Banking Supervision, *Guidelines. Corporate Governance Principles for Banks* (Basel, Bank for International Settlements, 2014).

[143] ibid, para 4.

[144] See also *Guidance for a Risk-Based Approach. The Banking Sector* (Paris, Financial Action Task Force, 2014).

The UK has had a principles-based approach to corporate governance since the 1992 Cadbury Report, which introduced a Code based on openness, integrity and accountability.[145] The 2009 Walker Review concluded that the UK's unitary board structure and Combined Code of the Financial Reporting Council, and its 'comply or explain' mode, remained fit for purpose for companies generally, and not just financial institutions.[146] New editions of the UK Corporate Governance Code were issued in 2010,[147] 2012[148] and 2014.[149] The Code calls for 'dialogue which is both constructive and challenging' and states that a key role for a board is to establish the culture, values and ethics of the company.[150] The Stewardship Code was issued by the Financial Reporting Council to enhance the quality of engagement between institutional investors and companies, give sharper emphasis on long-term company strategy, and tackle overly complex incentive schemes which encourage short-termism and tend to pay out asymmetrically.[151] Various statements were issued by investors' bodies,[152] including clarifying the principles on 'comply or explain'.[153]

The Kay report set out principles to provide a foundation for a long-term perspective in UK equity markets, and made recommendations to re-establish equity markets that work well for their users.[154] The recommendation that work should be done to identify how investors can work together better in engaging with companies, fostering trust and building constructive relationships, was taken forward by an ad hoc group.[155] The group noted some improvement by bodies such as ABI (Association of British Insurers) and the Local Authority Pension Fund Forum (LAPFF), and that many individual asset managers and asset owners had improved the seriousness of their stewardship efforts though others have principally ticked boxes. The group launched an Investor Forum from 2014 to improve accountability in the investment chain, extend participation and form Engagement Action Groups. Creation by leading institutional investors of an Investor Forum was encouraged

---

[145] *Report of the Committee on Financial Aspects of Corporate Governance* (1992) para 3.2, at http://www.ecgi.org/codes/documents/cadbury.pdf.

[146] Walker Review (n 9).

[147] *Combined Code on Corporate Governance* (Financial Reporting Council, 2010).

[148] *The UK Corporate Governance Code* (Financial Reporting Council, 2012). By the end of 2013 compliance was reported to be high: *Developments in Corporate Governance 2013. The Impact and Implementation of the UK Corporate Governance and Stewardship Codes* (Financial Reporting Council, 2013). See also *The Accountancy Regulations* (Financial Reporting Council, 2014); *The Actuarial Scheme* (Financial Reporting Council, 2014); *Sanctions Guidance* (Financial Reporting Council, 2014).

[149] *The UK Corporate Governance Code* (Financial Reporting Council, October 2014).

[150] ibid, Preface paras 3 and 4.

[151] Financial Reporting Council, *The UK Stewardship Code* (Financial Reporting Council, 2010); *Developments in Corporate Governance 2013: The Impact and Implementation of the UK Corporate Governance and Stewardship Codes* (Financial Reporting Council, 2013) (finding that companies were responding in a positive manner to the changes introduced in October 2012, but with less uptake of new reporting recommendations on the activities of audit committees).

[152] *Corporate Governance Policy and Voting Guidelines* (National Association of Pension Funds, 2013).

[153] *Comply or Explain: Investor Expectations and Current Practices* (Association of British Insurers, 2012) available at http://www.abi.org.uk/content/contentfilemanager.aspx?contentid=65367.

[154] *The Kay Review of UK Equity Markets and Long-term Decision Making: Final Report* (Department for Business, Innovation & Skills, 2012). See also JA McCahery and EPM Vermeulen, 'Understanding the Board of Directors after the Financial Crisis: Some Lessons for Europe' (2014) 41(1) *Journal of Law and Society* 121–51 (arguing for the remuneration criterion of value creation through sustainable growth and innovation, and the ongoing involvement on boards of venture capitalists).

[155] *Report of the Collective Engagement Working Group* (Collective Engagement Working Group, 2013).

by the government so as to develop effective collective engagement, regarded by Kay as a vital step in shifting the culture of equity markets to support long term corporate views.[156]

The EU framework for listed companies is a combination of legislation and 'soft law', including recommendations and corporate governance codes.[157] Post-crisis reforms aimed at strengthening corporate governance in general[158] focused on the following elements:[159]

— Enhancing transparency—Companies need to provide better information about their corporate governance to their investors and society at large. At the same time companies should be allowed to know who their shareholders are and institutional investors should be more transparent about their voting policies so that a more fruitful dialogue on corporate governance matters can take place. Accordingly, measures were taken on disclosure of board diversity policy and management of non-financial risks; improving corporate governance reporting; shareholder identification; and strengthening transparency rules for institutional investors.

— Engaging shareholders—Shareholders should be encouraged to engage more in corporate governance. They should be offered more possibilities to oversee remuneration policy and related party transactions, and shareholder cooperation to this end should be made easier. In addition, a limited number of obligations will need to be imposed on institutional investors, asset managers and proxy advisors to bring about effective engagement. Accordingly, measures were taken to give better shareholder oversight of remuneration policy; better shareholder oversight of related party transactions; regulate proxy advisors; clarify the relationship between investor cooperation on corporate governance issues and the 'acting in concert' concept; and on employee share ownership.

— Supporting companies' growth and their competitiveness—A need was perceived to simplify cross-border operations of European businesses, particularly in the case of small and medium-sized companies. Accordingly, measures were taken on transfer of seat of companies; improving the mechanism for cross-border mergers; enabling cross-border divisions; smart legal forms for European SMEs; promoting and improving awareness of the European Company (SE) and the European Cooperative (SCE) Statutes; and groups of companies.

---

[156] *Building a Culture of Long-Term Equity Investment: Implementation of the Kay Review: Progress Report* (Department for Business, Innovation & Skills, 2014).

[157] Dir 2006/46/EC promotes the application of codes by requiring that companies refer in their corporate governance statement to a code and that they report on their application of that code on a 'comply or explain' basis. However, a study showed that the informative quality of explanations was not satisfactory and there was insufficient monitoring: *Study on Monitoring and Enforcement Practices in Corporate Governance in the Member States* (RiskMetrics Group, 2009), at http://ec.europa.eu/internal_market/company/docs/ecgforum/studies/comply-or-explain-090923_en.pdf.

[158] The EU corporate governance framework includes legislation in areas such as corporate governance statements, transparency of listed companies, shareholders' rights and takeover bids as well as 'soft law', namely recommendations on the role and on the remuneration of companies' directors.

[159] *Green Paper The EU Corporate Governance Framework* COM (2011) 164, 5.4.2011; Communication from the Commission to the European Parliament, the Council, the European Economic and Social Committee and the Committee of the Regions. Action Plan: European company law and corporate governance—a modern legal framework for more engaged shareholders and sustainable companies, COM(2012) 740/2; Green Paper on the EU corporate governance framework, COM(2011) 164 final.

Specific measures aimed at financial institutions highlighted issues of excessive remuneration of directors, especially where some investors focus on short-term performance.[160] Strengthening the status and authority of the chief risk officer, with independence from operational and business units and a close relationship with the board, was widely supported.[161] Companies are required to adopt the 'comply or explain' principle in relation to corporate governance codes.[162]

The review of governance issues by G30 is notable in including a number of strong statements on the importance of ethical practice as underpinning desirable culture in banks: These will be discussed further below.

D. Transparency

Transparency has been a general principle for the public sector by the UK government for some time,[163] and was re-emphasised in 2012.[164] Transparency of information about systemic risks, and companies' internal systems and their operation, follow as important topics from the reforms discussed above. The regulators (PRA and FCA) were required to have regard to two new regulatory principles[165] relating to transparency:[166]

—   The desirability in appropriate cases of each regulator publishing information relating to persons on whom requirements are imposed by or under this Act, or requiring such persons to publish information, as a means of contributing to the advancement by each regulator of its objectives;[167] and

—   the principle that the regulators should exercise their functions as transparently as possible.[168]

One move was to improve the quality of disclosure of financial information and its value to users, reducing clutter in financial reports.[169] A 2013 self-assessed survey of global systemically important banks (G-SIBs) and domestically systemically important banks (DSIBs), together with a review of a subset of the disclosures made in banks' 2012 Annual Reports and related documents, found that participating banks reported that they disclosed in

---

[160] *Green Paper, Corporate Governance in Financial Institutions and Remuneration Policies*, European Commission COM(2010) 284.

[161] *Summary of Responses to Commission Green Paper on Corporate Governance in Financial Institutions*, European Commission. 2010. Directorate General Internal Market and Services, Brussels.

[162] Dir 2013/34/EU, art 20 and Commission Recommendation of 9 April 2014 on the quality of corporate governance reporting ('comply or explain'), 2014/208/EU.

[163] See the Freedom of Information Act 2000.

[164] *Implementing Transparency* (National Audit Office, 2012).

[165] The regulator must 'have regard to' the regulatory principles when carrying out its work: FSMA, s 3B, as amended by the 2012 Act, s 6(1).

[166] See *Transparency as a Regulatory Tool*, Discussion Paper DP08/3; *Code of Practice on Regulatory Transparency* (FSA, 20xx); *Discussion Paper. Transparency* DP13/1 (FSA, 2013); *Transparency Discussion Paper DP13/01: Responses* (FCA, 2013).

[167] FSMA, s 3B(1)(g).

[168] FSMA, s 3B(1)(h).

[169] *Thinking about Disclosures in a Broader Context: A Road Map for a Disclosure Framework* (Financial Reporting Council, October 2012); *Feedback Statement. Thinking about Disclosures in a Broader Context. A Roadmap for a Disclosure Framework* (Financial Reporting Council, June 2013).

aggregate only 34 per cent of the information recommended by the Enhanced Disclose Task Force (EDTF) prior to the publication of its report in October 2012; but afterwards they made substantial effort to incorporate, and increased to 50 per cent disclosure at year ends, and expected to give 72 per cent in 2013.[170]

Another action was to strengthen transparency of complaints. The FCA publishes data provided by firms that report over 500 complaints in a six month period, and such firms are also required to publish the data on their websites.[171] A survey of 183 firms was found that exposing firms' complaint figures has focused their senior management's minds on improving the quality of complaint handling, and fears of lack of impact or unintended consequences (that the wrong firms would be targeted or that publication might incentivise firms to under report) did largely not materialise.[172] Trade associations agreed that firms were more focused on complaints and took actions to address the causes of complaints. 76 per cent of firms used complaints data to compare against peers and 59 per cent to review their own complaints performance. 22 per cent of consumers claimed to be aware of the complaints data, 38 per cent of whom said they used it when choosing a new financial services provider.

With the aim of enhancing the transparency of UK company ownership and increasing trust in UK business,[173] the government introduced requirements for companies to obtain and hold information on who owns and controls them; implement a central registry of company beneficial ownership information; and to review the use of bearer shares (which do not require the identity of the holder to be entered in the company's publicly available register of members) and nominee directors (which can be used to conceal the identity of the person really controlling the company).

The FCA was authorised to publish such information about the matter to which a warning notice relates as it considers appropriate. The principal purpose of the new power is to promote early transparency of enforcement proceedings.[174]

From April 2013 the Financial Ombudsman Service (FOS)'s policy[175] has been to publish ombudsman decisions in full, identifying the business, subject only to removing all reference to the identity of the consumer, and certain other clearly sensitive information, such as commercially sensitive information or information about a product or practice that would help fraudulent activities or frustrate a regulatory or criminal investigation. The outline issues and decisions of the ombudsman are described in full, but decisions vary considerably in form and length: Simpler, lower value decisions may be dealt with in a page, whilst more complex cases will require longer decisions.[176]

---

[170] *Progress Report on Implementation of Disclosure Recommendations* (Enhanced Disclosure Task Force, 2013); *Letter to M Carney, Chairman of the Financial Stability Board, Enhanced Disclosure Task Force* (2 July 2013); *Enhancing the Risk Disclosures of Banks—Progress Report* (FSB, 2013).

[171] See http://www.fca.org.uk/firms/systems-reporting/complaints-data/firm-level/firm-level-complaints-data-faq.

[172] *Discussion Paper. Transparency* DP13/1 (FSA, 2013) para 2.19.

[173] *Transparency & Trust: Enhancing the Transparency of UK Company Ownership and Increasing Trust in UK Business. Discussion Paper* (Department for Business, Innovation & Skills, 2013).

[174] Financial Services and Markets Act 2000, s391(1)(c); see *Publishing Information About Enforcement Warning Notices* CP13/9 (FSA, 2013); PS13/9 *Publishing Information about Enforcement Warning Notices*, FCA 2013-11-01.

[175] Financial Services and Markets Act 2000, s 230A, inserted by Financial Services Act 2012, Sch 11.

[176] *Publishing Ombudsman Decisions: Our Approach for 2013* (Financial Ombudsman Service, 2013).

E. Consumer Focus and Facilitating Redress

Many bodies supported strengthening consumer protection mechanisms.[177] The World Bank considers that the global financial crisis highlighted the importance of financial consumer protection for financial stability.[178] The FSB, endorsed by the G20, noted that

> [p]olicies that protect the interests of consumers of financial products and services contribute to enhanced risk management by households, more competitive financial markets, and greater financial stability. This financial crisis demonstrated the desirability of strengthening such policies and ensuring that the use (or misuse) of individual financial products do not become a source of financial instability.[179]

An emphasis on avoiding irresponsible lending and borrowing can be seen from the extensive regulatory provisions that were included in the EU's amendments to mortgage legislation.[180] The controls extend to financial education of consumers (responsible borrowing and debt management), extensive controls on creditors, credit intermediaries and appointed representatives, including remuneration policy and duties to behave honestly, fairly, transparently and professionally, taking account of the rights and interests of consumers.

In the UK, the Financial Services Compensation Scheme was strengthened[181] and, as described in chapter 13, the FOS continued with its crucial position and the FCA's powers to deliver redress were extended.

The FCA's policy statements since 2010 on achievement of its consumer protection goal, have emphasised the change in their approach from reactive to proactive interventions, with an outcomes-focused style of conduct supervision.[182] Consumer protection is strongly emphasised through imposing penalties, stopping firms from trading and securing redress for consumers.[183]

The FCA's consumer focus has included research into various aspects of the behaviour of consumers and sellers, applying behavioural economics to the prevention of consumers making predictable mistakes. One study examined the phenomenon that consumers choosing retail financial products and services are particularly prone to mistakes, and how firms can and should be expected to behave so as to avoid exploiting these traits and avoid

---

[177] See *Strategic Response to the Financial and Economic Crises* (Paris, OECD, 2009) 11.

[178] *Global Survey on Consumer Protection and Financial Literary: Results Brief. Regulatory Practices in 114 Economies* (The World Bank, 2013).

[179] *Consumer Finance Protection with Particular Focus on Credit* (FSB, 2011) http://www.financialstabilityboard.org/publications/r_111026a.pdf.

[180] Dir 2014/17/EU on credit agreements for consumers relating to residential immovable property and amending Dirs 2008/48/EC and 2013/36/EU and Reg (EU) No 1093/2010.

[181] Improvements to the FSCS are made to provide a single customer view (SCV) of aggregate protected deposits with a deposit taker: *Financial Services Compensation Scheme Reform—Single Customer View—Verification* (Financial Services Authority, 2009), available at http://www.fsa.gov.uk/pubs/policy/ps09_18.pdf, implemented in the PRA's COMP sourcebook: http://fshandbook.info/FS/html/PRA/COMP/17/3.

[182] *The Financial Conduct Authority: Approach to Regulation* (Financial Services Authority, 2011); *The FCA's Approach to Advancing its Objectives* (FCA, July 2013).

[183] *Business Plan 2014/15* (FCA, 2014).

mis-selling.[184] Taking account of behavioural analysis, the FCA stated that firms should design effective interventions:

Provide information. Require firms to provide specific information in a way that is not likely to exacerbate consumer weaknesses, or prohibit specific marketing or promotion materials or practices where they unfairly target such behavioural weaknesses, biases or mistakes. Example: require firms to give consumers data on past product usage or claims ratio.

Change the choice environment. Adjust how choices are presented to consumers to address biases. Example: set the default options for products by requiring consumers to make an active decision instead of being automatically 'opted in' to buying a product.

Control product distribution. Require products to be promoted or sold only through particular channels or only to certain types of clients. Example: require complex products to only be promoted with advice.

Control products. Ban specific product features or products that appear designed or otherwise likely to exploit consumer mistakes to their detriment, or require products to contain specific features to address the risk of detriment arising from such mistakes. Example: require firms to remove or limit product features, such as high exit charges.[185]

The FCA noted a series of early warning indicators that it would seek to identify:

1. Rip-offs. Uncompetitively high margins.
2. Suckers. Concentrated profits from a small group of consumers.
3. Bargains. Innovative products that appear very cheap.
4. Traps. Contract features that often target behavioural biases.

The new powers to achieve redress have been discussed in chapter 13 above.[186]

Experimentation by the FSA found that the design of letters to consumers notifying them of a possible right to claim compensation could have a marked effect on response rates.[187] In a test case in which a firm wrote voluntarily to almost 200,000 customers, an initial 1.5 per cent response rate was improved by over seven times to almost 12 per cent (equivalent to an additional 20,000 people responding to claim redress), by making various changes to the design of the letter. The most significant improvement was to use a number of salient bullet points in the text.

In 2014 the FCA published policy on improvements required in how banks deal with consumer complaints, after a review and discussions with 15 major retailing banks.[188] This found that: Firms did not always consider the impact on consumers when designing and implementing processes and procedures; there were inconsistencies in the amount of redress offered, particularly for distress and inconvenience; firms took a narrow approach to root cause analysis (which should enable them to determine, and fix, the underlying reason for a complaint), which may affect their awareness of wider issues; and there were weaknesses in some firms' management information.

---

[184] *Applying Behavioural Economics at the Financial Conduct Authority* (FCA, 2013). See also *How Does Selling Insurance as an Add-on Affect Consumer Decisions?* (FCA, 2014).
[185] ibid.
[186] See also *Changes to the Dispute Resolutions: Complaints Handbook* (Financial Ombudsman Service, 2013).
[187] *Encouraging Consumers to Claim Redress: Evidence from a Field Trial* (FCA, 2013).
[188] *Complaint Handling* (Financial Conduct Authority, 2014) TR14/18.

F. Controls on Remuneration

In 2012 the British Secretary of State for Business, Vince Cable, noted the fundamental change in attitudes from the statement of a predecessor, Lord Mandelson, that he was 'intensely relaxed about people getting filthy rich as long as they pay their taxes'.[189] Dr Cable noted that bonuses in the City of London tripled between 2002/03 and 2007/08, from £3.3 billion to £11.6 billion. He criticised the fact that excessive remuneration had encouraged the pursuit of short-term, sometimes illusory, returns rather than long-term value.

The Financial Stability Forum (FSF) identified compensation practices at large financial institutions as one factor among many that contributed to the financial crisis that began in 2007. The FSF said:

> High short-term profits led to generous bonus payments to employees without adequate regard to the longer-term risks they imposed on their firms. These perverse incentives amplified the excessive risk-taking that severely threatened the global financial system and left firms with fewer resources to absorb losses as risks materialised. The lack of attention to risk also contributed to the large, in some cases extreme absolute level of compensation in the industry.[190]

The European Commission noted that aligning

> directors' interests with those of these new categories of shareholder has amplified risk-taking and, in many cases, contributed to excessive remuneration for directors, based on the short-term share value of the company/financial institution as the only performance criterion.[191]

The Basel Committee on Banking Supervision issued principles in 2010 including:

Principle 10

> The board should actively oversee the compensation system's design and operation, and should monitor and review the compensation system to ensure that it operates as intended.

Principle 11

> An employee's compensation should be effectively aligned with prudent risk taking: compensation should be adjusted for all types of risk; compensation outcomes should be symmetric with risk outcomes; compensation payout schedules should be sensitive to the time horizon of risks; and the mix of cash, equity and other forms of compensation should be consistent with risk alignment.[192]

The FSF issued Principles for Sound Compensation Practices that aimed to ensure effective governance of compensation, alignment of compensation with prudent risk taking and effective supervisory oversight and stakeholder engagement in compensation.[193] Its 2011

---

[189] V Cable, 'Responsible Capitalism' speech to National Association of Pension Funds, November 2012.

[190] *FSF Principles for Sound Compensation Practices* (Financial Stability Forum, 2009).

[191] *Green Paper. Corporate Governance in Financial Institutions and Remuneration Policies* COM(1020) 284, 2.6.2010, at http://ec.europa.eu/internal_market/company/docs/modern/com2010_284_en.pdf.

[192] Basel Committee on Banking Supervision, *Principles for Enhancing Corporate Governance—Final Document* (Bank for International Settlements, Basel, 2010). See also *Compensation Principles and Standards Assessment Methodology*, Basel Committee on Banking Supervision, January 2010, available at www.bis.org/publ/bcbs166. htm. This document aims to guide supervisors in reviewing individual firms' compensation practices and assessing their compliance with the FSB Principles and Standards, and seeks to foster supervisory approaches that are effective in promoting sound compensation practices at banks and help support a level playing field.

[193] ibid. See also *FSF Principles for Sound Compensation Practices. Implementation Standards* (Financial Stability Board, 2009) and subsequent monitoring in *Thematic Review of Compensation* (Financial Stability Board, 2009); *Thematic Review of Compensation. Peer Review Report* (Financial Stability Board, 2010); *2011 Thematic Review on Compensation. Peer Review Report* (Financial Stability Board, 2011).

review found that large internationally active firms had roughly similar certain pay structure characteristics that were consistent with its standards, such as deferral rates, vesting
periods, variable pay fractions, the use of equity and the use of ex post adjustments like
malus and clawback.[194] In 2012, the FSB established a Compensation Monitoring Contact
Group (CMCG) comprising national experts from member jurisdictions with regulatory or
supervisory responsibility on compensation practices to monitor national implementation
of its principles and standards.[195]

The EU introduced requirements for Member State competent authorities to use
aggregate quantitative information on remuneration to benchmark remuneration trends
and practices. Such information must also be sent to the Committee of European Banking Supervisors (CEBS) (now EBA).[196] The UK strengthened disclosure in remuneration
reports[197] and later implemented two items:

a)   the Remuneration Benchmarking Information Report—significant banks, build-
     ing societies and investment firms, that have total assets of £50bn or greater, that are
     required to submit information on the structure of remuneration for its group.
b)   the High Earners Report—banks, building societies and investment firms, excluding
     solo limited employees in the group (excluding subsidiaries and branches established
     outside the EEA) with total annual remuneration of €1m or more.[198]

In 2013 the EU agreed that from January 2014 bonuses of 'material risk takers' in banks
would be restricted to 100 per cent of their salaries. This can be increased to 200 per cent if
shareholders agree, either by a 66 per cent majority of a quorum representing 50 per cent
of shares, or 75 per cent of shareholders present.[199] The UK challenged this in the Court of
Justice, while implementing it,[200] and withdrew its challenge in November 2014.[201]

ESMA issued Guidelines on sound remuneration policies under the Alternative Investment Fund Managers Directive (AIFMD)[202] and on Markets in Financial Instruments

---

[194] *2011 Thematic Review on Compensation. Peer Review Report* (Financial Stability Board, 2011).
[195] *Implementing the FSB Principles for Sound Compensation Practices and their Implementation Standards. Progress Report* (Financial Stability Board, 2012).
[196] Dir 2010/76/EU (Capital Requirements Directive 3: CRD3).
[197] Financial Services Act 2010, ss 4–6.
[198] *Data Collection on Remuneration Practices* (FSA, 2012) PS12/18.
[199] Dir 2013/36/EU of the European Parliament and of the Council of 26 June 2013 on access to the activity
of credit institutions and the prudential supervision of credit institutions and investment firms, amending Dir
2002/87/EC and repealing Dirs 2006/48/EC and 2006/49/EC; Reg (EU) No 575/2013 of the European Parliament
and of the Council of 26 June 2013 on prudential requirements for credit institutions and investment firms and
amending Reg (EU) No 648/2012 (CRD IV).
[200] *Legal Challenge Launched into New Rules on Bankers' Pay*, HM Treasury, 25 September 2013.
[201] After an adverse Opinion from Advocate General Jääskinen in Case C-507/13 *United Kingdom of Great
Britain and Northern Ireland v European Parliament, Council of the European Union.*
[202] Dir 2011/61/EU on Alternative Investment Fund Managers. *Guidelines on Sound Remuneration Policies
under the AIFMD. Final Report* (European Securities and Markets Authority, 11 February 2013) http://www.esma.
europa.eu/content/Guidelines-sound-remuneration-policies-under-AIFMD. See also *General Guidance on the
AIFM Remuneration Code (SYSC 19B)* (FCA, 2014).

Directive (MiFID)[203] in 2013. The latter included the following statements on governance and design of remuneration policies and practices:

13.   When designing or reviewing remuneration policies and practices, firms should consider the conduct of business and conflicts of interest risks that may arise. A firm's remuneration policies and practices should be aligned with effective conflicts of interest management duties (which should include the avoidance of conflicts of interests created by those remuneration policies and practices) and conduct of business risk management obligations, in order to ensure that clients' interests are not impaired by the remuneration policies and practices adopted by the firm in the short, medium and long term.

14.   Remuneration policies and practices should be designed in such a way so as not to create incentives that may lead relevant persons to favour their own interest, or the firm's interests (for example in the case of self-placement[204] or where a firm promotes the sale of products that are more lucrative for it), to the potential detriment of clients.

15.   Furthermore, where firms' remuneration policies and practices link remuneration directly to the sale of specific financial instruments or of a specific category of financial instrument, it is unlikely that such firms could, in this situation, demonstrate compliance with MiFID conduct of business or conflict of interest requirements.

It gave these examples of good practice:[205]

—   The variable part of the remuneration paid out is calculated and awarded on a linear basis rather than being dependent on meeting an 'all or nothing' target. In some cases, the firm decides to pay out the variable remuneration in several tranches over an appropriate time period, in order to adjust for and take into account the long term results.

—   A firm has fundamentally changed the components of variable remuneration. The variable component of the remuneration is now based on qualitative criteria and more closely reflects the desired conduct of the employees to act in the best interests of the clients.

—   References used in the calculation of variable remuneration of relevant persons are common across products sold and include qualitative criteria.

—   In the case of an open-ended investment with no investment term, the remuneration is deferred for a set number of years or until the encashment of the product.

—   Payment of variable remuneration may be aligned with the investment term or deferred in order to ensure that the product sold does in fact take into consideration the final return of the product for the client and, where applicable, an adjusted award of variable remuneration is made.

—   Employees are paid in relation to both volume of products sold and effective return of these products for the client over an appropriate timeframe. In this instance, the assessment of financial data is used as a measure of the quality of the service provided.

---

[203] Dir 2004/39/EC on Markets in Financial Instruments. *Guidelines on Remuneration Policies and Practices (MiFID). Final Report* (European Securities and Markets Authority, 2013), ESMA/2013/606, http://www.esma.europa.eu/system/files/2013-606_final_report_guidelines_on_remuneration_policies_and_practices_mifid.pdf. See also Guidelines on certain aspects of the MiFID compliance function requirements' (ESMA/2012/388), and the EBA Guidelines on Internal Governance.

[204] The practice of firms selling proprietary financial instruments—such as common equity shares, preference shares, hybrid securities and debt (in either the firm itself or in another entity within the same group)—to their own clients.

[205] Guidelines (n 203) para 27.

It specified the following examples of poor practice:[206]

— A firm has started offering advisers specific additional remuneration to encourage clients to apply for new fund products in which the firm has a specific interest. This often involves the relevant person having to suggest that their clients sell products that they would otherwise recommend they retain so they can invest in these new products.
— Managers and employees receive a large bonus linked to a specific product. As a result, the firm sells this specific product irrespective of the suitability of this product for the clients addressed. Warnings from the risk manager are ignored because the investment products generate high returns for the firm. When the risks that had been identified occur, the products have already been sold and the bonuses have already been paid out.
— The variable component of the total remuneration is based only on volumes sold, and increases the relevant person's focus on short-term gains rather than the client's best interest.
— Relevant persons engage in frequent buying and selling of financial instruments in a client's portfolio in order to earn additional remuneration without considering the suitability of this activity for the client. Likewise, rather than considering the suitability of a product for a client, relevant persons focus on the sale of products that have a short investment term in order to earn remuneration from re-investing the product after the short term.

The MiFID Guidelines also gave detailed controls for compliance through the design and operation of remuneration policies and committees.

Corporate remuneration has been an issue in the UK that has attracted consistent public disquiet, especially in the context of extensive public ownership of banks. Reforms by government in the UK introduced: Greater transparency; greater shareholder powers, such as the introduction of binding votes; increased diversity of boards and remuneration committees; and best practice led by the business and investor community. Respondees supported more shareholder and employee engagement, but a majority opposed having shareholders or employees on the remuneration committee.[207] The issues of remuneration for executives and sales will be considered separately below.

i. Executive Remuneration

A firm's business is often subject to future risk and uncertainty. Financial services products involve long time-frames, and customers may have asymmetric sophistication and knowledge with intermediaries, whose focus may be on short-term maximisation of rents rather than customers' long-term interests.[208] If variable remuneration is paid out without any link to future performance, employees have less incentive to take future risk into account, and firms are exposed to the risk of paying out variable remuneration which proves not to

---

[206] ibid, para 28.
[207] *Executive Remuneration. Discussion Paper: Summary of Responses* (Department for Business, Innovation & Skills, January 2012).
[208] Jaffer, Morris, Sawbridge and Vines (n 34).

be justified by results.[209] Two mechanisms that were strengthened were deferral and claw-back of remuneration. The Walker Review had said:[210]

> Deferral of incentive payments should provide the primary risk adjustment mechanism to align rewards with sustainable performance for executive board members and 'high end' employees in a BOFI included within the scope of the FSA Remuneration Code. Incentives should be balanced so that at least one-half of variable remuneration offered in respect of a financial year is in the form of a long-term incentive scheme with vesting subject to a performance condition with half of the award vesting after not less than three years and of the remainder after five years. Short-term bonus awards should be paid over a three-year period with not more than one-third in the first year. Clawback should be used as the means to reclaim amounts in circumstances of misstatement and misconduct.

The Third Capital Requirements Directive (CRD 3) lays down the fundamental principle whereby institutions are required to ensure that their 'remuneration policies and practices are consistent with and promote sound effective risk management'.[211] It required the Committee of European Banking Supervisors (CEBS)[212] to issue guidelines on remuneration.[213] The European Commission issues technical standards drafted by the EBA on criteria on the categorisation of staff whose professional activities have a material impact on an institution's risk profile (Material Risk Takers) and are subject to controls on remuneration.[214]

In its original consultation paper, the FSA emphasised its focus upon the *structure* of remuneration, rather than its *level*:

> We are not concerned with the levels of remuneration, which we regard as a matter for firms' boards and shareholders. None of the principles in our Code will prevent firms providing large remuneration packages to employees if such packages can be justified by their contribution to the success of the firm, adjusted appropriately for risk.[215]

Implementation was through a revision of the Code coming into force in January 2010, with 10 new principles to be reflected in the Handbook,[216] focusing on risk management: 'A firm must establish, implement and maintain remuneration policies, procedures and practices that are consistent with and promote effective risk management'.[217]

---

[209] A Clark and T Edmonds, *Banking Executives' Remuneration in the UK* (House of Commons Library note, 4 June 2013).

[210] *Final Report of Review team led by Sir David Walker: A Review of Corporate Governance in UK Banks and other Financial Industry Entities*, November 2009, Recommendation 33.

[211] Dir 2010/76/EU, art 22.

[212] CEBS is composed of high level representatives of bank regulators and central banks throughout the EU. It will form the core of one of the new European supervisory authorities recently established by the EU in response to the crisis.

[213] *Guidelines on Remuneration Policies and Practices* (CEBS, 2010).

[214] Regulatory Technical Standards for the definition of material risk takers for remuneration purposes, EBA/RTS/2013/11, 16 December 2013, issued under Dir 2013/36/EU, art 94(2).

[215] *Reforming Remuneration Practices in Financial Services*, Consultation Paper 09/10 (FSA, 2009) 6. This was also supported in *The Turner Review* (n 13).

[216] *Reforming Remuneration Practices in Financial Services* (FSA, 2009) Policy Statement 09/15.

[217] *Reforming Remuneration Practices in Financial Services* (n 215) 28.

The key principles were:

Principle 1: Role of bodies responsible for remuneration policies and their members

A remuneration committee should:

(a)   exercise, and be constituted in a way that enables it to exercise, independent judgment;
(b)   be able to demonstrate that its decisions are consistent with a reasonable assessment of the firm's financial situation and future prospects;
(c)   have the skills and experience to reach an independent judgment on the suitability of the policy, including its implications for risk and risk management; and
(d)   be responsible for approving and periodically reviewing the remuneration policy and its adequacy and effectiveness.

Principle 2: Procedures and input of the risk and compliance functions

Procedures for setting remuneration within a firm should be clear and documented, and should include appropriate measures to manage conflicts of interest.

A firm's risk management and compliance functions should have significant input into setting remuneration for other business areas.

Principle 3: Risk and compliance function remuneration

Remuneration for employees in risk management and compliance functions should be determined independently of other business areas.

Risk and compliance functions should have performance metrics based on the achievement of the objectives of those functions.

Principle 4: Profit-based measurement and risk-adjustment

Assessments of financial performance used to calculate bonus pools should be based principally on profits.

A bonus pool calculation should include an adjustment for current and future risk, and take into account the cost of capital employed and liquidity required.

Principle 5: Long-term performance measurement

The assessment process for the performance-related component of an employee's remuneration should be designed to ensure assessment is based on longer-term performance.

Principle 6: Non-financial performance metrics

Non-financial performance metrics should form a significant part of the performance assessment process.

Non-financial performance metrics should include adherence to effective risk management and compliance with the regulatory system and with relevant overseas regulatory requirements.

Principle 7: Measurement of performance for long-term incentive plans

The measurement of performance for long-term incentive plans, including those based on the performance of shares, should be risk-adjusted.

Principle 8: Fully flexible bonus policies

The fixed component of remuneration should be a sufficient proportion of total remuneration to allow a firm to operate a fully flexible bonus policy.

Principle 9: Deferment of the majority of any significant bonus

The majority of any bonus should be deferred with a minimum vesting period if, when compared with the fixed component of an employee's remuneration, the bonus is a significant proportion of that fixed component.

Principle 10: Linking deferred elements to the firm's future performance

Any deferred element of the variable component of remuneration should be linked to the future performance of the firm as well as the employee's division or business unit.[218]

A revised Code was published in December 2010 to include changes required by the EU in the CRD3.[219] From 1 October 2013, a quoted companies' directors' remuneration report[220] has to contain:[221]

i.   A statement by the chair of the remuneration committee.
ii. The company's policy on directors' remuneration (the 'remuneration policy').[222] The remuneration policy must set out how the company proposes to pay directors, including every element of remuneration that a director will be entitled to and how it supports the company's long-term strategy and performance. The policy must also include details of the company's proposed approach to recruitment and loss of office payments.
iii. In information on how the remuneration policy was implemented in the financial year being reported on (the 'implementation report'), including a single figure for the total pay directors received that year. This is to allow shareholders to make comparisons year-on year and between companies.

Shareholders have a binding vote on a resolution to approve the directors' remuneration policy at least every three years.[223] If a company wishes to make any changes to the remuneration policy it has to put the new policy to shareholders for approval at a general meeting. Once a remuneration policy has been approved, a company is only able to make remuneration and loss of office payments which are permitted within the limits of the policy, unless the payment has been approved by a separate shareholder resolution.

Shareholders will also have an annual advisory vote on a resolution to approve the implementation report. If a company fails to pass this resolution in a year in which the remuneration policy was not put to a shareholder resolution, this will trigger the need for the company to put the remuneration policy to shareholders the following year.

---

[218] *Reforming Remuneration Practices in Financial Services* (n 216).

[219] Dir 2010/76/EU. See Consultation Paper 10/19, *Revising the Remuneration Code* (FSA, 2010).

[220] Required by the Companies Act 2006, s421, as amended by the Financial Services Act 2010, ss 4 and 5, and implemented in the Large and Medium-sized Companies and Groups (Accounts and Reports) Regs 2008, SI 2008/410.

[221] See *Directors' Remuneration Reforms—Frequently Asked Questions* (Department for Business, Innovation & Skills, 2013) available at https://www.gov.uk/government/uploads/system/uploads/attachment_data/file/158048/13-727-directors-remuneration-reforms-faq.pdf.

[222] Enterprise and Regulatory Reform Act 2012, s 79, amending the Companies Act 2006, ss 421 and 422.

[223] Enterprise and Regulatory Reform Act 2012, s 79(4), amending the Companies Act 2006, s 439A; Large and Medium-sized Companies and Groups (Accounts and Reports) Amendment Regs 2013, amending the Companies Act 2006, by substituting Sch 8. A Private Members' Bill, the Executive Pay and Remuneration Bill, would require that companies' remuneration committees have employee representation, and hold an annual binding shareholder vote on executive remuneration.

To further improve transparency around loss of office payments, from 1 October 2013, whenever a director leaves office, companies need to publish a statement setting out what payments the director has received or may receive in future. This statement must be published as soon as reasonably practicable.

Principles on remuneration were also issued on behalf of various major institutional investors, including insurers[224] and pension funds.[225] It was reported that 14 per cent fewer people receiving any kind of bonus in 2012–13 than 2011–12 (82 per cent down to 68 per cent).[226]

The Government initiated reform of the UK Corporate Governance Code on provisions for all quoted companies for clawing back remuneration from directors,[227] and amendment from 2015 of the Remuneration Code to require the inclusion in employment contracts for all PRA-authorised firms to include clawback of vested variable remuneration.[228]

Ongoing public criticism of excessive fees reduced the number of bonuses paid in 2014 but payment of large fines had some impact on the size of bonuses.[229]

In 2014 UK proposals were published that[230] at least 60 per cent of awards for directors and other high-earners (with total variable remuneration of £500,000 or more) firms must be deferred for a minimum of seven years (previously five years), with first vesting of deferred remuneration no earlier than the third anniversary of the award, and vesting no

---

[224] *ABI Principles of Remuneration*: November 2012 available at: http://www.ivis.co.uk/ExecutiveRemuneration.aspx; this expressed a clear preference for simple remuneration structures (ie one annual bonus incentive and one long term incentive), whilst not seeking to prescribe or recommend any particular type of scheme. *ABI Remuneration Principles* (ABI, November 2013), available at http://www.ivis.co.uk/ExecutiveRemuneration.aspx; this set out substantial guidance in the light of reporting regulations produced by the GC 100 and Investor Group (GC100 is the Association of General Counsel and Company Secretaries working in FTSE 100 Companies), covering the role of shareholders; the role of the board and directors; the role of the remuneration committee in protecting and promoting shareholders' interests; the function of remuneration policies in promoting value creation through transparent alignment with the agreed corporate strategy, supporting performance, encouraging the underlying sustainable financial health of the business and promoting sound risk management for the benefit of all investors; and remuneration structures in avoiding payment for failure and promoting a long-term focus, by including a high degree of deferral and measurement of performance over the long-term, and including provisions that allow the company, in specified circumstances, to forfeit all or part of a bonus or long-term incentive award before it has vested and been paid ('performance adjustment' or 'malus'); and/or recover sums already paid (clawback). See later *IMA Principles of Remuneration* (Investment Management Association, 2014).

[225] *Remuneration Principles for Building and Reinforcing Long-term Business Success* (National Association of Pension Funds and Hermes Equity Ownership Services, February 2013) available at http://www.napf.co.uk/Press-Centre/NAPFbuzz/~/media/Policy/Documents/0290-Hermes-EOS-NAPF-Pay-Principles.ashx; this stated that pay should be aligned to long-term success and the desired corporate culture throughout the organisation; pay schemes should be simple, understandable for both investors and executives, and ensure that rewards reflect long-term returns to shareholders; and remuneration committees should fully explain and justify how their decisions operate to deliver long-term business success. This was revised in *Remuneration Principles for Building and Reinforcing Long-term Business Success* (Hermes / EOS / NAPF and others, November 2013).

[226] Report by Morgan McKinley, May 2013. See also D Sahäfer, 'Rabobank to Eradicate Board Bonuses Voluntarily' *Financial Times* (London, 18 October 2013).

[227] *Directors' Remuneration: Consultation Document* (FRC, October 2013); see *Executive Remuneration* (House of Commons, January 2012), available at http://www.publications.parliament.uk/pa/cm201212/cmhansrd/cm120123/debtext/120123-0001.htm#12012313000002.

[228] *Consultation Paper CP6/14. Clawback* (Prudential Regulatory Authority, 2014).

[229] J Armitage and J Prynn, 'City Divided with Many Bonuses for the Few not the Many' *The Independent* (London, 11 January 2014); J Armitage and M Tadeo, 'JP Morgan's Bonus Pot Shrinks 4% as it Pays Off Billions in Fines' *The Independent* (London, 15 January 2014).

[230] Strengthening the alignment of risk and reward: new remuneration rules. PRA CP15/14/FCA CP14/14 (Bank of England Prudential Regulation Authority and Financial Conduct Authority, 2014).

faster than pro rata in years three to seven. For other senior staff, at least 40 per cent should be deferred, the deferral period would be five years (previously three), first vesting no earlier than the first anniversary of the award, and vesting no faster than pro rata. Previous rules were continued that a minimum of 50 per cent of the deferred remuneration must be paid in the form of shares or other instruments, such as bail-in debt, the value of which will reflect the firm's performance.

ii. Sales Incentives

The FSA also attacked sales incentives generally for more junior staff, in order to address practices that had produced extensive and repeated damage to consumers.[231] Whilst no specific changes were outlined, the FSA reminded firms that they should make sure that they have sufficient management information, business quality monitoring and controls on inappropriate behaviour and governance arrangements to counteract poor behaviour.

> Consumer trust and confidence in financial services is at an all-time low. A lack of trust and confidence is perpetuated every day when frontline staff sell products driven predominantly by financial incentives and profits for firms, rather than the needs of consumers.

> We know that the way sales staff are paid influences how and what they sell to consumers and can encourage a culture of mis-selling. For example, we have seen a sales person intentionally lie about the price of a product to increase his bonus; another adviser cut corners to rush through six sales in the last few days of a quarter to avoid his pay being reduced; and, staff able to double their bonuses even if they were mis-selling. Incentives may also be used to skew sales to more profitable products, for example we have seen advisers at one firm earn a significantly higher incentive for the more profitable products. This culture must change.

> While we recognise that firms may want to incentivise their staff to sell, this must never be at the customer's expense. Consumers must be confident they are being sold a product for the right reasons rather than just because it adds to the profits of the firm or individual sales person's pay.[232]

A review across a variety of authorised firms found that incentive schemes with high risk features and the potential for sales staff to earn significant bonuses were common across the firms assessed. Most firms did not have effective systems and controls in place to adequately manage the increased risks of mis-selling arising from their incentive schemes. The review uncovered a range of serious failings, such as:

— Firms failing to identify how incentive schemes might encourage staff to mis-sell, suggesting they had not sufficiently thought about the risks or had turned a blind eye to them.
— Firms failing to understand their own incentive schemes because they were so complex, therefore making it harder to control them.
— Firms not having enough information about their incentive schemes to understand and manage the risks.
— Firms relying too much on routine monitoring, rather than taking account of the specific features of their incentive schemes.
— Sales managers with clear conflicts of interest that were not properly managed.

---

[231] *Final Guidance. Risks to Customers from Financial Incentives* (FSA, 2013).
[232] *Guidance Consultation. Risks to Customers from Financial Incentives* (FCA, 2012).

— Firms having links to sales quality built into their incentive schemes that were ineffective.
— Firms not doing enough to control the risk of mis-selling in face-to-face situations.

The guidance stated that the likelihood of mis-selling increases when the value of incentives available to sales staff increases, or when incentives make up a high proportion of a remuneration package for sales staff. Firms will be expected to:

— Properly consider if their incentive schemes increase the risk of mis-selling and, if so, how;
— review whether their governance and controls are adequate;
— take action to address any inadequacies—this might involve changing their governance and/or controls, and/or changing their schemes;
— where risks cannot be mitigated, take action to change their schemes; and
— where a recurring problem is identified, investigate, take action and pay redress where consumers have suffered detriment.[233]

It stated that customers are likely to lose out if:

— Firms reward staff through material incentive schemes based on sales volumes, fee income or similar measures;
— firms' incentive schemes include features that are harder to manage;
— management do not understand how the specific features, complexity and value of their incentive schemes could increase mis-selling; and/or
— poor quality sales or mis-selling are not adequately reflected in the eligibility for, or level of, incentive payments.

Examples of unacceptable practices given in the Guidance were:

— Disproportionate rewards for marginal sales; a retrospective accelerator; first past the post; incentive bias; variable salaries
— Incentive scheme features that might reduce the risk of mis-selling
— Emphasising quality
— Claw back
— Capped or decreasing incentives
— Deferral of incentive payments
— Rolling target thresholds
— Balanced scorecards

In relation to Guidance on managing the risks and governance of incentive schemes, it was said that effective controls and governance may include:

— Robust risk-based business quality monitoring and adequate controls to mitigate the risk of inappropriate behaviour during sales conversations;
— Management information (MI) to identify, and act upon, trends or patterns in individual sales staff activity that could indicate an increased risk of mis-selling as a result of features in the incentive scheme. Using this MI to inform the approach to monitoring sale staff incentive risks;

[233] As set out in DISP 1.3.6 G. Principle 3 of the FSA's Principles for Businesses states that 'a firm must take reasonable care to organise and control its affairs responsibly and effectively, with adequate risk management systems'. The Senior Management Arrangements, Systems and Controls sourcebook (SYSC) of the Handbook sets out organisational and systems and controls requirements for firms.

— proper management of sales managers' conflicts of interest;
— effective oversight of incentive schemes by appropriate senior management, including approval of the incentive schemes; and
— an effective risk identification and mitigation process, including regular reviews of incentive schemes and the effectiveness of controls, taking into account customers' interests.

In December 2013 the FCA fined two prominent banks for serious failings in the systems and controls governing the financial incentives that they gave to sales staff in branches in selling over 1,094,000 protection and investment products to over 692,000 customers on an advised basis.[234] Its 2014 review found significant change in practices but roughly one in 10 firms with sales teams had higher-risk incentive scheme features where it appeared they were not managing risk properly.[235]

G. Culture and Values

In setting an agenda for future governance of financial institutions, the G30 issued a notable report in 2012 in which it set out that behaviour 'appears to be key' and that to achieve the right behaviours a shift is required from the 'hardware' of governance (structures and processes) to the 'software' (people, leadership skills, and values).[236]

> Values and culture may be the keystone of FI governance because they drive behaviors of people throughout the organization and the ultimate effectiveness of its governance arrangements.
>
> Suitable structures and processes are a necessary but not a sufficient condition for good governance, which critically depends also on patterns of behavior. Behavioral patterns depend in turn on the extent to which values such as integrity, independence of thought, and respect for the views of others are embedded in the institutional culture.
>
> In a great FI, positive values and culture are palpable from the board to the executive suite to the front line. Values and culture drive people to do the right thing even when no one is looking.[237]
>
> 1. Honesty, integrity, proper motivations, independence of thought, respect for the ideas of others, openness/transparency, the courage to speak out and act, and trust are the bedrock values of effective governance.
> 2. It is for the board of directors to articulate and senior executives to promote a culture that embeds these values from the top to the bottom of the entity. Culture is values brought to life.
> 3. Well-functioning boards set, promulgate, and embed these values, commonly in the form of a code, so that directors, senior executives, and all other employees in an entity are fully aware of the standards of behavior that are expected of them.
> 4. Because of their power to influence behaviour and the execution of the FI's strategy, values and culture are essential dimensions of inquiry and engagement for supervisors. Major shareholders or their fund managers should be attentive to the culture of an entity when making their investment decisions and engaging with an investee board.[238]

---

[234] *Final Notice to Lloyds TSB Bank plc and Bank of Scotland plc, 10 December 2013* (FCA), http://www.fca.org.uk/static/documents/final-notices/lloyds-tsb-bank-and-bank-of-scotland.pdf.
[235] *Risks to Customers from Financial Incentives—An Update* (FCA, 2014) TR14/4.
[236] *Toward Effective Governance of Financial Institutions* (Group of 30, 2012).
[237] ibid, 14 (original emphasis).
[238] ibid, s 7.

Absent impeccable personal values—honesty, personal integrity, and motivation—nothing is possible. Honesty and personal integrity are self-explanatory and important in any business, but especially in FIs, where public trust and a reputation for honesty and integrity are essential to the value proposition.[239]

It regarded a customer-centered focus as driving business behaviours, and to be a strategic choice, not a governance issue, which is then translated into operational discipline. Financial institutions, it said, had societal responsibility, since they are licensed by society to serve the needs of society.

In 2013, the G30 followed up their 2012 report by describing 'a new paradigm' for interaction between supervisors and boards of major financial institutions across the globe, based on interviews with more than 60 senior supervisors and board members of some of the largest global and domestic banks in 15 countries.[240] It noted that much attention had been given to new regulations in areas such as risk-based capital, liquidity, resolution, and risk management. But 'not enough attention had been placed on "softer" issues that rules alone cannot address, such as enhancing supervisor–board relations to improve supervisor

---

Box 20.1: G30: Supervision and Regulation are Different, and High-Quality Supervision Matters to Financial Stability

Supervision is assessing inherent risk in financial institutions and whether appropriate corporate governance, management capability, and operational processes are in place at the board and senior-executive level to oversee, understand, measure, and manage that risk. Supervision includes early intervention by the supervisor to have the institution rectify deficiencies, and choosing appropriately from a variety of informal and formal tools to be effective and to avoid unnecessary costs. High-quality, timely supervision makes institutions more resilient. It reduces the likelihood and severity of material financial or operational problems, thus enhancing financial stability.

Supervision is not regulation, which is the setting of rules that apply to the institution. And supervision is much more than assessing compliance with rules, although compliance is essential. Rather, supervision deals with behaviors that rules cannot.

Supervision requires qualitative monitoring and assessing of the capability and behavior at the board and senior-executive level. It requires considerable judgment on the part of the supervisor, and deep knowledge about the institution. Supervision is not running the institution, and supervisors must rely on governance, risk management, and control processes of the institution while testing to confirm whether reliance is well placed.

Supervision cares whether financial institutions are successful—which is the best assurance of their safety and soundness. Supervision is not designed to prevent all losses or failures.

---

[239] ibid, 77.
[240] *A New Paradigm. Financial Institution Boards and Supervisors* (Group of 30, 2013).

and board effectiveness, or on the culture of firms'.[241] The approach should be based on mutual respect and trust, and involve a particular culture.

> Realism is important. The goal is not a partnership. The fact that it is the responsibility of super-visors to assess boards means there will inevitably be occasional tension, and the new paradigm requires a substantial increased time commitment from many board members and supervisors. But the potential payoff is large. What is needed is not more of the same, rather it is a step change in the level and quality of the interaction between boards and supervisors, and having the right people who take the time to make that happen.[242]

The G30 argued that supervision is different from regulation (see its statements in Box 20.1).[243] It considered that boards remain with primacy for the implementation of effective corporate governance, emphasising the leadership role of the chairman, the need for adequate board skill sets, regular board effectiveness reviews and good visibility on risk/prudential matters for the board. But boards and supervisors should adopt a paradigm of trust-based interaction based on clear mutual expectations, with a focus on examining business model vulnerabilities, governance effectiveness and culture. The goals were effec-tive two-way communication, predictability and no surprises from either party.

> Boards of financial institutions need to welcome interaction with high-quality supervisors, view such interaction as contributing to board effectiveness, and understand that it is the responsibility of the supervisor to seek reasonable assurance that the board is effective and the institution's risk culture is appropriate and to help the supervisors fulfill that responsibility. Boards need to make enhancing supervisory relations a priority and take specific action to support the new paradigm recommended in this report.[244]

In emphasising the importance of culture and ethical standards, the G30 said:

> Boards must understand the culture of their organization, in conjunction with their business model. While an institution's broader culture affects its attitude toward risk taking, it is important to prioritize attention to risk culture since it has the most direct connection to safety and sound-ness of financial institutions. Boards should identify and deal seriously with risky culture, ensure their compensation system supports the desired culture, discuss culture at the board level and with supervisors, and periodically use a variety of formal and informal techniques to monitor risk culture. Supervisors should share their observations about the institution's risk culture with the board, and should watch for serious culture issues that need rectification. Supervisors and policy makers should be cautious about writing rules or guidance about culture, and should set realistic expectations about what is achievable.[245]

The report noted that systems and messages can reinforce or undermine the culture of understood behaviours and attitudes within an organisation.

---

[241] ibid, 11.
[242] ibid, 5.
[243] The distinction was also made by the de Larosière Report (n 56 above), para 38: 'Regulation is the set of rules and standards that govern financial institutions; their main objective is to foster financial stability and to protect the customers of financial services. Regulation can take different forms, ranging from information requirements to strict measures such as capital requirements. On the other hand, supervision is the process designed to oversee financial institutions in order to ensure that rules and standards are properly applied. This being said, in practice, regulation and supervision are intertwined ...'
[244] (n 240) 18.
[245] *A New Paradigm. Financial Institution Boards and Supervisors* (Group of 30, 2013).

The G30's Effective Governance report states that 'values and culture may be the keystone of FI governance because they drive behaviors of people throughout the organization and the ultimate effectiveness of the governance arrangements'.[246]

> Culture is the internal compass that guides individuals' behaviors when no one is looking. It involves soft features that defy quantitative measurement, but they cannot be ignored.
>
> There is no one culture that is appropriate for a major FI. Any culture can fail....
>
> Culture is closely aligned with business model. Management, boards, and supervisors should carefully consider whether the business model reinforces a healthy culture. Business strategies and models that focus on sales rather than customers, short-term results rather than long-term value, growth rather than sustainability, and low cost rather than efficiency, can create unhealthy cultures. It can be very difficult to change the culture without also changing the business model.
>
> The risk culture of individual institutions will naturally be embedded in the institution's overall culture and in the financial culture of the country....
>
> The realistic expectation of supervisors' interventions should be to deal with potentially seriously problematic cultures (outliers) that are not adequately mitigated and that boards have not dealt with. Understanding culture more broadly at major institutions is valuable. But supervisors should avoid attempts to make granular cultural distinctions between one firm and another. There is no one FI cultural ideal. To expect more than this is to ask for the undoable, to waste scarce resources, and to lead to excessive intrusion into how banks are run.[247]

The report recommended that supervisors and boards should use a short list of simple descriptors of culture.

> Useful descriptors of desired culture include: valuing risk awareness across the FI; sustainability; client-focused; integrity; accountability; independence of thought; respect for the views of others; transparency; doing the right thing; balanced decision making; open to constructive challenge, including from subordinates; viewing risk management and compliance as adding value; culture of ownership of risk and compliance in both the business and control functions; collaboration across functional groups; innovation; excellence in execution; learning from mistakes; inclusion of others; conservative; and prudent or cautious.
>
> While these traits appear to be uniquely desirable, they can also be problematic in certain circumstances; for example, too conservative or cautious a culture can lack the dynamism needed for success, which in turn is a key bulwark of safety and soundness. Again, as an example, the organizational culture literature has identified that an excess of collaboration can produce groupthink, which itself can pose risks.
>
> In contrast, various people interviewed for this report suggested elements of culture that can be problematic. Examples include: growth for growth's sake, an excessive sales- or cost-focused culture, an overbearing CEO (or business line head), an unduly deferential culture, an excessively aggressive culture that does not adequately consider whether the identified goal is the right thing to do, cultures that push business while disregarding risks and controls, an ego-driven or star-performer culture, hubris, seeing policies and limits as items to be gamed, siloed cultures, and excessively valuing autonomy over control and adherence to policies.

---

[246] *Toward Effective Governance of Financial Institutions* (n 236) 79.
[247] ibid, 38.

Aspects of culture that could prove problematic can be mitigated. For example, some bemoan the powerful short-term-performance-driven-CEO culture. But organizations do need active, engaged CEOs who can push change and achieve complex strategies for success (which is important for safety and soundness). The downsides of this culture can be mitigated by an equally strong board, with highly effective challenge, including the counterweight of a very strong chair....[248]

Statements by the FCA from the same time also emphasised the fundamental importance of a firm's culture.[249] The Director of Supervision at the FCA, Clive Adamson, noted that it was difficult to set criteria for an acceptable culture, but it was possible to observe outcomes and actions that indicated this, and to identify the key drivers of culture at a firm, which include:

— Setting the tone from the top;
— translating this into easily understood business practices; and
— supporting the right behaviours through performance management, employee development, and reinforcing through reward programmes.[250]

This approach can be contrasted with the policy of focusing on individuals in a different way, noted above, through rules on accountability and criminalisation. It remains to be seen whether this conflict can be viewed as a successful two-pronged strategy or wholly inconsistent and ineffective.

A 2013 report by Anthony Salz into the business practices of a major bank, in the light of the emergence of ongoing scandals, noted that

A bank's licence to operate is built on the trust of customers and of other stakeholders, such as its staff, regulators and the public as a whole. Trust is built from experience of reasonable expectations being fulfilled—a confidence that an organisation will behave fairly. Successful banks acquire a reputation for being trustworthy. This can take decades to build. Yet it can be destroyed quickly and, in global organisations, by events almost anywhere in the world. Some companies have greater reputational resilience than others. They get the benefit of the doubt when things go wrong—partly because of the far greater number of things that go right and partly because of the way they respond to problems. Public opinion also tends to be more generous to those organisations that seem to be trying to do the right thing, or that have an appreciable social purpose.[251]

The bank had itself noted that trust in banks had been 'decimated and needs to be rebuilt' and that its own behaviours had elicited significant criticism.[252] The bank's culture had favoured 'transactions over relationships, the short term over sustainability, and financial over other business purposes'.[253] Salz found that that culture had predominantly shaped the unacceptable business practices. He laid the responsibility for leading a transformation

---

[248] ibid, 39–40.

[249] *The FCA's Approach to Advancing its Objectives* (FCA, 2013).

[250] C Adamson, 'The Importance of Culture in Driving Behaviours of Firms and how the FCA will Assess this', speech by Director of Supervision at the CFA Society UK Professionalism Conference, 19 April 2013, http://www.fca.org.uk/news/regulation-professionalism.

[251] *The Salz Review of Barclays' Business Practices report to the Board of Barclays PLC* (2013), para 2.4; www.salzreview.co.uk, https://www.salzreview.co.uk/c/document_library/get_file?uuid=557994c9-9c7f-4037-887b-8b5623bed25e&groupId=4705611.

[252] ibid, paras 2.5 and 2.7.

[253] ibid, para 2.13.

in culture with the Board and the Group Chief Executive.[254] He recommended that the design and operation of the ways in which the bank managed and developed its people was crucial to supporting a desirable culture, and that the human resources function should be given sufficient status to stand up to the business units on a variety of people issues, including pay. Pay had been seen as the primary tool to shape behaviour, and insufficient attention had been given to personal development and leadership skills (as opposed to technical training).[255] The bank must improve its openness and transparency in order to facilitate trust, but this would involve a fundamental change in attitude and mindsets, rather than mere reporting[256] Fundamental change was also in relationships with key stakeholders, including moving from a confrontational approach with regulators to one that is more open and cooperative.[257]

Perceptive scholars also noted a shift in the analysis of financial markets from economics to a social conception.[258] This would necessitate a shift in the style of regulation from rules to a social dimension. A major group of investment firms noted: 'The Group is unanimously and firmly of the view that beyond our formal recommendations, the greatest need is for deep cultural change'.[259]

The Corporation of the City of London was particularly concerned that the ongoing sequence of financial scandals would undermine confidence in the City and lead to significantly deterioration in the ranking of London as a financial and corporate centre.[260] The Lord Mayor spearheaded an initiative to restore the City's 'trust and values', recalling the traditional adage 'my word is my bond'. This produced a series of agreements on improving business culture and behaviour, based around the following actions:[261]

— *Leadership with Integrity*. A new research and education programme at Cass Business School.
— *Performance with Integrity*. Recruitment, appraisal and development would be linked to ethics and behaviour. A new policy guide and best practice toolkit in performance management was prepared to help employers embed values at three crucial stages: Recruitment, performance appraisal and development. The toolkit particularly addresses the needs of the individual who delivers short term financial results but does not work by the organisation's values and creates excessive risk. The work was cross-referenced to published professional standards, regulatory requirements and internal disciplinary processes.
— *Governing Values*. Designed to enable Boards to ensure that values are observed and 'lived'.

---

[254] ibid, para 2.21.
[255] ibid, para 2.25.
[256] ibid, para 2.32.
[257] ibid, para 2.34.
[258] J Black, 'Seeing, Knowing, and Regulating Financial Markets: Moving the Cognitive Framework from the Economic to the Social', LSE Legal Studies Working Paper No 24/2013.
[259] *Report of the Collective Engagement Working Group* (Collective Engagement Working Group, 2013), available at http://www.investmentuk.org/assets/files/press/2013/20131203-cewginvestorforum.pdf.
[260] *Report on The Lord Mayor's Conference on Trust and Values*, November 2011.
[261] *Investing in Integrity. The Lord Mayor's Conference on Trust and Values*, City Values Forum, October 2012, http://tomorrowscompany.com/governing-values.

654   *Financial Services*

— *The City Obligation.* A personal pledge to be taken voluntarily by those working in the City to uphold the City's enduring values, the highest standards of integrity and professional behaviour, with a focus on obligations to clients and other stakeholders. Similar to 'My Word is My Bond'.
— *Integrity Resources.* Defining and sharing best practice, including: Next generation leaders; remuneration and regulation; diversity and inclusion; training and development; corporate social responsibility.

A group of interested parties issued a report in late 2014 that identified culture as cause and solution of problems for retail banking.[262] It stated that an aggressive sales culture was a major driver of bank failure, that policy interventions addressed structural issues but left culture change to the banks, that all banks had some kind of culture change process underway, but that change remained fragile and many expected bad practices to continue. Culture was said to be better in the new, smaller challenger banks. It called on banks to commit themselves to continuous and consistent delivery of culture change.

IV. Conclusions

The global financial crisis spawned a series of fundamental reforms in the regulatory architecture and approaches. Fourteen issues are worthy of comment in the context of this book.

First, perhaps the most fundamental observation is that the regulation of financial services before the crisis *failed to adapt* to changing circumstances. A senior regulator has observed that the modern market is global in nature, featuring highly mobile capital; is characterised by fierce competition among financial service providers; no longer features barriers between historically separate financial products, sectors and actors; features increasing cost to investors, financial entities and regulators of monitoring conduct and risk due to increasing use of complex products; features large and relatively liquid unregulated institutional financial markets paralleling the regulated markets; and has rapidly incorporated advanced technologies.[263]

Second, a major concern is that the *entire system* failed. The financial crisis was ultimately a crisis of markets and the system, rather than of institutions or individual products.[264] The system of checking that fair practices were achieved in outcomes was not in place, important signals were not observed, ongoing bad practices were not identified, the objective of regulation was to support growth rather than safe and fair conduct, and the regulators did not have appropriate powers to intervene. A number of these problems can and now have been addressed. Thus, a focus on outcomes should identify bad practices more readily and swiftly and enable regulators and markets to address them: This is the purpose of the empowerment of conduct regulation.

---

[262] *A Report on the Culture of British Retail Banking* (New City Agenda and Cass Business School, 2014). Founders of New City Agenda were Lord McFall of Alcluith, David Davis MP and Lord Sharkey.
[263] E Tafara, 'Foreword. Observations about the crisis and reform' in Ferran, Moloney, Hill and Coffee, Jr (n 21).
[264] A Turner, 'Reforming Finance: Are we being Radical Enough?' Speech February 1, 2011; Moloney (n 21) 122.

This leads to the third point, which concerns the absolute requirement for financial services regulatory systems to be *global and comprehensive* in scope. There is universal realisation that 'global governance of financial markets calls for global institutions to be able to coordinate and internalize local diversities determined by public but also private regulatory cultures'.[265] Regulation of financial services can no longer be national or regional, but global. Opportunities for forum shopping to exploit differences in regimes need to be eliminated.[266] But both 'varieties of capitalism' theory[267] and 'public choice' theory[268] postulate that differences will remain as nations and regulators seek to specialise according to their comparative advantages and to protect their autonomy. Indeed, some scholars argue that regulatory diversity is a virtue, since harmonisation can increase systemic risk, rather than decrease it.[269]

Fourth, it follows that there has been an *extension 'upwards' in regulatory control* from national bodies to regional bodies or higher. The current position is that a range of supranational governance structures and regulatory approaches exist, which have been considered to vary with two dimensions: (a) The degree of centralisation of regulation, which includes networks, meta-organisations and single central authorities; and (b) the degree of invasiveness of regulation, which ranges from sunshine regulation to command and control approaches.[270] In contrast to the EU competition law model, the newly established financial European Supervisory Authorities (ESAs) are part of a complex structural development, in which the separation between a highly invasive regulatory approach and a decentralised supervisory structure adds further complexity.[271] Power amongst public bodies has been transferred upwards to international bodies, including political and technical standards bodies.[272] This is, at this stage, an incomplete shift, since the EBA is argued to have had insufficient powers, and there is a need for clarification of the roles and responsibilities between the EBA, the ECB and the national authorities.[273] However, the involvement of

[265] Miller and Cafaggi (n 119) 8.
[266] This has given rise to jurisdictional contests between, for example, US and EU authorities: see JC Coffee Jr, 'Extraterritorial Financial Regulation: Why ET Can't Come Home' (2014) 99(6) *Cornell Law Review* 1259.
[267] PA Hall and D Soskice, 'An Introduction to Varieties of Capitalism' in PA Hall and D Soskice (eds), *Varieties of Capitalism: The Institutional Foundations of Comparative Advantage* (Oxford, Oxford University Press, 2001) 1–68; B Hancké, 'Introducing the Debate' in B Hancké (ed), *Debating Varieties of Capitalism: A Reader* (Oxford, Oxford University Press, 2009) 5. See also H Macartney, 'Variegated Neo-Liberalism: Transnationally Oriented Fractions of Capital in EU Financial Market Integration' (2009) 35 *Review of International Studies* 451–80, 452–56; B Amable, *The Diversity of Modern Capitalism* (Oxford, Oxford University Press, 2003); M Aoki, *Towards a Comparative Institutional Analysis* (Cambridge MA, MIT Press, 2001).
[268] JR Macey, 'The "Demand" for International Regulatory Cooperation: A Public-Choice Perspective' in GA Bermann, M Herdegen and PL Lindseth, *Transatlantic Regulatory Cooperation: Legal Problems and Political Prospects* (Oxford, Oxford University Press, 2000).
[269] R Romano, 'For Diversity in the International Regulation of Financial Institutions: Redesigning the Basel Architecture' Yale Law & Economics Research Paper No 452 ECGI—Law Working Paper, at http://papers.ssrn.com/sol3/papers.cfm?abstract_id=2127749.
[270] GS Castellano, A Jeunemaître and B Lange, 'Reforming European Union Financial Regulation: Thinking Through Governance Models' (2012) 23(3) *European Business Law Review* 409.
[271] ibid.
[272] Miller and Cafaggi (n 119) ch 5. 'The legitimacy and accountability of the IASB as an international standard setter'; T Büthe and W Mattli, *The New Global Rulers. The Privatisation of Regulation in the World Economy* (Princeton and Oxford, Princeton University Press, 2013).
[273] *Special Report. European Banking Supervision Taking Shape—EBA and its Changing Context* (European Court of Auditors, 2014).

both regional and national regulators and of individual firms remains essential. The system has become more complex as well as more intense.

Fifth, effective regulation needs to have a suitably strong level of *intensity*. The prior regime was demonstrably far too lax. This was the result of two factors: The assumption that markets were sufficiently competitive and that the banks' commercial self-interest would engender sensible and reliable behaviour, and deliberate political decisions by national governments in the major financial centres not to annoy financial institutions, so as to avoid the risk of institutions relocating away from major host jurisdictions. Regulatory supervision was therefore 'light touch'. Intervention and enforcement were reactive. Orthodox thinking was that banks and the market would regulate themselves. However, the climate enabled banks to make huge mistakes that neither they nor regulators were able to anticipate nor control, or even identify. One aspect of subsequent reform was simply to introduce a significantly strengthened regulatory system, in which controls and reporting were more onerous, so that intervention could now be pro-active and frequent.

In this respect it is interesting to *compare* the general architecture of the regulatory systems for financial services with those reviewed in the previous chapter for product safety, such as for pharmaceuticals. The types of controls introduced in 2009–2014 for the former had all existed for some time in the latter. There was nothing particularly novel in the techniques. This highlights the fact that the depth and breadth of regulation are primarily political choices rather than flow from technical or scientific considerations. But it also reveals that regulatory systems have developed in silos with little cross-reference between different models, and no over-arching planning or review. Both policy papers and academic comment on the nature of the financial sector reforms has come almost exclusively from officials and scholars who focus only on that sector, rather than from a wider cohort.

That observation on the narrowness of the debate can be illustrated by a sixth point, which concerns the nature of a series of debates within financial services experts. The point concerns the degree of *objectivity* that is brought to bear, the breadth of vision and ability to learn by making as wide comparisons as possible. One argument has been based on the premise that regulation has failed, so private enforcement should be preferred. A second premise—which contrasts with the first—is that the crucial failure was in self-regulation, so more regulation should be prescribed. A third premise is whether the system failed because it is too reliant on either rules or principles (depending on one's point of view). A fourth premise is that there should be more deterrence on corporations and individuals. Those who are familiar with regulatory systems other than just financial services might frame or answer each of these issues differently from those who are within the particular system. On the first two points, for example, a common response might be that the regulatory system was simply insufficiently globalised and lacking in intensity and cohesion, and the fact that it suffered catastrophic failure should be no surprise. Accordingly, the response should be to globalise, intensify and coalesce the regulatory system.

Seventh, comments can be made on the point that the financial services regulatory and supervision system highlights a perennial *conflict between rules and principles*. The system comprises very many detailed rules, which are largely unmappable and impenetrable to all but expert insiders. By contrast, the rules are based on simple principles of fairness, transparency and accountability. Nevertheless, the endless progression of long-submerged scandals show that many industry personnel lost sight of the core values, and the regulatory system was inadequate to identify or control such behaviour. Political fixes have been put in place by strengthening rules, but rules fail to address the conundrum of how to ensure that values are observed.

It is widely accepted that the previous model incorporated extensive freedom from intrusive regulatory requirements by banks, described by many as self-regulation,[274] and a complete absence of regulation by the 'shadow banking' sector, and that such mechanisms failed.[275] Whilst club-style self-regulation may have been adequate in an era when the market was constituted by a closed elite that could operate on reputation for reliability and trust, the Big Bang sought to impose a mass of detailed rules and codes.

Some scholars consider that a key issue is the difference between rules and principles, in that reliance on rules gives rise to avoidance through arbitrage and exceptions, and failure to apply principles.[276] The approach enabled 'capture by complexity'.[277] Interestingly, capture by regulatees has not been asserted, but capture by politicians ('support growth, don't annoy the banks or drive them away') has support. Campbell and Loughrey note that the excessively detailed rules and codes emptied financial services regulation of moral content, and hence failed to include regard for the legitimate interests of the client.[278] They argue that it is *in principle* impossible to ex ante specify the rules because such specification must create the possibility of gaming those rules, as the process of rule-following is reflexive.[279]

But the financial services regulatory system *did* include principles, albeit ones that it failed to apply, or to recognise were being widely flouted.[280] The rules provided, and were based on the assumption, that firms would operate on the moral principle of *fairness*.[281] Indeed, the FSA's 2001 Treating Customers Fairly (TCF) initiative[282] *should* have worked, but it was based on trusting the regulated community to establish and apply to itself 'basic moral norms' in day-to-day business.[283] Sharon Gilad's analysis is that TCF failed for a series of reasons.[284] First, the meaning of the TCF initiative was framed by the FSA as a 'principles-based initiative' but its implementation was 'managerialised' by the relevant

---

[274] It is significant that the term 'self-regulation' is used by financial services scholars rather than 'co-regulation', which would be used by regulatory scholars. The statement by the European Commissioner that 'self-regulation has failed' itself fails to recognise that public regulation existed previously but was inadequate: M Barnier, 'Financial Regulation in Europe-Where Next?' speech March 31, 2010.

[275] Gennaioli, Shleifer and Vishny (n 14); Gorton and Metrick (n 14); Pacces (n 2).

[276] J Black, 'Forms and Paradoxes of Principles-Based Regulation' (2008) 3 *Capital Markets Law Journal* 425–57; J Black, M Hopper and C Band, 'Making a Success of Principles-Based Regulation' (2007) 1(3) *Law and Financial Markets Review* 191–206; CL Ford, 'New Governance, Compliance, and Principles-Based Securities Regulation' (2008) 45 *American Business Law Journal* 1–60.

[277] Moloney (n 21).

[278] D Campbell and J Loughrey, 'The Regulation of Self-Interest in Financial Markets' in J O'Brien and G Gilligan (eds), *Integrity, Risk and Accountability in Capital Markets. Regulating Culture* (Oxford, Hart Publishing, 2013) 69.

[279] ibid.

[280] H Sants, 'Creating the FCA', speech, BBA Conference, 2 March 2011.

[281] The FSA's principles required firms to pay due regard to customer interests and to treat customers fairly (Principle 6) and to pay due regard to clients' information needs by communicating information in a way which is clear, fair and not misleading (Principle 7).

[282] FSA, *Treating Customers Fairly After the Point of Sale*, DP7 (June 2001); *Policy Statement 7/11, The Responsibilities of Providers and Distributors for the Fair Treatment of Customers* (FSA, 2007). See S Gilad, 'Institutionalizing Fairness in Financial Markets: Mission Impossible?' (2011) 5 *Regulation and Governance* 309.

[283] A Georgosouli, 'The FSA's "Treating Customers Fairly" (TCF) Initiative: What Is So Good About It and Why It May Not Work' (2011) 3 *Journal of Law and Society* 405, 412; Campbell and Loughrey (n 278).

[284] S Gilad, 'Beyond Endogeneity: How Firms and Regulators Co-Construct the Meaning of Regulation' (2014) 36(2) *Law & Policy* 134–64.

professionals in the banks, who re-framed it as a requirement to produce management information. The information was to evidence their belief that the purpose was to demon\ strate that they delivered a 'great customer experience' rather than to show that customers were sold products that were appropriate for them. (The difference in emphasis in understandings might be illustrated by changing the emphasis: From treating customers *fairly*, to *treating* them fairly.) Second, banks perceived their practices as already fair to customers. They were incapable of realising the gap between internal and external ethical standards. Third, the entrenched hard-sell practices were embedded in industry practice and remuneration schemes and product development practices. Fourth, although the FSA realised after a year or two that the initiative was not producing the desired results, and mounted a fresh attack, the combination of factors two and three above defeated achievement of substantial change in banks' practices until the tsunami of allegations of mis-selling built up over several years. It has also been argued that because the objectives and principles in the old rules *operated at a general level*, rather than in relation to specific actions, and also were expressed in an open-textured way, they were not well-suited to the role of being a mechanism for formal accountability through the judicial system.[285]

O'Brien argues that approaches based on rules and principles *both* failed, and what is needed is to add further principles and controls, namely *permissibility* (whether a particular product can be sold and if so to whom and on what basis),[286] *responsibility* (who carries the risk if the investment sours and on what terms) and *legitimacy* (does the product serve a legitimate purpose and who should determine it).[287] O'Brien argued for the dynamic integration of rules, principles and social norms within an interlocking responsive framework.[288]

The eighth point concerns the correct analysis of *the nature of the regulatory system*, and to what extent it comprises 'regulation', self-regulation, or other forms, and how the forms have changed or should change. Niamh Maloney notes that traditional, rules-based 'command and control' regulation is replacing the variants of self-regulation which dominated in certain market sectors pre-crisis.[289] She is right that there has been a retreat into hierarchical regulation. However, the system is so large and complex, and involves so many actors at different levels, that a regulatory system based solely on 'command and control' could never succeed. Eilís Ferran notes:

> [T]he delivery of 'good' supervision, which is now perceived to be characterized by an approach that is 'intrusive, skeptical, proactive, comprehensive, adaptive, and conclusive',[290] is simply too complex and too important a task for even the most self-confident and sure-footed supervisory authority not to need significant support. [291]

---

[285] E Lomnika, *The Financial Services and Markets Act: An Annotated Guide* (London, Sweet & Maxwell, 2002) 39; E Ferran, 'The New Mandate for the Supervision of Financial Services Conduct' (2012) *Current Legal Problems* 1–43.

[286] Hence the addition of a power for supervisors to ban products: Financial Services Act 2012, s 22, inserting FSMA s137C.

[287] O'Brien (n 43).

[288] ibid.

[289] Moloney (n 21).

[290] J Viñals and J Fiechter, 'The Making of Good Supervision: Learning to Say "No"' IMF Staff Position Note, 18 May 2010, SPN/10/08.

[291] Ferran (n 285) 11–12.

Such a complex system has no option but to enlist and rely on the active involvement of actors at every level, with effective inter-relation between their various management systems. This approach corresponds to Christine Parker's multi-centred regulatory model,[292] which includes 'command and control' elements but also many other elements of control. Geoffrey Miller and Fabrizio Cafaggi identify the importance of management-based information,[293] given that firms ought to have better information about their businesses than external regulators,[294] and identify the strengthening of tools such as internal audit, compliance, risk management, internal ratings-based methodologies under the Basel guidelines, house rules and contracts.

The financial services system, unlike for example the medicines system but like the general products system, does not require ex ante approval of individual products or marketing statements. The New Framework system requires firms to approve product safety systems and individual product types. The new financial services approach is not based on ex ante licensing of retail market products, but is 'pitched between a strategy that relies on point-of-sale interventions and one that relies on product pre-approval'.[295] It is argued that there are too many financial services products to permit individual external approval and that that would impede innovation, so the regulatory equivalent has to be reliance on internal controls, extensive ex post monitoring and regulatory power to prohibit products[296] and practices and impose requirements. An observation by Elizabeth Warren in proposing the establishment of the US Consumer Financial Protection Bureau has been much cited.[297] She noted that the regulatory system supported the post-marketing withdrawal of a toaster that had been identified as dangerous, so as to reduce the risk of fire, whereas no such system operated in relation to post-marketing safety of financial products, for which ex post litigation remained the only option to try to clear up the mess. It would appear that systemic comparison between regulatory regimes has rarely occurred, and is overdue. Post-sale duties on suppliers and monitoring systems involving users, suppliers, intermediaries (ombudsmen) and regulators are well established in other sectors, but are only now being incorporated into financial services regulation as 'risk monitors'.[298]

The ninth point is that the focus should be on *results* (*outcomes*), as has now been recognised in financial services regulation. It is necessary to deliver services fairly, through products that are appropriate for their users, and on the basis that the entire system will operate as intended. The perceived tension between systemic stability and consumer protection justified concentrating on the former as the principal objective and largely ignoring the latter goal.[299] That view has been shown to be poor policy for two main reasons: First,

---

[292] C Parker, *The Open Corporation: Effective Self-regulation and Democracy* (Cambridge, Cambridge University Press, 2002).

[293] Miller and Cafaggi (n 119) ch 1.

[294] C Coglianese and D Lazer, 'Management-Based Regulation: Prescribing Private Management to Achieve Public Goals' (2010) 37 *Law & Society Review* 691; KA Bamberger, 'Technologies of Compliance: Risk and Regulation in a Digital Age' (2010) 88 *Texas Law Review* 669.

[295] *Discussion Paper 11/1, Product Intervention* (FSA, 2011) 21.

[296] Financial Services Act 2012, s 24 inserting FSMA s 137C.

[297] E Warren, 'Unsafe at Any Rate' (2007) 5(8) *Democracy* 8.

[298] J Black, 'Enrolling Actors in Regulatory Processes: Examples from UK Financial Services Regulation' [2003] *Public Law* 63–91.

[299] Tafara (n 263).

concentrating on consumer (or user) protection itself supports systemic stability by reveal-ing weaknesses in the system and, second, ignoring the basic societal purpose of financial services leads to not only failure to achieve social ends (because economic ends are not achieved) but also a collapse of trust in financial service providers and intermediaries when behaviour is shown to be unethical.

Tenth, it is clear that *incentives* play a role in behaviour. Various scholars argue that since the purpose of businesses is to make profits, it makes sense for shareholders to incentivise managers and sales staff to maximise profits consistent with the desired attitude for risk and innovation in the particular business. Certainly, a widely held mantra holds that fierce com-petition is good for markets, innovation, customers and society. In some firms, the appetite for one or more of the values of risk, competition and sales will be high. But how far should a drive for sales be allowed if it gives rise to anti-social practices? It may be questioned whether capping pay or bonuses in any sector will merely achieve changes in behaviour unless the same cap is applied to the overwhelming majority of workers in the same sector globally and possibly also other business sectors. Some consider that the problem is one of timing: By the time undesirable consequences of the taking of unacceptable risk have come to light, individual managers responsible will have left the firm's employment. Thus, the 'problem is not that bankers earn too much money, but that they may take their money and run before the bank goes bankrupt [or] bailed out'.[300] Hence, the rational arrangement is to defer bankers' performance pay until well after the end of their term.[301]

An eleventh point relates to the attempt to hold individual managers, especially sen-ior directors, *accountable* for actions and, in particular, for failures. This has been done by specifying their responsibilities, so that if failures occur the 'responsible' manager can be punished and pursued for compensation, including by having remuneration clawed back. The evidence base as to whether such an approach works appears to be entirely lacking. This absence appears to be connected with the fact that the adoption of this policy of sanc-tioning individuals for systemic failures was largely initiated, in the UK at least, by parlia-mentarians. Its simplistic approach is easy to put across in a speech or newspaper headline.

However, the policy of threatening to punish individuals is at odds with a different idea that has emerged from senior regulators and bankers themselves. That is the idea that (the twelfth point) it is in fact a commercial organisation's *culture* that matters, and which is fundamentally important in driving the behaviour of all of its staff. Corporate culture is difficult to regulate, but references are beginning to appear not just to 'culture' but to good or bad cultures, and how they can be created or avoided. These thoughts deserve consider-ably more attention. If the notion is correct, then the most important objective of a regu-latory system should be to require and nurture a culture in which virtuous decisions and outcomes occur.

It has, however, been observed that not only is it difficult to define an organisation's culture, but it is possibly impossible to regulate it, at least through traditional tools such as encapsulating it in rules that will identify when it does not exist and justify imposition

---

[300] Pacces (n 2); citing LA Bebchuk and H Spamann, 'Regulating Bankers' Pay' (2010) 98(2) *Georgetown Law Journal* 247–87.

[301] S Bhagat and R Romano, 'Reforming Executive Compensation: Focusing and Committing to the Long-term' (2009) 26(2) *Yale Journal on Regulation* 359–72.

of some sanction.[302] Furthermore, culture varies between organisations, understandably related to the underlying purposes of the organisation, its structure and modes of operation.[303] Obvious differences can be expected between organisations that are, for example, public entities, charities, private businesses. An important observation is that 'While banking regulation is designed to control and, to a certain extent, suppress risk taking, securities regulation is, in stark contrast, designed to facilitate it.'[304] In many situations within democratic capitalist states firms are required to make profits.

The thirteenth point is to make a link between culture and *ethics*, so as to be able to identify the particular *nature of the culture* that an organisation has and exhibits through its actions. Differences in cultures are connected with variations in what are regarded in relation to humans as personal intentions, which can range from altruism to negligence, recklessness, wilful to malignity.[305] In relation to organisations, Sorensen argues that the issue is the degree to which egregious conduct is informed by a disconnect between stated and lived values.[306] The focus on an ethical mode of action has, therefore, given rise to suggestions that what should be required is 'truth-telling'[307] and 'other-regarding action'.[308] Julia Black has issued a strong call for reorientation of regulating financial markets in terms of *social networks*.[309]

Eilís Ferran notes that public policy has gone back to basics in recalling that *core functions* of financial institutions are to provide payment mechanisms and deposit-taking facilities, and to channel resources to where they are most needed by making loans: Financial services should support the real economy.[310] Westbrook has argued that finance is *social*, given that many social goods on which people and their relationships rely (education, health care, employment opportunities and retirement) are provided by the financial system, and that the nature of regulation should be viewed not as permissive but as custodial, involving custody of social assets.[311] This chimes with bankers' 'radical pledge' of corporate responsibility to society.[312] Similarly, Seumas Miller notes that the proximate end of (retail) banks

---

[302] Campbell and Loughrey (n 278) (questioning whether concrete regulation can directly address so vague a task as changing culture).

[303] Miller (n 27).

[304] Tafara (n 263) xxv.

[305] G Rossouw and L van Vuuren, 'Modes of Managing Morality: A Descriptive Model of Strategies for Managing Ethics' (2003) 46 *Journal of Business Ethics* 389 (noting a five-stage process in which corporate activity moves from (1) immorality; (2) reactivity; (3) compliance; (4) integrity; (5) total alignment: at 391.

[306] J Sorensen, 'The Strength of Corporate Culture and the Reliability of Firm Performance' (2002) 47 *Administrative Science Quarterly* 70, 72 (defining culture narrowly as a system of shared values and norms that define appropriate attitudes and behaviours for organisational members).

[307] DC Langevoort, 'Global Securities Regulation after the Financial Crisis' (2011) 13 *Journal of International Economic Law* 799–815.

[308] D Awrey, W Blair and D Kershaw, 'Between Law and Markets: Is There A Role for Culture and Ethics in Financial Regulation?' (2013) 38(1) *Delaware Journal of Corporate Law* 191.

[309] Black (n 258).

[310] Ferran, Moloney, Hill and Coffee, Jr (n 21) 10.

[311] DA Westbrook, 'The Culture of Financial Institutions: The Institution of Political Economy' in J O'Brien and G Gilligan (eds), *Integrity, Risk and Accountability in Capital Markets. Regulating Culture* (Oxford, Hart Publishing, 2013); S Miller, *The Moral Foundations of Social Institutions: A Philosophical Study* (New York, Cambridge University Press, 2010).

[312] M Agius et al, 'Financial Leaders Pledge Excellence and Integrity' *Financial Times* (London, 29 September 2010).

might be to maximise shareholder value, but their ultimate purpose is to provide a safe and secure place for depositors' savings and (relatedly) to loan funds to enable families to buy homes, businesses to expand, long-term infrastructure investment needs to be met, and so on.[313] Accordingly, he suggests that collective moral responsibility is required:

> The point here is not that the majority of individuals themselves engage in corrupt or unethical practices, but rather that in certain cultural or ideological contexts, they may well refrain from reporting them or otherwise preventing a minority from doing so. Many key elements of integrity systems such as ethics codes, codes of practice, education programs and the like, do not exist, for the most part, to directly prevent or deter the few people who are wrongdoers from doing wrong, but rather to ensure that the many are intolerant of the wrongdoing of the few.[314]

He considers that an important potential engine of ethno-cultural education is the 'professionalization' process at the occupational level,[315] and that

> The process of occupational ethical acculturation in large banking organisations would consist of such things as the establishing an independent occupational association for the occupational group in question, reward and remuneration systems designed to realise the ultimate institutional purposes of the organisation rather than to maximise short-term profits and share process (or line the pockets of executive managers), establishing of complaints processes conducted by the association, independent (of management) and well-resourced anti-corruption units within the banking organisation itself, appropriate whistle-blowing legislation (including legal protections) and the like. Such measures can assist in the generation and maintenance of a culture of collective moral responsibility and, not the least, one that is intolerant of corruption.[316]

Such an approach can clearly be seen in the City of London's City Values programme noted above. The conclusion is that a culture is necessarily based on both individual personal responsibility and also organisational integrity, and a joint commitment to achieving market integrity.

Finally, a fourteenth point is to note a *tension between technical and political considerations*. The Basel Core Principles are the product of supervisory professionals, whereas the EU system that has been constructed is—as always—the product of a political legislative process in which features can be distorted, omitted or enhanced.[317] In the UK, a series of reports by professional or academic experts have been influential but so have the views of the Government and of the Parliamentary Committee. The observation that law is influenced by political and constitutional constraints is far from new, but when the operational integrity of legal systems is absolutely required in order to deliver physical and economic safety, it would seem to be important that the right decisions are taken. This idea raises the problem of the balance of influence between experts, the general populace and political representatives.

---

[313] Miller (n 27) 116.

[314] ibid, 127.

[315] See A Alexandra and S Miller, *Integrity Systems for Occupations* (Aldershot, Ashgate, 2010).

[316] Miller (n 311) 127.

[317] E Ferran, 'European Banking Union: Imperfect, But It Can Work' University of Cambridge Faculty of Law Research Paper 30/2014, available at http://papers.ssrn.com/sol3/papers.cfm?abstract_id=2426247.

Table 20.2: Basel Core Principles for Effective Banking Supervision[318]

Supervisory powers, responsibilities and functions
— *Principle 1—Responsibilities, objectives and powers*: An effective system of banking supervision has clear responsibilities and objectives for each authority involved in the supervision of banks and banking groups. A suitable legal framework for banking supervision is in place to provide each responsible authority with the necessary legal powers to authorise banks, conduct ongoing supervision, address compliance with laws and undertake timely corrective actions to address safety and soundness concerns.
— *Principle 2—Independence, accountability, resourcing and legal protection for supervisors*: The supervisor possesses operational independence, transparent processes, sound governance, budgetary processes that do not undermine autonomy and adequate resources, and is accountable for the discharge of its duties and use of its resources. The legal framework for banking supervision includes legal protection for the supervisor.
— *Principle 3—Cooperation and collaboration*: Laws, regulations or other arrangements provide a framework for cooperation and collaboration with relevant domestic authorities and foreign supervisors. These arrangements reflect the need to protect confidential information.
— *Principle 4—Permissible activities*: The permissible activities of institutions that are licensed and subject to supervision as banks are clearly defined and the use of the word "bank" in names is controlled.
— *Principle 5—Licensing criteria*: The licensing authority has the power to set criteria and reject applications for establishments that do not meet the criteria. At a minimum, the licensing process consists of an assessment of the ownership structure and governance (including the fitness and propriety of Board members and senior management) of the bank and its wider group, and its strategic and operating plan, internal controls, risk management and projected financial condition (including capital base). Where the proposed owner or parent organisation is a foreign bank, the prior consent of its home supervisor is obtained.
— *Principle 6—Transfer of significant ownership*: The supervisor has the power to review, reject and impose prudential conditions on any proposals to transfer significant ownership or controlling interests held directly or indirectly in existing banks to other parties.
— *Principle 7—Major acquisitions*: The supervisor has the power to approve or reject (or recommend to the responsible authority the approval or rejection of), and impose prudential conditions on, major acquisitions or investments by a bank, against prescribed criteria, including the establishment of cross-border operations, and to determine that corporate affiliations or structures do not expose the bank to undue risks or hinder effective supervision.
— *Principle 8—Supervisory approach*: An effective system of banking supervision requires the supervisor to develop and maintain a forward-looking assessment of the risk profile of individual banks and banking groups, proportionate to their systemic importance; identify, assess and address risks emanating from banks and the banking system as a whole; have a framework in place for early intervention; and have plans in place, in partnership with other relevant authorities, to take action to resolve banks in an orderly manner if they become non-viable.

(continued)

---

[318] Basel Committee on Banking Supervision, *Core Principles for Effective Banking Supervision* (Bank for International Settlements, 2012).

Table 20.2: *(Continued)*

— *Principle 9—Supervisory techniques and tools*: The supervisor uses an appropriate range of techniques and tools to implement the supervisory approach and deploys supervisory resources on a proportionate basis, taking into account the risk profile and systemic importance of banks.
— *Principle 10—Supervisory reporting*: The supervisor collects, reviews and analyses prudential reports and statistical returns from banks on both a solo and a consolidated basis, and independently verifies these reports through either on-site examinations or use of external experts.
— *Principle 11—Corrective and sanctioning powers of supervisors*: The supervisor acts at an early stage to address unsafe and unsound practices or activities that could pose risks to banks or to the banking system. The supervisor has at its disposal an adequate range of supervisory tools to bring about timely corrective actions. This includes the ability to revoke the banking licence or to recommend its revocation.
— *Principle 12—Consolidated supervision*: An essential element of banking supervision is that the supervisor supervises the banking group on a consolidated basis, adequately monitoring and, as appropriate, applying prudential standards to all aspects of the business conducted by the banking group worldwide.
— *Principle 13—Home-host relationships*: Home and host supervisors of cross-border banking groups share information and cooperate for effective supervision of the group and group entities, and effective handling of crisis situations. Supervisors require the local operations of foreign banks to be conducted to the same standards as those required of domestic banks.
Prudential regulations and requirements
— *Principle 14—Corporate governance*: The supervisor determines that banks and banking groups have robust corporate governance policies and processes covering, for example, strategic direction, group and organisational structure, control environment, responsibilities of the banks' Boards and senior management, and compensation. These policies and processes are commensurate with the risk profile and systemic importance of the bank.
— *Principle 15—Risk management process*: The supervisor determines that banks have a comprehensive risk management process (including effective Board and senior management oversight) to identify, measure, evaluate, monitor, report and control or mitigate all material risks on a timely basis and to assess the adequacy of their capital and liquidity in relation to their risk profile and market and macroeconomic conditions. This extends to development and review of contingency arrangements (including robust and credible recovery plans where warranted) that take into account the specific circumstances of the bank. The risk management process is commensurate with the risk profile and systemic importance of the bank.
— *Principle 16—Capital adequacy*: The supervisor sets prudent and appropriate capital adequacy requirements for banks that reflect the risks undertaken by, and presented by, a bank in the context of the markets and macroeconomic conditions in which it operates. The supervisor defines the components of capital, bearing in mind their ability to absorb losses. At least for internationally active banks, capital requirements are not less than the applicable Basel standards.

Table 20.2: *(Continued)*

— *Principle 17—Credit risk*: The supervisor determines that banks have an adequate credit risk management process that takes into account their risk appetite, risk profile and market and macroeconomic conditions. This includes prudent policies and processes to identify, measure, evaluate, monitor, report and control or mitigate credit risk (including counterparty credit risk) on a timely basis. The full credit lifecycle is covered including credit underwriting, credit evaluation, and the ongoing management of the bank's loan and investment portfolios.
— *Principle 18—Problem assets, provisions and reserves*: The supervisor determines that banks have adequate policies and processes for the early identification and management of problem assets, and the maintenance of adequate provisions and reserves.
— *Principle 19—Concentration risk and large exposure limits*: The supervisor determines that banks have adequate policies and processes to identify, measure, evaluate, monitor, report and control or mitigate concentrations of risk on a timely basis. Supervisors set prudential limits to restrict bank exposures to single counterparties or groups of connected counterparties.
— *Principle 20—Transactions with related parties*: In order to prevent abuses arising in transactions with related parties and to address the risk of conflict of interest, the supervisor requires banks to enter into any transactions with related parties on an arm's length basis; to monitor these transactions; to take appropriate steps to control or mitigate the risks; and to write off exposures to related parties in accordance with standard policies and processes.
— *Principle 21—Country and transfer risks*: The supervisor determines that banks have adequate policies and processes to identify, measure, evaluate, monitor, report and control or mitigate country risk and transfer risk in their international lending and investment activities on a timely basis.
— *Principle 22—Market risks*: The supervisor determines that banks have an adequate market risk management process that takes into account their risk appetite, risk profile, and market and macroeconomic conditions and the risk of a significant deterioration in market liquidity. This includes prudent policies and processes to identify, measure, evaluate, monitor, report and control or mitigate market risks on a timely basis.
— *Principle 23—Interest rate risk in the banking book*: The supervisor determines that banks have adequate systems to identify, measure, evaluate, monitor, report and control or mitigate interest rate risk in the banking book on a timely basis. These systems take into account the bank's risk appetite, risk profile and market and macroeconomic conditions.
— *Principle 24—Liquidity risk*: The supervisor sets prudent and appropriate liquidity requirements (which can include either quantitative or qualitative requirements or both) for banks that reflect the liquidity needs of the bank. The supervisor determines that banks have a strategy that enables prudent management of liquidity risk and compliance with liquidity requirements. The strategy takes into account the bank's risk profile as well as market and macroeconomic conditions and includes prudent policies and processes, consistent with the bank's risk appetite, to identify, measure, evaluate, monitor, report and control or mitigate liquidity risk over an appropriate set of time horizons. At least for internationally active banks, liquidity requirements are not lower than the applicable Basel standards.

(continued)

Table 20.2: *(Continued)*

— *Principle 25—Operational risk*: The supervisor determines that banks have an adequate operational risk management framework that takes into account their risk appetite, risk profile and market and macroeconomic conditions. This includes prudent policies and processes to identify, assess, evaluate, monitor, report and control or mitigate operational risk on a timely basis.
— *Principle 26—Internal control and audit*: The supervisor determines that banks have adequate internal control frameworks to establish and maintain a properly controlled operating environment for the conduct of their business taking into account their risk profile. These include clear arrangements for delegating authority and responsibility; separation of the functions that involve committing the bank, paying away its funds, and accounting for its assets and liabilities; reconciliation of these processes; safeguarding the bank's assets; and appropriate independent internal audit and compliance functions to test adherence to these controls as well as applicable laws and regulations.
— *Principle 27—Financial reporting and external audit*: The supervisor determines that banks and banking groups maintain adequate and reliable records, prepare financial statements in accordance with accounting policies and practices that are widely accepted internationally and annually publish information that fairly reflects their financial condition and performance and bears an independent external auditor's opinion. The supervisor also determines that banks and parent companies of banking groups have adequate governance and oversight of the external audit function.
— *Principle 28—Disclosure and transparency*: The supervisor determines that banks and banking groups regularly publish information on a consolidated and, where appropriate, solo basis that is easily accessible and fairly reflects their financial condition, performance, risk exposures, risk management strategies and corporate governance policies and processes.
— *Principle 29—Abuse of financial services*: The supervisor determines that banks have adequate policies and processes, including strict customer due diligence rules to promote high ethical and professional standards in the financial sector and prevent the bank from being used, intentionally or unintentionally, for criminal activities.

Part F

Conclusions

21

Business Values: Culture, Commitment, Trust and Ethics

This chapter examines the importance of values in business, regulation and law. It begins by recalling the findings of chapter 20 in relation to the catastrophic collapse in the global finance system caused by the collapse in ethical culture that dominated the financial services industry. It appears that regulation has reached its limits in effectively controlling behaviour in the financial services sector, and the issue of culture is critical. It then examines two extremes of business values, first the maximisation of shareholder value, which has dominated modern business, and second, the values that a number of leading commentators have recently noted as being absent from modern business practice, namely commitment and trust. It then notes the desirable relationship between ethics and values.

Economic models of principal–agent assume a simple binary (or similar) relationship. The reality is that businesses exist in structures that have both hierarchical tiers and horizontal 'groups' of 'agents', and that the individuals involved are subject to multiple influences. The collective effect of these influences creates organisational culture—in fact, a series of sub-cultures. It is wholly misleading to frame the motivations for action by individual staff, which occur in many different situations, as if they were all equal agents of a principal, whether shareholders or the company as employer.

I. Selfishness

Economic orthodoxy has interpreted Adam Smith's analysis of economic actors[1] as being based on *self-interest* as being that they are—and should always be—*selfish*. As Gold noted,[2] the development of this idea in the nineteenth century led to extensive preoccupation with mechanisms that align (only) the economic interests of intermediaries with those of their supposed principals (agency theory),[3] and paved the way for a utility-maximising model to become an all-encompassing theory of human behaviour.[4]

---

[1] A Smith, *Theory of Moral Sentiments* (1759).

[2] N Gold, 'Trustworthiness and Motivations' in N Morris and D Vines (eds), *Capital Failure; Rebuilding Trust in Financial Services* (Oxford, Oxford University Press, 2014).

[3] FY Edgeworth, *Mathematical Physics: An Essay on the Application of Mathematics to the Moral Sciences* (London, Kegan Paul, 1881) 12.

[4] SB Lewin, 'Economics and Psychology: Lessons for Our Own Day from the Early Twentieth Century' (1996) 34(3) *Journal of Economic Literature* 1293–323; M Mandler, 'A Difficult Choice in Preference Theory: Rationality Implies Completeness or Transitivity But Not Both' in E Millgram (ed), *Varieties of Practical Reasoning* (Cambridge MA, MIT Press, 2001) 373–402.

Sedgwick charts the following history.[5] In 1943, Schumpeter defined the principal goals of entrepreneurial culture as profitability and growth, with innovative strategic practices.[6] The entrepreneur was expected to decline but this did not occur. In 1967 Galbraith argued that the entrepreneur was being replaced by 'the technosphere', namely individuals bringing specialised knowledge, talent or experience to group decision making.[7] Management theory then underwent significant development, bringing the idea that individuals would no longer work for life in one firm or skill but those with expertise would have increased movement within and between economic units.[8] Even by 1992, capitalism was being attacked for 'greed, selfishness, exploitation and a crude disregard for any interests but one's own.'[9]

Collins and Porras' study of high achieving companies found that highly successful companies all had an all-consuming internal vision that was shared by all staff and drove them to excel.[10] Offer's analysis is that since the 1980s public policy has been guided by two doctrines: Selfishness and that the primacy of self-regard is good.[11] The behaviour demonstrated across the financial services industry, and also increasingly by other business leaders, has been essentially selfish, arrogant and greedy.[12] These values have been instilled by inherent weaknesses in business school MBA education, through focusing on profit-maximisation and ignoring ethics.[13] There has been a complete dislocation between the values of society and practice in some industries. Regulatory and liability systems have proved wholly incapable of addressing this problem. Deterrence was defective and ineffective.[14] Self-reporting, even when required, is vulnerable to opportunistic behaviour, cherry-picking.[15] Leniency policies have not addressed cultures.

As Jaffer, Morris, Sawbridge and Vines have recently analysed,[16] a series of serious consequences follow from the situation described above. Shareholders have held other stakeholders to ransom.[17] Risks have been misallocated and service providers have extracted

[5] P Sedgwick, *The Enterprise Culture* (London, SPCK, 1992).

[6] J Schumpeter, *Capitalism, Socialism and Democracy* (New York, Harper & Row, 1943).

[7] JK Galbraith, *The New Industrial State* (London, Hamish Hamilton, 1967).

[8] eg C Handy, *The Age of Unreason* (London, Business Books, 1989).

[9] Sedgwick (n 5) 126.

[10] J Collins and JI Porras, *Built to Last: Successful Habits of Visionary Companies* 12th edn (London, HarperCollins, 1994, 2005).

[11] A Offer, 'Regard for Others' in N Morris and D Vines (eds), *Capital Failure; Rebuilding Trust in Financial Services* (Oxford, Oxford University Press, 2014).

[12] P Cammock, 'Vocational Calling and the Search for a New Approach to Business Leadership' in J Buckingham and V Nilakant (eds), *Managing Responsibly. Alternative Approaches to Corporate Management and Governance* (Aldershot, Gower, 2012).

[13] E Krell, 'Why Character is Destiny for Business Schools—And the MBAs they Groom' (2010) 28(2) *Baylor Business School* 4.

[14] J O'Brien, 'Professional Obligation, Ethical Awareness, and Capital Market Regulation' in N Morris and D Vines (eds), *Capital Failure; Rebuilding Trust in Financial Services* (Oxford, Oxford University Press, 2014) 213.

[15] MW Toffel and JL Short, 'Coming Clean and Cleaning Up: Does Voluntary Self-Reporting Indicate Effective Self-Policing?' *Journal of Law and Economics* (forthcoming); AA Pfaff and W Sanchirico, 'Big Field, Small Potatoes: An Empirical Assessment of EPA's Self-Audit Policy' (2004) 23(3) *Journal of Policy Analysis and Management* 415–32.

[16] S Jaffer, N Morris, E Sawbridge and D Vines, 'How Changes to the Financial Services Industry Eroded Trust' in N Morris and D Vines (eds), *Capital Failure; Rebuilding Trust in Financial Services* (Oxford, Oxford University Press, 2014).

[17] L Stout, *The Shareholder Value Myth* (San Francisco, Berrett-Koehler Publishers, 2012); C Mayer, *Firm Commitment* (Oxford, Oxford University Press, 2012).

huge rents:[18] Pay was significantly higher than justified by long-term performance.[19] The equity market was overcome by short term maximisation of profits.[20] Remuneration structures involved annual performance fees for asset managers, with large bonuses based on short-term profits. Sandel's conclusion was that an era of market triumphalism came to a devastating end.[21]

Corporations are not static bodies, their cultures and 'DNA' evolve. Organisations are susceptible to *cultural drift*.[22] In fact the IMF (International Monetary Fund) has pointed out in their most recent Global Stability Report that the *tendency* for corporate culture to drift may be more evident with financial firms since 'corporate culture plays an important role in banks because to a much larger extent than other sectors, bank employees often face decisions in situations for which rules are ambiguous or allow for discretion, which may lead to an expectation that bad behavior will go unpunished and good behavior unrewarded.'[23] Mandis, in recording organisational drift in the financial industry, warns of firms incrementally moving away from their intended culture.[24] He also warns that this slow drift often goes unnoticed unless direct and deliberate control is taken to guide that evolution. Mandis points out that the financial industry, both collectively and individually, has over the years surrendered an ethical standard for a legal one, in other words, ethical values for technical compliance. The proliferation of laws, regulations and guidelines has an obfuscatory effect here and can substitute for reputation and ethics.[25]

Despite statements that culture was changed after 2008, there has been glaring evidence that that assertion is incorrect. Kay commented that the American model of lightly regulated capitalism and liberal democracy supposedly controlled large financial institutions when in reality the floors beneath were occupied by a rabble of self-interested individuals determined to evade any controls on their own activities.[26] Manipulation of the foreign exchange markets took place long after the banks had said they had sorted out their cultures and approaches, and had been fined for abusing interbank interest rate benchmarks. Fines were imposed on banks for operating ineffective controls that allowed their traders to manipulate the G10 spot foreign exchange (FX) market between January 2008 and October 2013.[27] The Governor of the Bank of England commented: 'The repeated nature of these

---

[18] R Sandler, *Medium and Long-Term Retail Savings in the UK: A Review* (HM Treasury, 2002).

[19] IH Cheng, H Hong and J Scheinkman, 'Yesterday's Heroes: Compensation and Creative Risk Taking' (2009), unpublished working paper, Princeton University, cited in H Davies *The Financial Crisis: Who is to Blame?* (Cambridge UK and Malden MA, Polity Press, 2010).

[20] Stout (n 17); Mayer (n 17).

[21] MJ Sandel, *What Money Can't Buy: The Moral Limits of Markets* (London, Penguin, 2013).

[22] J Shipton, *Integrity in Financial Markets—Challenges from Asia*, Speech to the FCA International Regulators' Seminar, London, 24 November 2014.

[23] *Global Financial Stability Report. Risk Taking, Liquidity, and Shadow Banking. Curbing Excess while Promoting Growth, October 2014* (International Monetary Fund, 2014) 129.

[24] S Mandis, *What Happened to Goldman Sachs: An Insider's Story of Organizational Drift and its Unintended Consequences* (Boston, Harvard Business Review Press, 2013).

[25] J Macey, *The Death of Corporate Reputation: How Integrity has been Destroyed on Wall Street* (London, FT Press, 2013).

[26] J Kay, *Obliquity* (London, Profile Books, 2010) 174.

[27] Fines totalling £1,114,918,000 were imposed in Novemner 2014 on five banks for failing to control business practices in their G10 spot foreign exchange (FX) trading operations: Citibank NA £225,575,000 ($358 million), HSBC Bank Plc £216,363,000 ($343 million), JPMorgan Chase Bank NA £222,166,000 ($352 million), The Royal

fines demonstrates that financial penalties alone are not sufficient to address the issues raised. Fundamental change is needed to institutionalise culture, to compensation arrangements and to markets.'[28]

A number of studies suggest that group decision making can make members of the group willing to accept stupid ideas or hazardous risks[29] that they would reject if making the same decision alone.[30] Evidence exists from various sectors that serious wrongdoing can emerge in small, tight groups of individuals. Chapter four noted that point in relation to cartels. This appears true of the PIP breast implant fraud.[31] The FCA (Financial Conduct Authority)'s FX investigation found that:

> traders at different banks formed tight knit groups in which information was shared about client activity, including using code names to identify clients without naming them. These groups were described as, for example, 'the players', 'the 3 musketeers', '1 team, 1 dream', 'a co-operative' and 'the A-team'.

> Traders shared the information obtained through these groups to help them work out their trading strategies. They then attempted to manipulate fix rates and trigger client 'stop loss' orders (which are designed to limit the losses a client could face if exposed to adverse currency rate movements). This involved traders attempting to manipulate the relevant currency rate in the market, for example, to ensure that the rate at which the bank had agreed to sell a particular currency to its clients was higher than the average rate it had bought that currency for in the market. If successful, the bank would profit.[32]

The sum of these failings has been failure of the financial services sector to understand not just that there has occurred a dislocation between the values of society and the values of that have driven the behaviour of many in the sector, but also that this dislocation has endangered the whole global economic system. The Archbishop of Canterbury said that the banking system should return to 'a broad sense of promoting the wellbeing' of those whom it serves.[33] The action of destroying trust in financial services as a sector crumbles its social licence to operate.[34] Research on individual traders and firms shows that success follows a

---

Bank of Scotland Plc £217,000,000 ($344 million) and UBS AG £233,814,000 ($371 million): Press release, *FCA Fines Five Banks £1.1 Billion for FX Failings and Announces Industry-wide Remediation Programme* 12 November 2014. See subsequently Press release *FCA Fines Barclays £294,432,000 for Forex Failings* 20 May 2015. Perhaps 20 traders communicated through an internet chat room between 2007 and 2013 sending 'comically self-incriminating messages' such as 'If you ain't cheating, you ain't trying' *The Economist* (London, 23 May 2015) 6.

[28] M Carney, Speech 'The Future of Financial Reform', 2014 Monetary Authority of Singapore Lecture, 17 November 2014.

[29] See IL Janis and M Mann, *Decision Making* (New York, Free Press, 1977) 423, where, however, it is also pointed out that there are some studies that an initially dominant risk-averse viewpoint within a group may shift an individual away from risk.

[30] B Fisse and J Braithwaite, *Corporations, Crime and Accountability* (Cambridge, Cambridge University Press, 1993).

[31] See http://www.bbc.co.uk/news/health-16391522 and *Poly Implant Prothèse (PIP) Silicone Breast Implants: Review of the Actions of the Medicines and Healthcare Products Regulatory Agency (MHRA) and Department of Health* (London, Department of Health, 2012) at https://www.gov.uk/government/publications/pip-silicone-breast-implants-review-of-the-actions-of-the-mhra-and-department-of-health; 'Restoring Confidence in Medical Devices. Reporting on the Success of the PIP Action Plan, European Commission', June 2014, at http://ec.europa.eu/health/medical-devices/regulatory-framework/pip-action-plan/index_en.htm.

[32] Press release (n 27).

[33] J Welby, 'How Do We Fix This Mess?' speech given on Monday 21 April 2013, http://www.archbishopofcanterbury.org/articles.php/5050/how-do-we-fix-this-mess-archbishop-justin-on-restoring-trust-and-confidence-after-the-crash.

[34] Carney (n 28): 'A trusted system can retain its social licence to support the real economy in innovative and efficient ways'.

customer focus, involving asking what innovations, products or services customers need and value, and then satisfying that demand and gaining a justified reputation for doing so. A supplier or self-intermediary that believes that their position and function is more important than their customers is not on solid ground. The problem with the financial services sector was that selfishness became endemic, and a sense of the value of financial services to the wider society was lost. The fact that a whole sector can focus on external values such as ensuring the absolute safety of their customers, is demonstrated by the civil aviation industry, as discussed in chapter 19, in which the quality of humility is notably present.

II. The Business Objectives of Profit and Shareholder Value

The classic theory runs as follows. It is axiomatic that capitalism is a political and economic system in which enterprises compete to make profit. Firms are owned by shareholders, who choose to invest their capital in a firm in exchange for, and with the expectation of, making profit.[35] Since many investors lack detailed information or expertise (asymmetry) to control or monitor the decisions being taken in relation to their money, managing agents take operational decisions on their behalf, as directors and professional managers of a company. Avoidance of conflicts between the interests of owners and managers (agency problem) is minimised or avoided where the interests of both groups are aligned, and managers are incentivised by being paid by results. This is the model of maximising shareholder value.

The model has been modified in some jurisdictions to take account of wider interests than just those of shareholders, namely those of employees and other stakeholders. Thus, under the 'enlightened shareholder value' model of the UK Companies Act,[36] Directors must promote the success of the company for the benefit of its members and in doing so have regard to various factors, for example

— the likely consequences of any decision in the long term;
— the interests of employees;
— the need to foster the company's relationships with; suppliers, customers and others;
— the impact of operations on the community and the environment;
— the desirability of the company maintaining a reputation for high standards of business conduct.

---

[35] AA Berle and GC Means, *The Modern Corporation and Private Property* (New York, Harcourt, Brace & World, 1923); M Friedman, *Capitalism and Freedom* (Chicago IL, University of Chicago Press, 1962); RE Freeman, *Strategic Management: A Stakeholder Approach* (Boston MA, Pitman/Ballinger, 1984); A Sen, *On Ethics and Economics* (Oxford, Blackwell, 1987); JR Boatright, 'Business Ethics and the Theory of the Firm' (1996) 34(2) *American Business Law Journal* 217; JE Stiglitz, 'Evaluating Economic Change' (2004) 133(3) *Daedalus* 18; T Donaldson and LE Preston, 'The Stakeholder Theory of the Corporation: Concepts, Evidence, and Implications' (1995) 20(1) *Academy of Management Review* 65; AL Friedman and S Miles, 'Developing Stakeholder Theory' (2002) 39(1) *Journal of Management Studies* 1; TM Jones, W Felps and GA Bigley, 'Ethical Theory and Stakeholder-related Decisions: The Role of Stakeholder Culture' (2007) 32(1) *Academy of Management Review* 137; RK Mitchell, BR Agle and DJ Wood, 'Toward a Theory of Stakeholder Identification and Salience: Defining the Principle of Who and What Really Counts' (1997) 22(4) *Academy of Management Review* 853.

[36] Companies Act 2006, s 172.

Nilakant and Lips-Wiersma record the following changes.[37] Corporate control shifted from owners to non-owning professional managers in the early twentieth century (the managerial revolution) but the dominance of professional managers was challenged around the mid-1980s.[38] Shareholding shifted from a large number of small shareholders to institutional investors.[39] An ideology of neo-liberalism emerged during the mid-1980s, which viewed individual freedom as both the mark and aim of human progress. This coincided with deregulation, technological change and globalisation.[40] The contractarian perspective became the model, viewing an organisation not as a social institution, but as a nexus of contracts.[41] A modified version of utilitarianism, normative economic theory drawing on consequentialism and welfarism emerged, with the argument that all choices must be evaluated by their outcomes, and outcomes must enhance individual utilities or personal well-being.[42]

It is widely agreed that business behaviour became narrowly focused on maximising shareholder value from the 1980s,[43] linked with a widening of citizens' shareholding (and so a dilution of external control by individual shareholders) and a political ideology that influenced individualism[44] and individual liberty.[45] Governance arrangements were changed so as more closely to align managerial incentives with investor interests.[46] Some have criticised that approach as being, contrary to humans' better nature, to be selfish and greedy, to ignore civic responsibilities and to cause society to descend to amorality.[47] Porter and Kramer have criticised an outdated approach to value creation, and he argues that the solution lies in the idea of shared value.[48]

---

[37] V Nilakant and M Lips-Wiersma, 'The Duty of Corporate Management: From the Perspective of Dharma' in J Buckingham and V Nilakant (eds), *Managing Responsibly. Alternative Approaches to Corporate Management and Governance* (Aldershot, Gower, 2012).

[38] M Useem, *Investor Capitalism* (New York, Basic Books, 1996).

[39] C Brown, 'Rise of the Institutional Equity Funds: Implications for Managerialism' (1998) 32(3) *Journal of Economic Issues* 803.

[40] M Chen, 'Post-crisis Trends in Asian Management' (2002) 1 *Asian Business & Management* 39.

[41] S Baiman, 'Agency Research in Managerial Accounting: A Survey' (1982) 1 *Journal of Accounting Literature* 154; JL Bradach and R Eccles, 'Price, Authority, and Trust' (1989) 15 *Annual Review of Sociology* 97; L Donaldson, 'The Ethereal Hand: Organizational Economics and Management Theory' (1990) 15(3) *Academy of Management Review* 369; L Donaldson, *American Anti-management Theories of Organization: A Critique of Paradigm Proliferation* (Cambridge, Cambridge University Press, 1995); KM Eisenhardt, 'Agency Theory: An Assessment and Review' (1989) 14(1) *Academy of Management Review* 57; EF Fama and MC Jensen, 'Agency Problems and Residual Claims' (1983) 26 *Journal of Law and Economics* 327; M Jensen and W Meckling, 'Theory of the Firm: Managerial Behaviour, Agency Costs and Ownership Structure' (1976) 3 *Journal of Financial Economics* 305; F Lafontaine, 'Agency Theory and Franchising: Some Empirical Results' (1992) 23(2) *RAND Journal of Economics* 263; D Levinthal, 'A Survey of Agency Models of Organizations' (1998) 9 *Journal of Economic Behaviour and Organization* 153; J Pfeffer, *New Directions for Organization Theory: Problems and Prospects* (New York, Oxford University Press, 1997).

[42] A Sen, *Development as Freedom* (New York, Alfred A Knopf, 1999).

[43] W Werner, 'Management, Stock Market and Corporate Reform: Berle and Means Reconsidered' (1977) 77(3) *Columbia Law Review* 388; A Kaufman, L Zacharias and M Karson, *Managers vs Owners: The Struggle for Corporate Control in American Democracy* (Oxford, Oxford University Press, 1995); WW Bratton, 'Berle and Means Reconsidered at the Century's Turn' (2001) 26 *Journal of Corporation Law* 737.

[44] FA von Hayek, *The Constitution of Liberty* (London, Routledge & Kegan Paul, 1960).

[45] J Rawls, *A Theory of Justice* (Cambridge MA, Harvard University Press, 1971).

[46] Useem (n 38).

[47] M Ridley, *Origins of Virtue* (London, Penguin Science, 1998).

[48] ME Porter and MR Kramer, 'Creating Shared Value' (2011) at https://hbr.org/2011/01/the-big-idea-creating-shared-value.

In any event, a policy of pursuing the maximisation of shareholder value has recently drawn strenuous criticism from leading scholars, and has especially been held to have been a root cause of the global financial crisis. First, Armour and Gordon have argued that the extent to which two key assumptions necessary to support the maximisation of the value of shareholders' claims fail to do so has been underappreciated. The assumptions are, first, that the share price does in fact give the best available estimate of the value of shareholders' claims and, second, that a range of mechanisms—contracts, liability rules, and regulation—act to ensure that any costs a firm's activities impose on other parties are internalised into that firm's profit function. Armour and Gordon argue that the shareholder value norm in fact creates incentives for firms systematically to undermine the efficacy of regulatory internalisation mechanisms, thereby failing to avoid the significant externalities that were thought to be avoided.[49] They suggest that directors and officers should have liability for negligence causing significant loss *to the firm*, and thereby to its shareholders.[50]

Second, Mayer has argued that the structure of Anglo-American companies enables and incentivises short-termism, such that business continuity is systemically disrupted in pursuit of the realisation of instant profit by incentives to create mergers, and asset strip by hedge funds.[51] When these trends are aligned with remuneration of managers on the basis of their short-term results, the resulting focus on making decisions so as to produce short-term profitability undermines investment, continuity and business sustainability, and generates a significant shift in power from long-term investors towards short-term investors and their agents, who seek to make instant profits. Mayer asserts that Vermaelen's defence of shareholder value[52] is misguided. He argues that shareholders are vulnerable to the performance of the corporation to a greater degree than any other party. Directors must uphold the interests of their shareholders, who are weaker. In reality, Mayer observes, managers, shareholders, employees, creditors and society are all in ongoing relations with each other. Although some parties can protect themselves through contracts, the plurality of interests and objectives is not fully recognised in English or United States law—although better embedded in German law.

Collins' analysis of highly successful companies[53] noted that their executive compensation patterns were not systematically different relative to comparison companies in the use of stock (or not), high salaries (or not), bonus incentives (or not), or long-term compensation (or not). The only significant difference was that the executives in the former category received slightly *less* total cash compensation 10 years after the transition than their counterparts at the still-mediocre comparison companies.[54] They concluded that 'It's not how

---

[49] J Armour and JN Gordon, 'Systemic Harms and the Limits of Shareholder Value' in N Morris and D Vines (eds), *Capital Failure; Rebuilding Trust in Financial Services* (Oxford, Oxford University Press, 2014). For an absence of voice in corporate environmental responsibility, see C Bradshaw, 'The Environmental Business Case and Unenlightened Shareholder Value' (2012) 1 *Legal Studies* 141.

[50] J Armour and JN Gordon, 'Systemic Harms and Shareholder Value' (2014) 6(1) *Journal of Legal Analysis* 35. For officers and other controllers liability would arise where there had been lack of candor in risk committee review or for a deficient risk review process, and for directors for lack of care in risk-oversight.

[51] Mayer (n 17).

[52] T Vermaelen, 'Maximizing Shareholder Value: An Ethical Responsibility?' in C Smith and G Lenssen (eds), *Mainstreaming Corporate Responsibility* (Chichester, Wiley, 2009).

[53] J Collins, *Good to Great* (New York, Harper Business, 2001).

[54] ibid, 49.

you compensate your executives, it's which executives you have to compensate in the first place.' 'The purpose of a compensation system should not be to get the right *behaviors* from the wrong people, but to get the right *people* on the bus in the first place, and to keep them there.'[55] Collins and Porras had earlier quoted George Merck II: 'We never try to forget that medicine is for the people. It is not for the profits. The profits follow, and if we have remembered that, they have never failed to appear. The better we have remembered it, the larger they have been'.[56]

Kay adopts the observation that the most profitable businesses are not the most profit-oriented and argues that happiness is not achieved through the pursuit of happiness ('Happiness is not a red Ferrari').[57] Similarly, Mayer points out that shareholder value is an outcome, not an objective.[58] Mayer suggests that the reason why senior executives insisted on paying themselves so much was to sustain their sense of their own importance ('bonuses come to matter as much for the kudos they confer as the cash they generate').[59] He states that a 'corporate culture that extols greed is, in the end, unable to protect itself against its own employees. Nor does the business with such a culture attract public sympathy when things go wrong.'[60]

Analyses of the sources of corporate power reveal competing interests, and hence how to balance and align them.[61] Alternatives to the shareholder primacy theory[62] are director primacy, team production theory (requiring mediation by directors of the competing interests of the various relevant stakeholders)[63] and managerialism.[64] Against this background, the emergence of corporate *social* responsibility, and now a call for corporate *ethical* responsibility, are unsurprising.

In response to the self-interest of maximising individual remuneration or shareholder value it has been pointed out that wealth creation is a collective effort.[65] Individual greed comes at the expense of exploitation of others, and is essentially unethical. It constitutes an affront to the values of all stakeholders and society generally. It also undermines sound business practice. In 1998 Pfeffer stated seven 'high performance practices' that can lead to innovation, productivity and sustained profitability: Employment security, selective hiring, self-managed teams and decentralisation, extensive training, reduction of status differences, sharing of information, and high and contingent compensation.[66] However, in 2007 he found little evidence of the widespread use of these practices in contemporary

---

[55] ibid, 50.
[56] Speech to Medical College of Virginia, 1 December 1950, quoted in Collins and Porras (n 10) 49.
[57] Kay (n 26). See 'Unilever: In search of the Good Business' *The Economist* (London, 9 August 2014) 69.
[58] Mayer (n 17) 167.
[59] Kay (n 26) 36.
[60] ibid, 37.
[61] SJ Padfield, 'Corporate Social Responsibility & Concession Theory' *William & Mary Business Law Review* (forthcoming).
[62] LA Bebchuk, 'The Myth That Insulating Boards Serves Long-Term Value' (2013) 113 *Columbia Law Review* 1637.
[63] MM Blair and LA Stout, 'A Team Production Theory of Corporate Law' (1999) 85 *Virginia Law Review* 247, 280.
[64] U Rodrigues, 'A Conflict Primacy Model of the Public Board' (2013) *University of Illinois Law Review* 1051.
[65] J Buckingham and V Nilakant (eds), *Managing Responsibly. Alternative Approaches to Corporate Management and Governance* (Farnham, Gower, 2012).
[66] J Pfeffer, *The Human Equation* (Boston MA, Harvard Business School, 1998).

organisation.[67] Exclusive focus on shareholder wealth creates organisations typically characterised by a culture of compliance and control.[68] Employees, particularly those with high aspirations, are likely to find the culture constraining, and the culture itself tends to stifle innovative thinking from the lower ranks.[69]

The financial services sector was not unique in creating conflicting pressures. Conflict could arise between performance goals, such as achievement of performance or time targets or cost control, and maintaining safe or ethical operation. This could expose employees to irreconcilable stresses, often under intense time pressure.[70]

Offer places the blame firmly on economics, in having 'arrived at what appears to be a blind alley: The doctrines of efficient markets and the policy norms they endorsed have failed repeatedly and badly.'[71]

III. Commitment and Trust

Even before the financial crisis, academic distrust of corporate culture was growing. Since the global financial crisis it has erupted against individualism, unbalanced self-interest and the maximisation of shareholder value. Scholars have instead asserted the need to balance the interests of all stakeholders in pluralist structures, based on values of sustainable commitment and trust.

Economists have long noted the rationality of trusting others, rather than acting selfishly, where exchange transactions are repeated. Adam Smith also argued that solidarity that appears in trust networks grows from sympathy bred by long-term familiarity, and this forms stronger bonds within households than across kin groups or neighbourhoods.[72] A member of a network will rely on the network's connectedness to assure that a cheater faces shunning by all network members.[73] Tilly studied 'trust networks' which consist of ramified interpersonal connections, consisting mainly of strong ties, within which people set values, consequential, long-term resources and enterprises at risk to the malfeasance, mistakes or failures of others.[74] Examples are fourteenth century Waldensian heretics who faced a threat of denunciation,[75] and sixteenth century English credit networks.[76] Tilly concluded

---

[67] J Pfeffer, *What Were They Thinking? Unconventional Wisdom about Management* (Boston MA, Harvard Business School, 2007).

[68] J Buckingham and V Nilakant, 'Introduction: Globalizing Corporate Social Responsibility—Challenging Western neo-Liberal Management Theory' in J Buckingham and V Nilakant (eds), *Managing Responsibly. Alternative Approaches to Corporate Management and Governance* (Farnham, Gower, 2012).

[69] CC Manz and HP Simms, *Business Without Bosses* (New York, John Wiley, 1993).

[70] D McCune, C Lewis and D Arendt, 'Safety Culture in Your Safety Management System' in AJ Stolzer, CD Halford and JJ Goglia (eds), *Implementing Safety Management Systems in Aviation* (Farnham, Ashgate, 2011) 143.

[71] Offer (n 11) 155.

[72] Smith (n 1).

[73] A Greif, 'Cultural Beliefs and the Organization of Society: A Historical and Theoretical Reflection on Collectivist and Individualist Societies' (1994) 102 *Journal of Political Economy* 912, 936.

[74] C Tilly, *Trust and Rule* (New York, Cambridge University Press, 2005).

[75] ibid, 1–4.

[76] C Muldrew, *The Economy of Obligation* (London, Macmillan, 1998) 148; see C Muldrew, 'Interpreting the Market: The Ethics of Credit and Community Relations in Early Modern England' (1993) 18 *Social History* 163.

that trust consists in placing valued outcomes at risk to others' malfeasance, mistakes or failures. He suggested that trust relationships cluster in distinctive networks, and that it is critical to the future of democracy not just that such small networks are sustained but also that they are sufficiently connected with large public politics. Where this occurs, it supports a governmental shift away from coercion toward combinations of capital and commitment promotes contingent consent.[77]

An analysis of human biology notes that individual human genes have coagulated into cooperative teams, and individual humans have coagulated into societies that are based on cooperation. Socialisation involves large groups with complex inter-relationships, in which divisions of skills and labour support exchange, trade and specialisation. 'Cooperation is a frequent feature of human society; trust is the very foundation of social and economic life.'[78] However, reciprocity only works if people recognise each other, and can rationally trust commitments.[79] Our emotions are guarantees of our commitment. Frank argues that emotions are a way of settling the conflict between short-term expediency and long-term prudence in favour of the latter.[80] 'Trust is as vital a form of social capital as money is a form of actual capital.'[81] Ridley argues for 'a society built on voluntary exchange of goods, information, fortune and power between free individuals in small enough communities for trust to be built. I believe such a society could be more equitable, as well as more prosperous, than one built on bureaucratic statism.'[82]

Collins and Porras' 2005 study of high achieving companies did not find any specific ideological content essential to being a visionary company.[83] They thought that the *authenticity* of the ideology and the extent to which a company attains consistent alignment with the ideology counts more than the *content* of the ideology. However, Collins' 2001 analysis of 'great' companies did conclude that they all involved creating 'a climate where truth is heard', based on open dialogue and debate, and not coercion or authoritarian leadership or bureaucracy. Consensus is *not* specifically sought, but discussion and challenge is encouraged. The great firms also selected people who are self-motivated (and not *de*-motivated) to work passionately within a cultural framework of freedom and responsibility to fulfil their responsibilities.[84] National cultures may vary across a multinational company but the firm's values can still be unified.[85]

Later comparison of the companies in Collins' cohort with others indicated that focusing on 'strategies for success' was significantly less important to long-term value than concentrating on 'cultures for success', in particular on 'conscious capitalism' expressed by concentration on being values driven, higher purpose, stakeholder orientation, conscious

---

[77] Tilly (n 74) 135.
[78] Ridley (n 47) 57.
[79] ibid, 69.
[80] RH Frank, *Passions within Reason* (New York, Norton, 1988).
[81] Ridley (n 47) 250.
[82] ibid, 263.
[83] Collins and Porras (n 10).
[84] Collins (n 53).
[85] L Hoecklin, *Managing Cultural Differences: Strategies for Competitive Advantage* (Wokingham, Addison-Wesley, 1995) 4 (rather than embracing a standardised way of behaving, the company's French, German and British managers 'had values and behaviours more French, more German and more British than those of their compatriots working for local, domestic companies'.

leadership and conscious culture.[86] Barrett firmly supports the idea that focusing on the needs of employees and the culture of the company is much more important than focusing on strategies for success.[87] Since culture drives performance by unleashing human potential, he argues that organisation should be firmly values-driven.

Sandel's critique of the supremacy of the market and of reliance solely on economics as a means of its control concludes that markets crowd out morals, and this leads to corruption and degradation in the moral worth of society's goods.[88] He calls for strenuous reassertion of public goods, such as altruism, generosity, solidarity and civic spirit.[89] He worries about the kind of society that single-minded pursuit of markets has produced.

Drawing on JS Mill,[90] Kay proposed a principle of obliquity: The process of achieving complex objectives indirectly.[91] He also noted Lindblom's principle of 'muddling through': An oblique approach characterised by successive limited comparison.[92] Kay noted that obliquity contradicted the hugely influential theory of rational choice,[93] and instead supported a policy of constant adaptation based on 'trial and error'[94] He also went further by arguing that

> Business exists to serve social purposes and enjoy legitimacy in the short term and survival in the long term only to the extent that such business meets these purposes. Profit cannot then be the 'defining purpose' of a business. [95]

Mayer's analysis of the global financial crisis focused on the notion of the corporation as a mechanism for providing commitment to others, and the evidence that the Anglo-American models of corporations have destroyed essential trust and commitment.[96] Most relationships are based on trust, not contracts, and that to establish trust it is necessary to demonstrate commitment. In this he echoes Michel Albert's conclusion first published in 1991 that rejected the neo-American model of individual achievement and short-term profits in favour of the 'Rhine model' in which the keys to success are collective achievement and public consensus.[97]

Amongst the evidence Mayer cited was the following. First, he argued that the market fails to police itself. The market can reward and discipline corporations through the power of reputation. Thus, when the FSA (Financial Services Authority) discloses that a corporation

---

[86] R Sisodia, D Wolfe and J Sheth, *Firms of Endearment: How World-class Companies Profit from Passion and Purpose* (Upper Saddle River NJ, Wharton School Publishing, 2007).

[87] R Barrett, *The Values-Driven Organization: Unleashing Human Potential for Performance and Profit* (London, Routledge, 2014) 29.

[88] Sandel (n 21).

[89] ibid, 130.

[90] JS Mill, *Autobiography* (1873) ed (London, Penguin, 1989) 117: 'Those only are happy (I thought) who have their minds fixed on some object other than their own happiness; on the happiness of others, on the improvement of mankind, even on some art or pursuit, followed not as a means, but as itself an ideal end. Aiming thus at something else, they find happiness by the way.'

[91] Kay (n 26).

[92] C Lindblom, 'The Science of "Muddling Through"' (1959) 19(2) *Public Administration Review* 79; see also C Lindblom, 'Still Muddling, Not Yet Through' (1979) 39(6) *Public Administration Review* 517.

[93] P Samuelson, *Foundations of Economic Analysis* (Cambridge MA, Harvard University Press, 1947) 172.

[94] 'If it fails, admit it frankly, and try another.': FD Roosevelt, *Looking Forward* (London, William Heinemann Ltd, 1933) 150.

[95] Kay (n 26) 154.

[96] Mayer (n 17).

[97] M Albert, *Capitalism Against Capitalism* (English edition, London, Whurr Publishers, 1993).

has engaged in some form of misconduct, the decline in its market value is approximately 10 times that of the fine levied.[98] But this disciplining mechanism only works for misconduct that is against the interests of customers or investors, and there is no such effect in relation to some other party.[99] Indeed, there is evidence that the share price of the corporation actually rises in such circumstances.[100] In environmental disasters, the share price losses are no larger than the direct penalties imposed by regulatory authorities, without any further reputational effect;[101] but the victims are third parties—communities, wildlife, the atmosphere. Mayer argued that the market promotes good conduct in a very specific sense: In relation to things that it itself values.[102] His solution is to defer payment until true performance has been revealed.[103]

Second, Mayer argued that regulation promotes immoral conduct. Regulation leads to gaming against rules so as to circumvent or minimise their effects, diverts attention from the moral substance to details of rules, is pro-cyclical, confuses rules with standards, compliance with compassion, and obedience with integrity.[104] He argued that moves to strengthen corporate governance would merely raise the authority of shareholders, and banks would take more risks to please their more powerful shareholders, as had happened in the run-up to the financial crisis.[105]

Mayer then contrasted different models of corporations. He criticised the Anglo-American model on the basis that a combination of diversified shareholding[106] and pursuit of shareholder value had produced mergers or hostile takeovers aimed at short-term realisation of profit by hedge funds.

> The underlying principle of the corporation is perceived to be to promote shareholder interests, but these have come at the expense of other stakeholders who have significant interests in the corporation. Market incentives and reputation intensify the focus on shareholder interests and distort the allocation of resources in an economy to those that yield the greatest benefits for shareholders at the expense of other parties.[107]

Mayer argued that the British financial system

> systematically extinguishes any sense of commitment—of investors to companies, of executives to employees, of employees to firms, of firms to their investors, of firms to communities, or of this generation to any subsequent or past one.[108]

---

[98] ibid, 46.

[99] ibid, 47.

[100] J Armour, C Mayer and A Polo, 'Regulatory Sanctions and Reputational Damage in Financial Markets' European Corporate Governance Institute, Finance Working Paper Series, No 300 (2011).

[101] J Karpoff, J Lott and E Wehrly, 'The Reputational Penalties for Environmental Violations: Empirical Evidence' (2005) 48 *Journal of Law and Economics* 653.

[102] Mayer (n 17), 49.

[103] ibid, 53.

[104] ibid, ch 4.

[105] Studies reporting that banks that tied executive remuneration closely to their corporate earnings performed worse and took greater risks during the financial crisis than other banks: R Fahlenbrach and R Stulz, 'Bank CEO Incentives and the Credit Crisis' (2010) 99 *Journal of Financial Economics* 11; Cheng, Hong and Scheinkman (n 19).

[106] Mayer (n 17) 85. In contrast to diversification, in 50% of Austrian, Belgian, German and Italian corporations a single investor or group of investors controls more than 50% of the voting shares in corporations. In 50% of Dutch, Spanish and Swedish corporations a single shareholder controls over 30% of the voting shares. In UK they control less than 10% of votes.

[107] ibid, 115.

[108] ibid, 143–44.

Economics does not recognise the fundamental role of commitment in all aspects of our commercial as well as social lives and the way in which institutions contribute to the creation and preservation of commitment.[109]

Based on the claim that family values create stability and commitment to other stakeholders that dispersed shareholders cannot provide, Mayer's prescription to restore companies' ability to make trusted commitments is that corporate governance mechanisms are needed that promote commitment and stronger managerial oversight, and ownership arrangements that encourage both longer-term and more active shareholdings. He suggested that corporations need to exhibit morality, based on three sets of principles. First, companies need values that are credible, consistent and moral. The values will be those of the corporation's customers, investors and employees. Public and private values can be integrated. Second, since self-restraint, reputation and regulation are ineffective, a corporation needs third parties (trust boards) to restrain it from defaulting on its values. Third, the shareholding structure should allow enhanced control to be conferred on shareholders who commit to invest in the corporation for a long period.[110]

The British Standards Institute's code of practice for customer service states the principle that 'good customer service should result in the customer's complete satisfaction with the product or service that they have received'.[111] It continues:

> In order to establish good customer service the organization should show commitment and credibility to its customers and offer an experience that achieves increased customer satisfaction and loyalty. In order to achieve this the organization should demonstrate commitment to providing effective customer service by all employees within the organization, starting with the board, chief executive officer and top management.

> Promises should be kept, service should be delivered at times that suit customers and robust and reliable systems should be in place for every aspect of an organization's transactions with its customers.[112]

Ethical trading is intrinsic to business in Germany. Every trader must by law join the local Chamber of Commerce (*Handelskammer*) and is subject to a legal requirement to ensure the decency and morality of the 'honourable merchant' or 'honourable businessman'.[113] The national Association of Industry and Chambers of Commerce expands on the concept thus:

> The 'honourable businessman' is a concept which should not be dealt with in Sunday sermons. The aim is to fill the 'honourable businessman' with life. The DIHK is therefore committed to acting against unfair competition, as well as product and brand piracy, works to prevent and combat corruption and supports commercial mediation and arbitration.[114]

Trust is a moral virtue, which is internally driven.[115] The crucial element that underpins both human contracting and regulation is an ability to trust the people one is dealing with. Contracts and regulatory systems are proxies and supports for uncertainty in trustworthiness.

---

[109] ibid, 144.
[110] ibid, 246. See also 'Family Firms: Business in the Blood' *The Economist* (London, 9 August 2014) 55.
[111] BS 8477:2014, para 3.1.
[112] ibid, paras 3.1.4 and 3.1.5.
[113] Chamber of Commerce and Industry Law (IHKG) art 1.1.
[114] *DIHK—We are Business* (Deutscher Industrie- und Handelskammertag, 2012) p 11.
[115] R Holton, 'Deciding to Trust, Coming to Believe' (1994) 72(1) *Australasian Journal of Philosophy* 63, 66.

Trust gives sufficient confidence to overcome risk and bridge vulnerability.[116] 'Trust is redundant where I have effective guarantees or control of outcomes.'[117] Trust is stronger than mere reliance, the latter being behaviour that is motivated by the pursuit of rewards or the avoidance of punishment.[118] However, it is no longer credible that compliance can be ensured by reliance on formalised structures of accountability and legal duties of accountability. O'Neill argues that '*except in rare and atypical cases* (the infantile case) both placing and refusing trust is a matter of judging either *truth claims* or *commitments to action (promises)*. Trust in others' truth claims is *well placed* if their words are, or turn out to be, true of the world.'[119] Hence, in order to constitute an intelligent response to evidence of trustworthiness, adequate evidence is needed of non-self-regarding motivation and other-regarding commitment,[120] but this need not be complete evidence, let alone proof.[121] She considers that the benchmarks for intelligent accountability are *informed* and *independent* judgement of performance, complemented by *intelligible* communication of those judgements.

The shift that is required is, therefore, away from reliance on legal (liability or regulatory) or economic (deterrent or rational actor) theories and controls to a system based on ethical behaviour. The construction of mechanisms by which an independent judgement may be made of the expectation of ethical behaviour can apply to contracting parties, regulatory scrutiny, stakeholder expectations and firms' internal arrangements.

What could be the sources of such evidence? Mere personal claims will not suffice. They might include evidence of a deep and consistent adherence to ethical principles;[122] a high proportion of satisfied customers; consistent application of compliance systems and audits; transparency; ethical governance structures; belonging to an external professional structure that has high ethical principles and provides ongoing training, auditing and sanctions; and structures enabling decisions to be debated to test ethical compliance, evaluated against external views, and made transparent. These sources of evidence will be mutually reinforcing, so as to provide density.[123]

Lucas argues that with morals there is an ultimate emphasis on authenticity—individual motives and intentions matter—whereas with the law the ultimate emphasis is on conformity.[124] Studies suggest that the obligation to obey the law may be stronger in a country with a longer tradition of democracy and trust in the legal system.[125]

---

[116] Gold (n 2) 135.

[117] O O'Neill, 'Trust, Trustworthiness, and Accountability' in N Morris and D Vines (eds), *Capital Failure; Rebuilding Trust in Financial Services* (Oxford, Oxford University Press, 2014) 178.

[118] A Baier, 'Trust and Antitrust' (1986) 96(2) *Ethics* 231, 234.

[119] O'Neill (n 117).

[120] K Hawley, 'Trust, Distrust and Commitment' (2012) 48(1) *Noûs* 1.

[121] ibid.

[122] H Sants, 'Delivering Intensive Supervision and Credible Deterrence', speech delivered at the Reuters Newsmaker Event, London, 12 March 2009: 'a principles-based approach does not work with people who have no principles'.

[123] CA Heimer, 'Explaining Variation in the Impact of Law: Organizations, Institutions, and Professions' (1996) 15 *Studies in Law, Politics and Society*, 29–59, 37 (the law's shadow is likely to be 'densest' within organisations when it 'largely coincides with the shadow cast by professional bodies').

[124] JR Lucas, 'The Phenomenon of Law' in PMS Hacker and J Raz (eds), *Law, Morality and Society* (Oxford University Press, 1977) 89.

[125] PB Smith et al, 'Cultural Values, Sources of Guidance, and their Relevance to Managerial Behaviour: A 47 Nation Study' (2002) 33 *Journal of Cross-Cultural Psychology* 188–208. It is interesting to note the view that, in comparison with Europe, the USA is a more polyglot and fragmented society: M Thomas, 'In Search of Culture: Holy Grail of Gravy Train' (1985) September *Personnel Management* 24.

IV. Ethics

Hofstede describes culture as a person's 'mental programming'. It begins at childhood, and results in patterns of thinking, feeling and acting. This programming forms the basis of what a person considers to be right and wrong, and to be normal, rational and logical. He believes that such programming is a product of two factors: Social environment and the experiences collected during life.[126] Hofstede has talked of a series of cultural dimensions, and orientations: Individualism–collectivism; uncertainty–avoidance; power–distance; masculinity–femininity; long–short-term.[127] Trompenaars proposes that there are five orientations that shape behaviour when relating to others: (1) The extent to which rules prevail over relationships; (2) the degree to which the group is valued over the individual; (3) the range of feelings that are expressed; (4) the range of involvement that is appropriate; and (5) how status is ascribed.[128] He creates a typology of corporate cultures, which need to be distinguished, for example in reconciling differences between corporate culture and local culture in multinational companies.[129]

Many of the regulatory and scholarly documents that highlight the importance of *culture* in business behaviour refrain from going further and clarify that the ideal that is meant is *ethical* culture. It is no longer acceptable, for example, that a leader's actions should exert aggressive strength whilst maintaining lip service to an ethical high ground.[130] Both the claims and the actions have to be seen to be ethical. The Oxford English Dictionary defines ethics as moral principles that govern a person's behaviour. The cardinal virtues of hope, faith, charity, justice, courage, temperance and prudence,[131] constituted foundations of the development and flourishing of free-market capitalism in the West and also Eastern wisdom traditions.[132] Values that sustain relationships and lives are all about *how*, not *how much*.[133] Pleasure, wealth and happiness do not appear in this list. As the best companies found (chapter 18), success and rewards come as a by-product to those who seek to achieve their (ethical) goals.

[126] G Hofstede et al, *Cultures and Organizations: Software of the Mind—Intercultural Cooperation and Its Importance for Survival* 3rd edn (New York, McGraw Hill, 2010).

[127] G Hofstede, *Culture's Consequences: International Differences in Work-related Values* (1984); M Minkov and G Hofstede, 'The Evolution of Hofstede's doctrine' (2011) 18(1) *Cross Cultural Management: An International Journal* 10.

[128] F Trompenaars, *Riding the Waves of Culture: Understanding Diversity in Global Business* (New York, Irwin, 1993) 156.

[129] C Mills, 'Navigating the Tension between Global and Local: A Communication Perspective' in J Buckingham and V Nilakant (eds), *Managing Responsibly. Alternative Approaches to Corporate Management and Governance* (Farnham, Gower, 2012).

[130] N Macciavelli, *The Prince* (trans (T Parks, London, Penguin Books, 2009).

[131] T Aquinas, *Treatise on the Virtues* ((trans JA Oesterle, Notre Dame IN, University of Notre Dame Press, 1270/1984).

[132] DN McCloskey, *The Bourgeois Virtues: Ethics for an Age of Commerce* (Chicago IL, University of Chicago Press, 2006).

[133] D Seidman, *How: Why HOW we do anything means everything* (Hoboken NJ, John Wiley & Sons, 2007) xviii.

For Aristotle, the character and disposition of the moral agents are as important as the knowledge they are able to assimilate and execute.[134] Aristotle distinguishes between the intellectual and moral virtues.

> [Practical] Wisdom and Understanding and Prudence are intellectual, Liberality and temperance are moral virtues.[135]

> Virtue, then, is of two kinds, intellectual and moral. Intellectual virtue owes both its inception and its growth chiefly to instruction, and for this very reason needs time and experience. Moral goodness, on the other hand, is the result of habit, from which it has got its name, being a slight modification of the word *ethos*. This fact makes it obvious that none of the moral virtues is engendered in us by nature.[136]

Similarly, Justinian's Institutes begin by stating the simple proposition: 'The precepts of the law are these: to live honestly, to injure no one, and to give every man his due.'[137]

Modern empirical evidence tends to support these ideas.[138] Leading modern philosophers MacIntyre and Hauerwas suggest that ethics is only meaningful within the context of a moral community and the moral leadership within that community.[139] Reflecting on the subversion of morality through Nazism and international terrorism, Buchanan called for a systematic comparative evaluation of alternative institutional arrangements and social practices as to their efficacy and efficiency in promoting beliefs that are especially important for the proper functioning of the moral powers (social moral epistemology), and an account of the epistemic virtues of social institutions.[140] In modern life, however, the global community is enormous, composed of a multitude of smaller and overlapping communities, and there is no unified leadership. Steare notes a general decline in religious beliefs and practices, which have historically moderated selfish appetites.[141] Two possible ways forward here are to ensure that communities are sufficiently *small* as to be able to sustain ethical inter-dependence, and to build or reinforce global ethical values, leaders and structures.

Pirie's recent survey of legal anthropology across global cultures through time finds strong emphasis on the relationship between law as a concept and ethics.[142] There are striking examples. In Ladakh, villages saw a dispute as a tear in the fabric of the community, which must be mended with the payment of fines and a ceremonial process of mediation,

---

[134] See J Alexander, 'Cultivating Character: The Challenge of Business Ethics Education' in J Buckingham and V Nilakant (eds), *Managing Responsibly. Alternative Approaches to Corporate Management and Governance* (Farnham, Gower, 2012).

[135] Aristotle, *Nicomachean Ethics, Book I* (trans JAK Thompson, London, Penguin Books, 1978) 90.

[136] ibid, 91.

[137] *The Institutes of Justinian*, Book I, Title I, para 3.

[138] TM Jones, 'Can Business Ethics be Taught? Empirical Evidence' (1990) 8(2) *Business and Professional Ethics Journal* 73; FH Gautschi and TM Jones, 'Enhancing the Ability of Business Students to Recognize Ethical Issues: An Empirical Assessment of the Effectiveness of a Course in Business Ethics' (1998) 17(2) *Journal of Business Ethics* 205; H Gardner, 'The Ethical Mind' (2007) March *Harvard Business Review South Asia* 33.

[139] A MacIntyre, *After Virtue* (London, Gerald Duckworth & Co, 1981); S Hauerwas, *A Community of Character: Towards a Constructive Christian Social Ethic* (Notre Dame IN, University of Notre Dame Press, 1981).

[140] A Buchanan, 'Philosophy and Public Policy: A Role for Social Moral Epistemology' (2009) 26(3) *Journal of Applied Philosophy* 276, 287.

[141] R Steare, *Ethicability: How to Decide what's Right and Find the Courage to do it* 5th edn (Roger Steare Consulting Limited, 2013) 74.

[142] F Pirie, *The Anthropology of Law* (Oxford, Oxford University Press, 2013).

rather than regarding a dispute as a clash of rights.[143] In the Hindu world the *dharmas-utras* of the sixth century BC concern rituals that are necessary to maintain the cosmic and moral order. *Dharma* is a Hindu concept that refers to both appropriate conduct and one's duty.[144] Islamic *shari'a* gives a sense of a divine vision for the world and the individual's duties towards God. Law was divinely ordained, its authority provided by God, a product of a marriage between revelation and reason. Islamic law enjoyed a prestige and authority that was essentially independent of any political or governmental power and authority. Different forms of social order may exist in one society.[145]

Pirie concludes that legal rules and categories specify the way society ought to be; at their most basic, they are a public expression of moral order.[146] 'Law provides a language for expressing what is right and just. It is by encapsulating values that transcend power and politics that it can serve both to legitimate power and to resist or control it.'[147] 'At their most basic, laws create moral standards. They can be read as public statements of the principles upon which their adherents act…'[148] Law is an expression of moral values, as much as an instrument of government, a means of conflict resolution, or a technique of power. 'As well as justice and equity, law tends to invoke an ideal order … something that its rules and categories represent, but can never fully realize.'[149] She notes that Berman emphasised the necessary connections between law and morality, their 'fundamental unity', and laments their separation in the contemporary world. When the lines are broken, he says, a society becomes demoralised; law without religion loses its basis for commitment.[150] The particular form that law takes in our culture is to some degree the product of our beliefs about it and our attitudes toward it.[151] Similarly, Finnis asserts that the task of a legal philosopher is evaluative in a moral sense, not just descriptive.[152] Zizioulas has argued that moral rules are hard to follow if they are separated from religious beliefs.[153]

Sedgwick's theological analysis of enterprise focuses on themes of work and social justice, treating these not as being anti-wealth but fair non-exploitative exchange.[154] He suggests that creation, and hence the creation of wealth, is celebrated, and hence so is innovation. But wealth must be shared amongst the community. It is the *use* of wealth that creates problems. Under a doctrine of stewardship, freedom is understood in relation to membership of, contribution to, and cooperation within, the collective society. This is freedom to create anew and contribute to the active ordering and re-ordering if things.[155]

---

[143] F Pirie, *Peace and Conflict in Ladakh: The Construction of a Fragile Web of Order* (Leiden, Brill, 2007) ch 4.

[144] Nilakant and Lips-Wiersma (n 37); PV Kane, *History of Dharmashastra* (Poona, Bhandarkar Oriental Research Institute, 1968); WD O'Flaherty and DJ Derrett (eds), *The Concept of Duty in South Asia* (New Delhi, Vikas, 1978).

[145] SF Moore, 'Law and Social Change: The Semi-Autonomous Social Field as an Appropriate Subject of Study' (1973) 7 *Law and Society Review* 719–46.

[146] Pirie (n 142) 110.

[147] ibid, 13.

[148] ibid, 175.

[149] ibid, 226.

[150] H Berman, *The Interaction of Law and Religion* (London, SCM Press, 1974) 21.

[151] G Lamond, 'Coercion and the Nature of Law' (2001) 7 *Legal Theory* 35–57, 37.

[152] J Finnis, *Natural Law and Natural Rights* (Oxford, Clarendon, 1980) 3.

[153] JD Zizioulas, 'Preserving God's Creation' in M Palmer and E Breuilly (eds), *Christianity and Ecology* (London, Cassel, 1992).

[154] Sedgwick (n 5) ch 6.

[155] K Barth, *Church Dogmatics* (Edinburgh, T & T Clark, 1965).

In Christian religious foundations a strong association has been noted between the experience of work as a calling and the sense that the work is meaningful.[156] Bunderson, Thompson and Cammock note that the protestant conception of a vocation or 'calling' contains two discrete strands: The first involves the discovery of one's unique 'gifts and talents', and the second the recognition of invitations to deploy those gifts and talents in the service of others.[157]

Philosophers have suggested that a moral issue is present where a person's actions, when freely performed, may harm or benefit others.[158] It follows that the action must have *consequences* for others and must involve the decision maker exercising *choice*. However, that analysis does not ideally fit a view of accidents where the role of an individual actor is viewed as occurring within a wider systemic context, and where that context is of more fundamental significance in relation to causation and prevention of accidents, as discussed in chapter 19 particularly in relation to aviation. The wider view chimes with the well-recognised legal problem of identifying the actor to whom liability should—and should not—be attributed as having legally 'caused' harm, when many possible causes could scientifically be identified.

Rest's overview of research on the performance of moral acts included the following conclusions.[159] First, moral judgement changes with time and formal education. Age/education accounts for 30–50 per cent of the variance in results. Second, for most people, it is not specific moral experiences that foster development (eg education) but rather becoming more aware of the social world in general and one's place in it. The people who develop moral judgement are those who love to learn, who seek new challenges, who enjoy intellectually stimulating environments, who are reflective, who make plans and set goals, who take risks, who see themselves in the larger social contexts of history and institutions and broad cultural trends, who take responsibility for themselves and their environs. The people who develop are advantaged by receiving encouragement to continue their education and their development, who are in stimulating and challenging environments, and who operate in social milieus that support their work, endeavour to interest them, and reward their accomplishments. Third, moral education programmes designed to stimulate moral judgement do produce modest but significant gains. This is particularly so for programmes emphasising peer discussion of controversial moral dilemmas. Education programmes designed to foster general personality development are also effective. But discipline-oriented, information-laden courses on traditional academic topics seem not to be so effective. Fourth, similarities across cultures are more striking than dissimilarities.

Various scholars have expanded Rest's analysis. Particularly useful is Jones' notion of *moral intensity*.[160] He first adopts previous views that an *ethical decision* is defined as a

[156] AM Grant, 'Employees without a Cause: The Motivational Effects of Prosocial Impact in Public Service' (2008) 11(1) *International Public Management Journal* 48; DT Hall and DE Chandler, 'Psychological Success: When the Career is a Calling' (2005) 26(2) *Journal of Organizational Behaviour* 155; KS Cameron, *Positive Leadership: Strategies for Extraordinary Performance* (San Francisco CA, Berrett-Koehler, 2008); P Cammock, *The Spirit of Leadership: Exploring the Personal Foundations of Extraordinary Leadership* (Christchurch, Leadership Press, 2009).

[157] S Bunderson and JA Thompson, 'The Call of the Wild: Zookeepers, Callings, and the Double-edged Sword of Deeply Meaningful Work' (2009) 54(1) *Administrative Science Quarterly* 32; Cammock (n 12).

[158] MG Velasquez and C Rostankowski, *Ethics: Theory and Practice* (Englewood Cliffs NJ, Prentice-Hall, 1985).

[159] JR Rest, *Moral Development: Advances in Research and Theory* (New York, Praeger, 1986).

[160] TM Jones, 'Ethical Decision Making by Individuals in Organizations: An Issue-Contingent Model' (1991) 16(2) *Academy of Management Review* 366.

decision that is both legal and morally acceptable to the community.[161] He then suggests that ethical decision making is issue contingent; that is, characteristics of the moral issue itself, collectively called *moral intensity*, are important determinants of ethical decision making and behaviour. Jones identifies six such characteristics: Magnitude of consequences, social consensus, probability of effect, temporal immediacy, proximity and concentration of effect.[162] He argues that the intensity of these features will tend to make moral issues more frequently recognised, although he accepts that some cognitive processes will affect moral decision making and behaviour in general, without regard to the moral intensity of the issue itself.[163]

Ethical principles have to be applied in practice, and it is here that problems arise. In practical terms, it includes *not* selling a mortgage to someone who will never be able to repay it, *not* selling an insurance policy for which the customer has no realistic need, *not* promoting a product through inaccurate or misleading fashion, *not* selling or continuing to sell a dangerous product, *not* on-selling bonds that have no value, *not* having an undisclosed or major conflict of interest, *not* paying oneself or others more than they deserve.

These examples can all be described in terms of a lack of fairness. Treating customers fairly has for some years been a legal requirement under EU law on financial services,[164] and general consumer trading.[165] The FSA ran a programme from 2003 specifically on 'Treating Customers Fairly' but, as noted in chapter 20, it was not applied by banks, one reason for this being that it was mis-framed in translation, another being that it was deliberately antithetical to the banks' culture of selling and simply misapplied through 'creative compliance'. So there is nothing new about a requirement of fairness, and it would be widely held to be true as a general principle, but the *context* leads to people not observing it in practice. As was found in relation to compliance with sometimes extensive and complex regulatory regimes by SMEs (small and medium sized enterprises), owner-managers might think they are in compliance but it needs an external person in a position of trust to point out that they are wrong and should make changes.[166]

The examples given above can also be attributed to a moral stance that is selfish and not *other-regarding*. It has been called a pro-social attitude, defined as altruism, or the concern for the outcomes of another or others.[167] In some, it may be deeply held, in others it may be driven by care about being esteemed by others (selfish but other-regarding),[168] but will not be driven by fear of sanctions.

Ethical conduct is a cornerstone of many professions and membership of professional associations. The Hippocratic Oath (I will take care that they suffer no hurt or damage; … Further, I will comport myself and use my knowledge in a godly manner) is instilled in

[161] Following HC Kelman and VL Hamilton, *Crimes of Obedience: Toward a Social Psychology of Authority and Responsibility* (New Haven CT, Yale University Press, 1989).
[162] Jones (n 160) 372.
[163] ibid, 389.
[164] See ch 20; *Treating Customers Fairly After the Point of Sale*, DP7 (FCA, 2001).
[165] Dir 2005/29/EC on unfair commercial practices.
[166] See ch 18.
[167] DA Collard, *Altruism and Economy: A Study in Non-Selfish Economics* (Oxford, Martin Robertson, 1978); E Fehr and U Fischbacher, 'The Nature of Human Altruism' (2003) 425(6960) *Nature* 785–91.
[168] G Brennan and P Pettit, *The Economy of Esteem: An Essay on Civil and Political Society* (Oxford, Oxford University Press, 2004); A Offer, 'Between the Gift and the Market: The Economy of Regard' (1997) 50(3) *The Economic History Review* 450–76.

medical students at an early stage and underpinned by subsequent training. The Institution of Engineering and Technology promotes and encourages ethical behaviour through its Knowledge Network and commitment to shared Rules of Conduct, thereby seeking 'to raise the level of public trust and confidence in the positive contribution to society made by science, engineering and technology'.[169] The Rules of Conduct 'aim to support members to take an ethical stance when balancing the often conflicting interests and demands of employers, society and the environment'.[170] The Institution requires both Bachelor and Incorporated Engineer qualifications to include that candidates are able to demonstrate 'understanding of the need for a high level of professional and ethical conduct in engineering'.[171] This will require familiarity with the Code of Conduct, ethical theory and awareness of ethical dilemmas through case studies.[172]

V. Mechanisms for Supporting Ethical Behaviour

The objective is to enable business to behave on the basis of commitment. It should provide evidence of a deep and consistent adherence to ethical principles, so as to be able to identify which individuals, businesses and systems can and cannot be trusted, and appropriate action taken. The mechanisms set out at the end of the previous section will now be discussed in greater detail.

The ideal is that ethical principles should be held and applied by both the individuals in the group and expressed in the actions of the organisation to which they belong. However, it is not possible to tell others what to believe. The issue is how we can access sufficient evidence on which to decide whether or not to trust an organisation and its personnel.

A Gallup study found that organisations with highly engaged employees have 3.9 times the earnings per share growth rate compared with organisations with low engagement in the same industry.[173] Data from 5,000 German establishments demonstrated that firms that adopt trust-based work contracts tend to be between 11 to 14 per cent more likely to improve products.[174] The same positive relationship was found in relation to flexible working time arrangements. The psychology research (chapter one) tells us that the two key points are that values that are applied must conform to individuals' internal value system, and that the norms must be made and applied in fairly and consistently.

At a structural level, Mayer's form of corporate governance and ownership—the 'trust firm'—combines responsibility with power and denies power without responsibility. It therefore defines the notion of a moral corporation and imbues the corporation with a degree of morality which exceeds that of the individual.[175] But ethical governance structures

---

[169]   *Rules of Conduct* (The Institution of Engineering and Technology, 2012).
[170]   ibid.
[171]   *IET Learning Outcomes Handbook incorporating UK-SPEC for Bachelors and MEng Degree Programmes* (The Institution of Engineering and Technology, 2009).
[172]   ibid, 28.
[173]   *Employee Engagement: What's Your Engagement Ratio* (Gallup Consulting).
[174]   ON Godart, H Görg and A Hanley, 'Trust-based Work-time and Product Improvements: Evidence from Firm Level Data' Kiel Institute for the World Economy Working Paper No 1914, 2014.
[175]   Mayer (n 17) 8.

would not stop at board level. A range of publications are now appearing on how to grow an ethical culture within a business.[176]

Public statements made by an organisation of their official position on how ethics apply to their activities are clearly relevant, especially if the statement is that the organisation will always seek to act ethically.[177] Statements of corporate goals should be enfused with statements that the enterprise espouses ethical values.[178] It can assist to view corporate goals in wide social terms, such as ideals of advancement of medical science and of service to humanity, as this celebrated statement by Merck:

> We never try to forget that medicine is for the people. It is not for the profits. The profits follow, and if we have remembered that, they have never failed to appear. The better we have remembered it, the larger they have been.[179]

The review of the policies of public authorities in Part C above found that the objectives and activities of agencies have widened from focusing solely on economic market aspects to encompassing responsibility for maintaining market balance and for delivering fair outcomes. In a parallel approach within firms, successful businesses have focused not on profit but on adopting the ethical standpoint of fairly delivering high quality outcomes for customers. Similarly, philosophical investigation of corporate accountability finds that corporate decisions can be immoral, illegal or just bad because no one feels personal responsibility for the ultimate outcome.[180] Encouraging individuals—in private or public employment—to feel responsible for outcomes appears to be sound policy. Ariely noted in relation to the game of golf, where there is no referee and people have to decide for themselves what is acceptable, the further people are from the action, the greater it is to indulge in mild dishonesty.[181] As discussed above, Barrett's recent conclusion of the evidence is that focusing on values to drive an organisation, expressed through addressing the needs of employees and the culture of the company, is paramount to long-term success.[182]

A review of codes of ethics in finance found they are built on seven core principles or values: Integrity, objectivity, competence, fairness, confidentiality, professionalism and diligence.[183] Statements of corporate goals and ethics have both external and internal value. But they may be mere window dressing and not applied in practice. Whilst much attention has been devoted to 'the tone from the top', values need to be applied throughout an

[176] See particularly P Montagnon, *Ethics, Risk and Governance* (Institute of Business Ethics, 2014); F Coffey, *The Role and Effectiveness of Ethics and Compliance Practitioners* (Institute of Business Ethics, 2014); L Tansey Martens, *Globalising a Business Ethics Programme* (Institute of Business Ethics, 2012).

[177] A study in 1982 found that only 18 of 80 companies had clearly articulated sets of qualitative (non-financial) beliefs: T Deal and A Kennedy, *Corporate Cultures: The Rites and Rituals of Corporate Life* (Reading, MASS, Addison Wesley, 1982).

[178] T Levitt, 'Marketing Myopia' (1960) 38(4) *Harvard Business Review* 45.

[179] Collins and Porras (n 10) 47. The authors cite a number of company credos and ideologies, such as that of Johnson & Johnson: ibid, 59–71.

[180] M Bovens, *The Quest for Responsibility: Accountability and Citizenship in Complex Organizations* (Cambridge, Cambridge University Press, 1998).

[181] D Ariely, *The (Honest) Truth about Dishonesty. How We Lie to Everyone—Especially Ourselves* (New York, HarperCollins, 2012) ch 3.

[182] Barrett (n 87) 29.

[183] JA Ragatz and RF Duska, 'Financial Codes of Ethics' in J Boatright (ed), *Finance Ethics: Critical Issues in Theory and Practice* (Hoboken, John Wiley, 2010) 297.

organisation in multiple discrete sub-groups.[184] Employees should feel they are trusted by their managers: The converse will provoke misconduct.[185] Negative experiences are much more salient, memorable and influential than positive ones.[186] Feelings of shame may lead to distancing, resistance and a dismissive, antagonistic stance.[187]

Applying fair values fairly and consistently can include the following aspects. Dealings between all staff, supervisors, stakeholders and the public should be honest and open. Information should be freely shared, in a no blame culture, on a constant feedback basis, with the objective of constant learning. When things go wrong, one should apologise, share all relevant information and make redress when harm is caused to others. Praise should be given not just for good works and success but for honesty and openness. Difficult issues could be raised in an ethics hotline, or discussed with ethics committees (not just at board levels and involving external stakeholders) and with internal 'ethics ambassadors'.[188] Surveys can reveal how the employees perceive the company on fairness and openness issues.[189]

Evidence from earlier chapters is that many people believe that they are doing the right thing until it is pointed out to them by someone they respect, that this is not the case, and they could improve certain activities. This is particularly true of small businesses, who do not have the resource to devote to detailed compliance knowledge or systemic activities. The nature of the communication is best undertaken in an educational, supportive fashion, rather than an aggressive, authoritarian fashion. Hence, useful techniques can be education, low key visits from officials, but also auditors, notified bodies and trade associations. The enlistment of groups and trade associations as lines of communication between officials and multiple dispersed firms in UK Primary Authority scheme is an example of this. Ethics training programmes alone appear to be minimally effective.[190]

Opportunities for reflection, introspection, seeking advice and open discussion are preferable to authoritarian decision making.[191] Working with devil's advocates, Cassandras and multiple advocacy[192] can counter a tendency for conformity in groups that have strong

---

[184] S Killingsworth, 'Modeling the Message: Communicating Compliance through Organizational Values and Culture' (2012) 25 *Georgetown Journal of Legal Ethics* 961.

[185] *Compliance and Ethics Leadership Roundtable, 2007.* Corporate Executive Board research; M Griffin and T Davis, *Corporate Executive Board Research Alert, Sourcing Competitive Advantage from Organizational Integrity: the Hidden Cost of Misconduct,* at https://www.celc.executiveboard.com/public/CELC_ResearchAlert. html; Ethics Resource Center, *National Business Ethics Survey,* 2 (2007), http://www.ethics.org/resource/2007-national-business-ethics-survey.

[186] RF Baumeister et al, 'Bad is Stronger than Good' (2001) 5 *Review of General Psychology* 323.

[187] V Braithwaite, 'Is Reintegrative Shaming Relevant to Tax evasion and Avoidance?' in H Elffers, P Verboon and W Huisman (eds), *Managing and Maintaining Compliance* (The Hague, Boom Legal Publishers, 2006).

[188] R Steinholtz, 'Ethics Ambassadors: Getting Under the Skin of the Business' (2014) *Business Compliance* 16–28.

[189] LK Treviño et al, 'Managing Ethics and Legal Compliance: What Works and What Hurts' (1999) 41 *California Management Review* 131.

[190] EP Waples, AL Antes, ST Murphy, S Connelly and MD Mumford, 'A Meta-Analytic Investigation of Business Ethics Instruction' (2009) 87(1) *Journal of Business Ethics* 133–61, 146.

[191] J Elkington and S Fennel, 'Partners for Sustainability' in J Bendell (ed), *Terms for Endearment: Business, NGOs and Sustainable Development.* (Sheffield, Greenleaf Books, 2010) 150–62; CL Hartman and ER Stafford, 'Green Alliances: Building New Business with Environmental Groups' (1997) 30(2) *Long Range Planning* 184; JW Selsky and B Parker, 'Cross-Sector Partnerships to Address Social Issues: Challenges to Theory and Practice' (2005) 31(6) *Journal of Management* 1; Alexander (n 134).

[192] AL George, *Presidential Decisionmaking in Foreign Policy: The Effective Use of Information and Advice* (Boulder CO, Westview Press, 1980) 191–208; J Habermas, 'Political Communication in Media Society: Does Democracy Still Enjoy an Epistemic Dimension? The Impact of Normative Theory on Empirical Research' (2006) 16(4) *Communication Theory* 11.

internal cohesion.[193] This chimes with recent political theory on widening of democratic involvement in governance and deliberation.[194]

The introduction of checklists in clinical practice, such as the World Health Organisation Surgical Safety Checklist, has been shown to improve communication,[195] preparedness,[196] teamwork[197] and attitudes to safety.[198] Such introduction in five different medical specialties at each of two hospitals under a randomised trial basis resulted in decreases in postoperative complication rates, patients' length of stay and mortality.[199]

Employment policies can seek to identify non-psychopaths,[200] since they are trust-responsive.[201] Indications on the views of staff and customers can be obtained through blind surveys, complaint mechanisms and external ombudsmen. Metrics can demonstrate satisfaction, such as employee turnover, illness records, performance levels and the proportion of satisfied customers.

Auditing, checking and internal due diligence have been found to identify problems. The medical device sector has learned the importance of unannounced inspections.[202]

The City Values project proposed that all workers in the City of London should undergo initial and continuing professional training in ethics, and be asked to sign a voluntary pledge.[203] Some have even suggested that all bankers should swear a Bankers' Oath.[204] Belonging to an external professional organisation that has high ethical principles and

---

[193] IL Janis, *Groupthink: Psychological Studies of Policy Decisions and Fiascoes* 2nd edn (Boston, Wadsworth, 1982).

[194] J Dryzek, *Deliberative Democracy and Beyond: Liberals, Critics, Contestations* (Oxford, Oxford University Press, 2000); HS Richardson, *Democratic Autonomy. Public Reasoning about the Ends of Policy* (Oxford, Oxford University Press, 2002).

[195] AHK Fudickar, J Wiltfang and B Bein, 'The Effect of the WHO Surgical Safety Checklist on Complication Rate and Communication' (2012) 109 *Deutsches Arzteblatt International* 6; RJ Kearns, V Uppal, J Bonner J, et al 'The Introduction of a Surgical Safety Checklist in a Tertiary Referral Obstetric Centre' (2011) 20 *BMJ Quality and Safety* 818, L Nilsson, O Lindberget, A Gupta et al, 'Implementing a Pre-operative Checklist to Increase Patient Safety: A 1-year Follow-up of Personnel Attitudes' (2010) 54 *Acta Anaesthesiologica Scandinavica* 76; RSK Takala, SL Pauniaho, A Kotkansalo et al, 'A Pilot Study of the Implementation of WHO Surgical Checklist in Finland: Improvements in Activities and Communication' (2011) 55 *Acta Anaesthesiologica Scandinavica* 1206.

[196] AB Böhmer, P Kindermann, U Schwanke U et al, 'Long-term Effects of a Perioperative Safety Checklist from the Viewpoint of Personnel' (2013) 57 *Acta Anaesthesiologica Scandinavica* 150.

[197] AB Böhmer, F Wappler, T Tinschmann et al, 'The Implementation of a Perioperative Checklist Increases Patients' Perioperative Safety and Staff Satisfaction' (2012) 56 *Acta Anaesthesiologica Scandinavica* 332; P Helmiö, K Blomgren, A Takala et al, 'Towards Better Patient Safety: WHO Surgical Safety Checklist in Otorhinolaryngology' (2011) 36 *Clinical Otolaryngology* 242.

[198] AB Haynes, TG Weiser, WR Berry et al 'Changes in Safety Attitude and Relationship to Decreased Postoperative Morbidity and Mortality following Implementation of a Checklist-based Surgical Safety Intervention' (2011) 20 *BMJ Quality and Safety* 102.

[199] A Steinar Haugen, E Søfteland, SK Almeland, N Sevadalis, B Vonen, GE Eide, MW Nortvedt and S Harthug, 'Effect of the World Health Organization Checklist on Patient Outcomes: A Stepped Wedge Cluster Randomized Controlled Trial' (2015) 261(5) *Annals of Surgery* 821–28.

[200] Gold (n 2).

[201] M Bacharach, G Guerra and DJ Zizzo, 'The Self-Fulfilling Property of Trust: An Experimental Study' (2007) 63(4) *Theory and Decision* 349.

[202] *Restoring Confidence in Medical Devices. Reporting on the Success of the PIP Action Plan, European Commission* (European Commission, 2014).

[203] *Investing in Integrity. The Lord Mayor's Conference on Trust and Values* (City Values Forum, 2012) http://tomorrowscompany.com/governing-values.

[204] DT Llewellyn, R Steare and J Trevellick, *Virtuous Banking: Placing Ethos and Purpose at the Heart of Finance* (London, ResPublica, 2014).

provides ongoing training, auditing and sanctions can be an indicator or reliability through training and peer support.[205] However, as with all aspects discussed here, reliance on professional organisations alone may be unreliable.[206] Reliance on external support is likely to be critical. In 2014 the Archbishop of Canterbury invited financial workers to spend a gap year in a new quasi-monastic community at Lambeth.[207]

External actions can demonstrate internal values, such as Merck's giving away Mectizan to cure 'river blindness'. Individuals and firms that demonstrate that they deserve trust should be rewarded. Commercial reward should follow reputations. Regulatory rewards should also be made. Rewards might be in terms of public awards,[208] honours or esteem,[209] or might be grant of an earned lower regime of regulatory scrutiny. Communication of ethical issues should enable market-based reputational sanctions to operate more readily.[210] Ethical criteria might be applied in insurance, similar to current credit being given for factors such as external technical accreditation. Actors' reputations could be adjusted in response to their cooperative or uncooperative behaviour.[211]

In relation to remuneration, it should be obvious that bonuses tied to performance are not well-suited to inducing honest and trustworthy behaviour.[212] Paying executives on the basis of performance has attracted strong criticism as a practice.[213] In fact, whilst experience from the Enron and WorldCom crises underlined the risks which flawed incentives can pose to market efficiency (and was not adequately learnt),[214] and various theoretical arguments on how particular schemes *might* induce particular behaviour,[215] there is

[205] J Coffee, *Gatekeepers: The Professions and Corporate Governance* (Oxford, Oxford University Press, 2006); CJ Cowton, 'Accounting and the Ethics Challenge: Re-membering the Professional Body' (2009) 39(3) *Accounting and Business Research* 177–89; J Loughrey, *Corporate Lawyers and Corporate Governance* (Cambridge, Cambridge University Press, 2011); O'Neill (n 117) 186; O'Brien (n 14).

[206] O O'Neill, 'Accountability, Trust and Professional Practice' in N Ray (ed), *Architecture and its Ethical Dilemmas* (London, Taylor & Francis, 2005); A Alexandra and S Miller, *Integrity Systems for Occupations* (Aldershot, Ashgate Publishing, 2010).

[207] *Archbishop Appoints Prior to Oversee Radical New Community at Lambeth Palace* (Archbishop of Canterbury, 2014) at http://www.archbishopofcanterbury.org/articles.php/5440/archbishop-appoints-prior-to-oversee-radical-new-community-at-lambeth-palace-video.

[208] Trust marks.

[209] G Brennan and A Hamlin, *Democratic Devices and Desires* (Cambridge, Cambridge University Press, 2000).

[210] J Armour, C Mayer, and A Polo, 'Regulatory Sanctions and Reputational Damage in Financial Markets', Oxford Legal Studies Research Paper No 62/2010 (2012). *Australian Securities and Investments Commission v Rich* 44 ACSR 431 (2003). *Australian Securities and Investments Commission v Healey* 278 ALR 618 (2011). *Australian Securities and Investments Commission v Healey (No2)* FCA 1003 (2012).

[211] JT Scholz, 'Cooperative Regulatory Enforcement and the Politics of Administrative Effectiveness' (1991) 85 *American Political Science Review* 115–36.

[212] T Noe and HP Young, 'The Limits to Compensation in the Financial Services Sector' in N Morris and D Vines (eds), *Capital Failure; Rebuilding Trust in Financial Services* (Oxford, Oxford University Press, 2014).

[213] M Dorff, *Indispensable and Other Myths: Why the CEO Pay Experiment Failed and How to Fix It* (Oakland CA, University of California Press, 2014).

[214] JC Coffee Jr, 'Understanding Enron: It's the Gatekeepers, Stupid' (2002) 57 *The Business Lawyer* 1403–20; Coffee, Jr (n 205).

[215] See eg S Bhagat, BJ Bolton and R Romano, 'Getting Incentives Right: Is Deferred Bank Executive Compensation Sufficient?' European Corporate Governance Institute (ECGI)—Law Working Paper No 241/2014 Yale Law and Economics Research Paper No 489 (arguing to retain equity-based incentive pay, to reform bank capital structure to reduce the probability of a tail event, and mandatory issuance of contingent convertible capital–debt that converts to equity under specified adverse states of the world).

very little empirical evidence on how different bonus schemes affect traders' propensity to trade and which bonus schemes improve traders' performance. Recent studies suggest that bonuses may be detrimental for performance, at least when threshold and linear compensation schemes are compared.[216] However, those involved in markets appear not to favour regulation of remuneration.[217]

From 2015, GSK Plc revised its remuneration scheme for all sales employees, dropping individual sales targets and changing remuneration from being based on targets to evaluation on technical knowledge, the quality of the service they deliver to support improved patient care and the overall performance of GSK's business.[218] The CEO said that in providing doctors with information about medicines 'this must be done clearly, transparently and without any perception of conflict of interest'.[219]

VI. Conclusions

Economic orthodoxy has been allowed to run away with the idea that human society and especially a politico-economic capitalist system is based on selfishness. That is not what the founding god Adam Smith actually said: He referred to the fact that self-interest in economic utility-maximising relationships would have major self-regulating effects. In fact, he also noted the importance of inter-personal social concern and altruism, but such virtues have been largely overlooked, both in Smith's writing and in the obsessive focus of economic thought on self-interest. Economic theorists in the twentieth century have asserted that companies will self-regulate because the economic interests of principals and agents (shareholders and managers) are aligned. Maximisation of shareholder value has been a mantra in business for some decades now. Yet these theories have been shown to be seriously flawed.

The global financial crisis from 2008 has vividly demonstrated that corporate values based on selfish maximisation of profit, whether for individual employees or businesses or shareholders, carries huge risks for society. In the 2000s scandals such as BCCI, Enron, Worldcom or Nick Leeson,[220] were dismissed as idiosyncratic rogues that were not representative of the majority of traders. The collective and systemic activities of the financial services sector in threatening the viability of global economic stability have, however, revealed that the uncontrolled capitalist system has serious flaws. This is not an ideological issue of communism or socialism against capitalism. It is that capitalism needs to put its house in order. Uncontrolled selfishness and individual freedom cause harm to others and to the self.

---

[216] E Pikulina, L Renneboog, J Ter Horst and P Tobler, 'Bonus Schemes and Trading Activity' *TILEC Discussion Paper No 2013-007.*

[217] J-M Hitz and S Müller-Bloch, 'Market Reactions to the Regulation of Executive Compensation' at http://papers.ssrn.com/sol3/papers.cfm?abstract_id=2434580 (reporting weak evidence of an average negative reaction to proposed legislation in Germany, and negative stock price reactions on firms most exposed).

[218] Press release, 17 December 2013, available at http://www.gsk.com/en-gb/media/press-releases/2013/gsk-announces-changes-to-its-global-sales-and-marketing-practices-to-further-ensure-patient-interests-come-first/.

[219] Sir Andrew Whitty, ibid.

[220] *How Leeson Broke the Bank* (BBC News Online, 22 June 1999).

Regulatory systems can do a great deal, but are not enough. One needs to revert to some basic premises. Values, commitment and trust have always been essential to markets, and need to be reinvented in modern globalised markets. The problems in the financial services sector should not be seen in isolation. Various other sectors pose risks. Some sectors have demonstrated outstandingly impressive reliability. Debates about culture in financial services too often fail to connect with the fact that *ethical* values are required. The history of ethics in business, professional and general human life is not new and has a very long history. Sound roots can be found at least in Ancient Greek philosophers and revered eighteenth century philosophers. The ideas are neither new nor complex. Ethics means identifying conflicts of interest and acting in a way that shows consideration for others, especially customers and those for whom one is responsible. It is those simple propositions that have been forgotten and need to be reinforced in modern business structures.

Three types of changes are essential. First, the objectives and structures of business organisations need to be re-examined. The idea that many businesses exist for the long term and need to be based on sound social values is intrinsic to the German trust structures advocated by Mayer. Second, business arrangements need to avoid incentives that promote unethical behaviour, such as remunerating employees or shareholders on a short term basis as opposed to a long term basis based on sound success in providing useful value to society. Third, structures can be put in place to support ethical conduct. Many of these ideas are based on the avoidance of the risks identified by cognitive and behavioural psychology, such as promoting System 2 thinking, avoiding herd behaviour, reassessment of risks and so on. Thus, psychology—and not economics—can provide a rational theory of ethical business. The development of ethical business is only a small step from the approach developed under the mantra of corporate social responsibility. There is some evidence that ethical businesses succeed in producing outstanding commercial performance as well as—and because of—integrating with the social behaviours desired by the wider society in which they operate.

22

Conclusions: Ethical Regulation

It is now time to summarise the findings from previous chapters, to take an overview and draw conclusions. The analysis above has established the following points.

I. The Basis of Decisions

Much is known about how individuals make decisions, either alone or in groups. Behavioural psychology suggests that voluntary human actions are made on the basis of emotions and heuristics (mental shortcuts). They are not usually the product of deliberative, rational evaluative processes. People often make decisions that do not maximise their own utility.[1] They have a limited ability to think rationally when potential outcomes involve uncertainty.[2] They tend to discount the importance of ambiguous information.[3] They exhibit a related 'availability heuristic' bias, and tend to predict the probability of an event based on how easily an example can be brought to mind (WYSIATI).[4] They have selective optimism and over-confidence, and tend to perceive positive outcomes as more probable than negative ones, especially when they have a certain level of control over actions associated with the outcome.[5] They often follow what other people are doing, or what seems easiest.

Better decisions can be promoted by making a human stop a heuristic short-cut and use a longer and more rational and evaluative thought process, so that risk is not underevaluated, and the behaviour of others can be evaluated for whether it is positive or negative. Prompting openness to external influences, and discussion, is positive.

Where humans belong to groups, the objectives and dynamics of the group have a major effect on behaviour. A criminal gang will adopt a certain pattern of behaviour. A professional association that values a reputation for skilled, consistent and ethical conduct will

---

[1] RB Korobkin, and TS Ulen, 'Law and Behavioral Science: Removing the Rationality Assumption from Law and Economics' (2000) 88 *California Law Review* 1051–144.

[2] M Faure, *The Impact of Behavioral Law and Economics on Accident Law* (The Hague NL, Boom Jurisdiche Uitgevers, 2009).

[3] E Van Dijk and M Zeelenberg, 'The Discounting of Ambiguous Information in Economic Decision Making' (2003) 16(5) *Journal of Behavioral Decision Making* 341; SP Curley, FJ Yates and RA Abrams, 'Psychological Sources of Ambiguity Avoidance' (1986) 38(2) *Organizational Behavior and Human Decision Processes* 230; C Camerer and M Weber, 'Recent Developments in Modeling Preferences: Uncertainty and Ambiguity' (1992) 5(4) *Journal of Risk and Uncertainty* 325; G Keren and LEM Gerritsen, 'On the Robustness and Possible Accounts of Ambiguity Aversion' (1999) 103(2) *Acta Psychologica* 149.

[4] What you see is all there is: A Tverksy and D Kahneman, 'Judgment Under Uncertainty: Heuristics and Biases' (1974) 185 *Science* 1124: See ch 1 above.

[5] C Jolls, 'Behavioral Economics Analysis of Redistributive Legal Rules' (1998) 51(6) *Vanderbilt Law Review* 1653; Faure (n 2).

tend to support achievement of such behaviour. A business unit in which achieving financial targets or individual recognition is paramount will inevitably be influenced by such objectives. People often belong to multiple groups, each with differing objectives, cultures and ethics. So conflicts may occur. It will clearly be beneficial if the objectives and cultures of the various groups to which an individual belongs are open, clearly stated, able to be evaluated and form a consistent matrix of ethical values.

Two theories of influencing people are entrenched in law and economics and deserve to be upended from legal thinking. Deterrence and rational actors focus on ideas about how people and organisations make decisions and act that turn out to be largely false. An approach based on instilling fear through deterrence turns out to have limited empirical support, and to raise a series of undesirable consequences. It is rare that a decision by a normal person or a business will be strongly influenced by considerations of formal sanctions. An individual might be influenced by the *perception* of being identified and exposed, but this is rare. The objective risk of imposition of a high penalty is unlikely to result in a decision in which that factor plays a role in a calculation. A rare exception would be where a criminal risks another long period of imprisonment, or where a company faces a further massive fine, in both cases after similar punishments have been imposed several times. Overall, however, deterrence has a very limited place in affecting behaviour, and possibly only affects certain personality types, who appear to exist in small numbers in society. As a central theory of affecting behaviour, and therefore law, deterrence is hopeless, and it produces unjust results.

An economic approach assumes that every decision is made on the basis of a prior conscious and deliberate evaluation of the risks and benefits of different options, and that the actor will (almost) always base the decisions and action on maximising personal benefit and minimising personal cost. Accordingly, the state can affect decisions by ensuring that, for certain actions, costs will be increased to an extent that makes the action sufficiently unattractive. But the findings of psychology research challenge these ideas head on.

For some time, positions on enforcement have been polarised between supporters of the two distinct 'schools' of economists and psychologists.[6] Debate has not been assisted by the fact that the evidence on both sides can be difficult for non-specialists in one or other discipline to understand (each has its own language and reference points), and the fact that few expert scholars outside each specialism are aware of the totality of the evidence. Attempts to integrate psychology into the economic model, as behavioural economics, miss the point. The problem with behavioural economics is that economists continue to frame most decisions in terms of rational and calculated decisions, so that subsuming psychology

---

[6] Fukuyama summarises the opposing giants by noting that economics, the study of markets, is primarily concerned with the rules of rational, spontaneous exchange, and that economists' game theoretical understanding of the origins of social norms is essentially a vast elaboration of the views of classical liberals like Hobbes, Locke and Rousseau on the origins of society, who characterised the state of nature as one populated by isolated, self-regarding individuals. On the other hand, he notes that Durkheim argued that sociology, which is concerned with arrational norms, trumps economics in getting to the most fundamental layer of human motivation. F Fukuyama, *The Great Disruption* (New York, Simon & Schuster, 1999) 151. Given the dominance of economic rationalism, there is no shortage of critics of 'behavioural economics', notably R Posner, 'Rational Choice, Behavioural Economics and the Law' (1998) 50 *Stanford Law Review* 1551–75; R Romano, 'A Comment on Information Overload, Cognitive Illusions and their Implications for Public Policy' (1986) 59 *Southern California Law Review* 313–28.

into a model that remains essentially based on economic calculations is thought to continue to capture reality. The fact that many decisions with economic consequences can be affected by incentives and considerations of rational irrationality, and hence nudged, does not overcome the inability of founding socio-legal structures on the reality of how people make decisions and what in fact affects their behaviour. We should be talking essentially about psychology not economics in looking at the basis of influences on behaviour. And we should be looking at organisations and multiple social, psychological and economic influences in relation to behaviour of individuals within groups.

We need to re-evaluate legal theories based on the evidence of psychology and what we know about how individuals and organisations make decisions, and how the desired behaviour can be supported and improved. What is set out in this book might turn out to be wrong, and will almost certainly be incomplete and refined as more behavioural research comes to light. The essential point is that it is on that learning that we should start to construct behavioural systems, and therefore legal and regulatory systems.

II. Culture

The unfettered pursuit of individual freedom has to be modified where groups of individuals form a social system. The society will break down unless individual behaviour is modified to take account of the need for common cooperation and respect. The key values here involve respect for others and a conception of social solidarity. Where the social activity involved is the pursuit of commerce and employment, through operation of a market, the pursuit of success should ultimately be communal and holistic, rather than the unfettered pursuit of individual benefit (whether corporate profits or individual remuneration). The pursuit of individual benefit has considerable motivational force. But the benefits (return on capital, profit, remuneration, pensions, employment) should only be achieved through fair exchange. At the other extreme, unfair exchange is extortion, and should be banned. Where it occurs, there should be correction and redress.

People will obey rules where the rules conform to their internal value systems, where the rules are made and applied in fair processes. If a Western democratic market society wishes for its rules to have wide observance and legitimacy, the substance of the rules should be ethical.

Law and legal systems can never be the ultimate means of controlling behaviour. It is the ethical values of the group in which the rules are applied, and of the individuals in that group, which ultimately matter. Law can have a symbolic value in establishing the base-line rules for a society, and supporting the underlying ethical values.[7] People might obey the law because it is the law, and is enforced by the society's organs as such, but they might not respect its values and thus withhold genuine allegiance to either the law or the society. Evidence from repressive regimes repeatedly shows this. But if the society and its citizens wish to command respect, laws should be based on the fundamental ethical values of the society. If so, people will be self-motivated by their ethical programming to respect the rules and institutions.

---

[7] R Cooter, 'Expressive Law and Economics' (1998) 27 *Journal of Legal Studies* 585.

Cognitive Evaluation Theory notes that a person's self-perception of her competence and autonomy is vital for her motivation to undertake voluntary activities.[8] Factors that support a sense of self-worth, such as receiving positive feedback, may strengthen subjects' intrinsic motivation to act.[9] Conversely, factors that undermine, such as negative feedback, tend to weaken subjects' intrinsic motivation,[10] and can prompt resentment and hostility.[11]

Avoiding problems before they arise, through an ex ante approach, is far more effective than trying to address future behaviour ex post an individual disaster in the hope that that might affect things in future. When an adverse event occurs, we should aim to learn from it and apply the lessons ex ante in relation to future activity, but not expect that punitive responses will, by themselves, have much effect on general future behaviour. In fact, we should establish systems and cultures so that we constantly learn from events and ideas on how to improve performance and reduce risk.

The law focuses to a considerable extent not on creating a positive code but on things one should *not* do, and on the problems that arise when things go wrong. So it limits its ability to have a positive influence on behaviour, and can lose sight even of the existence of positive behaviour, and the means of promoting the normal position that the considerable silent majority of people in an ethical democracy observe most of the rules most of the time on a daily basis. Law is always trying to catch up. By focusing on problems—criminal behaviour or regulatory non-compliance—legal and economic thought have gone down blind alleys.

People need to be not only instructed in the basic ethical norms but also regularly reminded of them by ways that relate to the issues that they face in their daily lives. This means that providing education, training and information not just in ethical principles but also in practical examples that are relevant to the context in which people operate. But providing instruction is far from being enough to support ethical behaviour in practice, and peer support in identifying and validating the outcome that actions are ethical is vital. As Fukuyama has said, transparency policies are effective only when the information they produce becomes 'embedded' in the everyday decision-making routines of information users and information disclosers.[12] Since highlighting particular behaviour tends to remind people of it, highlighting bad behaviour instead of good behaviour can be self-defeating.

The bigger the organisation, the fewer are the individuals that can be held responsible by outside scrutiny,[13] and the lower will be the willingness of individual staff to feel responsibility for what occurs. In order to overcome this problem of a sense of responsibility, organisations should be arranged in groups that are small enough to enable a sense of belonging and mutual support to be generated, and open enough to enable ideas and decisions to be

---

[8] M Gagné and EL Deci, 'Self-Determination Theory and Work Motivation' (2005) 26 *Journal of Organizational Behavior* 331–62; LW Porter and EE Lawler, *Marginal Attitudes and Performance* (Homewood IL, Dorsey Press, 1968).

[9] eg EL Deci, 'Effects of Externally Motivated Rewards on Intrinsic Motivation' (1971) 18 *Journal of Personality and Social Psychology* 105.

[10] CD Fisher, 'The Effects of Personal Control, Competence, and Extrinsic Reward Systems on Intrinsic Motivation' (1978) 21(3) *Organizational Behaviour & Human Performance* 273.

[11] E Bardach and RA Kagan, *Going by the Book: The Problem of Regulatory Unreasonableness* (Philadelphia PA, Temple University Press, 1982) 123.

[12] D Weil, A Fung, M Graham and E Fogotto, 'The Effectiveness of Regulatory Disclosure Policies' (2006) 25(1) *Journal of Policy Analysis and Management* 155.

[13] HR van Gunsteren, *Denken over politieke verantwoordelijkheid* (Alphen aan den Rijn, Rijksuniversiteit Leiden, 1974) 3.

debated and questioned. The previous chapter has outlined some ideas on reconstructing ethical underpinning into cultures. Regulatory systems—whether public administrative regimes or internal business compliance systems—will not be enough to ensure the safety of a system, as the financial services sector has shown.

There needs to be integration between ethical values and compliance systems. Those businesses whose internal values differ from those of the society in which they operate should be challenged to change them so as to comply with the society's values, such as in the payment of remuneration benefits that society regards as excessive.

Reflecting on the current world, Fukuyama reached the following conclusions:

> That children will learn certain things at certain times according to a certain structure is set by biology; what they learn is the province of culture.[14]

> Capitalism places self-interest ahead of moral obligation, and endless innovation constantly destroys bonds within communities.[15]

> Ideally, the best form of crime control is not a large and repressive police force, but a society that socializes its young people to obey the law in the first place and to steer violators back into the mainstream of society through informal community pressures.[16]

III. Regulation and Compliance

Compliance with the norms of a social system is produced by ethical values and systems. It is not produced directly by rules (laws) and their enforcement. Systems can be risk-based, but behaviour is value-based.

In seeking to support and maximise good behaviour, it is self-defeating to focus on 'wrongdoing', or on a distinction between compliance and non-compliance. *Performance* is the most desired level of behaviour.[17] All modern control systems seek to ensure consistently high levels of performance against set standards, and encourage constant improvement. This can be seen from the business management systems outlined in chapter 18 and the regulatory systems in chapters 19 and 20. The FCA (Financial Conduct Authority) has created a unit that focuses on how consumers make *predictable mistakes* when choosing and using financial products, and how firms' responses to such behaviour can itself be modified.[18] The civil aviation safety structure is entirely focused on constant learning, rather than on blaming individuals for errors. The CQC (Care Quality Commission) also focuses essentially on improving the quality and safety of healthcare in a vast organisational structure by supporting learning and improvement rather than by constantly wielding a big stick.

---

[14] Fukuyama (n 6) 159.

[15] ibid, 251.

[16] ibid, 28.

[17] Y Feldman and HE Smith, 'Behavioral Equity' (2014) 170 *Journal of Institutional and Theoretical Economics* 137.

[18] *Applying Behavioural Economics at the Financial Conduct Authority* (FCA, April 2013); *How does Selling Insurance as an Add-on Affect Consumer Decisions?* (FCA, 2014).

Both structures and language have historically divided regulation and enforcement (by officials) from compliance (by firms internally). They are the same thing, and should be joined up both functionally, operationally and linguistically. In various sectors, firms have internal regulators, in the form of employed experts who exercise independent professional judgement in approving activities (such as doctors or pharmacists in the pharmaceutical industry in their 'qualified person' function). It is time that the internal and external functions were regarded as holistic and joined up. They need to operate in partnership.

The role of many regulators has for many years rested on assisting compliance by providing information and advice to firms on how to do things better and so improve their compliance. It has not rested on a general punitive or deterrent approach. All UK regulators have been forced by developing government policy to publish their 'enforcement' policies, and this has revealed that many adopt a responsive and soft approach to most businesses. Only where there is intentional wrongdoing do most regulators rely on strong punitive responses. One reason for this is that only in such cases do individuals demonstrate a seriously anti-social disregard for others (and the law), and not only does society respond by marking the seriousness of such threatening behaviour, but the perpetrators' attitude tends to indicate that they are unresponsive to receiving support directed at modifying their future behaviour. Currently, there is, however, not complete unanimity of approach between all regulatory bodies, and some maintain adherence to a deterrent policy alone: This position raises questions of why such differences in approach can any longer be justified.

Multiple British regulators are inextricably involved in attempting to control business behaviour, and almost all have been engaged in this activity for some decades. There is a striking absence of any claim by a regulator that private enforcement—litigation—can realistically affect the behaviour of any business—with the sole exception of competition regulators worldwide, for which such a proposition is orthodoxy. No other regulatory body in the UK in any sector ascribes to such a view. Litigation is about delivering compensation for harm, not about affecting behaviour. Virtually no regulatory body outside competition is calling for more litigation: On the contrary, the shift in dispute resolution is towards ombudsmen, who function as part dispute resolution body, part consumer adviser, and part regulatory information officer.[19]

Business, regulators and governments all rely on *systems* for control and compliance. A concentration on systems risks losing sight of the ethics that can drive behaviour. But we should be thinking about how to combine ethics and systems. In any event, technology is enabling us to access large amounts of aggregated data about behaviour and the occurrence and causes of problems, so that we can learn how to improve. If we are going to gain these benefits, removing impediments such as fear of reporting will be critical.

Modern regulatory systems have multiple layers of control and action. For example, many have global informal coordinating committees, EU-level oversight committees of various kinds, networks of national regulators, national self-regulatory bodies, firms' regulatory and compliance functions, market and external auditors and commentators and internal and ethical influences. All of these cogs make up a holistic system. Lack of contribution or performance by any of them will lead to problems. Each element deserves respect for its

---

[19] C Hodges, 'Consumer Ombudsmen: Better Regulation and Dispute Resolution' (2015) *ERA Forum*, DOI: 10.1007/s12027-014-0366-8.

function and performance. Meta regulation and governance is an accurate description, and open communication is essential. Every element in the system has an impact on controlling risk. Every element needs to function effectively, if the regulatory, commercial and social systems are to operate as intended.

Regulatory systems should not be thought of as opposing public officials and firms. Both of those groups—but also many other stakeholders—are all integral parts of learning and hence compliance and successful systems. In the same way that UK regulators are now required to taper their actions to support growth, firms need to assist rather than confront regulators and enforcers. An open culture generates debate and information, from which everyone can learn and improve how they operate.

Regulatory systems should function so as to provide continuous collection, evaluation and response to appropriate (usually complete) transparent information and ideas for improvement. Organisations (public and private) should be constantly open to suggestions for improvement, and should be able to apply them, so as constantly to identify risks and raise standards.

Black's analysis of five seemingly unrelated regulatory disasters in different countries and domains identified common elements that manifested six contributory causes, operating alone or together: The incentives on individuals or groups; the organisational dynamics of regulators, regulated operators and the complexity of the regulatory system in which they are situated; weaknesses, ambiguities and contradictions in the regulatory strategies adopted; misunderstandings of the problem and the potential solutions; problems with communication about the conduct expected, or conflicting messages; and trust and accountability structures.[20] The correct way to approach these problems is to frame them from the viewpoint that all of them are systemic: To analyse each one in terms of individual fault misses the point about how they were caused and how the risk that they might recur can be reduced.

In a complex system, who is accountable? In political terms, there is aggregate accountability.[21] In legal terms, no single actor can be responsible for every aspect, and every person is responsible for trying their best to ensure that their part of the whole functions. The 'new modes of governance' rely on non-hierarchical and informal instruments, based upon mutual learning, persuasion and administrative coordination.[22] In personal terms, motivating people to take personal accountability for outcomes not only focuses on the need for achieving outcomes, but can also instil increased commitment and output.

Accountability lies in providing an open, honest and timely explanation of what one has done and the reasons for it. In most situations, it should not be focused on producing the consequence of external blame but of comprehensive learning and improvement.

Psychology suggests that providing peer support assists ethical behaviour. There are various examples of peer support in regulatory systems. In the vertical dimension, the activities of many enforcement officials, as noted, largely support learning. Horizontal

---

[20] J Black, 'Learning from Regulatory Disasters' (2014) LSE Legal Studies Working Paper No 24/2014.

[21] J Freeman, 'The Private Role in Public Governance' (2000) 75 *New York University Law Review* 543.

[22] E Chiti, 'The Governance of Compliance' in M Cremona (ed), *Compliance and the Enforcement of EU Law* (Oxford, Oxford University Press, 2012); G Majone, *Regulating Europe* (London, Routledge, 1996); D Gerardin, R Muñoz, N Petit (eds), *Regulation through Agencies in the EU. A New Paradigm of European Governance* (Cheltenham, Edward Elgar, 2005).

professional networks support ethics through their training, codes and opportunities to discuss responses to problems and appropriate behaviour, and counteract undesirable/conflicting self-motivated or corporate-profit-motivated behavior. We should develop more of these networks, especially in financial services. Some examples from other sectors are: Collaboration between national competent authorities in the EU, the Faculty of Pharmaceutical Medicine for medics in the pharmaceutical industry, Qualified Persons groups, Ethical Compliance Committees that operate across national and European sectors, Notified Body groups, and so on.

Peer review has proved to be a highly effective learning technique when used by EU regulators, notified bodies and firms. The 'inspection' of a notified body or firm turns into an opportunity for learning to go in all directions for all of the participants. This technique is also a useful anti-bribery device. The constant peer review practised by pilots is the same: A question by a junior might be an opportunity for training or it might assist the senior person to engage the slow brain and evaluate more carefully the options, risks and decision to be taken.

Regulatory systems should be reviewed to ensure that they comply with the lessons from cognitive and behavioural psychology and the theory of group behaviour so that design features that maximise the likelihood of compliance are included, and features that encourage non-compliance are excluded.

IV. Responses or Enforcement

In considering enforcement, we should again join up internal and external thinking—with ethical values. The combined contributions of all actors and systems are needed to maximise the outcome that the right thing is done as often as possible. A holistic approach is needed.

Every regulatory system should include a stated enforcement policy. The enforcement policy that is appropriate for a society and political system such as contemporary Europe should be based primarily on supportive, responsive enforcement. A holistic approach to 'enforcement' focuses on outcomes. (Response is perhaps a better word than enforcement.) That means two things. First, in order to apply ethical norms fairly, problems cannot be ignored and must be addressed. Second, responses to problems need to be fair. The essence of a response should be forward looking: To improve the situation, to reduce the risk, including serious measures to reduce risk or to protect society from rogues if appropriate.

The primary response to non-compliance should be to respond to the behaviour and the risk of its repetition by the particular individuals who have committed it. The primary response should not be punitive or retributive. A systematic approach that is based on a theory that future behaviour is controlled by the imposition of sanctions that respond to the seriousness of the behaviour and so will deter future non-compliance has no real empirical support. However, in serious circumstances a retributive tariff response will be appropriate and proportionate.[23] Where the motivation for non-compliant behaviour is sufficiently

---

[23] Organisations that were fined for a serious contravention of a data protection principle (that was of a kind likely to cause substantial damage or substantial distress, where the data controller knew or ought to have known

serious, the tariff response should include imposition of serious sanctions. Thus, behaviour that is motivated by deliberate intentions to break the criminal law and wrongly deprive others should be met with criminal sanctions (ultimately imprisonment, loss of licence to operate, disqualification) and by serious internal sanctions (dismissal, loss of professional accreditation, loss of gains or clawback of assets).

The primary aim should be to achieve and exceed compliance. This means that the response to non-compliance should be based on selection of a response from a hierarchical tariff of options that start with information, education, advice and support, and move upwards in the pyramid in response to the nature of the problem, the character and ethics (willingness to comply) of the target, the culture of the infringing organisation, the seriousness of the non-compliance, and the risk of continued non-compliance. Much compliance is improved by provision of advice and education. This can be done by experts internally or externally, and by private consultants or trade associations or by public inspection. In this context, punitive or deterrent responses to non-compliance have no function.

Separate responses should be made in relation to the behaviour of individuals who have committed the non-compliance, to other individuals who have some oversight responsibility for it, and to the organisation whose system is revealed as inadequate to give rational control over such behaviour in future.

Responses should be integrated between actions that occur within the relevant organisation and those that are external and applied by state organs. The form (internal or external; social, organisational, administrative or criminal) of the individual responses is irrelevant in relation to maximising compliant behaviour. What matters from the behavioural perspective is the effectiveness of the combination of responses.

The understanding of responsibility and accountability that has been generated in the airline industry is based on the rule that everyone has a duty to contribute relevant information, including information on personal actions that might be embarrassing, so that lessons can be learnt and safety improved by all. The culture accepts that people can do things that appear silly, for all sorts of reasons, but the important point is that an action was taken in good faith based on relevant information (ie the process and the basis), and how one might improve the process and basis of future decisions. Dividing actions based on the consequences of which of them caused damage and whether they constituted a breach of a theoretical legal duty is arbitrary and does not assist learning. It is clear that fear of criticism systematically strangles sharing of valuable information. We need to rethink this barrier and construct a new approach.

It is ethical that those who cause harm to others should put it right. This points to establishing a new basis of compensating or cleaning up that does not carry the problems of the tort system. If the tort system has little, if any, relevance to behaviour, the consequence is liberating, at least for Europe, if not for the entrenched USA. If litigation is not a regulatory system, and the objective is merely to provide rectification of harm caused, then a new approach can be taken, based on insurance, ADR (alternative dispute resolution) systems

there was a risk that the contravention would occur and would be of a kind likely to cause substantial damage or substantial distress, but failed to take reasonable steps to prevent the contravention) subsequently took their data protection obligations more seriously and instituted revised practices and policies, and increased staff training. Knowledge of the fine served as a reminder for other peer organisations of their own obligations. *Review of the Impact of ICO Civil Monetary Penalties* (Information Commissioner's Office, 2014).

such as ombudsmen, personal injury compensation schemes and other mechanisms. The successes that some regulators have achieved when they began to require redress to be made by firms are revolutionary and very welcome. As the UK financial regulator and ombudsman have shown, designing those two organisations to work together can achieve swift and effective results that have advantages for consumers and businesses, and save transactional costs for all (not least on regulatory enforcement).

Further, the ability of an enforcer to oversee resolution of *all* legal aspects of a case swiftly and at the same time is of great value. It can produce outcomes for ongoing behaviour modification, redress and sanctioning if appropriate. The ability to resolve all aspects through negotiation (in the DPA (Deferred Prosecution Agreement) process, calling on outside technical assistance if required, such as in evaluation of the level of redress to be made) can save costs for all involved, and engage swift remedial action to be taken. The outcome of process should usually be transparent and overseen as appropriate, for example by a judge.

Deterrence is both an illusory and irrelevant idea in most situations, but brings with it wholly negative, repressive connotations. The language of deterrence should be dropped. But are there situations in which deterrence might be relevant? It is ethical that a sanctioning system should be based on a range of sanctions that enable responses that are proportionate to the offence. We do not apply capital punishment in Europe, but we can ethically remove firms' licences to operate and individuals' freedom to circulate. Having a sanction that constitutes the top of the pyramid is sensible. Perhaps four per cent of the population is non-responsive to emotive embarrassment, whose decisions may be influenced by rational calculation or fear of serious consequences.

A responsive policy should be promoted across all regulators and enforcers, as well as firms. The following should be the expected standard steps:

1. Identify the non-compliance,
2. Stop the infringement,
3. Share all relevant information so as to conclude what caused the problem, how to improve, and prevent the problem recurring,
4. Make changes to prevent recurrence,
5. Restore any harm caused,
6. Disgorge unjustified gains.

In order to achieve these ends, those who are in supervisory roles (whether in public authorities, businesses supervisors or professional bodies) should have comprehensive and extensive systems and powers. Such systems should enable information on performance and problems constantly to circulate, be evaluated and be fed back. Such powers should enable behaviour to be affected, and good behaviour be supported and rewarded, whilst responding appropriately to rare instances of unacceptable behaviour. Powers should also enable harm to be put right as swiftly as possible. The various systems, powers and responses (criminal, regulatory, professional, employment, stakeholders, trade and consumer bodies) should be integrated, so that an effective and proportionate approach is taken. The objective should be to resolve all aspects of future and past behaviour, and the consequences, as swiftly, fairly and comprehensively as possible. The operation of the systems, powers and responses should be transparent, monitored and overseen, to ensure that all aspects, procedures and decisions are fair and timely. Monitoring of ethical and actual performance should exist. Performance and outcomes need to be achieved swiftly and fairly, and be fair.

Voluntary and negotiated responses should be encouraged and rewarded. Solutions should be holistic, encompassing behaviour, accountability, and restoration. The system itself should be constantly evaluated, as well as decisions on behaviour and responses.

Tort law is of almost no utility as a means of affecting the future behaviour of either individuals or organisations. Tort law has long ago ceased to have any relevance to establishing, maintaining or improving levels of safety or performance. To the extent that any such role ever existed in modern times, it has now clearly been replaced by the requirements of regulatory systems and compliance systems—and by ethical cultures. The two primary claimed justifications for liability law have been compensation and deterrence. Since it has long been known that liability law is an inefficient, expensive and selective means of delivering compensation, and it is now clear that deterrence from tort is illusory, there should, therefore, be reform of the legal means and processes by which compensation for harm is delivered.

In what situations should sanctions be imposed? In an ethical system it is better to think in terms of 'steps to prevent recurrence' rather than 'sanctions', in order to avoid a general culture of repression or retribution. We should aim to get to an ethical system, and maybe there is a period of transition to go through in getting there. But if we adhere to the ideas that in most situations harm occurs because systems can be improved and it is not the fault of individuals, that we will not learn how to improve systems or how to assist individuals to behave so as to avoid causing recognised harm, that deterrence is irrelevant and bars honesty and learning, what role do sanctions or penalties play?

Punitive sanctions would be relevant for actions that are classed as so objectionable as to constitute criminal behaviour. They should be a useful signal of the relative severity of an action, on a proportionate scale. But the primary justification for imposition of a serious sanction is defensive of ethical, civilised society, rather than punitive and repressive. Those who base their enforcement policies on deterrence alone need to justify that policy. Imposition of serious punitive sanctions may be justified where there appears to be no effective means of affecting the offender's behaviour, so that society should be protected from the risk of the offender's conduct by imprisonment or removal of licence to operate. This is essentially protective. A response that is simply punitive constitutes mere revenge by the society that has been harmed, and an expression of the frustration of failure. Such a response does not dignify the society as an expression of its values.

Future behaviour can in most cases only be influenced by imposition ex post of strong deterrent sanctions where the subject perceives that the risk of being caught and sanctioned is particularly high. There is very little evidence that imposition of weighty punitive sanctions affects the behaviour of most people, and such practice is abusive of human rights as they are now understood in Europe.

If we are serious about identifying serious wrongdoing, such as cartels or fraud, we should all contribute relevant information, rather than turn a blind eye. Auditors and unannounced inspections are required and should be regarded as normal. Where a firm is behaving ethically but encounters an unexpected and undesired problem, it should be sufficient that an enforcer ensures that an activity is ceased, redress is paid, and systems are changed, and a company fined £1, as some regulators have done recently. Why should this not be appropriate and fair—if there has been no unethical behaviour or intent?

If any sanctions are imposed, they need to start with the individuals involved, and then address the deficiencies in the organisational system that permits an unacceptable culture and unethical behaviour. Banks that demonstrate unacceptable culture should be reconstructed. Imposing penalties on firms is pointless when the firms have done all they could to support compliance and identify wrongdoing: Such a response is unjust, and does not deserve support. Individuals who demonstrate selfish unethical behaviour need to be identified as such. Responses might be internal (disciplinary, ultimately termination of employment), professional (disciplinary, striking off), public (prosecution), or removal of remuneration (better as removal of long-term right to unpaid remuneration) but there should be a mechanism for each of these responses to be coordinated. It may be that internal responses are all that are required. In cases of serious unethical behaviour, a professional response is required. Traditional thinking might be that the plurality of all these responses constitutes collective and alternate forms of deterrence. But if deterrence is not the currency, a different approach is required. In many instances, punitive responses are unfair, and impede learning.

Redress needs to be integrated as a normal integral response to non-compliance. Redress should be instituted on a voluntary, speedy and fair basis, rather than through an adversarial system in which the object is to negotiate the lowest settlement. In this respect, redress achieved through the involvement of voluntary arrangements, compensation schemes, regulators, ombudsmen or other ADR systems has many advantages. The implication is that new procedures for redress are required.

In short, individuals and organisations deserve their place in society on the basis of doing the right thing. The basis of humans living and operating together in social groups is based on the expectation that we and other group members will behave according to the norms of behaviour of the group. In contemporary European society, such norms are based on a particular code of ethics and supported by a particular culture. Such ethics and culture can be summarised as 'doing the right thing'. We should expect that the behaviour of individuals, businesses and public bodies should be consistent in applying the ethical values that society expects, as expressed through its laws and social norms. All parts of the system should adopt and observe the same approaches. This is ethical, integrated behaviour.

Firms, or groups of firms, that establish sufficient trust that they intend to and do operate on ethical lines should be given credit in regulatory and enforcement terms. The onus should be on firms to take sufficient steps to embed ethical values and performance into their culture and behaviour. This is an added but more fundamental dimension to the focus over the past 50 years on regulatory compliance. Ethical business needs particular structures and features (codes, peer support, ethics committees, openness and so on). But the consequence of establishing it should support not only ethical behaviour but also a vibrant, competitive market and economic health through high levels of trust between traders and consumers.Individuals and firms who do not behave ethically should expect not to gain the reputations, professional or commercial, that would follow ethical businesses. They should also not expect ethical responses to evidence of infringements, but should expect a more authoritarian and exclusive response.

The ultimate question that should be debated is: If we wish to establish an ethical society and legal system, what needs to change? A certain amount of rethinking is called for.

APPENDIX 1: A CONSUMER REDRESS SCHEME UNDER THE FINANCIAL SERVICES AND MARKETS ACT 2000 AS AMENDED

S 404 Consumer redress schemes

(1) This section applies if—
  (a) it appears to the Authority that there may have been a widespread or regular failure by relevant firms to comply with requirements applicable to the carrying on by them of any activity;
  (b) it appears to it that, as a result, consumers have suffered (or may suffer) loss or damage in respect of which, if they brought legal proceedings, a remedy or relief would be available in the proceedings; and
  (c) it considers that it is desirable to make rules for the purpose of securing that redress is made to the consumers in respect of the failure (having regard to other ways in which consumers may obtain redress).

(2) "Relevant firms" means—
  (a) authorised persons;
  (b) payment service providers. or
  (c) electronic money issuers.

(3) The Authority may make rules requiring each relevant firm (or each relevant firm of a specified description) which has carried on the activity on or after the specified date to establish and operate a consumer redress scheme.

(4) A "consumer redress scheme" is a scheme under which the firm is required to take one or more of the following steps in relation to the activity.

(5) The firm must first investigate whether, on or after the specified date, it has failed to comply with the requirements mentioned in subsection (1)(a) that are applicable to the carrying on by it of the activity.

(6) The next step is for the firm to determine whether the failure has caused (or may cause) loss or damage to consumers.

(7) If the firm determines that the failure has caused (or may cause) loss or damage to consumers, it must then—
  (a) determine what the redress should be in respect of the failure; and
  (b) make the redress to the consumers.

(8) A relevant firm is required to take the above steps in relation to any particular consumer even if, after the rules are made, a defence of limitation becomes available to the firm in respect of the loss or damage in question.

(9)   Before making rules under this section, the Authority must consult the scheme operator of the ombudsman scheme.

(10)   For the meaning of consumers, see section 404E.

404A Rules under s.404: Supplementary

(1)   Rules under section 404 may make provision—
   (a)   specifying the activities and requirements in relation to which relevant firms are to carry out investigations under consumer redress schemes;
   (b)   setting out, in relation to any specified description of case, examples of things done, or omitted to be done, that are to be regarded as constituting a failure to comply with a requirement;
   (c)   setting out, in relation to any specified description of case, matters to be taken into account, or steps to be taken, by relevant firms for the purpose of—
      (i)   assessing evidence as to a failure to comply with a requirement; or
      (ii)   determining whether such a failure has caused (or may cause) loss or damage to consumers;
   (d)   as to the kinds of redress that are, or are not, to be made to consumers in specified descriptions of case and the way in which redress is to be determined in specified descriptions of case;
   (e)   as to the things that relevant firms are, or are not, to do in establishing and operating consumer redress schemes;
   (f)   securing that relevant firms are not required to investigate anything occurring after a specified date;
   (g)   specifying the times by which anything required to be done under any consumer redress scheme is to be done;
   (h)   requiring relevant firms to provide information to the Authority;
      (i)   authorising one or more competent persons to do anything for the purposes of, or in connection with, the establishment or operation of any consumer redress scheme;
   (j)   for the nomination or approval by the Authority of persons authorised under paragraph (i);
   (k)   as to the circumstances in which, instead of a relevant firm, the Authority (or one or more competent persons acting on the Authority's behalf) may carry out the investigation and take the other relevant steps under any consumer redress scheme;
   (l)   as to the powers to be available to those carrying out an investigation by virtue of paragraph (k);
   (m)   as to the enforcement of any redress (for example, in the case of a money award, as a debt owed by a relevant firm).

(2)   The only examples that may be set out in the rules as a result of subsection (1)(b) are examples of things done, or omitted to be done, that have been, or would be, held by a court or tribunal to constitute a failure to comply with a requirement.

(3)   Matters may not be set out in the rules as a result of subsection (1)(c) if they have not been, or would not be, taken into account by a court or tribunal for the purpose mentioned there.

(4)   The Authority must exercise the power conferred as a result of subsection (1)(d) so as to secure that, in relation to any description of case, the only kinds of redress to be made are those which it considers to be just in relation to that description of case.

(5)   In acting under subsection (4), the Authority must have regard (among other things) to the nature and extent of the losses or damage in question.

(6)   The provision that may be made under subsection (1)(h) includes provision applying (with or without modifications)—
   (a)   any provision of section 165; or
   (b)   any provision of Part 11 relating to that section.

(7)   The reference in subsection (1)(k) to the other relevant steps under any consumer redress scheme is a reference to the Authority making the determinations mentioned in section 404(6) and (7) (with the firm still required to make the redress).

(8)   If the rules include provision under subsection (1)(k), they must also include provision for—
   (a)   giving warning and decision notices, and
   (b)   conferring rights on relevant firms to refer matters to the Tribunal,
   in relation to any determination mentioned in section 404(6) and (7) made by the Authority.

(9)   Nothing in this section is to be taken as limiting the power conferred by section 404.

404B Complaints to the ombudsman scheme

(1)   If—
   (a)   a consumer makes a complaint under the ombudsman scheme in respect of an act or omission of a relevant firm, and
   (b)   at the time the complaint is made, the subject-matter of the complaint falls to be dealt with (or has been dealt with) under a consumer redress scheme,
   the way in which the complaint is to be determined by the ombudsman is to be as mentioned in subsection (4).

(2)   If a consumer—
   (a)   is not satisfied with a determination made by a relevant firm under a consumer redress scheme, or
   (b)   considers that a relevant firm has failed to make a determination in accordance with a consumer redress scheme,
   the consumer may, in respect of that determination or failure, make a complaint under the ombudsman scheme.

(3)   A complaint mentioned in subsection (1) or (2) is referred to in the following provisions of this section as a "relevant complaint".

(4)   A relevant complaint is to be determined by reference to what, in the opinion of the ombudsman, the determination under the consumer redress scheme should be or should have been (subject to subsection (5)).

(5)   If, in determining a relevant complaint, the ombudsman determines that the firm should make (or should have made) a payment of an amount to the consumer, the amount awarded by the ombudsman (a "money award") must not exceed the monetary limit (within the meaning of section 229).

(6)   But the ombudsman may recommend that the firm pay a larger amount.

(7)   A money award—

    (a)   may specify the date by which the amount awarded is to be paid;

    (b)   may provide for interest to be payable, at a rate specified in the award, on any amount which is not paid by that date; and

    (c)   is enforceable by the consumer in accordance with Part 3 or 3A of Schedule 17 (as the case may be).

(8)   If, in determining a relevant complaint, the ombudsman determines that the firm should take (or should have taken) particular action in relation to the consumer, the ombudsman may direct the firm to take that action.

(9)   Compliance with a direction under subsection (8) is enforceable, on the application of the consumer, by an injunction or, in Scotland, by an order for specific performance under section 45 of the Court of Session Act 1988.

(10)   In consequence of the provision made by this section, sections 228(2) and 229 do not apply in relation to relevant complaints; but all other provision made by or under Part 16 applies in relation to those complaints.

(11)   The compulsory jurisdiction of the ombudsman scheme is to include the jurisdiction resulting from this section.

(12)   Nothing in subsection (1) is to be taken as requiring the ombudsman to determine a complaint in any case where (apart from that subsection) the complaint would not fall to be determined (whether as a result of rules made under Schedule 17 or otherwise).

(13)   Nothing in subsection (2) is to be taken as conferring an entitlement on a person who, for the purposes of the ombudsman scheme, is not an eligible complainant in relation to the subject-matter of the determination mentioned there.

404C Enforcement

The following provisions—
(a)   Part 14 (disciplinary measures), and
(b)   so much of this Act as relates to any provision of that Part,
(which apply only in relation to authorised persons) are also to apply in relation to relevant firms which are not (or are no longer) authorised persons.

404D Applications to Tribunal to quash rules or provision of rules

(1) Any person may apply to the Tribunal for a review of any rules made under section 404.

(2) The Tribunal may—
    (a) dismiss the application; or
    (b) make an order (a "quashing order") quashing any rules made under section 404 or any provision of those rules.

(3) An application may be made only if permission to make it has first been obtained from the Tribunal.

(4) The Tribunal may grant permission to make an application only if it considers that the applicant has a sufficient interest in the matter to which the application relates.

(5) The general rule is that, in determining an application, the Tribunal is to apply the principles applicable on an application for judicial review.

(6) If (or so far as) an application relates to an example set out in the rules as a result of section 404A(1)(b), the Tribunal may determine whether the example constitutes a failure to comply with the requirement in question.

(7) If (or so far as) an application relates to a matter set out in the rules as a result of section 404A(1)(c), the Tribunal may determine whether the matter should be taken into account as mentioned in that provision.

(8) In the case of an application within subsection (6) or (7), the Tribunal's jurisdiction under that subsection is in addition to its jurisdiction under subsection (5).

(9) A quashing order may be enforced as if it were an order made, on an application for judicial review, by the High Court or, in Scotland, the Court of Session.

(10) The Tribunal may award damages to the applicant if—
    (a) the application includes a claim for damages arising from any matter to which the application relates; and
    (b) the Tribunal is satisfied that an award would have been made by the High Court or, in Scotland, the Court of Session if the claim had been made in an action begun in that court by the applicant when making the application.

(11) An award of damages under subsection (10) may be enforced as if it were an award made by the High Court or, in Scotland, the Court of Session.

(12) In the case of any proceedings under this section, the judge presiding at the proceedings must be—
    (a) a judge of the High Court or the Court of Appeal or a judge of the Court of Session; or
    (b) such other person as may be agreed from time to time by—
        (i) the Lord Chief Justice, the Lord President or the Lord Chief Justice of Northern Ireland (as the case may be); and
        (ii) the Senior President of Tribunals.

(13)   Section 133 does not apply in the case of an application under this section, but—

    (a)   Tribunal Procedure Rules may make provision for the suspension of rules made under section 404 or of any provision of those rules, pending determination of the application; and

    (b)   in the case of an application within subsection (6) or (7), the Tribunal may consider any evidence relating to the application's subject-matter, whether or not it was available at the time the rules were made.

(14)   If—

    (a)   the Tribunal refuses to grant permission to make an application under this section, and

    (b)   on an appeal by the applicant, the Court of Appeal grants the permission,

(15)   The Court of Appeal may go on to decide the application under this section.

404E Meaning of "consumers"

(1)   For the purposes of sections 404 to 404B "consumers" means persons who—

    (a)   have used, or may have contemplated using, any of the services within subsection (2); or

    (b)   have relevant rights or interests in relation to any of the services within that subsection.

(2)   The services within this subsection are services provided by—

    (a)   authorised persons in carrying on regulated activities;

    (b)   authorised persons in carrying on a consumer credit business in connection with the accepting of deposits;

    (c)   authorised persons in communicating, or approving the communication by others of, invitations or inducements to engage in investment activity;

    (d)   authorised persons who are investment firms, or credit institutions, in providing relevant ancillary services;

    (e)   persons acting as appointed representatives;

    (f)   payment service providers in providing payment services. or

    (g)   electronic money issuers in issuing electronic money.

(3)   A person ("P") has a "relevant right or interest" in relation to any services within subsection (2) if P has a right or interest—

    (a)   which is derived from, or is otherwise attributable to, the use of the services by others; or

    (b)   which may be adversely affected by the use of the services by persons acting on P's behalf or in a fiduciary capacity in relation to P.

(4)   If a person is providing a service within subsection (2) as a trustee, the persons who have been, or may have been, beneficiaries of the trust are to be treated as persons who have used, or may have contemplated using, the service.

(5)   A person who deals with another person ("B") in the course of B providing a service within subsection (2) is to be treated as using the service.

(6)   In this section—
  — "accepting", in relation to deposits, includes agreeing to accept;
  — "consumer credit business" has the same meaning as in the Consumer Credit Act 1974 (see section 189(1));
  — "credit institution" has the meaning given by section 138(1B);
  — "engage in investment activity" has the meaning given by section 21;
  — "electronic money" has the same meaning as in the Electronic Money Regulations 2011 and any reference to issuing electronic money must be read accordingly;
  — "payment services" has the same meaning as in the Payment Services Regulations 2009;
  — "payment service provider" means a person who is a payment service provider for the purposes of those regulations as a result of falling within any of paragraphs (a) to (e) of the definition in regulation 2(1);
  — "relevant ancillary services" has the meaning given by section 138(1C).

404F Other definitions etc

(1)   For the purposes of sections 404 to 404B—
     "redress" includes—
     (a)   interest; and
     (b)   a remedy or relief which could not be awarded in legal proceedings;
     "specified" means specified in rules made under section 404.
(2)   In determining for the purposes of those sections whether an authorised person has failed to comply with a requirement, anything which an appointed representative has done or omitted as respects business for which the authorised person has accepted responsibility is to be treated as having been done or omitted by the authorised person.
(3)   References in those sections to the failure by a relevant firm to comply with a requirement applicable to the carrying on by it of any activity include anything done, or omitted to be done, by it in carrying on the activity—
     (a)   which is in breach of a duty or other obligation, prohibition or restriction; or
     (b)   which otherwise gives rise to the availability of a remedy or relief in legal proceedings.
(4)   It does not matter whether—
     (a)   the duty or other obligation, prohibition or restriction, or
     (b)   the remedy or relief,
     arises as a result of any provision made by or under this or any other Act, a rule of law or otherwise.

(5)   References in sections 404 to 404B to a relevant firm include—

    (a)   a person who was at any time a relevant firm but has subsequently ceased to be one; and

    (b)   a person who has assumed a liability (including a contingent one) incurred by a relevant firm in respect of a failure by the firm to comply with a requirement applicable to the carrying on by it of any activity.

(6)   References in those sections to the carrying on of an activity by a relevant firm are, accordingly, to be read in that case with the appropriate modifications.

(6A)   References in sections 404 and 404E to an "electronic money issuer" are references to a person mentioned in paragraph (a), (b), (c), (d), (h) or (i) of the definition of "electronic money issuer" in regulation 2(1) of the Electronic Money Regulations 2011.

(7)   If the Authority varies a permission or authorisation of a person so as to impose requirements on the person to establish and operate a scheme which corresponds to, or is similar to, a consumer redress scheme, the provision that may be included in the permission or authorisation as varied includes—

    (a)   provision imposing requirements on the person corresponding to those that could be included in rules made under section 404; and

    (b)   provision corresponding to section 404B.

(8)   In subsection (7) the reference to the variation of a permission or authorisation by the Authority is a reference to—

    (a)   the variation under section 44 or 45 of a Part IV permission;.

    (b)   the variation under regulation 8 or 11 of the Payment Services Regulations 2009 of an authorisation under those regulations. or

    (c)   the variation under regulation 8 or 11 of the Electronic Money Regulations 2011 of an authorisation under those regulations.

APPENDIX 2: GUIDANCE FOR ENFORCERS OF CONSUMER LAW

Department
for Business
Innovation & Skills

ENHANCED CONSUMER
MEASURES

Guidance for enforcers of
consumer law

MAY 2015

Contents

1. Introduction

1.   This guidance is aimed principally at Trading Standards Officers to help them understand what the new enhanced consumer measures (ECMs) are, how they are intended to work and when it might be appropriate for them to be used. Trading Standards Officers are referred to in this guidance as 'the enforcer'.

2.   While this guidance may be helpful to other enforcers of consumer law who also have access to ECMs, they will have a range of different powers, duties and polices, and will need to carefully consider these before taking a decision on whether or not to use ECMs.

3.   The guidance can also be used by business to help them understand what the measures are and what they can expect if they have breached the law and an enforcer is seeking to use them.

4.   The guidance sets out when and how ECMs should be used and what might be appropriate measures. This includes the use of illustrative case studies. Please note these are not actual cases and are only included to give a flavour for how and when the measures might be used. Ultimately only the courts can decide if the use of ECMs is appropriate in a particular case and whether or not they should be included in an enforcement order or undertaking.

5.   The guidance has been written in consultation with business representatives, public enforcers and consumer organisations. It is not a detailed breakdown of the rules and procedures in the civil courts.

6.   ECMs give enforcers of consumer law greater flexibility to get better outcomes for consumers who have been the victims of a breach of the law.

7.   The main formal sanction for dealing with the most serious breaches of consumer law will remain criminal prosecution. Enforcers can seek a civil injunction (interdict in Scotland) under Part 8 of the Enterprise Act 2002 against infringements of consumer protection legislation.

8.   ECMs widen the orders that the enforcer can seek in the civil courts, giving the flexibility to seek orders aimed at achieving one or more of:

- redress for consumers who have suffered loss from breaches of consumer law;
- remedies from traders who have breached consumer law to improve their compliance and reduce the likelihood of future breaches;
- remedies to give consumers more information so they can exercise greater choice and help improve the functioning of the market for consumers and other businesses.

9.   The measures should always be just, reasonable and proportionate[1]. Details of possible measures are not included in the legislation. This ensures that the enforcer or the court retain the flexibility to find the most appropriate measure or measures to deal with a business that has broken the law. It may also take away the flexibility for a person who is subject to enforcement orders or undertakings to put forward their own measures, which could be deemed suitable, to the court or enforcer.

10.   Whilst criminal courts have the power to award compensation to victims of crime, the experience is that often criminal prosecutions do not lead to all consumers who have suffered loss receiving compensation.

11.   The enforcer will take a number of factors into account before deciding on the most suitable way of dealing with a case including, for example, what is in the public interest[2].

12.   In Scotland decisions about whether to prosecute in any case will be taken by the procurator fiscal, in the public interest, and not by the enforcer. Any references in this Guidance to decisions about prosecutions should be read subject to this exception.

Case Study 1 - How the measures give greater flexibility

Trading standards receive a number of complaints from consumers who had made payments to a business offering online courses. The courses were never delivered.

Using the company's own records and details of complaints made to trading standards and citizens advice it is established that 130 consumers have suffered loss in the region of £550.

Actions available before enhanced consumer measures

Criminal Prosecution
- fine, imprisonment, disqualification etc.

Civil action
- to stop the offending behaviour and prevent it's re-occurrence.

---

[1] An explanation of these terms is contained below

[2] The reference to the public interest reflects the requirements of section 21 of the Legislative and Regulatory Reform Act 2006 to act in a way that is transparent, accountable, proportionate, and consistent and target cases in which action is needed and the practice of many public enforcers of having regard to the principles of the Code for Crown Prosecutors in determining whether or not to bring a criminal prosecution. http://www.cps.gov.uk/publications/code_for_crown_prosecutors/codetest.html. For prosecutions in Scotland, a similar Code can be found at:
http://www.crownoffice.gov.uk/images/Documents/Prosecution_Policy_Guidance/Prosecution20Code20_Final20180412__1.pdf

Actions after enhanced consumer measures

Criminal Prosecution
- fine, imprisonment, disqualification etc.

Civil action
- to stop the offending behaviour
- to pay consumers redress;
- to increase business compliance;
- to provide more information to consumers about the breach.

FAQ 1 - What are enhanced consumer measures?
- Measures designed to give public enforcers greater flexibility to get the best outcomes for consumers. Measures must aim to achieve one or more of the following: redress for consumers, enabling consumer choice or a reduction in reoffending.

FAQ 2 - What if a business does not comply with the measures?
- If they don't comply with a court order or undertaking individual traders and directors or officers of a company, who have failed to ensure compliance by the company, can be committed for contempt of court. This is punishable by up to 2 years imprisonment.
- In addition, individual traders, directors or officers of companies and the company itself can have property sequestered or be given an unlimited fine.

FAQ 3 - Are the measures an alternative to criminal prosecution?
- An enforcer should aim to use the measures whenever they deem them to be appropriate.
- In most cases, they will be used as an alternative to criminal prosecution.
- However, there may be cases where the offences are serious enough to warrant them being used in conjunction with criminal prosecution.
- The enforcer will take a number of factors into account before deciding on the most suitable way of dealing with a case including, what is in the public interest.

2.   The Enterprise Act 2002

13.   Part 8 of the Enterprise Act 2002 (EA 2002) allows certain enforcers to seek a civil remedy against a trader for infringement of consumer protection legislation. The key power is an enforcement order. Through an enforcement order, a civil court can order that the trader does not engage in the conduct in question. Enforcers can also seek an undertaking from business that they will not engage in that conduct.

Enforcement Orders

14.   EA 2002 enables enforcers to apply to the civil court for an order to stop a trader from breaching certain legislation, where the breach harms the collective interests of consumers. The enforcement procedure is set out at sections 214 to 223 of the EA 2002 with applications for an enforcement order set out under section 215.

15.   Section 214 of the EA 2002 requires an enforcer to consult the person against whom the enforcement order would be made and not to apply for an order until 14 days (or 28 days where under the new extended consultation period applies, see below) after the request for consultation is received by the person concerned in respect of an enforcement order or 7 days in respect of an interim enforcement order. Prior consultation is not required if the CMA thinks that an application for an enforcement order or an interim enforcement order should be made without delay.

16.   Enterprise Act 2002 (Part 8 Request for Consultation) Order 2003 lays down the rules in respect of the making and receipt of an enforcer's initial request for consultation to the person concerned.

17.   If the consultation is not successful and the enforcer seeks an enforcement order, the application must name the person the enforcer thinks has engaged is engaging or is likely to engage in conduct that infringes relevant consumer protection legislation.

18.   Following consultation an application can be made to the court who can then consider the merits of issuing an order (under section 217).

19.   Section 217 sets out the detail relating to the enforcement order, which must direct the business to comply with the prohibitions set out in the order. As an alternative to issuing an order, the court may accept an undertaking from the business under section 217(9).

20.   Enforcement orders made under Part 8 will apply throughout the UK. It will therefore be capable of stopping a person who is the subject of an order in one jurisdiction of the UK from harming the collective interests of consumers in the other parts of the UK.

Undertakings

21.   As an alternative to an enforcement order the enforcer can seek an undertaking from the business that they will stop engaging in practices that infringe consumer protection legislation. The scope of such undertakings mirror the scope of the enforcement order, see sections 217(6) and section 219(4) EA 2002.

22.   Where such undertakings are accepted, and the enforcer goes on to make an application for an enforcement order the court must have regard as to whether such an undertaking has been given and whether they have failed to comply with it (section 217(4)).

What has changed?

23.   The Consumer Rights Act 2015 amends EA 2002 to widen the scope of the measures that an enforcer can apply for in the civil courts. Rather than being constrained to seeking an order to stop certain practices, the ECMs allow a much wider range of measures and enable the enforcer to consider on a case by case basis the best way of dealing with a breach of the law.

24.   For example, enforcers can now seek an order for a business to pay consumers redress, change their practices to stop a repeat of the breach and/or put measures in place to increase consumer choice.

FAQ 4 – What is an undertaking/enforcement order?

- A business can agree with an enforcer to put measures in place to put right their breach of the law, known as an undertaking.
- If the enforcer and business do not agree that there has been a breach or cannot agree an appropriate response to a breach of the law, the enforcer can seek an enforcement order from the court that will require the business to put measures in place.

---

3. Overview

25.   Consumers and markets do best in a climate of strong consumer confidence where there is a robust framework of law allowing consumers to defend their own rights where possible and providing support and protection where not. This encourages enterprise, innovation, choice and efficiency, and helps reduce prices and improve quality, ultimately creating conditions that support economic growth.

26.   Business compliance with the law is an important element of any enforcement regime, as it helps to ensure that consumers do not continue to suffer from breaches of the law.

27.   The Government believes that there is a lack of flexibility in the ways that enforcers can achieve the best outcomes for consumers. Prosecutions in the criminal courts can lead to a fine or even imprisonment, while actions in the civil courts under EA 2002 can stop the infringing conduct. However, neither option tends to lead to positive outcomes for consumers, for example getting their money back, nor does the person who has broken the law have to take positive steps to put right the damage they have caused.

28.   ECMs are designed to allow public enforcers to seek a wider range of innovative and positive measures in the civil courts. In the first instance the enforcer should seek to work with the trader that has breached the law to identify suitable measures to deal with the breach. If the trader refuses to co-operate or disagrees that the measures put forward by the enforcer are just, reasonable and proportionate, the enforcer will have to present their case to the court. It will be for the court to decide, after hearing from both parties, if the measures being proposed by the enforcer, but being rejected by the trader, are just, reasonable and proportionate.

29.   The legislation does not contain a list of what might constitute suitable measures. This is to ensure that the enforcer has as much flexibility as possible to identify the most suitable approach to dealing with a breach or potential breach of the law. This also gives the business the opportunity to put forward their own suggested measures to address their behaviour.

30.   The measures became available to enforcers on the 1st October 2015.

4. Scope

31. Use of ECMs is open to all public enforcers under Part 8 EA 2002[3]. This includes specialist enforcers who operate within a particular market, for example the CAA, whereas others like Trading Standards Services, who this guidance is aimed at, have a far broader remit.

32. A power is included in the Act that can, subject to certain safeguards, extend the use of the measures to private designated enforcers[4].

33. ECMs can be used to address domestic and Community infringements of legislation set out at Annex A to this guidance.[5]

34. The decision on whether or not use of the measures is appropriate to deal with a breach or suspected breach rests with the enforcer. The enforcer will need to evaluate the detriment caused and use this to decide on the best way of dealing with the business, taking into account their enforcement policies and prioritisation principles.

When can they be used?

35. The measures should be used to address breaches or potential breaches of consumer law, for example the Consumer Protection Regulations (CPRs). . As stated, the decision whether or not to use the measures rests with the enforcer. However, there are conditions on when and how the redress part of the enhanced consumer measures can be used. In short, they can only be used when consumers have suffered loss[6].

36. There may be cases where it is appropriate that ECMs are used in addition to a criminal prosecution. For example, where an individual has caused considerable detriment to a number of elderly consumers, criminal prosecution might be suitable. However, it may also be appropriate for the enforcer to use the measures to seek an order for the individual to pay those consumers, who had suffered loss, redress.

---

[3] Competition and Markets Authority, Trading Standards Services in Great Britain, Department for Enterprise, Trade and Investment in Northern Ireland, Civil Aviation Authority, the Northern Ireland Authority for Utility Regulation, Ofcom, Ofwat, Ofgem, Phonepay Plus, The Information Commissioner, Office of Rail Regulation, the Financial Conduct Authority, community enforcers under the Injunctions Directive, Secretary of State for Health, Department of Health, Social Services and Public Safety in Northern Ireland.
[4] Only Which? are designated as a private enforcer.
[5] List up to date as at 1st October 2015
[6] See the section on redress measures below for further information.

How should the measures be used?

37.   Before deciding whether or not to seek to use the measures the enforcer will need to take a number of factors into account, for example whether or not it is in the public interest and whether use of the measures would be just, reasonable and proportionate.

In the first instance the enforcer should seek to agree appropriate measures with the trader. At this stage it should be made clear to the trader, and confirmed in writing, what measures the enforcer is seeking and what the trader will have to do to put them in place. A public enforcer cannot impose the measures on a business, what they can do is seek an undertaking from the business that they will put the measures in place.

38.   It is open to the trader to suggest alternative measures to the enforcer. If the enforcer considers them appropriate, they can accept an undertaking with measures suggested by the trader instead or together with measures suggested by the enforcer.

39.   If the trader and enforcer cannot agree suitable measures that address the breach of the law, the enforcer will have to present their case to the court and the court will decide if the measures are just, reasonable and proportionate.

40.   An enforcer or the court will have to consider the likely benefit to consumers of the proposed measure. They will also have to consider the cost to the business of putting the measures in place and whether there will be a cost to consumers of obtaining the benefit of the measures. As part of the measures the trader can also be required to provide information to show that they have carried out the agreed measures. The enforcer will need to play a key role in ensuring that the measures are being complied with and, if ordered, consumers are receiving redress.

The extended consultation period

41.   The Consumer Rights Act 2015 extends in certain circumstances from 14 to 28 days the consultation period before an enforcer can seek to use the enhanced consumer measures.

42.   The extended period applies in those cases where the person that may be subjected to the enforcement order or undertaking using the measures is a member of, or represented by, a trade association or other business representative body that operates a consumer code of practice that has been approved by a public enforcer or a community interest company whose role includes the approval of consumer codes, such as the Trading Standards Institute.

43.   The extended consultation period may be used, for example, by the person that may be subject to the enforcement order or undertaking to propose their own measures to address the detriment caused and be based on the requirements of the relevant consumer code. Depending on the circumstances of the case, this may be an indicator that the infringement will not be repeated. At the end of the 28 day period, the enforcer may take further action if they consider it appropriate. They can either commence court action to seek an enforcement order and/or seek to work with the person to agree undertakings.

Case Study 2 – Using the measures alongside criminal prosecution.

A number of complaints are received by trading standards regarding a business specialising in selling mobility aids to vulnerable consumers. The complaints allege that the business is cold calling consumers and arranging to visit them at home.

Once at the address the salesmen are using high pressure sales techniques to get the consumer to sign up to purchase a mobility aid. In many cases the aid is unfit for the purpose it was being sold for and the price eventually being paid by consumers is much more than that originally quoted.

Following investigation, due to the serious nature of the offences a criminal prosecution against the company and its directors is commenced[7].

The vulnerable nature of the victims means it is unlikely that they will be able to take their own civil actions to try and recover money lost. Due to the complexity of the case, after the criminal prosecution has been successfully completed, the enforcer launches a civil action seeking an enforcement order using the redress category of ECMs.

The enforcer contacts the affected consumers and establishes that 25 consumers have suffered detriment. Of these 20 want to return the aid and receive a full refund while 5 wish to keep the aid but only pay what they were originally quoted.

Using the redress measures in the ECMs the enforcer obtains a civil order that orders the Directors of the company to:

- Give a full refund to the 20 consumers who want to return the mobility aid and get their money back. The order states that the consumers must make the aid available for collection;
- Pay the difference between what the consumers were originally quoted and the money they eventually paid by the 5 consumers who wish to keep the aid.

---

[7] In Scotland, any criminal prosecution would be a decision for the procurator fiscal

5.   The Measures – Redress, Compliance and Information

44.   Enhanced consumer measures give enforcers greater flexibility to get better outcomes for consumers. Measures must be based around achieving one or more of:
- Redress – giving consumers who have suffered loss their money back
- Compliance - reducing the likelihood of future breaches;
- Information – enabling consumers to exercise greater choice in the market.

45.   The legislation specifically leaves out a list of possible measures. This enables the enforcer to choose the most appropriate measure to deal with a breach. It also enables the business to have the flexibility to suggest their own measures to put right the detriment they have caused.

46.   A list of potential measures was included in the consultation. These are included here as suggested measures only. The decision on the most suitable way of dealing with a breach of the law remains with the enforcer. Possible remedies could include the business doing one or more of:

- Setting up a redress scheme and advertising/notifying it to customers;
- Detailing their breach and what they are doing to put it right, for example on their website, in the press or in store.
- Signing up to a Primary Authority scheme;
- Appointing a compliance officer;
- Providing better staff training/guidance to staff;
- Undertaking internal spot checks (and maintaining records of these);
- Improving record-keeping;
- Collecting (and acting on) customer feedback;
- Introducing a robust customer complaints-handling scheme;
- Signing up to a certified ADR scheme and committing to be bound by its decisions.

47.   It is open to the enforcer to seek measures that are specific to a particular case. For example, a second hand car dealer found to be selling 'clocked' cars, could, under the compliance measures, have to make specified millage checks on all cars obtained for sale.

Case Study 3 – Using the three categories of measures

A large furniture shop advertises that it is *'never beaten on price'* and goes on to explain that it matches at the till all offers and discounts offered by its competitors on any given day ensuring their customers always pay the lowest price available. The adverts are displayed prominently in the press, on their website and in large advertisements outside their stores

The Local Trading Standards Service receives complaints from consumers that the advertising is misleading and on a particular weekend an online competitor was offering a discount that was not matched at the till. Following investigation, it is established that the store was not including online retailers in the deal, but had decided not to make this clear to consumers unless they asked.

What is just, reasonable and proportionate?

Redress measures?
- Yes, consumers who purchased furniture that could have been brought cheaper from an online retailer could be offered the difference between the price paid and that charged by the online retailer.

Compliance measures to reduce re-offending?
- Yes. It would be appropriate to seek an order changing the internal practices of the company to ensure there was not a repeat, for example updating their training materials or advertising material to ensure all offers are properly explained to customers and designed to comply with the law.

Measures to give consumers more information?
- Yes. It would be appropriate to seek an order requiring the business to advertise their breach in the press, on their website and in store.
- It may also be appropriate for trading standards to name the company on their own website and to publicise details of the breach.

FAQ 5 - Is there a list of appropriate measures?
- A list of possible appropriate measures is not included in the legislation as it is not possible to list each and every measure that might be appropriate in a particular circumstance.
- Business may also want to come up with their own innovative measure to put right a breach of the law.

FAQ 6 - Can the measures contain financial penalties?
- The measures should aim to achieve one of more of redress for consumers, more information for consumers or increasing business compliance with the law.
- Whilst a business might be required to spend money in order to pay redress to consumers, or to increase compliance or provide information to consumers, a financial penalty payable to the Treasury cannot be imposed under the measures.

The Redress measures

48.   ECMs give the enforcer the opportunity to seek redress for consumers who have suffered loss as a result of the actions of a business. If using measures under all three categories would be disproportionate to the breach, then the enforcer should first consider whether using the redress measures to get consumers their money back should take priority.

49.   Use of the redress category is limited to those cases where consumers have suffered loss as a result of the breach of consumer law. There is no minimum or maximum of loss that must be suffered by consumers before the measures are used.

50.   The enforcer or the court must be satisfied that the cost to the business of putting a redress scheme in place is unlikely to be more than the losses suffered by consumers. However, this does not include the administrative cost of putting a redress scheme in place for example accessing consumers details and getting in contact with them to make an offer of redress. Although the administrative cost must be included in the overall assessment of proportionality.

Case Study 4 – Costs to business of putting a redress scheme in place.

Over a 12 month period a business causes £10,000 of loss to 1000 consumers. Each consumer is owed £10 by the business.

Scenario 1 – A redress scheme may be proportionate.
- The business has digital records of all of their customers and it is easy for them identify which consumers are owed money as a result of their actions. The business employs 5 staff and the owner estimates it will take one of them 2 days to access the records and process the redress claims.
- There is minimal cost to the business of putting the redress scheme in place. The business does not have to close and the administrative cost of the scheme is estimated at £500.

> **Scenario 2 – A redress scheme may not be proportionate.**
> - The business is small and does not employ any staff other than a family member at weekends. It does not have detailed records of its customers but does retain delivery information. However, all files are paper based and do not show which customers might be owed money as a result of the actions of the business.
> - To identify the customers who may be owed £10 the business owner estimates that they would have to close the business for an initial 5 days to process their records. They will have to write to all their previous customers to check whether they are owed the £10. Following that the business owner estimates it will take a further 6 days to process the claims.
> - The business owner estimates that the 11 days that they will have to close the business will cost them £11,000, they also estimate that the administrative cost of the scheme at £1000.
> - After checking the accuracy of the information given by the business, the enforcer is satisfied that a redress scheme is not proportionate. As an alternative the enforcer has the option of seeking measures that are in the 'Collective interests of consumers[8]' to ensure that the business does benefit from their actions.

51. In the first instance the enforcer should work with the business to identify whether or not consumers have suffered loss, and if so, whether the business is prepared to be subject to an undertaking to pay them redress.

52. It is for the enforcer to decide if redress is appropriate in a case. If the business disagrees then the enforcer will have to prove the case in court and show what redress is appropriate.

53. The enforcer will have to consider the following when deciding if a redress scheme is appropriate:

Consideration	Explanation
The likely benefit to consumers if the measures are used.	• Have consumers suffered loss? • How much loss have they suffered? • Are they likely to receive any money back?
The cost likely to be incurred by the business of putting the measures in place.	• The reasonable costs of putting the redress scheme in place i.e. if a large number of consumers have lost a small amount of money a full redress scheme may not be proportionate. • Will the cost of the redress scheme be more than the loss caused to consumers?
The likely cost to consumers of obtaining the benefits of the measures being used.	• Will it cost consumers more to collect redress. Is the business being clear about what they are offering as part of a redress scheme?

---

[8] See page 19 below.

Making an offer of redress

54. It is recognised that each case will be different. The legislation does not say how much a consumer should lose before redress becomes appropriate The enforcer should consider the following questions:

   - Have consumers suffered loss?
   - How much loss have they suffered?
   - How will consumers who have suffered loss be identified, does the business have records?
   - How will consumers be contacted?
   - How will the redress be paid?

55. The enforcer has responsibility for deciding whether a redress scheme is proportionate and how much each consumer should be offered by the business. The administrative cost of a redress scheme will not fall to the enforcer. This is the responsibility of the business.

56. The enforcer could use information given direct to them by consumers or information supplied by the trader.

57. The enforcer should agree with the business who has responsibility for contacting consumers with an offer of redress. In most cases it will be for the business to contact consumers to make the offer of redress. However, there will be cases, for example when the offence is particularly serious or when the consumers are vulnerable, where it may be more appropriate for the enforcer to contact the consumer.

58. As part of a redress scheme the business can include a condition that if a consumer accepts it, they waive the right to take additional action to get their money back. However, the business cannot include a condition that the consumer agrees to waive their right to take any action in relation to other conduct against the business. For example a consumer could accept redress for money owed, but it would still be open to them to take their own civil action for compensation if they believed that other actions of the business had caused them harm. They would though, not be able to seek additional damages in relation to conduct for which they had already received redress.

59. It is recognised that some consumers may not get back 100% of the loss they have suffered. For example, when a large number of consumers have suffered different amounts of loss it may be appropriate to work out an average of the loss suffered and for the enforcer or business to make consumers an offer of redress based on that. In these circumstances it will be up to individual consumers to decide whether or not to accept this offer of redress.

60.   In these situations the enforcer should ensure that the offer of redress acknowledges that the redress being offered may not cover the total loss suffered by the consumer and the consumer is free to reject the offer of redress and take their own civil court action to recover the total amount they have lost. The business could also include a condition that if the offer of redress is accepted, the consumer waives their right to take additional action to recover the difference between the amount being offered and the actual loss suffered, but only in respect of the conduct that gave rise to the enforcement order or undertaking.

Case Study 5 – Using the redress measures

Trading standards receive a number of complaints regarding a business. Consumers are complaining that they have paid a deposit but the goods are subsequently not delivered. Consumers are struggling to get their deposits back.

Trading standards visit the business to investigate the complaints.

The enforcer establishes that the business has only recently been set up and the owner is struggling to keep up with the number of customers and orders. The enforcer confirms that the complaints are due to poor practices in the business, rather than them actively seeking to mislead and scam consumers.

The enforcer works with the business to establish the level of loss suffered. Using the business' own records, including details of payments made by credit and debit cards, and details of complaints, the enforcer is able to establish that 75 consumers have lost amounts in the region of £100.

Using ECMs the enforcer seeks an undertaking from the business that they will:
- Change their internal processes to give accurate delivery dates when orders are placed and reduce the chances of the business re-offending;
- Improve the training given to their staff on deposits, delivery dates and refunds; and
- Repay those consumers who do not want to wait any longer for delivery 100% of the money owed to them.

The business agrees to the first two measures and these are included in an undertaking. However, while accepting that consumers have suffered loss, the owner insists that the costs of processing the deposits should be deducted from the balance owed. The enforcer disagrees and brings a civil action for an enforcement order with ECMs in the redress category requiring the business to contact all the consumers who have suffered loss and repay them 100% of the money owed.

The enforcer sets out to the court:
- Details of the business' behaviour;
- Why the order is required;
- Details of the consumers who have suffered loss and how much each of them is owed;
- How long the enforcer believes the business should take to carry out each of the measures; and
- What information the business should lodge with the court to prove it has carried out these measures.

The court grants the order and the owner of the business is required to comply.

Measures in the collective interest of consumers

61. The redress category of ECMs allows enforcers to seek measures that are in the 'collective interest of consumers'. This means that in circumstances where a business has caused consumer loss, but it is impossible to identify some or all of the consumers who have been affected, the enforcer can , for example, seek a measure requiring the business to pay the equivalent of the loss suffered to a consumer charity.

62. Using measures that are in 'the collective interest of consumers' might also be appropriate when it is disproportionate for the trader to contact all the consumers who may have suffered loss. This could be in cases where a large number of consumers have suffered a small amount of loss.

63. In the first instance the enforcer should seek to identify a suitable charity with the business. If the business refuses to co-operate it will be for the enforcer to identify a suitable consumer charity for the redress to be paid to. In instances where there is unclaimed redress the enforcer could also seek an order for the business to pay this to a consumer charity. However, in circumstances when the consumer has declined the offer of redress in anticipation of bringing their own civil action, the enforcer should not seek to include that money in a payment to a consumer charity.

64. The measures must serve the collective interests of "consumers", so it must benefit people in their capacity as consumers. This might include consumer charities like the Citizens Advice Service, but not charities solely aimed at, for example, medical research or protecting animals. The charity could be one that supplied vulnerable or elderly consumers with help choosing the best energy supplier or broadband provider or one that gave educational talks to young people explaining their consumer rights.

> ## Case Study 6 - Using the redress measures to pay money to a consumer charity
>
> A trading standards officer makes a routine visit to a petrol station. They find that three of the twelve pumps are wrongly calibrated and are dispensing a quarter of a litre less than the amount shown on the pump when the consumer comes to pay.
>
> The petrol station has records of the pumps being checked and being correct two weeks before.
>
> Initially the owner is keen to put right the detriment they have caused. Using records of the fuel dispensed from the pumps the enforcer and the business are able to establish that the three pumps had been used around five thousand times in the last two weeks with each customer being overcharged by an average of £3.
>
> Following investigations the enforcer establishes that it would not be just, reasonable and proportionate to seek an order for the business to pay back individual consumers as it is not possible to identify individual consumers who used the defective pumps. A number of consumers paid by cash and the records from the cash register do not show which credit card payments relate to the defective pumps.
>
> Once it is established that it is impossible to identify the consumers who have suffered loss, the owner becomes less co-operative.
>
> Using the redress part of the ECMs the enforcer brings a civil action and obtains an order for the business to pay £15,000 to a local consumer charity.

Terminating Contracts

65.   Under the redress category, enforcers also have the option of seeking an order to allow consumers to terminate a contract. For example, a consumer might have been misled as to the price of an annual subscription for a certain good. It was advertised at one price but when they signed up to it, it turned out that more money was being debited from their bank account. The measures allow the enforcer to seek an order for the contract to be terminated in addition to the consumer receiving redress.

> **FAQ 7 – What is a loss case?**
> * Each case will be different but loss in respect of the redress measures is likely to be financial loss suffered by a consumer or consumers as a result of the actions of a trader.

FAQ 8 - How will consumers get their money back?
- Each case will be different. In some cases the business will have customers credit card details so they may be able to pay redress simply by reimbursing the cards. In others they will have address and telephone numbers, for example on invoices, warranties and letters of complaint. It may also be possible for the business to use social media to identify consumers who may have suffered loss to pay them their redress.

- In others they may have no details so the business and the enforcer will have to agree on the best way of paying redress. Only when the enforcer is satisfied that the trader has made an appropriate effort to identify consumers who have suffered loss should the option of paying money to a consumer charity be considered.

FAQ 9 - What if some consumers accept redress but others don't?
- Consumers do not have to accept the offer of redress. They are free to take their own action against the trader if they think the offer of redress is not appropriate for the losses they have suffered.

FAQ 10 - What if there are hundreds or thousands of consumers who have suffered loss and it is impossible to work out exactly how much each individual consumer has lost?
- Each case will be different but in cases that involve a large number of consumers who have all lost a small amount of money and where they are not easily identifiable, then it might not be appropriate or proportionate to offer them individual redress.
- Enforcers should bear in mind that in cases where consumers have lost a small amount of money they might be more unlikely to bring their own civil actions to recover money lost
- In these circumstances the business could agree with the enforcer that a payment to a consumer charity is most appropriate.

FAQ 11 - Should all consumers get 100% of their money back?
- Ideally, all consumers who have suffered loss should get back 100% of the loss. However, we recognise that this will not be possible in all cases and the enforcer will have to make a decision on whether use of the measures is appropriate.

FAQ 12 - What if some consumers have lost more than others?
- In some cases it will be possible for the enforcer to calculate what each consumer has lost and ensure that they get their money back.
- In other cases it will not be possible to work out exactly how much each consumer has lost so the enforcer will have to work out how much each consumer should be offered.
- This might be less than a particular consumer has lost so it will be up to the individual consumer whether or not they accept the offer of redress.

FAQ 13 - How much loss must consumers suffer before they get any redress?
- Each case will be different. It will be up to the enforcer to decide whether a redress scheme is appropriate.

FAQ 14 - Can a business offer consumers more/less than the detriment caused?
- A business will have to agree with the enforcer on what an appropriate level of redress should be. If they want to offer additional redress on top of that then that is up to them.

FAQ 15 – Can a business use their own redress scheme?
- There is nothing to stop a public enforcer agreeing in an undertaking that a business can use their existing redress scheme to give consumers redress

FAQ 16 – Can a business declare themselves bankrupt to avoid paying redress?
- If the redress order was against the company director then the order to pay redress remains in place, regardless of whether the company is in liquidation.
- If the order is obtained against a sole trader who declares bankruptcy[9], the redress order becomes a debt in the bankruptcy.
- If the order is against company and it goes into liquidation, the redress order becomes a debt in the liquidation

FAQ 17 – Who will decide what is an appropriate consumer charity?
- The enforcer will decide what is an appropriate consumer charity. However, there is nothing to stop the business suggesting a local charity that they have supported in the past.

FAQ 18 –What if a business has paid money to a consumer charity and consumers later come forward seeking redress?
- This will be a risk the enforcer will have to consider before seeking to use measures that are in the 'collective interests of consumers'.
- They will need to consider how likely it is that a consumer will take their own court action to seek redress. For example, a consumer would be less likely to bring a civil action to recover their money if they were owed £1 than if they were owed £100.
- If they think it is necessary, the enforcer could include in the order that the business pays 50% of the money to a consumer charity immediately, and that they must hold the rest in reserve for say 12 months to guard against consumers coming forward to claim redress. After this period the business could pay the remaining balance to the consumer charity.

---

[9] In Scotland, whose estate is sequestrated.

The Compliance Measures

66.　Business compliance with the law is an important element of any enforcement regime. It helps to ensure that consumers do not continue to suffer from breaches.

67.　Measures under the compliance category must be designed to prevent or reduce the risk of further breaches of the law. This includes a repeat of the conduct that led to the original complaint.

68.　As with the use of the other categories of ECMs the enforcer will have to decide if seeking a measure to ensure business compliance with the law is just, reasonable and proportionate. This is particularly important when considering the compliance measure. For example, the enforcer will have to take into account the size of the business and the possible impact on them that the measures might have. It would not be proportionate for the enforcer to seek to use ECMs to make a small business employ a full-time compliance officer.

Case Study 7 - Using the compliance measures to reduce the risk of re-offending

Trading standards receive a number of complaints regarding an online retailer. Some consumers have paid an additional fee for next day delivery but the goods are being delivered late. They are also complaining that their complaints are not being taken seriously enough by the firm.

The enforcer visits the firm and establishes that while some orders are being delivered late, they are being delivered. The delivery delays are due to short term staff shortages and poor staff training.

The business has already refunded the additional fee charged for next day delivery to those consumers whose goods were delivered late. They have also advertised for temporary staff to cover the staff shortages.

However, the enforcer is concerned that the internal problems relating to staff training and not taking customer complaints seriously remain. The business refuses to accept that there is a risk of a repeat of the delivery delays issue.

To ensure there is no repeat of the breach the enforcer seeks a civil order for the business to:

- Change and improve staff training; and
- Designate a member of staff to act as a customer complaints manager.

The enforcer explains to the court that if the original consumer complaints had been dealt with promptly, the issue of late deliveries would not have snowballed as it did. The court accepts that the compliance measures are just, reasonable and proportionate and will ensure that there is not a repeat of the breach.

69.   Again a list of possible measures is not included in the legislation, but measures could include a business having to sign up to the Primary Authority Scheme, appointing a compliance officer or updating internal processes to ensure there is no repeat of the breach. It may also be appropriate to seek a measure that improves the training the business gives to its staff to ensure that there is no repeat of the breach.

Consumer information measures

70.   A key element of a purchasing decision by consumers is the past performance of a business. Enabling consumers to see whether a business has broken the law and what action they have taken to put right any detriment caused will enable consumers to make better informed purchasing decisions.

71.   If consumers are not aware of a business' past performance, there is no incentive for that business to change their practices and put consumers first. Informing consumers about businesses that have broken the law will encourage switching behaviour. This benefits not only consumers but also legitimate businesses who can find it hard to compete against businesses who flout the law.

72.   The choice category gives the enforcer the flexibility to seek orders for the business to give consumers more information on the businesses past performance on complying with consumer law. This could include a business having to advertise their breach of the law and what they are doing to put the situation right on a business's own website, in the press, on social media or in store. It could also include the enforcer advertising the breach of the law and details of the business on their own website.

Case Study 8 - Using the consumer information measures.
Trading standards receive a number of complaints regarding a business that advertised prominently in the press that they were closing down and offering price reductions of 25% for 'this weekend only'.

When customers visited the business there was no sale and the business was not closing down. Goods were being sold at their usual price.

Trading standards establish that the business had purposely set out to mislead consumers that it was closing down.

Due to the actions of the business the enforcer seeks an order using the consumer information measures.

The court orders that the business displays a notice both in store, on their website, on social media and in the local press notifying consumers of their actions.

FAQ 19 – Can the measures be used to name a business on an external website, for example one set up to give consumers more information on businesses that have breached consumer law?

- As long as the measure is just, reasonable and proportionate, there will be nothing to stop an enforcer using the measures to name a business.
- This could be the enforcer putting the business, the details of their behaviour and the actions they are taking to put right any detriment caused on an external website. Consumers could use this information to decide whether or not they wish to buy from that particular business

6. Roles and responsibilities

The Enforcer

73.   ECMs are flexible and to some extent this extends to the roles and responsibilities of those involved. Whilst we expect in most cases that the enforcer will propose the measures to be put in place, each case will be different and if possible the enforcer should seek to work with the business to put in place measures that put right any detriment they have caused.

74.   In the first instance the enforcer will seek to establish the best way of dealing with a breach or potential breach of the law, whether this should involve criminal prosecution, action under Part 8 EA 2002 and/or use of ECMs. The enforcer will be best placed to decide on the most appropriate way to proceed. The enforcer will have to decide whether it is proportionate for the measures to be used.

75.   If the enforcer decides to use the measures their role will be to set out clearly what they expect the business to do to comply with them. They will also be expected to ensure c

76.   Compliance and bring the case back to the civil court if the business is not complying with the undertaking or enforcement order.

Redress Measures

77.   The enforcer will be responsible for making an initial assessment to establish whether or not using the redress measures is appropriate. They will need to take into account the amount of loss suffered by consumers and whether a redress scheme would be proportionate.

78.   This should be done by using the available information including details of complaints from consumers, the companies own records or other information supplied by the business.

79.   If the business refuses to cooperate then the enforcer will have to decide whether or not to seek an order from the court for the disclosure of documents.

The business

80.   The business will have to decide if they believe that the enforcer is seeking to use ECMs in a just, reasonable and proportionate way. If they do not believe that they are or they do not think that they have done anything wrong, then they can reject the use of the measures and the enforcer will have to seek an enforcement order in the civil court. The business will have an opportunity to put their side of the case and the enforcer will have to present whatever evidence they have. The court will then be responsible for deciding whether the enforcer is using the measures in a just, reasonable and proportionate way.

81.   When redress measures are being used, in the majority of cases, it will be for the business to contact consumers who have suffered loss to make them an offer of redress.

FAQ 20 – How does the trader show they have carried out the measures?
- A trader will discuss in advance with the enforcer or the court what they will do to put the measures in place. It should be made as clear as possible to the trader what they have to do and the outcomes that the measures should achieve.
- What the business has to do to comply with an undertaking or enforcement order should be set out in writing.

FAQ 21 - Can a court order the trader to prove they have carried out the measures?
- Yes, a court can require the trader to show that they have carried out the agreed measures.
- The enforcer would also be expected to take a role in ensuring the measures were carried out as agreed or ordered.

7. Definitions

What is a just, reasonable and proportionate?

82.   Whatever measures the enforcer is seeking to put in place to deal with a breach, they must be just, reasonable and proportionate to the behaviour of the trader and the detriment caused to consumers. The enforcer will have to weigh up the different aspects of the particular case and put in place measures to address the trader's behaviour and the impact that it has had on consumers.

83.   Enforcers such as trading standards officers are already guided by the Regulators Code[10] when deciding on appropriate enforcement action. The measures should be used in conjunction with the Code and the same considerations should be used when deciding whether or not using the measures is appropriate.

84.   The Code puts a duty on the enforcer to act transparently and proportionately. Enforcers should have the necessary knowledge and skills to support those they regulate, including having an understanding of those they regulate that enables them to choose proportionate and effective approaches.

85.   Enforcers also need to act proportionately, clearly explain what the non-compliant activity is, the advice being given, actions required or decisions taken, and the reasons for these. Enforcers should also provide an opportunity for dialogue in relation to the advice, requirements or decisions, with a view to ensuring that they are acting in a way that is proportionate and consistent.

---

[10] https://www.gov.uk/government/publications/regulators-code

Case Study 9 – Measures that are not just, reasonable and proportionate.

Consumers complain that a small white goods retailer is mispricing its products. Goods such as fridges and freezers are advertised in store at a lower price than consumers are eventually charged when they purchase the product. Some consumers may not have realised they were charged extra but the majority did not suffer loss as once they complained they were either charged the correct price or returned the product.

Following investigation the enforcer establishes that the goods are not being purposely mispriced and the fault lies with a new computer system the retailer has recently had installed. The enforcer also establishes that around 20 consumers had lost on average £6. The retailer has managed to contact 15 customers and repaid them the money lost.

The retailer has already been through their records in an attempt to locate and identify the 5 consumers who have suffered loss. They have established that their delivery records are incomplete and are able to show the enforcer the gaps in their records.

The enforcer seeks to use ECMs to put in place the following measures:
- A redress scheme requiring the retailer to go through records of thousands of transactions again in an effort to identify the 5 consumers who have not had their money returned.
- Employ a compliance officer to ensure that there is no repeat of the breach.
- Advertise in the local press detailing what the store did and what they are doing to put right the detriment caused.

The measures the enforcer is seeking to put in place are not just, reasonable and proportionate. The detriment was caused by an honest mistake and it would cost the retailer more to put the redress scheme in place than the loss suffered by consumers. In the circumstances described above the court would be likely to find that the measures are not just, reasonable and proportionate and refuse to make an enforcement order that includes them. It would be more proportionate for the enforcer to work with and advise the business to ensure that there was not a repeat of the breach.

FAQ 22 - What does an enforcer have to consider when deciding if a measure is just, reasonable and proportionate?
- An enforcer or the court will have to consider all the facts of the case including the likely benefit to consumers of the proposed measure. They will also have to consider the cost to the business of putting the measures in place and the cost to consumers of obtaining the benefit of the measures.

INDEX

Abbott, Carolyn 58
ABTA Code (Travel Association)
  Code of Conduct Committee 479, 500
  Consumer Codes Approval Scheme 469–70
  logo 479
  standards 479–80
abuse of dominant position 87–8, 111, 420, 434
accountability
  Accountability for Regulator Impact initiative 208
  air safety 585, 590–1, 703
  capture, risk of 458
  cartels 102
  competition 439
  consumer protection 416
  corporate responsibility 36, 520
  culture and values 35
  decision-making 195
  disasters, common elements of regulatory 701
  ethics 689
  financial services 626–7, 652, 656, 660
    consumer redress 283
    EU law 622
    Financial Conduct Authority 627
  health and safety 574
  health and social care 605–6
  independent and informed judgments 682
  legitimacy 29
  liability law 54
  meta-regulation 174
  Principles for Economic Regulation 195
  railway safety 323
  Regulators' Compliance Code 191
  responsive regulation 705
  safety, regulating 604
  self-regulation 498–501
  structure of regulation 174, 185, 196–7, 206
  teams 35
  trust 682, 701
  United States 102
  whistleblowing 526–7
accreditation 464, 467–9, 480, 554–5, 692
Adamson, Clive 652
  administrative penalties 164–5, 184–5, 205–6,
    257–8, 426
ADR see alternative dispute resolution (ADR)
Advanced Risk-Responsive Operating framework
  (ARROW) 617
adversarial model 67, 84, 156, 218, 490, 706
advertising and marketing see also Advertising
  Standards Authority (ASA)
  cartels 104
  consumer protection 407

disclosure of complaints 473
engineering products 549–54
financial promotions 290, 473, 624
Germany 494–6
medicinal products 8, 464, 489–93, 500, 538–46
safety, regulating 531, 533–4, 555, 607–8, 659
  engineering products 549–54
  medicinal products 8, 464, 489–93, 500, 538–46
Advertising Standards Authority (ASA) 8, 482–9
  advice and support 484, 487, 489–90
  Audiovisual Media Services Directive 483
  briefings 489
  Broadcasting Committee on Advertising Practice
    Code 483–6, 487–9
  child protection 485–6, 489
  codes 469, 483–9
  Committee of Advertising Practice Code 483–9
  complaints 483–4, 488–9
  Compliance and Marketing Team 489
  confidentiality 484, 489
  consumer protection 374, 485
  co-regulation 469
  electronic communications 486, 488
  established means of regulation, as 464, 483
  evidence, production of 488–9
  feedback 485
  Financial Services Authority 488
  freedom of information 489
  funding 485
  Independent Review procedure 489
  Internet/websites 484, 489
  investigations 488–9
  learning, education, and training 487
  levy on industry members 485
  monitoring 484
  Nolan Principles for public appointments 484
  non-broadcast adverts 485–6
  Ofcom 482–4
  Office of Fair Trading 464, 488
  On Demand Programme Services 483
  online complaints 488
  one-stop shop for complaints 484
  organisation 483–9
  precedent bank 489
  Press Complaints Commission 488
  pre-vetting 484–5
  product placement 483
  publication of adjudications 489
  racial hatred 483
  referrals 488
  Research Reports 489
  reviews 489

negligence   217
private enforcement   72–4, 81
profit and shareholder value, business objectives
    of   673, 676
public authorities   627
remuneration   73
disasters   36–7, 701
discrimination
    class actions   83
    electricity and gas services   307
    employees   69, 83
    Equal Employment Opportunity Commission
        69, 84
    Ofwat   320
    United States   69
    whistleblowing   523
disgorgement *see* **restitution/disgorgement**
dispute resolution *see also* **alternative dispute
    resolution (ADR)**
    ABTA Code   479–80
    electricity and gas services   308, 314–15, 319
    financial services   274, 276–7
disqualification orders   3, 364, 422–3, 432, 627
distributive justice   51
divestiture   111–12
DPAs *see* **deferred prosecution agreements (DPAs)**
drink driving   146
drug trafficking   221
due diligence   11, 217, 342, 518–19, 691
Duff, David   146

Eckard, E Woodrow   127
economic approaches *see also* **economic costs**
    behavioural/cognitive psychology   696–7
    competition   87, 90, 105, 132
    consumer protection   352, 355, 359, 388, 402
    decision-making   153–4, 696–7
    deterrence   7, 107–11, 154
    economic analysis of law   52, 56–61
    financial penalties   125
    incentives   697
    law and economics approach   25, 62, 696
    liability law   107–11
    maximising personal benefits   696
    nudging   697
    OECD   257
    Principles for Economic Regulation   195–6
    private enforcement   71
    rational actor, theory of economic   1, 5, 15
    Regulators' Compliance Code   187
    restorative justice   219
    self-regulation   466
    selfishness   693
economic costs
    Better Regulation   179–80
    class actions   78–81
    competition   126
    costs-benefit analysis
        decision-making   155, 570
        design of systems   193, 380
        deterrence   56–61, 107–10, 144

estimates   173
inertia and procrastination   19
settlements   81
damages   78–81
design of systems   193, 380
deterrence   56–61, 78–81, 107–10, 144, 155
fraud   339
health and safety   561–2, 566
legal liability   78
litigation tax   79
local authorities   204
OECD   263
private enforcement   78–81, 155
public enforcement   81
research   78–80
securities law   81
settlements   78
statistics   78–9
structure of regulation   179–80, 193
United States   78–81, 155
EDF Energy   316
Edlin, Aaron S   70
education *see* **learning, education, and training**
**Effective Open Voluntarism initiative (European
    Commission)**   520, 528
**electricity and gas services, enforcement policy
    relating to**   8, 269–70, 307–19
    ADR   310
    agencies, enforcement policies of individual
        8, 269–70, 307–19
    Better Regulation   309
    Capacity Market and Contracts for Difference
        mechanisms   319
    compensation   316–17, 456
    Competition and Markets Authority   308
    Consumer Futures, investigations by   317
    consumer outcomes   316–18
    consumer redress   270, 308–10, 312, 315–18,
        408, 453
    culture of customers first policy   454
    direct redress to customers   317
    discrimination   307
    dispute settlement   308, 314–15, 319
    Enforcement Decision Panel   314
    Enforcement Guidelines (Ofgem)   311–13
    Enforcement Oversight Board   315
    Enforcement Vision and Strategic Objectives   313
    Environment and Climate Change
        Committee   309
    EU law   318–19
    final compliance orders   312, 317
    financial penalties   308, 309–10, 315–19, 453
    Gas and Electricity Markets Authority   308,
        310–12
    Gas Safety Register   469
    greenhouse gases   308, 309, 316
    insider trading   318
    investigations   308, 314, 317
    licences   308, 310, 316
    market manipulation   318
    mis-selling   316–17